Routledge Handbook on Consumption

Consumption research is burgeoning across a wide range of disciplines. The *Routledge Handbook on Consumption* gathers experts from around the world to provide a nuanced overview of the latest scholarship in this expanding field. At once ambitious and timely, the volume provides an ideal map for those looking to position their work, find new analytic insights and identify research gaps. With an intuitive thematic structure and resolutely international outlook, it engages with theory and methodology; markets and businesses; policies, politics and the state; and culture and everyday life. It will be essential reading for students and scholars across the social and economic sciences.

Dr. Margit Keller is a senior researcher in social communication in the Institute of Social Studies, at the University of Tartu, Estonia. She chairs the Research Network of Sociology of Consumption in the European Sociological Association.

Dr. Bente Halkier is a professor of sociology in the Department of Sociology, at the University of Copenhagen, Denmark.

Dr. Terhi-Anna Wilska is a professor of sociology in the Faculty of Social Sciences, at the University of Jyväskylä, Finland.

Dr. Monica Truninger is a senior research fellow in the Institute of Social Sciences, at the University of Lisbon, Portugal.

Routledge Handbook on Consumption

Edited by Margit Keller, Bente Halkier, Terhi-Anna Wilska and Monica Truninger

ROUTLEDGE
Routledge
Taylor & Francis Group
LONDON AND NEW YORK

First published 2017 by Routledge

2 Park Square, Milton Park, Abingdon, Oxfordshire OX14 4RN
52 Vanderbilt Avenue, New York, NY 10017

Routledge is an imprint of the Taylor & Francis Group, an informa business

First issued in paperback 2019

British Library Cataloguing-in-Publication Data
A catalogue record for this book is available from the British Library

Library of Congress Cataloging-in-Publication Data
Names: Keller, Margit, editor.
Title: Routledge handbook on consumption / edited by Margit Keller, Bente Halkier, Terhi-Anna Wilska and Monica Truninger.
Description: Abingdon, Oxon ; New York, NY : Routledge, 2017.
Identifiers: LCCN 2016037842 | ISBN 9781138939387 (hardback) | ISBN 9781315675015 (ebook)
Subjects: LCSH: Consumption (Economics) | Consumers.
Classification: LCC HC79.C6 R68 2017 | DDC 339.4/7—dc23
LC record available at https://lccn.loc.gov/2016037842

ISBN: 978-1-138-93938-7 (hbk)
ISBN: 978-0-367-33585-4 (pbk)

Typeset in Bembo
by Apex CoVantage, LLC

Contents

Figures and tables

Figures

Tables

List of contributors

Duygu Akdevelioglu is a PhD Candidate at the Paul Merage School of Business, University of California, Irvine, USA. Her research focuses on Social Networks and Social Media. She has made presentations at various conferences, American Marketing Association, Association for Consumer Research and Social Networks.

Eric J. Arnould is an omnivorous anthropologist who has been writing and practicing social science since 1973. He is a devotee of Maussian social theory and interested in applying cultural theory to wicked social problems. He has taught consumer culture theory and qualitative research methods on every continent. He is a Professor at University of Southern Denmark (DK) and EMLYON, France.

Søren Askegaard, Professor of Marketing at the University of Southern Denmark. His research lies in the domain of Consumer Culture Theory where he has published widely. He is co-author of the book Consumer Behaviour. A European Perspective (now in its 6th edition) and co-editor of the forthcoming *Routledge Companion to Canonical Authors in Social Theory on Consumption*.

Lívia Barbosa is Associate Professor at Fluminense Federal University and Invited Researcher at Pontifica Universidade Católica do Rio de Janeiro, Brazil. She has published widely in the areas of Brazilian Society and Culture and Consumption, particularly about food, in Portuguese as well as in English and among others Cultura, Consumo e Identidade, in co-authorship with Colin Campbell, *Rice and Beans* in co-authorship with Richard Wilk, Sociedade de Consumo and Tendências da Alimentação Contemporânea.

Russell Belk is a York University Distinguished Research Professor and Kraft Foods Canada Chair of Marketing. He has published extensively in consumer research including papers and books on sharing, gift-giving, collecting, materialism, extended self, the meanings of possessions, and digital consumption. Recent books include *Consumer Culture Theory: Research in Consumer Behavior* (Emerald, 2015), *The Routledge Companion to Identity and Consumption* (Routledge, 2013), and the 10-Volume set *Russell Belk, Sage Legends in Consumer Behavior* (Sage, 2014).

Rishi Bhardwaj is a PhD candidate in the Faculty of Management at University of British Columbia, Canada. His research area is Consumer Culture Studies. He is the recipient of a University Graduate Fellowship as well as MITACS Globalink Travel grant for his research. He also holds an MBA in Marketing.

Matthias Bode is Associate Professor of Marketing at the University of Southern Denmark. His research focus on the historical, cultural, social and aesthetic production of marketing practices where he has published widely, amongst other "The Wild and Wacky Worlds of Consumer Oddballs: Analysing the Manifestary Context of Consumer Culture Theory" in Marketing Theory and as a co-author a book about the German marketing & consumption history (Marketing und Konsum: Theorie und Praxis von der Industrialisierung bis ins 21. Jahrhundert).

David Buckingham is Emeritus Professor at Loughborough University, UK, and was formerly Visiting Professor at the Norwegian Centre for Child Research. He has directed numerous research projects on young people's interactions with media, and on media literacy education. He is the author, co-author or editor of 30 books, including most recently *The Material Child: Growing Up in Consumer Culture* (2011), *The Civic Web: Young People, the Internet and Civic Participation* (2013) and *Youth Cultures in the Age of Global Media* (2014). His website and blog are at: davidbuckingham.net.

Melissa L. Caldwell. Professor of Anthropology, University of California, Santa Cruz. Editor of *Gastronomica: The Journal of Critical Food Studies*. Her research, teaching, and publications focus on practices of everyday life in postsocialist societies, with particular emphasis on Russia, the former Soviet Union, and Eastern Europe. Has published widely on poverty, welfare, food politics, and social justice, including *Living Faithfully in an Unjust World: Compassionate Care in Russia, Dacha Idylls: Living Organically in Russia's Countryside, Food and Everyday Life in the Postsocialist World*, and the co-edited volume *Ethical Eating in the Postsocialist and Socialist World.*

Cecilia Díaz-Méndez is Professor of Sociology in the Department of Sociology at the University of Oviedo. She has been teaching Sociology of Consumption since 1993 and since 2000 she has been the director of the Research Group on Sociology of Food http://www.unioviedo.es/socialimen. She has published widely in international journals. She has carried out the National Survey of Food Habits (Ministerio de Agricultura, Alimentación y Medio Ambiente, 2013) with her colleagues in the Department of Sociology and has applied her knowledge to social studies, like those on Food in Times of Crisis carried out for the Spanish Red Cross (2014).

Arne Dulsrud is PhD and Research Director at Consumption Research Norway (SIFO). He has published widely on consumer policy issues, economic sociology and food policy both in books and journals including Journal of Consumer Policy and Acta Sociologica.

Adrian Evans is a Senior Research Fellow at The Centre for Agroecology Water and Resilience (CAWR) at Coventry University. His current research focuses on the ethics, sustainability and resilience of different types of food systems. He has developed new theoretical approaches for understanding food consumption behaviours and his work seeks to foster improved science-society dialogue around food and farming issues. He recently published in *Environment and Planning D* and has a chapter in Harvey, M., 2015. *Drinking Water: A Socio-economic Analysis of Historical and Societal Variation.* Routledge Taylor & Francis Group, with Mark Harvey.

David Evans is a professorial Research Fellow, Geography, University of Sheffield, UK. He has published extensively on consumption, food and sustainability. He is the author of *Food Waste: Home Consumption, Material Culture and Everyday Life* (Bloomsbury, 2014).

Güliz Ger, Professor of Marketing at Bilkent University, Turkey. She has published on the sociocultural and global dimensions of consumption and markets, particularly in transitional societies/groups. Her recent publications include: Türe, Meltem and Güliz Ger "Continuity through Change: Navigating Temporalities through Heirloom Rejuvenation," *Journal of Consumer Research*, 2016; Kuruoğlu, P. Alev and Güliz Ger "An Emotional Economy of Mundane Objects," *Consumption Markets & Culture*, 2015, 18:3, 209-238. Karababa, Eminegül and Güliz Ger, "Early Modern Ottoman Coffeehouse Culture and the Formation of the Consumer Subject," *Journal of Consumer Research*, 2011, 37:5, 737-760 and Sandıkcı, *Özlem and Güliz Ger*, "Veiling in Style: How Does a Stigmatized Practice Become Fashionable?" *Journal of Consumer Research*, 2010, (June), 37:1, 15-36.

Olga Gurova is a Academy of Finland research fellow at the Department of Social Research, University of Helsinki, Finland. Has published in the areas of sociology of consumption, sociology of fashion, socialist and postsocialist cultures of consumption. She is the author of the books Fashion and the Consumer Revolution in Contemporary Russia (Routledge, 2015) and Soviet Underwear: Between Ideology and Everyday Life (New Literary Observer, 2008).

Bente Halkier is a professor in sociology at Department of Sociology, University of Copenhagen, Denmark. Her empirical research focuses on food consumption in everyday life, and social contestation of knowledges and practices. She has published widely on contested consumption and everyday life, e.g. the book *Consumption Challenged: Food in Medialised Everyday lives* (Ashgate, 2010).

Pernille Hohnen, Associate Professor in Culture and Consumption studies, Aalborg University. Pernille Hohnen has a PhD in Social Anthropology and has published widely on vulnerable groups and forms of marginalization in relation to Welfare, Work life and Consumption. She is the author of *A Market out of Place? Remaking Economic, Social and Symbolic Boundaries in Post-Communist Lithuania* (Oxford University Press) and a number of articles on vulnerability and consumption in the Nordic Welfare States. Her most recent research concentrates on credit consumption and debt and new forms of vulnerability in credit markets.

Eivind Jacobsen is a sociologist with a PhD in Science Studies from the University of Oslo, Norway. Since the late 1980thies he has been working at the National Institute for Consumer Research (SIFO) recently renamed to Consumption Research Norway (SIFO). He has published on a broad set of topics - mostly in Norwegian - related to food consumption, power in distribution chains, political consumption, consumer power and everyday kitchen practices. Jacobsen is currently Institute Director at SIFO.

Annamma Joy is Professor of Marketing at the University of British Columbia, Canada. Her research interests are primarily in the area of consumer behaviour and branding with a special focus on luxury brands in the PRC and India, fashion brand experiences, wine marketing and aesthetic consumption. She has published several articles in the Journal of Consumer Research, Journal of Consumer Psychology, International *Journal of Research in Marketing, Journal of Cross-cultural Psychology, Journal of Economic Psychology, Canadian Journal of Administrative Sciences and Consumption, Markets and Culture.*

Tally Katz-Gerro is a Reader in Sociology at Sustainable Research Institute, University of Manchester, UK. Her work focuses on comparative culture consumption research, gender differences in cultural consumption, cultural omnivorousness, material consumption, and environmental concern and behavior. Recent projects include cultural policy of the performing arts, cultural economics of the artistic canon in museums, and cultural cosmopolitanism in divided societies.

Margit Keller is a Senior Researcher at the University of Tartu, Estonia. She has studied the development of post-socialist consumer culture, young people and children's consumption and is at present focusing on the change of everyday practices and institutional interventions. She has published in Environmental Policy and Governance, Marketing Theory, International Journal of Consumption Studies, Journal of Consumer Culture as well as co-authored a book "From Intervention to Social Change" (Routledge 2015). She is currently the chair of the Research Network of Sociology of Consumption of the European Sociological Association.

Carol Kelleher. Lecturer in Marketing at University College Cork, Ireland. Has published widely in the areas of service marketing and consumer culture theory, including in the Journal of Service Research, Marketing Theory and Advances in Consumer Research.

Mikael Klintman is a professor of Sociology at Lund University, Sweden. He has published in areas of green, ethical, and political consumption as well as on the interdisciplinary for managing environmental problems. Klintman's publications include 'Citizen-Consumers and Evolution' (Palgrave, 2012) and 'Human Sciences and Human Interests: Integrating the Social, Economic, and Evolutionary Sciences' (Routledge, 2016).

Sebastian Koos is Assistant Professor of Corporate Social Responsibility at the University of Konstanz, Germany. His research focuses on ethical consumption, corporate social responsibility, industrial relations as well as pro-social behaviour. He recently coauthered the monograph "Looking behind the label: global industries and the conscientious consumer" 2015 at Indiana University Press.

Robert V. Kozinets is an academic innovator who has developed important methods and theories that are widely used around the world. In 1995, he invented netnography, and since that time, he has applied, developed, written about, and taught digital research methods and branding theories to academics as well as to a range of global companies and nonprofits. He is the Hufschmid Chair of Strategic Public Relations and Business Communication at the University of Southern California, US.

Mikko Laamanen is Postdoctoral Researcher at Grenoble École de Management, France. His research on everyday politics and practices of organizing work and consumption has been published in management and consumer studies journals, and in the *Palgrave Handbook of Volunteering, Civic Participation, and Nonprofit Associations*. He's a co-editor of recent special issues on Consumption, Lifestyle and Social Movements in the *International Journal of Consumer Studies* as well as Alternative Economies in the *Journal of Macromarketing*.

Pauline Maclaran, Professor of Marketing & Consumer Research at Royal Holloway University of London. She has published widely on the symbolic and experiential aspects of consumer culture, particularly in relation to gender issues. She is a co-editor of *Marketing & Feminism: Current*

Issues & Research (2000) and *Motherhoods, Markets & Consumption: The Making of Modern Mothers in Contemporary Western Culture* (2013).

Laurie A. Meamber is an Associate Professor of Marketing, School of Business, George Mason University, Virginia, USA. Her research focuses on the aesthetics of consumption, and the arts in consumer culture. She is the Regional Editor – North America for *Arts and the Market.*

Mara Miele. Her research addresses the geographies of ethical foods consumption and the role of animal welfare science and technology in challenging the role of farmed animals in current agricultural practices and policies. In recent years her work has developed in conversation with cultural geography and STS scholars. Recent publications appeared in *Environment and Planning A, Environment and Planning D, Theory, Culture & Society, Food Ethics.*

Cele C. Otnes, Investors in Business Education Professor at the University of Illinois at Urbana-Champaign; also Professor of Advertising and Professor of Recreation, Sport and Tourism. In addition to publishing on gender and consumption, she explores the intersection of ritual at all levels (individual, social-network, cultural) and consumer culture. She has most recently co-authored *Royal Fever: the British Monarchy in Consumer Culture* with Pauline Maclaran (Univ. of California Press, 2016), and co-edited *Gender, Culture, and Consumer Behavior* (Routledge, 2012).

Jessica Paddock is Research Associate at the Sustainable Consumption Institute, University of Manchester, UK. Jessica's research interests intersect across areas of consumer culture, food and environment. She has published in the discipline areas of sociology, consumer culture and rural sociology amongst others. Her recent publications include: Paddock, J. 'Positioning Food Cultures: Alternative Food as Distinctive Consumer Practice', *Sociology* DOI: 10.1177/0038038515585474 and Paddock, J. (2015) 'Invoking Simplicity: 'Alternative' Food and the Reinvention of Distinction', *Sociologia Ruralis* 55 (1) pp.22-40

Siwarit Pongsakornrungsilp is Assistant Professor of Marketing at Walailak University, Thailand. He founded the Consumption and Sustainable Economy Research Cluster (CSE) in order to co-create research collaboration across Thailand and the region. His research interests focus on value co-creation, consumer culture theory, working consumers, brand culture, and brand co-creation. These also include how consumers employ spirituality and superstition to co-create brand value. He received his PhD from University of Exeter.

Laura T. Raynolds is a professor of Sociology and Co-Director of Center for Fair & Alternative Trade, Colorado State University, US. She has authored numerous articles on globalization and agro-foods including Raynolds, L. (2012). Fair Trade: Social Regulation in Global Food Markets. *Journal of Rural Studies*, 28 (3), 276-87, and is the Co-Editor of Raynolds, L. & Bennett, E. (Eds.). (2015). *Handbook of Research on Fair Trade*. Edward Elgar.

Lucia A. Reisch is a Behavioural economist, Professor of Consumer Research and Consumer Policy at Copenhagen Business School, Denmark. She has published widely in the field of consumer research in general and sustainable consumption in specific, as well as behavioural economics, nudging and sustainability politics. She also is active in policy consulting in these areas.

George Ritzer is Distinguished University Professor at the University of Maryland, USA. His major publications are in the areas of social theory and the sociologies of production, consumption and prosumption. His best-known book is The McDonaldization of Society (eighth edition, 2015). Over the last decade his work has focused on prosumption. His latest (2015) essay on that topic is entitled "Prosumer Capitalism."

Minna Ruckenstein is Principal Investigator at the Consumer Society Research Center, University of Helsinki, Finland. She holds a Ph.D. in cultural anthropology and the title of docent in consumer economics. She has studied consumer culture from the perspectives of childhood and technology engagements. Current projects focus on self-tracking technologies, data practices and datafication. She has published widely, for instance, in the *Journal of Consumer Culture* and *Information, Communication and Society.*

Lisa Peñaloza. Professor of Marketing. Kedge Business School, France. Her ethnographic studies of cultural formations in markets with a focus on elderly, ethnic, and gender dynamics are featured in journals, edited books, and film.

Roberta Sassatelli is Associate Professor of Sociology at the University of Milan, Italy. She has published widely on the sociology of consumer practices and the politics of contemporary consumer culture as well as sociology of leisure and sport, sexuality and gender. Her works are translated into Spanish, Portuguese, German, Greek, Check, Finnish, Polish, Korean and Chinese. Among her recent books in English you may find "Consumer Culture. History, Theory and Politics, Sage, 2007; "Fitness Culture. Gyms and the Commercialisation of Discipline and Fun", Basingstoke, Palgrave, 2010 [2014 paperback].

Jonathan Schroeder is the William A. Kern Professor in the School of Communication at Rochester Institute of Technology in New York, USA. His books include *Visual Consumption* and *From Chinese Brand Culture to Global Brands: Insights from Aesthetics, Fashion and History* (co-author). He is editor at large of the interdisciplinary journal *Consumption Markets & Culture.*

Sue Scott is a sociologist and honorary professor, University of York and Visiting Professor University of Helsinki. She has held Chairs in four UK Universities and has undertaken research and published widely in the areas of: Sexuality; Gender; the body, childhood, and risk. See for example: Jackson, S and Scott, S (2010) *Theorising Sexuality* Open University Press/McGraw Hill; Jackson, J. and Scott, S. (2016) Practice Theory and Interactionism: an integrative approach to the sociology of everyday sexuality? in A. King, A. Cristina Santos and I. Crowhurst (Eds) *Sexualities Research: Critical Interjections, Diverse Methodologies and Practical Applications*, London Routledge.

Jennifer Smith Maguire is senior lecturer of Cultural Production and Consumption in the School of Management, University of Leicester, UK. Her research examines the construction of markets, tastes and value, primarily in relation to the commercial fitness and premium wine markets. She has published in such journals as *Consumption, Markets & Culture, International Journal of Cultural Studies*, and the *European Journal of Cultural Studies*, and she is the author of *Fit for Consumption: Sociology and the Business of Fitness* (Routledge, 2008) and co-editor of *The Cultural Intermediaries Reader* (Sage, 2014).

Dale Southerton is a professor of Sociology and Director of the Sustainable Consumption Institute, The University of Manchester, UK. He has published extensively on consumption, social change and sustainability. He is editor of the 'Encyclopedia of Consumer Culture

(Sage, 2011) and (with Alistair Ulph) 'Sustainable Consumption: multi-disciplinary perspectives' (OUP, 2015).

Gert Spaargaren is a professor on 'Environmental Policy for Sustainable Lifestyles and Patterns of Consumption' at the Environmental Policy Group of Wageningen University, The Netherlands. His main research interests and publications are in the field of environmental sociology, sustainable consumption and behavior, and the globalization of environmental reform. His most recent book project is *Social Practices and Research on Social Change* (with Don Weenink and Machiel Lamers), Routledge, 2016.

John B. Thøgersen is a Professor of Economic Psychology at Aarhus University, Denmark. Has published widely in the area of sustainable consumption, including food, energy, transport and labelling, including the "Handbook of research on sustainable consumption," Edward Elgar 2015 (with Lucia A. Reisch) and "Unsustainable consumption: Basic causes and implications for policy," European Psychologist, 2014.

Vebjørg Tingstad is Professor at Norwegian Centre for Child Research at Norwegian University of Science and Technology (NTNU) in Trondheim, Norway. She has been the director of the centre, and has directed several research projects on children's day care institutions, education, consumption and media culture. She is the author and co-author/editor of books and journal articles, including the most recent ones (in English), *Children, Food and Identity in Everyday Life* (2009), *Childhood and Consumer Culture* (2010) and *Researching children in a digital age. Theoretical perspectives and observations from the field* (2013).

Monica Truninger is senior research fellow at the Instituto de Ciências Sociais da Universidade de Lisboa, Portugal. Her research interests include food (in)security, children and families; school meals and children's food practices; domestic technologies and cooking practices, sustainable consumption and food provisioning systems. She has published widely in national and international journals, e.g. Journal of Consumer Culture; International *Journal of Sociology of Agriculture and Food; Young Consumers; Ecology and Society; Journal of Community Development, Gastronomica.*

Linda Tuncay Zayer, Associate Professor of Marketing at Loyola University Chicago. She has published in the areas of gender, marketing and consumer behavior as well as transformative consumer research in journals such *as Journal of Consumer Research, Journal of Retailing, Journal of Advertising, Journal of Service Research, Journal of Product Innovation Management*, among others. She is also the co-editor of the book, *Gender, Culture and Consumer Behavior*, Routledge, 2012.

Alladi Venkatesh is a Professor at the Paul Merage School of Business, University of California, Irvine, USA. He has published widely in the area of technology diffusion in such journals as the Journal of Marketing, Management Science, Journal of Marketing Management, JACR, Communications of the ACM and others. His papers on consumer culture and postmodernism have appeared in the Journal of Consumer Research (Best paper award), International Journal of Research in Marketing, Marketing Theory and others.

Triin Vihalemm is a professor Communication Research at the University of Tartu, Estonia. Her main field of research is social change and communication. In her recent publications she analyses the people's mundane, everyday habits and underlying structural nexuses on the various fields of consumption domestic energy use, health (risks), managing economic crises etc. She co-authored the book "From Intervention to Social Change: A Guide to Reshaping Everyday Practices" (Routledge 2015).

Marta Vilar Rosales is a research fellow at the Instituto de Ciências Sociais da Universidade de Lisboa. She has a PhD in Anthropology (2007) and her main areas of research concern contemporary material culture and consumption practices (particularly focusing on the domestic context), food, contemporary migrations and media anthropology.

Bas van Vliet is an associate Professor at Wageningen University at the Environmental Policy Group, The Nethelands. He has published on urban infrastructures of energy, water, and sanitation, amongst others *Urban Waste and Sanitation Services for Sustainable Development* (Routledge, 2014) and *Urban Infrastructures of Consumption* (Earthscan, 2005).

Stefan Wahlen is Assistant Professor at Wageningen University, The Netherlands. He studies consumption governance with particular focus on eating, sharing, and households as primary contexts of consumption and everyday life. He has published in the *Journal of Consumer Policy* and the *International Journal of Consumer Studies* as well as co-edited a special issue on Consumption, Lifestyle and Social Movements in the *International Journal of Consumer Studies.*

Alan Warde is Professor of Sociology in the School of Social Sciences and Professorial Fellow of the Sustainable Consumption Institute at the University of Manchester, UK. His research interests include the application of theories of practice to the sociological analysis of culture, consumption and food. He recently published *The Practice of Eating* (Polity, 2016).

Matt Watson is a senior Lecturer in Human Geography at the University of Sheffield, UK. He has published widely in the field of sustainability and practice theory, including co-authoring *The Dynamics of Social Practice* (Sage 2012).

Daniel Welch is a Research Associate at the Sustainable Consumption Institute, University of Manchester, UK. His research focuses on novel articulations between the the sociology of consumption, social theory, sustainability, cultural economy and economic sociology. Recent publications include Welch, D. and Warde, A. (2017) 'How should we understand 'general understandings'?' in A. Hui, T.R. Schatzki and E. Shove (eds.) *The nexus of practice: connections, constellations and practitioners*. London: Routledge.

John Wilkinson is Associate Professor at the Graduate Centre for Development, Agriculture and Society at the Rural Federal University, Rio de Janeiro, Brazil. He co-authored *From Farming to Biotechnology (Blackwell, 1987)*, co-edited and *Fair Trade (Routledge, 2007)* and is the author of many articles on the agrifood system and economic sociology in European and US Journals. He has been a consultant to the EU, OECD, FAO, OXFAM, and Actionaid and to a variety of public and private bodies in Brazil.

Terhi-Anna Wilska is professor of Sociology at the University of Jyväskylä, Finland. Her expertise areas are consumption and lifestyles from many perspectives, currently focusing on age, generations, digitalization, well-being and sustainability. She has published widely on these topics in international journals and edited volumes. She is a co-editor of *Digital Technologies* *and Generational Identity. ICT Usage Across the Life Course (Routledge, 2017)*, and also co-edited a special issue: *Environmental governance and communication meet everyday life: the (im)possibilities of sustainable consumption in Europe*, in *Environmental Policy and Governance (2016)*.

LiAnne Yu. PhD Anthropologist and independent consumer research strategist. Author of *Consumption in China: How China's new consumer ideology is shaping the nation*, and has published widely in areas of technology, business, and culture for various publications including *Hawaii Business Magazine*.

Preface

This book was born out of a need to combine within a single volume answers to one main question – what is the state of the art in consumption studies? Consumption research is a burgeoning, yet a fragmented terrain. This handbook is a comprehensive edited collection, a "one-stop shop" and a benchmark for readers interested in social scientific consumption studies, featuring authors from all over the world.

The handbook's objective is to give a thorough and nuanced overview of the cutting-edge research and recent debates of the field. We believe that a critical review of consumption studies is timely in terms of the burning issues societies face globally: climate change, economic crisis, sharpening inequalities, population ageing, obesity epidemic, food insecurity and poverty as well as the strengthening foothold of digital technologies in everyday lives. One of the major goals of the book is to unpack the latest knowledge on how consumers' everyday practices of consumption are enacted within the complexities and conundrums of today's world, where clashing forces (e.g. commercial marketing and behavior-change campaigns; contradictory medialized environmental and health messages; the lethargic impacts of policy interventions to change consumers' practices given the time pressures posed by the challenges of climate change) often draw people, markets and governments schizophrenically in opposing directions. The handbook surveys existing work in the field, also raising new and emerging topics and approaches, thereby providing a solid grounding for future progress.

We invite a worldwide audience of scholars and students interested in research on consumption, with varying disciplinary backgrounds from sociology to marketing. The work also caters for a wider readership outside academia, namely marketers, educators, policy-makers and various intervention programme practitioners.

This book has been a joint effort of many people. The initial idea came to life in a fruitful conversation between professor Alan Warde and the Routledge editor Catherine Gray. We wish to thank them for setting the ball rolling and helping at different stages of the book. Also, Gerhard Boomgarden and Alyson Claffey at Routledge have been most supportive in making this volume happen. The editing work of post-graduate student Benedicta Ideho Omokaro at the University of Jyväskylä, Finland, was invaluable at the final stages of preparing the manuscript for submission. Credit is also due to an inspiring and relaxing spa weekend of brainstorming ideas and chapters' revisions in the fabulous landscape and surroundings of Laulasmaa in Estonia.

The editors also wish to thank members of the Research Network of Sociology of Consumption of the European Sociological Association for inspirational conferences and cooperation, as well as many contributions to this book. Without the good spirit of this network the handbook would not have been possible.

Margit Keller wishes to thank her colleagues and postgraduate students of the Institute of Social Studies at the University of Tartu, Estonia, with whom ideas in this book have been discussed, molded and tried out. She is grateful for the funding of the grant IUT20–38 by the Estonian Research Council that has made work for this volume possible.

Bente Halkier wishes to thank her former colleagues at the Department of Communication and Arts, Roskilde University, Denmark, for constructive discussions of some of the ideas which ended up in this book.

Terhi-Anna Wilska wishes to thank her colleagues at the Department of Social Sciences, University of Jyväskylä, Finland, particularly the researchers in the research group "Digital Life", for fruitful discussions around the themes that gave inspiration to this book. She also thanks the Faculty of Social Sciences at the University of Jyväskylä for financial support in the preparation of the book at different stages.

Monica Truninger would like to acknowledge the fruitful and engaging discussions with her various colleagues from different disciplinary backgrounds at the Institute of Social Sciences, at the University of Lisbon, Portugal. Such an interdisciplinary and lively environment greatly inspired some of the ideas contained in this book. She is also pleased and very grateful to be the recipient of an FCT Investigator grant (IF/01057/2012) awarded by FCT – the Portuguese national funding agency for science, research and technology.

Finally, we want to thank our brilliant and enthusiastic authors for all the time and effort they gave for this book. Without your insightful and impressive contributions this *Handbook on Consumption* would never have been materialized and enacted.

1

Consumption research revisited

Charting of the territory and introducing the handbook

Bente Halkier, Margit Keller, Monica Truninger and Terhi-Anna Wilska

A multi-disciplinary research field

In *Keywords*, Raymond Williams describes the historical development in the uses of the words *consumer* and *consumption*: "To consume" dates back to the fourteenth century and meant "to destroy, to use up, to waste, to exhaust" (Williams, 1987, pp. 78–79), whereas "to consume", "consumer" and "consumption" gained the meaning of the use of market-provided goods and services from the eighteenth century onwards, alongside the development of capitalism and political economy, but also with Romanticism (Campbell, 1987). Both meanings of *consumption* are still with us today in so far as the understanding of consumption as part of market relations dominates popular discourse as well as research definitions. Seeing consumption as something potentially problematic is also part of the recent consumption research history and the current societal challenges to the environment, health, well-being and equality.

To researchers of consumption, it is of course no surprise that important terms have different meanings and definitions. In the introduction to the Sage four-volume book titled *Consumption*, Warde (2010) argued that the research field is characterized by the lack of consistent, agreed-upon and workable definitions of its core concepts. Earlier, Warde had given a definition of consumption that is sociological in its disciplinary background, yet encompassing and nuanced enough to provide a field for versatile problem framings and empirical agendas: "Consumption is a process whereby agents engage in appropriation and appreciation, whether for utilitarian, expressive or contemplative purposes, of goods, services, performances, information or ambience, whether purchased or not, over which the agent has some discretion" (2005, p. 137).

In *Consumption* the contributions are grouped under three headings, reflecting three interrelated aspects of consumption processes, bearing close affinity to the above-quoted definition: *acquisition, appropriation* and *appreciation* (Warde, 2010). Acquisition refers to the dynamics, arrangements and conditions of economic and social exchange in consumption whereby goods and services are procured. Appropriation covers the variations of how consumers use goods and services and what is being done with goods and services in which processes. Appreciation concerns the meaning-making made in relation to consumption activities. We are suggesting that these terms are helpful in structuring the broad questions to be asked about consumption. We are adding *disposal* (Cappellini, Marshall & Parsons, 2016) since the ways in which consumers get rid of things, empty them of meaning, throw out, re-use and re-craft them have been a focus of research for some time and have gained momentum especially in the context of sustainable consumption. These terms might be used to express the recognitions of the above-outlined common – or at least cross-disciplinary and cross-perspective – ideas and potentially used for conceptual work.

Some researchers will see a search for a conceptual core or synthesis of consumption research as possible and as something worth striving for across the different intersecting disciplines of the field. This view parallels an understanding of a field such as consumption research as being potentially trans-disciplinary, whereby different disciplines meet around complex subjects and attempt to renegotiate and re-draw traditional disciplinary boundaries (Klein, 1990, pp. 27–28). As far as we can see, there is only a little of this type of research going on, primarily in parts of anthropology, sociology, critical marketing and cultural geography.

Other consumption researchers will perhaps see their research as contributing to a much more specific field of research, under the big umbrella of consumption research, and therefore perhaps not in need of conceptual synthesis. This view is parallel to an understanding of a research field as being multi-disciplinary, where the disciplines to a large degree work independently "next to" each other (Klein, 1990, pp. 56–57). It can be argued that consumption research is dominated by multi-disciplinarity across e.g. sociology, cultural studies, marketing, anthropology, communication and information, economics, psychology, nutrition and health sciences, history, and cultural and economic geography. This obviously contributes to the degree of differentiation of theoretical perspectives, concepts, methodological designs and types of empirical questions and conclusions. Moreover, multi-disciplinary studies of consumption share a lot of their theoretical and methodological foundations with the research on other topics in social, cultural and political research, such as different divisions and inequalities, leisure and lifestyles, social and political transformations, the use and meanings of technology, mobility and transport, ethnicity and multiculturalism, learning and education, social and political participation, and health, well-being and happiness – to mention only a few.

We hope that consumption researchers of both kinds find this handbook a useful partner in conversation.

Rationale of the handbook

The purpose of this handbook is not to decide whether or not to aim for conceptual syntheses across disciplines, subfields and perspectives. Rather, its main objective is to bring together and represent broadly the state-of-the-art across these variations in order to make this handbook a "one-stop shop" and a benchmark for readers interested in social scientific consumption studies. The aim of this chapter is to set the scene.

On top of this variation across the field, consumption is also part and parcel of many central societal issues, which leads to it often being treated in an unrealistic manner, as either god of the market or victim of economic, cultural and social conditions. The handbook's objective is to give a thorough and nuanced overview of cutting-edge research and recent debates of the field. It is meant to operate as a map for scholars and students to position their work, to find new analytic nodes and research gaps. The handbook takes sociology of consumption as its main focus, yet also covers and engages with debates in adjacent disciplines in the field such as marketing research, anthropology, psychology, cultural studies, communication, cultural geography and education.

The handbook stages a series of conversations on consumption, covering different sectors of society: markets and businesses; policies, politics and the state; civil society and culture. Special attention will be given to social divisions, constraints as well as opportunities and solutions that varying consumption cultures and societies afford. We also cater for readers interested in particular sub-fields by relating consumption to sustainability, body, age, gender, cultural issues and lifestyles, information and communication technologies (ICTs), consumer policies, global challenges and specific emerging markets such as Russia, China, Brazil and Turkey.

A critical review of consumption studies is timely given the burning issues societies face globally: climate change, economic crisis, sharpening inequalities, population ageing, obesity epidemic, food insecurity and poverty as well as the strengthening foothold of ICTs in everyday lives. In all these areas consumption processes play key roles, yet are often taken for granted, or rendered invisible, consumers seen as passive or isolated recipients by commercial marketing and policy rhetoric, as well as fragmented and often contradictory research results. This handbook has three specific aims. First, to encourage readers to delve deeper into issues related to consumption, and especially to fascinate the more uninitiated reader – a graduate student perhaps – with the burgeoning and intriguing field of consumption studies. Second, to persuade that much high-level analysis and theoretical thinking is done in this diverse field and deserves careful attention. This is to avoid focusing only on a few narrow analytical levels and perspectives that may become ossified in the vast and rich literature on consumption. Third, we should aim to de-ossify studies on consumption and be open to the surprising interstitial spaces of innovation and imagination.

A brief story across stories of consumption research

Attempting to tell one story of the analytical development and theoretical distinctions in an inherently multi-disciplinary research field such as consumption studies is of course almost impossible. Hence, the ambition of this section is much more humble: to set a scene for sharing the different versions of what consumption research entails by pulling together some of the often-referred-to overviews in our framing. Thus, our brief story draws upon the following accounts of different parts of the consumption research field: Arnould & Thompson, 2005; Askegaard & Linnet, 2011; Bauman, 1988, 1998, 2007; Featherstone, 1990, 1991; Fine & Leopold, 1993, Gabriel & Lang, 2015; Gronow, 1997, Gronow & Warde, 2001; Lury, 2011; McGregor & Murnane, 2010; Miller, 1998; Paterson, 2006; Ratneshwar & Mick, 2005; Ritzer & Slater, 2001; Sassatelli, 2007; Slater, 1997; Soper & Trentmann, 2008; Sulkunen, Holmwood, Radner & Schulze, 1997; Trentmann, 2016; Warde, 1994, 2010, 2014. Looking across these accounts makes it possible to see a trajectory of diversification in the international studies on consumption, and also the mainstreaming of certain ideas across perspectives and disciplines.

Within recent social science, the study of consumption has roughly followed a trajectory of working mainly from economistic assumptions in the beginning, then moving towards and including first socio-cultural structuralism, then embracing a cultural turn, and lately also covering practice and materiality turns.

The economistic strand of consumption research originally resided in two quite different research perspectives. The first was the neo-liberal economic perspective of the consumer as individual and somewhat rational decision-maker with fixed preferences, choosing on the basis of various kinds of self-interest, utility and other individual motivations. Moreover, consumption is treated abstractly, all commodities under the term *consumer goods*, and consumption in aggregate level as one single consumer, ignoring cultural and social aspects of consumption. Income and prices are principal factors in the consumption process in economist theories, such as

Milton Friedman's permanent income hypothesis (1957) or Engel's law on the relation between income and food expenditure (Fine & Leopold, 1993). This perspective dominated theoretical and empirical social scientific interest in consumption from the 1950s on, and was particularly strong in the US, where consumption research became associated more closely with marketing research and business studies.

The other standpoint in consumer research based on economistic assumptions is the neo-Marxist critical theory perspective on consumption, which tended to see consumers rather differently at one level, namely as alienated, dependent upon and manipulated by and into participation in superficial, even trivial activities of mass consumption and mass culture. Mass culture was produced and dominated by a concentrated culture industry whose sole motive was profit. This perspective, originally introduced by Frankfurt School theorists Max Horkheimer and Theodor Adorno in the 1940s (Horkheimer & Adorno, 1981/1944), was particularly strong in European theoretical discussions about consumption in the 1960s and 1970s. The two otherwise different perspectives on consumption, however, shared one assumption: that the social and cultural practices and relations involved in consumption were dependent upon economic mechanisms.

Reactions to understanding consumption mainly as a function of economic dynamics came first from anthropology and sociology, where a perspective of seeing consumption as expressions of cultural and social relations and the reproduction of social structures came forward in the late 1970s and early 1980s. The classic work by Jean Baudrillard published in the 1970s, *The Consumer Society* (1998), is illustrative of this shift. Baudrillard acknowledged the highly symbolic nature of consumption, arguing also that symbols and signs do not only express pre-existing sets of meanings, but also create meanings during the consumption process. Another classic representative of this perspective, but from the 1980s, would be Mary Douglas' (Douglas & Isherwood, 1980) anthropological approach to consumption as rituals that reflect social order and reproduce cultural markers and classifications. One last prominent example comes from sociology with Pierre Bourdieu's approach to consumption as reproduction of patterns of cultural tastes, reflecting the place of consumers in the social hierarchy based on their habitus and forms of capital (Bourdieu, 1984). The inclusion of this perspective in consumption research meant that consumption and consumers could be defined in terms of social and cultural categories, and thus the unit of analysis was significantly broadened out, being neither only the individual consumer nor the capitalist system, but also more meso-level collective units such as cultural orders and social hierarchies.

During the 1980s and into the 1990s however, reactions towards the alleged structuralism of the above perspective formed part of a broader so-called "cultural turn" (Gronow, 1997; Warde, 1994, 2014) which strongly influenced research on consumption. The empirical study of different types of consumption was taken up across a broader range of disciplines than marketing, sociology and anthropology – e.g. cultural studies and media and communication studies. The cultural turn in studying consumption gained momentum within marketing, sociology and anthropology. It consisted in giving priority to the symbolic (and often discursive) cultural dynamics and experiential expressions of modern mass consumption activities. Theoretically, the term *consumer culture* was a programmatic part of the cultural turn, even giving name to a whole research program, Consumer Culture Theory, and establishing a journal, *Journal of Consumer Culture*. Empirically, there was a large growth in studies on detailed consumption activities, lifestyle and subculture, creative ways of engaging with consumer goods and services, semiotic meanings of material culture objects, and relations between consumption activities and consumer identities. The unit of analysis varied from the individual consumer to collective cultural dynamics.

But importantly, the cultural turn paved the way for consumption activities themselves being appreciated as meaningful and enjoyable, as well as being measured, categorized and criticized.

Much-quoted examples connected with this perspective are e.g. Colin Campbell's sociological analysis of consumers as modern hedonists (Campbell, 1987), Paul Willis' cultural studies description of symbolic consumption in youth culture (Willis, 1990), Elisabeth Hirschman and Morris Holbrook's article on hedonic consumption (Hirschman & Holbrook, 1982) and a book on postmodern consumer research in marketing (Hirschman & Holbrook, 1992). In the 1980s and early 1990s, postmodernist theorists in sociology regarded consumption as the central element in the formation of the arguably fluid and changeable self-identity of a consumer in the conditions of reflexive modernization (Bauman, 1988; Featherstone, 1991; Giddens, 1991). Equally important was the growth in amount and diversity of empirical studies and publications on consumption and consumers in their socio-cultural contexts, paving the way for the potential of conducting comparative research across different places.

Although disciplines defined consumer culture and cultural aspects of consumption differently, researchers from around the year 2000 began to argue that the cultural turn, despite its many empirical and theoretical achievements, also had neglected particular social dynamics in consumption, namely the more inconspicuous, practical, routine, embodied and material aspects of and conditions for consumption. The emergence of this fourth broad perspective on consumption has several labels, such as the practice turn or materiality turn, and has been particularly rooted in sociology and anthropology, but also critical marketing and cultural geography. Theoretically, there has been a focus on practices and arrangements into which consumption is seen as embedded. Empirically, there has been a growth in studies on routine consumption, flows of mundane conduct in and around consumption, and processes of reproduction and change of consumption patterns. A much-stressed assumption has been that the unit of analysis should not be the individual consumer.

An early example of this practice-informed perspective is the edited collection with empirical sociological studies of different forms of so-called "ordinary consumption" by Jukka Gronow and Alan Warde (2001), which worked as a precursor to Warde's programmatic article on practice theories and consumption (Warde, 2005). A new example could be Calvignac and Cochoy's ANT-inspired study of consumer logistics within marketing research (Calvignac & Cochoy, 2016).

All four broad perspectives on consumption co-exist today in various versions, and they are all represented in this handbook, if not directly, then in dialogue with some other approach. A huge field of consumer behavior research works with much more sophisticated assumptions about individual motives to consume than the traditional neo-liberal economistic perspective. In the field of economics, behavioral economics and economic psychology, in particular, have recently attracted public attention when explaining individual consumption. Moreover, neurosciences are increasingly deemed as a disciplinary field to turn to in order to get comprehensive insight of consumer behavior. This poses challenges to current research traditions of social sciences and marketing studies. Also, even if accounts of consumers within markets are critical and acknowledge the power of the capitalist system in creating needs and lifestyles, today's writing is not uni-dimensional; it weaves in both structural factors and the agency of consumers. Bourdieusian-inspired studies of social and cultural distinctions in consumption seem to be as popular as ever (possibly boosted by the practice turn). Consumer culture studies in many different versions are going strong, and empirical studies based on practice theories are spreading across disciplines. Hence, the field of consumption research has diversified as part of its multidisciplinary character as well as inside its contributing disciplines.

At the same time, some ideas seem to have caught on and become part of a certain mainstreaming across the four broad perspectives and the disciplines involved. First, it has become increasingly difficult to ignore, regardless of perspective or discipline, the analytical importance of social and cultural dynamics for the shaping of consumption. This also involves relating to societal consequences of consumption, such as environmental, health and inequality issues. Second, there seems to be recognition across perspectives and disciplines that consumption theoretically cannot be defined only as buying activities – although in individual studies, an operationalization of consumption still frequently turns out to be defined narrowly as buying or shopping. Third, across perspectives and disciplines, empirical studies of consumption phenomena tend to show that consumption is meaningful and many times enjoyable for consumers themselves.

A dialogical research field?

Other consumption researchers could or would have produced a different story across stories. In our view, it is less important exactly what the different perspectives are called or who makes the typology. The important point is that the field of consumption research is diversified. On the one hand, this can be viewed as a strength, because the research field sheds light upon many different angles of a highly complex social and cultural phenomenon. It would be a problem to have a field of consumption studies closed around one theoretical and methodological truism. On the other hand, if there is too little agreement and attempts at syntheses across perspectives, the research field can come across as weakly defined, because of the lack of clarity about core categories. Maybe the diversity of perspectives is inescapable, due to the dominance of multi-disciplinary consumption research? Diversity however, ought not necessarily be the same as doing our research and publication in separate silos, where we read and refer to only work within a single perspective.

To return to the main purpose of the handbook, the aim is to bring together and represent a state-of-the-art research collection covering the multiplicity of the consumption research field. By doing this, we hope to encourage all our colleagues and readers to consider each other's research *across* perspectives – be it termed consumption studies, consumer culture theory or consumer behavior research – rather than only staying in our theoretical, methodological and collegial comfort zones. We are certainly *not* hereby arguing that new trans-disciplinary consumption theory or studies ought to emerge. There are many difficulties involved in trans-disciplinary research, such as different if not contradictory or even incompatible theoretical assumptions and epistemological research practices, and the concept "trans-disciplinary" is invoked much too easily and empty of content in e.g. research applications. However, if we as consumption researchers do not show a degree of openness towards reflecting upon our own analytical assumptions, signs of potential syntheses in relation to core concepts of consumption will remain far away, even if this is what some researchers might wish for. Furthermore, knowing works across perspectives also enhances chances of establishing more comparative and systematic empirical studies of consumption.

If we, as consumption researchers, think that conceptual and analytical integration across perspectives or disciplines does not seem worthwhile, and we, as researchers, want to retain our multi-disciplinarity, we could at least refrain from attempting to patent our own perspective as *the* only or "correct" understanding of how consumption should be defined and researched. As consumption researchers, we will probably go on disagreeing on meta-theoretical discussions, but inside each of the empirical subfields, also represented in this handbook, we have to acknowledge and relate to the works of each other across perspectives. Otherwise, too much unnecessary re-invention of existing knowledge and categories of consumption will prevail, bringing cacophony rather than conceptual clarity in the diversity.

Thus, we recommend more academic dialogue across the multiplicity of perspectives and disciplines in consumption research for the purpose of heightening the quality of research. Yet, we are not calling for a theoretical and methodological omnivorousness for its own sake, rather for openness and dialogue, still being aware that different ontological and epistemological premises provide for different sorts of questions to be asked, problem framings and empirical solutions to research tasks. Thus, search for synergies and conversations among sub-fields of consumption studies do not mean an uncritical mix-and-match to please our deepest eclectic tastes. It does mean instead a substantial amount of academic self-reflection on one's own points of departure as well as affiliations of various kinds. In this vein, this handbook is a contribution to make visible and clearer such points of departure and affiliations to guide both the beginner and the mature researcher.

The contents of the handbook

This handbook consists of seven parts, each of which encompasses a subfield of consumption studies, which have some tentative coherence and common issues and themes tackled. Each section comes with a brief sub-theme-specific introduction encapsulating the main topics of each part. Here we only provide a bird's eye view of the whole handbook and rationale of its organization to ease the pathway for the reader.

Part I, *Theoretical and methodological perspectives on consumption*, demonstrates the kinds of questions that have been asked within consumption studies and theoretical and methodological concepts and tools – especially the more recent and innovative ones. Part II is entitled *Consumers and markets* and opens with chapters on how the market "interpellates" consumers via the ubiquitous processes of marketing and branding. Also, the authors look at hybrid and new forms of market activity, where established mechanisms are brought in question: prosumption and sharing economy. Part III, *Global challenges in consumption*, shifts attention away from the global North and advanced markets onto the tension between north and south, global and local, as well as onto emerging consumer societies of China, Brazil, Turkey and Russia. Part IV, *Politics and policies of consumption*, links two streams of thinking: firstly debates in political and ethical consumption focusing on social movements of consumers and their ethically and politically motivated consumption choices (or lack thereof); and secondly, current discussions on how various policy interventions can or should encourage and empower, or perhaps discipline, consumers to live more healthy, sustainable and economically sensible lives, as well as to protect individuals from the powers of the market. Part V, *Consumption and social divisions*, concentrates on how consumption creates divisions and how various social differences (e.g. income, gender, age, ethnicity) are embedded, at sometimes reinforced and at others downplayed in varying contexts. Part VI, *Contested consumption*, weaves together debates on how consumption has become challenged and critiqued on various grounds, be they related to sustainable development, health, morality, well-being or socially constructed taste. (Im)possibilities of environmental sustainability, as one of the most prominent research areas in today's consumption studies, are paid particular attention in this part. Consumption and the body is another tension-ridden terrain given attention in this section. A premise that unites these chapters is the starting point of consumers' everyday lives in which embodied and material aspects are prominent alongside cognitive ones. Part VII, *Culture, media and consumption*, embraces the vibrant field of cultural consumption studies in the broad sense, covering themes like lifestyle, leisure, luxury and fashion as well as more particular cultural preferences as manifestations of various socio-cultural contexts and consumption patterns. As many of the latter have become mediatized in today's world, specific chapters are devoted to ICTs and digitalized consumption that have become important pillars of lifestyle creation.

Potential futures

Consumption is paradoxical: It is ubiquitous in today's world, where most goods and services for the bulk of the world's population have some relation to mass production and markets. And if we follow Alan Warde's rather wide definition of consumption in which purchasing is not the only means to consume, it is quite hard to imagine human activity that does not entail any consumption. Undoubtedly this makes the aims of consumption researchers more complex. Another twist is added by a wide strand of everyday life research in which consumption is not conceived of as anything specific, a stand-alone phenomenon, but rather a thread that permeates everyday routines and daily life, while the processes of acquiring, appropriating, appreciating and disposing are not viewed as consumption per se. Everyday contexts entail many different activities which overlap and are shifted between such as working, parenting, socializing and acting as citizens. In today's societies, social participation and full "citizenship" mean a wide range of everyday consumption activities, both in work and leisure. Also private relations inside families and between generations are mediated through consumption, from everyday purchases and communication to major life events, cultural traditions and rituals. In high-involvement shopping situations or when something goes wrong with goods and services, consumer rights, in particular, have to be exercised. Thus consumption is everywhere, which makes studying consumption and intervening into consumption for policy purposes exceedingly difficult and elusive, or "unmanageable" as Gabriel and Lang (2015) have aptly put it.

We believe that the field of consumption research has to preserve its strong theoretical, multidisciplinary foundations, but simultaneously to remain open and receptive to new concepts and theoretical approaches across the intersecting disciplines and perspectives. Consumption research should also expand and deepen its themes, e.g. consumption at workplace in addition to home, consumption by collectivities in addition to individuals, vicarious and virtual consumption in addition to personal and material consumption, consumption perhaps not fully done, but at least mediated by non-humans (e.g. robots, technologies, animals, plants, inorganic matter) in addition to humans, consumption under several constraints, limits and shocks (e.g. sustainability, sufficiency, frugality, crisis and disruption), among others. Due to the major environmental, political, economic, and social crises, and deepening inequalities, it is likely that the research focus will shift more and more into global and cross-cultural issues. The development of ICTs and the digitalization of everyday life will make profound changes in consumption, production and marketing in the future as well as enlarge the channels of marketing and spaces of consumption. Also, the conversations and cooperation between consumption researchers (from anthropology and sociology to marketing) and various actors within the markets and political fields have to be loud and clear, since all societal challenges analyzed and tackled by and with the help of the research community have a bearing on consumption.

The diversification of consumption and the complexity of consumption contexts also pose challenges to research methodologies. The mixed-method approach of the future does not only mean mixtures of survey or register data and ethnographic methods. The relevance of the well-established methods will definitely not vanish, but the consumption studies of the future must also adapt more innovative methods such as big data techniques, different online analyses, process analysis and experimental research. However, as noted above, this is not necessary solely for the sake of methodological pluralism, but rather to utilize more sensitive ways to tackle the increasingly complex global and local challenges associated with consumption.

References

Arnould, E. & Thompson, C. J. (2005). Consumer culture theory (CCT): Twenty years of research, *Journal of Consumer Research*, 31, 868–82.

Askegaard, S. & Linnet, J. T. (2011). Towards an epistemology of consumer culture theory: Phenomenology and the context of context, *Marketing Theory*, 11, 381–404.

Baudrillard, J. (1998, first published 1971). *The Consumer Society: Myths and Structures*. London: Sage.

Bauman, Z. (1988). *Freedom*. Milton Keynes: Open University Press.

Bauman, Z. (1998). *Work, Consumerism, and the New Poor*. Milton Keynes: Open University Press.

Bauman, Z. (2007). *Consuming Life*. Cambridge: Polity Press.

Bourdieu, P. (1984). *Distinction: A Social Critique of the Judgement of Taste*. London: Routledge and Kegan Paul.

Calvignac, C. & Cochoy, F. (2016). From "market agencements" to "vehicular agencies": Insights from the quantitative observation of consumer logistics, *Consumption Markets & Culture*, 19, 133–47.

Campbell, C. (1987). *The Romantic Ethic and the Spirit of Modern Consumption*. Oxford: Basil Blackwell.

Cappellini, B., Marshall, D. & Parson, E. (Eds) (2016). *The Practice of the Meal: Food, Families and the Market Place*. Abingdon: Routledge.

Douglas, M. & Isherwood, B. (1980). *The World of Goods: Towards and Anthropology of Consumption*. Harmondsworth: Penguin Books.

Featherstone, M. (1990). Perspectives on consumer culture, *Sociology*, 24, 5–22.

Featherstone, M. (1991). *Consumer Culture and Postmodernism*. London: Sage.

Fine, B. & Leopold, E. (1993). *The World of Consumption*. London: Routledge.

Friedman, M. (1957). The permanent income hypothesis. In M. Friedman (Ed), *A Theory of the Consumption Function*. Princeton: Princeton University Press, 20–37.

Gabriel, Y. & Lang, T. (2015). *The Unmanageable Consumer*. London: Sage.

Giddens, A. (1991). *Modernity and Self-Identity*. Cambridge: Polity Press.

Gronow, J. (1997). *The Sociology of Taste*. London: Routledge.

Gronow, J. (2015). Main currents in recent consumer studies. In P. Strandbakken & J. Gronow (Eds), *The Consumer in Society*. Oslo: Abstrakt Forlag, 39–58.

Gronow, J. & Warde, A. (2001). *Ordinary Consumption*. London: Routledge.

Hirschman, E. C. & Holbrook, M. B. (1982). Hedonic consumption: Emerging concepts, methods and propositions, *Journal of Marketing*, 46 (3), 92–101.

Hirschman, E. C. & Holbrook, M. B. (1992). *Postmodern Consumer Research*. Newbury Park, CA: Sage.

Horkheimer, M. & Adorno, T. (1981, first published 1944). *The Dialectic of Enlightenment*. New York: Continuum.

Klein, J. T. (1990). *Interdisciplinarity: History, Theory & Practice*. Detroit: Wayne State University Press.

Lury, C. (2011). *Consumer Culture*. Cambridge: Polity Press.

McGregor, S. L. T. & Murnane, J. A. (2010). Paradigm, methodology and method: Intellectual integrity in consumer scholarship, *International Journal of Consumer Studies*, 34, 419–27.

Miller, D. (1998). *A Theory of Shopping*. Cambridge: Polity.

Paterson, M. (2006). *Consumption and Everyday Life*. London: Routledge.

Ratneshwar, S. & Mick, D. G. (2005). *Inside Consumption: Consumer Motives, Goals and Desires*. London: Routledge.

Ritzer, G. & Slater, D. (2001). Editorial, *Journal of Consumer Culture*, 1, 5–8.

Sassatelli, R. (2007). *Consumer Culture: History, Theory, and Politics*. London: Sage.

Slater, D. (1997). *Consumer Culture and Modernity*. Cambridge: Polity Press.

Soper, K. & Trentmann, F. (2008). *Citizenship and Consumption*. Houndmills: Palgrave.

Sulkunen, P., Holmwood, J., Radner, H. & Schulze, G. (Eds) (1997). *Constructing the New Consumer Society*. Houndmills: Macmillan.

Trentmann, F. (2016). *The Empire of Things: How We Became a World of Consumers, from the Fifteenth Century to the Twenty-First*. London: Allen Lane/Penguin.

Warde, A. (1994). Consumption, identity-formation and uncertainty, *Sociology*, 28 (4), 877–98.

Warde, A. (2005). Consumption and theories of practice, *Journal of Consumer Culture*, 5, 131–53.

Warde, A. (2010). *Consumption*. London: Sage.

Warde, A. (2014). After taste: Culture, consumption and theories of practice, *Journal of Consumer Culture*, 14, 279–303.

Williams, R. (1987). *Keywords*. London: Fontana.

Willis, P. (1990). *Common Culture: Symbolic Work at Play in the Everyday Cultures of the Young*. Buckingham: Open University Press.

Part I

Theoretical and methodological perspectives on consumption

2
Consumer culture theory

Russell Belk

Despite the label, consumer culture theory (CCT) is not a theory. Rather, it is the name given to a field studying consumption from an ethnographic, conceptual, and qualitative perspective. An article by Arnould and Thompson (2005) summarized twenty years of research in this area that had been published in the *Journal of Consumer Research* (*JCR*). They define CCT as research that "focuses on the experiential and sociocultural dimensions of consumption that are not plainly accessible through experiments, surveys, or database modeling" (p. 870). They note that as a result CCT research tends to be qualitative and pluralistic, often using methods such as observation and depth interviews.

In 2006 the first annual CCT conference was held. These conferences spawned an association: the Consumer Culture Theory Consortium. It currently has several hundred members and several thousand followers of CCT's Facebook site. As Arnould and Thompson (2007) wrote in a subsequent paper, a more accurate label would have been Consumer Culture Theoretics, inasmuch as the intent was merely to provide a framing device or "brand name" for a then loosely associated group of researchers who challenged the positivist information-processing experimental paradigm that dominated *JCR*.

Historical emergence of consumer culture theory

While the label of CCT emerged with the 2005 invited article by Arnould and Thompson, the field has a longer heritage. For Levy (2006), qualitative consumer research can be traced to Jean Brillat-Savarin's (1825) *Physiologie du gout*. Fullerton (1990) cites Paul Lazarsfeld's ninety-eight-page 1933 report, "Shoe Buying in Zurich." Others point to Haire's (1950) "shopping list" projective measure employed to study consumer resistance to adopting instant coffee (e.g. Kassarjian & Goodstein, 2010). Desmond (2013), Levy (2006), and Tadajewski (2010, 2013) all highlight Ernest Dichter's controversial work with "motivation research" in the 1950s as a predecessor to CCT work. Levy (2006) also emphasizes the qualitative work of Chicago-based Social Research, Inc., started in 1946 and in which he was a principle.

But the 1980s and early 1990s were the formative period for qualitative consumer research by scholars who were primarily located within American university business and communication schools. Previous consumer research within these schools was (and remains) dominated by quantitative survey and experimental studies. In 1980 Elizabeth Hirschman and Morris Holbrook (1980) hosted a conference on consumer aesthetics and symbolic consumption and included some of their conceptual work on experiential consumption that would subsequently appear in *JCR* (Holbrook & Hirschman, 1982) and the *Journal of Marketing* (Hirschman & Holbrook, 1982). In 1984 Michael Solomon organized a conference on fashion that included qualitative papers by Rebecca Holman, Grant McCracken, Ernest Dichter, Dennis Rook, Michael Solomon, Morris Holbrook, and other qualitative pioneers.

As described in Belk (1991b, 2014), a group of nearly two-dozen of us launched a major qualitative consumer research project with a 1985 pilot study at a swap meet (Belk, Sherry & Wallendorf, 1988) and a 1986 summer-long data collection effort that involved travelling across the US in a rented van, observing and interviewing consumers, aided by still and video cameras (Belk, Wallendorf & Sherry, 1989). It was dubbed the Consumer Behavior Odyssey. In addition to the journal papers, the Odyssey produced a number of conference papers and a book containing sixteen papers from participants (Belk, 1991a). Moreover, it helped to precipitate the field of Consumer Culture Theory, as Bode and Østergaard (2013) observe:

> The history of CCT, starting with the Symbolic Consumer Behavior Conference and building up towards the Consumer Behavior Odyssey can be told as a history of manifestos, rousing the troops, getting attention in the field of consumer research and heralding new phases in the social drama of the 1980s and 1990s
>
> *(p. 178).*

The Odyssey project is now widely seen to be a critical event in the formation of what came to be called CCT (e.g. Askegaard & Scott, 2013; Bradshaw & Brown, 2007; Thompson, Arnould & Giesler, 2013).

Arnould and Thompson (2005) also sought to correct some then-dominant myths about the field by those in other sub-disciplines studying consumers. Three interrelated myths were singled out:

1. Consumer culture theorists study specific contexts with a descriptive goal rather than specific concepts with an interpretive and theoretical goal.
2. CCT researchers employ a particular methodology rather than taking a pluralistic approach often involving using multiple methods in a single study.
3. CCT research involves "a sphere of creative expression, voyeurism, entertaining esoterica, and sonorous introspection of limited relevance to consumer research's broader theoretical projects or the pragmatic interests of managers of public policy makers."

(p. 870).

Besides introducing the CCT label and classifying prior CCT research in *JCR* into overarching categories, an avowed purpose of the Arnould and Thompson (2005) paper was to deconstruct these myths and thereby forge a more accurate understanding of the nature of the papers gathered under the CCT heading. They argued that formative CCT work in the 1980s was opposed to managerially relevant research because at the time this was seen to equate with a rational choice paradigm and with emphasis being placed on purchase behavior rather than consumption activity. However, the article ignored the anti-establishment ethos that was characteristic of the era and that was a part of early qualitative researchers' opposition to the establishment positivist information processing research orientation that was dominant at the time and that still prevails to a large degree in the Association for Consumer Research and *JCR*.

Debates and divisions within consumer culture theory

In an effort to counter the anti-business image of CCT, Arnould and Thompson (2005) pointed to a number of CCT studies that exemplify relevance for managers (e.g. Deighton & Grayson, 1995; Fournier, 1998; Holt, 2002, 2004; Levy, 1959; Luedicke, Thompson & Giesler, 2010; Muñiz & O'Guinn, 2000; Peñaloza, 2000; Price & Arnould, 1999; Price, Arnould & Tierney, 1995; Schouten & McAlexander, 1995; Sherry & McGrath, 1989). There have also been numerous subsequent CCT papers that display a seemingly purposeful attempt to negate the image of the field as producing papers of limited relevance to managerial concerns (e.g. Arnould, 2007; Arsel & Bean, 2013; Bernthal, Crockett & Rose, 2005; Cayla & Arnould, 2013; Cayla & Eckhardt, 2008; Dolbec & Fischer, 2015; Giesler, 2012; Humphreys & Thompson, 2014; Izberk-Bilgen, 2012; Martin & Schouten, 2009; Thompson & Arsel, 2004). This pro-business bias has, in turn, provoked a backlash by those CCT scholars who see such efforts as reinforcing a neoliberal capitalist agenda without considering alternative economic systems or problems with such an establishment agenda (e.g. Cova, Maclaran & Bradshaw, 2013; Earley, 2014; Fitchett, Patsiaouras & Davies, 2014). This side of the debate within the CCT field is able to point to work that takes a more critical perspective on global corporate practices and systems (e.g. Kozinets & Handelman, 2004; Murray, 2002; Varman & Belk, 2008, 2009; Varman, Skålén & Belk, 2012; Varman, Vikas & Belk, 2015; Zwick, Bonsu & Darmody, 2008).

A further criticism that might be addressed to the foundational article by Arnould and Thompson (2005) is that it pursues a modernist taxonomic project of naming and classifying the substantive focus of CCT studies. Their initial classification scheme listed four categories of CCT research: "the sociohistoric patterning of consumption," "mass-mediated marketplace ideologies and consumer interpretive strategies," "consumer identity projects," and "marketplace cultures." To this they subsequently added four other categories: "the ontological conception of culture as distributed networks," "the politics of consumption," "consumer marketing theoretics," and "regional cultural theoretics" (Arnould & Thompson, 2015). This nominal approach is a descriptive exercise. This is not to suggest that taxonomic efforts are necessarily mere ordering efforts; there are more productive and generative theoretical taxonomies like Holt's (1995) classification of consumption practices. But the classifications of Arnould and Thompson serve more to mark out a playing field in a descriptive and triumphalist manner.

In part too, this taxonomic approach illustrates and reinforces an unfortunate trend in the field to follow what might be regarded as the theory-of-the-month club. That is, it celebrates and encourages faddish trends comprised of importing theories and concepts from other fields, one after another, in an effort to appear progressive. Theoretical anchors for recent cyclical fads have included Bourdieu's Cultural Capital Formation, Foucault's Self-Governance, Latour's Actor Network Theory, Deleuze and Guattari's Assemblage Theory, Bourdieu's Taste Regimes, Scott's and Meyer's Institutional Theory, Bourdieu's Practice Theory, and others. These are all great theories, but they are all borrowed.

A more productive approach might be to outline some of the more original theoretical and conceptual contributions of consumer culture theory. They include, for example, possession attachment (Belk, 1992a; Kleine & Baker, 2004; Watkins & Molesworth, 2012), experiential consumption (Carù & Cova, 2007; Hirschman & Holbrook, 1982; Holbrook & Hirschman, 1982; Lindgreen, Vanhamme & Beverland, 2009), extended self (Ahuvia, 2005; Belk, 1988a, 2013a), consumer-brand relationships (Belk & Tumbat, 2005; Cova, Kozinets & Shankar, 2007; Fournier, 1998; Muñiz & O'Guinn, 2001; Schouten & McAlexander, 1995; Schroeder & Salzer-Mörling, 2006), consumer desire (Belk, Ger & Askegaard, 2003), gift-giving (Otnes & Beltramini, 1996; Sherry, 1983), sharing (Bardhi & Eckhardt, 2012; Belk, 2010), agapic love (Belk & Coon, 1993; Giesler, 2006), historical consumption (Belk, 1992b; Karababa & Ger, 2011), death (O'Donohoe & Turley, 2000; Turley, 1995), cool (Belk, Tian & Paavola, 2010; Warren & Campbell, 2014; Wooten, 2006), the experience of place (Hirschman, Ruvio & Belk, 2012; Sherry, 1988; Sherry, Kozinets, Storm, Duhachek, Nuttavuthisit & DeBerry-Spence, 2001), benign envy (Belk, 2011a; van de Ven, Zeelenberg & Pieters, 2011), and consumption rituals (Belk, 1987; McCracken, 1988; Otnes & Lowrey, 2003; Otnes & Pleck, 2009; Rook, 1985). These are rich theoretical treatments of concepts where CCT researchers have made unique contributions. Rather than theories in search of an application to consumption, these papers can be seen as consumption phenomena and concepts in search of a theoretical understanding. If the CCT perspective is to be about generating rather than applying theories, this sort of research seems a far more productive pursuit than merely borrowing perspectives from the theory-of-the-month club.

In addition, the approach of describing CCT research by Arnould and Rose (2015) and Arnould and Thompson (2005, 2015) champions empirical work rather than conceptual and theoretical work. A number of recent critiques in marketing and consumer research have documented the decline of conceptual work within consumer research and lamented the decrease in original generative formulations that has resulted (e.g. MacInnis, 2004, 2011; Yadav, 2010, 2014). Indeed, it is through conceptual contributions, including some of the work cited in the previous paragraph, that CCT has the best chance of emerging as a foundational discipline rather than a field that merely applies concepts and theoretical perspectives developed in other social sciences. It is likely that in the long run, the contribution of CCT research will not be in how well it is able to apply concepts and theories developed in other disciplines, but instead in what it is able to offer in terms of conceptual and theoretical contributions of its own.

Another emerging area of disagreement within CCT is with regard to the focus on the individual versus the culture as a way of understanding consumption. Askegaard and Linnet (2011), Moisander, Peñaloza and Valtonen (2009), and Moisander, Valtonen and Hirsto (2009) called for a non-individual unit of analysis. They also called for at least partially reconciling CCT with classical economics and psychology "emphasizing the rational, universal, individual consumer" (Moisander, Valtonen & Hirsto, 2009, p. 8), notwithstanding the epistemological and ontological opposition of this perspective to most CCT work. Another paper picking up this theme is Thompson, Arnould and Giesler (2013), who argue that a shift has already taken place to "a multilayered CCT heteroglossia that features a broad range of theorizations integrating structural and agentic levels of analysis" (p. 149). They go on to suggest that:

> In conjunction with their valorization of the autotelic, noninstrumental, esthetic, symbolic, and experiential aspects of consumption, humanist/experientialist discourses also accepted the methodological individualistic assumption that the consumer subject is the fundamental unit of analysis. Accordingly, many of the foundational CCT studies, discursively constructed consumer culture as a kind of symbolic supermarket in which autonomous consumers made selections, chose identities, and extended their core selves through the ownership and use of material goods. . . . Holbrook and Hirschman's (1982) treatise on the experiential aspects of consumption – and their companion piece on hedonic consumption (Hirschman & Holbrook, 1982) – and the high profile consumer behavior Odyssey (Belk, 1991[a]; Belk et al., 1988, 1989) stand as key inflection points through which these methodological individualist motifs crystallized as an organized discursive system
>
> *(p. 156).*

They argue that instead, CCT should be more attuned to cultural context, class, and gender formations, although there is no reason that these perspectives should be seen as opposed to one another or as mutually exclusive.

A core CCT theme

Many of the debates and alternative perspectives highlighted in the preceding section can be seen as struggling to define the substantive focus of CCT as being consumer culture rather than the consumer. While this was the focus of only a minority of the studies cited by Arnould and Thompson (2005, 2015), it is nevertheless an implicit part of the arguments that CCT should be more about culture, more critical, and more macro in focus. It is consistent with the call for more work on political economies, institutional theory, and cultural, conceptual, and theoretical perspectives. Clearly, a number of CCT papers have explicitly addressed the origin and effects of consumer cultures from historical and cultural perspectives (e.g. Belk, 1988b, 1992b, 1995, 1996, 2007, 2010, 2013b, 2014; Belk, Groves & Østergaard, 2000; Belk, Wallendorf, Sherry & Holbrook, 1991; Belk & Zhao, 1987, 2012; Ger & Belk, 1999, 2005; Karababa & Ger, 2011; Kimura & Belk, 2004; Minowa, Khomenko & Belk, 2011; Mish, 2007; Nguyen & Belk, 2012; Otnes & Pleck, 2009; Sobh, Belk & Gressel, 2014; Speck & Peterson, 2010; Sredl, 2007; Strizhakova, Coulter & Price, 2008; Tse, Belk & Zhou, 1989; Varman & Belk, 2008; Zhao & Belk, 2008a, 2008b).

Consumer cultures are composed of people who define themselves and often gain a sense of community through their consumption practices. Thus a CCT focus on consumer culture can also be found in studies of global, local, and hybrid consumption practices (Askegaard, Arnould & Kjeldgaard, 2005; Ger & Belk, 1996; Kjeldgaard & Askegaard, 2006), religious aspects of consumption (Belk, 1987; Belk et al., 1991; Belk & Wallendorf, 1990; Bonsu & Belk, 2010; Izberk-Bilgin, 2012; Muñiz & Schau, 2005; Rinallo, Scott & Maclaren, 2013), philosophies of consumption and non-consumption (Belk, 2011b; Schor, 2011), and the adoption of stigmatized consumption practices (Luedicke, Thompson & Giesler, 2010; Sandikci & Ger, 2010). Furthermore, studies of consumption communities and related practices (Alon & Brunel, 2007; Arsel & Bean, 2013; Belk, 2013a; Belk & Tumbat, 2005; Canniford, 2011; Molesworth & Denegri-Knott, 2012; Muñiz & O'Guinn, 2000; Schouten & McAlexander, 1995; Thomas, Price & Schau, 2013; Wood & Solomon, 2009), sharing (Bardhi & Eckhardt, 2012; Belk, 2010), gift-giving (Belk & Coon, 1993; Otnes & Beltramini, 1996; Sherry, 1983), and striving to become a part of consumer cultures (Üstüner & Holt, 2007, 2010; Varman & Belk, 2012) can all be seen to focus on constructing and participating in communities organized through and focusing on consumption.

It might be expected that studies published in the *Journal of Consumer Culture* (*JCC*) are also all about consumer culture. Indeed, there are a number of such studies in this journal focusing on the origin and effects of consumer cultures from historical and cultural perspectives (e.g. Bauman, 2007; Caldwell, 2004; Campbell, 2005; Delhaye, 2006; Van Bavel, 2003) and on collateral perspectives (e.g. Alexander & Ussher, 2012; Goldstein-Gidoni, 2005; Gong, 2014; Guschwan, 2012; Hilton, 2004; Keller, 2005; Luthar, 2006; Possamaï, 2002; Trentmann, 2007, 2009). However, with rare exceptions (e.g. Thompson, 2011), these authors are unlikely to consider themselves CCT researchers, as judged by their lack of participation in CCT conferences and their affiliations with other organizations and disciplines. Thus, while *JCC* has published consumer culture papers with some frequency, the focus on communities and cultures defined by consumption practices has, ironically, been a more dominant, if not defining, characteristic of CCT research.

Gaps and directions for future CCT research

Given its dominant focus on consumer culture from historical and cultural perspectives, CCT can do much more from a historical perspective. More work is needed on both the long-term global origins of consumer cultures and shorter-term phenomena such as the shift from communism and socialism to capitalist systems since the late 1970s. Similarly, while some CCT work is emerging from the less affluent and emerging or newly affluent worlds, the majority of CCT research is still conducted in North America, Europe, Australia, and New Zealand. Cultures that are rapidly changing economically, ethnically, and culturally are especially fertile areas in which to study the impact of consumer culture.

With its focus on construction and participation in consumption-based communities, CCT should also be poised to further research online and virtual communities. Again, there have been some studies of social media participation, but much remains to be done in this area. For example, our basic relationship with possessions likely changes as these possessions become digital rather than material. The same is true of our relationships with other people as an increasing amount of interpersonal communication moves from face-to-face to online. The accelerating pace of technological change is another factor that has received only scant attention. The others with whom we interact may soon include humanoid robots and artificially enhanced cyborgs, yet these developments and related reformulations of what it means to be human, animal, or machine have received very little research attention from CCT scholars.

A further glaring gap and opportunity for future CCT scholarship is in doing more conceptual and theoretical work rather than merely empirical studies. As noted earlier, there have been several recent calls for more conceptual work on consumption in the face of declining proportions of journal pages devoted to concepts and theory development (MacInnis, 2004, 2011; Yadav, 2010, 2014). These papers as well as a recent analysis of the most influential articles in forty years of *JCR* show that CCT research and conceptual papers draw the greatest number of citations and have received a heavily disproportionate number of awards (Wang, Bendle, Mai & Cotte, 2015). If there is ever to be a cashing out of the premise that CCT research is about the pursuit of theory, then such work is essential.

References

Ahuvia, A. (2005). Beyond the extended self: Loved objects and consumer identity narratives. *Journal of Consumer Research*, 32, 171–184.

Alexander, S. & Ussher, S. (2012). The voluntary simplicity movement: A multinational survey analysis in theoretical context. *Journal of Consumer Culture*, 12, 66–86.

Alon, A. & Brunel, F. (2007). Dynamics of community engagement: The Role of interpersonal communicative genres in online community evolutions. In R. Belk & J. F. Sherry, Jr. (Eds.), *Consumer culture theory: Research in consumer behavior, Vol. 11* (pp. 371–400). Bingley, UK: Elsevier.

Arnould, E. (2007). Service-dominant logic and consumer culture theory: Natural allies in an emerging paradigm. In R. Belk & J. F. Sherry, Jr. (Eds.), *Consumer culture theory, Vol. 11* (pp. 57–78). Bingley, UK: Elsevier.

Arnould, E. & Rose, A. (2015). Mutuality: Critique and substitute for Belk's 'sharing.' *Marketing Theory*, 16, 75–99.

Arnould, E. & Thompson, C. (2005). Consumer culture theory (CCT): Twenty years of research. *Journal of Consumer Research*, 31, 868–882.

Arnould, E. & Thompson, C. (2007). Consumer culture theory (and we really mean *theoretics*): Dilemmas and opportunities posed by an academic branding strategy. In R. Belk & J. F. Sherry, Jr. (Eds.), *Consumer culture theory, research in consumer behavior, Vol. 11* (pp. 3–22). Amsterdam: Elsevier.

Arnould, E. & Thompson, C. (2015). Introduction: Ten years gone (and beyond). In A. Thyroff, J. Murray, & R. Belk (Eds.), *Consumer culture theory, research in consumer behavior, Vol. 17* (pp. 1–21). Bingley, UK: Elsevier.

Arsel, Z. & Bean, J. (2013). Taste regimes and market-mediated practice. *Journal of Consumer Research*, 39, 899–917.

Askegaard, S., Arnould, E. & Kjeldgaard, D. (2005). Postassimilationist ethnic consumer research: Qualifications and extensions. *Journal of Consumer Research*, 32, 160–170.

Askegaard, S. & Linnet, J. (2011). Towards an epistemology of consumer culture theory: Phenomenology and the context of context. *Marketing Theory*, 11, 381–404.

Askegaard, S. & Scott, L. (2013). Consumer culture theory: The ironies of history. *Marketing Theory*, 13, 139–147.

Bardhi, F. & Eckhardt, G. (2012). Access-based consumption: The case of car-sharing. *Journal of Consumer Research*, 39, 881–898.

Bauman, Z. (2007). Collateral casualties of consumerism. *Journal of Consumer Culture*, 7, 147–158.

Belk, R. (1987). A child's Christmas in America: Santa Claus as deity, consumption as religion. *Journal of American Culture*, 10 (1) Spring, 87–100.

Belk, R. (1988a). Possessions and the extended self. *Journal of Consumer Research*, 15, 139–168.

Belk, R. (1988b). Third world consumer culture. In E. Kumcu & A. F. Firat (Eds.), *Research in marketing: Marketing and development: Toward broader dimensions* (pp. 103–127). Greenwich, CT: JAI Press.

Belk, R. (Ed.) (1991a). *Highways and buyways: Naturalistic research from the consumer behavior odyssey.* Provo, UT: Association for Consumer Research.

Belk, R. (1991b). The history and development of the consumer behavior odyssey. In R. Belk (Ed.), *Highways and buyways: Naturalistic research from the consumer behavior odyssey* (pp. 1–12). Provo, UT: Association for Consumer Research.

Belk, R. (1992a). Attachment to possessions. In I. Altman & S. Low (Eds.), *Human Behavior and environment: Advances in theory and research, Vol. 12, place attachment* (pp. 37–62). New York: Plenum Press.

Belk, R. (1992b). Moving possessions: An analysis based on personal documents from the 1847–1869 Mormon migration. *Journal of Consumer Research*, 19, 339–361.

Belk, R. (1995). *Collecting in a consumer society*. London: Routledge.

Belk, R. (1996). Hyperreality and globalization: Culture in the age of Ronald McDonald. *Journal of International Consumer Marketing*, 8, 23–38.

Belk, R. (2007). Consumption, mass consumption, and consumer culture. In G. Ritzer (Ed.), *Blackwell encyclopedia of sociology* (pp. 737–746). Oxford: Blackwell.

Belk, R. (2010). Sharing. *Journal of Consumer Research*, 36, 715–734.

Belk, R. (2011a). Benign envy. *Academy of Marketing Science Review*, 1, 117–134.

Belk, R. (2011b). Philosophies for less consuming societies. In K. Ekström & K. Glans (Eds.), *Beyond the consumption bubble* (pp. 205–220). London: Routledge.

Belk, R. (2013a). Extended self in a digital world. *Journal of Consumer Research*, 40, 477–500.

Belk, R. (2013b). The sacred in consumer culture. In D. Rinallo, L. Scott, & P. Maclaren (Eds.), *Spirituality and consumption* (pp. 69–80). London: Routledge.

Belk, R. (2014). The labors of the odysseans and the legacy of the odyssey. *Journal of Historical Research in Marketing*, 6, 379–404.

Belk, R. & Coon, G. (1993). Gift-giving as agapic love: An alternative to the exchange paradigm based on dating experiences. *Journal of Consumer Research*, 20, 393–417.

Belk, R., Ger, G. & Askegaard, S. (2003). The fire of desire: A multi-sited inquiry into consumer passion. *Journal of Consumer Research*, 30, 311–325.

Belk, R., Groves, R. & Østergaard, P. (2000). Aboriginal consumer culture. In R. Belk (Ed.), *Research in Consumer Behavior, Vol. 9* (pp. 1–45). Greenwich, CT: JAI Press.

Belk, R., Sherry, J. F. Jr. & Wallendorf, M. (1988). A naturalistic inquiry into buyer and seller behavior at a swap meet. *Journal of Consumer Research*, 14, 449–470.

Belk, R., Tian, K. & Paavola, H. (2010). Consuming cool: Behind the unemotional mask. In R. Belk (Ed.), *Research in Consumer Behavior, Vol. 12* (pp. 183–208). Bingley, UK: Emerald.

Belk, R. & Tumbat, G. (2005). The cult of Macintosh. *Consumption, Markets and Culture*, 8, 205–217.

Belk, R. & Wallendorf, M. (1990). The sacred meanings of money. *Journal of Economic Psychology*, 11, 35–67.

Belk, R., Wallendorf, M. & Sherry, J. F. Jr. (1989). The sacred and the profane in consumer behavior: Theodicy on the odyssey. *Journal of Consumer Research*, 16, 151–138.

Belk, R., Wallendorf, M., Sherry, J. F. Jr. & Holbrook, M. (1991). Collecting in a consumer culture. In R. Belk (Ed.), *Highways and buyways: Naturalistic research from the consumer behavior odyssey* (pp. 178–215). Provo: Association for Consumer Research.

Belk, R. & Zhou, N. (1987). Learning to want things. *Advances in Consumer Research*, 14, 478–481.

Belk, R. & Zhao, X. (2012). Advertising and consumer culture in old Shanghai versus contemporary China. In S. Okazaki (Ed.), *Handbook of research in international advertising* (pp. 137–157). Cheltenham, UK: Edward Elgar.

Bernthal, M., Crockett, D. & Rose, R. (2005). Credit cards as lifestyle facilitators. *Journal of Consumer Research*, 32, 130–145.

Bode, M. & Østergaard, P. (2013). The wild and wacky worlds of consumer oddballs': Analyzing the manifestary context of consumer culture. *Marketing Theory*, 13, 175–192.

Bonsu, S. & Belk, R. (2010). Marketing a new African god: Pentecostalism and material salvation in Ghana. *International Journal of Nonprofit and Voluntary Sector Marketing*, 15, 305–323.

Bradshaw, A. & Brown, S. (2007). Scholars who stare at goats: The collaborative circle cycle in creative consumer research. *European Journal of Marketing*, 42, 1396–1414.

Brillat-Savarin, J. (1825 [1989]). *Gastronomy as a fine art*. R. E. Anderson, trans., London: Chatto & Windus.

Caldwell, M. (2004). Domesticating the French fry: McDonald's and consumerism in Moscow. *Journal of Consumer Culture*, 4, 5–26.

Campbell, H. (2005). Chicano lite: Mexican-American consumer culture. *Journal of Consumer Culture*, 5, 297–333.

Canniford, R. (2011). A typology of consumption communities. In R. Belk, K. Grayson, A. Muñiz, & H. Schau (Eds.), *Research in Consumer Behavior, Vol. 13*. (pp. 57–76). Bingley, UK: Emerald.

Carù, A. & Cova, B. (Eds.) (2007). *Consuming experience*. London: Routledge.

Cayla, J. & Arnould, E. (2013). Ethnographic stories for Market Learning. *Journal of Marketing*, 77, 1–16.

Cayla, J. and Eckhardt, G. (2008). Asian brands and the shaping of a transnational consumption community. *Journal of Consumer Research*, 35, 216–230.

Cova, B., Kozinets, R., & Shankar, A. (Eds.) (2007). *Consumer tribes*. London: Routledge.

Cova, B., Maclaran, P. & Bradshaw, A. (2013). Rethinking consumer culture theory from the postmodern to the communist horizon. *Marketing Theory*, 13, 213–225.

Deighton, J. & Grayson, K. (1995). Marketing and seduction: Building exchange relationships by managing social consensus. *Journal of Consumer Research*, 21, 660–676.

Delhaye, C. (2006). The development of consumption culture and the individualization of female identity: Fashion discourse in the Netherlands 1880–1920. *Journal of Consumer Culture*, 6, 82–115.

Desmond, J. (2013). *Psychoanalytic accounts of consuming desire: Hearts of Darkness*. London: Palgrave Macmillan.

Dolbec, P.Y. & Fischer, E. (2015). Refashioning at field? Connected consumers and instsitutional dynamics in markets. *Journal of Consumer Research*, 41, 1447–1468.

Earley, A. (2014). Connecting contexts: A Badiouian epistemology for consumer culture theory. *Marketing Theory*, 14, 73–96.

Fitchett, J., Patsiaouras, F. & Davies, A. (2014). Myth and ideology in consumer culture theory. *Marketing Theory*, 14, 495–506.

Fournier, S. (1998). Consumers and their brands: Developing relationship theory in consumer research. *Journal of Consumer Research*, 24, 343–373.

Fullerton, R. (1990). The art of marketing research: Selections from Paul F. Lazarsfeld's 'Shoe buying in Zurich' (1933). *Journal of the Academy of Marketing Science*, 18, 319–327.

Ger, G. & Belk, R. (1996). I'd like to buy the world a Coke: Consumptionscapes of the 'less affluent world'. *Journal of Consumer Policy*, 19, 271–304.

Ger, G. & Belk, R. (1999). Accounting for materialism in four cultures. *Journal of Material Culture*, 4, 183–204.

Ger, G. & Belk, R. (2005). Emergence of consumer cultures: A cross-cultural and (art) historical comparison. In *The future of marketing's past: Proceedings of the 12th conference on historical analysis and research in marketing (CHARM)*, 337.

Giesler, M. (2006). Cybernetic gift giving and social drama: A netnography of the Napster file-sharing community. In M. Ayers (Ed.), *Cybersounds: Essays on virtual music culture* (pp. 21–56). New York: Peter Lang.

Giesler, M. (2012). How doppelgänger brand images influence the market creation process: Longitudinal insights from the rise of Botox cosmetic. *Journal of Marketing*, 76, 55–68.

Goldstein-Gidoni, O. (2005). The production and consumption of 'Japanese culture' in the global cultural market. *Journal of Consumer Culture*, 5, 155–179.

Gong, R. (2014). From grassroots to digital ties: A case study of a political consumerism movement. *Journal of Consumer Culture*, 14, 343–364.

Guschwan, M. (2012). Fandom, brandom and the limits of participatory culture. *Journal of Consumer Culture*, 12, 19–40.

Haire, M. (1950). Projective techniques in marketing research. *Journal of Marketing*, 14, 649–656.

Hilton, M. (2004). The legacy of luxury: Moralities of consumption since the 18th century. *Journal of Consumer Culture*, 4, 101–123.

Hirschman, E. & Holbrook, M. (Eds.) (1980). *Symbolic consumer behavior: Proceedings of the conference on consumer esthetics and symbolic consumption*. New York, NY: Association for Consumer Research and New York University Institute for Retail Management.

Hirschman, E. & Holbrook, M. (1982). Hedonic consumption: Emerging concepts, methods, and propositions. *Journal of Marketing*, 46, 92–101.

Hirschman, E., Ruvio, A. & Belk R. (2012). Exploring space and place in marketing research: Excavating the garage. *Marketing Theory*, 12, 269–289.

Holbrook, M. & Hirschman, E. (1982). The experiential aspects of consumption: Consumer fantasies, feelings, and fun. *Journal of Consumer Research*, 9, 132–140.

Holt, D. (1995). How consumers consume: A typology of consumption practices. *Journal of Consumer Research*, 22, 1–16.

Holt, D. (2002). Why do brands cause trouble? A dialectical theory of consumer culture and branding. *Journal of Consumer Research*, 29, 70–90.

Holt, D. (2004). *How brands become icons: The principles of cultural branding*. Cambridge, MA: Harvard Business School Press.

Humphreys, A. & Thompson, C. (2014). Branding disaster: Re-establishing trust through the ideological containment of systematic risk anxieties. *Journal of Consumer Research*, 39, 877–910.

Izberk-Bilgin, E. (2012). Infidel brands: Unveiling alternative meanings of global brands at the nexus of globalization consumer culture, and Islamism. *Journal of Consumer Research*, 39, 663–687.

Karababa, E. & Ger, G. (2011). Early modern Ottoman coffeehouse culture and the formation of the consumer subject. *Journal of Consumer Research*, 37, 737–760.

Kassarjian, H. & Goodstein, R. (2010). The emergence of consumer research. In P. Maclaran, M. Saren, B. Stern, & M. Tadajewski (Eds.), *The Sage handbook of marketing theory* (pp. 58–73). London: Sage.

Keller, M. (2005). Needs, desires and the experience of scarcity. *Journal of Consumer Culture*, 5, 65–85.

Kimura, J. & Belk, R. (2004). The process of assimilation of foreign consumer culture: Reproduction of culture in Japan (in Japanese). *Journal of Marketing and Distribution*, September, npn.

Kjeldgaard, D. & Askegaard, S. (2006). The globalization of youth culture: The global youth segment as structures of common difference. *Journal of Consumer Research*, 33, 231–247.

Kleine, S. & Baker, S. (2004). An integrative review of material possession attachment. *Academy of Marketing Science Review*, 1, 1–35.

Kozinets, R. & Handelman, J. (2004). Adversaries of consumption: Consumer movements, activist, and ideology. *Journal of Consumer Research*, 31, 691–704.

Levy, S. (1959). Symbols for sale. *Harvard Business Review*, 37, 117–124.

Levy, S. (2006). History of qualitative research methods in marketing. In R. Belk (Ed.), *Handbook of qualitative research methods in marketing* (pp. 3–16). Cheltenham, UK: Edward Elgar.

Lindgreen, A., Vanhamme, J. & Beverland, M. (Eds.) (2009). *Memorable customer experiences: A research anthology*. Farnham, UK: Gower.

Luedicke, M., Thompson, C. J. & Giesler, M. (2010). Consumer identity work as moral protagonism: How myth and ideology animate brand-mediated moral conflict. *Journal of Consumer Research*, 36, 1016–1032.

Luthar, B. (2006). Remembering socialism: On desire, consumption and surveillance. *Journal of Consumer Culture*, 6, 229–259.

MacInnis, D. (2004). Where have all the papers gone? Reflections on the decline of conceptual articles. *Association for Consumer Research News*, 75, 1–3.

MacInnis, D. (2011). A framework for conceptual contributions in marketing. *Journal of Marketing*, July, 136–154.

Martin, D. & Schouten, J. (2009). Engineering a mainstream market for sustainability: Inside Wal-Mart's perfect storm. In J. Sherry & E. Fischer (Eds.), *Explorations in consumer culture theory* (pp. 150–168). New York: Routledge.

McCracken, G. (1988). *Culture and consumption: New approaches to the symbolic character of consumer goods and activities*. Bloomington, IN: Indiana University Press.

Minowa, Y., Khomenko, O. & Belk, R. (2011). Social change and gendered gift giving rituals: A historical analysis of Valentine's Day in Japan. *Journal of Macromarketing*, 31, 44–56.

Mish, J. (2007). A heavy burden of identity: India, food, globalization, and women. In R. Belk & J. F. Sherry, Jr. (Eds.), *Consumer culture theory: Research in consumer behavior, Vol. 11* (pp. 165–186). Oxford: Elsevier.

Moisander, J., Peñaloza, L. & Valtonen, A. (2009). From CCT to CCC: Building consumer culture community. In J. F. Sherry, Jr. & E. Fischer (Eds.), *Explorations in consumer culture theory* (pp. 7–33). New York: Routledge.

Moisander, J., Valtonen, A. & Hirsto, H. (2009). Personal interviews in consumer Culture research – Post-structuralist challenges. *Consumption, Markets and Culture*, 12, 329–348.

Molesworth, M. & Denegri-Knott, J. (Eds.) (2012). *Digital virtual consumption*. London: Routledge.

Muñiz, A. & O'Guinn, T. (2000). Brand communities. *Journal of Consumer Research*, 27, 412–432.

Muñiz, A. & Schau, H. (2005). Religiosity in the Abandoned Apple Newton Brand Community. *Journal of Consumer Research*, 31(4), 737–747.

Murray, J. (2002). The politics of consumption: A re-Inquiry on Thompson & Haytko's (1997). 'Speaking of Fashion.' *Journal of Consumer Research*, 29, 427–440.

Nguyen, D. & Belk R. (2012). Vietnamese weddings: From Marx to market. *Journal of Macromarketing*, 32, 109–120.

O'Donohoe, S. & Turley, D. (2000). Dealing with death: Art, mortality and the marketplace. In S. Brown & A. Peterson (Eds.), *Imagining marketing: Art, aesthetics and the avant-garde* (pp. 86–106). London: Routledge.

Otnes, C. & Beltramini, R. (Eds.) (1996). *Gift giving: A research anthology*. Bowling Green, OH: Bowling Green State University Popular Press.

Otnes, C. & Lowrey, T. (Eds.) (2003). *Contemporary consumption rituals: A research anthology*. Mahwah, NJ: Lawrence Erlbaum.

Otnes, C. & Pleck, E. (2009). *Cinderella dreams: The allure of the lavish wedding*. Berkeley, CA: University of California Press.

Peñaloza, L. (2000). The commodification of the American west: Marketers' production of cultural meanings at a trade show. *Journal of Marketing*, 64, 82–109.

Possamai, A. (2002). Cultural consumption of history and popular culture in alternative spiritualities. *Journal of Consumer Culture*, 2, 197–218.

Price, L. L. & Arnould, E. (1999). Commercial friendships: Service provider-client relationships in social context. *Journal of Marketing*, 63, 38–56.

Price, L. L., Arnould, E. & Tierney, P. (1995). Going to extremes: Managing service encounters and assessing provider performance. *Journal of Marketing*, 59, 83–97.

Rinallo, D., Scott, L. & Maclaran, P. (Eds.), (2013). *Consumption & spirituality*. London: Routledge.

Rook, D. (1985). The ritual dimension of consumer behavior. *Journal of Consumer Research*, 12, 252–264.

Sandikci, Ö. & Ger, G. (2010). Veiling in style: How does a stigmatized practice become fashionable? *Journal of Consumer Research*, 37, 15–36.

Schor, J. (2011). *True wealth: How and why millions of Americans are creating a time rich, ecologically light, small-scale, high-satisfaction economy*. New York: Penguin.

Schouten, J. & McAlexander, J. H. (1995). Subcultures of consumption: An ethnography of the new bikers. *Journal of Consumer Research*, 22, 43–61.

Schroeder, J. & Salzer-Mörling, M. (2006). *Brand culture*. London: Routledge.

Sherry, J. F., Jr. (1983). Gift giving in anthropological perspective. *Journal of Consumer Research*, 10, 157–168.

Sherry, J. F., Jr. (Ed.) (1988). *ServiceScapes: The concept of place in contemporary markets*. Chicago: NTC Business Books.

Sherry, J. F., Jr., Kozinets, R., Storm, D., Duhachek, A., Nuttavuthisit, K. & DeBerry-Spence, B. (2001). Being in the zone: Staging retail theater and ESPN Zone Chicago. *Journal of Contemporary Ethnography*, 30, 465–510.

Sherry, J., Jr. & McGrath, M.A. (1989). Unpacking the holiday presence: A comparative ethnography of two gift stores. In Elizabeth Hirschman (Ed.), *Interpretive Consumer Research* (pp. 148–167). Provo, UT: Association for Consumer Research.

Sobh, R., Belk, R. & Gressel, J. (2014). Mimicry and modernity in the Middle East: Fashion invisibility and young women of the Arab Gulf. *Consumption, Markets and Culture*, 17, 392–412.

Speck, S. & Peterson, T. (2010). Socialization of adult and young consumers into materialism: The roles of media and church in Peru. In R. Belk (Ed.), *Research in consumer behavior* (pp. 133–160). Bingley, UK: Emerald.

Sredl, K. (2007). Consumption and class during and after state socialism. In R. Belk & J. F. Sherry, Jr. (Eds.), *Consumer culture theory: Research in consumer behavior, Vol. 11* (pp. 197–205). Oxford: Elsevier.
Strizhakova, Y., Coulter, R. & Price, L. (2008). Branded products as a passport to global citizenship: Perspectives from developed and developing countries. *Journal of International Marketing*, 16, 57–85.
Tadajewski, M. (2010). Contesting motivation research: Intellectual primacy and interpretive consumer research. In S. Schwarzkopf & R. Gries (Eds.), *Great persuader: Ernest Dichter and the making of postwar consumer culture* (pp. 91–106). London: Palgrave.
Tadajewski, M. (2013). Promoting the consumer society: Ernest Dichter, the cold war and FBI. *Journal of Historical Research in Marketing*, 5, 192–211.
Thomas, T., Price, L. & Schau, H. (2013). When differences unite: Resource dependence in heterogeneous consumption communities. *Journal of Consumer Research*, 39, 1010–1033.
Thompson, C. (2011). Understanding consumption as political and moral practice: Introduction to the special issue. *Journal of Consumer Culture*, 11, 139–144.
Thompson, C., Arnould, E. & Giesler, M. (2013). Discursivity, difference, and disruption: Genealogical reflections on the consumer culture theory heteroglossia. *Marketing Theory*, 13, 149–174.
Thompson, C. & Arsel, Z. (2004). The Starbucks brandscape and consumers' (anticorporate) experiences of glocalization. *Journal of Consumer Research*, 31, 631–642.
Trentmann, F. (2007). Citizenship and consumption. *Journal of Consumer Culture*, 7, 147–158.
Trentmann, F. (2009). Crossing divides: Consumption and globalization in history. *Journal of Consumer Culture*, 9, 187–220.
Tse, D., Belk, R. & Zhou, N. (1989). Becoming a consumer society: A longitudinal and cross-cultural content analysis of print advertisements from Hong Kong, People's Republic of China and Taiwan. *Journal of Consumer Research*, 15, 457–472.
Turley, D. (1995). Dialogue with the departed. *European Advances in Consumer Research*, 2, 10–13.
Üstüner, T. & Holt, D. (2007). Dominated consumer acculturation: The social construction of poor migrant women's consumer identity projects in a Turkish squatter community. *Journal of Consumer Research*, 34, 41–56.
Üstüner, T. & Holt, D. (2010). Toward a theory of status consumption in less industrialized countries. *Journal of Consumer Research*, 37, 37–56.
Van Bavel, R. (2003). Understandings of consumerism in Chile. *Journal of Consumer Culture*, 3, 343–362.
Van de Ven, N., Zeelenberg, M. & Pieters R. (2011). The envy premium in product evaluation. *Journal of Consumer Research*, 37, 984–998.
Varman, R. & Belk, R. (2008). Weaving a web: Subaltern consumers, rising consumer culture, and television. *Marketing Theory*, 8, 227–252.
Varman, R. & Belk, R. (2009). Nationalism and ideology in an anti-consumption movement. *Journal of Consumer Research*, 36, 686–700.
Varman, R. & Belk, R. (2012). Consuming postcolonial shopping malls. *Journal of Marketing Management*, 28, 62–84.
Varman, R., Skålén, P. & Belk, R. (2012). Conflicts at the bottom of the pyramid: Profitability, poverty alleviation, and neoliberal governmentality. *Journal of Public Policy and Marketing*, 31, 19–35.
Varman, R., Vikas, R. & Belk, R. (2015). Status, caste, and markets in a changing Indian village. *Journal of Consumer Research*, 42, 472–498.
Wang, X., Bendle, N., Mai, F. & Cotte, J. (2015). The journal of consumer research at 40: A historical analysis. *Journal of Consumer Research*, 42, 93–108.
Warren, C. & Campbell, M. (2014). What makes things cool? How autonomy influences perceived coolness. *Journal of Consumer Research*, 41 (2), 543–563.
Watkins, R. & Molesworth, M. (2012). Attachment to digital virtual possessions in videogames. In R. Belk, S. Askegaard, & L. Scott (Eds.), *Research in consumer behavior, Vol. 4* (pp. 153–170). Bingley, UK: Emerald.
Wood, N. & Solomon, M. (Eds.) (2009). *Virtual social identity and consumer behavior*. Armonk, NY: M. E. Sharpe.
Wooten, D. (2006). From labeling possessions to possessing labels: Ridicule and socialization among adolescents. *Journal of Consumer Research*, 188–198.
Yadav, M. (2010). Enhancing theory development in marketing. *Academy of Marketing Science Review*, 4, 1–4.
Yadav, M. (2014). The decline of conceptual articles and implications for knowledge development. *Journal of Marketing*, 74, 1–19.

Zhao, X. & Belk, R. (2008a). Advertising consumer culture in 1930s' Shanghai: Globalization and localization in yue fen pai. *Journal of Advertising*, 37, 45–56.

Zhao, X. & Belk, R. (2008b). Politicizing consumer culture: Advertising's appropriation of political ideology in China's social transition. *Journal of Consumer Research*, 35, 231–244.

Zwick, D., Bonsu, S. & Darmody, A. (2008). Putting consumers to work: Co-creation and new marketing governmentality. *Journal of Consumer Culture*, 8, 163–196.

3

Studying consumption through the lens of practice

Alan Warde, Daniel Welch and Jessica Paddock

Introduction

In this chapter we describe how the application of current popular theoretical interest in the concept of practice has affected the study of consumption.

Although the study of consumer behavior, grounded in psychology and economics, got underway earlier, the interpretive social sciences (anthropology, sociology, human geography, etc.) were slow to engage in empirical study of consumption. Prior to the 1980s normative macro-level critique was the dominant mode of engagement among sociologists; for instance, the Frankfurt School's analysis of mass culture and Veblen's notion of conspicuous consumption were frequently reiterated. The cultural turn in the humanities and social sciences from the 1970s had a huge impact on contemporary understanding of consumption. There was an explosion of interest in issues of lifestyle, identity, meanings, experience and taste. This led to more extensive empirical research. Consumption came to be celebrated rather than denigrated, underpinned by a robust defense of the virtues of popular culture and a proclamation of the value of the opportunities delivered by mass production for populations. Spearheaded by cultural studies, research concentrated on cultural communication, both on institutions like the media and the shopping mall, and also on how consumption expressed self-identity and group belonging. Most research was conducted in the light of cultural theories which, opposing both the utilitarian and the classical sociological norm-orientated models of social action, typically highlighted symbolic and cognitive structures and found the locus of the social in those structures. Consequently, while never totally eclipsed, the unequal distribution of resources and Bourdieusian concerns with distinction were minimized. Furthermore, the cultural turn, in emphasizing the role of the symbolic aspects of communication, tended to support a model of consumption that foregrounded the 'reflexive individualism' of the consumer (Warde, 2014).

The development of theories of practice

Despite the burgeoning volume of empirical research, towards the end of the twentieth century social scientists seemed to get little closer to a satisfactory general or synthetic theory of consumption. Recently, however, a sustained attempt was made to commandeer theories of practice as a potential source of re-orientation and synthesis.

Davide Nicolini (2012) offers the most comprehensive review of the current state of theories of practice which social scientists might employ. He notes the origins of the concept in the social philosophy of antiquity, but pays attention primarily to contemporary variants. His book is directed primarily to applications in the field of work and organizations, and hence some of the approaches which he identifies have no current significance for the analysis of consumption. Nevertheless, his classification of approaches is a sound starting point. He identifies six discrete bodies of theorizing: a praxeological approach, which he associates with Pierre Bourdieu and Anthony Giddens; the 'communities of practice' tradition associated with Etienne Wenger; cultural historical activity theory (CHAT) deriving from Marxism and Lev Vygotsky; ethnomethodology, which seeks to account for the practical accomplishment of everyday life; the ontological theory of the philosopher Theodore Schatzki, which draws on Heidegger and Wittgenstein; and theories of discourse deriving from the work of Michel Foucault. These are in many ways different and it is therefore hard to say what theories of practice hold in common. Nicolini suggests that their implications for methodology and empirical investigation are similar. Schatzki (2001), asking himself the same question, said, 'Practice accounts are joined in the belief that such phenomena as knowledge, meaning, human activity, science, power, language, social institutions and historical transformation occur within and are aspects of components of the field of practices' (2001, p. 2). He adds that a central core conception is that practices are embodied, materially mediated arrays of human activity centrally organized around shared practical understanding which depend on shared skills or understandings (2001, pp. 2–3). The scale of the problem of integration is, however, indicated by Schatzki's remark that practice theory has proved appealing for proponents of post-functionalism, post-structuralism and post-humanism! Of Nicolini's six approaches, neither Wenger nor Vygotsky have had much impact on studies of consumption, but the others crisscross the field.

Bourdieu and Giddens operated with post-Marxist, primarily sociological, theories of praxis or social praxeology. Practice theories were one source of critique of the dominant structural-functionalist framework which had pervaded American sociology and which emphasized value consensus as the basis of social order. Bourdieu and Giddens were authors dealing with central problems of social theory, most clearly the unresolved oppositions between structure and agency, and holism and individualism (see Rouse, 2007). Bourdieu's *Distinction* (1984), his major study relevant to consumption, was couched in terms of a theory of practice, but the empirical analysis used concepts of habitus and capitals to understand taste and the distribution of cultural capital (see Warde, 2016). Giddens's early work (1984) made practice central to his theory of structuration, but later work discussing lifestyles (1991) tended to emphasize choice rather than the constraints presented by practices. The legacy of these two authors is very visible in subsequent empirical research on consumption.

Somewhat less evident is the legacy of Foucault, who was an important influence on the wider 'cultural turn'. The appropriation of his work in the Anglophone world initially tended towards what Reckwitz (2002a) terms 'textualism', in which the linguistic is privileged. More recently, and especially following the publication in 2004 of his late College de France lectures, the 'Birth of Biopolitics' and 'Security, Territory, Population' (Foucault, 2004a, 2004b), there has been a growing appreciation of his distinctive approach. In his later works he was especially concerned with heterogeneous apparatuses of discourses, practices and institutional arrangements ('dispositifs') and the congruence of practices of self-conduct and techniques of power in 'governmentality' (Collier, 2009).

A third set of resources for the renewal of theories of practice was found in SSK (the sociology of scientific knowledge) and STS (science and technology studies). Both contested dominant views of the nature of pure and applied science. SSK offered a radical critique of the philosophy of scientific knowledge. Observational study of the mundane processes of scientific investigation and reportage poured considerable doubt on idealized Enlightenment representations of both the procedures of investigation and status of science (Latour and Woolgar, 1986). While previous standpoints assumed that technologies were firmly subordinated to the pursuit of human objectives, STS emphasized that technologies shape, steer and script people's activities. Problematizing voluntarist accounts, technologies can be seen not only to empower individuals, but also to take over projected futures, to determine what is worth accomplishing, and to prescribe ends to which human endeavor should be directed. The strong version of the account, in Actor Network Theory (ANT), is controversially post-humanist. ANT demands symmetrical treatment of persons and things. Agency is not solely the prerogative of people, but a function of intricate networks of objects and persons wherein people's relationship to their material possessions, and their uses of things, is at least as important as their symbolic meanings. The increasing attention paid to the materiality of the objects which circulate as commodities in modern economies allows things themselves to be traced, their effects isolated, their biographies written, and their contribution to everyday life, for example in cementing social relationships and organizing household activity, to be documented. Material culture studies, promoted most notably by Daniel Miller (e.g. 2008), further elaborated the importance of things for studies of consumption specifically.

The end of the 1990s saw self-conscious and programmatic concentration of academic endeavor around the concept of practice. While Bourdieu, Giddens and Foucault – the first generation of the revival (Bräuchler and Postill, 2010) – accorded the concept a foundational role in explaining social phenomena, they did not hold as a central intellectual objective the advancement of a theory of practice. A subsequent generation was more attentive to theory development. A collection of essays, *The Practice Turn in Contemporary Theory* (Schatzki, Knorr Cetina and Savigny, 2001), was symptomatic of a determination to operate with theories of practice for their own sake. Theodore Schatzki, joint editor of this collection of essays, clearly sought an alternative to dominant forms of cultural analysis. The essays in the collection indicated some new theoretical contributions to the practice approach. STS was prominent, but the collection also drew a good deal on ethnomethodology and to some degree the sociology of culture. In association, two intricate and detailed volumes by Schatzki (1996, 2002) presented an extended social ontology in which practices are the locus of the social. His *The Site of the Social* (2002) was addressed to showing how his Wittgensteinian account could be relevant for social sciences. He came to have a major impact on studies of consumption partly because he was championed in two essays by Andreas Reckwitz.

Reckwitz (2002a, 2002b) located theories of practice in relation to dominant schools of cultural analysis, arguing primarily that the latter's focus on symbolic aspects failed to appreciate the material attributes of social life. This hinted at how the profound entanglement of consumption with culture might be unwound. Signs of discontent with the preponderance of attention in the study of consumption to culture were already in evidence. Campbell (1994) and Falk and Campbell (1997) argued against the tendency to treat consumption solely as a process of communication. Gronow and Warde (2001) coined the term 'ordinary consumption' to direct attention to those episodes of consumption which conveyed almost no symbolic meaning. Extrapolating the specific implications of this account of practice theory for consumption, Warde (2005) suggested that consumption might be better approached as a moment in practices rather than as acts of purchase. In particular, by observing social differentiation among the ways in which people engaged in practices it became possible to reconnect with sociological themes of distinction and collective identity.

Debates within theories of practice

It is hard to specify exactly what different theories of practice have in common beyond a commitment to understanding social order and action as transpiring primarily through the medium of social practices (Schatzki, 2001). Put briefly, they challenge the role of individual decision making and ideas of consumer choice, and the underpinning alternative models of the sovereign and expressive consumer. As Warde (2014, p. 286) says, theories of practice emphasize different aspects of action usually obscured by cultural analysis by underscoring routine and sequencing (Southerton, 2013), dispositions, practical consciousness and embodiment (Wilhite and Wallenborn, 2013), as well as the materials implicated in consumption (Shove, Pantzar and Watson, 2012). The appropriateness of these emphases has generated significant general debate. In the analysis of consumption, where Giddens, Bourdieu and Schatzki have had most impact on empirical investigation, a number of debates are currently live.

The legacy of Giddens and Bourdieu

Giddens (1984) was initially found appealing because his clear and elegant account of the duality of structure appeared to solve the structure–agency problem. His emphasis on routinization and on the role of practical rather than discursive consciousness provided a background against which to explain inconspicuous, regularized and repetitive episodes of consumption. However, Giddens did not pursue further themes about practice after his major contribution in 1984, and actually he became more interested in the expressive aspects of lifestyles, stressing reflexive and voluntary engagement. Moreover, his concepts rarely seemed to throw new light on explanatory problems. So while both Shove (2004) and especially Spaargaren (2003) and Spaargaren and Vliet (2000) wrote instructively about issues of sustainable consumption against the framework of structuration theory, few of their valuable insights seemed to be directly attributable to the theory. Gradually, as studies of consumption began to recognize more roles for the body, habits and material devices, the categories of structuration theory had decreasing purchase. The associated dilemmas of reflexivity and routine, structure and agency, and practical and discursive consciousness remained relevant nevertheless.

Bourdieu was better equipped to deal with issues of habit and embodiment. His key concept of habitus stands for a set of, not necessarily conscious, predispositions and dispositions which people acquire as a function of their social location and experience (see Bourdieu, 1977 and 1990). Critics charge habitus with a tendency to pander too much to processes of reproduction rather than change, but it nevertheless captures vital aspects of the capacity for people mostly to be able to continue to operate fluently and confidently on a daily basis without need to pause to deliberate or make conscious decisions. It captures many automatic, repetitive and distracted aspects of daily conduct which subtend patterns of consumption. Bourdieu also typically emphasizes the role of collective actors as a source of dynamism, and locates them and their practices within the 'games' that define stakes and allocate rewards within social fields. His concepts make it easier to think of practices as entities rather than simply an aggregate of discrete performances. Many applications of practice theory go no further than describing performances, thus ignoring the ways in which practices may be organized and coordinated. Whether practices are best considered entities, just such a strong version is proposed by Schatzki (1996, 2002) and Shove et al. (2012), or whether they are merely the sum of multiple performances is one point of dispute. Methodologically, how best to access performances and practices is a subsidiary controversy.

Neither Giddens nor Bourdieu paid a great deal of attention to technologies, infrastructures, objects and machines, which they treated as instruments employed by human agents going about their daily practice. However, many in the early twenty-first century propose that the objects and devices of material culture exert a significant determining, and partially autonomous, role in patterns of behavior. How much power to attribute to material artefacts is now a major source of disagreement. The post-humanist strand of practice theory and much analysis in STS find that machines script performances. The strong Actor Network Theory version proposes that people and things should be treated in an equivalent manner when explaining social processes (Latour, 2005). Schatzki (2002) is skeptical of the post-humanist position and addresses material phenomena by making a distinction between practices and material arrangements, thereby to signify the importance of objects and technology. Who or what exercises agency – individuals, collectivities, objects – remains an active field of debate.

Competence or teleology?

An important contribution of contemporary theories of practice for the study of consumption has been to understand the organization of human activity as nexuses of generic types of components (e.g. Schatzki, 1996, 2002; Shove and Pantzar, 2005; Shove et al., 2012; Warde, 2005). Such a conceptualization of the heterogeneous arrays of ideational, discursive, material, embodied and affective elements that compose practices typically places them into discrete conceptual categories. Schatzki (2002, p. 86) conceives of practices as being made up of 'practical understandings' ('know how', understanding 'how to go on' with an activity); 'rules' (explicit directions, instructions, admonishments etc.); 'teleoaffective structures' (normatively ordered arrays of ends, orientations, and affective engagements); and 'general understandings', which are common to many practices and condition the manner in which practices are carried out. Shove et al.'s (2012) widely reproduced model offers three elements, 'meanings', 'competences' and 'materials'. Models of generic components do much useful conceptual work and have afforded methodological and analytical innovation (see Browne, Pullinger, Medd and Anderson, 2013; Halkier and Jensen, 2011; Halkier, Martens and Katz-Gerro, 2011). Equally, however, such schemas inevitably inflect understandings of praxis *per se*. Shove et al.'s (2012) foregrounding of 'competence' tends to occlude the end-orientation of activity (teleology), by emphasizing the competent performance of practice as an end in itself. Schatzki's (2002) highlighting of 'teleoaffective structure', by contrast, emphasizes ends and purposes as the prime axis of praxis, as well as affective and motivational engagement (cf. Schatzki, 2010). Schatzki's category 'general understandings' also gestures towards the conditioning of practices by discursive formations that possess their own forms of organization exogenous to those practices (Welch and Warde, 2016).

The contrast between Shove et al.'s (2012) emphasis on competence and Schatzki's (2002, 2010) emphasis on teleology reveals different orientations towards the ends of practices. A focus on the competence of performance draws our attention to the practice as an end in itself. For some kinds of practice, perhaps particularly those readily thought of as skills, including many enthusiast or leisure activities pertinent to consumption (e.g. skateboarding, Nordic walking, hula-hooping), the emphasis on an internal orientation to competent performance may be appropriate. The performance of skateboarding, for example, may be orientated purely towards the end of developing skill as a skateboarder. However, there are many forms of activity where the practice is a means to another end rather than being the end in itself. Ends external to the specific practice are often simultaneously the object of multiple practices conjoined through the pursuit of that end. For example, practices of listening to music and following fashion, along with the adoption of a particular argot and engagement in specific types of leisure activity, may conjoin in the heterotelic pursuit of subcultural identity. A useful distinction can therefore be made between two kinds of orientation: autotelic (activity having an end, purpose or meaning not apart from itself) and heterotelic (having an end, purpose or meaning outside itself). These orientations are not mutually exclusive, nevertheless, for subcultural members may get aesthetic enjoyment from music while skilled skateboarding can afford kudos amongst peers.

Collective activity and politics

Considering the orientations of practices also helps us marshal a practice-theoretical account of purposive collective activity. The long history of consumer movements, where 'the consumer' has been mobilized in wider social and political fields, indicates the broad range of collective projects pertinent to consumption (Hilton, 2009; Trentmann, 2008, 2010). Studies of brand management within a broadly practice-theoretical framework reveal understandings of 'the consumer' as active co-producer of value and posit consumption as an economically productive activity, often framed through the Foucauldian concept of 'governmentality' (e.g. Arvidsson, 2007; Zwick, Donsu and Darmoddy, 2008). Parallel notions of governmentality appear also in the analysis of sustainable consumption (e.g. Rumpala, 2011) and accounts critical of the 'responsibilisation of the consumer' (e.g. Barnett, Clarke, Cloke and Malpass, 2011).

Governance projects also affect the integrity and autonomy of practices. Contemporary projects of governance often construct socio-technical objects, through (increasingly digital) processes of monitoring, feedback and statistical aggregation, which orient everyday practices, public discourse and institutional-organization arrangements. Shove et al. (2012, p. 110) see the socio-technical object of 'obesity' as 'simultaneously reproduced in "micro" and "macro" forms as data recorded on such humble instruments as bathroom scales are added, analysed and aggregated' into the datasets from which the World Health Organization formulates policy. Hence does moralizing public discourse find its way back to the bathroom scales.

The interconnection of practices

A further pressing issue for practice-theoretical accounts is how practices relate to one another. If the social world is nothing but practices, understanding their interaction is vital. One can consider how much autonomy any practice exerts. Some practices are heavily dependent on the organization of others. They may be effectively subordinated to others, or highly inter-dependent within larger configurations or fields (e.g. economic, material, temporal, spatial). Also, collective projects frequently configure multiple practices towards a common end. Consequently, some practices will hold greater determining power than others for particular social phenomena. The scheduling and location of working practices, for example, strongly determines eating practices. However, exogenous temporal factors will exert less pressure on the consumption-related practices of enthusiast groups, which have relative autonomy from such institutional pressures. Whilst the scheduling of ballroom dancing or battle re-enactment will inevitably be subject to wider societal temporal patterns, endogenous factors play a greater role in explaining their trajectories.

Applications of theories of practice to consumption

The substantial differences at the general theoretical level among competing schools often matter rather less at the operational level when employing concepts in empirical analysis. The insights of practice theory have, to date, been applied to a number of research areas in consumption including food preparation and eating (Halkier, 2009; Jackson, 2015; Warde, 2016), recreational enthusiasms (Arsel and Bean, 2013; Pantzar and Shove, 2010; Spaargaren, Osteveer and Loeber, 2013) and listening to music (Magaudda, 2011). Attention is paid to the humdrum and functional properties of things, which Reckwitz (2002a) had complained were often neglected. Mundane activities like washing bodies and clothes (Shove, 2004), gardening (Hitchings, 2007), heating and cooling (Shove and Walker, 2014), using electronic devices (Røpke, Christensen and Jensen, 2010) and waste disposal (Evans, 2011) require generic commodities like water and electricity which are invisible to paradigms concerned with symbolic display and the presentation of self, and yet have much to do with environmental degradation. These raise issues of the mitigation of environmental effects which require changed patterns of consumption.

It is to this topic of sustainable consumption that we turn (see also chapter 30) in order to illustrate selectively how practice theory has been operationalized in empirical research (cf. Welch and Warde, 2015). We delineate three areas of focus – socio-technical evolution, temporal ordering, and the direct critique of a dominant policy paradigm.

First, in response to an external critique deeming practice theory weak when explaining social change, some research now goes beyond attention to micro-scale everyday life phenomena. Advocating a 'systems of practice' approach, Watson (2012) illustrates interaction between socio-technical systems and practice performances by considering interventions that could affect transition towards decarbonized transport. The key focus is the role of technology, materials and artefacts in reshaping elements of practice and how they connect with others (Shove and Spurling, 2013; Spurling, McMeekin, Shove, Southerton and Welch, 2013). In such fashion, Hand, Shove and Southerton (2005) explain the evolution of private showering through innovations in plumbing, heating and electrification. Novel technologies and infrastructures have thus enabled new ideas of comfort, cleanliness and convenience (Shove, 2003). Similar studies account for the domestic uptake of electric irons and washing machines (Gram-Hanssen, 2011), lighting (Jensen, 2013), mechanical cooling (Shove, Walker and Brown, 2014), cooking appliances (Truninger, 2011) and even low-temperature washing of laundry (Yates and Evans, 2016).

What each of these examples has in common in their empirical accounts of practice transformation is their concentration on technologies, artefacts and materials. This is not to say they afford greater power to these. Shove et al. (2012) argue that change and stability is best understood by how three elements of a practice are related, and in turn, how practices are related to each other. Home cooking, showering and driving each require materials (ovens, mixers, water pipes, cars and roads), competences (techniques, skills and practical knowledge) and meanings (aspirations, ideas and symbolic meaning). What may look like the diffusion of Nordic walking in Northern European countries is in fact a localized reinvention of 'doing walking' with a new artefact, the Nordic walking stick (Shove and Pantzar, 2005). At the next level, practices are dependent on their connection with others. Cooking and eating rely upon synchronization with working and travelling practices, not to mention the performances of other social actors, both proximate and distant.

Second, Southerton, Díaz-Méndez and Warde (2012) explain cross-cultural variation and the importance of understanding the temporal order of practices through a study of the timing of eating events in Spain and the UK. For commensality to occur, eating events must synchronize with the rhythms and routines of other practices. Temporality matters similarly to laundry where flows and sequences of activities in sorting, washing, drying, preparing and finally storing clean laundry are important. Underscoring these examples is the strength of habit and routine (Warde and Southerton, 2012), which are similarly studied in practices of eating (Warde, 2016), food growing in urban gardens (Veen, Derkzen and Visser, 2014), home energy consumption (Gram-Hanssen, 2011), control of ambient indoor workplace temperatures (Hitchings, 2011) and showering (Browne et al., 2013). The social patterning of routines and rhythms points not only to their steadfastness but, under the right circumstances, their potential to be unlocked (Paddock, 2015), for the crossing points of practices may offer the most suitable opportunity for intervention.

Third, despite internal tensions within practice theory, it is generally agreed that empirical cases challenge the foundations of contemporary policy interventions aimed at changing consumer behavior. Novel approaches to policy intervention arise from frustration with 'the ABC' – attitude, behavior, choice – model (Shove, 2010; Welch, 2016). For example, the information deficit approach underpinning use of smart-energy monitors in the home is too simple, for making energy visible does not account for the dynamism of practices that demand energy (Hargreaves, Nye and Burgess, 2013). Strengers and Maller (2015) cite further examples extending from mobilities and low-carbon housing to the divestment of domestic goods. Such approaches typically neglect the ways in which the practices of domestic life are entangled with one another (Ozaki and Shaw, 2014). Crosbie and Guy (2008), examining changing household lighting practices, conclude that policies aimed at promoting energy-efficient lighting would benefit from enlisting support from wider industry stakeholders. Echoing this advice, while championing a practice theoretical approach to designing policy interventions, Vihalemm, Keller and Kiisel (2015) argue that because practices in daily life are interdependent, so too must the policy programmes aiming to bring forth change. 'Wicked' policy problems, such as climate change, public health nutrition, alcohol and drug abuse, or obesity, demand multi-stakeholder, multi-issue approaches to intervention which aim, for example, to disrupt one or more practices or to substitute one element of a practice with another.

Conclusions

Theories of practice have seriously challenged orthodox social scientific accounts of consumption. They raise controversial questions about an appropriate conceptualization of the relationship between mind, body, things, social context and action. They adopt an unconventional model of action which is bolstered from a distance by developments in cognitive neuro-science and pragmatist philosophy. To focus on habits, routines and conventions, and on embodied dispositions, disrupts the dominant ideology of consumer choice (Sahakian and Wilhite, 2014; Warde and Southerton, 2012). Some critics are suspicious that theories of practice cannot handle social change, especially macro-level change, although doubts have been assuaged by Shove et al. (2012) and Warde (2014). In fact, many studies have successfully deployed narrative forms of explanation to account for change within practices.

Many other questions remain open. Should practices be examined as entities with powers? How much emphasis should be attributed when analyzing performances to agency and deliberation, and how much to habit, social environment and practical sense? What are the methodological consequences: are some methods, for example observation and ethnography, to be privileged, or can all the methods and techniques in the social science toolbox be useful?

Practice theories have clarified these matters, although the returns to theory from the recent wave of empirical studies have yet to be consolidated. Internal disputes and external critiques continue to throw up unresolved theoretical issues. Meanwhile however, recent empirical inquiries have cast valuable new light on a range of activities, processes and political issues. Novel suggestions about modes of intervention, for instance for the purposes of mitigating the effects of climate change, have emerged. Hidden determinants of patterns of consumption have been revealed. The role of acquired goods and objects in the accomplishment of everyday activities has become clearer, as has the importance of embodied experience in the formation of tastes and behavior. The extent of possible innovation is not yet settled, but there can be little doubt that theories of practice have moved debates about consumption forward.

References

Arsel, Z. and Bean, J. (2013), 'Taste regimes and market-mediated practice,' *Journal of Consumer Research*, Vol. 39, no. 5, pp. 899–917.

Arvidsson, A. (2007), *Brands: meaning and value in media culture*. London and New York: Routledge.

Barnett, C., Clarke, N., Cloke, P. and Malpass, A. (2011), *Globalizing responsibility: the political rationalities of ethical consumption*. Chichester: Wiley-Blackwell.

Bourdieu, P. (1977), *Outline of a theory of practice*. Cambridge: Cambridge University Press.

Bourdieu, P. (1984), *Distinction: a social critique of the judgement of taste*. Cambridge, MA: Harvard University Press.

Bourdieu, P. (1990), *The logic of practice*. Stanford, CA: Stanford University Press.

Bräuchler, B. and Postill, J. (eds.) (2010), *Theorising media and practice*. New York: Berghahn Books.

Browne, A. L., Pullinger, M., Medd, W. and Anderson, B. (2013), 'Patterns of practice: a reflection on the development of quantitative/mixed methodologies capturing everyday life related to water consumption in the UK,' *International Journal of Social Research Methodology*, Vol. 17, no. 1, pp. 27–43.

Campbell, C. (1994), 'Consuming goods and the good of consuming,' *Critical Review: A Journal of Politics and Society*, Vol. 8, no. 4, pp. 503–520.

Collier, S. J. (2009), 'Topologies of power: Foucault's analysis of political government beyond "governmentality",' *Theory, Culture & Society*, Vol. 26, no. 6, pp. 78–108.

Crosbie, T. and Guy, S. (2008), '"Enlightening" energy use: the co-evolution of household lighting practices,' *International Journal of Environmental Technology and Management*, Vol. 9, no. 2, pp. 220–235.

Evans, D. (2011), 'Blaming the consumer – once again: the social and material contexts of everyday food waste practices in some English households,' *Critical Public Health*, Vol. 21, no. 4, pp. 429–440.

Falk, P. and Campbell, C. (1997), *The shopping experience*. London: Sage.

Foucault, M. (2004a), *The birth of biopolitics: lectures at the Collège de France 1978–1979*. New York: Picador.

Foucault, M. (2004b), *Security, territory, population: lectures at the Collège de France 1977–1978*. New York: Picador.

Giddens, A. (1984), *The constitution of society: outline of the theory of structuration*. Cambridge: Polity.

Giddens, A. (1991), *Modernity and self-identity: self and society in the late modern age*. Cambridge: Polity.

Gram-Hanssen, K. (2011), 'Understanding change and continuity in residential energy consumption,' *Journal of Consumer Culture*, Vol. 11, No. 1 pp. 61–78.

Gronow, J. and Warde, A. (2001), *Ordinary consumption*. London: Routledge.

Halkier, B. (2009), 'Suitable cooking? Performances and positionings in cooking practices among Danish women,' *Food, Culture and Society*, Vol. 12, no. 3, pp. 357–377.

Halkier, B. and Jensen, I. (2011), 'Methodological challenges in using practice theory in consumption research: examples from a study on handling nutritional contestations of food consumption,' *Journal of Consumer Culture*, Vol. 11, no. 1, pp. 101–123.

Halkier, B., Katz-Gerro, T. and Martens, L. (2011), 'Applying practice theory to the study of consumption,' *Journal of Consumer Culture*, Vol. 11, no. 1, pp. 3–13.

Hand, M., Shove, E. and Southerton, D. (2005), 'Explaining showering: a discussion of the material, conventional, and temporal dimensions of practice,' *Sociological Research Online*, Vol. 10, no. 2. Online article: *http://www.socresonline.org.uk/10/2/hand.html* Last accessed on 26/10/2016.

Hand, M., Shove, E. and Southerton, D. (2007), 'Home extensions in the United Kingdom: space, time, and practice,' *Environment and Planning D*, Vol. 25, no. 4, pp. 668–681.

Hargreaves, T., Nye, M. and Burgess, J. (2013), 'Keeping energy visible? exploring how householders interact with feedback from smart energy monitors in the longer term,' *Energy Policy*, Vol. 52, pp. 126–134.

Hilton, M. (2009), *Prosperity for all: consumer activism in an era of globalization*. Ithaca, NY: Cornell University Press.

Hitchings, R. (2007), 'How awkward encounters could influence the future form of many gardens,' *Transactions of the Institute of British Geographers*, Vol. 32, no. 3, 363–376.

Hitchings, R. (2011), 'Researching air-conditioning addiction and ways of puncturing practice: professional office workers and the decision to go outside,' *Environment and Planning A*, Vol. 43, no. 12, pp. 28–38.

Jackson, P. (2015), *Anxious appetites: food and consumer culture*. London: Bloomsbury.

Jensen, C. L. (2013), Social practices in energy related transitions? The complex example of electrical lighting. *UEA Working Paper Series*.

Latour, B. (2005), *Reassembling the social: an introduction to actor-network-theory*. Oxford: Oxford University Press.

Latour, B. and Woolgar, S. (1986), *Laboratory life: the construction of scientific facts*. Princeton, NJ: Princeton University Press.

Magaudda, P. (2011), 'When materiality "bites back": digital music consumption practices in the age of dematerialization,' *Journal of Consumer Culture*, Vol. 11, no. 1, pp. 15–36.

Miller, D. (2008), *The comfort of things*. Cambridge: Polity.

Nicolini, D. (2012), *Practice theory, work, and organization: an introduction*. Oxford: Oxford University Press.

Ozaki, R. and Shaw, I. (2014), 'Entangled practices: governance, sustainable technologies and energy consumption,' *Sociology*, Vol. 48, no. 3, pp. 590–605.

Paddock, J. (2015), 'Household consumption and environmental change: rethinking the policy problem through narratives of food practice,' *Journal of Consumer Culture*. Online First, 1–18, doi: 10.1177/1469540515586869.

Pantzar, M. and Shove, E. (2010), 'Understanding innovation in practice: a discussion of the production and re-production of nordic walking,' *Technology Analysis & Strategic Management*, Vol. 22, no. 4, pp. 447–461.

Reckwitz, A. (2002a), 'The status of the "material" in theories of culture: from "social structure" to "artifacts",' *Journal of the Theory of Social Behaviour*, Vol. 32, no. 2, pp. 195–211.

Reckwitz, A. (2002b), 'Toward a theory of social practices: a development in culturalist theorizing,' *European Journal of Social Theory*, Vol. 5, no. 2, pp. 243–263.

Røpke, I., Christensen, T. H. and Jensen, J. O. (2010), 'Information and communication technologies–a new round of household electrification,' *Energy Policy*, Vol. 38, no. 4, pp. 1764–1773.

Rouse, J. (2007), 'Practice theory.' *Handbook of the philosophy of science*. Paper 43, pp. 499–540. Division I Faculty Publications: WesScholar.

Rumpala, Y. (2011), '"Sustainable consumption" as a new phase in a governmentalization of consumption,' *Theory and Society*, Vol. 40, no. 6, pp. 669–699.

Sahakian, M. and Wilhite, H. (2014), 'Making practice theory practicable: towards more sustainable forms of consumption,' *Journal of Consumer Culture*, Vol. 14, no. 1, pp. 25–44.

Schatzki, T. (1996), *Social practices: a Wittgensteinian approach to human activity and the social*. New York: Cambridge University Press.

Schatzki, T. (2001), 'Introduction: practice theory'. In T. Schatzki, K. Knorr Cetina and E. Savigny (eds.), *The practice turn in contemporary theory*, pp. 10–23. London: Routledge.

Schatzki, T. R. (2002), *The site of the social: a philosophical account of the constitution of social life and change*. University Park: Pennsylvania State University Press.

Schatzki, T. R. (2010), *The timespace of human activity*. Lanham: Lexington Books.

Schatzki, T. R., Knorr Cetina, K. and Savigny, E. (2001), *The practice turn in contemporary theory*. London: Routledge.

Shove, E. (2003), *Comfort, cleanliness and convenience: the social organization of normality*. Oxford: Berg.

Shove, E. (2004), Converging conventions of comfort, cleanliness and convenience. *Journal of Consumer Policy*, Vol. 26, no.4, pp. 395–418.

Shove, E. (2010), 'Beyond the ABC: climate change policy and theories of social change,' *Environment and Planning A*, Vol. 42, no. 6, pp. 1273–1285.

Shove, E. and Pantzar, M. (2005), 'Consumers, producers and practices: understanding the invention and reinvention of Nordic walking,' *Journal of Consumer Culture*, Vol. 5, no. 1, pp. 43–64.

Shove, E., Pantzar, M. and Watson, M. (2012), *The dynamics of social practice: everyday life and how it changes*. London: Sage.

Shove, E. and Spurling, N. (eds.). (2013), *Sustainable practices: social theory and climate change*. Oxon: Routledge.

Shove, E. and Walker, G. (2014), 'What is energy for? Social practice and energy demand,' *Theory, Culture & Society*, Vol. 31, no. 5, pp. 41–58.

Shove, E., Walker, G. and Brown, S. (2014), 'Transnational transitions: the diffusion and integration of mechanical cooling,' *Urban Studies*, Vol. 51, no. 7, pp. 1506–1519.

Southerton, D. (2013), 'Habits, routines and temporalities of consumption: from individual behaviours to the reproduction of everyday practices,' *Time and Society*, Vol. 22, no. 3, pp. 335–355.

Southerton, D., Díaz-Méndez, C. and Warde, A. (2012), 'Behavioural change and the temporal ordering of eating practices: a UK-Spain comparison,' *International Journal of Sociology of Agriculture and Food*, Vol. 19, no. 1, pp. 19–36.

Spaargaren, G. (2003), 'Sustainable consumption: a theoretical and environmental policy perspective,' *Society and Natural Resources*, Vol. 16, no. 8, pp. 687–701.

Spaargaren, G., Osteveer, P. and Loeber, A. (2013), *Food practices in transition: changing food consumption, retail and production in the age of reflexive modernity*. London: Routledge.

Spaargaren, G. and Vliet, B.V. (2000), 'Lifestyles, consumption and the environment,' *Environmental Politics*, Vol. 9, no. 1, pp. 50–76.

Spurling, N., McMeekin, A., Shove, E., Southerton, D. and Welch, D. (2013), *Interventions in practice: re-framing policy approaches to consumer behaviour*. Sustainable Practices Research Group Report, September 2013.

Strengers, Y. and Maller, C. (eds.). (2015), *Social practices, intervention and sustainability*. Oxon: Routledge Earthscan.

Trentmann, F. (2008), *Free trade nation: commerce, consumption and civil society*. Oxford: Oxford University Press.

Trentmann, F. (2010), 'Multiple spaces of consumption: some historical perspectives'. In M. K. Goodman and M. Redclift (eds.), *Consuming space: placing consumption in perspective*, pp. 41–56. Farnham: Ashgate.

Truninger, M. (2011), 'Cooking with Bimby in a moment of recruitment: exploring conventions and practice perspectives,' *Journal of Consumer Culture*, Vol. 11, no. 1, pp. 37–59.

Veen, E. J., Derkzen, P. and Visser, A. J. (2014), 'Shopping versus growing: food acquisition habits of Dutch urban gardeners,' *Food and Foodways*, Vol. 22, no. 4, pp. 268–299.

Vihalemm, T., Keller, M. and Kiisel, M. (2015), *From intervention to social change: a guide to reshaping everyday practices*. Farnham: Ashgate.

Warde, A. (2005), 'Consumption and theories of practice,' *Journal of Consumer Culture*, Vol. 5, no. 2, pp. 131–153.

Warde, A. (2014), 'After taste: culture, consumption and theories of practice,' *Journal of Consumer Culture*, Vol. 14, no. 3, pp. 279–303.

Warde, A. (2016), *The practice of eating*. Cambridge: Polity Press.

Warde, A. and Southerton, D. (2012), 'The habits of consumption,' *COLLeGIUM: Studies Across Disciplines in the Humanities and Social Sciences*. Helsinki Collegium for Advanced Studies, Vol. 12, pp. 1–25.

Watson, M. (2012), 'How theories of practice can inform transition to a decarbonised transport system,' *Journal of Transport Geography*, Vol. 24, pp. 448–496.

Welch, D. (2016), 'Social practices and behaviour change'. In F. Spotswood (ed.), *Beyond behaviour change*, pp. 237–256. Bristol: Policy Press.

Welch, D. and Warde, A. (2015), 'Theories of practice and sustainable consumption'. In L. Reisch and J. Thøgersen (eds.), *Handbook of research on sustainable consumption*, pp. 84–100. Cheltenham: Edward Elgar Publishing.

Welch, D. and Warde, A. (2016), 'How should we understand "general understandings"?' In A. Hui, T. Schatzki and E. Shove (eds.), *The nexus of practice: connections, constellations and practitioners*, pp. 183–196. London: Routledge.

Wilhite, H. and Wallenborn, G. (2013), Articulating the body in the theorizing of consumption. *Proceedings from the ECEEE 1999 summer study on energy efficiency in buildings*.

Yates, L. and Evans, D. (2016), 'Dirtying linen: re-evaluating the sustainability of domestic laundry,' *Environmental Policy and Governance*, Vol. 26, no.2, pp. 101–115.

Zwick, D., Donsu, S. K. and Darmoddy, A. (2008), 'Putting consumers to work "co-creation" and new marketing govern-mentality,' *Journal of Consumer Culture*, Vol. 8, no. 2, pp. 163–196.

4

Methods and methods' debates within consumption research

Bente Halkier

Introduction

The international social scientific research on consumption and consumers is such a wide and interdisciplinary field that it is almost a mission impossible to construct an overview of all the different approaches to methodological design and use of methods applied within the field, which range from highly quantitative consumer behaviour analysis to deeply qualitative ethnographic consumption process studies. Thus, this chapter attempts to do something much more humble.

In this chapter, I am proposing four different analytical "families" which I see as the main different groupings in researching consumption in and across the social and cultural sciences. The consumption research in each grouping tends to display a particular portfolio of typical methodological assumptions and choices, and I am using the groupings as a lens to structure the current methods varieties and debates through. Methodological assumptions, strategies and choices in empirical research are (or ought to be) consistent with the theoretical perspective taken to the research and the specific knowledge interest framing the research (Blaikie, 2007). In other words, the kinds of different typical research questions asked in studies on consumption and consumers are analytically closely related to the types of methodological arrangements in the empirical research projects.

How to carve up a research area is always contested, especially since this chapter looks at the broader area of research on consumption, attempting to somewhat include sociology, anthropology, geography, cultural studies and marketing. However, a number of international overview publications over the years have come to similar or parallel distinctions of different approaches to consumption research: Consumption as dependent upon economic dynamics; consumption as dependent upon cultural dynamics; consumption as identity-construction; and consumption as everyday life (e.g. Gronow & Warde, 2001; Paterson, 2006; Sassatelli, 2007; Soper & Trentmann, 2008; Warde, 2002).

The first three of these approaches resonate with the distinctions in approaches from the programmatic article on sociology of consumption by Mike Featherstone, called "Perspectives on consumer culture," in the journal *Sociology* in 1990 (Featherstone, 1990). Varieties of the four approaches can be traced in the first editorial for *Journal of Consumer Culture* (Ritzer &

Slater, 2001). The four approaches can also be seen as somewhat overlapping with or parallel to the distinctions in consumer culture theory (CCT – see chapter 2) made by Eric Arnould and Craig Thompson in their influential article from 2005 in *Journal of Consumer Research* (Arnould & Thompson, 2005), where they divide the CCT approaches into consumer identity, marketplace cultures, socio-historic patterning, and meetings of mediated marketplace ideologies with consumers' interpretative strategies.

A recent overview article in a special issue about "new approaches to consumer research" (Lyon, 2010) in *International Journal of Consumer Studies* (McGregor & Murnane, 2010) distinguishes between approaches to consumer research based on research methodologies, and argues that there are three main methodological approaches being used: positivistic, interpretive and critical. In their article, each of these methodological approaches is linked with theoretical assumptions about consumption as well as a range of preferred methods for each of them.

This chapter builds upon the insights of these and other relevant overview publications as well as a systematic search for methods' debates in nine journals for consumption research. I have constructed four rough groupings of consumption research around which the methods' descriptions and discussions are organized: 1) Consumption as behaviour, 2) Consumption as identity, 3) Consumption as cultural dynamics and 4) Consumption as part of social configurations. The four groupings do contain an element of research historical sequence, but on the other hand all four currently thrive and contribute to consumption research.

The structure of the chapter is as follows: First, stretching over four sub-sections, the typical methodological strategies of each of the four groupings in consumption research are described. Second, a number of current methods' debates in consumption research which tend to go across some of the groupings are discussed. Finally, some methodological potential in consumption research is discussed.

Consumption as behaviour

In this grouping of consumption research, the sub-strands would cover the main part of consumer behaviour studies and parts of marketing (see also e.g. chapter 6 in this volume). The kinds of research questions that are typically asked are: What are the individual motives to consume? Which economic, psychological, informative, normative, emotional, social and cultural factors influence consumer attitudes and choices and to which degrees? How wide-spread are particular types of consumer behaviour patterns among different kinds of populations? How can the existence of particular patterns of consumer behaviour be explained? How can marketing strategies be organized in order to fit the motives and choices of consumers? How do consumers react to different kinds of stimuli?

Embedded in such kinds of research questions are some of the positivistic epistemological assumptions such as logic of discovery in relation to consumption phenomena, the objectivity of scientific knowledge about consumption phenomena, and the goal of providing systematic explanation to consumption phenomena. Methodologically, the main assumptions cover strategies of deduction and testing of theories of consumer behaviour as well as methodological individualism, that the unit of analysis is the individual consumer. The typical kinds of methods used in consumption as behaviour research are surveys and different types of experiments (Arnould & Thompson, 2005, p. 869; McGregor & Murnane, 2010, pp. 422–3, 425–7; Sassatelli, 2007, pp. 57–64; Slater, 1997, pp. 61–2), although examples of using qualitative methods such as focus groups do exist. Here follow two current examples of consumption studies, belonging to this grouping of research, which are respectively drawing upon survey methods and experimental methods.

The first example consists in a review study of twenty-nine existing cross-country survey studies on the usefulness of the theory of planned behaviour in explaining as different types of consumer behaviour as purchasing organic food, adopting mobile data service and using condoms (Hassan, Shiu & Parry, 2015). The study focuses on the impact of a national culture factor on the other explanatory elements that are assumed to be involved in patterns of consumer behaviour such as intention, attitude, subjective norm and perceived behavioural control, and the relationships between these elements. The method in the study consists in comparing the statistical findings in the twenty-nine cross-country surveys on consumer behaviour, in making extra statistical tests where possible and making the across-studies comparison through statistical multilevel modelling. The results of the study consist in showing that there are significant differences across countries in the ways in which subjective norms influence consumption behaviour intention, and thus, cultural differences in consumption behaviour can be explained more precisely. This example is typical in the consumption as behaviour grouping with regards to its use of quantitative survey data, statistical modelling and a purpose of testing and strengthening a popular theory, in this case the theory of planned behaviour, in order to provide an improved explanation.

The second example consists in an experimental study of how consumers' preferences and willingness to pay for organic food are influenced by sensory experiences (Bi, Gao, House & Hausmann, 2015). The focus of the study is to determine and explain how sensory evaluations and labelling of conventional and organic orange juice affects consumer preferences and hypothetical choices. The methods used are a combination of two different kinds of experimental set-ups with ninety-eight American university campus students and staff participating: one blind sensory evaluation experiment and one discrete choice experiment. Data from the experiments are statistically and econometrically analyzed. The results indicate that there are differences in the degree of influence of the consumers' sensory experiences on the willingness to pay extra for organic food. This second example of consumption as behaviour research is also typical of its grouping in so far as it uses quantitative methods, observable experimentation, and has a purpose of contributing to the explanation of particular elements of consumer behaviour. Here consumers' use of different cues is related to goods and consumers' preferences and intentions, in a more explanatory manner and thus with more cautious inference claims.

Consumption as identity

The identity grouping of consumption research would cover as sub-strands a large part of consumer culture theory (CCT – see chapter 2 in this volume), and some of the qualitative sociology of consumption. Recognizable research questions within this group of consumption research would be: What kind of experiences with consumption do consumers have? How do consumers make sense of different kinds of consumption? How do consumers interpret their own and others' consumption? In which ways are consumption activities part of people's personal (and perhaps cultural) identities? What kind of relations with consumer goods and services do consumers display? What kind of identity-negotiation processes do consumers take part in?

These kinds of research questions imply interpretive epistemological assumptions, such as logic of interpretation and perspective in relation to consumption phenomena, the intersubjective character of scientific knowledge about consumption, and the goal of providing systematic and socio-culturally sensitive understandings of consumption phenomena. Parts of the consumption as identity research explicitly mentions e.g. phenomenology as the epistemological inspiration. The main methodological assumptions cover an inductive or an abductive research strategy, depending upon the degree of exploration in the relation between empirical data and theoretical concepts, and the analytical unit is intersubjectively embedded individuals. The most used methods in consumption as identity research are qualitative individual interviewing, focus groups and mixed methods (Arnould & Thompson, 2005, pp. 871–3; Askegaard & Linnet, 2011, pp. 384–7; Gronow & Warde, 2001, pp. 3–5; McGregor & Murnane, 2010, pp. 422–3, 425–7; Sassatelli, 2007, pp. 80–2).

One of the classic methodological publications in consumption as identity research is probably the article by Thompson, Locander and Pollio about existential-phenomenology and the phenomenological interview. The stated purpose in the article is to bring back the focus on consumers' experience and meaning-making into consumer research by way of a methodology that is different from the one in the dominant consumer behaviour research (Thompson, Locander & Pollio, 1989). In the following, I have picked three recent examples of studies within this grouping, which represent each choice of methods.

The first example – a study of consumers who purposively and frequently change place of living and how they form relations with material possessions – builds on qualitative individual interviews (Bardhi, Eckhardt & Arnould, 2012). The focus in the study is on the different ways in which attachment to material possessions becomes an anchor of consumers' identities, when they are engaged in their frequently relocated lifestyles. The theoretical perspective in the study builds partly upon Zygmunt Bauman's understanding of liquid modernity, nomadic lifestyles and their implications for consumption. The methods used are individual qualitative interviews with sixteen elite mobile professionals from different countries, which are analyzed by way of iterative coding and interpretation in combination with theoretical concepts belonging to the study. The main result consists in identifying three different liquid relationships with material possessions seeing those as expressions of nomadic consumption. This consumer as identity example clearly belongs to the grouping methodologically with its focus on individual consumer experiences and narratives on identification.

The second example is a research project on meaning and identity in relation to holiday consumption among mature Danish couples (Therkelsen & Gram, 2008). The focus is on the identity construction of couples through their tourism activities, and theoretically draws upon the debates about consumer identification. The methods chosen are a combination of five couple interviews with mature couples, and two focus groups. The main result is to show that consumer identification is not only an individual process, but that a couple can also be the identifying unit through their discursive negotiations of belonging to as well as differentiating from particular kinds of holiday consumption. This consumer as identity example highlights the analytical unit as being intersubjective individuals, which is reflected in the choice of methods as couple and group methods.

The last example consists in a study about identity production among retired consumers in the US (Schau, Gilly & Wolfinbarger, 2009). The research focuses on the amount of and changes in old consumers' identity work, and draws theoretically on a social constructivist interpretation of the CCT tradition for consumer identity projects. The methods in the study are a combination of in-depth individual interviews with retired people, naturalistic and participant observation at senior centers, and discussion threads in online forums for older people. The main result is to show that consumption forms an inspiration for extension and renewal of older consumers' identities. This example of consumption as identity research explicitly frames itself methodologically as part of CCT, and at the same time reflects critically upon the unit of analysis perhaps sliding back into the individual consumer, in spite of the mixed methods in the project.

Consumption as cultural dynamics

This grouping of consumption research is slightly more composite than the two first ones when it comes to uses of research methods, which may or may not be related to the greater mixing and overlapping of different sub-strands. In these quarters of consumption research, one will usually find parts of CCT (research interested in marketplace cultures, in socio-historic patterning of consumption, and in meetings of marketplace discourses with consumers' sense-making), as well as parts of material culture (see e.g. chapter 24 in this volume), parts of sociology of consumption, parts of cultural geography and parts of critical marketing. The typical research questions in consumption as cultural dynamics would be the following: What characterizes the cultural context of a particular kind of consumption? What characterizes the symbolic and material processes of consumption? How are consumer subject positions discursively produced? Which cultural orders are implied in consumption? How have particular consumption patterns developed historically? What are the implications for power relations in society from consumption arrangements?

Here it seems to be a mixture of critical realist and social constructivist types of epistemological assumptions being embedded in the typical kinds of research questions. Thus, these two epistemological perspectives tend to share a logic of interpretation and a goal of providing systematic, context-sensitive and theoretically informed analyses of consumption phenomena. However, there are also disagreements over important epistemological questions such as the status of scientific knowledge on consumption phenomena. The social constructivist perspective tends to favor situationism, co-construction and the instability of knowledge, whereas the critical realist perspective tends to argue for cultural transferability, critical questioning and slightly more stability of knowledge (Høijer, 2008; Sayer, 1992). Regarding the main methodological assumptions, abductive and retroductive research strategies (Blaikie, 2007) are preferred, and the analytical unit is the cultural dynamics. The methods most often chosen in consumption as cultural dynamics research covers a number of techniques from ethnographic fieldwork methods and active interviewing to surveys, semiotics, discourse analysis and action research (Arnould & Thompson, 2005, pp. 873–5; Bell & Valentine, 1997, pp. 16–18; McGregor & Murnane, 2010, pp. 223–3, pp. 225–7; Sassatelli, 2007, pp. 92–101; Slater, 1997, pp. 153–63; Slater & Miller, 2007, pp. 7–8; Tadajewski, 2010, pp. 216–17; Warde, 2014, pp. 281–4).

It is slightly more difficult to pick a "classic" methodological publication in consumption as cultural dynamics research. Some would highlight Holt's article on how to construct a typology of how consumers consume on the basis of a Goffinan approach to participant observation (Holt, 1995). Others would perhaps pick Miller's book *A Theory of Shopping* (Miller, 1998) for its demonstration of the embeddedness of larger cultural structures in situated consumption processes. Others again prefer a publication focusing on the more text-analytical kinds of methods in analyzing consumption as cultural dynamics (Hirschman & Holbrook, 1992). In the following, I have chosen three current empirical examples within consumption as cultural dynamics research that illustrate some (but not all) of the variation in the research methods applied.

The first example is a study about consumption as voluntary simplicity among Israeli consumers (Zamwel, Sasson-Levy & Ben-Porat, 2014). The focus of the research is on potential political implications of the private consumption strategy of voluntary simplifiers, and draws theoretically on the debates about the overlapping and ambivalences of private, public and political dimensions in conscious consumption. The methods in the research consist in a combination of long-term, field-based participant observation and qualitative interviewing with thirty-five consumers who have chosen to restrict their consumption. The main result amounts to identifying four characteristics of voluntary simplicity consumption which point to their political character. This example shows the attention in the consumption as cultural dynamics research to analyzing larger cultural structures embedded in situated contexts of particular consumption types.

The second example does not consist in an actual empirical research project, but is rather an article with a firm methodological argument (Moisander, Valtonen & Hirsto, 2009). I have included it here as an example, because it shows clearly some of the differences between the use of qualitative interviewing in consumption as cultural dynamics research compared to the use of qualitative interviewing in the second grouping, consumption as identity. The article criticizes the uses of the classical phenomenological interviewing in research on consumer culture, because of its sliding into methodological individualism, both with regard to unit of analysis and when describing and using techniques of interviewing. Instead, the authors suggest using active interviewing (Holstein & Gubrium, 2003), which is a social constructivist type of interviewing where it is assumed that all participants (including the interviewer) perform socially and enact cultural meanings. Active interviewing includes e.g. the uses of materials and texts, and purposeful shifts of cultural positions.

The last example of consumption as cultural dynamics research is a study about environmental advertising discourses aimed at pregnant women (Atkinson, 2014). The focus of the research is on how the advertising discourses frame expectant mothers as consumers, and draws theoretically on the debates about motherhood and sustainable consumption. The method applied here is critical discourse analysis of one year's advertising in a US pregnancy magazine. The main result is to show the ambivalences of the framing of parental consumption choices, where mothers are both constructed as becoming empowered by the environmental discourse, and at the same time the commercial brands are constructed as sources of expert knowledge. This example draws attention to the importance of the discursive dimensions of cultural dynamics in this type of consumption research.

Consumption as part of social configurations

This last grouping of consumption research consists of fewer sub-strands than the previous grouping insofar that it seems to be mainly based within sociology of consumption, anthropology of consumption, material culture and geographies of consumption, but with threads to CCT. The typical research questions would be like the following: How is the context of particular types of consumption socially and spatially organized? In which ways are particular consumption activities embedded in social practices? How are the uses of materials embodied in routines? How do patterns of consumption become socially, spatially and materially reproduced and changed? Which social dynamics are involved in the normalization of consumption activities? How are consumption patterns embedded across different social practices and across trajectories of practices?

These recognizable research questions cover a mix of epistemological understandings, like the previous grouping of consumption research. Thus, a mixture of critical realist and social constructivist assumptions tend to be drawn upon in this kind of consumption research, such as logics of description, interpretation and production of knowledge. There is a shared goal of providing systematic, context-sensitive and theoretically informed analyses of consumption phenomena. At the same time, there are also variations in the status ascribed to scientific knowledge on consumption phenomena, mostly to do with situationism versus generalizability, tacit versus discursive knowledge types, and the challenges of what counts as knowledge about collective categories. Methodologically, abductive research strategies are preferred, and the unit of analysis is social practices, which means that this kind of consumption research tends to strive for working in an anti-methodological-individualist manner. Furthermore, it seems as if this kind of consumption research adheres to what might be called "non-consumption-centric" consumption research insofar that the analytical unit is neither consumers nor consumption, but the socially, materially and spatially organized contexts of these. The typical methods used in consumption as part of social configuration research are nearly always combinations of several methods. The favorite methods are e.g. participant observation, sensory and visual ethnographic methods, different types of qualitative interviewing, and different kinds of structural data such as time-use surveys, material measurements and digital tracking (Goodman, Goodman & Redclift, 2012; Halkier, Katz-Gerro & Martens, 2011; Jackson, 2009; Martens, 2012; Martens, Pink & Halkier, 2014; Pink, 2012; Shove, Pantzar & Watson, 2012; Warde, 2005, 2014).

A classic methodological publication within this grouping of consumption research has not yet crystallized; the classic publications are more oriented towards theory and are commenting on practice theories and consumption (see chapter 3 in this volume). I have chosen four examples to illustrate the big variation in methods. The first example is a study of the activities of a pro-environmental consumption change team in a UK workplace (Hargreaves, 2011). The focus of the study is to describe the importance of social negotiations and collective organization of workplace practices in relation to initiating and sustaining changes to consumption activities regarding e.g. use of resources. The theoretical perspective is practice theoretical, and the methods consist in a combination of nine months' participant observation at the workplace and thirty-eight in-depth interviews with sixteen members of the change team. The main results point to the difficulties in achieving change of consumption patterns stretching beyond the practical contextual barriers towards the construction of a "normal" everyday workplace life and its power relations. This example shows the probably most typical methods combination within this grouping of consumption research; some kind of participant observation and some kind of qualitative interviewing.

The second example is a study on the consumption aspects of sport fishing in Finland (Valtonen, Markuksela & Moisander, 2010). The focus here is on the ways in which the senses play a central role in the consumption patterns involved in performing sport fishing, and the theoretical perspective is a practice theoretical one. The methods employed are all in all called sensory ethnography, but involve multiple methods such as participant observations, interviews, conversations, visual materials and autobiographical narratives. One main result is here a more methodological one, showing that visual methods enable consumption researchers to attend to the multi-sensorial manifestations of consumption processes. Thus, this study exemplifies the ambitions of this type of consumption research in including as many relevant dimensions as possible, also the ones that seem particularly hard to register and interpret, for analyzing consumption.

The third example consists in research about food consumption and issues of health and environment among French consumers (Plessz, Dubuisson-Quellier, Gojard & Barrey, 2014). The focus in the study is on potential changes in food practices and the possible links with public health and environment prescriptions, and theoretically the study is based on practice theories. The methods used in this study are a slightly unusual combination in this consumption research grouping, because they combine quantitative and qualitative data, consisting in analysis of quantitative opinion and purchase data from a representative consumer panel, and individual re-interviewing with members of thirty households, plus ten shopping-tours. The main result is that food practitioners seem to be more likely to change consumption habits when they are at life-course turning points. This example shows the tendency in this consumption research grouping to mix methods from all corners within single research projects.

The last example does not present an actual study, but discusses the potentials and pitfalls in including methods such as digital tracking as data-material in studies of consumption patterns (Pantzar & Ruckenstein, 2015). The consumption example discussed is digital ways of monitoring heart-rate in everyday life, based on a tracing of the historical development in the self-tracking market, and the theoretical perspective is practice theoretical. The methods reflections conclude among other things that the visualizations in this type of consumption due to the media can open new possibilities to access rhythms and patterns of more intimate parts of consumption otherwise difficult to register and interpret. This example shows the grappling with new kinds of structural-ish data-types in the consumption as part of social configurations research.

Some current methods' debates in consumption research

Doing justice to all methodological debates is impossible (see also chapter 5 in this volume). Thus, for this section on current methods' debates, I have chosen to focus on three debates that seem to go across some of the four groupings of consumption research and their methodological main assumptions. For example, I could have also discussed the debate about using neuro-scientific methods in consumer behaviour research and marketing (e.g. Morin, 2011). But this methods' debate seems to be taking place only inside of consumption as behaviour research discussions.

The first of the three debates is about *how to investigate collective categories in consumption*, and it often takes a starting point in criticizing methodological individualism (Jepperson & Meyer, 2011), such as working with the individual consumer as analytical unit as it is explicitly done in large parts of consumer behaviour research and parts of CCT. An example on a recent publication that brings this debate to the consumption as behaviour research is an article that argues for using more discourse analysis in marketing and consumer research (Fitchett & Caruana, 2014). Other quarters of consumption research such as cultural dynamics and the social configurations versions argue that they do work with more collective analytical units. However, it is discussed whether this is the case or whether concrete uses of data-production methods such as individual interviewing and data-analysis inspired by performance-focused categories tend to make concrete research slide towards more individualist, agentic, empirical claims (Warde, 2014, p. 295). At least two different proposals have been brought forward for strengthening the methods strategies for investigating collective categories of consumption. One of them is the suggestion to use so called "big data" much more in the data-production, such as quantitative digital tracking and pattern visualization and other kinds of quantitative material measurement of big flows of patterns of consumption (e.g. Pantzar & Ruckenstein, 2014). Another proposal is more of a theoretical kind, but pertains to the data-analysis strategies, which is using a "strong" practice theory approach (Warde, 2014, pp. 285–6) to interpret consumption patterns, thus focusing on Bourdieusian categories of e.g. dispositions and field.

The second debate is about *how to balance the tacit and material dimensions of consumption with the discursive ones* in empirical methods is as long-standing as it is current. It is one of the points of several current fashionable theoretical perspectives in consumption research – such as Actor Network Theory (ANT) and practice theories – that the material and tacit routinized parts of consumption have been under-researched by earlier approaches to consumption research which have focused too much on discursive and symbolic dimensions of consumption. Thus, a number of methods suggestions in consumption research about how to achieve a better balance come from these quarters. For example, there is the classical argument that observational methods are better at producing knowledge about the practical and tacit activities implying consumption, compared with interview-based methods (Martens, 2012), here made in relation to an empirical study on kitchen hygiene consumption. Another example, which expands the observational methods argument further, is the argument that more different senses and modalities should be used actively for producing and representing data-patterns on consumption in order to understand consumption processes and contexts, such as the visual (Pink, 2012) and the olfactory ones (Valtonen, Markuksela & Moisander, 2010). An example of a quantitative methods suggestion in how to include the material and tacit dimensions of consumption better is to use quantitative observations of consumer logistics based on video recordings in public space from an ANT perspective (Calvignac & Cochoy, 2016).

The third debate is on *non-representational or more-than-representational methodologies* in consumption research, and it is related to the previous discussions about how to investigate tacit and material elements of consumption insofar that tacit and material dimensions of data-materials can be difficult to represent. But the methods discussions relating explicitly to non-representational theory (e.g. Law, 2004) within consumption research also argue for the importance of focusing on movement and flow by way of the methods, thus linking up with the so-called "mobilities turn" in the social sciences generally (Urry, 2007) and creating interesting challenges for data-production, analysis and representation. In a recent special issue of *Consumption, Markets & Culture* on "Moving consumption", the editorial article underlines the potential many new kinds of methods choices that might be implied in researching consumers as "a fleeting entity" (Brembeck, Cochoy & Moisander, 2015, p. 2), such as visual methods, shadowing, experiments and quantitative ethnography. One methods suggestion in this type of consumption research consists in what is named "onflow of the everyday" (Hill, Canniford & Mol, 2014) and covers e.g. following actors (and things) around in the processes and on the move and extending traditional interviewing with visual and introspective elements. The focus here is on the messiness of consumption and market arrangements, and consumption categories and practices as well as things are not seen as impossible to represent, but rather that researchers should recognize the epistemological incompleteness of their attempts to do so. Another slightly more radical version of such methodological argumentation comes from those consumption researchers who seem to want to use ANT to get rid of what is framed as counterproductive theoretical assumptions about consumption and existing methods tools, and instead follow what they call enactments of heterogeneous and precarious networks that make up consumption (Bajde, 2013, p. 239).

Future methods' potentials in consumption research?

As a way of rounding off this chapter about methods in consumption research, I will argue that there is especially one methodological avenue which seems particularly promising for future consumption studies. This is *methodological multiplicity*. It is becoming less and less common to see interesting and theoretically innovative consumption research being based on only one method. The degree of complexity in consumption conduct, identifications, dynamics and arrangements is calling for combinational methodological designs (see e.g. Brembeck, Cochoy & Moisander, 2015). In my view, methodological multiplicity can consist in at least three different and overlapping ways of linking several methods in data-production and analysis. First, different methods can complement each other by producing knowledge about different questions and categories in the consumption research. For example participant observation with visual elements and informal interviewing can shed light upon the more situational dimensions of e.g. healthier cooking, while institutional mapping and text analysis can shed light upon more structuralized dynamics and conditions for healthier cooking. Second, different methods can be combined to produce different kinds of knowledge about the same questions and categories. To e.g. use digital tracking and focus groups to produce knowledge about normalization of exercising could shed light upon patterns of exercising as well as the social negotiations of these patterns. Third, different methods can be mixed by being integrated into each other in the data-production. For example, observing while interviewing, photo and film elicitation as input to interviewing, and using socially recognizable materials in socially recognizable network focus groups (Halkier, forthcoming).

Obviously, the strategy of methodological multiplicity also has its pitfalls as well as promises. Examples of such potential pitfalls could be the illusion of being able to produce "complete" knowledges of a field of consumption by covering as much as possible; the risk of becoming seduced by the endless possibilities in digital media when including digital tracking and representation of consumption; and the danger of not keeping the categories for comparing consumption processes across the different data-types sufficiently clear. The future will show how much and in which manners methodological multiplicity will be embraced by consumption research.

References

Arnould, E. & Thompson, C.J. (2005). Consumer culture theory (CCT): Twenty years of research, *Journal of Consumer Research*, 31, 868–82.

Askegaard, S. & Linnet, J.T. (2011). Towards an epistemology of consumer culture theory: Phenomenology and the context of context, *Marketing Theory*, 11, 381–404.

Atkinson, L. (2014). Green moms: The social construction of a green mothering identity via environmental advertising appeals, *Consumption Markets & Culture*, 17, 553–72.

Bajde, D. (2013). Consumer culture theory (re)visits actor-network theory: Flattening consumption studies, *Marketing Theory*, 13, 227–42.

Bardhi, F., Eckhardt, G.M. & Arnould, E.J. (2012). Liquid relationship to possessions, *Journal of Consumer Research*, 39, 510–29.

Bell, D. & Valentine, G. (1997). *Consuming geographies: We are what we eat*. London: Routledge.

Bi, X., Gao, Z., House, L.A. & Hausmann, D.S. (2015). Tradeoffs between sensory attributes and organic labels: The case of orange juice, *International Journal of Consumer Studies*, 39, 162–71.

Blaikie, N. (2007). *Approaches to social enquiry* (2nd ed.). Cambridge: Polity Press.

Brembeck, H., Cochoy, F. & Moisander, J. (2015). Moving consumption, *Consumption Markets & Culture*, 18, 1–9.

Calvignac, C. & Cochoy, F. (2016). From "market agencements" to "vehicular agencies": Insights from the quantitative observation of consumer logistics, *Consumption Markets & Culture*, 19, 133–47.

Featherstone, M. (1990). Perspectives on consumer culture, *Sociology*, 24, 5–22.

Fitchett, J. & Caruana, R. (2014). Exploring the role of discourse in marketing and consumer research, *Journal of Consumer Behaviour*, 14, 1–12.

Goodman, M.K., Goodman, D. & Redclift, M. (2012). *Consuming space: Placing consumption in perspective*. Farnham: Ashgate.

Gronow, J. & Warde, A. (2001). *Ordinary consumption*. London: Routledge.

Halkier, B. (forthcoming). Questioning the "gold standard" thinking in qualitative methods from a practice theoretical perspective: Towards methodological multiplicity. In M. Jonas, L. Lassnigg, B. Littig and A. Wroblewski (Eds.), *Methodological reflections on practice oriented theories*. Berlin: Springer.

Halkier, B., Katz-Gerro, T. & Martens, L. (2011). Applying practice theory to the study of consumption: Theoretical and methodological considerations, *Journal of Consumer Culture*, 11, 3–13.

Hargreaves, T. (2011). Practiceing behaviour change: Applying social practice theory to pro-environmental behaviour change, *Journal of Consumer Culture*, 11, 79–99.

Hassan, L.M, Shiu, E. & Parry, S. (2015). Addressing the cross-country applicability of the theory of planned behaviour (TPB): A structured review of multi-country TPB studies, *Journal of Consumer Behaviour*, 14.

Hill, T., Canniford, R. & Mol, J. (2014). Non-representational marketing theory, *Marketing Theory*, 14, 377–94.

Hirschman, E.C. & Holbrook, M.B. (1992). *Postmodern consumer research*. Newbury Park, CA: Sage.

Höijer, B. (2008). Ontological assumptions and generalizations in qualitative (audience) research, *European Journal of Communication*, 23, 275–94.

Holstein, J.A. & Gubrium, J.F. (2003). Active interviewing. In J.F. Gubrium and J.A. Holstein (Eds.), *Postmodern interviewing*. London: Sage, 67–80.

Holt, D. (1995). How consumers consume: A typology of consumption practices, *Journal of Consumer Research*, 22, 1–16.
Jackson, P. (2009). *Changing families, changing food*. Basingstoke: Palgrave Macmillan.
Jepperson, R. & Meyers, J.W. (2011). Multiple levels of analysis and the limitations of methodological individualism, *Sociological Theory*, 29, 54–73.
Law, J. (2004). *After method: Mess in social science research*. London: Routledge.
Lyon, P. (2010). Editorial: New approaches to consumer research, *International Journal of Consumer Studies*, 34, 367–68.
Martens, L. (2012). Practice "in talk" and talk "as practice": Dish washing and the reach of language, *Sociological Research Online*, 17, 3.
Martens, L., Pink, S. & Halkier, B. (2014). Introduction to special issue on researching habits: Advances in linguistic and embodied research practice, *International Journal of Social Research Methodology*, 17, 1–9.
McGregor, S.L.T. & Murnane, J.A. (2010). Paradigm, methodology and method: Intellectual integrity in consumer scholarship, *International Journal of Consumer Studies*, 34, 419–27.
Miller, D. (1998). *A theory of shopping*. Cambridge: Polity.
Moisander, J., Valtonen, A. & Hirsto, H. (2009). Personal interviews in cultural consumer research – post-structuralist challenges, *Consumption Markets & Culture*, 12, 329–48.
Morin, C. (2011). Neuromarketing: The new science of consumer behaviour, *Society*, 48, 131–35.
Pantzar, M. & Ruckenstein, M. (2014). The heart of everyday analytics: Emotional, material and practical extensions in self-tracking market, *Consumption Markets & Culture*, 18, 92–109.
Paterson, M. (2006). *Consumption and everyday life*. London: Routledge.
Pink, S. (2012). *Situating everyday life: Practices and places*. London: Sage.
Plessz, M., Dubuisson-Quellier, S., Gojard, S. & Barrey, S. (2016). How consumption prescriptions affect food practices: Assessing the roles of household resources and life-course events, *Journal of Consumer Culture*, 16, 101–23.
Ritzer, G. & Slater, D. (2001). Editorial, *Journal of Consumer Culture*, 1, 5–8.
Sassatelli, R. (2007). *Consumer culture: History, theory and politics*. London: Sage.
Sayer, A. (1992). *Method in social science: A realist approach*. London: Routledge.
Schau, H.J., Gilly, M.C. & Wolfinbarger, M. (2009). Consumer identity renaissance: The resurgence of identity-inspired consumption in retirement, *Journal of Consumer Research*, 36, 255–76.
Shove, E., Pantzar, M. & Watson, M. (2012). *The dynamics of social practices: Everyday life and how it changes*. London: Sage.
Slater, D. (1997). *Consumer culture and modernity*. Cambridge: Polity.
Slater, D. & Miller, D. (2007). Moments and movements in the study of consumer culture, *Journal of Consumer Culture*, 7, 5–23.
Soper, K. & Trentmann, F. (2008). *Citizenship and consumption*. Houndmills: Palgrave.
Tadajewski, M. (2010). Critical marketing studies: Logical empiricism, "critical performativity" and marketing practice, *Critical Marketing*, 10, 210–22.
Therkelsen, A. & Gram, M. (2008). The meaning of holiday consumption: Construction of self among mature couples, *Journal of Consumer Culture*, 8, 269–92.
Thompson, C.J., Locander, W.B. & Pollio, H.R. (1989). Putting consumer experience back into consumer research: The philosophy and method of existential-phenomenology, *Journal of Consumer Research*, 16, 133–46.
Urry, J. (2007). *Mobilities*. Cambridge: Polity.
Valtonen, A., Markuksela, V. & Moisander, J. (2010). Doing sensory ethnography in consumer research, *International Journal of Consumer* Studies, 34, 375–80.
Warde, A. (2002). Setting the scene: Changing conceptions of consumption. In S. Miles, A. Anderson and K. Meethan (Eds.), *The changing consumer*. London: Routledge, 10–24.
Warde, A. (2005). Consumption and theories of practice, *Journal of Consumer Culture*, 5, 131–53.
Warde, A. (2014). After taste: Culture, consumption and theories of practice, *Journal of Consumer Culture*, 14, 279–303.
Zamwel, E., Sasson-Levy, O. & Ben-Porat, G. (2014). Voluntary simplifiers as political consumers: Individuals practising politics through reduced consumption, *Journal of Consumer Culture*, 14, 199–217.

5

Ruminations on the current state of consumer ethnography

Robert V. Kozinets and Eric J. Arnould

This chapter takes an open look at how researchers are using new topographies, technologies, and technocultural rituals and routines in order to reconceptualize what market actors are and do, and most especially, how they should be studied. We are interested in the latest developments in consumer ethnography, as we have experienced and visualized them being practices in our native fields of anthropology, marketing and consumer research, and as it has touched upon industry market researchers and their workings. We do not rehash classic treatments easily available to interested scholars (e.g. Arnould & Wallendorf, 1994; Kozinets, 2010; Spradley, 1979, 1980; Mariampolski, 2006).

We are interested in consumers and consumer ethnography in the current time. Consumers, communications and consumption are all swept up in an anthropocenic streaming and scaping of various sorts, but particularly in our current time as regards the technological. It may be that the rapid pace of technological change and consumption defines our current times better than any other, except perhaps the related condition of perpetual crisis. Consumers extend themselves in more networks of data and information than ever before and are incorporated into supra individual networks. Brands take on new roles in the fantasy lives and media vocabulary of families and individuals. Data, that wonderful word and construct, is everywhere. A share of everyone's life is being digitized and animated, taking on new, independent life as digital biography and aggregated digiculture.

And there are few to chronicle these massive extensions and diminutions of human life except for the social scientists using polysemic analysis and applying it to sensuous spaces of material communication and to material archives both carnal and digital. Applied to this latter domain, ethnography shades effortlessly to include netnography (Kozinets, 2015), but it also remains simply ethnography, literally, "writing the ethnos". But the carnal-digital hybrid ethnos should permeate every element of anthropology now, as it does every discipline, every field, every idea, everybody, although resistance to the holistic writing of what Mauss called "the Complete Human" (l'Homme Total) persists in foundationalist corners of neuro-this, evolutionary-that, and Frank(einsteinian)onomics.

Writing the consumer ethnos usually and perhaps inevitably submits the overflowing richness of the superorganic anthropocentric ecosystem to a logos of logos, terms, and constructs. To ordering, reducing, and diverse figurations, consumer ethnography involves an always-problematic assertion of authority whether practiced as thick description, inscription, or translation, only ever justified in pursuit of edification. Turning human lifeways into figures and representations both includes and excludes, hence the inevitable contestation provoked by ethnographic interpretations, configuring, writing, depicting the ethnos. This is surely better than reductionism, irrelevance, or undisciplined sophistry.

This short chapter hesitantly ruminates on an ethnographic present for ethnography which, just recently, seemed like a distant future. For, during the dot-com boom bust around the time of the Millennium, a cyborg anthropology had been proposed, propagated, and then pretty much forgotten. However, the time of the cyborg never really changed; the agenda continued, like a forgotten clock, to run. Consumer cyborgs are ever more ubiquitous, but their anthropology is not. As human beings rely increasingly on ever-more-intelligent algorithms and information sharing networks, and when increasingly self-organizing intelligence apparatuses and networks of information processing devices rely more and more upon us in a liquid matrix of mutual affordances, we may need more systematic insights in order to perform more appropriate ethnography. Cyborg ethnographies may be simpler than we once thought. To dance with the cyborg. To dine with her. To run with him. The harder part about cyborg ethnographies, perhaps, is that writing them is made so much more difficult by the fact that so many of us have already gone native. By the time we got around to really writing them, we had forgotten, pretty much, what it meant before we started changing into them. Perhaps being a human, like being a consumer, is now too slippery of a signifier to be treated as if it were obvious.

Ethnographers have not feared to enter daunting precincts, cross forbidden thresholds, take up residence with kings and fools, sorcerers and magicians, the desperately privileged and the simply desperate. Tracing networks of meaning along pathways of commerce, art, warfare, and technology has ever been the province of ethnographers, the new electronically self-organizing networks no more daunting than the self-organizing networks of kula and potlatch that challenged analog ethnographic forebears. And yet, we cannot explain it, they hover at the doorway, these old women and men, weighted down beyond their years with decades of recordings, cartons of cannistered films and fading photographs, and boxes of file folders in their basements, afraid to fully enter these nonspaces, nonplaces, these echo chambers where they will be so well exposed.

We concern ourselves in this short chapter with the nature of the consumer and how to study her or him. Who or what is this cyborg consumer, who reclaims from other actants so many practices of extraction, transformation, secretion, and circulation in the consumer ethnography? What does it mean in a technological world to "be" a consumer and an ethnographic subject? What sort of presence and participation does this imply? How should we now best study consumers and consumption? What methods would we recommend or at least pay attention to? What special sorts of rituals and routines would they allow us access to? What do we need to know and think in order to act effectively as consumer ethnographic agents? And finally we wonder where it is taking us. What is the full extent of market-oriented ethnography today? What must be constituted as the ethnographic subject when the subject's identity projects are those of "consumer" and "entrepreneur" and others? What does this realization suggest, or insist, that we do differently? We consider these questions in the following set of shared public and private exchanges, primarily constituted in emails exchanged between the two co-authors. We mean this representation to indicate how we move and shade between types of representation, between private email and publicly published chapter, as easily as everyday consumers move between Facebook, TV, their smartphone apps, and their telephone. We found that these exchanges and the concerns which spur them naturally fit into three broad and overlapping categories of research-related tensions: those between big data and small data, between immateriality and materiality, and between disembodiment and embodiment.

Tension 1: Big data versus small data

Eric: I have been super inspired and kind of terrified by Maxwell (2013). He is advocating for a kind of ethnographic analytics in commercial applications, driven by a host of new tools for analyzing big textual data. I do not know how to do this or how to approach it, but as more of "culture" migrates to the virtual world, it seems that ethnography must also evolve and rather far beyond your early vision of netnography. What experience do you have with ethnographic analytics? And what do you think about it? How should we train students differently; is studying the material world becoming an anachronism as the immaterial occupies a large share of the consumer imaginary?

Rob: Those are thought-provoking questions. I have not read Maxwell's chapter, but am familiar with these sorts of ideas. Richard Rogers of the University of Amsterdam, for instance, has been writing about digital ethnography using only "digital native" methods, in other words, no in-person ethnographic work at all, too. Citing Miller and Slater's (2000) work in Trinidadian cybercafés and dismissing its findings as "typical" and obvious, Rogers (2010, pp. 242–243) critiques the adaptation of existing social science methods to study contemporary "digital" society and offer his own solutions. He suggests, in short, that the "classic social scientific armature, which includes interviews, surveys, observation, and others" is being moved online, but this is insufficient. What he offers, he claims, is nothing short of the introduction "a new era in Internet-related research", which, of course, is something totally new and vague, but which looks a lot like adaptations of analytic things we did before, like statistics on big sample surveys. The claim itself, I think, is more interesting than what is being claimed.

What I see here is a conflation of several things. In the first case, the idea that taking the notion of the interview to online communications is a "digitization" of an offline method and somehow less appropriate to use in such circumstances strikes me as odd. Personal interviews have historically been conducted via mail, and certainly via phone. Those techniques have always been adapted. If the adaptations are sensible and helpful, why would the technique itself be dismissed? Simply because it was deemed to be "non-native"?

Eric: In Roger's broadside I see a host of compelling but contradictory points. One point with which I concur is resonant with an earlier moment in ethnography in which compelling emic constructs like mana, kula, potlatch, shaman, even fetish, among others, were incorporated into the social science lexicon. So should it be with emic concepts that emanate from various digital tribes, a project that William Gibson seems to have seized.

Similarly, Rogers offers an implied critique of the theory ladenness of method. Classic ethnographic methods are more or less alien modes of discourse, as I learned in my Nigerien ethnography. Handicraft tanners would not or could not submit to my efforts to inventory their production and sales but were far more tolerant of conveying this sort of information through my apprenticeship with them. And no one in the villages could or would comprehend a seven-point Likert scale, clearly an artifact of an alien cultural environment in which meticulous choice-making impregnated the cultural repertoire.

And finally perhaps there is a complaint about mediation. Consider our concerns in classic ethnographic practice about the use of interpreters or surrogates. Boas' British Columbian ethnography has been criticized on both counts, and it seems we often lionize the ethnographer who has mastered the local language over one who has not. Indeed the practice of "lone wolf" participant observation is a revolt against methodological mediation in the relationship between ethnographer and the human milieu in which she is operating. Hence, perhaps we may sympathize with Rogers' call for a native netnography dealing in emic method and content.

Rob: In the second case, this notion of digital groundedness, where claims about society or culture in general are grounded exclusively in online data, is problematic. Although there are many things we may be able to study using online data, to make that assumption about everything seems foolhardy.

Eric: I guess that unless we are talking about an ethnography of operating systems like Samantha in the film *Her* or the machine world of *The Matrix* I am hard pressed to support an epistemological claim for the superiority of digital groundedness. On the other hand, are we far from such a prospect?

Rob: Rogers (2010, p. 242) dismisses Miller and Slater (2000) in some ways, but he also makes a claim that their research "set a methodological agenda: [Internet researchers] had to go offline; you had to go to the offline, or the ground, in order to study the online. One had to study users. And, indeed, this has been the social scientific project [in Internet research]". Indeed, there have been many social scientific projects in Internet research, and the one that Rogers explains has certainly not been the only one operating in our field of consumer and marketing research. As examples of exemplary research he has conducted, Rogers (2010) provides numerous analyses of websites using traffic data, page ranks, and word clouds. Ethnography in Rogers' world becomes SEO. There's no "there" there, which is a critique that has often been levelled, in different forms, against netnography. And I find that interesting.

I am not sure how statistical analyses that were first developed in order to count physical objects are any more natively digital than interviews, surveys, or observational techniques, but that is not really my point. My two main points are more about being ecumenical in Internet research, and in being rigorous. First, why and how would we exclude particular methods as examples of "a classic social scientific armature" that one "tries" to move online by "accounting for some small differences", making "slight changes" and "small amendments". Indeed, this is a classic rhetorical move, where one creates a strawperson without any evidence and argues how one's own approach is vastly superior to it. Yet there is a considerable amount of diversity in regards to how ethnography has been adapted and brought online, as Garcia et al. (2009) explore. And in terms of being rigorous, where is the ethnographic participation in the SEO exercise that Rogers (2010) advocates as a substitute for ethnography? How is this ethnography?

Eric: Ok, I think I am with you Rob, and rather critical of Rogers' claim along the same lines as you. To grossly oversimplify, if we pose the question of the point of method in ethnography, it is to facilitate pattern recognition of the orderly superorganic in human life. Perhaps one could make two points: First, the larger the number of data points, the more useful are tools that can find patterns in large data sets; and two, the more chaotic the patterning in data, the greater the usefulness of better tools of pattern recognition. Fair enough, although I am not convinced that the digital world contains more information than the analog world. Of course you and I probably also agree that statistics are no insurance against false positives, the indeterminacy of pattern recognition having been usefully explored by William Gibson in *Pattern Recognition* and Thomas Pynchon way back in *The Crying of Lot 49*. So like you I am suspicious of analytics absent an anthropologically and ethnologically grounded concept of culture as in the classic anthropological project, and which thus drives my unease with Maxwell, an engineer; and Roberts, a technologist.

Rob: The early work on netnography that I conceptualized and wrote up, for the most part in the 90s, was obviously for a very different world. My work in the last few years has been based on developing various new ways of thinking about these evolving issues. I do not shy away from including, not excluding, a panoply of data mining and analysis techniques into netnography when it makes sense, from a research question perspective (not an ideological one) to do so. In Kozinets (2015, p. 254) I am very specific about these inclusions, stating that not only is netnography a technique of observation, interviews, and participation, but one that also includes "web-crawling, tag clouds, sentiment analysis, PageRanks and other algorithms, crowdsourcing, semantic analysis, network analysis and much more". Ethnographers and netnographers of online experiences and interactions should feel limited in their techniques only by their imaginations and abilities, not by some imposed thou-shalt-not strictures.

I have been using "big data" analytic-type approaches obviously since the beginning of netnography, because search engines are one form of this, and using more social search types of tools such as NetBase, Crimson Hexagon, Radian6, Sysomos, and so on, since they began appearing around 2006. Those who are interested might consult the white paper I wrote with NetBase in 2010 that talks about combining methods (Kozinets, 2010).

Tension 2: Materiality versus immateriality

Rob: Let's reflect a little on this chapter. This text is itself an organic thing, like the Internet, moving both backwards and forwards in time from the present, seemingly aware of itself, where it thinks right now it is going, where it will think in future that it has been. In an earlier email exchange on which it was based, you raised the idea of digital immateriality, and an immaterial world. I countered by saying that there is no immaterial world. There is only the material world, even if it is server farms, smartphone screens, and people self-immobilized, eyes darting back and forth, fingers over-extended. Or, if you prefer it so, language, words, utterances are all immaterial. Then where do we go? Into silly models that try to chart how people move back and forth between the material and the immaterial, as words fly out of their mouths. . . . ? No, culture is often embodied, embodied into practices and things. Ethnography is even more relevant, even more necessary than ever. That has been my guiding instinct, and I don't think I am wrong. This is a BIG issue, not only for us, for marketing, for anthropology, but I believe for society itself.

Eric: You say "There is no immaterial world. There is only the material world, even if it is server farms, smartphone screens, and people self-immobilized, eyes darting back and forth, fingers over-extended". Evidently the material-immaterial is an over-simplified binary. Interestingly, in some sort of terms, it's an emic binary for some, equally evidently not for others. But perhaps it makes sense to talk of analogue and digital worlds, or synchronous and a-synchronous ones. Or perhaps it doesn't make sense to draw such distinctions at all, but to simply follow people where and how they go. It is perhaps of interest to consider the energy or resources people commit to such "fields." But then, I was also thinking of *Otaku* (the book), *Transcendence*, *Tron*, *Lawnmower Man*, (the films) and the like that evoke certain moral images of these fields too. At the same time, I wonder if the nature of the physicality of engagement with these worlds like the mental engagement is of more than passing significance to ethnography and especially anthropology of consumption, taken in its material sense as Miller (1987) discussed it. Ethnography can deal with the ways in which human subjects are distinctively configured through their practices of materiality I suppose, perhaps a point lost in the big data frenzy of mere pattern recognition. Surprisingly I didn't see much at the most recent AAA meetings in Denver that suggested a massive push toward a grand ethnographic incursion into whatever all this is. Perhaps I am too out of the loop.

Rob: No, I don't think it is that you are out of the anthro-loop. I think it is that anthropology as a field has never been and still is not a place where these conversations are happening in any sort of major or central way. Gabriella Coleman's (2010) excellent summary of ethnographic approaches to digital media aside, it still seems very much on the periphery of business as usual in anthropology, and that has left the topic to others, such as ourselves and our fields. Business and communications schools seem to be on the cutting edge of this conversation. I'm not sure about sociology, but I'd be surprised if some of it is not happening there. Emic-etic divisions abound, absolutely.

Blanchette (2011, p. 1043) talks about the "trope of immateriality", which confounds thinking about digital communications technologies. He finds that this trope has been present not only in more recent portrayals of the Internet as a type of nonspace, but also in the introduction of past communications technologies such as the telegraph: "The promise of telegraphy is metaphysical: by annihilating space and time, it allows humankind to escape physical limitations. The power and ubiquity of electricity are metaphorically attached to a newly disembodied consciousness" (Rosenheim, 1997, p. 93). Thinkers and writers such as William Gibson, John Perry Barlow, Nicholas Negroponte, and Kevin Kelly, among others, perpetuated through allusion and metaphor the trope that digital communications technologies were somehow immaterial, that information had finally broken free of matter, like a ghost that had thrown off its fleshy coat. Miller and Horst (2012) made the point, among several others, that keeping things on this apparently "virtual" and "immaterial" level actually hides massive amounts of resource use and redistribution, which is entirely correct.

In fact, the trope of immateriality seems to be a bit of a shell game, and I wonder if many ethnographers have fallen for it. "The more effective the digital technology, the more we tend to lose our consciousness of the digital as a material and mechanical process, evidence in the degree to which we become almost violently aware of such background mechanics only when they break down and fail us" (Miller & Horst, 2012, p. 25). Kirschenbaum (2008, p. 135) notes that computers are unique communications instruments in that "they present a premeditated material environment built and engineered to propagate an illusion of immateriality". It is fascinating to read about the many small glitches which are constantly present in digital media that send, transmit, and read data. However, they have algorithms that correct these glitches. They are rendered invisible. Unlike the typos in newspapers, the snow on TV, the hiss on a cassette tape, they provide us with a seductive illusion of perfection. But, Kirschenbaum (2008) argues, it's an engineered orchestration, a performance of perfection. Backstage, digital technologies are just as imperfectly material as anything else.

The same is true of virtual people or communities. People do not simply disappear when they are standing on their mobile phones pushing keys on its screen – as anyone knows who has bumped into one of them while walking. Those people and those screens are physical, and they are backed by mechanisms with a host of toxic chemicals and rare metals, as well as more mundane ones. There is nothing virtual about the amount of energy that Google uses, or the radical transformation of industries that the Internet engenders. Technology, even digital technology with its unsupportable tropes, is matter and bodies. And it is materiality and bodies that should still matter to ethnographers, no matter the age we live in.

Tension 3: Embodiment versus disembodiment

Eric: Reading your text, I realized that perhaps a better point of contrast and one worthy of a lot of investigation is one you mention in passing, the embodied versus disembodied, or perhaps varying degrees of and locations for embodiment. I like this because I am reminded of the whole self-tracking side of the digital world that entails an interesting sort of auto ethnography. I agree with your point about where the conversation is taking place. And it is interesting that it should take place in communications. Let's remember to point out that the ethnographic imagination is engaged in an ongoing struggle with the forces of essentialisms and reductionisms that wish to disenchant the human world, as you also point out in your introduction to Netnography 2.

The issues of embodiment and of technologically mediated ethnography concern me. Because my own experiences of ethnography that are the most trenchant for me are those in which I was a participant observer interacting with other embodied actors with a minimum of technological mediation, that feels like ethnography to me. Evidence from the early days – e.g. Boas' interest in video of the Kwakiutl and in dance, Mead's use of film in Bali, Rouch's incredible films among the Songhai, Cushing with the Zuni, and Flaherty's Nanook about Inuit hunters – shows powerful, often amazing and compelling representations of ethnographic material. But at the same time as they render culture vividly, they foreclose its potential to be otherwise. It reminds me, by contrast, of the experience I often have doing fieldwork that no matter how interesting and compelling the events unfolding before me, something equally compelling is happening just out of the range of my senses. And often it was so; I would round a corner or peer through a fence or wall or enter a field, and lo and behold something amazing was happening. I recall stumbling on possession dances, one in Dahomey in 1970 and one in Niger in 1978, in this way. But with online data in all its proliferation; I don't feel that way. Perhaps because it lacks sensory qualities, sensory depth, it feels like film; flat and like a kind of endless surface.

Rob: My stance is grounded in very different sets of experiences and thoughts. First of all, my interactions with people move through different communication channels. Some of the most powerful interviews that I had with people during my dissertation work in 1995–1996 took place over email, a medium where perhaps people felt more comfortable making confessions. One of my key informants, who I felt very close to, turned out to be a woman, while for about eighteen months I had kind of assumed she was a man. Was it disembodiment, or some sort of impartiality, a gender net neutrality, or both?

In your email you first talk about video and film, and its power to represent ethnographic materials. Then you talk about online data being "like film; flat. . . . ". I will remind you that online data includes film, YouTube video, iTunes podcasts, Instagram photos, and of course Skype interviews in real time. What is "real" and what is not real? What is disembodied about a Skype interview may not be what is disembodied about an email exchange. We are not yet adept at talking and thinking about these nuances and differences. However, if we are going to talk in any sort of general way about ethnography and where it is headed, I think we need to include that it is becoming more multidimensional in its forms and must continue to do so. Films, audio, photographs, hyperlinks, and so on are exciting and important ways to represent ethnographic data and ethnographic understandings. I think the cutting edge of ethnography is already moving to meet the cutting edge of the digital humanities and engage in major projects that represent the lifeways and experiences of specific groups of people.

In terms of online research contracting opportunities for discovery, I do not see why it needs to be so. This sense might be a function of the amount of time you spend openly exploring online, wandering from one server and site to another, so to speak, as compared with wandering places in the physically embodied world. Within a very short amount of time doing netnography I stumble serendipitously upon all sorts of surprising material. Online spaces are like rivers; they branch and turn. You can spend days following them, getting more and more lost until you find something that fascinates you.

To say that someone's videos or words are less "sensory" than the experience of being in the room with them is no doubt true. But having access to their photo albums, to videos they made on YouTube and posted over the last six years, to the texts of their articles and books also gives me a massive amount of understanding of them that I might not get simply sitting down with them in a room. But do we really need to choose one or the other? Why in the world would any researcher in their right mind choose to press the mute button on so much that is going on in human communications now?

Online or offline ethnography? Embodied or digital field research, interviews, and sites? It is never *either or.* It is always *both and.* If we want to understand contemporary experience, which I would think has changed a lot, at least for young people, in Dahomey and Niger as well as in Odense and Los Angeles, since 1970, then don't we need to follow the path of communications wherever it lead us, through all media? Netnography was never meant to stand alone, although it certainly can do this. Like interviews or archival analysis, it was always intended to complement existing approaches and help to systematically explore questions of human culture(s).

Eric: I take your points and particularly like your comments about following digital rivers. Perhaps a useful "how to" would be more a "Notes and Queries" about becoming such a digital flaneur rather than merely how one uses various pattern recognition tools. This could be a very useful come back to the promoters of pattern recognition. Thus; I could not agree more with your comment "We are not yet adept at talking and thinking about these nuances and differences," which is precisely why it is still pedagogically useful to talk about them, I think.

Rob: I agree wholeheartedly that we need more flaneur's guides to the digital trail. There has been a lot of pressure to write netnography as if it was a manual for a piece of magical software. Others have been doing so, and others have eschewed anthropological values entirely. I like where this conversation is heading and hope we can continue it, and maybe start to build out some of the bits and pieces of that flaneur's guide.

Our thoughts are public

This chapter has centered on a particular topic: who are the new "consumers" and how should we, as ethnographers, study them? This short introductory conversation has inspired us to dip our toes into three areas of tension around the ethnographic enterprise as it looks at consumers: using big data versus small data in our ethnographies, embracing disembodied netnography versus versus embodied ethnography, and considering the merits and indeed veracities of immateriality versus the familiar ones of materiality.

In this new world of disembodied, immaterial researchers and consumers interacting as digital ghosts, what does it mean to study consumption in a natural setting? What meaning, exactly does that term natural have, when the definition of what it means to be a functioning member of human society shifts every few years? People who were viable and fully functioning while in their fifties two decades ago are in an anachronistic form of self-exile unless they have kept up with technology and own a smartphone and a tablet. And does anyone, anyways, really want to like the selfie of some random old guy?

Professors are old. Academia is ancient. Ethnography is beyond geriatric. There is a well-earned, heartily-honed, heartfelt fear of the techno-future in anthropology and some other parts of academia that young people simply do not subscribe to. They are happy to dive into digital waters populated by corporate predators and prey, swim in them every day, make them a part of their world, their dreams, their lives. But does this mean that the anthropology which seeks to understand their world must also do so?

We think not. The range and scope of the routines and rituals that may be apprehended from the most intimate and intrapersonal to the most public and interpersonal is virtually infinite. Why would we only choose one, or a few? Or even a bounded subset? I would rather be a cyborg than a god, but if I had the choice, I would be a cyborg action hero T-Rex superhero god, and many other things beside.

Ethnographic aims may be edifying, answering the full range of journalistic questions about what, how, where, when and why, but may also be proscriptive, reflecting the persuasive ends of public policy makers, NGOs, commercial firms, and ever more frequently, consumers themselves.

Indeed, it may well be that increasingly the most credible, most legitimate, most desirable, and most seductive "things" are those that are crowdsourced into existence. The system is interesting which makes all of this possible. So too are the habits, the routines, the thoughts and emotions that drive the individual, that propel her through keyboard and smartphone routines into realms of significance and satisfaction. Where ethnographic techniques meet their biggest challenges occurs at this extreme micro and extreme macro scale of analysis, perhaps partially mitigated by the flow of information provided by personal tracking devices at one end or new techniques of visual representation of big data at the other end. As we have discussed, these elements might be seen to be threats to ethnographic understanding. We choose, instead, to see them as opportunities for a synthetic understanding, an anthropology of cyborgs, by cyborgs, for cyborgs.

Mapping the terrain of a cyborg-infused, market-oriented ethnography is virtually impossible, but also vitally important. The ethnographic gaze extends its purview towards the most intimate and the most public of environments. And perhaps more importantly, overturns a narrow conception of consumer as one who passively purchases amongst an array of market offerings. Who is this cyborg consumer, we have asked? It seems obvious that the weight of the term *consumer* is too much to bear, even before obfuscating it with the silly term *cyborg*. The contemporary consumer is of course a cyborg. She is of course part of a new networked society. Perhaps even something on its way to becoming a new form of species, a posthuman. Perhaps it is silly to speak of such things because they are already so obvious. And yet it still seems worth mentioning that this cyborg consumer is one who intervenes actively and collectively at almost any point in a given value-creating chain of relationships, and thus becomes consumer/designer, consumer/developer, consumer/entrepreneur, consumer/maker, consumer/distributer, consumer resister, and so on by turns. Yet always the cyborg. Making money. Designing products. Developing software. Commenting, critiquing, cataloguing emergent or ephemeral netstensive experiences. Selling to and being sold to by her followers, friends and family.

Can ethnography include the nonhuman world? Should we think about an agenda in which ethnographies explore the agency, if not the intentionality, of things? In general, we think not insofar as such things are not sentient. When they do become sentient, they should be the ones typing their own "machinography" stories, not us. We will probably be very busy at that point trying to define, perhaps defend, our own humanity.

Ethnography is and always will be about human understanding. A human understanding of consumption must focus on the nature of humanity and its relation to the non-human, however it might be changing. Let us leave the participant-observational work among the bots and AIs to the bots and AIs. The materiality of consumption on the one hand, and on the other ethnographies that investigate the relationship between various modes of circulation, mutuality, gifting, access, purchase, and lateral cycling, are powerful enough topics for human beings to consider and ponder in such dynamic and heady times as these.

Perhaps surprisingly, perhaps not, what remains a less-visited country are the vast territories occupied by the poorer billions, both mobile and sedentary, nonetheless each and all entirely swallowed up into the infrastructure of global market capitalism. And many are on the forefront of the digital, from the mad PR genius of ISIS to the fraught precincts of crowdsourced microfinance. Where do we enlist their voices? How do we represent them? How do we understand the pathway out, if we never truly understand the path not taken?

References

Arnould, E. J. & Wallendorf, M. (1994). Market oriented ethnography: Interpretation building and market strategy formulation. *Journal of Marketing Research*, 31 (November), 484–504.

Blanchette, J.-F. (2011). A material history of bits. *Journal of the American Society for Information Science and Technology*, 62 (6), 1042–1057.

Coleman, E. G. (2010). Ethnographic approaches to digital media. *Annual Review of Anthropology*, 39, 487–505.

Garcia, A. C., Standlee, A. I., Bechkoff, J. & Cui, Y. (2009). Ethnographic approaches to the internet and computer-mediated communication. *Journal of Contemporary Ethnography*, 38 (1), 52–84.

Kirschenbaum, M. G. (2008). *Mechanisms: New media and the forensic imagination*. Cambridge, MA: MIT Press.

Kozinets, R.V. (2015). *Netnography: Redefined*. London: Sage.

Kozinets; R.V. (2010). *Netnography: Doing ethnographic research online*. London and Thousand Oaks: Sage.

Mariampolski, H. (2006). *Ethnography for marketers*. Thousand Oaks and London: Sage.

Maxwell C. R. (2013). Accelerated pattern recognition, ethnography, and the era of big data. In B. Jordan (Ed.), *Advancing ethnography in corporate environments* (pp. 175–192). Walnut Creek: Left Coast Press.

Miller, D. (1987). *Material culture and mass consumption*. Oxford: Basil Backwell.

Miller, D. & Horst, H. A. (2012). The digital and the human: A prospectus for digital anthropology. In H. A. Horst & D. Miller (Eds.), *Digital anthropology* (pp. 3–15). London and New York: Berg.

Miller, D. & Slater, D. (2000). *The internet: An ethnographic approach*. Oxford: Berg.

Rogers, R. (2010). Internet research: The question of method – a keynote address from the YouTube and the 2008 election cycle in the United States conference. *Journal of Information Technology & Politics*, 7 (2/3), 241–260.

Rosenheim, S. J. (1997). *The cryptographic imagination: Secret writing from Edgar Poe to the internet*. Baltimore, MD: Johns Hopkins.

Spradley J. P. (1979). *The ethnographic interview*. Belmont, CA: Wadsworth.

Spradley, J. P. (1980). *Participant observation*. New York: Holt, Rinehart and Winston.

Part II

Consumers and markets

Introduction

Modern consumer culture is often defined by the mediation of meanings and resources on markets. The latter is thus the meeting place of consumption and production, which enmeshes a complex mix of power relations, symbols, practices and material objects. Economics tends to analyse capitalist markets as adhering to universal laws, whereas a long sociological tradition sees markets and their actors as inherently embedded in socio-cultural contexts. This part of the book, although its headline could call for different interpretations, does not take a managerial approach, characteristic to the bulk of studies on markets and marketing, but a deliberately sociological one by problematizing markets as socio-economic and cultural sites. That is networks of power relations and objects, within which resources are provided for consumers for leading their everyday lives, forging their identities and giving meaning to the world, on the one hand, and within which resources are extracted from consumers in the form of money, time, attention and symbolic labour for value co-creation with and for consumer goods and brands, on the other hand.

The classic question whether those who hold power – namely corporations and other providers – manipulate consumers into satisfying needs that "really" do not exist, that is, are false, or whether consumers are independent actors who outwit the corporate marketer by being subversive, streetwise or just fickle looms in the background but does not take centre stage in here; the main agenda is to shed light onto the complexity of the relationships between consumers and markets, especially in the context of various new or recently theorised phenomena and processes such as value co-creation, prosumption, sharing economy as well as crises of the markets that make a deep imprint on ways of consumption.

As in the other sections of this book, some chapters deal with consumers and markets more directly, while others talk about concepts, disciplines and the winding road of research.

This section opens with chapters on how the market "interpellates" consumers via the ubiquitous processes of marketing and branding and how these phenomena have been dealt with by scholars. Chapter 6 by Matthias Bode and Søren Askegaard plunges head on into the "uneasy" relationship between marketing studies, done to a large extent in business schools, and consumer research that has more epistemological than managerial ambitions. They do not look at marketing or consumer research practices, but the academic disciplines and their interaction. They define consumer research "as the distinctly individualized decision science approach" while acknowledging that this version of studying consumers has changed significantly over the years. The chapter charts the timeline of the development of the field of consumer research with its search for autonomous self-identity against the parallel discipline of marketing, as well as its mutations from strictly cognitive dominance towards more humanistic and sociological scientific logics. Readers of this chapter have to bear in mind the specific definition of "consumer research" provided in the text, to avoid collating this particular sub-discipline with the whole of consumption studies that is a much more varied complex of approaches, as the whole volume witnesses.

Chapter 7, authored by Siwarit Pongsakornrungsilp and Jonathan Schroeder, asks how consumers co-create with brands. Their particular interest lies with two concepts: culture and value. They address the dynamic relations between consumers and brand owners, managers and employees, i.e. both strategic and casual interactions that generate brand meaning. The authors also unpack some tensions that have been highlighted by scholars, namely between the concept of working consumers and their unpaid labour for brands. The chapter gives detailed attention to various consumer roles in the co-creation process.

Chapter 8 is a somewhat unorthodox handbook chapter: while charting the emergence and use of the concept of prosumption, it also narrates the personal and serendipitous research journey of its author, George Ritzer. Prosumption is postulated as an umbrella term which incorporates both production and consumption, because the latter are inherently impossible to unequivocally distinguish from one another. G. Ritzer also provides a detailed map of more explicitly linked concepts, such as co-creation and service-dominant logic, as well as more implicit relatives by such diverse authors as Stuart Hall, Henry Jenkins and Michel de Certeau. Ritzer retains in this contribution his critique of the co-optation and control of the prosumer by capitalist forces, while calling for more research attention to prosumption, especially in the light of the advent of the "smart prosuming machines" that may well proclaim the death of the prosumer.

The authors of chapter 9, Stefan Wahlen and Mikko Laamanen, look at hybrid and new forms of market activity, where established mechanisms are brought in question: namely collaborative consumption and sharing economy. The authors do not hail the dawn of a new era shattering the foundations of capitalist economy; they rather offer a more sobering account which states the status of these phenomena – alternative to, better than, or even worse than traditional forms of capitalism – it is not clear yet. A tension exists between the potential of sharing economy to foster sustainability, lessen inequalities and empower consumers, on the one hand, and on the other, the role and actions of corporate players within sharing economy, that may in the worst-case scenario undermine its positive potential. The chapter provides a historical perspective of economic collaboration, thus questioning the total novelty of sharing economy. Wahlen and Laamanen juxtapose sharing based on kinship structure with networks of exchange between strangers that make use of modern information and communication technology. As a valuable reference to read further, the chapter offers an overview table of recent research and debates around sharing economy based on a SCOPUS search.

Chapter 10 by Sebastian Koos contributes to highlighting present-day problems and challenges to markets, namely issues related to economic crises – disruptive economic events that have a detrimental effect on consumers – both on a societal level and an everyday micro-level. As there is relatively little social scientific research on crises and consumers, this compact treatment of how economic shocks impact consumption is very welcome. The author outlines two basic impact mechanisms: resources (by decreasing income) and beliefs (primarily by inflicting uncertainty about the future). Amongst other things, Koos provides a review of empirical studies of how consumers react to crises, as well as goes a long way in contextualizing the impact of crises in terms of their type, national context and temporality. Even though crises lessen excessive consumption and thus potentially the ecological footprint, Koos concludes that economic shocks are not a straightforward route towards sustainability given their adverse effects on the most vulnerable socio-economic groups. This chapter is a good complementary reading of other chapters in Part V – *Consumption and social divisions*.

6

Marketing and consumer research

An uneasy relationship

Matthias Bode and Søren Askegaard

The first thing to note, when addressing the relationship between marketing and consumer research, is that the link between promotional practices for advancing specific exchange processes and insight into the sociological (and psychological) factors guiding engagement in such social exchange processes can be found in market relations from the dawn of markets (Graeber, 2012). That the systematic relationship between understanding the population as consumers and usage of such knowledge for target marketing and advertising purposes has proliferated in scope and intensity and has become a significant social institution during the twentieth century, is also obvious (Trentmann, 2016). In short, it is beyond the scope of this short chapter to treat relations between marketing and consumer research as social practices. Instead, we have chosen to look at the relationship between marketing and consumer research as institutionalized academic disciplines. It should be noted right away that when we talk about "consumer research" in the following, we are referring to the consumer research organized mainly through the Association for Consumer Research (ACR) and predominantly working in marketing departments, since the nexus between marketing and consumer research is the topic of this chapter. The term *consumer research* underlines the distinctly individualized decision science approach that has dominated this discipline throughout the years, albeit with significant change over the last decades, mainly represented by the Consumer Culture Theory version of consumer research. The use of the term *consumer research* in this narrow sense by no means is an indication that research on consumers and consumption does not take place in other disciplines, as this volume is witnessing.

Seen from the outside, the relationship between marketing and consumer research must seem fairly straightforward. One seminal article about the subject suggests that marketing as a business orientation and a research discipline can be understood as developing "criteria which we would use in determining which product to market. *And these criteria were, and are, nothing more nor less than those of the consumer herself*" (Keith, 1960, emphasis in original). If this is so, then the case is straightforward. There can be no marketing without consumer research. Inside the world of business education and marketing professionalism, it is less obvious, however, that marketing and consumer research are two sides of the same coin. To this day, for example, whereas most business educational programs include marketing as a compulsory part of the curriculum, much fewer include a compulsory consumer behavior class.

Thus, it might be conceived – paradoxically – to have marketing without consumer research. Conversely, it has been equally problematic for consumer researchers to define their discipline in relation to marketing. Concluding his 1981 presidential address for the ACR, Jerry Olson pondered on the future (lack of direct) relationship between consumer research and marketing:

"My final suggestion is somewhat more specific. I think that we should expand our beginning efforts to develop concepts and theories of consumer behavior from different perspectives than that of the marketing manager. For instance, what would a theory of brand loyalty look like from the perspective of the consumer as an effort minimizer? Or, what would individual difference theories of consumers be like if they were not consciously constructed to be useful for market segmentation? Until we start explicitly contrasting our marketing-oriented theories with theories based on different values and objectives, we probably won't realize how limiting the marketing perspective is" (Olson, 1982, p. ix).

Thus, a certain critical reflection on an attitude towards what is considered to be an epistemological "straightjacket", of being reduced to an auxiliary discipline to marketing, is far from new to consumer researchers. Here, it can also be noted that the highly prestigious *Journal of Consumer Research* does not consider itself a managerial journal. However, since by far the largest number of ACR members are employed in business schools, this pursuit of a certain distance between marketing and consumer research usually is not reflected in terms of institutional organization.

This chapter explores the history of this uneasy relationship between marketing and consumer research, and concludes with some prospective reflections on the future of this relationship. Our approach centers on the birth of consumer research as a discipline. Here we make a conceptual first stop in the continuous flow of events. From there we will first turn backwards, to develop the undercurrents for the birth, and then we focus on the aftermath of the birth. This approach acknowledges the intertwined relations in historicizing between the *res facta* (the actual events) and *res ficta* (the narrated events): What happened in the development in consumer research cannot be separated from how the story is told. In breaking up the allegedly "normal" structure of events we intend to avoid the illusion of a linear and teleological development. Disciplinary developments are not necessarily that way, and they do not advance from the naïve to the sophisticated. Rather, consumer research developed in contingent forms of interconnectedness and reciprocal resonances.

Birth: The institutionalization of consumer research

The field of consumer research, encompassing specialized researchers, dedicated academic courses, textbooks, journals and associations, was born in the end of the 1960s in the USA. While there was research on the behavior of consumers before, a process of institutionalization excogitated at this time. One consequence was a rapid increase in published research. In one of the leading consumer behavior textbooks at that time, the authors Engel, Kollat and Blackwell (1972, p. 662) claimed that more research has been published between 1968 and 1972 than during all the years prior to 1968.

In 1969, the already mentioned textbook author James Engel invited several scholars to discuss the state of affairs for consumer research. This led to the foundation of the Association of Consumer Research (ACR) (e.g. Mittelstaedt, 1990). In the invitation letter, Engel formulated the goal: "We need a new organization cutting across the lines of various disciplines and organizations which are currently involved in or concerned with consumer behavior research. The organization is intended to bring in people from psychology, economics, all phases of industry, home economics, and other areas" (cited in Pratt, 1974, p. 4).

The ACR conference proceedings became an additional outlet for publications, besides the already existing *Journal of Marketing* (founded in 1936), *Journal of Advertising Research* (founded in 1961) and especially the *Journal of Marketing Research* (founded in 1964). However, in the founding sessions of the ACR, the need for a specialized journal for consumer research was articulated. There was on the other hand concern within AMA that another academic journal would lead to losing the link with marketing practitioners. For the new *Journal of Consumer Research* (*JCR*), the opposition towards being exclusively defined by marketing became a core of the founding vision, with ten different disciplinary organizations functioning as the board: "Consumer research was not marketing research, or public-opinion research, or psychological research, or sociological research, but all of these – and more" (Kernan, 1995, p. 440). The institutionalization of consumer research, and the articulation of a future vision, went hand in hand with an emerging sense of identity, a self-consciousness and feeling of responsibility for a disciplinary field in becoming. As an "invisible college" (Crane, 1972), a communicative and social network was established that offered a forum for advancing consumer research, and producing a shared sense of norms and practices. These interactions centered on the issues of "who are we?" and "who do we want to become?" For consumer research this self-reflexivity started with an identity crisis, in particular with the philosophy of science debates in the 1980s (Sherry, 1991), that has lasted into the new millennium (Simonson, Carmon, Dhar, Drolet and Nowlis, 2001).

The evaluation of the state of consumer research in the institutionalization phase was bleak, sometimes even bordering at self-flagellation: There is no theory of consumer behavior (Sheth, 1967), the research so far is a "flood of triviality" (Pollay, 1972, p. 595), 90% of the findings are probably wrong (Kollat, Blackwell and Engel, 1972), the problems researched are insignificant with the "proverbial 1-ply vs. 2-ply toilet tissue decision" and research strategies are dominated by opportunism and reductionism (Arndt, 1976). In the same breath, the future looked bright concerning the growing need for consumer research knowledge for a variety of users due to affluent societies. In such circumstances, consumers can now "buy what they 'want' rather than what they 'need'" (Twedt, 1965, p. 269). Such volatile and hard-to-predict behavior would increase the necessity for marketers and governments to have a better understanding of consumers.

The "immaturity" of consumer research was linked to the pre-paradigmatic *science status* (e.g. Pollay, 1972). The question was surprisingly treated less as a *philosophy of science* issue, but as a *sociology of science* one. The philosophy of science question about the defining qualifications of knowledge products as science seemed to have been solved: Science is based alone on the hypothetico-deductive method (Kernan, 1995) established by natural science. The more pressing issue at that point was the development of science as a sociological issue, dependent on external and internal conditions and power relations: How can disciplines gain reputation and legitimacy?

The different models for the organization of science at hand were the anarchistic, the market and the organized model. The *anarchistic model* was seen as the actual reality: Research is based on idiosyncratic preferences and convenience of data availability, and it leads to a lack of interrelatedness (Pollay, 1972). In the *market model*, the "invisible hand" could theoretically improve science by the market success of "better" knowledge products. However, while consumer researchers were predominantly employed in business schools, they did not trust the market as a solution for science (e.g. Mittelstaedt, 1990). In an ironic twist, a few years later Peter and Olsen (1983) would demonstrate the actual relevancy of the market model for science by reversing the pressing question about the scientific status of marketing: "Is science marketing?" The only alternative was therefore the *organized model*. Hereby, the development of science was achieved by having a core comprehensive theory, and research that is derived from such model to further refine the variables and their links. At that time, the most influential comprehensive models were developed by Engel, Kollat and Blackwell (1968) and Howard and Sheth (1969). These neo-behavioristic S-O-R models were process-oriented, incorporated internal constructs in form of hypothetical constructs and intervening variables, as well as external variables which were taken as a given. The models emphasized cognitive processes and shaped the consumer research until the 1980s (Bettmann, 1979).

One major question remained unanswered: Who should be in charge of determining the general direction of research and research priorities (Arndt, 1976)? One way to solve that issue was to refer to the needs of consumer research knowledge users. In the institutionalization phase, these were primarily marketing management, government, consumerist advocates, consumers and academics. However, this led to what Robertson and Ward (1972) called the "payoff dilemma". For an applied discipline like consumer research, a role conflict was seen in meeting both the long-term goals for scientific knowledge production and a short-term goal of responding to the so-called "action needs" of knowledge users. On the one hand, especially the link to marketing managers was seen as a defining element of consumer research, awarding a sense of relevancy and identity to the consumer discipline. This territory was threatened by applied and commercial market research. As Guest (1962, p. 316) warned, researchers employed by business have the advantage of being closer to real consumer problems and having more resources at their disposal than academic researchers. Yet, they lack in the methodological skills. Arndt (1976) suggested calling such research "customer analysis" to emphasize the difference from consumer research. In this way, the payoff dilemma characterized the complex relation between consumer research and marketing. Marketing was a primary reference point as the academic affiliation and as a practical research context to differentiate consumer researchers from members of other disciplines who were all invited to contribute to the knowledge corpus. At the same time, a distance had to be established to secure the scientific development of the discipline.

The category of the "consumer" was used as a decisive anchor for defining consumer research, while at the same time this anchor was left surprisingly unexplored. Pragmatically, this had the advantage of uniting factions that favored a close link between marketing and consumer research, as well as factions that opted for a more independent status. Theoretically, it shows a lack of awareness of how the concept of the consumer came into being as a master category for collective and individual subjectivities. Only a few scholars addressed at that time the influence of the knowledge user's perspective and interests in the conceptualization of the consumer. Examples are Kover (1967) and Arndt (1976). From a marketing perspective, the consumer emerged as an isolated, individual decision-making unit considering mainly commercially offered products and services. It was Tucker (1974, p. 31) who most clearly expressed the consequence of a narrow marketing perspective towards the consumer: The consumer " ... was always studied in the ways that fishermen study fish rather than as marine biologists study them."

Prequel: The state of consumer research before the institutionalization

Historical phenomena have no inherent starting points. Here we may rather speak of a reconstructive process which is framed by the interests of the observers. For consumer researchers, the late 1960s constitute the birth of consumer research as a formal and informal institutionalized network. For sociologists, origins in research on consumption and consumers lead back to works by Marx, Weber, Simmel, Sombart or Veblen (Zukin and Maguire, 2004; Warde, 2015). Feminists emphasize related fields as household economics and commercial market research in the early twentieth century, where gendered consumption activities in the household like doing laundry or food preparation were researched (Caterall, Maclaran and Stevens, 2005, see e.g. Frederick, 1929).

As for "marketing", it was first introduced in the beginning of the twentieth century, with university courses about the distribution, pricing and retailing of mainly farm products (e.g. Maynard, 1941; Bartels, 1988) following the impetus of new forms of advertising, products and retail systems. Methodologically, simple secondary data processing was the dominant approach until the 1920s. When the active market cultivation was becoming more obvious in the 1920s, survey methods gained popularity, and for consumer research as a part of marketing research, the methodological refinement of surveys was dominant. More advanced impulses at that time were coming from business sectors, with media research, public opinion polling organizations and advertising agencies. This included readership analyses, observing consumers at the point-of-sale, weekly brand barometers or consumer testing departments, where consumers were observed on how they use products (Lockley, 1974).

Up to World War II, new influences for consumer research were often coming from European scholars who emigrated because of the rise of Nazism in Germany, like George Katona (who developed the economic psychology field), Kurt Lewin (developing social psychology with his field theory) or Paul Lazarsfeld (who developed radio research in Europe) (e.g. Kassarjian, 1994). Lazarsfeld also brought with him a student named Ernest Dichter, a key figure in motivation research, who in multiple ways shaped the field of consumer research before the birth of the discipline (Fullerton, 1990; Stern 2004).

Motivation research was positioned against a descriptive research of consumers, which was denigrated as "superficial nose counting" and naïve empiricism: "It is not enough to know that young women use more hand lotions than older women. The point is to find out *why* people have these preferences" (Britt, 1950, p. 669). The biggest problem for consumer research at that time was a possible consumer bias in survey answers, where they might not tell the truth or be aware of the "hidden motives" behind their consumption behaviour. Attempts to optimize such research were primarily methodologically and not theoretically based. Here a researcher like Dichter went away from the economic theory of rational decision and utilized psychoanalytical and psychological theories of human behaviour. The socio-cultural atmosphere was supportive: Freud and psychoanalysis were widely discussed in urban America during the 1950s; McCarthyism was raising fear of communist brainwashing tactics and mind control, and the myth of subliminal advertising was widely spread (Tadajewski, 2006). In this climate, Dichter's methods of depth interviews, Rorschach personality tests, Thematic Apperception Tests or role playing to uncover hidden motives for not only describing but understanding behavior were widely used in consulting work for big corporations (Dichter, 1960; Schwarzkopf and Gries, 2010). The majority of academic researchers, however, distanced themselves from motivation research, as it lacked in shared scientific standards.

However, the decisive reason for the decline was the development of the marketing discipline at that time, characterized by the scientification of marketing and the rise of the marketing concept. An evaluation of business schools in the US by the Ford Foundation and the Carnegie Foundation was heavily critical about the state of affairs (Gordon and Howell, 1959), stating that to become more relevant for business needs, teaching and research had to become more scientific by incorporating especially the behavioural sciences, mathematics and statistics. With big grants, the foundations changed the marketing landscape, increasing laboratory research, experimental design, operations research, advanced mathematics and computer simulations (e.g. Bartels, 1988; Kerin, 1996; Staelin, 2005). At the same time, the rise of the marketing concept increased the relevance of consumer research as a sub-discipline of marketing. The marketing concept claims that the consumer is the foundation of a business and prescribes an organisational focus on the consumer to achieve its goals. In a seminal article, Levitt (1960, p. 50) stated: "Selling focuses on the needs of the seller, marketing on the needs of the buyer". The developing cognitive approaches in psychology, replacing a former behavioural dominance, were more in line with the general changes in marketing. They came from a scientifically accepted discipline (psychology); they promised more realistic assumptions than any economic theories; they were able to be integrated in more quantitative marketing models and finally shared the now accepted goals of marketing with the prediction, explanation and control of individual behavior (Mittelstaedt, 1990).

It was only in the 1980s, when researchers revived a more qualitative research tradition and took up again the "why question", that they could connect to the forgotten traditions of motivation research (Tadajewski, 2006).

Sequel: Consumer research and marketing as "parallel disciplines"

After its birth, consumer research was supposed to reach a point of maturity in the 1970s and 1980s. More work was empirically based, with a strong psychological foundation and proudly anchored on the pillars of the consensual experimental, deductive-nomological logics of scientific explanations (Leong, 1989). Despite the founding ideals, the accepted status of consumer research was now as a subdiscipline of marketing (Mittelstaedt, 1990). The psychological orientation secured a scientific status, and the marketing affiliation guaranteed the social and professional legitimacy. Furthermore, psychology's disciplinary objectives of prediction, explanation and control of individual behaviour framed the compatibility of consumer research and marketing. Rossiter (1989, p. 410) stated as the hegemonic norm for consumer researchers to effectively use "psychological theories of how to better produce responses to marketing stimuli".

During the 1980s a new generation of consumer researchers attacked the dominant consensus about what consumer research should be. Under labels like interpretive, humanistic, or post-positivistic scholarship, they first criticized the cognitive dominance, and then advanced towards a methodological criticism, stating that consumer research should utilize the scientific logics of humanities and social science instead of the natural sciences. Dilthey's distinction between "understanding" for social behaviour and "explaining" for natural phenomena was a shared reference (Hudson and Ozanne, 1988).

This insurgency defined new goals for consumer research. Instead of being "handmaidens of business", consumer research should aspire to an independent status from marketing (Holbrook, 1985; Belk, 1986). As Sanders (1987, p. 73f.) phrased it: "Rather than providing marketing managers with information which they can use to more effectively manipulate consumers, the interpretive/ethnographic approach can (and should be) used as a source of humanizing and liberating knowledge". As the official line, Lutz (1989) hoped in his presidential address to the field of consumer researchers for a tolerant, respectful pluralism of diverse approaches in a united consumer research discipline with continued links to marketing.

When the dust of the paradigm debate had settled, consumer research emerged in the 1990s and early 2000s as a field characterized by multidisciplinary pluralism (MacInnis and Folkes, 2010). The insurgent tradition developed into Consumer Culture Theory (see Belk, this volume), a research stream now firmly established next to more psychological research streams such as information.

Processing and behavioural decision theory

Overall, research on consumption and consumers has been relatively marginalized outside of the marketing discipline, the most notable exception possibly being the sociology of consumption community in Europe. Insofar, recognition, legitimization and individual work environments mainly still justify the characterization of consumer research as a subfield of marketing. This general positioning can however allow wide variations in the degree of contiguity to marketing. Contributing factors in this variety are changes in marketing theory and practice. Marketing theory, for example, has opened up to understandings that also include views of marketing as a social institution, embedded in wider socio-cultural contexts. In the 1980s, consumer research proponents of the independence status feared a dependency on the straightjacket of supporting business in their profit maximization strategies. Meanwhile, marketing theory has been discussing wider social and ethical issues, and for example social and environmental goals may potentially gain priorities besides profit maximization. This allowed new alliances and developments, which transcend easy "for or against marketing" positions. One example is the service-dominant logic (Vargo and Lusch, 2004), as one of the most profound paradigmatic changes in recent marketing theory. Here, services rather than products become the main reference point for exchanges, which leads to a process view and the acknowledgement of an active consumer role in value co-creation (see chapter 7). This resonated with the ideas of consumer researchers who were coming from the independence tradition to engage in new discussions within marketing to establish a stronger political role in the discipline (Lusch and Vargo, 2006).

Hence, it is obvious that both within consumer research and within marketing, there continues to be significant movements that challenge the firm-centric view. As we have already outlined, this has been a defining characteristic for the field of consumer research and its leading journal for decades. However, this has not prevented leading scholars within the field to suggest a trans-disciplinary movement within the field, named Transformative Consumer Research (TCR), as a venue for research-oriented problem solving for consumers rather than for firms (Mick, 2006). A look at the history of publications in *JCR* during the first thirty years of its existence (1974–2004) shows a general decline in articles dealing with central issues for consumer welfare such as energy and conservation, sustainability, credit and debt, and consumer education (Mick, 2008). Mick's conclusion is that consumer research has "generally underprioritizied scholarship for alleviating problems and advancing opportunities for well-being" (Mick, 2008, p. 377). Consumer research is transformative insofar as it tries to go against this tendency.

A similar tendency can be spotted in marketing, although it is arguably considerably less powerful in terms of setting agendas. The predominantly British tradition of Critical Marketing studies (e.g. Tadajewski and Brownlie, 2008) has tried to pave the way for a marketing discipline that operates with respect for consumer-citizens, underlining that the critical scrutiny of the marketing institution and its practices should first and foremost be beneficial to consumer interests rather than to managerial interests. A parallel attempt to demonstrate the critical and beneficial potential of marketing as a discipline is the group of marketing scholars from University of Notre Dame arguing for the positive societal impact of marketing for the common good (rather than for individual corporate benefit) (Murphy and Sherry Jr., 2014).

However, such exceptions should not conceal the general truth that the overwhelming majority of marketing and consumer research is embedded in the paradigm of economic growth and a neoliberal logic of "what is good for business is good for society". Even if it is acknowledged that there are numerous global, climatic, political, social and economic problems to be solved, the fundamental premises of free market relations and the sovereign consumer are not questioned (Giesler and Veresiu, 2014).

Epilogue: Back to the future of marketing and consumer research

What might be the future relationship between marketing and consumer research? According to one recent report, the economic benefits from marketing based on consumer data are one of the main sources of growth in the American economy (Deighton and Johnson, 2016). Marketing, it seems, continues to believe in and celebrate its own consumer-centric world view. However, the question is what such information actually means? Since, from a philosophy of science perspective, we have to assert that the consumer data referred to are constructed representations of people-as-consumers, it is uncertain to what degree the alleged successes in navigating markets are due to both such data's ability to reveal tendencies and preferences in the marketplace and the ability of consumer data to structure and strengthen marketing performativity in complex global markets. It is useful to remind ourselves of the validity not just in the narrow but in a very general sense of Marx's (1973 [1859]) observation, that production not only produces an object for the subject but also a subject for the object, and Weick's (1995, p. 54) observation that "when you're lost, any old map will do".

The creation of the consumer subject not least through marketing's own performativity (Mason, Kjellberg and Hagberg, 2015) must therefore be the starting point for a reflection of the future relationship between marketing and consumer research. Questions about the context of knowledge generation and, as we have seen, the subject and object of research are becoming increasingly salient in a contemporary marketing world. This is true not least when one considers the changes in technological devices for the construction of consumer knowledge.

One of the most significant changes in the relationship between marketing and consumer research in recent years is the upsurge of neuro-marketing. Neuro-marketing is referring to the usage of medical scanner techniques such as electroencephalography or functional magnetic resonance imaging for eliciting consumer response to strategic marketing communications, product or brand cues and the like. This is a domain where we presumably have only just begun to see very preliminary results of things to come, and while there are calls for caution in terms of the potential hype of finding the "buying button" in the consumers' brains, there are equally pronounced hopes for cracking some codes of consumer behavior through neurological insights (e.g. Ariely and Berns, 2010) and, not least, providing consumer research with a halo of scientific – or is it scientistic? – legitimacy.

Another domain where technological development is altering the relation between marketing and consumer research is the myriad of digital traces that we as consumers leave through our usage of the numerous electronic devices that are used to facilitate our lives as citizens and consumers. The summary construct "big data" has become one of the most alluring in the contemporary marketing scene. The question is, however, whether large-scale search data will "help us create better tools, services, and public goods? Or will it usher in a new wave of privacy incursions and invasive marketing" (Boyd and Crawford, 2012, p. 662)? Marketing and marketers generally have embraced the potential of big-data-based insights without reservation. But as Boyd and Crawford suggest, beyond technology and analysis there is also a heavy element of mythology in big data: a belief that big data represents access to hitherto hidden dimensions of social life, an access that espouses objectivity and accuracy (Boyd and Crawford, 2012, p. 663).

However, as Boyd and Crawford make it clear, such claims to objectivity and accuracy are misleading since they are ontologically and epistemologically unsustainable. What is more, the allure of scientism and truth – just like is the case with neuro-scientific information – risks altering the very definition of knowledge. Who needs all kinds of uncertain interpretations of consumer motivations when "factual and objective" information about what people do are readily at hand? As the editor-in-chief of the magazine *Wired* is quoted for saying, "Massive amounts of data and applied mathematics replace every other tool that might be brought to bear" (cit. in Boyd and Crawford, 2010, p. 666). The problematic ethical consequences in terms of either manipulative power from an increased focus on neurological data among marketers or the big-brother-like scrutiny of all our electronic traces left for Google,

Facebook or other commercial agents to exploit are obvious and discussed elsewhere. What we would like to point out as a risk is the potential expropriation of consumer research as an institutionalized discipline from being the authority in producing consumer knowledge. How that might affect the scientific landscape around marketing and consumer research remains to be seen.

Not all that moves and shakes in the world of marketing is reflexive of scientists' dreams of objectivity and mathematization. The growing success of usage of ethnographic methods in industry settings, as witnessed by the globalizing EPIC (Ethnographic Praxis in Industry Conference) organization and the increased demand for complex cultural approaches to market systems, is testifying to a significant countertrend to contemporary marketing scientism. The increased cultural and social complexities which marketers must navigate in markets where global and local forces mold practices and imaginaries have provoked a growing demand for cultural and anthropological analytical insights in market systems (and correspondingly emerging degrees in Market Anthropology), a trend that also includes analytical competences for interpretation of emerging patterns in big data. This demand is further sustained by the increasingly complex conditions for navigating a universe of critical consumers and critical journalism concerning the ethical dimensions of market operations.

To summarize, the cult(ure) of the customer (du Gay and Salaman, 1992) is not a tired old religion. It is as vivid and dynamic as ever and it takes many shapes and forms, from the most objectivist and scientist to the most humanistic and empathic – from neoliberal apologies to critical and transformative approaches where marketing efforts, at least in principle if not in practice, serve the interests of consumers before the interests of corporate structures. Consumer research and marketing continue to affirm their complex relationship in the sense given to complexity by Edgar Morin (e.g. 2005) as a systemic relationship between elements that are concurrent, complementary and antagonistic.

References

Ariely, D. and Berns, G. S. (2010), 'Neuromarketing: The hope and hype of neuroimaging in business,' *Nature Reviews Neuroscience*, vol. 11, no. 4, pp. 284–292.

Arndt, J. (1976), 'Reflections on research in consumer behavior,' in B. B. Anderson (ed), *Advances in consumer research*, pp. 213–221. Cincinnati, OH: Association for Consumer Research.

Bartels, R. (1988), *The history of marketing thought* (3rd ed.). Columbus, OH: Publishing Horizons.

Belk, R.W. (1986), 'What should ACR want to be when it grows up,' in R. J. Lutz (ed), *Advances in consumer research*, pp. 423–424. Provo, UT: Association for Consumer Research.

Bettman, J. R. (1979), *An information processing theory of consumer choice.* Reading, MA: Addison-Wesley.

Boyd, D. and Crawford, K. (2012), 'Critical questions for big data: Provocations for a cultural, technological, and scholarly phenomenon,' *Information, Communication & Society*, vol. 15, no. 5, pp. 662–679.

Britt, S. H. (1950), 'The strategy of human motivation,' *Journal of Marketing*, vol. 14, no. 5, pp. 666–674.

Crane, D. (1972), *Invisible colleges: Diffusion of knowledge in scientific communities.* Chicago, IL: University of Chicago Press.

Deighton, J. and Johnson, P. (2016), *The value of data: Driving insight, innovation and efficiency in the US economy.* New York: Direct Marketing Association.

Dichter, E. (1960), *The strategy of desire.* New York: Doubleday.

du Gay, P. and Salaman, G. (1992), 'The cult[ure] of the customer,' *Journal of Management Studies*, vol. 29, no. 5, pp. 615–633.

Engel, J. F., Kollat, D.T. and Blackwell, R. D. (1968), *Consumer behavior.* New York: Holt, Rinehart & Winston.

Engel, J. F., Kollat, D. T. and Blackwell, R. D. (1973), *Consumer behavior* (2nd ed.). New York: Holt, Rinehart & Winston.

Frederick, C. (1929), *Selling Mrs. Consumer.* New York: The Business bourse.

Fullerton, R. A. (1990), 'The art of marketing research: Selections from Paul F. Lazarsfeld's "Shoe buying in Zurich",' *Journal of the Academy of Marketing Science*, vol. 18, no. 4, pp. 319–327.

Giesler, M. and Veresiu, E. (2014), 'Creating the responsible consumer: Moralistic governance regimes and consumer subjectivity,' *Journal of Consumer Research*, vol. 41, no. 3, pp. 840–857.

Gordon, R. A. and Howell, J. E. (1959), *Higher education for business*. New York: Columbia University Press.

Graeber, D. (2012), *Debt: The first 5,000 years*. London: Melville.

Guest, L. (1962), Consumer analysis. *Annual Review of Psychology*, vol. 13, no. 1, pp. 315–344.

Holbrook, M. B. (1985), 'Why business is bad for consumer research: The three bears revisited,' in E. C. Hirschman and M. B. Holbrook (eds), *Advances in consumer research*, pp. 145–156. Provo, UT: Association for Consumer Research.

Howard, J. A. and Sheth, J. N. (1969), *The theory of buyer behavior*. New York: Wiley.

Hudson, L. A. and Ozanne, J. L. (1988), 'Alternative ways of seeking knowledge in consumer research,' *Journal of Consumer Research*, vol. 14, no. 4, pp. 508–521.

Kassarjian, H. H. (1994), 'Scholarly traditions and European roots of American consumer research,' in G. Laurent, G. L. Lilien and B. Pras (eds), *Research traditions in marketing*, pp. 265–287. Dordrecht, NL: Springer.

Keith, R. J. (1960), 'The marketing revolution,' *Journal of Marketing*, vol. 24, no. 1, pp. 35–38.

Kerin, R. A. (1996), 'In pursuit of an ideal: The editorial and literary history of the journal of marketing,' *Journal of Marketing*, vol. 60, no. 1, pp. 1–13.

Kernan, J. B. (1995), 'Framing a rainbow, focusing the light: JCR's first twenty years,' in F. R. Kardes and M. Sujan (eds), *Advances in consumer research*, pp. 488–496. Provo, UT: Association for Consumer Research.

Kollat, D. T., Blackwell, R.D. and Engel, J. F. (1972), 'The current status of consumer behavior research: Developments during the 1968–1972 period,' in M. Venkatesan (ed), *Proceedings of the third annual conference of the association for consumer research*, pp. 576–585. Chicago, IL: Association for Consumer Research.

Kover, A. J. (1967), 'Models of man as defined by marketing research,' *Journal of Marketing Research*, vol. 4, no. 2, pp. 129–132.

Leong, S. M. (1989). 'A citation analysis of the *Journal of Consumer Research*,' *Journal of Consumer Research*, vol. 15, no. 4, pp. 492–497.

Levitt, T. (1960), 'Marketing myopia,' *Harvard business review*, vol. 38, no. 4, pp. 45–56.

Lockley, L. (1974), 'History and development of marketing research,' in R. Ferber (ed), *Handbook of marketing research*, pp. 1.3–1.15. New York: McGraw-Hill.

Lusch, R. F. and Vargo, S. L. (eds). (2006), *The service-dominant logic of marketing: Dialog, debate, and directions*. Armonk, NY: M.E. Sharpe.

Lutz, R. J. (1989), 'Positivism, naturalism, and pluralism in consumer research: Paradigm in paradise,' in T. K. Srull (ed), *Advances in consumer research*, pp. 1–8. Provo, UT: Association for Consumer Research.

MacInnis, D. and Folkes, V. (2010), 'The disciplinary status of consumer behavior: A sociology of science perspective on key controversies,' *Journal of Consumer Research*, vol. 36, no. 6, pp. 899–914.

Marx, K. (1973), *Karl Marx: Grundrisse*. London: Penguin Classics. (Original work published 1859).

Mason, K., Kjellberg, H., & Hagberg, J. (2015), 'Exploring the performativity of marketing: theories, practices and devices,' *Journal of Marketing Management*, vol. 31, no. 1–2, pp. 1–15.

Maynard, H. H. (1941), 'Marketing courses prior to 1910,' *Journal of Marketing*, vol. 6, no. 2, pp. 382–384.

Mick, D. G. (2008), 'Introduction: The moment and place for a special issue,' *Journal of Consumer Research*, vol. 35, no. 3, pp. 377–379.

Mittelstaedt, R. A. (1990), 'Economics, psychology, and the literature of the subdiscipline of consumer behavior,' *Journal of the Academy of Marketing Science*, vol. 18, no. 4, pp. 303–311.

Morin, E. (2005), *Introduction à la pensée complexe*. Paris: coll. Points essais.

Murphy, P. E. and Sherry, J.F., Jr. (eds). (2014), *Marketing and the common good*. New York: Routledge.

Olson, J. C. (1982), 'Presidential address: Towards a science of consumer behavior,' in A. Mitchell (ed), *Advances in consumer research*, pp. v–x. Ann Arbor: MI: Association for Consumer Research.

Peter, J. P. and Olson, J. C. (1983), 'Is science marketing?' *Journal of Marketing*, vol. 47, no. 4, pp. 111–125.

Pollay, R. W. (1972), 'A model for research planning, in consumer behavior,' in M. Venkatesan (ed), *Proceedings of the third annual conference of the association for consumer research*, pp. 594–601. Chicago, IL: Association for Consumer Research.

Pratt Jr., R.W. (1974), 'ACR: A Perspective,' in S. Ward and P. Wright (eds), *Advances in consumer research*, pp. 1–8. Ann Abor, MI: Association for Consumer Research.

Robertson, T. S. and Ward, S. (1972), 'Toward the development of consumer behavior theory,' in B. W. Becket and H. Becker (eds), *Combined proceedings of the American marketing association 1972*, pp. 57–64. Chicago, IL: American Marketing Association.

Rossiter, J.R. (1989), 'Consumer Research and Marketing Science,' in *Advances in Consumer Research*, vol. 16, ed. Thomas K. Srull, Provo, UT: Association for Consumer Research, 407–413.

Sanders, C. R. (1987), 'Consuming as social action: Ethnographic methods in consumer research,' in M. Wallendorf and P. Anderson (eds), *Advances in consumer research*, pp. 71–75. Provo, UT: Association for Consumer Research.

Schwarzkopf, S. and Gries, R. (eds). (2010), *Ernest Dichter and motivation research*. Basingstoke: Palgrave Macmillan.

Sherry, J. F. Jr. (1991), 'Postmodern alternatives: The interpretive turn in consumer research,' in T. S. Robertson and H. H. Kassarjian (eds), *Handbook of consumer behavior*, pp. 548–591. Englewood Cliffs, NJ: Prentice Hall.

Sheth, J. N. (1967), 'A review of buyer behavior,' *Management Science*, vol. 13, no. 12, pp. B718–B756.

Simonson, I., Carmon, Z., Dhar, R., Drolet, A. and Nowlis, S.M. (2001), 'Consumer research: In search of identity,' *Annual Review of Psychology*, vol. 52, no. 1, pp. 249–275.

Staelin, R. (2005), 'Eras III and IV my reflections,' *Journal of Public Policy and Marketing*, vol. 24, no. 1, pp. 146–149.

Stern, B. B. (2004), 'The importance of being Ernest: Commemorating Dichter's contribution to advertising research,' *Journal of Advertising Research*, vol. 44, no. 2, pp. 165–169.

Tadajewski, M. (2006), 'The ordering of marketing theory: The influence of McCarthyism and the cold war,' *Marketing Theory*, vol. 6, no. 2, pp. 163–199.

Tadajewski, M. and Brownlie, D. (2008), *Critical marketing: Issues in contemporary marketing*. Chichester, UK: Wiley.

Trentmann, F. (2016), *Empire of things: How we became a world of consumers, from the fifteenth century to the twenty-first*. London: Allen Lane/Penguin.

Tucker, W. T. (1974), 'Future directions in marketing theory,' *Journal of Marketing*, vol. 38, no. 2, pp. 30–35.

Twedt, D.W. (1965), 'Consumer psychology,' *Annual Review of Psychology*, vol. 16, no. 1, pp. 265–294.

Vargo, S. L. and Lusch, R. F. (2004), 'Evolving to a new dominant logic for marketing,' *Journal of Marketing*, vol. 68, no. 1, pp. 1–17.

Warde, A. (2015), 'The sociology of consumption: Its recent development,' *Annual Review of Sociology*, vol. 41, no. 1, pp. 12.1–12.18.

Weick, K. (1995), *Sensemaking in organizations*. London: Sage.

Zukin, S. and Maguire, J. S. (2004), Consumers and consumption. *Annual Review of Sociology*, vol. 30, no. 1, pp. 173–197.

7

Consumers and brands

How consumers co-create

Siwarit Pongsakornrungsilp and Jonathan E. Schroeder

Introduction

The digital age has wreaked havoc on traditional models of branding. Social media has become a key platform for branding activity, including online brand communities, promotion, and branded content, as well as a powerful forum for brand celebration, commentary, and critique. Two issues seem critically important for this new branding environment: culture and value. Culture intersects with contemporary brands in many ways. Fundamentally, one can speak of a brand culture that underlies brands. The brand concept long ago transcended traditional definitions of *logo*, *name*, and *slogan*; brands embody cultural, ideological, and psychological value, providing representational and rhetorical power that shape brand meaning and value (Schroeder, 2009). Furthermore, the relationships between consumers and producers in branding process are blurred – consumers tend to be creative, unmanageable, active, and productive players in the market. Therefore, brand researchers have begun to understand brands through a cultural lens.

Within traditional perspectives of branding, a brand was often viewed as a marketing tool for communicating with consumers; consumers played only reactive roles in responding to marketing or branding messages. However, advances in information technology allow consumers to digitally interact with other consumers through global social networks, and create platforms for participating, interacting, discussing, and 'curating' their consumption, including their use, preferences, and evaluation of brands (Pongsakornrungsilp & Schroeder, 2011). Thus, the foundation of branding theory has shifted to acknowledge the consumers' role in branding processes, meaning production, and value creation. Of course, such co-creation is not entirely new. In the 1920s, the Kodak film corporation encouraged consumers to send in their own photographs, and published a selection in various company magazines and newsletters (Pretelin Rios, 2011). Moreover, like-minded fans have gathered around their favored brands for decades, such as the nineteenth-century bicycle clubs that offered aficionados a chance to share stories, information, and comradery (Burr, 2012). The digital age, however, has greatly transformed the co-creation process, and has placed consumers at the center of brand value creation and nurturance.

Value creation represents a key aspect of consumer-brand relationships (e.g. Ritchins, 1994; Fırat, Dholakia, & Venkatesh, 1995; Brown, 1996; Wikström, 1996; Vargo & Lusch, 2004, 2008; Schroeder, 2005; Holbrook, 2006; Woodruff & Flint, 2006; Sánchez-Fernández & Iniesta-Bonillo,

2007; Schroeder, Borgerson & Wu, 2015). Consumer research on branding has identified various forms of value co-creation, including co-production, prosumption, working consumers, consumer involvement, cultural hijacking, consumer agency, consumer resistance, and so on (Schroeder, 2015). Although value can be difficult to conceptualize and measure, from a consumer perspective value co-creation generally includes such processes as relationships, engagement, interaction, and experience, to name a few.

Brands benefit from celebrity endorsements, enthusiastic selfies, and knowledgeable reviews that consumers post online (see Borgerson & Miller, 2016). However, consumers often criticize brands, posting negative comments and nasty reviews on social media, using the Internet to call attention to perceived negative aspects of brands, engaging in boycotts, and 'culture jamming' brands by co-opting brand logos, advertisements, and other aspects of the brand in derogatory – and often humorous – ways. In other words, consumers have been empowered as brand critics. In this way, consumers are important players in co-creating brand value, meaning, and culture. But when and why do consumers devote themselves to such work for brands? How are consumers motivated and rewarded in co-creation processes? This chapter provides an overview of current thinking about brand culture, brand communities, brand co-creation, and so-called 'crowdculture.'

Consumers and brands: Challenges in the era of brand culture

Several typologies of branding have been proposed by brand researchers. For example, Schroeder has proposed four different perspectives of brand research: *corporate* perspectives, *consumer* perspectives, *cultural* perspectives, and *critical* perspectives (Schroeder, 2015). These perspectives demonstrate the growing interdisciplinary interest in brands, and how brand research illuminates central issues of consumer agency, consumer behavior, and consumer culture. Focusing on brand management, Holt classified branding strategies into four perspectives: *mindshare* branding, *emotional* branding, *viral* branding, and *cultural* branding (Holt, 2004). Each perspective provides a distinctive lens: mindshare branding focuses on brand DNA, building a set of abstract associations, and communicating the brand's essence; emotional branding attempts to appeal to consumers' emotional states, desires, and motivations; viral branding emphasizes deploying social media to enhance brand awareness and evaluation; and cultural branding stresses how brands tap into cultural tensions, myths, or stories to create meaning and value (Holt, 2004).

Although these two typologies emphasize different aspects of branding and brand research, they both converge on the importance of a cultural perspective that highlights myth making, iconic brands, and brand stories in consumer-brand co-creation processes. In addition, they signal a shift in thinking about brands. As Holt argues in a recent article in *Harvard Business Review*, 'While crowdculture has deflated conventional branding models, it actually makes an alternative model – cultural branding – even more powerful. In this approach, brands collaborate with crowdcultures and champion their ideologies in the marketplace' (Holt, 2016, p. 5). The cultural approach to brands focuses on such ideology: 'the cultural codes of brands – history, images, myths, art, and theatre – that influence brand meaning and value in the marketplace' (Schroeder, 2009, p. 124). Within this perspective, the power of brand value creation is not confined to corporations; it also involves stakeholders, including consumers, media, suppliers, and watchdogs – all of whom increasingly operate in digital space. Consumers, in particular, play important roles in co-creating brand meaning, myth, and culture (e.g. Schroeder & Salzer-Morling, 2006; Pongsakornrungsilp & Schroeder, 2011; Schroeder et al., 2015; Holt, 2016; Schembri & Latimer, 2016).

The brand culture perspective highlights how brand meaning is co-created among consumers and brands, how consumers form relationships with brands, and how brands interact with culture (e.g. Fournier, 1998; Muñiz & O'Guinn, 2001; Holt & Cameron, 2010; Pongsakornrungsilp, Pusaksrikit & Schroeder, 2011; Wu, Borgerson, & Schroeder, 2013). In other words, brand culture refers to consumer response toward the cultural codes of brands, including linguistic codes. For example, Starbucks coffee houses present a coded language for ordering coffee, referring to their drink sizes as *grande*, *venti*, and *trenta* rather than small, medium, or large, and offering a somewhat bewildering range of coffee choices, such as doppio, mocha light Frappuccino, caramel macchiato, and flat white; caffeinated or decaffeinated, with milk, half and half, or soy milk. Such linguistic brand codes can create a feeling of anxiety for new customers, as a well as a sense of insider knowledge for regulars, and are regular topics of coffee-focused brand communities (Rodriguez, 2016; see also WikiHow, 2016). The Starbucks brand so dominates the coffee landscape that it shapes how consumers interpret 'coffee language,' as it emphasizes consumers' experiential meaning as much as their products (Thompson & Arsel, 2004).

From a cultural perspective, co-creation is a crucial process in which consumers play dynamic roles to co-create value through interaction, dialog, and consumption (e.g. Schau, Muñiz & Arnould, 2009; Schroeder, 2011; Pongsakornrungsilp & Schroeder, 2011). Lawrence and Phillips (2002) have suggested that we are living in the era of the cultural industries, which rely on 'meaning' and 'interpretation' for their core brand values. Thus, consumers have to be increasingly taken into account in branding strategy because they play creative roles for brands – curating, sharing, and performing brand stories in seemingly authentic ways. In other words, they co-create branding meaning and value. Fournier's work on brand relationships showed how co-creation works – consumers are seen to have relationships with brands (Fournier, 1998). Further, brands can be thought of as *partners* – working with the consumer – or *servants* – working for the consumer (Dong & Aggarwal, 2014).

Co-creation refers to consumers and producers – so-called *brand actors*, including brand owners, managers and branded employees – working together in ways that are both casual and strategic, to create brand meaning and value. For example, brands within the tourism sector increasingly depend upon online consumer reviews. Sites like Amazon, TripAdvisor, Zomato, Yelp, and Hotels.com include thousands of consumer reviews, with comments, evaluations, and ratings, as well as photographs that provide detailed documentation of consumer experiences with brands. These ratings produce dynamic rankings of hotels, restaurants, and tourist attractions in each market. Consumer 'curations' – collections that feature images of brands, objects, lifestyles, and consumption – posted on social media sharing sites such as Instagram, Pinterest, and Tumblr also provide platforms for value creation and creating brand awareness. (These sites are also important outlets for branded content – including stories, photographs, and press releases produced by brands for strategic purposes.) Thus, consumers help build key aspects of tourist industry brand reputations in a co-creative process, apart from the strategic communication of the particular brand. In this way, the brand culture of social media impacts brand meaning and value.

Co-creation has also attracted critical responses from scholars. A stream of research on consumers' brand relationships has focused on tensions between the concept of working consumers and the unpaid labor they perform for brands (Zwick, Bonsu & Darmody, 2008; Cova & Dalli, 2009), in the form of aesthetic labor (e.g. Pettinger, 2004; Carah, 2014) and consumer co-creation and value production (Pongsakornrungsilp & Schroeder, 2011; Healy & McDonagh, 2012). This tension is reflected within the wider marketing discipline, where terms such as *co-production*, *prosumption*, and *service-dominant logic* each capture aspects of the interactions between brands and consumers, and how consumers help build brand value.

Co-creation is not limited to the consumer sector. The global conglomerate General Electric (GE) calls itself 'the world's largest digital industrial company.' GE's social media strategy is 'all about innovation, new technology, or looking at science with a new perspective. It's GE's vision for its company and for the world' (Gomez, 2016). Their digital initiatives revolve around digital storytelling – creating branded content about their products and initiatives and encouraging their buyers, suppliers, and other stakeholders to share this material on social media platforms (see GE Social Hub, 2016). For example, GE Canada publishes *GE Reports*, which features news stories, written by GE staff and independent journalists, that promote the brand. Their social media strategy includes working with LinkedIn, Twitter, Instagram, and Google, as well as producing podcasts for their highly successful *the Message* program for GE Podcast Theater. One of their many Instagram feeds offers high-quality photographs of GE products and employees in action, in an effort to 'align GE with science innovation and forward looking technology' by showcasing 'the stunning beauty of GE products' (Thorbun, 2016). GE's social media success, of course, depends upon liking, sharing, and commenting on content – fundamental co-creation activities. Across many market sectors, brands rely heavily on customer input and sharing of branded content that shapes brand identity and reputation. In the next section, a look at the micro processes within brand communities sheds light on co-creation.

Consumer roles in brand co-creation

The active role of consumers represents a hallmark of culturally oriented brand research (e.g. Vargo & Lusch, 2004; Arnould & Thompson, 2005; Schroeder, 2009; Pongsakornrungsilp and Schroeder, 2011). Consumers interact with brands in many ways, including brand communities (Muñiz & O'Guinn, 2011), subcultures (Schouten & McAlexander, 1995), consumer tribes (Cova & Cova, 2002), and online brand evaluation and review sites (e.g. Reagle, 2015). Research has revealed a diversity of processes underlying consumers' relationships with brands, including 'working' as consumers (Zwick et al., 2008; Cova & Dalli, 2009), value co-creation in co-consuming groups (Pongsakornrungsilp & Schroeder, 2011; Healy & McDonagh, 2012), cultural branding (Holt, 2004; Schroeder, 2009), and brand volunteering (Cova, Pace & Skålén, 2015). This chapter focuses primarily on value co-creation within brand communities. Muñiz and O'Guinn defined brand community as 'a specialized, non-geographically bound community, based on a structured set of social relations among admirers of a brand' (2001, p. 412). Within brand communities, relationships between consumers and brand have changed from dyadic – between consumer and producer – to more complex triadic or networked relationships. Brand communities provide a value platform for co-consuming groups to organize around particular brands in order to co-construct 'we-ness', 'culture', and 'reciprocity'.

Many scholars have discussed the definition of value, and much research has focused on how value emerges. A key tenet of the service-dominant logic of marketing approach (S-D logic) concerns how the ecology of value creation has changed (Vargo & Lusch, 2004). From this perspective, consumers are empowered to co-create value through interaction, dialog, and consumption (Pongsakornrungsilp & Schroeder, 2011; Healy & McDonagh, 2012). However, from a critical perspective, this process turns them into 'working consumers', who are exploited by corporations who gain from co-creation, but do not compensate consumers for the value they help create (Zwick et al., 2008).

Co-creative consumers dedicate their energy, knowledge, time, or resources to brands, providing marketing resources, ideas, and data to help develop marketing strategy, but they still have to pay for purchasing products or services. Further, consumers often offer help and useful information to other consumers on brand community sites, performing free 'customer service' for brands (e.g. Thompson, Kim & Smith, 2016). Pongsakornrungsilp and Schroeder (2011) have argued that consumers may not consider themselves as 'unpaid workers' because they also gain something from their 'work' for brands – emotional benefits, valuable experience and information, or friendship. From this viewpoint, each party benefits in the value co-creation process. Another variant of this process has been called 'brand volunteering' (Cova et al., 2015). Brand volunteering centers on the willingness of many consumers to engage in value co-creation. Thus, the question of exploitation versus positive co-creation is complicated, and may depend upon the particular framework adopted by brand researchers.

From a brand culture perspective, value within brand co-creation is both dynamic and multidimensional (e.g. Sánchez-Fernández & Iniesta-Bonillo, 2007; Vargo & Lusch, 2008; Pongsakornrungsilp & Schroeder, 2011). In order to understand the process of brand co-creation, we need to understand how consumers play crucial roles in brand co-creation. An in-depth study of a large online brand community focused on the Premier League Liverpool Football Club (LFC) shed light on the processes by which consumers interact with brands.

Reactive Consumers can be found in many co-consuming groups and tend to co-create the flow of experience with their fellows. Like a member of a brand community (see also Muñiz & O'Guinn, 2001), reactive consumers play an important role to drive community by complying with written and unwritten codes of conduct (Pongsakornrungsilp & Schroeder, 2011). Within ThisisAnfeld (TIA) – an unofficial Liverpool Football Club brand community named after the club's celebrated stadium – reactive consumers can be classified into two groups: less experienced members and more experienced members (Pongsakornrungsilp & Schroeder, 2011). The former group tends to be 'newbies,' loosely linked to a brand relationship, and 'pointless posting' members of the brand community. Less experienced reactive consumers have a tendency to believe rumors or negative news about the featured brand. On the other hand, they can quickly perceive positive brand stories, and are important players in spreading good news. In contrast, more experienced reactive consumers generally enjoy positive relationships with other community members and always join in the flow of conversation with regular engagement and interactions. However, they are merely reactive consumers because their responses to the brand and the brand community are generally limited to replying to particular issues. Therefore, they are qualified to be active consumers, who enjoy the community phenomenon, but also share and provide something back to the community.

Creative Consumers are experienced consumers who have more knowledge and experience with a particular brand, and frequently share their resources to other brand community members with valued information. In contrast with reactive consumers, they spend more time interacting and sharing brand stories – characterized as 'celebrating the history of a brand' (Muñiz & O'Guinn, 2001). Their participation can enrich brand resources because they often provide persuasive information to steer community discussion and win arguments. These stories and arguments are crucial resources of brand co-creation processes – consumers are seen as authors of brand stories. Creative consumers possess important brand resources: knowledge of past glory and triumph, the myth and culture of brand, which they make available to brand communities.

These creative consumers can be found in most brand communities, including communities that might not be considered typical. For example, research on brand communities organized around religious amulets in Thailand revealed similar patterns to other, more conventional brand communities (Pongsakornrungsilp, Pusaksrikit & Schroeder, 2011). The online Thai amulet community Palungjit.com is the largest Buddhist community in the world where religious amulets are bought, sold, and traded. Amulets have formed an important part of Thai cultural society since the nineteenth century, and wearing amulets is quite common among contemporary Thai Buddhists. Amulets come in all styles and shapes and they can be made from a variety of materials including gypsum, clay, metal, wood, bone, or plaster. The ingredients often include sacred incense ash, colored dust from a temple's bricks, and venerable monks' hair or bones. Evolving from the original forms of the image of Buddha, amulets today come in many different forms – such as lockets, statuettes, and coins. Today, amulets feature prominently on Thai social media, where consumers play major roles in value creation through sharing experiences and providing information about amulet myths and legends (Pongsakornrungsilp et al., 2011). In this way, creative amulet consumers help perform the myth of amulet 'brands' by sharing their knowledge and stories and celebrating the history of amulets via a process of crowdculture. Their activity not only nurtures brand relationships among members of the amulet community; it also co-creates faith in the religious properties of amulets.

Brand Warriors are one of the crucial players in brand culture. Brand warriors contribute their knowledge, experience, information, and time to the brand community, and help co-create the 'cult' of a brand (Belk & Tumbat, 2005). Brand warriors enforce the cultural codes of a brand, protecting it from dilution and enforcing the 'rules' of the brand. Additionally, brand warriors serve as 'brand knights' against competitors or negative media messages. For example, the TIA brand warriors have co-created the ritual of LFC fans against the *Sun* newspaper – which had harshly criticized Liverpool Football Club after the1989 Hillsborough disaster when many fans were crushed to death from overcrowding during a Liverpool versus Nottingham Forest game. Brand warriors began a campaign; 'LFC fans do not read the *SUN*,' which called for a boycott of a perceived brand threat, and taught newer community members about a singular event in the brand's history (Pongsakornrungsilp & Schroeder, 2011). Brand warriors also remind other fellows about authentic brand culture by sharing unique, extraordinary, and impressive stories to arouse the passion of community members. Interestingly, to be recognized as a brand warrior, one needs to accumulate adequate cultural capital about brand history, myth, and rituals (Kjeldgaard, Askegaard & Eckhardt, 2015).

Understanding active consumers sheds light on the 'working consumers' controversy, and helps address a key question: 'Why do consumers work to co-create brand value?' (Cova & Dalli, 2009). By serving as creative consumers or brand warriors, consumers can obtain something more than wages: they can experience social interaction, satisfaction, friendship, a sense of belonging, creativity, and fun.

Brand co-creation in the co-consuming group

Brands rely on collaborative networks of consumers who can be seen as creative, but uncontrollable and unmanageable (see Figure 7.1). The concept of 'resource integrator' from service-dominant (S-D) logic also is useful in understanding how co-consuming groups contribute to brand co-creation. Resource integrators are participants in value co-creation processes who contain resources that contribute benefits to others (Vargo & Lusch, 2008). According to Vargo & Lusch (2008), all parties in an exchange system, e.g. company, customer, supplier, distributor, financial institution, and so on, are resource integrators. Cooperation from these parties contributes to strengthening the value chain of a brand. However, in brand co-creation processes, consumers can collaborate as independent resource integrators to discuss, argue, extend, and share brand culture. Within this framework, there are three main processes of brand co-creation: engaging, educating, and enriching.

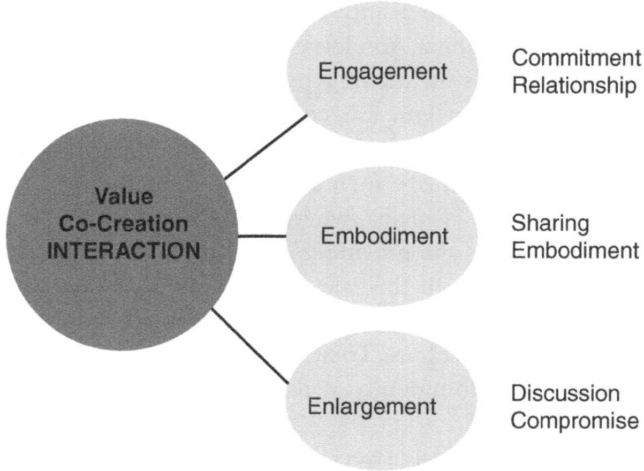

Figure 7.1 Processes of brand co-creation

Engaging

To collaborate with brand community members in co-creating brand value, brand managers need to co-create strong relationships, both individual and collective, within the community. For their part, consumers have to commit themselves by dedicating time, resources, experience, and knowledge to interactions with the brand and other consumers. Thus, creative consumers are key players in this process, because a vibrant brand community requires flows of experiences, discussions, and participation. The more interaction, the more consumers bond with the community. Within many brand communities, conversations or co-creative contexts are not limited to the particular brand context, but also include mundane issues of everyday life, family, travel, and so forth. This wide-ranging co-creation can increase the passion toward brand (Wenger & Snyder, 2000). As found in the Liverpool Football Club TIA community, creative consumers can be recognized as 'highly committed members' with cultural capital, who play an important role in uniting fellow consumers through regular interactions, activities, and collaboration (Pongsakornrungsilp & Schroeder, 2011). It is worth noting that this collective process contributes to strengthen 'consciousness of kind' within the brand – forming 'we-ness' among the consumers, which, in turn, develops consumers' passion for the brand (Muñiz & O'Guinn, 2001).

Educating

Educating includes telling and retelling brand stories, recounting brand myths, and articulating brand community rules, and it represents another important activity in the co-creation process. Educating brand community members requires strong relationships among consumers; often community members never meet in person, and the brand plays an important role as the center of interaction. In this situation, it is inevitable that conflicts will emerge among consumers who have different knowledge and experience. Thus, often educating is a process of harmonization – forming and observing rituals and traditions. One of three foundational brand community markers, rituals and traditions require sharing and embodiment (Muñiz & O'Guinn, 2001). To foster brand rituals, experienced brand community members need to share knowledge and experience, such as information about the brand story, to new consumers in order to allow them to learn and accumulate brand resources. As mentioned by Pongsakornrungsilp (2010), experienced consumers believe that sharing brand resources with fellow consumers is a way to continue and maintain the brand culture. The more experienced consumers share, the more embodiment new consumers can accumulate and embed into brand rituals and traditions.

Enriching

Enriching marks a process of evolution with brand communities. Brand community requires discussion and compromise among consumers. Discussion among consumers about the brand story can extend brand resources from different consumers who have different knowledge, experience, and information. To participate in controversial or sensitive issues, consumers can learn and share resources that enrich the discussion with new knowledge or information. Importantly, to keep conversations in line, brands need rituals and traditions. Therefore, compromise is a crucial process to harmonize brand co-creation – compromise often enriches and harmonizes the brand community's interaction. Often, high cultural capital consumers dominate such interaction. Brand warriors can support this continuing learning process by sharing their resources or directing the ritual of discussion and argument. However, compromise does not always result in avoiding confrontation among consumers; instead, it fosters dialogue – respectful disagreements that can lead to an enriched community.

Understanding consumer participation in brand co-creation

To extend our understanding of how brand management can work with co-consuming groups to co-create brand culture, we need to explore consumer movement in brand co-creation. To co-create brand culture, two main dimensions come into play: *resource intensity* and *engagement*, which can be combined into a typology of four consumer types of brand co-creation (see also Pongsakornrungsilp, 2010).

The first dimension consists of consumer engagement toward a particular brand, where engagement includes both commitment and relationship. Engagement forms an elementary component of brand co-creation; it contributes to the 'we-ness' within co-consuming groups. A second dimension is resource intensity, including brand knowledge as well as discussion issues (brand context *versus* other contexts). To plot consumer participation in brand co-creation, we need to consider whether consumers are interacting around the brand context – for example, TIA members discuss the story of LFC; or out of the brand context – about everyday of life, travelling, jobs, family, politics, and so on. These dimensions produce four types of consumer participation: arrival, player, resident, and stranger, which depend upon how consumers interact with the brand community in terms of regular participation, context of interaction, and recognition among consumers.

Arrival is the primary stage of each consumer's participation, when they have relatively low engagement and low resource identity. Arrivals tend to be newcomers who are not regular members of the co-consuming group. They have some knowledge about the brand and its consumers, and focus mainly on the brand context. A key turning point is when they have to decide to stay or leave the brand community. In the second stage, *player*, brand community members evolve into 'regulars.' They become engaged with the culture of community, but remain largely focused on the brand context. If and when brand community members are able to accumulate resource intensity and play a role as creative consumers or brand warriors, they may emerge as *residents* who are highly committed consumers with high resource intensity. They do not focus only on the brand context, but also bring up mundane life events and other 'out of brand content.' If brand community members lose their commitment or stop regularly visiting the community, they may become *strangers*. Strangers may have high resource intensity, but they do not demonstrate familiarity with the brand community and its members. However, strangers can shift back into the resident mode if they increase their commitment and visits to the community.

It is possible to describe five strategies for transforming consumers through these participatory stages: bonding, boosting, holding, refreshing, and resigning. *Bonding* is the main strategy for arrivals and strangers to increase their engagement with the brands and other brand community members. This strategy not only helps increase brand recognition among other consumers, it also communicates about brand rituals and traditions. *Boosting* is a player's strategy for moving on to the resident stage by accumulating relevant knowledge and experience about either the brand or its brand culture. *Holding* marks a strategy for consumers to preserve their brand community status by maintaining their level of participation, mostly by regularly interacting with the community. *Refreshing* can be applied by consumers when they find themselves 'downgraded' in stature within the brand community, by demonstrating their brand commitment and regularly interacting with the brand and the brand community. *Resigning* offers another option – leaving the community for good.

Conclusion

Future research on branding will be faced with a number of challenges, including dealing with the 'big data' that Internet use generates, pursuing insights into brands via algorithms and analysis of code; accommodating the rise of global brands from emerging economies, such as China, India and Brazil; understanding the growing importance of branded content – including branded content within video games – amidst a rapidly changing media and entertainment landscape; and focusing on personal branding. Brand models must acknowledge the social media environment where branding logics and techniques permeate daily life, exemplified by the ubiquitous presence of the selfie – which serves as a branding tool for consumers and companies alike (see Iqani & Schroeder, 2016).

Further, brands and brand loyalty may be threatened by a number of cultural trends, including inconspicuous consumption, the maker movement – where consumers produce their own goods, such as furniture, beer and wine, and clothing – and downshifting, which may involve consumers dropping out of corporate careers to take on more socially conscious jobs, giving up automobile ownership in favor of car sharing, or moving from large single-family homes to smaller apartments. Of course, each of these trends has spawned a growing number of brand communities that offer consumers new ways to co-create knowledge and value around their lifestyle choices.

The rise of the Internet, and particularly the rapid adoption and proliferation of social media, exerted a profound influence on how brands are understood, researched, and managed. In the digital age, consumers co-create value for brands. Brands now interact with and depend upon brand communities, brand tribes, working consumers, and crowdculture. A cultural approach offers distinctive insights into how these consumer groups co-create meaning and value with brands, why consumers engage with brands, and the processes of consumer participation with brand communities.

References

Arnould, E.J., & Thompson, C.J. (2005). Consumer culture theory (CCT): Twenty years of research. *Journal of Consumer Research, 31(4)*, 868–82.

Belk, R.W., & Tumbat, G. (2005). The cult of Macintosh. *Consumption Markets & Culture, 8(3)*, 205–17.

Borgerson, J., & Miller, D. (2016). Scalable sociality and "how the world changed social media": conversation with Daniel Miller. *Consumption Markets & Culture, 19(6)*, 520–533.

Brown, S. (1996). Art or science?: fifty years of marketing debate. *Journal of Marketing Management, 12*, 243–67.

Burr, T. (2012). National market communities: bicycle use and civil society in France and the United States, 1867–1910. *Consumption Markets & Culture, 15(1)*, 63–85.

Carah, N. (2014). Brand value: how affective labor helps create brands. *Consumption Markets & Culture, 17(4)*, 346–66.

Cova, B., & Cova, V. (2002). Tribal marketing: The tribalization of society and its impact on the conduct of marketing. *European Journal of Marketing, 36(5)*, 595–620.

Cova, B., & Dalli, D. (2009). Working consumers: the next step in marketing theory? *Marketing Theory, 9(3)*, 315–39.

Cova, B., Pace, S., & Skålén, P. (2015). Brand volunteering: value co-creation with unpaid consumers. *Marketing Theory, 15*, 465–85.

Dong, P., & Aggarwal, P. (2014). Partner versus servant relationship and its influence on brand evaluation: the moderating role of warmth versus competence trait. Paper presented at the Society for Consumer Psychology Conference, February 22–24, Miami, FL.

Fırat, A.F., Dholakia, N., & Venkatesh, A. (1995). Marketing in a postmodern world. *European Journal of Marketing, 29(1)*, 40–56.

Fournier, S. (1998). Consumers and their brands: developing relationship theory in consumer research. *Journal of Consumer Research, 24*, 343–73.

General Electric (2016). *Social hub.* Accessed May 23, 2016. http://www.ge.com/digital/social-hub

Gomez, A. (2016). What we can learn from GE's digital marketing strategies. *Kissmetrics Blog: A blog about analytics, marketing and testing.* Accessed May 21, 2016. https://blog.kissmetrics.com/learn-from-ge-digital-marketing/

Healy, J., & McDonagh, P. (2012). Consumer roles in brand culture and value co-creation in visual community. *Journal of Business Research, 66*, 1528–40.

Holbrook, M. (2006). Consumption experience, customer value, and subjective personal introspection: an illustrative photographic essay. *Journal of Business Research, 59(6)*, 714–25.

Holt, D. (2004). *How brands become icons: the principles of cultural branding.* Boston: Harvard Business School.

Holt, D. (2016). Branding in the age of social media. *Harvard Business Review, March*, 3–11.

Holt, D., & Cameron, D. (2010). *Cultural strategy: using innovative ideologies to build breakthrough brands.* New York: Oxford University Press.

Iqani, M., & Schroeder, J. E. (2016). #selfie: digital self-portraits as commodity form and consumption practice. Consumption Markets & Culture, 19 (5), 405–415.

Kjeldgaard, D., Askegaard, S., & Eckhardt, G. M. (2015). The role of cultural capital in creating "glocal" brand relationships. In S. Fournier, M. Breazeale, & J. Avery, (Eds.), *Strong brands, strong relationships* (pp. 48–60). New York: Routledge.

Lawrence, T.B., & Phillips, N. (2002). Understanding cultural industries. *Journal of Management Inquiry, 11(4)*, 430–41.

Muñiz, A.M., Jr., & O'Guinn, T.C. (2001). Brand community. *Journal of Consumer Research, 27(1)*, 412–32.

Pettinger, L. (2004). Brand culture and branded workers: service work and aesthetic labour in fashion retail. *Consumption Markets & Culture, 7(2)*, 165–84.

Pongsakornrungsilp, S. (2010). *Value co-creation process: reconciling S-D logic of marketing and consumer culture theory within the co-consuming group.* Ph.D. Dissertation. University of Exeter.

Pongsakornrungsilp, S., Pusaksrikit, T., & Schroeder, J.E. (2011). Co-creation through fear, faith, and desire. In A. Bradshaw, C. Hackley, & P. Maclaran (Eds.), *European advances for consumer research* (pp. 333–40). Duluth, MN: Association for Consumer Research.

Pongsakornrungsilp, S., & Schroeder, J.E. (2011). Understanding value co-creation in a co-consuming brand community. *Marketing Theory, 11(3)*, 303–24.

Pretelin Rios, C. (2011). Usted apretaba un botón, Kodak hacía el resto [You press the button, Kodak does the rest]. *Alquimia, 42*, 15–21.

Reagle, J.M. Jr. (2015). *Reading the comments: likers, haters, and manipulators at the bottom half of the web.* Cambridge, MA: MIT Press.

Richins, M.L. (1994). Special possessions and the expression of material values. *Journal of Consumer Research, 21(3)*, 522–33.

Rodriguez, I. L. (2016). I speak Starbucks: a netnographic study on brand codes. Paper presented at the Brands and Brand Relationships Conference, Toronto, May 18–20.

Sanchez-Fernandez, R., & Iniesta-Bonillo, M.A. (2007). The concept of perceived value: a systematic review of the research. *Marketing Theory, 7(4)*, 427–51.

Schau, H.J., Muñiz, A.M., Jr., & Arnould, E.J. (2009). How brand community practices create value. *Journal of Marketing, 73(5)*, 30–51.

Schembri, S., & Latimer, L. (2016). Online brand communities: constructing and co-constructing brand culture. *Journal of Marketing Management, 32(7–8)*, 628–651.

Schouten, J.W., & McAlexander, J.H. (1995). Subcultures of consumption: an ethnography of the new bikers. *Journal of Consumer Research, 22(1)*, 43–61.

Schroeder, J.E. (2005). The artist and the brand. *European Journal of Marketing, 39(11/12)*, 1291–1305.

Schroeder, J.E. (2009). The cultural codes of branding. *Marketing Theory, 9(1)*, 123–26.

Schroeder, J.E. (2015). Introduction. In J.E. Schroeder (Ed.), *Brands: interdisciplinary perspectives* (pp. 1–10). New York: Routledge.

Schroeder, J.E., Borgerson, J., & Wu, Z. (2015). A brand culture approach to Chinese culture heritage brands. *Journal of Brand Management, 22*, 261–79.

Schroeder, J.E., & Salzer-Morling, M. (eds.) (2006). *Brand culture.* London: Routledge.

Thoburn, P. (2016). Matchstick: a social media marketing agency. Paper presented at the Brands and Brand Relationships Conference, Toronto, May 18–20.

Thompson, C.J., & Arsel, Z. (2004). The Starbucks brandscape and consumers' (anticorporate) experiences of glocalization. *Journal of Consumer Research, 31(December)*, 631–642.

Thompson, S.A., Kim, M., & Smith, K.M. (2016). Community participation and consumer-to-consumer helping: does participation in third party–hosted communities reduce one's likelihood of helping? *Journal of Marketing Research, 53(2)*, 280–295.

Vargo, S.L., & Lusch, R.F. (2004). Evolving to a new dominant logic for marketing. *Journal of Marketing, 68*, 1–17.

Vargo, S.L., & Lusch, R.F. (2008). Service-dominant logic: continuing the evolution. *Journal of the Academic Marketing Science, 36*, 1–10.

Wenger, E.C., & Snyder, W.M. (2000). Communities of practice: the organizational frontier. *Harvard Business Review, January – February*, 139–45.

WikiHow. (2016). How to order at Starbucks. *WikiHow to do anything.* Accessed May 25, 2016. http://www.wikihow.com/Order-at-Starbucks

Wikström, S. (1996). The customer as co-producer. *European Journal of Marketing, 30(4)*, 6–19.

Woodruff, R.B., & Flint, D.J. (2006). Marketing's service-dominant logic and customer value. In R.F. Lusch and S.L. Vargo (Eds.), *The service-dominant logic of marketing: dialog, debate, and directions* (pp. 183–95). Armonk, NY: M.E. Sharpe.

Wu, Z., Borgerson, J., & Schroeder, J. (2013). *From Chinese brand culture to global brands: insights from aesthetics, fashion and history.* Basingstoke: Palgrave Macmillan.

Zwick, D., Bonsu, S.K., & Darmody, A. (2008). Putting consumers to work: "co-creation" and new marketing govern-mentality. *Journal of Consumer Culture, 8(2)*, 163–96.

8

From production and consumption to prosumption

A personal journey and its larger context

George Ritzer

Review essays in handbooks are generally pitched at a general, impersonal level. However, I will deviate from that model here in dealing in very personal terms with production, consumption, and prosumption. My career in sociology has encompassed and progressed through those three areas and journal articles, monographs, textbooks, edited volumes, and special journal issues devoted to them. A practical reason for sticking close to my career interests is that the literatures on these areas has exploded, making it nearly impossible to offer an overview of one of them, let alone all three, in a single review essay. However, this is not merely an overview of the three topics, but it is embedded in a larger narrative on the ways in which dealing with the concepts and processes of production and consumption are in the process of being subsumed – and arguably should have always been subsumed – by prosumption. What we historically have conceived of as production and consumption will remain important, but they need to be reconceptualized as aspects of prosumption.

Personal journey

My earliest substantive scholarly focus was on production, specifically in the area of industrial sociology. I had worked in industry before returning to Cornell for my PhD. My dissertation on the personnel manager drew on that experience (Ritzer and Trice, 1969). I began my career teaching industrial sociology, but I quickly found that what I was really interested in was the broader area of the sociology of occupations (occupations are clearly central to production). I came to realize that my research on the personnel manager was an occupational study and that led me into broader issues in the sociology of occupations such as occupational commitment and professionalization.

What most attracted me to the sociology of occupations was its strong theoretical orientation (especially symbolic interactionism) as well as its reliance on ethnographic studies championed by the Chicago School of Sociology, especially Everett Hughes. His best-known book was *Men and Their Work* (Hughes, 1958), and to show its lineage the first edition of my occupations text (Ritzer, 1972) was entitled *Man and His Work* (later changed to *Working* [Ritzer and Walczak, 1986] because of the sexism inherent in the title). However, the sociology of occupations, like sociology in general, was undergoing a major transformation in the 1970s and 1980s with ethnographic research giving way to more quantitative, statistical studies. The field was also growing less theoretical at a time when my interest in occupations, as well as my more general orientation, was growing increasingly theoretical. I remained (and remain) focally interested in the economy, but my interest in occupations was flagging.

During this period I was writing a great deal about and teaching sociological theory, especially the work of Max Weber, including his general theory of the rationalization of society. His paradigm of the rationalization process was a key work setting – the bureaucracy. However, bureaucracies were changing dramatically and were under attack for their irrationalities; they no longer seemed so paradigmatic. I began asking this question: Is there another organizational form in the late twentieth century that is a better example of rationalization? Over time, I came to the conclusion that the fast food restaurant was that organizational form, and based on Weber's rationalization of society, I began thinking and writing about the McDonaldization of society. An early article with that title drew little interest, but a decade later the book was published at a more propitious time; it is now in its eighth edition (Ritzer, 1983; 2015a).

At first, I thought about McDonaldization in terms of Weber's theory and the fast food restaurant as a setting for production and (service) work. My early thinking on this was not consciously and overtly related to consumption since I was still immersed in the sociology of occupations, and at the time there was little or no sociology of consumption in the United States. The book was a great success not only in the United States, but globally; it led to fifteen translations, as well as a number of speaking engagements throughout the world, especially Europe. During those trips I first learned about the sociology of consumption and that my work was seen by those in that field as a contribution to it. Thus, I had inadvertently become a sociologist of consumption, a specialty that was attractive because it had the characteristics that I felt the sociology of occupations had lost – strong ethnographic research and a powerful theoretical orientation.

I wrote two other books that were primarily about consumption even though I had not yet fully assimilated work on the sociology of consumption. One was on credit cards (Ritzer, 1995) and the other dealt with the "cathedrals of consumption" (Ritzer, 1999/2010). I thought of these as further works in applied theory with the credit card book building on Simmel's (1907/1978) thinking on money and credit and the cathedrals of consumption book returning to Weber (1921/1968), but mainly this time to his thinking on the enchantment of the world.

Another bit of serendipity that will become important later in this narrative is the fact that included in *The McDonaldization of Society* was a section entitled "Putting the Customers to Work". My interest in the sociology of work led me to the realization that fast food restaurants had created new ways of getting customers to do work (e.g. bus their dishes, clean their tables) – to "prosume" – for no pay that was previously and in other settings done by paid employees. While this had occurred previously in other consumption settings such as cafeterias, it was raised to new heights and importance by the fast food restaurant. While I had read Alvin Toffler's (1980) work, it was his broad theory of social change that interested me. At the time, his thinking on the prosumer had not resonated with me, and I did not relate it to the work that consumers were doing in fast food restaurants. It would take another decade and another serendipitous event to lead me to that revelation.

By the early 2000s I had finally come to think of what I was doing as a sociology of consumption. Actually, it was others, especially scholars in Europe, who led me to think in those terms. Especially notable was the influence of Chris Rojek, a sociologist of leisure and, more importantly, sociology editor at Sage of England. He invited me to publish an edited book on consumption, which brought together my work on consumption (essays, book excerpts) in a single volume (Ritzer, 2001). More importantly, he invited me to be one of the founding editors (with Don Slater) of *The Journal of Consumer Culture*, a position I held for almost a decade. Thus, by the early 2000s I was a full-fledged sociologist of consumption and much of my attention came to be devoted to it.

Then, in 2007, yet another serendipitous development led to another significant change in my orientation. I was invited to speak at a 2007 conference on prosumption in Frankfurt, Germany. The presentations at the conference, as well as preparation for my talk, led to a dramatic shift in my work, this time from consumption to prosumption. Since that time my scholarly attention has focused almost exclusively on prosumption in a number of journal articles, book chapters, and encyclopedia entries.

This recent work has revolutionized my thinking, especially in allowing me to see that production and consumption are not clearly distinct from one another or from prosumption. This, in turn, has allowed me to conceive of my work over the years on production, consumption, and prosumption as a coherent whole rather than a series of discrete stages.

Among the lessons of this discussion for young scholars is that what interests one early in one's career may not remain one's focal interest. Substantive interests do change, and they should as the social world, and the study of it, changes. Furthermore, those changes are often serendipitous and can take a scholar in interesting and surprising new directions.

Clarifying the concept of prosumption

The addition of the concept of prosumption – defined as the interrelationship of production and consumption where it becomes difficult, if not impossible, to clearly and unequivocally distinguish one from the other – to the traditional concepts of production and consumption leads to some false impressions. For one thing, it leads to a sense that these are three separable processes when it is prosumption that is the overarching process, and production and consumption can be seen as extreme types of prosumption (as depicted below in Figure 8.1).

Second, the recent outburst of attention to the process of prosumption (especially in the last decade), and the many very contemporary changes demanding and expediting it, leads to the impression that prosumption is something very new. Indeed, there is a "new prosumer" associated with recent developments, especially the new "means of prosumption", most notably on the internet (Ritzer, 2015b). However, people have always prosumed; for example, the earliest hunters and gatherers typically consumed what they produced and produced what they consumed; they were in main "pure" prosumers. Over time, especially after the Industrial Revolution, we came to think of those who went to work in the early factories, and later other work settings, as "producers" even though they had to consume (e.g. raw materials) as they produced. As distinct settings for consumption evolved, many of the activities that took place in them came to be thought of as consumption and those involved as "consumers" while they, of course, had to produce (e.g. shop, create definitions of various products and brands, etc.) as they consumed. Throughout the late nineteenth and twentieth centuries the distinctions between these activities and types of actors tended to harden and solidify. While Marx (1867/1967) is often thought of as having focused on production, he had a more integrated sense of production and consumption. However, some of his followers (e.g. economic determinists; Agger, 1978) did come to focus on production, while later others (e.g. Baudrillard, 1970/1998) focused on consumption. In sociology, the production-oriented fields of industrial and occupational sociology developed separately from the sociology of consumption. Lost sight of in these developments was the fact that all acts of production require at least some consumption (e.g. production workers must use, even use up, raw materials) and all acts of consumption necessitate some production (e.g. travelers using Expedia.com must perform all the steps involved in arranging and paying for their trips).

The early stages of a variety of social changes (e.g. the arrival of the internet; the invention of the modern fast food restaurant) contributed to Toffler's thinking about and coining of the term *prosumer* in 1980. While some analysts have grown more likely to think in terms of prosumers, the concepts of producers and consumers remain preeminent and are likely to continue to be so. It will be difficult to shake our attachment to these terms, especially since there is virtually no discussion of prosumption (and cognate terms; see below) outside of limited academic circles. Such discussion is especially lacking in the popular media. This is the case even though an increasing amount of scholarly attention is being paid to prosumption (Jacobs, 2015) and cognate terms because the kinds of social changes that first motivated Toffler have expanded and exploded since he first created the term.

To the degree that we seem to be destined to continue to think in terms of production and consumption, we need to conceptualize both as sub-types, and in terms of, prosumption. Rather than thinking, as we normally do, in terms of production and consumption, we should think (admittedly somewhat awkwardly) – we should have always thought – in terms of "prosumption-as-production" (p-a-p) and "prosumption-as-consumption" (p-a-c) (Ritzer, 2015c). It is these concepts (not production and consumption) that constitute the two ends of the prosumption continuum (see Figure 8.1) that lies at the base of this discussion and analysis. The fact is that all economic processes and societies have always involved and continue to involve a mix of production and consumption.

P-a-p involves what we have traditionally thought of as "production" and "producers" (but conceived of here as both producing and consuming workers; as those who must inevitably consume various goods and services in the process of production). P-a-p is clear in Marx's work and is the primary meaning associated with the concept of prosumption by most analysts. As a result of Marx's (and many others') prioritization of production, work on p-a-p, and on prosumption more generally, tends to have a productivist bias. To Marx, producers, that is the proletariat, must consume a variety of goods and services in order to produce. For example, workers must consume raw materials, tools and machines, the services provided by many others, as well as their own labor time. There can be no production without consumption in the factories of interest to Marx. Indeed, it is safe to say that there can never be any production without consumption.

However, it is important to accord similar if not equal weight to p-a-c (prosumption-as-consumption). To the degree that it has been recognized, at least implicitly, p-a-c has been subordinated to p-a-p because of that overwhelming productivist bias. Just as p-a-ps (prosumers-as-producers) must consume, p-a-cs (prosumers-as-consumers; or producing consumers) must produce (Dujarier, 2014) or work (Rieder and Voss, 2010; Dunkel and Kleeman, 2013). This has always been the case (at the minimum, p-a-cs must produce some of the meanings associated with what it means to be consumers, what they consume, where they consume it, as well as the process by which they consume it). However, the production associated with consumption is especially important in the case of contemporary prosumption. That is, by far the greatest recent change in this area involves the increasing importance of p-a-cs who are, in a variety of domains (supermarkets, fast food restaurants, and especially the internet), doing most of the work and in most cases for no pay. As a result, they are now replacing paid workers (e.g. in banking) and leading to a future where fewer and fewer paid workers will be hired to

Prosumption-as-Production (p-a-p)..."Balanced" Prosumption...Production-as-Consumption (p-a-c)

Figure 8.1 The prosumption continuum

work in them, at least on a full-time basis (e.g. full-time taxi drivers being replaced by transient Uber drivers; Ritzer, 2015c).

Work on prosumption has boomed in recent years; it would require a separate essay to do justice to it, but among the topics covered recently under this heading are Bitcoin, Silk Road, Mechanical Turk, selfies, citizen science, collaborative mapping, social media, Wikipedia, YouTube, eBay, Internet of Things, 3-D printing, translations, active learning, and MOOCs.

Given this brief overview of the perspective on prosumption that informs this essay, I turn to an abbreviated review of the broader and wider context of this topic and to the burgeoning work on some of the most important concepts that overlap in various ways with prosumption.

The broader context

The broadest context of these conceptual developments is the move away from modern thinking, especially the tendency to think in binary terms (Ritzer, 1997). Production was at the heart of modernity, while late modernity and even postmodernity were seen as increasingly characterized by consumption. However, as we can now see, especially from the vantage point of the literature on prosumption, the production-consumption binary is indefensible, as are many such modern binaries.

This move away from binary thinking, and in the direction of more integrative concepts (such as prosumption), is explicit in a variety of literatures on topics such as, among others, the produser, co-creation, service-dominant logic, pro-ams (Leadbeater and Miller, 2004), DIY (Watson and Shove, 2008), craft consumers (Campbell (2005), and the like. In addition, it is more implicit in other work, especially that dealing with the media, the social factory, the internet, and branding and the "ethical surplus" associated with it (Arvidsson, 2005). However, because of space constraints we can focus on only a few of these here.

Explicit conceptual similarities

While he acknowledged their resemblance to the concepts of the prosumption and the prosumer, Axel Bruns (2008; see also Grinnell, 2009) created the concepts of produsage and the produser as alternatives to them. As is true of many of those who work in this area, Bruns has a productivist bias, although he seeks to move beyond the traditional concepts of producers, products, and production. He re-imagines production as user-led (or commons-based) and this leads him to the concept of "produsage as an alternative to production". Because of his focus on production and the fact that he sees produsage as an alternative to production but not consumption, Bruns gives short shrift, despite his emphasis on the user, to the process of consumption, especially as it occurs in the process of production. In other words, his approach may offer an alternative to prosumption-as-production, but it is not an alternative to prosumption-as-consumption. However, what is in fact needed is not an alternative to either, but an approach that encompasses both. Bruns' approach stands in contrast to the main thrust of work on prosumption, which involves the fusion of more-or-less co-equal processes of prosumption-as-production and prosumption-as-consumption. Whatever approaches and concepts we create in this area, they must deal with both of these in a balanced manner and not prioritize one or the other. They must deal not only with consumption as being productive (as Bruns does), but also with production as involving consumption (as Marx, among many others, understood).

Perhaps the best-known of the work on concepts similar to prosumption is that which deals with co-creation (Prahalad and Ramaswamy, 2004a; 2004b; Ramaswamy and Ozcan, 2014).

This work, largely based in the business literature (in contrast, Bruns' work is oriented to media studies), offers a view and model of the relationship between connected, informed, empowered, and active consumers. In this case the binary in question is primarily the distinction between the creators employed by the firm and its creative customers. Instead of being distinct, and even being in conflict with one another over profits and cost, firms and customers are viewed as being involved in the process of co-creation. They are seen as collaborators in the production of an experience (or a product that offers an experience) rather than being adversaries in the process of sale and purchase, especially over the price to be paid for goods and services.

Closely related to the idea of co-creation is a concept – service-dominant logic – largely based in the field of marketing. The central figures in work on this idea are Stephen L. Vargo and Robert F. Lusch (2004). They put their thinking in the context of what they describe as a paradigm shift from a focus on goods-centered systems to those that center on services. Furthermore, while goods and services were in the past treated as distinct from one another, they view the provision of goods in the context of service provision. That is, goods provision involves services of various kinds. For our purposes the key to this argument is the distinction between the positions of customers in these two systems. In goods-centered systems customers are defined as "operand resources" who are "acted on to create transactions with resources". In contrast, in service-centered systems customers are "operant resources" and as such are "active participants in relational exchanges and coproduction" (Vargo and Lusch, 2004, p. 7). The idea that customers are active participants and co-producers brings us very close to the ideas of prosumption and co-creation.

The key premise of service-dominant logic is that the "the Customer is always a Coproducer" (Vargo and Lusch, 2004, p. 10). As part of a wide-ranging service process, the customer is always involved in the production of value. Even goods are seen as part of this process as they, in interaction with customers, are seen as providing services to the latter. Service is not something that is simply provided by the goods producer, but it also involves a number of activities provided by the customer. Among other things, customers must learn to use the product, figure out how to maintain it, repair it as needed, and adapt the product to their particular needs. This relationship between customers and tangible goods continues over a considerable period of time. Vargo and Lusch (2004, p. 11) summarize their view in this way: "The customer becomes primarily an operant resource (coproducer) rather than an operand resource ("target") and can be involved in the entire value and service creation chain in acting on operand resources". As a result, the value of a product is not embedded in the tangible product itself but rather in the relationship between producer and consumer; in other words, value is co-produced by producer and consumer.

Vargo and Lusch explicitly link their thinking on service-dominant logic to Prahalad and Ramaswamy's work on co-creation. The two ideas have recently been combined under the broader heading of "collaborative capitalism" (Cova, Dalli and Zwick, 2011).

More implicit linkages

While those involved have not often used the term, it is in media studies that the prosumer (and producer) has perhaps been of greatest concern. Of central importance here is the work of the Birmingham Centre for Cultural Studies (founded in 1964), especially that of its best-known figure, Stuart Hall. This body of work was a reaction against the Frankfurt School of critical theory, which focused on the "culture industry" and famously viewed the consumers of its products as passive recipients of what it had to offer; as "dupes" or "cultural dopes". The critical theorists operated with a one-way model with the cultural industry (radio, the movies, etc.), imposing its messages on the audience (consumers), who had little or no capacity to adapt, let alone reject, those messages (Jay, 1973, p. 216). Not only was the audience passive, but it was the passive recipient of a phony culture.

Hall (1980) responded with his famous distinction between encoding and decoding. Broadcasting structures such as those associated with television emit "encoded" messages, which are embedded in specific programs. However, to have an effect, these programs and their meanings must be "decoded" by the audience. In other words, the audience must do interpretive work in order to understand the meanings of a TV program and for those meanings to have an effect on them. Indeed, the objective fact of TV discourse and the subjective interpretive work of the audience cannot be clearly separated from one another; they are dialectically related.

While Hall approaches the issue of prosumption in the media and communications from the more subjectivist (or culturalist) perspective associated with the Frankfurt School, Dallas Smythe (1977) operates from a more traditional Marxian materialist perspective. He believes that Marxian scholars have neglected to do a materialist analysis of communications, or the "consciousness industry". Such an analysis of audiences (and readerships) leads him to conclude that under monopoly capitalism "all non-sleeping time of most of the population is work time" (Smythe, 1977, p. 3). Included in the "work" done during this period is "essential marketing functions for the producers of consumers' goods" (Smythe, 1977, p. 3). Advertisers are seen as buying the marketing services of the audience. Audiences work for advertisers by creating the demand for their products. They "learn to buy particular 'brands' of consumer goods, and to spend their income accordingly" (Smythe, 1977, p. 6). In so doing, they "complete the production process of consumer goods" (Smythe, 1977, p. 6).

Also within media studies is the work of Henry Jenkins (1992). In his early work on textual poachers, Jenkins takes on the idea that fans are "brainless consumers". Textual poachers, following Foucault and especially de Certeau (see below), are seen as those who extract from texts that which they find useful or pleasurable and use them to create texts of their own. However, the term *poachers* better reflects the media realities of the early 1990s than it does today. That is, the media owned and controlled the means of producing texts and fans had to "poach" them in order to produce their own texts. However, in the age of the internet the media have much less control over those means of producing texts and fans exercise greater control over them and are able to produce texts largely on their own (e.g. on blogs, Facebook pages, and on Twitter).

It is important to digress for a moment and mention de Certeau's important ideas on poaching. They are part of de Certeau's (1984, p. 30) very explicit sense of the consumer as a producer, the "labor of consumption", or of consumption as an entirely different kind of production, but of production nonetheless. Consumers are experts in the art of using what is imposed on them. In other words, they poach what is imposed on them and use it in their own ways and for their own purposes. De Certeau (1984, p. 34) has a romantic and powerful image of consumers as "unrecognized poets of their own affairs" and as "trailblazers in the jungles of functionalist rationality." They are accorded considerable power and independence as "poets" and "trailblazers", but we must not forget that they operating within the constraints of a structure that is in accord with, and the product of, functionalist rationality.

In the process of writing *Textual Poachers*, Jenkins (2006) developed the broader ideas of participatory and convergence culture which inform much of his more recent work. Participatory culture is one where fans are not mere spectators but active participants; fandom is a specific form of participatory culture. He defines convergence culture as one involving unpredictable interaction between the power of the media producer and the power of the media consumer. His primary interest is in counteracting the idea of the passive media spectator and emphasizing, instead, the ideas of spectators performing work and as consumers engaged in active participation. This is especially the case with new technologies empowering audiences who are demanding the right to participate.

Another neo-Marxian approach sees production, especially of immaterial phenomena, occurring throughout society rather than only in designated settings such as factories (Hardt and Negri, 2000). One group of contemporary Marxian theorists – the autonomist Marxists – have developed a perspective that offers a more integrative sense of the producer-consumer, albeit without using the term *prosumer*. This thinking has its origin in the fact that much production has moved outside of the walls of the factory and into society as a whole, creating the "social factory", or the "factory without walls" (Negri, 1989). This has been made possible by the fact that a great deal of production now involves little or no material labor (Lazzarato, 1996). Instead, we now see more and more immaterial production. The actual material production of cars by automobile workers is now of less importance than the immaterial production of ideas to improve the manufacturing, marketing, or design of the product by those who work in and around the automobile industry. More generally, there are now many industries (in software, marketing, and advertising) that are primarily about the production of ideas. Since immaterial production takes place in the realm of ideas, and these ideas are part of what is called the "General Intellect", it becomes increasingly possible (although as pointed out above it always was) for consumers to draw on this general fund of knowledge and information. As they draw upon – or consume – this knowledge, they produce and further contribute to it. For example, the open-source movement involves the production of computer software (e.g. Linux, Firefox) by those who use the software. In addition, consumers have increasingly been asked to provide ideas for advertisements and some of them have been adopted by producers.

As we will see below, perhaps the ultimate social factories are the Web 2.0 sites where prosumers simultaneously consume and produce ideas on, for example, wikis, blogs and social networking sites. From a Marxist perspective, capitalist systems are able to extract value from the unpaid labor of the prosumers on Web 2.0 sites and elsewhere (e.g. in the creation of brand meaning). In the view of some, they are able to exploit consumers and in the process earn even greater profits than they would from the exploitation of workers (Fuchs, 2010; Ritzer and Jurgenson, 2010; Rey, 2012). After all, even the lowest-paid workers are paid something; many prosumers work without any financial compensation.

The prosumer is implicit, and sometimes quite explicit, in various key works on the internet. This is largely because the internet is today the site par excellence of prosumption. Tapscott and Williams (2006, p. 18) define Wikinomics as the "art and science of collaboration". The term *collaboration* implies prosumers since it is they who are collaborating. In addition, Tapscott and William operate with an explicit conception of the prosumer (chapter 5 is entitled "The Prosumers"). Another key and similar term in Wikinomics is *peer production*, and this makes it clear that the authors are focusing on the prosumption-as-production end of the prosumption continuum and have little to offer on prosumption-as-consumption.

They correctly argue that the internet is crucial in this development, especially the transition from Web 1.0 to Web 2.0. While most of what took (takes) place on Web 1.0 was "produced" by those in control of the sites (e.g. Yahoo), Web 2.0 is "about the communities, participation, and peering" (Tapscott and Williams, 2006, p. 19). To put it another way, people were largely passive on Web 1.0, but are active participants on Web 2.0 sites such as Flickr, YouTube, Google Maps, and Craigslist, as well as in activities that inherently involve prosumption such as remixing and mashups.

Jeff Howe (2008) deals with crowdsourcing and the fact that inherent in it is prosumption. The "crowd", after all, is to a large extent those outside the organization who have traditionally been thought of as consumers. They are an object and resource for those "producers" within the organization. However, Howe (2008, p. 71) recognizes that "the line between producer and consumer has begun to blur".

While Howe pays no attention to the fact that producers are consumers, he is clear that consumers are increasingly becoming producers. He attributes this to the fact that the "means of production" (really the "means of prosumption") are increasingly widely available, including to consumers. He concludes quite rightly that as a result of this, "the 'consumer,' as traditionally conceived, is becoming an antiquated concept" (Howe, 2008, p. 71).

Much the same argument can be made about James Surowiecki's "The Wisdom of Crowds" (2004), especially the crowds associated with the internet and sites such as Wikipedia. It is clear that large numbers of people can collaborate and put together, say, definitions of key ideas more quickly and at least as accurately as those created by experts. The wise crowd, in this case, is composed largely of amateurs who we would more likely think of as, and would more likely be, consumers of the material on Wikipedia. Yet, in many cases they are more than consumers; they are producers of the text on Wikipedia; they are its prosumers. A large number of prosumers is likely to be as effective, if not more effective, than those we have historically thought of producers.

A similar argument applies to "everybody" in Clay Shirky's (2008) *Here Comes Everybody*. For example, he argues that we are witnessing a process of mass amateurization (to a large extent, consumers) of areas that were previously dominated by professionals (production). The dialectical nature of the web makes it clear that there is a dialectical relationship between producers and consumers whereby the (false, at least in our view) distinction between them erodes. This argument is even clearer in the subtitle of Shirky's (2010) *Cognitive Surplus: How Technology Makes Consumers into Collaborators*.

In sum, there is a great deal of work in a number of fields that deals with the prosumer, albeit in different ways and using different terms. When all of that work is taken together and seen as a whole, the increasing importance of the concept of prosumption and of the process of prosumption becomes quite evident.

Conclusion

This essay began with a brief overview of the fields of the sociology of production, consumption, and prosumption through the lens of my personal experience with them. I concluded by arguing that prosumption is the process that overarches the other two and that work on that topic is booming. This boom is traceable to a variety of social and intellectual changes. Among the key social changes are new economic settings (e.g. fast food restaurants, IKEA, online sites of all types) where the lines between work and consumption are eroding and new technologies are allowing, even forcing, consumers to work. At a theoretical level, key developments included the Autonomist Marxists who moved us in the direction of thinking of the "social factory" and, more importantly, postmodern theorists who helped us see the limitations and distortions of binary thinking (production and consumption), making room for, even demanding, more integrative, "liquid" ways of thinking such as prosumption (Bauman, 2000).

I then reviewed works in a variety of fields that deal with a similar set of concepts and conclusions. Some of that work is largely conceptual and neutral (e.g. that on the produser and the internet), but a good deal of it is slanted in either a positive (e.g. on co-creation and service-dominant logic) or in a critical direction (e.g. much of the literature on the mass media and the social factory). My own work in this area tends to be either purely conceptual and descriptive or critical of the way prosumption has come to be controlled and coopted by capitalist forces which increasingly prefer unpaid or poorly paid prosumers (e.g. Uber drivers) to paid workers such as taxi drivers and bank tellers (Ritzer, 2015c, 2015d). This is also leading to the classic pattern of the replacement of human (prosumers in this case) by non-human technologies, especially smart prosuming machines, including the sensor-laden technologies now coming together on the Internet of Things. Ironically, just as the importance of the concept of the prosumer is growing increasingly evident, we may be on the verge of the "death of the prosumer" amidst the rise of such smart prosuming machines (Ritzer, 2015e). Thus, while a good deal of my work on this topic is mainly theoretical and conceptual, I have become increasingly critical of recent developments in this domain. As a result, my view has drawn closer to the neo-Marxian perspective on this issue.

The explosion of the new means of prosumption and the associated prosumers presages the fact that we will see more scholarly attention devoted to them. Needed beyond additional attention, at least in the short run, is an effort to bring together the diverse strands of work that deal with, or relate to, prosumption. The goal must be to develop a more coherent and overarching perspective on this wide-ranging and very important development.

References

Agger, B. (1978), *Critical Social Theories: An Introduction.* Boulder, CO: Westview Press.
Arvidsson, A. (2005), 'Brands: A Critical Perspective.' *Journal of Consumer Culture*, Vol. 5, pp. 235–258.
Baudrillard, J. (1970/1998), *Consumer Society*. London: Sage.
Bauman, Z. (2000), *Liquid Modernity*. Cambridge, England: Polity.
Bruns, A. (2008), *Blogs, Wikipedia, Second Life, and Beyond: From Production to Produsage*. New York: Peter Lang.
Campbell, C. (2005), 'The Craft Consumer: Culture, Craft and Consumption in a Postmodern Society.' *Journal of Consumer Culture*, Vol. 5, pp. 23–42.
Cova, B., Dalli, D. and Zwick, D. (2011), 'Critical Perspectives on Consumers' Roles as "Producers": Broadening the Debate on Value Co-Creation and Marketing Processes.' *Marketing Theory*, Vol. 11, pp. 231–241.
De Certeau, M. (1984), *The Practice of Everyday Life.* Berkeley: University of California Press.
Dunkel, W. and Kleeman, F. (eds.) (2013), *Customers at Work: New Perspectives on Interactive Service Work*. Palgrave Macmillan.
Dujarier, M-A. (2014), 'The Three Sociological Types of Consumer Work.' *Journal of Consumer Culture*, published online April 2014, DOI: 10.1177/1469540514528198
Fuchs, C. (2010), 'Class, Knowledge and New Media.' *Culture and Society*, Vol. 32, pp. 141–150.
Grinnnell, C. K. (2009), 'From Consumer to Prosumer: Who Keeps Shifting My Paradigm? (We Do!).' *Public Culture*, Vol. 21, pp. 577–598.
Hall, S. (1980), "Encoding/Decoding." In S. Hall, D. Hobson, A. Lowe, and P. Willis (eds.) *Culture, Media, Language*, pp. 117–127. London: Unwin Hyman.
Hardt, M. and Negri, A. (2000), *Empire*. Cambridge, MA: Harvard University Press.
Howe, J. (2008), *Crowdsourcing*. NY: Three Rivers Press.
Hughes, E. (1958), *Men and Their Work*. Glencoe, IL: Free Press.
Jacobs, J. (2015), 'Top Cited Articles in Sociology Journals, 2010–2014.' *Footnotes*, December: 9.
Jay, M. (1973), *The Dialectical Imagination*. Boston: Little Brown.
Jenkins, H. (1992), *Textual Poachers: Television Fans and Participatory Culture*. NY: Routledge.
___ (2006), *Convergence Culture: Where Old and New Media Collide*. New York: New York University Press.
Lazzarato, M. (1996), "Immaterial Labor." In M. Hardt and P. Virno (eds.) *Radical Thought in Italy: A Potential Politics*, pp. 133–147. Minneapolis: University of Minnesota Press.
Leadbeater, C. and Miller, P. (2004), *The Pro-Am Revolution: How Enthusiasts are Changing Our Economy and Society*. London: Demos.
Marx, K. (1867/1967), *Capital: A Critique of Political Economy*, Vol. 1. NY: International Publishers.
Negri, A. (1989), *The Politics of Subversion. Malden:* MA: Polity Press.
Prahalad, C. K. and Ramaswamy, V. (2004a), 'Co-creation Experiences: The Next Practice in Value Creation.' *Journal of Interactive Marketing*, Vol. 18, pp. 5–14.
___ (2004b) *The Future of Competition: Co-Creating Unique Value with Customers*. Cambridge, MA: Harvard Business School Press.
Ramsawamy, V. and Ozcan, K. (2014), *The Co-Creation Paradigm*. Stanford: Stanford Business Books.

Rey, P.J. (2012), 'Alienation, Exploitation, and Social Media.' *American Behavioral Scientist*, Vol. 56, pp. 399–420.
Rieder, K. and Voss. G.G. (2010), 'The Working Customer: An Emerging New Type of Consumer.' *Journal Psychologie des Alltagshandelns / Psychology of Everyday Activity*, Vol. 3, No. 2, pp. 2–10.
Ritzer, G. (1972), *Man and His Work: Conflict and Change*. NY: Appleton-Century-Crofts.
___ (1983), 'The McDonaldization of Society.' *Journal of American Culture*, Vol. 6, No. 1, pp. 100–107.
___ (1995), *Expressing America: A Critique of the Global Credit Card Society*. Newbury Park, CA: Pine Forge Press.
___ (1997), *Postmodern Social Theory*. NY: McGraw-Hill.
___ (1999/2010), *Enchanting a Disenchanted World*. Thousand Oaks, CA: Pine Forge Press.
___ (2001), *Explorations in the Sociology of Consumption: Fast Food Restaurants, Credit Cards and Casinos*. London: Sage.
___ (2015a), *The McDonaldization of Society*. 8th ed. Thousand Oaks, CA: Sage.
___ (2015b), 'The New World of Prosumption: Evolution, Return of the Same, or Revolution?' *Sociological Forum* Vol. 30, pp. 1–17.
___ (2015c), 'Prosumer Capitalism,' *Sociological Quarterly*, Vol 56, pp. 413–445.
___ (2015d), 'Jobless Recovery or Ever-More Joblessness,' *Contexts*, Vol. 14, pp. 58–59.
___ (2015e) 'Automating Prosumption: The Decline of the Prosumer and the Rise of the Prosuming Machines.' *Journal of Consumer Culture*, Vol. 15, pp. 407–424.
___ and Jurgenson, N. (2010), 'Production, Consumption, Prosumption: The Nature of Capitalism in the Age of the Digital "Prosumer".' *Journal of Consumer Culture*, Vol. 10, pp. 13–36.
Ritzer, G. and Trice, H. (1969). *An Occupation in Conflict: A Study of the Personnel Manager.* Ithaca, NY: NYSSILR, Cornell University Press.
Ritzer, G. and Walczak, D. (1986), *Working: Conflict and Change*, 3rd edition. New Jersey: Prentice-Hall.
Shirky, C. (2008), *Here Comes Everybody*. NY: Penguin.
___ (2010), *Cognitive Surplus: How Technology Makes Consumers into Collaborators*. NY: Penguin.
Simmel, G. (1907/1978), *The Philosophy of Money*. London: Routledge and Kegan Paul.
Smythe, D. W. (1997) 'Communications: Blindspot of Western Marxism.' *Canadian Journal of Political and Social Theory*, Vol. 1, pp. 1–27.
Surowiecki, J. (2004) *The Wisdom of Crowds*. NY: Anchor Books
Tapscott, D. and Williams, A.D. (2006), *Wikinomics: How Mass Collaboration Changes Everything*. New York: Portfolio.
Toffler, A. (1980), *The Third Wave*. NY: William Morrow.
Vargo, S. L. and Lusch, R.F. (2004), 'Evolving to a new dominant logic for marketing.' *The Journal of Marketing*, Vol. 68, pp. 1–17.
Watson, M. and Shove, E. (2008), 'Product, Competence, Project and Practice: DIY and the Dynamics of Craft Consumption".' *Journal of Consumer Culture*, Vol. 8, pp. 69–89.
Weber, M. (1921/1968), *Economy and Society*, 3 vols. Totowa, NJ: Bedminster Press.

9

Collaborative consumption and sharing economies

Stefan Wahlen and Mikko Laamanen

Introduction

Recently, various newer, older and revived forms of living, producing and consuming have gained ground in academic and societal debates. Collaborative consumption (CC) and sharing economies (SE) have become part of a nomenclature describing and conceptualizing developments promising different forms of prosperity cemented in new types of economic revitalization and good life with minimized dependence on material possessions and ownership. A common denominator of CC and SE initiatives is the mediating role of new digital technologies connecting various actors and modes of transfer. Consequently, CC and SE effectively delineate and concern new forms of consumption and consumers. Some forms of CC and SE illustrate new types of consumer activism and alternative lifestyles with a heightened awareness of the consequences of unfettered capitalism whereas others emerge as new forms of business activity. Both can be oriented towards sustainable development: the former in (militant) opposition of growth and injustice, the latter in seeing market-mediated provisioning as a source of collective benefit. In this chapter we offer a critical reading of contemporary CC and SE literatures and attempt to delineate possible boundaries by referring to classical and contemporary theories and empirical research in these areas. We address the broad array of ideas that are bundled under CC and SE: given that these concepts are continuously (re-)defined, it increasingly becomes muddled as to what they stand for. While CC and SE can be seen challenging current social, cultural, economic, and sometimes, political institutions, it's not clear whether these new forms of economic activity are an alternative, better than, or even worse than traditional forms of capitalism and consumption.

The interdependency of CC and SE is, to our understanding, manifested in the former being embedded in the latter. At the core, CC can be considered a form of economic collaboration where idling resources are made available – shared – with others in a larger community – the sharing economy. The acts of sharing take place between those who need and those who can provide resources leading to the effective use of existing, often dormant resources, while simultaneously building connections and developing participants' skills. Differentiation can be drawn between global corporate SE platforms (such as AirBnB and Uber) and more localized systems based on business, public administration, and community initiatives as well as their hybrids (these initiatives are connected among others to sharing transportation, everyday tasks, commodities, time, space; see table 9.1, p. 124).

In what follows, we discuss CC and SE as forms of socio-economic order and technical systems that connect to historical, cultural, and technological developments in society and economic collaboration. Also, given the variety of what can be understood as being part of CC and SE, we delineate the cornerstones – the somewhat contradictory confluence of the economy and consumption with collaboration and sharing. The meta-level aim of our analysis in the chapter overall is to question the supposed novelty of CC and SE in relation to social, cultural, and economic forms of human conduct. Two central questions span the chapter: (1) To which extent do consumers behave differently in contexts of CC and a SE? and (2) What is the nature of consumer agency in these assumingly novel forms of conduct? Even though an increasing amount of literature on CC and SE focusses on the potential for commercial applications, we consider an elaboration of such business models as beyond the scope of the chapter. In what follows, we first consider a historical perspective presented through economic collaboration and reciprocities in archaic community exchange. Then, we critically assess the current state of CC and SE including the techno-believers' hope in a networked society underlying much of CC and SE as well as the potentiality of societal challenges, increased democracy, inclusive participation, and sustainable environmental development. In conclusion, we feature room for further engagement and provide avenues for future investigation.

Collaboration and the economy: A historical perspective

In contemporary debate, particularly in the public domain, CC and SE become discursively framed as alternative and novel. Indeed, as phenomena of consumption and economic activity, the alternative character of CC and SE is a major political catalyst. Yet, much of the jubilee and debate around CC and SE is pertinent to ahistoricism. In order to better understand CC and SE, we examine historical developments from a long-term perspective considering the processes through which the current monetized economy and consumer culture have emerged. We explore how modes of transfer took place in and between antediluvian communities, such as clans and kinship-based structures, which might still be found in emerging societies.

Further, we are interested in how the breakdown of traditional communities and commons, including the development of commercialism, led to the rationalization and marketization of economic exchange. Households, families, and other communities that are built on relationships can assist us in understanding the non-market aspect of CC and SE. All of this is done without the aspiration of providing a complete history of sharing and collaboration, but more to pinpoint particular important developments.

Classically, economy stood for the localized form of social and economic collaboration. Economic collaboration, i.e. the social ties and exchange in and between groups in 'primitive', premodern times, connects to proximity, togetherness, and solidarity as opposed to the individual survival. Solidarity and 'communistic' distribution translates to organizing for group survival due to in-group needs and the possibility of external threats (Coates, 2007). In *The Great Transformation* Karl Polanyi discusses how in antediluvian exchange the individual interests were effectively suppressed by community. Social relations and economic needs were met, balancing reciprocity and parity as mechanisms of social order in and between groups. To a lesser degree, these exchange relationships related to quantity, quality, and temporalities of exchange. Polanyi (2001) argues how various economic principles may exist in a society or community simultaneously without taking prevalence and/or being subordinate to other principles and mechanisms. For instance, reciprocity gives symmetry to social organization of exchange and regulates expectations and outcomes whereas redistribution rests on centricity of authority in resource allocation. Householding locates production and consumption in households as the immediate use contexts (related to the Greek meaning of an economic social unit or *oikos*).

Where the returns of hunting, gathering, pastoralism, and farming could be distributed through the symmetrical, centralized, or privatized mechanisms of reciprocity, redistribution, and householding respectively, these were not markets, but rather orderings of economic collaboration. In pre-modern times, markets as known today had a very limited role in organizing and regulating economic life (Polanyi, 2001); the emergence of barter institutionalized a market and a valuation mechanism. Analogously, though monetary exchange was part of economic interaction with primitive currencies, such as salt, gold dust, or sea-shells as currency, barter endured even within monetary systems (Braudel, 1992). With the issue of modern money, a measure of parity emerged at the cost of community. Maurer (2006) argues that the great transformation embedded in money was the liberation of individuals from communality, yet money also became the only mechanism for valuation of any social or natural production. In other words, money was (and is) the source of alienated emancipation.

Capitalism, commercialization, and an associated consumer culture are inextricably linked to the development of what is termed *modernity* (cf. Slater, 1997) and *the great transformation* by Polanyi. In industrializing societies, further distinction was drawn between the productive and consumptive aspects of the economy, where the former is seen as the creation and the latter the destruction of goods. Whilst this may represent a theoretical distinction, it allowed for the emergence and evolution of the modern understanding of consumerism and the consumer (Trentmann, 2006). Mass production required mass consumption. Gabriel and Lang (2015) describe how a Fordist deal then lead to quiescent labor force in exchange for increasing standard of living. While this welfare paternalism aimed to improve local employment conditions and avoid organized labor, it wasn't an act of pure altruism, but a means to generate demand and markets for products. Still, the early labor movement fought to balance the unevenly distributed economic gains that industrialization brought to society by levelling income differentials, moderating working hours, and consequentially stimulating the economy through consumption (Lichtenstein, 2002). This provided a form of redistribution from a more democratic orientation. Similarly, the consumer cooperative movement has been authoritative in contributing to the development of consumer policy guaranteeing stable prices and secure livelihoods (Wahlen & Huttunen, 2012). The cooperative movement further bridges the divide between production and consumption through joint ownership and rights to the common good.

In current societies, institutions for economic collaboration can be coercive or altruistic; for instance, taxation and philanthropy in distinct degrees represent contemporary forms of householding, redistribution, and reciprocity. Nevertheless, these mechanisms do not seem to be able to effectively alter the divisions that we have inherited from modernity or the ever-increasing societal differentials that resemble those in the early twentieth century. This is partly due to the uninterrupted dominance of economics with its inherent dualism and separation of production and consumption as well as its rationality-based conceptualization of the consumer (Trentman, 2006). Consumption, in its narrow, colloquial understanding, equates with market exchange, that is, the acquisition of goods and services for use. In this individualist understanding, consumption is an economic and rational action, not a socio-cultural phenomenon. Rationality designates the consumer as a calculative agent in the economy, a leaf in the wind making do with the little agency it has.

In advanced capitalist societies, the logic of individuality disavows communalities that would otherwise emerge as natural human conduct. The consumer economy is the pinnacle of individuality and economic growth, and the consumer becomes wooed to desire and acquire over and above their means and the capacities of the planet with regards to resources and waste. Furthermore, with affluence divided unequally, current societies are polarizing to haves and have-nots with access to material, cultural, and political resources allocated unevenly (Albo, 2013; Gilbert, 2014; Heinrichs, 2013). In these conditions of inequality, the question is why do people come together in social and/or economic co-operation? Central to these considerations is how the organization and reproduction on social life takes place in economic relations. For instance, where local collaboration revives 'communistic' tendencies in models of sharing and collaborative consumption, it also brings with it a new post-industrial model that is based on the wisdom of crowds and the many actively providing appropriable commodities. Referring back to a longue durée, we can see that a so-called "sharing economy" is as such neither new nor innovative per se.

According to Sahlins (1972), the location of production in the domestic, familiar context and distribution in the local community differentiates an antediluvian economy from the modern, which concerns itself with the ownership of the means and outcomes of production. The sharing economy can indeed represent a relocation and moralization of economic activity in the former perspective (e.g. Molz, 2013) while simultaneously being scaled up to a global community owing to connective network technologies. Comparably, yet to a lesser degree relying on network technologies, social and solidarity economies also offer ways in which socio-cultural changes have come to challenge wasteful and unequal economic structures and practices of the past. It is to be shown to what extent these concepts collude with the sharing economy. As such, the advances of the past decade come apparent in the re-emergence of the sharing groundswell.

Deconstructing collaborative consumption and sharing economy

The re-emergence of interest in collaboration and sharing in the recent past has been described as groundswell and heralded as a socially and ecologically sustainable form of living and business with the upcoming of novel, digital network technologies. In what follows we describe and evaluate the causes and nature of the newly found importance of collaboration in consumption and sharing as an economic activity.

Sharing and the economy

The ever-increasing pools of unused resources may incentivize individuals to connect in the community and live more attuned to sustainability. Also, the breakdown of economic structures and associated growing inequalities give impetus to the increasing emergence of alternative or complementary modes of transfer emerging from everyday challenges and economic subordination. Alternatives are aided by non-monetary exchange, DIY, and reuse on networking technology platforms. *Sharing* is the term that can be used for the acts and practices through which people gain access to resources, both material and immaterial, in a given (virtual) network, group, or community. Sharing can be understood as possessing and appropriating things or services with others or letting others use. The concept of sharing can be linked to specific ways of understanding what is property and more generally as a way of organizing social life (Widlok, 2013). The structure of sharing is such that abides to the common understandings and rules of the participants as to what and to which extent resources are available.

As such, sharing can be understood not only as a mode of exchange or transfer of ownership, as in commercial exchange, but also as a form of co-ownership. In this manner, John (2013) distinguishes three different spheres of sharing: first, sharing in intimate interpersonal relationships of time, emotions, and feelings; second, sharing commodities and resources in socio-economic contexts as in household consumption and production; and third, sharing in a virtual sphere where photos, music, films, data, and others are exchanged on social networking and peer-exchange platforms. While proximity and close physical ties aid conventional sharing in households and families, network technologies have removed physical and temporal boundaries of sharing activities. Hence, in the first two spheres, sharing is not a novel or innovative economic activity and some degree of reciprocity and mutuality is fundamental. Sharing as alternative mode of transfer has been tightly linked to the notion of gift-giving, opposing the dominant logic of commercial exchange (Widlok, 2013). In terms of the virtual sphere, the past decades have witnessed peer platforms amassing: used for sharing work and workflows (Taskrabbit, Google Drive), commodities (e.g. torrent-sharing on Pirate Bay), experiences (Yelp, Tripadvisor, Instagram), interests of various kinds (e.g. on Twitter), and personal details (Myspace, Facebook). These various ways of connecting with others and sharing with them transcend physical proximity.

As briefly illustrated, sharing certainly has economic implications, yet is seen as either complementary or alternative to the dominant commercial economy. The difference between complementary and alternative economic forms can, respectively, be made in considering whether these by nature exist parallel to or in challenge of the dominant (capitalist market) economy as for instance in the moral household economy. We see the sharing economy to stand for a particular form of social and economic organization centered around the practice of sharing and accessing of pooled resources via network technologies. Resources can be dormant, unused material possessions or skills and competences, and become accessible through participation in a particular collectivity and/or engagement in a relevant lifestyle. Community structures, such as the membership and composition of sharing groups, form boundaries to sharing practices. Sharing economy, however, appears as a paradox (Richardson, 2015; Slee, 2015). In current neoliberal capitalism, cooperative sharing and the market economy exist in opposed ideational and practical dimensions.

Collaborative consumption

Analogously to the ancient Greek understanding of the economy, consumption can be perceived as both on a dichotomy of private and public, and individual and collective. Individual sustenance relates to meeting personal needs and wants in their essential and superfluous nature. The latter particularly relates to the expression of individuality in society through conspicuous consumption. The individual, both in private and public lifestyle, is the epitome on which the consumer society rests upon. Conspicuous consumption is the mechanism of distinction – of elaborating difference and illustrating individual lifestyles and practice repertoires (Bourdieu, 1984). Giddens (1991) considers lifestyle more than utilitarian, as self-narrating and identity-creating practices adopted from a plurality of options routinely consolidated into the everyday – in Giddens' (1991) words, '. . .[Everyday] choices (as well as in larger and more consequential ones) are decisions not only about how to act, but who to be. The more post-traditional the settings in which an individual moves, the more lifestyle concern the very core of self-identity, its making and remaking' (p. 81).

Households as collectives are institutions of mutual dependency and functional similarity between their participant members; their activities organize both production and consumption towards the aim of individual and collective sustenance. From the early treatise of collaborative consumption by Felson and Spaeth (1978), which saw the phenomenon as cooking and drinking beer in a neighbourly reference group, emerged later an entirely revamped version of collaborative consumption. The private aspects of collective sustenance and householding build the groundwork for collaboration in collaborative consumption and more publicly oriented lifestyles.

Here, the notion of collaborative consumption re-emerged as a groundswell, which Botsman and Rodgers (2010, pp. 71–75) divide into three particular systems: (1) product service systems, (2) redistribution markets, and (3) collaborative lifestyles. The product service systems challenge the concept of ownership through sharing or renting of corporate or privately owned products. In the redistribution markets pre-owned products are exchanged for free or sold, whereby recycling and reusing products is supported. Finally, collaborative lifestyles illustrate sharing space, skill, time, currencies in local contexts spanning, amongst others, work and farming spaces, local currencies, work assignments, etc. The systems can be global or local, market- or non-market mediated, economizing or politicizing lifestyles (cf. Eckhardt & Bardhi, 2016; Laamanen, Wahlen & Campana, 2015), with connective technologies scaling up spaces and networks.

Networked society and the mechanisms of sharing

In an increasingly networked society, powered by the Internet and mobile applications, collaborative ways of sharing, pooling and using resources have gained momentum. Instead of a kinship structure, networks of exchange are constructed between strangers on virtual platforms. New information technologies widen the temporal and spatial parameters of community and exchange. Communicative technologies are just one mechanism amongst many, yet central to various conceptualizations of both CC and SE. Particularly they offer efficient ways of communication. These new means of communication blur the boundaries between producers and consumers in a traditional commercial and economic understanding. Consumers themselves start acting to offer products and services and coming across with the agency that is traditionally ascribed to the producer, thus taking over the role of the prosumer (see previous chapter in this volume). In this vein, Stephany (2015) argues that SE renders underutilized assets accessible online, reducing the need for ownership and increasing the convenience of 'being able to access most of our essential needs like food, shelter, and transportation from share platforms direct from a smartphone' (p. 185). This is in line with Castells' (2010) characteristics of a network society, being demarcated as connected by information technology that electronically processes information in networks. Social networks are a very old phenomenon of social organization, but the novelty is considered to be located in the information-processing and communication technology. Information is a key, being more easily accessible in virtual networks and social media.

The newly acquired agency of the consumer in terms of using the Internet also raises hope for new opportunities for democratic processes and liberating potential of increased political participation and fighting social inequalities. Indeed, technological solutions can assist in solving social problems and increasing inclusion. Taylor (2014) considers technology as an important tool in giving power and culture back to a broad societal basis, while keeping overreliance and romantics of technology in check (Morozev, 2011). For instance, what is the role of big data and matters of trust and privacy? How are social relationships changing in the reputation economy? Can we even speak of a new digital divide including new inequalities considering social, economic and political implications in the use of new technologies and the way these influence everyday life?

Illustrative examples of collaborative consumption and the sharing economy

A variety of ideas are currently attached to the concepts of collaborative consumption and sharing economies: the mesh; peer, circular, rental or on-demand economy; access-based consumption and access economy; collaborative production; collaborative lifestyles; commercial sharing systems; p2p platforms, to name but a few. Particularly new connective technologies that offer distinctive tools to connect and 'get things done' diffuse the boundaries between roles and positions of market participants (the blurring of boundaries between production and consumption). In this field it is possible to witness a variety of activities and initiatives representing different categories in the study of SE and CE. These can be clustered according to shared core phenomena: what and/or how is shared. Table 9.1 (below) provides an overview of studies that we identified through a systematic search in SCOPUS using the keywords *collaborative consumption* and *sharing economy* in title, keyword or abstract. This list is not exhaustive, but gives an indications of current debates.

As elaborated, CC and SE are a broad and diverse field of initiatives with a clear focus on sharing spaces, mobility and exchanging commodities. In tabularizing these studies, we considered the most significant area of empirical illustration: the categories outlined are illustrative whereby it is possible and indeed probable that studies transcend rigid categories (see e.g.

Table 9.1 Studies in collaborative consumption and sharing economy

	CC / SE categories	*Illustrative studies*
Physical space	Co-housing, co-working, community gardening, and facilities, such as storage	German Molz, 2013 Gould Ellen, 2015 Forno & Garibaldi, 2015 Hong & Vicdan, 2016 McArthur, 2015 Seyfang, 2007
Mobility and transport	Ridesharing, car sharing, bike sharing, public transport, agencies for arranging lifts	Bardhi & Eckhardt, 2012 Cohen & Kietzmann, 2014 Möhlmann, 2015
Commodities	Exchange and recycle of various goods including book and clothing libraries, free cycling, pre-owned goods (eBay, Craigslist), tools, barter, food as in community gardens, food sharing	Ozanne & Ballantine, 2010 Corciolani & Dalli, 2014 Martin et al., 2015 Piscicelli et al., 2015 Pedersen & Netter, 2015
Time/skills	Skills sharing, for instance, in local communities (complementary currencies such as time banking or TaskRabbit)	Seyfang, 2007 Laamanen et al., 2015
Finances and peer-to-peer banking	Crowdfunding and crowdsourcing, social lending and social currencies, complementary currencies (e.g. Bitcoin and Blockchain models)	Bauer & Gegenhuber, 2015
Open-source software development, virtual consumption	Wikipedia, open government	John, 2013 Aaltonen & Lanzara, 2015 O'Neil, 2015

inter-contextual comparison of sharing; Harvey, Smith & Golightly, 2014) and can be included in various categories. Interestingly, all the studies focus on advanced capitalist societies, whereas it could prove interesting to consider emerging countries as contexts as well.

Further, the variety in commercial promise and application illustrates how CC and SE are easily marketable, low-hanging fruit for market development. We see this in particular as critique towards Botsman and Rodgers' (2010) conclusions. For instance, community exchange of commodities, such as food, are attempts to reduce food waste with a societal spillover effect (considering e.g. the recent legislation banning food waste in France). However, the ever-increasing inquiry into the various social and commercial applications has not lead to consensus about the impact and outcomes of CC and SE. This is what we turn to next.

Capitalism amplified or serious mobilization for emancipation?

Finally, in questioning both the conceptual coherence and novelty of the supposedly new ways of understanding contemporary consumption, the question remains whether or not CC and SE are but misnomers. The harbingers of these new empowered and collaborative ways of consuming in the sharing economy have become accused of consumer/worker exploitation and tax avoidance (prominent examples are Airbnb and Uber; see e.g. Slee, 2015). One conclusion could be that CC and SE are nothing but the emperor's new clothes, capitalism amplified and crowdsourced – capitalism 2.0. The other possibility highlights CC and SE embedded in an inclusive and solidarity-based economy. These questions are central to the future as we are noticing how and whether CC and SE can actually provide the context and outcomes for challenging neoliberal capitalism, empowering communities and individuals, reducing inequalities, and protecting the environment and the consumers, that is, impacting social, economic, cultural and political transformation.

Martin (2016) questions whether the sharing economy provides an innovative disruption of sustainable consumption or whether it is merely an extended form of neoliberal capitalism. His discursive analysis resulted in supportive frames, talking about economic opportunities, more sustainable consumption in particular, and an opportunity for a decentralized and equitable access to resources. On the other hand, there are opposing frames that consider SE models as unregulated marketplaces and as such are bolstering a neoliberal paradigm, an incoherent spectrum of innovation, and a winner-takes-all-marketplace (see e.g. Slee, 2015). In a similar vein, Richardson (2015) explains that CC and SE are capitalist and alternative economy at the same instance, holding '. . . seemingly paradoxical potential to both shake up and further entrench "business-as-usual" in a variety of areas of economic activity' (p. 127). For instance, community holds the potential to be inclusive as well as exclusive, and common resource pools may concentrate rather than diffuse in CC and SE contexts. It is thus an opportunity and critique by blurring some boundaries, ideologies and conventions that have not been combinable before. Indeed, SE may equal an exploitation economy, whose mechanisms gainfully appropriate consumer work and extract value from consumers' collaborative tendencies.

Avenues for future research

Based on the aforesaid, we would like to address avenues for future research. There are different streams of investigation, often from different disciplinary angles, approaching CC and SE. Networking, the Internet, Web 2.0 and mobile applications are central aspects of SE and CC; there is an increasing amount of literature at the cross section of social and technological disciplines. In social science research we can distinguish two streams: one that is focusing on advancing new business models and another one that is addressing social and environmental problems that are addressed in CC and SE. For the readership, we stick to the latter (for the former we in general refer to Stephany, 2015; for mobility to Cohen & Kietzmann, 2014; for clothes to Pedersen & Netter, 2015). Estimated solutions can address social inequality but also relate to sustainable development; therefore we highlight contingencies and distinct avenues for further investigation. Hence, there are three possible avenues: first, a consumer (user) agency perspective; second, a consumer (supplier) agency perspective and third, that of grander transformations.

As is outlined in this chapter, sharing in kinship relations is not new, so then what are the mechanisms that promote proximity? Central from a user perspective, what is the nature of what is being shared? Are cases of short-term rental or gig-economy (getting access to goods and services) sharing, particularly if enabled by apps? Are apps and platforms representative of (virtual) communities? What about a sharing economy as an urban phenomenon? Does concentration make an economy? What about rural lifestyles – do these allow for collaborative consumption? How are CC and SE taken up in less developed countries with different kinship and community structures? There are still a lot of uncertainties and opportunities as to the implications of CC and SE to community transformation. There is insufficient evidence of CC and SE as true social innovations and therefore it would prove an engaging endeavor to examine disadvantage in communities in order to establish to what extent SE and CC are possible solutions (cf. McArthur, 2015).

From the perspective of the consumer as provider of commodities and services, exploitation of consumers as workers is a central critique of CC and SE (see e.g. Gabriel & Lang, 2015; Slee, 2015). Is contemporary sharing a creation of a new, hypercapitalist version of an economy beyond traditional regulation of markets? The phenomenon of #WeWashing illustrates how corporate players in the fields of CC and SE are assumed to misuse the terms of sharing for renting. With the formal distinctions and institutional arrangements, such as collective representation, not applicable to the new forms of economy, commodification of private spheres of individual lives as well as matters of responsibility become opaque. This leads to another aspect that has not been researched, which is the legal position of those involved in SE and CC. Who or what is a consumer in legal terms? How can regulating CC and SE take form? For instance, what can be done to the independent contractor loophole and the reality of CC and SE participants working below minimum wages, without insurance and basic employment protection? With CC and SE embracing an entrepreneurial ethos, how are the positive overtones of economic innovation and new job opportunities comparable with harsh realities of precarious employment? Finally, what about consumer protection?

A central societal question is how CC and SE might contribute to a reduction of social inequalities and empowerment of localities. Meeting needs and sharing resources is a paradox for the societal collective good. While above the focus on regulation relates to protecting individuals, on a larger level, where are the borders between community self-help and the creation of underground economies drawn? What is the societal impact of reduced consumption and local procurement (e.g. in the form of downshifting and voluntary simplicity)? For instance, Heinrichs (2013) suggests further scrutiny of materialist and post-materialist values in SE and CC. Here it might be possible to question the dominant economic growth paradigm with the limits of growth or the liberating character of post-materiality. Likewise, new technologies enable collaboration by bringing different parties together, parties that would otherwise unlikely be connected via regular markets, and engage them in many ways. While social media provide entertainment and connect participants, they also provide spaces for collective action through elaborating and framing identities, worthy causes and subsequent action (e.g. Dubuisson-Quellier, 2015).

There is still limited to no research about considering CC and SE from perspectives of a solidarity economy as radical transformations of the economy beyond the status quo. Solidarity economy consists of 'forms of economic activity that prioritize social and often environmental objectives, and involve producers, workers, consumers and citizens acting collectively and in solidarity' (Utting, 2015, pp. 1–2). A solidarity economy approach does not invigorate a capitalism 2.0 perspective, but moves toward critical perspectives on the politics of the everyday, local action (Gibson-Graham, 2006; Wahlen & Laamanen, 2015). To this point, Wahlen and Laamanen (2015, p. 401) call for research on how people 'enact alternatives, practice change and "do politics" in the everyday in a way that does not necessarily relate to the hegemonic understanding of the consumer as market participant or citizen as political actor'. Finally, the possible impact of CC and SE in emerging economies remains under-researched. SE and CC seem to be phenomena related to individualized advanced capitalist societies, whereas it would prove interesting to reflect on the more archaic societal history with the social structures, possibilities and challenges of economic, regional and democratic development. Would it be possible that alternative, moral and democratic paths in economic progress – drawing on economic experimentation and innovative technologies – build and extend on moral economies?

Concluding remarks

In the beginning of this chapter, we posed two questions: to which extent do consumers behave differently in contexts of CC and a SE, and what is the nature of consumer agency in these assumedly novel forms of conduct? Our approach brought to the fore the historical embedding, current state and future prospects of what has emerged in the past years as CC and SE. As we have shown, economic collaboration as contemporary collaboration and sharing illustrates and is reminiscent of historical forms of individual and collective economic collaboration. With regards to the first question, we illustrate a continuum on which economic collaboration evolves through time and conclude that, while forms of interaction and mediation of resource transfer are novel, the current forms of CC and SE have a historical lineage. CC and SE generate boundaries around communal redistribution and reciprocity which are combined with open access and connectivity of network technologies. The consequent potential of the CC and SE form of householding extends far beyond the immediate context. Alongside other contemporary forms of alternative economic experimentation, CC and SE hold the potential of increasing consumer agency. Consumers can be empowered to change the structures of contemporary capitalism in mutual benefit and solidarity. However, big corporate players and venture capitalism in the sharing economy can undermine the utopian potentials and foundations of civil society. Through CC and SE, this hyperliberalism infiltrates spheres of everyday life previously not affected by commercial activity. As many commentators have noted, the question is whether *the sharing economy* is the correct term for commercial activities where mutualism and reciprocity of users can be colonized by platform owners. This question is left open: the future will show whether CC and SE promote solidarity and mindful use of resources and consequently sustainable consumption, an exploitative business model innovatively appropriating local resources and activities, or a hybrid form of the two. For the critically inclined observers, the most interesting research in this framework relates to the duality of emancipation and domination ingrained in the social, cultural and economic practice of CC and SE.

References

Aaltonen, A., & Lazara, G. F. (2015). Building governance capability in online social production: Insights from Wikipedia. *Organization Studies*, 36 (12), 1649–1673. doi:10.1177/0170840615584459

Albo, G. (2013). The crisis and economic alternatives. *Socialist Register*, 49, 1–25.

Bardhi, F., & Eckhardt, G. (2012). Access-based consumption: The case of car sharing. *Journal of Consumer Research*, 39 (4), 881–898.

Bauer, R., & Gegenhuber, T. (2015). Crowdsourcing: Global search and the twisted roles of consumers and producers. *Organization*, 22 (5), 661–681. doi:10.1177/1350508415585030

Botsman, R., & Rodgers, R. (2010). *What's mine is yours: The rise of collaborative consumption*. New York, NY: HarperCollins.

Bourdieu, P. (1984). *Distinction: A social critique of the judgement of taste*. Cambridge, MA: Harvard University Press.

Braudel, F. (1992). *The structures of everyday life: The limits of the possible. (Civilization and Capitalism 15th – 18th century, Vol. 1)*. Berkeley, CA: University of California Press.

Castells, M. (2010). *The rise of the network society. (The information age: Economy, society and culture, Vol. 1.) (2nd ed.)*. Malden, MA: Blackwell.

Coates, R. (2007). Solidarity. In G. Ritzer (Ed.), *The Blackwell encyclopedia of sociology* (pp. 4620–4623). Malden, MA: Blackwell.

Cohen, B., & Kietzmann, J. (2014). Ride on! Mobility business models for the sharing economy. *Organization & Environment*, 27 (3), 279–296. doi:10.1177/1086026614546199

Corciolani, M., & Dalli, D. (2014). Gift-giving, sharing and commodity exchange at Bookcrossing.com: New insights from a qualitative analysis. *Management Decision*, 52 (4), 755–776. doi:10.1108/MD-03-2012-0241

Dubuisson-Quellier, S. (2015). From targets to recruits: The status of consumers within the political consumption movement. *International Journal of Consumer Studies*, 39 (5), 404–412. doi: 10.1111/ijcs.12200

Eckhardt, G. M., & Bardhi, F. (2016). The relationship between access practices and economic systems. *Journal of the Association of Consumer Research*, Advance online publication. doi:10.1086/684684

Felson, M., & Spaeth. J. E. (1978). Community structure and collaborative consumption: A routine activity approach. *American Behavioral Scientist*, 21 (4), 614–624. doi:10.1177/000276427802100411

Forno, F., & Garibaldi, R. (2015). Sharing economy in travel and tourism: The case of home-swapping in Italy. *Journal of Quality Assurance in Hospitality & Tourism*, 16 (2), 202–220. doi:10.1080/1528008X.2015.1013409

Gabriel, Y., & Lang, T. (2015). *The unmanageable consumer (3rd ed.)*. London: Sage.

Germann Molz, J. (2013). Social networking technologies and the moral economy of alternative tourism: The case of Couchsurfing.org. *Annals of Tourism Research*, 43, 210–230.

Gibson-Graham, J. K. (2006). *A postcapitalist politics*. Minneapolis, MN: University of Minnesota Press.

Giddens, A. (1991). *Modernity and self-identity: Self and society in the late modern age*. Stanford, CA: Stanford University Press.

Gilbert, J. (2014). *Common ground: Democracy and collectivity in an age of individualism*. London: Pluto Press.

Gould Ellen, I. (2015). Housing low-income households: Lessons from the sharing economy? *Housing Policy Debate*, 25 (4), 783–784, doi:10.1080/10511482.2015.1042204

Harvey, J., Smith A. & Golightly D. (2014). Giving and sharing in the computer-mediated economy. *Journal of Consumer Behavior*, doi:10.1002/cb.1499

Heinrichs, H. (2013). Sharing economy: A potential new pathway to sustainability. *GAIA*, 22 (4), 228–231.

Hong, S., & Vicdan, H. (2016). Re-imagining the utopian: Transformation of a sustainable lifestyle in ecovillages. *Journal of Business Research*, 69 (1), 120–136. doi:10.1016/j.jbusres.2015.07.026

John, N. (2013). The social logics of sharing. *The Communication Review*, 16 (3), 113–131, doi:10.1080/10714421.2013.807119

Laamanen, M., Wahlen, S., & Campana, M. (2015). Mobilizing collaborative consumption lifestyles: A comparative frame analysis of time banking. *International Journal of Consumer Studies*, 39 (5), 459–467. doi:10.1111/ijcs.12190

Lichtenstein, N. (2002). *State of the union: A century of American labor*. Princeton, NJ: Princeton University Press.

Martin, C. (2016). The sharing economy: A pathway to sustainability or a nightmarish form of neoliberal capitalism? *Ecological Economics*, 121 (January 2016), 149–159. doi:10.1016/j.ecolecon.2015.11.027

Martin, C., Upham, P., & Budd, L. (2015). Commercial orientation in grassroots social innovation: Insights from the sharing economy. *Ecological Economics*, 118 (October 2015), 240–251. doi:10.1016/j.ecolecon.2015.08.001

Maurer, B. (2006). The anthropology of money. *Annual Review of Anthropology*, 35, 15–36.

McArthur, E. (2015). Many-to-many exchange without money: Why people share their resources. *Consumption Markets & Culture*, 18 (3), 239–256. doi:10.1080/10253866.2014.987083

Möhlmann, M. (2015). Collaborative consumption: Determinants of satisfaction and the likelihood of using a sharing economy option again. *Journal of Consumer Behavior*, 14 (3), 193–207. doi:10.1002/cb.1512

Morozov, E. (2011). *The net delusion. The dark side of Internet freedom*. New York, NY: Public Affairs.

O'Neil, M. (2015). Labour out of control: The political economy of Capitalist and ethical organization. *Organization Studies*, 36 (12), 1627–1647. doi:10.1177/0170840615585339

Ozanne, L. & Ballantine, P. (2010). Sharing as a form of anti-consumption? An examination of toy library users. *Journal of Consumer Behavior*, 9, 485–498. doi:10.1002/cb.334

Pedersen, E. R. G., & Netter, S. (2015). Collaborative consumption: Business model opportunities and barriers for fashion libraries, *Journal of Fashion Marketing and Management*, 19 (3), 258–273. doi:10.1108/JFMM-05-2013-0073

Piscicelli, L., Cooper, T., & Fisher, T. (2015). The role of values in collaborative consumption: Insights from a product-service system for lending and borrowing in the UK. *Journal of Cleaner Production*, 92, 21–29. doi:10.1016/j.jclepro.2014.07.032

Polanyi, K. (2001/1947). *The great transformation: The political and economic origins of our time. (2nd ed.)*. Boston: Beacon Press.

Richardson, L. (2015). Performing the sharing economy. *Geoform*, 67, 121–129.

Sahlins, M. (1972). *Stoneage economics*. Chicago: Aldine-Atherton.

Seyfang, G. (2007). Growing sustainable consumption communities: The case of local organic food networks. *International Journal of Sociology and Social Policy*, 27 (3/4), 120–134. doi:10.1108/01443330710741066

Slater, D. (1997). *Consumer culture & modernity*. Cambridge, UK: Polity Press.

Slee, T. (2015). *What's yours is mine. Against the sharing economy*. New York, NY: OR Books.

Stephany, A. (2015). *The business of sharing*. Basingstoke, UK: Palgrave Macmillan.

Taylor, A. (2014). *The people's platform: Taking back power and culture in the digital age*. New York, NY: Metropolitan Books.

Trentmann, F. (2006). The modern evolution of the consumer: Meanings, knowledge, and identities before the age of affluence. In J. Brewer & F. Trentmann (Eds.), *Consuming cultures, global perspectives: Historical trajectories, transnational exchanges* (pp. 19–69). Oxford, UK: Berg.

Utting, P. (2015). Introduction: The challenge of scaling up social and solidarity economy. In P. Utting (Ed.), *Social and solidarity economy: Beyond the fringe* (pp. 1–37). London, UK: Zed Books.

Wahlen, S., & Huttunen, K. (2012). Consumer policy and consumer empowerment: Comparing the historic development in Finland and Germany. *International Journal of Consumer Studies*, 36 (1), 2–9. doi:10.1111/j.1470-6431.2011.01007.x

Wahlen, S., & Laamanen, M. (2015). Consumption, lifestyle and social movements. *International Journal of Consumer Studies*, 39 (5), 397–403. doi:10.1111/ijcs.12237

Widlok, T. (2013). Sharing: Allowing others to take what is valued. *HAU: Journal of Ethnographic Theory*, 3 (2), 11–31. doi:10.14318/hau3.2

10
Crises and consumption

Sebastian Koos

Introduction

When the recession hit the small community of Marienthal, the main industry had to close its gates, leaving most workers unemployed, fully depending on public support by the welfare state. The crises had severe impacts on life in general and on consumption in particular. The unemployed, mostly men, would walk slower, spent less time in public clubs, changed their diet and borrowed fewer books from the public library (Jahoda, Lazarsfeld, and Zeisel, 2002 [1933]). Families needed to develop coping strategies to provide for their basic needs. The seminal "sociography of an unemployed community", published in 1933 by Marie Jahoda, Paul Lazarsfeld and Hans Zeisel, today reads like a timely description of how economic crises impact the life of people. This hallmark study is a blueprint of how macro-economic shocks translate into personal hardship for the people of a community. The recent 2008 global financial crises, followed by the 2010 fiscal crises of many European states, have been the largest economic shocks since the Great Depression of the 1930s. They once again showed the detrimental effect of disruptive economic events for the everyday lives of citizens.

Crises have severe impacts on the consumption patterns of people, their life chances and well-being; therefore the sociology of consumption has devoted some attention to this topic, yet contributions so far remain rather isolated and disciplinarily separated (Alonso, Rodríguez and Rojo, 2015; Ang, 2001; Hampson and McGoldrick, 2013; Kaytaz and Gul, 2014; McKenzie, 2003; Shama, 1978). In this chapter I seek to give an overview of basic analytical frameworks to the study of crises and consumption and review the respective empirical literature. I aim to highlight what has been found and point towards shortcomings and gaps in an effort to establish a research agenda for the study of the impact of major shocks on consumption and social resilience in the everyday (Hall and Lamont, 2013).

In the following I start by briefly unpacking the notion of crisis, defining what it means and distinguishing between different types of shocks (Gundel, 2005), while generally limiting myself to the literature on economic crises. Next, in studying the actual impact of crises on consumption, I first provide two mechanisms that relate crises to practices: a basic "economic" and a "cognitive/emotional" mechanism. Second, I discuss existing conceptual frameworks for analysing consumption changes. Thereafter a review of empirical studies on individual consumer reactions to crises is provided. Finally, I outline the context of crises and their potential effect on coping strategies, referring to the nature of crises, their unfolding in different institutional contexts and the temporal dimension of crises adjustments. In the conclusion I discuss existing research gaps and the need for future research.

Varieties of crises

In general, a crisis can be understood as some unforeseen event that creates uncertainty, threatening daily routines and putting the accomplishment of certain personal ends at a risk (Kutak, 1938). According to Kutak (1938, p. 66) crises have the potential to result in "the breakdown of the general organization of the community. New problems are faced, new needs arise and the every-day system of organization fails to meet the new situation." Crises may also entail some psychological strain and a sense of "confusion".

A number of different situations fit such a description, but vary in their very nature, number of people affected, temporal impact and predictability. First of all, crises can have natural causes or be man-made. While an earthquake cannot be prevented from happening, an oil crisis is to a certain degree the responsibility of certain market actors and the failures of people that govern such markets. Given the complex social, economic and technological systems characteristic for modern societies, such man-made "normal accidents" are inevitable (Perrow, 2011, p. 5). Second, crises differ in whether they affect an individual, a small group, a whole community, society or even world society. People experience personal crises, for instance when getting laid off, confronted with the death of a relative or being involved in any type of accident. Such events are disruptive to routines and the everyday, but usually do not change the organization of a whole community. On the contrary societal crises, like economic downturns, natural disasters, wars or system transformations, affect a whole society or at least a large group of people. Obviously the former is not independent of the latter. Societal crises often translate into individual hardship and thus have a direct impact on people. Third, depending on the type of crisis, its temporal impact can vary strongly. Some crises have potential long term effects, while for instance economic shocks mostly are temporary. Finally, crises differ in the extent to which they are predictable or likely (Gundel, 2005). The predictability of a crisis may have important effects on the coping strategies applied. Crises that are rather common, such as recessions, industrial accidents, or in some regions even earthquakes, can to a certain degree be expected and insured or attenuated. Big natural crises, like a tsunami, are by far more difficult to predict and the consequences therefore more difficult to govern. The very nature, level and predictability of a crisis is very likely to shape the effects it has on social life and the coping strategies.

There has been a multitude of research on different types of crises and their influence on consumption. A systematic and coherent overview covering the variety of crises is well beyond the limits of this chapter. Therefore, I confine myself to the study of macro-economic crises, their impact on consumption behavior and coping strategies. An economic crisis can be associated with a recession, thus a period of economic stagnation or decline. Recessions are often characterized by high inflation – rising prices for products – stagnating wages, and rising unemployment. Reasons for economic recessions are multifold, such as long economic cycles, wars or financial crises. Driven for instance by credit bubbles, the failure of a banking system, the devaluation of a currency or default on sovereign debt by a country, financial crises are a frequent source of recessions all over the world. Since the 1970s, Laeven and Valencia (2013) report 211 currency crises, 147 banking crises, and 66 sovereign debt crises, some of which overlap. Studies focusing on crises' impact on consumption span from the impact of the recent financial crisis in the US and Europe to the Mexican peso crises, the Argentinian sovereign debt crises, the oil crises in the 1970s and the decline of the Asian economy in the early 2000s.

How do crises affect consumption?

Two mechanisms: Resources and beliefs

Most basically there are two major ways by which aggregate crises translate into individual consumption: a direct objective and an indirect cognitive/emotional mechanism. First, crises can have direct ramifications on the resources available to people for their daily consumption decisions. Stagnating or declining wages and becoming unemployed reduce the actual monetary income of people and thus put direct limits to their consumption options. At the same time, crises may lead to a decline of social transfers by the state and might constrain financial transfers within families and households and thus impact available resources, beyond direct personal market income. Moreover, inflation might lead to products becoming more expensive and even to shortages in products, due to unfavorable exchange rates (Zurawicki and Braidot, 2005). Thus, crises affect the degrees of freedom in consumption decisions in a number of ways. In general, this resource-based mechanism is rather simple, but powerful. Depriving people of monetary resources or devaluing these puts direct limits to their purchasing decisions on markets. Empirical studies show that the recent economic recession had detrimental effects on employment and income. According to a report by the OECD, the 2008 crises led to rising unemployment especially among young workers aged fifteen to twenty-four and among temporary workers, with part-time and limited-term contracts (Brian and Patrick, 2010, p. 5). Obviously, these effects varied across countries, having specifically bad effects in the US, Ireland, Spain, Portugal and Greece. Reeskens and van Oorschot (2014) find that self-reported financial deprivation varies widely across Europe, with people in Eastern and Southern European countries being most affected. They show that the unemployed, the welfare dependent and people with lower income are most strongly affected by crises induced deprivation. On the contrary, McKenzie (2003), studying the effects of the Mexican peso crises, found that people in more advantaged socio-economic positions are most affected by crises in terms of income loss.

Second, crises do not need to have direct tangible effects on people to impact their consumption practices. Crises inflict a sense of uncertainty; thus beliefs about potential future impacts of a crisis on one's life can lead to changing behavior. For instance, Alonso et al. (2015, p. 69) cite a Spanish interviewee mentioning that as a consequence of the financial crisis "uncertainty is now a part of us". Such a predominantly cognitive mechanism is likely to be also infused with emotional strains, like fear or confusion. Hence, an economic recession might lead to consuming less and differently, while not directly being affected by unemployment or even a wage cut, but fearing some potential future job loss. Crises, thus, have the potential to undermine the innate belief in the stability and structure of our life world, the trust in the very institutions enabling human conduct, and therefore increase uncertainty about the future. Chung and Van Oorschot (2011) show that the recent financial crisis had strong effects on the subjectively perceived job insecurity across Europe. This varies strongly across countries. Interestingly they find that "the economic forecast of the financial crisis was more influential in explaining the employment insecurity perceptions of individuals than the actual labour market consequences of it" (Chung and Van Oorschot, 2011, p. 297). This quote underlines the importance of crises' influence on subjective beliefs and perceptions.

Generally, both of the described mechanisms interact in multiple ways and in reality are often mingled. In the first instance, where a crisis has a direct objective impact on available resources, this will also inevitably be linked to cognitive and emotional reactions. Yet, in the second mechanism, a resource constraint need not be observed to have consequences. Generally, the distinction is important to understand that crises can play out in the everyday despite real material deprivation. Beliefs, as irrational as they might be, can well result in very real behaviour sometimes with critical consequences. In a classical example, rumours of a bank crisis spurred a bank run – people trying to withdraw all their money from their bank – which as a self-fulfilling prophecy in turn led to a real bankruptcy of the bank, now deprived of all assets (Merton, 1968). The change of aggregate demand, through both mechanisms in times of economic recessions, can itself worsen the general economic situation of a country, setting a vicious circle in motion. Therefore some governments have taken efforts to keep consumption high during crises, for instance in the US during the Second World War (Covert, 2003), or in Turkey in the recent financial crisis (Kaytaz and Gul, 2014). Yet, which aspects of consumption change?

Conceptual frameworks for analyzing changes in consumption patterns

The central question of this chapter is if and how economic crises affect consumption. Most economic shocks have important effects on the everyday lives of people. Yet, the way people cope with a crisis can be very different, ranging from organized reactions of consumers to individual sacrifices, saving of resources or consuming even more due to lower prices. Such coping strategies also vary widely across different socioeconomic groups and national contexts. Lekakis (2015) distinguishes between three broader reactions to the crisis: resistance, reinforcement and resilience. Resistance refers to the usage of consumption as a means to stop objectionable market practices fueled by the economic crisis, like boycotts targeting poor labor conditions. The notion of reinforcement describes consumption patterns focusing on the purchase of national products to support the economy, favoring a culture of ethnocentrism. Finally, resilience refers to a creative reorganization of markets, for instance by direct trade networks and cooperatives. This nicely illustrates that the notion of coping or, more recently, "social resilience" is fundamental to dealing with economic shocks (Hall and Lamont, 2013). Thus, crises do not evoke passive reactions, but people have to actively rethink, restructure and reorganize their everyday lives. Social resilience then can be understood, not only as a psychological trait of people, but rather as the adaptive capacity of a social system "to absorb disturbances and re-organize while undergoing change", while at the same time opening up opportunities for "recombination of both structures and processes, renewal of the system and emergence of new trajectories" (Folke, 2006, p. 259).

On a more individual or household level, people react to economic shocks most basically by either stopping to consume certain goods, reducing purchases or buying different goods, prolonging certain purchases and using some goods longer. In an early attempt to model consumer reactions to economic crisis Shama (1978, 1981) distinguishes between five reactions of consumers: general adjustments, price, product, place and promotion adjustments. General adjustments refer to whether people have changed their consumption practices at all and, if so, how they changed them. For instance, whether people consume less, are more energy conscious, seek more information on shopping or discuss purchases with a partner. Price relates to all financial aspects of purchasing decisions including comparing prices, shopping for bargains and using credit. Product adaptions denote all changes of the types and quality of products consumed, like temporarily avoiding the purchase of durables or substituting branded goods with private label products. Place refers to the outlet at which products are obtained, for instance buying at market stalls, general retailers, wholesale outlets or discount stores. Finally, promotion adjustments denote the use of and trust in promotions. While this framework makes intuitive sense, the meaning and distinctiveness of the categories remain somewhat arbitrary. To date the framework, mainly informed by a marketing perspective, has been widely used in studies on the impact of crises on consumption (Alimen and Bayraktaroglu, 2011; Ang, 2001; Ang, Leong, and Kotler, 2000; Hampson and McGoldrick, 2013). Using factor analytical techniques, Alimen and Bayraktaroglu (2011) analyze the partitioning of different dimensions of crisis adaptations, but find seven somewhat different factors. In their empirically informed classification, responses of consumers vary from cautious spending, simplicity in purchase and distribution, product adjustments, quest for low price, and financial anxiety to promotion adjustments and awareness. Urbonavicius and Pikturniene (2010) develop a somewhat different framework distinguishing between six behavioral patterns in response to a crisis. First, some consumers might not change their consumption at all. Second, some consumers need to drastically reduce spending in order to get by. Others might decrease consumption in order to build up savings, as a protection against potential future loss. Some consumers might even spend more money to increase the life quality on a short-term basis as long as it can be afforded. Finally, some groups that are objectively not affected by the crisis might even buy more or higher quality products, since prices are usually lower. If this is combined with the two above-described mechanisms that translate crises into behavior, it could be expected that objective impacts of crises will lead to more severe and far-reaching changes, while the cognitive/emotional mechanism will lead to some more limited reactions related to building up savings.

Changes in consumer practices might also be related to the types of products and services consumed. Some authors distinguish between necessities and supplementary goods (McKenzie, 2003). Others distinguish between durables, like furniture, and semi-durables, like clothes and food items (Zurawicki and Braidot, 2005). These differences might become important in the face of an economic shock, since according to Engel's law declining income will lead to a relative increase of expenditure for necessities (McKenzie, 2006). Thus people will spend the largest share on food and basic goods, but will postpone or abstain from buying durables and luxury goods.

Empirical studies on changing consumption patterns

Empirical studies on the impact of crises on consumption behavior are varied. Urbonavicius and Pikturniene (2010), studying two generations of Lithuanian consumers after the 2008 recession, find that these mostly decreased spending, either in order to get by or to build up some savings, while only some continue their shopping routines unchanged. Different than expected, people who are better off seem not to take advantage of lower prices. Likewise, in Portugal, the two main strategies of consumers to deal with the crisis are to sacrifice consumption (63%) and to build up savings (23%) (Lopes and Frade, 2012, p. 489). Studying the stagflation in the US, which resulted from the oil crisis in the 70s, Shama (1978) found that 65% of customers had changed their consumption preference and habits; 86% became less wasteful and 89% engaged more often in comparative shopping; 60% of respondents looked for cheaper products; and 66% shopped more in "cut-rate stores" than before the crisis. Around 25% claimed to believe less in advertising claims. Thus, Shama found that consumers changed their consumption practices on most dimensions surveyed, resulting in a new lifestyle of voluntary simplicity (Shama, 1981). In a different study analyzing the effect of the Argentinian economic recession of the 90s, D. McKenzie and Schargrodsky (2011) actually confirm that people do buy less, but that they spend more time shopping. This contrasts with the research of Ironmonger (2012), who finds that people in the US in general spend less time shopping after the financial crisis. Ang and colleagues (2000) and Ang (2001) adopt Shama's framework to the Asian economic crisis of the late 90s. They also find consumers to be opting for a simpler lifestyle, reducing expenditures on luxury goods and durables. The greatest adjustments have been price related, where consumers buy less, bargain for lower prices, buy in cheaper outlets and postpone the purchase of durables (Ang, 2001, p. 280). Compared to US consumers in the crisis of the late 70s, Asian shoppers consulted spouses more often in shopping decisions and searched more for information. One limitation of the studies by Ang and Shama is that they do not link the changes in consumption behavior back to different socio-economic groups or social classes. Thus it remains unclear to which extent different groups engage in different strategies. Moreover, from these studies we learn little about adoptions for different types of products.

Some research is also concerned with the socio-demographic underpinnings of reactions to crises. In a study on the impact of the recent financial crisis, Alimen and Bayraktaroglu (2011) not only analyze empirically the partitioning of different crises adoption dimensions (finding seven somewhat different dimensions), but also link these back to socio-demographic variables. Using a non-representative sample of Turkish consumers, Alimen and Bayraktaroglu (2011) find that respondents with low income react significantly stronger to financial adjustments than do people better off. In addition, they find women to purchase more cautiously and quest more for low prices than do men. Unfortunately, they do not test the impact of these determinants in a multivariate statistical analysis. In their qualitative study of Spanish consumers' reaction to the recent financial crisis, Alonso et al. (2015) find important differences between social classes in their interpretation of and reaction to the 2008 financial crisis. While people in lower-class positions have to cut back, they report that their consumption behavior has not changed drastically. Being the group "least influenced by the pressure of excessive consumption and imitation" (p. 72), changes for them seem to be less meaningful. The middle and higher classes, more strongly engaged in conspicuous consumption and a culture of "keeping up with the Joneses" experience the crisis as something new and more threatening (Alonso et al., 2015). The qualitative approach of this research allows getting a better understanding of the meanings and understandings of crisis-related consumption changes. Thus, while people in lower socio-economic positions seem to change their behavior more drastically, these changes to them seem to be less problematic and threatening. One reason for this disparity is that these consumers had often experienced scarcity at times and thus can draw on past routines.

Focusing on the effects of age, Alonso et al. (2015) show for the Spanish case that especially younger consumers are affected. On the contrary Urbonavicius and Pikturniene (2010) report for a Lithuanian sample of two generations, that younger generations are less affected than older ones. The difference might well be related to the different timing of the fieldwork as the crisis evolves. A study about food consumption that focused specifically on older citizens in Europe (fifty years and older) found that elderly eat out less when income decreases during the crisis. This decline is more pronounced in countries that have been specifically hit hard by the economic recession like Spain or Poland (Angelini, Brugiavini, and Weber, 2013).

A couple of researchers are also sensitive to the changes in the types of products and services bought. In a research note on the changes in the European Union, Gerstberger and Yaneva (2013) show that consumers have mostly cut back on durables and semi-durables, like furniture and textiles, but also on eating out and travelling. Studying the impact of the Mexican peso crises, McKenzie (2006) finds that consumption expenditures decrease for all kind of goods, but expenditures are cut back the least on food. Providing support for Engel's law, the relative share of expenditure for food consumption increases, as do consumption focuses on "basic staples, such as grains, eggs, milk, oil and vegetables, whereas fruit consumption and out-of- house dining decrease" (McKenzie, 2006, p. 147). This is more pronounced in less-affluent households.

Interviewing people from different social classes in Britain during the 2008 financial crisis, Atkinson (2013) shows how it is especially the poor "who are jolted closer to necessity at a disproportionate rate" (p. 29). In a study on the consequences of the Argentinian economic crisis for the consumption of the middle classes, Zurawicki and Braidot (2005) find them especially abstaining from consuming cultural goods, like movies and theatre or the purchase of magazines. Unlike people in lower-class positions, they do not have to concentrate their means on obtaining necessity goods, but rather substitute within the "broad categories replacing pricy items with similar cheaper ones" (Zurawicki and Braidot, 2005, p. 1108). Decreasing expenditures on cultural consumption is also a central aspect of changing consumer patterns to be observed during the economic recession in Greece (Barda and Sardianou, 2010).

In line with the notion of social resilience as an active reaction to crises, some research addresses consumer activism. Concerned with consumption as a political practice, Lekakis (2015) shows that in Greece many initiatives have started to reclaim the economic sphere, for instance through solidarity purchase groups (p. 6). Others have started to engage in consumer boycotts more frequently, as a means to penalize producers that treat workers unfairly. Barda and Sardianou (2010) find that 49% of a non-representative sample of Greek consumers had participated in a boycott during the economic recession. Vihalemm, Keller and Pihu (2016) do not observe similar consumer activism in their study of the Estonian media discourse in the financial crisis. Finally, Lekakis (2015) points out that economic crises potentially spur nationalist sentiment leading to ethnocentric consumption. For instance, Smyczek and Glowik (2011) find that economic recessions directly impact the intent of ethnocentric consumption among Polish consumers. Such a form of political consumption creates symbolic national boundaries on markets (Lekakis, 2015), which are often paralleled by political nationalism.

A final set of studies focuses on the impact of economic shocks on consumer bankruptcy. Generally, economic crisis strongly increases the number of bankrupt consumers not able to pay back their debts (Lopes and Frade, 2012; Lown, 2008; Marsellou and Bassiakos, 2016). Marsellou and Bassiakos (2016) find that during the crisis less-affluent households are not necessarily at a greater risk of consumer bankruptcy than more affluent ones. The main reasons for consumer bankruptcy are job problems, the usage of credit cards and trouble managing money, as well as unexpected illness and family problems (Lown, 2008, p. 237). Thus, other than is often voiced, consumer bankruptcy is not the consequence of careless and excessive spending, but is grounded in real life problems that are propelled by economic shocks.

Contextualizing the impact of crises: Type of crisis, national context and temporality

Few studies have addressed whether the impact of crisis on consumption varies according to the nature of a crisis, the institutional set-up in which it unfolds and the temporality of the crisis. As the decline of consumption can have detrimental effects on the local or national economy and thus further amplify economic crisis, it seems key to better understand the contexts in which crises evolve and the opportunities to bolster their effects.

Research on the effect of different economic or man-made versus natural crises has yet to be carried out. Only Ang (2001) explicitly compares the Asian crises to the US oil crises, finding somewhat limited differences. Yet, he also points to the importance of understanding the context's effects on moderating crises' impact on purchasing decisions. Gerstberger and Yaneva (2013) provide a comparative assessment of the impact of the 2008 economic recession on consumption patterns in Europe. They show that especially Eastern and Southern European countries, as well as Ireland have been affected and that the crises had more long-term effects on consumption in Greece, Ireland and Portugal than in all other countries. Yet, the authors provide no analyses on the determinants of these effects.

The institutional context in which a crisis emerges might have important implications for consumption adaptions. In countries where people have far-reaching social rights in a developed welfare state, they might react very differently than in countries lacking such arrangements. According to classical typology by Polanyi (1992 [1957]) there are three types of instituted exchange, which are central in bolstering the effects of a crisis, namely, redistribution, market exchange and reciprocity. Redistribution by a (welfare) state helps people to cope with crises, for instance by providing unemployment benefits or social assistance. Market exchange helps by providing private insurance schemes that can be purchased on markets and insure against all kind of risks, from sickness to death. Reciprocity allows sharing resources, as, for instance, found in family exchange. Thus the effect of crisis on consumption also depends on the institutional infrastructure available in different nation states. Bentolila and Ichino (2008) study how becoming unemployed in different institutional settings is related to different coping strategies. In countries with a well-established welfare state, unemployment benefits and social assistance help to keep the basic living standard. If such institutions are absent or less developed, like in Southern Europe, family support to some degree substitutes for the lack of market and state transfers (Bentolila and Ichino, 2008). Similarly, Paugam (2016) nicely shows how the norm of receiving familial support in case of unemployment is widespread in Southern European countries, but is disapproved of in Germany and France.

Finally, a central, but rarely acknowledged, dimension in the research on consumption adaptions to crisis is the timing and temporality of reactions. Do consumers quickly change their consumption patterns, or wait until they cannot suspend such a decision anymore? Some evidence exists that in the Asian context some people will retain the old spending patterns despite the loss of income at the initial stage of the crisis (Ang et al., 2000). A different question relates to the durability of changes in consumption patterns. Do consumers return to old routines once the crisis is over? To my knowledge this has hardly been studied. Some evidence seems to suggest that rising income does not automatically translate into increased spending, yet income reductions often directly lead to reductions in consumption (Bricker, Bucks, Kennickell, Mach and Moore, 2012). Thus, crises' effects on consumption might be sticky, and the end of a crisis will not lead to a direct return on pre-crisis levels of spending.

Conclusion and future research

Economic crises seem to be an inherent characteristic of capitalist market economies. On a global scale over the last decades, literally hundreds of financial crises evolved and provoked consumer reactions. As shown by the example of the citizens of Marienthal, and the other studies reported here, economic recessions can have detrimental effects on the consumption of citizens. While economic crisis need not have direct material effects on consumers to become effective in changing their behavior, crisis often creates a strong sense of uncertainty and thus a threat to personal life worlds. Existing research has studied many different crises, their impact on income, unemployment and changes in consumption practices. Existing frameworks of consumer reactions to crises focus more or less systematically on different types of behavioral changes. Existing models are descriptively rich, yet mostly not theoretically grounded. Especially the marketing literature has not been interested in linking changes back to specific socioeconomic groups. Nevertheless, as some of the discussed studies show, consumers are very differently affected by crises and also differ in their consumption adaptations. In general, consumers seem to adopt a more rational and pragmatic approach to consumption. Future research needs not only to develop more systematic frameworks of crises reactions, but also of the underlying explanations of who changes what and why.

As indicated, there is also a lack of comparing the effect of different types of crises and comparative analysis of the impact of the same crises in different institutional and cultural contexts. Such studies could also shed light on which institutions and policies can help to bolster the effects of crises on consumption. Given that changes in consumption and thus in aggregate demand can accelerate crises, this seems specifically important (Kaytaz and Gul, 2014). Moreover, we still lack an understanding of the temporality of crises. When does the effect of crises on consumption wear off and how willing are consumers to go back to their old routines? One framework that could be used to develop a more encompassing and less individualistic approach to consumer reactions is the notion of social resilience.

Some studies argue that changing consumption patterns are not only a consequence of an economic crisis, but excessive, conspicuous and overconsumption might well have contributed to the emergence of the crisis in the first place (Alonso et al., 2015). While crises induce consumption restraint and potentially decrease the ecological footprint, crises are not a valid route to increased sustainability, disproportionally penalizing the socio-economically most-vulnerable groups (Nielsen and Holm, 2016). This chapter is a first effort to tie together the loose ends of existing research on crisis and consumption. Yet, much work remains to be done to better understand the effects of crises on consumption.

References

Alimen, N. and Bayraktaroglu, G. (2011), 'Consumption adjustments of Turkish consumers during the global financial crisis,' *Ege Academic Review*, vol. 11, no. 2, pp. 193–203.

Alonso, L. E., Rodríguez, C. J. F. and Rojo, R. I. (2015), 'From consumerism to guilt: Economic crisis and discourses about consumption in Spain,' *Journal of Consumer Culture*, vol. 15, no. 1, pp. 66–85.

Ang, S. H. (2001), 'Crisis marketing: a comparison across economic scenarios,'. *International Business Review*, vol. 10, no. 3, pp. 263–284.

Ang, S. H., Leong, S. M. and Kotler, P. (2000), 'The Asian apocalypse: crisis marketing for consumers and businesses,' *Long Range Planning*, vol. 33, no. 1, pp. 97–119.

Angelini, V., Brugiavini, A. and Weber, G. (2013), 'Household consumption and the crisis,' in A. Börsch-Supan, M. Brandt, H. Litwin, and G. Weber (eds), *Active ageing and solidarity between generations in Europe: First results from SHARE after the economic crisis*, pp. 19–26. Berlin: Walter de Gruyter.

Atkinson, W. (2013), 'Economic crisis and classed everyday life: Hysteresis, positional suffering and symbolic violence,' in Atkinson, W., Roberts, S., & Savage, M. (eds), *Class inequality in austerity Britain*, pp. 13–32. Basingstoke: Palgrave Macmillan.

Barda, C. and Sardianou, E. (2010), '"Analysing consumers""activism"in response to rising prices,' *International Journal of Consumer Studies*, vol. 34, no. 2, pp. 133–139.

Bentolila, S. and Ichino, A. (2008), 'Unemployment and consumption near and far away from the Mediterranean,' *Journal of Population Economics*, vol. 21, no. 2, pp. 255–280.

Brian, K. and Patrick, L. (2010), *OECD insights from crisis to recovery the causes, course and consequences of the great recession: The causes, course and consequences of the great recession*. Paris: OECD Publishing.

Bricker, J., Bucks, B., Kennickell, A., Mach, T. and Moore, K. (2012), 'The financial crisis from the family's perspective: Evidence from the 2007–2009 SCF panel,' *Journal of Consumer Affairs*, vol. 46, no. 3, pp. 537–555.

Chung, H. and Van Oorschot, W. (2011), 'Institutions versus market forces: Explaining the employment insecurity of European individuals during (the beginning of) the financial crisis,' *Journal of European Social Policy*, vol. 21, no. 4, pp. 287–301.

Covert, T. A. (2003), 'Consumption and citizenship during the second world war product advertising in women's magazines,' *Journal of Consumer Culture*, vol. 3, no. 3, pp. 315–342.

Folke, C. (2006), 'Resilience: The emergence of a perspective for social–ecological systems analyses,' *Global Environmental Change*, vol. 16, no. 3, pp. 253–267.

Gerstberger, C. and Yaneva, D. (2013), Analysis of EU-27 household final consumption expenditure – Baltic countries and Greece still suffering most from the economic and financial crisis. *Eurostat Statistics in Focus 2/2013*. pp. 1–7. Luxembourg: Eurostat.

Gundel, S. (2005), 'Towards a new typology of crises,' *Journal of Contingencies and Crisis Management*, vol. 13, no. 3, pp. 106–115.

Hall, P. A. and Lamont, M. (2013), *Social resilience in the neoliberal era*. Cambridge: Cambridge University Press.

Hampson, D. P. and McGoldrick, P. J. (2013), 'A typology of adaptive shopping patterns in recession,' *Journal of Business Research*, vol. 66, no. 7, pp. 831–838.

Ironmonger, D. (2012), 'Research note: What happened to time use during the global financial crisis?' *Australian Journal of Social Issues*, vol. 47, no. 4, pp. 527–540.

Jahoda, M., Lazarsfeld, P. F. and Zeisel, H. (2002 [1933]), *Marienthal: The sociography of an unemployed community*. New Brunswick: Transaction Publishers.

Kaytaz, M. and Gul, M. C. (2014), 'Consumer response to economic crisis and lessons for marketers: The Turkish experience,' *Journal of Business Research*, vol. 67, no. 1, pp. 2701–2706.

Kutak, R. I. (1938), 'The sociology of crises: The Louisville flood of 1937,' *Social Forces*, vol. 17, no. 1, pp. 66–72.

Laeven, L. and Valencia, F. (2013), 'Systemic banking crises database,' *IMF Economic Review*, vol. 61, no. 2, pp. 225–270.

Lekakis, E. J. (2015), 'Economic nationalism and the cultural politics of consumption under austerity: The rise of ethnocentric consumption in Greece,' *Journal of Consumer Culture*, doi: 10.1177/1469540515586872. pp. 1–17.

Lopes, C. A. and Frade, C. (2012), 'The way into bankruptcy: market anomie and sacrifice among Portuguese consumers,' *Journal of Consumer Policy*, vol. 35, no. 4, pp. 477–496.

Lown, J. M. (2008), 'Consumer bankruptcy in Utah (USA): who files and why?' *International Journal of Consumer Studies*, vol. 32, no. 3, pp. 233–240.

Marsellou, E. and Bassiakos, Y. (2016), 'Bankrupt households and economic crisis: Evidence from the Greek Courts,' *Journal of Consumer Policy*, vol. 39, no.1, pp 41–62.

McKenzie, D. and Schargrodsky, E. (2011), 'Buying less but shopping more: the use of nonmarket labor during a crisis,' *Economia*, vol. 11, no. 2, pp. 1–35.

McKenzie, D. J. (2003), 'How do households cope with aggregate shocks? Evidence from the Mexican peso crisis,' *World Development*, vol. 31, no.7, pp. 1179–1199.

McKenzie, D. J. (2006), 'The consumer response to the Mexican peso crisis,' *Economic Development and Cultural Change*, vol. 55, no. 1, pp. 139–172.

Merton, R. K. (1968), *Social theory and social structure*. New York: The Free Press.

Nielsen, A. and Holm, L. (2016), 'Making the Most of Less: Food Budget Restraint in a Scandinavian Welfare Society,' *Food, Culture & Society*, vol. 19, no. 1, pp. 71–91.

Paugam, S. (2016), 'Social bonds and coping strategies of unemployed people in Europe,' *Italian Sociological Review*, vol. 6, no. 1, pp. 27–56.

Perrow, C. (2011), *Normal accidents: Living with high risk technologies*. Princeton: Princeton University Press.

Polanyi, K. (1992 [1957]), 'The Economy as Instituted Process,' in M. Granovetter and R. Swedberg (eds), *The sociology of economic life*, pp. 29–51. Boulder: Westview Press.

Reeskens, T. and van Oorschot, W. (2014), 'European feelings of deprivation amidst the financial crisis Effects of welfare state effort and informal social relations,' *Acta Sociologica*, vol. 57, no. 3, pp. 191–206.

Shama, A. (1978), 'Management & consumers in an era of stagflation,' *The Journal of Marketing*, vol. 42, no. 3, pp. 43–52.

Shama, A. (1981), 'Coping with stagflation: Voluntary simplicity,' *The Journal of Marketing*, vol. 45, no. 3, pp. 120–134.

Smyczek, S. and Glowik, M. (2011), 'Ethnocentrism of Polish consumers as a result of the global economic crisis,' *Journal of Customer Behaviour*, vol. 10, no. 2, pp. 99–118.

Urbonavicius, S. and Pikturniene, I. (2010), 'Consumers in the face of economic crisis: Evidence from two generations in Lithuania,' *Economics & Management*, vol. 15, pp. 827–834.

Vihalemm, T., Keller, M. and Pihu, K. (2016), 'Consumers during the 2008–2011 Economic Crisis in Estonia: Mainstream and grass roots media discourses,' *Italian Sociological Review*, vol. 6, no. 1, p. 57.

Zurawicki, L. and Braidot, N. (2005), 'Consumers during crisis: Responses from the middle class in Argentina,' *Journal of Business Research*, vol. 58, no. 8, pp. 1100–1109.

Part III

Global challenges in consumption

Introduction

This book contests the conceptualization of the development of diverse global and local ways of consumption as a straightforward trajectory of adopting a "Western" or "northern" consumerist way of life. In the so-called developing world, levels of consumption have undoubtedly risen, but it would be too simplistic to understand it as a linear catching up with the global North. There are very many diverse, hybrid and creative ways of consumption across the globe. However, acknowledgement of this multiplicity should not eclipse analysis and problematization of clashing dynamics: how consumerism gives opportunity and raises standards of living, how it dismantles and re-creates boundaries between the advanced and the developing, how it reinforces inequalities, redefines whatever may be termed as authentic, genuine or normal and how it sharpens environmental degradation that could change our planet beyond recognition. It is well known that the so-called industrial countries have produced most of the ecological effects by rampant production and consumption and the so-called developing world has to participate in, or in some cases bear the brunt of, ills that result from this.

It is hypocritical of academics and other well-off professionals who maintain a relatively comfortable standard of living to admonish others – whoever fits into the definition of an "other" in a given case – to consume less or more responsibly. Thus, whenever scholars write about "global challenges of consumption" it is inevitably always a search of ways of analyzing, conceptualizing and verbalizing so that justice is done to the complexity of various consumption cultures and consumer lifeworlds, at the same time not shadowing the larger structural power dynamics and developments, and above all, without reproducing hypocrisy and dominance of the global North societies.

The objective of this part of the handbook is to shift attention onto the tension between north and south, as well as onto emerging consumer societies of China, Brazil, Turkey and Russia. The chapters below aim to do both – to give an overview of the contours and patterns of consumption cultures in these societies, as well as provide a meta-level overview (though not exhaustive) of academic consumption studies conducted in and by scholars from these countries.

In chapter 11 Güliz Ger reflects on how consumption is associated with tensions embedded in globalization and neoliberal marketization, taking a closer look at Turkey and zooming in on two themes in particular: dynamics of global-local and local-local relations and the interplay of change and continuity. The chapter takes issue with the widely used hybridity discourse and "flow-speak" that is refreshingly non-essentialist and provides for a dynamic understanding of culture and identity on the one hand, yet has the danger of losing touch with belonging, social relations, power differences, historicity and local "others". These debates are shed light upon and illustrated with vivid examples from research on Turkey.

Chapter 12, written by LiAnne Yu, takes the reader to China and delves into the problematics of its emerging consumer power. Since market reforms were instituted in 1978, consumption practices in China have been transformed at an unprecedented pace and scale. Looking at four emerging consumer practices: the shift from conspicuous consumption to experiential consumption; the influence of social media and the formation of virtual neo-tribes; consumption as a form of nationalism; and finally, the influence of the Global East on Chinese consumer practices, LiAnne Yu gives a sense of China's particular form of consumer culture. She argues that it features a hybrid consumer culture that de-centers the West, and privileges Global Eastern models of modernity.

Chapter 13 by Lívia Barbosa and John Wilkinson gives an elaborate picture of the development of consumption and consumption studies within the historical context of Brazil. The chapter's particular focus is on the new middle class and its relations with the "old" middle class, the latter analyzed in search of signs of being the vanguard of new responsible consumption. In this vein, citizenship and alternative social movements have been recently considered by consumption researchers. However, the situation is bound to change with the present unstable status of Brazilian politics and economics. As the country plunges into what could be a prolonged recession in the next years, issues related with credit indebtedness and the renegotiation of consumer contracts are shifting the attention to aspects of consumer access and citizen rights to education and health.

In chapter 14 Olga Gurova writes about post-socialist transformations in Russia and asks how Soviet legacy impacts today's consumption in this country by providing a bird's eye view of the consumption scholarship in and on Russia from the early 1990s to 2015. She narrates the development from early research on post-socialist consumption and "consumer revolution" through the transformation of the retail landscape, advance of consumer media and marketing, as well as structural and class-related issues. The chapter ends with zooming in onto conundrums faced by the consumptionscapes of Russia today. Of particular attention is how the ideology of glamour has become to be replaced with the ideology of patriotism (exacerbated by economic difficulty and sanctions imposed on Russia), how the authoritarian state influences consumption and how to understand the nascent sharing economy and sustainability agenda.

Chapter 15 by Laura T. Raynolds wraps up this section by drawing theoretically on political economy to explain North/South inequalities in production/consumption networks, on the one hand, and on social movement conceptualizations to highlight what consumers do and can do to promote global social justice, on the other. Her analysis is grounded in the case study of fair trade, its historical evolution and present challenges. The chapter elaborates on the limitations – namely the reaffirmation of North/South power divisions, control by large corporations and commercial intermediaries, and threat of re-commodification – on fair trade's progressive potential to bridge consumers and producers in the global North and South. Raynolds also takes the perspective of the consumers by problematizing the ethical and political motives (or their absence) of fair trade purchases. She calls for cooperation between consumption scholars and activists to theorize, empirically analyze and practically pursue most fruitful ways of consumer engagement in advancing global justice.

The selection of areas on which a more detailed account is given is definitely not exhaustive or fully objective by some universal criteria. The reader can ask critically, why is there no chapter on India, South Africa or Central and Eastern Europe outside Russia? What about those countries in Africa, Asia, the Middle East, South-America or parts of Oceania that have not (yet) been termed as "emerging markets", but remain lumped into the notion of the "developing world"? Indeed, this is a book and selection that is inevitably idiosyncratic to particular editors, authors and debates that have been clustered together. We acknowledge these limitations and the more modest ambition of this section to shed light onto some of the conversations, ask some questions (rather than provide resolute answers) and call for (as we do in our introductory chapter) de-ossifying boundaries and comfort zones of research groups and themes. However, doing so we admit that there are always frameworks of particular research areas and epistemologies, networks and funding that enable and constrain the global and local research questions that can be posed.

11

Consumption in the web of local and global relations of dominance and belonging

Güliz Ger

In this essay I reflect on how consumption serves to build and resolve tensions amplified by globalization and, its escort, neoliberal marketization, in the so-called emerging markets, in particular in Turkey. When scholars allude to "globalization," or global consumer culture, there is typically an implicit opposition between the global versus the local. The foreign global is associated with change, modernity, novelty, innovation, commodification; the familiar local with tradition and stubbornly old or romantically authentic ways of life. In addition, there are internal tensions between, for example, the rural and the urban or the dominated and the dominant, which are impacted by transnational relations. Contrary to a position "that sees the local from the outside, as a place continuously impinged upon by and encapsulated within external forces" (Lambek, 2011, p. 200), I take the perspective of the local. I examine how the consumers in a locality experience their encounters with people, things, ideologies, and images global, within the structural enablers and disablers, and if and how their ways and patterns of consumption change or not; how they define and differentiate themselves from internal Others that emerge or become amplified with globalization. My deliberations are framed by two considerations: domination and affiliation dynamics in global-local and local-local relationships and the dialogue of change and continuity.

I discuss the main approaches in the literature and offer directions for future research on consumption. The works I cite are representative, but not comprehensive. The first section reviews the diverse consumer experiences of and responses to their global encounters, as they navigate local social structures, embedded in asymmetrical global flows and a structure of common differences (Wilk, 1995). The second section presents criticisms of hybridity and "flow speak." The third section focuses on the Others within the local as it navigates the global: the rural other, class-based Others, and multiple Others of the faithful or the Islamists in Turkey. Finally, I offer suggestions for research on consumption in a global world.

Encounters of consumers in emerging markets with global products and ideas

Emulation and resistance, along with their opposite predictions for global homogenization and heterogenization, have been the earliest accounts of consumer responses. The issues with these engendered diverse arguments such as mimicry, hybridity, global flows, local appropriations and recontextualization of things global, and reinvented traditions. Criticisms of "flowspeak" and hybridity speak have bred yet more intricate theses.

Emulation and resistance and their discontents

Emulation thesis, along the lines of linear convergence theories, viewed globalization akin to modernization-as-Westernization, as a wave that spreads from the origin, typically from the "West to the Rest." This spread is fueled at the individual level by the emulation of aspirational consumption lifestyles seen on television and films, which parade imaginaries and discourses of global neoliberal consumerist ethos and deeds. Imitative learning is expected to result in a homogenized (thus Westernized) world to which the locals will assimilate. Sometimes called Coca-colonization or McDonaldization (Ritzer, 1993), emulation-based diffusion view has a palpable reflection in the consumptionscapes all over the world where consumers are being bombarded by the Cokes, Levi's, Disney toys, and look-alike shopping malls (Abaza, 2001; Ger and Belk, 1996; Howes, 1996).

On the other hand, resistance thesis argues that locals will resist the global consumer culture and maintain their local, "traditional" patterns of consumption. Refusal to buy foreign products is one example where nationalist or religious ideologies deploy moral sensibilities to induce resistance. Consumer resistance has been framed by broader notions of "clash of civilizations" (Huntington, 1996) or McDonaldization and Jihad (Barber, 1996), which pit tribal – nationalist, ethnic, and religious – identities against global marketization, as forces which cannot co-exist. Furthermore, religious fundamentalism has been argued to be a threat to consumerist ideology (Turner, 1994). Hence, instead of homogenization, the prediction here is that the world will confront revitalized forms of nationalism, parochialism, and religious fundamentalisms that will challenge the Western hegemony.

Emulation and rejection accounts suffer from linear and essentialist logic. Moreover, they fail to explain observed consumption patterns. There is ample evidence that neither religion nor nationalism pose a challenge to global marketization and consumerism. The growth of Islamic markets, marketing, and fashions (Gökarıksel and Secor, 2009; Sandikci and Jafari, 2013; Sandikci and Ger, 2007, 2011; Sandikci and Rice, 2011), at the junction of global capitalism and global Islam, is an instantiation of the global condition and part and parcel of global capitalism and consumerism. Islam is very much embedded in and coexists with global markets, consumption, and, politics (Ger, 2013). Neoliberalism couples symbiotically with Islamism in Turkey and elsewhere (Karaman, 2013). As Karaman argues, while neoliberalism and Islamism are distinct normative political rationalities, they are collaborative logics. Besides, Islam is not the only tribalism that collaborates with global markets and consumerism. Hindu nationalism also seems to happily coexist with the form global marketization takes in India (Rajagopal, 2001).

Furthermore, particular observed forms of resistance and emulation defy their simple definitions. Consider voluntary simplicity, anti-consumption, and anti-brand movements. Consumers engaged in such movements in Turkey do not partake in any "clash of civilizations." Instead, they participate in local manifestations of global movements. Similarly, local consumerism is more than an emulation of the global. A consumer in Turkey may well be using her smart phone and wearing her fashionable branded goods of "normal" modernity (Kravets and Sandikci, 2014) while at the same time carrying a "traditional" blue-white evil eye bead in her purse. She is likely to decorate a Christmas tree in December and pray to Allah and fast during Ramadan. There is ample evidence, from Belize to Turkey, that globalization can be comprehended neither as a unidirectional emulation nor a simple rejection process (e.g. Abaza, 2001, 2007; Ger and Belk, 1996; Howes, 1996; Kjeldgaard and Askegaard, 2006; Miller, 1995; Sandikci and Ger, 2001, 2002, 2005, 2007, 2011; Wilk, 1995, 1998). Persons pursuing social position and belonging yield locally shaped multiple consumer cultures. These consumer cultures, embedded in dominance relations, materialize change tamed by continuity and continuity powered by transformations, which in turn breed co-existent and co-nourishing homogeneity and heterogeneity.

Postcolonial relationships: The alluring foreign and the authentic local

Despite their pitfalls, the emulation and resistance accounts accentuate the very real dominance relationships. Feelings of exclusion from and desire for First World affluence and sophistication have a historical background (de Koning, 2009). In that historical context, advertisements announce that "the world" has arrived and claim that this exclusion is being overcome – if only for the elite or the middle classes, if only in consumption.

In postcolonial studies (e.g. Bhabha, 1994; Eaton, 2004; Taussig, 1993), rather than two preexisting essences – us-Other (or local – foreign/global) – there is entanglement of "unequal times – contingent, shifting, and unstable orderings" (Bhabha, 1994, p. 140). Bhabha (1994) describes mimicry as ironic and mocking emulation by dominated groups, which animates postcolonial imaginations after the end of colonization. Taussig (1993) argues that "meaning and hence power, ricocheting from West to Other, from mimesis to alterity, and back again . . . can only be thought of as endless mobility" (p.249). Taussig suggests that mimesis is *the* basis of knowledge about the Other. Accordingly, Wilk (1999) argues that appetite for foreign goods is an upshot of the desire to know about the world. Mimetic learning about the world at any particular moment is permeated with the us-other tension, however mobile and entwined it may be.

Then, the struggle between "seductive globalism" and "authentic localism," "*our* culture versus the powerful and dangerous *other*" (Wilk, 1999, p. 248) permeates consumptionscapes. On the one hand, there is an "allure of the foreign" (Orlove, 1997), a fascination with and a trust in the foreign global. Ger, Askegaard, and Christensen (1999) report that Turkish middle class consumers regard foreign goods to be superior and using them to be a part of the world. To them, the "West" signifies modernity, advancement, orderliness, innovation, comfort, and freedom. As they eat KFCs and text with their iPhones, consumers feel they are a part of such a global modern world. Global brands are arguably embraced as a passport to global citizenship (Strizhakova, Coulter and Price, 2008). The preference for the foreign is also reflected in the adoption of foreign or foreign-sounding names for domestic products (Ger, Kravets and Sandikci, 2011).

On the other hand, there is an ambivalence about the Western Other, rooted in the history of relations with dominant Others (Bhabha, 1994; Chatterjee, 1993). The occidental has been seen as a bearer of moral threat as well as a source of innovation (Creighton, 1995) in formerly colonized geographies and elsewhere. In contemporary Turkey, the imagery of the West conjures up desire as well as fear of moral dangers and its destructive potential, and frustration, due to the EU membership process. Juxtaposed to such danger is the "authentic local." The familiarity with local products and forms deliver a sense of warmth, comfort, and security (Ger, 2005). The words of one middle class Turkish consumer is telling: "Our hearts say 'stay here, you are members of the East,' but our mind, our direction is always facing West" (Ger et al., 1999, p. 166).

Local consumers who struggle navigating seductive globalism and authentic localism are embedded in the neoliberal marketplace of global media, transnational corporations and the global-facing and local-facing local actors. The particular interplay between the desirable and/or the dangerous foreign/global and the downgraded and/or exalted local rests on the past and present of particular dominance relations. Such contestations make for interactive homogenization and heterogenization, set in Taussig's "endless mobility." Accordingly, consumption reveals adaptations of transnational structures and ideologies in local contexts – "glocalization" (Robertson, 1995). In Wilk's (1995) terms, "structures of common difference," a globally common set of formats and structures controlling what is to be produced and consumed "put diversity in a common frame" (p. 111). Such structures of global dominance relations and neoliberal transnational capitalism give rise to certain similarities in consumption patterns, which show heterogeneity in their meanings and manifestations and limits.

Reinvented localization and revival of imagined roots

One way to navigate the seductive global and the comforting local is to re-form localizations (Ger and Belk, 1996; Sandikci and Ger, 2001, 2002; Ustuner, Ger and Holt, 2000). These localizations entail a search for authenticity and revival of reimagined roots, yet in a dialogue with the modern global world and its marketplace.

The last couple of decades in Turkey witnessed a revival of interest in objects and customs constructed to represent "our traditions". One fashionable "traditional" ritual is the new "henna night" – a party preceding the wedding night. Henna is a reddish brown plant-based dye used, in this case, to color brides' hands. Henna night used to be an all-female party, which used to (and still does among lower classes) reproduce patriarchy. However, the meanings produced at the new henna night entail creatively retooled old meanings, now portraying modern urban sensibilities (Ustuner, Ger and Holt, 2000). The ritual is performed in a more theatrical and playful manner with a combination of "traditional" and "modern" implements and props. While their urban middle-class parents had a simpler party on their wedding night, the offspring now want a big "traditional" wedding, including a "henna night" and a day in the Turkish baths, frolicking with nostalgia, before their party, organized by a professional firm, consistent with global trends in themed weddings yet nothing like the Turkish weddings of the past.

Like the henna night ritual, although not particularly Turkish or Islamic, but rather pagan and prevalent in the broader region, the blue-and-white evil eye bead is imagined to be "ours". Customarily, small evil eye beads have been attached on children's clothing and larger ones hung over the door, for protection against evil spirits. Now, variously sized and shaped beads, used in new forms and ways, inserted in silver or porcelain decorative objects, even on gift items for an imported celebration, Valentine's Day, are prominent.

In addition to reinvented rituals and objects construed to be Turkish, there has been a recent interest in Ottoman restaurants and cookbooks, highly popular television series on the golden era of the empire, home accessories such as cushion cases with Ottomanesque embroideries, *nargile* (hookah) cafés where Turkish coffee is made in coffee machines rather than the traditional pots, marbling and calligraphy classes, and buying Ottoman art at Sotheby's, London. Other examples of this Ottomania (Sandikci and Ger, 2002) include luxury hotels which make a direct reference to the Ottoman past with their architecture and decoration, restaurants serving old Ottoman cuisine, and performances named "Sultan's Night," featuring Ottoman music and belly dancing. As Öncü (2007) argues, the current interest in "our" Ottoman past cannot be divorced from transnational trends: "in the world of late capitalism . . . the display and promotion of 'cultural heritage' as a marketable commodity" (p. 233) is commonplace.

A more potent sense of roots has been located in Islam, accompanying its political rise in legally secular Turkey (Balkan, Balkan and Öncü, 2015; Keyman, 2007; White, 2002). Islamic firms prospered with their novel products and services such as Islamist television channels, books, music, luxury resorts, recreations clubs, and *halal* (lawful, by Islamic law) foods (Demir,

Acar and Toprak, 2004; Sandikci and Ger, 2007). While these are Islam-appropriate, they are not conventional. For example, Islamic music today has hip-hop, techno, or rap, as well as the classical mystical versions. The luxury resorts have discos where all-female guests dance to Shakira or Timberlake. In urban Turkey, even the Ramadan rituals are being reinvented with a market logic and consumerist ideology (Sandikci and Omeraki, 2007).

Perhaps the most visible in everyday life has been the rise of new and fashionable veiling (Navaro-Yashin, 2002; Sandikci and Ger, 2001, 2005, 2007, 2010; Saktanber, 1994; Secor, 2002). Whereas covering used to be a mostly rural habit, now many urban women cover, and cover fashionably. For urbanites that grew up in the 1960s and 1970s Turkey and its secular ideology, covering was not a practice that they had socialized into in homes and schools. Yet, many educated middle-class women, whose mothers were not covered, chose to cover in the 1990s and 2000s, at a time of a growing neoliberal market and rising political power of Islam. Concurrent with the emergence of a new Islamist middle class, aesthetics and personalization of the scarf has become as important as its politics and religiosity. The new veiling is a modern practice of choice that seeks continuity in religion and is fueled by the opportune neoliberal market and politics.

Whether in the form of Turkish coffee made with electric appliances, reinterpreted rituals, Islamic fashions, or *halal* goods, such reinventions materialize novel localizations. What are being revived are not anything that was, either in a national or religious sense, but rather a reconstructed past, origin, or authenticity, reformulated and framed in light of global relations. "Ours" is defined by drawing from many different imaginaries of pasts. Then, as Keyder (1999) argues, the main question is not what is local, but what is being reformulated as local, after years of westernization/modernization, or globalization.

The consumers and producers of these revivals are agents of change instead of solely gatekeepers of continuity. Feeding from global flows, they also construct hybrids, which are either celebrated as expressions of creativity and appropriation or disparaged as unauthentic emulative mishmashes. Some of the above examples, such as Sandikci and Ömeraki's (2007) Christmasy Ramadan, are as much hybrids as reinventions.

Global flows and local appropriation: Hybridity and recontextualization

Other consumer navigations of the seductive global and the comforting local engender hybrids and recontextualizations. Hybridization or creolization (Bhabba, 1994; Ger and Belk, 1996; Hannerz, 1992, 1996) refer to an intercultural process of mixing and matching things from different sources and underscore the interlinked nature of cultures. They involve local appropriation of global products, technologies, and images. The mixtures entail as much struggle as fusion. Recontextualization (Ger and Belk, 1996) is another form of local appropriation where meanings and functions are transformed in ways not intended by their producers. Examples include old washing machines being used to make butter in villages in Turkey and Christmas trees decked with Disney figures decorating living rooms of the Muslim working class in Uzbekistan, year round, to make the children happy.

Hybridization is now ubiquitous. Coca-Cola served with "döner kebap" at neighborhood eateries, Islamic hip-hop, or a Monet reproduction framed with verses from the Kuran, hung on the wall of an upper middle class Islamist's home, illustrate hybrid compositions in Turkey. Such co-existent and mixed patterns, which appeared jarring twenty years ago, are now so prevalent that they no longer surprise.

Globalization-as-hybridization perspective (Pieterse, 2001) intersects with the view that globalization entails interconnectivity (Hannerz, 1996), organized by flows and scapes – mediascapes, finanscapes, ideoscapes, ethnoscapes, technoscapes (Appadurai, 1990). The global flows of products, media images, technologies and information, people, money, and ideas allow movement across boundaries, making them fluid. Scapes are navigated and negotiated by consumers in ways that serve their own life goals, help resolve the contradictions they face in their daily lives, such as the struggle between the allure of the foreign and the comfort of the authentic, or establish identity and difference in local social hierarchies. In this view, the local reception of global flows is creative. Flows can increase the availability of meanings and lead to an increasing globalization of fragmentation (Firat, 1997) in which the consumer has access to a multitude of resources (Jafari and Goulding, 2013) for dealing with everyday life. Hence, the multiple and decentered flows engender fragmentation, mixing, and co-existence, rather than any synthesis in the sense of resolution of opposites.

The literature has tended to either condemn (lack of purity) or celebrate (creativity and local appropriation) hybridity. However, as Pieterse (2001) argued, hybridity (and global consumptionscapes) needs to be theorized rather than celebrated or condemned.

Beyond hybridity and "flow speak"

Hybridity and global flows emphasize interplay (Pieterse, 2001) and provide a non-essentialist, non-dualistic, and dynamic notion of culture and identity that problematize boundaries. However, the entailed fluidity notions ignore the importance of having a coherent sense of belonging to one's class, religion, ethnicity, or nation. The prevailing overemphasis on mobility and deterritorialization overlooks issues of belonging and social relations. "Flow speak," by simply including people in "ethnoscapes", "precludes the question of social participation and the deeper meaning of social existence" (Bude and Dürrschmidt, 2010, p. 482).

Secondly, the flow and hybridity speak sidestep power differences. However, flows are not symmetric: there are more flows from the dominant to the dominated locales than the other way around – more KFCs in Turkey than Turkish restaurants in the USA. In addition to importing popular culture from the dominant center (Ger, 1997), cultural practices are re-appropriated in their places of origin "after a process of sanctioning in (what is most often) the Western hotbed of consumer culture production" (Askegaard and Eckhardt, 2012, p. 46). For example, homemakers in Turkey switched from their usual olive oil to the advertised new Western sunflower oil in the 1980s and then back to olive oil in the 2000s, after it was reformulated to be a fashionable and healthy Mediterranean item. Although the periphery is "allowed" to talk back in cultural production, the conversation is not symmetrical. Moreover, taking notice of a local culture usually morphs into commodification of that culture (Spivak, 1988), dependent on notions of "cultural and aesthetic authenticity" (Root, 1996, p. 69), which are again defined by the core.

In addition, flows involve a series of symbolic translations across locations rather than mechanistic movement along inert channels of passage (Rajagopal, 2001). In such translations, disjunctures in flows are used to the advantage of those powerful in transnational networks. Dominant "global structures of common difference" (Wilk, 1995) such as market institutions and their consumerist ideology define what types of diversity and hybrids will diffuse and what kinds will be submerged or suppressed. Consumers and producers come to organize their lives along similar institutional arrangements created by globalizing power blocs, such as transnational corporations.

Furthermore, while flows of multiple and counterveiling discourses leave space for consumer resistance and creativity (Thompson and Haytko, 1997), at least for consumers with appropriate cultural capital, they also reinforce structures of inequality, globally and locally. Global flows "feed into local social hierarchies and are taken up as forms of cultural distinction" (de Koning, 2009, p. 194). Globalization amplifies awareness of a first (class) world and the experience of exclusion from it as well as the social and economic polarization within cities: parts of the city that serve global networks are increasingly disconnected from national economies, and integrated into the global networks (de Koning, 2009). Given that consumption can empower and connect people depending on resources such as time, skill, and knowledge, the dominated, the migrant, the lower class, the less refined rural are excluded form social links to the local or the global world. Thus, we circle back to transnational and domestic power and affiliation relations.

Thirdly, "flow speak" and hybridity speak forget the historicity of the local and fail to note the multiple internal Others and tensions. Yet, the accelerating impact of globalization forces inhabitants of a country to position their own identities vis-à-vis others in that country (Keyder, 1999). The real clash may well occur not between the local and global, but between the local and local systems of meanings (Jafari and Goulding, 2013). Identity being relational, the hybridized identity needs its others. Hence, what needs to be accounted for are the formation and interaction of Others within a society that encounters marketization and globalization – changes which interrogate sociocultural ideals, norms, and notions of normality.

Internal tensions and "Others" within the local as it navigates the global

Studies from Turkey (e.g. Kandiyoti and Saktanber, 2002; Kravets and Sandikci, 2014; Kuruoglu and Ger, 2015; Türe and Ger, 2016) reveal the role of the historical context in forming the relevant Others that pertain to consumption anxieties, desires, and patterns. The historical relations with Europeans, Arabs, and Iranians, interpreted with diverse ideologies, serve different political purposes in the present. These imaginaries entail the good old days of Islamic ways of life and the glamour of the Ottoman past, or the purity of the Anatolian (or Turkish) peoples, or the backwardness of the Late Ottomans versus the progressive and enlightened reforms of Atatürk. Such a past is in this present (Friedman, 1992) intertwined with asymmetrical global flows, which further dominance structures. The "global" imaginaries include the USA and Europe in the minds of Western-oriented seculars, the Gulf States and Muslim Asian countries as well as the USA and Europe in the minds of Islamists. Such pasts in presents and ensuing imaginations of different futures set the stage for inclusion and exclusion relations between the urbanites and the peasants, the upscale and the downscale, and the secular-religious groups.

The rural Other in Turkey

A basic clash since the nineteenth- and twentieth-century modernizations has been between the city, the center, and the countryside, the periphery (Mardin, 1973). Whereas the city connotes progressive modernity, the village signifies ignorant backwardness (Türe and Ger, 2016). Given that literacy continues to be a serious issue, the relative deprivation of villagers in education, health services, and transportation increases the social distance between the city and the village. Globalization fosters that distance and self-Orientalization tendencies. New imported products, shopping malls, five-star hotels, gated communities, and foreign cuisine restaurants proliferated in the 1990s in the cities (Kravets and Sandikci, 2014), further dissociating urban lives from rural ones (and middle classes from lower classes).

A rapid urbanization, along with the 1980s economic liberalization, raised the urban population from 30% to 70% in four decades (Icduygu, 2004). Rural migrants typically settled in squatter houses at the periphery of the city and worked in the informal economy. With increasing urban poverty, many of these now-urban families faced deprivation and became subject to social exclusion (Bugra and Keyder, 2003). Today, over 50% of the urban population in Ankara, Istanbul and Izmir, the three biggest cities, resides in squatter settlements, which have been stigmatized as ghettos and their residents as the "threatening Other," attacking the city's modern values and social order (Erman, 1998). Despite recent improvements in infrastructure and hence their living conditions and legal recognition of their status (Baslevent and Dayoglu, 2005), they remain socially and economically excluded. As Ustuner and Holt (2007) demonstrate, the hegemonic urban culture conflicts with the rural culture. They find that some rural-to-urban migrants reconstitute the village culture in the city; others engage in the urban consumer culture and try to adopt urban consumption patterns. However, rural-to-urban migrants remain dominated (Ustuner and Holt, 2007). They remain the Other in the eyes of the urbanites who want to distance themselves from the rural past and still-rural scenes. A recent youth subculture who struggle to differentiate themselves from the squatter area culture with their clothing and grooming styles have become subjects of mockery among their own parents and the urbanites (Yaman, 2013).

As cities became crowded with rural immigrants and rural aesthetics, urban middle classes moved to gated communities (Datta, 2014; Öncü, 1997). Öncü suggests that this is a strategy to protect their middle/upper-class status and move away from the cultural pollution, vulgarity, and ugliness of what once used to be their city. Ger and Yenicioglu (2004) note the links between attributions of dirtiness and rural-urban status as well as social class status. Hence, the rural-urban tension and Othering the peasants are as much a matter of modernizing urbanization as social class.

Class-based Others in Turkey

Social class continues to be germane to the formation of individual identities to the extent that people construct their identities in relational terms (Karademir-Hazir, 2014a, b). Consumers use global products, brands, and styles to articulate local social distinctions. Karademir-Hazir finds that, despite the presence of multiple ways to be modern and traditional, despite the proliferating commercial services aiming to manage appearance based on global images, "there are still compelling conditions hindering one's playful engagement with the related consumption domains" and class remains embodied in Turkey (Karademir-Hazir, 2014a, p. 17). She uncovers four embodiment clusters: conspicuous modern (upper middle class, with ties to Western cultural patterns and global brands), reserved traditionals (low brow), modern and modest (pious), and constrained display. These four clusters are apt to be the Other for each other.

Even within one social class there appear to be subgroups that are each other's Other. Turkish middle class consumers with larger volumes of capitals draw stronger boundaries built upon judgments of "good taste", by distancing themselves from the "uncultured" Others of the same class (Karademir-Hazir, 2014b). Similarly, Üstüner and Holt's (2010) investigation of two factions of Turkish upper middle class women indicates that high culture consumers use Western lifestyles to distinguish themselves from low culture consumers who mimic the lifestyles of the domestic elites.

Kravets and Sandikci (2014) report yet another recipe for distinction, which simultaneously provides a sense of global belonging, employed by the new middle class (NMC). Through "formulaic creativity" (rather than emulation or resistance) consumers attempt to align with the global middle. NMC consumers "seek a secure place in a new society by embracing the shared standard, which includes . . . a modern apartment and a set of goods (e.g. a Volkswagen car, an iPhone, a Louis Vuitton bag, a Samsung television)" (p. 137). In this case, "consumers assimilate one another into 'people like us' and imagine the middle as a site of normality and comfort" (p. 126). If attained, global normality provides a consumption-driven social connection to the world, among those who are included.

Rare exceptions to such exclusionary inclusions include the democratizing tea (Ger and Kravets, 2009) and the "high-society bazaars," which evolved from conventional lower class versions (Vicdan and Firat, 2015). Like the tea, the "high-society bazaar," where lower classes and omnivore middle classes experience each other, are social levelers.

Others of the urban faithful and Islamists in Turkey

The rising clash between the seculars and faithful/Islamists is a political, moral, and normative issue. After over a century of westernization, the secular modernization has yielded to an Islam-laden neoliberal globalization. To Islamists, secularism connotes a rejection of religion – absence of Islamic law. To secular urbanites, separation of state and religion, and hence relocation of religion from the public to the private sphere, is a condition of modernity. For them, not Islam itself, but Islamic ways of life are associated with the past, the village, and retrogression. Hence, the so-called "secularists" and "Islamists" adhere to very different worldviews, ideals, lifestyles and consumption practices. With the populist and Islamist Justice and Development Party (JDP) at the helm, in the last couple of decades Islamist ideology and ways of life moved from the peripheries of Turkey to its urban centers and has eventually become dominant (Balkan, Balkan and Öncü, 2015; Karaman, 2013; Keyman, 2007; Toprak, 1984). Under JDP, neoliberalism became entrenched, so did a new Muslim elite; everyday lives have become marketized as well as Islamized with a renewed conservatism: neoliberal and Islamist values, practices, and codes of conduct have become normalized, routinized, mainstream, and hegemonic.

The Islamist elite and middle class, aligned with the local and global networks of economic and political power, and the urban seculars Other each other with a vengeance. This struggle, shaped locally and globally, is far more substantial than with any global Other. Drawing from Islam and local and global cultural resources and claiming their own modernity, the Muslim elite crafts new consumption patterns – modern, casual, and trendy clothes, natural goods, traditional cuisine, Ottoman artifacts, alternative vacations, and traveling. They adopt fashionable styles of covering to distinguish their modern selves morally from secular moderns, and employ fashion to routinize covering. Sandikci and Ger (2010) reveal that there is now a new habitus, "informed by Islamic as well as modern sensitivities" (p. 31). Accordingly, the so-called secular and Islamist taste structures are in competition.

Moreover, the secular urbanites are not the only Others for the Islamist elites. They seek to distance themselves from other faithful or Islamist groups in the way they consume. While they favor *halal* products like all other Muslims, they simultaneously seek progress and modernization, construed in terms of shopping malls, global brands, smart phones, and Facebook. Their Muslim Others include three groups: the more strict and "backward" Muslims who wear the "nonsensical" black chador and who reject Western brands (Izberk-Bilgin, 2012); the "traditional" villagers and the rural-to-urban migrants who live their lives in habitual manners; and the Islamist "new rich" who display "gaudy and pretentious" styles.

How to study always-local global consumption?

The issues identified suggest that, to understand global-local encounters, we need to shift the perspective from flows and interplay to *dominance and belonging relations* – from hybridity as a mere blend to hybridity embedded in and embodying power relations (as Kjeldgaard and

Askegaard [2006] have done) and social bonds. Appadurai's flows "have to be located in global and local histories of inequality and dominance" (de Koning, 2009, p.194). This is critical given that local inequalities have been rising under current politics of neoliberal globalization (Pieterse, 2001).

Moreover, we have to emphasize the dominance and belonging relations *within* societies as they navigate intensifying global connections. In doing so, we have to take materiality (Kravets and Örge, 2010; Türe and Ger, 2016) and emotionality (Kuruoglu and Ger, 2015) as seriously as we do meanings and narratives. Consumption of global brands and reinvented, recontextualized, or appropriated hybrid products entail very material and affective dominance and belonging relations – and not merely symbolic and fluid play.

While studying the global-local encounters in consumption, we must start with the lived experiences as well as the structuring context (Askegaard and Linnet, 2011; Venkatesh, 1995), considering consumers' agentic capabilities and the limits thereof. A focus on experiences in configuring structures calls for historicity and a temporal perspective: the locals' multiple imaginaries of their pasts, presents, and futures (Türe and Ger, 2016). Actually, neither of these are novel ideas: Friedman wrote "cultural realities are always produced in specific sociohistoric contexts" and discussed "the past in the present" and "the past in the future" in 1992. Lambek (2011) provides further ideas as to how to be "attuned to the temporality and depth of the local" (p. 209). As he argues, we must rethink "the local" "as a structure of feeling, affect, temporality and relatedness" (p. 197) and understand local consumers through the "sedimentation of acts" (p. 216) and their consequences.

"Catching the local" (Lambek, 2011) does not only apply to the peripheries of the world such as Turkey, but also to the dominant centers such as the USA. It would be telling if we study how, for example, North Americans navigate their encounters with, for instance, Chinese products, brands, and images. So far, consumer researchers examined North American locals usually as cosmopolitans and expats (e.g. Thompson and Tambyah, 1999). An exception is Thompson and Arsel's (2004) study of a hegemonic brandscape, structuring consumer experiences of glocalization. It is perhaps timely to conduct such refreshing studies, for example, of Asian brandscapes in the USA.

Just like remembering Friedman, recalling multi-sited ethnography (Marcus, 1995) is also timely. Consider Mintz's (1985) brilliant historical work on the taste for sugar and the underlying colonial relations, and more recently Foster's (2008) study following the social life of soft drinks from New York to New Guinea. We consumer researchers (see Ger and Csaba, 2000; and Kjeldgaard, Csaba and Ger, 2006 for exceptions) have not yet taken full advantage of this methodology.

Finally, as Bude and Dürrschmidt (2010) argue, we must complement the overemphasis on mobility and deterritorialization with a focus on issues of belonging. We have seen examples of consumers' pursuit of belongingness, being part of the world – even if merely with their consumption, or global citizenship via global brands, or reinventing authenticities to attain the comfort of local social links. A focus on social connections as well as fluidity converges with the suggestion that we should probe the continuities within changes and vice versa.

We can revive the stifled consumer research on globalization by examining the lived experiences of consumers *and* teasing out the historical and current structures that make an experience and/or a consequence what it has come to be (Karababa and Ger, 2011; Sandikci and Ger, 2010), continuities as well as discontinuities (Schatzki, 2002; Türe and Ger, 2016), similarities as well as differences (Kravets and Sandikci, 2014), affective structures (Ahmed, 2004; Kuruoglu and Ger, 2015), and dominance and belonging relations. Teamwork across different locales will make such investigations more reflective, fruitful, and fun.

References

Abaza, M. (2001), 'Shopping Malls, Consumer Culture and the Reshaping of Public Space in Egypt,' *Theory, Culture and Society*, vol. 18, no. 5, pp. 97–122.

Abaza, M. (2007), 'Shifting Landscapes of Fashion in Contemporary Cairo,' *Fashion Theory*, vol. 11, no. 2–3, pp. 281–98.

Ahmed, S. (2004), 'Affective Economies,' *Social Text*, vol. 22, no. 2, pp. 117–139.

Appadurai, A. (1990), 'Disjuncture and Difference in the Global Cultural Economy,' *Theory, Culture and Society*, vol. 7, pp. 295–310.

Askegaard, S. and Eckhardt, G.M. (2012), 'Glocal Yoga: Re-appropriation in the Indian Consumptionscape,' *Marketing Theory*, vol. 12, no. 1, pp. 45–60.

Askegaard, S. and Linnet, J. T. (2011), 'Towards an Epistemology of Consumer Culture Theory: Phenomenology and the Context of Context,' *Marketing Theory*, vol. 11, no. 4, pp. 381–404.

Balkan, N., Balkan, E. and Öncü, A. (eds) (2015), *The Neoliberal Landscape and the Rise of Islamist Capital in Turkey*, New York: Berghahn Books.

Barber, B. R. (1996), *Jihad vs. McWorld: How Globalization and Tribalism are Reshaping the World*, New York: Ballantine.

Baslevent, C. and Dayoglu, M. (2005), 'The Effect of Squatter Housing on Income Distribution in Urban Turkey,' *Urban Studies*, vol. 42, no. 1, pp. 31–45.

Bhabha, H. (1994), *The Location of Culture*, London: Routledge.

Bude, H., and Dürrschmidt, J. (2010), 'What's Wrong with Globalization?: Contra "Flow Speak"-Towards An Existential Turn in the Theory of Globalization,' *European Journal of Social Theory*, vol. 13, no. 4, pp. 481–500.

Bugra, A. and Keyder, C. (2003), *New Poverty and the Changing Welfare Regime of Turkey*, Ankara: UNFP Office in Turkey.

Chatterjee, P. (1993), *The nation and its fragments: Colonial and postcolonial histories* (Vol. 11), Princeton: Princeton University Press.

Creighton, M. R. (1995), 'Imagining the Other in Japanese Advertising Campaigns,' in J. G. Carrier (ed) *Occidentalism: Images of the West*, Oxford: Clarendon Press, pp. 135–160.

Datta, A. (2014), 'Gendered Nature and Urban Culture: The Dialectics of Gated Developments in Izmir, Turkey,' *International Journal of Urban and Regional Research*, vol. 38, no. 4, pp. 1363–1383.

de Koning, A. (2009), *Global Dreams: Space, Class, and Gender in Middle-Class Cairo*, Cairo: American University in Cairo Press.

Demir, Ö., Acar, M. and Toprak, M. (2004), 'Anatolian Tigers or Islamic Capital: Prospects and Challenges,' *Middle Eastern Studies*, vol. 40, no. 6, pp. 166–188.

Eaton, N. (2004), 'Between Mimesis and Alterity: Art, Gift, and Diplomacy in Colonial India, 1770–1800,' *Comparative Studies in Society and History*, vol. 46, no. 4, pp. 816–844.

Erman, T. (1998), 'Becoming 'Urban' or Remaining 'Rural': The Views of Turkish Rural to Urban Migrants on the 'Integration' Question,' *International Journal of Middle Eastern Studies*, vol. 30, no. 4, pp. 541–561.

Firat, A. F. (1997), 'Globalization of Fragmentation: A Framework for Understanding Contemporary Global Markets,' *Journal of International Marketing*, vol. 5, no.v2, pp. 77–86.

Friedman, J. (1992), 'The Past in the Future: History and the Politics of Identity,' *American Anthropologist*, vol. 94, no. 4, pp. 837–859.

Foster, R. J. (2008), *Coca-Globalization: Following Soft Drinks from New York to New Guinea*, New York: Palgrave MacMillan.

Ger, G. (1997), 'Human Development and Humane Consumption: Well-Being Beyond the Good Life,' *Journal of Public Policy and Marketing*, vol. 16, no 1, pp. 110–125.

Ger, G. (2005), 'Warming: Making the New Familiar and Moral,' *Ethnologia Europea: Journal of European Ethnology*, vol. 35, no. 1–2, pp. 19–22.

Ger, G. (2013), 'Islamic Marketing at the Nexus of Global Markets-Religions-Politics and Implications for Research,' *Marketing Theory*, vol. 13, no. 4, pp. 493–499.

Ger, G., Askegaard and S. Christensen, A. (1999), 'Experiential Nature of Product-Place Images: Image as a Narrative,' in E. Arnould and L. Scott (eds) *Advances in Consumer Research*, Provo, UT: Association for Consumer Research, vol. 26, pp. 165–169.

Ger, G. and Belk, R.W. (1996), 'I'd Like to Buy the World a Coke: Consumptionscapes of the "Less Affluent World",' *Journal of Consumer Policy*, vol. 19, no. 3, pp. 271–304.

Ger, G. and Csaba, F.F. (2000), 'Flying Carpets: The Production and Consumption of Tradition and Mystique,' in S. J. Hoch and R. J. Meyers (eds) *Advances in Consumer Research*, Provo, UT: Association for Consumer Research, vol. 27, pp. 132–137.

Ger, G. and Kravets, O. (2009), 'Special and Ordinary Times: Tea in Motion,' in E. Shove, F. Trentmann and R. Wilk (eds) *Time, Consumption and Everyday Life*, Oxford: Berg, pp. 189–202.

Ger, G., Kravets, O. and Sandikci, O. (2012) 'International Marketing at the Interface of the Alluring Global and the Comforting Local,' in L. Peñaloza, N. Toulouse, L. M. Visconti (eds) *Marketing Management: A Cultural Perspective*, London: Routledge, pp. 30–42.

Ger, G. and Yenicioglu, B. (2004), 'Clean and Dirty: Playing with Boundaries of Consumer's Safe Havens,' in B. E. Kahn and M. F. Luce (eds) *Advances in Consumer Research*, Provo, UT: Association for Consumer Research, pp. 2462–2467.

Gökarıksel, B. and Secor, A.J. (2009), 'New Transnational Geographies of Islamism, Capitalism and Subjectivity: The Veiling-Fashion Industry in Turkey,' *Area*, vol. 41, no. 1, pp. 6–18.

Hannerz, U. (1992), *Cultural complexity: Studies in the social organization of meaning*, New York: Columbia University Press.

Hannerz, U. (1996), *Transnational Connections*, London: Routledge.

Howes, D. (ed) (1996), *Cross-Cultural Consumption*, London: Routledge.

Huntington, S. P. (1996), *The Clash of Civilizations and the Remaking of World Order*, New York: Simon & Schuster.

İçduygu, A. (2004), 'From Nation-Building to Globalization: An Account of the Past and Present in Recent Urban Studies in Turkey,' *International Journal of Urban and Regional Research*, vol. 28, no. 4, pp. 941–951.

Izberk-Bilgin, E. (2012), 'Infidel Brands: Unveiling Alternative Meanings of Global Brands at the Nexus of Globalization, Consumer Culture, and Islamism,' *Journal of Consumer Research*, vol. 39, no. 4, pp. 663–687.

Jafari, A. and Goulding, G. (2013), 'Globalization, Reflexivity, and the Project of the Self: A Virtual Intercultural Learning Process,' *Consumption Markets and Culture*, vol. 16, no. 1, pp. 65–90.

Kandiyoti, D. and Saktanber A. (2002), *Fragments of Culture: The Everyday of Modern Turkey*, London: IB Tauris.

Karababa, Eminegül and Güliz Ger (2011), 'Early Modern Ottoman Coffeehouse Culture and the Formation of the Consumer Subject,' *Journal of Consumer Research*, vol. 37, no. 5, pp. 737–760.

Karademir-Hazir, I. (2014a), 'How Bodies are Classed: An Analysis of Clothing and Bodily Tastes in Turkey,' *Poetics*, vol. 44, pp. 1–21.

Karademir-Hazir, I. (2014b), 'Boundaries of Middle-Class identities in Turkey,' *The Sociological Review*, vol. 62, no. 4, pp. 675–697.

Karaman, O. (2013), 'Urban Neoliberalism with Islamic Characteristics,' *Urban Studies*, vol. 50, no. 16, pp. 3412–3227.

Keyder, C. (ed) (1999), *Istanbul, Between the Global and the Local*, Lanham, Boulder, New York, Oxford: Rowman and Littlefield Publishers.

Keyman, F. (2007), 'Modernity, Secularism and Islam: The Case of Turkey,' *Theory, Culture and Society*, vol. 24, no. 2, pp. 215–34.

Kjeldgaard, D. and Askegaard, S. (2006), 'The Glocalization of Youth Culture: The Global Youth Segment as Structures of Common Difference,' *Journal of Consumer Research*, vol. 33, pp. 231–247.

Kjeldgaard, D., Csaba, F.F. and Ger, G. (2006), 'Grasping the Global: Multi-sited Ethnographic Market Studies,' in R. W. Belk (ed) *Handbook of Qualitative Research Methods in Marketing*, Cheltenham, UK: Edward Elgar Publishing, pp. 521–533.

Kravets, O. and Örge, Ö. (2010), 'Iconic Brands: A Socio-Material Story,' *Journal of Material Culture*, vol. 15, no. 2, pp. 205–232.

Kravets, O. and Sandikci, Ö. (2014), 'Competently Ordinary: New Middle Class Consumers in Emerging Markets,' *Journal of Marketing*, vol. 78, pp. 125–140.

Kuruoglu, P. A. and Ger, G. (2015), 'An Emotional Economy of Mundane Objects,' *Consumption Markets & Culture*, vol. 18, no. 3, pp. 209–238.

Lambek, M. (2011), 'Catching the Local,' *Anthropological Theory*, vol. 11, no. 2, pp. 197–221.

Marcus, G. E. (1995), 'Ethnography in/of the World System: The Emergence of Multi-sited Ethnography,' *Annual Review of Anthropology*, vol. 24, pp. 95–117.

Mardin, S. (1973), 'Center-Periphery Relations: A Key to Turkish Politics?' *Daedalus*, vol. 102 (Winter), pp. 169–90.

Miller, D. (1995), *Worlds apart: Modernity Through the Prism of the Local*, London: Routledge.

Mintz, S.W. (1985), *Sweetness and Power*, New York: Viking.

Navaro-Yashin, Y. (2002), 'The Market for Identities: Secularism, Islamism, Commodities,' in D. Kandiyoti and A. Saktanber (eds) *Fragments of Culture: The Everyday of Modern Turkey*, London: I. B. Tauris, pp. 221–53.

Öncü, A. (1997), 'The Myth of the Ideal Home Travels Across Cultural Borders to Istanbul,' in A. Öncü and P. Weyland (eds) *Space, Culture, Power: Struggles Over New Identities In Globalizing Cities*, London: ZED, pp. 56–72.

Öncü, A. (2007), 'The Politics of Istanbul's Ottoman Heritage in the Era of Globalism: Refractions through the Prism of a Theme Park,' in B. Drieskens, F. Mermier and H. Wimmen (eds) *Cities of the South: Citizenship and Exclusion in the 21st Century*, London, Beirut: Saqi Books, pp. 233–264.

Orlove, B. (1997), *The Allure of the Foreign: Imported Goods in Postcolonial Latin America*, Ann Arbor: University of Michigan Press.

Pieterse, J. N. (2001), 'Hybridity, So What? The Anti-Hybridity Backlash and the Riddles of Recognition,' *Theory, Culture & Society*, vol. 18, no. 2–3, pp. 219–245.

Rajagopal, A. (2001), *Politics After Television: Hindu Nationalism and the Reshaping of the Public in India*, Cambridge: Cambridge University Press.

Ritzer, G. (1993), *The McDonaldization of Society*, NewBury Park, CA: Pine Forge Press.

Robertson, R. (1995), 'Glocalization: Time-Space and Homogeneity-Heterogeneity,' in M. Featherstone, S. Lash and R. Robertson (eds) *Global Modernities*, London: Sage, pp. 25–44.

Root, D. (1996), *Cannibal Culture: Art, Appropriation, and the Commodification of Difference*, Boulder, CO: Westview Press.

Saktanber, A. (1994), 'Becoming the 'Other' as a Muslim in Turkey: Turkish Women vs. Islamist Women,' *New Perspectives on Turkey*, vol. 11 (Fall), pp. 99–134.

Sandikci, Ö. and Ger, G. (2001), 'Fundamental Fashions: The Cultural Politics of the Turban and the Levi's', in J. Meyers-Levy and M. Gilly (eds) *Advances in Consumer Research*, Provo, UT: Association for Consumer Research, vol. 28, pp. 146–150.

Sandikci, Ö. and Ger, G. (2002), 'In-Between Modernities and Postmodernities: Theorizing Turkish Consumptionscape,' in S. Broniarczyk and K. Nakamoto (eds) *Advances in Consumer Research*, Provo, UT: Association for Consumer Research, vol. 29, pp. 465–470.

Sandikci, Ö. and Ger, G. (2005), 'Aesthetics, Ethics and the Politics of the Turkish Headscarf,' in S. Kuechler and D. Miller (eds) *Clothing as Material Culture*, Oxford: Berg, pp. 61–82.

Sandikci, Ö. and Ger, G. (2007), 'Constructing and Representing the Islamic Consumer in Turkey,' *Fashion Theory*, vol. 11, no. 2–3, pp. 189–210.

Sandikci, Ö. and Ger, G. (2010), 'Veiling in Style: How Does a Stigmatized Practice Become Fashionable?' *Journal of Consumer Research*, vol. 37, no. 1, pp. 15–36.

Sandikci, Ö. and Ger, G. (2011), 'Islam, Consumption and Marketing: Going Beyond the Essentialist Approaches,' in O. Sandikci and G. Rice (eds) *Handbook of Islamic marketing*, Cheltenham, UK: Edward Elgar, pp. 484–501.

Sandikci, Ö. and Jafari, A. (2013), 'Islamic Encounters in Consumption and Marketing,' *Marketing Theory*, vol. 13, no. 4, pp. 411–420.

Sandikci, Ö. and Ömeraki, S. (2007), 'Globalization and Rituals: Does Ramadan Turn Into Christmas?' *Advances in Consumer Research*, vol. 34, pp. 610–15.

Sandikci, Ö. and Rice, G. (eds) (2011), *Handbook of Islamic Marketing*, Cheltenham, UK: Edward Elgar Publishing.

Schatzki, T. R. (2002), *The Site of the Social: A Philosophical Account of the Constitution of Social Life and Change*, University Park, PA: The Pennsylvania State University Press.

Secor, A. J. (2002), 'The Veil and Urban Space in Istanbul: Women's Dress, Mobility and Islamic Knowledge,' *Gender, Place and Culture*, vol. 9, no. 1, pp. 5–22.

Spivak, G. C. (1988), *In Other Worlds: Essays in Cultural Politics*, New York: Routledge.

Strizhakova, Y., Coulter, R. and Price, L.L. (2008), 'Branded Products As a Passport to Global Citizenship: Perspectives from Developed and Developing Countries,' *Journal of International Marketing*, vol. 16, no. 4, pp. 57–85.

Taussig, M. (1993), *Mimesis and Alterity: A Particular History of the Senses*, New York: Routledge.

Thompson, C. J. and Arsel, Z. (2004), 'The Starbucks Brandscape and Consumers' (Anticorporate) Experiences of Glocalization,' *Journal of Consumer Research*, vol. 31 (Dec), pp. 631–642.

Thompson, C. J. and Haytko, D. L. (1997), 'Speaking of Fashion: Consumers' Uses of Fashion Discourses and the Appropriation of Countervailing Cultural Meanings,' *Journal of Consumer Research*, vol. 24 (June), pp. 15–42.

Thompson, C.J. and Tambyah, S.K. (1999), 'Trying to Be Cosmopolitan,' *Journal of Consumer Research*, vol. 26 (December), pp. 214–241.

Toprak, B. (1984), 'Politicisation of Islam in a Secular State: The National Salvation Party in Turkey,' in S. A. Arjomand (ed) *From Nationalism to Revolutionary Islam*, New York: SUNY Press, pp. 119–133.

Türe, M. and Ger, G. (2016), 'Continuity through Change: Navigating Temporalities through Heirloom Rejuvenation,' *Journal of Consumer Research*, vol. 43, no. 1, pp. 1–25, forthcoming.

Turner, B. (1994), *Orientalism, Postmodernism and Globalism*, London: Routledge.

Üstüner, T., Ger, G., and Holt, D. (2000), 'Consuming Ritual: Reframing the Turkish Henna-Night Ceremony,' in S. J. Hoch and R. J. Meyers (eds) *Advances in Consumer Research*, Provo, UT: Association for Consumer Research, Vol. 27, pp. 209–214.

Üstüner, T. and Holt, D.B. (2007), 'Dominated Consumer Acculturation: The Social Construction of Poor Migrant Women's Consumer Identity Projects in a Turkish Squatter,' *Journal of Consumer Research*, vol. 34, no. 1, pp. 41–55.

Üstüner, T. and Holt, D.B. (2010), 'Toward a Theory of Status Consumption in Less Industrialized Countries,' *Journal of Consumer Research*, vol. 37 (June), pp. 37–56.

Venkatesh, A. (1995), 'Ethnoconsumerism: A New Paradigm to Study Cultural and Cross-Cultural Consumer Behavior,' in J. Arnold Costa and G. Bamossy (eds) *Marketing in a Multicultural World: Ethnicity, Nationalism, and Cultural Identity*, Thousand Oaks, CA: Sage Publications, pp. 26–67.

Vicdan, H. and Firat, A.F. (2015), 'Evolving Desire to Experience the Social 'Other': Insights from the High-Society Bazaar,' *Journal of Consumer Culture*, vol. 15, no.2, pp. 248–276.

Wilk, R. (1995), 'Learning to be Local in Belize: Global Systems of Common Difference,' in D. Miller (ed) *Worlds Apart: Modernity through the Prism of the Local*, London: Routledge, pp. 110–133.

Wilk, R. (1998), 'Emulation, Imitation, and Global Consumerism,' *Organization & Environment*, vol. 11, no. 3, pp. 314–333.

Wilk, R. (1999), '"Real Belizean Food": Building Local Identity in the Transnational Caribbean,' *American Anthropologist*, vol. 101, no. 2, pp. 244–255.

White, J. B. (2002), *Islamist Mobilization in Turkey: A Study in Vernacular Politics*, Seattle: University of Washington Press.

Yaman, Ö. M. (2013), *Apaci Genclik*, Istanbul: Acilim Kitap.

12

China – the emerging consumer power

LiAnne Yu

In the three decades after Deng Xiaoping proclaimed that "to get rich is glorious," China has gone from being one of the poorest and most isolated nations to becoming the world's second largest economy, second only to the US. China's new rich are attracting the attention of the world's companies, who vie for market dominance in everything from soft drinks to smartphones. Messages to consume more emanate from everywhere. Advertisements are as relentless and ubiquitous as socialist propaganda posters once were in China's public spaces. Even the Chinese state encourages its citizens to spend more on vacations, cars, homes, and raising children, as a way to stimulate its economy. Chinese consumers are, in ever greater numbers, buying luxury goods, traveling abroad, and even celebrating the very un-Communist holiday of Christmas by shopping.

This chapter is based on over two decades of ethnographic research in China, and highlights five key dynamics that characterize the country's consumer revolution. While these dynamics have aspects that reflect broader, global themes around consumption, they also reflect the uniqueness of China's transformation, suggesting that not all consumer cultures necessarily follow the same path.

The first dynamic is what I call "conspicuous accomplishment." Thorsten Veblen coined the term *conspicuous consumption* in the nineteenth century to describe how the nouveau riche behaved (1899). He observed that the acquiring of and display of luxury items signified economic power, social status, and in relation to these, a life of leisure rather than work. The term *conspicuous consumption* has entered the general lexicon and is often used to describe Chinese consumer desires for luxury brands, and in particular European and Japanese ones (Podoshen et al., 2011). However, what I will argue is that Chinese consumption practices are characterized not by the desire to appear idle and indulgent, but to appear successful through one's personal efforts and hard work. What Chinese consumers seek to display through the symbolism of luxury items is in fact their own capacity for accomplishment.

The second dynamic is what I call "brand ideologies." While the state has retreated from several corners of citizens' lives, including daily household management, educational choices, and work (Davis, 2000), it has nonetheless remained a strong force in shaping the consumer experience. Furthermore, although political ideologies do not necessarily dominate everyday discourse in China anymore, they have been replaced by what I call brand ideologies, as China's new consumers seek forms of belonging and expression through the global companies.

The third dynamic is what I call "multiple nodes of cosmopolitanism." China's consumer revolution is shaped by a complex set of cultural influences, emerging from both the West and the Global East. As such, Korean pop music and fashion sensibilities, for example, play as great a role, if not greater, than the consumer practices of the West (Zhang & Zhang, 2015). Such dynamics open up the possibilities of a kind of hybrid modernity that does not follow one particular evolutionary path, but reflects a new kind of Asian modern consumer figure.

The fourth dynamic is what I call the "public sphere of consumption." Analyses of Chinese society today are often focused on whether there is the possibility of a "true" public sphere to emerge (Habermas, 1989). Within this public sphere, Chinese citizens can, hypothetically, exercise some political power that is separate from the state. What I have found is that while a public sphere in the traditional sense of the phrase has not emerged, what we do see is a limited, albeit rich, sphere where people speak freely in their roles as consumers. Thus, while critique of the Chinese Communist Party is still censored, individuals can, in their role as consumers, critique companies for their product quality or treatment of customers. While this is admittedly a limited sphere, and not a true public sphere, it does open up some possibilities for Chinese consumer forms of expression and political action that were not possible before (Herold & Marolt, 2011).

The fifth dynamic is what I call "virtu-real spaces." For consumers, the internet is one of the richest "places" to be in China. Although most Western studies of the role of online access in China tends to explore it in terms of censorship, it is a space that is, in many ways, more advanced than what we see in the so-called developed world. What I argue is that we should not review it as a space that is separate or distinguished from the "real" world. In fact, consumer practices have developed in such a way that they transition fluidly from one realm to the next, as people shop, play, communicate, and express themselves in both all throughout the day. An analysis of the virtu-real can help us better understand the particularities of China's consumer revolution, and how it may be charting a different kind of path (Yu, 2014).

Conspicuous accomplishment

Does China have a "real" middle class? A strictly economic or objectivist approach defines middle class in terms of household income. In these terms, figures for annual income range from 10,000 to 60,000 US dollars a year (Li, 2010). A more subjectivist approach also considers occupation, ownership of certain commodities such as a house and a car, and lifestyle (see Weber, 2005 for interaction of economic wealth, social status, and professional prestige in modern societies). Estimates of the size of China's middle class range anywhere from 5% to 25% of the population. The most optimistic predict that by 2030, 70% of the population will reach the middle class (Li, 2010).

Although the term *conspicuous consumption* is often used to refer to Chinese consumer habits, it is in fact not an accurate way to conceptualize social distinction in China. According to Thorstein Veblen, conspicuous consumption entailed not just the display of luxury items, but also the display of a leisurely lifestyle (1899). In the context of his writing, which was the turn-of-the-century US, being independently wealthy was considered an important social distinguisher. Thus, in striving to build status, people displayed not only what they could afford to buy but also the lifestyle of being idle and not having to get involved in the unsavory business of making money. Veblen observed that those who had to work to make a living nonetheless strove to give off the impression of idleness, through participating in country clubs and the like. He called this "conspicuous leisure." His interrelated concepts reflect a particular social and historical context, in which being idle and wealthy was the most desirable status.

What we see in China is actually quite different. Instead of conveying idleness, China's new consumers tend to frame status in terms of the ability to create opportunities. People who demonstrate more upward mobility – the ability to nurture, create, and realize their own success – are perceived as having higher status. In this sense, social distinction is not so much about markers of "having made it" but rather, markers of "moving on up." As such, some of the most important markers of status should reveal that one is upwardly mobile and entrepreneurial. Being busy and sought after, for example, is an important social distinguishing trait. Reflecting Veblen's original concept, I call this emerging phenomenon in China "conspicuous accomplishment."

The importance of demonstrating one's accomplishment through work, and not just wealth, connects consumption to production within Chinese perceptions of social status. This is significant in light of the artificial distinction between production and consumption within the body of consumption work. Marx's work on commodity fetishism and alienation addressed the experiences of the consumer, but his focus was in fact people's roles at work, whether they were at the top of the hierarchy or were the exploited workers (1990). Early consumption theory, influenced by Marx, continued to privilege production as a focus. More recent work, influenced by postmodern theory (Ong, 1997), has seen the shift towards the perspective of consumers as active, self-aware agents who, through their acquisition and use of products, experiment with subjectivities and social distinctions. However, some have argued that each perspective on its own artificially separates people's consumer behaviors from their money-making activities.

Thus, instead of attempting to force fit a framework for defining class, it is important to understand how Chinese consumers themselves experience and define social distinctions. As Mark Liechty argues, "The middle class is a constantly renegotiated cultural space – a space of ideas, values, goods, practices and embodied behaviors – in which the terms of inclusion and exclusion are endlessly tested, negotiated, and affirmed. From this point of view, it is the process, not the product, that constitutes class" (2003, p. 15).

Instead of assuming the existence of a middle class in China, we need to investigate consumers' actual strategies of inclusion and exclusion, as Liechty (2003) puts it. What we see is a desire by Chinese consumers themselves to frame status differently in terms of one's potential for accomplishment, as opposed to purely one's income and related lifestyle. Among consumers in China, there is no attempt to hide hard work or the fact that one has come from a difficult or humble background. In fact, such narratives of upward mobility and entrepreneurialism are valued over the appearance of idleness. Feeling satisfied as a consumer is linked to feeling fulfilled as a producer. Conspicuous accomplishment is the emerging form of status distinction (Yu, 2014).

Brand ideologies

Chinese consumers are the world's top spenders when it comes to luxury goods. In just the past decade, China has become the biggest market for such established, global prestige brands as Louis Vuitton, Chanel, and Gucci (D'Arpizio, 2012). When it comes to luxury brands, however, the bulk of these items are purchased not by the millionaire elites, but rather, by those with fairly average urban professional incomes. These tend to be middle-income professionals who splurge on a few luxury items every year – but there are enough of these en masse to help create the world's largest luxury market. A second fact that surprises most is the relative youth of these shoppers, who are between 25 and 28 years old, a good 15 years younger than similar consumers from Europe, and 25 years younger than those from the US (Gomel et al., 2012). The typical profile of the luxury brand shopper is an unmarried young adult, still living at home with his or her parents. While their incomes are not especially high, they have no expenses as they are expected to live at home until they get married. In addition to being able to spend their own salaries any way they like, as singletons, they are the sole recipient of any discretionary income from their parents and grandparents. Thus, while wealthy political elite and business owners certainly buy luxury goods, it is these younger, middle-income shoppers that are shaping the market for global high-end brands.

Does the tremendous increase in the number of things people can purchase mean that Chinese consumers have more agency in their daily lives? The Chinese state has retreated, in some ways, from its heavy-handed structuring of people's everyday lives, which characterized the decades under Mao's rule. The academic postmodern consumption literature (Bird et al., 2012) focuses heavily on how consumers forge and experiment with new identities through their consumption behaviors. Such scholars (Miller, 1998) emphasize the pleasure, enjoyment, and escape of consumption, challenging earlier frameworks that focused on structure and social hierarchy. From such a theoretical vantage point, consumption is viewed as liberating and a space for democratic expression (see Fiske, 2000).

Michel de Certeau argued against the idea that consumers were passive victims of corporate brainwashing, and posited that their everyday "tactics of consumption" can lead to self-realized, resistant, and creative selves (1984). Likewise, what we see in China is a growing sense of agency connected to consumption, as consumers reinvent and reimagine themselves through their consumer choices. As Daniel Miller observed in London malls, shopping, place, and identity are closely intertwined concepts (1998).

The reality that I have observed in China over the last few decades, however, is not quite as uniformly positive (Yu, 2014). While the state has retreated in some aspects of people's daily lives, it has been replaced by a new kind of structuring power, represented by product and service brands. When people, and especially young people, talk about their social affiliations, their aspirations, and their own identities, they more often than not refer to brands. They refer to themselves in relation to these brands – what it means to be a Jeep owner, an iPhone user, or a Gucci wearer. Global corporations continuously feed into the seemingly insatiable desire to associate one's self with brands that represent different facets of identity in new, "modernizing" China (Wang, 2008).

As the state once created structure of status as part of its holistic ideology, corporations now fill that void through the use of brand ideologies. Individuals use brands – and in particular, global luxury or status brands – to signify their values and aspirations. They use brands as entrees into new forms of belonging. Brands have thus become a kind of shortcut way of describing one's self (see Lukacs, 2010). Chinese consumers are not unique in the world in terms of their desire to associate themselves with brands. French sociologist Michel Maffesoli described the move from traditional tribes, based on static and unified notions of geographic and kinship, to neo-tribes, which can come into being as occasions arise (1996).

The incredible desire for branded products has led to some controversial behaviors, which have become topics of national conversation through social media. Well-publicized examples such as the teenager who sold a kidney to buy an iPhone, the couple who sold an infant daughter to buy luxury clothing, and the young woman on a reality TV show who declared she would rather be unhappy in the back of a BMW than in love on the back of a bike underscore the new kind of structuring force that brands play in everyday consumer lives. They represent desired lifestyles (Yu, 2014).

Nonetheless, while brands represent a new kind of structure and ideology, consumers are also engaging in actively reinventing these brands. In turn, corporations are adapting to mirror back what their customers seek from them. We see this in the way consumers in China have inverted some of the meanings around Western fast food brands, associating them with quality, wholesomeness, and modernity (Jing, 2000). These brands have responded by recasting their own identities in China, offering different products, and most importantly, continually inviting consumers in China to actively participate in these brand experiences. In this sense, brand identities can be viewed as the outcomes of conversations between producers and consumers, rather than simply the imposition of one's strategies upon the other.

Whether individuals are exercising more agency or not as consumers in China today, brands represent the new ideologies that play a significant role in structuring desire and daily lifestyles. Gone are the Communist propaganda posters, exhorting people to strive towards a socialist utopia. They are replaced by advertisements that connect beauty, success, and love not only to consumption, but more importantly, to specific brands. Whether consumers are walking around with knockoffs or saving up for a trip to Paris to shop at the real Gucci store, they are not only desiring the objects, but the lifestyles that these objects represent. To understand consumption in China today, we must view their engagement with products and services as brand experiences, with their own logics and structuring capabilities (Wang, 2008).

Multiple nodes of cosmopolitanism

Chinese lives are increasingly touched by globalization, "the process in which consumers, corporations and government are increasingly interconnected across national borders through the media, capital exchanges, production and consumption" (Hall, 2002, pp. 25–31). While there is little argument around the phenomena, it is the outcomes of globalization that are hotly contested within academia (Appadurai, 2001). On one end of the spectrum are studies that view globalization as a destroyer of the local and authentic. These studies focus on the so-called "McDonaldization" of urban spaces, as the authentic makes way to a mass, global culture originating from the West (Ritzer and Ovadia, 2000). On the other end of the spectrum are studies that celebrate globalization and transnational processes, focusing on the "freely" flowing stream of media, information, cultures, people, and money across borders (Appadurai, 1990).

For Chinese consumers, the reality spans the spectrum. China's cities are becoming increasingly homogenized, looking more like other cities in developed Asia as older neighborhoods are torn down to build the same kinds of malls and skyscrapers one can find in Singapore, Seoul, and Taipei. On the other hand, globalization has led to increased opportunities for education, career, and self-expression. The desire to become more knowledgeable about the world outside of their immediate experience is a strong motivator of consumer behaviors in China. People are looking to travel as a way to make them "modern" in the sense of being more knowledgeable through physical as well as social mobility. In *Desiring China*, Lisa Rofel explores the themes of postsocialist modernity and identity constructions. In it, she offers a conceptual connection between cosmopolitanism and consumption. "Consumption is about embodiment, embodying a new self. At the heart of this embodiment is desire. A properly cosmopolitan self is supposed to be desirous and this desire is supposed to be open and unconstrained" (2007, p. 118).

The forms of cosmopolitanism in China are multi-sited and multi-cultural. The ubiquity of McDonald's, Starbucks, and other American brands in the urban landscape, as well as the strong interest among young people in particular to learn English, all seem to point to the desire to become Westernized. However, the reality is that Chinese forms of cosmopolitanism incorporate multiple nodes of influence. These include the West for sure, but also integrate the "Global East" as well as transnational China.

In particular, South Korean culture has had a growing presence in China since the late 1990s. Chinese consumer interest in Korean pop, or k-pop, soap operas, movies, fashion, and celebrities has been dubbed the "Korean Wave" (Chua & Iwabuchi, 2008). South Korea's TV novellas have swept China's imagination. Popular television dramas are broadcast both over the air and on internet TV in China. Korean superstars, including Kwon Sang-woo, Jang Seo-hee, and Jang Woo-hyuk appear in Chinese dramas. K-pop artists such as Big Bang enjoy number one status on Chinese music charts. Korean movies, such as *Late Autumn*, starring Hyun Bin, become instant hits at the box office. Korean stars such as Rain have also become the obsession of teen girls in China, and in several household ethnographies I found posters of him lovingly taped to bedroom walls.

Perceptions of Japan, however, are more complex. On the one hand, since economic reforms, an ever-increasing array of Japanese products has become available in China. Japanese technology, in particular, is often thought of as superior to any domestic or Western brands. Japanese cosmetics brands, such as Shiseido, enjoy high prestige among female consumers. Japanese food is among the most popular among foreign cuisines in China's largest cities. At the same time, there is still a pervasive sense of distrust of the Japanese. Older Chinese have much stronger feelings, typically citing the Nanjing Massacre (1937), and what they feel is a history of hostility between the two nations. Younger Chinese tend to say that such historical events do not affect them, yet they do cite issues such as the dispute between China and Japan over the sovereignty of a set of islands, known as Diaoyu in China, as proof of Japan's aggression. In 2012, the tension between Beijing and Tokyo around the status of those islands erupted into consumer boycotts of Japanese products. At the height of tensions, Japanese cars were vandalized, and retailers took down Japanese products in their stores. Japanese manufacturers closed their factories for several weeks in order to protect their property and employees. Yet as soon as quickly as these protests rose up, they also died down. In some ethnographic research I conducted in late 2012 on conspicuous consumption, consumers in China were back to buying luxury Japanese products as if there had been no international tensions (Yu, 2014).

Restaurants that represent modern Asian cultures – Japanese, Korean, Taiwanese – are also becoming popular as spaces that embody desirable consumer experiences. Taiwanese cuisine, in particular, has elicited a lot of interest from consumers in China, who flock to Taiwanese tea shops, noodle stands, and fast food restaurants to experiment with the cuisine from a place that was, until the last few decades, a mystery to them.

The experiences of consumers in China, as well as throughout modern and modernizing Asia, throw into question the common assumption that there is a global consumer culture with the US model as the ultimate endpoint (Sassatelli, 2007). In order to properly understand the effects of globalization on China and emerging forms of cosmopolitanism, we need to disentangle multiple cultural influences and forms of knowledge. What casual observers of China may take as Westernization is in fact a complex mix of Global East, Global West and uniquely Chinese sensibilities, stewing together to create emerging forms of desire. Instead of merely emulating the West, Chinese forms of cosmopolitanism are complex, multi-nodal, and characterized by the desire to express both globalism and "Chineseness" at the same time. As Aihwa Ong and Donald Nonini argue, within the global capitalist economy are competing modernities (1997).

Virtu-real spaces of consumption

In China, virtual and real spaces of consumption have become important staging areas for the expression of sociality and subjectivity. The number of internet users in China is fast approaching 700 million. Not only does China have more people online than any other country in the world, it has the world's largest population of gamers, online shoppers, social networkers, and smartphone users. Another significant fact to note is the relative youth of China's online population. Sixty percent of Chinese netizens are under thirty, in contrast to the US, where the average age is 42 (Herold & Marolt, 2011). Online commerce sites, selling everything from electronics to cosmetics to bottled water, make the virtual world a critical part of any analysis of China's consumer culture.

While computer penetration in China still lags behind most developed countries, over 600 million people in the country are accessing the internet via smartphones. Such devices foster "always on" forms of communication and consumption, as acts in the "real world" become conversational pieces in the virtual world, and decisions in the virtual world become enacted in the real world (Yu, 2014). The ecosystem of online resources in China connected to commerce – ranging from social media to review sites to photo sharing sites to mobile wallet apps – creates consumption processes that interconnect physical and virtual realms in an increasingly seamless way. What we see among China's hip, urban, socially connected and technologically savvy consumers is potentially what we may see in other countries as their populations begin to adopt mobile internet devices.

China's virtual landscape is also rich with media content – always for free. Tudou and Youku are similar to YouTube in that they feature videos posted by users. Unlike YouTube, however, they feature full-length movies for free. Music, movies, and books are commonly free downloads, as China has yet to institute a consistently enforced digital rights management policy. Copyright violations are not enforced in China with the same discipline as they are elsewhere, and the casual shopper can easily find pirated DVDs of movies that are still in theaters, as well as all forms of pirated software.

Despite the richness of China's online universe, when it comes to sites of consumption, the academic literature tends to privilege the physical realms of shopping malls, supermarkets, and entertainment destinations. Analyses of online activities are growing, but still tend to be treated as secondary and separate from the "primary" realms of shopping in the "real" world (Hjorth & Khoo, 2015).

In my observations of internet behavior in China, consumers move fluidly between online and offline spaces when they consume. They use their smartphones to access the mobile internet, and move back and forth between social media and physical spaces to discuss, plan, experience, and share their consumption activities. For younger Chinese in particular, consumer activities are incomplete without the component of online social sharing. In fact, I have found that consumers in China do not distinguish between virtual and real spaces when it comes to their daily consumer practices. Rather, they move seamlessly between the two throughout the day, initiating consumption in one realm and continuing it into the other. The virtual and the real are experienced as a continuum of consumer experiences. In fact, for many, consumer activities do not feel complete until both the physical and the virtual aspects are satisfied. I call these emerging forms of consumption "virtu-real" to signify the fact that consumers themselves have developed behaviors that span across both (Yu, 2014).

The spaces of consumption for Chinese consumers are, thus, fluid, encompassing online and offline practices, in an often seamless way that doesn't differentiate between one realm and the other. Geographer Doreen Massey offers a direction to follow for a more fluid way of conceptualizing space, which allows for the inclusion of multiple forms. As she puts it, space is not just the flat land upon which we walk, but also a dimension of multiplicity. Space, in this more conceptual form, is made up of our relations and connections with each other, which are, of course, fraught with inequality and power differentials (2005). Following Massey's suggestion, we can frame the intersections between the virtual and the physical as a social space, within which consumer connections are expressed, fostered, harnessed, and exploited. As consumers develop new paths through these emerging spaces, they create different forms of social dynamics and desire fulfillment.

The public sphere of consumption

Freedom of expression when it comes to politics and religion is severely restricted in China. Journalists, book publishers, and even ordinary citizens who happened to post something politically sensitive on social media have been detained or arrested. Attorneys fighting for civil liberties have been attacked by officials. While China's online universe is rich with social media, online shopping, and music and movie sites, it is also a heavily censored space, where access to global news and conversations via sites such as Facebook and Twitter are restricted.

Jurgen Habermas defined the public sphere as "private people coming together as a public to debate the general rules governing relations in the basically privatized but publicly relevant sphere of commodity exchange and social labor" (1989, p. 27). Scholars have, over the last few decades since reforms were instituted in China, explored the question of whether a true public sphere would emerge. Most agree that it has not, at least not broadly and not consistently (Davis, 2000). While the internet has played a huge role in creating a free space of dissent and discussion, it is also fraught with restrictions and censorship.

Although there may not be a true public sphere in China, the consumer sphere is an interesting space to consider. Sharon Zukin offers a framework for understanding consumer spaces that goes beyond the mere pleasure of consumption. "The revolutionary achievement of mass consumption has been to construct another space between the self and civil society – and by shopping, we place ourselves in this space. Neither completely free nor completely democratic, the public sphere of shopping is a space of discussion and debate. It is a space of manipulation and control, but also of discretion and fulfillment. It is, in fact, an ambiguous or a heterotopic space, where we struggle to combine principles of equality and hierarchy, and pleasure and rationality, to create an experience we value" (2004, p. 32).

We see consumer spaces in China becoming these places of discussion and debate, particularly around the topic of food safety (Wu & Zhu, 2014). In 2008, over 300,000 babies fell ill after being fed Chinese-made formula that had been adulterated with melamine (Huang, 2014). The melamine was added to boost the protein content of the formula. At least six infants died from consuming this baby milk. The scandal caused immense outrage about the lack of food safety standards among domestic companies, which do not have the same strict requirements that global corporations impose. Anxious parents purchased international brands over domestic ones, even buying out all of the baby formula in Hong Kong, where food safety standards are thought to be much higher.

The baby formula scandal was only one of several cases that became widely talked about in the general public. Just a few years earlier, a domestic brand of soy sauce was found to be made of hair clippings. Ink and paraffin were found in instant noodles. Pork buns were discovered to be so loaded with bacteria that they glowed in the dark. Formaldehyde has been found in cabbage, and chlorine in the soft drinks (McDonald, 2012). In May 2013, officials arrested 904 suspects for passing off bogus beef, which was in fact made out of fox, mink, and rat.

Food contamination stories show up almost daily in social media. Nascent but quickly growing forms of consumer activism are spreading, especially online. The China Survival Guide iPhone app was downloaded 200,000 times within the first week of its launch. It gives out daily updates on issues, organizing them into the categories of health, nutrition, dairy, and beverages. Wu Heng's "Throw it out the window" is a food scandal database that alerts the public to the dangers at the supermarket and in restaurants. His thirty volunteers help him post information on food safety scandals around the country, which are also broadcast over Weibo (Jackson, 2015).

It would be a mistake to be overly optimistic about the potential for China's consumer sphere to lead the way towards a sphere that is truly free from the state. The economy has grown and consumption has expanded enormously not in spite of the Communist state, but *because of* the CCP's concerted efforts to grow the economy and its consumer base. The Chinese Communist Party has not been laissez faire in any sense – through carefully crafted and controlled policies, it has created a vibrant, consuming population. Thus, while consumer culture appears to be ruled by pure market forces, it is in fact closely regulated by the state.

Yet even within this context of a strong state that seeks to control consumer behavior and corporations that seek to entice shoppers to buy more, consumers themselves are nonetheless asserting their agency. In online forums, consumers challenge corporate greed, demand compensation for products that do not fulfill their promises, and expose companies selling counterfeit products. They in fact demand more information about their producers, defying the logic of commodity fetishism. Within the public space of consumption, consumer identities are created and expressed, frustrations are vented, and netizens discuss what is moral and ethically correct. People may not be entirely "free" within the space of consumption, but they have used their consumer identities to push for more rights vis-à-vis states and corporations that seek to assert their dominance (Hjorth & Koo, 2015).

Conclusion: Consumption with Chinese characteristics

China's consumer revolution is characterized by several unique dynamics. This chapter has explored five in particular. First, status distinctions are evolving in ways that defy established frameworks around class, as the upwardly mobile seek to differentiate themselves not only by what they consume but what they produce. Second, while consumers are increasingly identifying themselves via brands, we see that brand meanings have become another form of ideology, replacing political ones. Third, the influence of the Global East, and in particular, South Korea, Japan and Taiwan, calls into question the notion of the West being the model of modern consumption practices. Fourth, the fact that consumer culture and internet usage are so deeply intertwined makes it imperative to understand the role of the virtual world, not as a secondary, but as a primary place of consumption. And finally, the development of a public sphere of consumption, one that is neither completely free nor completely controlled, is a unique feature of China's consumer culture within the context of restrictions on political speech.

Other phenomena that need further attention include the tension between Chinese consumer practices and environmental degradation (Carter & Mol, 2013; Shapiro, 2016). What are the consequences of having more autos on the road, more packaging needing disposal, and more strain on China's land and water resources? Secondly, migration from rural to urban areas is also a phenomenon that may have far reaching consequences on social forms in China, as there are now over 125 cities with populations over one million. How do these migrants participate in the urban economy? What role does technology play in their connections back to "home," and how are they defining their identities within urban consumption practices (Ren, 2013; Wu et al., 2013)?

While China's consumer practices validate a great deal of what we know about consumption from case studies around the world, the particularities of China's economic and social development demand that we acknowledge the Western-centric frameworks that have so far dominated consumption theory. Following Garon and Maclachlan (2006), I would argue that we should not assume that the ultimate endpoint is that Chinese consumers will evolve like those in the

West. What we see emerging is, to paraphrase Deng Xiaoping, "consumption with Chinese characteristics." Consumption in China is much more than just the "triumph" of a Western-style free market. It is the new ideology in China, replacing that of socialism. Like its predecessor, this new ideology has changed the fabric of society, creating new structures, power hierarchies, subjectivities, and futures.

References

Appadurai, Arjun. (2001). *Globalization*. Durham, NC: Duke University Press.

Appadurai, Arjun. (1990). Disjuncture and difference in the global cultural economy. In M. Featherstone (Ed.), *Global Culture*. London: Sage, 295–310.

Bird, Jon, Barry Curtis, Tim Putnam & Lisa Tickner. (1993). *Mapping the Futures: Local Cultures, Global Change*. London: Routledge.

Carter, Neil & Arthur P.J. Mol. (2013). *Environmental Governance in China*. Abingdon: Routledge.

Certeau, Michel. (1984). *The Practice of Everyday Life*. Berkeley: University of California Press.

Chua, Beng Huat & Koichi Iwabuchi. (2008). *East Asian Pop Culture: Analyzing the Korean Wave*. Hong Kong: Hong Kong University Press.

D'arpazio, Claudia. (2012). Chinese shoppers world's top luxury goods spenders. In *Bain and Company*. (online) December 12, 2012. Available at http://www.bain.com/about/press/press-releases/bains-china-luxury-market-study-2012.aspx (accessed October 24, 2013).

Davis, Deborah (2000). Introduction: A revolution in consumption. In Deborah S. Davis (Ed.), *The Consumer Revolution in Urban China*. Berkeley: University of California Press, 1–22.

Fiske, John. (2000). Shopping for pleasure: Malls, power, and resistance. In Juliet B. Schor & Douglas B. Holt (Eds.), *The Consumer Society Reader*. New York: The New Press, 306–328.

Garon, Sheldon & Patricia L. Maclachlan. (2006). Introduction. In Sheldon Garon & Patricia L. Maclachlan (Eds.), *The Ambivalent Consumer: Questioning Consumption in East Asia and the West*. Ithaca: Cornell University Press, 1–15.

Gomel, Giorgio, Daniela Marconi, Ignazio Musu & Benjamino Quintieri. (2012). *The Chinese Economy: Recent Trends and Policy Issues*. New York: Springer Science and Business Media.

Habermas, Jurgen. (1989). *The Structural Transformation of the Public Sphere*. Trans.by Thomas Burger. Cambridge: MIT Press.

Hall, Stuart. (2002). Political belonging in a world of multiple identities. In Steve Vertovecn and Robin Cohen (Eds.), *Conceiving Cosmopolitanism: Theory, Context, and Practice*. Oxford: Oxford University Press, 25–31.

Herold, David Kurt & Peter Marolt (Eds.) (2011). *Online Society in China: Creating, Celebrating, and Instrumentalising the Online Carnival*. New York: Routledge.

Hjorth, Larissa & Olivia Koo (Eds.) (2015). *Routledge Handbook of New Media in Asia*. Abingdon: Routledge.

Huang, Yanzhong. (2014). 'The 2008 Milk Scandal Revisited.' In *Forbes Asia*. (online) July 16, 2014. Available at http://www.forbes.com/sites/yanzhonghuang/2014/07/16/the-2008-milk-scandal-revisited/#3fe3593a4428

Jackson, Peter. (2015). *Anxious Appetites: Food and Consumer Culture*. London: Bloomsbury Academic.

Jing, Jun. (2000). Introduction: Food, children, and social change in contemporary China. In Jun Jing (Ed.), *Feeding China's Little Emperors: Food, Children, and Social Change*. Redwood City, CA: Stanford University Press, 1–26.

Li, Cheng (Ed.) (2010). *China's Emerging Middle Class: Beyond Economic Transformation*. Washington, DC: Brookings Institution Press.

Liechty Mark. (2003). *Suitably Modern: Making Middle-Class Culture in a New Consumer Society*. Princeton: Princeton University Press.

Lukacs, Gabriella. (2010). *Scripted Affects, Branded Selves*. Durham, NC: Duke University Press.

Maffesoli, Michael. (1996). *The Time of the Tribes: The Decline of Individualism in Mass Society*. London: Sage Publications.

Marx, Karl. (1990). *Capital: A Critique of Political Economy*. London: Penguin Books.

Massey, Doreen. (2005). *For Space*. Thousand Oaks, CA: Sage Publications, Ltd.

McDonald, Mark. (2012). From milk to peas, a Chinese food safety mess. In *International New York Times*. (online) June 21, 2012. Available at http://rendezvous.blogs.nytimes.com/2012/06/21/from-milk-to-peas-a-chinese-food-safety-mess/?_r=0 (accessed October 24, 2013).

Miller, Daniel. (1998). *A Theory of Shopping*. Ithaca, NY: Cornell University Press.

Podoshen, Jeffrey S., Lu Li & Junfeng Zhang. (2011). Materialism and conspicuous consumption in China: A cross-cultural examination. In *International Journal of Consumer Studies*. 35(1) 17–25.

Ong, Aihwa. (1997). Chinese modernities: Narratives of nation and of capitalism. In Aihwa Ong & Donald Nonini (Eds.), *Ungrounded Empires: The Cultural Politics of Modern Chinese Transnationalism*. New York: Routledge, 171–202.

Ren, Xuefei. (2013). *Urban China*. Cambridge, UK: Polity Press.

Ritzer, George & Seth Ovadia. (2000). The process of McDonaldization is not uniform, nor are its settings, consumers, or the consumption of its goods and services. In Mark Gottdiener (Ed.), *New Forms of Consumption: Consumers, Culture, and Commodification*. Lanham: Rowman and Littlefield Publishers, Inc., 33–50.

Rofel, Lisa. (2007). *Desiring China: Experiments in Neoliberalism, Sexuality, and Public Culture*. Durham, NC: Duke University Press.

Sassatelli, Roberta. (2007). *Consumer Culture: History, Theory and Politics*. London: Sage.

Shapiro, Judith. (2016). *China's Environmental Challenges*. Cambridge, UK: Polity Press.

Veblen, Thorstein. (1899). *Theory of the Leisure Class: An Economic Study of Institutions*. New York: Macmillan Company.

Wang, Jing. (2008). *Brand New China*. Cambridge: Harvard University Press.

Weber, Max. (2005). *Economy and Society*. Redwood City, CA: Stanford University Press.

Wu, Fulong, Fangzhu Zhang & Chris Webster. (2013). *Rural Migrants in Urban China: Enclaves and Transient Urbanism*. Abingdon: Routledge.

Wu, Linhai & Dian Zhu. (2014). *Food Safety in China: A Comprehensive Review*. Boca Raton: CRC Press.

Yu, LiAnne. (2014). *Consumption in China: How China's New Consumer Ideology is Shaping the Nation*. Cambridge, UK: Polity Press.

Zhang, Weiyu & Lize Zhang. (2015). Fandom of foreign reality TV shows in the Chinese Cyber Sphere. In Wenhong Chen & Stephen D. Reese (Eds.), *Networked China: Global Dynamics of Digital Media and Civic Engagement: New Agendas in Communication*. Abingdon: Routledge.

Zukin, Sharon. (2004). *Point of Purchase: How Shopping Changed American Culture*. New York: Routledge.

13

Consumption in Brazil – the field of new consumer studies and the phenomenon of the "new middle classes"

Lívia Barbosa and John Wilkinson

Introduction

In this chapter we review and interpret the development of consumer studies as a field of research in Brazil. Academic debates and intense media coverage of the emergence of a "new middle class" in the middle of the first decade of the 2000s drew attention to Brazil as a consumer society. This focus coincided with the diffusion of a range of translations of key international authors in New Consumer Studies (NCS) and led to a surge of dissertations, theses and publications exploring a range of consumer practices and experiences. At the same time, we see the beginnings of an institutionalization of this thematic area both inside and outside the Brazilian Social Science Associations.

An understanding of the debates on the new middle class in Brazil and the multifaceted dynamic which consumption has assumed requires that we adopt a longer historical perspective focusing on the stabilization and opening of the economy in the 1990s and the consolidation of diverse rights in this same period on the basis of the New Constitution of 1988 marking the end of the long twenty-year dictatorship. Brazil's classical debates on the model of industrialization and the characteristics of its domestic market have heavily influenced the way consumption has been analyzed, particularly the notion that modern consumption practices were the exclusive preserve of a privileged middle class.

Mostly within a Marxist or Frankfurt School perspective, consumption was predominantly analyzed as an expression of regressive income distribution and social exclusion. The urban low income population was consequently viewed from the point of view of what it lacked and the way it served to reproduce the luxury consumption of an exclusive minority.

The debates on the new middle class in the first decade of the 2000s focused rather on the new purchasing capacity of the urban lower strata which was now seen as an indicator of social inclusion, although this view was subject to vigorous sociological critique. Occurring as they did, at a moment when the NCS contributions were becoming widely known, these debates stimulated a new concern to study these consumer practices in all their detail.

While classical approaches, whether harnessing Marxist notions of alienation and fetishism, the Frankfurt school, or the analysis of consumption in terms of distinction and positional goods, continue to be influential, new lines of consumer research can be identified which focus on consumption and material culture as a constitutive aspect of social life and as expressions of individual and social reproduction and identity. In addition, the impact of democratization has transformed consumption into a terrain where rights can be affirmed and citizenship defended. It is in this context also that alternative forms of consumption in defense of the environment are beginning to be articulated.

The chapter is divided into four parts in which we first characterize the emergence of consumer studies as a thematic area under the influence of a new generation of international authors who analyze consumption as a fundamental component of material culture and social reproduction. We then examine the antecedents to current discussions of consumption in Brazil focusing on the transformations since the end of the dictatorship and the debates on the Brazilian industrialization model. The specific features of the new consumer studies in the first decade of the 2000s are then highlighted through two surveys of publications and papers presented to the main social science forums in Brazil. In the final section, we discuss in detail the debates on the concept of the new middle classes and explore the range of themes and consumer segments which are currently being studied and to which NCS and related theoretical currents are making an important contribution. The chapter closes with a summary of the main arguments, a consideration of the strengths and weaknesses of NCS in the Brazilian context, and a call for attention to the very different economic and political conditions facing consumption and the new middle classes when viewed from the standpoint of 2016.

The emergence of consumer studies in Brazil and the influence of New Consumer Studies (NCS)

Studies on consumption and correlated themes in Brazil can be divided into two phases, the first from the academic consolidation of the social sciences up until around the end of the twentieth century and the second, which can be identified with the expansion of New Consumer Studies (NCS) in Europe and the United States, from the first decade of the new millennium until today. Both phases are important for understanding discussions related to the middle classes in general and particularly to the so called new middle classes, themselves part of broader changes in Brazilian society which were making themselves felt in these years. The NCS began to appear in Brazil around the end of the 1990s, almost twenty years later than in Europe and the United States, and were marked by the translation of some key works: Colin Campbell (1987/2002), Daniel Miller (1995/2000), Don Slater (1997/2001) and Grant MacCracken (1988/2003), followed a little later by Mary Douglas and Baron Isherwood (1979/2004), Pierre Bourdieu, (1979/2007) and Arjun Appadurai (1988/2008). The participation of some of these authors in academic events organized in Brazil around this time and the simultaneous presence of Brazilian students in European centers in exchange programs with some of these key figures were also fundamental for the development of this area in Brazil.

However, other seminal works from this same period by Daniel Miller (1987), and the whole range of contributions that redesigned the historical origins of consumer culture and society, including Neil McKendrick et al. (1982), Rosalind Williams (1991), Stuart Ewan, Chandra Mukerji (1983) and M. Miller (1981), are still not translated and have not received significant attention.

The sequence of these translations, however, does not follow the appearance of these classical works in Europe or in the United States, when we compare the original dates of publication of those works and their translation in Brazil. The delay of more than twenty years in the translation of these works, and the late establishment of an approach to studying consumption in Brazil within the new perspective developed by the NCS, does not mean that some of these authors were not previously known or read in Brazil. Some were very popular as is the case of Mary Douglas and Pierre Bourdieu. Although widely cited and known among Brazilian social scientists since the 1970s, they were read and integrated in contexts not directly related to consumption

Other classics in anthropology, such as *The Gift*, by Marcel Mauss (1967), originally integrated into discussions of exchange and the gift economy became reinterpreted after 2000, with the popularization of NCS, as a precursor of consumption studies. Veblen's (1966) concept of conspicuous consumption, previously more appropriated by economists in Brazil, became, together with Pierre Bourdieu, a key historical reference for studies in consumption and identity, distinction, lifestyles and status in Brazil.

From the institutional point of view, it was also only after 2000 that Brazilian social scientists and students began to organize and promote courses and seminars (Barbosa and Gomes, 2000, Barbosa, 2006). According to Portilho, Castañeda and Galindo (2010), between 1980 and 2009,[1] 250 articles were identified that had the word *consumption* in either the title, the key words or in the abstracts. As many as 236 of these appeared after 2004, when the National Meeting of Consumer Studies (ENEC) was also created.[2] The absence of the term, however, does not mean that the subject of consumption was not dealt with through other theoretical lenses and concepts prior to 2000. In the next section we will explore the different ways in which consumption was analyzed in the Brazilian context in this period.

Consumption studies before 2000

While anthropologists (DaMatta, 1981; Gilberto Freyre, 1990) and historians (Sergio Buarque de Holanda, 2001; Raymundo Faoro, 1984) have played a decisive role in composing a framework for understanding Brazilian society, economists and social scientists within a Marxist perspective have dominated discussions on the Brazilian (and Latin American) model of development. Whether in the industrial import substitution economic model of the ECLA, the United Nations organization for Latin America, (Furtado, 2007) or the social science dependency theories (Cardoso and Faletto, 1981), consumption was subsumed within the problematic of the growth of the "domestic market". In the classical debates of the 50s and 60s (Guimaraes, 1963; Caio Prado, 1996), when Brazil was still predominantly an agrarian society, the impediment to development was identified with the exclusion of the rural population from the money economy and the need for an agrarian reform. In the 70s and 80s, in the face of an industry-led economic boom and a massive rural-urban exodus industrialization was argued to be stunted by the "marginalization" of the urban poor, cordoned off in shanty towns. In both cases, a functionalist analysis argued that the excluded sector, whether rural or urban, made the development model possible, either by proving cheap food or cheap labour (Quijano, 1978; Oliveira, 2002).

Whether this model of industrialization was seen as condemned to stagnation (Furtado, 2007), or whether a more diffusionist outcome was envisaged which would eventually expand consumption to lower income sectors (Coutinho, 1979), the actual development model was identified with a privileged middle class benefitting from "luxury" consumption, while the mass of the population had to survive on wage levels repeatedly shown to be below basic reproduction costs by the trade union statistical studies unit, DIEESE. Although some analyses (Medeiros, 1992) recognized that this was a distorted reproduction of the US model which was geared to mass consumption, growth based on the development of a consumer market in Brazil was from the outset identified as illegitimate, focused on luxury consumption in the face of widespread misery and associated with US capitalism. The fact that the economic boom of the 70s and 80s occurred during the military dictatorship and in a period characterized by anti-imperialist sentiment further confirmed the negative interpretations of the Brazilian consumer dynamic.

It is not surprising in this context that, to the extent that consumption practices were discussed, it was the Frankfurt School and Baudrillard which provided the theoretical template, with the focus on fetishism and alienation, publicity and the culture industry. This School and Baudrillard were widely read and studied in the social sciences in Brazil and, therefore, provided an already digested theoretical perspective for studies on consumption.

When not adopting this line of cultural critique, social science studies focused primarily on the "marginal" aspects of the different categories of poor. An abundant literature on riverside populations, fishing communities, urban working classes, peasants, blacks and many other groups was produced. Beyond the immediate preoccupation of registering the material living conditions of these groups, perceived as deprived, the underlying preoccupation of most of these studies was the condemnation of the capitalist system and all its alleged distortion, from both economic and moral points of view.

These analyses of the material life conditions of these groups and their social reproduction were generally described from a negative perspective. What they lacked in material terms was seen as more relevant than what they possessed and perceived themselves to be. Changes in their way of life, idealized as authentic and original, were identified with cultural loss, subjugation and marginality under the pressure of more powerful processes. As Sahlins previously pointed out in his Cosmologies of Capitalism (1994), and transposing this to Brazilian reality, these groups – natives, poor blacks – were not analyzed as having dynamic of their own. They were perceived, not as acting, but only as reacting to the outside stimulus of the capitalism system and oppression. Since their material deprivation was their defining characteristic, they did not live; they merely survived. What they consumed did not matter; rather what did matter was what they did not consume (Barbosa and Gomes, 2000; Zaluar, 2002; Sarti, 2003; Sahlins, 2007).[3]

In this context, however, the field of anthropology deserves a specific mention. Due to its ethnographic tradition certain themes related to everyday life and social reproduction have been present all along, as is the case of consumption patterns in food, clothes, lifestyles, the body and identity of different communities and social groups. In parallel, a line of academic production relating to the lifestyle of middle range segments and their individualistic ethos emerged which was very much intertwined with the development of an urban anthropology in Brazil (Velho, 1981).

Consumption studies after 2000

If that was the state of "consumption studies" in Brazil before 2000 and its engagement with the middle classes, the current situation is entirely different. A general appraisal of the field easily identifies a flourishing academic production. Themes range from a historic perspective on consumption (Monteleone, 2013) to political consumption, passing by fashion, clothing, food, body, technology, communications, propaganda and marketing, sustainability, contested markets and of course, the "new middle classes" (Mezabarba, 2012; Barbosa, Portilho, Wilkinson and Dubeux, 2014; Yaccoub, 2011).

In a preliminary survey of the Education Ministry database which was made publicly available, we identified 323 works which included the word *consumption* in the list of keywords, from 33 different disciplinary fields (Barbosa and Soares, 2015).[4] Selecting only works from social sciences and communication, 18 theses/dissertations were identified from 2004 to 2007, and 143 from 2007 to 2011. The CAPES data base, also from the Ministry of Education, for the years 2011 and 2012, registers 180 works which could be considered to fall within the broad field of social sciences and communication studies, with 61 in the areas of anthropology and sociology and 91 in communication and propaganda.[5]

The survey carried out by Portilho et al. (2010), to which we referred above, identified 16 different themes among the 250 papers analyzed, of which the most frequent were cultural consumption, identity and political or sustainable consumption.[6]

Further insights can be drawn from another survey carried out by Barbosa and Soares (2015) of more than 3000 references cited in 13 books on consumption edited by researchers from different graduate courses located in different geographical regions of Brazil, between the years of 2006 and 2015[7] and involving a total of 183 authors. The survey computed how many times authors identified theoretically with research in the area of consumption; material culture, consumer culture and society were mentioned among the references.[8]

What can we gather from this preliminary survey? First, the introduction of NCS in Brazil legitimated an expansion of themes and authors that are now subsumed under the term *consumption, material culture* or both, when they probably would not have been so some few years ago. The phenomenon of the "new middle classes" is one case in point. Their sudden increase in buying power and the discussion that followed it, coupled with the political appropriation of the phenomena by the Lula Government, raised an interest in all aspects of their lives as testimony of their existence beyond the category of poor, which until very recently, had rendered them invisible to the rest of society.

Secondly, the survey also suggests that the theoretical influence of authors linked to the NCS favored new interpretations of the meaning of consumption in Brazilian academic production. Thirdly, studies related to cultural products, communication, media studies, consumer culture and society are still very much approached from a Marxist or Frankfurt School tradition. A significant number of these works privilege the reading of empirical material as texts or discourses, applying a semiotic approach, and also an exegesis of authors and concepts.

Consumer studies and the new middle classes

Brazilian society underwent a radical change in the 1990s. The end of inflation and the stabilization of the economy had an immediately beneficial impact on the salaried poor. The minimum wage was increased above inflation in all but one year, formal employment increased on average by over half a million each year and by over one million at the end of the decade. Brazil adhered to the WTO and the economy was opened to imports (Doria, 2013). The banking system was reformed and opened to global capital and strategic sectors of future consumer goods, such as telecommunications, were privatized and similarly opened up to the global players. The press called attention to the emergence of new consumer habits among the poor. Yoghourts were identified as a new icon of food consumption, indicating the integration of low income families into modern retail shopping and consumer durables, in this case, fridges. These changes were best captured in the pioneering study by Sorj entitled the *New Brazilian Society* (2000), and particularly in his third chapter: "Brazil: a consumer society" in which he also emphasized the importance of consumer rights as a new expression of citizenship.

As early as the 80s, a number of authors had contested the stark dualism of the dependency version of economic development (Fishlow, 1972; Coutinho, 1979; Saboia, 1983). From different and often conflicting perspectives these authors showed how market segmentation, the existence of a "hand-me-down", often informal, second-hand market, and the increasing availability of consumer credit were incorporating large sectors of the presumed-to-be excluded urban population into modern consumer practices, particularly the world of consumer durables.

Globally, international organizations and initiatives focused on the possibilities of integrating the poor into the market economy, either through Hernando de Soto´s strategy of turning shanty town dwellers into house owners or through the Bangladesh Grameen-style small credit associations. In Brazil, a national program to strengthen the family farm (PRONAF) increasingly narrowed the gap between the town and the countryside for hundreds of thousands of small farmers.

Business studies and marketing, which, from an opposite perspective, had also excluded the urban poor from their focus, were now paying attention to these changes as a supposed "market exhaustion" of the A and B classes stimulated the search for new sources of market dynamism. Prahalad and Hammond's (2002) article "Serving the world's poor, profitably" was the game changer here, proposing market integration as the key to alleviating poverty. These ideas were later consolidated in an article by Prahalad and Hart (2002), translated in Portuguese in 2005, that became very popular in Brazil, where he indicated the possibilities of profit hidden among the people "at the base of the pyramid". The market potential of the "bottom billion" which became a global target of business consultants and international organizations alike reinforced the attention given to the urban poor as the next new consumer market. The financial innovation of pre-paid cell phones became perhaps the most iconic expression of this integration.

While a "new middle class" was already germinating and was beginning to draw attention in the 90s, a combination of years of high growth riding on China´s voracious commodity demand and a mix of social and economic policies favoured a rapid and striking improvement in the well-being of low-income households. An ambitious cash transfer programme and a rapid expansion of formal employment deepened and extended their purchasing power which was further stimulated by low interest credit directed to consumer durables.

Integration into the modern consumer market now became a legitimate object of concern since it was widely interpreted as the transformation of what had been condemned as a privilege for the few into a right for the bulk of the population, achieved through the social and economic policies of a Workers' Government. Although many would remain critical of this conflation of consumer and citizen, market inclusion as a proxy for social inclusion was endorsed as the Workers' Government´s key achievement (Neri, 2011). Consumer practices now became an important object of study as the above-mentioned surveys demonstrate and, although the Frankfurt traditions remained strong, the NCS authors now came into their own as is clear in the weight they assume in the bibliographical references to which we have referred.

A series of studies from the middle of the 2000s, accompanied by extraordinary media coverage, placed the notion of the new middle classes at the centre of discussions. The most euphoric of these analyses by Neri (2011) became incorporated into the official publicity of the government. Neri defined the new middle class, or the "C class" in Brazil´s income stratification, in terms of the country´s median household income. Based on this stratification, Brazil should now be considered a middle class country with a total "C strata" of some 90 million people. Of these some 29 million were argued to have been brought out of poverty into the new middle class since 2003 on the basis of a combination of the economic and social policies indicated above.

This definition of class in terms of income categories suffered a serious critique at the hands of Souza (2010) and Pochmann (2012). These authors argued that we were dealing with segments of the working class which were barely making ends meet at the cost of increasing personal indebtedness, and were largely without adequate access to basic social services (sanitation, transport, medical care and education).

Whatever the analysis, the spotlight was firmly turned on the phenomenon of these new "middle classes" which became privileged objects of the media, stimulated the emergence of specialized consultancy firms and reinforced the autonomization of consumer studies as an area of research and teaching.

Ethnographic studies of this new middle class (itself a striking process of social construction, not only in Brazil but globally in relation to the "emerging" world), have become the order of the day: life styles, consumer practices, economic and financial strategies, tastes, shopping practices, cultural expressions, housing conditions. The consumer world, previously dismissed as luxury made possible by social exclusion, has now become a legitimate object of study revealing a new "them", no longer defined by social exclusion, and in the process throwing a new light on "us" (Mattoso, 2005; Rocha e Silva, 2009). Authors have also insisted on the heterogeneity of these social groups and have drawn attention to the emergence of new market sectors – in music (country music in the rapidly growing new agricultural regions; funk and rap in the metropolitan suburbs and favelas), sports, food services, personal services, the keep-fit culture – which have all become objects of consumer studies (www.estudosdeconsumo.com.br).

Perhaps the most significant transversal theme has been that of colour and Afro-Brazilian identity, which has been reinforced by the introduction of colour-based quota systems in education and public services, but which has also stimulated the development of market segments particularly in fashion and personal care (Sansome, 2000; Oliveira, 2002).

The Brazilian Constitution of 1988, reflecting the break with the long period of military dictatorship, was notable for its defense of the rights of "minorities". The following decades witnessed an increasing affirmation of "minority" rights – indigenous communities, ex-slave communities, gay rights and above all women´s rights – promoted particularly through the vigorous activity of the NGO world, itself another key feature of the emerging democracy. Defense of indigenous and ex-slave communities and above all the promotion of family farming, which included agrarian reform initiatives, was reinforced by the identification of these social categories with the defense of the environment (Portilho, 2005). On the one hand, these new identities were increasingly picked out as potential objects of market segmentation by publicity and a new generation of green firms. On the other, social movements and NGOs began to use the market to further social and environmental demands (Wilkinson, 2007).

The Brazilian Constitution also established the notion of consumer rights and a Consumer Protection Code became law in 1990. Government consumer protection offices have since been established throughout the country. The defense of consumer rights has also had a very active civil society presence, particularly through the Brazilian Institute in Defence of the Consumer, (IDEC) which has focused on campaigns identified with key issues mobilizing social movements – GMOs and consumer information, internet access – and with a special focus on food and health (Sorj, 2000). Among these, publicity geared to stimulating consumption among children has been a particularly focus of campaigning and has built on the well-established Frankfurt critique of the culture industry which as we have seen has characterized Brazilian analyses of consumption in the 80s and 90s and continues as a strong component of consumer studies.

Social movements based on the defense of social and environmental and the alternative markets which emerged in their wake comprise an important segment of consumer studies, most notably in the case of food products where defense of the "traditional" and the environment is associated with the promotion of personal health and well-being (Menasche, 2007). It is not surprising, in this context, that discussions of citizenship and the political consumer, which was a key theme of the ENEC Meetings in this period, have also assumed an important place in consumer studies (Portillo, 2005), and the work of Micheletti (2003) has become a key reference. In the Brazilian context, the connections between consumption or alternative consumption and markets has led to an approximation with the "new economic sociology" and discussions of social networks *a la* Granovetter, the solidarity economy in the writings of Polanyi and Laville and social money drawing on the work of Zelizer are now frequent in consumer studies.

Conclusions

In addition to this central focus on the new middle classes, Brazilian consumption studies are being heavily influenced by the emergence of new social groups, whose rights were defined in the post-dictatorship constitution and promoted by an increasingly active civil society. Notions of citizenship are, therefore, key themes in current consumer studies. The orientation of social movements to market outcomes has similarly expanded consumer studies as new patterns of desired consumption are associated with the promotion of alternative actors and alternative markets, with pride of place here for food studies. In this context, consumer studies draw also on the new economic sociology literature, some of whose authors we have referred to above. The "old" middle class, previously seen as the privileged consumer of luxury, positional goods, is now studied for signs of the emergence of the political or conscientious consumer as the vanguard of new green and healthy consumption practices.

As Brazil plunges into what threatens to be a prolonged recession combining increasing unemployment and inflation, consumer studies will have to confront the political and economic factors underpinning consumer practices. At the level of individual consumption the issue of credit indebtedness and the renegotiation of consumer contracts is already becoming a major concern. Perhaps more importantly, questions of collective consumption, whether relating to public transport, access to education and health are beginning to problematize the relation between consumer access and citizen rights. It remains to be seen whether new consumer studies can rise to this challenge.

Notes

1 The events analyzed were the meetings of the Brazilian Society of Sociology (SBS), the Brazilian Association of Anthropology, and the National Graduate Social Science Association (ANPOCS).
2 ENEC is an international seminar, bringing together Portuguese and Latin American researchers around the theme of consumer studies on a biannual basis. The ENEC also gave rise to a research group, Consumer Studies: www.estudosdoconsumo.com.br registered with the National Research Council (CNPq).
3 For instance, in the case of the "black community", most research focused on questions of political identity. Little or nothing was said about this group as consumers and citizens. Already by 2000, data from IBGE (Brazilian Institute of Geography and Statistics), indicated that the "black community" made up 25% of the middle class in Brazil. The most outstanding work in this tradition was "A Integração do Negro na Sociedade de Classes" by Florestan Fernandes (2008), one of the "founders" of sociology in Brazil.
4 The medical and natural sciences were excluded.
5 We would like to thank Cecilia Soares for her research into these data bases: http://portal mec.gov.br/dominio-publico and http://www.bce.unb.br/2013/11/banco -de-teses-da-capes/
6 Brazilian social sciences journals are another source of reference At least two of them have organized special thematic issues about consumption as it is the case of Antropolítica (2004) and Horizontes Antropológicos (2007) e (2011).
7 The books analyzed are Barbosa and Campbell (2006), Leitão et al (2006), Migueles (2007), Baccega (2008), Bueno et al (2008), Rial et al (2012), Prado et al (2013), Freitas, et al (2014), Correa et al (2015).
8 We did not consider authors, Brazilian or non-Brazilians, who were principally relevant for only a specific field of interest, such as food, technology, and so on.

References

Appadurai, A. (1986), *The Social Life of Things: Commodities in Cultural Perspective.* Cambridge: Cambridge University Press.

Baccega, M.A. (Edit) (2008), *Comunicação e Cultura do Consumo.* São Paulo, Editora Atlas S.A.

Barbosa, L. and Campbell, C. (2006), *Cultura, Consumo e Identidade* (org.). Rio de Janeiro: FGV Editora.

Barbosa, L. and Gomes, L. (2000), *Projeto Apresentado ao CNPQ e ao British Council Sobre Consumo e Identidade*. Rio de Janeiro. Unpublished Manuscript.

Barbosa, L., Portilho, F., Wilkinson, J. and Dubeux, V. (2014), 'Trust, participation and political consumerism among Brazilian Youth,' *Journal of Cleaner Production and Consumption*, 63, 93–101.

Barbosa, L. and Soares, C. (2015), *Levantamento Sobre a Produção Acadêmica em torno do tema Consumo*. Rio de Janeiro. Unpublished Manuscript.

Bourdieu, P. (2007), *A Distinção: Crítica Social do Julgamento*. São Paulo, Edusp.

Buenos, M. L. and Camargo, L. O. de Lima, (2008), *Cultura e Consumo. Estilos de Vida Na Contemporaneidade*. São Paulo, Editora do Senac.

Campbell, C. (2002), *A Ética Romântica e o Espírito do Consumismo Moderno*. Rio de Janeiro, Editora Rocco.

Cardoso, F. and E. Falleto (1981), *Dependência e Desenvolvimento na América Latina*. Zahar, Rio de Janeiro.

Correa, S. B., Pinto, M. L. and Dubeux, V. (Eds.). (2015), 'Consumo e Sociabilidades. Espaços, Significados e Reflexões'. Rio de Janeiro, Escola Superior de Propaganda e Marketing. Coleção Contextos e Pesquisas. E- papers.

Coutinho, M. (1979), 'Distribuição de Renda e Padrões de Consumo: alguns autores em torno da tradição cepalina,' *Ensaios FEE*, 1(1), 139–152.

DaMatta, R. (1981), *Carnavais, Malandros e Heróis*. Zahar, Rio de Janeiro.

Doria, R. M. Soares (2013), *Evolução do Padrão de Consumo das Famílias Brasileiras no Período 2003–2009 e Relações com a Distribuição de Renda*, Masters Dissertation, Institute of Economia, Federal University, Rio de Janeiro.

Douglas, M. and Isherwood, B. (2004), *O Mundo dos Bens*. Rio de Janeiro, Editora da UFRJ.

Ewen, S. (1988), *All Consuming Images: The Politics of Style in Contemporary Culture*, New York, Basic books.

Faoro, R. (1984), *Os Donos do Poder*. São Paulo, Globo Editora.

Fernandes, F. (2008), *A Integração dos Negros na Sociedade de Classes*, vols 1 and 2. Globo Editora: São Paulo.

Fishlow, A. (1972), 'Brazilian Size Distribution of Income', *The American Economic Review*, 62(2), 391–402.

Freyre, G. (1990), *Casa Grande e Senzala*. Record, Rio de Janeiro.

Freitas, R. F., Ferreira, F.R., Carvalho, M. C.V. S. and Prado, S. D. (2014), *Corpo e Consumo na Cidade*. Série Sabor Metrópole: Curitiba, Editora CRV.

Furtado, C. (2007), *A Formação Econômica do Brasil*. Companhia das Letras: São Paulo.

Guimaraes, A. P. (1963), *Quatro Séculos do Latifundio*. Paz e terra, São Paulo.

Holanda, S. Buarque de. (2001), *Raízes do Brasil*. Companhia das Letras, São Paulo.

Leitão, D. K., Lima, D.N.O and Machado, R. P. (2006), *Antropologia e Consumo. Diálogos entre Brasil e Argentina*. Porto Alegre, Editora AGE.

Mattoso, C. L. Q. (2005), *Me Empresta seu nome? Um estudo sobre os consumidores Pobres e seus problemas financeiros*. Rio de Janeiro, Mauad X.

Mauss, M. (1967), *The Gift. Forms and Functions of Exchange in Archaic Societies*. New York, Norton & Company.

McCracken, G. (2003), *Cultura e Consumo*. Rio de Janeiro, Editora Maud.

McKendrick, N; Brewer, J.; Plumb, J. H. (1982), *The Birth of a Consumer Society*. London: Hutchinson.

Medeiros, C. A. (1992), *Padrões de Industrialização e Ajuste Estrutural*. UNICAMP, São Paulo.

Menasche, R. (2007), *Agricultura Familiar e a Mesa*. Buscapé, São Paulo.

Micheletti, M. (2003), *Political Virtue and Shopping*. Palgrave, MacMillan, New York.

Migueles, C. (Edt.) (2007), *Antropologia de Consumo*. Rio de Janeiro, FGV.

Migueles, C. (org) (2007), *Antropologia de Consumo*. FGV, Rio de Janeiro.

Miller, D. (1987), *Material Culture and Mass Consumption*. London, Basil Blackwell.

Miller, D. (1995), Consumption as the Vanguard of History. A Polemic by Way of an Introduction. In: Miller, D. *Acknowledging Consumption*. Routledge, London, pp. 1–57.

Miller, D. (1998), *A Theory of Shopping*. Oxford, Polity Press.

Miller, M. (1981), *The bon Marché: Bourgeois Culture and the Department Store, 1869-1920*. Princeton: Princeton University Press.

Mezabarba, S. (2012), *Vestuário e Cidades: Ethos, Consumo e Apresentação de Si no Rio de Janeiro e em São Paulo Niterói*. Unpublished PhD Thesis in Social Anthropology, Niterói: Universidade Federal Fluminense.

Monteleone, J. (2013), *O Circuito das Roupas. A Corte, o consumo e a moda. Rio de Janeiro 1840–1889*. Doctoral Thesis, University São Paulo.

Mukerji, C. (1983), *From Graven Images. Patterns of Modern Materialism*. New York, Columbia University press.

Neri, M. C. (2011), (Coord). *A nova classe média.* Rio de Janeiro: FGV/ IBRE, CPS, 2008. Disponível em: <http://www3.fgv.br/ibrecps/M3/M3_ A Nova Classe Media_Port_2.pdf>. Acesso em: 20 fev. 2011.

Oliveira, L. C. M. (2002), 'Negros em Ascenção Social. Poder de Consumo e Visibilidade'. Mastes Thesis, Niterói.

Pochmann, M. (2012), *Nova Classe Média?* Boitempo Ed. São Paulo.

Portilho, F. (2005), *Sustentabilidade Ambiental, Consumo e Cidadania.* Cortez Editora, São Paulo.

Portilho, F., Castañeda, M. and Galindo, F. (2010), *Estudos de consumo no Brasil. A construção de um novo campo nas ciências sociais brasileira.* X ENEC, Rio de Janeiro.

Caio Prado, Jnr. (1996), *Formação do Brasil Contemporâneo.* Brasiliense, São Paulo.

Prahalad, C. K. (2002), 'Serving the World's Poor, Profitably,' *Harvard Business Review*, September, 48/57.

Prahalad, C. K. and Hart, S. L. (2002), 'O Pote de ouro na base da pirâmide,' *HSM Management*, 32, maio-junho, 14/27.

Prado, S. D., Freitas, S. D., Ferreira, F. R. and Carvalho, M.C.S (Edts.) (2013), *Alimentação, Consumo e Cultura.* Curitiba, Editora CRV.

Quijano, A. (1978), 'Dependência e Mudança Social e Urbana na América Latina', In: Almeida, F. L. (org) *A Questão Urbana na América Latina.* Rio de Janeiro: Forense, 9–60.

Rial, C., Silva, S. R. and Souza, A. M. (Edts.) (2012), *Consumo e Cultura Material.* Perspectivas Etnográficas. Florianópolis, Editora da UFSC.

Rocha, A. and Silva, J. F. (2009), *Consumo na Base da Pirâmide: estudos brasileiros.* Rio de Janeiro, Maud.

Saboia, J. (1983), 'As causas da Difusão da Posse dos Bens de Consumo Duráveis no Brasil', *National Programme of Economic Research, Série Fac-Simile*, 4, pp. 3–45.

Sahlins, M. (1994), 'Cosmologies of Capitalism: the trans-pacific sector of "The World System"'. In: Dirks, N. Eley, G. & Ortner, S. *Culture/ Power/ History. A Reader in Contemporary Social Theory.* Princeton, Princeton University Press, pp. 412–456.

Sahlins, M. (2007), 'A Sociedade Afluente Original'. In: Sahlins, M. *Cultura na prática.* Rio de Janeiro: Editora UFRJ, pp. 105–152.

Sansome, L. (2000), 'Os Objetos de Identidade Negra: consumo, mercantilização, globalização e a criação de culturas negras no Brasil'. *MANA*, 6(1): 87–119.

Sarti, C. A. (2003), *A Família como Espelho*: um estudo sobre a moral dos pobres. São Paulo: Cortez.

Slater, D. (1997), *Consumer Culture and Modernity.* Cambridge: Polity Press. (English)

Slater, D. (2001), *Cultura do Consumo e Modernidade.* São Paulo, Nobel. (Portuguese)

Sorj, B. (2000), *A Nova Sociedade Brasileira.* Zahar, Rio de Janeiro.

Sousa, J. (2010), *Os Batalhadores Brasileiros: nova classe média ou nova classe trabalhadora?* UFMG, Belo Horizonte.

Torquato, S. (2009), *Entre o prazer e o drama*: consumo e distinção social na nova classe média. Paper presented to the IV Students Days, Graduate Programme in Anthropology, Federal University Fluminense. Rio de Janeiro.

Veblen, T. (1966), *A Teoria da Classe Ociosa: Um Estudo Econômico das Instituições.* Pioneira, São Paulo.

Velho, G. (1981), *Individualismo e Cultura.* Zahar, Rio de Janeiro.

Wilkinson, (2007), 'Fair Trade. Dynamic and Dilemmas of a Market Oriented Global Social Movement', *Journal of Consumer Policy*, 30(3), pp. 219–239.

Williams, R. (1991), *Dream Worlds: Mass consumption in Late Nineteenth-Century France.* Berkeley, University of California Press, 1991.

Yaccoub, H., A Chamada, (2011),'Nova Class Média'. Cultural Material, Inclusão e Distinção Social. *Horizontes Antropologicos*, 17(36), 197–231, jul/dez.

Zaluar, A. (2002), *A máquina e a revolta.* São Paulo, Brasiliense.

14
Russia
Postsocialist consumer culture

Olga Gurova

Introduction

After the dissolution of the Soviet Union in 1991 and transition from a state-planned to market-driven economy, the sphere of consumption in Russia has drastically changed. Among the changes are the proliferation of global media and advertising, transnational corporations, brands and commodities. Russia also became better integrated in the global economy and culture. Therefore, the question is raised: how did these changes affect consumption in Russia at a structural level and in everyday life? How did the Soviet legacy inform consumption in postsocialist Russia? This chapter addresses these questions through exploration of scholarship on consumer culture in Russia from the beginning of the 1990s to 2015. The chapter contributes to discussion on postsocialist consumerism, global consumer culture and the effects of global capitalism on former non-market economies.

The article is structured as follows. First, I discuss the approaches to consumer culture in Russia and provide a brief literature review. After that I proceed to topical discussions that exist in scholarship on Russian consumption, namely, state and patriotic consumption, evolution of the retail trade, transformations in class structure and consumer practices. In conclusion, I will address recent developments in consumption in Russia in the context of prospective topics for future research.

Consumer culture and postsocialism

Whether Russia was and is a consumer society is a controversial question. Some scholars reserve the concepts of consumer society and consumer culture for western societies (Sassatelli, 2007; Slater, 2008). Consumer culture can be considered as a set of values, norms and meanings that is built around individual consumption. Thus, consumption is a central activity in such a culture; that is, identity construction is based on consumption; social organization, social relations and daily life are market-driven. Few scholars who studied consumption in Soviet Russia share this view and argue that Soviet society was not a consumer society because Soviet people were not active consumers as there were no conditions for expressing consumer choice in the "society of shortages" that characterized Soviet Russia (Humphrey, 1995). An alternative view, however, is that socialist societies, including Russia, were "indisputably consumer societies because citizens were compelled to find creative ways to negotiate the existing system" (Caldwell, 2002, p. 298). Moreover, consumerism has "long occupied a key role in consumers' relations to each other, the state, and the world" (Patico and Caldwell, 2002, p. 287).

In the 1990s Russia had survived the so-called "consumer revolution", which was understood as a shift from necessary consumption to overconsumption, from production-driven to consumption-driven modernity (Caldwell, 2002, p. 298; Il'in, 2005; Gurova, 2015). The consumer revolution was not a result of a gradual process of modernization, but rather a sea change, a reaction to liberal reforms (so-called "shock therapy") and the introduction of a market economy; therefore, scholars focus their attention on the changes and on an analysis of the "reaction to marketization" (Patico, 2008). There are at least two points of view on how to interpret a consumer revolution. According to the first point of view, which is common among Russian sociologists (for instance, Il'in, 2005), Russia went from being a "society of shortage" (Kornai, 1992) to a western-type consumer society. This transition was accompanied by such processes as globalization, westernization, homogenization and glocalization. The second viewpoint, more common among anthropologists (for example, Caldwell, 2002; Patico and Caldwell, 2002), considers former socialist countries along with western countries as different types of consumer cultures formed by different political, economic and cultural conditions. Nevertheless, these scholars point out similar processes that affected local consumer cultures with the onset and proliferation of capitalism.

Postsocialist consumption: Previous research

The topic of consumption and postsocialism was studied mostly in the fields of sociology, anthropology of consumption, cultural history and social history. The cultures of consumption in postsocialist countries, including Russia, have been explored since the beginning of the 1990s, mostly by American and British anthropologists who applied an ethnographic approach to study daily life in the context of expanding capitalism in the former socialist states. The majority of these researchers describe market transformations and the consequences of the consumer revolution. The shared argument is that postsocialist consumer culture represents "configurations of old and new cultural products and practices, and the complex articulation of global commodities in local settings" (Patico and Caldwell, 2002, p. 285; Shevchenko, 2009; see also Humphrey and Mandel, 2002; Patico, 2008). Indeed, the market economy appeared in a society with existing forms of consumption. Thus, the transformation was not a "clash of two systems", socialism and capitalism, but a complex encounter of systems with specific, culturally embedded institutions and practices (Humphrey and Mandel, 2002, p. 2).

Unlike previously discussed research, scholarship devoted to consumption in the 2000s is focused on what can be called "really existing capitalism" and mostly belongs to the fields of sociology of consumption, cultural and media studies, gender studies and marketing. This scholarship continues to utilize the argument about the legacy of socialism and its effects on the culture of consumption, yet there is a shift in the discussions from the transition to capitalism to newly emergent phenomena studied in the context of the peculiarities of Russian capitalism. Several interdisciplinary volumes that touch upon the themes related to consumption in the 2000s explore issues of media and the ideology of consumption in the first decade of the 2000s such as glamour (Rosenholm, Nordenstreng and Trubina, 2010; Goscilo and Strukov, 2011). The peculiarities of branding, advertising and, in general, consumer culture in Russia as an emerging market (Roberts, 2016) have been researched. In addition, clothing consumption and its changes since the 1990s at several levels of retail trade and the ideology of consumption and daily practices have also been explored (Gurova, 2015). In Russian-language academic discourse, consumer culture is mostly studied by sociologists and is approached from the point of view of application of the concept of consumer society to Russia (see, for instance, Volchkova, Gronow and Minina, 2001; Il'in, 2005). In addition, a broad set of studies of various empiric phenomena in the sphere of consumption (shopping, lifestyles, consumer public and downshifting) in relation to social structure (class, gender and age) are explored (see, for instance, Echevskaia, 2011; Zhurnal, 2011).

As can be seen, consumer culture in Russia is a topic that attracts scholarly attention. However, this attention is rather incomplete. There are certain themes that recur, such as the transition to a market economy and capitalism and the role of media in the formation of the ideology of consumption, yet these discussions often belong to area studies, such as Russian studies, and do not transfer to other fields in order to contribute to broader theoretical or thematic discussions on global consumption.

State and patriotic consumption

In Russia, the state takes an active part in shaping consumption. This situation is not new and specific to contemporary Russia. The "top-down" approach to consumption was a feature of the socialist era when the state regulated the production and distribution of consumer goods, discourse on consumption and daily behaviour (see, for instance, Osokina, 2001). In the 1990s, liberal reforms lessened the role of the state when market mechanisms took over the sphere of consumption. At the same time, state-citizen relations in the context of a market economy have been studied in the frameworks of patriotic consumption, which reflects the choice of one's own country's brands and products rather than imports (Caldwell, 2002; Gromasheva and Brunori, 2014; Gurova, 2017).

Anthropologists explore how attitudes towards domestic and imported products changed in postsocialist Russia because of the process of globalization (Humphrey, 1995; Caldwell, 2002; Patico, 2008). At the beginning of the 1990s, imported goods that had not been widely available in socialist times poured into the country because of the liberalization of trade, and consumers rushed to buy them. They perceived the goods in terms of a dichotomy: "ours" or "not ours" (Humphrey, 1995; Caldwell, 2002; Patico, 2008, p. 107). Initially consumers were curious and often found that the taste and quality of imported – "not our" – goods were superior (Caldwell, 2002, p. 302). As Humphrey (1995) notes, already in 1993 the attitude toward imported consumer goods was more complex. Muscovites preferred domestically produced goods – "our" goods – at least in the case of food; consumption of "our" goods became a new form of political statement (Patico, 2008).

In her study of Muscovites, Caldwell (2002, p. 297) argues that Russians express their national belonging through such food choices not only in reaction to globalization, but also, more specifically, in a way of refashioning consumer market capitalism practices in a more familiar socialist manner in order to maintain the values of sociality and collective responsibility recognizable as socialist ethics. Caldwell calls this phenomenon "commercialized nationalism", by which she means the purchase of goods that "reflect specifically Russian values and attributes" (pp. 296–297). According to Caldwell, through these shared consumer choices, consumers commit to a collective and publicly situate themselves within an imagined national community of Russians (p. 297).

Alternatively, according to Patico (2008), her interviewees (teachers from St. Petersburg) at the end of the 1990s rarely justified their choice from the point of view of "patriotic duty". Rather, they applied many other criteria when choosing consumer goods: geographical origin helped them to assess the quality of consumer goods while they also considered longevity and taste. Similarly, the dichotomy of "our/not our" products did not work equally in categorizing or considering all goods. For food, preferences were given to "our" products. As for non-food items, shoppers continued to prefer foreign consumer goods. Clothing made in Western Europe was seen to be of higher quality in comparison to the clothing from China, South Korea or Turkey (p. 112). In addition, as Shevchenko (2009) noted, in the 1990s the domestic technologies and electronic equipment of "white assembly" (in Europe and Northern America) were higher in the hierarchy than the technology of "yellow" assembly (Asia, except for Japan) (p. 101). In turn, research on consumer ethnocentrism, purchases based on information about the country of origin, consistently stated that Russians did perceive differences in product quality based on the country of origin (for instance, see Huddleston, Good and Stoel, 2000; Karpova, Nelson-Hodges and Tullar, 2007).

After the first decade of the 2000s, the state control over consumption became more noticeable. In a forthcoming article (Gurova, 2017), I discuss the participation of the state, business and citizens in political consumerism, which are understood as strategies to affect the decision-making process by means of and in the sphere of consumption. The state applies embargo as a political strategy: Russia banned many products during the past ten years, including Georgian wines and mineral water, Polish meat, Moldovan wine, Latvian fish and Ukrainian sweets and also promoted a discourse on the formation of a patriotic subject. Business plays along with these rules providing and selling products advertised in line with this ideology of patriotism. Consumers also express their views and citizenship through consumption or non-consumption, acting in line with or against the ideology of consumer patriotism promoted by the state.

Therefore, the researchers discussed state-citizens' relationships to consumption with the focus on "our/not our" commodities. The purchase of locally produced items was considered a sign of anti-global or nostalgic sentiments in the 1990s and early 2000s, whereas later, in the second decade of the 2000s, the state has become heavily involved in promoting patriotism through consumption. A greater number of people have recognized consumption as a way of expressing their views and patriotism.

Media, glamour and gender representations

Changes in the sphere of media, such as the emergence and proliferation of glossy magazines in the 1990s and digital media in the 2010s and, as a consequence, a growing variety of discourses and transformations of the ideology of consumption and representations of masculinity and femininity are popular topics of research in sociology, media studies and gender studies (Gudova and Rakipova, 2010; Rosenholm, Nordenstreng and Trubina, 2010; Goscilo and Strukov, 2011; Ratilainen, 2015).

In Soviet Russia the state was responsible for the formation of the dominant discourse and ideology of consumption and the set of socially proven norms and attitudes. The media market has evolved significantly since the mid-1990s with the proliferation of glossy magazines contributing to the development of market-driven consumer culture. The arrival of glossy magazines announced a change in the politics of style, imagery, gender representations and consumption practices (see Bartlett, 2006, p. 176). The journals also served as educational tools for mastering new patterns and norms of a new consumer culture (Bartlett, 2006; Gurova, 2015).

Glossy magazines in Russia and the ideology of glamour that they channel became a popular topic of research. The glamorous lifestyle promoted by glossy magazines is understood as a lifestyle that appreciates larger- or smaller-scale luxuries as a recurrent source of pleasure (Ratilainen, 2015). In the scholarship glamour is presented not only as a lifestyle, but also as the new dominant ideology of the first decade of the 2000s (Gusarova, 2008; Menzel, 2008; Mesropova, 2008;

Rudova, 2008; Gudova and Rakipova, 2010; Goscilo and Strukov, 2011). Luxury, wealth and conspicuous consumption as tropes of this ideology have become a national ideal and "a matter of national pride" (Menzel, 2008, p. 4; Rudova, 2008, p. 2). The ideology of glamour represents a mix that unites the past, present and future of the country with global and local tendencies. This serves as a sign of the increased well-being of the country, and a consequent "dramatic upsurge of consumerism" (Goscilo and Strukov, 2011) occurred after the upheavals of the 1990s.

Glamour is linked to the class structure of Russian society. Initially it reflected the lifestyle of the elites that trickled down to the masses (Gusarova, 2008). Scholars portray glamour as a part of the lifestyle of the new elite (Ratilainen, 2012) and middle class (Klingseis, 2011; Gurova, 2015). They also depict the glamour of the working class (Kuleva, 2015). The trickling down of glamour to the lower classes occurs because glamour not only gives a sense of belonging to contemporary consumer culture, but through visual symbols, it also offers an illusion of upward social mobility, which is otherwise hindered in Russia (Gusarova, 2008, p. 16).

Glamour is connected to politics, and scholars discuss "peaceful co-existence" (Mesropova, 2008). On the one hand, being a new national idea of the early 2000s, based on well-being and the expression of wealth, glamour has become a convenient means for fostering people's non-participation in politics (Mesropova, 2008, p. 13). On the other hand, politicians themselves have become a part of the glamorous discourse with the president, Vladimir Putin, as the ultimate celebrity (see Goscilo and Strukov, 2011). This status quo, however, was disrupted in 2011 when political protests after election frauds revealed that not all citizens were ready to exchange their material well-being for political passivity. This was a sign of the decline of the ideology of glamour and the rise of patriotic consumption, which was discussed in the previous section of this chapter (see Gurova, 2015, p. 164).

Glossy media productions convey new representations of femininity compared to the Soviet magazines. Postsocialist Russia's media discourse promoted the "beauty myth", reclaiming traditional femininity after years of prescribed gender equality between men and women. Furthermore, in the 1990s, the sexualisation of popular culture occurred and resulted in the shift towards commodified and objectified female body representations (Ratilainen, 2015, p. 95). As a result, the demand to beautify oneself, to care about the body and physical appearance became key components of performing femininity in Russia (Porteous, 2013). At the same time, recent post-feminist discourse has been formed in the media in which beauty practices and consumption are considered as a means of empowerment of women, because they give them freedom of self-expression (Gudova and Rakipova, 2010, p. 95). For men, especially those involved in business, belonging to the middle and upper class, consumption has also become an important manifestation of dominant masculinity. Therefore, men's magazines in Russia pay attention to symbols of status (cars, watches, ties, etc.) that embody prestige, success and power (Yurchak, 2001; Pietilä, 2010).

Thus, scholarship in media and consumer culture, focused on glamour, portrays this new dominant ideology of consumption of the beginning of the 2000s as transmitted ideas of luxury, wealth and beauty as well as promoted images of consumer-oriented femininity and masculinity.

Retail trade: New formats and retail outlets

Changes in organizational forms of retail and in the culture of service are scrutinized by scholars, with attention to how new spaces of consumption proliferate and replace old retail spaces (Zhelnina, 2009, 2011; Pachenkov, 2011; Gurova, 2015). Scholars discuss the so-called "retail revolution" (Radaev, 2007) as retail has been one of the leading sectors of postsocialist economies in the 1990s and 2000s (see Gurova, 2015, p. 34).

One new phenomenon in the retail realm of the 1990s that gained scholarly attention was the rise of the shuttle traders, that is, individual entrepreneurs, mostly women, who travelled for shopping outside of Russia (mostly to Turkey, China and Poland), shopped for consumer goods, brought them back and sold them at open-air markets, in kiosks or via other vendors (Yükseker, 2007; Mukhina, 2014). Shuttle traders emerged in the process of transition from a socialist to a capitalist economy and by the mid-1990s retailing in Russia was in the hands of individual entrepreneurs before it was taken over by large-scale retail chains and corporations. By the end of the 1990s, shuttle traders had disappeared because of the economic crisis of 1998, the collapse of the national currency and newly introduced regulations governing the transit of goods.

The major tendency since the beginning of the 2000s is the proliferation of so-called "civilized retailing" which replaced individual trade and the "uncivilized" and "dirty" open-air-markets that flourished in Russia in the 1990s (Zhelnina, 2009, p. 51; 2011; Pachenkov, 2011). In the 1990s, when free trade was allowed, many people became involved in trading activities, which were often concentrated in the open-air markets. Vendors there were rarely legal and did not pay taxes. They were not only ambitious in developing their own businesses, but they were also "survivors" who wanted to get immediate cash in the times of economic hardship. Zhelnina (2009) explores how these open-air markets were closed down in St. Petersburg by the authorities and replaced with organized large-scale retail. Although the authorities considered such change in a positive way, as the modernization of trade, Zhelnina (2009, p. 54) argues that from many perspectives they were not positive. For instance, not only did certain retail formats disappear and people lose their jobs, but the new shopping malls affected the face of the city as their aesthetics did not always conform to the style of the historical surroundings. Flea markets faced the same difficulties as open-air markets. However, for instance, the fate of the *Udel'nyi* flea market in St. Petersburg differs from the fate of the other open-air markets. It was reinvented as a cultural and historical phenomenon important to St. Petersburg as a European city and the so-called "cultural capital" of Russia. This flea market is considered a "place of nostalgia" and an "open-air museum", which corresponds to the image of the city (Pachenkov, 2011, p. 198).

Shopping malls as a popular retail format are seen as celebrating the middle-class culture of consumption in which class, brands, leisure and pleasure matter (Zhelnina, 2011; Gurova, 2015). Being the space symbolically owned by the middle class, the malls create boundaries for those who do not belong; hence, they are privatized and commercialized quasi-public spaces meant for particular groups of people (Zhelnina, 2011).

In general, scholars emphasize the conceptual changes that occurred in relation to the shopping experience. In socialist times the process of purchasing goods was hindered by shortages, because demand exceeded supply; therefore, consumers had to expend considerable effort in order to obtain the goods. During postsocialist times, the birth of the "hedonistic consumer" led by desire and pleasure rather than need and necessity was observed (Gurova, 2015, p. 67); a shift to recreational shopping occurred. However, the consumers still perceive shopping as a "hard job", because it is a time-consuming practice in the context of increased choice (Gurova, 2015, p. 45). As for customer service, scholars mostly point out shifts in retail during postsocialist times and do not often compare socialist and postsocialist service. The highlighted shifts are in the standardization and depersonalization of service that characterizes modern retail formats, such as shopping malls (Zhelnina, 2009; Pachenkov, 2011).

Thus, the evolution of retail formats in a former socialist state illustrates the spread of transnational corporations, the take-over of local markets by global retailers who bring a standardized service culture. It also shows how shopping malls formed the middle-class culture of consumption and how boundaries are produced by and reflected in retail formats.

Everyday consumer practices and social structure

The issue of social differences in consumption is covered by scholars with attention to the emergence of a postsocialist middle class and its lifestyles (Gladarev and Tsinman, 2009). In addition, scholars study consumer practices in the consumption of food (Ganskau, 2001; Gromasheva and Brunori, 2014); fashion (Klingseis, 2011; Gurova, 2015); home and housing (Gladarev and Tsinman, 2009); leisure (Roshchina, 2007) and communication technologies (Lonkila and Gladarev, 2008).

During socialism Russia had been a society with relatively homogenous income distribution. At the beginning of the 1990s, it was a country with a growing gap between the rich and the poor (Kalabekov, 2015, p. 746). The attention of scholars was attracted to the newly rich, the so-called New Russians, a group of entrepreneurs who gained their capital, not necessarily legally, during the transitional period of the 1990s (Oushakine, 2000; Patico, 2008; Ratilainen, 2012). The New Russians were notorious for their attachment to expensive labelled goods, crimson suits, thick gold chains and Mercedes automobiles; in general, they flaunted their wealth in public. Oushakine (2000) called their consumption strategy "the quantitative strategy" in the context of "symbolic shortage" because they demonstrated their money by multiplying in quantity the former socialist symbols of well-being; thus, they exaggerated symbols that were already familiar signs of success: super-thick golden chains or multiple rings on every finger, or wearing a very expensive suit or tie (pp. 107–109).

During the 1990s, a new postsocialist middle class emerged. It included a group of "mass intelligentsia" that belonged to the Soviet middle class, new professionals (managers, bank clerks, IT specialists, etc.) and small business owners. Jennifer Patico (2008) explores the middle-class lifestyle, taking as an example a particular group: teachers in St Petersburg. The teachers were the representatives of the Soviet "mass intelligentsia", who in the 1990s experienced downward mobility in terms of income, but belonged to the postsocialist middle class based on their cultural capital (p. 12). Patico identifies two tropes that characterized the lifestyle and consumption patterns of the middle class: "culturedness", which draws on Soviet norms of modesty and propriety, and "civilization", which articulates the anxieties related to, on the one hand, the process of globalization and, on the other hand, the desire for greater access to consumer commodities from the west. Thus, a middle-class person is viewed as someone who aspires to both material well-being and, at the same time, the kind of moral virtues and certain taste that money cannot buy (Patico, 2008; Gurova, 2015).

In the scholarship of the 2000s, the middle class is defined according to four criteria: education (a college degree or higher), occupation (white collar or entrepreneurial), income (higher than average in the region) and self-identification with the middle class (Gladarev and Tsinman, 2009). According to estimates, from 20 to 22 percent in 2006 to 42 percent in 2014 belonged to the middle class (see Gurova, 2015, p. 3). The middle class is seen as one that shares patterns of a common lifestyle that is evolving (Gladarev and Tsinman, 2009; Patico, 2008; Gurova, 2015). In terms of food, scholars showed how food consumption practices of the middle class shifted from widespread home-cooked meals in the mid-1990s (Ganskau, 2001) to meals eaten in fast-food restaurants and cafes (Caldwell, 2002, 2009). Clothing consumption is studied from the point of view of communicating a "sense of belonging" and also a "sense of superiority" that is a form of symbolic violence and aids in the construction of class boundaries (Klingseis, 2011). Recently, new trends in sustainable consumption and fashion have emerged in the middle-class lifestyle (Gurova, 2015, pp. 149–151). In general, Gladarev and Tsinman (2009, pp. 200–201) explored the lifestyle of the St. Petersburg middle class in the first decade of the 2000s and found that its representatives "invest in the future", as they spend money on real estate, education and health.

The middle-class citizens in Russia prefer to have a flat that has been recently renovated according to both modern standards and individualized design. They invest in education and self-development, because cultural capital is as important to them as income. They also put money into private health care and sports and recreational practices for the purpose of maintaining good health. For similar reasons, leisure and free time are important; therefore, home duties are sometimes outsourced to hired labour (nannies, cleaning ladies). Vacation, as a rule, is an obligatory part of the urban middle-class lifestyle, often spent in the form of an annual family tour abroad.

According to the studies of consumption of the lower classes (Echevskaia, 2011, pp. 90–97), it was found that lower classes purchase consumer goods according to plan, only rarely practise spontaneous purchases, prefer to buy habitual rather than unexpected goods and opt for home production of food instead of eating out or buying prepared food. Kuleva (2015) in her study of working class youth noted that its representatives use consumption and fashion to imitate the consumer patterns of the middle class. The working-class youth prefer to shop at the shopping malls and avoid alternative retail channels, such as second-hand stores and flea markets that are popular among the middle-class youth, as those channels are not seen by the working-class youth as source of fashionable things. They draw boundaries between classes through not accepting some of the middle-class subcultural styles, such as hipsters or emo, in which clothing transgresses the traditional gender order (on postsocialist youth cultures, see Omelchenko and Sabirova, 2015).

Thus, the research on consumption and social structure illustrates how lifestyles are formed as derivatives of economic and cultural capital. The major attention is given to middle-class consumption, which embodied values of postsocialist consumer culture. So far little research has been done on the rich and the poor. Such spheres as the consumption of digital media or new means of communications are also yet to be researched (see, however, Ratilainen 2016).

Conclusion: Current issues and future research

In conclusion, what are the current topical issues on consumption in Russia? First and foremost, the main tendency, which I already mentioned above, is the replacement of the ideology of glamour with the ideology of patriotism. The ideology of glamour has dominated since the beginning of the 2000s and began to slowly decline after the economic crises of 2008–2009. A discourse on patriotic consumption has become more intense in the context of sanctions introduced by the Russian authorities in response to western sanctions and the politics of phasing out imports (*importozameshchenie*) in 2014–2015. Anti-American and anti-European sentiments, transmitted in the official discourse of the state, have added to citizens' patriotic feelings. The question is, how do citizens perceive this politics and how have their practices been changed? The general issue of state influence on consumption in the case of the contemporary authoritarian state is also of interest: to what extent does the state affect consumption in a market-driven economy? Second, Russia is currently facing an economic crisis due to the decline of oil prices and, as a consequence, the country's income, which has led to a collapse of the national currency. The question is, how will people cope with this economic crisis and adjust consumption practices to new circumstances? According to reports, currently the main strategy of households is to reduce consumption (Razgovory, 2015). However, a more nuanced analysis perhaps could reveal new emerging practices as happened earlier in 2008–2009, when collaborative consumption had been pushed by economic crisis. Third, various forms of collaborative consumption that have been developed in Russia (as well as in other countries) during the past several years could be explored in comparison with practices of sharing goods that were wide-spread in socialist times. Fourth, in Russia, the discourse on sustainable consumption has been emerging, but is still nascent. At the same time, the discussion on the decline of food quality and the use of new technologies in food production (GMO) is a new critical discourse that is growing and can affect both institutions and practices of consumption in the future.

References

Bartlett, D. (2006), In Russia, at last and forever: The first seven years of Russian vogue. *Fashion Theory*, vol. 10, no. 1–2, pp. 175–204.

Caldwell, M. (2002), The taste of nationalism: Food politics in postsocialist Moscow. *Ethnos*, vol. 67, no. 3, 295–319.

Caldwell, M. (2009), 'Tempest in a coffee pot. Brewing incivility in Russia's public sphere,' in M. Caldwell (ed), *Food and everyday life in the postsocialist world*, pp. 101–129. Bloomington & Indianapolis: Indiana university press.

Echevskaia, O. (2011), *Potreblenie i razlichie: Sotsial'nye znacheniia i praktiki potrebitel'skogo povedeniia gorozhan* [Consumption and distinctions: Social meanings and consumer practices of urban dwellers]. Novosibirsk: Novosibirskii gosudarstvennyi universitet.

Ganskau, E. (2001), 'Obraztsy potrebleniia produktov pitaniia v sankt-peterburgskikh sem'iakh [Patterns of food consumption of families in St. Petersburg],' in L.T. Volchkova, J. Gronow, & V.N. Minina (eds), *Sotsiologiia potrebleniia*, pp. 109–129. St. Petersburg: Sotsiologicheskoe obshchestvo im. Kovalevskoi.

Gladarev, B. and Tsinman, Zh. (2009), 'Dom, shkola, vrachi i muzei: potrebitel'skie praktiki srednego klassa [A home, a school and a museum: Consumer practices of the middle class],' in E. Zdravomyslova, A. Rotkirch, & A. Tiomkina (eds), *Novyi byt v sovremennoi Rossii: gendernye issledovaniia povsednevnosti*, pp. 189–221. St. Petersburg: European University at St. Petersburg press.

Goscilo, H. and Strukov, V. (eds.) (2011), *Celebrity and glamour in contemporary Russia*. New York & London: Routledge.

Gromasheva, O. and Brunori, G. (2014), Proizvodstvo, sbyt i potreblenie v Sankt-Peterburge: plodorodnaia pochva dlia razvitiia korotkikh tsepochek postavok fermerskikh produktov? [Production, distribution and consumption favorable environment for development of short food supply chains?]. *Labirint*, vol. 2, pp. 35–51.

Gudova, M.Y. and Rakipova, I. (2010), *Zhenskie gliantsevye zhurnaly: khronotop voobrazhaemoi povsednevnosti* [Women's glossy magazines: Imagined everyday reality] Ekaterinburg: Izdatel'stvo Ural'skogo universiteta.

Gurova, O. (2015), *Fashion and the consumer revolution in contemporary Russia*. London and New York: Routledge.

Gurova, O. (2017, forthcoming), 'Political consumerism in Russia after 2011', in A. Etkind, B. Beumers, S. Turoma, & O. Gurova (eds), *Cultural mechanisms of political protest in Russia*. London & New York: Routledge.

Gusarova, K. (2008), 'The deviant norm: Glamour in Russian fashion,' *Kultura*, vol. 6, pp. 14–19.

Huddleston, P., Good, L.K., and Stoel, L. (2000), Consumer ethnocentrism, product necessity and quality perceptions of Russian consumers. *The International Review of Retail, Distribution and Consumer Research*, vol. 10, no. 2, pp. 167–181.

Humphrey, C. (1995), 'Creating a culture of disillusionment: Consumption in Moscow, a chronicle of changing times,' in D. Miller (ed), *Worlds apart: Modernity through the prism of the local*, pp. 43–68. London: Routledge.

Humphrey, C. and Mandel, R. (2002), 'The market in everyday life: Ethnographies of postsocialism,' in R. Mandel, & C. Humphrey (eds), *Markets and moralities. Ethnographies of postsocialism*, pp. 1–16. Oxford & New York: Berg publishers.

Il'in, V. (2005), 'Obshchestvo potrebleniia: teoreticheskaia model' i rossiiskaia real'nost' [A consumer society: Theoretical model and reality in Russia],' *Mir Rossii*, vol. 14, no. 2, pp. 3–40.

Kalabekov, I.G. (2015), *Rossiiskie reformy v tsifrakh i faktakh* [Reforms in Russia in numbers and facts]. Retrieved from http://refru.ru/

Karpova, E., Nelson-Hodges, N., and Tullar, W. (2007), 'Making sense of the market. An exploration of apparel consumption practices of the Russian consume,'. *Journal of Fashion Marketing and Management*, vol. 11, no. 1, pp.106–121.

Kornai, J. (1992), *The socialist system: the political economy of communism.* Princeton, New Jersey: Princeton University press.

Klingseis, K. (2011), 'The power of dress in contemporary Russian society: On glamour discourse and the everyday practice of getting dressed in Russian cities,' *Laboratorium*, vol. 3, no. 1, pp. 84–115.

Kuleva, M. (2015), *Constructing identities and boundaries: Fashion and clothing of working and middle-class youth in contemporary Russia.* Working papers by Basic Research Programme. Series HUM "Humanities", 85. Retrieved from http://www.hse.ru/data/2015/02/03/1105972777/85HUM2015.pdf

Lonkila, M. and Gladarev, B. (2008), Social networks and cellphone use in Russia: Local consequences of global communication technology. *New Media & Society*, *10*(2), 273-293.

Menzel, B. (2008), Russian discourse on glamour, *Kultura*, vol. 6, pp. 4–8.

Mesropova, O. (2008), 'I choose Russia – I choose glamour!' *Kultura*, vol. 6, pp. 12–14.

Mukhina, I. (2014), *Women and the birth of Russian capitalism. A history of the shuttle trade.* DeKalb, IL: Northern Illinois University press.

Omelchenko, E. and Sabirova, G. (2015), 'Youth cultures in contemporary Russia: Memory, politics, solidarities,' in M. Schwartz, and H. Winkel (eds), *Eastern european youth cultures in a global context*, pp. 253–270. New York: Palgrave Macmillan.

Osokina, E. (2001), *Our daily bread: socialist distribution and the art of survival.* Armonk, NY, London, England: M.E. Sharpe.

Oushakine, S.A. (2000), 'The quantity of style. Imaginary consumption in the New Russia,' *Theory, Culture and Society*, vol. 17, no. 5, pp. 97–120.

Pachenkov, O. (2011), 'Every city has the flea market it deserves: The phenomenon of urban flea markets in St. Petersburg,' in T. Darieva, W. Kaschuba, & M. Krebs (eds), *Urban spaces after socialism: Ethnographies of public places in Eurasian cities*, pp. 181–206. Frankfurt/New York: Ed. Campus Verlag.

Patico, J. (2008), *Consumption and social change in a post-soviet middle class.* Stanford: Stanford University press.

Patico, J. and Caldwell, M. (2002), 'Consumers existing socialism: Ethnographic perspectives on daily life in post-communist Europe,' *Ethnos*, vol. 67, no. 3, pp. 285–294.

Pietilä, I. (2010), 'Eastern cowboys: Masculine selves and coping with stressful life in the Russian edition of Men's Health magazine,' in A. Rosenholm, K. Nordenstreng, & E. Trubina (eds), *Russian mass media and changing values*, pp. 115–133. London & New York: Routledge.

Porteous, H. (2013), 'There are no ugly women, only lazy ones' – The duty of beauty labour in contemporary Russian women's magazines,' in H. Ehlers, G. Linke, N. Milewski, B. Rudlof & H. Trappe (eds), *Körper – geschlecht – wahrnehmung: sozial- und geisteswissenschaftliche*, pp. 133–156. Berlin: Verlag.

Radaev, V. (2007), Zakhvat rossiiskikh territorii: novaia konkurentnaia situatsiia v roznichnoi torgovle [Takeover of Russian territory: A new situation in retail trade]. Moskva: Izdatel'skii Dom GU-VSHE.

Ratilainen, S. (2012), 'Business for pleasure: Elite women in the Russian popular media,' in S. Salmenniemi (ed), *Rethinking class in Russia*, pp. 45–65. London: Ashgate.

Ratilainen, S. (2015), 'Old title, new traditions. Negotiating ideals of femininity in *Krest'ianka* magazine,' *Feminist Media Studies*, vol. 15, no. 1, pp. 92–112.

Ratilainen, S. (2016) 'Russian Digital Lifestyle and the Construction of Global Selves,' in M. Suslov, M. Bassin (eds.), Eurasia 2.0. Russian Geopolitics in the Age of New Media, pp. 3-24. Lanham: Lexington books.

Razgovory v pol'zu srednikh [Talks in favor of middle class] (2015), Retrieved from: http://www.levada.ru/2015/12/14/razgovory-v-polzu-srednih/

Roberts, G.H.J. (2016), *Consumer culture, branding and identity in New Russia.* London & New York: Routledge.

Rosenholm, A., Nordenstreng, K., and Trubina, E. (eds) (2010), *Russian mass media and changing values.* London & New York: Routledge.

Roshchina, Y. (2007), 'Differentsiatsiia stilei zhizni v pole dosuga [Differentiation of lifestyles in the field of leisure],' *Sotsiologicheskie issledovaniia*, vol. 8, no. 4, pp. 23–42.

Rudova, L. (2008), 'Uniting Russian glamour', *Kultura*, vol. 6, pp. 2–3.

Sassatelli, R. (2007), *Consumer culture. History, theory and politics.* London: Sage publications.

Shevchenko, O. (2009), *Crisis and the everyday in postsocialist Moscow.* Bloomington: Indiana University press.

Slater, D. (2008), *Consumer culture and modernity.* Cambridge: Polity press.

Volchkova, L.T., Gronow, J., and Minina, V.N. (eds) (2001), *Sotsiologiia potrebleniia* [Sociology of consumption]. St. Petersburg: Sotsiologicheskoe obshchestvo im. M.M. Kovalevskogo.

Yükseker, D. (2007), 'Shuttling goods, weaving consumer tastes: Informal trade between Turkey and Russia,' *International Journal of Urban and Regional Research*, vol. 31, no. 1, pp. 60–72.

Yurchak, A. (2001), 'Muzhskaia ekonomika: "Ne do glupostei, kogda kar'eru kuesh'" [Men's economy: No time for silly things when building a career],' *Neprikosnovennyi zapas*, 5. Retrieved from: http://magazines.russ.ru/nz/2001/5/ur.html

Zhelnina, A. (2009), 'From barakholka to shopping mall: Transformation of retail spaces in St. Petersburg,' *Anthropology of East Europe Review*, vol. 27, no. 1, pp. 51–56.

Zhelnina, A. (2011), '"It's like a museum here": The shopping mall as public space,' *Laboratorium*, vol, 2, pp. 132–136.

Zhurnal. (2011), *sotsiologii i sotsial'noi antropologii* [Journal of sociology and social anthropology], vol. 15. no. 5.

15

Bridging North/South divides through consumer driven networks

Laura T. Raynolds

Introduction

Scholars and activists have sought to identify avenues for addressing rising global disparities, focusing largely on reconfiguring production. This chapter shifts our focus to the realm of consumption, exploring the challenges and opportunities for consumers and consumption activities to help bridge global North/South divides. How can consumers confront growing inequalities and foster global social justice through their consumption activities? My analysis builds theoretically on political economy approaches to explaining North/South inequalities in production/consumption networks and social movement approaches to explaining the role of consumers and their actions in promoting global social justice. I propose that a theoretical synthesis of these approaches is essential for understanding the possibilities for bridging North/South divides, since a political economy approach best explains the historically rooted structures that undergird global inequalities while a social movement perspective identifies most clearly the power of social actors to challenge those inequalities.

To ground this analysis, I draw on the case of fair trade.[1] Fair trade illuminates the intersection of structural market forces and social movement agency and the promise and pitfalls for consumer driven networks in challenging global inequalities. In principle, *fair trade* refers to a critique of the historical inequalities inherent in international trade and to a belief that trade can be made more socially just. In practice, it is best known for the work of Fairtrade International affiliates in creating new consumer/producer networks for labeled commodities, most popularly coffee, chocolate, and tea, produced by disadvantaged farmers and workers in the global South for sale in the global North. With US$7 billion in annual sales (FTI, 2014), Fairtrade certification represents one of the most successful contemporary efforts to harness consumer power in challenging global inequalities. This chapter explains how fair trade, and Fairtrade International in particular, work to bridge global North/South divides through consumer/producer networks, identifying the successes, but also the limitations in escaping colonial-based trade relations, top-down regulation, corporate dominance, and the privileging of consumer purchasing power.

Contributions from political economy

Political economy scholars focus on understanding the intersecting political and economic forces that generate inequalities in national and international arenas. An extensive literature seeks to explain the nature and consequences of ongoing globalization, identifying historical-political economic continuities and discontinuities. Research highlights ways in which capitalist economic relations and international political relations uphold patterns of inequality established in the colonial era, evidenced to this day in the division between affluent countries of the global North and poorer countries of the global South. International political economy theories locate the genesis of the global North/South divide within the structures of political hegemony established under colonialism and the international division of labor which positioned the global South as a supplier of low-value products to be consumed in the global North. In addition to explaining the historically rooted structures that undergird global inequalities, political economy has sought to identify the novel facets of globalization transforming the world economy (McMichael, 2008).

Analysis of the embeddedness of economic transactions within broader societal dynamics of production and consumption deepens our understanding of globalization and inequality. Polanyi challenges a neo-classical view of the autonomous self-regulating market, arguing that economic activity is always shaped by social and political institutions. As he asserts, the "human economy is an instituted process" that is "embedded and enmeshed in institutions, economic and noneconomic" (1957b, p. 250). Recent studies demonstrate how political and economic spheres are mutually constituted and embedded within society (Block & Evans, 2005). Gereffi (1994) develops an institutionalist view of the embedded nature of "global commodity chains," which involve the interlinking of products and services in a sequence of value-added activities, organizational and spatial ties between enterprises comprising global networks, and governance structures which allocate resources among network participants. Global commodity/value chain analysis has been used extensively to reveal the transnational organization of production, trade, and retail activities in industrial (Gereffi, Humphrey, & Sturgeon, 2005) and agro-food sectors (Raynolds, 2004). Gereffi argues that over time power has shifted from producers to buyers, with distributors exerting increasing control over their suppliers through "buyer-driven" global chains. Validating this argument, Dolan and Humphrey (2000) demonstrate how dominant retailers in the global North control international supply chains and the market opportunities of producers. A key strength of the commodity/value chain framework lies in the injunction to analyze relations from production to consumption, yet, reflecting political economy's production focus, buyers in "buyer-driven" chains are typically identified as retailers, not consumers.

Veblen's (1899) classic work helps develop a political economy of consumption. Veblen supports an institutionalist and embedded view of the economy, locating consumers within economic networks which are simultaneously political arenas for upholding class divides. As he argues, consumption is not simply a mechanism for satisfying wants; it is a form of strategic action to reflect, protect, and gain social standing. Veblen shows how the upper class pursues "conspicuous consumption," purchasing and displaying luxury goods to signal their superior class position, and the lower class seeks, as budgets permit, to emulate this consumption. Veblen is concerned with how consumption thus solidifies national class boundaries, but his insights can logically be extended to explain how in the current era wealthy Northern consumers drive global consumption patterns, shape worldwide aspirations, and cement North/South divides between the few who can and the majority who cannot afford to engage in conspicuous consumption. Although Veblen's contributions have not been fully appreciated in international political economy (Archer & Fritsch, 2010), Sklair (2002) for example demonstrates the transnational nature of the capitalist class, consumerist culture, and consumers' position in commodity chains.

While Veblen augments the political economy perspective through a social view of consumption (Reisman, 2012), most consumption scholars favor Bourdieu's (1984) constructivist cultural theory. Bourdieu argues that people's tastes are shaped by an internal schema (habitus) rooted in cultural, social, and economic experiences which uphold class-based consumption practices and lifestyles. From this vantage point, consumption is seen as a central field for individual and collective self-expression and identity creation, and consumer products are defined as much by their symbolic as their material value. An extensive literature builds on Bourdieu's insights regarding class culture, consumption, and everyday social distinction. Research finds that in the global North, consumption by high cultural capital consumers is guided by cosmopolitanism which for many includes social and environmental principles (Holt, 1998). As Bourdieu argues, food is a key arena in which social differentiation is affirmed and revealed, and a rising number of Northern consumers purchase specialty food items to proclaim their values (Clarke, Barnett, Cloke, & Malpass, 2007) and perform their distinctive, often privileged, lifestyle (Johnston, 2008).

Lamont (2012) argues that a constructivist view should be re-aligned with political economy concerns through "sociology of valuation and evaluation." From this perspective, goods are transformed into consumer products through qualification processes which render them valuable to consumers. Consumer products are thus valued not simply for their utility, but their morality (Zelizer, 2011). Analysis of the normative foundations of consumption aligns with Polanyi's view that economic activity is not always guided by rational economic logic (Beckert, 2013). Convention theorists argue that specific and potentially variable norms underpin economic networks, fundamentally shifting the nature of products, exchange relations, and organizational forms (Boltanski & Thévenot, 2006). This approach illuminates the industrial and commercial norms which prioritize product standardization and price competition in mainstream market relations, privileging transnational corporations and maintaining historical North/South inequalities, as well as the nature of alternative consumer/producer networks founded on ethical, ecological, and place-based values which configure product standards, market relations, and institutions (Barham, 2002; Raynolds, 2002, 2004).

Contributions from social movement theory

Social movement analysis focuses on how collective action fosters social change, emphasizing the contentiousness of economic and other arenas. An extensive literature focuses on how social movements challenge and potentially transform markets (King & Pearce, 2010). Social movement theory concurs with a political economy view of markets as inherently political, embedded within social structures of inequality, and marked by competition over resources. To illuminate these connections it is helpful to return to Polanyi (1957a, p. 3), who argues that since the "self-adjusting market . . . could not exist for any length of time without annihilating the human and natural substance of society," movements arise to re-assert social control over economic activity and limit the destruction caused by commodification. Diverging from Marx's (1867) argument that commodification leads to revolution, Polanyi suggests that market encroachment fuels national governmental regulation. In the contemporary era a wide range of initiatives seek to curb commodification and promote de-commodification (Vail, 2010).

Although traditional social movements are generally motivated by economic interests and oriented to legislative changes, "new" social movements address diverse social and ecological concerns and are oriented to multiple centers of power (Buechler, 2000). With the intensification of global market rule, countermovements of social protection have similarly come to operate in global arenas. Keck and Sikkink (1998) demonstrate the importance of "transnational advocacy networks" in linking local movements to global campaigns coordinated by international non-governmental organizations (NGOs). Rather than lobbying for government regulations, social movements and NGOs have in recent years pressured corporations directly to improve their practices by "naming and shaming" poor performers, a strategy that has proved particularly effective in areas with high identity content like food and fashion (O'Rourke, 2006; Raynolds, 2004). Working to promote corporate accountability, social movements and NGOs have fostered product certification as an avenue to address human rights, environmental and other concerns. There is now a large and growing market for products which are certified for their ethical and environmental attributes (Raynolds, Long, & Murray, 2014).

An insightful literature merges political economy and social movement theories, showing how collective social and economic actors compete in strategic action fields, like markets, and through negotiation create expectations and institutions (Fligstein & McAdam, 2012). Bartley (2007) reveals how conflict between social movement groups and corporations led to the rise of transnational certification systems. Numerous studies explore the roles of corporations, industry groups, NGOs, and social movements in creating and maintaining social and environmental certification programs (Auld, 2014; Fransen, 2012). This institutionalist literature locates consumers in certified networks for organic foods, sweat-free clothing, ecological forest products, and other items from the top-down, looking at how consumers are drawn to certified products.

The political consumption literature reverses this orientation, analyzing the role of consumers as strategic actors in market arenas who may help forge new market expectations and institutions.[2] While consumption is traditionally viewed as an arena for pursuing individual self-interest, Micheletti and colleagues argue that people use the market to advance their values (Micheletti, 2003; Stolle, Hooghe, & Micheletti, 2005). Research suggests that by "voting with their dollars" a growing number of ethically minded consumers promote social justice, animal rights, and environmental concerns (Barnett, Cloke, Clarke, & Malpass, 2010). Much of this work builds on Bourdieu's (1984) view that consumption is a reflexive activity, involving a process of self-expression, value affirmation, and everyday class distinction (Adams & Raisborough, 2008). Food is a central arena of political consumption, since it is here that social and environmental concerns intersect and purchasing patterns appear most clearly to advance a progressive agenda (Barham, 2002; Raynolds, 2000). For example, DuPuis (2000) shows how reflexive consumers generated demand for organic milk in response to rising concerns over the health, safety, and sustainability of the mainstream dairy industry. Conscientious consumers have fueled markets for a range of naturally and socially responsible foods through "buycotts" where products with positive attributes are sought out and "boycotts" where products viewed negatively, like genetically modified grains and hormone intensive milk, are avoided (Goodman, DuPuis, & Goodman, 2012).

In addition to shopping in line with their values, political consumers are seen as acting strategically in choosing "particular producers or products because they want to change institutional or market practices" (Stolle et al., 2005, p. 246). From this perspective, consumption represents a form of everyday political action through which individual consumers pursue the rights and responsibilities of citizenship. Johnston (2008) reveals the complexities and contradictions in this "citizen-consumer" hybrid. Some authors fear that political consumption individualizes responsibility for social and environmental problems and can undermine more effective forms of collective political action. Yet research finds that consumers often see their purchasing as a form of collective engagement (Thompson & Coskurer-Balli, 2007), and ethical consumption is significantly and positively related to consumers' involvement in a range of political activities (Willis & Schor, 2012). Stolle and Micheletti (2015) analyze the role of Northern consumers in addressing global problems, and conclude that consumers are an increasingly important and organized political force able to bring significant changes.

Fair trade: Bridging global North/South divides

Fair trade challenges historically unequal international trade relations and seeks to foster more equitable relations by linking marginalized producers in the global South with progressive consumers in the global North. This initiative works to transform North/South trade, creating more egalitarian commodity networks particularly for colonial based agro-exports like coffee, cocoa, tea, and sugar, which historically forged global divides. Fair trade fosters fairness in the global South by alleviating poverty and empowering farmers and workers, and in the global North by fueling ethical consumption and the availability of socially responsible products. While fair trade's critique is akin to that of other social justice movements, what accounts for its success is the linking of visionary goals with practical engagements in creating ethical markets (Raynolds, Murray, & Wilkinson, 2007; Raynolds & Bennett, 2015). Millions of producers and consumers participate in the US$7 billion fair trade market.

Given its critique of capitalist economic relations and effort to re-embed international markets, fair trade can be characterized as a Polanyian countermovement of social protection (Jaffee, 2007; Raynolds, 2000, 2002). In the words of its major proponents (FINE, 2001):

> Fair Trade is a trading partnership, based on dialogue, transparency and respect, that seeks greater equity in international trade. It contributes to sustainable development by offering better trading conditions to, and securing the rights of, marginalized producers and workers – especially in the South. Fair Trade organisations (backed by consumers) are engaged actively in supporting producers, awareness raising and in campaigning for changes in the rules and practice of conventional international trade.

Fair trade thus seeks to transform capitalist relations, where products are valued based on abstract prices which devalue human and natural resources, and redefine international trade around partnership principles, where products are valued for their social and ecological content (Raynolds, 2000). In convention theory terms, fair trade questions the legitimacy of "industrial" and "commercial" norms, grounded in efficiency, standardization, and competition, and fosters alternative economic relations based on "civic" and "relational" values rooted in collective responsibility for global social and ecological well-being and personal commitment to people and places (Raynolds, 2002; Renard, 2003).

A key contradiction for fair trade is that it operates "in and against the market," working through market channels to create new trade networks for ethical products while simultaneously working against conventional market forces that generate global inequalities (Raynolds, 2000, 2002). Contestations between social movement and market principles, practices, and actors have shaped the nature and dynamics of fair trade's development along two paths: the original yet smaller direct trade model and the newer yet now dominant certification model.

NGOs and faith-based solidarity groups pioneered fair trade, purchasing handicrafts at favorable prices from Southern producers to sell to concerned Northern consumers. Informed by political economy views of the role of unequal exchange in fueling global poverty, these forerunners created direct trade channels, cutting out middlemen to increase producer returns. Fair trade was bolstered by 1960s and 1970s international social justice movements, and handicraft shops spread across North America and Europe. Direct trade was extended to coffee and tea by mission-focused companies which promoted relational ties between Southern producers and Northern consumers and civic values through support for disadvantaged producers and social justice advocacy (Raynolds, 2009, 2012). Fair trade organization sales have seen modest growth in recent years (EFTA, 2013).

What is now the dominant fair trade model was established in the 1980s using formal product certification and labeling. Social movement groups initiated this strategy to increase fair trade involvement in key agro-export sectors, where the majority of impoverished producers in the global South work, and in mainstream market venues, where the majority of Northern consumers do their shopping (Raynolds, 2009). Fairtrade International (previously Fairtrade Labelling Organizations International) was established to coordinate the certification and labeling of products by NGO market country members. Fairtrade International establishes standards for producers, who must be organized into democratic associations, uphold International Labor Organization standards, and promote ecological practices, and for importers, who must pay minimum prices and a social premium and offer producer credit and long-term contracts (FTI, 2014). An autonomous NGO, FLO-Cert, oversees compliance. The range and volume of Fairtrade certified products has risen dramatically over recent years as outlined in Table 15.1. Colonial-based agro-exports, particularly coffee, tea, and cocoa, provide the core of the Fairtrade system, supplemented by other key Southern exports like bananas, rice, and flowers.

Although fair trade has made important advances in bridging global divides and challenging North/South trade inequalities, its progressive potential is limited in three related ways. First, while fair trade originated in and remains aligned with social justice movements, it has been increasingly defined by certification and market interests in the global North. Some groups remain strongly committed to fair trade's activist agenda of supporting social justice advocacy and maximizing returns to Southern producers. But in Fairtrade certified networks, social movement ties and commitments have been eroded by mainstream market priorities and practices. Fairtrade upholds rather than overturns Southern producer dependence on agro-export markets and, as in other programs (Auld, 2014), certification maintains global power inequalities

Table 15.1 Top Fairtrade International commodities (volume, metric tons)

	2004	*2006*	*2008*	*2010*	*2012*[a]
Bananas	80,640	135,763	299,205	286,598	331,980
Sugar	1,960	7,159	56,990	126,810	158,986
Coffee	24,222	52,064	65,808	87,576	77,429[b]
Cocoa	4,201	7,913	10,299	35,179	40,559
Other Fresh Fruit	–	–	26,424	18,396	12,259
Tea	1,965	3,883	11,467	12,356	11,869
Rice	1,384	2,985	4,685	5,048	5,623
Total[c]	126,160	217,628	505,152	601,244	651,900

Source: Adapted from Raynolds and Greenfield (2015) using data from Fairtrade International.

Notes: a Column excludes Fair Trade USA sales, thus understating total certified sales.
b Figures for prior years are for roasted coffee; this is for green coffee.
c Includes other labeled commodities measured by weight.

by having a European-based standard organization dictating standards for Southern producers (Bacon, 2010; Raynolds, 2009).

The second major limit to fair trade's efforts to bridge North/South divides relates to its goal of shortening the distance between producers and consumers. Fair trade's direct trade model proposed that by eliminating intermediaries between Southern producers and Northern consumers, trade exploitation could be abolished and producers could reap greater profits. Mission-focused groups typically maintain direct trade supply chains. Yet as mainstream companies have adopted Fairtrade certified products and labeled items have multiplied, middlemen have reemerged. In coffee, corporations like Starbucks and Nestlé typically source certified beans from their regular suppliers (Bacon, 2010; Raynolds, 2009). In Fairtrade products like bananas and sugar, which involve expensive cool chains and capital-intensive processing, intermediaries play a prominent role (Raynolds, 2007). Fairtrade remains the only major certification that addresses trade inequities, yet the involvement of mainstream corporations and middlemen makes fostering trade fairness very difficult (Raynolds, 2012).

The third major barrier to fair trade's efforts to bridge North/South divides involves the challenges of de-commodification. While fair trade was founded on a critique of commoditization and alternative vision grounded in civic and relational values, its operation in, as well as against, the market has threatened these principles. Mission-focused organizations work hard to uphold social priorities, but to remain in business they must incorporate market expectations (Raynolds, 2009). Fairtrade certification's price guarantees foster de-commodification by absorbing market risks and bolstering producer returns (Hudson & Hudson, 2003; Raynolds, 2000), but do not pull producers out of poverty (Bacon, 2010; Jaffee, 2007). Fairtrade certified items are now largely sold in supermarkets, where they are held to conventional volume, quality, and price guidelines. Thus, while certification accounts for fair trade's commercial success, its imposition of conventional industrial and market values and practices threatens the movement's alternative relational and civic conventions (Raynolds, 2002, 2012; Renard, 2003).

Fair trade: Consumer-driven networks

Fair trade markets have grown across the global North. Certified agro-food products account for most sales, which generate over US$6 billion annually and are growing at 12 percent per year (FTI, 2013). Handicraft sales bring in an additional US$379 million (EFTA, 2010). As noted in Table 15.2, the United Kingdom has the world's largest fair trade market. Germany, France, Switzerland, and the Netherlands also have well developed markets. Fairtrade's twenty certified commodities and numerous composite products are readily available across Europe. Certified products are not stocked as widely in North America and many US fair trade organizations prefer not to use the certification label. Still due to its market size the United States has the second highest certified sales.

Fair trade's growth reflects Northern consumers' mounting social and environmental concerns with sales increasing alongside other ethical and environmentally certified products (Bartley, 2007; Fransen, 2012). Fair trade is often seen as an exemplar of how people use the market to voice their ethical commitments, since consumers receive no objective returns from their product selection and often pay higher prices. The purchase of Fairtrade certified food products, like organic and local foods, represents a rejection of the mainstream agro-industrial food system and an embrace of alternative values (Barham, 2002; Raynolds, 2000, 2002). Numerous studies analyze the socio-demographic profile of ethical and fair trade shoppers, confirming that social class is positively related with ethical purchasing (Bartley, Koos, Samel,

Table 15.2 Fairtrade International sales in lead countries (value, US$1,000,000)[a]

	2004	*2006*	*2008*	*2010*	*2012*
UK	256	514	1,297	1,872	2,654
USA	267	627	1,116	1,305	1,436[a]
Germany	71	138	313	474	743
France	87	209	376	423	482
Switzerland	169	179	248	306	434
Canada	22	68	190	271	275
Australia/NZ	1	8	27	175	262
Netherlands	43	51	90	166	259
Total[b]	$1,034	$2,039	$4,351	$5,728	$7,985

Source: Adapted from Raynolds and Greenfield (2015) using data from Fairtrade International.

Notes: a Figure is for 2011, prior to Fair Trade USA departure from Fairtrade International. b Includes countries not listed.

Setrini, & Summers, 2015). Following Bourdieu, reflexive Northern consumers can be seen as selecting fair trade products to express and promote their cosmopolitan, ethical, and ecological values (Barnett et al., 2010) and foster everyday class distinctions (Adams & Raisborough, 2008; Johnston, 2008). Pursuing Veblen's conceptualization, the consumption of Fairtrade and other expensive certified products can be characterized as conspicuous consumption, where Northern consumers flaunt their discretionary income and fuel global consumer aspirations (Sklair, 2002).

Fair trade can also be seen as a key arena of political consumption which transforms conventional consumer/producer relations. As articulated by one pioneer, this initiative seeks to "humanize the trade process–making the producer-consumer chain as short as possible" (EFTA, 1998, p. 23). Within the agro-food sector, producer-consumer chains are typically shortened through local production and face-to-face sales which foster trust and place attachment (Murdoch et al., 2000). In creating relations based on trust and partnership, fair trade works to narrow the social distance between consumers and producers globally, humanizing trade by infusing products with information about the peoples and places engaged in production (Raynolds, 2002). Fair trade thus heightens the moral worth of, and consumer attachment to, particular products (Lamont, 2012; Zelizer, 2011). From a political economy perspective, fair trade can be seen as fueling de-commodification whereby products are valued not simply by price but by their human, ecological, and place-based attributes (Raynolds, 2002; Watson, 2006). While fair trade organizations humanize economic relations through direct trade and extensive consumer interaction, de-commodification is far more difficult in certified networks where consumer contact is reduced to a Fairtrade product label (Raynolds, 2012).

Political economy and political consumption perspectives concur that it is not sufficient for consumers to simply recognize the social dimensions of commodities; they must work to actively challenge market rule. While ethical pioneers who purchased expensive, hard-to-find fair trade products, volunteered in fair trade shops, and petitioned businesses to carry certified goods certainly acted politically, this may be less true for contemporary consumers who select Fairtrade certified items off supermarket shelves (Raynolds, 2012). Yet consumers continue to see their purchasing as consequential political action. Thirty-seven percent of US consumers perceive their purchasing decisions as "making a difference;" not much less than the forty-five percent that identify voting as "making a difference" (Hartman, 2009). Over half of European and North American consumers think that their "shopping choices can make a positive difference for workers and farmers in poor countries" (FTI & Globespan, 2011).

For consumers to foster a Polanyian countermovement, they must engage politically and in some sense collectively. Although consumption is typically seen as a form of atomistic behavior, individual choices are often argued to, through aggregation, promote change. Fair Trade USA's tag line, "every purchase matters," heralds this consumer choice model. As Raynolds (2012) argues, fair trade may go beyond this aggregationist consumer choice model by promoting collective identity in two ways: In keeping with the narrative of North/South partnership, Northern consumers may come to align themselves with Southern producers creating an "imagined community" (Anderson, 1983) of "global citizens"; or in keeping with a political consumption perspective (Micheletti, 2003), they may align themselves with other ethical consumers, creating an imagined community of "citizen consumers" (Johnston, 2008). Fair trade movement groups have played a central role in "mobilizing the ethical consumer" (Barnett et al., 2010), enrolling consumers as both global citizens and citizen consumers (Raynolds, 2012). Although fair trade pioneers had an easier time fostering collective consumer responsibility amongst the small ranks of highly motivated Northern consumers, Fairtrade labeling groups and their movement allies still promote communities of global responsibility and collective consumer voice though public events and media campaigns which mobilize supporters and justify their cause (Raynolds, 2012). While shopping is not in itself collective political action, ethical consumers' engagement does not end when they leave the supermarket, for as Willis and Schor (2012) demonstrate, they are more likely than their peers to engage in other political activities.

This analysis suggests that consumers can play a central role in bolstering fair trade's progressive potential, but they must work politically with social movement groups to counter the privileging of Northern consumer purchasing power and to address the central market challenges identified earlier: the reassertion of North/South power relations, dominance of mainstream corporations and intermediaries, and threat of re-commodification. To ensure that fair trade does not reproduce North/South power inequalities, Northern consumers must support Southern producers' interests in producing for household consumption and local markets and in shaping Fairtrade International certification. Bridging global divides also requires that the Northern consumer/Southern producer hierarchy be dismantled by fostering connections between ethical consumers in the North and South and socially responsible producers in both North and South. Consumers must work to forestall fair trade's takeover by mainstream corporations reasserting market rule, by fostering efforts to humanize trade and shorten the substantial distance between Northern consumers and Southern producers and the lesser distance between domestic consumers and producers. Consumers everywhere can bolster progressive alternatives, steering their purchases to mission-focused businesses and supporting more participatory certification. To ensure that Fairtrade certified markets are not driven by dominant supermarkets and corporate brands seeking to profit through re-commodification, consumers must uphold the normative value of products and engage in the politics of de-commodification and global social justice.

Conclusion and future research directions

This chapter reveals the challenges and opportunities for consumers to help bridge global North/South divides. I argue that to understand how consumers can foster global social justice, we must link a structural view of consumption and its role in maintaining or transforming global inequalities with a political view of consumers as individual and potentially collective strategic actors. My analysis combines political economy theory, to explain North/South inequalities, and social movement theory, to explain consumer agency in fostering social justice. As I demonstrate this synthesis acknowledges the powerful economic interests upholding global inequalities, thereby avoiding an overly naïve view of the role of shopping in bridging North/South divides, and the contentiousness of markets, thereby revealing how diverse social actors engage individually and collectively in forging market relations.

My case study of fair trade illuminates the intersection of structural market forces and social justice initiatives and the promise and pitfalls for consumer driven networks. Fair trade represents the most successful contemporary initiative challenging historical trade inequities and fostering more equitable relations between Southern producers and Northern consumers. Despite its robust critique of conventional market norms and success in fostering alternative civic and relational values, fair trade's alternative principles are being strongly challenged by mainstream corporate engagement and the rapid growth in certified markets. Fairtrade's operation in, as well as against, the market makes it difficult to escape North/South inequalities in trade, top-down regulation, and corporate domination. While Northern consumers have helped drive fair trade markets and promote more equitable market relations, bridging North/South divides requires extensive collaboration between progressive consumers, producers, NGOs, and social movement groups.

Further theoretical and empirical investigation is needed to help identify the most fruitful avenues for consumer engagement in progressive efforts to bridge North/South divides and foster global social justice. Scholars and activists must acknowledge the difficulties in overcoming the privileging of consumer purchasing power and the structural rigidities of colonial-based trade relations, top-down regulation, and corporate dominance. Consumption researchers can advance this agenda by reorienting their analysis away from the traditional emphasis on consumers as individuals and consumption as representational, and developing a more collective understanding of consumers and more structural view of consumption. Theoretical work in this area can help elaborate the political and global nature of consumption, link consumption studies to other social science research on global divides, and unravel the Northern consumer/Southern producer conceptual hierarchy. Empirically oriented studies can also contribute greatly to this research agenda by analyzing lessons learned from ongoing collaborative initiatives which link progressive consumers and producers and merge local and global efforts to bridge North/South divides and pursue social justice for all.

Notes

1 "Fair trade" refers to multiple initiatives pursuing a common vision. "Fairtrade" refers specifically to the certification system governed by Fairtrade International.

2 For more on political consumption see chapter 4.1, this volume.

References

Adams, M., & Raisborough, J. (2008). What can sociology say about Fairtrade? *Sociology*, *42*(6), 1165–1182.

Anderson, B. (1983). *Imagined Communities: Reflections on the Origin and Spread of Nationalism*. London: New Left Books.

Archer, C., & Fritsch, S. (2010). Global fair trade: Humanizing globalization and reintroducing the normative to international political economy. *Review of International Political Economy*, *17*(1), 103–128.

Auld, G. (2014). *Constructing Private Governance: The Rise and Evolution of Forest, Coffee, and Fisheries Certification*. Hartford: Yale University Press.

Bacon, C. (2010). Who decides what is fair in fair trade? *Journal of Peasant Studies*, *37*, 111–147.

Barham, E. (2002). Towards a theory of values-based labeling. *Agriculture and Human Values*, *19*(4), 349–360.

Barnett, C., Cloke, P., Clarke, N., & Malpass, A. (2010). *Globalizing Responsibility: The Political Rationalities of Ethical Consumption*. London: Blackwell, Oxford.

Bartley, T. (2007). Institutional emergence in an era of globalization: The rise of transnational private regulation of labor and environmental conditions. *American Journal of Sociology*, *113*(2), 297–351.

Bartley, T., Koos, S., Samel, H., Setrini, G., & Summers, N. (2015). *Looking Behind the Label: Global Industries and the Conscientious Consumer*. Bloomington: Indiana University Press.

Beckert, J. (2013). Capitalism as a system of expectations. *Politics & Society*, *41*(3), 323–350.

Block, F., & Evans, P. (2005). The state and the economy. In N. Smelser & R. Swedberg (Eds.), *Handbook of Economic Sociology* (pp. 505–526). Princeton: Princeton University Press.

Boltanski, L., & Thévenot, L. (2006). *On Justification: Economies of Worth*. Princeton, NJ: Princeton University Press.

Bourdieu, P. (1984). *Distinction: A Social Critique of the Judgment of Taste*. Cambridge, MA: Harvard University Press.

Buechler, S. (2000). *Social Movements in Advanced Capitalism*. London: Oxford University Press.

Clarke, N., Barnett, C., Cloke, P., & Malpass, A. (2007). Globalising the consumer: Doing politics in an ethical register. *Political Geography*, *26*(3), 231–249.

Dolan, C., & Humphrey, J. (2000). Governance and trade in fresh vegetables. *Journal of Development Studies*, *37*(2), 145–176.

DuPuis, E. M. (2000). Not in my body: RBGH and the rise of organic milk. *Agriculture and Human Values*, *17*(3), 285–295.

EFTA (European Fair Trade Association). (1998). *Fair Trade Yearbook: Towards 2000*. Netherlands: EFTA.

EFTA (European Fair Trade Association). (2010). *Fair Trade Facts and Figures*. Netherlands: EFTA.

EFTA (European Fair Trade Association). (2013). *European Fair Trade Association*. Netherlands: EFTA.

FINE (FLO, IFAT, News!, EFTA). (2001). *Fair Trade Definition*. Bonn: FLO.

Fligstein, N., & McAdam, D. (2012). *A Theory of Fields*. New York: Oxford University.

Fransen, L. (2012). *Corporate Social Responsibility and Global Labor Standards*. New York: Routledge.

FTI (Fairtrade International). (2013). *Annual Report 2012–2013*. Bonn: FTI.

FTI (Fairtrade International). (2014). *Annual Report 2013–2014*. Bonn: FTI.

FTI & Globespan. (2011). *Shopping Choices Can Make a Positive Difference to Farmers and Workers in Developing Countries*. Bonn: FTI.

Gereffi, G. (1994). The organization of buyer -driven global commodity chains. In G. Gereffi & M. Korzeniewicz (Eds.), *Commodity Chains and Global Capitalism* (pp. 95–122). Westport, CT: Praeger.

Gereffi, G., Humphrey, J., & Sturgeon, T. (2005). The governance of global value chains. *Review of International Political Economy*, *12*(1), 78–104.

Goodman, D., DuPuis, E. M., & Goodman, M. (2012). *Alternative Food Networks: Knowledge, Practice and Politics*. London: Routledge.

Hartman Group. (2009). *Sustainability: The Rise of Consumer Responsibility*. www.hartman-goup.com.

Holt, D. B. (1998). Does cultural capital structure American consumption? *Journal of Consumer Research*, *25*(1), 1–25.

Hudson, I., & Hudson, M. (2003). Removing the veil? Commodity fetishism, fair trade, and the environment. *Organization & Environment*, *16*(4), 413–430.

Jaffee, D. (2007). *Brewing Justice: Fair Trade Coffee, Sustainability, and Survival*. Berkeley: University of California Press.

Johnston, J. (2008). The citizen-consumer hybrid: Ideological tensions and the case of Whole Foods Market. *Theory and Society*, *37*(3), 229–270.

Keck, M., & Sikkink, K. (1998). *Activists Beyond Borders: Advocacy Networks in International Politics*. Ithaca: Cornell University Press.

King, B., & Pearce, N. (2010). The contentiousness of markets. *Annual Review of Sociology*, *36*, 249–267.

Lamont, M. (2012). Toward a comparative sociology of valuation and evaluation. *Annual Review Sociology*, *38*, 201–221.

Marx, K. ([1867]1976). *Capital Volume 1*. New York: Vintage Books.

McMichael, P. (2008). *Development and Social Change*. Thousand Oaks, CA: Pine Forge Press.

Micheletti, M. (2003). *Political Virtue and Shopping*. New York: Macmillan.

Murdoch, J., Marsden, T., & Banks, J. (2000). Quality, nature, and embeddedness. *Economic Geography*, *76*(2), 107–125.

O'Rourke, D. (2006). Multi-stakeholder regulation: Privatizing or socializing global labor standards? *World Development*, *34*(5), 899–918.

Polanyi, K. (1957a). *The Great Transformation: The Political and Economic Origins of Our Time*. Boston: Beacon Press.
Polanyi, K. (1957b). The economy as instituted process. In K. Polanyi, C. M. Arensberg, & H. W. Pearson (Eds.), *Trade and Market in the Early Empires: Economies in History and Theory*. Glencoe, IL: The Free Press, 243–270.
Raynolds, L. T. (2000). Re-embedding global agriculture: The international organic and fair trade movements. *Agriculture and Human Values, 17*, 297–309.
Raynolds, L. T. (2002). Consumer/producer links in fair trade coffee networks. *Sociologia Ruralis, 42*(4), 404–424.
Raynolds, L. T. (2004). The globalization of organic agro-food networks. *World Development, 32*(5), 725–743.
Raynolds, L. T. (2007). Fair trade bananas: Broadening the movement and market in the United States. In L. T. Raynolds, D. Murray, & J. Wilkinson (Eds.), *Fair Trade: The Challenges of Transforming Globalization* (pp. 63–82). London: Routledge.
Raynolds, L. T. (2009). Mainstreaming fair trade coffee: From partnership to traceability. *World Development, 37*(6), 1083–1093.
Raynolds, L. T. (2012). Fair trade: Social regulation in global food markets. *Journal of Rural Studies, 28*(3), 276–287.
Raynolds, L. T., & Bennett, E. (Eds.). (2015). *Handbook of Research on Fair Trade*. Cheltenham: Edward Elgar.
Raynolds, L. T., & Greenfield, N. (2015). Fair trade: Movement and markets. In L. T. Raynolds & E. Bennett (Eds.), *Handbook of Research on Fair Trade* (pp. 24–44). Cheltenham: Edward Elgar.
Raynolds, L. T., Long, M. A., & Murray, D. L. (2014). Regulating corporate responsibility in the American market. *Competition & Change, 18*(2), 91–110.
Raynolds, L. T., Murray, D., & Wilkinson, J. (Eds.). (2007). *Fair Trade: The Challenges of Transforming Globalization*. London: Routledge.
Reisman, D. (2012). *The Social Economics of Thorstein Veblen*. Cheltenham: Edward Elgar.
Renard, M.-C. (2003). Fair trade: Quality, market and conventions. *Journal of Rural Studies, 19*(1), 87–96.
Sklair, L. (2002). The transnational capitalist class and global politics. *International Political Science Review, 23*(2), 159–174.
Stolle, D., Hooghe, M., & Micheletti, M. (2005). Politics in the supermarket: Political consumerism as a form of political participation. *International Political Science Review, 26*(3), 245–269.
Stolle, D., & Micheletti, M. (2015). *Political Consumerism: Global Responsibility in Action*. Cambridge: Cambridge University Press.
Thompson, C. J., & Coskuner-Balli, G. (2007). Enchanting ethical consumerism: The case of community supported agriculture. *Journal of Consumer Culture, 7*(3), 275–303.
Vail, J. (2010). Decommodification and egalitarian political economy. *Politics & Society, 38*(3), 310–346.
Veblen, T. (1899 (1973)). *The Theory of the Leisure Class*. Boston: Houghton Mifflin Company.
Watson, M. (2006). Towards a Polanyian perspective on fair trade. *Global Society, 20*(4), 435–451.
Willis, M., & Schor, J. (2012). Does changing a light bulb lead to changing the world? *Annals of the American Academy of Political and Social Science, 644*(1), 160–190.
Zelizer, V. (2011). *Economic Lives: How Culture Shapes the Economy*. Princeton, NJ: Princeton University Press.

Part IV

Politics and policies of consumption

Introduction

Consumption was probably never ever an entirely economic or private endeavor. The interweaving of consumption, politics and policies has roots back into history. Political consumption activity appeared already in the eighteenth and nineteenth centuries with the Boston Tea Party in the American Revolution where Americans protested over a British tea law by destroying tea, and the struggle between the Irish Land League and Captain Boycott, where farmers refused to have economic transactions with Boycott, laying the ground for the now well-known term for deliberately avoiding specific goods. Likewise, political regulation of consumption has run somewhat parallel with regulation of markets, thus also dating back in history, but the specific policy area of consumer laws and consumer protection was introduced only after the Second World War.

Today, the areas of research on e.g. political consumption and consumer policies criss-cross the alleged boundaries between public and private. But to think of consumption and politics explicitly together is not taken for granted, neither in all quarters of consumption research, political science and political sociology research, nor among political actors in society.

In this section, the chapters cover both political consumption and political regulation of consumption, as well as interventions stemming from particular policy-making efforts to improve ways people lead their everyday lives, be it towards more environmental sustainability, better health or some other societally acceptable and beneficial goal.

In chapter 16, Eivind Jacobsen introduces the discussions in the research about political consumption, covering the popular term *consumer-citizens*, discussing the debates about the public-private boundaries in relation to political activism, and highlighting the disagreements in the research field about whether to focus on the individual political or conscious consumer, or to focus on politically related consumption activities and how they are socially and culturally embedded.

Chapter 17 authored by Adrian Evans and Mara Miele focuses on ethical food labelling and looks more closely at organic, fair-trade and animal welfare-friendly products to contend that labelling practices need to be understood in situated contexts and have plural effects. They are both the reflection of the socio-political environment where consumption is embedded, functioning here as *icons*; but they are also political and politicized intervention tools, working as *devices* that act upon the entire agro-food system, triggering shifts and changes to it. The chapter offers novel and insightful connections between the literature on this topic and presents a strong and persuasive approach to food labelling by looking at the *origins* and *effects* of ethical food labels.

Chapter 18 brings us head on into consumption policies and regulation of consumption. Dale Southerton and David Evans outline the research discussions about different theoretical underpinnings of consumption policies: on the one hand, what they call the theoretical orthodoxy, where consumption policies are framed as regulation of the individual consumer, and on the other hand, theoretical heterodoxy, where consumption policies are framed as relations between different processes of societal changes, involving multiple types of actors at different scales.

In chapter 19 Arne Dulsrud unpacks the notion of consumer-citizen in great detail, focusing on how citizenship and consumption practices interweave and overlap. He also looks at how different consumer protection regimes are linked to the understanding that consumer mobilization and empowerment are always limited, since consumers' and corporations' powers and capabilities to exercise their interests are very uneven. The chapter provides a useful and systematic account of different types of consumer protection regimes. Dulsrud acknowledges that consumer movements as well as consumer protection are international affairs, highlighting their achievements and less successful aspects. The chapter ends on a sobering note problematizing the future of consumer-citizenship suited to the affluent Western model in case the basic premises of that no longer work as they used to.

Chapter 20 picks up the thread of chapter 18 on consumption policies and regulation of consumption by more concretely elaborating upon one of the heterodox ways of analysing consumption policies – namely the relations between interventions and practice changes in everyday life. Margit Keller and Triin Vihalemm discuss and demonstrate how consumption policy interventions can use practice theoretical underpinnings for designing attempts for social change via consumption activities. The chapter follows the logic of an intervention planning from background research to programme design and evaluation and, as such, caters for a wider audience of practitioners and policy-makers in addition to fellow academics.

Finally, in chapter 21 Lucia Reisch and John Thøgersen offer yet another approach – behavioural economics – that contests the theoretical orthodoxy of a rational *homo economicus* that underpins much of consumption policies. Their account takes a deeper look at how consumers act in decision-making situations, in particular how they make decisions deemed important for the private realm as opposed to those that belong to the moral domain and are governed by motivations to benefit others. Reisch and Thøgersen zoom in on two aspects of behaviourally informed regulation: firstly, choice architecture that provides the background framework in which decisions are made and, secondly, libertarian paternalism that attempts to steer or "nudge" people to make more beneficial decisions for themselves as individuals and for the society at large. The authors acknowledge the need for more research and debate to find and agree upon accepted rules for behaviourally informed regulation.

Chapters 20 and 21 have in common the premise that consumers do not always act as rational-decision-makers and both seek other approaches to policy and intervention than just persuading individuals to make better choices. Yet their theoretical points of departure are different: while chapter 20 takes a social practice as an entity as the focus of intervention, for chapter 21 the main locus of change is an individual, even though he or she is steered into better behaviour by regulators and interveners.

16

Political consumption – citizenship and consumerism

Eivind Jacobsen

The term *political consumption* is often used for practices of consumption pertaining to aims beyond consumerist, utilitarian considerations – like that of balancing quality to price in buying decisions. People subscribing to these kind of practices see them "in relation to a broader palette of concerns" (Thompson & Coskuner-Balli, 2007, p. 138), such as e.g. ecological sustainability, animal welfare, biodiversity, energy conservation, workers' safety, living wages and/or ethnic and national affiliation. In the last two decades this phenomenon has been given considerable attention in the global North, academically (e.g. Friedman, 1999; Micheletti, Føllesdal & Stolle, 2004; Jacobsen & Dulsrud, 2007; Carrier & Luetchford, 2012), politically (e.g. EU Green Paper on CSR, 2005; UNEP, 2015) and commercially (e.g. Unilever, 2015; HM, 2014; Williams, 2015). In pace with economic growth there has also been an increasing interest in these issues for the aspiring middle class of the global South (e.g. Chan, 2004; Nejati, Salamzadeh & Salamzadeh, 2011; Ariztia, Kleie, Brightwell & Barholo, 2012; Ibok & Etuk, 2014; McEwan, Hughes & Bek, 2015).

Moral judgements and actions

The term implies that some forms of consumption are seen to involve acts of moral judgement and are attempts to influence matters and issues normally assigned to political institutions and processes. Using the term therefore implies subscribing to a wide definition of politics, pertaining to power, governance and authority in general and beyond the representative institutions of the political system of nation-states, as in Ulrich Beck's writings about subpolitics, Giddens' on life politics or Melucci's on social movements (e.g. Melucci, 1989; Giddens, 1991; Beck, 1997; see also Dahlgren, 2006). A narrower definition reserving politics to activities relating to political institutions hardly makes sense in this regard. However, using the term also implies that there are acts of consumption that are non-political, and these latter are seen as the "normal", the standard against which political consumption is a kind of deviation.

In the literature – which spans most social science disciplines – the term has often been used more or less synonymously with ethical consumption (e.g. Clark, 2004; Loureiro, 2011; Micheletti, 2011), critical consumerism (e.g. Sassatelli, 2006, p. 220) or green consumption (e.g. Miller, 2001). We will also do that, though the terms do carry somewhat different connotations:

ethical consumerism points in the direction of more personal lifestyle considerations (e.g. Pringle & Thompson, 1999), while especially political consumption and critical consumption points more towards community oriented collective action (e.g. Whatmore & Clark, 2008).

The phenomenon of political consumption is obviously much older than the term itself. The term was first time used in Denmark in the mid-1990s in relation to the Shell Brent Spar boycott (cf. Micheletti, 2011) and the boycott of French wines due to the nuclear tests in the Pacific (Halkier & Holm, 2008). In the historical literature there are hundreds of accounts of politically motivated boycotts of specific products and/or their providers, e.g. tea in colonial New England (1776) (see Carp, 2010), slave-sugar from the West Indies in eighteenth-century England (1791) (see Mintz, 1985), salt in Colonial India (1930) (see Dalton, 1993), Jewish shops in Nazi Germany (1933) (see Kreutzmüller, 2012), grapes in California due to poor working conditions of immigrant farm laborers (1966) (see Shaw, 2008), Nestle breastfeeding milk (1977 and ongoing) and boycotts of French wines due to nuclear tests in the Pacific (1995). Likewise, many studies have documented so-called "buycotts", the deliberate buying of specific products and support of certain providers in order to sponsor certain interests/values/concerns.

Consumer-citizens

The actors involved in political consumption have often been denoted *consumer-citizens* (Micheletti, 2003), implying not only that they use a consumer role to express concerns usually ascribed to a citizen-role, but even more literally, that they vote at the check-out (see also Dickinson & Carsky, 2005). This voting metaphor suggests that products and providers correspond to political parties, and that consumers make deliberate and more or less informed moral choices based on interests and values. The mundane everyday practice of shopping is equaled to the moral act of voting.

The literature identifies various motivations for boycotting and buycotting (e.g. Micheletti, 2004). Most obviously, and of course given priority in most of the literature, political consumption is assumed to aspire to change unwanted behavior and conditions among producers and sellers, or to support worthy causes and actors. Such motivations imply that the consumers in question believe their singular buying or non-buying decisions can make a difference. Implicitly this infers a belief in the workings of the market and hence in consumer sovereignty. The political scientist Michele Micheletti (2011, p. 1098) points out that the concept of the citizen consumer involves two claims; first, that consumers must view their consumption as involving public considerations (e.g. about how the world is governed) and second, that consumers should use their consumption practices to address these concerns. The latter implies that there are relevant and available alternatives and that consumers believe they have latent power that can be mobilized for these purposes.

As e.g. Føllesdal (2004) points out, consumers may be motivated to act ethically even when they don't believe they can make a difference in regard to changing unwanted behaviors or helping worthy ones. For instance, consumers may have a desire to have "clean hands", to construct and support some kind of self-identity and/or have an ambition to influence other consumers by putting moral pressure on them (Føllesdal, 2004).

The empirical literature on political consumption, mostly based on quantitative survey data, has identified political consumers to be more upper or middle class, to be white, to have children, to live in Northern Europe or North America, and to be on average more politically left-leaning than the average population. Women are also more likely to be political consumers than men are, and – interestingly – political consumers are in general more concerned with prices and qualities of consumer products (e.g. Gilg, Barr & Ford, 2005; Micheletti & Stolle, 2005;

Strømsnes, 2005; Micheletti, 2004; 2011; Goul Andersen & Tobiasen, 2004; Worcester & Dawkins, 2005; cf. Lindén & Carlsson-Canyama, 2007, see also Boström & Kintman, 2008). In some of these studies as much as twenty or thirty percent of consumers are estimated to practice some kind of political consumption (e.g. Kjærnes, Harvey and Warde, 2007, p. 167; Goul Andersen & Tobiasen, 2004, p. 2007; Boström & Klintman, 2008, p. 6). Accordingly, the social and political significance of the phenomenon is seen to be considerable.

Contingent practices

However, the very existence of a distinct category of citizen-consumers has been questioned in studies based on more qualitative data (e.g. Halkier & Holm, 2008). Actions like boycotts and buycotts are entangled in the ordinary everyday routines of consumers (Halkier, 1999, 2004) and the political is therefore difficult to distinguish from other aspects of consumption activities. They are often contingent in webs of conflicting expectations of practical as well as emotional nature, and consumers often experience considerable ambivalence in their everyday dealings with these issues (Halkier, 2001). Hence, to construct a distinct category of political/ethical consumers based on simple survey questions tends to undervalue the contingent nature of consumption. For instance, more attention should be given to the national institutional contexts of consumption (see also Kjærnes, Harvey & Warde, 2007).

Moreover, due to a too-inclusive definition of this phenomenon most quantitative survey-based studies tend to overestimate the prevalence of the phenomenon. As Halkier and Holm (2008) point out, it should take both intentionality – "the carrying out of actions with intention of some societal consequence" – and autonomy – "whether the conditions for actions are structured in ways that make it likely for them to be carried out" – for consumer's actions to be classified as political consumption (Halkier & Holm, 2008, p. 669). Using such a restrictive definition on their own survey data on food consumption, they found that fewer than one in ten Danish food consumers qualified as political consumers (Halkier & Holm, 2008, p. 671). This is far less than supposed in other studies.

The universality of an active moral consumerist model has also been questioned (e.g. Jacobsen & Dulsrud, 2007). Comparative surveys suggest that there may be systematic differences between countries regarding what kind of responsibilities people assign to their consumer role. For instance, the more neo-liberal Brits seem more likely to think that individual consumers have moral responsibilities towards producers and production conditions than do their in general more social democratic Scandinavian counterparts, who on their part think such responsibilities should be taken care of collectively by the state (Kjærnes et al., 2007). Likewise, a lot of studies have documented that high-income and high-education consumers are more likely to think they have such responsibilities than their less affluent and less educated counterparts (e.g. Kjærnes, Harvey & Warde, 2007; Miller, 1998; Bostrøm, Fællesdal, Micheletti & Sørensen, 2005).

Substitute for public politics?

The effectiveness of political consumption has also been questioned. The scope open for political consumption is limited to the range of products and services deliberately chosen by consumers. As such e.g. infrastructural arrangements and a wide range of habitual, ordinary consumption practices fall outside the area of issues and relations approachable through acts of consumption (Gronow & Warde, 2001). Thus, political consumption can only be a viable instrument for citizens' power and active influence in restricted topical areas. Some, like Gjerris, Gamborg and Saxe (2016), go even further in their criticism, claiming e.g. current environmental challenges to be much too complex to be addressed by way of changing individual consumption practices, and that as such critical consumerism may give way to false expectations as the complexity of choices transpires. As such it may serve to preserve – rather than undermine – dominant and destructive consumerist capitalism (Carrington, Zwinck & Neville, 2016).

In line with this some, perhaps especially on the left side of politics, fear that political consumption is promoted as a substitute for ordinary politics. They see political consumption as a concession to neo-liberal politics, where difficult issues are lifted out of regular political bodies to be left to individual consumers to handle (Jacobsen & Dulsrud, 2007). A strong, active responsible consumer role is congruent with neo-liberal models of governance (Braithwaith, 1997; Giesler & Veresiu, 2014). Choosing consumers are assumed to exert the power to choose between what is supposed to be morally distinct market alternatives, catered for by companies' private standards and codes of conduct. Thereby both consumers and producers/sellers are assigned responsibilities that would otherwise be the prerogative of states to take care of (Jordana & Levi-Faur, 2004). This is putting too much responsibility on weak consumer shoulders, and it is politically ineffective, producing frustration and guilt among consumers (Coff, 2006; Sassatelli, 2006).

Others are more optimistic, pointing to the didactic and mobilizing potential of bringing ethical and political alternatives into the everyday life of ordinary people. This may in turn serve to put issues on the agenda in more regular political arenas (Micheletti, 2011, Micheletti & Stolle, 2015). They also point to the limited reach of nation-state-based politics in an interconnected world of information and trade. The British Parliament has no legal instruments available for influencing workers' rights in Bangladesh, and the Norwegian government can hardly influence conditions for Costa Rican coffee farmers, but HM, Nike and importers of coffee may, if pushed by conscious and demanding consumers.

Micheletti (2011, p. 1098) also points out that boycotts and buycotts have increasingly been supplanted by new forms of political consumerism. What she calls "discursive political consumerism" concerns the active communication of values. It differs from traditional political consumerism as it involves actions beyond the market, like lobbying, active use of social media, emails and postcard campaigns, cultural jamming and ad-busting in order to influence retailers, producers and/or politicians in regard to the relevant issues. The use of social media to target global brands like Nike, HM or McDonalds for promoting sustainability in commodity chains and corporate social responsibility is part of this new form of political consumerism. Another form is what she calls "lifestyle political consumerism". This form involves more personal commitments, like veganism or downshifting overall private consumption (see e.g. Schor, 1998). These are paradigmatic practices that may work to promote social change. Micheletti (2011) explains the growth of these other forms of political consumerisms, pointing to how the Internet and social media have opened up for communicating about lifestyles and how consumer culture in general has been more associated with identity politics.

The consumer sovereignty implied in this argument has been questioned (e.g. Coff, 2006; Jacobsen & Dulsrud, 2007). Sassatelli (2006) points to the role played by activist NGO groups, like e.g. environmentalists groups, in promoting an active, conscious, choosing consumer (see also Micheletti & Stolle, 2015; see also Southerton & Evans in this volume, chapter 18). In their rhetoric, consumers have duties rather than rights, and they are potentially powerful rather than vulnerable.

Commercial interests have also promoted an active consumer role, making room for market differentiation by appealing to a willingness to pay higher prices in certain market segments. As Jacobsen and Dulsrud (2007) have pointed out, the alternatives open for consumers to choose among have been arranged by supply side actors as well as regulators. There is a choice architecture framing every act of consumption, and in markets this setup is very much arranged by commercial considerations. Information about products is selected and designed in order to sell. The latter has often been helped by designated labelling schemes (see chapter 17 in this volume by Evans and Miele), referring to e.g. organic farming methods, fair trade, workers' rights in manufacturing, animal welfare, local food production, country of origin (e.g. Dinnie, 2004), sustainable land-use practices in rainforest areas, sustainable fishing practices or carbon footprints. Moreover, the packaging, the physical presentation of products and their accessibility in relevant choice situations are also designed for sale. In-store marketing is a commercial craft, increasingly helped by clever digital monitoring techniques and applied sales psychology (e.g. Jacobsen & Dulsrud, 2007; Wansink, 2014; see also Cochoy, 2010). The promotion and selling of political or ethically virtuous products are no exception in this regard. Their commercial success or failures depend a lot on sellers' motivation to prioritize them in their overall sales strategies. Alas, consumer autonomy is at best partial, contingent on commercial strategies.

Political consumption embedded

This approach, focusing on choosing individuals, is predominant in contributions from within political science, social psychology, economics, marketing and philosophy. Empirical contributions very much discuss the uniqueness of this kind of consumption and these kinds of consumers, how they deviate from what is supposed to be a universal consumerist standard model.

This approach has been challenged by human geographers, social-anthropologists, historians and certain sociologists more concerned with the commonalities political consumption has with other processes, movements and sets of beliefs. As such, they have focused more on the embedding of political consumption in respectively supply chain relations, everyday social practices, history and culture. Social geographers like Whatmore and Clark and (2008) point to the spatial and temporal situatedness of political consumption. Historians like Frank Trentmann (2006) have noted that the very language and identity of the consumer and non-political consumerism as such have been discursively constructed. Social anthropologists like James Carrier (2012) have pointed to how ethical consumption involved other ways of drawing borders between "economy" and "society" and sociologists like Bente Halkier (2009) have discussed ambivalent political consumption practices in everyday life.

The social-anthropologist James Carrier (2012, pp. 13–15) has also noticed the middle class profile of what he calls ethical consumers, which in many ways (but not all) appears to cover the same persons we so far have called political consumers. He also notes that ethical consumption often tends to be a NIMBY (not-in-my-back-yard) kind of phenomenon, involving products from far-away places. Carrier notices that ethical shoppers seldom care for the working conditions of the clerks that stock the shelves and the drivers who deliver the pallet loads from the warehouse to the shops (Carrier, 2012, p. 15). Instead, focus is on products that can be imagined or presented as having been produced by a person. However, even though ethical consumers seem to have a preference for direct trade, they very seldom confront the real makers of what they buy. Accordingly, consumers may freely imagine the makers of the products to be congenial people who share their values (Carrier, 2012, p. 15). Hence, for Carrier ethical consumption is a Western middle-class way of trying to overcome the alienating anonymity of the marketplace and mass consumption. Ethical consumers seek out products that already carry an identity, that of their makers.

This contrasts the working-class women studied by Daniel Miller (1998), who preferred their products to be more like impersonal blank slates that could more easily be appropriated into private social worlds. For Miller the main contrast isn't between ethical and non-ethical ways of consumption, but rather between an ethics of how to relate to far-away-producers and the morals of caring for family, kin and friends (Miller, 2001, p. 111). However, according to Carrier, both the middle-class ethical shopping and the working-class clean-slate strategies have the same aim, that of maintaining a social sphere in the face of an expanding economic sphere and its products (Carrier, 2012, p. 10; see also Polanyi, 1957, p. 130; Zelizer, 1989).

The social geographer Nigel Clark (2008) notices that people buying fair-trade products "think of themselves less as consumers and more like activists, campaigners, Christians etc." (Clark, 2008, p. 1873). And this is also how they tend to be approached by campaigning organizations, not as consumers, but as socially and geographically situated beings with concerns far beyond utilitarian price-quality considerations and with awareness and thoughts about their moral responsibilities in regard to these concerns (Barnet & Land, 2007). Organizations in this field approach people by providing narrative storylines acknowledging the complexities of subjectivity while connecting them to themes like environmental degradation, injustice and exploitation (Littler, 2005). Storytelling like this has the capacity to provoke empathy and mobilize for actions. Moreover, as Miller has noticed, this way of emotional mobilization thrives especially well in new media, like those supported by the Internet (Miller, 2003).

However, the role of narratives in modern ethical consumption has also been criticized for serving to rework, rather than de-fetishize, the commodities in question, whereby ethical products, like organic food or fair-trade products, come with their own mystifications (Gutman, 2014). Behind their counter-cultural image, poor labor conditions, exploitations and oppression may hide (Goodman, 2003; Bryant & Goodman, 2004). Such storylines are often formalized in production standards and codes of conduct, to be imposed on producers in the South by Western supermarkets, brand owners, social movements and international certification bodies. As Freidberg (2003) has pointed out this can in many ways be reminiscent of past colonial projects aimed at "cleaning up" in the South – new versions of the "white man's burden". She also notes that the extra costs involved with these standards are met by producers in the South rather than by Western consumers (see also Lien, 2004 and Raynolds in this volume, chapter 15).

For future research

Political consumption very much mirrors the dynamics of society at large. Therefore, when economy, technology and culture change, new agendas for research open up. Here are four fields worth studying closer.

Today the role of the Internet and especially the use of social media should be given more attention. How are activists using social media to mobilize consumers, and what are producers' and retailers' strategies to fight back? In this regard, does it matter that the Internet – with all its apps – has become portable, to be carried along in your smartphone and be consulted during shopping? Likewise, how does the growth in Internet shopping influence political consumption? Alternative information – e.g. from activists – is easily accessible, but on the other hand the very act of shopping becomes rather private. Does that mean anything for mobilization processes? Moreover, how does collaborative consumption fit into this picture? How does perto-per collaborative consumption, with its blurring of the lines between supplier and consumer, fit into what Micheletti calls lifestyle consumerism?

Another field worth looking closer at is political consumerism in the global South. Are Southern consumers simply copying Northerners or are things evolving differently there? To what extent are mobilizations taking place across borders, and to what extent are old imperialistic North-South relations activated – or reversed – in these mobilizations? Moreover, is political consumption viable only for the more well-off, or does it apply also for more marginalized consumer groups?

A third field relates to more non-liberally oriented forms of political consumption. Most research has focused on liberal "good causes", perhaps because these are what scholars themselves believe in. However, we need more research on non-democratic, illiberal, nationalistic, racist, non-sustainable and otherwise less "sympatric" forms of mobilizations and the role played by consumption in these cases. Who are the activists and the followers in these cases, and how is consumption used? Does it differ from what is going on in the left and more liberal span of politics?

A fourth field worth looking more empirically into is what we above called lifestyle political consumerism (see above). Downshifting, for instance, implies more or less retreating from consumer markets, perhaps even from capitalism. This way it stands in stark contrast to the active embracing of the market associated with boycotts and buycotts. Hence, we need to learn more about this phenomenon, and what it implies in social, political and economic terms. Given that downshifters actively try not to be consumers, is it then right to include them in a discussion about political consumerism? Moreover, to what extent do they represent a serious challenge to capitalism as such? Do they carry the potential to form scalable parallel societies and economies built on alternative principles and relations? Or are they just to be regarded as another lifestyle soon to be exploited by creative capitalistic entrepreneurs? We need more studies, especially comparative case studies, to start answering such questions.

References

Ariztia, T., Kleine, D., Brightwell, G. & Barholo, R. (2014). Ethical consumption in Brazil and Chile: Institutional contexts and development trajectories. *Journal of Cleaner Production*, Vol. 63, January 2014, 84–92.

Barnett, C. & Land, D. (2007). Geographies of generosity: Beyond the 'moral turn'. *Geoforum*, Vol. 38, No.6, 1065–1075.

Beck, U. (1997). Subpolitics. *Organization & Environment*, Mars 1997, 10, 1.

Boström, M. & Klintman (2008). *Eco-standards, Product Labelling and Green Consumerism*. Houndmills: Palgrave.

Boström, M., Føllesdal, A., Micheletti, M. & Sørensen, M.P. (Eds.) (2005). Political Consumerism: Its Motivation, Power, and Conditions in the Nordic Countries and Elsewhere. Proceedings from the Second International Seminar on Political Consumerism, Oslo Aug. 26.-29. 2004. TemaNord 2005: 517. København: Nordisk Ministerråd.

Braithwaite, J. (1997). 'On Speaking Softly and Carrying Big Sticks: Neglected Dimensions of a Republication Separation of Powers'. University of Toronto Law Journal 47, 305–361.

Bryant R. L. & Goodman, M. K. (2004). Consuming narratives: The political ecology of 'alternative' consumption. *Transactions of the Institute of British Geographers*, New Series, Vol. 29, No. 3, 344–366.

Carp, B. L. (2010). *Defiance of the Patriots: The Boston Tea Party and the Making of America*. New Heaven: Yale University Press.

Carrier, J. (2012). Introduction. In J. Carrier & P. Luetchford (Eds). *Ethical Consumption: Social Value and Economic Practice*. New York: Berghahn.

Carrier, J. & Luetchford, P. (Eds.). (2012). Ethical Consumption: Social Value and Economic Practice. Oxford: Berghahn Books.

Carrington, M. J., Zwinck, D. & Neville, B. (2016). The ideology of the ethical consumption gap. *Marketing Theory*, March 2016, Vol. 16, No. 1, 21–38.

Chan, R.Y.K. (2004). Consumer responses to environmental advertising in China. Marketing, Intelligence & Planning, Vol. 22, No. 4, 427–437.

Clark, D. (2004). *Rough Guide to Ethical Shopping*. London: Rough Guide.

Clarke, N. (2008). From ethical consumerism to political consumption. Geography Compass, Vol. 2, No. 6, 1870–1884.

Cochoy, F. (2010). "How to build displays that sell": The politics of performativity in American grocery stores. Journal of Cultural Economy, July 2010, 1–16.

Coff, C. (2006). *The Taste for Ethics. An Ethic of Food Consumption.* Dordrecht: Springer Verlag.

Dahlgren, P. (2006). Doing citizenship: The cultural origins of civic agency in the public sphere. European Journal of Cultural Studies, Vol. 9, No. 3, 267–286.

Dalton, D. (1993). *Mahatma Gandhi: Nonviolent Power in Action.* New York: Columbia University Press.

Dickinson, R. D. & Carsky, M. L. (2015). The Consumer as Economic Voter. In R. Harrison, T. Newholm, & D. Shaw (Eds.). *The Ethical Consumer.* London: SAGE.

Dinnie, K. J. (2004). Country-of-origin 1965–2004: A literature review. *Journal of Customer Behaviour*, Vol. 3, No. 2, 165–213.

Dulsrud, A. and Jacobsen, E. (2009). In-store Marketing as a Mode of Discipline. *Journal of Consumer Policy*, Vol. 32, No. 3, 203–218.

EU (2005): Green Paper - Promoting a European framework for Corporate Social Responsibility [COM(2001) 366 - Not published in the Official Journal]. http://eur-lex.europa.eu/legal-content/EN/TXT/HTML/?uri=URISERV:n26039&from=EN (Downloaded Oct 26, 2016)

Føllesdal, A. (2004). Introduction. In M. Micheletti, A. Føllesdal, & D. Stolle (Eds.), Politics, Products and Markets: Exploring Political Consumerism Past and Present, New Brunswick and London: Transaction Publishers.

Freidberg, S. (2003). Cleaning up down South: supermarkets, ethical trade and African horticulture. *Social & Cultural Geography*, Vol. 4, No. 1, 27–43.

Friedman, M. (1999). Consumer Boycotts: Effecting Change through the Marketplace and the Media. New York: Routledge.

Giddens, A. (1991). Modernity and Self-identity. Polity Press: London.

Giesler, M. & Veresiu, E. (2014), 'Creating the responsible consumer: Moralistic governance regimes and consumer subjectivity,' *Journal of Consumer Research*, vol. 41, no. 3, pp. 840–857.

Gilg, A., Barr, S. & Ford, N. (2005). Green consumption or sustainable lifestyles? Identifying the sustainable consumer. Futures, Vol. 37, 481–504.

Gjerris, M., Gamborg, C. & Saxe, H. (2016). What to buy? On the complexity of being a critical consumer. Journal of Agricultural and Environmental Ethics, February 2016, Vol. 29, No. 1, 81–102.

Goodman, D. (2003). The quality 'turn' and alternative food practices: Reflections and agenda. Journal of Rural Studies, Vol. 19, 1–7.

Goul Andersen, J. & Tobiasen, M. (2004). Who Are These Political Consumers Anyway? Survey Evidence from Denmark. In M. Micheletti, A. Føllesdal, & D. Stolle (Eds.). *Politics, Products, and Markets. Exploring Political Consumerism Past and Present.* London: Transaction Publishers.

Gronow, J. & Warde, A. (2001). *Ordinary Consumption.* Hove, UK: Psychology Press.

Guthman, J. (2014). *Agrarian Dreams. The Paradox of Organic Farming in California.* Oakland: University of California Press.

Halkier, B. (1999). Consequences of the politicization of consumption; the example of environmentally friendly consumption practices. *Journal of Environmental Policy and Planning*, Vol. 1, 25–42.

Halkier, B. (2001). Consuming ambivalences: Consumer handling of environmentally related risks in food. *Journal of Consumer Culture*, Vol. 1, 205–224.

Halkier, B. (2004). Consumption, Risk, and Civic Engagement: Citizens as Risk-Handlers. In M. Micheletti, A. Føllesdal & D. Stolle (Eds.). *Politics, Products, and Markets. Exploring Political Consumerism Past and Present*, 223–244. London: Transaction Publishers.

Halkier, B. (2009). A practice theoretical perspective on everyday dealings with environmental challenges of food consumption. In *Anthropology of Food* (online), S5, September 2009.

Halkier, B. & Holm, L. (2008). Food consumption and political agency: On concerns and practices among Danish consumers. *International Journal of Consumer Studies*, Vol. 32, 667–674.

HM (2014). Conscious Actions. Sustainability Report. http://sustainability.hm.com/

Ibok, N. I. & Etuk, S. G. (2014). Socio-economic and demographic determinants of green consumption. *Int. J. of Managerial Studies and Research*, Vol. 2, No. 9, 47–56.

Jacobsen, E. & Dulsrud, A. (2007). Will consumers save the world? The framing of political consumerism. *Journal of Agricultural and Environmental Ethics*, Vol. 20, 469–482.

Jordana, J. & Levi-Faur, D. (Eds.). (2004). *The Politics of Regulation: Institutions and Regulatory Reforms for the Governance Age.* The CRC Series on Regulation, University of Manchester, Manchester: Edward Elgar.

Kjærnes, U., Harvey, M. & Warde, A. (2007). *Trust in Food. A Comparative and Institutional Analysis.* New York: Palgrave.

Kreutzmüller, C. (2012). *Final Sale – The Destruction of Jewish Owned Businesses in Nazi Berlin 1930–1945.* Berlin: Metropol-Verlag.

Lien, M. E. (2004). Dogs, Whales and Kangaroos: Transnational Activism and Food Taboos. In M. E. Lien & B. Nerlich (Eds.). *The Politics of Food*, 179–198. London: Berg.

Lindén, A-L. & Carlsson-Kanyma, A. (2007). Energy efficiency in residences – A challenge for women and men. *Energy Policy*, Vol. 35, 2163–2172.

Littler, J. (2005). Beyond the boycott: anti-consumerism, cultural change and the limits of reflexivity. *Cultural Studies, 19*(2). pp. 227-252

Loureiro, M. (2011). Ethical considerations and food demand. In J. L. Lusk, J. Roosen, & J. F. Shogren (Eds.). *The Oxford handbook of the Economics of Food Consumption and Policy*. Oxford: Oxford University Press.

Melucci, A. (1989). *Nomads of the Present: Social Movements and Individual Needs in Contemporary Society*. Philadelphia: Temple University Press.

McEwan, C., Hughes, A. & Bek, D. (2015). Theorizing middle class consumption from the global south: A study of everyday ethics in South Africa's Western Cape. *Geoforum*, Vol. 67, 233–243.

Micheletti, M. (2004). Why More Women? Issues of Gender and Political Consumerism. In M. Micheletti, A. Føllesdal, & D. Stolle (Eds.). *Politics, Products, and Markets. Exploring Political Consumerism Past and Present*. London: Transaction Publishers.

Micheletti, M. (2011). Political and Ethical Consumption. In D. Southerton (Ed.). *Encyclopedia of Consumer Culture, Part III, 1097–1100*. London: Sage Publications.

Micheletti, M., Føllesdal, A. Stolle, D. (2004). Politics, Products, and Markets: Exploring Political Consumerism Past and Present, New Brunswick: Transaction Publishers.

Micheletti, M. & Stolle, D. (2005). Swedish Political Consumers: Who they are and why they use the market as an arena for politics? In M. Boström, A. Føllesdal, M. Micheletti, & M. P. Sørensen (Eds.). *Political Consumerism: Its Motivation, Power, and Conditions in the Nordic Countries and Elsewhere*. Proceedings from the Second International Seminar on Political Consumerism, Oslo Aug. 26–29 2004. TemaNord 2005: 517. København: Nordisk Ministerråd.

Micheletti, M. & Stolle, D. (2015). Consumer Strategies in Social Movements. In D. della Porta & M. Dani (Eds.). *The Oxford Handbook of Social Movements*. Oxford: Oxford University Press.

Miller, D. (1998). *A Theory of Shopping*. Ithaca, New York: Cornell University Press.

Miller, D. (2001). *The Dialectics of Shopping*. Chicago: University of Chicago Press.

Miller, D. (2003). Could the Internet defetichise the commodity? Paper presented at the SIFO-conference: The social meaning and the political importance of consumption in modern societies, April 2003.

Mintz, S.W. (1985). *Sweetness and Power: The Place of Sugar in Modern History*. New York: Viking Penguin.

Nejati, M., Salamzadeh, Y. & Salamzadeh, A. (2011). Ecological purchase behavior: Insights from a Middle Eastern country. *Int. J. Environment and Sustainable Development*, Vol. 10, No. 4, 417–432.

Polanyi, K. (1957). *The Great Transformation*. London: Octagon Books.

Pringle, H. & Thompson M. (1999). *Brand Spirit: How Cause Related Marketing Builds Brands*. Chichester: Wiley.

Sassatelli, R. (2006). Virtue, responsibility and consumer choice. Framing critical consumerism, in Consuming Cultures, Global Perspectives, edited by J. Brewer & F. Trentmann. Oxford: Berg.

Schor, J. B. (1998). *The Overspent American. Upscaling, Downshifting, and the New Consumer*. New York: Harper Perennial.

Shaw, R. (2008). *Beyond the Fields: Cesar Chavez, the UFW, and the Struggle for Justice in the 21st Century*. California: Oakland: University of California Press.

Strømsnes, K. (2005). Political Consumption in Norway: Who, Why – And Does It Have Any Effect? In M. Boström, A. Føllesdal, M. Micheletti & M. P. Sørensen (Eds.). *Political Consumerism: Its Motivation, Power, and Conditions in the Nordic Countries and Elsewhere*. Proceedings from the Second International Seminar on Political Consumerism, Oslo Aug. 26–29 2004. TemaNord 2005: 517. København: Nordisk Ministerråd.

Thompson, C. J. & Coskuner-Balli, G. (2007). Enchanting ethical consumerism. The case of community supported agriculture. *Journal of Consumer Culture*, November 2007, Vol. 7. No. 3, 275–303.

Trentmann, F. (2006). The Modern Genealogy of the Consumer: Meanings, Identities and Political Synapses. In J. Brewer & F. Trentmann (Eds.). *Consuming Cultures, Global Perspectives. Historical Trajectories. Transnational Exchanges*. London: Berg.

UNEP (2015). *Sustainable Consumption and Production*. Global edition. https://sustainabledevelopment.un.org/content/documents/1951Sustainable%20Consumption.pdf

Unilever Sustainable Living Plan: Scaling for Impact. Summary of progress 2014. https://www.unilever.com/Images/uslp-unilever-sustainable-living-plan-scaling-for-impact-summary-of-progress-2014_tcm244-481642_en.pdf (downloaded 26.10.2016).

Wansink, B. (2014). *Slim by Design: Mindless eating solutions for everyday life.* Carlsbad, Cal.: Hay House, Inc.
Whatmore, S. & Clark, N. (2008). Good Food: Ethical consumption and global change. In N. Clark, D. Massey, & P. Sarre (Eds.). *Material Geographies: A World in the Making.* London: Sage.
Williams, E. F. (2015). *Green Giants: How Smart Companies Turn Sustainability into Billion-Dollar Businesses.* New York: Amacom.
Worcester, R. & Dawkins, J. (2005). Surveying Ethical and Environmental Attitudes. In R. Harrions, T. Newholm, & D. Shaw (Eds.). *The Ethical Consumer.* London: Sage.
Zelizer, V. (1989). The social meaning of money: "Special Monies". *The American Journal of Sociology*, Vol. 95, No. 2, 342–377.

17

Food labelling as a response to political consumption

Effects and contradictions

Adrian Evans and Mara Miele

Introduction

Food labels have become an important medium through which many consumers come to understand and appreciate foods. In contemporary Western supermarkets foods are frequently adorned with a plethora of information on origins, allergens, nutritional content, health benefits, environmental credentials, expiry dates and cooking instructions, to name but a few examples. We are confronted with a range of different logos and symbolic devices (traffic lights, footprints, tractors and frogs) designed to grab our attention, influence our emotions and purchasing decisions and to channel our ethics and politics along certain pre-set paths.

In this chapter we focus attention on ethical food labels,[1] such as organic, fair-trade and animal-welfare friendly, and we examine both the context in which these labels emerge and the effects that these labels exert in the marketplace and beyond. Ethical food labels are far from inevitable; indeed they emerge from and represent a particular set of social and economic circumstances, and they enshrine a particular set of relations between consumers and producers. Ethical food labels are not merely labels; rather they are *icons* that encapsulate a particular form of food provisioning. Indeed, they stand for a particular socio-economic ordering of the food system, in which more intimate connections between producers and consumers have been dissolved and in which the origin, provenance and even the substance of foods emerging from complex globalised supply chains need affirmation. Furthermore, the growth of ethical food labelling reflects other changes in the food system, such as the growth of heavily processed foods, the growth of food packaging and the growth of particular versions of food quality. Finally, and crucially, ethical food labels reflect a socio-political environment in which consumption is deemed to be an appropriate, if not a preeminent, field through which to exert influence over the ethics of the entire food system. This of course has implications for other forms of governing, resisting, intervening in or proposing radical alternatives to the current food system.

This is not to contend that ethical food labelling is necessarily incompatible with other forms of political and ethical engagement around food (indeed authors such as Clarke et al., 2007 have interpreted ethical labelling as part and parcel of a range of more traditional political strategies for influencing food production), nor is it to contend that attempting to exert ethical or moral influence through consumption is an entirely new or totally inappropriate phenomenon (see for example Trentmann, 2007), nor is it to contend that ethical food labels necessarily inhibit other more embodied/aesthetic ethical evaluations of food (see Eden, Bear, & Walker, 2008). However, it is to suggest that ethical food labels warrant critical appraisal both in terms of how they come to be (and the types of psycho-economic, pedagogical and neoliberal ideologies that bolster them) and in terms of what they function to do (how they do not merely reflect but also help to shape agro-food systems).

This chapter provides an overview of some of the current academic literatures on ethical food labelling. In particular, we draw on research from a range of different academic disciplines, including human geography and sociology. Rather than attempting to produce a comprehensive overview, we have instead attempted to highlight those studies which we believe generate the most interesting and critical insights into this important phenomenon. Furthermore, we have sought to develop novel connections between these studies and to present a novel synthesis of ideas concerning both the *origins* and the *effects* of ethical food labels. The remainder of the chapter is divided into four sections. In the first section we discuss work that critically situates ethical food labelling within its broader socio-economic context. In particular, we draw on the academic literature to identify a range of precursors for the emergence and growth of ethical food labels. In the second section, we turn to focus on the *effects* of ethical food labels, and we discuss how these labels can function both to increase the market share of ethically produced foods but also, and perhaps more significantly, to provide support for traditional political mechanisms, such as influencing public opinion, shoring up current support and lobbying producers, retailers and policy makers. In the third section we look more broadly at the economic, ethical and aesthetic impacts of ethical food labels. Finally, we draw some conclusions about the ways in which ethical food labels function both as *icons* (which embody the socio-economic circumstances in which they emerge) and as devices (which act upon, rather than merely represent, the food supply chain behind a given food product).

The contexts behind ethical food labelling

Ethical food labels, such as fair-trade, organic, welfare-friendly and halal, are now a common feature on the shelves of shops in the UK, across Europe and America and increasingly in the Asia-Pacific region (see Agriculture & Agri-Food Canada, 2011). Clearly, these ethical food labels did not emerge from a vacuum, and in this section we ask how and why shopping for food has become such a semiotic feast. More specifically, we review research that sheds light on the broader political, economic and social contexts in which food labelling has gained traction as an appropriate mechanism for influencing shopping behaviours and for addressing ethical, environmental and health concerns. We believe that the academic literature addresses the contexts behind the growth of ethical food labels on four different levels. Firstly, on an *historical level*, we discuss work which positions ethical food labelling within long-running historical trends, and we consider the extent to which ethical food labelling represents an entirely new means for 'caring at a distance' or whether it is best considered as part of a longer-running moral economy of commerce. Secondly, on a *systemic level*, we identify four broad socio-economic and ideological drivers that underlie the recent growth in ethical food labelling across Europe and beyond. Thirdly, on a *national level*, we draw on the example of the ethical market for animal-welfare-friendly foods across Europe to illustrate complexities and variations in the ways in which labelling is (and is not) used as a means of governing farm animal welfare. Finally, on a *micro-level* we show how differences between food products (such as sugar and chicken) and between specific types of labelling (e.g. producer-led versus NGO-led) also need to be taken into consideration if we are to account for the presence and variety of ethical food labels.

Turning first to consider the broader *historical contexts* behind the emergence of ethical food labelling, Trentmann (2007) contends that the majority of the literature on ethical food labelling is either blind to the broader historical contexts in which these labels emerge or presents an overly simplistic view of ethical food labels as a response to soulless neoliberal forms of capitalism which are inherently devoid of values. In contrast, Trentmann urges us to adopt a moral economy approach, in which markets are viewed as always already ethical. He states: '. . . for large chunks of modernity, people goods and services have been mobile, and . . . many men and women looked to commercial exchange as a vehicle of civil society, reciprocity, and social solidarity' (Trentmann, 2007, p. 1093). Seen in this light, ethical food labels and ethical consumption practices do not represent a radical departure from previous forms of consumption but rather an extension of the broader ways in which economic activities of all kinds are influenced by moral dispositions and norms (see Jackson, Ward, & Russell, 2009; Kaiser & Lien, 2006; Sayer, 2000; Smith, 2005). By adopting this moral economy approach and through a detailed historical analysis, Trentmann is able to produce new critical insights into the development of fair-trade goods. More specifically, he contends that fair-trade goods should be placed within a 'longer and more troubled genealogy of consumption and power' (Trentmann, 2007, p. 1080), which does not consider only the more obvious pre-cursors to fair-trade movements, such as anti-slavery boycotts and cooperative groups, but also takes into account other, more morally ambiguous, pre-cursors such as the 'Buy Empire Goods' campaign and campaigns supporting free trade.

Whilst 'caring at a distance' might not be an entirely new feature of globalised food markets, the literature shows that the recent unprecedented growth in ethical food labelling can be attributed to a number of *systemic factors*. In particular, it is possible to identify four broad socio-economic and ideological drivers that underlie the recent growth in ethical food labelling. Firstly, the nature of the contemporary agro-food system has meant that many, but certainly not all, consumers have become increasingly detached (both physically and mentally) from agricultural production. Fewer people are employed in food production; food chains have become increasingly complex; food production is becoming increasingly informed by techno-science (including biotech, machinery, information technology, etc.); food scares are becoming commonplace and the food distribution and retail sector is becoming more concentrated and delocalised (see for example, Eden et al., 2008). Within this context it is easy to see why consumer reassurance is needed and equally easy to see why labelling might offer a relatively status-quo-friendly way of achieving this. Ethical food labels work well within this world of processed food packaging, supermarket aisles and corporate social responsibility and whilst labels might be able to nudge this world in more beneficial directions their very existence is inextricably interwoven with that which they seek to critique. Secondly, the growing influence of neo-liberal political agendas has led to both a re-evaluation of the role of the state in governing agro-food and a redistribution of responsibility, culpability and blame throughout the food chain. Whilst there is some debate as to whether neo-liberalism involves a simple rollback of the state from traditional duties to allow a free-market to flourish or rather a re-positioning of state power in relation to the market, it is still clear that traditional forms of state regulation are being increasingly complemented by private standards and assurance schemes. Once again ethical food labelling fits well within this model. Thirdly, the persistence of a mainstream, yet entirely unrealistic, psycho-economic model of consumer behaviour has also lent support to labelling as a means for influencing consumption. Within this model consumption and particularly shopping is viewed as a predominantly cerebral and rational activity, in which consumers exercise their choices by carefully evaluating the different options available to them in the marketplace. This model has been disparagingly termed the 'ABC' or 'attitudes, behaviour, choice' model by Shove (2010) and the 'knowledge fix' model by Eden et al. (2008). Other academics have also been highly critical of this overly rational model of food consumption and have instead drawn attention to the importance of non-reflexive, embodied and social practices in shaping food preparation, shopping and eating routines. There is now a growing international literature focusing attention on social and embodied food practices, including studies in Europe (see for example Evans & Miele, 2012; Warde, 2005; Wheeler, 2012), in Asia (Law, 2001), in Australasia (Longhurst & Johnston, 2009) and in Africa (Mathee, 2004). Furthermore, food producers, retailers and labelling bodies clearly have a far more sophisticated understanding of how shopping for food works in practice, as evidenced by their focus on product aesthetics, product and price differentiation, packaging design and emotional branding. Despite these critiques, there is still a widely held belief, especially amongst policy makers, that labelling operates primarily at a rational-reflexive level to offer the possibility of both influencing consumer 'choice' and 'fixing' consumer ignorance. Fourthly, Freidberg (2004) has pointed to the importance of the relationships between the media, NGOs and retailers in driving the ethical labelling agenda. Indeed, she coined the term 'ethical complex' to depict these relations in the UK context. She states: 'We need to consider . . . the relationships between NGOs and certain kinds of media actors, how these relationships have shaped the British mass media's coverage of food and agriculture, and how, in turn, Britain's corporate food retailers have had to overhaul the practice of public relations' (Freidberg, 2004, p. 518). She contends that this relationship has developed to such an extent in the UK that the CSR (corporate social responsibility) efforts of supermarkets have become reliant on NGOs for information, advice, joint initiatives and public displays of approval (such as awards and favourable press-releases).

Having considered some of the systemic factors which have driven the ethical labelling agenda, we would like to turn to consider how different *national contexts* affect the use and prominence of ethical food labels. Clearly, many of the broad trends identified above are played out unevenly across space. At a global scale many, if not a majority, of consumers are still dependent on traditional forms of small-scale subsistence agriculture or local food supply chains.[2] Even at the European scale there are clear differences in the prominence of neo-liberal agendas, the perceived role of the state in governing food supply, and the perceived wisdom in shifting ethical responsibility to the market place. Drawing on the example of animal welfare governance across Europe, Miele and Lever (2014) contend that there are significant differences in the prominence and use of ethical labelling in different national contexts. For example, they contrast a 'supermarket model' prevalent in the UK and the Netherlands (where animal-welfare-friendly labels are frequently employed), to a 'welfare state' model in Scandinavia, in which there is widespread public belief that animal welfare issues are already sufficiently addressed through state regulation and in which NGOs tend to focus on influencing policy and public debate rather than consumption. They also outline a 'terroir model' of ethical labelling, which they believe is dominant in France and Italy. Within this model specific ethical issues, such as farm animal welfare, are often bundled together with concepts of tradition and typicality when communicating quality characteristics to consumers.

Finally, more micro-level contextual factors such as the specific nature and history of a particular food product also help to explain the presence and variety of ethical food labels. As a recent Euromonitor report noted: 'Values that resonate with consumers are highly country and product specific. For example, for a chocolate manufacturer in the UK, Fairtrade is the label to invest in, whilst for a sugar confectionary player in the US, the kosher label has become a must have . . .' (Euromonitor, 2016, p. 2). Jackson et al. (2009) also draw a poignant comparison between the labelling of sugar and chicken products in the UK. Whilst the former is 'sold like cement' with little attempt at product differentiation, or demonstration of provenance (it is often not even possible to tell whether it is cane or beet), the latter is often adorned with labels showing origin, welfare friendliness and environmental credentials. The authors attribute these differences to the specific history and nature of chicken as a product, pointing out that chickens were once sentient beings deserving of care; that chicken meat comes with significant health risks (such as salmonella); and that agricultural intensification has led to significant differences between traditionally reared birds and their intensively farmed counterparts allowing for product differentiation (Dixon, 2002). In addition to these differences between products, labelling schemes themselves differ in relation to a variety of factors, such as whether they are led by retailers, producers, manufacturers or NGOs (see Roe, Murdoch, & Marsden, 2005); their legal status (e.g. mandatory versus voluntary); and their specific histories. Furthermore, even within specific designations such as 'halal' or 'organic', there is competition between different versions of these standards and debate over who has the authority and credibility to set them (see Lever & Miele, 2012; Reed, 2001). This type of competitive certification can occur in contexts in which a lack of state intervention and leadership creates an overly fertile environment for private standards to flourish (Bain, Ransom, & Higgins, 2013; Miele, 2016).

Thus, one can see that ethical food labels do indeed emerge from a specific set of circumstances and that, more than this, they can be viewed as 'icons' that are interwoven with and emblematic of certain forms of agriculture and food provisioning. In the next section, we move away from the contexts in which ethical food labels emerge to consider the different effects of these labels in the marketplace and beyond.

The effects of ethical food labels: Growing the market or growing debate?

In this section we consider some of the more apparent and immediate effects of ethical food labels. Advocates of ethical food labelling claim that it helps to empower consumers; to improve food choices; to increase consumer knowledge of food production; to reconnect consumers with distant producers; to increase transparency in food chains; to change consumption and shopping behaviours; to address consumer concerns; and ultimately to grow the market for ethical foods and achieve ethical improvements across the entire agro-food system. In contrast to this view of ethical labelling, we draw on the academic literature to produce a more nuanced understanding both of the effectiveness of ethical food labels and of the mechanisms through which they work. In particular, we show that when viewed solely from the perspective of consumption, there are a series of structural and practical constraints that prevent consumers from 'voting with their wallets'. However, we also show that ethical labels can have important effects beyond the marketplace, as they can be used as a means of bolstering more traditional political and lobbying activities.

If we begin by adopting a narrow focus on consumption, it is clear to see that ethical food labels have enjoyed significant market success. In the UK, sales in 'ethical' food and drink, including organic, fair-trade, free range and freedom foods rose to £8.4 billion in 2013, which represents 8.5% of all household food sales (DEFRA, 2015). Despite the economic downturn, DEFRA (2015) also reports that sales of ethical produce have increased year on year since 2007, although this overall growth hides a 33% decline in the sale of organic food and drink since its peak in 2008. Looking at global trends in the ethical food sector, a report by the Canadian government indicates that Germany has one of the largest markets for organic food and beverage products in Europe, totalling around US$9 billion in 2009, followed by the UK and France (Agriculture & Agri-Food Canada, 2011). The report also notes that the organic food and drink market in China grew by 27.1% from 2004 to 2009 and that Japan has the largest organics market in the Asia-Pacific region, totalling US$4.3 billion in sales in 2009 (Agriculture & Agri-Food Canada, 2011).

Hence, one can see that, whilst ethical food labels are undoubtedly an important feature of contemporary global foodscapes, they still occupy a rather small niche when compared with mainstream alternatives. Furthermore, a large body of research also indicates that there is frequently a big discrepancy between the number of people who state that they are concerned about a given ethical issue and the number of people who are prepared to act upon this concern by purchasing ethical products. This difference is referred to as the 'attitude-behaviour' or 'value-action' gap. For example, Miller (2001), in his well-regarded ethnography of shopping in North London, notes that even consumers who discussed their environmental and social concerns while pushing their trolleys through the aisles rarely bought ethically marked products. Researchers have also identified value-action gaps in relation to the consumption of sustainable foods (Vermeir & Verbeke, 2006), organic foods (Padel & Foster, 2005), animal-welfare-friendly foods (Kjaernes, 2012), and in relation to waste recycling (Chung & Leung, 2007; Evans, Campbell, & Murcott, 2012; Evans, 2014) and sustainable energy use (Flynn, Bellaby, & Ricci, 2009). It would seem that taking certain ethical concerns from the arena of abstract discussion and transferring them to the arena of the marketplace causes new barriers to emerge.

One of these barriers relates to the fact that willingness-to-pay for a given product is constrained by ability-to-pay, which is of course an important consideration given that the majority of ethically labelled products retail for higher prices than their non-labelled alternatives (on this point, see Koos [2012] for an interesting discussion regarding the geographies of ethical consumption). Another significant potential barrier to changing consumption habits relates to the fact that many are social and habitual rather than cognitive and rational (see Shove, Trentmann, & Wilk, 2009; Warde, 2005). Moreover, as we have previously contended, consumer 'choice', if it does exist, is severely constrained by systems of provisioning and access to commodities. This is especially important in relation to ethically labelled products, where access appears to be very uneven in both geographical and social space. A further complication arises due to the fact that shopping always already embodies a whole series of competing ethical and moral imperatives (not to mention a degree of self-interest), so that any label prompting us to purchase a given product, if it is considered at all, will be evaluated in relation to issues such as health, family well-being, thrift, standards of hospitality etc. (see Miele & Evans, 2010; Miller, 2001). Similarly, the credibility of any claims made on product labels will also be considered in relation to a whole series of other ethical proxies, such as the aesthetic qualities of the product and the nature of the shop from which it was purchased (Eden et al., 2008). Finally, those consumers who do pay attention to food labels will not necessarily use them in the way in which they were intended; as Eden et al. (2008) contend, consumers are not passive recipients of knowledge and the information presented on product labels can be re-interpreted, validated, received, resisted or ignored.

So it would seem that whilst ethically-labelled food products have achieved a great deal of market success, there are substantial barriers which might prevent future market growth. However, this might not be as big a problem as one might first suspect because ethical labels can produce beneficial effects outside of the marketplace. Indeed, several academics have highlighted the role of ethical product labels as part of broader strategies for exerting political influence. For example, Freidberg (2004) doesn't primarily view ethical labels as tools for influencing markets, but rather as the outcome of advocacy groups and the media forcing companies to take more responsibility for their products and business practices. Similarly, Clarke et al. (2007) have argued that what we have termed *ethical consumption* throughout this chapter should be more accurately termed *political consumption*, as in their view the existence of labelled produce is more about registering importance and collective organisation than about expressing individual morality though the marketplace (see also Clarke, 2008). These authors contend that ethical/political consumption is 'indicative of a type of "politics of shame" in which one set of collective actors (campaigns, NGOs, charities) engage with other collective actors (retailers, suppliers, corporations) through the real and discursive figure of the ethical consumer' (Clarke et al., 2007, p. 238). They see ethical/political consumption not primarily as a means for recruiting new consumers to a given cause but rather as a way of enabling people who already support a given issue to extend their concerns and commitments to their shopping practices. Furthermore, they argue that demonstrating a growth in sales is a 'relatively low-cost strategy available to organisations for performing their legitimacy in the wider public realm, as well as validating themselves to members and supporters' (Clarke et al., 2007, p. 241).

Thus one can see that academics have made some important observations regarding both the effectiveness of ethical food labels and the mechanisms through which they can exert influence. In the next section we want to expand this focus on the effects of ethical food labels to consider how they exert influence in less apparent ways, not just over consumers and over the broader politics of lobbying but also over a range of other important issues, such as producers' access to markets, the broader ethics of food and broader understandings of what constitutes food quality.

The broader economic, ethical and aesthetic impacts of ethical food labels

In this section we consider the ways in which ethical food labels exert broader influences over the entire food chain and beyond. In particular, we contend that ethical food labels should be treated as 'devices' which do not merely *represent* but also *intervene* in matters of food production and in relation to the broader ethics and aesthetics of food.

How ethical labels intervene in food production

In addition to their impact on consumers, food labels also work to reshape the landscape of food production. Ethical labels do not just reward producers for the 'good work' that they are already doing but they also function to control access to markets and to set up new divisions between producers. Thus, for example, if you were a small producer farming your land in accordance with agro-ecological principles, it would not necessarily be an obvious decision to seek organic accreditation. On the positive side you would be able to gain access to new markets and to charge a premium for your product and you would receive recognition for your environmental stewardship, but on the negative side you would have to adhere to uncompromising standards, some of which might be costly to implement, and you would have to pay for the privilege of certification. As such, labelling and accreditation schemes like organic help to set up a three-fold division of the market between 'organic' producers, non-organic producers and those hidden 'inbetweeners' who adhere to stricter self-imposed standards but who do not seek accreditation.

Authors such as Guthman (2007; 2014) have also highlighted the potentially damaging effects that ethical labels, and more specifically accreditation by third parties, can have on the broader organisation of production. In particular, through her detailed analysis of organic agriculture in California, Guthman contends that because certification agencies charge fees they tend to favour well-capitalised producers. More worryingly, she contends that the fees charged by certification agencies are dependent on organic foods fetching higher prices and that this is in turn dependent on their scarcity; all of which create a potential barrier to the spread of sustainable agriculture (see also Dupuis & Goodman, 2005). Freidberg (2003) is also critical of certain ethical accreditation schemes and she notes that many of the additional costs associated with British supermarkets meeting higher ethical standards have been borne by producers in less-economically developed countries. Du Toit (2001) also notes that in order to gain access to British food markets, Zambian producers were obliged to comply with strict national and international codes which required significant investments in hygiene, environmental management and facilities such as crèches, schools and on-farm clinics. This in turn has meant that 'ethical' production has become unaffordable except for the biggest producers, a situation which has led to the formation of 'ethical enclaves'. Mutersbaugh (2002) also outlines similar problems for small producers in relation to organic certification in Mexico.

Recent academic scholarship has also drawn attention to a range of other undesirable consequences of ethical labelling. In particular, authors have highlighted the ways in which ethical food labels such as organic and fair trade can function to reproduce further social injustices and power imbalances in the food system. For example, Trauger and Murphy (2013) in their study of banana production in the Domican Republic contend that organic certification led to a series of political, environmental and social outcomes which were contrary to consumer expectations. In particular, they show how organic certification helped to encourage the entrance of transnational corporations, such as Del Monte, into the marketplace. They also argue that the price premiums that consumers paid for organic produce might not flow through to farmers or agricultural labourers. Furthermore, they maintain that the high prices attained for organic bananas drew more producers into the market and encouraged existing producers to intensify their production. Ironically, this intensification was partly responsible for the increased incidence of fungal diseases such as Black Sigatoka, which in turn forced producers to use fungicides and, as a result, to lose their organic accreditation. There is also a growing 'critical fair trade literature' which raises similar issues in relation to fair-trade certification. For example, Philips (2014) draws attention to some of the unintended consequences of fair-trade certification in relation to sugar producers in Malawi. Furthermore, Staricco and Ponte (2015) pointed out that fair-trade certification had the effect of further marginalising the most vulnerable producers in the Argentinean wine market. Finally, Elias and Saussey (2013), in their study of fair-trade shea butter produced by women in Burkina Faso, inferred that the low returns earned by these women for their product casts doubt on the fairness and solidarity aspects of fair-trade certification. Thus one can see that ethical labels and especially their associated certification schemes can exert great influences over production as well as consumption.

How ethical labels intervene in the broader ethics of food

Ethical food labels do not only depict or reinforce pre-existing ethical concerns; they also help to generate new ones. More specifically, the very form of *product labels* as both a medium for expression and a device for influencing opinion helps to shape the broader ethical terrain around food. For example, labels help to shape what matters of concern around food can and cannot be; they separate and group together different matters of concern in new ways; and they help to determine who has the right to be concerned.

Much academic debate around ethical food labels has focused on whether their increasing prevalence represents a broader 'marketization of ethics'. For example, Bauman (1999) and Needham (2003) view ethical food labels as symptomatic of a democratic crisis in which public participation and civil engagement is being replaced by private expressions of concern through the marketplace. If this were indeed the case, then they would represent a wholesale transformation of the ethical field. Crucially, it would imply that one's ability to engage in this new form of marketised ethics would be dependent on one's access to the market for ethical produce. This in turn would be structured not only by income and social class but by a whole range of other social and geographical factors, such as distance from farm shops or whether your local supermarket stocks these foods. In contrast, other authors have viewed the growth of ethical labelling as a positive sign of democratic renewal; in their accounts labelling is a non-bureaucratic and low-threshold way to express concern (see Follesdal, 2004; Micheletti, 2003).

These debates are certainly important. However, as we have argued previously, the effects of food labels extend well beyond the marketplace to influence public debate and to help bolster the lobbying power of NGOs. In some ways this is reassuring, as it means that we can be less worried about a wholesale marketisation of food ethics, yet in other ways it is more disconcerting, as it reflects the extended power and reach of these 'ethical devices' beyond the marketplace. This is important, because ethical labels and their associated certification schemes are not neutral or transparent mediums for expressing ethics, but rather they help to shape what foods ethics can be. For example, if we consider the ethical issue of farm animal welfare, then one could argue that this ethical concern has been framed and reshaped in different ways, as it has been incorporated into different labelling schemes. The very nature of what farm animal welfare can be is then, to some extent, shaped by whether it is treated as a standalone ethical issue in a dedicated assurance scheme (such as Freedom Food in the UK), or whether it forms part of an organic certification, or whether it is integrated with broader quality labels. What is more, these are not just issues for the market, as these types of classifications and groupings help to inform broader public opinion and debate. Furthermore, ethical food labels do not just represent the most important or pressing ethical issues that we face; rather they represent a pragmatic mixture of what are genuine matters of concern, what might work in the marketplace and the specific history of a particular ethical issue or product. This helps to explain why fair-trade labels are more closely associated with certain products, such as bananas, coffee and chocolate but not with other foods. It also helps to explain why some important ethical issues remain unlabelled.

How ethical labels intervene in food quality

Issues of food quality (see Harvey, McMeekin, & Warde, 2004) and more broadly 'economies of quality' (see Callon, Méadel, & Rabeharisoa, 2002) have become an important feature of the academic literature around food. In this section we want to identify two ways in which ethical food labels can impact upon food quality. Firstly, from the point of view of consumers, ethical food labelling provides a relatively novel indicator of food quality, which has become increasingly important as consumers have become more detached from producers. However, rather than replacing traditional signals of food quality, such as appearance and taste, we believe that these new symbolic devices sit alongside and interact with more aesthetic indicators. As Evans and Miele (2012, p. 311) state: '. . . just as consumers make inferences about the animal welfare credentials of products based on their sensorial qualities, so they also make assumptions about the sensorial qualities of products based on their animal welfare credentials. . . . Food labels have the potential not only to influence how we think about certain foods but also to influence how we experience them, how they taste to us'. Eden et al. (2008) also propose that ethical labels such as organic are not evaluated in isolation but rather in relation to a whole series of proxy indicators of quality, such as the appearance of the product and the type of shop from which it was purchased. Secondly, ethical food labels and their associated certification schemes function to standardise food quality in sometimes problematic ways. Whilst this is not always the case, food labels can help to perpetuate more uniform notions of what constitutes food quality at the cost of more nuanced understandings of how different versions of good quality are embedded in different places and settings.

Conclusions: Ethical food labels as icons and devices

Throughout this chapter we have attempted to show that ethical food labels do not merely *represent* specific types of food and food production but rather they function as both *icons* and *devices*. They are *icons* because they encapsulate a particular form of food provisioning and they embody the socio-economic circumstances through which they emerge. They are *devices* because they act upon and intervene with, not only consumption practices and forms of political lobbying, but also with broader economic, ethical and aesthetic dimensions of food.

With regards to the *contexts* in which ethical food labels emerged, we drew on the academic literature to identify a set of historical, systemic, national and micro contexts, which either acted as necessary precursors for ethical labelling to emerge, or which helped to shape the specific forms that ethical labels adopted. In particular, we showed how ethical labelling is inextricably interwoven with certain contemporary types of food provisioning, especially those in which there is a disconnection between consumers and producers. Furthermore, we showed how neoliberal governance strategies and rational-cerebral models of consumption also helped to promote ethical food labelling as a way of reshaping foodscapes. Finally, we illustrated how these systemic influences are played out unevenly through space by drawing on the example of national variations in farm-animal-welfare labelling.

With regards to the *effects* of ethical food labels, we considered whether the main function of these labels was to grow the market for ethical produce or to grow debate around ethical and unethical systems of food production. We contended that if the success of ethical food labels was to be judged solely in terms of market share, then there were significant structural and practical constraints that might prevent the mainstreaming of these products (e.g. ability to pay, the routinized nature of consumption, the nature of systems of provisioning etc.). However, we also contended that ethical food labels can have important effects beyond the marketplace, as they can be used as a means of bolstering more traditional political and lobbying activities (Clarke et al., 2007). In addition to these more apparent effects of ethical food labelling, we also considered how ethical food labels exert influence over a range of other important issues, such as producers' access to markets, the broader ethics of food and broader understandings of what constitutes food quality. In particular, we argued that ethical food labels do not just represent the most important or pressing ethical issues that we face; rather they represent a pragmatic mixture of what are genuine matters of concern, what might work in the marketplace and the specific history of a particular ethical issue or product.

Finally, we would like to end by posing the question of whether ethical food labels are sufficient to achieve the types of changes that are required to reshape global agro-food systems to face the substantial and imminent threats of climate change, soil degradation and global food security. We suspect that they might not be up to the task and that what is really needed are more radical state-led reforms of the agro-food sector, including the widespread adoption of agro-ecological farming techniques and the re-localisation of food provisioning. Bearing this in mind we believe that there is a need for further critical research into the role and effectiveness of food labels and into potential alternatives for bringing about positive ethical and environmental changes within the food system. Important areas of further investigation are the origins of food labelling and the broader social and political contexts from which ethical food labelling emerges and gains its efficacy. Additionally, there is still important research to be conducted on the unintended social and environmental consequences of ethical labelling schemes and on the ways in which labelling as a strategy reaches well beyond its initial ethico-commercial context to shape broader ethical and political debates in sometimes helpful and sometimes unhelpful ways.

Notes

1 We use the term 'ethical food labels' rather than 'political food labels' throughout the text; however, in section 3 we draw attention to authors such as Clarke, Barnett, Cloke and Malpass (2007) who explicitly debate whether these types of labels operate on a primarily ethical or political register.

2 According to recent research, family farms constitute over 98% of all farms, and work on 53% of agricultural land (see Graeub et al., 2015). Altieri (1999, p. 197) also notes that 'the great majority of farmers in Latin America are peasants who still farm small plots of land, usually in marginal environments utilizing traditional and subsistence methods'.

References

Agriculture & Agri-Food Canada. (2011). *Global trends. Sustainable Food and Beverages Market Analysis Report* (AAFC Publication No. 11428E). Ottawa: Agriculture and Agri-food Canada.

Altieri, M.A. (1999). Applying agroecology to enhance the productivity of peasant farming systems in Latin America. *Environment, Development and Sustainability*, *1*(3–4), 197–217.

Bain, C., Ransom, E. & Higgins, V. (2013). Private agri-food standards: Contestation, hybridity and the politics of standards. *International Journal of Sociology of Agriculture and Food*, *20(1)*, 1–10.

Bauman, Z. (1999). *In search of politics*. Stanford: Stanford University Press.

Callon, M., Méadel, C. & Rabeharisoa, V. (2002). The economy of qualities. *Economy and Society*, *31*(2), 194–217.

Chung, S. S. & Leung, M. M.Y. (2007). The value-action gap in waste recycling: the case of undergraduates in Hong Kong. *Environmental Management*, *40*(4), 603–612.

Clarke, N. (2008). From ethical consumerism to political consumption. *Geography Compass*, *2*(6), 1870–1884.

Clarke, N., Barnett, C., Cloke, P. & Malpass, A. (2007). Globalising the consumer: Doing politics in an ethical register. *Political Geography*, *26*(3), 231–249.

DEFRA. (2015). *Food statistics pocketbook 2015 in year update*. London: Department for Environment food and Rural Affairs.

Dixon, J. (2002). *The changing chicken: chooks, cooks and culinary culture*. Sydney: University of New South Wales Press.

DuPuis, E. M. & Goodman, D. (2005). Should we go "home" to eat?: toward a reflexive politics of localism. *Journal of rural studies*, *21*(3), 359–371.

Du Toit, A. (2001). *Ethical trading: a force for improvement, or corporate whitewash*? London: Overseas Development Institute. Retrieved from http://www.odi.org.uk/nrp/

Eden, S., Bear, C. & Walker, G. (2008). Mucky carrots and other proxies: problematising the knowledge-fix for sustainable and ethical consumption. *Geoforum*, *39*(2), 1044–1057.

Elias, M. & Saussey, M. (2013). "The Gift that Keeps on Giving": Unveiling the Paradoxes of Fair Trade Shea Butter. *Sociologia Ruralis*, *53*(2), 158–179.

Euromonitor (2016). *Introducing passport ethical labels*. Retrieved May, 2016, from Euromonitor Passport Database.

Evans, A. B. & Miele, M. (2012). Between food and flesh: how animals are made to matter (and not matter) within food consumption practices. *Environment and Planning D: Society and Space*, *30*(2), 298–314.

Evans, D. (2014). *Food waste: home consumption, material culture and everyday life*. London: Bloomsbury Publishing.

Evans, D., Campbell, H. & Murcott, A. (2012). A brief pre-history of food waste and the social sciences. *The Sociological Review*, *60*(S2), 5–26.

Flynn, R., Bellaby, P. & Ricci, M. (2009). The "value-action gap" in public attitudes towards sustainable energy: the case of hydrogen energy. *The Sociological Review*, *57*(S2), 159–180.

Follesdal, A. (2004). Political consumerism as chance and challenge. In M. Micheletti, A. Follesdal, & D. Stolle (Eds) *Politics, products and markets: exploring political consumerism past and present* (pp.3–20). London: Transaction Publishers.

Freidberg, S. (2003). Cleaning up down South: supermarkets, ethical trade and African horticulture. *Social & Cultural Geography*, *4*(1), 27–43.

Freidberg, S. (2004). The ethical complex of corporate food power. *Environment and Planning D: Society and Space*, *22*(4), 513–531.

Graeub, B. E., Chappell, M. J., Wittman, H., Ledermann, S., Kerr, R. B. & Gemmill-Herren, B. (2015). The state of family farms in the world. *World Development*. http://dx.doi.org/10.1016/j.worlddev.2015.05.012
Guthman, J. (2007). The Polanyian way? Voluntary food labels as neoliberal governance. *Antipode, 39*(3), 456–478.
Guthman, J. (2014). *Agrarian dreams: the paradox of organic farming in California*. Oakland: University of California Press.
Harvey, M., McMeekin, A. & Warde, A. (2004). *Qualities of food*. Manchester: Manchester University Press.
Jackson, P., Ward, N. & Russell, P. (2009). Moral economies of food and geographies of responsibility. *Transactions of the Institute of British Geographers*, 34(1), 12–24.
Kaiser, M. & Lien, M. E. (Eds.). (2006). *Ethics and the politics of food: preprints of the 6th Congress of the European Society for Agricultural and Food Ethics*, EurSAFE 2006, Oslo, Norway, June 22–24, 2006 (6). Wageninggen: Wageningen Academic Publishers.
Kjærnes, U. (2012). Ethics and action: a relational perspective on consumer choice in the European politics of food. *Journal of Agricultural and Environmental Ethics*, 25(2), 145–162.
Koos, S. (2012). What drives political consumption in Europe? A multi-level analysis on individual characteristics, opportunity structures and globalization. *Acta Sociologica*, 55(1), 37–57.
Law, L. (2001). Home cooking: Filipino women and geographies of the senses in Hong Kong. *Ecumene*, 8, 264–283.
Lever, J. & Miele, M. (2012). The growth of halal meat markets in Europe: an exploration of the supply side theory of religion. *Journal of Rural Studies, 28*(4), 528–537.
Longhurst, R., Johnston, L. and Ho, E. (2009). A visceral approach: cooking "at home" with migrant women in Hamilton, *New Zealand. Transactions of the Institute of British Geographers, 34*, 333–345.
Mathee, D. D. (2004). Towards an emotional geography of eating practices: an exploration of the food rituals of women of color working on farms in the Western Cape *Gender, Place and Culture: A Journal of Feminist Geography, 11* 437–443.
Micheletti, M. (2003). Shopping with and for virtues. In M. Micheletti (Ed.), *Political virtue and shopping. individuals, consumerism and collective action* (pp. 149–168). New York: Palgrave Macmillan US.
Miele, M. (2016). Killing Animals for food: how religion, science and technology affect the debate about and halal and conventional slaughter, *Food Ethics, 1*(1) 47–60.
Miele, M. & Evans, A. (2010). When foods become animals: ruminations on ethics and responsibility in care-full practices of consumption. *Ethics, Place and Environment, 13*(2), 171–190.
Miele, M. & Lever, J. (2014). Improving animal welfare in Europe: cases of comparative bio-sustainabilities. In T. Marsden & A. Morley (Eds.), *Sustainable food systems building a new paradigm*, (pp. 143–165). London: Routledge.
Miller, D. (2001). *The dialectics of shopping*. Chicago: University of Chicago Press.
Mutersbaugh, T. (2002). The number is the beast: a political economy of organic-coffee certification and producer unionism. *Environment and Planning A, 34*(7), 1165–1184.
Needham, C. (2003). *Citizen-consumers: new labour's marketplace democracy*. London: Catalyst.
Padel, S. & Foster, C. (2005). Exploring the gap between attitudes and behaviour: understanding why consumers buy or do not buy organic food. *British Food Journal, 107*(8), 606–625.
Phillips, D. P. (2014). Uneven and unequal people-centered development: the case of Fair Trade and Malawi sugar producers. *Agriculture and human values, 31*(4), 563–576.
Reed, M. (2001). Fight the future! how the contemporary campaigns of the UK organic movement have arisen from their composting of the past. *Sociologia Ruralis, 41*(1), 131–145.
Roe, E, J., Murdoch, J. & Marsden, T. (2005). The retail of welfare-friendly products: A comparative assessment of the nature of the market for welfare-friendly products in six European Countries. In A. Butterworth (Ed.). *Proceedings from the Welfare Quality Conference: Science and Society improving Animal Welfare*, 17–18th November 2005, Brussels.
Sayer, A. (2000). Moral economy and political economy. *Studies in Political Economy, 61*, 79–104.
Shove, E. (2010). Beyond the ABC: climate change policy and theories of social change. *Environment and Planning A*, 42(6), 1273–1285.
Shove, E., Trentmann, F. & Wilk, R. (2009). *Time, consumption and everyday life: practice, materiality and culture*. Oxford: Berg.
Smith, S. J. (2005). States, markets and an ethic of care. *Political Geography, 24*(1), 1–20.
Staricco, J. I. & Ponte, S. (2015). Quality regimes in agro-food industries: a regulation theory reading of Fair Trade wine in Argentina. *Journal of Rural Studies, 38*, 65–76.

Trauger, A. & Murphy, A. (2013). On the moral equivalence of global commodities: placing the production and consumption of organic bananas. *International Journal of Sociology of Agriculture and Food*, *20*(2), 197–217.

Trentmann, F. (2007). Before "fair trade": empire, free trade, and the moral economies of food in the modern world. *Environment and Planning D: Society and Space*, *25*(6), 1079–1102.

Vermeir, I. & Verbeke, W. (2006). Sustainable food consumption: exploring the consumer "attitude–behavioral intention" gap. *Journal of Agricultural and Environmental Ethics*, *19*(2), 169–194.

Warde, A. (2005). Consumption and theories of practice. *Journal of Consumer Culture*, *5*(2), 131–153.

Wheeler, K. (2012). The practice of Fairtrade support. *Sociology*, *46*(1), 126–141.

18

Consumption policies within different theoretical frameworks

Dale Southerton and David Evans

Introduction: Regulating consumers and shifting consumption patterns

This chapter critically examines consumption-oriented policies with reference to the theoretical frameworks upon which they are founded. We use the term *consumption policies* to capture the diversity of ways in which consumption and policy can be understood. More usually, terms like *consumer* or *consumer behavior* are used to prefix the term *policy*. Both are problematic and draw from a wide range of academic fields (from law to neuro-science). Consumer policies tend to refer to legislative measures designed to protect individual consumers in various ways. These can include health and safety regulations, product labeling to advise on risks (such as the voltage capacity on electronic goods), the prohibition of particular forms of consumption during designated times (for example, the sale of alcohol) or in public spaces (for example, smoking bans), or policies that seek to give vulnerable citizens greater access to consumer markets (see Kjaernes, 2011 for a discussion of consumer regulation; Everson, 2011 on consumer rights and the law). Consumer behavior policies tend to refer to initiatives that have a more voluntaristic element. These are policies that seek to change patterns of consumption by influencing the way that people live their lives, and can include social marketing to influence purchase decisions (McKenzie-Mohr, 2000), the provision of infrastructures to encourage particular activities (such as cycle lanes; see Watson, 2012), or incentivizing producers to innovate new products whose consumption might yield societal benefits (such as energy-efficient domestic appliances). Consumer policies affect consumer behavior and vice versa, and both approaches tend to reduce consumption to a matter of the purchasing choices made by individuals (Shove, 2010), who are then assumed to be responsible for the consequences of their consumption (cf. Clarke, Barnett, Cloke & Malpass, 2007).

This chapter examines the relationship between theoretical understandings of consumption and how they frame policy approaches. We begin by discussing 'orthodox' framings of consumption policies, which privilege the consumer as a 'sovereign' market actor (Southerton, Hand & Warde, 2004). Core theoretical approaches are examined with examples of how they have been applied within consumption policy frameworks. These include economic theories that focus policies around price mechanisms, taxation and incentives (Southerton & Ulph, 2014); psychological theories that emphasize how values and attitudes shape consumption and focus policies around information and marketing campaigns (Stern, 2000); and behavioral economics that modifies neo-classical economics to encompass insights from other fields (including social psychology and neuroscience) and focus policies on changing choice architecture and default choice sets (Sunstein & Reisch, 2014).

We then discuss 'heterodox' framings of consumption policy, which are based on theoretical approaches that emphasize the inter-connections between different processes of societal change across a number of scales (McMeekin & Southerton, 2012). Three approaches are examined, again with reference to the forms of consumption policy associated with each. First are governance approaches to citizen consumers, consumer protest, and the responsibilisation of the consumer. Associated policies focus on embracing or mobilizing the ethical concerns of consumers and rendering them 'responsible' for societal change (cf. Barnett, Cloke, Clarke & Malpass, 2011). Second are political economy approaches that focus on the relationship between production and consumption (Fine, 2002), highlighting the critical role of intermediaries (e.g. retailers or consumer associations) in changing consumption (Spaargaren, 2003), with a focus on policies such as the standardization of products, product labeling to stimulate upstream innovation, and grassroots initiatives to foster niche innovation (Seyfang, 2004). Third are theories of practice (see chapter 3), a broad body of theory that explores the social organization of everyday practices that are often routine and inconspicuous in the forms of consumption involved. Such approaches seek to encourage shifts in *practice* through policies that simultaneously affect the material, cultural, pragmatic, and temporal ordering of practices by changing their trajectories (see Spurling, McMeekin, Shove, Southerton & Welch, 2013).

To conclude, we briefly consider the grand societal challenge presented by climate change, and environmental sustainability more specifically, to illustrate and summarize the principal distinctions between theoretical understandings of consumption and their attendant policy approaches. It is argued that grand societal challenges require changes to consumption beyond the sovereign individual, and on scales far greater than orthodox theoretical framings of consumption policies can deliver, and that this represents the critical future challenge for consumption policies (see also Geels, McMeekin, Mylan & Southerton, 2015).

Orthodox framings: Consumer-directed policies

Orthodox framings of consumption policies, drawn principally from economic and psychological theory, take as their ontological starting point the actions of individual consumers. When applied to consumption they present the individual as a sovereign consumer, where consumption is largely a matter of personal decision making within commercial markets that, in turn, respond to (aggregate) consumer demands and provide the sovereign consumer with a range of product choices from which to shape their lifestyle (see Southerton at al, 2004). Within this portfolio model of action, consumer choices are the outcome of an individual's values and attitudes in relation to the utility and quality of the products available for acquisition. This model implies linear processes of cause and effect: to change behaviour (for example, towards more sustainable ways of life or healthier diets), and therefore what people consume, requires changes in the attitudes that shape, and values that frame, their consumer choices (see Shove, 2010).

Economic theory: Price and taxation

A basic principal of economic theories of consumption is that individuals seek to maximize their utility (well-being) subject to the constraints of wealth, income, and time (for a detailed discussion see Southerton & Ulph, 2014). This approach assumes the consumer has rational preferences vis-à-vis all the goods available in the economy. This does not imply that that the consumer's choices need be conscious; they could reflect automation of the utility function. By *rational* economists mean that choices are made on the basis of perfect information, and that preferences are complete (they cover any possible set of choices that might be made) as well as transitive (they are mutually consistent). These preferences are represented by the consumer's utility function and it is assumed that beyond a certain point, additional units of consumption for a particular good or service do not yield proportional increases in well-being. For example, the additional utility derived from consuming a third scoop of ice cream is assumed to be less than the utility derived from consuming the first scoop. One possible interpretation of diminishing marginal utility is that consumption policies ought to favor the additional consumption of poorer people (for example, through policies of welfare provision) over the additional consumption of wealthy people (Birchenhall, 2011).

This model of behavior underpins many policies on consumption. Accepting that consumers make rational choices between goods and services within markets on the basis of their marginal utility and costs, it follows that pricing is an obvious mechanism for shaping consumer preferences. At a micro-level smoking policies underpinned by price increases to the cost of cigarettes (via taxation) are a classic example. Economic theory would suggest that increasing price will reduce demand. However, tobacco is an addictive substance meaning that people may not respond quickly to changes in price. In cases like this, when products and services are resilient to price shocks, economic theory suggests that demand is inelastic (see De Marchi, 2011). At a macro level, this model suggests that societal levels of consumption are influenced by income and wealth. It follows that consumer policies that wish to stimulate demand, for example in response to economic shrinkage, are premised on the assumption that people will consume more if they are richer. Government policies around interest rate reduction are based on the logic that rational consumers will decide that it is in their interests to spend more in the present than to save for future consumption (Bernheim & Whinston, 2008).

Not all of the goods that affect the consumer's well-being are necessarily traded privately via market exchanges. Public goods, which are non-excludable (those who have not paid cannot be denied access to it) and non-rivalrous (consumption by a given individual does not reduce the amount available for other consumers), would be undersupplied if left to market-mechanisms. For example, if the residents of a given street agree to pay for lighting in public areas, the benefit that any individual derives from having it – greater security and visibility – is unaffected by the benefit that their neighbors derive (non-rivalrous). Similarly, if a particular resident refuses to pay their share they still have access to these benefits (non-excludable). This is known as the free rider problem, and it is the reason why public goods are usually provisioned by national governments and financed by taxation (Kemp, 2002).

A second reason why a number of goods are not traded in markets is because it is hard to ascertain property rights. Examples include clean air and fish stocks. The use of such resources can have significant deleterious impacts, but these are not reflected in the private costs faced by firms or households – rather they are external costs. Economists argue that the existence of externalities is a market failure that provides another role for government intervention in the economy through taxes and subsidies. For example, in the case of environmental externalities it would be suggested that the price of air travel be increased to reflect the 'true' cost of emitting high levels of carbon, which in turn would cause a reduction in air travel and carbon emitted. Similarly, it has been suggested that a set of tradeable property rights (e.g. permits for fishing or carbon emissions) could be established to incentivize the reduction of such costs (Lovell,

Bulkeley & Liverman, 2009). The fundamental problem underpinning non-market traded goods is correctly estimating the value and externalities of these goods (Schor, 2005).

Psychology: Values, attitudes, and consumer choice

Psychological theories, like economics, view consumption as an individual matter but suggest it is shaped by a different set of factors (see also chapter 20). For example, the individual consumer might be influenced by those around them – who influence their attitudes and values – or by intermediaries such as advertising and marketing. Policies on consumption often draw together the core premise of both economic and psychological theories; however, psychological theories bring the limitation of purely economic mechanisms into sharp relief. Other than the difficulties of interfering with market mechanisms, three further problems can be identified. First, as has been noted, certain activities are relatively 'inelastic' when it comes to price rises. Second, incentives do not necessarily foster long-term changes in behaviour. For example, a study conducted as part of the Danish Environmental Research programme gave free one-month bus passes to 400 car-driving commuters. Following a significant increase in the number of journeys made by bus rather than car, the number of bus journeys declined and people largely reverted back to driving their cars after the trial period (Thøgerson and Moller, 2008). Third, monetary penalties or disincentives can work to legitimate the behaviour being discouraged. For example, when parents at a kibbutz school were fined for turning up late to collect their children the number of late pick-ups rose, because parents felt that they were paying for the right to be late (Gneezy and Rustichini, 2000).

A second approach is to assume that consumers already possess particular values and attitudes (i.e. those that the analyst or policy maker would wish for them to hold), and to inform them of the available opportunities to address their consumption and exercise their preferences accordingly. Such approaches can be expensive in relation to their effectiveness. For example, during the 1980s Californian utility companies spent $200 million to advertise residential energy efficiency measures, but household energy use changed only marginally. In one case, the Pacific Gas and Electricity Company spent more money advertising the benefits of home insulation in California than it would have cost to install the insulation directly into the homes of every person it was trying to reach (McKenzie-Mohr, 2000).

Partly in response to the limited success of price-incentive and information policies, and partly to counter the perceived influence of commercial marketing on consumer attitudes, social marketing has emerged as an influential approach to consumption policy. It seeks to encourage individuals to conform to a model of rational behavior by recognizing that it would be sensible to modify their ways of life to contribute to a public good (like helping to save the planet). Such approaches often employ segmentation models on the basis that information campaigns are most effective when tailored and targeted at particular groups. Targeted marketing also opens the opportunity to develop campaigns attached to values that are not necessarily based on the assumption that people already possess or practice the specific values that the campaigns are intended to foster. A principal focus in this approach is using behavioral prompts, commitments to community-based schemes, and appeals to social norms in order to overcome perceived attitudinal barriers to change. An useful example (Evans, McMeekin & Southerton, 2012) is the application of social marketing to bring about a 10% reduction in residential water use focused on garden watering in Ontario, Canada. Four test groups were chosen: a control group that received no intervention; a second group that received an information brochure; a third group that had access to 'master gardener' volunteers; and a fourth group selected for a community-based social marketing approach. This latter group received a visit from a student who explained the initiative in detail, were given a sign to be hung on the outside water tap reminding them when not to water their gardens, and were asked to sign a pledge to reduce water and inform their neighbors about the initiative. The results were revealing. The group that was given informational brochures actually increased the amount of water they used when watering their lawns, whereas the group selected for the social marketing approach decreased their watering by 54%.

One fundamental problem with psychological approaches is that apparently pro-social values (whether towards the environment or health) do not seem to translate into pro-social actions. For example, DEFRA (2008) demonstrates that pro-environmental attitudes are consistently higher than the percentage of people who take measures to change their behavior. While this discrepancy can be explained partly by survey respondents not being sure about what steps they could take, the evidence suggests that the relationship between 'attitudes', 'values', and 'behavior' is not straightforward. The 'value–action gap' reveals a critical lacuna in policies for changing patterns and forms of consumption.

Behavioral economics: Habit, automaticity, and nudge

The persistence of the value–action gap brings the limitations of price, information, and social marketing policies into focus. This in turn has forced some recent revisions to the fundamental theoretical premises of orthodox economics and psychology. This shift is generally referred to as 'behavioral economics' and at the core of this loose constellation of perspectives is recognition that people in market situations (and by analogy, other situations of 'choice' and decision) do not calculate rationally on the basis of perfect knowledge or in light of fixed intransitive preferences (Sunstein & Reisch, 2014).

Rather, as Thaler and Sunstein (2008) illustrate, behavioral economics adopts insights from cognitive science to the effect that that the brain has two systems generating behavior. One is 'automatic', uncontrolled, effortless, associative, fast, unconscious, and skilled. The other is 'reflective', controlled, effortful, deductive, slow, self-aware, and rule following. The first, argue Thaler and Sunstein, is far more important. Much behavior is governed by automatic mental processes and involves little deliberation or rationality. The result is said to be biased judgments, difficulties in resisting temptation, and a strong tendency to social conformity. Accordingly, Thaler and Sunstein advocate the importance of better 'choice architecture' – favorable default settings, good infrastructural design, feedback on the outcomes of actions, and purposefully aligned economic incentives – to steer people away from the detrimental consequences of their naturally rash behavior, and to 'nudge' their automated propensities towards pro-social ends:

> A nudge, as we will use the term, is any aspect of the choice architecture that alters people's behavior in a predictable way without forbidding any options or significantly changing their economic incentives. To count as a mere nudge, the intervention must be easy and cheap to avoid. Nudges are not mandates. Putting fruit at eye level counts as a nudge. Banning junk food does not.
>
> *(Thaler & Sunstein, 2008, p. 6)*

Other classic examples are the automatic opt-in for pensions schemes and organ donations or the use of housefly images in urinals to prevent men from urinating on the floor. While a rather obtuse solution, since it uses rational individual choice as the yardstick for remedial action, it nevertheless emphasizes the normality of repetition and the absence of deliberation in everyday conduct and points to how the external environment steers behavior.

Orthodox policy framings and the resilience of methodological individualism

Common to all the perspectives presented above is a view – whether implicit or explicit – of consumption as a matter of the individual engaging in very many discrete events, typically understood to be purchasing behaviors. Of course, all disciplinary approaches admit to contextual influences on individual decision making, and attention has variously been drawn to income, subjective norms, socio-demographic characteristics, lifestyle group membership, and emotional factors. Nevertheless, individual choice – both 'automatic' and 'reflective' – is the core presupposition, with contextual influences considered secondary to the main analytic focus. Even in accounts that seemingly query the basis of deliberative action, such as behavioral economics, methodological individualism – a view of social phenomena as the aggregate of individual actions – remains hegemonic in policy framings of consumption.

The application of methodological individualism to understandings of consumption has been challenged on many grounds, but five concerns are particularly germane with respect to policy approaches (for a full discussion see Warde & Southerton, 2012). First and foremost, these approaches largely equate consumption with purchase, without reference to the manner in which goods, services, and experiences are appropriated in people's everyday lives. Second, the extensive evidence of the social patterning of purchase suggests that 'preferences' are not a simple function of personal financial resources. Rather, people conform to the norms of groups to which they are attached, and social groups differ in their views (or tastes) of what is valuable and desirable. Third, choices are not independent of one another. Past purchases preclude some options and leave gaps for new ones. People learn from experience, which items give them pleasure or satisfaction. Fourth, many items are acquired repetitiously but not necessarily as a consequence of automation. Firms make very strategic investments, through advertising and branding, to try to ensure that repeat purchases happen. Fifth, the role of deliberation is easily exaggerated. Much of the most environmentally problematic features of consumption (such as energy or water use) are invisible at the point of purchase or use, and a great deal of consuming occurs in contexts where someone else does the purchasing (as in the case of women purchasing food to be consumed by household members). Each of these five reservations undermines perspectives that approach consumption as principally a matter of individual discretionary actions.

Heterodox framings: Changing consumption

Heterodox framings of consumption policies derive from an altogether different ontological starting point. Where orthodox perspectives proceed via a focus on the actions of individual consumers, heterodox perspectives draw attention to a broader range of actors (both human and non-human) in order to theorize the heterogeneous elements that together configure the organization of consumption. In this view, consumption cannot be understood as the linear outcome of determining and constraining factors. Heterodox approaches recognize that consumption results from the interconnections between multiple processes including (but not limited to) markets, policies, industry structures, infrastructures, conventions, and technologies. These perspectives are broadly sociological in orientation but draw from a range of allied disciplines such as science and technology studies, political science, geography, anthropology, and innovation studies. Put crudely, the task of changing consumption or developing policies is not a matter of changing what individuals do. Rather, as Urry (2011) points out in his discussion of climate change policies, it is a matter of 'changing whole systems of economic, technological and social practice'.

Governing consumption: The responsibilzation of 'the consumer'

Consumption has traditionally been understood as incongruous with the ideals of citizenship (Trentmann, 2007). Whereas orthodox perspectives present consumption as individualized, self-interested and frivolous, citizenship is typically associated with collective activity, civic duty, and activity in the political sphere. To the extent that 'consumers' are conventionally understood as 'citizens', the emphasis is on the obligations of the state to provision certain goods, services, or experiences (such as education, healthcare, or housing) for consumption (see also chapter 4.1). These understandings are potentially problematic from the point of view of consumption policies that have the responsibilities of 'citizen–consumers' (whether for their own health or for public goods such as the environment) firmly in their sights. A resolution to this tension might be found in the growing recognition – both intellectually and politically – that consumption is a site through which people can exert and assert their political and activist positions (Dubuisson-Quellier, 2013). Whether these developments are understood as 'ethical consumption' (Newholm, Shaw & Harrison, 2005) or 'political consumerism' – the basic logic is that consumers 'make choices among producers and products with the goal of changing objectionable institutional or market practices' (Micheletti, 2003, p. 2).

One possible interpretation of ethical and political consumerism is that consumers are voluntarily assuming responsibilities and demonstrating solidarity with distant others. It is nevertheless instructive to situate the contemporary figure of the 'responsible consumer' in relation to the broader history of consumer activism. Gabriel and Lang (2015) usefully suggest that the 'alternative' consumer represents the fourth wave of consumer activism that builds on previous waves of the co-operative movement (consumers co-operating with one another to take control of production); the value for money movement (providing consumers with authoritative information on products); and Naderism (concerned with the power of large corporations as compared to the power of individuals). Crucially, they suggest that these four waves have a number of features in common, principally an emphasis on collective action and recognition of the need for organization. In addition to providing an important historical caveat to claims that consumption has spontaneously become politically and ethically charged, this highlights the importance of processes that reach beyond the ethical dispositions of individual consumers.

From a slightly different angle, there are good reasons to question the legitimacy of maneuvers that locate responsibilities for responding to complex and systemic challenges (such as obesity or climate change) at the level of individual consumers. Governmentality theories (Foucault, 1977) address techniques of government when power is distributed and decentralized by focusing on the co-evolution of the modern state and the idea of the autonomous individual. In this view, contemporary forms of governing involve creating – and working through – the capabilities of freely choosing subjects in order to achieve particular outcomes. Central to this endeavor is the autonomous individual's capacity for self-control, together with the existence of multiple authorities and agencies below the level of the state to provide the expertise and knowledge required to ensure that people act as they are required to act. For example, people are increasingly governing themselves in relation to health promotion by regulating calorific intake, exercising, and smoking less. This can be viewed as an active accomplishment of a number of actors (public health campaigners, medical professionals, gym trainers) and their associated knowledge practices (information on populations, Body Mass Index statistics, healthy eating guidelines).

Drawing on these ideas, Barnett et al. (2011) suggest that the growth of ethical consumption cannot be attributed to the agency of individual consumers. They posit a focus on the efforts and repertoires of organizations and institutions such as campaigners, lobby groups, and ethical trading associations in working the consumer up to the surface of government. Their analysis draws attention to the way in which the strategies and tactics of governmental and non-governmental actors work to problematize everyday consumption, provide opportunities for individuals to reflect on their own ethical dispositions, and offer practical and moral instruction (in the form of 'how to' guides) on how to consume more ethically. They also suggest that the politics of consumption is about how 'one set of collective actors (campaigns, NGOs, charities) engage with other collective actors (retailers, suppliers, corporations) through the real and discursive figure of "the ethical consumer"' (Clarke et al., 2007, p. 238). In addition to suggesting that consumption policies might usefully focus on a range of strategic and collective actors, these insights intimate the persistent rhetorical focus on the consumer need not result in the responsibilisation of individuals by these actors (Evans and Welch, 2015).

Political economy: Connecting consumption and production

Attention to the relationships and interactions between multiple collective actors who affect consumption is at the core of political economy approaches, which insist that consumption cannot be fully understood without accounting for its relationship with the domain of production. Fine's (2002) systems of provision perspective provide a powerful critique of the 'horizontal' accounts of consumption that generalize causal effects (e.g. the significance of price) across all types of commodities. By way of corrective, Fine posits a 'vertical' approach to the study of consumption in which explanations are specific to particular commodities and focused on the distinct economic and social processes that underpin their production, distribution, and circulation. In this view, for example, changes in food consumption would not be sufficiently explained by the consumers' love of variety or the need for convenience; rather it would also call for (amongst other things) a focus on agricultural policies, relationships between various actors along the supply chain, and international regulatory frameworks. It follows that societal problems such as obesity are less to do with individual choices but with the historical evolution of the food system and the intersection between agricultural policies and the economic interests of food businesses.

One possible implication of this approach for consumption policies is to view the analysis of commodity chains as the basis for consumer mobilization. For example, studies that pick up the injunction to 'follow the thing' and trace the biography of particular commodities (Cook, 2006) sit comfortably with the genre of activist documentary films that expose the (typically unfavorable labor) conditions under which everyday consumer items – such as chocolate, apparel, coffee, and electrical goods – are produced. This approach also draws attention to the role of commercial actors and intermediaries in shaping and potentially changing patterns of consumption. For example, supermarkets are well understood as powerful actors in the food chain with the ability to influence activities both 'upstream' (with suppliers) and 'downstream' (with consumers). In terms of consumption, Dixon (2007) suggests that supermarkets have positioned themselves as actors who are able to help their customers solve problems (related, for example to healthy diets) and/or leverage their powerful position in the food system to take action on behalf of their customers (for example by reforming supply chains in response to issues that consumers care about, such as animal welfare).

Theories of socio-technical transitions (Geels, 2002) provide another way of exploring the relationships between production and consumption. In this view, socio-technical regimes (such as food, energy, and mobility systems) represent configurations of actors (companies, governments, NGOs, consumer groups, and so on) that are stable as a consequence of economic and technological interdependencies, and the dominance of the prevailing political and economic landscape.

Societal change occurs through disruptions to socio-technical regimes, either from external shocks and disruptions (e.g. economic crises) or through niche innovations. Niche innovations relate to entrepreneurial activity and the practices of vanguard consumers or 'early adopters'. Consumption policies could address these by stimulating organizational and technological innovations via incentivizing start-up firms, investing in R&D facilities, and facilitating localized grassroots initiatives (Seyfang, 2004).

Theories of practice: The dynamics of everyday life

Theories of practice (see also chapter 3) – which have been hugely influential in the development of contemporary consumption scholarship (following Warde, 2005) – have only recently been applied to consumption policies (Evans et al., 2012; Vihalemm, Keller & Kiisel, 2015). These approaches take 'practices' – each practice is defined as a 'nexus of doings and sayings' (Schatzki, 1996) – as the central unit of analysis for social phenomena. Practice theories are diverse and in many their similarities relate to little more than an ontological orientation toward explanation focused on the ways in which everyday activities form into sets of practices that are reproduced in particular ways. The distinction between practices as 'entities' and as 'performances' is particularly instructive. Practices as entities exist 'out there', involve the co-ordination of disparate elements, and refer to recognizable and shared social phenomena. Practices as entities are reproduced via their often habituated and routine performance by practitioners (for a full discussion see Shove, Pantzar & Watson, 2012).

In their report on practice theory and policy interventions, Spurling et al. (2013) identify three principal ways that these theoretical approaches can be applied to consumption policy. The first focuses on 're-crafting' practices. For example, the New Nordic Diet programme – which aimed to develop a healthy, environmentally sustainable diet based on the consumption of regional foods (Mithril et. al, 2012) – changed the elements of practices via the provision of cookery classes (thus intervening in practicable knowledge) and seeking to shift shared understandings of good food. The second focuses on 'substituting' practices to discourage current unsustainable practices and substituting them with existing or new alternatives. An example can be found in new-build flats in the UK which often have no bath, simply a shower-room, 'locking-in' trends towards showering (see also Hand, Shove and Southerton, 2005). Finally, they suggest a focus on the ways that practices 'interlock'. Practices are interconnected, often through the socio-temporal rhythms that affect their timing and coordination. For example, school timetables, the working day, and shop opening hours shape rush hours, dinner times, leisure, and times of entertainment. The premise of many practice theory applications to policy approaches is that the connections between practices – via the orchestrating role of institutions and organizations – can be reconfigured to produce very different consumption outcomes (see also chapter 20).

Conclusion and future challenges

This chapter has presented an overview of key theoretical approaches to consumption and how they translate into the framing of policies. The distinction between orthodox and heterodox policy framings reflects a foundational division between theories which understand change through the lens of 'methodological individualism' and those that consider change as resulting from multiple, inter-connected, and context-dependent 'processes'. Methodological individualism is of clear appeal to governments and policy-makers as they ultimately locate the locus of change in the hands and minds of individuals. Such approaches have some purchase when it comes to changing behavior. Price mechanisms, information campaigns, social marketing, and nudges have an effect on some discrete acts of consumption. But, as the value–action gap shows, not all forms of consumption are amenable to such policy mechanisms. Unfortunately, the major societal challenges of our time – such as climate change and obesity – have continually shown themselves resilient to orthodox consumption policies. The scale of change required – with respect to the extent, speed, and geographical reach – call for policy approaches that can move beyond individual discretionary acts of purchasing behavior (see Geels et al., 2015). The main challenge for consumption policy concerns how process theories and the translation of heterodox framings into coherent and actionable policy activities, and how those activities could be assessed to determine their efficacy in tackling societal challenges such as climate change (see also Vihalemm et al., 2015).

References

Barnett, C., Cloke, P., Clarke, N. & Malpass, Alice (2011), *Globalizing Responsibilities: The Political Rationalities of Ethical Consumption*, Oxford: Wiley-Blackwell.

Bernheim, B.D. & Whinston, M.D. (2008), *Microeconomics*, Boston: McGraw-Hill.

Birchenhall, C. (2011), Economics. In D. Southerton (Ed.) *Encyclopedia of Consumer Culture* (pp 502–509), Thousand Oaks, CA: Sage.

Clarke, N., Barnett, C., Cloke, P. & Malpass, A. (2007), Globalising the consumer: Doing politics in an ethical register, *Political Geography* 26(3): 231–249.

Cook, I. (2006), Geographies of food: Following, *Progress in Human Geography* 30(5): 655–666.

Defra. (2008), A Framework for Pro-Environmental Behaviours, Department for Environment, Food and Rural Affairs Report, January.

De Marchi, N. (2011), Consumer Demand. In D. Southerton (Ed.) *Encyclopedia of Consumer Culture* (pp 256–258), Thousand Oaks, CA: Sage.

Dixon, J. (2007), 'Supermarkets as New Food Authorities', in D. Burch & G. Lawrence (Eds.) *Supermarkets and Agri-Food Supply Chains: Transformations in the Production and Consumption of Foods*, Cheltenham: Edward Elgar, 29–50.

Dubuisson- Quellier, S. (2013), *Ethical Consumption*, Halifax: Fernwood.

Evans, D., McMeekin, A. & Southerton, D. (2012), Sustainable Consumption, Behaviour Change Policies, and Theories of Practice. In A. Warde & D., Southerton (Eds.), *The Habits of Consumption*, Helsinki: Open Access Book Series of the Helsinki Collegium of Advanced Studies, 113–129.

Evans, D. & Welch, D. (2015), *Food Waste Transitions: Consumption, Retail and Collaboration towards a Sustainable Food System*, SCI: University of Manchester.

Everson, M. (2011), Consumer Rights and the Law. In D. Southerton (Ed.) *Encyclopedia of Consumer Culture* (pp 314–318), Thousand Oaks, CA: Sage.

Fine, B. (2002), *The World of Consumption: The Material and Cultural Revisited*, London: Routledge.

Foucault, M. (1977), *Discipline and Punish: The Birth of the Prison*, Harmondsworth, UK: Penguin.

Gabriel, Y. & Lang, T.M. (2015), *The Unmanageable Consumer*, 3rd edition, London: Sage.

Geels, F.W. (2002), *Understanding the Dynamics of Technological Transitions: A Co-Evolutionary and Socio-Technical Analysis*, Enschede: Twente University Press.

Geels, F., McMeekin, A., Mylan, J. & Southerton, D. (2015), 'A critical appraisal of Sustainable Consumption and Production research: The reformist, revolutionary and reconfiguration agendas', *Global Environmental Change*, 34: 1–12.

Gneezy, U. & Rustichini, A. (2000), 'Pay enough or don't pay at all', *The Quarterly Journal of Economics*, 115(3): 791–810.

Hand, M., Shove, E. & Southerton, D. (2005), Explaining Showering: A Discussion of the Material, Conventional, and Temporal Dimensions of Practice, *Sociological Research Online* 10. http://www.socresonline.org.uk/10/2/hand.html

Kemp, S. (2002), *Public Goods and Private Wants: A Psychological Approach to Government Spending*, Cheltenham, UK: Edward Elgar, 2002.

Kjaernes, U. (2011), 'Consumer Regulation', In D. Southerton (Ed.) *Encyclopedia of Consumer Culture* (pp 305–309), Thousand Oaks, CA: Sage.

Lovell, H., Bulkeley, H. & Liverman, D. (2009), 'Carbon Offsetting: Sustaining Consumption?', *Environment and Planning A*, 41: 2357–2379.

McKenzie-Mohr D. (2000), Promoting Sustainable Behavior: An Introduction to Community-based Social Marketing, *Journal of Social Issues*, 56: 543–554.

McMeekin, A. & Southerton, D. (2012), 'Sustainability Transitions and Final Consumption: Practices and Socio-Technical Systems', *Technology Analysis & Strategic Management*, 24(4): 345–361.

Micheletti, M. (2003), *Political Virtue and Shopping: Individuals, Consumerism, and Collective Action*, New York: Palgrave.

Mithril, C., Dragsted, L. O., Blauert, E., Holt, M. K. & Astrup, A. (2012), 'Guidelines for the New Nordic Diet', *Public Health Nutrition*, 15(10): 1941–1947.

Newholm. T., Shaw, D. & Harrison, R. (Eds.) (2005), *The Ethical Consumer*, London, Thousand Oaks and New Delhi: Sage.

Schor, J. (2005), 'Prices and quantities: Unsustainable consumption and the global economy', *Ecological Economics*, 55: 309–320.

Seyfang, G. (2004), 'Consuming values and contested cultures: A critical analysis of the UK strategy for sustainable consumption and production', *Review of Social Economy*, 62(3): 323–338.

Schatzki, T. (1996), *Social Practices: A Wittgensteinian approach to human activity and the social*, Cambridge: Cambridge University Press.

Shove, E. (2010), 'Beyond ABC: Climate change policy and theories of social change', *Environment and Planning A*, 42: 1273–1285.

Shove, E., Pantzar, M. & Watson, M. (2012), *The Dynamics of Social Practice*, London: Sage.

Southerton, D. & Ulph, A. (Eds.) (2014), *Multi-Disciplinary Approaches to Sustainable Consumption*, Oxford: Oxford University Press.

Southerton, D., Warde, A. & Hand, M. (2004), 'The Limited Autonomy of the Consumer: Implications for Sustainable Consumption', in D. Southerton, H. Chappells & B. Van Vliet (Eds.) *Sustainable Consumption: The Implications of Changing Infrastructures of Provision* (pp 32–48), London: Edward Elgar.

Spaargaren, G. (2003). 'Sustainable consumption: A theoretical and environmental policy perspective', *Society & Natural Resources: An International Journal*, 16(8): 687–701.

Spurling, N., McMeekin, A., Shove, E., Southerton, D. & Welch, D. (2013) 'Interventions in practice: reframing policy approaches to consumer behaviour', SPRG Report, Sept.

Stern, P. (2000), 'Toward a coherent theory of environmentally significant behavior', *Journal of Social Issues*, 56(3): 407–424.

Sunstein, C. & Reisch, L. (2014), 'Automatically green: Behavioral economics and environmental protection', *Harvard Environmental Law Review*, 38(1), 127–158.

Thaler, R. & Sunstein, C. (2008), *Nudge: Improving Decisions About Health, Wealth, and Happiness*, New Haven, CT: Yale University Press.

Thøgersen, J. & Berit Møller, B. (2008), 'Breaking car use habits: The effectiveness of a free one-month travelcard, *Transportation*, 35(3): 329–345.

Trentmann, F. (2007), 'Citizenship and consumption', *Journal of Consumer Culture*, 7: 147–158.

Urry, J. (2007), *Mobilities*, Cambridge: Polity.

Urry, J. (2011), *Climate Change and Society*, London: Polity.

Vihalemm, T., Keller, M. & Kiisel, M. (2015), *From Intervention to Social Change: A Guide to Reshaping Everyday Practices*, London: Ashgate.

Warde, A. (2005) 'Consumption and theories of practice', *Journal of Consumer Culture*, 5(2): 131–153.

Warde, A. & Southerton, D. (2012), 'Social Sciences and Sustainability', in A. Warde & D., Southerton (Eds.) *The Habits of Consumption*, Helsinki: Open Access Book Series of the Helsinki Collegium of Advanced Studies, 1–25.

Watson, M. (2012), 'How theories of practice can inform transition to a decarbonised transport system', *Journal of Transport Geography*, 24: 488–496.

19

Citizen-consumers

Consumer protection and empowerment

Arne Dulsrud

The making of a citizen-consumer

Historically, the idea of a consumer identity has been associated with the advent of the market economy and the growing mountain of commodities in the eighteenth and nineteenth centuries. Since then the market has been an arena through which citizens as consumers have expressed their visions of social justice, politics, the state and the government. Historians have demonstrated that political activism in terms of consumer boycotts against imported goods became a significant force during the American Revolution in the eighteenth century (Breen, 2004). Throughout the nineteenth century citizens protested against slavery in British colonies by not purchasing at shops that sold sugar produced by enslaved labor. People's concern for basic needs, access to necessities and resistance to exploitation by dominant sellers led to the establishment of the consumer cooperative movement in England in 1844 whereby consumers organized and controlled their own provision of goods and services. According to the historian Frank Trentmann (2006) it was not until the late nineteenth century – after a number of serious protests – that a new social identity of being a consumer emerged. Citizens realized that they could voice their interest as consumers and vice-versa.

The awareness of consumers having a critical role in the society accentuated in the aftermath of World War II, as many Western economies gradually shifted from austerity to affluence (Mayer, 1989; Hilton, 2008). If consumers were to contribute to the goals of macro-economic growth introduced by planners and politicians, increased consumer spending was crucial. Lizbeth Cohen accounts how the logic of mass consumption emerging in post-war America involved a certain sense of civic responsibility as "(p)rivate consumption and public benefit, it was widely argued, went hand in hand" (Cohen, 2004, p. 237). While traditional sociology allocated consumers and citizens to separate spheres, recent research has dissolved this conceptual boundary and generated reflection on the figure of the citizen consumer (Warde, 2015, p. 127). Cohen identifies citizen-consumers as "consumers who take on the political responsibility we usually associate with citizens to consider the general good of the nation through their consumption" (Cohen, 2003, p. 204).

If consumers were to fulfill their role as the engine driving up the growth rate of the economy, they needed to know that their spending would result in greater utility for themselves and their households. Citizens had to be assured that they could operate efficiently in their assumed role as consumers. Western governments explored new regimes of consumer protection aimed at providing consumers with the confidence to enter and participate in the market. Although states responded in different ways according to national regulatory traditions, there was an astonishing growth in consumer protection measures throughout Western economies during the 1960s and 1970s in such areas as automobile industry, product safety, food and drugs regulation, package labelling, consumer credit and trading practices. Several issues – among them the thalidomide scandal during the 1960s[1] and the campaigning of the consumer advocate Ralph Nader against the unsafety of American cars[2] – revealed that modern industrial economy could not be viewed as an arena of balanced exchange relationships between sellers and consumers. Several incidents involving harmful marketing practices of multinational corporations in developing countries – such as the promotion of breast milk formula in Africa by the Swiss-based Nestlè food company – demonstrated that consumers in less developed economies were in need of consumer protection as much as their Western counterparts (Sethi, 1994). Deregulation of domestic import restrictions and the increased flow of consumer goods across national borders illustrated that the empowerment of consumers through politics had to stretch beyond national barriers in order to become efficient.

Glickman introduces "three core elements of consumer politics [. . .] consumer activism, the consumer movement and consumer regimes . . . [as] distinct sites of politics" (quoted in Warde, 2015, p. 127). While chapter 16, "Political Consumption and Citizenship and Consumerism", mainly focuses on consumer activism, this chapter explores how consumers came to understand their own role and identity and how this led to struggles for political acceptance of citizens as consumers in need of a policy (Mayer, 1989). In more general terms, citizen-consumer refers to an acknowledgement that the economic sphere and consumption cultures are closely interlinked with respective political systems.

The concept of the citizen-consumer also introduces dilemmas and conflicting identities of consumers that stretch beyond the antagonism inherent in the transactional relationship between consumer and providers of goods and services. Everson and Joerges (2007) account how consumer identity challenges identities related to the role of being a merchant, a farmer or a laborer both in terms of economic interests and in terms of legal rights. There is also a long line of critique of consumption in Anglo-American and Western scholarship running back to the previous turn of the century. Among them are Torstein Veblen's critique of wasteful lifestyles amid the American leisure class from 1899 (Veblen, 1994), Theodore Adorno's Marxist critique of mass consumption (Adorno, 1991), Vance Packard's attack on wasteful consumerism (Packard, 1960) and Zygmunt Bauman's critique of consumerism as an ideology of individualism (Bauman, 1997). Similarly, consumer organizations agitating for more choice and better value for money have been accused of individualism and promoting shallow materialism without considering collective values. While the term *consumerism* initially referred to the efforts by activists for improved consumer conditions, it later became synonymous with indulgence, excess and waste. Although this critique overlooks the achievements of consumer movements advocating for social justice and better access to consumer goods for everybody at a global level, it is also part of a continuing debate on the role of consumption in society (Sassatelli, 2006). Frank Trentmann suggests that instead of regarding the citizen and the consumer as contradicting entities in separate systems of commerce and politics, we should focus on "the flow of knowledge between these systems, the interaction and overlap between ideas and practices of consumption and citizenship and the multiple forms of identities therefrom" (Trentmann, 2006, p. 18).

Consumer empowerment

In a general sense, empowerment not only rests on consumers' ability to acknowledge their identity as consumers, but also their capacity to organize themselves, exercise power and achieve their own goals. There are fierce debates on what can be expected from such mobilization. In his influential book on the logic of collective action, the economist Mancur Olson (1965) argues that there is no presumption that consumers will act in their own interest as a collective. On the contrary, "(t)he multitude of workers, consumers, white collar workers, farmers, and so on are only organized in special circumstances, but business interests are organized as a general rule" (Olson, 1965, p. 143). Olson explains differences by the fact of size. Whereas the business in many industries consists of oligopoly-sized groups and industries that are small in numbers, consumers, on the other hand, are many and difficult to organize and mobilize – they are a typical latent group. An individual in a large group will not be willing to make sacrifices to achieve common benefits that others will achieve in any case. It is more rational to be a free rider. Consumers are, by the words of Olson, examples of "forgotten groups" – one of those who suffer in silence. Olson finds support for his argument in his contemporary America where consumers' level of organization rate during the 1960s was less than one percent.

There are many responses to Olson's accounts on the limiting factors of consumer mobilization. One is the empirical evidence signifying that consumption has been a reason for collective action across time and across countries where social justice has been a driving factor. As mentioned above, they have protested, boycotted, established their own distribution of goods and utilities through cooperatives; they have sought for protection regimes to defend their role as consumers. Consumers have, to use the words of Hilton (2008), been everything but a silent majority. Furthermore, it can be argued that consumption by nature is something more than rational choices taking place in the market. To a certain extent, this critique can be directed against the rational actor model in general as postulated in the Homo economicus model. There is also a more explicit critique originating from careful empirical studies of consumption practices in mundane settings and everyday life. According to Warde, consumption is embedded in everyday practices involving planning, purchasing, consumption and disposal (Warde, 2005, 2015). In social life, therefore, the distinction between being a consumer or a citizen is blurred as individuals tend to switch between various tasks and roles according to context. Understanding consumer interests requires that we consider a mix of motivations and rationalities that tend to be overlooked by modeled and abstract visions of the consumer.

Although empirically and theoretically contested, the insights from Olson have been important for understanding the restricting mechanisms of consumer empowerment. For politicians, consumer advocates and regulators it became clear that the relationship between sellers and consumers involved an uneven capability to mobilize and to voice interests in order to exercise power. This acknowledgement served as a legitimation for governmental intervention into markets on behalf of consumers (Rask Jensen, 1986; Grønmo & Olander, 1991; Trentmann 2016).

Consumer protection regimes

Although consumer polices in industrialized societies have similarities, several studies demonstrate the significance of national institutions in processes of consumer identity formation, role expectations and interpretations (Trentmann, 2006; Stolle & Micheletti, 2015). What appears as evident from these studies are accounts of a distinct citizen-consumer relationally bound within certain national contexts.

Attempts have been made to construct typologies of consumer protection regimes. Gunnar Trumbull (2010) argues that we can identify three basic models. First, a model of economic citizenship – as adopted in Britain, Germany, Austria and Japan – saw consumers more as partners and less as adversaries to the supply side of the market economy. Consumers were interpreted as economic actors with a legal status analogous to workers or suppliers. As long as the conditions for market failure were eliminated, consumer protection should remain as a private contractual matter. Government policies emphasized programs that educated consumers to become well-informed and rational consumers so that they could exert their role in the market in an efficient and sensible manner. The role of the state was to provide clear and meaningful pricing policies, clear contract terms and comparative product testing. Regulatory policies sought to strengthen consumer protection through the improvement of existing competition and commercial regulations. The reformation of British consumer policy in recent years illustrates this point. As an outcome of several reforms in recent years, British authorities have merged consumer policy with competition policy under the same governmental body. Since 2014, Competition and Markets Authority (CMA) enforces consumer protection legislation "to tackle practices and market conditions that make it difficult for consumers to exercise choice" (CMA, 2016).

In Scandinavia, a second more "associational" and corporativist approach has been pursued emphasizing a view of consumers as a legitimate societal group. The model rests on recognition that consumers, similar to other interest groups in the society such as workers, business groups, fishermen, etc. need to be involved as partners in decision-making processes at equal level with the government. In order to defend their interests through ongoing negotiations with other interest groups, consumers must be adequately organized. Swedish and Norwegian governments in particular saw it as their responsibility to assist consumers in their efforts to represent their own interests. Consumer representatives should be granted access to negotiation processes between government and producers – such as farmers. The state moved early into consumer affairs, through institutions like the consumer ombudsman and the introduction of special market courts and dispute resolution mechanisms that mediated between consumers and sellers. Scandinavian consumer protection has pioneered many forms of state interventions that have been adopted by governments around the world. These early state interventions have made the need for an independent consumer movement less apparent.

Third, a model of consumer protection emphasized a political approach to consumer citizenship recognizing the right of consumers as political actors. To some extent, this model was adopted in France and the United States. Consumer rights were regarded as rights of citizenships to be incorporated in the existing legal and institutional framework of the country. The challenge of the consumers was to mobilize politically and push for new legal protections, as in the case of Ralph Nader's advocacy for automobile safety. For consumers, according to Trumbull, this approach called for consumer mobilization, grassroots activism and an up-front confrontation with industry to draw attention to problems requiring regulatory intervention. Product-related risks would be allocated to producers through strict standards of liability and product recall actions. On the background of an increasingly more active consumer movement, President John F. Kennedy presented the Consumer Bill of Rights in 1962 to the United States Congress in which he recognized the responsibility of government to respond to the key concerns of consumer activists. He introduced four basic consumer rights: the right to safety, the right to be informed, the right to choose and the right to be heard. The International Organization of Consumer Unions later adopted The Consumer Bill of Rights as their pillar of policy[3].

As Trumbull argues, the various models of consumer protection give a very different role to consumers and consumer mobilization. In the US, consumer mobilization has close ties with a confronting grass-root activism. In Britain, the existence of the comparative testing magazine

Which? has meant that state has been excused from taking on a more proactive role for the consumers. In Scandinavia the opposite has been observed with a state that itself established consumer institutions and incorporated consumer mobilization into the apparatus of the state (Rask Jensen, 1986; Stø, 2015). In France, a strong central state framework existed together with a highly politicized aspect of citizenship. In Japan, the consumer movement had to fit in with a strong state and the existence of a producer-political power at the center. To some extent, Japan failed to adopt the model by which consumer organizations achieve political independence through membership fees or sale of consumer magazines providing comparative testing (Inoue, 2015, p. 280). In spite of similarities, there are national variations when it comes to definitions of consumer role, its rights, responsibilities and agency (Jacobsen & Dulsrud, 2007).

Consumer protection has become an international phenomenon in which states have learnt from another and adopted "best practices" that take measures successful in one national setting to another. In spite of national peculiarities, consumer protection, information, redress and safety all remain as the basic claims for the consumer movement and for governments at national and international levels.

However, as emphasized by several scholars, a shift in consumer policies and priorities has taken place over the last decades across the consumer protection regimes of developed economies. The driving motive for the pre-war consumer movement was that of access for every citizen to basic consumer goods, such as clean water, electricity and food (Trentmann, 2006). For the period when the consumer movement was regarded to have reached its maturity during the first decades after World War II, access to consumer goods for all and creating a more equitable marketplace were major concerns. Access to consumer goods were associated with an increase in standard of living. National policies of economic deregulation, liberalization of trade and new governance following the economic crisis of the 1980s led to a new approach of consumer policy. According to Mathew Hilton, "(The) . . . model of consumer protection has been dictated by the broader goal of market reform, ensuring that consumerism as a regulatory regime has been diluted if not replaced with a notion consumerism emphasizing choice, competition and ever expanding markets" (Hilton, 2008, p. 70). As will be discussed below, the tensions between consumer policy emphasizing equitable access and improved consumer choice has also been a major concern issue at a European and global level.

The international citizen-consumer

If the burgeoning consumer movement of the post-war period was going to be an influential player in the global society, it needed to manifest itself across the developed capitalist world. It needed to attract the attention and make its message attractive to all – rich and poor. In 1960 several consumer activists met in Hague to form the International Organization of Consumer Unions (IOCU), later termed as Consumer International (CI). IOCU was originally initiated as a body for international collaboration on product testing. Today it is the principal coordinating body of the international consumer movement, representing 240 members from 120 countries around the world (Consumers International, 2016). It was granted consultative status by the Economic and Social Council of the UN in 1963 and IOCU has become the basis for consumer protection regimes all over the world. In order to receive the support from its member organizations, it was necessary for IOCU and later CI to respond to a diversity of interests, from the consumer groups of the affluent West to consumer groups in the South campaigning for access to basic necessities such as clean water and energy for everybody. In the policy papers of CI, both perspectives are represented (Consumers International, 2015).

IOCU also played an important role in supporting national consumer organizations in Asia and Africa. Some examples may illustrate both the challenges and the concerns that consumer organizations in these countries face. In India, the roots of consumer mobilization can be traced back to the beginning of the twentieth century (Cheriyan, 2015), particularly related to improvement of transport services. The Indian consumer movement gained momentum during the 1970s and 1980s with the formation among others of Consumer Unity and Trust Society (CUTS) in Jaipur, which has become an international organization operating in several overseas locations including Southeast Asia and Eastern and Western Africa. Their legitimacy as a consumer movement rests on their ability to balance between the concerns of a growing affluent urban middle class and the needs of a large section of the population that still are below the poverty line. CUTS' own-declared vision illustrates this duality by emphasizing "consumer sovereignty in the framework of social justice, economic equality and environmental necessity, within and across borders" (CUTS, 2013).

China has the world second-largest economy and its export-led economy has dramatically shrunk the income gap between China and developed countries and increased the size of the Chinese middle class. A number of consumer problems including food adulteration, unsafe products and polluted drinking water have shaken the trust of Chinese consumers in domestic products. Still, according to Ying Yu (2015), China's consumer protection program is lagging far behind of what is found in developed countries and in some developing countries as well. The Chinese Consumers' Association (CCA) is a quasi-governmental consumer organization handling a huge number of consumer complaints each year through a hotline service. Nevertheless, CCA is restrained from playing a role as an independent consumer watchdog because it does not synthesize complaints into policy issues or mobilize for policy reforms (Yu, 2015). At the same time, Trentmann (2006) argues that the recognition of consumer rights by the Chinese authorities has generated political awareness and demands from citizens, not least in the housing and community politics.

Consumer organizations have adjusted their policy in various ways. Malaysia has been one of the leading advocates for a more development-oriented consumer policy that focuses more on the needs of the poor rather than the demands of the affluent. The country remains an important center for the international consumer movement. Even in the Middle East, where consumer issues have been regarded as secondary compared to "more important" political problems, consumer grievances have had large political impacts as was demonstrated during the Arab Spring (Mourassilo, 2015).

Independence from commercial interests has remained a key principle of global consumer movement; independence from the state has been more complicated, as illustrated by the case of China. The Indian consumer movement, operating as independent NGOs, faces similar challenges as consumer organizations in the West. Their success depends on their ability to attract the attention of politicians and regulators on issues requiring intervention in sharp competition with producer interests.

The consumer-citizen relationship is under continuous contestation also at the global level. On the one hand, consumption represents a language of material culture of a more mundane nature that does not immediately challenge the political regimes around the world. From this perspective, there has been a tendency to downplay consumer concerns as trivialities taking place within the household involving the role of housewives and females. On the other hand, there are enough examples throughout history of how aggravated consumer conditions and increased cost of living, such as hiking bread prices, have spurred civil riots, unrest and anti-regime critique as with the case of the Arab Spring fresh in memory. This illustrates that the mobilization potential of consumption when related to social justice, equity and equal access to consumer goods remains high.

Global challenges

Although the consumer movement has enjoyed considerable achievements on a number of policy issues, there are policy areas where the consumer voice has been less successful. According to Hilton (2008), a new anti-regulatory agenda emerged during the 1980s, first in the US during the Reagan administration, and later in other Western countries, resulting in a number of setbacks for consumer protection regulations both at a national and international level. Whereas the United Nations infrastructure had been responsive to claims from NGOs such as the consumer movement, the establishment of the World Trade Organization (WTO) in 1995 and the successive rounds of trade negotiations gave lesser room for consumer representation. Few opportunities were offered to consumer advocates to have real effects on rules governing global business. Frustration over not being heard or taken into account by the agreements governed by WTO, or talks taking place among the world's leading economic powers at the G7 summit meetings, resulted in a series of anti-globalization demonstrations the following decade, where consumer activists joined forces with the environmental movement.

The international body of consumer unions, Consumers International (CI), does not oppose WTO per se on the reason that multilateral trade bodies are a better alternative than "destructive bilateralism" (Consumers International, 2003). The basic concern of consumer advocates and the anti-globalization movement has been that the gains from free trade should not only benefit the profit of the few, but ensure that consumers, workers and small producers also get a fair share. A similar critique has been raised against the current trade talks taking place between trading blocs, particularly in the negotiation over the Transatlantic Trade and Investment Partnership (TTIP) and TiSA (Trade in Services Agreement) between the EU Commission and the US government. This agreement is about regulatory issues and non-tariff trade barriers. Negotiations have already been concluded in the Trans-Pacific Partnership (TPP) between the US and eleven countries in the Pacific region. The future of these agreements are questioned due to a more protectionist climate reflected in the victory of Brexit and Donald Trump as the elected president of USA, but their connection with the the consumer movement is not direct or obvious.

Both CI and the European Consumer Organization (BEUC) have questioned whether the proclaimed potential benefits of TTIP would be at the expense of consumer protection, health, environmental, labor and safety standards in Europe. Consumer organizations suspect that the logic of the least common denominator will be decisive, meaning that the standards of consumer protection in Europe must give way to a lower American protection standard. Therefore, CI has argued that consumers will gain only if the consequent international agreements harmonize on the highest levels of consumer protection and welfare practicable.

The post-national consumer

EU and US negotiators are facing growing demands from civil society, especially concerning transparency and the way consultation with stakeholders is handled. There is widespread concern of BEUC that the consumer protection standards achieved in the EU, such as the precautionary principle of food risk management, will lose against the US approach to food risk analysis that tends to be more like a cost-benefit one.

Through the introduction of the EU internal market by the Treaty of Maastricht in 1993, consumer choice was to be extended in order to promote a figure of the active European consumer – providing a "bottom-up" integration of European markets. From this point of view, the identity as a consumer, devoid of cultural, political and social conflicts, was approached as building bloc for a more tight-knit and integrated Europe. The Treaty of Lisbon (2007) defined consumer protection as an area where the European Commission shares responsibility with its member states.

In recent policy papers the dual ambitions of EU consumer policy have become evident. On the one hand, consumer policy has become an important contribution to the Europe 2020 process and its general purpose of reviving the European economy through "smart, sustainable, inclusive growth" (European Commission, 2012). A long-term goal of the EU has been to strengthen economic integration of member states through a removal of barriers to cross-border shopping. Consumers play a significant role in this. In order to realize the potential of the Single Market and drive forward economic growth, empowered and confident consumers are regarded as crucial factors. Empowerment of consumers, according to the Commission, will not take place without a high level of protection that enables consumers to benefit from the social and economic progress of Europe. Working through European Consumer Agenda, the Commission has put forward consumer policy initiatives such as safety for products and services, information and education, rights and redress and enforcements at the top of the list (European Commission, 2012).

Compared to distinction criteria as social class, ethnicity, language or national identity, consumer identity appears as a less contentious term, as both class and national identity have been sources of fierce conflicts and contradictory interests. Consumption serves as a source of identification that is neutral to national borders. Critics have argued that contrasted to "class society", the idea of a consumer society depicts consumers as a uniform group of people with similar interests. Whether the modern notion of citizen-consumer is insensitive to class distinctions and class identities is a matter of debate (Mort, 2006), as the post-war citizen-consumer in the West has been closely associated with middle-class values. Neither is the citizen-consumer devoid of national connotations. Public-sponsored marketing campaigns such as "Buy British", "Enjoy Norway" or "Made in France" are part of a national narrative shaping that appeals to the civic responsibility of the national consumer.

The end of consumer policy?

Looking back at the first decades after World War II, consumer policy in many industrialized countries seemed to reflect a genuine ambition among politicians to increase consumer welfare through a strengthened regulatory agenda. We have already mentioned that the notion of the citizen-consumer was related to the egalitarianism of the post-war welfare state which secured the idea of welfare for everybody, an expectation that all citizens could benefit from economic growth taking place. At the same time, consumer policy became a remedy to boost economic growth and improve citizen welfare in areas such as public health, nutrition or economic development.

In spite of certain setbacks for the consumer movement, as in the global trade negotiations, there are legitimate reasons to ask whether consumer leaders have already achieved what they have been campaigning for, at least in the affluent West. Basic protections are provided to consumers in the marketplace and consumer protection is part of public policy in most nations. Consumer protection is high on the political agenda, and political parties claim to represent the consumers. Regulatory mechanisms are in place to protect consumers against the risks of dangerous and unreliable goods. Consumer organizations are no longer the only ones to offer unbiased consumer information. Product testing and independent information on goods and services appear through newspapers and magazines, TV, the Internet, blogs and social media.

One response to the question on the future of a consumer movement is that consumer policy is more needed than ever. The economic growth taking place in China (1.3 billion people) and India (1.2 billion people) implies that a huge number of people will expect the same standard of living as consumers living in Europe and North America. Their increased demand for consumer goods in combination with a growth of global population amounting to 75 million annually will put an immense pressure on the global resources, including food and energy. Sustainability, in terms of the responsibility of the individual consumer, has become a key element in the consumer critique emphasizing that consumers should be a part of the solution.

Consumerism remains a controversial issue. By taking consumerism for granted, we tend to overlook the fact that consumerism does not only unite, but splits the world. The logic of choice has created a division between those who can and those who cannot participate in the consumer society. We have seen movements of an oppositional logic to the liberal capitalist democracy in the Middle East, in Africa and in Asia that are fundamentalist in character and hostile to consumerism based on Western lifestyles. Recent events, particularly after the so-called Arab Spring, provide examples of a polarization based on nationalism, religious extremism and ethnic particularism. For those who do not have access to the benefits of a consumer society – or ever see the opportunity to achieve this, oppositional visions to the Western model of a consumer society will remain as attractive.

The post-war concept of a citizen-consumer identity was formed by the political efforts to overcome class distinctions and to leave behind the turmoil that threatened to tear apart the industrialized societies during the mid-war period. The citizen-consumer of the affluent West symbolized an underlying contract between citizens and politicians. In exchange for support and stability, politicians provided for steady economic growth and a distribution of wealth that could embrace the majority of the population – if not always on equal terms. A set of consumer policy measures including protection, representation and legal rights were introduced in order to provide for and to empower the position of consumer in society.

Questions can be raised on the future robustness of this model. To be more precise: what if the basic premises no longer are present or fail to perform? Questions may be asked on the future of the post-war consumer protection regime. More than any other, Thomas Piketty's book *Capital in the Twenty-First Century* revealed that evolution of income and wealth inequalities not only took place in France but in Europe and the US since the eighteenth century (Piketty, 2014). Piketty's central thesis is that inequality is a persistent feature of capitalism. He predicts a future of low economic growth and argues that unless capitalism is reformed, democratic order will be challenged. Piketty's prospective also affects ideals of equal opportunities and democracy. In what manner will these scenarios influence upon our ideas as citizen-consumer and the role of consumer policy protection? In the absence of more aggressive state intervention to redistribute wealth from rich to poor, Piketty's economic law means that we will see an acceleration of inequality since the rich will always own a disproportionate share of capital. What does this increase in inequality mean for democracy? The legitimacy of democracy depends, at least in part, on producing outcomes that citizens think are fair. A rapid growth in inequality risks undermining this implicit contract between citizens. Will increased social inequality in the US and Europe affect current consumer policy priorities emphasizing consumer choice?

We should remind ourselves that citizens' lives in most parts of the world are structured by consumption. In their everyday lives, consumers will be concerned with the procuring of necessities and with making ends meet. As such, consumption is entangled in overlapping and conflicting moral expectations, care and power relations, economic concerns, nutritional concerns, tastes and preferences and various practical considerations that will continue to contest the identity of the citizen consumer.

Notes

1 Thalidomide was used against nausea and to alleviate morning sickness in pregnant women. Thalidomide became an over-the-counter drug in several Western countries since the late 1950s. Throughout the world, about 10,000 cases were reported of infants with phocomelia (malnutrition of limbs) due to thalidomide; only 50 percent of the 10,000 survived (Wikipedia).

2 Ralph Nader (1991) wrote the book *Unsafe at Any Speed* in 1965, in which he claimed that many American automobiles were unsafe to drive. Corvair, manufactured by General Motors (GM), had been involved in fatal accidents involving spins and rollovers. Nader's advocacy of automobile safety, along with concern over escalating nationwide traffic fatalities, contributed to Congress' passage of the 1966 National Traffic and Motor Vehicle Safety Act.

3 International Organization of Consumer Unions added four more rights to its list: the right to redress, the right to consumer education, the right to healthy environment and the right to basic goods and services.

References

Adorno, T.W. (1991). *The Culture Industry: Selected Essays on Mass Culture.* London: Routledge.

Bauman, Z. (1997). *Work, Consumerism and the New Poor.* London: Open University Press.

Breen, T.H. (2004). *The Marketplace of Revolution: How Consumer Politics Shaped American Independence.* Oxford: Oxford University Press.

Cheriyan, G. (2015). Indian Consumer Movement. In S. Brobeck & R.N Mayer (Eds.). *Watchdogs and Whistleblowers: A Reference Guide to Consumer Activism* (pp. 245–247). Santa Barbara: Greenwood.

CMA (2016). *Competition and Market Authorities. Consumer protection.* Accessed January 25th 2016. https://www.gov.uk/government/organisations/competition-and-markets-authority

Cohen L. (2003). *A Consumers' Republic: The Politics of Mass Consumption in Postwar America.* New York: Knopf.

Cohen, L. (2004). A Consumers' Republic: The Politics of Mass Consumption in Postwar America. *Journal of Consumer Research*, 31(1), 236–239.

Consumers International (2003). Globalization for All – Reviving the Spirit of Bretton Woods. An Examination of Developments in Global Financial Markets. *Consumersinternational.org.*

Consumers International (2015). The State of Consumer Protection around the World. *Consumersinternational.org.*

Consumers International (2016). *Frontpage.* http://www.consumersinternational.org. Accessed January 25th 2016.

CUTS (2013). CUTS@50. A Vision Document. CUTS International, Jaipur, India.

European Commission (2012). A European Consumer Agenda – Boosting confidence and growth. *Communication from the Commission*, Brussels, 22.5.2012. 225 final.

Everson, M. & Joerges, Chr. (2007). Consumer Citizenship in Postnational Constellations. In K. Soper & F. Trentmann. *Citizenship and Consumption* (pp.154–171). New York: Palgrave Macmillan.

Grønmo, S. & Olander, F. (1991). Consumer Power: Enabling and Limiting Factors. *Journal of Consumer Policy*, 14, 141–169.

Hilton, M. (2008). *Prosperity for All: Consumer Activism in the Era of Globalization.* Itacha, NY: Cornell University Press.

Inoue, T. (2015). Japanese Consumer Movement. In S. Brobeck & R.N. Mayer (Eds.). Watchdogs and Whistleblowers. *A Reference Guide to Consumer Activism* (pp.276–280). Santa Barbara: Greenwood.

Jacobsen, E. & Dulsrud, A. (2007). Will Consumers Save the World? The Framing of Political Consumerism. *Journal of Agricultural and Environmental Ethics*, 20, 469–482.

Mayer, R.N (1989). *The Consumer Movement: Guardians of the marketplace.* Boston, MA: Twayne.

Mort, F. (2006). Competing Domains: Democratic Subjects and Consuming Subjects in Britain and the United States since 1945. In F. Trentmann (Ed.). *The Making of the Consumer. Knowledge, Power and Identity in the Modern World* (pp.225–249). Oxford: Berg.

Mourassilo, A. (2015). Middle Eastern Consumer Movements. In S. Brobeck & R.N. Mayer (Eds.). Watchdogs and Whistleblowers. *A Reference Guide to Consumer Activism* (pp. 307–310). Santa Barbara: Greenwood.

Nader, R. (1991). *Unsafe at Any Speed: The Designed in Dangers of the American Automobile.* Mass: Knightbridge Publishers.

Olson, M. (1965). *The Logic of Collective Action. Public Goods and the Theory of Groups.* Cambridge: Harvard University Press.

Packard, V. (1960). *The Wastemakers.* Brooklyn, NY: Ig Publishing.

Piketty, T.P. (2014). *Capital in the Twenty-First Century.* Cambridge, MA: Harvard University Press.

Rask Jensen, H. (1986). The relevance of alternative paradigms as guidelines for consumer policy and organized consumer action. *Journal of Consumer Policy, 9*(17), 389–405.

Sassatelli, R. (2006). Virtue, Responsibility and Consumer Choice: Framing Critical Consumerism. In J. Brewer & F. Trentmann, F. (Eds), *Consuming Cultures, Global Perspectives: Historical Trajectories, Transnational Exchanges* (pp. 219–250). Oxford: Berg.

Sethi, P.T. (1994). *International Corporations and the Impact of Public Advocacy on Corporate Strategy: Nestlè and Infant Formula Controversy.* New York: Kluwer Academic Publishers.

Stø, E. (2015). Norwegian Consumer Movement. In S. Brobeck & R.N Mayer (Eds.). Watchdogs and Whistleblowers. *A Reference Guide to Consumer Activism* (pp.343–347). Santa Barbara: Greenwood.

Stolle, D. & Micheletti, M. (2015). *Political Consumerism. Global Responsibility in Action.* Cambridge: Cambridge University Press.

Trentmann, F. (Ed). (2006). *The Making of the Consumer. Knowledge, Power and Identity in the Modern World.* Oxford: Berg.

Trentmann, F. (2016). *Empire of Things. How We Became a World of Consumers, from the Fifteenth Century to the Twenty – First.* UK: Penguin Random House.

Trumbull, G. (2010). Consumer Policy: Business and the Politics of Consumption. In D. Coen, W. Grant & G. Wilson, G. (Eds.). *The Oxford Handbook of Business and Government.* Oxford: Oxford University Press, 622–642.

Veblen, T. (1994). *The Theory of the Leisure Class.* Hammondsworth: Penguin.

Warde, A. (2005). Consumption and Theories of Practice. *Journal of Consumer Culture*, 5, 131–153.

Warde, A. (2015). The Sociology of Consumption: Its Recent Development. *Annu. Rev. Sociol.*, 41, 117–134.

Yu, Y. (2015). Chinese Consumer Movement. In S. Brobeck & R.N. Mayer (Eds.). Watchdogs and Whistleblowers. *A Reference Guide to Consumer Activism* (pp. 88–92). Santa Barbara: Greenwood.

20

Practice change and interventions into consumers' everyday lives

Margit Keller and Triin Vihalemm

This chapter deliberately deviates from the standard genre of a handbook chapter and takes the liberty to take a vantage point of a policy intervention designer. It is best read together with chapter 18 on consumption policies and their theoretical underpinnings on which we build upon. Since the above-mentioned chapter charts the broader conceptual map of policies, this chapter will zoom in on particular issues for an intervention designer, taking social practice theory (SPT) as the basis. Although it is a bundle of related theories and using a singular does not do justice to this multiplicity, we use it as a broader umbrella term for a set of approaches that have several commonalities (see e.g. chapter 3).

In the area of climate change, sustainability and, in particular, sustainable consumption, so-called practice-based analyses and policy implications that appear at the end of journal articles are most advanced and versatile (as can be seen in chapters 18 and 30; see also their references lists). Here studies on food, water and energy consumption (particularly energy use at homes and mobility) stand out. Providing even a very tentative overview of those is beyond the scope of this chapter. For excellent recent collections of sustainable consumption and SPT studies see Shove and Spurling, 2013 and Strengers, Moloney, Maller, Horne, 2014. SPT-based and policy-relevant research has also recently been making inroads to public health scholarship and debates (e.g. Blue, Shove, Carmona, and Kelly, 2016; Harries and Rettie, 2016; Maller, 2015). Here the two prominent examples analyzed are smoking as a unhealthy social practice and walking as a healthy one.

The SPT approach is promising for explaining consumption's impact on the environment, health, etc. However, its actual application in intervention policies and programmes is challenging for several reasons. Practice theoreticians have hotly debated with mainstream individual behavior change approach (e.g. Shove, 2010 vs. Withmarsh, O'Neill and Lorenzoni, 2011). Yet a certain rigidity and "unpracticality" of SPT for applied programmes paradoxically stems from the theory itself – it does not address directly the agency of the potential intervener and sometimes even discourages the application of the practice theoretical approach. At a theoretical level (de)construction of the entity of the practice into the nexuses and elements sounds convincing as an explanation of social order and change, but on the applied level it can be very problematic, not least because it requires an "enlightened monarch", who has legitimacy, power and resources for holistic solutions to complex issues and multi-agential challenges that SPT-informed social change design requires. Below we will discuss the potentials to apply SPT in today's fractionalized public sphere and policy-making practices, by focusing, in particular, on consumption-related issues.

Everyday life perspective of social change – consumers, responsibility and "ownership" of problems

SPT literature conceptualizes consumption as a "moment in everyday practices" (Warde, 2005, see also chapter 3), not as a set of practices per se. From a policy-maker's or intervener's point of view the essence of the matter is to take neither the individual, nor broader social structures, nor isolated activities as the focus – attention is shifted rather to the social practices as meaningful patterns of activities.

Warde and Southerton (2012, see also chapter 18) have elaborated on the main tenets about consumption that link the everyday life perspective and practice thinking. Let us just mention some points: consumption is rarely only an individual matter, but it is often done collectively or for the sake of the others or by others (families and organizations are cases in point); consumption cannot be reduced to isolated purchase episodes, and it abounds in repetition (e.g. empty shampoo bottles need replacing) and sequences (e.g. loyalty cards make people visit the same supermarket over again). The marketing concept of "purchasing behavior" can lead the analyst astray – consumption is a network of buying, using, disposing and buying again (see about consumption rituals McCracken, 1986). Thus, if consumption is woven through the fabric of everyday life in multiple and complex ways, a workable focus for intervention programmes can be a problematic social practice or a complex of practices.

We first make a brief detour into a somewhat broader conceptual debate about the responsibilization of the consumer in the context of consumer and citizen practices (about the latter see also chapters 16 and 19). The question boils down to the following: who and what are responsible for environmental degradation, excessive waste, climate change or obesity and who and what should provide solutions to these conundrums?

Welch and Warde (2015) refer to the influences of Foucault, who has been "providing resources for a small body of work addressing sustainable consumption as 'green governmentality' implicated in the neoliberal project of 'responsibilization of the consumer'" (p. 87). It is maintained that various interventions, notably communication campaigns, nominate some everyday practices explicitly as practices of consumption (which diverges from the "consumption as distributed activities and moments in everyday practices" view). Halkier (2010) contends that in some cases, responsible consumption activities merge into an integrative practice in Schatzki's (2002) sense, having a recognizable pattern of its own. It may be useful to set an objective for a policy to engender and nourish such sustainable or healthy practices in their own right. But, for present purposes we contend that consumption is dispersed in various social practices and the task is to analyze wherein lies the problem and which practices are connected to it.

It is necessary to bear in mind the dynamic between a practice as *performance* (an everyday enactment done by concrete people) and practice as *entity* (a pattern of doings and sayings which has some consistency over time and can be described to have some unity) proposed by Schatzki (2002). Some proponents of a "stronger version" of practice theory suggest that the main site to galvanize change are social practices as entities and their historical development. For example, Shove, Pantzar and Wattson (2012) and Blue, Shove, Carmona and Kelly (2016) provide useful insights into how the practices of driving (in the context of climate change) and the practice of smoking (in the context of public health) can be made sense of for policy makers and social change. These patterns are easy to track post-hoc, but in order to anticipate or design the future, delineating the patterns within larger sets of compound practices (Warde, 2013) is challenging.

There is a stream of practice-based research that scrutinizes everyday enactments (both bodily and discursive) of various practices (Aro, 2016, Halkier, 2010; Dubuisson-Quellier and Gojard, 2016; Keller and Halkier, 2014) using ethnographic methods and interviews to understand how social practices unfold in everyday lives. It is tempting to conclude that the stronger version calls for more structural and larger-scale policy interventions, because only governments and their coalitions with for example large enterprises can affect transformations on that scale. And the more everyday-life, "closer-to-individual" perspective permits smaller-scale projects and that address communities, workplaces, organizations, families and perhaps, in some cases, individuals. However, when looking more closely – and persisting with the "practical" needs of the actual policy-maker or intervener – there are no exclusive alternatives of "big" and "small" interventions. There is always an interaction of various dualities of agencies and structures in the Giddens' sense (1984).

Sustainability and health-oriented social change is always a mix of more wide-ranging political agreements (e.g. made at the UN or OECD level) and more local programmes and everyday steps towards these goals, sometimes with significant results and sometimes with none whatsoever. Therefore, from the vantage point of the organization whose aim is to affect change, let alone an individual policy or programme maker, a rallying call to intervene into complex sets of overlapping and intersecting social practices may be enlightening, yet too daunting. Thus even the most macro-level technological or regulative changes that in their inception may not have the end-consumer in mind at all, will affect people's everyday lives (and this does not mean subscribing to methodological individualism, which is one of the main criticisms of SPT proponents towards behavior-change approaches; see Shove, 2010).

There are always agents with varying coordinating powers of practice involved, and every intervention programme needs some knowledge of them and their activity. For example, political changes are often communicated by addressing the inhabitants of a particular country as consumers, not as citizens. In the field of energy efficiency, scholars have reported a very narrow conceptualization of the public on the part of political decision-makers as users/refusers of ready-made solutions without foreseeing any community empowerment and bottom-up innovation (Brondi, Sarrica, Caramis, Piccolo, Mazzara, 2015; Cotton and Devine-Wright, 2012; Vihalemm and Keller, 2016). The responsibilization issue is crucial in terms of what type and of what strength agency is attributed to a certain position. With discursive practices characteristic to the political field (Bourdieu, 1991), construction of inhabitants as mass consumers legitimizes constraining their agency and delegating power to political, business and technological professionals. The scholarly construction of "energy citizenship", for example, is a sort of re-responsibilization of people, who seek to change the existing social structure of energy production and distribution (Kunze and Becker, 2014; Devine-Wright, 2007; Sarrica, Brondi, Cottone and Mazzara, 2016; Strengers, 2012). Today the concept of citizenship itself is under transformation and scholars propose new concepts of temporary, flexible and horizontal forms of engagements that are based on "personally meaningful causes" in parallel with or as a replacement to declining traditional forms of citizenship (e.g. Norris, 2002, Sloam, 2014), as well as about quotidian "acts of citizenship" (Bennett, 2012, Isin and Nielsen, 2008). Thus the borders between consumers and citizens are blurred. On the one hand, it renders the field of action for interveners more intricate, but, on the other hand, expands possibilities for synergistic coalitions between potential agents of change.

Interveners and key actors

Next, the dynamics between bottom-up and top-down change attempts deserve a brief mention, even though this limited chapter cannot delve deeply into this enormous discussion (e.g. Sulkunen, 2009 for a reflection on the role of the state in prevention policies). The distinction between grassroots social innovations (Wahlen and Laamanen, 2015) and consumer movements (chapter 16) and institutional interventions can be a useful one, although in actual social change programme design, a less rigid categorization and an open attitude to potential coalition building with versatile actors may be more fruitful. Another twist into this complex picture is added by "resolutely ordinary" yet transformational everyday routines that consumers engage in (Lewis, 2015, p. 348), be they informal re-use and goods-swap schemes between neighbors or setting up carpenters' clubs. The concept of *social innovation* is helpful here in conceptualizing more collective and purpose-oriented initiatives than simply totally individualized healthy or sustainable activities (which in their turn may be the aim or result of a social intervention programme, once the new practices have become habituated). For a proposed typology of sustainable consumption-oriented social innovations see Jaeger-Erben, Rückert-John and Schäfer, 2015, who advocate more strategic political and financial support for these initiatives as well as more systematic planning and goal setting by change agents themselves.

Closely related with the discussion above is the issue of who intervenes. Vihalemm, Keller and Kiisel (2015) examine the concepts of *key actors*, *coordinating agents* and *coalitions*, highlighting the concept of agents more than do stronger versions of practice theory, which sometimes tend to elide people and organizations from the scene. The relationship between the intervening body and the so-called target group may be a complex one. It would be more worthwhile to chart a network of key actors and their capacity to effect change, as well as the depth and intensity of a potential change for them. Some of these actors may be the end-consumers, while others may be various intermediaries (manufacturers, sellers, service providers, experts, community organizations or lifestyle bloggers). The coordinating agent notion (put forward by Warde in 2013) can be utilized here. These are individuals or organizations that have power (either symbolic and material) to catalyze or hinder change. In policy documents such agents are often referred to as "stakeholders", but this term may be misleading, because of the assumed reflexivity and awareness by the agents of their roles and responsibilities (or of the "stakes" involved), which may not exist at all. Whereas Vihalemm et al. offer a tool for mapping the capacities of key actors; earlier, Gardner, Rachlin and Sweeney (1986) have presented a matrix of stakeholder power/influence and interest, which in various adapted forms has been widely employed in strategic communications planning research and practice.

This leads us to the need to unpack the notion of coalitions of intervention. According to SPT-based writing, it is beyond the capacity of any single actor to simultaneously transform all elements of practices in focus; thus there must be many actors joining their forces. Evans, McMeekin and Southerton (2012, p. 128) argue that this provides an opportunity for policy makers to set the agenda, co-ordinate activities and mobilize legislative and financial support to variously sustainable practices, no matter whether they are initiated by "official" change agents or are emerging informally on a grassroots level. This emphasizes the "distributed and versatile intervener" concept (Strengers, Moloney, Maller, and Horne, 2014). Coordination and mediation between miscellaneous actors with varying power and funding is a challenge. Yet searching for synergies may be a less demanding strategy in the long term than the narrow silo-approach, in which other programmes are treated as competitors.

In addition, according to Macrorie, Foulds and Hargreaves (2014, p. 96), there is "glaring omission" in studying the professional practices of those who govern, even though some analyses exist (see Hargreaves, 2011; Ozaki and Shaw, 2014). This deserves attention for two reasons: firstly, if we proceed from the distributed intervener it is obvious that various professionals from engineers to salespeople implement interventions every day, whether they are conscious of it or not. And, secondly, deeply entrenched work routines, sometimes strongly regulated and coordinated (see Warde, 2013) by formal rules, may be crucial components of the (im)possibility of transition. Also, work-related practices are often aligned to serve a higher objective – be it economic profit, efficient public service or quality of education. For instance, a study by Huttunen and Oosterveer (2016) looked at Finnish farmers and found "fertilization practices to be subordinate to general farming, showing that it is useful to consider practices as forming hierarchies, particularly in the case of production activities. . . . A core purpose stabilizes a practice by streamlining other elements around it and reinforces tight connections between the elements" (p.17).

One possible option to foster change of professional practices may be Public Procurement for Innovation (PPI) (e.g. https://www.innovation-procurement.org/), which demands customers to replace their earlier and "safe" practices with new practices with unforeseen effects.

SPT scholarship has been accused of limiting its scope on the home and domestic everyday life, but as people spend long hours at work, attempts to unfreeze workplace habits and procedures would be a promising way forward, particularly taking into account the extent to which professionals (from property managers and human resources specialists to work environment controllers) can act as partners (or enemies) in various change processes. Also, workplace consumption practices as such are a relatively under-explored area in consumption studies, meriting much more effort from scholars (Hargreaves, 2011).

Analyzing problematic practices

So, the puzzle for the change agent consists in the questions of wherein lies the problem, who does it affect and how to analyze it. Policy makers deal with large concepts like "public health" and "climate change", whereas consumers' and citizens' everyday lives are ridden with totally different concerns of one's immediate surroundings, daily schedules and important others, which may sometimes intersect with these policy agendas, but often do not.

We may say that even the most ardent attempts at responsibilization of the consumer can hit the complex network of everyday do-abilities and normativities (Halkier, 2010) – i.e. the boundaries within which consumers deem various activities feasible, acceptable and normal to perform – that set limitations to free choice and dig gaps between evinced values and actual habits. Awareness-raising programmes may be of negligible impact, because the immediate surroundings of an individual whom the problem framings stipulated in policy documents remain distant and irrelevant. Our recent research has shown that the involved and socially and economically active (often better-off and better-educated) people have to manage very busy schedules, multitask and experience acceleration of both individual and social time (Uibu and Vihalemm, 2016, Vihalemm, Lauristin and Harro-Loit, 2016). Therefore their networks of things, people and activities may not accommodate another obligation of for example going with one's own mug to a local festival to lessen the environmental footprint of public events by reducing plastic disposable packaging usage. Or they may be engaged temporarily and deflect from the suggested action because competition for their attention is high and they will take up something new. Following the classical diffusion of innovations (Rogers, 1962) model, these consumer-citizens may be early adopters, who could involve the early and late majority before they became disengaged.

Such more-empowered consumers may also be less reachable to behavior change attempts and employ their agency in socially innovative or resistant ways that may not coincide with public agendas of health promotion or environmentalism. Ideally, practice changes need also interaction and public sense-making, a public sphere in the classical Habermasian sense. The fractionalization of the public sphere into a diverse and ever-dynamic complex of partly overlapping and temporarily interconnected sub-spheres (Keane, 1995), the group escapism into the sphericules (Gitlin, 1998) and digital homophily (Rasmussen, 2014) hinder the possibility that the people with different lifestyles meet and share new ways of "doing and saying". These limitations to interventions may also be a reason why the so-called "nudge" (see chapter 21) appeals to policy-makers.

On the other hand, those who are relatively inactive and have more spare time may have low capacity for change, because of lack of access, skills and interest to engage in various healthy and green behaviors (Keller and Kiisel, forthcoming, Seppel and Kiisel, 2016). At the same time, paradoxically, shortage of resources may keep people embedded in sustainable practices despite their low environmental awareness (Orru and Lilleoja, 2015). Having resources in socioeconomic terms does not necessarily result in transformation of lifestyles towards sustainability. Improvement of the socio-economic position of the less-advantaged population groups may paradoxically re-surface non-sustainable lifestyle practices that have so far been structurally suppressed.

Thus the analysis of agency and the actors or target groups vis-á-vis intervention programmes, especially public communication campaigns, as one of the most widespread methods, poses complex questions about who is addressed and what is suggested to people as the right thing to do (e.g. "eat five a day" as a common slogan in healthy eating campaigns). Are these docile and disciplined consumers, who are educated to learn the necessary skills within a new framework, e.g. cope within a liberalized electricity market or use smart meters and thus (perhaps inadvertently) cut short of developing any citizenship practices with more substantial change potential (e.g. setting up an energy cooperative)? Or are these citizens, who are expected to engage in transformative civic practices? Or hybrid combinations of both? Thus the question for the intervener also has a bearing on the continuum of responsibility, agency and engagement on which there may appear different combinations of routine and transformation, "revolutionary" and ordinary (see Halkier, in press a; Lewis, 2015). The social change road is always winding with unpredictablities and non-scalability and non-transferrability of a previous solution to a new context (Shove et al., 2012, Vihalemm et al., 2015). Various forms of "everyday agency" with multiple degrees of taking responsibility and potentials of connectiveness and engagement with the public campaigns by the consumers have to be born in mind (Halkier, in press a); Keller and Halkier, 2014).

All this makes a case for the use of sociological, anthropological and communication studies knowledge alongside economic, technological, environmental and health studies in policy design. There are vibrant methodological debates in SPT circles on how researchers can gain access to both practices as entities and their change over time, to real-time unfolding of performances, as well as discursive accounts of both (for a recent collection on this topic see Jonas, Litting, Wroblewski, in press; see also chapters 4 and 5). The bulk of SPT research has employed qualitative methods, and observation has been treated as the "gold standard" (Halkier, in press b), yet the methodological palette is quickly widening to embrace quantitative surveys (see Gram-Hanssen, 2014; Jallinoja, Niva and Latvala, 2016; John, Rückert-John and Jaeger-Erben, 2016; Yates and Evans, 2016). Also, there are exciting first experiments in visualizing and diagramming practice elements with network analysis (for the case of laundry practices see Higginson, McKenna, Hargreaves, Chilvers and Thomson, 2015).

In addition, recent developments in employing different kinds of "big data" (for example, based on mobile positioning or electricity billing) on people's everyday activities in such areas as mobility, shopping, watching TV and energy use could be one solution to some of the methodological problems, but this is definitely not a cure-all. The issue how practical problems faced by policy-makers are to be operationalized and researched remains pressing. For example, the Nexus network in the UK (combining researchers on food, water and energy) searches for ways of investigating practices with multiple methods and "translating" this knowledge into policy-making language (Leck, Conway, Bradshaw, Rees, 2015). A methodological design that combines different qualitative data-production methods or even combines quantitative with qualitative methods, including the potentials in visual and digital registration, is definitely preferable. However, in practical programme design the most vulnerable points are time and funds. Extensive studies are costly and time-consuming; thus in some cases one has to resort to quick ethnography (Penn Handwerker, 2001) or simply expert assessments and secondary data.

Aims of interventions

Different authors have outlined slightly varying conceptualizations of practice change. For example, Spurling, McMeekin, Shove, Southerton and Welch (2013, pp. 9–12) elaborate on different problem framings, which can be understood as intervention aims. Firstly, re-crafting practices is meant to change practice elements – meanings, materials and skills – or their relationships to make existing practices more sustainable or healthy. Vihalemm et al. (2015, pp. 60–61) follow a similar route in proposing practice modification – e.g. when alcohol consumption is shifted towards active monitoring of alcohol units by consumers. This embraces introducing new skills and material means (unit measures on bottle labels). The second option is substituting practices, where more sustainable or healthy alternatives are encouraged (eating bean protein instead of beef or cycling instead of car-driving) (see Spurling et al., 2013, p. 11; Vihalemm et al., 2015, pp. 63–64). In addition Spurling et al. discuss changing, how practices interlock, focusing on sequences (e.g. car driving home from work and an evening supermarket trip) and synchronizations (energy peak loads because of people's daily schedules).

Vihalemm et al. (2015, pp. 57–58) also dwell on the creation of new practices, describing how in Estonia pedestrians wearing hanging reflectors was made normal during dark hours to enhance traffic safety. In theory at least, total disruption of practices is also possible. However, that would require a major societal upheaval (change of political regime or war) or at least a ban (state ban on alcohol; see Vihalemm et al., 2015, pp. 65–66 for a recap on how M. Gorbachov tried to introduce a systematic anti-alcohol policy in the Soviet Union in the 1980s).

Thus a SPT-inspired goal setting of any programme or policy is the creation of a new normality. Of course, there are different scales; climate change is an issue to be tackled with the grandest possible momentum like the COP21 at the end of 2015 showed. Yet strategic documents adopted on an international or national level alone do not cause change. They have to be implemented by concrete people in specific ways and timespaces. The overall aims of large-scale programmes are often enormous – for example to make consumption sustainable. Therefore, tangible and manageable smaller projects are needed to translate grand policy goals to everyday life. The role of these smaller projects can be interpreted as being accelerators of processes. For example, Jallinoja, Niva and Latvala (2016) inquire: "The question is, to what extent is it possible to accelerate the process of turning plant proteins into a normal component of Finnish diets and meals and, finally to be frequently consumed?" (p. 10). This brings one back to the coalition-building and distributed-intervener discussion stressing the need to see any governance response embedded in a wider context of multiple (and sometimes competing) change attempts.

Tools and approaches based on practice elements

A very multi-faceted part of practice-based intervention design is the question of "how", or the strategic implementation plan. Most of the SPT-based studies outline some policy implications at their concluding sections, stressing the overlapping nature of social practices and the complexity of everyday lives, as well as reiterating the central postulate of transforming practices rather than influencing individuals. But more often than not these are broad and abstract recommendations that are not exactly "policy-amenable" in the applied sense. Keller, Halkier and Wilska (2016, pp. 84–85) have provided a series of more concrete recommendations that synthesize earlier studies' suggestions.

In recent years a few guides for practitioners that either more directly or indirectly make use of the SPT thinking have been published as well. Vihalemm et al., 2015 is a theory-driven guidebook whose usability is yet to be proven. In addition, Darnton and Horne (2013) have worked out a so-called ISM-tool (I-individual, S-social, M-material) for the Scottish Government. It seeks to move "beyond" (the individual), yet it still takes the individual behavior as the basic "unit" of intervention. However, considerable attention is dedicated to material and social aspects. Its strength lies in encompassing other issues besides sustainable consumption (e.g. health, driving safety). While being quite a wide-ranging analytic guide, its actual counsel on how to design an intervention programme is compressed into one box titled "take action".

A recent report for the European Commission (Umpfenbach, 2014), titled "Influences on consumer behavior. Policy implications beyond nudging", pays considerable homage to social practice theory-based research and acknowledges, for example, the importance of "lock-ins" of consumers' behavior, as well as the power of habit. Notably a new document titled *Sustainable Consumption and Production. A Handbook for Policymakers* by UNEP (2015) also features a small section on social practice theory and is influenced by it in its practical recommendations' mentality and wording. All this demonstrates the influx of SPT thinking into actual policy and intervention circles, even though practical guidelines of programme design are few and far between. What is still almost totally lacking are analyses of interventions that have been conducted bearing practice thinking in mind. The simple reason is that cases of such programmes are still very rare. There are SPT-inspired accounts of change programmes (see analyses of New Nordic Cuisine, the Japanese Cool Biz initiative and Manchester Cycling Hubs in Spurling et al., 2013), but these projects themselves have taken a social practice view inadvertently.

The following section draws to some extent on the guidebook of Vihalemm et al., 2015, which has quite a thorough chapter on programme implementation design taking the three elements of practices – meanings, skills and objects/material environments (Shove et al., 2012) – as the point of departure, asking what sorts of tools and approaches can the intervener choose from? There is always an interweaving dynamic between intervention and self-regulation/"natural" evolution of social change. We briefly discuss awareness campaigns, technological innovations and product design and skills and competences enhancement.

Chapter 18 of this handbook proposes a clear distinction between regulation and behavior change. As the present chapter is driven by the idea to provide theory and research-informed guidance to potential practitioners, we ask: how useful is this distinction in professional practice of intervention design? We tend to think that both these strands of policy tend to blur and intermingle (as regulation influences behavior change and vice versa) and should do so, if we take the consumer everyday life trajectories as the point of departure.

The three elements – materials, meanings and skills – are inextricably interwoven, and SPT scholars tend to be rather unanimous in asserting that in order to step up change, intervention into all practice elements, as well as the ways how practices interlock and intersect, is necessary.

But again, coming some steps down from that academic high ground, a professional intervention designer or policy maker does need a focus and a strategic approach. A larger-scale policy or strategy (be it on the global, regional or national level) can address all these requirements; a single programme seldom can. Nevertheless, the component elements scheme must be held as a guiding light. To provide an example by Maller (2015, pp. 61–62), "To encourage eating a healthy breakfast, interventions could target the meanings of breakfast (what to eat, when to eat), the materials involved (food, places to eat, recipes) and competences (how to prepare, cook, eat breakfast). What is important is that all three elements are the focus of attempts to intervene. . ." But again, it would be overtly simplistic to assume that well-synergized, SPT-inspired strategic programmes could predict outcomes for healthy and sustainable consumption practices, let alone guarantee them. An intervener has to reconcile with the knowledge that practice performances may be uneven, trajectories unpredictable and experience acquired in an earlier programme non-transferrable into a new context.

Meanings and communication

To address meanings, communication campaigns are pervasive. Particularly the ones centering on individuals' awareness hoping to prompt behavior change have been a target of severe criticism by SPT scholars (see Warde and Southerton, 2012). The SPT view assures that in most cases communication campaigns alone cannot effect change, yet there is no need to demonize or totally dismiss them. SPT draws attention to the limitations of the theoretical groundings such campaigns are often based upon (even though in many cases campaigners do not explicitly draw upon any theory, their professional routines and language are at least indirectly influenced by them). One such concept is the theory of planned behavior (Ajzen, 1991), which has enjoyed a near-hegemonic status in public health. For a very instructive discussion on this see Holm and Gronow, 2015. They stress that "the actions people perform are not merely single events determined by individual cognition. They are also elements in practices that are guided by social conventions and cultural norms and influenced by social and material structures" (Holm and Gronow, 2015, p. 146).

Also, the conceptualization of hierarchy of effects (Lavidge and Steiner, 1961), which has been one of the pillars of mainstream approaches to communications planning that assume a linear relationship between different cognitive (knowledge), affective (attitudes, preferences) and conative states (behavior), can be considered limited and rather unhelpful in actual change planning. The value-action gap (see Warde and Southerton, 2012) between purported attitudes and actual activities is widely acknowledged.

But it must be noted that even though in the background there exists a body of literature on practice and discourse (see e.g. Rouse, 2006), SPT-inspired research, which explicitly addresses communication and social interaction, is still making its first steps (see Christensen and Røpke, 2010; Keller and Halkier, 2014; Welch, 2012). So for SPT-minded professionals who seek to re-shape the meanings of problematic social practices, there is not much to rely on in terms of theory-informed and empirically grounded guidance.

In addition, Welch and Warde (2015) highlight the inadequacy of practice theories in their current state of development for providing "analytical or explanatory resources" (p. 13) to fully grasp supra-practice discourses such as "obesity" or "sustainable consumption" to the extent that the structuring effects of such discourses upon practices may be obscured. Thus, to put it simply, there are practice-specific orders of meaning which particular intervention programmes may address, but they are always in some way linked to supra-practice networks of meanings, cultural discourses which have to be paid attention to in programme design.

Another aspect worth stressing here is the so-called deficit model of the audiences (Halkier, 2015, Brondi et al., 2015, Sarrica et al., 2016) that constructs citizens as passive recipients of information and as having knowledge gaps that need to be filled by technical or scholarly expertise. At the same time, for example, dialogic approaches to participatory research as well as various interventions postulate communication processes not as diffusion and transmission, but as interaction and co-construction of meaning (Phillips, 2011). Halkier (2015) directly investigates the implications of the practice approach to communication by proposing a "practice theoretical understanding" of audiences in which citizen-consumers are made sense of as being "active and embedded in contextual potentials and conditions of everyday life" (2015, p. 9). How exactly to employ the practice theoretical understanding in actual applied communication is a further step that needs to be taken in the cooperation of scholars and practitioners.

Skills and learning

Another crucial practice element is skills, having an obvious link to training and education. Although the present chapter cannot plunge into an elaborate discussion on that, a few remarks are made. An SPT view grounds its understanding of learning on the interplay between discursive and practical consciousness (see Giddens, 1984). Lizardo (2009) has elaborated on "practical socialization", which points to developments also in cognitive neuroscience according to which learning takes place, to a large extent, based on implicit, embodied experiences and representations in which doing, rather than much speaking, thinking or listening (the cornerstones of a linguistic and representational formal education), takes center stage.

In discussing interventions into strong habits, Wilhite (2012) advocates social learning theory: "Learning through participation in practices such as sporting activities is an example of social learning. . . . Another form for social learning is purposive learning through apprenticeship, involving exposure to and participation in practices along with guidance and feedback" (2012, p. 95). The examples of "permablitzes" (creating permaculture gardens in urban people's backyards) offered by Lewis (2015, p. 359) is a case in point, where people acquire competences of social practices (permaculture-gardening) through collective "embodied sensory engagement".

Objects and material environments

Critics have pointed out that much of the current techno-rational paradigm in sustainability transitions (McMeekin and Southerton, 2012) utilizes or proposes large-scale technological innovations (electric cars, renewable energy, etc.) on a high policy level without much mobilizing or analyzing consumer agency or the effect of technological innovations in everyday lives. The Multi-Level-Perspective with the Socio-Technical Transitions theory (Geels and Schot, 2007; Geels, 2011) provides one avenue for conceptualizing components of socio-technical systems, without eclipsing the everyday practice level. Also, Mylan (2015) makes a contribution to the Sustainable Product-Service System's literature by building a bridge with sociology of consumption and practice theory. She discusses the cases of low-temperature laundry and energy-efficient light-bulbs and asserts that "The two cases illustrate the importance of looking beyond acquisition to explain the demand-side dynamics underpinning the diffusion of innovations" (p. 18). She proposes to reframe the SPSS agenda not to meet consumer needs, but to transform them. The former understanding stems from an assumed independence and stability of consumer need outside the configurations of social practices. Thus SPSS innovations "should be approached as a transformational alignment process in which practices (and needs) co-evolve with new products, business models and infrastructures" (p. 19). Thus there is evidence of some cross-fertilization of the productionist-technological understanding of change and the sociological consumer-based approach.

There is an emerging literature on *practice-oriented design* concentrating on how material objects and environments can be innovated to re-craft or substitute consumer practices (Nilstad Pettersen, 2015). Scott, Bakker and Quist (2011) outline a methodology, based on interviews and experimentation, of how practice-oriented designers may work together with consumers in reshaping practices, using the example of bathing. They admit that such a participatory lab type design may at least in the early stages remain within academic design research for being impracticable for industrial product design. Yet this is a start and may offer considerable inspiration for reconceptualising design and human-artefact relationships in social situations. In a later article Kuijer and Bakker (2015, p. 9) suggest, "In practice-oriented design, the designer is seen as a facilitator or catalyser of change in practice that is eventually a concerted, emergent achievement of a variety of stakeholders." This view stresses that designers of products and environments definitely have a crucial role in steering habits of everyday life, yet this relationship is not linear and the objects cannot single-handedly induce good or bad behaviors, "as people creatively reconfigure practices in everyday performance"(p. 9).

In the area of public health studies, bio-metric self-tracking (Harries and Rettie, 2016) has been analyzed to look at human and non-human configurations and their relation to the change of practices (walking in that particular work) which open another intriguing avenue to discuss how technological objects can and cannot be used in galvanizing change in consumer lifestyles.

Impact evaluation – a mission (im)possible?

Lastly the chapter offers a brief note on intervention programme evaluation or impact assessment, as it is often termed.

"Social impact" is an "effect of an activity on the social fabric of a community and the well-being of individuals and families" (Business Dictionary, n.d.) that refers to the collective and socio-cultural nature of expected change and calls for a search of evidence regarding social structure, social relations and subjects' well-being. Providing proof on change of practices as collective patterns of action induced by a single intervention programme or even a policy is exceedingly difficult, if not impossible.

Practice change can be observed when a certain way of doing something is acknowledged as a group norm as well as considered personally follow-able by single performers (Vihalemm et al., 2015); when key actors (e.g. the management board of an organization or the staff of a service provider) have accepted and internalized particular procedures; or when a service delivered by an NGO is upscaled as a public service concept. But always there are many contributing factors that impact the returns on investments, and extraction of very definitive causalities is dubious. Instead, multiple-method approaches are suggested (e.g. by European Evaluation Society), both qualitative and quantitative (Saunders, 2011).

Funders' expectations towards "monetization" of results of intervention programmes can be met in collecting evidence about short-term effects, i.e. outputs (interactive or safer things and improved environments) and outcomes (what changes beneficiaries' experience in terms of skills, knowledge, understanding and mutual relations), but these may not tell much about the persistence of the achieved changes beyond the programme's completion.

Continuation of change depends on the viability of the produced things, environments and interactions vis-á-vis the socio-material network that helps to disrupt, substitute or modify problematic practices. This potential to maintain and reshape the socio-material network that supported earlier unwanted practices is called the *provisional stability* (Saunders, 2011) of interventions. The maintenance is more likely when the agents or designers of change build strong coalitions, as well as public legitimacy and legal framework with a potential to reorganize social spaces and rhythms. We suggest to base evaluation of the programme's possible long-term impact on a combination of outcomes, viability and positive contributing effects of factors outside the programme – how the socio-material network that practices are embedded in is shaped, in order to enable self-reproduction of the desired activities.

Summary

To sum up – single interventions have usually little effect in tackling large-scale problems and strong consumer habits, yet as the social problems related to consumer lifestyles are embedded in intricate socio-material networks, so must intervention programmes be symbiotic and form a mutually supportive network of steps and measures that try to shift normalities in the desired direction, to accelerate changes in practices as entities, yet acknowledging the volatility and versatility in lived practice performances. An SPT-based approach does not invent a package of completely novel implementation methods to step up change, but it tries to offer a fresh and potentially helpful way of framing problems and mobilizing ways and tools (some of them tried and tested and some of them creatively emergent) of change in new combinations.

Potential future avenues for research that might be most valuable for applied intervention could deal with workplace and professional practices of consumers and interveners, practice-oriented design as well as impact analysis of practice-minded interventions. Also, it is probable and welcome that SPT-based studies of change in consumers' lives expand from the hitherto dominant focus on sustainability to health, financial literacy, various safety-related topics as well as other areas of well-being and quality of life.

Acknowledgement

The work underlying this chapter has been funded by the research grant IUT20-38 by the Estonian Research Council.

References

Ajzen, I. (1991), 'The theory of planned behavior,' *Organizational Behavior and Human Decision Processes*, vol. 50, pp. 179–211.

Aro, R. (2016), 'Normality against sustainability – Mobility practices of well-to-do households,' *Environmental Policy and Governance*, vol. 26, no. 2, pp. 116–128.

Bennett, L. (2012), 'The personalization of politics: Political identity, social media, and changing patterns of participation,' *AAPSS Annals*, vol. 644, pp. 20–39.

Blue, S., Shove, E., Carmona C. and Kelly, M. P. (2016), 'Theories of practice and public health: Understanding (un)healthy practices', *Critical Public Health*, vol. 26, no. 1, pp. 36–50.

Bourdieu, B. (1991), 'Political Representation: Elements for a Theory of the Political Field.' In J. P. Thompson (ed.), *Language and Symbolic Power. chapter* (pp. 203–219). Cambridge, MA: Harvard University Press.

Brondi, S., Sarrica, M., Caramis, A., Piccolo, C. and Mazzara, B. (2015), 'Italian parliamentary debates on energy sustainability: How argumentative "short-circuits" affect public engagement,' *Public Understanding of Science 25*(6), 737–753. doi: 10.1177/0963662515580067.

Christensen, T.H. and Røpke, I. (2010), 'Can practice theory inspire studies of ICTs in everyday life.' In B. Bräucher and J. Postill (eds.), *Theorizing Media and Practice* (pp. 233–56). New York, NY: Berghahn Books.

Cotton, M. and Devine-Wright, P. (2012), 'Making energy networks "visible": Industry actor representations of "publics" and public engagement in infrastructure planning,' *Public Understanding of Science*, vol. 21, no.1, pp. 17–35.

Darnton, A. and Horne, J. (2013), *Influencing Behaviors. Moving Beyond the Individual. A guide to the ISM Tool.* The Scottish Government. Edinburgh. http://www.scotland.gov.uk/Publications/2013/06/8511/downloads [17 Nov 2014].

Devine-Wright, P. (2007), 'Energy Citizenship: Psychological Aspects of Evolution in Sustainable Energy Technologies.' In J. Murphy (ed.), *Framing the Present, Shaping the Future: Contemporary Governance of Sustainable Technologies* (pp. 63–86). London: Earthscan.

Dubuisson-Quellier, S. and Gojard, S. (2016), 'Why are food practices not (More) environmentally friendly in France? The role of collective standards and symbolic boundaries in food practices', *Environmental Policy and Governance*, vol. 26, no. 2, pp. 89–100.

Evans, D., McMeekin. A. and Southerton, D. (2012), 'Sustainable consumption, behavior change policies and theories of practice,' In *The Habits of Consumption*, Warde, A. and Southerton, D. (eds.), *COLLeGIUM: Studies Across Disciplines in the Humanities and Social Sciences*, vol. 12, pp. 113–129. https://helda.helsinki.fi/handle/10138/34226 [21 January 2015].

Gardner, J. R., Rachlin, R. and Sweeney, H. W. A. (1986), *Handbook of Strategic Planning*. New York, NY: John Wiley and Sons.

Geels, F. (2011), 'The multi-level perspective on sustainability transitions: Responses to seven criticisms,' *Environmental Innovation and Societal Transitions*, vol. 1, no.1, pp. 24–40.

Geels, F. and Schot, J. (2007), 'Typology of sociotechnical transition pathways,' *Research Policy*, vol. 36, pp. 399–417.

Giddens, A. (1984/1989), *The Constitution of Society: Outline of the Theory of Structuration*. Cambridge, England: Polity Press.

Gitlin, T. (1998), 'Public Sphere or Public Sphericules?'. In Liebes, T. and Curran, J. (eds.), *Media, Ritual and Identity*. London: Routledge, 168–174.

Gram-Hanssen, K. (2014), 'New needs for better understanding of households' energy consumption – behavior, lifestyle or practices?', *Architectural Engineering and Design Management*, vol. 10, pp. 91–107.

Gronow, J. and Holm, L. (2015), 'Explaining Consumer Choice: A Critique ofTheory of Planned Behavior.' In P. Strandbakken and J. Gronow (eds.), *Consumer in Society*. Abstrakt Forlag, 229–249.

Halkier, B. (2010), *Consumption Challenged. Food in Medialized Everyday Lives*. Farnham: Ashgate.

Halkier, B. (2015), 'Mundane science use in a practice theoretical perspective: Different understandings of the relations between citizen-consumers and public communication initiatives build on scientific claims,' *Public Understanding of Science*, doi: 10.1177/0963662515596314.

Halkier, B. (2016), 'Civic Engagement by Invitation? Citizen Negotiations About Public Media Framings of Everyday Life Responsibilities for Societal Problems.' In H. K. Nielsen (ed.), *The Democratic Public Sphere*. Aarhus Universitetsforlag, 289–317.

Halkier, B. (in press), 'Questioning the "Gold Standard" Thinking In Qualitative Methods from a Practice Theoretical Perspective: Towards Methodological Multiplicity.' In M. Jonas, B. Littig and A. Wroblewski (eds.), *Methodological Reflections on Practice Oriented Theories*. Springer.

Hargreaves, T. (2011), 'Practice-ing behavior change: Applying social practice theory to pro-environmental change,' *Journal of Consumer Culture*, vol. 11, no. 1, pp. 79–99.

Harries, J. and Rettie, R. (2016), 'Walking As a Social Practice: Dispersed Walking and Theorganisation of Everyday Practices', In *Sociology of Health and Illness*. doi: 10.1111/1467–9566.12406.

Higginson, S., McKenna, E., Hargreaves, T., Chilvers, J. and Thomson, M. (2015), 'Diagramming social practice theory: An interdisciplinary experiment exploring practices as networks,' *Indoor and Built Environment*, vol. 27, no.7, pp. 950–969.

Huttunen, S. and Oosterveer, P. (2016), ' Transition to Sustainable Fertilisation in Agriculture, A Practices Approach,' *Sociologia Ruralis*, DOI: 10.1111/soru.12118.

Isin, E. and Nielsen, G. (2008), *Acts of Citizenship*. London and New York: Zed Books.

Jäger-Erben, M., Rückert-John, J. and Schäfer, M. (2015), 'Sustainable consumption through social innovation: A typology of innovations for sustainable consumption practices,' *Journal of Cleaner Production*, vol. 108, pp. 784–798.

Jallinoja, P., Niva, M. and Latvala (2016), 'Future of sustainable eating? Examining the potential for expanding bean eating in a meat-eating culture,' *Futures*, doi:10.1016/j.futures.2016.03.006

John, R., Jäger-Erben, M., and Rückert-John, J. (2016), 'Elusive Practices: Considerations on limits and possibilities of environmental policy for sustainable consumption,' *Environmental Policy and Governance*, vol. 26, no. 2, pp. 129–140.

Jonas, M., Littig, B. and Wroblewski, A. (eds.) (in press), *Methodological Reflections on Practice Oriented Theories*. Springer.

Keane, R. (1995), 'Structural transformations of the Public Sphere,' *The Communication Review*, vol. 1, no. 1, pp. 23–25.

Keller, M. and Halkier, B. (2014), 'Positioning consumption: A practice theoretical approach to contested consumption and media discourse,' *Marketing Theory*, vol. 14, pp. 35–51.

Keller, M., Halkier, B. and Wilska, T.-A. (2016), 'Policy and governance for sustainable consumption at the crossroads of theories and concepts', *Environmental Policy and Governance*, vol. 26, no. 2, pp. 75–88.

Keller, M. and Kiisel, M. (forthcoming), 'Tarbimine: võimalused, eneseväljendus ja sääst/ Consumption: opportunities, self-expression and saving,' [in Estonian], in P. Vihalemm, M. Lauristin, T. Vihalemm and V. Kalmus (eds), *Eesti ühiskond kiirenevas ajas: eesti elaviku muutumine 2001–2014 uuringu Mina.Maailm. Meedia tulemuste põhjal/ Estonian society in an accelerating time: change of Estonian lifeworld based on the findings of the Me. The World. The Media survey.* Tartu: Tartu University Press.

Kuijer, L. and Bakker, C. (2015), 'Of chalk and cheese: Behaviour change and practice theory in sustainable design,' *International Journal of Sustainable Engineering*, http://dx.doi.org/10.1080/19397038.2015.1011729.

Kunze, C. and Becker, S. (2014), *Energy Democracy in Europe. A Survey and Outlook*. Brussels: Rosa-Luxemburg-Stiftung & Van Ruys Printing.

Lavidge, R. J. and Steiner, G. A. (1961), 'A model for predictive measurements of advertising effectiveness,' *Journal of Marketing*, vol. 25, pp. 59–62.

Leck, H., Conway, D., Bradshaw, M. and Rees, J. (2015), 'Tracing the water–energy–food nexus: Description, theory and practice,' *Geography Compass*, vol. 9, no. 8, pp. 445–460.

Lewis, T. (2015), '"One city block at a time": Researching and cultivating green transformations', *International Journal of Cultural Studies*, vol. 18, no. 3, pp. 347–363.

Lizardo, O. (2009), 'Is a 'special psychology' of practice possible? From values and attitudes to embodied dispositions,' *Theory and Psychology*, vol. 19, pp. 1–15.

Macrorie, R., Foulds, C. and Hargreaves, T. (2014), 'Governing and governed by practices. Exploring interventions in low-carbon housing policy and practice. In Social Practices, Intervention and Sustainability: Beyond Behaviour Change, Strengers, Y. and Maller, C. (eds), *Social Practices, Intervention and Sustainability: Beyond Behavior Change*. Abingdon, UK: Routledge, 95–111.

Maller, C.J. (2015), 'Understanding health through social practices: performance and materiality in everyday life', *Sociology of Health and Illness*, vol. 37, no. 1, pp. 52–66.

McCracken, G. (1986), 'Culture and consumption: A theoretical account of the structure and movement of the cultural meaning of consumer goods,' *Journal of Consumer Research*, vol. 13, no. 1, pp. 71–84.

McMeekin A. and Southerton, D. (2012), 'Sustainability transitions and final consumption: Practices and socio-technical systems,' *Technology Analysis & Strategic Management*, vol. 24, pp. 345–361.

Mylan, J. (2015), 'Understanding the diffusion of sustainable product-service systems: Insights from the sociology of consumption and practice theory,' *Journal of Cleaner Production*, vol. 97, pp. 13–20.

Nilstad Pettersen, I. (2015), 'Fostering absolute reductions in resource use: The potential role and feasibility of practice-oriented design,' *Journal of Cleaner Production*, doi:10.1016/j.jclepro.2015.02.005.

Norris, P. (2002), *Democratic Phoenix: Reinventing Political Activism*. New York: Cambridge University Press.

Orru, K. and Lilleoja, L. (2015), 'Contextual drivers of environmental values cross-culturally: Evidence from Europe between 2004 and 2012,' *Studies of Transition States and Societies*, vol. 7, no. 3, pp.38–51.

Ozaki, R. and Shaw I. (2014), 'Entangled practices: Governance, sustainable technologies, and energy consumption,' *Sociology: The Journal of the British Sociological Association*, vol. 48, pp. 590–604.

Penn Handwerker, W. (2001), *Quick Ethnography: A Guide to Rapid Multi-Method Research*. Plymouth, UK: Altamira Press.

Phillips, L. (2011), *The Promise of Dialogue: The Dialogic Turn in the Production and Communication of Knowledge*. Amsterdam: John Benjamins Publishing Company.

Rasmussen, T. (2014), 'Internet and the political public sphere,' *Sociology Compass*, vol. 8, no. 12, pp. 1315–1329.

Rogers, E. M. (1962), *Diffusion of Innovations*. New York: Free Press of Glencoe.

Rouse, J. (2006), 'Practice Theory'. In D.M Gabbay, P. Thagard and J. Woods (eds.), *Handbook of the Philosophy of Science. Volume 15: Philosophy of Anthropology and Sociology.* Amsterdam: Elsevier, 500–540.

Sarrica, M., Brondi, S., Cottone, P. and Mazzara, B. (2016), 'One, no one, one hundred thousand energy transitions in Europe: The quest for a cultural approach,' *Energy Research and Social Science*, vol. 12, 1–14.

Saunders, M. (2011), 'Capturing effects of interventions, policies and programmes in the European context: A social practice perspective,' *Evaluation*, vol. 17, pp. 89–102.

Schatzki, T. (2002), *The Site of the Social. A Philosophical Account of the Constitution of Social Life and Change.* Pennsylvania, USA: Pennsylvania State University Press.

Scott, K., Bakker, C. and Quist, J. (2011), 'Designing change by living change,' *Design Studies*, vol. 33, pp. 279–297.

Seppel, K. and Kiisel, M. (forthcoming), 'Ootused maailma tuleviku ja riskide suhtes. [in Estonian] Expectations towards the future of the world and global risks,' in P. Vihalemm, M. Lauristin, T. Vihalemm and V. Kalmus (eds), *Eesti ühiskond kiirenevas ajas: eesti elaviku muutumine 2001–2014 uuringu Mina.Maailm. Meedia tulemuste põhjal/ Estonian society in an accelerating time: change of Estonian lifeworld based on the findings of the Me. The World. The Media survey.* Tartu: Tartu University Press.

Shove, E. (2010), 'Beyond the ABC: Climate change policy and theories of social change,' *Environment and Planning A*, vol. 42, pp. 1273–1285.

Shove, E., Pantzar, M. and Watson, M. (2012), *The Dynamics of Social Practice: Everyday Life and How It Changes.* London: Sage.

Shove, E. and Spurling, N. (2013), 'Sustainable practices: Social theory and climate change,'. In E. Shove, N. Spurling (eds.), *Sustainable Practices: Social Theory and Climate Change*, (pp. 1–13). Oxon: Routledge.

Sloam, J. (2014), '"The outraged young": Young Europeans, civic engagement and the new media in a time of crisis,' *Information, Communication & Society*, vol. 17, no. 2, pp. 217–231.

Social impact. (2016), In *Business Dictionary*. Retrieved from http://www.businessdictionary.com/definition/social-impact.html

Spurling, N., McMeekin, A., Shove, E., Southerton, D. and Welch, D. (2013), Interventions in practice: Re-framing policy approaches to consumer behaviour. Sustainable Practices Research Group Report. http://www.sprg.ac.uk/uploads/sprg-report-sept-2013.pdf [12 April 2016].

Strengers, Y. (2012), 'Peak electricity demand and social practice theories: Reframing the role of change agents in the energy sector,' *Energy Policy*, vol. 44, pp. 226–234.

Strengers, Y. and Maller, C. (eds.) (2014), *Social Practices, Intervention and Sustainability. Beyond Behaviour Change.* London: Routledge.

Strengers, Y., Moloney, S., Maller, C. and Horne, R. (2014) 'Practical Applications of Social Practice Theory in Behaviour Change Programmes.' In Y. Strengers and C. Maller (eds.), *Social Practices, Intervention and Sustainability: Beyond Behaviour Change* (pp. 63–77). Oxon: Routlege.

Sulkunen, P. (2009), *The Saturated Society. Governing Risk & Lifestyles in Consumer Culture.* London: Sage.

Sustainable Consumption and Production. A Handbook for Policymakers. A Global Edition. (2015), United Nations Environment Programme. https://sustainabledevelopment.un.org/content/documents/1951Sustainable%20Consumption.pdf. URL accessed April 15, 2016

Uibu, M. and Vihalemm, T. (forthcoming), 'Tervisepüüdlused ühiskonna polariseerijana? [in Estonian] Will striving for health polarize Estonian society? in P. Vihalemm, M. Lauristin, T. Vihalemm and V. Kalmus (eds), *Eesti ühiskond kiirenevas ajas: eesti elaviku muutumine 2001–2014 uuringu Mina.Maailm.Meedia tulemuste põhjal/ Estonian society in an accelerating time: change of Estonian lifeworld based on the findings of the Me. The World. The Media survey.* Tartu: Tartu University Press.

Umpfenbach K. (2014), Influences on consumer behaviour. Policy implications beyond nudging. Ecologic Institute, Berlin. http://ec.europa.eu/environment/enveco/economics_policy/pdf/Behaviour%20Policy%20Brief.pdf [27 November 2014].

Vihalemm, T. and Keller, M. (2016), 'Consumers, citizens or citizen-consumers? Domestic users in the process of the Estonian electricity market liberalization,' *Energy Research and Social Sciences*, vol. 13, 38−48.

Vihalemm, T., Keller, M. and Kiisel, M. (2015), *From Intervention to Social Change. A Guide to Reshaping Everyday Practices.* London: Ashgate.

Vihalemm, T., Lauristin, M. and Harro-Loit, H. (forthcoming). 'Personaalse aja tihenemine ja Eesti elanikkonna ajakapital. [in Estonian] Acceleration of personal time and time as capital among the Estonian population,' in P. Vihalemm, M. Lauristin, T. Vihalemm and V. Kalmus (eds), *Eesti ühiskond kiirenevas ajas: eesti elaviku muutumine 2001–2014 uuringu Mina.Maailm.Meedia tulemuste põhjal/ Estonian society in an accelerating time: change of Estonian lifeworld based on the findings of the Me. The World. The Media survey.* Tartu: Tartu University Press.

Wahlen, S. and Laamanen, M. (eds.) (2015), 'Consumption, lifestyle and social movements,' *International Journal of Consumer Studies*, vol. 39, no. 5, pp. 397–403.

Warde, A. (2005), 'Consumption and theories of practice,' *Journal of Consumer Culture*, vol. 5, no. 2, pp. 131–153.

Warde, A. (2013), 'What Sort of a Practice is Eating?' In E. Shove and N. Spurling (eds.), *Sustainable Practices: SocialTtheory and Climate Change*, (pp. 17–30). Oxon: Routledge.

Warde, A. and Southerton, D. (2012), 'Introduction. Preamble: Social Sciences and Sustainable Consumption.' In A. Warde and D. Southerton (eds.), *The Habits of Consumption. COLLeGIUM: Studies Across Disciplines in the Humanities and Social Sciences* (pp. 1–25). https://helda.helsinki.fi/handle/10138/34226 [11 April 2016].

Welch, D. (2012), *Understanding the Commercial Field of Sustainability Communications.* PhD dissertation. University of Manchester.

Welch, D. and Warde, A. (2015), 'Theories of Practice and Sustainable Consumption.' in L. Reisch and J. Thøgersen (eds.), *Handbook of Research on Sustainable Consumption* (pp. 84–100). Cheltenaham: Edward Elgar Publishing.

Whitmarsh, L., O'Neill, S. and Lorenzoni, I. (2011), 'Commentary,' *Environment and Planning A*, vol. 43, pp. 258–261.

Wilhite, H. (2012), 'Towards a Better Accounting of the Roles of Body, Things and Habits in Consumption.' In A. Warde and D. Southerton (eds.), *The Habits of Consumption. COLLeGIUM: Studies Across Disciplines in the Humanities and Social Sciences* (pp. 87–99). https://helda.helsinki.fi/handle/10138/34226 [11 May 2016].

Yates, L. and Evans, D. (2016), 'Dirtying Linen: Re-evaluating the sustainability of domestic laundry,' *Environmental Policy and Governance*, vol. 26, no. 2, pp. 101–115.

21

Behaviorally informed consumer policy

Research and policy for "humans"

Lucia A. Reisch and John B. Thøgersen

The myth of the "econ" consumer

Consumer policy has long been based on a view of the consumer as a rational *homo oeconomicus* who actively engages in a search for the best available product/service option, knows and considers all cost and benefits and follows her true preferences. In this view, consumer behavior is largely determined by individual preference orders (based on information provided and prior learning) and individual income, as well as the goods and prices available. The formal economic model expressing this approach is essentially a constrained optimization situation for a set of considered consumption bundles. It does account for some factors that influence choices beyond prices, primarily time (current availability), other goods (opportunity costs), and consumption circumstances (including diminishing marginal utility); yet it assumes that attitudes, values, social norms, and other mental representations are all included in a consumer's preferences (Thaler, 1980). While such consumption models recognize potential "anomalies" – such as bandwagon or cascade effects, Veblen effects, habits, addiction, limited information processing – they assume that the human biases and heuristic strategies that have been identified in empirical consumer research and the specific choice situations are generally "irrelevant" and can hence be neglected (Reisch & Sunstein, 2015). However, as we will see, this is not a helpful assumption for the real world; empirical studies have shown that these "supposedly irrelevant factors" (SIFs) (Thaler, 2015) are – quite to the contrary – rather decisive (Halpern, 2015).

Economic models are theoretically underpinned by the assumption that humans, and indeed consumers, behave in a generally rational and consistent manner in the sense that: they are motivated (solely) by expected utility maximization, are generally governed by purely selfish concerns, and have consistent time preferences and fungible income and assets. That means that decisions are logically planned and implemented, with a clear decision criteria used to enable the consumer to make the best possible decision for them, weighing pros and cons (Brennan, Binney, Parker, Aleti, & Nguyen, 2014). The empirical truth is, however, that consumers often display "bounded rationality" (Kahneman, 2003; Simon, 1956), in the sense that they depart from the standard account in predictable and systematic ways. Because of those departures, consumers can make serious errors by their own lights, even in the absence of externalities (the typical justification for political corrective measures of internalization of external costs), and even compromising their own interest (Luth, 2010; Scharff, 2009). Behavioral economics captures such losses that hurt people's future selves in the term *internalities* (Allcott, Mullainathan, & Taubinsky, 2014). If we understand human beings as a series of selves extending over time, internalities can be seen to create a kind of intrapersonal collective action problem whose solution could provide significant benefits (Thaler & Sunstein, 2003; for a critique of such an approach see: Whitman, 2006).

Later versions of the standard *homo oeconomicus* model partly incorporate the notion of cognitive limitations in economic actors, mainly the fact that information is not free but bears costs in itself (bounded rationality), the existence of unselfish motivations (as found in game theory), and the influence of formal and informal institutions on markets. This is reflected in two economic theories that serve as theoretical ground for most of consumer regulation to date:

> The economics of information analyses market failures which occur due to imperfect information of market processes (so-called asymmetric information) as well as the corresponding (inefficient) behavior of market players (namely: moral hazard and adverse selection). Information has an invisible price tag, at least in the form of time and effort (Akerlof, 1970; Nelson, 1970; Stigler, 1961). In this worldview, "the economics of consumer protection is the economics of information."
>
> *(Shapiro, 1983, p. 528)*

New Institutional Economics focuses on the institutional framework on which consumers as well as producers of goods and services base their decision making. The notion of an "institution" is understood as both formal (e.g. actors, contracts) and informal (e.g., shared mental models; social norms), and covers both markets and non-markets. Human decisions are viewed to be influenced by acquired thought patterns or ideologies that are characterized by incompleteness, uncertainty, and imperfectness in the light of the complex environment and an individual's limited cognitive abilities (Williamson, 2000). The focus is on institutional arrangements designed to mend market failures that occur due to information asymmetries, mental models, principle-agent problems, external effects, and problems of collective action (Furubotn & Richter, 1998). Consumer policy instruments aim at correcting existing institutional regulations and their (negative) incentive effects for consumer behavior.

In spite of the behavioral elements in these two influential theories, the model of the consumer as rational actor is still impactful in today's consumer research and theory (Bartels & Johnson, 2015). It lies at the root of major cognitive theories such as the theory of planned behavior, the theory of interpersonal behavior, and the willingness model of behavior (Brennan et al., 2014). In consumer policy, the leitbild of "consumer sovereignty" and the "information paradigm" still reign (Reisch, 2011). These key beliefs nourish the assumption that if consumers are better informed and if markets are transparent and functioning, consumers will act upon their true preferences and hence in their own best interest. Consequently, consumer information, education, and advice have been and are the major policy tools to educate, enable, encourage, and empower consumers. Harder regulatory tools (law and regulation) as well as financial incentives (subsidies and transfers) and disincentives (taxes and fees) are typically reserved for the protection of life and health (OECD, 2010).

This almost exclusive cognitive-deliberative approach to consumer policy has only recently been challenged by scholars stemming mainly from two research fields: social practice theory on the one hand (see chapter 20) as well as economic psychology, behavioral economics, and behavioral law on the other hand. The present chapter concentrates on the latter. The growing field of behavioral decision research has contributed a lot to the evidence base, comparing normative (how people should make decisions), descriptive (how people actually decide), and prescriptive (how decisions can be improved) analyses of choice and their underlying processes (e.g. Kahn, Luce, & Nowlis, 2006). Scholars refer to the well-researched systematic influence of biases and heuristics as well as to the importance of situation and choice contexts (LeBoeuf & Shafir, 2012; Reis, 2008; Shafir, 2013) and call for a radical departure from the standard economic model that still dominates economic policy consulting and most of policy thinking. A shift from a concept of "econs" to one of real-life humans (Thaler & Sunstein, 2003) promises to extend explanatory power and practical relevance of consumer policy research. In this empirically informed view on regulation (Sunstein, 2011), consumers are not seen as "irrational"; rather, empirical evidence suggests that heuristics and biases as well as situational dependency are decisive and present both challenges and opportunities for policymakers (Chetty, Friedman Leth-Petersen, Nielsen, & Olsen, 2012; Thaler & Sunstein, 2008).

Behavioral economics: An empirical view on the consumer

Fundamentally, behavioral economics is concerned with the question of how people actually behave in decision-making situations and how their choices can be improved. A primary focus is placed on two aspects: first, on what are referred to as decision heuristics and biases on the part of consumers, and second, on the specific effect of the situation or decision context (Thaler & Sunstein, 2008).

Decision heuristics and biases come into play in situations involving uncertainty, which is a relevant factor in many if not most decisions. Empirical research has shown that in our everyday consumption we humans rarely follow up our own preferences and intentions and generally inform ourselves to a far lesser extent than is suggested by the prevailing model of the rational consumer. Rather, during the search phase of the consumption process, we only perceive selective product characteristics, and because of our limited processing capacities, we restrict our search criteria to just a few (or more precisely, to "seven plus or minus two," see Miller [1956], meanwhile empirically well supported by neuroeconomics). The presence of a large variety of (actual or claimed) product alternatives is likelier to confuse us than to generate optimal buying decisions (i.e., producing a situation referred to as choice overload or hyperchoice); this is why fewer (pre-chosen) alternatives often end up being better (Mick, Broniarczyk, & Haidt, 2004).

Moreover, consumers are strongly influenced by earlier decisions, behavioral lock-ins, and habits, even if these have not proven to be optimal (Thøgersen, 2006). To some extent, we allow ourselves to be swayed by emotions and are often influenced simply by the way that product information is presented (i.e., by the framing of the product) (Bolderdijk, Steg, Geller, Lehman, & Postmes, 2013). Even the sheer name of a product – whether a food item "sounds" healthful or not – influences our choice (Irmak, Vallen, & Robinson, 2011). At the moment of purchase, there are a number of decision heuristics and biases that systematically undermine idealized decision behavior. The anchor effect leads us to overvalue the information we obtained first; the source effect draws greater attention to the source of information and leads to assumptions about its credibility that may not necessarily be correct; and herd behavior makes us adopt products just because others purchase them (Baumeister, Sparks, Stillman, & Vohs, 2008).

Alongside these effects, we are relatively bad at estimating probabilities, and thus, objective risks. We tend to overestimate our capacity for self-control and discipline. At the same time, we are quite gifted at cheating in the way we conduct our mental bookkeeping and excuse our low level of self-regulation ("Today I ate too much junk, but I'll just exercise tomorrow"). Overall, we tend to select current enjoyment (i.e., a piece of cake now) over conditions we wish for later (i.e., an attractive figure), which behavioral economists explain in terms of the hyperbolic discounting of future conditions. And yet, depending on factors such as situation, educational level, our involvement in and importance of the task, and our strength of self-regulation, we can formally and informally develop self-commitment strategies that help to counteract such disadvantageous behavioral tendencies, sometimes with the help of significant others and their group pressure (Bénabou & Tirole, 2004; Kim, 2006).

The decision-making situation itself has a systematically undervalued effect on behavior (Reis, 2008). Environmental psychology in general and the psychology of architecture in specific have long pointed to the power of "affordances"[1] (Gibson, 1979; 1986) of the immediate – built and social – environment (Withagen, De Poel, Araújo, & Pepping, 2012). The eminent role of such contexts has been demonstrated in human ecology models (Story, Neumark-Sztainer, & French, 2002) that are well-established in socialization and public health research (e.g. Reisch & Gwozdz, 2013). Research findings from behavioral economics can be usefully combined with this human ecological-setting approach. They demonstrate that the triple A (i.e., affordability, availability, and accessibility) factors associated with an action or purchasing alternatives have a major impact on decisions, and also help to explain the value-action gap (Reisch & Gwozdz, 2013). Thus, marketers have long understood that how a product is positioned in the spatial architecture of the store (for example, at eye level on the shelf) has a major impact on sales. The same is true for the perception of rapid availability (i.e., "ready-to-eat" dishes) and the product's or brand's potential of reward. In fact, most preferences are much less stable than postulated in cognitive models of consumer behavior; rather, many preferences are first constructed at the place where the decision is made (constructive preferences) (Payne, Bettman, & Johnson, 1992) and only then influence the decision.

Another robust finding from behavioral economics is the power of default options in decision-making situations, such as the standard menu in a cafeteria, the default in organ donation or the default when deciding whether or not to accept remote regulation of electricity-consuming equipment in the home to balance the electricity grid (Johnson & Goldstein, 2003; Sunstein & Reisch, 2014; Toft, Schuitema, & Thøgersen, 2014). Studies have shown that people generally follow the default and that defaults "stick" – interestingly (almost) no matter what the decision is about and how the study has been conducted (e.g. via experiments, questionnaires, secondary evaluations) (Sunstein, 2013a). It does not come as a surprise that a number of incentive systems have been developed in practice based upon "hard" and "soft" defaults (Johnson & Goldstein, 2013). To prevent ethical reservations, however, defaults (i.e., "choice without awareness") must obey to rules of good governance, such as full transparency and openness to public debate (Sunstein, 2015c).

The rise of behavioral economics in studying, explaining, and modelling consumer behavior can be traced to the 1970s (Camerer, & Loewenstein, 2004; Kahlil, 2009). In 1974, Nobel laureate Daniel Kahneman and Amos Tversky showed that people use mental shortcuts in evaluating risks, including, for example, the availability heuristic, which means that people assess probabilities based on how readily events come to mind (Tversky & Kahneman, 1974). A few years later, the two made another seminal contribution with their work on prospect theory, which proposed an alternative to expected utility theory (Kahneman & Tversky, 1979). In prospect theory, it is assumed that people dislike losses more than they like equivalent gains (i.e., loss aversion), which has been shown empirically to greatly affect their choices. What counts as a gain or loss is determined by the reference point, which can be manipulated by, for example, sellers or regulators (Ölander & Thøgersen, 2014). The 1980s, 1990s, and 2000s witnessed a stream of ground-breaking research on human biases and on the power of contexts, defaults, priming, and framing (Jolls, Sunstein, & Thaler, 1998; Kahneman, 2011).

Behavioral economics experienced broad public recognition in the mid-2000s, when public officials became interested in new policy instruments: Behaviorally informed regulation

(Sunstein, 2011) was introduced into academic discourse and was soon applied to policy in fields ranging from healthy eating and weight loss to saving for retirement, standard terms in consumer contracts, acceptance of off-shore wind farms, energy conservation, and many more. For about a decade, nudging has increasingly been applied to consumer policy problems (e.g. Lunn, 2014; Luth, 2010; OECD, 2006, 2007, 2010; Ölander & Thøgersen, 2014; Reisch & Sandrini, 2015). Consumer policy seems to be natural starting point since the concept of nudging is well known in consumer research and practice – even if under different labels – and the instruments of consumer policy do offer various entry points. Nudges are defined as low-cost, choice-preserving, behaviorally informed approaches to regulatory problems, including disclosure requirements, default rules, simplification and use of salience and social norms (Thaler & Sunstein, 2008; see also: Allcott, 2011; Sunstein, 2013b).

As indicated above, behaviorally informed regulation mainly explores two concepts (Sunstein, 2015a). The first is choice architecture, understood as the background (social and natural) against which consumer decisions are made (Thaler & Sunstein, 2003). Consumers do not decide in a vacuum, but always in a choice context that bears "affordances" (Gibson, 1979; see above). Choice architecture is ubiquitous and always present. The question is not whether there should be a choice architecture or not, but rather, who designs the architecture with which goals and whether and how this choice architect (e.g. the state, businesses, schools) is democratically legitimized. If, for example, one nation has a far more serious pollution problem than another or a far higher organ donation rate than other nations, it may well be because of differences in the relevant choice architecture, not because of any fundamental differences between the preferences or values of the citizens of the two nations (Jones, Bettman, & Whitehead, 2013; Sunstein & Reisch, 2014).

The second concept is libertarian paternalism, understood to include approaches that preserve freedom of choice but nonetheless incline or steer people in a particular direction (Sunstein, 2014c; Thaler & Sunstein, 2003). The hope of libertarian paternalism is that inexpensive and seemingly modest policy initiatives – in practice, forms of positive reinforcement and indirect suggestions to try to achieve non-forced compliance – can have large and highly beneficial effects on motives, incentives, and decision making of consumers; these stimuli (soft paternalism) or nudges are typically at least as effective, and sometimes even more effective, than direct instruction, legislation, or enforcement (hard paternalism) (Chetty et al., 2012; Chetty, Looney, & Kroft, 2009; Shafir, 2013). Nudges used as a policy tool are by definition always transparent and open for public discourse, and they have to be accepted and supported by the same democratic processes, public debate, and critical scrutiny of their costs and benefits as other political instruments (Sunstein, 2014a). Interestingly, it seems that nudges do not lose their effectiveness when made transparent and are communicated to subjects, at least in study contexts (Loewenstein, Bryce, Hagmann, & Rajpal, 2014). Sunstein (2014b) recently proposed a list of the ten most important nudges to influence consumer behavior (see Table 21.1).

Behavioral economics is sometimes criticized for being "empirically rich, but theory poor" – a claim that is hard to substantiate considering both the rich psychological and economic body of theoretical work on which it is built and the fact that it remains a nascent field. In consumer research, consumer policy, and environmental policy, behavioral economics has refreshed and expanded the debate on behavioral assumptions, consumption models, and effective and efficient policy instruments. Moreover, behavioral economics is closely related to other recently developing areas of economics, primarily neuroeconomics and experimental economics, both of which contribute innovative methodological approaches to the development of this research and policy application (Reisch & Sunstein, 2014, 2015).

Table 21.1 The ten most important nudges

No	*Nudges*
1	Default rules
2	Simplification
3	Use of social norms
4	Increase ease of access and use
5	Disclosure and transparency
6	Warning signs (visual or other)
7	Self-binding tools
8	Reminders
9	Trigger intentions to change
10	Feedback on earlier choices

Source: Adapted from Sunstein, C. R. (2014b). Nudging: A very short guide, *Journal of Consumer Policy* 37(4), 583–588.

Some critics point to the fact that it is often unclear how sustained and long running the effects of behavioral interventions really are. As is the case with other policy tools such as information, advice, or even financial incentives, the answer is an empirical one: some nudges have long-term effects (e.g. since they enable and encourage consumption experiences that ultimately become accepted habits); others might have more short-term or even one-off effects that vanish after a short while if not repeated often enough (Allcott & Rogers, 2012). To our knowledge, there is no substantiated evidence that shows that nudges are on principle less effective in the long run than other policy instruments. Ideally, nudges can change habits and social norms, and will in the best case be simply integrated – and become superfluous.

Self-interest vs. moral norms

An important premise of the model of the consumer as rational actor is that people are driven only by self-interest, and actions that appear unselfish are either self-interest in disguise, of marginal importance, or simply an error. However, mounting evidence suggests that most people distinguish between decisions and actions that are (only) privately important and moral actions and that they apply different decision rules for actions in these two domains (e.g. Bolderdijk et al., 2013; Thøgersen, 1996). Moral actions belong to the "domain of morality" (Schwartz, 1970), in contrast to only privately important actions where it is culturally and socially approved to strive to maximize personal outcomes. This distinction receives support from decision research studying the importance of social norms against trading off moral and selfish concerns (Janis & Mann, 1977) and from research into the undermining effect of economic and other extrinsic incentives on the intrinsic motivation to perform acts for the benefit of others or the society (e.g. Bowles, 2008).

On the other hand, the assumption is, of course, a simplification. Sometimes the distinction between moral and selfish decision problems gets blurred. It is abundantly revealed by empirical studies on conscious and political consumption (e.g. De Barcellos et al., 2014; Micheletti & Stolle, 2012) and also part of common human experience – for most of us both first and second hand – that moral norms are frequently set aside in cases where the costs of behaving morally (or the gains from behaving immorally) are perceived as too high (Mansbridge, 1990). When the personal stakes are high, decision making in the moral domain indeed seems to involve some kind of trade-off between costs and benefits: the ideal of decision making in the economic domain.

Consciously breaking one's moral norms arouses unpleasant emotions (guilt, bad consciousness). To avoid or dampen these emotions, people may employ various mental defense strategies, re-framing a moral act as non-moral (Gruber & Schlegelmilch, 2014; Schwartz, 1977). Schwartz (1977) suggests that the most common mental defense strategies are convincing oneself either that the moral consequences of the act are really not that serious or that it is somebody else's responsibility to solve the problem (see e.g. Gosling, Denizeau, & Oberlé, 2006).

Another possible cause of amoral conduct in a seemingly morally laden situation is that the actor fails to perceive the situation as morally laden. This may happen either because of idiosyncratic or subcultural properties of a person's value and norm structure or because he or she fails to make the connection between situational characteristics and his or her moral values and norms. In these cases, the actor has either no moral norm fitting the situation, or the moral norm is not activated. For example, an intervention informing students at a Dutch university about the negative environmental impacts of bottled water and at the same time making norms about avoiding bottled water salient led to a significant decrease in intentions to buy bottled water compared to a control condition (van der Linden, 2015). A baseline study before the intervention revealed only a weak correlation between students' assessment of the environmental impact of bottled water and bottled water consumption, a relatively new topic on the political agenda in the Netherlands.

Even if situational cues activate the actor's moral values, a feeling of moral obligation to act in a certain way may not be evoked due to ambiguity. Given the combination of prior knowledge and information provided in the situation, the actor may be uncertain, for instance, whether the case is really moral (Is the beggar really in need or just lazy? Is the claimed environmentally friendly product really environmentally friendly?), or uncertain as to which response is appropriate (Plastic or paper bag? Vote or donate money?), who should respond (Is there a physician present?), or to whether his or her choice of action makes any difference (If I don't catch the fish, somebody else will). Due to uncertainty about the appropriate behavior, the actor's moral values may provide insufficient guidance for behavior. If the pressure to make a decision is low, inaction is likely to follow (which typically means not doing the morally prescribed thing, like helping someone, donating time or money to a cause, or using extra precaution in handling a waste item). If the pressure is high, an attitude towards the act may be formed (or a stored one activated) based on an evaluation of salient (selfish and moral) consequences, as suggested by applications of the reasoned action approach to morally laden behaviors (e.g. Beck & Ajzen, 1991).

Uncertainty is more likely to characterize behaviors that have recently become morally laden (like polluting the natural environment or buying goods produced by child labour) than behaviors with a long-established status in the domain of morality (like lying or stealing). In addition, some of the newcomers in the moral domain are technically complicated, in some cases to a degree where even qualified scientists disagree about the preferable behavior (Gardner & Stern, 2008). If an action of the latter type is recurrent, learning may gradually strengthen the actor's certainty about the morally appropriate behavior (Grønhøj & Thøgersen, 2011) as well as his or her feeling of obligation to perform this behaviour, especially if he or she decides to try the morally prescribed act, in spite of the uncertainty (Lin, Zhang, & Hauser, 2015).

Behaviourally informed consumer policy

The strength of behavioral economics lies in the fact that it is based on an empirically and theoretically well-grounded set of psychological principles and derives its results from empirical methods such as field and lab experiments, as well as survey research. It explicitly revises rational choice models by identifying specific departures from them. While rational choice models continue to have explanatory power, psychological plausibility is producing more realistic models of consumer behavior. Studies in behavioral economics paint a more realistic picture of an overstrained, less capable, not-always-disciplined consumer with little time and with limited interest – a multiply bounded consumer facing different "scarcities" (e.g. Mullainathan & Shafir, 2013).

However, more complex models and a better evidence base come at a price: Consumer policy is expected to become more target-group and target-behaviour specific to be effective, less "one-size-fits-all", and hence more challenging and "messy". Adding to this complexity is the extended scope of consumer policy such as sustainable consumption (Reisch, 2004a; Thøgersen, 2005), the digital world, the sharing economy, lifestyle risks, well-being, and more (see also Reisch & Thøgersen, 2015). This entails a wider view of the consumer, beyond her role as market actor, as citizen consumer, entrepreneur, innovator, household manager, prosumer, and so forth. To date, behaviorally informed regulation has primarily been applied to regulating lifestyle risks (Alemanno & Garde, 2015), healthy eating (Wansink, 2014), and environmental and climate policy (Sunstein, 2015a). It has recently also been discovered as an effective tool for development policy (World Bank, 2014).

Consumer policy research has identified three distinctive types of consumers that generally may occur in any person in various situations but can also be linked to sociodemographic groups of consumers (Micklitz, Oehler, Piorkowsky, Reisch, & Strünck, 2011): (1) the "confident" consumer who basically trusts in markets and who limits time and effort to meta information (such as consumer reports, labels, brands) or simple heuristics; (2) the "vulnerable" consumer who for diverse reasons (such as age, language, capability, money and time poverty, ill health) has no full access to the potentials of the markets and hence needs special support and protection; these disadvantaged consumers do typically profit particularly from pre-set arrangements and choice architecture that softly and easily guides them to good and simple choices for them (Banerjee & Duflo, 2011; Mullainathan & Shafir, 2013); and (3) the "responsible" or "ethical" consumer, who has a specific interest in making consumer decisions in line with environmental, social, or ethical values. While this type is most prone to be interested in information and transparency, she will also have an interest in time-saving meta-labels and trustworthy information brokers (Nuttavuthisit & Thøgersen, 2015; Thøgersen, Jørgensen, & Sandager, 2012). Depending on the situation and the subject area, consumers will show characteristics of all of these patterns that also partially overlap. For policymakers, it is a challenge to meet the interests and needs of these three archetypes when designing effective policy toolkits. Behaviorally informed regulation is typically "micro" and inquires empirically into the problem to solve, the actors involved, and the potential policies to take. With such a case-by-case approach, it seems to create more target-group-specific, effective policies than more "macro" approaches such as taxes, levies, and incentives schemes.

One approach to meet these challenges of case-specific policies is to adapt a more flexible, evidence-based, trial-and-error policy approach, including testing tools and programmes in the field in pilot projects and evaluating them for potentials and pitfalls. The British Behavioral Insights Team (BIT), the first behavioral unit installed by and for a state government worldwide, calls this their "test-learn-adapt" approach (Halpern, 2015; Jones et al., 2013). One of the key learnings in the past years is that before policies should be rolled out, they should be tested for effectiveness and cost benefits (BIT, 2015). Experimental settings, for instance in living labs, with feedback and feedforward loops allow for such policy learning; exchanging experiences and results on such trials, e.g. in a European database, would be most helpful to bring behaviorally informed tools forward.

There is no doubt that further progress in shaping consumer demand will require the continued use of traditional tools of consumer information and advice, economic incentives and regulation; however, all of these tools can benefit from knowledge about how to make them more efficient (Sunstein, 2013b). Also, to avoid misunderstandings, no one contends that nudges are sufficient in this domain. The more modest suggestion is that an understanding of choice architecture and libertarian paternalism significantly expands the policy toolbox and has the potential to make programmes and strategies more effective (Jones et al., 2013). What is urgently needed – and constitutes a clear research gap to be solved by political science and consumer policy research – to avoid unfounded criticism of manipulation and disrespect of sovereign people (Sunstein, 2015b), are accepted and tested rules for a "good governance" for behaviorally informed regulation. There is an excellent conceptual base to start from as well as much practical experience from behavioral units worldwide; however, the concept has to be translated and adapted to both the political structure and cultural sensitivities of the respective national states – their institutions and political systems (i.e., their "polity"), the level of acceptance of paternalism and welfare politics, the specific historical aftermaths and earlier experience of a people with manipulation and transparency in non-democratic societies (as in former Eastern Europe, in some Asian states and South America).

Note

1 Gibson (1979) defines affordances as all "action possibilities" latent in the environment, objectively measurable and independent of the individual's ability to recognize them, but always in relation to agents and therefore dependent on their capabilities.

References

Akerlof, G. A. (1970). The market for 'lemons': Quality uncertainty and the market mechanism. *Quarterly Journal of Economics*, 84, 488–500.

Alemanno, A., & Garde, A. (Eds.) (2015). *Regulating lifestyle risks: The EU, alcohol, tobacco and unhealthy diets.* Cambridge, UK: Cambridge University Press.

Allcott, H. (2011). Social norms and energy conservation. *Journal of Public Economics*, 95(9), 1082–1095.

Allcott, H., Mullainathan, S., & Taubinsky, D. (2014). Energy policy with externalities and internalities. *Journal of Public Economics*, 112, 72–88.

Allcott, H., & Rogers, T. (2012). The short-run and long-run effects of behavioral interventions: Experimental evidence from energy conservation. *NBER Working Paper No. 18492.* Retrieved from: http://www.nber.org/papers/w18492 (29.07.2015).

Banerjee, A. V., & Duflo, E. (2011). *Poor economics: A radical rethinking of the way to fight global poverty.* New York: PublicAffairs.

Bartels, D. M., & Johnson, E. J. (2015). Connecting cognition and consumer choice. *Cognition*, 135, 47–51.

Baumeister, R. F., Sparks, E. A., Stillman, T. F., & Vohs, K. D. (2008). Free will in consumer behaviour: Self-control, ego depletion, and choice. *Journal of Consumer Psychology*, 18, 4–18.

Beck, L., & Ajzen, I. (1991). Predicting dishonest actions using the theory of planned behavior. *Journal of Research in Personality*, 25, 285–301.

Behavioural Insights Team (2015). *Update report 2013–2015.* London: BIT. Retrieved from: http://www.behaviouralinsights.co.uk/wp-content/uploads/2015/07/BIT_Update-Report-Final-2013-2015.pdf (20.07.2015).

Bénabou, R., & Tirole, J. (2004). Willpower and personal rules. *Journal of Political Economy*, 112, 848–886.

Bolderdijk, J. W., Steg, L., Geller, E., Lehman, P., & Postmes, T. (2013). Comparing the effectiveness of monetary versus moral motives in environmental campaigning. *Nature Climate Change*, 3, 413–416.

Bowles, S. (2008). Policies designed for self-interested citizens may undermine "the moral sentiments": Evidence from economic experiments. *Science*, 320, 1605–1609.

Brennan, L., Binney, W., Parker, L., Aleti, T., & Nguyen, D. (2014). Rational economic models (cognitive models). In L. Brennan, W. Binney, L. Parker, T. Aleti, & Dang Nguyen (Eds.), *Social marketing and behaviour change: Models, theory and applications* (pp. 17–37). Cheltenham, UK: Edward Elgar.

Camerer, C. F., & Loewenstein, G. F. (2004). Behavioral economics: Past, present, future. In C. Camerer, G. F. Loewenstein & M. Rabin (Eds.), *Advances in behavioral economics* (pp. 3–51). Princeton, MA: Sage.

Chetty, R., Friedman, J., Leth-Petersen, S. Nielsen, T., & Olsen, T. (2012). Active vs. passive decisions and crowdout in retirement savings accounts: Evidence from Denmark. *NBER Working Paper No. 18565*. Retrieved from: http://www.nber.org/papers/w18565 (29.07.2015).

Chetty, R., Looney, A., & Kroft, K. (2009). Salience and taxation: Theory and evidence. *American Economic Review*, 99(4), 1145–1177.

De Barcellos, M. D., Teixeira, C. M., & Venturini, J. C. (2014). Personal values associated with political consumption: an exploratory study with university students in Brazil. International *Journal of Consumer Studies*, 38, 207–216.

Furubotn, E. G., & Richter, R. (1998). *Institutions and economic theory: The contribution of the new institutional economics* (2nd ed.), Ann Arbor, MI: University of Michigan.

Gardner, G. T., & Stern, P. C. (2008). The short list. The most effective actions U.S. households can take to curb climate change. *Environment*, 50(5), 12–24.

Gibson, J. J. (1979/1986). *The ecological approach to visual perception*. Boston, MA: Houghton Mifflin.

Gosling, P., Denizeau, M., & Oberlé, D. (2006). Denial of responsibility: A new mode of dissonance reduction. *Journal of Personality and Social Psychology*, 90, 722–733.

Grønhøj, A., & Thøgersen, J. (2011). Feedback on household electricity consumption: Learning and social influence processes. *International Journal of Consumer Studies*, 35, 138–145.

Gruber, V., & Schlegelmilch, B. (2014). How techniques of neutralization legitimize norm- and attitude-inconsistent consumer behavior. *Journal of Business Ethics*, 121, 29–45.

Halpern, D. (2015). *Inside the nudge unit. How small changes can make big differences*. London: Ebury Publ.

Irmak, C., Vallen, B., & Robinson, S. R. (2011). The impact of product name on dieters' and nondieters' food evaluations and consumption. *Journal of Consumer Research*, 38(2), 390–405.

Janis, I. L., & Mann, L. (1977). *Decision making: A psychological analysis of conflict, choice, and commitment*. New York: Free Press.

Johnson, E. J., & Goldstein, D. (2003). Do defaults save lives? *Science*, 302, 1338–1339.

Johnson, E. J., & Goldstein, D. (2013). Decisions by default. In E. Shafir (Ed.), *Behavioral foundations of public policy* (pp. 417–428). Princeton, NJ, USA: Princeton University Press.

Jolls, C., Sunstein, C. R., & Thaler, R. (1998). A behavioral approach to law and economics. *Stanford Law Review*, 50, 1471–1550.

Jones, R., Bettman, J., & Whitehead, M. (2013). *Changing behaviour: On the rise of the psychological state*. Cheltenham, UK: Edward Elgar.

Kahlil, E. L. (2009). *The new behavioral economics, 1–3. The international library of critical writings in economics, 238*. Cheltenham, UK: Edward Elgar.

Kahn, B. E., Luce, M. F., & Nowlis, S. M. (2006). Debiasing insights from process tests. *Journal of Consumer Research*, 33, 131–138.

Kahneman, D. (2003). Maps of bounded rationality: Psychology for behavioral economics. *The American Economic Review*, 93, 1449–1475.

Kahneman, D. (2011). *Thinking fast and slow*. New York: Farrar, Straus and Giroux.

Kahneman, D., & Tversky, A. (1979). Prospect theory: An analysis of decision under risk. *Econometrica*, 47(2), 263–291.

Kim, J. (2006). Hyperbolic discounting and the repeated self-control problem. *Journal of Economic Psychology*, 27, 344–359.

LeBoeuf, R. A., & Shafir, E. (2012). Decision making. In K. J. Holyoak & R. G. Morrison (Eds.), *The Oxford handbook of thinking and reasoning* (pp. 301–21). Oxford, UK: Oxford University Press.

Lin, S., Zhang, J., & Hauser, J. R. (2015). Learning from experience, simply. *Marketing Science*, 34, 1–19.

Loewenstein, G., Bryce, C., Hagmann, D., & Rajpal, Sachin (2014). Warning: You are about to be nudged. *Working Papers Series*. Retrieved from http://ssrn.com/abstract=2417383 (29.07.2015).

Lunn, P. (2014). *Regulatory policy and behavioral economics*. Paris: OECD Publishing.

Luth, H. A. (2010). *Behavioral economics in consumer policy: The economic analysis of standard terms in consumer contracts revisited*. Antwerp: Intersentia.

Mansbridge, J. J. (1990). *Beyond self-interest*. Chicago: University of Chicago Press.

Micheletti, M., & Stolle, D. (2012). Sustainable citizenship and the new politics of consumption. *The ANNALS of the American Academy of Political and Social Science*, 644(1), 88–120.

Mick, D. G., Broniarczyk, S. M., & Haidt, J. (2004). Choose, choose, choose, choose, choose, choose, choose, choose: Emerging and prospective research on the deleterious effects of living in consumer hyper-choice. *Journal of Business Ethics*, 52, 207–211.

Micklitz, H.-W., Oehler, A., Piorkowsky, M.-B., Reisch, L. A., & Strünck, C. (2011). The consumer – trusting, vulnerable or responsible? Plea for a differentiated strategy in consumer policy. In *Statement by the Scientific Advisory Council on Consumer and Food Policy at the Federal Ministry for Food, Agriculture and Consumer Protection (BMELV)*. Berlin, Germany: BMELV. Retrieved from: http://www.bmelv.de/SharedDocs/Downloads/EN/Ministry/Trusting-Vulnerable-Responsible-Consumer.html (29.07.2015).

Miller, G. (1956). The magical number seven, plus minus two: Some limits on our capacity for processing information. *Psychological Review*, 63, 81–97.

Mullainathan, S., & Shafir, E. (2013). *Scarcity: Why having too little means so much*. New York: Time Books/Henry Holt.

Nelson, P. (1970). Information and consumer behavior. *Journal of Political Economy*, 78, 311–329.

Nuttavuthisit, K., & Thøgersen, J. (2015). The importance of consumer trust for the emergence of a market for green products: The case of organic food. *Journal of Business Ethics*. doi:10.1007/s10551-015-2690-5

OECD (Organization for Economic Co-operation and Development) (2006). *Report on a roundtable on demand-side economics for consumer policy. OECD Digital Economy Papers*, 116. Paris, France: Organization for Economic Co-operation and Development (OECD) Publishing.

OECD (Organization for Economic Co-operation and Development) (2007). *Report on the second roundtable on economics for consumer policy. OECD Digital Economy Papers*, 132. Paris, France: Organization for Economic Co-operation and Development (OECD) Publishing.

OECD (Organization for Economic Co-operation and Development) (2010). *Consumer policy toolkit. Paris.* Organization for Economic Co-operation and Development (OECD) Publishing.

Ölander, F., & Thøgersen, J. (2014). Informing versus nudging in environmental policy. *Journal of Consumer Policy*, 37, 341–356.

Payne, J. W., Bettman, J. R., & Johnson, E. J. (1992). Behavioral decision research: A constructive processing perspective. *Annual Review of Psychology*, 43, 87–131.

Reis, H. T. (2008). Reinvigorating the concept of situation in social psychology. *Personality and Social Psychology Review*, 12(4), 311–329.

Reisch, Lucia A. (2004a). Sustainable consumption as a consumer policy issue. In L. A. Reisch & I. Røpke (Eds.), The ecological economics of consumption. *Edward Elgar series current issues in ecological economics* (pp. 175–189). Cheltenham, UK: Edward Elgar.

Reisch, L. A. (2011). Consumer sovereignty. In D. Southerton (Ed.), *Encyclopedia of Consumer Culture* (pp. 323–325). Thousand Oaks, CA: Sage.

Reisch, L. A., & Gwozdz, W. (2013). Smart defaults and soft nudges: How insights from behavioral economics can inform effective nutrition policy. In J. Scholderer & K. Brunsø (Eds.), *Marketing, food, and the consumer: Festschrift in Honour of Klaus Grunert* (pp. 189–200). New Jersey, NJ: Pearson Custom Publishing.

Reisch, L. A., & Sandrini, J. (2015). *Nudging in der Verbraucherpolitik: Ansätze verhaltensbasierter Regulierung.* Baden-Baden, Germany: Nomos.

Reisch, L. A., & Sunstein, C. R. (2014). Redesigning cockpits: Introduction to the Special issue of journal of consumer policy on "Behavioural Economics, environmental policy and the consumer". *Journal of Consumer Policy*, 37(3), 333–339.

Reisch, L. A., & Sunstein, C. R. (2015). Behavioral economics and consumption. In D. T. Cook & J. M. Ryan (Eds.), *The Wiley Blackwell encyclopedia of consumption and consumer studies* (pp. 41–42). Hoboken, NJ: Wiley-Blackwell.

Reisch, L. A., & Thøgersen, J. (Eds.) (2015). *Handbook of research on sustainable consumption*. Cheltenham, UK: Edward Elgar Publishing.

Scharff, R. L. (2009). Obesity and hyperbolic discounting: Evidence and implications. *Journal of Consumer Policy*, 32(1), 3–21.

Schwartz, S. H. (1970). Elicitation of moral obligation and self-sacrificing behavior. *Journal of Personality and Social Psychology*, 15, 283–293.

Schwartz, S. H. (1977). Normative influence on altruism. In L. Berkowitz (Ed.), *Advances in experimental social psychology*, Vol. 10 (pp. 221–279). New York: Academic Press.

Shafir, E. (Ed.) (2013). *The behavioral analysis of public policy*. Princeton, NJ: Princeton University Press.

Shapiro, C. (1983). Consumer protection policies in the United States. *Journal of Institutional and Theoretical Economics*, 139, 527–544.

Simon, H. (1956). Rational choice and the structure of the environment. *Psychological Review*, 63, 129–138.

Stigler, G. J. (1961). The economics of information. *Journal of Political Economy*, 69, 213–225.

Story, M., Neumark-Sztainer, D., & French, S. (2002). Individual and environmental influences on adolescent eating behaviors. *Journal of the American Dietetic Association*, 102, 40–51.

Sunstein, C. R. (2011). Empirically informed regulation. *The University of Chicago Law Review*, 78(4), 1349–1429.

Sunstein, C. R. (2013a). Deciding by default. *University of Pennsylvania Law Review*, 162(1), 1–57.

Sunstein, C. R. (2013b). *Simpler: The future of government*. New York: Simon and Schuster.

Sunstein, C. R. (2014a). Nudges.gov: Behavioral economics and regulation. In E. Zamir, & D. Teichman (Eds.), *Oxford handbook of behavioral economics and the law* (pp. 719–747). Oxford, UK: Oxford University Press.

Sunstein, C. R. (2014b). Nudging: A very short guide. *Journal of Consumer Policy*, 37(4), 583–588.

Sunstein, C. R. (2014c). *Why nudge? The politics of libertarian paternalism*. New Haven, CT: Yale University Press.

Sunstein, C. R. (2015a). Behavioral economics, consumption and environmental protection. In L.A. Reisch, & J. Thøgersen, (Eds.). *Handbook of research on sustainable consumption* (pp. 313–327). Cheltenham, UK: Edward Elgar Publishing.

Sunstein, C. R. (2015b). Nudges do not undermine human agency. *Journal of Consumer Policy*, 38(3), 207–210.

Sunstein, C. R. (2015c). The ethics of nudging. *Yale Journal on Regulation*, 32, 413–420.

Sunstein, C. R., & Reisch, Lucia A. (2014). Automatically green: Behavioral economics and environmental protection. *Harvard Environmental Law Review*, 38(1), 127–158.

Thaler, R. H. (1980). Toward a positive theory of consumer choice. *Journal of Economic Behavior and Organization*, 1, 39–60.

Thaler, R. H. (2015). *Misbehaving: The making of behavioral economics*. New York, NY, USA: Norton.

Thaler, R. H., & Sunstein, C. R. (2003). Libertarian paternalism. *The American Economic Review*, 93(2), 175–179.

Thaler, R. H., & Sunstein, C. R. (2008). *Nudge: Improving decisions about health, wealth, and happiness*. New Haven, CT: Yale University Press.

Thøgersen, J. (1996). Recycling and morality. A critical review of the literature. *Environment and Behavior*, 28, 536–558.

Thøgersen, J. (2005). How may consumer policy empower consumers for sustainable lifestyles? *Journal of Consumer Policy*, 28, 143–177.

Thøgersen, J. (2006). Understanding repetitive travel mode choices in a stable context: A panel study approach. *Transportation Research Part A: Policy and Practice*, 40, 621–638.

Thøgersen, J., Jørgensen, A.-K., & Sandager, S. (2012). Consumer decision making regarding a "green" everyday product. *Psychology & Marketing*, 29, 187–197.

Toft, M. B., Schuitema, G., & Thøgersen, J. (2014). The importance of framing for consumer acceptance of the smart grid: A three country study. *Energy Research and Social Science*, 3, 113–123.

Tversky, A., & Kahneman, D. (1974). Judgment under uncertainty: Heuristics and biases. *Science*, 185, 1124–1131.

Van der Linden, S. (2015). Exploring beliefs about bottled water and intentions to reduce consumption: The dual-effect of social norm activation and persuasive information. *Environment and Behavior*, 47, 526–550.

Wansink, B. (2014). *Slim by design: Mindless eating solutions for everyday life*. New York: Harper Collins.

Whitman, G. (2006). Against the New Paternalism. Internalities and the economics of self-control. *Policy Analysis, CATO Institute*, 563, 1–16.

Williamson, O. E. (2000). The new institutional economics: Taking stock, looking ahead. *Journal of Economic Literature*, 38(3), 595–613.

Withagen, R., de Poel, H. J., Araújo, D., & Pepping, G.-J. (2012). Affordances can invite behavior: Reconsidering the relationship between affordances and agency. *New Ideas in Psychology*, 30, 250–258.

World Bank (2014). *Mind, society, and behavior. World development report 2015*. Washington, DC: The World Bank Group.

Part V

Consumption and social divisions

Introduction

Two strands of consumption research have been discussed at length over the last decades: one towards fluidity, circulation, mobility, homogeneity and standardization of consumption practices, triggered, according to some, by the increasing demise of longstanding structures of social differentiation and positioning (see the work of Bauman, Beck, Giddens among others); and another that concentrates on how consumption creates divisions and how social differences (e.g. income, gender, sexuality, age, ethnicity) are embedded in a diversity of contexts, sometimes erupting and gaining symbolic and material visibility, other times reproduced imperceptibly in everyday life. Here, several important bodies of work have shed light on the need for renewal, revisiting and critiquing the apparent fluidity and homogenization of consumption practices, claiming that varieties of consumption (and of taste) exist and have never been totally effaced (the sociologist Pierre Bourdieu is often hailed as offering a prominent account of the role of taste as a marker and reproducer of social division).

In Part V, *Consumption and social divisions*, the aim is not so much to opt for one or another flank of the literature or asses their main gaps or contributions, but instead show how consumption research has tackled empirically and conceptually issues related to processes of social differentiation around gender, sexuality, generations, age, ethnicity, migration and income. Rather than solely bringing forward the relevance of looking at these issues and giving an account of the effects and outcomes of social divisions (unfairness, exclusion, discrimination, inequality, conflict and struggle), the chapters pay attention to the tensions, paradoxes and ambiguities that derive from the plural, fragmented, multiple and invariably juxtaposed social divisions across social groups with disparate access to resources, goods and services.

Chapter 22, authored by Pernille Hohnen, brings forward three different aspects on the theme of poverty, financing and social exclusion in consumption research. First, she looks at the lack of attention from consumption research on issues related to poverty, financing and inequality. Secondly, she offers a critical account of the main empirical research on consumption and financing among poor consumer households. Third, she addresses the recent developments and effects of credit consumption and debt, looking at emerging processes of financial inequality. Hohnen contends that future research on consumption should more consistently include poor consumers (instead of mostly focusing on the middle classes), an aspect that is even more prominent and urgent in face of the impacts of recent economic crises in several global North (but also South) countries.

Chapter 23 follows nicely from Hohnen's plea for more research on consumption and poor households by noticing that there is a bias in current studies on poverty and food security towards food production issues. The chapter analyses the concept of food security and its emergent context, and then offers a review of empirical studies across three important debates: the relationship between poverty, food insecurity and "bad" eating habits; the link between poverty and obesity; and finally the effects of food aid in low-income families. Together with Hohnen, Truninger and Díaz-Méndez also claim more insightful and consistent connections between the consumption research and the poverty literatures, to make a double rectification: a bias towards consumption research on the middle classes, and a bias towards production research, especially when looking at food (in)security matters.

Chapter 24 takes a material culture approach to consumption to look at the contemporary significant movements of things and people, paying attention to cultural diversity and the different ways things affect and are appropriated in the lives of migrants in their journeys. By intersecting two bodies of literatures that are often disconnected (material culture and migration studies), Marta Rosales offers a novel look at how things participate in migrants' experiences and journeys – how things make people on the move confront themselves with novel and outmoded material items. Stuff that is left behind, that is brought along or acquired (again or anew) may work as stabilization devices that help deal with cultural diversity but also as disruptive devices of migrants' perceptions of themselves and of the others.

Pauline Maclaran, Cele C. Otnes and Linda Tuncay Zayer in chapter 25 review and discuss the work on gender within consumer research through the lens of marketing. They split this work in two different periods – pre 1990s and post 1990 – taking into account the influence of feminist perspectives in this literature. Two emergent fields that can benefit from more systematic and consolidated exploration in consumption research are masculinity and LGBT consumption. These fields have the potential to open up stimulating lines of enquiry that should be examined in future studies.

Also coming from a marketing perspective, David Buckingham and Vebjørg Tingstad in chapter 26 offer an insightful and critical account of contemporary debates about children and consumer culture. For marketers, children are important because they are increasingly seen as key participants in consumption processes, not only shaping and influencing their own markets but also the adults' markets. However, concerns of risk and the commercialization of children open up new debates that often fall between a view of children as agents or children as victims (especially of manipulative publicity and advertisements). The authors advance a critical perspective to this debate, going beyond dichotomous thinking and offering a fresh and novel approach that unsettles some of the basic assumptions of consumer culture theory.

In chapter 27, "Youth and Generations in Consumption", Terhi-Anna Wilska highlights the main perspectives of different disciplines in the research on youth, generations and consumption. Acknowledging young people's importance for consumption and consumer cultures over time, the chapter specifically focuses on the generational approach to the research on consumption and youth. This approach, which has gained even more momentum with the digitalization of consumption, emphasizes a gap between consumer generations. The chapter challenges the over-emphasis of generational differences, as several social, economic and developmental aspects affect young people's consumption. In conclusion, a more versatile global and multi-cultural approach into the research on youth and consumption is called for, as well as for more-sensitive research methods, with regard to young people's fragile social and economic positions in many societies.

In chapter 28, Carol Kelleher and Lisa Peñaloza offer a rich review of studies on aging and consumption, tapping into a group (age 65 and older) that is rapidly growing in contemporary societies, opening up a whole field of consumption research, which is going to be increasingly important in the future. By taking a multi-perspective approach (socio-cultural, physiological, psychological) it addresses a plurality of issues, namely consumption patterns and practices, identity and subjectivity issues, social relationships, family and service providers, social representations of ageing in markets and in popular discourse, market experiences and ethics, among other issues. This is a rich and insightful chapter that concludes with future directions in consumption research regarding this challenging and prominent topic.

22

Poverty, financing and social exclusion in consumption research

Pernille Hohnen

Introduction

> While the world is made up mostly of poor people, the marketing field in general and the consumer behavior subfield in particular have given such citizens limited attention.
>
> *(Hill, 2015: 474)*

Poor consumers have generally not occupied a very prominent position in recent decades of consumption research. This has been the case in social sciences as well as in marketing (cf. Hill, 2015; Ekström & Hjort, 2009; Hohnen, 2007). This omission seems moreover rather paradoxical, because most of the research which does focus on low-income citizens suggest that in terms of consumption this group occupies a very different position and faces a specific set of dilemmas compared to mainstream or middle-class consumers. Consumers with limited budgets face specific consumption choices and limited access to markets; hence, they develop specific financial practices (Martin & Hill, 2012; Hjort & Salonen, 2010; Hamilton, 2009). In addition, this group of consumers is subject to a set of restrictions both in terms of limited purchasing power and in terms of (often indirect) market restrictions imposed by suppliers (Hill & Stephen, 1997). In terms of social inequality in markets, moreover, it is of particular relevance to include the recent development of and changes in credit markets and credit-based consumption (Langley, 2014), as access to credit and loans is particularly significant for poor households (Hill, 2008). Finally, poor consumers are subject to a particular morally invested public gaze often picturing them as 'inadequate', 'unwanted', 'abnormal', 'blemished', 'defective', 'faulty' and 'deficient', 'flawed consumers' and 'non-consumers' (Bauman, 2005: 38, 112–13). Poor consumers, by being exposed to a mainstream 'culture of consumption', therefore experience what Bourdieu (1999) has called *la petite misère* (the little misery) by being subject to the rhetoric of affluence and material welfare among other social groups, but being themselves only to a limited extent able to take part in consumerism (Hohnen, 2006).

The present chapter discusses prevailing insights in and approaches to poverty, financing and processes of social exclusion in contemporary consumption research aiming to depict research gaps and future research challenges. The general argument builds on different types of insights and the chapter is structured accordingly. First, contemporary theoretical approaches to issues of poverty, financing and inequality in consumption and in particular the (lack of) inclusion of these topics in approaches to consumption research are outlined and discussed. Second, empirical insight from studies on consumption and financing among poor consumer households are presented. Third, the role of recent developments in credit consumption and debt is described, and implications in terms of emerging processes of financial inequality are examined. The chapter concludes with a discussion of the main theoretical challenges and research gaps related to these three discussions.

Critical debates on the invisibility of poor consumers in consumption research

The following section focuses on selected critical debates concerning the position of poor consumers, inequality and money in consumption research. The debates are mainly covering the period of what Warde (2015) has termed 'the cultural turn' in consumption studies, i.e., from the 1980s to the mid-2000s. Although according to Warde this 'culturalist era' is running to an end and theories commonly addressed by the umbrella concept 'practice theory' seem to be replacing it, the prevailing critique on 'culturalist studies' provides a number of more general insights into the relationship between poverty, financing and consumption which are of relevance also for 'practice theories'. In addition, although practice theory seems to be gaining ground in the sociology of consumption, the extent of this 'turn' may be debated, and the culturalist perspective still prevails in the adjoining fields of consumption in marketing (Ekström & Hjort, 2009) and anthropology (see Carrier, 2006).

Around the early 2000s a number of researchers raised concern with what then appeared as a theoretical bias in most consumption research in terms of an overemphasis on symbolic and spectacular consumption and a lack of concern with inequality and the material basis of consumption, e.g. money. These critiques took different directions. In the following, three such areas of critique in relation to culturalist consumption research will be addressed: '*Assuming affluence*', '*Consumption as an ideological and moral battlefield*' and finally '*Context and political economy*'.

Assuming affluence

In 2002 Lodziak launched an attack on what he terms 'the myth of consumerism'. His critique was based on theoretically pinpointing a set of assumptions which he claimed dominated the larger research field. Some of these, such as the assumption of consumer sovereignty and the prevailing focus on symbolic value rather than use value or functional value, are now more widely acknowledged (cf. Halkier, 2010; Warde, 2005, 2014). However, Lodziak's criticism also covered a lack of concern with inequality, uneven and constrained access to markets and a more basic acknowledgement that the issue of money and financing were by and large absent in most studies of consumption. The fact that low-income consumers tend to focus their consumption on fulfilling 'needs' rather than more conspicuous consumption of 'wants' was also emphasized as largely ignored in this theoretical discourse. Lodziak therefore argued, along with Chin, that 'Much consumption theory founders on the question of poor consumers because it implicitly assumes that consumers are first and foremost, middle class' (Chin, 2001: 11). Lodziak found a theoretical consensus portraying the realm of consumption as being about self-identity, lifestyle and freedom of choice whereas the economic dimension was not allocated any explanatory role and general prosperity thereby taken for granted. In addition, he argued for a widening of scope in consumption research and suggested to include the role of the market in consumption, arguing along with Bauman that all choice is really about 'choosing among' and that the set of items to be chosen from is seldom in itself a matter of choice (Bauman, 1999: 72). A final dimension of Lodziak's critique was also largely based on Bauman (1999) to confront the methodological individualism inherent in some, though not in all, culturalist theorizing by emphasizing the role of normative discourses and prevailing issues of legitimacy (code of conduct, Bauman, 1999) as constituting as well as constraining individual consumption. Issues of legitimacy and moral dilemmas were, however, addressed more elaborately by others.

Consumption as an ideological and moral battlefield

Prevailing notions on poor consumers indicate that this group of citizens is not only struggling financially in today's consumer society, but also that their consumption tends to be either unrecognized or framed as morally problematic (Power, 2005; Salonen, 2016). However, ideology has hitherto not occupied a central place in consumption research (Martin & Hill, 2012). The Swedish ethnologist Löfgren (1996) was one of the first to address a lack of concern with ideology and morality in consumption studies. Much in line with Lodziak above and later Gronow and Warde (2001), Löfgren was concerned with the preoccupation of symbolic meanings and what he termed '. . . slithering around in a semiotic jungle of whispers and shouts . . .' (Löfgren, 1996: 120). However, he also specifically addressed the omission of studies of poverty, downward social mobility and other socially relevant issues as generally being ignored in consumption research. Not only did he find this omission unfortunate for general sociological and social policy insights, he also found it theoretically problematic not to acknowledge the field of consumption as an ideological battlefield, where some consumption patterns are constituted as 'right' and others as 'wrong'. In Löfgren's view the lack of concern with moral and ideological dimensions in consumption research resulted not only in a gradual 'narrowing down' of the study of consumption, but also a theoretical bias by 'overtaking' commonsense ideological and moral values largely associated with neo-liberalism.

Context and political economy

The final theoretical critique related to 'culturalist' consumption research (having broader implications for the research on poor people's consumption) concerns the issues of scope and context and was launched by Carrier in a contribution to the collection *The Making of the Consumer* edited by Frank Trentmann (2006). Building partly on Carrier and Heyman (1997), Carrier (2006) discusses what he considers a failure to locate consumption in a broader framework of political economy. Carrier develops his argument on a discussion of consumption research in social anthropology; however, he claims to identify issues that are of relevance to consumption studies more generally. The anthropological angle, however, is pointed out as a particularly advantageous starting point in identifying issues of scope, because, following Carrier, social anthropology as a discipline 'advertises itself as being concerned with contextualizing what it studies, to show how it is linked to other things' (Carrier, 2006: 271). In line with this, Carrier proposes the aim of consumption studies to be a vehicle for understanding society, not merely to understand consumption patterns or practices in themselves. Having an interest in poverty and social exclusion, Carrier initiates a discussion of the 'culturalist' orientation in consumption research by referring to the fact that at the time where consumption research was flourishing, inequality was increasing in the US and elsewhere. Although acknowledging that there were also alternative anthropological perspectives on consumption at the time, Carrier emphasizes the lack of concern in 'culturalist' consumption research with this overall social and political context of inequality:

> The fervor with which anthropologists and others embraced the study of consumption in that decade [mid-1980s to mid-1990s] would have been understandable, if it had reflected this problematic state of affairs, or at least taken cognizance of it. However, this was not the case. The big names and the big ideas that motivated a lot of anthropological work on the topic construed a world of choice among a world of goods by a world of people constrained only be the need to decide which object among all those available, they wanted. I find this unsettling. . .
>
> *(Carrier, 2006: 272).*

Carrier sees three fundamentally problematic issues involved in 'culturalist' consumption research: the 'location of meaning making', i.e. the assumption that meanings are attached to goods by advertisers and ordinary people – hence that meaning making is individually construed rather than socially structured; the idea that the relevant time frame for understanding consumption is 'the moment of purchase' hence ignoring other longer timescales in people's lives which could be relevant in understanding consumption patterns and practices; and finally and more generally tied to the other two, that prevailing theoretical perspectives ignore that people's choices are shaped by the material, social and cultural constraints of their situations, i.e. labour market relations, family relations or national/international political contexts (regarding the latter issue, Carrier specifies Bourdieu as an exception). In sum, therefore, Carrier suggests including a broader focus on political systems in order to understand meaning making and consumer practices, hence framing individual consumer choices as inherently collective and as a consequence of political-economic forces (Carrier, 2006: 275).

To conclude, the three areas of discussion outlined above highlight different forms of critique of what has been termed 'culturalist' consumer research (Warde, 2015) and was initially addressing research in social anthropology, sociology and marketing from the mid-1980s to mid-2000s. Although each of these were initially targeting the broader research field they also pinpoint areas of specific relevance for understanding the way social inequality, poverty and money have been represented in much prevailing consumer research. In addition, each of these discussions has highlighted different types of theoretical bias in the legacy of dominant consumer research up to the mid-2000s. The assumption of affluence and the lack of concern with how consumption is financed, the lack of reflections on consumption as an ideological/political and moral battlefield within which poor consumers tend to become socially and morally stigmatized and the lack of inclusion of the wider cultural, temporal and political framing of consumption all have consequences for the ways poor people's consumption has been addressed, represented and explained.

Insights from studies on consumption and financing in poor consumer households

> *'I think it is a lie that money doesn't buy you happiness'.*
>
> Low-income Irish parent quoted in Hamilton (2009: 45)

Prevailing research on poor people's consumption points to several defining characteristics. Some of these have already been touched upon in the previous discussion. The aim of the following section is to highlight prevailing approaches in and empirical insights from consumption studies which focus explicitly on poverty and processes of social exclusion. Some of these studies apply a micro-sociological approach focusing on consumer behavior and experiences within households (cf. Hill, 2003, Hill & Gaines, 2007) while others hold a more macro-oriented and/or poststructuralist approach focusing on processes of inequality and the social, economic and cultural conditions that poor families face (cf. Hjort, 2004; Power, 2005). However, most studies on poor consumers seek a combination of the two pursuing a structure/agency approach and position household consumption in a wider sociocultural and structural context of consumerism (e.g. Hohnen, 2006; Hohnen & Hjort, 2009; Hamilton, 2009, 2012; Salonen, 2016). For the sake of clarity, however, the outline of these studies begins with a discussion of consumption patterns and household strategies in low-income families and then proceeds to the structural market conditions and societal discourses.

Consumption patterns and strategies in low-income households

Studies of everyday consumption of poor consumers not surprisingly points to financing as a key aspect in consumption and strategies, and money matters as a continuous concern for low-income consumers. Bonke et al. (2005) in a study comparing low-income and middle-class consumers in the Nordic countries found that whereas middle-class consumers tend to regard consumption as 'fun' and would laugh and joke during interviews, people from low-income families were nervous and uncomfortable when talking about consumption; the interview situation reflected obvious unease as well as conveyed an image of consumption as being a burden rather than as pleasurable (see also Hohnen, 2006, 2007 and Hohnen & Hjort, 2009). Hamilton (2009) in a study on Northern Irish low-income consumers reports similar findings emphasizing the role of money as crucial for low-income consumers (as the vignette above suggests). Moreover, Hamilton emphasizes that for these low-income consumers shopping was not considered an enjoyable activity but a 'nightmare', 'stressful, 'a struggle' or even 'hateful' (Hamilton, 2009: 45). In most of these studies, low-income consumption is reported as including tedious planning rather than impulse spending as well as a series of economizing strategies, i.e. making lists, searching for bargains and even 'hurrying' in and out of shops in order to avoid any temptations (Hamilton, 2009; Hohnen, 2007). Basically everyday consumption in poor households is aimed at 'making ends meet' in order not to have to borrow money at the end of the month (cf. Kempson, 1996, 2002). Consumption in low-income households is also described as temporally structured, and studies of budgeting reveal that in the beginning of the month there may be slightly more 'room' in the budget, e.g. for going to McDonalds, whereas towards the end of the month spending is more strictly aimed at basic necessities (Hohnen, 2006). Finally, low-income consumption patterns are challenged by the fact that although the fulfilling of everyday necessities holds priority, poor households are also faced with the dilemmas of living in a consumer culture of affluence where the consumption of basic necessities is generally not considered sufficient (cf. Hill & Gaines, 2007). Following this most research emphasizes how poor households are stuck between their ambition to make ends meet by refraining from buying anything but the most basic things such as food and utilities, and their exposure to a consumer culture of affluence where extra's – e.g. organic food consumption, the pursuit of branded goods/lifestyle purchases, etc. – are regarded as common. In order to capture this dilemma, Hjort (2004) developed the term 'social necessity', reflecting the social urgency that many of these goods seem to convey not only directly, e.g. having money for gifts, mobile phones or generally socializing, but also indirectly, for example by being able to purchase the same style of goods, e.g. certain brands, in order not to deviate too much from others. As a result of the dilemmas they face, low-income consumers tend to develop different strategies of consumption control. One such strategy is an unequal division of resources within the household privileging children's consumption and creating what Kochuyt (2004) has termed 'artificial affluence' among children and 'artificial poverty' for parents. Another strategy to cope is discussed by Hamilton (2012), who shows how low-income parents may decide to engage in conspicuous consumption in an attempt to avoid social stigmatization of their children, however, often with the consequence that this eventually fuels further stigmatization rather than promoting social inclusion. A more recent strategy of control and saving among low-income households is 'secondary consumption' understood as consuming market surplus which is not considered acceptable to most of the middle class (Hill, 2003). The recent development of food banks may be considered an institutionalized form of such secondary consumption; however, it also creates ambiguity in terms of being dependent on those things which are regarded as superfluous by others (Salonen, 2016).

Social conditions and market hindrances

In addition to the particular consumer patterns characterizing poor consumers, most studies highlight structural inequality in terms of getting access to consumer markets. Many refer back to Caplovitz' (1963) study 'The poor pay more' and report on recent empirical examples of poor people's structural disadvantages in contemporary markets. Hjort and Salonen (2010) conceptualize two forms of market hindrances: *explicit hindrances and barriers* and *indirect expectations*. Explicit mechanisms refer to explicit restrictions to specific markets based on consumers' social economic positions (Hjort & Salonen, 2010.). The lack of housing ownership, for example, makes it difficult to get access to low-interest loans, hence consumers are obliged to look at more expensive solutions (see also Kempson & Collard, 2005). Certain living areas result in marketplace restrictions resulting in 'fringe banking' in poor neighborhoods (Hill, 2008). Hill talks about three such different types of fringe banking: subprime mortgages with high-interest loans, car-title pawn or car-title lending, where the car owner turns over the title to their vehicles in exchange for a (high-interest) loan, and finally, rent-to own (RTO) industry which also eventually results in overpriced purchases (Hill, 2008: 78). In addition to these examples of market differentiation, Hjort and Salonen (2010) also mention access to transportation (having a car), access to the internet and finally the fact that low income results in a lack of savings, and hence lack of possibilities to take advantage of market offers, as significant explicit market hindrances for low-income consumers.

The second type of market differentiation refers to what Hjort and Salonen (2010) call *indirect expectations*. These refer to a broader set of dominant social and moral discourses about 'normal consumption' in consumer society as well as to the specific expectations for those with scarce financial resources (Hjort & Salonen, 2010). Expectations of normal consumption are linked to common ideas about how to be rational and economical as well as to dominant ideas about 'healthy', 'ethical' or 'responsible' consumption' – hence reflecting dominant discourses about responsible parenting and citizenship via consumption. These normative expectations also epitomize the significance of the field of consumption and consumption patterns for social role, social status, identity and citizenship in what Rose (1999) calls 'advanced liberalism' (see also Seestoft, 2002, 2008). For low-income households deviating from consumption patterns generally assumed to be both rational and reasonable creates a sense of shame (Hjort & Salonen, 2010: 353). Low-income consumers become subject to a particular set of moralizing. In the cases where they try to consume like mainstream consumers fulfilling obligations of 'good parenthood' or 'ethical consumption', their choices are generally labeled unnecessary and wasteful which may lead to further stigmatization (Salonen, 2014). If they try to be thrifty and aim to consume basic needs and the cheapest goods only, they are looked upon as 'flawed consumers' (Bauman, 1999) e.g. not being able to fulfill general citizen or parent responsibilities (Hohnen & Hjort, 2009).

Credit consumption and debt – changing markets and implications for poor consumers

> '. . .managing and spending money is no longer simply a matter of making the cash go round, but an electronic activity which is shaped by complex social and economic processes. The effect is to create a global financial system which privileges some individuals and households and from which others are partly or completely excluded' (Pahl, 1999: 2).

Credit and loans play a significant role in the budgeting strategies of consumption in poor households; however, most studies also emphasize the fear of debt. Hamilton (2009) found that most of her poor Irish respondents did everything possible to avoid credit, fearing that it would get them into debt that would spiral out of control. Despite this, many were actually forced to make use of credit in order to make ends meet and several reported to have credit cards which were 'all maxed out' (Hamilton, 2009: 45). Previous studies on financing and budgeting supports the view that poor households are often forced to use credit – in spite of the fact that they often only have access to unfavorable loans with high interest rates (Kempson, Bryson & Rowlingson, 1994; Kempson, 1996; Kempson & Collard, 2005; Poppe & Böcker Jakobsen, 2009). The field of credit and debt therefore is presented as ambiguous for poor consumers. On the one hand it is necessary to have access to 'payday' loans; on the other, debt is regarded as very risky out of fear of losing control, and cash is preferred to credit cards or other electronic forms of money (Kempson & Collard, 2005). In addition, poor consumers' consumption of credit reflects their structurally unfavorable position as the available short-term (micro) loans are generally with very high interest rates (Kempson & Collard, 2005).

The following and last section of the chapter addresses the role of credit consumption and debt in consumption research in general and in research focusing on poor consumers in particular. First, the section focuses on recent developments in the role of credit and debt as the new drivers in contemporary consumption where consumption has to some extent been cut loose from consumption and where (in spite of unequal access) credit for consumption is becoming more readily available as a consumer product (Poppe & Böcker Jakobsen, 2009; Hohnen & Böcker Jakobsen, 2014). Second, prevailing approaches to the consumption of credit are outlined and discussed. Last but not least, as the vignette formulated by Pahl (1999) above suggests, the development of credit markets and emerging forms of financial inequality and exclusion will be addressed (Pahl, 1999, 2008).

Emerging markets of credit

Deregulation of credit markets and the widespread use of credit have become increasingly pervasive since the 1980s across many Western countries (cf. Marron, 2012; Poppe, 2008; Lazzaretto, 2012). Marron (2012) suggests that '. . .the credit card represents the consumption mirror image of post-Fordist, just-in-time production, enabling and facilitating the immediacy of consuming experiences' (Klein, 1999:16 quoted in Marron, 2012: 408). In Britain over 75% of households have access to at least one credit card (Kempson, 2002) and consumer credit is now an integral component in contemporary consumer practices (Kempson, 2002). In contemporary markets, credit takes a range of different forms, e.g. short-term payday loans, bank overdrafts or revolving lines of credit that don't necessarily have to be repaid at the end of each month, and furthermore interest rates vary (Langley, 2014). Even the Scandinavian welfare states, traditionally subject to a high degree of state legislation, have witnessed a comprehensive deregulation of credit markets during the last decades (Poppe & Böcker Jakobsen, 2009; Østrup, 2010).

Although, as Langly (2014) has pointed out, credit has a long history, the contemporary financial markets differ by having made credit widely available as well as by epitomizing the consolidation of financing based on market conditions. Maurer (2014) conceptualizes this change as a general shift from credit as a means of consumption which he calls consumption *for* credit to credit as an object of consumption itself which he calls consumption *of* credit. (Maurer, 2014: 512).

Theorizing new forms of credit consumption

Although studies on credit consumption are still relatively sparse, the area has recently received some attention from researchers. Langley (2014), in an editorial introduction to a special issue of *Consumption, Markets & Culture* on markets and cultures of consumer credit, highlights some recent trends. He suggests that studies of credit consumption have hitherto been characterized by what he perceives as an 'instrumental' perspective, focusing on credit merely as a way of 'bridging' consumer income and consumer demands. The problem with such an approach is that the new ways consumer credit is now being manufactured as part of a deregulated financial market reflecting emerging business models in financing as well as new consumer roles is theoretically kept out of view (Langley, 2014).

Alternatively, Langley (2014) proposes to understand the development of consumer credit (and consumer debtors) in terms of the creation of new market relationships and new consumer subjectivities, i.e. as a form of governmentality (Foucault, 1991, Rose, 1999). From this perspective credit is understood as a part of a market relationship shifting focus on credit (and debt) from being merely a question of fulfilling repayment obligations, to analyzing how financial market actors install new forms of discipline. Maurer (2014), also focusing on shifts in credit regimes, suggests that the shifting regime epitomizes that credit is not necessarily about money, but about consumers (and consumption) increasingly 'becoming rent'. By the use of credit and the borrowing of money for everyday consumer purchases, Maurer suggests that people are essentially renting their own future incomes (Maurer, 2014: 514). What these approaches suggest is to look at the development of financial markets and political discourses surrounding them as forms of discipline and as ways to create certain long-term customer relationships. The shift from money to credit therefore is not merely instrumental but is here viewed as a means to promote prolonged consumption by creating post-purchase relationships where credit works as a vehicle for further transactions, for example by the 'harvesting' of personal data (Maurer, 2014).

In a similar vein, but from an anthropological perspective, Gregory (2012) also approaches the renewed role of credit in consumption. The focus by Gregory is on how what he terms 'credit-card-like' forms of payments have complicated the boundaries between debt and credit. The granting of a request for credit does not necessarily result in immediate debt (having a credit card does not automatically result in using it); however, it does create a right to obtain credit which abolishes the traditional notion of fixed-term debt, hence theoretically renders debt effectively perpetual (Gregory, 2012: 384). What Gregory suggests here resembles Maurer's notion of consumers 'becoming rent'. By conceptualizing contemporary notions of credit (and debt) as prolonged by a liminal phase of either not obtaining debt or having the right not to repay it, the time frame of the creditor/debtor relationship is prolonged. Finally, and directly related to the issue of social exclusion, Gregory discusses the process of boundary-making between credit and debt in this prolonged credit/debt time-frame. Building on existing research on cultural discourses of credit and debt, which suggests that credit is usually considered to be positive, while being in debt carries negative connotations, he suggests focusing on the semantic differences as empirical evidence of moral economy. In other words, the empirical differences in terms of whom and when consumers are considered to be in debt as opposed to merely having obtained credit highlight cultural notions as well as social and moral hierarchies (Gregory, 2012).

Studies of inequality in credit consumption and financial exclusion

As the above discussion has emphasized, a range of issues have been addressed in studies focusing on emerging forms of credit: the deregulation of credit markets including changing forms of discipline, subjectivities and consumer agency. However, although research on low-income budgeting has a long history (cf. Kempson, 1996; Kempson, Shyley, Caskey & Collard, 2000; Kempson & Collard, 2005) only a few studies focus specifically on new forms of social exclusion and/or on mechanisms which could indicate how the development of new forms of money and credit may reproduce and/or transform processes of financial exclusion.

In an early study on family finances in the electronic economy based on a mixed-method British study, Pahl (1999) suggests that financial arrangements epitomize other social aspects, hence that the study of financial arrangements may serve as a methodological starting point for understanding broader social organization. Pahl (1999) finds that those who are credit rich also tend to be education rich, as well as information rich and work rich, while the credit poor tend to be education poor, information poor and work poor. She moreover concludes that low-income households often having less secure jobs find new forms of digital money by way of credit cards as well as debit cards to be a source of anxiety because they are more difficult to control (Pahl, 1999). Similar anxieties among low-income households are found by Hohnen (2007), suggesting that digital money is more difficult to earmark (Zelizer, 1997), while earmarking is simultaneously a significant strategy in low-income budgeting (Hohnen, 2007). In a more recent study Pahl (2008) suggests that the use of credit cards can be understood as an individualized form of money which privileges those with good credit ratings, while disadvantaging those who have not.

Pahl (2008), therefore, along with Langley (2014) above, suggests that financing is no longer simply a matter of making the cash to round, but a specific credit-based regime. Low-income households – who are depending on credit in order to make ends meet – experience the development of the new credit regime including the digitalization of money as being at odds with their preferred way of budgeting which is based on strategies of control. Finally, emerging credit systems must be understood in terms of the types of subjectivities, organization of temporality and discipline, which poses new demands – in particular on poor consumers.

Conclusion

Insights from the three fields of study discussed above suggest that the prevailing lack of concern with poor consumers and social exclusion has had a number of empirical as well as theoretical implications not only for the subfield of poverty and inequality, but also for the field of consumption studies at large.

First, critical debates of theoretical bias in what Warde (2015) has called 'culturalist' consumption studies have highlighted three areas of concern: the assumption of affluence, consumption as an ideological and moral battlefield, and finally context and political economy, which have been either neglected or indirectly biased towards middle-class consumption patterns. To some extent, the recent 'practice turn' (Warde, 2014, 2015) might resolve the problems mentioned. The fact that focus is now moving beyond issues of identity and aestheticization towards more ordinary and mundane practices, emphasizing '. . . doing over thinking, the material over the symbolic, and embodied practical competence over expressive virtuosity' (Warde, 2015) shifts the 'location of meaning' to social practice, hence countering some of the critique of the 'semiotic jungle' forwarded by Lodziak (2002) and Löfgren (1996). However, the mere fact that the focus of attention has shifted to routine practices does not necessarily resolve other parts of this critique. There may be as much tendency to neglect poor consumers and inequality in mundane activities of 'washing bodies', or 'disposing of waste' (Warde, 2015: 127) as we saw in the culturalist studies, and although it is probably too early to say, we have yet to see the booming literature on poverty and exclusion in recent practice-oriented studies. Furthermore, practice studies are not automatically inclined to privilege other issues significant for the understanding of low-income consumption, such as issues of legitimacy, ideology and conflicting moral discourses. Finally, Carrier's (2006) proposal to position consumption in a broader context of political economy is not necessarily resolved, although the boundaries between consumption practices and other social practices are probably less rigid in studies which are conducted from a practice-oriented perspective.

The second body of literature, studies on poor people's consumption and inequality debated above, suggests a number of empirical differences in consumption patterns of poor compared to more affluent consumers. Prevailing studies on poor people's consumption – albeit sparse – have highlighted how poor people's consumption strategies are developing in response to differentiated markets and shown how poor consumers are being challenged and even trapped by the task of trying to combine prevailing normative assumptions and expectations of good and responsible consumption on the one hand and limited resources and a disadvantaged market access on the other. In this way prevailing studies not only clearly show that 'money matters' and needs to be taken into account in consumption studies; they also indicate that this is not purely a matter of limited finances. Emerging consumer areas such as sustainable and ethical consumption may therefore need to consider such possible lines of inequality. Poor consumers' preoccupation with money and their strategies of control show how financial inequality is closely related to prevailing social, cultural and moral discourses. Empirical studies of poor consumers' practices may therefore help to identify emerging types of social structuring and moral hierarchies in contemporary consumer markets, hence pinpointing areas and social processes of concern for other groups of consumers as well.

The outline of the third and most recent research area, credit consumption, confirms the picture that poverty and inequality are no central research areas in consumption research. This literature also (indirectly) points to emerging areas of concern. First, the increase in credit consumption in itself seems to render consumers with low and irregular incomes increasingly financially vulnerable. Although the notion of 'becoming' rent outlined above results in increasing financial risks for all, households in unstable and unfavorable financial situations are most likely to be directly affected (getting unemployed, getting sick, etc.). In addition, as the need for short-term credit in the form of payday loans is greater for low-income consumers, the risk of getting caught in spiraling debt in financial markets with easy access seems greater as well. Second, the perspective of governmentality applied in much research on credit consumption has been more concerned with carving out the contours of an emerging credit regime than with what Power (2005) has termed 'the unfreedom of being other', referring to the fact that the development of governmentality in credit as well as in other areas rests on the judgment of self-discipline, i.e. on the fact that those who are not evaluated as self-disciplining enough are governed by other disciplinary methods. The point in this discussion is that although credit is presumably available to all, the more implicit boundaries between those acknowledged to be part of and those who are considered to be outside the credit card regime are still by and large unaddressed. This leads to the third area of relevance for the study of credit consumption and social exclusion, which is what Gregory (2012) calls the increasing complexity of boundary-making between credit and debt, suggesting that such boundary-making reproduces social and moral hierarchies. Those whose credit is considered morally problematic are presented as being in debt, while those who are considered capable are never in debt but merely obtain credit. These insights suggest that the semantic production of credit/debt distinctions is crucial in understanding the development of social exclusion in new credit markets. They also give more general theoretical knowledge about social and cultural aspects of emerging credit markets.

In sum, the three areas in different ways suggest that a research focus on poverty, inequality and social exclusion may yield broader empirical and theoretical insights. A more consistent inclusion of poor consumers in consumption research may therefore shed light on empirical as well as theoretical issues which have hitherto remained unaccounted for also in mainstream consumption studies.

References

Bauman, Z. (1999). *In Search of Politics*, Oxford: Polity Press.

Bauman, Z. (2005). *Work, Consumerism and the New Poor*, 2nd edition, Buckingham: Open University Press.

Bonke, J., Bortgeraas, E., Døving, R., Hjort T., Hohnen, P., Montesino, N., Rysst, M., Salonen, T. (2005) *Udsathed og forbrug i de nordiske velfærdsstater*, København: Socialforskningsinstituttet.

Bourdieu, P. (1999). *The Weight of the World*, Cambridge: Polity.

Caplovitz, D. (1963). *The Poor Pay More*, New York, NY: Free Press.

Carrier, J. G. (2006). The Limits of Culture. Political Economy and the Anthropology of Consumption, in Trentmann, Frank (Ed). *Making of the Consumer: Knowledge, Power and Identity in the Modern World* (pp. 271–289). Oxford, GBR: Berg Publishers.

Carrier, J. & Heyman, J. (1997). Consumption and political economy. *Journal of the Royal Anthropological Institute*, 3(2), 355–373.

Chin (2001). *Purchasing Power: Black Kids and American Consumer Culture*, Minneapolis, MN and London: Mineapolis University Press.

Ekström, K. & Hjort, T. (2009). Hidden consumers in marketing – the neglect of consumers with scarce resources in affluent societies. *Journal of Marketing Management*, 25(7–8), 697–712.

Foucault, M. (1991). Governmentality. In G. Burchell, C. Gordon & P. Miller (Eds.), *The Foucault Effect: Studies in Governmentality*, (pp. 87–104). Chicago, IL: University of Chicago Press.

Gregory, C. A. (2012). On money, debt and morality: some reflections on the contributions of Economic Anthropology. *Social Anthropology*, 20(4), 380–396.

Gronow, J. & A. Warde (2001). Introduction. In J. Gronow & A. Warde (Eds.), *Ordinary Consumption*. London and New York: Routledge, 1–8.

Halkier, B. (2010). *Consumption Challenged: Food in Medialised Everyday lives*. Surrey: Ashgate Publishers.

Hamilton, K. (2009). Those Left Behind: Inequality in Consumer Culture. *Irish Marketing Review*, 20(2), 40–54.

Hamilton, K. (2012). Low-income Families and Coping through Brands: Inclusion or Stigma? *Sociology*, 46(1), 74–90.

Hill, R. P. (2003). Homelessness in the US: An Ethnographic Look at Consumption Strategies. *Journal of Community and Applied Social Psychology*, 13, 128–137.

Hill, R. P. (2008). Disadvantaged Consumers: An Ethical Approach to Consumption by the Poor. *Journal of Business Ethics*, 80(1), 77–83.

Hill, R. P. (2015). Materializing Poverty: How the Poor Transform Their Lives, (Book Review). *Consumption, Markets and Culture*, 18(5), 474–478.

Hill, R. P. & Gaines J. (2007). The Consumer Culture of Poverty: Behavioural Research Findings and Their Implications in an Ethnographic Context. *The Journal of American Culture*, 30(1), 81–95.

Hill, R. P. & Stephens, D. L. (1997). Impoverished Consumers and Consumer Behavior: The Case of AFDC Mothers. *Journal of Macromarketing*, 17(2), 32–48.

Hjort, T. (2004). *Nödvändighetens Pris*. Lund: Lund University.

Hjort, T. & Salonen, T. (2010). Consumption and Inequality. In K. Ekström (Ed.). *Consumer Behaviour – A Nordic Perspective*, (pp. 341–359). Lund: Studentlitteratur.

Hohnen P. (2006). Consumers without Money. A Qualitative Analysis of Consumption Patterns and New Forms of Citizenship among Low-income Families in Scandinavian Welfare Societies. In Glendinning, C. & Kemp P. (Eds.), *Cash and Care, Understanding the Evidence Base for Policy and Practice*, (pp. 79–94). Bristol: Policy Press.

Hohnen, P. (2007). Having the Wrong Kind of Money. A Qualitative Analysis of New Forms of Financial, Social and Moral Exclusion in Consumerist Scandinavia. *The Sociological Review*, 55(4), 748–767.

Hohnen, P. & Böcker Jakobsen (2014). Forbrug og gæld. In J. Elm Larsen, B. Greve, & Jørgensen A. Andersen (Eds.), *Det danske samfund*, (pp. 413–46). Copenhagen: Hans Reitzel.

Hohnen, P. & Hjort, T. (2009). Citizens as Consumers: A Discussion of New Emergent Forms of Marginalisation in the Nordic Welfare States. *European Journal of Social Security*, 11(3), 271–291.

Kempson (1996). *Life on a Low Income*. York: The Joseph Rowntree Foundation.

Kempson E. (2002). *Over-Indebtedness In Britain*, A report to the Department of Trade and Industry, http://www.pfrc.bris.ac.uk/Reports/Overindebtedness_Britain.pdf

Kempson E., Bryson, A. & Rowlingson K. (1994). *Hard Times: How Poor Families Make Ends Meet*. London: PSI.

Kempson, E. & Collard, S. (2005). *Affordable Credit: The Way Forward*, Bristol: Policy Press.

Kempson, E., Whyly, C., Caskey, J. & Collard, S. (2000). In or Out? Financial Exclusion a Literature and Research Review. *Consumer Research*, 3. Financial Services Authority.

Klein, L. (1999). *It's in the Cards: Consumer Credit and the American Experience*, Westport: Praeger.

Kochuyt, T. (2004). Giving Away One's Poverty. On the Consumption of Scarce Resources Within the Family. *The Sociological Review*, 52(2), 139–161.

Langley, P. (2014). Consuming Credit. *Consumption, Markets and Culture*, 17(5), 417–428.

Lazzareto, M. (2012). *The Making of the Indebted Man: An Essay on the Neoliberal Conditions*, (J. D. Jordan, Trans.). Cambridge, MA: MIT Press.

Lodziak, C. (2002). *The Myth of Consumerism*. London: Pluto Press.

Löfgren O. (1996). Komsumption som vardaglig praktik og ideologiskt slagfält. *Socialvetenskaplig tidskrift*, 1(2), 116–27.

Marron, D. (2012). Producing Over-indebtedness. *Journal of Cultural Economy*, 5(4), 407–421.

Martin, K. D. & Hill, R. P. (2012). Life Satisfaction, Self-Determination and Adequacy at the Bottom of the Pyramid. *Journal of Consumer Research*, 38(6), 1155–1168.

Maurer, B. (2014). Postcript: Is There Money in Credit? *Consumption Markets & Culture*, 17(5), 512–518.

Østrup, F. (2010). *Det finansielle System*. København: Thomson Reuters.

Pahl, J. (1999). *Invisible Money: Family Finances in the Electronic Economy*. Bristol: The Policy Press.

Pahl, J. (2008). Family Finances, Individualization, Spending Patterns and Access to Credit. *The Journal of Socio-Economics*, 37, 577–591.

Poppe, C. (2008). *Into the Debt Quagmire. How Defaulters cope with Severe Debt Problems*. Oslo: University of Oslo.

Poppe, C. & Böcker Jakobsen, T. (2009). *Lånefest? Betydningen af kreditfinansieret forbrug blandt udvalgte grupper i den danske middelklasse*, København: Thomson Reuters.

Power, E.M. (2005). The Unfreedom of Being Other: Canadian Lone Mothers' Experiences of Poverty and 'Life on the Cheque'. *Sociology*, 39(4), 4643–4660.

Rose, N. (1999). *Powers of Freedom: Reframing Political Thought*. Cambridge: Cambridge University Press.

Salonen, A. S. (2016). The Christmas Celebration of Secondary Consumers: Observations from Food Banks in Finland. *Journal of Consumer Culture*, 16(3), 870–886.

Sestoft, C. (2002). *Med hensyn til den politiske forbruger*. København: Akademisk.

Sestoft, C. (2008). *Forbrugeradfærd i et stats- og livsformsteoretisk perspektiv*, København: Copenhagen Business School. Ph.d. series.

Warde, A. (2005). Consumption and Theories of Practice. *Journal of Consumer Culture*, 5(2), 131–153.

Warde, A. (2014). After Taste: Culture Consumption and Theories of Practice. *Journal of Consumer Culture*, 14(3), 279–303.

Warde, A. (2015). The Sociology of Consumption: Its Recent Development'. *Annual Review of Sociology*, 41, 117–134.

Zelizer, V. (1997). *The Social Meaning of Money. Pin Money, Paychecks, Poor Relief, and Other Currencies*, Princeton: Princeton University Press.

23

Poverty and food (in)security

Monica Truninger and Cecilia Díaz-Méndez

Introduction

The concept of food security has been the subject of various debates and reconfigurations over time (Carolan, 2013). Such diversity of conceptualizations explains the lack of clarity in use of terms such as *food poverty*, *food insecurity* and *food sovereignty*. According to the influential work by Dowler, Turner and Dobson (2001, p. 12), food poverty "is the inability to acquire or consume an adequate quality or sufficient quantity of food in socially acceptable ways, or the uncertainty that one will be able to do so; it is thus the opposite of food security". Such conceptualization makes more visible a concern with diet and consumers. This definition echoes the one mentioned by Borch and Kjaernes (2016) wherein food insecurity "exists when people have limited or uncertain availability of nutritionally adequate and safe foods, or limited or uncertain ability to acquire acceptable foods in socially acceptable ways, for example without resorting to emergency food supplies, begging, scavenging, stealing, or other coping strategies" (p. 138). Hence, it is not surprising they are often used interchangeably. And yet, poverty and food insecurity are not the same phenomenon. If we take lack of income as a fundamental feature of poverty, then we find that income is a necessary condition but not sufficient to guarantee food security. High-income families may go through periods of food insecurity when facing a transient income shortfall (e.g. due to an economic crisis) and are forced to prioritise other expenses accumulated over time (e.g. transportation, mortgages, children's education), whereas low-income people may have sufficient social and cultural capitals and skills that enable them to prepare good-quality food on a tight budget (Borch & Kjaernes, 2016, p. 137).

If we turn to the policy discourse on food security, then the Food Agriculture Organization (FAO) of the United Nations defines it as when "all people, at all times, have physical, social and economic access to sufficient, safe and nutritious food to meet their dietary needs and food preferences for an active and healthy life" (2009, p. 8).

As to food sovereignty, it taps onto another issue: the entitlement to food framed by social and human rights, and the sustainability of livelihoods at the local community level (Dwiartma & Piatti, 2016, p. 153). Nowadays the definition encompasses four dimensions: the right to food; access to productive resources; mainstreaming of agroecological production; and trade and local markets. All four dimensions are entangled in the literature on food security, which often takes a political economy perspective (Midgley, 2013). Such debates gained momentum in recent years and are prominent in the *Journal of Peasant Studies; International Journal of Sociology of Food and Agriculture, Journal of Rural Studies* and *Agriculture and Human Values* (see also Patel, 2009; Trauger, 2015). However, despite the bourgeoning of this literature on food sovereignty, it is still greatly oriented towards production issues, overlooking consumers and consumption matters (Borch & Kjaernes, 2016).

Thus, such varied and nuanced conceptualizations uncover a lack of consistent terminology to pinpoint a social problem that greatly affects consumption practices – i.e. food in the context of social inequalities – that has been tackled in various forms, at different paces, by disparate disciplinary traditions (e.g. agricultural sciences, development studies, nutrition, public health, sociology, social policy, anthropology, geography), using both quantitative and qualitative methods, and objective and subjective indicators to measure it (Lambie-Mumford & O'Connell, 2015; Midgley, 2013; Maxwell, 1996).

The chapter is organized in three main sections. Firstly, we revisit the concept of food security and offer a brief historical account, concluding that there is a bias in the scientific literature towards production issues. Secondly, we look at poverty and food insecurity from a consumption perspective by addressing three prominent debates: the relationship between poverty, food insecurity and "bad" eating habits; the link between poverty and obesity; and finally the effects of food aid in low-income families. The third section summarizes the main arguments and offers pointers for future research.

Food security, insecurity and poverty: A brief historical account

Taking the FAO definition to close scrutiny, the concept of food security includes four dimensions: availability, access, stability and utilization, articulating the production (availability of food stocks and dealing with threats such as climate change impacts and biochemical risks of contamination), the market (access, affordability and stability) and consumption (appropriation and utilization of food according to nutritional adequacy and social acceptance). This conceptualization brings forward a concern with production and markets (the primary focus) but also with diet and food consumption (a later addition). The food security concept has originated at the World Food Conference of 1974 and it was framed by a productionist perspective, centred on food supply, availability and price stability monitored though the objective language of calories, prices and yields. In the 1980s the debate of food insecurity and tackling hunger as a matter of distribution instead of food production emerged, especially with the work by Amartyan Sen, *Poverty and Famines* (1981). This has brought a new shift to the concept, from production to markets and food access (Carolan, 2013). In the 1990s, another debate contributed to shift yet again this concept framing. Markets and distribution were important, but in some cases their mechanisms hugely hampered local communities' access to a nutritionally adequate and socially acceptable diet aimed at achieving well being, an active and healthy life.

This new frame introduced a new shift of scale – from the global and nation-state to the community and individual levels – encompassing multi-scalar levels, but also introducing subjective indicators such "as feelings of insecurity and deprivation among the poor", revealing the potential of a more solid link with the consumption arena and also to the daily experiences of poverty and food insecurity among local communities, families and individuals (Dwiartma & Piatti, 2016, p. 155). Since 1995 the US Department of Agriculture (USDA) has supported an annual survey to measure the prevalence of food (in)security among family households. It categorizes food (in)security according to risk groups: from food secure to low or very low food insecure, the latter when hunger afflicts households and individuals (Nord, Coleman-Jensen, Andrews & Carlson, 2010). In some countries such surveys are being implemented (for example, Portugal has had a similar survey since the mid-2000s, together with Australia and Canada), whereas countries such as the UK still lack such systematic and regular monitoring (Lambie-Mumford & O'Connell, 2015). Despite such efforts, consumption is taken as an individualized activity, mostly explained through psychological or biological factors, and focused on individuals. Such bias towards the individualization of food security may be a feature of the disciplinary background that informs these studies, which come mostly from nutrition, medicine and psychology. Political and social explanations also feature occasionally, but are less visible (Borch & Kjaernes, 2016, p. 144).

The combination of the recent economic and financial crisis coupled with the instability of food prices that were felt with particular impact during 2007-2008, has broadened the debate on food (in)security from developing to developed countries, bringing this issue to the policy and research agendas of industrialized and modern economies that were affected by austerity measures during the economic crisis (Kneafsey, Dowler, Lambie-Mumford, Inman & Collier, 2013).

The recent crisis led to civil unrest in several regions and has required an institutional response (Kneafsey et al., 2013, p. 101). Thus, it increasingly witnessed a shift of focus to the problems of hunger and food insecurity from the global South (that the journal *Food Policy* among others has for decades competently covered) to the global North, challenging the idea that residents in the most advanced economies are not affected by food insecurity. In this vein, recent studies begin to focus on other geographical areas, in addition to the traditional research on famine, malnutrition and food insecurity in Africa, Asia and South America, and take their analytical lens onto other realities such as the United States, Australia and Europe (Kirwan & Maye, 2013; Carolan, 2013; Riches & Silvasti, 2014; Dowler & Lambie-Mumford, 2015; Richards, Kjaernes & Vik, 2016).

In the social science literature on food security there has been hitherto a clear emphasis on food production (supply) and distribution (market), it being less-visible issues of access and consumption – a gap that recent studies are trying to fill (Kneafsey et al., 2013; Nielsen & Holm, 2016; Borch & Kjaernes, 2016). The food security concept is increasingly being appropriated by different frames and demonstrating its flexible and even contradictory use. If the productionist perspective brings forward the need to increase food production to feed the future population growth with lower resource inputs (e.g. sustainable intensification is deemed as a way to achieve this), the same concept is used to encourage local and alternative food movements (Kirwan & Maye, 2013) to tap into the capacity of communities, family households and individuals to have access to sustainable and resilient food systems that empower consumers and small producers to resist the vagaries of the market, and the injustice of food access and distribution.

While the academic literature on food (in)security has focused mostly on production issues, the food poverty literature is more oriented to explore the consumption and access issues. It is not surprising that recent calls to bring to the front consumption matters onto the food (in) security literature resource to the long tradition of social sciences studies on poverty and food poverty (Lambie-Mumford & O'Connell, 2015; Dowler, Turner & Dobson, 2001). The latter bringing to the fore issues of unequal access and the experiences of consumers in low-income families, although not necessarily taking a consumption-only focus (see chapter 22). This chapter links the food security literature with the food poverty one to strategically gain an orientation towards consumption issues. This strategy of connection is not to subsume food security to poverty issues, making it vanish behind a much more consolidated body of work, but instead to correct a bias in food security literature towards production, and open up the potential of exploring food security in its own right from a consumption perspective, which is severely lacking in academic studies. Moreover, due to the current economic crisis, the increasing income differences and the awareness of real hunger, we look more closely to empirical studies in developed countries (global North or First World countries) following a recent move in the literature on food security, hunger and food banks (Richards, Kjaernes & Vik, 2016; Nielsen, Lund & Holm, 2015; Riches & Silvasti, 2014). Yet, whenever pertinent, the chapter offers pointers to the reader regarding a much more bourgeoning and well-covered literature on poverty and food insecurity in the global South.

Consumption, poverty and food insecurity

Social studies on poverty and food insecurity in developed countries share a common framework of analysis, all focusing on the relationship between food and inequality. The issue of the unequal distribution of resources affects consumers' experiences, both in the global South and the global North. However, in developed countries this is perhaps more surprising, and especially since the recent economic crisis, as there are more clear indications that food insecurity is experienced in countries where food is abundant (clearly not the case of countries in the global South, where tackling hunger and malnutrition have been much more visible in the concerns of the international policy agendas – e.g. UN Millennium Development Goals). Some authors have put forward theoretical approaches for the analysis of food-related inequality (Murcott, 2002). However, the aim of this chapter is to offer a review of empirical studies and show how low-income families are affected by food problems.

A review of such studies entails certain difficulties. The economic and social improvements of the last few decades have modified how poverty is experienced and conceived. What is more, in countries where cases of malnutrition and hunger have ceased to exist and poverty is measured in relative terms, data regarding food privation is no longer considered important (OECD, 2001; Dominguez & Caraballo, 2006; Edin & Kissane, 2010; FAO, 2011). In order to understand the new face of food inequality and to draw attention to current problems and the debates arising from them, this chapter reviews empirical studies dealing with inequality and food. The relationship between poverty and food and the associated problems can be divided into three lines of study.

The first of these focuses on the causal relationship between poverty and "bad" eating habits. Several studies confirm that poorer households follow a monotonous, relatively unhealthy diet and are the ones with greatest prevalence of illnesses associated with malnutrition. However, the direction of this relationship is difficult to establish.

The second line of studies deals with one of the effects of the above-mentioned relationship: obesity. The debate revolves around whether obesity is a structural phenomenon associated with poor living conditions and nutritional contexts which favour inappropriate eating habits or, conversely, is the result of inappropriate individual practices.

A third debate involves how permanent situations of poverty are. It addresses whether social aid generates dependence and results in the situation of those receiving it becoming chronically poor, or whether, on the contrary, people take active measures to overcome the problem of food deprivation.

Food poverty and "bad" eating habits: "Bad" habits or "bad" social conditions?

The study which many researchers in this field look to as a reference model was published by Charles and Kerr in the 1980s (Charles & Kerr, 1986). It involved a qualitative analysis of a group of low-income households (single-parent families and families in which two members were out of work) and confirmed two hypotheses: that when a household is poor, the composition of the diet of that household is affected, but equally that diet is the last thing to be affected by a situation of material privation (see also chapter 10).

Subsequent studies have confirmed that certain characteristics of the diets of those affected by poverty do indeed differ from those of other social groups. Low-income families are associated with a reduction in the consumption of fish and vegetables and with a greater intake of processed and fried products, pasta, rice, bread, potatoes and sweet products and in general of foods with a high percentage of fats and sugar. Although the exact composition of the diet varies according to where the studies are carried out, it is confirmed that low-income households have a less healthy diet and that the higher the income, the greater the amount of vegetables, fruit and fish that is consumed. It is suggested that the poor prefer economical, energy- and calory-dense products and that subsequently fruit, fish and vegetables do not fulfil their criteria (Aguirre, 2000; Hoisington et al., 2002; Bhattacharya et al., 2003; Bowman, 2007; Peretti et al., 2009; Espeitx & Cáceres, 2011; Hérnandez et al., 2013).

Poverty appears to have a major effect on food-related decisions. As affirmed by Hoisington et al. (2002, p. 330), "when you don't have the money, you can't think nutritionally" or, as Aguirre states (2000, p. 11), "one learns to like what allows one to survive". However, criteria regarding price, and how filling food is, coexist with choices based on taste; furthermore, the sociable element of eating is not lost. It has been shown that even in households where food is scarce, there exists a desire to bring members of the family together around the table and to transmit patterns of nutritional education to the children in order to prevent "bad" eating habits (Fitchen, 1987; Aguirre, 2000; Hoisington et al., 2002; Peretti et al., 2009).

Regarding the second hypothesis advanced by Charles and Kerr (1986), more recent studies have shown that diet is affected when households face a crisis situation. It has been shown, for example, that at times of the year when heating is required in the house, the diets of low-income American families are affected whilst there is no change in those of higher-income families (Bhattacharya et al., 2003). Similar conclusions were reached in Spain and Portugal during the recent economic crisis, with those affected confirming that food is of secondary importance when it becomes difficult to pay the mortgage or the rent (Espeitx & Cáceres, 2011; Truninger et al., 2017).

These studies confirm the relationship between low incomes and imbalanced diets. They show that those affected by poverty eat differently, their choices being conditioned by their economic circumstances, not by their food preferences. They also show that, even in a situation of material privation, underlying cultural criteria regarding what constitutes a proper meal continue to exist, even though it may be difficult to put them into practice. Further to this, there is an emergent line of studies that challenge the idea of low-income and "poor" eating habits to be always linearly related, showing evidence that food insecurity and poverty are not the same phenomenon, and one cannot be reduced to the other (Borch & Kjaernes, 2016). A recent study conducted in a Scandinavian welfare state shows that "it is not only those with the lowest income or levels of education that experience food budget restraint. It is particularly noticeable that single-parent households were at relatively high risk of experiencing severe types of food budget restraint" (Nielsen, Lund & Holm, 2015, p. 439). This shows that food insecurity is the outcome of complex conditions, that a situation of economic crisis in high-income countries exacerbates. It is the outcome of the combined effects of "labour market politics, social security systems and food price regulation" that "produce very different food entitlements . . . and new situations of food insecurity" in places never before imagined to be possible to exist (Richards, Kjaernes & Vik, 2016, p. 68).

The physical and mental effects of poverty

Situations of food budget restrain have a negative effect on health, even in societies where there is no shortage of food. It has been shown that poor households undergo greater stress. The mere need to provide daily meals generates tension and distress and has a negative effect on mental health. The instability and uncertainty of the food supply makes the poor psychologically vulnerable, particularly if they have children under care (Hoisington et al., 2002; Whiting & Ward, 2010; Caron, 2011). Stress is also produced by awareness of the gap which exists between these families and society as a whole. Consequently, the more visible the situation of poverty is to the rest of society, the greater the stress for those affected and the greater their social isolation (Edin, 1991; Whiting & Ward, 2010; Hernández et al., 2013; Sales & Lafuente, 2014).

With regard to physical health, economic difficulties in a household are associated with diabetes and cardiovascular diseases, both linked to obesity. Obesity appears to be associated with low-income groups with a low level of education and affects women more than men (Costa-Font & Gil, 2007; Devaux et al., 2011; Álvarez-Castaño et al., 2012). In order to confirm whether this is the result of the situation of economic privation or of inappropriate individual decisions, some authors have used certain sociodemographic variables to study particularly vulnerable collectives with clear signs of obesity. The term *food deserts* is used to refer to the difficulties faced by poorer sections of the rural population in accessing healthy food, this in turn clearly linked to obesity. Other studies refer to the high percentage of homeless people suffering from obesity (Morton et al., 2008; Schafft et al., 2009; Walker et al., 2010; Smith et al., 2010). It is suggested that an imbalanced diet and being overweight or obese is the price these households or individuals must pay if they are to eat on a regular basis (Aguirre, 2000; Peretti et al., 2009; Gracia-Arnáiz, 2014). These authors offer data which points to obesity as being the new face of poverty in the twenty-first century.

Some authors have gone further and are beginning to ask themselves whether it is food aid itself that is contributing to obesity amongst those groups which receive social welfare benefits. This relationship has been found particularly amongst participants in the Food Stamp Programs (FSP) in the United States. The majority of studies confirm that participation in the FSP increases the risk of obesity in women, albeit studies including men are less conclusive (Gibson, 2003; Zick & Stevens, 2009; DeBono et al., 2012). Other authors reject this hypothesis and argue that it is possible that obesity increases participation in FSPs, given that those who are obese have greater calorie requirements and therefore a greater need for food vouchers in order to obtain more food (Fan, 2010). Again, it is possible to affirm that there exists a relationship between obesity and poverty since obesity affects those with least resources and who require social aid, but it is not easy to determine the direction of this relationship.

Coping strategies in the face of food insecurity

The long-term dependence on welfare aid of low-income social groups has become a cause for concern. Analysts have attempted to explain this situation by providing evidence to show that the attitude of those suffering from food deprivation is not a passive one. However, they have also pointed out that a profound understanding of the situation is not possible using traditional means of measuring poverty (Edin & Lein, 1997a; Coleman, 2010). Edin and Lein (1991; 1997b) analyse how people receiving social welfare benefits, single mothers with low levels of education, cope with their situation of privation. They do not study food specifically, although it is mentioned, but present a dynamic model in which poor households are shown to adopt at least three strategies in order to cope with privation. These involve private institutional support, provided by religious institutions (*agency-based strategies*); other informal support, involving the help of friends, neighbours or relatives (*network-based strategies*); and *work-based strategies*, involving supplementing welfare benefits with informal side jobs which they did not declare (Edin, 1991; Edin & Lein, 1997b).

This classification has also been used in more recent studies involving similar groups (Hill and Kaudd, 2001; Heflin et al., 2011) to show how poor households deal with nutritional needs. One such case is that of Morton et al. (2008), who apply it to both urban and rural American households and explain that the poor obtain food in two ways: firstly, using the *reciprocity mechanism*, that is, by exchanging food with those close to them; and secondly, by using the *redistribution mechanism*, in reference to the use of state aid or official organizations, which redistribute taxes according to criteria of need. Both strategies are non-economic patterns, used to solve nutritional necessities of poor households. They are not exclusive but simultaneous, and how they are used depends on the gravity of the situation. Households evaluate the available options and combine formal and informal aid. Consequently, it is not possible to speak of passivity when facing situations of nutritional need. People simply try to make the most of the available options, choosing one or another depending on various factors. For example, the type of aid selected may vary according to place of residence, with urban dwellers using more redistribution mechanisms (food stamps, food banks or soup kitchens) and those living in rural areas using more reciprocity ones (informal aid or even growing their own fruit and vegetables). In general, there is evidence of clear action on the part of low-income families to resolve their food needs by managing the aid which is available (Morton et al., 2008; Whiting & Ward, 2010; Heflin et al., 2011).

It is not only the environment that determines how food is obtained. In serious situations all the available resources are required and if informal means of support fail, or are not available, it is necessary to resort to formal means. However, attempts are made to avoid those support mechanisms which stigmatize users, and consequently the help of family and friends is preferred to institutional aid, which is only resorted to in extreme cases. The most onerous thing for those in this situation is to resort to soup kitchens, since this type of aid not only highlights nutritional need but also a lack of social support (Whiting & Ward, 2010; Sales & Lafuente, 2014).

Some authors have suggested that use of welfare aid is conditioned by awareness of its availability since in disadvantaged areas with high levels of unemployment, low incomes and a population with a low educational level, a large percentage of those eligible for state benefits do not claim them (Slack & Myers, 2012). Cultural background also plays a part, and it has been observed that Hispanics use family help and informal social networks more frequently than do other ethnic groups (Carney, 2012). Another factor affecting decisions is the structure of the household, especially the presence of minors. When people have children they make choices that they would not otherwise in order to prevent privation and affecting the minors (Whiting & Ward, 2010; Espeitx & Cáceres, 2011; Heflin et al., 2011).

These studies emphasize those structural aspects which condition the manner in which food deprivation is dealt with and show that structural factors impose themselves on individuals, who are forced to take decisions which, in other circumstances, they would not have taken. The fact that these people continue to depend on the social welfare system is the result of their difficult living conditions and the situation of material privation and poverty in which they are immersed. Indeed, some studies have shown unsuccessful attempts to escape poverty in which young mothers try to complement welfare benefits with paid jobs, but to no avail; neither the low wages nor the welfare benefits are sufficient (Edin & Lein, 1997b). This simply confirms the idea that working does not allow people to escape situations of material deprivation and consequently they continue to take advantage of social welfare programmes, not as a way of "living off the State" but because it is the only way to deal effectively with their situation.

Other studies show how saving strategies are sometimes applied when managing the food available in a household: dividing a meal into several courses, freezing in anticipation of shortages at the end of the month, organizing meals according to the food coupons available or the products received, repeating meals throughout the week or reducing the size of portions are some of the strategies adopted by those who manage the food in the household (Hoisington et al., 2002). Strategies become more sophisticated as hunger increases, and managing available food becomes more complex towards the end of the month when it becomes necessary to choose between paying the bills and eating (Hoisington et al., 2002; Heflin et al., 2011). Decisions are also harder when there are children in the household and the aim is to not deprive them of basic necessities. For this reason, unequal distribution of resources within the household is a practice commonly resorted to by mothers so that their children can eat, even if this implies they skip meals to feed their children (Carney, 2012). In a recent study it was found that "coping strategies such as using leftovers and cooking seasonal products, were common across all levels of budget restraint, while strategies affecting social life and taste preferences negatively", namely compromising food taste, inviting fewer guests for meals at home, "were mostly applied when restraint was more severe" (Nielsen, Lund & Holm, 2015, p. 429). It also showed that for some families the experience of food budget restraint was stressful and negative, while for others it was a form of expressing creativity, resilience and empowerment (e.g. learning a new skill such as cooking with seasonal vegetables, or going to local producers to buy food).

To sum up, it is clear that households affected by material deprivation experience it in different ways. Many make efforts to solve the daily problems that eating represents, and actively attempt to make ends meet, but equally it has been shown that reciprocity and redistribution are not effective ways of eliminating food insecurity.

Conclusion and future research

By linking the food security concept with the rich social sciences literature on poverty a shift of focus from production and markets to consumption and access was achieved. However, by subsuming the concept of food security onto the poverty literature we may risk overlooking that these two concepts are not synonymous, food insecurity being a problem that goes beyond income issues. Despite this risk, this review exercise served to contribute to a recent call to connect better food security with issues of access and consumption. By looking at the main food poverty debates, we hope to have inspired future studies to develop more the potential of looking at food (in)security in its own right, by interconnecting better production and consumption issues.

The first of these debates looked at the causal relationship between poverty and "bad" eating habits. Despite a strong link between low-income households and a monotonous and relatively unhealthy diet, there is further evidence that the direction of this relationship is difficult to establish. Recent studies challenge a linear connection between poverty and "bad" eating habits, opening up the possibility that high levels of food literacy and cooking skills may prevent low-income families from going through episodes of food insecurity. The second debate focuses on the links between food insecurity and obesity, and explores whether obesity is the modern manifestation of poverty. A third debate examines food aid and its effects in the maintenance of structural food poverty issues, instead of solving them. Some scholars openly suggest that food programmes are in part responsible for the problems of malnutrition faced by food aid recipients. One aspect that comes across all three debates is gender issues. Indeed, when analysing poverty and food insecurity, gender is a transversal factor since women are generally both the ones that manage all food-related matters, obtaining, organizing and preparing food and taking decisions that affect the whole household and, at the same time, play the role of carers, bearing responsibility for the family's health and nutrition, particularly that of any children in their care.

This chapter placed a bigger focus on poverty and food insecurity in developed countries due to the effects of the recent economic crisis. The financial crisis of 2008 triggered a renewed interest in food (in)security issues, and these debates became more connected not only with social inequality, poverty and health concerns, but also with climate change and sustainability.

The chapter started by discussing the lack of consistency in the use of terminology, an aspect in which future research should work towards conceptual clarity and consolidate theoretical perspectives on this topic. The recent crisis shed light on the need to look at consumption and access matters in developed countries when examining food insecurity, a shift that future studies should embrace through single-country analysis and comparative research of food practices and institutional arrangements (see Richards, Kjaernes & Vik, 2016). By fully agreeing with Lambie-Mumford and O'Connell (2015) we also believe that maintaining and fostering methodological and disciplinary diversity in this field is a welcome contribution in order to achieve a more robust evidence base on poverty and food (in)security.

References

Aguirre, P. (2000). Aspectos socioantropológicos de la obesidad en la pobreza. In Peña, M. & Bacallao, J. (Eds.) La obesidad en la pobreza: un nuevo reto para la salud pública (pp. 13–25). *Organización Panamericana de la Salud*, doc. 576.

Álvarez-Castaño, L. S., Goez-Rueda, J. D., & Carreño-Aguirre, C. (2012). Factores sociales y económicos asociados a la obesidad: los efectos de la inequidad y de la pobreza. *Revista Gerencia y Políticas de Salud*, 11(23), 98–110.

Bhattacharya, J., DeLeire, T., Haider, S., & Currie, J. (2003). Heat or Eat? Cold-weather shocks and nutrition in poor American families. *American Journal of Public Health*, 93(7), 1149–1154.

Borch, A., & Kjaernes, U. (2016). Food security and food insecurity in Europe: An analysis of the academic discourse (1975–2013). *Appetite*, 103(August), 137–147.

Bowman, S. (2007). Low economic status is associated with suboptimal intakes of nutritious food by adults in the National health and nutrition examination survey 1999–2002. *Nutrition Research*, 27(9), 515–523.

Carney, M. (2012). Compounding crises of economic recession and food insecurity: A comparative study of three low-income communities in Santa Barbara County. *Agriculture and Human Values*, 29(2), 185–201.

Carolan, M. (2013). *Reclaiming Food Security*. London: Routledge.

Caron, J. (2011). Predictors of quality of life in economically disadvantaged populations in Montreal. *Social Indicators Research*, 107(3), 411–427.

Charles, N., & Kerr, M. (1986). Eating properly, the family and state benefit. *Sociology*, 20(3), 412–429.

Coleman, A. J. (2010). US food insecurity status: Toward a refined definition. *Social Indicators Research*, 95(2), 215–230.

Costa-Font, J. & Gil, J. (2007). What lies behind socioeconomic inequalities in obesity in Spain? A decomposition approach. *Food Policy*, 33(1), 61–73.

DeBono, N. L., Ross, N. A., & Berrang-Ford, L. (2012). Does the food stamp program cause obesity? A realist review and a call for place-based research. *Health and Place*, 18(4), 747–756.

Devaux, M., Sassi, F., Church, J., Cecchini, M., & Borgonovi, F. (2011). Exploring the relationship between education and obesity. *OECD Journal: Economic Studies*, 5(1), 121–159.

Domínguez, J. D., & Caraballo, A.M. (2006). Medición de la pobreza: una revisión de los principales indicadores. *Revista de Métodos Cuantitativos para la Economía y la Empresa*, vol. 2 (Deciembre), 27–66.

Dowler, E., Turner, S., & Dobson, B. (2001). *Poverty Bites – Food, Health and Poor Families*. London: CPAG.

Dowler, E., & Lambie-Mumford, H. (2015). How can households eat in austerity? Challenges for social policy in the UK. *Social Policy and Society*, 14, 417–428.

Dwiartma, A., & Piatti, C. (2016). Assembling local, assembling food security. *Agriculture and Human Values*, 33, 153–164.

Edin, K. (1991). Surviving the welfare system: How Aids to families with dependent children recipients make ends meet in Chicago. *Social Problems*, 38(4), 462–474.

Edin, K., & Kissane, R.J. (2010). Poverty and the American family: A decade in review. *Journal of Marriage and Family*, 72(3), 460–479.
Edin, K., & Lein, L. (1997a). *Making Ends Meet: How Single Mothers Survive Welfare and Low-Wage work*. New York: Russell Sage Foundation.
Edin, K., & Lein, L. (1997b). Work, welfare, and single mothers' economic survival strategies. *American Sociological Review*, 62(2), 253–266.
Espeitx, E., & Cáceres, J. (2011). Los comportamientos alimentarios de mujeres en precariedad económica: entre la privación y el riesgo de malnutrición. *Zainak*, (34), 127–146.
Fan, M. (2010). Do food stamps contribute to obesity in low-income women? Evidence from the national longitudinal survey of youth 1979. *American Journal of Agricultural Economics*, 92(4), 1165–1180.
FAO (2011). *Una introducción a los conceptos básicos de la seguridad alimentaria*. Documenting electronic sources on the Internet: http://www.fao.org/docrep/014/al936s/al936s00.pdf
Fitchen, J.M. (1987). Hunger, malnutrition, and poverty in the contemporary United State: some observations on their social and cultural context. *Food and Foodways*, 2(1), 309–333.
Food and Agriculture Organization of the United Nations (2009). *State of Food Insecurity in the World*. Rome: FAO.
Gibson, D. (2003). Food stamp program participation is positively related to obesity in low income women. *The Journal of Nutrition*, 133(7), 2225–2231.
Gracia-Arnaiz, M. (2014). Comer en tiempos de "crisis": nuevos contextos alimentarios y de salud en España. *Salud Pública de México*, 56(6), 648–653.
Heflin, C., London, A. S., & Scott, E. K. (2011). Mitigating material hardship: The strategies low-income families employ to reduce the consequences of poverty. *Sociological Inquiry*, 81(2), 223–246.
Hernández, E., Pérez, D., & Ortiz-Hernández, L. (2013). Consecuencias alimentarias y nutricionales de la inseguridad alimentaria: la perspectiva de madres solteras. *Revista chilena de nutrición*, 40(4), 351–356.
Hill, H., & Kauff, J. (2001). *Living on little: case studies of Iow a families with very low income*. Washington, DC: Mathematica Policy Research, Inc.
Hoisington, A., Shultz, J. A., & Butkus, S. (2002). Coping strategies and nutrition education needs among food pantry users. *Journal of Nutrition Education and Behavior*, 34(6), 326–333.
Kirwan, J., & Maye, D. (2013). Food security framings within the UK and the integration of local food systems. *Journal of Rural Studies*, 29(0), 91–100.
Kneafsey, M., Dowler, E., Lambie-Mumford, H., Inman, A., & Collier, R. (2013). Consumers and food security: Uncertain or empowered? *Journal of Rural Studies*, 4, 101–112.
Lambie-Mumford, H., & O'Connell, R. (2015). *Food, Poverty and Policy: Evidence Base and Knowledge Gaps*, Report of the BSA Food Study Group-SPERI event. Sheffield: SPERI.
Maxwell, S. (1996). Food security: A post-modern perspective. *Food Policy*, 21(2), 155–170.
Midgley, J. (2013). Food (In)Security in the Global "North" and "South". In A. Murcott, W. Belasco, & P. Jackson (Eds.), *The Handbook of Food Research*. London: Bloomsbury, 425–438.
Morton, L.W., Bitto, E. A., Oakland, M. J., & Sand, M. (2008). Accessing food resources: Rural and urban patterns of giving and getting food. *Agriculture and Human Values*, 25(1), 107–119.
Murcott, A. (2002). Nutrition and inequalities. *The European Journal of Public Health*, 12(3), 203–207.
Nielsen, A., & Holm, L. (2016). Making the most of less: Food budget restraint in a Scandinavian welfare society. *Food, Culture and Society*, 19(1), 71–91.
Nielsen, A., Lund, T. B., Holm, L. (2015). The Taste of 'the End of the Month', and how to avoid it: Coping with restrained food budgets in a Scandinavian welfare state context. *Social Policy and Society*, 14(3), 429–442.
Nord, M., Coleman-Jensen, A., Andrews, M., & Carlson, S. (2010). Household food security in the United States, 2009. *Economic Research Report No. 108*, U.S. Department of Agriculture.
OCDE (2001). *Rising to the Global Challenge: Partnership for Reducing World Poverty*. Documenting electronic sources on the internet: http://www.oecd.org/dac/povertyreduction/1895254.pdf
Patel, R. (2009). What does food sovereignty look like? *Journal of Peasant Studies*, 36(3), 663–706.
Peretti, M. L., Romero, M. M., & Rovetto, A. (2009). Obesidad en la Pobreza. Prácticas y representaciones asociadas a esta patología en sectores de bajos recursos. *Invernio: Revista de investigación académica*, 23, 81–94.
Richards, C., Kjaernes, U., & Vik, J. (2016). Food security in welfare capitalism: Comparing social entitlements to food in Australia and Norway. *Journal of Rural Studies*, 43, 61–70.
Riches, G., & Silvasti, T. (Eds.) (2014). *First World Hunger Revisited: Food Charity or the Right to Food?*. London: Palgrave Macmillan.

Sales, A., & Lafuente, I. M. (2014). Ayuda alimentaria y descalificación social. Impacto de las diferentes formas de distribución de alimentos cocinados sobre la vivencia subjetiva de la pobreza en Barcelona. *Documentación Social*, 174, 171–190.

Schafft, K.A., Jensen, E. B., & Hinrichs, C. (2009). Food deserts and overweight schoolchildren: Evidence from Pennsylvania. *Rural Sociology*, 74(2): 153–177.

Sen, A. (1981). *Poverty and Famines. An essay on Entitlement and Deprivation*. Oxford: Clarendon Press.

Slack, T., & Myers, C. A. (2012). Understanding the geography of food stamp program participation: Do space and place matter? *Social Science Research*, 41(2), 263–275.

Smith, C., Butterfass, J., & Richards, R. (2010). Environment influences food access and resulting shopping and dietary behaviors among homeless Minnesotans living in food deserts. *Agriculture and Human Values*, 27(2), 141–161.

Trauger, A. (Ed.) (2015). *Food Sovereignty in International Context: Discourse, Politics and Practice of Place*. New York: Routledge.

Truninger, M.; Teixeira, J.; Augusto, F.; Cardoso, S.; Horta, A.; Fontes, A. (2017). *Alimentação em Tempos de Crise* [Food in Times of Crisis]. Lisbon: Imprensa de Ciências Sociais.

Walker, R. E., Keane, C. R., & Burke, J. G. (2010). Disparities and access to healthy food in the United States: A review of food deserts literature. *Health and Place*, 16(5), 876–884.

Whiting, E. F., & Ward, C. (2010). Food provisioning strategies, food insecurity, and stress in an economically vulnerable community: The Northern Cheyenne case. *Agriculture and Human Values*, 27(4), 489–504.

Zick, C.D., & Stevens, R. B. (2009). Is dinner ready yet? The time implications of participating in the food stamp program. American Time Use Research Conference, June 25–26, 2009, College Park, MD.

24

Materiality, migration and cultural diversity

Marta Vilar Rosales

Introduction

Contemporary social sciences define consumption as a complex and fascinating activity which encompasses a diverse set of practices, tastes and values (Brewer and Trentmann, 2006). If this feature makes it a vital and challenging object of research and reflection, it also poses significant challenges in terms of the best and more productive ways to address it. Given the great variety of practices and settings contemporary consumption entails, and the prolificness of existing theoretical frameworks at use in the social sciences, researchers are often confronted with the need to make choices which necessarily have great impact on their research and, most importantly, on how consumption is acknowledged in the wider spheres of public discussion.

This chapter addresses consumption as an aspect of material culture (Miller, 1987). It aims to challenge the perspectives that undertake consumption as synonymous of modern mass consumption and deal with contemporary uses of things as intrinsically different from use in prior times.

I will argue that a material culture approach to consumption constitutes a fundamental academic tool. Such approach privileges the analysis of the specificities of all objects, including mass-produced objects, in order to create a more profound understanding of a humanity which, as Miller states (2006), is inseparable from its materiality. It will be argued that such an approach brings light to the processes through which things are produced and appropriated, as well as to their contributions to the creation and recreation of social life (Mauss, 1924; Douglas, 1979). By turning away from too-broad approaches and towards the specificity of particular forms of consumption, that is the relationships of people with their things, material culture approaches become powerful and productive lenses (Rosales, 2010) to address the super diversity (Vertovec, 2007) that characterizes contemporary social and cultural life, as well as the communality which permeates it (Glick Schiller, 1995). The chapter will explore this main feature by focusing on the intersections of the movements of people and things. In fact, and even if most approaches tend to privilege other key aspects of contemporary global migration experiences and mobility policies and trends (e.g. positioning, belonging and integration strategies, networking practices, transnational practices and ties, border policies, diversity of push-and-pull factors at work in different parts of the world), all migrations are necessarily embedded in materiality (Basu and

Coleman, 2008). Migrating inevitably involves carrying, sending and receiving, as well as expropriations and appropriations, desires and expectations regarding a plural set of things which, in turn, are called to shape and actively participate in the migrants' daily experiences and are used as evaluation tools of what was accomplished during their migratory trajectories.

In fact, most contemporary objects are at least as potentially mobile as people. Things move or are moved from one location to the next, following, accompanying or being followed by people, and motion inevitably affects their social lives (Appadurai, 1986), value and cultural biographies (Kopytoff, 1986). The impacts of movement on material experiences reach further than attachments to objects from home. Migrants are constantly confronted with new material items whose processes of categorization, evaluation and domestication usually integrate their strategies for dealing with their new context. And if materiality can work as a significant stabilization device and promote security and recognition by means of dealing with familiar things, it can also change migrants' perceptions of themselves, restructure their patterns of social interaction, disrupt a sense of existential permanence or open space for a new sense of self through the introduction of new or unfamiliar objects in their daily routines and practices of consumption.

The chapter is organized in three parts. The first part summarizes a set of significant contributions which frame contemporary consumption practices as material culture. The second explores the intersections between migration and materiality and the third and concluding part examines the importance of this particular approach to explore the increasing specificities and complexities of contemporary global movements.

Consumption as material culture

The assumption of the term *consumption* as an alternative for *modern mass consumption* is fairly common. However, people have always consumed goods created either by themselves or by others. This is why consumption is emerging also in archaeological studies, which are more generally associated with material culture, as an increasingly significant research topic (Mullins, 2011). Crucial to this discussion is the question as to whether modern consumption is actually a different kind of activity in intention and nature from merely the use of goods in prior times.

Anthropological and sociological theories contributed to the debate by way of introducing alternative perspectives which stress the importance for observing what people do with the things with which they interact. In order to unfold and explain the present-day relationships between people and objects it is crucial to research, as it was in prior historical and cultural contexts, what part materiality plays in human interactions and rituals; how consumers appropriate, transform, and domesticate objects and attribute them meanings; and to what extent things integrate contemporary cosmologies; i.e. why and for what do people want their stuff?

Particularly important for the consolidation of a material culture approach to the study of contemporary consumption were the works of Mary Douglas and Baron Isherwood (1979) and Pierre Bourdieu (1979), followed by the seminal contribution of Daniel Miller (1987) and the noteworthy book *The Social Life of Things* edited by Arjun Appadurai (1986), both published one decade later.

The work of Mary Douglas (1921–2007), an English anthropologist, directly addresses the topic of the so-called distinctive nature of consumption in modern capitalist societies by exploring the concept of 'need'. In *The World of Goods. Towards an Anthropology of Consumption* (1979), Douglas and Isherwood call attention to the fact that economy seems unable to respond to the question of why people want things in industrialized capitalist societies. According to her, this happens because economy has cut off the social dimension off that critical concept for the study of contemporary consumption, an error that needs to be amended since consumption decisions have always constituted a vital source of culture in all times and contexts. According to Douglas, decisions involving things are the mainspring of culture and consumer choices, and activities are fundamental to one's own life, given that they necessarily reflect who consumers are and how they relate to others. In the end, consumption is a social and cultural activity of production of a universe of values. Then, instead of thinking that goods are, or once were, primarily needed for subsistence, Douglas asserts that they are fundamental for making visible and stable the categories of culture. Though some things sometimes serve physical needs, they also serve to communicate with others and to relate to them. People actively have been using them to speak about themselves and to learn things from others. Hence goods are for making sense, and consumption is about finding consistent meanings made visible through physical things. The objective of consumers today, as in the past, translates a concern for information about the changing cultural scene. In Douglas' words, in a finite social world, securely bounded, meanings echo and reinforce one another. Despite the differences in terms of the intensity of the changes happening in the market, the same is true in economies of scale. Consumers have to gain or keep control of the sources of information so that their interpretations, their cosmological synthesis, are consistent and secure.

Mary Douglas brought light to the complex connections and interdependences between the materialization of social life and the processes of exchange, acquisition and use, both in industrialized and non-industrialized societies. One of the most significant quests of collective life is the stabilization of meanings, i.e. the existence of a minimum consensual basis of shared meanings, for a certain period of time. Research approaches to consumption therefore allow the depiction of the mechanisms (their similarities and originalities) through which different societies produce shared meanings by using material culture.

Even if not primarily focused on contemporary consumption, the contributions of French sociologist Pierre Bourdieu to the study of contemporary consumption as material culture are also substantial. In *La Distinction. Critique Sociale du Jugement* (1979), Bourdieu explores the main mechanisms of stratification and reproduction of social distinction in France. Through an extensive approach to the patterns of consumption of all social classes he makes clear how everyday trivial consumption practices reflect and materialize the stratification system. Things actively participate in the maintenance of social order, and the different social groups strategically use things to materialize their positions in the overall social structure. Unlike Douglas, Bourdieu does not explore the existent similitudes between the social and the cultural work performed by material culture in pre-capitalist and capitalist societies. Still, *La Distinction* contributed significantly to unfold the plurality of social and cultural uses that different social groups could ascribe to ordinary mass consumption objects.

English anthropologist Daniel Miller's work constitutes a critical contribution to the rehabilitation of contemporary consumption as a major research field in anthropology. Miller's extensive production not only permanently places mass consumption in context of material culture studies but also, and most importantly, illuminates the scientific significance of everyday regular and ordinary human practices and the significant role materiality plays in them. His earlier research (1987) calls the attention to the fact that it is imperative to recognise industrialized mass consumption objects as one of the most significant features of contemporary material culture. Mass-produced things actively participate in the production of social and cultural life. Far from being neutral, they engage in meaningful relationships with subjects and participate in the making of the contexts which they inhabit. Furthermore, they still are one of the most significant tools to manage social relationships and belongings, as well as to appropriate and domesticate the increasingly global and potentially unfamiliar contexts in which we live. *Stuff* (2009), therefore, has got great cultural power, a power that resides in its ability to frame, in a very discrete though effective manner, one's daily practices and social relationships.

The Social Life of Things (1986), an edited volume by Arjun Appadurai (born 1949) constitutes another influential example in the field of anthropological theory of how the dichotomy which opposes pre-industrial (gift) societies to industrialized capitalist (commodity) ones failed in contributing to unfold the social role of contemporary consumption. Appadurai's introduction to the volume and the chapter by Igor Kopytoff (1986) explore the ability things have to move in and out of different contexts and identifications during their social lives in diverse historic settings. According to the authors, the biography of things discloses how material culture is subjected to constant change in terms of value and signification, how things adjust their performances according to the contexts they enter and the effectiveness of their work as carriers of identity markers and interpersonal power subjectivities. The trajectories of things, therefore, illuminate the contexts in which they circulate, influencing and directing beliefs, practices and obligations.

Material culture approaches to contemporary consumption fostered research out of the industrialised capitalist Western world, hence contributing to the debates on globalization with original theoretical and methodological approaches. In fact, all social sciences, and anthropology in particular, have been developing consistent research on the topic in other regions of the globe, analysing the impacts of capitalism, comparing its expressions and outcomes and exploring the originalities and contradictions, consistencies and inconsistencies, connections and disruptions of contemporary materiality. One of the most influential examples of these studies is the work of Sidney Mintz (1922–2015), *Sweetness and Power: The Place of Sugar in Modern History* (1985). His research, which inspired many others in different cultural contexts, explores how the production of sugar in one region became linked with consumption in another cultural and spatial setting, emphasizing the complex interplay between the growing heterogeneity and homogeneity in these encounters.

This line of work also contributed extensively to the consolidation of the *consumption as material culture* approach. It stressed further the main theoretical principles previously presented which conceptualized consumption as a complex activity that transcends purchase and involves the productive appropriation of objects and consequent creation of collective life. It also contributed to emphasizing the importance of cultural diversity in consumption studies, without overemphasising the subject or the object in their relationship. Following Miller (2006), a material culture analysis allows humanity back into consumption studies, without losing the focus on the object. It promotes an understanding of consumption practices as expressions of social relationships with others and with goods and validates the idea that people actively and strategically use objects for the production of meaning, as well as to mark their social actions and positioning strategies. By focusing on the cultural uses of things rather than in the political and economic mechanisms beyond the relationships amongst production and consumption, this framework situates the study of contemporary consumption in the realm of everyday naturalized practices and calls the attention to the constitutive and expressive potentials of ordinary and humble stuff.

Materiality and migration

Despite the intensity of the debate it has generated in the last decades, contemporary consumption is a relatively discrete research topic if compared with other major social sciences' topics, such as contemporary migrations. In fact, and according to the report of the UN Rio Summit of 2012, human mobility is at its highest levels in recorded history. And if in recent years international and internal migration has been recognized as a positive force for development, as migrants transfer knowledge and skills to both receiving and origin locations, channel investments and remittances, and foster economic linkages and business opportunities between countries and regions, it has also been increasingly acknowledged as a critical and potentially disruptive, if not a menace, to the western, richer and more stable regions of the world. Contemporary migration is under strong public scrutiny and all the visibility and passionate debate it generates at the present is matched by equally intense analysis and debate within the social sciences.

Many of the most influential references in the field point toward the necessity of thinking about the consequences of migration in terms of its macro and micro impacts in collective life. Structural dimensions as diverse as the impact of movement in cultural diversity, social reproduction, community life, economic stability and growth, transfer of knowledge and skills, economic linkages, border supervision and demographic management occupy a prominent position in the research agendas and are scrutinized by diverse theoretical and methodological lenses and perspectives. Even if occupying a less prominent position in the picture, research on micro topics directly focusing on the migrant and on the migration experience such as identity and belonging, aspirations and evaluations, positioning and negotiation processes have received considerable attention from all disciplines too and has generated significant contributions to the field of study.

In spite of its visibility and intensity, contemporary mobility does not necessarily entail fluidity, cosmopolitanism and openness. If for some groups, movement and transnational circulation are experienced as an enriching experience, the fact is that for most migrants movement is based on inequality and discrimination, is controlled and limited by states (Castles, 2010) and leads to confinement and exploitation (Portes and DeWind, 2004). Likewise, awareness of complexity, diversity and significance of context does not stand for postmodern fragmentation. Contemporary circulations of people present great diversity, but this diversity unfolds within increasingly universal relationships of power, translating the existence of global structures which Richard Wilk (2005) accurately describes as structures of common difference. Moreover, contemporary movement creates integrated systems, which should be addressed at a range of different, even if complementary, scales: the personal, the familiar, the communal, the national and the transnational scale formed by the constellation of countries linked by the ongoing migration flows and routes.

Social theory presents us today a multitude of concepts to capture and describe those on the move which stand as possible alternatives to the *migrant*. However, and despite the term in use, all migrants (and travellers, expatriates or cosmopolitans) as well all migrants' aspirations, beliefs and practices integrate multiple spatial networks and temporal linkages. This fact underlines the complexity of contemporary migrations' multiple layers and dimensions and calls the attention to the importance of the specificities entailed in each particular experience. In reality, all migrations are grounded on details with reference to who travels and who stays, when, how and in which circumstances the first journey occurs as well as the others that follow; what historic, economic, political and cultural conditions mark the spaces crossed and the trajectories traveled; what the impacts of the journey are over time on personal biographies; or how to characterize new and old relationships and networks, as well as the managing and displaying of belonging and affection.

The "transnational turn" (Vertovec, 2007) introduced significant changes in the debate about the articulation of these multiple dimensions of migration. It called attention to the fact that migrants maintain and manage their lives in spaces that go beyond national borders (Glick Schiller, 1995; Feldman-Bianco and Glick Schiller, 2011), and how institutions and states incorporated these movements and relations in order to control and manage them. Family and family ties emerged as especially significant in the structuring of transnational networks and relations. Transnationalism pulled research away from the approaches that portrayed those who migrated as passive reactors to the contexts and events that framed their journeys, and instead focused the research agenda on migration's lived experiences. Today there are numerous authors who call attention to crucial aspects of these experiences, and most particularly to the importance of exploring the disconnections between the ideal and the actual experiences in contexts of migration. Tackling and comparing the imaginaries and expectations of migrants with their narratives of concrete daily life experiences became a major topic of analysis and, this chapter argues, material culture and consumption practices can be a particularly productive lens to explore and analyse it. In fact, most modalities of migration are related to aspirations of *a better life*, a loose concept that integrates many dimensions and angles. Imaginaries may be defined as culturally shared. They are socially transmitted representational assemblages that interact with people's imaginings and expectations. Imaginaries are often used as meaning-making devices, as significant constellations of representations and values that work to justify and trigger migration. And even if most migration experiences fail to match the aspirations and imaginaries about the journey, the new context of living, the new daily routines or the relationships held with those who did not travel, they nonetheless work as important references to the evaluation of the outcomes of all effective migration experiences.

While human migration, movement and mobility, in general, and the migrants' lived experiences have most definitely caught the attention of all social sciences, their intersections with the movements of things, as well as the material dimensions involved in all migration process, are still underexplored. Yet, and as Paul Basu and Simon Coleman rightly state in the introduction of a thematic issue of the journal *Mobilities* (2008) dedicated to the theme, all migrations are highly embedded in materiality since they necessarily involve carrying, sending and receiving things, as well as expropriations and appropriations, desires and expectations regarding material items. Moreover, objects are at least as potentially mobile as people, and independently of whom they travel with or whom they encounter in their journeys, movement will always necessarily affect their social lives, their value and their cultural biographies.

As recent research demonstrates (e.g. Rosales, 2010, 2012; Parrot, 2012; Horst, 2011; Miller, 2008; Burrell, 2008; Sväsec, 2012, Povrzanović Frykman, 2009), ethnographic insights into mobile selves achieved through objects can work as particularly productive conceptual lenses. The impacts of movement on material experiences reach much further than attachments to objects from home. They also promote encounters with other and new material realities structured by original frames of values and rules, which necessarily affect the uses of things. Things from diverse cultural, spatial and temporal contexts establish complex relationships, not only with migrants, but also between themselves, creating new cosmological orders and dwelling contexts. Furthermore, things perform an important role in the management of relationships with those who stayed and with those whose daily lives also take place in the same context. They can materialize significant relationships with the past – the appreciation and recognition, or the abandonment of things "from home"; with the present – the incorporation of new things and/or the reconfiguration of patterns of consumption and with the future – access to more diverse/valued material universe or the inability to accomplish it.

Previously in this chapter, it was argued that a material culture approach to consumption was particularly productive to analyse contemporary identities. According to the inputs presented and explored here, things have the potential for and the capacity to promote changes in people's perceptions of themselves, participate in the restructuring of their patterns of social interaction, disrupt their sense of existential permanence or contribute to making space for a new sense of self to emerge. Hence, the complex and intense field of discussion of the impacts of migration and movement on contemporary identities would highly benefit from the inputs of a material culture based approach. Ranging from visual and literary representations of migration to gifts, remittances or the materiality of the means of transport and borders, things participate in the making, displaying and assessing of migrants' identities and frame migration experiences.

Following Burrell's (2008) contribution to the discussion, materiality is key to explore the intense ongoing relationships between the (changing) identity of places of mobility and the identities of those who travel. Burrell specifically calls attention to the importance of things in travelling experiences. According to her work, travel and border crossing are two key emotional, political, cultural and personal dimensions of all migration processes that are absent from many of the most influential research on contemporary migration. However, people develop in-situ travelling identities and relationships as they go "dwelling-in motion" (Burrell, 2008: 354) which should be integrated in the broader context of their migration experiences and explored as intensely material and used spaces and times. Far from being "in-between" spaces and times, journeys and borders are domesticated and experienced in multiple ways, and strategies and things play an important role in these particular processes. They take part of the migrants' journeys, embody significant aspirations and expectations directly related with migration and work to "customize" impersonal spaces such as transport seats or the waiting rooms of airports and stations.

Other contributions (e.g. Miller, 2008; Parrot, 2012; Rosales, 2012) emphasize the importance of materiality in the strategic processes of negotiation of migrants' identities. All migrations have significant impacts on identity since they necessarily entail a (sometimes major) reconfiguration of self, based on new cultural and social frames and settings. Things not only actively participate in these restructuring processes, but also constitute a particularly fertile terrain to observe how they unfold both in the public and the private spheres of migrants" lives. Moreover, migrants are most of the time confronted with the necessity of learning how to deal with new material worlds, a process which usually brings additional anxiety and difficulty since it implies evaluating not only *new things* introduced by migration, but also the things from the former cultural context. These processes often result in highly creative material environments, subjected to continuous evaluation and scrutiny, in which past and present come together to form new, even if sometimes instable, contexts of identity production and display.

Based on extensive ethnographic fieldwork, the material culture approach to this complex thematic goes beyond the analysis of the things that ground migration experiences, and it explores the diverse forms through which materiality provides ways of indexing the status and/or the agency of the migrant. The work of the authors cited above particularly illustrate the significance of how aspirations, transformations and past and present social positions are differently played and displayed both in the public and private domains of migrants' lives and, more importantly, how they progress and change over time. From contents of supermarket baskets and menus prepared to celebrate significant dates, to wardrobes or items used to set the table, everyday material culture becomes a crucial research site to explore how identity is objectified, produced and reproduced in the routines that form and shape most of what life is about. Things work as negotiation tools to perform these relational and positioning processes, but they can as well be explored as material testimonies of the transformations being performed and/or negotiated. Hence, things become productive translators, materializing different ways of seeing the world and crucially contributing to the management of belonging and *otherness* (and consequently *us*) and *self*.

Even if most research on migration focuses on uses and on the social and cultural work things are asked to perform in support of the migrant, it is important to call attention to the fact that materiality does not always work with subjects, favouring their intentions or helping to materialize their goals. In fact, sometimes things can resist appropriation by subjects, and consumption is experienced has a burden, i.e., a stressful and overwhelming activity which implies considerable effort and investment (Burrell, 2008, Rosales, 2015). Migrants are often confronted with the fact that some of their material belongings not only don't "fit in" in certain contexts, but are evaluated and/or used in different manners. Also, material culture can work in unexpected ways, exposing features of migrants' lives and identities that were meant to remain out of site, making visible their inability to master certain things and products and, most importantly, testifying the failures and unintended detours their migration experiences suffered (Parrott, 2012, Horst, 2011). Hence, the material realm of migration can also be a particularly useful tool to investigate the less positive, and perhaps more painful and blocked, dimensions resulting from movement and displacement – disruption, fragmentation and loss.

Conclusion

Even if the social sciences in general, and anthropology in particular, have always acknowledged materiality as a significant field of practice, only recently have objects regained centrality as a result of a set of theoretical productions which, as was discussed previously, emphasized the urgency of rethinking contemporary materiality and its relationships with subjects. Today, the capacity of contemporary materiality and consumption to generate culture and to do social and cultural work through processes of differentiation, objectification and integration is widely recognized and things are perceived as objectification devices, actively involved in processes of evaluation, positioning and mobility. As it was argued, objects participate in the co-production of reality. They compose a familiar frame, a subtle setting for social practice. And since social behaviour is cued by expectations and determined by frames, objects ensure appropriate behaviour without being open to challenge (Miller, 2010). Hence, materiality constitutes a "key-tool", i.e. a socialization device, for the definition of collective identities and ways of seeing the world, and interacting with things can therefore be understood as a learning process of collective norms (Miller, 2010).

Migration is intimately linked to human history. People have always moved, settled in new places and moved again, sometimes with great intensity and impact, causing major historical, political, cultural and social transformations, other times in a more discrete manner, producing perhaps less visible effects and public reactions. Contemporary migrations are at the centre of public debate. They are highly scrutinized by the media, occupy a significant position in academic, legal and political debate and constitute a core area of intervention of today's social institutions. However, and in spite of all this intense debate, migrations and migrants are still seen as problematic, complex and difficult to grasp, as most of social and cultural life dimensions also are. Social sciences have acknowledged by now that migration experiences present great diversity, as well as that many migrant groups are highly heterogeneous. They have also, however, acknowledged that it is imperative to compare migration experiences and bridge them in order to promote a wider understanding of the main outcomes of movement and their impacts on people, contexts and culture. As Glick Schiller's (2011) work amongst others stresses, the study of migration is particularly illustrative of the existing cultural diversity in contemporary urban settings, but it is also a crucial terrain to acknowledge the existing similarities between people, in spite of their migration experiences. So, migration ultimately underlines the "super diversity" of the social and cultural world while simultaneously reveals aspects of commonality and proximity between people. This aspect of contemporary migration needs to be further explored in the future, and material culture and consumption studies can give a solid contribution to the depiction of the existent differences and commonalities between migrants and non-migrants, in general, and how gender, age, class and religion mediate consumption practices, in particular. The analysis of consumption patterns through different migration generations should also be further explored since they could also bring light to analysis of both planned and unplanned strategies of integration and positioning. Things have the ability to bring people together and set people apart. Therefore, migration studies have much to gain in integrating consumption studies and dialoguing with them in order to address most of the main topics of their research agenda.

One can argue that material culture, in general, and the mundane realm of domestic stuff, in particular, constitutes a positive tool to explore, analyse and discuss these two main dimensions all migrations entail. On the one hand, things participate in migrants' experiences and journeys; work as significant resources and/or pose significant obstacles in the challenging task of restarting a life in a new and unfamiliar context; and constitute a powerful tool in the management of transnational relations and positioning strategies. But things, the movements they entail and the ways these intersect with the movements of people, can also work as a significant field of study to frame migration on a broader-scale analysis, that of the global connections that frame contemporary social life.

References

Appadurai, A. (ed.), (1986) *The Social Life of Things*, Cambridge: Cambridge University Press.

Basu, P. and S. Coleman (2008), "Introduction: Migrant Worlds, Material Cultures", *Mobilities*, vol 3, no 3, 313–330.

Bourdieu, P. (1979), *La Distintiction: Critique Sociale to Jugement*, Paris, Minuit.

Brewer, J. and F. Trentmann (2006), *Consuming Cultures, Global Perspectives*, London, Berg.

Burrell, K. (2008), "Managing, Learning and Sending: The Material Lives and Journeys of Polish Women in Britain", *Journal of Material Culture*, vol. 13, no.1, 63–84.

Castles, P. (2010), "Understanding Global Migration: A Social Transformation Perspective", *Journal of Ethnic and Migration Studies*, vol. 36, no. 10, 1565–86.

Douglas, M. and B. Isherwood (1979), *The World of Goods*, London, Routledge.

Feldman-Bianco B. and N. Glick Schiller (2011), "Una Conversación Sobre Transformaciones de la Sociedad, Migración Transnacional y Trayectorias de Vida", *Critica y Emancipación, Revista Latinoamericana de Ciencias Sociales*, vol. 5, no. 1, 9–42.

Glick Schiller, N. (2011), "Localized Neo-liberalism, Multiculturalism, and Global Religion: Exploring the Agency of Migrants and City Boosters", *Economy and Society*, vol. 40, no. 2, 184–210.

Glick Schiller, N., Basch, L. and Szanton, C. (1995), "From Immigrant to Transmigrant: Theorising Transnational Migration", *Anthropological Quarterly*, vol. 68, no. 1, 48–63.

Horst, H. (2011), "Reclaiming Place: The Architecture of Home, Family and Migration,", *Anthropologica*, vol. 53, no. 1, 29–39.

Kopytoff, I. (1986), "The Cultural Biography of Things: Commodisation as Process", in A. Appadurai (ed.) *The Social Life of Things*, Cambridge, Cambridge University Press, 64–91.

Mauss, M. (1924), *The Gift*, London, Cohen and West.

Miller, D. (1987), *Material Culture and Mass Consumption*, Oxford, Blackwell.

Miller, D. (2006), "Consumption", In C. Tilley, W. Keane, S. Kuchler, M. Rowlands, and P. Spyer (eds.) *Handbook of Material Culture*, London, Sage, 341–54.

Miller, D. (2008), "Migration, Material Culture and Tragedy: Four Moments in Caribean Migration", *Mobilities*, vol. 3, no. 3, 397–413.

Miller, D. (2010), *Stuff*, Cambridge, Polity Press.

Mintz, S.W. (1985), *Sweetness and Power: The Place of Sugar in Modern History*. New York, Penguin.

Mullins, P. R. (2011), "The Archaeology of Consumption", *Annual Review of Anthropology*, vol. 40, 133–44.

Parrott, F. (2012), "Materiality, Memories and Emotions: A View on Migration from a Street in South London", In M. Svasek (ed.) *Moving Subjects Moving Objects. Transnationalism, Cultural Production and Emotions*, Oxford, Berghahn Books, 41–54.

Portes, A. and DeWind, J. (2004), "A Cross-Atlantic Dialogue: The Progress of Research and Theory in the Study of International Migration", *International Migration Review*, vol. 38, no. 3, 828–851.

Povrzanović Frykman, M. (2009), "Material Aspects of Transnational Social Fields: An Introduction", *Dve domovini/Two Homelands*, vol. 29, 105–114.

Rosales, M.V. (2010), "The Domestic Work of Consumption: Materiality, Migration and Home Making", *Etnográfica*, vol. 14, no. 3, 507–525.

Rosales, M.V. (2012), "My Umbilical Cord to Goa: Food, Colonialism and Transnational Goan Life Experiences", *Food and Foodways: Explorations in the History and Culture of Human Nourishment*, vol. 20, no. 3–4, 233–256.

Rosales, M.V. (2015), *As coisas da casa: cultura material, migrações e memórias familiares*. Lisboa, ICS. Imprensa de Ciências Sociais.

Svasek. M. (2012), *Moving Subjects Moving Objects: Transnationalism, Cultural Production and Emotions*, Oxford, Berghahn Books.

Vertovec, S. (2007), "Introduction: New Directions in the Anthropology of Migration and Multiculturalism", *Ethnic and Racial Studies*, vol. 6, no. 6, 961–978.

Wilk, R. (2005), "Learning to be local in Belize: global systems of common difference", In Daniel Miller (ed). *Worlds Apart. Modernity through the Prism of the Local*, London, Routledge.

25

Gender, sexuality and consumption

Pauline Maclaran, Cele C. Otnes and Linda Tuncay Zayer

Marketers have long been aware that what we consume shapes our sense of who we are, and that a person's gender and sexuality associations comprise important parts of this identification. Having long treated biological sex as a key demographic variable to apply in market segmentation, marketers also play a major role in the gendering of consumption practices. In particular, activities positioning products and services for target segments – especially advertising – contribute to creating both positive and negative gender and sexuality stereotypes, and sometimes exacerbate sex differences regarding product usage and associations in spurious ways (e.g., creating Bic pens "for women").

The binary thinking typifying modernity privileged the male breadwinner and his production over the female consumer and her consumption. Unlike most other social sciences, marketing has been interested in gendered aspects of consumption since its inception in the 1900s, with (male) marketers typically targeting (female) consumers (Fischer & Bristor, 1994). Practitioners involved in early consumer research sought to open up new markets and more effectively hone marketing communications. When consumer research scholars looked at gender initially, they too tended to equate and essentialise sex differences with gender. In the 1980s, other disciplines (e.g., sociology, anthropology, women's studies) became interested in consumption, specifically focusing on its gendered nature. During the 1990s, scholars within consumer behavior infused these fresh perspectives into studies of the relationships between culture, gender and consumption.

In discussing the evolution of work on gender within consumer research, we focus on two time periods – pre 1990s and post 1990s – and specifically on how feminist perspectives shape the scholarship. We then detail two emerging research areas influencing contemporary debates on gender and consumption: 1) masculinity and consumption, and 2) LGBT consumption.

Pre 1990s

During this period, most consumer behavior research equated biological sex as a proxy variable for gender. Following Veblen (1899), this conflation of sex and gender reflected thinking in sociology and economics about gender roles, positioning men as producers/breadwinners and women as vicarious consumers representing the wealth of men. Drawing heavily from psychology, studies focused on how sex-role norms influenced individual and family decision making (Schneider & Barich-Schneider, 1979; Meyers-Levy, 1988, 1989; Meyers-Levy & Sternthal, 1991), and how gender identity could help researchers understand and predict consumer behavior. Pursuing these topics, scholars relied on Bem's (1974) sex-role inventory (BSRI) and the Personal Attributes Questionnaire (PAQ; see Spence et al., 1975) to measure the extent that people identified with masculine or feminine traits (Palan, 2001). Using either or both of these scales, many studies examined the effects of gender identity across product categories/activities, including cigarette brands (Vitz & Johnston, 1965), hairsprays (Morris & Cundiff, 1971), leisure activities (Gentry & Doering, 1979), food (Kahle & Homer, 1985) and Christmas gift shopping (Fischer & Arnold, 1990). Scholars pursuing the long-dominant information-processing perspective within marketing still rely on these scales to study sex differences and consumer behavior (i.e. Fischer & Dubé, 2005; Dommer & Swaminathan, 2013; Zhang, Feick & Mittal, 2014).

Pre 1990s, one key stream within advertising research was the representation of women. Feminist critiques of advertising from the late 1960s onwards shaped this scholarship (e.g., Grant, 1970). A particular concern for marketers through the 1970s–1980s was whether portrayals adequately reflected women's changing roles in society (Sexton & Haberman, 1974; Belkaoui & Belkaoui, 1976; Wagner & Banos, 1973). One often-cited study is Courtney & Lockeretz's (1971) content analysis of 729 advertisements in general-interest magazines. The authors show women are typically portrayed in non-professional roles, where men are much more likely to be depicted as professionals. They find four stereotypes, still salient in ads today, dominate women's depictions: as wives or mothers; engaged in less serious activities than men; dependent upon men; and objectified as sex objects. Other studies during the 1970s explore the effects of such stereotyping on women's self-image (Leigh, Rethans, & Whitney, 1987) and how such portrayals affect women's purchase intentions (Lundstron & Sciglimpaglia, 1977). In a more applied vein, Whipple and Courtney (1985) advocate adapting role portrayals for different product groups and market segments; e.g., they suggest household goods rely on traditional female-role portrayal, while career-oriented role models may be more effective for beauty products.

During the 1980s, negative stereotypes began to change as advertisers reacted to critiques from feminists and scholars such as the sociologist Erving Goffman, who explored the cultural significance of gender displays in his book *Gender Advertisements* (1976). Goffman revealed stark contrasts in male and female portrayals; men were depicted as confident and in charge, and women were shown as vulnerable and submissive. Similarly, Winship (1987) highlights the work of femininity, whereby women seek to achieve the ideals of beauty portrayed in the media. As Berger (1972, p. 134) puts it, "the publicity image steels a woman's love of herself as she is and offers it back to her for the price of the product". Thus many studies of this period report increasingly occurring depictions of women in professional or social settings (Lysonski, 1983), and more included in voiceovers or as product experts (Ferrante, Haynes and Kingsley, 1988). Still others, however, find that despite a lessening of traditional role portrayals, a concomitant increase occurs in women's portrayal as sex objects (Soley & Kurzbard, 1986).

Overall, research from this period is limited by its confounding of gender with biological sex differences, and its lack of recognition that people's gender identities can comprise a mix of masculine and feminine personality traits. In sum, this research comprises a surfeit of typically uncritical studies on sex-role stereotyping that aided practitioners interested in targeting the "women's movement" as an emerging market niche (Artz & Venkatesh, 1991). So although useful to marketers, this basically a-theoretical research provides little understanding of why gender differences exist, or what causes them (Catterall & Maclaran, 2001). Simply put, the study of gender issues in marketing needed to move beyond "superficial and self-evident inferences" (Artz & Venkatesh, 1991, p. 619).

Post 1990s

With emphasis on the social construction of meaning, the "cultural turn" pervading the social sciences during the 1990s likewise enriched consumer research. New perspectives on buying, having and being drew on sociology and anthropology, eschewing psychology and economics and conceptualizing humans as socially connected, emotional beings rather than merely purchasers who predictably process information. The new "Consumer Culture Theory" paradigm (Arnould & Thompson, 2005) accommodated postmodernism, poststructuralism, feminism and queer theory to offer more critical ways of viewing the relationship between consumption and the market. Overall, these perspectives challenge accepted meanings of gender, distinguishing it from the mere essentialization of male/female sex differences. These critiques deconstruct such universalizing categories, blur boundaries between masculinity and femininity, and argue for more fluid, malleable conceptualizations of gender and sexuality.

Postmodern perspectives expose the gendered nature of much marketing knowledge (Costa, 1991; Fischer & Bristor, 1994; Hirschman, 1993; Joy & Venkatesh, 1994). Through this lens, scholars began to more closely scrutinize the relationship between gender and consumption from a historical perspective. Firat (1991, p. 380) explores how the collapse between categories of sex and gender (male/masculine, female/feminine) in modernity parallels the separation between production (male/masculine) and consumption (female/feminine), and their association with public and private domains, respectively. Fischer and Bristor (1994) analyze the rhetoric of marketing relationships from a poststructuralist feminist perspective, revealing the patriarchal discourse inherent in marketing's construction of the consumer as female. In parallel, Stern and Holbrook (1994) leverage deconstruction theory to challenge the neutrality of advertising texts, while Hirschman (1993) emphasizes the masculinist ideology underpinning articles within the *Journal of Consumer Research*. She highlights how a machine metaphor dominates conceptualizations of the consumer, a theme Joy and Venkatesh echo (1994). These authors further illustrate the power relationships embedded in this metaphor – one built on homo economicus and that privileges mind/cognition over body/emotions. Peñaloza (1996) also suggests leveraging participatory feminist research to gain rich insights and move beyond an information-processing understanding of the consumer.

In the early 1990s, another key scholar pioneered programmatic approaches to gender scholarship. Janeen Costa established the Gender, Marketing and Consumer Research Conference (Costa, 1991), an influential academic consortium that continues to present times. It encouraged participants to plumb new insights on the relationships between gender and consumption through studies that challenge the still-dominant psychological paradigm, while revealing the gendered nature of the quest for objectivity in consumer research itself (Bristor & Fischer, 1991). Frequently using interpretivist methods, scholars broadened the range of topics significantly, exploring their gendered nature such as: symbolism and disposal (Milicic, 1991), possessions across cultures (Costa, 1991), identity as a socio-cultural concept (Venkatesh, 1993), narratives in fashion discourse (Thompson & Haytko, 1996), gay consumers (Kates, 1998), consuming sexuality (Schroeder, 1998), neo-traditional masculinity (Thompson and Holt, 1998), green consumerism (Moisander, 2000), male stereotypes (Otnes, 2000), shopping behaviors by transgender consumers (Hyatt, 2002) and performativity of identity (Schroeder & Borgerson, 2004; Arthur, 2006). Reflecting broader social-scientific debates interwoven with interest in identity politics during the 1990s, this work draws on more sophisticated understandings of gender, and recognizes multiple masculinities and femininities at the intersections of race, ethnicity, class and sexual orientation.

Initially responsible for a deeper critique of gender in consumer research, feminist perspectives became somewhat muted during the 2000s, subsumed into broader research on gender and identity projects, as reflected by the cultural turn (see Maclaran, 2015). A small, steady stream, however, emerged, through two books (Catterall, Maclaran & Stevens, 2000; Scott, 2005) and sporadic critiques. These included Dobscha and Ozanne's (2001) analysis of ecofeminists and their environmental agendas; Bettany and Woodruffe-Burton's (2009) agenda for reflexivity in marketing/consumer research; Brace-Govan's (2010) deconstruction of women's active embodiment in marketing communications, and Stevens, Kearney and Maclaran's (2013) ecofeminist exploration of brand mascots.

Much scholarship in consumer research still conflates biology and gender, emphasizing sex differences in relation to purchase decisions or message reception. Interpretivist studies contribute a much clearer appreciation of the social construction of gender and intertwined complexities with consumption, as Otnes and Tuncay Zayer's (2012) edited collection demonstrates. Furthermore, interest in the area of gender and consumption continues to grow, often at the intersection of sociology and consumer research (see, for example, Casey & Martens, 2007). Apart from the Gender, Marketing and Consumer Behavior Conference, the Macromarketing Conference featured its first gender track in 2014, followed by one in 2015. The Transformative Consumer Research Conference included its first gender track in 2015, exploring linkages between gender issues, social justice and public policy, and outlining what "gender justice" might look like in consumer research. Three special issues on gender in marketing and consumer research journals are in print, in *Consumption, Markets & Culture* (Schroeder, 2003), *Marketing Theory* (Bettany et al., 2010) and the *Journal of Marketing Management* (Arsel, Eraranta & Moisander, 2015). The premier-level publication, the *Journal of Consumer Research*, now boasts several articles exploring interrelationships between gender and consumption (i.e. Holt & Thompson, 2004; Moisio, Arnould & Gentry, 2013; Thompson & Üstüner, 2015), evidence the topic has become more mainstream. Yet as Hearn and Hein (2015) recently observe, much work remains to be done. They point to the absence of interdisciplinary theories on gender from scholarship in marketing/consumer research, including queer theory; material-discursive feminism; and critical race, intersectional and transnational feminisms (e.g., Olesen, 2008; Plummer, 2008).

We now focus on two key areas where post 1990s gender research is growing within consumer behavior, and where much potential exists for future exploration and expansion.

Masculinity

The last two decades have seen a surge of interest in understanding masculinity as it intersects with consumption, advertising, shopping behavior and branding. This new emphasis highlights the shift of men away from their perceived roles as producers to that of consumers (Schroeder and Zwick, 2004). Although not exploring discourses pertaining to gender, earlier studies examine men and consumption in extraordinary contexts, such as modern-day "mountain men" re-enactors (Belk & Costa, 1998) and within male-dominated subcultures (e.g., Schouten & McAlexander's [1995] ethnography of Harley-Davidson riders). As technology and the Internet became an even more salient force in consumers' lives, research also began to highlight the linkages between gender, technology and identity (Adam & Green, 2001) as well as the gendered nature of technology and cyberspace (e.g., Cockburn & Ormrod, 1994; Turkle, 1999).

At the turn of the twentieth century, media, advertising and academics delved into the "new" man and fluid forms of masculinity in society, as exemplified by Mark Simpson's (2002) now-famous essay on metrosexuality on Salon.com. Furthermore, television programs such as *Queer Eye for the Straight Guy* sought to provide heterosexual men with socialization and sensibilities pertaining to fashion, cooking and culture by a team of homosexual professionals. Marketers introduced new products to male audiences to support this new aesthetic (e.g., Procter & Gamble's $90 million introduction of Axe body spray; Neff, 2002). Advertising agencies attempted to capture the essence of the "new" man, through studies such as The Future of Men by Euro RSCG (now Havas) Worldwide. Popular culture proliferated a range of terms to capture ever-changing, popular notions of masculinity – from retrosexual to übersexual, and more recently, lumbersexual.

During the early 2000s, academic research focused on detailing traditionally masculine performances such as risk taking and competition in retail venues (e.g., Sherry et al., [2004] ESPN Zone study). Other scholars began to explore shared cultural spaces, such as male shopping behavior (Otnes & McGrath, 2001; however, see Campbell, 1997 for earlier discussion) and fashion (Frith & Glesson, 2004).

In 2004, Holt and Thompson focused on everyday consumption contexts as they relate to masculinity, putting forth the "man-of-action hero" ideal. They claim that this identity allowed men to resolve a dialectical tension between the traditional breadwinner ideal and its confinement within corporate bureaucracy, and the rebel, which touts a careless, free lifestyle. Nearly ten years later, Moisio, Arnould, and Gentry (2013) critique the generality of the man-of-action hero ideal by examining domestic masculinity along class lines within the do-it-yourself, home-improvement context. The authors advocate for a model which asserts that the masculine ideals influencing men's identity work are "class and identity-conflict bound" (2013, p. 300). Other scholarly work also focuses on capturing alternate expressions of masculinity (see Littlefield's [2010] and Littlefield and Ozanne's [2011] studies on hunters; Chen's [2012] work on the rise of soushokukei danshi in Japan; Modrak's [2015] study on urban woodmen).

Fatherhood enters the research spotlight through a series of studies attempting to capture the cultural tenor of shifting gender roles. Harrison, Gentry, and Commuri (2012) explore the consumption roles of single fathers, Coskuner-Balli and Thompson (2013) probe the lifestyles of stay-at-home dads, and Marshall et al. (2014) analyze how magazine ads depict fathers. Scholars also further unpack traditionally feminized domains, such as men's consumption and shopping behavior related to fashion and grooming (Tuncay & Otnes, 2008), their consumption of lingerie (Ourahmoune, 2012) and men's domestic foodwork (Klasson & Ulver, 2015). Importantly, this research illuminates the tensions coloring men's consumption practices as they negotiate their identities in the marketplace. Furthermore, some studies identify forms of cultural capital (e.g., Coskuner-Balli & Thompson, 2013) and examine a diverse range of masculinities.

Other research, mostly in the domain of media and advertising, attempts to capture masculine discourses in television (e.g., Zayer, Sredl, Parmentier & Coleman, 2012) and in fashion blogs and ads (Ostberg's [2010] study on gendered body-size ideals), even identifying a "male gaze" – extending earlier research conceptualizing how readers scrutinize women in ads, or the focus of attention from women models in ads (Patterson & Elliot, 2002). Cross-cultural studies investigate masculinity and femininity by seeking to understand cultural values across countries (e.g., Albers-Miller & Gelb, 1996; Chang, 2006; Nelson & Paek, 2008). Following Bettany et al.'s (2010, p. 17) call that "it is imperative that research moving forward continues to address equality and social justice issues for all genders", some researchers adopt a more critical tone in examining men/masculinities. Gentry and Harrison (2010) detail the lack of diversity in gender portrayals in advertising, while Zayer and Otnes (2012) outline men's responses to gender ideals, including experiencing feelings of vulnerability. Recent work also illuminates how stereotypical notions of gender and vulnerability regarding male and female audiences influence how some executives craft strategic/creative advertising decisions (Zayer & Coleman, 2015). Despite some of this recent critical work, some scholars note that power relations and dynamics are neglected in studies of men and masculinity (Hearn & Hein, 2015).

LGBT consumption

Fugate (1993) offers an early academic assertion of the practical and intellectual potential of understanding the LGBT market. Not surprisingly, recent inroads by gay-rights movements and the estimated buying power of LGBT consumers ($750–$900 billion in the US alone; Packaged Facts, 2010) is extending gender research into more "intersectional" topics, reflecting the complex impact of multiple social categories on identity (e.g., race, gender, sexuality; Gopaldas & Fischer, 2012). Compared to research on heterosexual masculinity, LGBT-consumption research remains relatively sporadic and dispersed across disciplines, due in part to the damper on scholarship associated with the AIDS crisis (Sender, 2002). Furthermore, the LGBT acronym implies scholars pay attention to four distinct sexual orientations, when in fact most focuses on the marketplace behavior of gay men, since the first edited volume on the topic (Wardlow, 1996). Kates follows his book on this segment (1998) with articles exploring the contested nature of the gay men's consumer subculture (Kates, 2002), and how gay men help brands achieve marketplace legitimacy (Kates, 2004). Some studies scrutinize specialized aspects of gay men's consumption, especially participation in cultural rituals (Newman & Nelson, 1996; Kates & Belk, 2001; Otnes & Pleck, 2003).

One research stream explores how advertising and other media (e.g., film; Ingraham, 1999) portrays gay men, women and most recently, gay families. Tsai's (2010) ideological textual analysis of ads articulates the stereotypes of gay and lesbian advertising characters. Other studies examine the portrayal of gay and lesbian characters through consumers' eyes, noting positive/negative attitudes toward homosexual ad characters are reflected in positive/negative attitudes toward portrayed products (Hester & Gibson, 2007), or that consumers sometimes ignore signals of gay portrayals, often interpreting characters as straight (Borgerson et al., 2006).

Another recent research stream explores LGBT consumers' usage of potentially harmful products (e.g., cigarettes, drugs). These studies assert that the stress associated with stigmatized and often closeted sexual identities contributes to substance-abuse levels among LGBTs that greatly exceed those of straight consumers (Stevens, Carlson & Hinman, 2004; Cochran, Peavy & Robohm, 2007; Heck, Flentje, &Cochran, 2011). Although located within public-health journals, this work is relevant to the Transformative Consumer Research movement, which shares advocacy-focused goals of enhancing consumer well-being and guiding social-justice policies. One recognition of the TCR interest in these issues is the recent inclusion of two articles about LGBT consumption in the *Journal of Public Policy & Marketing* (Hildebrand et al., 2013; Oakenfull, 2013).

With respect to transgender consumers (Griggs, 1998; Hyatt, 2002), research on this topic is just beginning to emerge, although coverage of (among others) Caitlyn Jenner's transition should spur interest. Extant studies focus on how transgender consumers cope with their ensuing vulnerability and stigmatization due to their increased social visibility (McKeage, Crosby & Rittenberg, 2015; Rowe & Rowe, 2015).

LGBT consumption is a key area for future research on gender, sexuality and consumption. It could benefit from an expanded research agenda – one extending beyond the rather narrow focus on how advertising and the media portray LGBT characters in the media. Instead, a reinvigorated agenda could build on earlier work exploring how LGBT consumers cope with stigma, discrimination and identity issues, integrating the interests of academics and policy-makers in public health, transformative consumer research, consumer culture theory, consumer psychology and applied marketing (e.g., LGBT consumers and stigmatization during service encounters; Ro & Olson, 2014).

Another key area for future research is in relation to feminism, now heralded as being in its fourth wave. Feminist perspectives are particularly relevant in order to bring a stronger critique of how consumption intersects with other social categories (race, class and so forth) to enable the enactment of different masculinities and femininities in the marketplace.

References

Adam, E., & Green, A. (2001). *Virtual Gender: Technology Consumption and Identity*. London: Routledge.

Albers-Miller, N. D., & Gelb, B. D. (1996). Business advertising appeals as a mirror of cultural dimensions: A study of eleven countries. *Journal of Advertising*, 25(4), 57–70.

Arnould, E. J., & Thompson, C. J. (2005). Consumer culture theory (CCT): Twenty years of research. *Journal of Consumer Research*, 31(4), 868–882.

Arsel, Z., Eraranta, K., & Moisander, J. (2015). Introduction: Theorizing gender and gendering theory in marketing and consumer research. *Journal of Marketing Management*, 31(15–16), 1553–1558.

Arthur, D. (2006). Hip Hop consumption and masculinity. In L. Stevens & J. Borgerson (Eds.), *Gender, Marketing and Consumer Behavior* 8 (p. 12). Edinburgh, Scotland: Association for Consumer Research.

Artz, N. & Venkatesh, A. (1991). Gender representation in advertising. In R. H. Holman & M. R. Solomon (Eds.), *Advances in Consumer Research* 18 (pp. 618–623). Provo, UT: Association for Consumer Research.

Belk, R. W. & Costa, J. A. (1998). The mountain man myth: A contemporary consuming fantasy. *Journal of Consumer Research*, 25(3), 218–240.

Belkaoui, A., & Belkaoui, J. (1976). A comparative analysis of the roles portrayed by women in print advertisements: 1958, 1970, 1972. *Journal of Marketing Research*, 12(2), 168–172.

Bem, S. L. (1974). The measurement of psychological androgyny. *Journal of Consulting and Clinical Psychology*, 42(2), 155–162.

Berger, J. (1972). *Ways of Seeing*. London: Penguin.

Bettany, S., Dobscha, S., O'Malley, L., & Prothero, A. (2010). Moving beyond binary opposition: Exploring the tapestry of gender in consumer research and marketing. *Marketing Theory*, 10(3), 3–28.

Bettany, S., & Woodruffe-Burton, H. (2009). Working the limits of method: The possibilities of critical reflexive practice in marketing and consumer research. *Journal of Marketing Management*, 12(7–8), 661–679.

Borgerson, J., Schroeder, J. E., Blomberg, B., & Thorssén, E. (2006). The gay family in the ad: Consumer responses to non-traditional families in marketing communications. *Journal of Marketing Management*, 22(9–10), 955–978.

Brace-Govan, J. (2010). Representations of women's active embodiment and men's ritualized visibility in sport. *Marketing Theory*, 10(4), 369–396.

Bristor, J. M., & Fischer, E. (1991). Objectivity and gender in consumer research: A feminist deconstructionist critique. In J. A. Costa (Ed.), *Gender, Marketing and Consumer Behavior Volume 1* (pp. 115–123). Salt Lake City, UT: Association for Consumer Research.

Campbell, C. (1997). Shopping, pleasure and the sex war. In Falk, P. & Campbell, C. (Eds.), *The Shopping Experience* (pp. 166–176), Thousand Oaks, CA: Sage.

Casey, E., & Martens L. (2007). *Gender and Consumption: Domestic Cultures and the Commercialisation of Everyday Life*. London: Ashgate Pub Co.

Catterall, M., & Maclaran, P. (2001). Gender perspectives in consumer behavior: An overview and future directions. *The Marketing Review*, 2(4), 405–425.

Catterall, M., Maclaran, P., & Stevens, L. (2000). *Marketing and Feminism*. London: Routledge.

Chang, C. (2006). Cultural masculinity/femininity influences on advertising appeals. *Journal of Advertising Research*, 46(3), 315–323.

Chen, S. (2012). The rise of Soushokukei Danshi masculinty and consumption in contemporary Japan. In Otnes, C. & Tuncay Zayer, L. (Eds.), *Gender, Culture, and Consumer Behavior* (pp. 285–310). New York: Routledge.

Cochran, B. N., Peavy, K. M., & Robohm, J. S. (2007). Do specialized services exist for LGBT individuals seeking treatment for substance misuse? A study of available treatment programs. *Substance Use & Misuse*, 42(1), 161–176.

Cockburn, C., & Ormrod, S. (1994). *Gender and Technology in the Making*. London: Sage.

Coskuner-Balli, G., & Thompson, C. J. (2013). The status costs of subordinate cultural capital: At-home fathers' collective pursuit of cultural legitimacy through capitalizing consumption practices. *Journal of Consumer Research*, 40(1), 19–41.

Costa, J. A. (1991). *Proceedings of the First Conference on Gender, Marketing and Consumer Behavior*. Salt Lake City: University of Utah Printing Service.

Courtney, A. E., & Lockeretz, S. W. (1971). A woman's place: An analysis of the roles portrayed by women in magazine advertisements. *Journal of Marketing Research*, 8(1), 92–95.

Dobscha, S.,& Ozanne, J. L. (2001). An ecofeminist analysis of environmentally sensitive women using qualitative methodology: The emancipatory potential of an ecological life. *Journal of Public Policy & Marketing*, 20(2), 201–214.

Dommer, S. L., & Swaminathan, V. (2013). Explaining the endowment effect through ownership: The role of identity, gender, and self-threat. *Journal of Consumer Research*, 39(5), 1034–1050.

Ferrante, C. L., Haynes, A. M., & Kingsley, S. (1988). Images of women in television advertising. *Journal of Broadcasting and Electronic Media*, 32(2), 231–237.

Firat, A. F. (1991). The consumer in postmodernity. In R. H. Holman, & M. R. Solomon, (Eds.), *Advances in Consumer Research* 18 (pp. 70–76), Provo, UT: Association for Consumer Rearch.

Fischer, E., & Arnold, S. J. (1990). More than a labor of love: gender roles and Christmas gift shopping. *Journal of Consumer Research*, 17(3): 333–345.

Fischer, E., & Bristor, J. (1994). A feminist poststructuralist analysis of the rhetoric of marketing relationships. *International Journal of Research in Marketing*, 11(4), 317–331.

Fischer, R. J., & Dubé, L. (2005). Gender differences in responses to emotional advertising: A social desirability perspective. *Journal of Consumer Research*, 31(4), 850–858.

Frith, H., & Gleeson, K. (2004). Clothing and embodiment: Men managing body image and appearance. *Psychology of Men & Masculinity*, 5(1), 40–48.

Fugate, D. L. (1993). Evaluating the US male homosexual and lesbian population as viable target market segment: Review with implications. *Journal of Consumer Marketing*, 10(4), 46–57.

Gentry, J. W., & Doering, M. (1979). Sex role orientation and leisure. *Journal of Leisure Research*, 11(2), 102–111.

Gentry, J. W., & Harrison, R. (2010). Is advertising a barrier to male movement toward gender change? *Marketing Theory*, 10(1), 74–96.

Goffman, E. (1976). *Gender Advertisements*. Cambridge, MA: Harvard University Press.

Gopaldas, A., & Fischer, E. (2012). Beyond gender: Intersectionality, culture, and consumer behaviour. In C. Otnes & L. Tuncay Zayer (Eds.), *Gender, Culture, and Consumer Behavior* (pp. 393–410). New York: Routledge.

Grant, D. (1970). Women's libs fume at 'insulting ads': ad gals unruffled. *Advertising Age*, 44(27), 1.

Griggs, C. (1998). *S/he: Changing sex and Changing Clothes*. New York: Berg.

Harrison, R. L., Gentry, J., & Commuri, S. (2012). A grounded theory of transition to involved parenting: the role of household production and consumption in the lives of single fathers. In C. Otnes & L. Tuncay Zayer (Eds.), *Gender, Culture, and Consumer Behavior* (pp. 337–367). New York: Routledge.

Hearn, J., & Hein, W. (2015). Reframing gender and feminist knowledge construction in marketing and consumer research: missing feminisms and the case of men and masculinities. *Journal of Marketing Management*, 31(15–16), 1–55.

Heck, N. C., Flentje, A., & Cochran, B. N. (2011). Offsetting risks: High-school gay-straight alliances and lesbian, gay, bisexual, and transgender (LGBT) youth. *School Psychology Quarterly*, 26(2), 161–174.

Hester, J. B., & Gibson, R. (2007). Consumer responses to gay-themed imagery in advertising. *Advertising & Society Review* 8(2), Advertising Educational Foundation. Project Muse. Retrieved October 29, 2016.

Hildebrand, D., DeMotta, Y., Sen, S., & Kongsompong, K. (2013). In-group and out-group influences on the consumption behavior of minority groups: the case of gay men. *Journal of Public Policy & Marketing*, 32(special issue), 70–78.

Hirschman, E. C. (1993). Ideology in consumer research 1980 and 1990: A Marxist and feminist critique. *Journal of Consumer Research*, 19(4), 537–555.

Holt, D. B., & Thompson, C. J. (2004). Man-of-action heroes: the pursuit of heroic masculinity in everyday consumption. *Journal of Consumer Research*, 31(2), 425–440.

Hyatt, E. M. (2002). An exploratory investigation of the shopping behavior of female-to-male consumers: Before, during, and after transition. In P. Maclaran & E. Tissiers-Desbordes (Eds.), *Gender, Marketing and Consumer Behavior* 6 (pp. 323–336). Paris: Association for Consumer Research.

Ingraham, C. (1999). *White Weddings: Romancing Heterosexuality in Popular Culture*. New York: Routledge.

Joy, A., & Venkatesh, A. (1994). Postmodernism, feminism, and the body: The visible and the invisible in consumer research. *International Journal of Research in Marketing*, 11(4), 333–357.

Kahle, L. R., & Homer, P. (1985). Androgny and midday mastication: Do real men eat quiche? In E. C. Hirschman & M. B. Holbrook (Eds.), *Advances in Consumer Research*, 12 (pp. 242–246). Ann Arbor, MI: Association for Consumer Research.

Kates, S. M. (1998). *Twenty Million New Customers! Understanding Gay Men's Consumer Behavior.* New York: Harrington Park.

Kates, S. M. (2002). The protean quality of subcultural consumption: An ethnographic account of gay consumers. *Journal of Consumer Research*, 29(3), 383–399.

Kates, S. M. (2004). The dynamics of brand legitimacy: An interpretive study in the gay men's community. *Journal of Consumer Research*, 31(2), 455–464.

Kates, S. M., & Belk, R. W. (2001). The meanings of lesbian and gay pride day. *Journal of Contemporary Ethnography*, 30(4), 392–429.

Klasson, M., & Ulver, S. (2015). Masculinising domesticity: an investigation of men's domestic foodwork. *Journal of Marketing Management*, 31(15–16), 1652–1675.

Leigh, T. W., Rethans, A. J., & Whitney, T. R. (1987). Role portrayals of women in advertising: cognitive responses and advertising effectiveness. *Journal of Advertising Research*, 27(5), 54–63.

Littlefield, J. (2010). Men on the hunt: Ecofeminist insights into masculinity. *Marketing Theory*, 10(1), 97–117.

Littlefield, J., & Ozanne, J. L. (2011). Socialization into consumer culture: Hunters learning to be men. *Consumption, Markets & Culture*, 14(4), 333–360.

Lundstron, W. J., & Sciglimpaglia D. (1977). Sex role portrayals in advertising. *Journal of Marketing*, 41(3), 72–79.

Lysonski, S. (1983). Female and male portrayals in magazine advertisements: A re-examination. *Akron Business and Economic Review*, 14(3), 45–50.

Maclaran, Pauline (2015). Feminism's fourth wave: a research agenda for marketing and consumer research. *Journal of Marketing Management*, 31(15–16), 1732–1738.

Marshall, D., Davis, T., Hogg, M., Schneider, T., Petersen, A. (2014). From overt provider to invisible presence: Discursive shifts in advertising portrayals of the father in Good Housekeeping, 1950–2010. *Journal of Marketing Management*, 30(15–16), 1654–1679.

McKeage, K., Crosby, E., & Rittenberg, T. (2015). *Living in a Gender-Binary World: Implications for a Revised Model of Consumer Vulnerability.* Working paper: department of marketing, Saint Paul, MN: Hamline University.

Meyers-Levy, J. (1988). The influence of sex roles on judgement. *Journal of Consumer Research*, 14(4), 522–530.

Meyers-Levy, J. (1989). Gender differences in information processing: A selectivity interpretation. In P. Cafferata & A. Tybout (Eds.), *Cognitive and Affective Responses to Advertising* (pp. 219–260), Lexington, MA: Lexington.

Meyers-Levy, J., & Sternthal, B. (1991). Gender differences in the uses of message cues and judgments. *Journal of Marketing Research*, 28(1), 84–96.

Milicic, B. (1991). Consumption and conservation: Disposal and gender in a Mediterranean community. In J. A. Costa (Ed.), *Gender, Marketing and Consumer Behavior Volume 1* (pp. 277–283), Salt Lake City, UT: Association for Consumer Research.

Modrak, R. (2015). Learning to talk like an urban woodsman: An artistic intervention. Consumption. *Markets & Culture*, 18(6), 539–558.

Moisander, J. (2000). Gender and green consumerism: Analyzing a case of domestication of women: The green-cleaners of the planet. In C. Otnes & J. Schroeder (Eds.), *Gender, Marketing and Consumer Behavior* 5 (pp. 193–204). Urbana, IL: Association for Consumer Research.

Moisio, R., Arnould, E. J., & Gentry, J. W. (2013). Productive consumption in the class-mediated construction of domestic masculinity: Do-it-yourself (DIY) home improvement in men's identity work. *Journal of Consumer Research*, 40(2), 298–316.

Morris, G. P., & Cundiff, E. W. (1971). Acceptance by males of feminine products. *Journal of Marketing Research*, 8, 372–374.

Neff, J. (2002). P&G shores up Old Spice with body-wash extension. *Advertising Age*, 73(51), 8.

Nelson, M. R., & Paek, H. J. (2008). Nudity of female and male models in primetime TV advertising across seven countries. *International Journal of Advertising*, 27(5), 715–744.

Newman Jr., P. J., & Nelson, M. R. (1996). Mainstream legitimization of homosexual men through Valentine's Day gift-giving and consumption rituals. *Journal of Homosexuality*, 31(1–2), 57–69.

Oakenfull, G. W. (2013). What matters: Factors influencing gay consumers' evaluations of "gay-friendly" corporate activities. *Journal of Public Policy & Marketing* 32(special issue), 79–89.

Olesen.V. L. (2008). Early millennial feminist qualitative research. In N. Denzin & Y. S. Lincoln (Eds.), *The Landscape of Qualitative Research* (pp. 311–370). Los Angeles, CA: Sage.

Ostberg, J. (2010). Thou shalt sport a banana in thy pocket: Gendered body size ideals in advertising and popular culture. *Marketing Theory*, 10(1), 45–73.

Otnes, C. (2000). Beyond the stereotypes of male consumption. In C. Otnes & J. Schroeder (Eds.), *Gender, Marketing and Consumer Behavior*, 5 (pp. 101–102). Urbana, IL: Association for Consumer Research.

Otnes, C., & McGrath, M. (2001). Perceptions and realities of male shopping behavior. *Journal of Retailing*, 77(1), 111–137.

Otnes, C., & Pleck, E. (2003). *Cinderella Dreams: The Allure of the Lavish Wedding*. Berkeley, CA: University of California Press.

Otnes, C., & Tuncay Zayer, L. (2012). *Gender, Culture and Consumer Behavior*. New York: Routledge.

Ourahmoune, N. (2012). Masculinity, intimacy, and consumption. In C. Otnes & L. T. Zayer (Eds.), *Gender, Culture, and Consumer Behavior* (pp. 311–335). New York, NY: Routledge.

Packaged Facts (2010). *The Gay and Lesbian Market. 6 ed.*, http://www.packagedfacts.com/Gay-Lesbian-2690458/

Palan, K. M. (2001). Gender identity in consumer behavior research: A literature review and research agenda. *Academy of Marketing Science Review*, 1(10), 1–25.

Patterson, M., & Elliott, R. (2002). Negotiating masculinities: Advertising and the inversion of the male gaze. *Consumption, Markets & Culture*, 5(3), 231–249.

Peñaloza, L. M. (1996). We're here, we're queer, and we're going shopping! *Journal of Homosexuality*, 31(1–2), 9–41.

Plummer, K. (2008). Critical humanism and queer theory. In N. Denzin & Y. S. Lincoln (Eds.), *The Landscape of Qualitative Research* (pp. 477–499), Los Angeles, CA: Sage.

Ro, H., & Olson, E. (2014). The effects of social justice and stigma-consciousness on gay consumers' service-recovery evaluation. *Journal of Business Research*, 67(6), 1162–1169.

Rowe, S., & Rowe, D. (2015). The politics of in/appropriate/d Others: Moving beyond the vulnerable consumer in the LBGT market/movement. In C. Schultz II, R. Benton & O. Kravets (Eds.), *Proceedings of the 40th Macromarketing Conference* (pp. 736–739), Chicago: Quinlan School of Business.

Schneider, K. C., & Barich-Schneider, S. (1979). Trends in sex roles in television commercials. *Journal of Marketing*, 43(4), 79–84.

Scott, L. (2005). *Fresh Lipstick: Redressing Fashion and Feminism*. New York: Palgrave Macmillen.

Schouten, J. W., & McAlexander, J. H. (1995). Subcultures of consumption: An ethnography of the new bikers. *Journal of Consumer Research*, 22(June), 43–61.

Schroeder, J. E. (1998). Consuming sexuality: A case study in identity marketing. In E. Fischer & D. Wardlow (Eds.), *Gender, Marketing and Consumer Behavior Volume 4* (pp. 27–40), San Francisco, CA: Association for Consumer Research.

Schroeder, J. E. (2003). Guest Editor's Introduction: Consumption, Gender and Identity. *Consumption, Markets & Culture*, 6(1), 1–4.

Schroeder, J. E., & Borgerson, J. (2004). Judith Butler, gender theorist: Philosophical and phenomenological insights into marketing and consumer behavior. In L. Scott & C. J. Thompson (Eds.), *Gender, Marketing and Consumer Behavior*, 7 (pp. 1–7), Madison, WI: Association for Consumer Research.

Schroeder, J. E., & Zwick, D. (2004). Mirrors of masculinity: Representation and identity in advertising images. *Consumption Markets & Culture*, 7(1), 21–52.

Sender, K. (2002). *Business, Not Politics: Gays, Lesbians, Bisexuals, Transgender People and the Consumer Sphere*. Commissioned paper for the Gay & Lesbian Alliance Against Defamation, Philadelphia: Annenberg School of Communications.

Sexton, D., & Haberman, P. (1974). Women in magazine advertisements. *Journal of Advertising Research*, 14(4), 41–46.

Sherry, J. F., Kozinets, R.V., Duhachek, A., DeBerry-Spence, B., Nuttavuthisit, K., & Storm, D. (2004). Gendered behavior in a male preserve: Role playing at ESPN Zone Chicago. *Journal of Consumer Psychology*, 14(1,2), 151.

Simpson, M. (2002). *Meet the Metrosexual*, http://www.salon.com/2002/07/22/metrosexual/, July 22.

Soley, L., & Kurzbard, G. (1986). Sex in advertising: A comparison of 1964 and 1984 magazine advertisements. *Journal of Advertising*, 15(3), 46–54.

Spence, J. X., Helmreich, R., & Stapp, J. (1975). Ratings of self and peers on sex role attributes and their relation to self-esteem and conceptions of masculinity and femininity. *Journal of Personality and Social Psychology*, 32(1), 29–39.

Stern, B. B., & Holbrook, M. B. (1994). Gender and genre in the interpretation of advertising text. In J. A. Costa (Ed.), *Gender Issues and Consumer Behavior* (pp. 11–47). Thousand Oaks, CA: Sage.

Stevens, L., Kearney, M., & Maclaran, P. (2013). Uddering the other: Androcentrism, ecofeminism, and the dark side of anthropomorphic marketing. *Journal of Marketing Management*, 29(1–2), 158–174.

Stevens, P., Carlson, L. M., & Hinman, J. M. (2004). An analysis of tobacco industry marketing to lesbian, gay, bisexual and transgender (LGBT) populations: Strategies for mainstream tobacco control and prevention. *Health Promotion Practice*, 5(3), 129S–134S.

Thompson, C. J., & Haytko, D. L. (1996). Narratives of "gendering": Poststructural analysis of consumers' fashion discourse and the negotiation of gender boundaries. In J. A. Costa (Ed.), *Gender, Marketing and Consumer Behavior Volume 3* (pp. 93–94). Salt Lake City, UT: Association for Consumer Research.

Thompson, C. J., & Holt, D. B. (1998). Consuming patriarchy: Consumption practices and the gender project of neo-traditional masculinity. In E. Fischer & D. Wardlow (Eds.), *Gender, Marketing and Consumer Behavior*, 4 (pp. 3–4), San Francisco, CA: Association for Consumer Research.

Thompson, C. J., & Üstüner, T. (2015). Women skating on the edge: Marketplace performances as ideological edgework. *Journal of Consumer Research*, 42(2), 235–265.

Tsai, W.-H. S. (2010). Assimilating the queers: Representations of gay men, bisexual and transgender people in mainstream advertising. *Advertising & Society Review*, 11(1), Advertising Educational Foundation. Project Muse. Retrieved October 29, 2016.

Tuncay, L., & Otnes, C. (2008). The use of Persuasion management strategies by identity-vulnerable consumers: The case of urban hetereosexual male shoppers. *Journal of Retailing*, 84(4), 487–499.

Turkle, S. (1999). *Liberating Cyberspace: Civil Liberties, Human Rights and the Internet*. London: Pluto Press.

Veblen, T. (1899). *The Theory of the Leisure Class: An Economic Study of Institutions*. New York: MacMillan.

Venkatesh, A. (1993). Gender identity in a socio-cultural construction Indian context of the female consumer. In J. A. Costa (Ed.), *Gender, Marketing and Consumer Behavior Volume 2* (pp. 119–132), Salt Lake City, UT: Association for Consumer Research.

Vitz, P. C., & Johnston, D. (1965). Masculinity of smokers and the masculinity of cigarette images. *Journal of Applied Psychology*, 49(3), 155–165.

Wagner, L., & Banos, J. (1973). A woman's place: A follow-up analysis of the roles portrayed by women in magazine advertisements. *Journal of Marketing Research*, 10(5), 213–214.

Wardlow, D., (Ed.) (1996/2014). *Gays, Lesbians, and Consumer Behavior: Theory, Practice, and Research Issues*. London: Routledge.

Whipple, W. T., & Courtney, A. E. (1985). Female Role Portrayals in Advertising and Communication Effectiveness: A Review. *Journal of Advertising*, 14(3), 4-8 and 17.

Winship, J. (1987). *Inside Women's Magazines*. London: Pandora.

Zayer, L. T., Coleman, C. (2005). Advertising professionals' perceptions of the impact of gender portrayals on men and women: A question of ethics? *Journal of Advertising*, 44(3), 264–275.

Zayer, L. T., & Otnes, C. C. (2012). Climbing the ladder or chasing a dream? Men's responses to idealized portrayals of masculinity in advertising. In C. Otnes & L. T. Zayer (Eds.), *Gender, Culture, and Consumer Behavior* (pp. 87–110). New York, NY: Routledge.

Zayer, L. T., Sredl, K., Parmentier, M., & Coleman, C. (2012). Consumption and gender identity in popular media: Discourses of domesticity, authenticity, and sexuality. *Consumption Markets & Culture*, 15(4), 333–357.

Zhang, Y., Feick, L., & Mittal, V. (2014). How males and females differ in their likelihood of transmitting negative word of mouth. *Journal of Consumer Research*, 40(6), 1097–1108.

26

Children as consumers

David Buckingham and Vebjørg Tingstad

Commercial marketing to children is by no means a new phenomenon. Indeed, historical studies show that children have been a key focus of interest at least since the inception of modern mass marketing (e.g. Cook, 2004; Cross, 1997; Denisoff, 2008; Jacobson, 2004). Nevertheless, in recent years, children have become increasingly important both as a market in their own right, as decision-makers within their families and as a means to reach adult markets. Marketers are targeting children more directly and at an ever-younger age; and they are using a much wider range of techniques that go well beyond conventional advertising.

Marketers often claim that children are becoming 'empowered' in this new commercial environment: the market is seen to be responding to needs and desires on the part of children that have hitherto been largely ignored or marginalized, not least because of the social dominance of adults. However, critics have expressed growing concern about the apparent 'commercialization' of childhood. Publications, press reports and campaigns have addressed what are seen to be the damaging effects of commercial influences on children's physical and mental health. Far from being 'empowered', children are typically seen here as victims of a powerful, highly manipulative form of consumer culture, producing needs, desires and 'materialistic' values that are almost impossible for them to escape or resist.

In this chapter, we aim to provide a critical account of contemporary debates about children and consumer culture. Most of the public concern we have described, and much of the academic research, relates primarily to children under the age of 12–13, with a particular focus on those in the 'tween' age group (roughly 7–12). We suggest that the terms of these debates are limited and problematic, in ways that reflect continuing difficulties in our conceptions of childhood. The debate about children's consumption rehearses binary views of children – as either agents or victims – and conflates important conceptual distinctions that need to be maintained. We also argue that these views of children fail to address the ways in which consumer culture itself is currently developing and changing. The more ubiquitous and 'participatory' techniques that are now being used by commercial companies reflect a new construction of the child consumer, which in turn requires us to rethink the terms of the debate, and some of the basic assumptions of consumer culture theory.

Children as consumers: Public debates

In the early years of the twentieth century, just as children were coming to be recognized as a distinct and special group, as innocent and in need of careful protection (Zelizer, 1985), they were also being seen as a potential market in their own right. Buying products especially for children became a way for parents to display values of care and 'good parenting'. Yet consumer culture also became a domain in which adults began to experience growing concerns about a loss of authority and control (Cross, 2004). This historical ambivalence has continued to inform debates at the start of the twenty-first century.

In the wake of Naomi Klein's influential *No Logo* (2001), there has been a flurry of popular critical publications about children and consumer culture: prominent examples include Susan Linn's *Consuming Kids* (2004), Dan Acuff and Robert Reiher's *Kidnapped* (2005) and Ed Mayo and Agnes Nairn's *Consumer Kids* (2009). The arguments in these publications are, by and large, far from new. One can look back to similar arguments being made in the 1970s, for example by groups like Action for Children's Television in the United States (Hendershot, 1998), or to announcements of the 'death of childhood' that have regularly recurred throughout the past two centuries (e.g. Postman, 1983). Even so, there now seems to be a renewed sense of urgency in these claims.

Such books typically presume that children used to live in an essentially non-commercial world, a kind of idyllic 'golden age'. Many of them link the issue of consumerism with other well-known concerns about media and childhood: as well as turning children into premature consumers, the media are accused of promoting sex and violence, obesity, drugs and alcohol, gender stereotypes and false values, and taking children away from other activities that are deemed to be more worthwhile. This is a familiar litany, which tends to conflate very different kinds of effects and influences. It constructs the child as innocent, helpless and unable to resist the power of the media. Thus, these texts describe children as being bombarded, assaulted, even subjected to 'saturation bombing' by the media: they are being seduced, manipulated, exploited, brainwashed, programmed and branded. And the predictable solution here is for parents to engage in counter-propaganda, to censor their children's use of media, or simply keep them locked away from corrupting commercial influences. These books rarely include the voices of children, or try to take account of their perspectives: this is essentially a discourse generated by adults *on behalf of* children.

Meanwhile, there has been a parallel growth in marketing discourse specifically focused on children. Again, there is a long history of this kind of material. As Dan Cook (2004) and Lisa Jacobson (2004) have shown, the early decades of the twentieth century saw marketers increasingly addressing children directly, rather than their parents. In the process, they made efforts to understand the child's perspective, and began to construct the child as a kind of authority, not least by means of market research. In recent years, however, this kind of marketing discourse has proliferated, most notably in relation to the newly-identified category of the 'tween', whose age can range anywhere between 7–8 to 12–13 (Cook & Kaiser, 2004). Examples here would include Gene del Vecchio's *Creating Ever Cool* (1997) and Anne Sutherland and Beth Thompson's *Kidfluence* (2003); although perhaps the most influential account is Martin Lindstrom and Patricia Seybold's *Brandchild* (2003), which is the basis of a major consultancy business that has effectively become a brand in its own right.

The most striking contrast between these accounts and those of the critics of consumer culture is their very different construction of the child consumer. The child is seen here as sophisticated, demanding and hard-to-please. Tweens, we are told, are not easily manipulated: they are an elusive, even fickle market, sceptical about the claims of advertisers, and discerning when it comes to getting value for money – and they need considerable effort to understand and to capture. Of course, given the political pressure that currently surrounds the issue of marketing to children (most notably around so-called 'junk food'), marketers are bound to argue that advertising has very little effect, and that children are 'wise consumers'. Yet this idea of the child as sovereign consumer often elides with the idea of the child as a citizen, or an autonomous social actor, and with the notion of children's rights; and it is often accompanied by a kind of 'anti-adultism' – an approach that is very apparent, for example, in the marketing of the global children's television channel Nickelodeon (Banet-Weiser, 2007).

Perspectives on consumer culture

These contrasting views of consumption are also played out in academic theories and debates. On the one hand, we have accounts that see consumerism as a kind of betrayal of fundamental human values. This argument stands in a long tradition of critical theory, from Adorno and Marcuse (and indeed more conservative critics like F.R. Leavis and Ortega y Gasset) through to contemporary authors such as Zygmunt Bauman (2007) and Benjamin Barber (2007).

On the other hand, there are accounts that emphasise the agency of consumers – that is, their ability to define their own meanings and pleasures, and to exercise power and control. Such accounts were particularly prominent in 'postmodernist' cultural studies at the beginning of the 1990s (e.g. Fiske, 1990, Featherstone, 1991), although they have arguably resurfaced with some more celebratory accounts of media fandom and so-called 'participatory culture' (Jenkins, 2006). Far from being passive dupes of the market, consumers are regarded here as active and autonomous, and commodities are seen to have multiple possible meanings, which consumers can select, use and rework for their own purposes. In appropriating the 'symbolic resources' they find in the marketplace, consumers are engaging in a productive and self-conscious process of creating an individual 'lifestyle' and constructing or 'fashioning' their identities. In the process, they are seen to be evading or resisting the control of what Fiske (1990) calls 'the power bloc'.

We have admittedly sketched these debates in somewhat stark and exaggerated terms here. Nevertheless, there is a clear polarization in accounts of consumer culture – and specifically of children as consumers – that replays a much wider polarization within the human sciences more broadly, between structure and agency. In relation to children, this typically results in a stand-off between two diametrically opposed views of children: the child as innocent victim versus the child as competent social actor. On the one hand, we have the call to protect children from exploitation and manipulation; and on the other, the call to extend their rights to self-determination and autonomy. This is an ambiguity that is also reflected in the UN Convention on the Rights of the Child (UNCRC). In relation to children's consumption, it leads to a series of binary oppositions that tend to dominate the debate. Are children active or passive consumers? Are they knowledgeable or innocent, competent or incompetent, powerful or powerless?

Later in this chapter, we will discuss some of the more theoretical problems with this debate, and point to some possible means of moving beyond what has become a kind of conceptual *impasse*. In some respects, the persistence of these problems reflects a continuing – and perhaps irreconcilable – tension between structure and agency that is characteristic of the human and social sciences much more broadly. However, we also want to suggest that popular criticisms of advertising and marketing fail to take account of the ways in which the children's market itself is changing. These changes reflect an apparently different way of conceiving of, or constructing, the child consumer; and this in turn means that we need to develop different theories and methodologies for research. New developments in the children's market, new techniques and marketing strategies, and new discourses about the child consumer seem to make redundant or problematic the binary oppositions we have outlined above, and require us to ask some new questions, which allow us to study child consumers in a wider context. Criticizing polarized views of consumption as either a capitulation to the industrial forces of corporate marketing or an act of resistance and cultural creativity, Pugh (2009) offers a 'third way' of viewing consumption, seeing it as part of children's meaning-making that borrows from but does not merely replicate corporate-made culture.

Children: A growing but uncertain market

From a marketing perspective, children are generally seen to play three main roles. They are an increasingly significant market in their own right through spending their own disposable income, gained from gifts and part-time work as well as regular allowances. However, they are also an important means of reaching adults: the influence that children exert on adults' purchases is more economically significant than what they buy themselves, and can inform choices of holidays, cars, new technology and other expensive goods. Thirdly, they are seen as a future market – a 'market potential' – with whom companies wish to establish relationships and loyalties that they hope will be carried through into adulthood (McNeal, 1999).

Nevertheless, the children's market is significantly more volatile and uncertain than adult markets. The failure rate for new products is much higher here than in the adult market (McNeal, 1999; Tingstad, 2012), and while enormous amounts of money can undoubtedly be made from successful brands and product ranges, there is also a high degree of risk. The unpredictable rise and fall of 'crazes' such as Pokémon or Ninja Turtles is a phenomenon that companies find hard to manage or predict.

One approach that marketers have used in attempting to manage risk in the children's market is segmentation, for instance in terms of age or gender. Yet even these differences may prove complex to manage. For example, segmenting children into a series of niche markets defined by age means that new products can be sold at different stages, while others are cast off or 'outgrown'; and the history of children's marketing has seen the ongoing construction of new age-defined categories such as 'toddlers', 'teenagers' and most recently 'tweens' (Cook, 2004). Yet children do not always 'act their age', or want the goods that appear to be targeted at them. In addition, the more segmented markets are, the smaller they become. The logic here points towards globalization: smaller national markets can be amassed into much larger markets if they are targeted on a global scale – although this in turn requires products to be produced for global rather than national consumption, which itself requires difficult calculations about cultural specificity (Buckingham, 2007). Many international companies are changing their brand portfolios so consumers can find the brands under the same name in multiple countries with generally similar and centrally coordinated marketing strategies (Steenkamp & de Jong, 2010). In order to succeed, companies typically pursue ways of 'localizing' global offerings that reflect local cultural preferences while simultaneously taking advantage of global economies of scale (Tobin, 2004).

Knowing consumers?

The increasing risks and uncertainties of the children's market place a new premium on knowledge. Marketers can never be sure that they can fully 'know' children or predict their behavior. As a result, a thriving research business has grown up around the children's market, which now seeks to access children's perspectives directly, rather than merely those of their parents. These 'commercial epistemologies' (Cook, 2000) often draw on the creative and ethnographic tools for accessing children's 'voice' developed within academic disciplines such as anthropology and cultural studies.

For example, in the practice known as 'cool hunting', young people may be recruited as 'consultants' (Tingstad, 2010) to supply their own views on products and advertisements, or employed to track trends among their peer groups. For example, Dubit, a UK-based youth research company, has a website aimed at young people that pays them to answer surveys about new ad campaigns, technologies or products, alongside chat and games. Digital media also provide new means of gathering and accessing data about consumer behavior. The practice of 'data mining' involves the gathering, aggregation and analysis of data about consumers, either based on their responses to online requests or questionnaires or (more covertly) through the use of 'cookies' that track their movements online. Such practices are widely used in social networking sites and online worlds, not only in online shopping or commercially branded sites. In these ways, the media that are often celebrated for their ability to 'empower' consumers also provide powerful means of surveillance.

Research companies operating in this market typically claim to offer privileged insights into the views and perspectives of young people. Their research is often aligned with the rhetoric of 'empowerment' identified above: young people are frequently described as self-determining, autonomous and innately 'savvy' in their dealings with the commercial world. Children, we are told, want to be in control, to be 'listened to, heard, respected and understood': they must not be patronized. They can recognize when advertisers are trying to manipulate them, and while they are quick to adopt new trends, they are also quick to move on. As such, they are extremely powerful and influential consumers: 'they get what they want when they want it' (Sutherland & Thompson, 2003). This new rhetoric of the competent, powerful child consumer is also aligned with a familiar discourse about young people and technology. Children are represented as 'digital natives', who are 'born with a mouse in their hands', as Lindstrom and Seybold (2003) put it. As such, it is argued, they can best be reached through these new kinds of 'participatory' techniques.

Yet while their methods and discourses might appear relatively innovative and in line with contemporary images of childhood, the theories on which such companies draw to explain young people are often much more traditional: Maslow's 'hierarchy of needs' and Piagetian developmental psychology are frequently cited, along with pop psychology and simplistic theories of generational change. For all the emphasis on novelty, marketers are also advised to address needs that are seen as somehow timeless and innate – needs for mastery, stability, fantasy, romance and rebellion and so on. Children at different ages are seen to be 'looking for an identity', seeking 'to identify with a role model', beginning 'to develop and understand their personal power in the world' or seeking 'power, freedom, fun and belonging' – assertions that seem to do little more than rehearse common-sense platitudes about childhood (see also Siegel, Coffey & Livingston, 2001).

New techniques, new questions

These new approaches are often invoked in justifying the need for new marketing techniques, especially those that involve digital media. Conventional advertising (for example, on television) is in decline, as marketers seek to employ new methods such as viral advertising, 'advergaming', peer-to-peer marketing and social networking. In many respects, these developments can be seen to represent a much more general paradigm shift in consumer culture, away from a 'mass marketing' model towards one that is significantly more pervasive, more personalized and more participatory.

These new approaches undoubtedly raise new ethical questions. Regulations that apply to advertising in 'old' media do not yet apply online, or to these more pervasive forms of marketing.

Many new marketing techniques, like product placement, blur the boundaries between promotional messages and other content, making it possible to embed advertising in contexts where it is less likely to be recognized as such. Online marketing often entails the gathering, aggregation and use of personal data about consumers without them necessarily being aware that this is taking place; and children may also be encouraged or required to provide personal information about others, for example parents or friends, without their knowledge, raising significant concerns about privacy (see Buckingham, 2007; Livingstone, 2006; Nairn & Monkgol, 2007).

These issues in turn raise new questions about children's understanding of commercial motivations and practices, and more broadly about their competence as consumers. Research suggests that children can understand the commercial intentions of conventional advertising from a fairly young age, but much less is known about their understanding of these new practices. There are justified concerns here, particularly about privacy and the potential for deception, yet the issues raised also go beyond questions about children's competence, or lack of it. Children (or indeed adults) may be more or less knowledgeable about such techniques, but that knowledge in itself does not necessarily confer the power to resist them. It is entirely possible that people might be active and sophisticated users of media, but might nevertheless still be influenced – or indeed that an *illusion* of autonomy and choice might be one of the pre-requisites of contemporary consumer culture. Yet *activity* is not necessarily the same thing as *agency*. The paradox of contemporary marketing is that it is bound to construct children as active, desiring and autonomous, and in some respects as resisting the imperatives of adults, while simultaneously seeking to make them behave in particular ways.

As such, it is positively misleading to see this in terms of a simple *opposition* between structure and agency, or as a kind of 'zero-sum game', in which more of one automatically means less of the other. Structure requires agency, but agency only works through structure: each, in this sense, actively produces the other. To this extent, easy oppositions of the kind with which we began – between active and passive, knowledgeable and innocent, competent and incompetent, powerful and powerless – are no longer useful. We need to look beyond such binary thinking, towards a more complex and critical understanding of children's consumer practices and participation, including seemingly children-and-youth-led 'authentic' content production which might be heavily commercialized and seemingly independent, yet the boundaries are very blurry.

Consumption out of context

The other recurring problem with this polarized debate is its tendency to displace attention away from other possible causes of the phenomena that are at stake. This arises largely because children's consumption is removed from the social contexts in which it occurs – and indeed which it helps to produce. Much of the research in this area focuses on children's responses to advertising – especially television advertising – rather than on other aspects of marketing or of consumption. A great deal of it is also concerned with purchasing behaviour, and relatively little with how children appropriate and use products in their everyday lives and in their peer-to-peer relationships. As such, this work focuses on a relatively narrow aspect of the broader nexus of production, distribution, circulation and consumption.

Much of the research in this field has been conducted by psychologists, working within two main traditions: media effects and consumer socialization. Both approaches have been widely challenged on methodological grounds, which do not need to be rehearsed here. More significant in this context are the theoretical and political problems of these approaches. Effects research is self-evidently premised on a view of children's relationship with media as a matter of cause and effect. A classic behaviorist perspective conceives of this process in terms of stimulus and response – of which the most obvious example would be imitation. From this perspective, television advertising would be seen to produce direct effects on viewers – not only in terms of purchasing behavior, but also in terms of attitudes and values. More sophisticated exponents of this approach posit the existence of 'intervening variables' (both individual differences and social factors) that come between the stimulus and the response and thereby mediate any potential effects, although the basic 'cause-and-effect' model continues to apply.

By contrast, consumer socialization research tends to draw on frameworks from developmental psychology in proposing a sequence of 'ages and stages' in maturation (John, 1999; McNeal, 2007). From this perspective, children's development as consumers is related to the development of more general cognitive skills and capacities, such as the ability to process information, to understand others' perspectives, to think and reflect in more abstract ways, and to take account of multiple factors that might be at play in decision-making. Influenced by parents and peers, as well as media and marketing, children's consumer behavior is seen to become gradually more autonomous, consistent and rational. While this approach might appear more child-centered, it tends to lead to a 'deficit model' of the ways in which children understand, interpret and act upon their world: they are seen simply in terms of what they lack. In common with developmental psychology more broadly, this approach also neglects the emotional and symbolic aspects of consumer behavior, in favor of cognitive or intellectual ones. By and large, children are not seen here as social actors: as sociologists of childhood would have it, they are seen not as *beings*, but only as *becomings* (cf. Qvortrup, 1991, Lee, 2001).

Critics of this approach argue that a more socio-cultural account of consumer socialization is required. Karin Ekström (2006), for example, proposes that consumer socialization is an ongoing, lifelong process, rather than something that is effectively concluded at the point of entry to adulthood; that it varies among different social and cultural groups, and over time; and that it involves different life experiences and contexts of consumption. As such, there can be no single definition of what counts as a 'competent' consumer. Ekström also argues that children should be seen as active participants in the process of socialization, not as passive recipients of external influences. Likewise, Dan Cook (2010) proposes that the notion of socialization should be replaced by the notion of 'enculturation', which he suggests would help to move beyond the normative, monolithic approach of consumer socialization research. He argues that children are already implicated in consumer culture from before the point of birth; and that rather than seeking to assess children's knowledge in the abstract, we need to consider how that knowledge is used (or not used) in everyday social practice. Learning to consume is seen here not as a matter of one-way transmission from parent to child, but on the contrary as a process of negotiation involving diverse social agents, in which multiple meanings are in play.

Dominant approaches based on media effects also feed into the familiar political game of 'blaming the media'. For example, there is a growing tendency in many countries to blame marketers and advertisers for the apparent rise in childhood obesity, and this is an issue that is also becoming an increasing preoccupation for researchers (see Buckingham, 2009a, b). Yet there may be many other complex reasons for this phenomenon. In fact, poor people are most at risk of obesity – and this clearly has something to do with the availability and price of fresh food, and the time that is available to people to shop and prepare their own meals. The rise of obesity might also be related to the rise of 'car culture', the fact that children (at least in some countries) are now much less independently mobile, and the increasing privatization of public leisure facilities. As with debates about media violence, blaming the media allows politicians to displace attention away from other potential causes, while also being seen to be 'doing something' about the problem.

Consumption in context

Our key point here is that it makes little sense to abstract children's relationship with advertising, or their consumer behavior, from the broader social and historical context. Indeed, the distinction between consumption and the 'context' in which it occurs may itself be misleading: it might be more appropriate to regard consumption as a form of *social practice*, and as a dimension of other social practices, which collectively *construct* 'contexts' within specific societies. In a capitalist society, almost all our social activities and relationships are embedded within economic relations. The children's market works through and with the family, the peer group and – increasingly – the school. We need to address how consumption practices are carried out in these different settings, how they help to define the settings themselves, and how they are implicated in the management of power, time and space. We also need to investigate how consumption is situated in practices of everyday life, politics, history and the markets, and address the complexities and contradictions in the ways in which consumption negotiates values (Sparrman, Sandin & Sjöberg, 2012; Sparrman, 2015). In the process, we need to move beyond the notion of the consumer as a self-contained individual, and beyond individualistic notions of desire, identity and lifestyle, to focus instead on relationships and reciprocity.

Johansson (2010) points to Actor Network Theory as an alternative to this individualistic view, by virtue of its emphasis on connections, networks and flows. Agency is seen here, not as a possession of the individual, but rather as something that is exercised in specific situations and events, and via 'assemblages' of human and non-human actors (including objects, artefacts and texts, as well as people). In our view, this approach has much in common with the 'circuit of culture' that is characteristic of cultural studies (see Buckingham, 2008), not least in that it moves beyond the dichotomy of structure and agency: power is not seen to lie either with consumers or with producers, but precisely in the interrelationships between them.

Anthropological and sociological studies of childhood have for some years begun to address these dynamics in other areas of children's lives (see Qvortrup, Corsaro & Sebastian-Honig, 2009); and in some studies, this approach been applied to children and parents' everyday consumption practices as well (see Martens et al., 2004). This work addresses central questions to do with the construction of childhood identities and the wider 'generational order', drawing on the sociology of childhood as well as on cultural studies and on anthropological studies of 'material culture' (see Buckingham & Tingstad, 2010; Buckingham, 2011; Lee & Motzkau, 2011).

One particular focus of interest here is how consumption produces and sustains hierarchies of status and authority in children's peer groups. Thus, some research shows how children's clothing purchases can be a site of anxiety about status and belonging as well as of play and creativity (Boden, Pole, Pilcher & Edwards, 2004). Other studies point to the operations of status and power in online spaces such as virtual-world games and social networks, where more participatory forms of advertising and cross-promotional marketing have developed (Willett, 2015). To what extent does knowledge of consumer culture function as a kind of cultural (or subcultural) capital for children in these contexts? How do the hierarchies of taste and 'cool' within the peer group relate to the hierarchies within adult culture (for example, of class, ethnicity or gender)? How might such hierarchies work with or against the imperatives of consumer culture (for example, by rendering the 'cool' uncool overnight)? How do we interpret the anti-consumerist rhetoric of some forms of youth culture – and the ways in which it has been appropriated for the purposes of so-called 'ethical' consumption?

Other studies have addressed the experience of young people who are excluded from peer group culture because of their lack of access to consumer goods (e.g. Chin, 2001; Croghan, Griffin, Hunter & Phoenix, 2006). Not all consumers are equally able to participate, since participation depends not just on one's creativity but also on one's access to material resources: the market is not a neutral mechanism, and the marketized provision of goods and services may exacerbate existing inequalities. In this context, it is particularly important to understand the consumption practices of children in disadvantaged communities, for whom 'consumer choice' may be a fraught and complex matter. While many children may be able to access some aspects of the goods that become the *lingua franca* of children's culture – for instance, by being part of the audience for the advertising that surrounds them – their experience of the actual products is likely to vary widely with material purchasing power. Elizabeth Chin's work (2001) on poor African-American children usefully challenges the idea that less-wealthy children are somehow more at risk from the seductions of consumer culture, exploring how their strikingly altruistic consumption practices – during a shopping trip she arranged as part of the research – are embedded within their social and familial relationships. Pugh (2009) introduces the concept of dignity to illustrate how very few families in her study, lower or upper income, were able to eschew their children's dignity for other priorities.

Conclusion

Children's involvement in consumer culture is a profoundly ambivalent phenomenon. Of course, there is always an economic 'bottom line': the global child market is a significant source of commercial profit – although, as we have argued, profit is by no means easy or straightforward to secure. On the other hand, the meanings and pleasures that consumer culture affords children – and the roles that it can play in the formation of childhood identities – are significantly more difficult to predict. The market clearly does have a considerable power to determine the meanings and pleasures that are available to children, but children themselves also play a key role in creating those meanings and pleasures, and they may define and appropriate them in very diverse ways. Despite the often melodramatic claims of campaigners and the generalized optimism of the marketers, the outcomes of children's increasing immersion in consumer culture are by no means the same for all. Seeing this in terms of a simple opposition between structure and agency is inadequate, especially in the changing context of contemporary consumer culture. The invisible and missing child in consumer research that Cook described more than ten years ago (Cook, 2007; Tingstad, 2007) is still a relevant criticism, given the fact that children's consumer culture seems to be moving rapidly toward an individualized niche marketing and brand and technology focus in multimedia formats (Chan, 2013). We undoubtedly need more adequate theoretical approaches, but we also need to account for the specificity of children's consumption practices in relation to various social contexts and circumstances of their daily lives (Gram, 2011; Tingstad, 2009; Jones & Reid, 2010), their participation in online networks (Willett, 2015; Jenkins, Ito & Boyd, 2016), the relations between global and local marketing, the ethics in marketing strategies towards children, and ways in which market relations may systematically favor already-affluent consumers above those who have fewer economic resources.

Note: This chapter includes material previously published in Buckingham (2011).

References

Acuff, D.S. & Reiher, R.H. (2005). *Kidnapped: How Irresponsible Marketers are Stealing the Minds of Your Children* Chicago: Dearborn.

Banet-Weiser, S. (2007). *Kids Rule! Nickelodeon and Consumer-Citizenship* Durham, NC: Duke University Press.

Barber, B. (2007). *Consumed: How Markets Corrupt Children, Infantilize Adults, and Swallow Citizens Whole* New York: Norton.

Bauman, Z. (2007). *Consuming Life* Cambridge: Polity.

Boden, S., Pole, C., Pilcher, J., & Edwards, T. (2004). New consumers: the social and cultural significance of children's fashion consumption. *Working Papers: Cultures of Consumption Series* 16.

Buckingham, D. (2007). Childhood in the age of global media. *Children's Geographies* 5(1–2): 43–54.

Buckingham, D. (2008). Children and media: a Cultural Studies approach. Drotner, K. & Livingstone, S. (eds.) *Handbook of Children, Media and Culture* London: Sage, 219–236.

Buckingham, D. (2009a). The appliance of science: the role of research in the making of regulatory policy on children and food advertising in the UK. *International Journal of Cultural Policy* 15(2): 201–215.

Buckingham, D. (2009b). Beyond the competent consumer: the role of media literacy in the making of regulatory policy on children and food advertising in the UK. *International Journal of Cultural Policy* 15(2): 217–230.

Buckingham, D. (2011). *The Material Child: Growing Up in Consumer Culture* Cambridge: Polity.

Buckingham, D. & Tingstad, V. (eds.) (2010). *Childhood and Consumer Culture* London: Palgrave Macmillan.

Buckingham, D., Whiteman, N., Willett, R., & Burn, A. (2007) *The Impact of the Media on Children and Young People* (review of the literature prepared for the DCSF Byron Review), at http://www.dcsf.gov.uk/byronreview/ (Annex G).

Chan, K. (2013). Children and consumer culture. Lemish, D. (ed.) *The Routledge Handbook of Children, Adolescents and Media Studies* (pp. 141–147), Oxon, UK: Routledge.

Chin, E. (2001). *Purchasing Power: Black Kids and American Consumer Culture*, Minnesota: University of Minnesota Press.

Cook, D.T. (2000). The other "child study": figuring children as consumers in market research. 1910s-1990s' *Sociological Quarterly* 41(3): 487–507.

Cook, D.T. (2004). *The Commodification of Childhood: The Children's Clothing Industry and the Rise of the Child Consumer*, Durham, NC: Duke University Press.

Cook, D.T. (2007). The disempowering empowerment of children's consumer "choice": cultural discourses of the child consumer in North America. *Society and Business Review* 2(1): 37–52.

Cook, D.T. (2010). Commercial enculturation: moving beyond consumer socialization. Buckingham, D. & Tingstad, V. (eds.) *Childhood and Consumer Culture* (pp 63–80), London: Palgrave Macmillan.

Cook, D.T. & Kaiser, S.B. (2004). Betwixt and between. Age ambiguity and the sexualization of the female consuming subject. *Journal of Consumer Culture* 4(2): 203–227.

Croghan, R., Griffin, C., Hunter, J. & Phoenix, A. (2006). Style failure: consumption, identity and social exclusion. *Journal of Youth Studies* 9(4): 463–478.

Cross, G. (1997). *Kids' Stuff: Toys and the Changing World of American Childhood.* Cambridge, MA: Harvard University Press.

Cross, G. (2004). *The Cute and the Cool*, New York: Oxford University Press.

Del Vecchio, G. (1997). *Creating Ever-Cool* Louisiana: Pelican.

Denisoff, C. (ed.) (2008). *The Nineteenth-Century Child and Consumer Culture* Aldershot: Ashgate.

Ekström, K. (2006). Consumer socialization revisited. Belk, R.W. (ed.) *Research in Consumer Behavior, 10* (pp. 71–98), Oxford: Elsevier.

Featherstone, M. (1991). *Consumer Culture and Postmodernism* London: Sage.

Fiske, J. (1990). *Understanding Popular Culture* London: Unwin Hyman.

Gram, M. (2011). Approaching children in experience advertising: Danish amusement parks 1969–2008. *Young Consumers* 12(1), 53–65.

Hendershot, H. (1998). *Saturday Morning Censors: Television Regulation Before the V-Chip.* Durham, NC: Duke University Press.

Jacobson, L. (2004). *Raising Consumers: Children and the American Mass Market in the Early Twentieth Century* New York: Columbia University Press.

Jenkins. H. (2006). *Convergence Culture* New York: New York University.

Jenkins, H., Ito, M. & Boyd, D. (2016). *Participatory Culture in a Networked Era* Cambridge: Polity Press.

Johansson, B. (2010). Subjectivities of the child consumer: beings and becomings'. Buckingham, D. & Tingstad, V. (eds.) *Childhood and Consumer Culture* London: Palgrave Macmillan.

John, D.R. (1999). Consumer socialization of children: a retrospective look at twenty-five years of research. *Journal of Consumer Research* 26(3): 183–213.

Jones, S.C. & Reid, A. (2010). Marketing to children and teens on Australian food company web sites. *Young Consumers* 11(1): 57–66.

Klein, N. (2001). *No Logo* London: Flamingo.

Lee, N. (2001). *Childhood and Society: Growing Up in an Age of Uncertainty* Buckingham: Open University Press.

Lee, N. & Motzkau, J. (2011). Navigating the bio-politics of childhood, *Childhood* 18(1): 7–19.

Lindstrom, M. & Seybold, E. (2003). *BrandChild* London and Sterling VA: Kogan Page.

Linn, S. (2004). *Consuming Kids* New York: Anchor Books.

Livingstone, S. (2006). Children's privacy online. R. Kraut, M. Brynin, & S. Kiesler (eds.) *Computers, Phones and the Internet* New York: Oxford University Press, 128–144.

Martens, L., Southerton, D. & Scott, S. (2004) Bringing children (and parents) into the sociology of consumption. *Journal of Consumer Culture* 4(2): 155–182.

Mayo, E. & Nairn, A. (2009). *Consumer Kids: How Big Business Is Grooming Our Children for Profit* London: Constable.

McNeal, J.U. (1999). *The Kids' Market: Myths and Realities* New York: Paramount.

McNeal, J.U. (2007). *On Becoming a Consumer: Development of Consumer Behavior Patterns in Childhood* Burlington, MA: Butterworth-Heinemann.

Nairn, A. & Monkgol, D. (2007). Children and privacy online. *Journal of Direct, Data and Digital Marketing Practice* 8: 294–308.

Postman, N. (1983). *The Disappearance of Childhood* London: W.H. Allen.

Pugh, A. (2009). *Longing and Belonging. Parents, Children, and Consumer Culture* Berkeley: University California Press.

Qvortrup, J. (1991.) Childhood as a social phenomenon – an introduction to a series of national reports. *Eurosocial* 36: 1–43.

Qvortrup, J., Corsaro, W. & Sebastian-Honig, M. (eds.) (2009). *The Palgrave Handbook of Childhood Studies* London: Palgrave.

Siegel, D.L., Coffey, T.J. & Livingston, G. (2001). *The Great Tween Buying Machine: Marketing to Today's Tweens* Ithaca, NY: Paramount Market Publishing.

Sparrman, A. (2015). Children's consumer culture. Cook, D.T. & Ryan, J.M. *The Wiley-Blackwell Encyclopedia of Consumption and Consumer Studies*. London: Wiley-Blackwell. http://eu.wiley.com/WileyCDA/WileyTitle/productCd-0470672846.html.

Sparrman, A., Sandin, B. & Sjöberg, J. (eds.) (2012). *Situating Child Consumption: Rethinking Values and Notions of Children, Childhood and Consumption* Lund: Nordic Academic Press.

Steenkamp, J.-B. E.M. & de Jong, M.G. (2010). A global investigation into the constellation of consumer attitudes toward global and local products. *Journal of Marketing* 74: 18–40.

Sutherland, A. & Thompson, B. (2003). *Kidfluence: The Marketer's Guide to Understanding and Reaching Generation Y* New York: McGraw Hill.

Tingstad, V. (2007). "Now it's up to you!" Children consuming commercial television. *Society and Business Review* 2(1): 15–36.

Tingstad, V. (2009). Discourses on child obesity and TV advertising in the context of the Norwegian welfare state. James, A., Kjørholt, A.T. & Tingstad, V. *Childhood, Food And Identity in Everyday Life* (pp. 172–191), London: Palgrave.

Tingstad, V. (2010). *Barndom under lupen. Å vokse opp i en foranderlig mediekultur.* (Exploring Childhood – Growing up in a Changing Media Culture) Oslo: Cappelen Akademisk 2nd edition.

Tingstad, V. (2012). Watching without voting: Norwegian child audiences questioning Idol's ethos Zwaan, K. & de Bruin, J.(eds.) *Adapting Idols: Authenticity, Identity and Performance in a Global Television Format* (pp. 195–206), London: Ashgate.

Tobin, J. (2004). *Picachu's Global Adventure* Durham, NC: Duke University Press.

Willett, R. (2015). Consumer literacies and virtual world games. *The Routledge Handbook of Literary Studies*, 382–395.

Zelizer, V. (1985). *Pricing the Priceless Child: The Changing Social Value of Children* New York: Basic Books.

27
Youth and generations in consumption

Terhi-Anna Wilska

Introduction

Young people's value as consumers increased rapidly in all Western consumer societies during the period after World War II. In post-socialist countries and emerging economies, young people's importance as consumers has grown particularly in the 1990s and 2000s, mainly due to the increase in middle-class standards of living, rising levels of education, increasing leisure time, and expanding markets of new technology (see chapters 12, 13, 14; Gbadamosi [ed.], 2016; Goodman [ed.] 2008; Li & Rainieri, 2010; Yin, 2005). Regardless of young people's usually limited economic resources and currently disadvantageous position in the labor market in many Western countries, especially in Europe, (e.g. Côté, 2014; de Lange, Gesthuizen & Wolbers, 2014), young people are still undoubtedly an important consumer group.

The public talk about youth in consumer society tells us a lot about the relative social, political, cultural and economic positions of different generations, as well as of the values of the generations who are in power. It also reflects the culture and traditions of the society, including consumer culture. Young people have always been seen as the vanguard of modernity and novelty: a group that first adapts new trends and innovations. The importance of youth in consumption in today's societies also lies in the phenomenon that youth itself has become a consumable item. In the commercial world and consumer market, youth and youthfulness are default characteristics of ideal lifestyles (Klein, 1999; Miles, 2000; Wyn & White, 1997). In consumer society, even adulthood and old age are evaluated by determinants associated with youth, such as vitality, flexibility, health, beauty, innovativeness, self-expression, openness to experiences, and mental growth and self-evaluation. This development has been accelerated in the recent consumer trends that value health and fitness and pursue youthful body and mind, regardless of age (see chapter 34; Sassatelli, 2010; Smith Maguire, 2008).

The cultural hegemony of youth in consumption and marketing is not a new phenomenon, though. Already in the 1980s, researchers noted that the age boundaries were becoming blurred in Western societies, as the post-war Baby Boomer generation entered middle age. This resulted in the idealization of youth and to the artificial expansion of the boundaries of youth, whereby the whole adult population must believe in its rejuvenation. Concepts such as *cognitive* or *subjective* age were invented to substitute chronological age. Subjective age was determined by one's individual physical feelings, appearance, and satisfaction with life (Featherstone & Hepworth, 1990). This illusion of eternal youth was also used in marketing and advertising. Consequently, the consumption styles of the middle aged began to resemble the youth consumption styles, particularly in fashion and leisure time (Baethge, 1989; Barak & Schiffman, 1981; Featherstone, 1991; Schiffman & Sherman, 1991; Lury, 1996). Along with this phenomenon, the transition to adulthood got delayed in the late 1980s and early 1990s, mainly due to economic recession in many countries (Côté & Allahar, 1996; Jones, 1995; Jones & Wallace, 1992; Wilska, 1999), and this situation seems to have become more or less permanent (e.g. Côté, 2014). The rejuvenation of adulthood also gradually affected the boundaries of childhood and youth. In the late 1990s and early 2000s, the lower boundaries of youth were stretched into childhood and a new market segment of "tweens" discovered (Quart, 2002; see also chapter 26).

As a result of more and more obscure boundaries between age categories, depending on the context, the definition of young people and youth is not straightforward. Most literature on the consumption of young people categorizes young people between the ages of 13–19. Particularly in studies focusing on the independent consumption and economic subsistence of young people, the upper limit of youth has been extended to the age of 30 or even higher. What is characteristic to the definition of "young consumer" is usually the unsettled life situation or at least semi-dependent life course stage (not yet permanently in labor market or having family and children). However, although the economic and social position of young people has varied across time periods and cultures, the symbolic value of youth in consumption seems to be rather salient.

In this chapter, I will first highlight some of the main perspectives of the research on youth, generations, and consumption. Then I will focus on the development of young people's position in Western consumer societies and also in the research on youth and consumption. After that I will analyze the ever-influential generational approach to the research on consumption and youth, also focusing on the way generational values and attitudes are seen as passing on to the next generation. Finally, I will discuss the new and emerging research perspectives and methods in the studies of young people and consumption.

Main perspectives of research on youth and consumption

In academic research, young people's importance as consumers has been explained from several perspectives in different disciplines, mainly in sociology, psychology, cultural studies, communication, marketing, and economics. The emphasis and significance of the approaches have varied over time. Psychologically oriented explanations stress the role of life course stages and physical and mental development in the formation of consumption patterns. Socio-cultural explanations often refer to *consumer generations*, pointing out the importance of the youth in the formation of generational values that affect consumption styles through the whole life. In current consumer research, these explanations are often intertwined.

The *psycho-social* and *developmental* perspectives particularly emphasize the connection between young people's mental and physical development and economic behavior in the transition to adulthood. In teenage and early adulthood, the increasing independence in teenage years, moving away from the parental home, participating in higher education, entering working life, forming a relationship and setting up a family, are all associated with economic resources and the use of them (e.g. Elder & Shanahan, 2007; Ranta, Chow & Salmela-Aro, 2013). The *economic socialization* perspective focuses on the development of economic agency in youth: learning the practices and principles of consumption and economic behavior in family and society (e.g. Gunter & Furnham, 1998). In marketing research, the impact of peer group influence on young people's economic socialization as well as the intra-family power relations in consumption decisions have been in focus for several decades (Dotson & Hyatt, 2005; Moschis & Moore, 1980).

The *social identity perspective*, which has been especially popular in sociology, focuses on young people's identity creation processes and changing social and economic roles in society. In teenage years and early adulthood young people become independent consumers and producers, and the role of different social communities is crucial in this process. Importantly, most transitions and related rites of passages on the way to adulthood contain certain kinds of consumption, thereby building young people's individual and social identities. In addition to the peer groups' influence, the general social and cultural changes in consumer society are regarded as crucial in the formation of young people's consumer identities (Furlong & Cartmel, 1997; Griffin, 1997; Miles, 2000; Wyn & White, 1997).

The *socio-cultural perspective* that dates back to the 1960s and 1970s sees young people's consumption as a manifestation of youth cultures and subcultures (e.g. Hebdige, 1979). In the 1990s and 2000s, along with the globalization of consumer markets and fragmenting lifestyles in the new millennium, the mainstream consumption styles in different cultural contexts are better acknowledged when explaining young people's consumption. The youth cultures of today are arguably revolving around specific consumption patterns and brands (e.g. Aledin, 2009; Quart, 2002; McCullough, Steward & Lovegreen, 2006), including "non-consumption" and sustainable consumption ideologies, such as shared economy communities (see e.g. chapter 9). Recently, revolutionized by the digitalization of consumption and the expansion of social media, the formation of consumption and brand-oriented subcultures of youth have taken new forms and arenas (see chapter 40).

Young people in consumer society over time

In the Western world, the key period in the formation of youth consumption was the decades after the World War II, the 1950s and 1960s, a period of a rapid economic growth and cultural change. In both the US and Britain, young people were discovered as an attractive consumer group already in the 1930s–1940s (Quart, 2002; Cook, 2004), but only after the war and the following economic boom were young people able to earn and use substantial amounts of their own money and thereby become independent consumers. More importantly, young people were able to spend money during their leisure time and thereby special youth markets were created (Miles, 2000; Osgerby, 1998). Mark Abrams's *Teenage Consumer* (1959) was among the first studies on the consumption of young people, but young people as consumers did not attract researchers yet, as young people's social and economic power in society was not yet established.

The post-war decades from the 1950s to the 1970s created youth sub-cultures that were characterized by specific music genres and clothing styles. In the 1950s and 1960s, the youth cultures were portrayed as "spectacular" in mass media (Miles, 2000) and represented the strengthening economic and cultural position in society. Young people were acknowledged as a consumer generation with distinctive lifestyle and consumption features.

In the 1970s, according to the popular Birmingham School interpretation (e.g. Hebdige, 1979; Clarke, Hall, Jefferson, & Roberts, 1976; Willis, 1977, 1990), the sub-cultures emerged to resist the hegemonic mainstream cultures. The interpretations of the Birmingham School also underlined the oppressed position of working-class youth in particular, and thus portrayed youth cultures in less idealistic and more objective ways. The role of consumption was incorporated in visual ways of resisting authorities, such as bricolage and recontextualization of objects (Miles, 2000). However, although youth cultures received a lot of attention in cultural studies research, consumption was still not regarded as a special interest in the research, but the interpretations mainly focused on class differences and generational tensions.

In the 1980s and 1990s, young people's significance as consumers was truly acknowledged, not only by marketers, but also by researchers in marketing and social sciences. During the economic boom in the Western world in the 1980s, the economic power of young adults, in particular, increased, along with the image of consumption-oriented, ambitious "yuppies" (e.g. Belk, 1986; Hammond, 1986), but the importance of fragmenting teenage youth cultures was fading (e.g. Förnäs & Bolin [eds.], 1995). The expansion of consumer culture and youth market as well as the global commercialization of lifestyles utilized the symbolic value of youth, which was also easily associated with the general image of a consumer in the postmodern era. The postmodern and cultural turn in social research praised individualization, hedonism, identity construction, creativity, and self-expression (e.g. Dittmar, 1992; Featherstone, 1991; Giddens, 1991), all elements that were central in young people's identity processes. Similarly, leisure and work were both expected to contain play, entertainment, and adventure (du Gay, 1996; Langman, 1992) in a youthful manner.

However, amidst the celebrated rejuvenation of consumer culture, and consumerism becoming the legitimate way of life for young people (Miles, 2000), the public talk of the 1990s also started to see young people as a marginalized group in the post-industrial risk-society with uncertain futures and increasingly diverse trajectories to adulthood (Furlong & Cartmel, 1997; Wyn & White, 1997). In the end of the 1990s, young people were better recognized as a diverse group of individuals rather than a homogeneous generation. Also, the significance of the micro-level factors such as socio-economic family background for young people's consumption styles was better taken into account than in previous decades, when young people's lifestyles were most often analyzed in relation to society and market, affected by peer groups rather than being socialized as consumers at homes (Furnham, 2001; Gunter & Furnham, 1998; McNeal, 1992).

Global changes in world economy and politics also started to enlarge the markets from young consumers in Western societies to young people in emerging economies. In post-socialist European countries, the significance of young people as consumers started to grow quickly in the late 1980s and early 1990s (e.g. Keller & Vihalemm, 2003; chapter 14). In the 2000s, developing countries and emerging economies such as Brazil, China, and India started to recognize young people as important consumer groups (De Castro, 2006). On the one hand, the globalization and increasing commercialization of young people's lives brought forth critics (e.g. Klein, 1999; Schor, 2004). On the other hand, the rapid development of ICTs and digital networks in the late 1990s and 2000s increased young people's relative importance in global consumption, as young people were the first to adapt the new technologies. Mobile phones and other digital devices became rapidly the symbolic icons of youth, resulting in the idealization of youth and young generations. Many researchers were fascinated by the ways young people used and appropriated ICTs. Thereby the position of young ICT consumers became almost mystified. The 'Net-Generation' or 'warp-speed generation' were argued (Gobé, 2001) to mature earlier and to be more knowledgeable than any of the previous generations (Ruskoff, 1996; Turkle, 1996; Tapscott, 1998; Wilska, 2003; Wilska & Pedrozo, 2007).

What was interesting in the discourse on young consumers in the 2000s was that the concept of *generation* in the context of consumption became popular again, after the late 1980s' and 1990s' talk about the collective rejuvenation of society and ageless youthful consumption styles. Still today, although young people are better recognized as varying in their social, demographic and cultural background, the talk about "consumer generations" that bundles together not only the young, but all age groups, remains salient. Next I will discuss the concept of generation in the context of youth and consumption in closer detail.

Young people as consumer generations

According to Karl Mannheim's well-known theory, each age cohort experiences certain social and cultural events from a distinct viewpoint. Mannheim stressed the importance of the events that have occurred in youth in the formation of collective identities of age cohorts. The collective consciousness of people who are born during certain periods becomes *social generations* that contain common values and cultural perceptions. (Mannheim, 1952). In other words, each generation carries the socio-historical world of their youth with them throughout their lives. This explanation has been particularly popular when explaining the values and behavior of the Baby Boomer generation who developed the first youth cultures in the 1950s and 1960s, and are thus also called the Sixties Generation. The Baby Boomer generation has been thought to be somewhat unique, as the age cohort experienced many historical and social shifts, such as worldwide economic boom, the rise of mass consumption and popular culture, as well as sexual liberation and political activism. Growing up during a period of revolutionary societal changes, Baby Boomers are also associated with untraditional and idealistic values. Moreover, the collective identity of the generation has been argued to be very strong (Jones, Higgs & Ekerdt [eds.], 2009; Karisto, 2007; Wilska, 2011). The Baby Boomers generally identify themselves with younger generations and distance themselves from the older ones. In empirical studies, Baby Boomers express subjective feelings of being much younger than their years. This is manifested in their consumption and leisure time which conspicuously aim at youthfulness (e.g. Biggs, Phillipson, Leach & Money, 2007), resulting in the collective rejuvenation and new conceptions of age, as described in the introduction above. According to Lury (1996) and Featherstone (1991), popular culture of the 1980s was particularly affected by Baby Boomers' "failure to grow up", which appeared especially in the popularity of Steven Spielberg's sci-fi and fantasy movies in the 1980s, for instance. Featherstone even cites a famous slogan of *The Face* magazine: "Nobody is a teenager, because everybody is" (1991, p. 100).

This subjective rejuvenation of the Baby Boomers has sometimes been interpreted as "capturing" youth from the next generation (Baethge, 1989). The next age cohort, born mainly in the 1960s and early 1970s, was regarded as an incalculable, passive, and fragmented youth generation in the 1980s and early 1990s. As the period of 1980s was rather stable in Western countries, lacking great historical events until the political and economic change in the socialist countries, the 1980s' youth generation was argued to lack strong collective values or identity. In the US, the young people of the 1980s were named "Generation X" after Douglas Coupland's novel (Wilska, 2011). Generation X became adults in the 90s, and consequently they encountered the financial recession in their early adulthood years. The lives of Generation X have been said to be influenced by economic uncertainties, which still affect their economic behavior (Smola & Sutton, 2002). Generation X also received a reputation of becoming culturally and socially trapped between the Baby Boomers and the younger age cohorts, Generations Y and Z, whose identities were seen as being constructed with ICTs.

The development of new media created new opportunities for civic commitment as well as new ways of forming social communities for young generations. Generation X is capable of using the new information and communication technologies, but that generation did not grow up with the ICT from early childhood as those born in the 1980s and early 1990s did. The generation of the young of the 2000s and 2010s is often called Generation Y, mainly by marketing researchers and companies marketing to youth. Also terms such as 'Net-Generation', 'E-Generation' and 'Millennials' are used, pinpointing the role of ICTs and digital media. Members of Generation Y have spent their early adulthood during a period of economic growth and emergence of new media, and consequently they appear as individualistic but well-educated and technologically skilled, with positive orientations towards consumer culture and new technological innovations (Paul, 2001). The Millennials have been said to grow up to a global mindset with unrestricted communication where mobile devices are instantly used for social networking. Generation Ys and Zs (those born in the late 1990s and 2000s) are often illustrated as '*digital natives*' that possess positive attitudes towards new technologies and carry well-developed technological skills. (Parment, 2011; 2012).

In consumer studies, it has been argued that different generations share common values and attitudes that significantly affect their daily consumption choices, preferences, and behaviors. The concept of generation is applied in marketing studies to understand consumer practices, arguing that generations differ in attitudes towards technology and practices towards sustainable consumption, as well as in adoption of novelties (Chhetri et al., 2014; Parment, 2011, 2012; Valentine and Powers, 2013). Also, management of personal finances and attitudes towards saving and debt have been argued to be generation-related in many studies (Carr, Gotlieb, Lee, and Shah, 2012; Lunt and Livingstone, 1992).

Explaining generation-specific consumption empirically is not unproblematic, though. Although generations have distinct values and attitudes, there is not much clear empirical evidence of generation-specific consumption which could not be determined by a certain life-course stage, biological age or period under examination. Among the few undoubtedly generation-specific preferences have been found aesthetic preferences and taste-formation. For example, music tastes are formed in a certain sensitive period of teenage and early adulthood. To some extent, this applies to preferences for fashion and apparel as well (Holbrook & Schindler, 1994). The use of mobile phones and ICT are proved to have clear generation-related differences, too. The "digital divide" between older and younger generations is obvious (e.g. Jones et. al [eds.], 2009). However, as digital devices penetrate the market during certain periods, they are also available to older generations. It has been often stressed that digital technologies and social communities and cultures formed within new technology have created a wider social and cultural gap between Generation Y and Generation X than the gap between Generation X and the Baby Boomers. In popular talk, Generation Z has also been argued to differ from the previous ones, precisely due to the digitalization of consumption, social networks, and other aspects of lifestyle.

The Mannheimian tradition that contains a gap or conflict between younger and older generations has also been contested. Lunt and Livingstone (1992) argue that the attitudes of older generations towards the behavior of younger generations are to a great extent a result of the "golden age" view of history, which tends to have a ring of nostalgia when talking about the past. The shift from the golden age to the present results often in a vision of a loss of values and standards. Alan France and Steven Roberts (2015) have questioned how the generations are "made" in the Mannheimian tradition, and criticized the traditional ways the "generational consciousness" is arguably formed in youth. According to France and Roberts, in late modernity there is a need to have an approach that accepts social change and continuity as critical parts of the life course of young people. According to DeMartini (1992), historically, generations traditionally adopted the values of previous generations. This is particularly obvious in the transmission of political or religious values. It is also likely that the new generations will derive their collective consciousness from communication practices, consumption and lifestyles, and new social networks rather than from contrasting values with previous generations.

The ways the values and attitudes related to consumption and economic issues are transmitted to the next generation have not been studied very much in social sciences. In studies of economic psychology and marketing, it is better acknowledged that money is a crucial mediator between today's parents and children, and also that consumerism is the key to all social involvement, and the key to consumerism is money (see West, Sweeting, Young & Robins, 2006; Wilska & Lintonen, 2016). Next, I will highlight some of these issues.

Across generations: Consumer socialization in the family

Although young people's economic position in society has become relatively worse than it was for previous generations in most Western countries (e.g. Côté, 2014), young people's purchase power has increased notably in the past decades. Teenagers' or young adults' own incomes have not increased very much (Lintonen, Wilska, Koivusilta & Konu, 2007; Wilska & Lintonen, 2016), but parents invest a lot of money in their offspring today. Teenagers and even children also have influence on the purchase decisions of the whole family, directly or indirectly (Brusdal, 2007; Buckingham, 2011; Pugh, 2009; Schor, 2004; Sharma, 2016). Therefore, the importance of the family, not only as source of money, but also as source of attitudes and values, should be better acknowledged in social sciences. According to the research in marketing and psychology, the parents' values and attitudes towards consumption have a great impact on the attitudes of young people, although parents are not the only ones to affect young people's consumption. Dotson and Hyatt (2005), name five major consumer socialization agents: peers, parents, TV, shops, and brands. The importance of each agent depends on the age and gender of the child as well as on time use, exposure to media, and spending money available.

Also socio-economic issues matter, but the effect of them is not straightforward. Young people's socialization as consumers in the family has been studied since the early 1980s. According to Adrian Furnham, the parents' values and attitudes affect the amounts and use of money of the teenagers even more than the socio-economic and demographic position of the family (e.g. Furnham, 1999; 2001; Furnham & Thomas, 1984). Many studies also reveal associations between materialism, consumption, and the high disposable income of young people. Paradoxically, these attitudes, as well as the income of young people, may be in contrast to the family income: young people from disadvantaged backgrounds may have more money at their own disposal than young people from better-off families. This suggests that parental values have a great impact on young people's income and consumption, as highly educated parents typically educate their children to become competent consumers by rationing pocket money (Kooreman, 2007; West et al., 2006; Wilska & Lintonen, 2016). Also, Anderson and Nevitte (2006) found correlations between parents' high education and income and teaching thrift to children and young people.

According to Webley and Nyhus (2006), communication between parents and young people, such as discussing economic matters, as well as the parents' future orientation, affect young people's attitudes towards money and saving. The effect of parents is visible even in young adulthood (Webley & Nyhus, 2013). In psychological studies, personality factors and behavioral problems are also seen as having an impact on young people's attitudes towards money and consumption. Personality dimensions such as goal-directedness, adult- and achievement-orientation, conscientiousness, and ability to defer gratification have been discovered to have a positive effect on thrifty values and ability to save. Conversely, emotional and behavioral problems, extraversion, impulsiveness, and agreeableness correlate positively with materialistic values. Cultural and religious background also have impact (e.g. Anderson & Nevitte, 2006; Nyhus & Pons, 2005; Sharma, 2016).

Empirical research also reveals gender differences in the consumption of young people. Research shows that the consumption of teenagers is still very traditionally determined: girls spend more money on their appearances, such as on clothes and accessories, whereas boys spend more on hobbies, activities, and particularly on technology, as well as on alcohol (Brusdal &

Berg, 2010; Kooreman, 2007; Wilska, 2005). There is contrasting evidence, though, as to whether the attitudes of parents today towards girls' and boys' consumption are different. In general boys are thought to be more rational consumers than girls, although most empirical studies suggest the opposite (Autio & Wilska, 2005; Brusdal & Berg, 2010; Ruspini, 2012). In some studies, teenage boys are even found to be more materialistic and more interested in brand products than girls (e.g. Wilska, 2005). However, in many studies it has been shown that the incomes of teenage boys are higher than the incomes of girls (e.g. Kooreman, 2007; Lintonen et al., 2007; Wilska & Lintonen, 2016). The social and demographic differences in consumption and income in youth are important to acknowledge, since having an appropriate level of personal money creates a sense of financial freedom, which in turn enhances subjective well-being and makes the transition to adulthood easier (Cunnien, MartinRogers & Mortimer, 2009; Ranta, Chow & Salmela-Aro, 2013).

Money also means social and economic power even in close relationships. Moreover, material inequalities and stereotypical consumer images that are created in youth, often affected by the attitudes of the previous generations, may pave the way to wider inequalities in later life. This is why the research on the effect of different socialization agents on income, consumption patterns, and attitudes towards consumption among young people are important also in the future. It is also crucial to better acknowledge the differences within young people, as there are enormous differences in young people's economic, social, and demographic background, and as a consequence, their consumption styles and consumer competences.

Conclusions and discussion

In this chapter, I have focused on the position of youth in consumption from different viewpoints. It can be concluded that the significance of youth and young people has remained high in consumption, although the real social, cultural, and economic position of young people has varied in different societies over time. Young people are always in the vanguard of social and economic changes and new innovations, and therefore their importance remains high at all times. Different disciplines have taken different approaches to young people's consumption, pointing out different contexts, such as society, social and cultural communities, peer groups and families, and generations with collective values. Particularly the conception of consumer generations with specific values has been influential for many decades. Recently, the generational approach has gained more momentum along with digitalization, which has arguably widened the gaps between generations. This is, however, something I would like to challenge below, bearing in mind that digitalization is causing more rapid changes in young people's consumption than ever before.

Particularly in terms of digital consumption, a post-Mannheimian conceptualization of generation acknowledges that all life stages can provide important building blocks for generational experiences, not only youth (Taipale, Wilska & Gilleard (eds.), *forthcoming*). Some age-related digital gaps are relatively short-lived. For example, during the first decade of the twenty-first century, age-cohorts of fifty years and older caught up with younger groups year by year in terms of mobile phone use in the United Kingdom (Gilleard, Jones & Higgs, 2015). Similar trends have been found in Finland (Statistics Finland, 2015). This suggests that generational identity, including that reflected in the integration of technology with individual lifestyles during youth, is not set in stone but keeps evolving over the life course (Taipale, 2016). New technology use, but also other kinds of consumption, could be means for bridging generations together rather than digging gaps between them. The ways of doing this are something that should be studied more in the future.

In addition to the conceptual comprehension of generations and digitalization, there should also be more research on the consumption of young people in different cultures, in both global and local contexts. Young people's economic and social position is getting weaker in Europe, due to the high unemployment rates and relatively small sizes of young age cohorts. In most Western countries, the relative economic position of today's younger age cohorts is evaluated to remain permanently worse than the position of older cohorts (e.g. Côté, 2014). As a consequence, the traditional conceptualization of youth as the vanguard of progress and new innovations is at stake in Western societies. In emerging economies, such as Russia, India, Brazil, and China, however, younger generations have much more spending power compared to older generations, and they also have distinctly different consumption patterns from the previous generations (e.g. Gurova, 2014; Yu, 2014: chapters 12, 13 & 14). This will change the traditional hierarchies of consumer generations. The significance of developing countries as consumer societies will grow in the future, and thus more research on the young people there is needed. Moreover, in both Western and developing countries, social and economic inequalities between young people, based on e.g. income, gender, area of residence, and education and cultural competences, are widening. Western societies are becoming increasingly multi-cultural, too, which is likely to change the national identities into more fragmented ones in the future. This necessarily affects young people's consumption patterns and attitudes towards consumption. This raises new research questions, but also demands more sensitive research methods.

Finally, understanding the formation of young people's consumption styles is of key importance when tackling global problems, such as ethical and environmental issues. When trying to enhance the transition into more sustainable lifestyles, a better understanding of young people's potential for change needs more innovative research methods, such as participatory practices and analyses of youth-led innovations and initiatives. Also, small, incremental changes in everyday life and marginal youth consumer cultures should be better recognized and utilized in future studies on the consumption of young people.

References

Abrams, M. (1959). *The Teenage Consumer.* London: London Press Exchange.

Aledin, S. (2009). *Teenagers' Brand Relationship in Daily Life: A Qualitative Study of Brand Meanings and Their Motivational Ground among Teenagers in Helsinki and London Metropolitan areas.* Series A-4: 2009. Turku: Turku School of Economics.

Anderson, C. L., & Nevitte, N. (2006). Teach Your Children Well: Values of Thrift and Saving. *Journal of Economic Psychology*, 27 (2), 247–261.

Autio, M., & T.-A. Wilska. (2005). Young People in Knowledge Society – Possibilities to Fulfil Ecological Goals. *Progress in Industrial Ecology*, 2 (3–4), 403–426.

Baethge, M. (1989). Individualization as Hope and Disaster. In: K. Hurrelmann & U. Engel, (eds.) *The Social World of Adolescence: International Perspective.* Berlin: DeGruyter, pp. 27–41.

Barak, B. & Schiffman, L.G. (1981). Cognitive Age: A Non-Chronological Age Variable. In: *NA-Advances in Consumer Research*, (pp. 602–606). Ann Abor, MI: Association for Consumer Research.

Belk, R.W. (1986). Yuppies as Arbiters of the Emerging Consumption Style. In: R. J. Lutz (Ed.), *Advances in Consumer Research*, (pp. 514–519). Provo, UT: Association for Consumer Research.

Biggs, S., Phillipson, C., Leach, R., & Money, A.-M. (2007). The Mature Imaginations and Consumption Strategies. Age and Generation in the Development of a United Kingdom Baby Boomer Identity. *International Journal of Ageing and Later Life*, 2 (2), 31–59.

Brusdal, R. (2007). If It Is Good for the Child's Development Then I Say Yes Almost Every Time: How Parents Relate to Their Children's Consumption. *International Journal of Consumer Studies*, 31 (4), 391–396.

Brusdal, R., & Berg, L. (2010). Are Parents Gender Neutral When Financing Their Children's Consumption? *International Journal of Consumer Studies*, 34 (1), 3–10. doi:10.1111/j.1470-6431.2009.00822.x.

Buckingham, D. (2011). *The Material Child. Growing Up in Consumer Culture.* London: Polity Press.

Carr, D.J., Gotlieb, M.R., Lee, N.J. & Shah, D.V. (2012). Examining Overconsumption, Competitive Consumption and Conscious Consumption from 1994 to 2004: Disentangling Cohort and Period Effects. *The Annals of the American Academy of Political and Social Science*, 664 (1), 220–233.

Chhetri, P., Hossain M.I. & Broom, A. (2014). Examining the Generational Differences in Consumption Patterns in South East Queensland. *City, Culture & Society*, 5(4), 1–9.

Clarke, J., Hall, S., Jefferson, T. & Roberts, B. (1976). Subcultures, Cultures, and Class: A Theoretical Overview. In: Hall. S. & Jefferson, T. (Eds.), *Resistance through Rituals*, London: Hutchinson, pp. 9–75.

Cook, D. (2004). *The Commodification of Childhood: The Children's Clothing Industry and the Rise of the Child Consumer*. Durham, NC: Duke University Press.

Côté, J. E. (2014). Towards a New Political Economy of Youth. *Journal of Youth Studies*, 14(4), 527–543. doi: 10.1080/13676261.2013.836592.

Côté, J. E. & Allahar, A. L. (1996). *Generation on Hold. Coming of Age in the Late Twentieth Century*. London: New Your University Press.

Cunnien, K. A., MartinRogers, N. & Mortimer, J. T. (2009). Adolescent Work Experience and Self-efficacy. *International Journal of Sociology and Social Policy*, 29 (3/4), 164–175.

De Castro, L. R. (2006). What is New in the "South"? Consumer Culture and the Vicissitudes of Poor Youth's Identity Construction in Urban Brazil. *Young*, 14 (3), 179–201. doi: 10.1177/1103308806065815.

de Lange, M., Gesthuizen, M. & Wolbers, M. H. J. (2014). Youth Labor Market Integration Across Europe. *European Societies*, 16 (2), 194–212. doi:10.1080/14616696.2013.821621.

DeMartini, J. (1992). Generational Relationships and social participation. *Sociological Inquiry*, 62 (4), 450–463.

Dittmar, H. (1992). *The Social Psychology of Material Possessions: To Have Is To Be*. Hemel Hempstead: Harvester Wheatsheaf.

Dotson, M. & Hyatt, E. (2005). Major Influence Factors in Children's Consumer Socialization. *Journal of Consumer Marketing*, 22 (1), 35–42.

du Gay, Paul. (1996). *Consumption and Identity at Work*. London: Sage.

Elder, G.H. & Shanahan, M.J. (2007). The Life Course and Human Development. In: W. Damon & R. M. Lerner (Eds.), *The Handbook of Child Psychology*, New York: Wiley, 665–715.

Featherstone, M. (1991). *Consumer Culture and Postmodernism*. London: Sage Publications.

Featherstone, M. & Hepworth, M. (1990). Images of Ageing. In: J. Bond & P. G. Coleman (Eds.), *Ageing in Society*, Sage: London, 170–96.

France, A. & Roberts, S. (2015). The Problem of Social Generations: A Critique of the New Emerging Orthodoxy in Youth Studies. *Journal of Youth Studies*, 18 (2), 215–230, http://dx.doi.org/10.1080/13676261.2014.944122.

Furlong, A. & Cartmel, F. (1997). *Young People and Social Change*. Buckingham: Open University Press.

Furnham, A. (1999). Economic Socialization: A Study of Adults' Perceptions and Uses of Allowances (Pocket Money) to Educate Children. *British Journal of Development Psychology*, 17 (4), 585–604. doi:10.1348/026151099165492.

Furnham, A. (2001). Parental Attitudes to Pocket Money/Allowances for Children. *Journal of Economic Psychology*, 22 (3), 397–422.

Furnham, A. & Thomas, P. (1984). Adult Perceptions of the Economic Socialization of Children. *Journal of Adolescence*, 7 (2), 217–231.

Förnäs, J. & Bolin, G. (Eds.) (1995) *Youth Culture in Late Modernity*. London: Sage.

Gbadamosi, A. (Eds). (2016). *Handbook of Research on Consumerism and Buying Behavior in Developing Nations*. Hershey (PA): IGI Global.

Giddens, A. (1991). *Modernity and Self-Identity. Self and Society in the Late Modern Age*. Cambridge: Polity Press.

Gilleard, C., Jones, I. & Higgs, P. (2015). Connectivity in Later Life: The Declining Age Divide in Mobile Cell Phone Ownership. *Sociological Research Online*, 20 (2), 3 http://www.socresonline.org.uk/20/2/3.html.

Gobé, Marc. (2001). *Emotional Branding: The New Paradigm for Connecting Brands to People*. New York: Allworth Press.

Goodman, D.S.G. (Ed.). (2008). *The New Rich in China: Future Rulers, Present Lives*. London: Routledge.

Griffin, C. (1997). Troubled Teens: Managing Disorgers of Transition and Consumption. *Feminist Review*, 55 (1), 4–21.

Gunter, B. & Furnham, A. (1998). *Children as Consumers: A Psychological Analysis of the Young People's Market*. London: Routledge.

Gurova, O. (2014). *Fashion and the Consumer Revolution in Contemporary Russia*. London: Routledge.

Hammond, J.L. (1986).Yuppies. *Public Opinion Quarterly*, 50 (4), 487–501. doi: 10.1086/268999.
Hebdige, D. (1979). *Subculture. The Meaning of Style*. New York: Methuen.
Holbrook, M. & Schindler, R. (1994). Age, Taste and Attitude toward the Past as Predictor of Consumers. Aesthetic Tastes for Cultural Products. *Journal of Marketing Research*, 31 (3), 412–422.
Jones, G. (1995). *Leaving Home*. Buckingham: Open University Press.
Jones, G. & Wallace, C. (1992). *Youth, Family, and Citizenship*. Buckingham: Open University Press.
Jones, I.R., Higgs, P. & Ekerdt, D.J. (Eds) (2009). *Consumption and Generational Change: The Rise of Consumer Lifestyles*. New Jersey: Transaction Publishers.
Karisto, A. (2007). Finnish Baby Boomers and the Emergence of the Third Age. *International Journal of Ageing and Later* Life, 2 (2), 91–108.
Keller, M. & Vihalemm, T. (2003). Return to the 'Consuming West'. Young people's Perceptions about the Consumerization of Estonia. *Young. Nordic Journal of Youth Research*, 11 (3), 195–215.
Klein, N. (1999). *No Logo*. Toronto: Knopf Canada.
Kooreman, P. (2007). Time, Money, Peers, and Parents: Some Data and Theories on Teenage Behavior. *Journal of Population Economics*, 20 (1), 9–33.
Langman, L. (1992). Neon Cages: Shopping for Subjectivity, In: Rob Shields (Ed.) *Lifestyle Shopping: The Subject of Consumption*, (pp. 40–82). London: Routledge.
Li, Y. & Ranieri, M. (2010). Are 'Digital Natives' Really Digitally Competent?—A Study on Chinese Teenagers. *British Journal of Educational Technology*, 41 (6), 1029–1042. doi: 10.1111/j.1467–8535.2009.01053.x_1.
Lintonen, T., Wilska, T.A., Koivusilta, L. & Konu, A. (2007). Trends in disposable income among teenage boys and girls. *International Journal of Consumer Studies*, 31 (4), 340-348.
Lunt, P. & Livingstone, S. (1992). *Mass Consumption and Personal Identity*. Milton Keynes: Open University Press.
Lury, C. (1996). *Consumer Culture*. Cambridge: Polity Press.
Mannheim, K. (1952). The Problem of Generations. In: K. Mannheim (Ed.) *Essays on the Sociology of Knowledge*. London: Routledge & Kegan, Paul, 276–320.
McCulloch, K., Stewart, A. & Lovegreen, N. (2006). 'We just Hang Out Together': Youth Cultures and Social Class. *Journal of Youth Studies*, 9 (5), 539–556.
McNeal, J. (1992). *Kids as Customes*. New York: Lexington Books.
Miles, S. (2000). *Youth Lifestyles in a Changing World*. Milton Keynes, UK: Open University Press.
Moschis, G. P. & Moore, R. L. (1980). Purchasing Behavior of Adolescent Consumers. *Proceedings of the Americal Marketing Association*, 45 (2), 89–92.
Nyhus, E.& Pons, E. (2005). The Effects of Personality on Earnings. *Journal of Economic Psychology*, 26, 363–385.
Osgerby, W. (1998). *Youth in Britain. Making Contemporary Britain*. Oxford: Wiley.
Parment, A. (2011). *Generation Y in Consumer and Labor Markets*. Routledge: New York.
Parment, A. (2012). Generation Y vs. Baby Boomers: Shopping Behavior, Byer Involvement and Implications for Retailing. *Journal of Retailing and Consumer Services*, 20 (2), 189–199.
Paul, P. (2001). Getting inside Generation Y. *American Demographics*, 23 (9), 42–49.
Pugh, A.J. (2009). *Longing and Belonging: Parents, Children and Consumer Culture*. Berkeley: University of California Press.
Quart, A. (2002). *Branded. The Buying and Selling of Teenagers*. Cambridge, MA: Perseus Publishing.
Ranta, M., Chow, A., & Salmela-Aro, K. (2013). Trajectories of Life Satisfaction and the Financial Situation in the Transition to Adulthood. *Longitudinal and Life Course Studies*, 4 (1), 57–77.
Rushkoff, D. (1996). *Playing the Future: How Kids' Culture Can Teach Us to Thrive in an Age of Chaos*. New York: HarperCollins.
Ruspini, E. (2012). Girls, Boys, Money. Economic Socialization, Gender, and Generations in Italy. *International Review of Sociology: Revue Internationale de Sociologie*, 22 (3), 514–529.
Sassatelli, R. (2010). *Fitness Culture: Gyms and the Commercialisation of Discipline and Fun*. Hampshire: Palgrave Macmillan.
Schiffman, L. & Sherman, E. (1991). Value Orientetions of New-Age Elderly: The Coming of an Ageless Market. *Journal of Business Research*, 22 (2), 187–194.
Schor, J. B. (2004). *Born To Buy. The Commercialized Child and the New Consumer Culture*. New York: Scribner.
Sharma, A. (2016). Exploring the Changing Role of Children as Consumers in India. Are They Learning from Us or Are They Teaching Us? In: Gbadamosi, Ayantunji (Eds.) *Handbook of Research on Consumerism and Buying Behavior in Developing Nations*, Hershey (PA): IGI Global, 283–310.
Smith Maguire, J. (2008). *Fit for Consumption: Sociology and the Business of Fitness*. London: Routledge.

Smola, K.V. & Sutton, C.D. (2002). Generational Differences: Revising Generational Work Values for the New Millennium. *Journal of Organizational Behavior*, 23 (4), 363–382.
Statistics Finland (2015). *More Mobile Internet Use, More Personal Devices.* http://tilastokeskus.fi/til/sutivi/2015/sutivi_2015_2015-11-26_tie_001_en.html. Accessed June 12, 2016.
Taipale, S. (2016). Synchronicity Matters: Defining the Characteristics of Digital Generations. *Information, Communication & Society*, 19 (1), 80–89.
Taipale, S., Wilska, T.-A. & Gilleard, C. (Eds.) (forthcoming). *Digital Technologies and Generational Identity: ICT Usage Across the Life Course.* London: Routledge.
Tapscott, D. (1998). *Growing up Digital. The Rise of the Net Generation.* New York: McGraw-Hill.
Turkle, S. (1996). *Life on the Screen. Identity in the Age of the Internet.* New York: Touchstone.
Valentine, D.B. & Powers, T.L. (2013). Generation Y Values and Lifestyle Segments. *Journal of Consumer Marketing*, 30 (7), 597–606.
Webley, P. & Nyhus, E. (2006). Parents' Influence on Children's Future Orientations and Savings. *Journal of Economic Psychology*, 27 (1), 140–164.
Webley, P. & Nyhus, E. (2013). Economic Socialization, Saving and Assets in European Young Adults. *Economics of Education Review*, 33 (1), 19–30.
West, P., Sweeting, H., Young, R. & Robins, M. (2006). A Material Paradox: Socioeconomic Status, Young People's Disposable Income and Consumer Culture. *Journal of Youth Studies*, 9 (4), 437–462. doi:10.1080/13676260600805739.
Willis, P. (1977). *Learning to Labor. How Working Class Kids get Working Class Jobs.* London: Saxon House.
Willis, P. (1990). *Common Culture. Symbolic Work at Play in the Everyday Cultures of the Young.* Milton Keynes: Open University Press.
Wilska, T.-A. (1999). *Survival with Dignity? The Consumption of Young Adults during Economic Depression: A Comparative Study of Finland and Britain, 1990–1994.* Publications of the Turku School of Economics and Business Administration. Serie 1999: A-3. Turku.
Wilska, T.-A. (2003). Mobile Phone Use as Part of Young People's Consumption Styles. *Journal of Consumer Policy*, 26(3), 441–463.
Wilska, T.-A. (2005). Gender Differences in the Consumption of Children and Young People in Finland. In: T.-A. Wilska & L. Haanpää (Eds.) *Lifestyles and Social Change. Essays on Economic Sociology.* Serie Discussion and Working Papers 11:2005. Turku School of Economics and Business Administration.
Wilska, T.-A. (2011). Generation. In D. Southerton (Ed.) *Encyclopedia for Consumer Culture.* Vol 1. London: Sage.
Wilska, T.-A. & Lintonen, T. (2016). The Gender Gap in Teenagers' Incomes. A 30-Year Trend in Finland 1983–2013. *Journal of Youth Studies*, 19 (4), 421–437.
Wilska, T.-A. & Pedrozo, S. (2007). New Technology and Young People's Consumer Identities: A Comparative Study between Finland and Brazil. *Young. Nordic Journal of Youth Studies*, 15 (4), 557–576.
Wyn, J. & White, R. (1997). *Rethinking Youth.* London: Sage.
Yin, X. (2005). New Trends of Leisure Consumption in China. *Journal of Family and Economic Issues*, 26 (1), 175–182. doi: 10.1007/s10834-004-1419-x.
Yu, L. (2014). *Consumption in China: How China's New Consumer Ideology Is Shaping the Nation.* Cambridge: Polity Press.

28
Aging and consumption

Carol Kelleher and Lisa Peñaloza

Introduction

Older people aged 65 and above comprise the most rapidly growing demographic in many parts of the world today, particularly but not exclusively in developed nations. Characterizing this growth over the past few decades are rapid and dramatic evolutions in consumption associated with active lifestyles and altered living arrangements, innovative medical technologies, changing pension and healthcare benefits, and increasingly interactive market accommodation and strategic targeting activities. This chapter provides an overview of research on aging and consumption (See Figure 28.1). As depicted in Figure 28.1, the chapter directs attention to the distinct theoretical perspectives that implicate a triumvirate of agents and institutions including elderly consumers, family, and the market, either separately or together, in aging and consumption phenomena, and it provides specific directives for future research. Specifically, the chapter begins by reviewing distinct theoretical perspectives, changes in research topics, in units of analysis, and in family, market and medical contexts over time. It proceeds to explore the intricate interrelations between consumption and aging in highlighting socio-cultural, physiological, and psychological perspectives; generational versus cohort categorical priorities; and third and fourth age distinctions. Topics include identity and subjectivity processes; social relationships, including family and service providers; individual information and decision making processes; specific consumption patterns and practices; popular cultural and market representations; and market experiences and ethics, including medical care. The chapter closes with future directions regarding the growing importance and challenges of disentangling the effects of aging people on consumption, and conversely, the increasingly pervasive aspects of consumer culture on understandings and treatments of aging, with emphases on intersectionalities of experience, market mediations, and social interventions.

Theoretical perspectives on aging and consumption

Overview

The overall body of work on elderly consumption is profoundly interdisciplinary, yet peppered with rather distinct socio-cultural, physiological, and psychological perspectives. In the field of

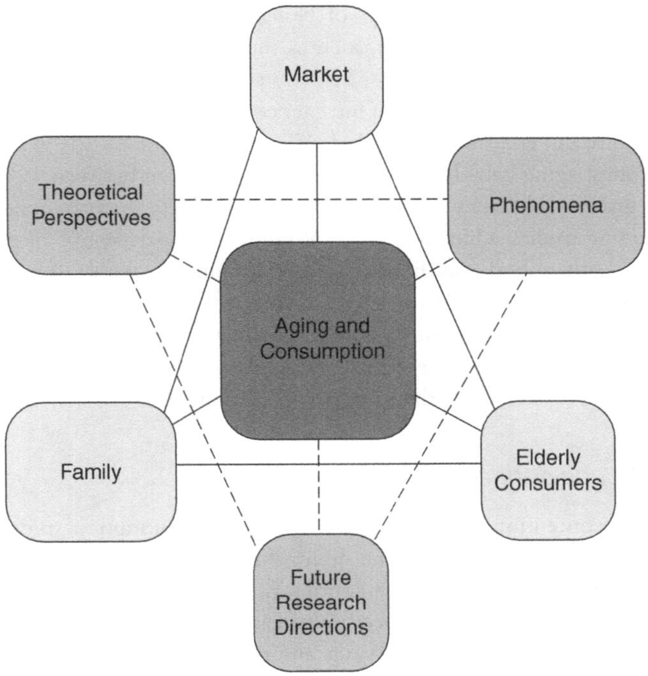

Figure 28.1 Aging and consumption

marketing, for example, early work positioned elderly consumers at the end of the family lifecycle, as empty nesters and solitary survivors marred with cognitive and physical deficits (Moschis, 1987). Over time, both marketing and sociology of aging discourses centred on "new aging" (Gergen and Gergen, 2000) and "successful aging" (Rowe and Kahn, 2015). Market research in particular has focused on mapping the consumption patterns of "mature" consumers for particular product and service categories (Moschis and Mathur, 1993), such as perfumes (Lambert-Pandraud and Laurent, 2010), fashion and cosmetics (Twigg and Majim, 2014), technology (Gilly, Celsi, and Schau, 2012; Nasi, Rasanen, and Sarpila, 2012), and alternative medical therapies (Fries, 2014). However, such segmentation and active targeting the lucrative grey market has been criticized. Specifically, Katz and Marshall (2003) observed, "aging as a diverse chronological process and age-related problems based on class, race, gender, and locality are obscured or disappear into coterminous market niches based on the vagaries of 'mature' consumer behavior" (p. 8). We next outline the different perspectives on aging and consumption in more detail.

Sociological perspectives

Sociologically oriented research on aging directs attention to social groupings, categorical distinctions, and stereotypes, which have arguably become more fluid in contemporary societies, as well as delineates how the third and fourth age impact elderly consumption.

Generational versus cohort priorities

A key distinction in this work is between cohort and generational perspectives. Research examining elderly consumers as a cohort aggregates by birthdate in order to identify and compare shared consumption experiences and ways of being. Cohort analysis has generated valuable insight into social changes (Ryder, 1997), such as the development of consumer culture and the social impact of technology. Examples of elderly consumption studies using cohort analysis include Gilleard and Higgs' (2008) study of internet consumption amongst elderly consumers in the United Kingdom, and Gilleard, Higgs, Hyde, Wiggins, and Blane's (2005) study of consumption patterns amongst aging baby boomers in Britain, those born between 1946 and 1967 who grew up and are growing old in an increasingly consumer society there. In contrast, generational approaches, including studies which adopt the Mannheimian perspective of generational units (Mannheim, 1952), situate both youth and elderly consumption within the socio-cultural and historic contexts in which consumers live and consume, as they grow old and age (Kertzer, 1983). For example, Higgs et al. (2009) foreground distinct, formative social and market conditions, such as changing life goals and living arrangements in association with evolving market targeting and media representations, in examining their impact on consumption patterns and practices.

Third and fourth age distinctions

A second point of contention in sociologically oriented consumption studies is the distinction between the third and fourth age. The dominant discourse of the third age valorises and promotes an attainable ageless self and the continuity of identity throughout life in consumption, albeit in a physically aging body. Specifically, Laslett (1989) characterized the "third age" in terms of improved quality of life, well-being, and positive and active aging. Kaufman (1986) explored how older persons continue to create new meanings and reformulate identities as they age. Along similar lines, Gergen and Gergen (2000) take a social constructionist perspective in emphasizing positive aspects of aging. Extending beyond this research, at the Taos Institute a team of scholars and practitioners offers a series of workshops, conferences, publications, and educational programs oriented to the development of positive aging and of skills for self-understanding and enhanced social relations in couples, families, and organizations.

Notably, marketers who target the "grey market" focus on these third age, active consumers with sufficient income and health to consume (Minkler, 1991). Indeed, market representations tend to almost exclusively highlight the positive, pleasurable, and seemingly unlimited consumption options of the third age in advertisements for a range of food and beverages (Williams, Ylänne, and Wadleigh, 2007), anti-aging products (Ellison, 2014), medical treatments (Katz & Marshall, 2003), and increased leisure consumption in retirement (McHugh, 2000, Ekerdt and Clark, 2001), while obscuring and rending invisible images of old age pain, malaise, and infirmity.

While not explicit commercial endorsements, academic discourses of the third age nonetheless affirm life states and conditions that readily align with people's hopes and assuage their fears and problems. Further, in emphasizing positive aging and neglecting its negative aspects, scholars help legitimize and normalize particular understandings and treatments of elderly persons. In a counter example, Blaikie (1999) noted that poor, infirm, and vulnerable elderly consumers are seldom investigated by researchers and not targeted by marketers, and as a result we know little about their consumption, except that limited financial means and privation are fairly widespread in old age.

Other critical aging researchers note the complicity of third age concepts with marketers' promises and with neoliberal economic arrangements. For example, examining utopian retirement communities in the Sunbelt states of the US, McHugh (2000) critiques their use of the ageless self in promotions promising elderly consumers long-lasting enjoyment and companionship as they age. Rudman (2015) notes how discourses of positive aging align in research and marketing practice with the neoliberal agenda of activation and individualization in institutional discourses and practices that govern how elderly consumers manage their bodies, health, finances, lifestyles, and retirement and become individually responsible for maintaining and attaining the unattainable ageless self.

Those advancing the fourth age begin with what the third age leaves out: qualities of deficiency, marginalization, degradation, and abjection. For example, while noting that aging in later years is not adequately addressed as a matter of the chronological passage of time, Twigg (2004) directed attention to the qualitative transition to deep old age, which is marked by serious infirmity. Gilleard and Higgs (2015) suggested possible future intra- and inter-generational age conflict as the result of juxtapositions of third age discourses and experiences of successful and active aging against the social realities of fourth agers. Suffering due to increased frailty is bad enough; worse still is the internalization of positive aging notions by those experiencing deep old age and being judged as having aged "unsuccessfully" by those in their social network and beyond in medical and eldercare. Yet fourth age discourses, for example social and healthcare policy debates, highlight the "crisis" or "tsunami" of ageing populations that play out with unintended consequences. Twigg (2004) cautioned that directing attention to older persons and their objectified treatment as "others" and "non-consumers" can further their marginalization in society and in public healthcare and policy.

Socio-cultural perspectives on aging and consumption

Treatment of the body and lived experience are other major issues in the literature on aging and consumption. Consumer culture studies direct attention to consumer rituals and practices, subjective understandings, and experiences of being old and aging. Topics of interest include the "life of things" in dispossession and bequeathing rituals. For example, De Witt, Campbell, Ploeg, Kemp, and Rosenthal (2013) examined interfamilial communication in inheritance decisions, while Ekerdt and Addington (2015) explored the dispossession rituals and strategies of downsizing elderly consumers. Much earlier, Price, Arnould, and Curasi (2000) detailed how elderly consumers look back on, make sense of, and bequeath to others a sense of their lives as they plan for, and dispose of, cherished positions.

Psychological perspectives on aging and consumption

In contrast, psychologically oriented studies of elderly consumption adopt a life cycle perspective or employ experimental scenarios and tasks to investigate the mental decision-making and information-processing capacities and skills of elderly persons. For example, Yoon et al. (2005) reviewed the consumer-behavior, neuroscience, and psychology literatures in order to examine how aging impacts consumer memory, persuasion, and decision making. Peters (2010) highlighted the use of accumulated experience, increased emotional focus, and selective use of deliberative capacity in characterising age-related changes in the decision-making processes of elderly consumers as compared with younger adults. Cole et al. (2008) attributed differences between older and younger consumers' brand choices to changes over time in cognition, affect, and goals. Yoon, Cole, and Lee (2009) showed that elderly consumers drew on previous knowledge and experience where there was a close fit between tasks and environment and engaged in adaptive decision making when this was not the case.

In summary, while the overall body of work on elderly consumption is profoundly interdisciplinary, rather distinct socio-cultural, physiological, and psychological perspectives emerge in aging and consumption studies. We next outline the main aging and consumption topics studied to date, followed by directions for future interdisciplinary and participatory studies.

Aging and consumption topics

A range of topics structures the literature on aging and consumption: identity and subjectivity negotiations; social relationships, including family and service providers; information and decision-making processes; specific consumption patterns and practices; market experience and ethics; popular cultural and market representations; and marketing experiences, including the medicalization of later life.

Identity and subjectivity negotiations

How changes in consumer culture come about, facilitate, and hinder elderly consumers in creating and/or re-fashioning aged identities are central topics in cultural studies of elderly consumption. Such changes are set against the backdrops of the increased targeting of "mature" consumers, the promotion of "agelessness," the perpetuation of youth subcultures, and a fixation on individual consumer responsibility to regulate consumption and the body in order to deny or delay loss of mental and physical ability. For example, Schau, Gilly, and Wolfinbarger (2009) detailed the intensive identity work of elderly consumers upon retirement, as they reinvigorated previously abandoned identities and crafted new ones. Earlier, examining gendered aspects of third and fourth age ideologies framing the elderly in marketing representations, and in turn elderly consumption, Silver (2003) noted a mix of altered gender identities, diminished gender differences, and blurred gender representations. She concluded that ageism and misogyny contributed to this "(de)gendered utopia" (p. 379). Most recently, Hearn and Wray (2015) highlighted the multiplicity and intersectionalities of ethnicity and sexualities framing elderly consumption in increasingly complex, heterogeneous, and multi-layered ways.

Noting the social construction of consumers as "old" and the reluctance of elderly consumers to identify with this social position, Barnhart and Peñaloza (2012) directed attention to how elderly consumers negotiate their age identity within elderly consumption ensembles (ECEs) of family members and service providers, and explained how old identity is implicated in consumption. Specifically, when they became aware of shortcomings in such consumption events as driving or paying bills by the elderly, family members and/or service providers imposed the conditions of being elderly on elderly persons. In turn, elderly consumers seldom accepted this designation. Building on this collective ECE understanding, Barnhart, Huff and Cotte (2014) showed how and when caregivers who were not family members were excluded versus included in performances of family involving eldercare in the home.

Social relationships with family and service providers

Early on, House, Landis, and Umberson (1988) identified social support as a key factor in elderly people's mental and physical health. Quadrello et al. (2005) examined elderly people's use of communication technologies enabling ongoing contact with grandchildren. Further, Castaño et al. (2012) detailed how elderly people relied on the help of their children in learning to use mobile phone technology, and used the teaching episodes to express their pride in the accomplishments of their children and to spend time together.

While a source of joy and support, social relations can also be a source of tension for elderly persons and those caring for them. Pettigrew and Moschis (2012) highlight positive implications when elderly consumers feel they have a productive or contributing role to society, for example, through volunteering or caregiving, and conversely, negative implications such as loneliness and a lost sense of role or purpose following loss of a spouse or shrinking social networks. Examining the expectations and experiences of baby boomer caregivers, Guberman, Lavoie, Blein, and Olazabal (2012) showed their categorization of caregiving responsibilities as work that should be supported and shared with public, social, and health services, and not just familial duty. In another example, Dean, Kellie, and Mould (2014) explored role reversal in families; as adult children become caregivers for their aging parents, family members negotiate collective decisions and related tensions regarding shopping, residential living arrangements, and financial resources.

Individual information and decision-making processes

Psychologically oriented elderly consumption studies examine age-related changes in cognitive abilities and processes in consumption meaning-making and goal formulation and attainment. Early on, Roedder John and Cole (1986) highlighted the way memory limitations negatively impact the information processing of elderly consumers, and recommended that marketers consider these information-processing limitations when they develop and convey product-related tasks. Later, Yoon (1997) noted that elderly consumers tended to use schema-based information processing strategies, as compared to the emphasis on information details among younger consumers, and recommended that marketers adapt their appeals accordingly when targeting elderly consumers. More recently, in a study of emotional appeals in advertising directed to elderly consumers, Williams and Drolet (2005) highlighted age-related differences in motivation and cognitive capabilities, while Drolet, Schwartz, and Yoon (2010) noted differences in the decision-making processes of older versus younger consumers.

Specific consumption patterns and practices

Many studies elaborate the consumption patterns and practices across a range of product and service categories for elderly consumers. For example, in their study of perfume purchase and consumption amongst French consumers, Lambert-Pandraud and Laurent (2010) found that older consumers were more likely to stay loyal to a small set of preferred brands and did so for a longer time than younger consumers. Risius, Thelwell, Wagstaff, and Scurr (2014) explored changes in brassiere preferences and self-perceptions of breasts and bodily changes among elderly women. Hurd Clarke and Korotchenko (2010) examined changes in women's hair styling and color in relation to aging. Castaño, Quintanilla, and Perez (2012) noted that elderly consumers discussed the importance of social relations and socialization at gaming casinos, while younger persons focused on their chances to win. In their study of Internet use, Gilly, Wolfingbarger, and Schau (2012) explained that the discomfort with the technology that elderly consumers expressed did not prevent them from adopting the technologies. Using UK consumption data collected from 1961–2011, Twigg and Majim (2014) noted increases in cosmetic, fashion, and clothing consumption amongst elderly women over this time period. Explaining the increase, the authors suggested that older women had become more concerned about appearance during this time, and, having controlled for period and cohort effects, they attributed such increases to the development of fast fashion and anti-aging products and categories.

Market experiences, ethics, and the medicalization of later life

Previous research has explored elderly consumers' interactions with commercial actors and environments. In some of the earliest studies, Bellenger and Korgaonkar (1980) noted that the recreational environment of a shopping mall alleviated feelings of loneliness amongst elderly consumers, while Block, Ridgway, and Nelson (1991) noted that interactions with service providers were an important source of social contact for elderly persons. In a follow-up study, Kang and Ridgway (1996) highlighted the importance of market access for elderly consumers, shopping in particular, in providing valuable opportunities for social interactions and consumer protection. In other work Price and Arnould (1999) noted that for some older consumers, commercial friendships between consumers and service providers complemented, and even superseded, their relationships with other people.

Other researchers have explored the ethical concerns of elderly consumers and related marketing and marketing research practices. Vitell, Lumpkin, and Rawwas (1991) noted a range of ethical beliefs and behaviours amongst elderly consumers, reflecting the heterogeneity amongst this consumer category that parallels society at large. Yet some issues, such as vulnerability due to loneliness, impaired or compromised information-processing ability, decreased financial means, and ageism in market representations and treatment merit particular attention in the case of elderly consumers. Grougiou and Pettigrew (2009) noted that elderly consumers were less likely to make complaints to service providers than their younger counterparts. Hill and Kozup (2007) explored elderly consumers' debt at the hands of predatory lenders. Griffith and Harmon (2011) elaborated ethical issues regarding the acquisition and reliability of informed consent for elderly consumers in relation to service encounters as a function of their cognitive abilities and their emotional connections to service providers. Clough (2015) explained the vulnerabilities of elderly consumers approaching fourth age, with anticipations and experiences of increasing frailty, dependence and resulting greater needs for care and social relations, while Johannesen and LoGiudice (2013) raised concerns regarding the abuse of elderly consumers by service providers. Reviewing these studies, we reemphasize the importance of monitoring and training service employees by managers and the oversight and regulation of these aspects of elderly consumption in public policy.

Finally, the consumerist desire to avoid or postpone aging, together with the promise of profit in the burgeoning grey market, together fuel the bio-medicalization of old age. In one of the earliest studies, Katz and Marshall (2003) illustrated the marketing of sexuality and sexual function to aid active seniors in rehabilitating and reinvigorating their aging bodies. Mykytyn (2008) explored business issues and ethical implications in the development of anti-aging products. Furthermore, Fries (2014) showed that some elderly consumers preferred alternative medical therapies in combination with self-care to commercial bio-medicalization.

Popular cultural and market representations

Popular cultural, market, and advertising representations both anticipate and reflect personal and social ideals and commercial interests. Particularly problematic is agelessness, an attainable state to which all consumers can aspire with the help of a range of market offerings. The implication that ageing does not exist results from the invisibility of older consumers in most market representations. For example, noting that elderly consumers were either conspicuously absent or appeared as ageist and negative stereotypes, Carrigan and Szmigin (2002) advocated for increased awareness of age discrimination by consumers and marketers and for its increased regulation in public policy. Ten years later Yoon and Powell (2012) noted in advertisements in the UK a mix of invisibility and negative stereotyping of elderly consumers, combined with more progressive and creative depictions featuring older celebrities. In her review of over 160 North American advertisements for anti-aging creams, Ellison (2014) highlighted campaigns that supported discourses of agelessness by reinforcing the myth that through consumption people could transcend the aging process and mask or deny its physical embodiment.

The situation was somewhat similar in other media. Lewis, Medvedev, and Seponski (2011) noted that despite constituting the majority of readers of fashion magazines, female consumers over forty were largely absent in them. The authors explained this absence as reflecting and contributing to ageist socio-cultural assumptions that aging female bodies are undesirable and asexual, and therefore should be less visible than young, white female ideals. In contrast, Hurd Clarke, Bennet, and Liu's (2014) visual and content analysis of portrayals of older male consumers in advertising found that they, too, were largely invisible; however, where represented, older male consumers and celebrities appeared as happy and healthy.

Future research directions

Reviewing the literature, we derive a number of future research challenges and opportunities, which we outline below.

A greater balance in studying positive and not-so-positive aspects of aging

First, noting that third age, positive representations and treatments of aging by far dominate those of the more difficult fourth age in academic studies and marketing practices, we call for greater attention to the latter. Third and fourth age distinctions in aging and consumption are partly a function of training and interest, and partly the result of cohort and generational differences among aging researchers, their baby boomer counterparts, and the incoming cadre of millennials. Each has had formative experiences, periods of abundance and recession, changing access to consumption and to medical services, that impact the phenomena we study as well as our perspectives and approaches.

It is valuable to emphasize positive aspects of ageing, whether due to conscious/ unconscious desires to bring them about, and/or to better understand the importance of will, perspective, and experience upon the aging process. As important for the elderly persons, for family members, for commercial establishments, and for public policy is the study of negative aging.

Gender, ethnic/racial, class, and third-world identities, social market formations, and intersectionalities

As consumers age, they experience a number of identity challenges and projects, and revisit current and former identity forms. We build upon Twigg's (2004) call for a "fuller and better account of the role of the body in deep old age, one that encompasses subjective feelings and experiences and that recognizes embodiment as its central topic" (p. 71). As important are racial/ ethnic and class dimensions and their interactions with gender in aging. Building on Barrett, Pai, and Redmond's (2012) study of the Red Hat Society, future studies might examine how particular gendered/ethnic/racial/class intersectionalities and subcultures of aging might promote social inclusion.

Regarding gendered aging bodies and selves, we encourage further studies examining the impacts of changing appearance on older consumers and consumption, with attention to these intersectionalities, to various consumption categories, and to media and technological interventions. Topics include the consumption strategies and rituals of elderly consumers in celebrating, denying, and/or masking changes in physical appearance, and when and how changing ageing bodies and appearance become more salient for certain consumption categories. Further studies might explore the degree to which elderly care is (still) women's work, the implications for female carers who typically live longer than the male relatives or dependents for whom they care, and eldercare funding, particularly for older women with breaks in employment history due to family and caring responsibilities.

Intergenerational perspectives on aging

Another pressing area of research and policy is the pressured sandwich generation, primarily baby boomers, who find themselves caring for aging parents, children, and sometimes even grandchildren. Future research could explore the experiences and expectations of the different generations in relation to eldercare provision, and parent/child role reversals for their impact on consumption and financial management.

Exploring further the intergenerational and interdependent aspects of elderly consumption as a group phenomenon within ECEs is another promising future research avenue. Research topics could include a deeper examination of family issues and intergenerational dynamics. Examples include the relations of adult children and grandchildren with elderly persons and caregivers in these ECEs, and the impact of these family and service relations on consumption.

Participatory research approaches with a greater focus on intersectionalities

Regarding methods, building on Silver's (2003) study, future studies could illuminate the meanings and experiences in aging intersectionalities using participatory approaches, such as ethnography (Degnen, 2015), participatory action research (Ozanne and Saatcioglu, 2008), and narrative biographical methods (Bornat, 2015). Critically, following Collins (2015) and Calasanti and King (2015), we also recommend that future studies engage elderly intersectionality as critical praxis.

Global, international, and developing markets perspectives

Studies in non-Western, third-world, and global contexts is desperately needed in better understanding the models, interpretations, and consumption practices of elderly consumers in different social and market circumstances and with various socioeconomic characteristics. Future research could explore the limited presence/absence of medical care, the activities of elderly in conjunction with family, friends, and/or service providers in assembling and exchanging resources, and allocating and engaging in specific tasks.

Critical and transformative marketing practice perspectives

In addition, research is required to help inform and implement future marketing practice and policy. Regarding marketing practice, future research could fruitfully explore how marketplace changes and specific marketing activity frames and impacts elderly consumption. Examples include the challenges in targeting members of a group who do not identify as such, codes of language, and direct versus subtle forms and manners of address. Another area of potential future studies is exploring the legitimation effect of increased targeting and market representation of elderly consumers to see whether it brings about greater incidence of elderly consumer identification. Conversely, ethical issues include exploring the long-term impacts on consumers, and their reactions to illusory marketing campaigns encouraging staying young and denying deep old age.

Elderly consumer-centric policy perspectives

Finally, from a policy perspective, topics of interest include how to measure and evaluate increasing health care and other elderly service costs, and how to deal with challenges of counseling, paying, and retaining service employees, with attention to nuances and differences across subcultures and various government and market institutions. While an empirical reality, the ECE does not align with the current policy focus on aging in place, which delegates sole and primary responsibility for caring with families as long as possible, regardless of family circumstances, geographic location, and occupations. Another pressing area where work is needed is how to manage and communicate end-of-life issues, particularly the right to die and assisted death, with their legality in various states in the US and in other nations.

Conclusion

In conclusion, diverse interdisciplinary perspectives inform studies on aging and consumption. As critical consumer researchers, it is incumbent on us to reflect the diversity, richness, and complexity of aging and consumption in order to fully embrace and meet the needs of elderly consumers. As Williamson (1978) noted decades earlier, commercial imagery sells to us our very selves, not as we are, necessarily, but rather as we want to be. It is understandable that marketers and advertisers provide to elderly consumers favourable and desirable imagery in their strategic materials that privileges positive ways of being old. Using the metaphor of the distorted mirror in describing advertising, Pollay (1986) explained that advertisers and marketers seek to employ imagery that is credible, if not realistic, as consumers must be able to see themselves and identify with the representations at some level. Adding another important insight relevant to aging consumption studies, Campbell (2004) detailed the ontological and constitutive aspects of consumption; in wanting things and experiencing their desire, consumers do more than recognize themselves; they produce their sense of themselves. The implications for research on aging and consumption share these properties. We need to constantly focus and readjust our gaze to critically study aging and consumption to deliver transformative research outcomes that will improve consumer lives, policies, and marketing practices of elderly consumers.

References

Barnhart, M., Huff, A.D. & Cotte, J. (2014), Like a member of the family: including and excluding paid caregivers in performances of family. *Journal of Marketing Management, 30(15–16)*, 1680–1702.

___ & Peñaloza, L. (2012), Who are you calling old? negotiating old age identity in the elderly consumption ensemble. *Journal of Consumer Research, 39*, 1133–1153.

Barrett, A. E., Pai, M. & Redmond, R. (2012), It's your badge of inclusion: the red hat society as a gendered subculture of aging. *Journal of Aging Studies, 26(4)*, 527–538.

Bellenger, D.N. & Korgaonkar, P.K. (1980), Profiling the recreational shopper. *Journal of Retailing, 56(Fall)*, 77–92.

Blaikie, A. (1999), *Aging and popular culture*, Cambridge, United Kingdom: Cambridge University Press.

Bloch, P.H., Ridgway, N.M. & Nelson, J.E. (1991), Leisure and the shopping mall. In R. H. Holman & M. R. Solomon (Eds.), *Advances in consumer research* (Vol. 18, pp. 445–452). Provo, UT: Association for Consumer Research.

Bornat, J. (2015), Ageing, narrative and biographical methods. In J. Twigg & W. Martin (Eds.), *Routledge handbook of cultural gerontology* (pp.113–120). New York: Routledge.

Calasanti, T. & King, N. (2015), Intersectionality and age. In J. Twigg & W. Martin (Eds.), *Routledge handbook of cultural gerontology* (pp.193–200). New York: Routledge.

Campbell, C. (2004), I shop therefore I know that I am: the metaphysical basis of modern consumption. In K. Ekstrom & H. Brembeck (Eds.), *Elusive consumption* (pp. 27–44). Oxford, United Kingdom: Berg.

Carrigan, M. & Szmigin, I. (2002), Advertising in an aging society. *Aging and Society*, *20*, 217–233.

Castaño, R., Quintanilla, C. & Perez, M.E. (2012), Aging and the changing meaning of consumption experiences. Documentary Film, 20 min., Association of Consumer Research Film Festival, Vancouver, Canada.

Clough, R. (2015), Older people: Citizens in a consumer society. In K. Hamilton, S. Dunnett, & M. Piacentini (Eds.), Consumer vulnerability: Conditions, contexts and characteristics (pp. 130–142). Abingdon: Routledge.

Cole, C., Laurent, G., Drolet, A., Ebert, J., Gutchess, A., Lambert-Pandraud, R., Mullet, E., Norton, M., & Peters, E. (2008), Decision making and brand choice by older consumers. *Marketing Letters*, *19:3/4 (July)*, 355–365.

Collins, P.H. (2015), Intersectionality's definitional dilemmas. *Annual Review of Sociology*, *41*, 1–20.

Dean, D., Kellie, J. & Mould, P. (2014), From pushchairs to wheelchairs: understanding tensions in family decision making through the experiences of adult children caring for aging parents. *Journal of Marketing Management*, *30(15/16)* (November), 1703–1721.

Degnen, C. (2015), Ethnographies of ageing. In J. Twigg & W. Martin (Eds.), *Routledge handbook of cultural gerontology* (pp.105–113). New York: Routledge.

De Witt, L., Campbell, L., Ploeg, J., Kemp, C. & Rosenthal, C. (2013), You're saying something by giving things to them: communication and family inheritance. *European Journal of Aging*, *10(3)*, 181–189.

Drolet, A., Schwartz, N. & Yoon, C. (2010), *The aging consumer: perspectives from psychology and economics*. New York: Routledge.

Ekerdt, D.J. & Addington, A. (2015), Possession divestment by sales in later life. *Journal of Aging Studies*, *34*, 21–28.

___ & Clark, E. (2001), Selling retirement in financial planning advertisements. *Journal of Aging Studies*, *15*, 55–68.

Ellison, K.L. (2014), Age transcended: a semiotic and rhetorical analysis of the discourse of agelessness in north American anti-aging skin care advertisements. *Journal of Aging Studies*, *29*, 20–31.

Fries, C. J. (2014), Older adults' use of complementary and alternative medical therapies to resist biomedicalization of aging. *Journal of Aging Studies*, *28*, 1–10.

Gergen, K. & Gergen, M. M. (2000), The new aging: self-construction and social values. In H.W. Schaie & J. Hendrick (Eds.), *The evolution of the aging self: the societal impact on the aging process* (pp. 281–306). New York: Springer.

Gilleard, C. & Higgs, P. (2008), Internet use and the digital divide in the english longitudinal study of aging. *European Journal of Aging*, *5(3)*, 233–239.

___, Hyde, M., Wiggins, R. & Blane, D. (2005), Class, cohort, and consumption: the british experience of the third age. *Journal of Gerontology*, *60B(6)*, S305–S310.

Gilly, M., Celsi, M.W. & Schau, H.J. (2012), It don't come easy: overcoming obstacles to technology use within a resistant consumer group. *Journal of Consumer Affairs*, *46* (Spring), 62–89.

Griffiths, M.A., & Harmon, T.R. (2011), Aging consumer vulnerabilities influencing factors of acquiescence to informed consent. *Journal of Consumer Affairs*, *45(3)*, 445–466.

Grougiou, V. & Pettigrew, S. (2009), Seniors' attitudes to voicing complaints: a qualitative study, *Journal of Marketing Management*, *25(9/10)* (November), 987–1001.

Guberman, N., Lavoie, J.P., Blein, L. & Olazabal, I. (2012), Baby boom caregivers: care in the age of individualization. *The Gerontologist*, *52(2)*, 210–218.

Hearn, J. & Wray, S. (2015), Gender: implications of a contested area. In J. Twigg & W. Martin (Eds.), *Routledge handbook of cultural gerontology* (pp.201–209). New York: Routledge.

Higgs, P. & Gilleard, C. (2015), *Rethinking old age: theorising the fourth age*. London, United Kingdom: Palgrave Macmillan.

___, Hyde, M, Gilleard, C.J., Victor, C.R., Wiggins, R.D. & Jones, I.R. (2009), From passive to active consumers? later life consumption in the UK from 1968–2005. *The Sociological Review*, *57(1)*, 102–124.

Hill, R. P. & Kozup, J. C. (2007), Consumer experiences with predatory lending practices. *Journal of Consumer Affairs*, *41*(1), 29–46.

House, J.S., Landis, K.R. & Umberson, D. (1988), Social relationships and health. *Science*, *241*, 540–545.

Hurd Clarke, L. & Korotchenko, A. (2010), Shades of grey: to dye or not to dye one's hair in later life. *Ageing and Society*, *30(6)*, 1011–1026.

___, Bennett, E.V. & Liu, C. (2014), Aging and masculinity: portrayals in men's magazines. *Journal of Aging Studies*, *31*, 26–33.

Johannesen, M. & LoGiudice, D. (2013), Elder abuse: a systematic review of risk factors in community-dwelling elders. *Age and Aging, 2*, 292–298.

Kang, Y.S. & Ridgway, N.M. (1996), The importance of consumer market interactions as a form of social support for elderly consumers. *Journal of Public Policy and Marketing, 15(1)* (Spring), 108–117.

Katz, S. & Marshall, B. (2003), New sex for old: lifestyle, consumerism, and the ethics of aging well. *Journal of Aging Studies, 17*, 3–16.

Kertzer, David I. (1983), Generation as a sociological problem. *Annual Review of Sociology, 9*, 125–149.

Kaufman, S.R. (1986), *The ageless self – sources of meaning in late life.* Madison, WI: University of Wisconsin Press.

Lambert-Pandraud, R. & Laurent, G. (2010), Why do older consumers buy older brands? the role of attachment and declining innovativeness. *Journal of Marketing, 74(5)* (September), 104–121.

Laslett, P. (1989), *A fresh map of life: the emergence of a third age*. London, United Kingdom: Weidenfeld and Nicolson.

Lewis, D.C., Medvedev, K. & Seponski, D.M. (2011), Awakening to the desires of older women: deconstructing ageism within fashion magazines. *Journal of Aging Studies, 25*, 101–109.

Mannheim, K. (1952), The problem of generations. In P. Kecskemeti (ed.) *Essays on the Sociology of Knowledge* (pp. 276–320). NY: Routledge.

McHugh, K.E. (2000), The "ageless self"? emplacement of identities in sun belt retirement communities. *Journal of Aging Studies, 14(1)*, 103–115.

Minkler, M. (1991), Gold in gray: reflections on business' discovery of the elderly market. In M. Minkler & C.L. Estes (Ed.), *Critical perspectives on aging: The political and moral economy of growing old* (pp. 81–93). Amityville, NY: Baywood.

Moschis, G. (1987), *Consumer socialization: a life-cycle perspective*. Lexington, MA: Lexington Books.

___, & Mathur, A. (1993), How they're acting their age: new research reveals hidden truths about marketing to the elderly. *Marketing Management, 2(2)*, 40–50.

Mykytyn, C.E. (2008), Medicalizing the optimal: anti-aging medicine and the quandary of intervention. *Journal of Aging Studies, 22*, 313–321.

Nasi, M., Rasanen, P. and Sarpila, O. (2012), ICT activity in later life: internet use and leisure activities amongst senior citizens in Finland. *European Journal of Aging, 9*, 169–176.

Ozanne, J. L., & Saatcioglu, B. (2008), Participatory action research. *Journal of Consumer Research, 35*(3), 423–439.

Peters, E. (2010), Aging-related changes in decision making. In Drolet, A., Schwartz, N. & Yoon, C. (Eds.), *The aging consumer: perspectives from psychology and economics* (pp.75–101). New York: Routledge.

Pettigrew, S. & G. Moschis (2012) Consumer well-being in later life. In D.G. Mick, S. Pettigrew, C. Pechmann & J.L Ozanne (Eds.), *Transformative consumer research: for personal and collective well-being* (pp. 565–582). USA: Routledge.

Pollay, R.W. (1986), The distorted mirror: reflections on the unintended consequences of advertising. *Journal of Marketing, 50(2)*,18–36.

Price, L.L. & Arnould, E.J. (1999), Commercial friendships: service provider-client relationships in context. *Journal of Marketing, 63(4)*, 38–56.

___ & Folkman, C. (2000), Older consumers' disposition of special possessions. *Journal of Consumer Research, 27(2)*, 179–201.

Quadrello, T., Hurme, H., Menzinger, J., Smith, P.K., Veisson, M., Vidal, S. & Westerback, S. (2005), Grandparents use of new communication technologies in a european perspective. *European Journal of Aging, 2(3)*, 200–207.

Risius, D., Thelwell, R., Wagstaff, C.R., & Scurr, J. (2014), The influence of ageing on bra preferences and self-perception of breasts among mature women. *European Journal of Ageing, 11*(3), 233–240.

Roedder John, D. & Cole, C. (1986), Age differences in information processing: understanding deficits in young and elderly consumers. *Journal of Consumer Research, 13(3)* (December), 297–315.

Rowe, J. W. & Kahn, R. L. (2015), Successful aging 2.0: conceptual expansions for the 21st century. *The Journals of Gerontology Series B: Psychological Sciences and Social Sciences, 70*(4), 593–596, doi:10.1093/geronb/gbv025. Advance Access publication April 15, 2015

Rudman, D.L. (2015), Embodying positive aging and neoliberal rationality: talking about the aging body within narratives of retirement. *Journal of Aging Studies, 34*, 10–20.

Ryder, N.B. (1965/1997), The cohort as a concept in the study of social change. In M.A. Hardy (Ed.), *Studying Aging and Social Change* (pp. 66–92), London, United Kingdom: Sage Publications.

Schau, H.J., Gilly, M.C. & Wolfinbarger, M. (2009), Consumer identity renaissance: the resurgence of identity-inspired consumption in retirement. *Journal of Consumer Research, 36(2)*, 255–276.

Silver, C.B. (2003), Gendered identities in old age: toward (de)gendering?. *Journal of Aging Studies, 17*, 379–397.

Twigg, J. (2004), The body, gender and age: feminist insights in social gerontology. *Journal of Aging Studies, 18*, 59–73.

___ & Shinobu Majim (2014), Consumption and the constitution of age: expenditure patterns on clothing, hair and cosmetics among post-war 'baby boomers. *Journal of Aging Studies, 30*, 23–32.

Vitell, S.J., J.R. Lumpkin & Rawwas, M.Y.A. (1991), Consumer ethics: an investigation of the ethical beliefs of elderly consumers. *Journal of Business Ethics. 10(5)* (May), 365–375.

Williams, P. & Drolet, A. (2005), Age-related differences in responses to emotional advertisements. *Journal of Consumer Research, 32(3)* (December), 343–354.

Williams, A., Ylänne, V. and Wadleigh, P.M. (2007), Selling the 'elixir of life': images of the elderly in an olivio advertising campaign. *Journal of Aging Studies, 21*, 1–21.

Williamson, J. (1978), *Decoding advertisements.* London, United Kingdom: Marion Boyars.

Yoon, C. (1997), Age differences in consumers' processing strategies: an investigation of moderating influences. *Journal of Consumer Research, 24(3)* (December), 329–342.

___, Laurent, G., Fung, H.H., Gonzalez, R., Gutchess, A.H., Hedden, T., Lambert-Pandraud, R., Mather, M., Park, D. C., Peters, E. & Skurnik, I. (2005), Cognition, persuasion and decision making in older consumers. *Marketing Letters, 16(3–4)*, 429–441.

___, Cole, C. & Lee, M.P. (2009), Consumer decision making and aging: current knowledge and future directions. *Journal of Consumer Psychology, 19(1)* (January), 2–16.

Yoon, H. & Powell, H. (2012), Older consumers and celebrity advertising. *Aging & Society, 32*, 1319–1336.

Part VI
Contested consumption
Introduction

Modern consumers in many different contexts sometimes get the impression that a lot of the ordinary things they go about doing in their everyday lives are being questioned. When you are taking your car to work, you contribute to the environmental problems. When you are serving fast food to your children, you behave in a morally questionable manner by not teaching them to enjoy proper meals. When you sit still and watch series on your tablet, you are damaging your own physical body shape and health.

A large number and broad variety of routinized ordinary ways of managing everyday contexts, activities and relations involve types of consumption, which are being publicly problematized and criticised in society. These public critiques are based on various grounds, for example sustainability, health and morality. Media discourses across genres and platforms amplify the different critiques and the negotiations about how to consume, and since media is present in most contexts, it is difficult for consumers to escape such discourses entirely, either themselves or within their social network interactions. This way, some types of consumption become contested: expectable and acceptable ways of consuming cannot necessarily be taken for granted, when particular consumer goods and consumption processes are being questioned normatively. As part of these contestation processes, responsibility for solving societal challenges tends to be placed on consumers as individuals, and thus, an important discussion in research is whether responsibility for collective political problems should be placed on the shoulders of individuals or should be for larger collective actors, such as governments or corporations, to tackle. All this renders consumption a thoroughly political issue even though consumers rarely contemplate on the larger-scale consequences of their routinized everyday activities (see also section 4 in this volume for consumer policies and politics).

This section covers two of the types of contested consumption that have received a lot of attention within consumption research, namely consumption contested on the basis of sustainability issues, and consumption contested on the basis of body issues. The approach to sustainability in this section takes a somewhat more general conceptual lens as a point of departure to carve some clarity into societal issues and theoretical debates going on in the field, leaving more empirical overviews of what has been studied regarding consumers' (non) sustainable behaviours in the background as there are several new volumes specifically on sustainable consumption on the book market today.

Naturally there are several more themes hotly discussed and studied under the wide umbrella of contested consumption today, such as coping with the increasing financialization of everyday life, i.e. ordinary money matters deeply embedded in global financial markets, or more specific health issues related to food or physical movement or lack thereof. Yet sustainability – mainly opened up through the topic of consumption's effect on environmental degradation and climate change (less so in terms of social and economic sustainability) – and the human body are hubs around which a bulk of the consumption studies discussion revolves, and this section aims to shed light to some of those conversations.

Chapter 29 is called "Sustainable consumption and changing practices", and it plunges the reader directly into a number of the key issues that have been researched and debated academically around sustainable consumption. In the chapter, Matt Watson argues that there are two main ways in which a practice theoretical approach has been used in research on sustainable consumption: a "weaker" version where more attention is paid to embodied skills, tacit knowledge and the habitual character of the practices which consumption forms part of, and a "strong" version where practices themselves take centre stage of analysis, and the individual consumer is thoroughly decentred from analysis. The chapter demonstrates implications for research on sustainable consumption from both versions.

The theme is also sustainable consumption in chapter 30, but here the focus is moving towards more structural dynamics. The chapter is called "Structural conditions for and against sustainable ways of consuming". Bas van Vliet and Gert Spaargaren underline that the research in sustainable consumption of energy and water has had a tendency to be separated into research on two different domains, namely research on energy and water consumption patterns, and research on infrastructural systems of energy and water. Instead, they argue that it is necessary to focus on the interplay through which consumption and infrastructure mutually reproduce each other and form structural conditions for consumption. Case-studies of drinking water, toilet use, medicine use and smart energy are presented and discussed.

Chapter 31 rounds off the chapters about sustainable consumption and is called "Retail sector facing the challenge of sustainable consumption". Here, Mikael Klintman explains and discusses the four main challenges that are coming out of the research on the retailing-consumption relationship for ways of moving consumption towards sustainability. These are strengthening the trustworthiness of the retail sector, to navigating among multiple sustainability-oriented values, reaching a sustainability-oriented dynamic between retailers and consumers, and handling the possible dominance of retail-based sustainability framings.

The body is another issue on the basis of which consumption is being contested, and where there is extensive consumption research literature. Chapter 32 does not beat about the bush with the title "Sexual embodiment and consumption". Sue Scott argues that although sex and bodies are clearly commodified, embodied "ordinary" sexuality has not been high on the agenda in consumption research. In the chapter, she discusses the various ways in which adult sexuality and embodiment have been related to consumption, and she examines in depth a case-study of childhood, consumption and sexualisation in order to show how a focus in research on the more exotic or problematic aspects of sexuality needs to be balanced by research on sexual embodiment as a mundane phenomenon – also in relation to consumption.

Chapter 33 goes classic in consumption research with a focus on taste as part of contested consumption. Melissa L. Caldwell, in her chapter called "Taste and embodied practice", outlines the different ways in which taste and its relationship to embodied practices have been differently accounted for and theorised in research about consumption. On the basis of this, she also discusses the potential societal and cultural implications from the relations between consumption, taste as classificatory dynamic and embodied practices.

The final chapter in the section moves towards the moving body. chapter 34, "Health, bodies and active leisure" is about the commercialization of physical bodily activity. Here, Roberta Sassatelli argues that fitness culture can be understood as primarily a commercial culture with a specific construction of the consumer as the chooser, and that the research shows how fitness users continuously intertwine processes of coping with body ideals with processes of gender play.

29

Sustainable consumption and changing practices

Matt Watson

So many of the ways in which consumption is contested gather around questions of sustainability. We can start this chapter with three of them. First, patterns of consumption are at the root of overall demands for resources and the goods and services they provide. That makes them problematic because those demands for resources are reckoned to total around 150% of the productive capacity of the planet (World Wide Fund for Nature, 2014). This represents the fundamental grounds of concern over the scale of contemporary global consumption. Definitions of sustainability are of course diverse and contested. But using up resources faster than they can be replaced is counter to the most foundational understandings of sustainability.

A second field of contestation relates to social equity. Even for any definitions that do not see social equity as a central plank of sustainability, the question of who consumes what matters for choosing where to seek change. 'Sustainable consumption' for someone surviving on less than the equivalent of $2 a day can be best understood as the challenge of making available and sustaining an adequate level of consumption to maintain well-being. Taking contributions to climate change as an indicator of overall responsibility for environmental damage through consumption, the around 10% of global population living at or below $2 a day (Cruz, Foster, Quillin, & Schellekens, 2015) accounts for approximately 1% of global anthropogenic greenhouse gas emissions (GHGs) (Oxfam, 2015). Meanwhile for someone in the top 10% of global income – along with most readers of this book, in the small minority which is reckoned to be responsible for about 50% of GHGs (Oxfam, 2015) – 'sustainable consumption' must be a matter of radical reduction in the resource intensity of ways of life.

A third related field of contestation of consumption that relates to sustainability is the relation of consumption to wellbeing. This can seem still further from any common core to different definitions of sustainability, but it becomes pertinent in light of the two points of contestation above. It is commonly accepted that, beyond a given level, increasing consumption in society does not benefit overall wellbeing (Pretty et al., 2015). Indeed, some argue that happiness and wellbeing are better served by reducing consumption from the levels characterising the world's relatively wealthy (Jackson, 2005).

These three key fields of contestation of consumption in relation to sustainability all point in a common direction: that the world's relatively wealthy should consume less stuff and services. Yet sustainable consumption research, and even more so policy in this field, only rarely focuses on that fundamental imperative. Commonly, consumption is considered as 'sustainable' where it involves purchase of a product or services which is somewhat less environmentally damaging that whatever is taken as 'normal'. That is, 'sustainable' consumption is that which makes a particular field of consumption at least a little bit less harmful, on at least some measures – for example by buying organically certified foods as a totemic act of environmental responsibility. There is a range of reasons why debate tends to stay within the relatively safe zone of incrementalism, from the unpalatability of challenging the standards of living that people have striven to achieve, to the fundamental logics of neoliberal democracies where gross domestic product continues to be the measure of social progress.

Conventional ideas of change in relation to consumption then are generally very incremental. Mainstream messages on sustainable consumption have it that many small changes in individual actions will add up to bigger change in overall resource consumption. What is needed are many big changes, across both systems of supply and situations of consumption, which add up to an enormous overall change. For consumption to be sustainable it is not enough that we make 'better choices' between one product and another at the checkout. We also need fundamental changes in how we live, how we work and how we play. Sustainable consumption demands changes to our practices.

Locating practice theory in sustainable consumption

The word *practice* commonly refers to concrete doing (rather than, say, abstract theorising). More specifically it refers to repetitively doing something to become better at doing that thing. Where researchers, including consumption researchers, talk of practice it is often to signal sensitivity to the lived experience of doing, the fine grain of human existence which escapes easy representation. However, as indicated in other chapters in this book (3, 18 and 20), a good number of researchers and theorists have practiced a lot of abstract theorising about practices. Practice theory, in its different manifestations, offers distinctive accounts of human actions and of social order, and of both how these stay the same over time, and how they change.

Thanks both to its radical implications for understanding human action, and for the slippery way that the term *practice* has both theoretical currency and readily accessible meanings, practice theory has had increasing prominence in recent years. What has for more than a century been largely a preserve of philosophy and abstract social theory has increasingly been brought into empirical and analytical operation. This has probably been true more in the field of sustainable consumption than anywhere else.

In this field, practice theory is used to challenge or overcome certain recurrent orthodoxies of both research and policy. Over recent decades attempts to make consumption more sustainable have principally been targeted through policy by focusing on helping individual consumers make better choices, whether through advertising, education, price signals or other incentives. Shove (2010) characterises the 'ABC' paradigm of environmental policy seeking to change what people do – where 'values and attitudes (the A) . . . are believed to drive the kinds of behaviour (the B) that individuals choose (the C) to adopt' (1274). This is manifested in the ways that behavior-change initiatives are enacted, targeting individuals to change particular behaviors through a limited suite of interventions, from public awareness campaigns (Windahl, Signitzer, & Olson, 1992) and financial incentives (Bolderdijk & Steg, 2015) to more sophisticated approaches to 'nudging' choices, inspired by behavioural economics (Thaler & Sunstein, 2009). This orthodoxy of sustainable consumption policy is often presented as the departure point, contestation of which provides the opening for introducing a practice approach.

However, as set out in chapter 3, the rise of practice theory research in relation to consumption also reflects broader intellectual currents, including the ways they have played out in relation to understanding consumption more generally. In the last decade, practice theory has grown in prominence as a means of approaching consumption. Indeed, within some subfields – not least within studies of sustainable consumption – it can feel like an established orthodoxy of its own.

This prominence results from the distinctive and challenging understanding of fundamental properties and bases of the social that result from a practice theory approach. Practice theory is claimed to represent a practicable means of moving beyond classic dualisms of social theory including between structure and agency, between voluntarism and determinism, and between individualism and holism. The principal move it makes in this is to decentre the individual from analysis, without resorting instead to focus on structure, but instead to consider practices as the central object of analytical concern. Practice approaches are often used for a focus on the details of doing, with a practice approach bringing sensitivity to aspects of doing which have often escaped analysis which focuses on representation or discourse. This means attention being paid to the role of embodied and tacit knowledge and skills, to the role of habits and routines and to the affective experience of being in the world. This way of engaging with practice theory has been a significant part of the approach's use in relation to sustainable consumption. However, for some working with practice theory, using practice theory to illuminate the details of doing is only going part way in realising the value of the approach, missing its more radical implications.

For Schatzki (1996: 13) 'both social order and individuality . . . result from practices', indicating the grander ambitions for practice theory, going well beyond understanding the details of human action. Rather, practices are centre stage. Understanding how the concept of practice can have such ambition in relation to accounting for social life demands more explanation of what constitutes a practice. A practice has a dual existence, both in the performance of the practice by a practitioner and as an entity, with enduring existence across individual moments of its enactment (Shove, Watson, Hand, & Ingram, 2007). As an entity a practice is something which can be spoken of, and it is possible to have an idea of the bunch of things it takes to be able to do the practice – the know-how, the things, the norms, rules and meanings it carries. In this sense a practice transcends individual moments of doing. However, as an entity it only has continued existence so long as it exists also as performances.

Through a focus on practices themselves, practice theory thoroughly decentres the individual person from analysis. Indeed, according to Reckwitz (2002), people are 'carriers' of practice. This implies a radically different understanding of the relationship between people and their actions than in dominant approaches to changing consumption behavior in fields such as behavioral economics (Sunstein, 2015) or psychology (Fishbein & Cappella, 2006). Individual attitudes and values are side-lined by attention to the meanings and purposes of the practices in which they engage and in which actions are only marginally and at times matters of reflective choice. As we see in the following sections, attention to mundane habits and doings has given rise to a range of critical insights, but what is increasingly called the 'strong' programme of practice theory (e.g. Welch & Warde, 2015) has further implications for approaching sustainable consumption and processes of change.

Rhythms, routines and the challenges of making consumption sustainable

The distinctive sensitivities that a practice approach brings have been applied to understanding consumption as embedded in the rhythms, routines and embodied goings-on of everyday life. We can exemplify insights here in relation to the field of food consumption. The global food system results in environmental harms that outweigh all other fields of human activity. In terms of climate change alone, taking a whole-systems approach, agriculture and food production account for up to one third of anthropogenic greenhouse gas emissions (Pretty et al., 2011). Together with the clear environmental dependencies of food production and the challenges of adequately feeding projected global populations of nine or ten billion (Godfray et al., 2010), food consumption is a significant area of concern. Indeed, at a global level processes of change are heading in very much the wrong direction as countries where significant proportions of the population are increasing in wealth are undergoing a 'nutrition transition' (Popkin, Adair, & Ng, 2012) to more environmentally burdensome diets, principally as a result of increasing meat and dairy consumption. While animal products provide less than one fifth of calorie intake worldwide (Food and Agriculture Organisation [FAO], 2010), livestock has been estimated to account for one half of greenhouse gas emissions resulting from the food system (FAO, 2006). However, food consumption is difficult to tackle. A practice approach helps to understand why across several dimensions, from which we can pick up three.

First, most human activity around food is profoundly routinized and mundane. It is through routinisation that we come to be able to cope with (and largely let go unnoticed) the complexity of keeping a household provided with food. The coordination of ingredients, hardware, skills, energy and more within the spaces and temporal rhythms of everyday life would by overwhelming if it demanded reflection at more than a superficial level. Routine enables the navigation of supermarket aisles and the bewildering choice they offer, without conscious choices between all of the options available being made, with the weighing of cost, economy, taste, pleasure and risk. In food as in so many other field of consumption (and life more generally) we are only able to navigate a path through and accomplish another day through reliance on routine (DeVault, 1994; Giddens, 1984; Warde, 2016). Of course people make reflective choices, buy something special, or try something new. But there is only space for novelty because the bulk of choices have been sedimented into routines of picking things from the shelf.

Second, and closely related to routine, is the extent to which food consumption is bound up with largely shared temporal rhythms, implicated in shared social conventions. Popular discourses identify processes of de-routinisation of eating patterns, associated with a sense of fragmentation and speeding up of social time, progress of individualisation and the breakdown of the 'traditional' family. However, time-use surveys show that, while there has been some change, conventions of eating prove remarkably resilient (Lund & Gronow, 2014; A. Warde, Cheng, Olsen, & Southerton, 2007). Meal times remain key to broadly shared temporal rhythms, with distinct profiles of temporal convergence between different national societies (Holm et al., 2012; A. Warde et al., 2007). For example, far fewer people eat simultaneously in Finland than in France (Shove, 2009). Conventions, however, go well beyond the timing of eating, going also into what makes a meal. Michel de Certeau and colleagues (1998) show repeatedly the convention-bound roles of food and drink in family life. For example, how the rules of conduct allow what could seem a random selection of goods from the shop to become the ordered entity of a family meal: "it is in the kitchen that they become a succession unfolding according to a pre-existing canonical order" (85). More broadly, though, conventions extend of course to gendered divisions of labour, tastes, table manners and more. Food is bound up with diverse norms of right conduct, many of which only become visible or problematized when they are transgressed, or are being actively passed on, as by parents to children.

Third, in addition to routine, rhythm and convention, a practice approach draws attention to the role of embodiment and tacit skills in relation to food. Of course, of all realms of consumption food is most clearly entwined with embodiment. It is after all what bodies are made from, its location in everyday lives inseparable from the ways in which it is incorporated into our bodies. A practice approach though is more concerned with how the body is part of the flow of action around food, which is of course shaped by the competencies and capacities that reside in our bodies as tacit skills and ways of going on, without being generally part of conscious reflection (Certeau, Giard & Mayol, 1998).

A practice approach, then – including through these three fields of concern – illuminates how food consumption is bound up with foundational processes of the reproduction of daily life and of key aspects of shared social order. Seeking to purposively change food consumption, for example to reduce meat consumption, means intervening into these complex and largely submerged relations around food. Of course food is represented. The mass of print, broadcast and digital media devoted to food is ample demonstration of that. A practice approach does not deny the significance of changing representations. Its frequent presentation as an alternative to representational approaches can easily lead to this impression, especially with many analyses using it to reveal aspects of phenomena beyond discourse. Halkier (2010) engages Warde's (2005) practice component categories of understanding, procedures and engagement to approach food practices in relation to media problematization of issues of health, sustainability and risk, emphasising the potential salience of such representations as interventions in the meanings comprising practices. Nevertheless, that prevalence of 'food media' is substantially a consequence of the extent to which food is part of the taken-for-granted substrate of social existence, which provides much of the stickiness of food practices.

In some ways, food can be argued to be a special case in relation to consumption given its centrality to human being and social life at many levels. Yet so much consumption of consequence for environmental sustainability shares key similarities. The mass of resource flows through the consumption that underpins everyday lives is less conspicuous, embedded in routines, rhythms, conventions and embodied actions. Electricity is demanded by appliances which provide services which have become needed or normally expected as part of the accomplishment of everyday life (Gram-Hanssen, 2011; Shove & Walker, 2014; Wallenborn & Wilhite, 2014). Water is used as part of routines and conventions bound up with historically contingent but deeply embedded norms of personal cleanliness and expectations of convenience (Allon & Sofoulis, 2010; Shove, 2003). Vehicle fuel is used up through the largely routinized travels (at given distances and speeds) that people come to structure their daily lives around to enable the performance of practices to be stitched together in the right times and places (Watson, 2012). Across fields of consumption, attention to practices reveals much of what makes obdurate the patterns of action that result in the use of resources and production of wastes. Against the range of relations that come to play a role in the making of doing, little wonder that interventions like education initiatives and price incentives often have uncertain or limited effect. So is practice theory a counsel of despair? Or can it help understand and inform meaningful change?

Practices and social change

The account of the implications of a practice approach as above already seems to speak more of stasis than of change. The emphasis of a 'strong' practice theory on practices themselves, rather than only the details of doing, makes change seem even more problematic. Reckwitz's (2002) representation of the entity of practice as a pattern to be filled by performance can be read to suggest human action is always scripted, shaped as if by a cookie cutter. Clearly, however, if practice theory could not accommodate change, it would lose all credibility in the face of empirical exploration. Food practices clearly vary across space and change over time, as do all practices.

In fact, rather than assuming permanence, as some critics seem to believe, practice theory starts from an understanding of all social relations as essentially mutable. As such practice theory is an account of the remarkable continuities and obduracies of social life – of individual lives, of institutions and of patterns of social order – those features being in much more need of explanation than is change. There is little reason to wonder that practice theory therefore has no difficulty in accommodating and accounting for change. To return to the practice of baking, the entity of baking provides the framing, encompassing the resources and patterns for a diversity of performances of baking. The entity of baking persists only through the innumerable moments of performance. Each performance is potentially unique, as performance depends on practitioners doing the active work of integrating the diverse elements of practice in a contingently effective configuration. There is always space for elements of innovation and spontaneity. Any such individual moment of innovation is always incremental, but through the accumulation of incremental innovations over successive performances the entity of baking shifts over time. Recent work in practice theory has sought to develop an account of different mechanisms through which practices change (Shove, Pantzar, & Watson, 2012), from which three present themselves as pertinent to thinking about change in relation to sustainable consumption.

First, there can be changes to the elements which comprise a practice. This makes immediate sense in relation to the material things comprising practices. Food practices have clearly been shaped and reshaped in part together with changing materialities and technologies. For example, fridges and freezers have changed the temporal demands of food provisioning, whether through enabling the preservation of surpluses from home food growing, or as a part of the changing systems of provisioning that lead to convenience foods (Shove & Southerton, 2000). The history of kitchens is littered with artefacts that once were innovations only to become obsolete, fossils of past patterns of kitchen practices (Shove & Pantzar, 2005). But meaningful change to practices can never be simply a story of technological change. Technical innovations have to be integrated to performances of a practice by a practitioner, with consequences for the meaning and the competencies which comprise the practice along with the technologies. Elements of meaning or of competence can also be sources of dynamism. For example, the rise of *The Great British Bake Off*, a surprisingly popular TV game show in the UK, has been part of dynamics in the meaning of baking, including the valorisation of conspicuous competence. Mostly, however, it is not easy to identify specific causes of change, or to predict the direction of change as the result of any specific moment of innovation. With any historical depth on a practice, the meanings, competencies and things comprising a practice co-evolve together. Innovation in relation to one sort of element reconfigures relations between elements such that spaces open up elsewhere for possible innovation. Change is endemic to practice.

A second location of change is in patterns of 'recruitment' and 'defection' to a practice – that is to the population of 'carriers' of the practice. While practice theory decentres the human subject from analysis, the practitioner is a distinctive and essential part of an account of practices. As in consideration of how elements change above, the active role of the practitioner is central. To understand the dynamics of practices, the capacities and active involvement of human individuals cannot be ignored. Ultimately, the fate of a practice depends on its success in recruiting and retaining practitioners ready to do the work of integrating together the elements of practice in moments of performance (Andersen, 2011; Meah & Watson, 2011).

After changes to elements and changes to practitioners, a third move opens up a whole new range of understandings of change. Attention to how practices relate to each other – how practices bundle together in spaces or in times, how they form complexes of interdependence – is clearly significant both for changes to elements comprising any one practice or to processes of recruitment or defection. Practices relate to each other at the level of how people perform them in the organisation of their days. So, for example, the rise of internet supermarket shopping enables shopping to fit into different moments and rhythms of the day, freed from its coordination with travel plans and opening hours. Such a change has implications for performances of practices elsewhere, such as of personal mobility, or of what gets done while TV-watching. Practices also bundle together in more tightly integrated ways, forming what can be termed *complexes of practices* (Shove et al., 2012). Particular patterns of food consumption are dependent on co-dependent practices continuing to be performed. For example, contemporary configuration of meat consumption at home depends on the practices comprising animal husbandry, livestock feed production, slaughtering and butchery, the practices of packaging and retail, amongst many others. The role of meat in contemporary Western diets is inseparable from the configurations of these practices. It is the industrialisation of meat production practices and the rationalisation of market practices which enable meat to be so very cheap despite the environmental costs of its production. Meanwhile it is the demand constituted through practices of shopping and food provisioning which sustains those practices of meat production and market provisioning. These interdependencies between practices across locales are constituted and sustained only through the performance of those practices. Recognising how the generally routinized, mundane actions underpinning consumption of resources are constituted through diverse relations with other practices across locales, and the arrangements those practices constitute, is the principal challenge, and opportunity, for advancing the contribution of practice theory to understanding how practices can change to enhance sustainability.

Frontiers of research on sustainable consumption and changing practices

It is clear that practice theory has gained remarkable traction in research and debates over sustainable consumption since the turn of the century. Over this chapter, a whole range of affordances of practice theory approaching for approaching change in consumption has been drawn out. Some of these affordances have already been worked well in empirical application. For example, attention to the role of routines in shaping the flow of daily action, or consideration of the effects of specific objects or technologies in reshaping practices, have been explored in a wide range of empirical fields. There is still plenty of room for development along these lines, as applications of practice theory illuminate challenges and opportunities for change in relation to different issues and fields of consumption.

However, the key frontier for practice theorists and the researchers who seek to operationalise it is to move beyond a focus on the practices and practitioners directly engaged with resource consumption. Consideration of the detail of individual practices lends itself to understanding the challenges and opportunities for changes in those particular practices with typically incremental implications for reducing resource consumption. Against the scale of challenges outlined at the top of this chapter, it is clear that to be genuinely useful for informing practice change to the extent required for sustainability means engaging with questions about understanding the broader collective shaping of specific consumption practices.

Practice theory does struggle to escape its corralling to understanding the detail of action. For example, Frank Geels (2010) identified the utility of practice theory only in relation to understanding the details of action at the lowest level of the multi-level perspective (MLP) model, a dominant approach to understanding socio-technical transition. However, appreciation of the shifting relations between practices is essential to understanding dynamics within practices (Shove et al., 2012). Processes of change to a practice are rarely, if ever, endogenous to that practice. Rather, they arise through shifting relations between practices, including across different apparent systemic scales. Through attention to the relations between practices, analysis can go beyond the details of mundane action to begin to account for forms of social relations which can be meaningfully understood as systemic in character.

In relation to sustainable consumption, a number of recent works have sought to explore the possibilities for articulating practice theory with established approaches to understanding sociotechnical system change. McMeekin and Southerton (2012) and Hargreaves, Longhurst and Seyfang (2013) each explore the potential of a practice-theory-informed understanding of consumption to usefully articulate with MLP. Neither of the articles, though, significantly challenges Geels' (2010) corralling of the value of practice theory to be limited to understanding end-user practices (see also Brand, 2010). The concept of 'systems of practice' (Watson, 2012) seeks to overcome this, with the contention that practices are substantially constituted by the socio-technical systems of which they are a part, and that those socio-technical systems are constituted and sustained by the continued performance of the practices which comprise them. Consequently, changes in socio-technical systems only happen if the practices which embed those systems in the routines and rhythms of life change, and if those practices change, then so will the socio-technical system. In principle, this understanding enables changes in consumption practices to be related with changes throughout the systems in which those practices are embedded. Looking to change consumption practices may mean looking to change practices comprising systems of provision, media or government, rather than intervening directly in consumption practices.

Recognising that the practices comprising governing are part of the same systems of practice as consumption practices that are the target of intervention challenges the dominant focus of practice research on sustainable consumption. As emphasised above, practice research is often framed as a critical engagement with policy preoccupations with technological or behaviourist interventions. Practice theory is presented as providing an alternative understanding of both human action and of possible grounds for intervention. However, the findings from such research have difficulty gaining purchase with policy makers and intervention designers. While practice theory has of late been finding its way into policy-oriented reviews and research documents in relation to sustainable consumption (e.g. Umpfenbach, 2014; UNEP, 2015), there is no clear evidence of its informing policy or intervention design. This is of little surprise. Particular ideas of human action, intention and subjectivity are embodied within the practices and arrangements comprising institutions of governing. It is naïve for practice theory scholars to expect different ways of thinking to easily take root in the practices of governing, which is ironic where those ways of thinking stress the need to fully understand the practices of consumption into which government seeks to intervene. Shove (2014: 43) contends that practice theory is 'paradigmatically at odds with the models of behaviour change and technological innovation on which much climate change policy depends'. Nevertheless, there increasingly are scholars who do the challenging work of holding on to the distinctive value of practice theory while articulating that value in ways relatively amenable for policy makers and intervention designers (Keller, Halkier, & Wilska, 2015; Spurling, McMeekin, Shove, Southerton & Welch, 2013; see also chapters 18 and 20 this volume).

If the apparent promise of practice theories to inform meaningful change for sustainability is to be realized, there remain substantial questions and issues to be confronted. Moving firmly beyond analysis of specific practices to meaningfully understand how practices are shaped by their mutual relations, across locales and social situations, poses substantial conceptual and empirical challenges. But doing so is necessary for practice theory to meaningfully engage with questions of equity and power, including recognizing how practices of consumption are bound up with societally shared ideologies aligning with the reproduction of capitalism and related models of individual and collective economic wellbeing. Practice theory analyses have some way still to go to realise the potential of a radical theoretical position and fully engage the broader debates over the changes needed for consumption to be sustainable.

References

Allon, F., & Sofoulis, Z. (2010). Everyday Water: Cultures in Transition. *Australian Geographer*, 37(1), 45–55.

Andersen, A. H. (2011). Organic Food and the Plural Moralities of Food Provisioning. *Journal of Rural Studies*, 27(4), 440–450.

Bolderdijk, J. W., & Steg, L. (2015). Promoting sustainable consumption: the risks of using financial incentives. In L. A. Reich & J. Thogersen (Eds.), *Handbook of Research on Sustainable Consumption* (pp. 328–243). Cheltenham: Edward Elgar Publishing.

Brand, K. W. (2010). Social Practices and Sustainable Consumption: Benefits and Limitations of a New Theoretical Approach. In M. Gross and H. Heinrichs (eds.), *Environmental Sociology: European Perspectives and Interdisciplinary Challenges*, (pp. 217–235) London: Springer Science & Business Media.

Certeau, M. de, Giard, L., & Mayol, P. (1998). *The Practice of Everyday Life: Living and Cooking. Volume 2.* Minneapolis: University of Minnesota Press.

Cruz, M., Foster, J., Quillin, B., & Schellekens, P. (2015). *Ending Extreme Poverty and Sharing Prosperity: Progress and Policies.* Washington, DC: World Bank Group.

DeVault, M. L. (1994). *Feeding the Family: The Social Organization of Caring as Gendered Work.* Chicago: University of Chicago Press.

FAO. (2006). *Livestock's Long Shadow.* Rome: FAO.

FAO. (2010). *Statistical Yearbook 2010.* Rome: FAO.

Fishbein, M., & Cappella, J. N. (2006). The Role of Theory in Developing Effective Health Communications. *Journal of Communication*, 56(s1), S1–S17.

Geels, F.W. (2010). Ontologies, Socio-Technical Transitions (to sustainability), and the Multi-Level Perspective. *Research Policy*, 39(4), 495–510.

Giddens, A. (1984). *The Constitution of Society: Outline of the Theory of Structuration.* Oakland: University of California Press.

Godfray, H. C. J., Beddington, J. R., Crute, I. R., Haddad, L., Lawrence, D., Muir, J. F., & Toulmin, C. (2010). *Food Security: The Challenge of Feeding 9 Billion People. Science* (New York, NY), 327(5967), 812–818.

Gram-Hanssen, K. (2011). Understanding change and continuity in residential energy consumption. *Journal of Consumer Culture*, 11(1), 61–78.

Halkier, B. (2010). *Consumption Challenged : Food in Medialized Everyday Lives.* Farnham: Ashgate.

Hargreaves, T., Longhurst, N., & Seyfang, G. (2013). Up, Down, Round and Round: Connecting Regimes and Practices in Innovation for Sustainability. *Environment and Planning* A, 45, 402–420.

Holm, L., Ekström, M. P., Gronow, J., Kjærnes, U., Lund, T. B., Mäkelä, J. & Niva, M. (2012). The modernisation of Nordic eating. Studying changes and stabilities in eating patterns. *Anthropology of Food*, S7. Retrieved from https://aof.revues.org/6997?lang=en

Jackson, T. (2005). Live Better by Consuming Less? Is there a "Double Dividend" in Sustainable Consumption? *Journal of Industrial Ecology*, 9(1–2), 19–36.

Keller, M., Halkier, B., & Wilska, T. (2015). Policy and Governance for Sustainable Consumption at the Crossroads of Theories and Concepts. *Environmental Policy and Governance*, 26(2), 75–88.

Lund, T. B., & Gronow, J. (2014). Destructuration or Continuity? The Daily Rhythm of Eating in Denmark, Finland, Norway and Sweden in 1997 and 2012. *Appetite, 82, 143–53.*

McMeekin, A., & Southerton, D. (2012). Sustainability Transitions and Final Consumption: Practices and Socio-Technical Systems. *Technology Analysis & Strategic Management*, 24(4), 345–361.

Meah, A., & Watson, M. (2011). Saints and Slackers: Challenging Discourses about the Decline of Domestic Cooking. *Sociological Research Online, 16*(2). Retrieved from http://socresonline.org.uk/16/2/6.html

Oxfam. (2015). *Extreme carbon inequality.* Oxford: Oxfam.

Popkin, B. M., Adair, L. S., & Ng, S.W. (2012). Global Nutrition Transition and the Pandemic of Obesity in Developing Countries. *Nutrition Reviews*, 70(1), 3–21.

Pretty, J., Barton, J., Bharucha, Z. P., Bragg, R., Pencheon, D., Wood, C., & Depledge, M. H. (2015). Improving Health and Well-Being Independently of GDP: Dividends of Greener and Prosocial Economies. *International Journal of Environmental Health Research*, 26(1), 11–36.

Pretty, J., Sutherland, W. J., Ashby, J., Auburn, J., Baulcombe, D., Bell, M., Pilgrim, S. (2011). The Top 100 Questions of Importance to the Future of Global Agriculture. *International Journal of Agricultural Sustainability, 8*(4), 219–236.

Reckwitz, A. (2002). Toward a Theory of Social Practices: A Development in Culturalist Theorizing. *European Journal of Social Theory*, 5(2), 243–263.

Schatzki, T. (1996). *Social Practices: A Wittgensteinian Approach to Human Activity and the Social*. Cambridge: Cambridge University Press.

Shove, E. (2003). *Comfort, Cleanliness and Convenience: The Social Organization of Normality*. Oxford: Berg.

Shove, E. (2009). Everyday Practice and the Production and Consumption of Time. In Shove, Trentmann and Wilk (Eds.) *Time, Consumption and Everyday Life: Practice, Materiality and Culture* (pp. 17–33). Oxford: Berg.

Shove, E. (2010). Beyond the ABC: Climate Change Policy and Theories of Social Change. *Environment and Planning A*, 42(6), 1273–1285.

Shove, E. (2014). Linking low carbon policy and social practice. In Y. Strengers & C. Maller (Eds.), *Social Practices, Intervention and Sustainability: Beyond Behaviour Change* (pp. 31–44). Abingdon: Routledge.

Shove, E., & Pantzar, M. (2005). *Fossilisation. Ethnologia Europaea, 25*(1–2), 59-63.

Shove, E., Pantzar, M., & Watson, M. (2012). *The Dynamics of Social Practice: Everyday Life and How It Changes*. London: Sage.

Shove, E., & Southerton, D. (2000). Defrosting the Freezer: From Novelty to Convenience: A Narrative of Normalization. *Journal of Material Culture*, 5(3), 301–319.

Shove, E., & Walker, G. (2014). What Is Energy for? Social Practice and Energy Demand Elizabeth Shove and Gordon Walker. *Theory, Culture and Society*, 31(5), 41–58.

Shove, E., Watson, M., Hand, M., & Ingram, J. (2007). *The Design of Everyday Life*. Berg: Oxford.

Spurling, N., Mcmeekin, A., Shove, E., Southerton, D., & Welch, D. (2013*). Interventions in Practice: Re-Framing Policy Approaches to Consumer Behaviour.* Manchester: Sustainable Practices Research Group.

Sunstein, C. (2015). Behavioural economics, consumption and environmental protection. In L. A. Reich & J. Thogersen (Eds.), *Handbook of Research on Sustainable Consumption* (pp. 313–327). Cheltenham: Edward Elgar Publishing.

Thaler, R., & Sunstein, C. (2009). *Nudge: Improving Decisions about Health, Wealth and Happiness*. London: Penguin.

Umpfenbach, K. (2014). *Influences on Consumer Behavior-Policy Implications beyond Nudging. Final Report of European Commission*. Brussels: European Commission.

UNEP. (2015). *Sustainable Consumption and Production Global Edition*. A Handbook for Policymakers. UNEP.

Wallenborn, G., & Wilhite, H. (2014). Rethinking Embodied Knowledge and Household Consumption. *Energy Research & Social Science*, 1, 56–64.

Warde, A. (2005). Consumption and Theories of Practice. *Journal of Consumer Culture*, 5(2), 131–153.

Warde, A. (2016). *The Practice of Eating*. Cambridge: Polity.

Warde, A., Cheng, S.-L., Olsen, W., & Southerton, D. (2007). Changes in the Practice of Eating: A Comparative Analysis of Time-Use. *Acta Sociologica*, 50(4), 363–385.

Watson, M. (2012). How Theories of Practice can Inform Transition to a Decarbonised Transport System. *Journal of Transport Geography, 24*, 488–496.

Welch, D., & Warde, A. (2015). Theories of practice and sustainable consumption. In Reich & Thøgersen (Eds.), *Handbook of Research on Sustainable Consumption*. Cheltenham: Edward Elgar Publishing, 84–100.

Windahl, S., Signitzer, B., & Olson, J. T. (1992). *Using Communication Theory: An Introduction to Planned Communication*. London: Sage Publications.

World Wide Fund for Nature. (2014). *The Living Planet Report*. Gland: WWF.

30

Structural conditions for and against sustainable ways of consuming

Bas van Vliet and Gert Spaargaren

Introduction

This chapter takes stock of social scientific research on consumption that involves the utilization of what we call infrastructures of consumption. These include the networks providing the universal and environmentally relevant services of water supply, electricity, heat and gas, as well as those collecting, transporting and treating our waste water. It is tempting to conceive these infrastructures of consumption as external moderators or impediments to sustainable ways of consumption and hence to study them as distinct domains: provisioning systems on the one hand and the behavior of consumers on the other. Especially concerning the latter, there is a long research tradition dominated by individualistic approaches, fuelled by social psychological theories of Bounded Rationality (Simon, 1955), Attitudes and Behavior (Fishbein & Ajzen, 1975), and Planned Behavior (Organ, Proverbs & Squires, 2013). Central in these approaches is that consumption is seen as a set of behavioral patterns which are the result of individual attitudes, norms and choices. Turning consumption into sustainable consumption would mean to inform consumers about the environmental consequences of their behavior, and to introduce and facilitate "green" choice in the supply of consumer goods and services. This so-called Attitude, Behavior, Choice perspective has been criticized for its reliance on consumers' supposedly rational, conscious decision making about a single behavior, which is in fact highly routinized, socially constructed and embedded in larger socio-technical systems of provision. (Shove, 2010)

Over the last century the availability of energy and water infrastructures and its services have indeed become a prime condition for everyday consumption. Hence a vast body of literature has been built on sustainable consumption that paints a more dualistic picture of consumption patterns on the one hand and systems of provision on the other (Verbong & Geels, 2010; Brand, 2013; O'Keefe, Lüthi, Tumwebaze & Tobias, 2015). The dynamics in consumption patterns involving services like energy, water or wastewater are analyzed against the background of changes taking place in the world of infrastructural systems. Typical research questions are how consumption patterns change as a consequence of liberalization of utility markets or make a shift in sources or technologies of provision; or how initiatives of consumers, like energy communities, may become the seeds of a transition in electricity systems.

Although these studies have produced valuable insights in sustainable consumption and in the dynamics of systems of provision, the analytical division between infrastructural systems and consumption patterns has also partly obscured the intricate relationships between the two domains. A dualistic view of structural conditions versus sustainable consumption has the tendency to equate "structure" with (only) physical infrastructural systems, while consumption remains a separate social domain.

Within a sociological view domestic routines and activities that involve water or energy use are pictured as much more complex than often suggested in the above-mentioned literature or than is often expected by policy makers and service providers (Gram-Hanssen, 2010; Shove, Pantzar & Watson, 2012; Strengers, 2012). Rather than focusing on individual attitudes, behaviors and choices as the main attributes of domestic consumption, or on infrastructures facilitating certain behavior, sociologists direct attention to the shared, routinized and intensely embedded nature of everyday consumption practices.

So in trying to grasp the structural conditions for or against sustainable ways of consumption, this chapter takes another perspective. In line with Giddens' structuration theory (Giddens, 1984) this perspective conceives both consumption patterns and infrastructures services as part of the same practices while they are mutually reproducing each other. So in this perspective "structural conditions for consumption" include the material, social, cultural and legal conditions that are shaping – and which are being shaped by – consumption practices. Rather than tearing "structure" and "consumption" apart, they are both analyzed as part of the same phenomenon. We suggest Social Practice theory is the best candidate to represent such a perspective in studying sustainable ways of consuming. Being a contextual rather than an individualistic approach, social practice theory adds valuable insights to conventional studies of domestic energy or water consumption "behavior". Rather than appliances, infrastructures or people, it is the performance of practices that helps to understand domestic energy or water consumption, including its "structural conditions" (Higginson, McKenna, Hargreaves, Chilvers & Thomson, 2015). With Shove et al.'s "slim-line version of practice theory" (Shove et al., 2012) social practices can be conceived as comprising three elements: firstly the material artefacts (including appliances, infrastructures and the physical flows they accommodate), secondly the related conventions or meanings that are socially constructed and shared and, thirdly, skills or competences employed in performing the practice. Social practices thus employ objects, flows and technologies while they are based upon and reproduce skills and social rules and norms. Analyzing dynamics in practices of sustainable consumption implies taking into account the co-shaping roles of objects, technologies, and infrastructures that are relevant for those practices. As such, a practice approach allows investigating the activities and interactions taking place in (situated) domestic and local settings, while including the systems of provision for water and energy not as an "external" structural condition, but as essential parts of a range of consumption practices.

To illustrate what such a perspective may add to our understanding of sustainable consumption, this chapter reports on research that uses (a slim version of) Social Practice Theory as a lens to study the dynamic relationships between conduct, meaning and systems of water and energy provision. In the case of drinking water supply we report on a study of Dutch water consumption practices and consumer expectations concerning public drinking water supply in the Netherlands. The study was commissioned by the Dutch water sector with the aim to explore the possibilities for innovation in water companies, from the perspective of water consumers (Hegger, Van Vliet, Spaargaren & Frijns, 2010). In revisiting those data, we will try to show that drinking water supply has many different roles to play in the performance of different domestic water practices.

Next, we illustrate and explain the dynamics in practices of toilet use and medicine use in an experimental case study involving 1,224 patients receiving a CT scan at a hospital in the Netherlands. This project, commissioned by a consortium of a water board and a hospital, aimed to assess the willingness of patients to contribute to source-oriented solutions for the problem of the occurrence of medicine residues in surface waters (Diels, Muis, Verhoef, Van Vliet, Hendriksen & Wijn, 2015). This section illustrates that the change of a highly routinized practice of toilet use is not just the result of persuading practitioners, but a deliberate change in the material circumstances, meanings and competences around toilet use and medicine consumption at the same time.

Lastly, energy-related practices will be discussed, and in particular the energy practices that emerge while major changes in electricity infrastructures towards "smart" energy configurations are taking place. A smart grid has been defined as "a socio-technical network characterized by the active management of both information and energy flows, in order to control practices of distributed generation, storage, consumption and flexible demand" (Wolsink, 2012, p. 824). It is a concept that has become increasingly popular amongst electricity grid operators and municipalities who aim to include renewable energy and storage options on a local level. So far, elements of smart grids have been experimented with in pilot settings, including smart metering, tariff differentiation and adapted timing of demand.[1] The emerging energy practices that we studied relate to generating renewable electricity, local storage, monitoring via smart meters and cooperating with neighboring households.

The three cases together will give insights into the performance of practices related to the provision of water and energy through infrastructures of consumption and how these performances change over time. Based on these insights, the conclusion of this chapter will outline how (structural) conditions should actually be understood to make them work for the greening of water and energy consumption practices. Next to this we turn to gaps in current research on sustainable consumption and provisioning infrastructures and future research ahead.

Water sector innovation and domestic water practices

The conventional way of displaying "domestic water consumption" is to present figures of water use on the annual water bills in cubic meters for individual households or aggregated domestic water consumption statistics in reports of the water supply sector.[2]

To consider domestic water practices means that one has to go beyond the different water appliances like the shower, the toilet and the kitchen tap but rather to focus on what water is used for in a household, by what means and with which skills and competences. Employing such a practice approach reveals that the consumption of drinking water is far from a uniform phenomenon. The practice of showering, for instance, involves cultural norms of personal hygiene, the skills and competences to shower and the material infrastructures of a bathroom, water pipes, a water heater and an energy system, a gutter and a sewer system. Except for water this practice of showering has very little in common with the practices of gardening or cooking. Such practices rely on different cultural norms, reproduced in distinct domains of society; they involve totally different skills and competences, and other sets of technological devices, infrastructures and resources.

Water supply thus forms one common element of (and sometimes the only link between) totally different domestic social practices. How water is used, for what purpose and with what meaning and level of appreciation depends on the practice. To investigate the structural conditions for or against sustainable ways of water consumption we would need to unpack a number of domestic practices involving water use and find out how the social and material structures would influence the dynamics in the practices at hand. Here we review a study we did on water consumers and innovation in the water sector that was commissioned by the Dutch drinking water sector (Hegger et al., 2010). The aim of this study was to reveal how water consumers would expect and accept some specified innovation strategies of water companies. The data on consumer preferences which are obtained from a questionnaire (n=3452) and two focus groups with average Dutch water consumers also inform us on the current meanings, competences and materials within diverse domestic water practices. We tested consumers' appreciation of innovations that were suggested by the water sector. Those innovations were related to flows (water flows, financial flows and informational flows) as well as to products and services ranging from offering wellness and convenience products to services like product certification, nature conservation and education about sustainability.

We found that water consumers were generally very positive about the drinking water quality and services of the water supply sector in the Netherlands. There was a strong preference for water companies to maintain their public position rather than trying to enter into commercialized markets of retail (water coolers, Jacuzzis) or consultancy. Consumers would allow their water companies to step out of their core business of bulk water supply as long as all those activities would remain public and related to secure, safe and healthy water provision (Hegger, Spaargaren, Van Vliet & Frijns, 2011). This is not to say that consumers conceived water consumption in any uniform way. While discussing water consumption in the focus groups, participants made their own distinctions between water-related domestic practices and reflected on the different qualities of water and roles of the suppliers in supporting those practices. The fact that toilets are flushed with big amounts of the same water that is otherwise so appreciated for its high quality when it comes to drinking and cooking led to suggestions for systems supplying rain water or otherwise lower water qualities to flush toilets. Also for gardening the use of a lower quality was suggested. Water companies were trusted not only in supplying water but also in informing consumers about water safety; the supply of rainwater systems, de-calcifiers and smart (water) meters. According to consumers, water companies would better stay away from supplying (centrally) heated water, comfort showers or water coolers.

In terms of how consumers reflect on different water practices in the home we made the following observations. Water clearly has different roles to play and received different connotations and meanings varying over the practices in which water is involved. In practices where water is directly consumed (drinking, cooking) water should be of the highest quality possible, delivered by a trusted, publicly controlled supplier. In other practices, where water is used as a medium (for cleaning, doing the laundry, gardening, flushing the toilet) we found less reluctance to change, both with respect to water quality and to technologies of supply. And for practices associated with luxury and convenience (such as outdoor bathing in a Jacuzzi, drinking cooled water) consumers do care for water quality, but leave it to private providers rather than water companies to advise them about or to supply them the materials, infrastructure and sometimes even the hot or cold water itself.

So the appreciation of a water supply company as a public company is well in line with those water practices that involve direct water consumption. Moving on from water practices that fulfil basic needs towards practices considered "luxurious", other suppliers of various materials may enter the scene. It shows that consumers conceive domestic water consumption as consisting of distinct domestic social practices. Their structural conditions for change differ widely and so are the possible innovation strategies and modes of provision for sustainable water consumption practices. This brings us to a special and yet related practice, that of toilet use, which the next section reports.

Capturing medicines in a road bag

Toilet use is a practice involving a rich set of each of the practice elements materials, competences and meanings. In terms of materials we should consider infrastructures of water supply and waste water transport and treatment, bathrooms, toilet bowls, seats, paper and soap. The competences involved are routinized at an early age and become entirely private affairs, until the stages of life when caretakers are needed to help one out. Around toilet use many culturally determined taboos have been built up. In Western cultures, one normally does not show or speak about one's toilet practices apart from jokes or in case of illness. The dominant cultural meaning that has been socially constructed around the use of toilets is that of a (last) taboo (Black & Fawcett, 2008). The water flush toilet (and its connection to the sewer system) is heralded as the preferred system to effectively remove human waste out of reach and out of sight: in other words, to flush and forget (Vliet & Spaargaren, 2010).

In a collaborate project of a water board and a hospital in Deventer, the practice of toilet use was deliberately modified with the aim to collect contrast medium that patients get injected just before getting a CT scan. In the twenty-four hours after the scan, patients were asked to urinate in "road bags", dispensable plastic bags containing grained material that transforms liquid into hardened gel substance. In this way the contrast medium ends up in solid waste containers and incinerators, instead of sewer pipes, treatment plants and, eventually, surface water bodies. In this experimental project the participation of 1,224 patients receiving a CT scan was assessed as an indicator for the willingness of medicine users to contribute to a solution for the problem of persistent medicine residues in surface waters. The routes of contrast medium into either the solid waste system (via the road bags) or the sewer system (via the toilet) served as a proxy for the fate of medicine residues in urine on its way in waste (water) systems (Diels et al., 2015).

As this is not the place to report on the quantitative findings the project delivered, we only present the findings and conclusions concerning the adapted practice of toilet use. Important to note is that the intervention (the use of road bags instead of toilets) started in the hospital, more precisely in the waiting room at the radiology department. Patients were approached by experienced volunteer workers at the hospital, with the request to participate in the experiment. This would involve the use of up to seven road bags in the twenty-four hours after the scan and filling a questionnaire afterwards. The used road bags were to be disposed of in the conventional waste bins at home or elsewhere. The (suggested) reason to participate was that all contrast medium that was prevented from entering the waste water system does not need to be treated.

The participation of patients in the experiment was high. 85% of the respondents who filled the questionnaire (n= 831) had used one or more road bags. Although urinating in a plastic bag means the opposite of a "flush and forget" mode of conduct, respondents' reflections on the practical use of road bags (competences), as well as what they mean to users and the wastewater system at large, were generally positive. As patients, people were willing to contribute to the solution of the problems medicine residues are causing in water bodies, although they also envisioned other parties in the chain co-responsible: the pharmacy industry in the first place (to produce medicines that are less harmful for the environment) and lastly the waste water treatment (to adapt treatment systems as to filter medicine residues).

This temporary, yet radical change of a toilet practice entailed not only the obvious "structural conditions" such as the toilet appliance (a road bag) or the infrastructure it is connected to (the solid waste system with the bins, waste collection companies, waste incinerators). Equally radical changes were accomplished in the competences (handling a road bag instead of a toilet means inventing new practical ways of avoiding contact with urine) and in the social and personal meanings achieved: peeing is not just to relieve oneself, but to contribute to a better environment, or to help the hospital in abating its environmental impact, or just to please the volunteers and doctors in the hospital.

We have thus observed the active disintegration of the routinized practice elements of materials, competences and meanings into quite another performance of a normal toilet practice. Toilet practices are very intimate, bodily experiences and yet they are serving and are being served by large provisioning infrastructures for water and waste water. Changing the practice means changing a very interrelated set of social and material elements of the practice within and beyond the toilet and its user. In this project it took much more than persuasion of patients or just the replacement of toilets with road bags; it was the partly deliberate construction of a combination of a hospital setting (which holds a de-routinization of a number of practices in itself), the personal approach by volunteers, the design of road bags, the information about the problems of medicines in waste water and what this meant to this group of patients receiving a CT scan in a regional hospital.

Whilst this is an account of a temporarily changed and intimate practice, the next section will deal with the emergence of new practices over the longer term: that of energy practices in evolving smart energy systems.

Emerging energy practices in the smart grid

Also in the field of electricity supply and demand a practice-based approach can be useful to analyse the structural conditions facilitating or constraining ways of sustainable energy consumption. We studied the developments and pilot projects of smart grids in the Netherlands and the energy-related domestic practices that we see emerging alongside these developments (Naus, Van Vliet & Hendriksen, 2015; Naus, Spaargaren, Van Vliet & Van der Horst, 2014). We revisit these studies to give an account of how domestic electricity consumption is conditioned not only by infrastructure but rather by the know-how of individuals that take part in a practice and the meanings they attribute to it, while taking into account the co-shaping roles of objects, technologies and infrastructures that are relevant for that practice. Individual norms, values and preferences are thus not considered in isolation, but shaped in a context of practices that are shared with others and that co-produce new value orientations of individuals. As such, a practice approach allows us to investigate in detail the dynamics of activities taking place in domestic and local settings over the longer term, while not losing sight of the broader context of systems of energy provision (Spaargaren & Van Vliet, 2000; Van Vliet, 2012).

Energy practices (or e-practices) are the (routinized) practices around the production, distribution, storage, monitoring and use of electricity in a domestic setting. Studying the e-practices while they are emerging in a very dynamic time era of a roll-out of smart meters, experimentation with smart grid concepts in pilot areas and the blooming of hundreds of local energy cooperatives and collectives in Europe means that we are dealing with moving targets. It is as yet not clear whether we indeed witness the emergence of new distinguishable e-practices as a consequence of enrolling citizen-consumers into smart energy systems. Or, rather, that we see changes in various existing domestic practices that involve the use of energy. For the time being, both the birth of new practices (i.e. the monitoring of domestic energy flows, the utilization of new smart meters and smart appliances) and the adaptations of existing practices (i.e. adapting the timing of laundry practices to moments of abundant solar energy supply) are included in our analysis of emerging e-practices.

Our studies were executed by means of online surveys, focus groups and interviews with experts and domestic electricity consumers that were in different ways involved in smart grid pilot projects, in renewable energy cooperatives or just as individuals interested in sustainable energy (Naus et al., 2014; Sedee, 2014; Naus et al., 2015). We assessed how smart grid attributes like smart meters and the new information flows they produce, renewable energy generators like solar panels, rescheduled timing of demand help to shape new or reconfigure existing e-practices.

What was found is that new information that is presented to consumers by means of the new "smart" devices and displays is not straightforwardly adopted and put into use as to make energy consumption more sustainable. In line with many other findings (Van den Burg, 2003; Wallenborn, Orsini & Vanhaverbeeke, 2011) on the effects of energy monitoring, it depends very much on the capability of consumers to access the information and to incorporate its meaning into the so-far routinized energy practices of cooking, washing or car-based transport. We also found that initial enthusiasm for performing energy monitoring practices tends to diminish over time, or can even fade away altogether. In some cases, newly generated information flows in smart grid configurations did help householders to change their routines and practices. Respondents reported the money saving it entails, the transparency, enjoying sustainable consumption and participating in new forms of solidarity among householders as motivation.

Apart from changing individual domestic energy practices, smart configurations and the information flows they produce also redefine practices and relationships within households, for example in the case of parents monitoring their children's activities through their energy use, once the monitoring devices has become available to do so. Other smart appliances allow for remote control of the heating system through the internet in order to arrive in a warm home after coming back from holidays. The practice of heating the home has been expanded over time and space and has started to include issues such as who is in control of the heater, from where and at what times.

Like all social practices e-practices also draw upon and contribute to shared social and cultural norms. These are for instance socially constructed rules about energy conservation, the use of lights and curtains, ideal indoor temperatures and related and shared norms of coziness, convenience and comfort. What is new is that the sharing of rules and norms is increasingly taking place at the level of neighborhoods and in much more explicit ways. Collectively shared systems of renewable electricity generation (a wind turbine or solar roofs) require householders to collaborate in terms of energy production and consumption and conservation. In energy cooperative meetings as well as in our focus groups we observed the exchange of information concerning the energy practices at home, practices that were until recently strictly performed in private.

Lastly, newly emerging e-practices around energy monitoring, renewable energy generation and storage show changes in how energy-related information is being exchanged between householders, grid operators and energy suppliers. The vertical relations between provider and consumer have from the beginning of grid-based electricity provision been mono-directional, with the energy supplier obtaining information from consumers by means of meter readings. But smart energy configurations make information flows both thicker (much more detailed information about energy consumption patterns is being generated and exchanged) and deeper; information is generated beyond both sides of the meter: on the level of appliances and timing of demand at the consumer side and on the level of various green or grey sources of energy production on the production side.

Emerging e-practices involving such new household internal, horizontal and vertical relations were shaped, impeded or even obstructed not so much by the design of appliances or infrastructures, or by required skills and competences but especially by considerations of autonomy and privacy encompassing multiple domains of life (Naus et al., 2015). Smart energy systems therefore do not "produce" new e-practices in any predictable or linear ways. Instead, these systems co-evolve with existing domestic practices and norms set in "dynamic and situated interactions between domestic actors and 'external' actors on the one hand, and between domestic actors and new (information) technologies on the other" (Naus et al., 2014, p. 444).

Conclusion

The admittedly wide-ranging empirical studies on water, toilet and energy practices presented in this chapter reflect the dynamics that can be studied in the interrelations between consumption and provisioning systems. Together they show what a practice perspective can offer in understanding relations and dynamics in consumption of infrastructure services. The case of drinking water practices and innovation in the water supply sector highlights how distinctive material elements of drinking water, use water and luxury water and their devices matter in the meaning and appreciation of changes in the system of provision. Rather than being "conditioned" by larger water systems, domestic practices serve and are being served by water systems of provision.

Social practices relate to and combine services of multiple systems of provision. The case of changing toilet practices by means of road bags in a hospital setting shows how a robust toilet practice is yet malleable when it is relocated in and combined with practices of medicine use and medical check-up. Changes in toilet practices and medicine use were established by a new connection between the systems of provision for water and health care. Lastly a range of new energy practices are discussed in the realm of smart and cooperative energy systems' development. This case also reveals that energy practices, rather than being "conditioned" by energy infrastructures, become constitutive to newly emerging systems of provision: shared, flexible and decentralized systems of energy supply and demand.

The three cases also have a lot in common. They investigate the dynamic relations between environmentally relevant systems of provision and practices of household consumption. The analyses show that "environmentally sound consumption" as a concept does not suffice to understand the complicated social and technical relations with the systems of provision that deliver the natural resources of water or energy. Nor does it take into account the particular handling of human waste in tune with the systems of wastewater collection and treatment. Employing a social practice perspective means to reframe what is usually referred to as "structural conditions" for sustainable consumption: namely the institutions and infrastructures encompassing the systems of provision. Structural conditions for sustainable consumption patterns should be conceived as inherent elements of the performance of domestic practices, and they encompass not only material infrastructures and appliances, but also robust cultural norms around domestic everyday life and considerations of privacy and autonomy.

Environmentally informed agendas to save or generate renewable water and energy resources should therefore not be addressed solely to consumers but to the socio-technical complex of actors, institutions and infrastructures in which consumption practices co-evolve with other bundles of practices performed in systems of water and energy services.

More contemporary research on sustainable consumption in relation to infrastructure services is deviating from conventional approaches of analyzing determinants of consumption behavior which are connected to certain systems of provision (i.e. water or energy or waste services). Instead, more contextual approaches addressing these interactions have been developed over the past fifteen years: from sociological accounts of "infrastructures of consumption" (Southerton, Chappells & Van Vliet [Eds], 2004) and the role of intermediaries in infrastructure service provision (Moss, 2009) to studies of and beyond the "networked city" (Coutard & Rutherford [Eds], 2016). Although most research has been oriented to Western cities and infrastructures, research into fast-growing urban infrastructures in the global South is on the increase (Bulkeley & Castán Broto, 2013; Brand, 2013; Van Vliet, Van Buuren & Mgana [Eds] 2013).

Social practice research in relation to urban infrastructures is blooming: the body of literature is fast growing in fields of energy and smart grids (i.e. Strengers, 2012; Naus et al., 2014; Wallenborn et al., 2011; Shove et al., 2012; Skjølsvold, Ryghaug & Berker, 2015), water services (Brown, 2015; van Vliet, 2012; Sofoulis, 2005) and food (Spaargaren, Oosterveer & Loeber (Eds), 2012). A challenging field of research to connect to in this respect is that of the urban nexus (Beck & Walker, 2013; Hoff, 2011; Stengers, 2005), in which combinations of water, energy and food provisioning systems are analyzed as co-constituting domestic social practices.

Notes

1 See the Smart Grids pilot project's overview of the Netherlands: http://www.netbeheernederland.nl/smartgrids

2 http://www.compendiumvoordeleefomgeving.nl/indicatoren/nl0037-Waterverbruik-per-inwoner.html?i=3–126

References

Beck, M.B. & Walker, R.V. (2013). On water security, sustainability and the water-food-energy-climate nexus, Front. *Environ. Sci. Eng.* 7, 626–639.

Black, M. & Fawcett, B. (2008). *The last taboo: opening the door on the global sanitation crisis.* London: Earthscan.

Brand, R. (2013). Facilitating sustainable behavior through urban infrastructures: learning from Singapore? *International Journal of Urban Sustainable Development*, 5, 225–240.

Browne, A. L. (2015). *Insights from the everyday: implications of reframing the governance of water supply and demand from 'people' to 'practice'.* Wiley Interdisciplinary Reviews: Water, 2, 415–424.

Bulkeley, H. & Castán Broto, V. (2013). Government by experiment? Global cities and the governing of climate change. *Transactions of the Institute of British Geographers*, 38, 361–375.

Coutard, O. & Rutherford, J. (Eds.) (2016). *Beyond the Networked City: Infrastructure Reconfigurations and Urban Change in North and South.* London and New York, Routledge.

Diels, J., Muis, J., Verhoef A., van Vliet, B., Hendriksen A., Wijn, G. (2015). *Getting a Grip on Drug Residues in our Waters.* Zwolle: Water Authority Groot Salland.

Fishbein, M. & Ajzen, I. (1975). *Belief, Attitude, Intention and Behavior.* Phillipines: Addision-Wesley Publishing Company Inc.

Giddens, A. (1984). *The Constitution of Society. Outline of the theory of structuration.* Berkeley and Los Angeles, University of California Press.

Gram-Hanssen, K. (2010). Residential heat comfort practices: understanding users. Building Research & Information, 38(2), 175-186. doi: 10.1080/09613210903541527

Hegger, D. L. T., Spaargaren, G., van Vliet, B. J. M., Frijns, J. (2011). Consumer-inclusive innovation strategies for the Dutch water supply sector: Opportunities for more sustainable products and services. *NJAS – Wageningen Journal of Life Sciences*, 58, 49–56.

Hegger, D. L. T., van Vliet, B. J. M., Spaargaren, G., Frijns, J. (2010). *Eerst water, maar ook denken aan later. Kwantificering van voorkeuren van de huishoudelijke klant voor activiteiten en rollen van het drinkwaterbedrijf.* Nieuwegein & Wageningen: KWR & Wageningen University.

Higginson, S., McKenna, E., Hargreaves, T., Chilvers, J., Thomson, M. (2015). Diagramming social practice theory: An interdisciplinary experiment exploring practices as networks. *Indoor and Built Environment*, 24, 950–969.

Hoff, H. (2011). *Understanding the Nexus. Background paper for the Bonn 2011 Nexus Conference.* Stockholm: Stockholm Environment Institute.

Moss, T. (2009). Intermediaries and the governance of sociotechnical networks in transition. *Environment and Planning A*, 41, 1480–1495.

Naus, J. Spaargaren, G., van Vliet, B.J.M., van der Horst, H.M. (2014). Smart grids, information flows and emerging domestic energy practices. *Energy Policy*, 68, 436–446.

Naus, J., van Vliet, B.J.M., Hendriksen, A. (2015). Households as change agents in a Dutch smart energy transition: On power, privacy and participation. *Energy Research & Social Science*, 9, 125–136.

O'Keefe, M., Lüthi, C., Tumwebaze, I. K., Tobias, R. (2015). Opportunities and limits to market-driven sanitation services: evidence from urban informal settlements in East Africa." *Environment and urbanization*, 27, 421–440.

Organ, S., Proverbs, D., Squires, G. (2013) Motivations for energy efficiency refurbishment in owner-occupied housing. *Structural Survey* 31, 101–120.

Sedee, C. (2014). *Lowering the Peaks, assessing the role of an energy cooperative on practices in the smart grid.* Wageningen, Wageningen University (MSc. Thesis)

Shove, E. (2010). Beyond the ABC: Climate change policy and theories of social change. *Environment and Planning A*, 42, 1273–1285.

Shove, E., Pantzar, M., Watson, M. (2012). *The dynamics of social practice: Everyday life and how it changes.* London: Sage Publications.

Simon, H. (1955). A Behavioral Model of Rational Choice. *The Quarterly Journal of Economics*, 69, 99–118.

Skjølsvold, T. M., Ryghaug, M., Berker, T. (2015). A traveler's guide to smart grids and the social sciences. *Energy Research & Social Science*, 9, 1–8.

Southerton, D., Chappells, H., B. J.M. van Vliet (Eds.) (2004). *Sustainable consumption: the implications of changing infrastructures of provision.* Cheltenham: Edward Elgar.

Sofoulis, Z. (2005). Big Water, Everyday Water: A Sociotechnical Perspective. *Continuum* 19, 445–463.

Spaargaren, G. & Van Vliet, B. (2000). Lifestyles, consumption and the environment: The ecological modernisation of domestic consumption. *Environmental Politics*, 9, 50–76.

Spaargaren, G., Oosterveer, P., Loeber, A. (Eds.) (2012). *Food Practices in Transition, Changing Food Consumption, Retail and production in the Age of Reflexive Modernity.* London: Routledge

Stengers, I. (2005) Introductory notes on an ecology of practices, *Cultural Studies Review* 11, 183–196.

Strengers, Y. (2012). Peak electricity demand and social practice theories: Reframing the role of change agents in the energy sector. *Energy Policy* 44, 226–234.

Van den Burg, S.W. K. (2003). Consumer-oriented monitoring and environmental reform. *Environment and planning. C, Government & policy* 21, 371–388.

Van Vliet, B. J. M. (2012). Sustainable Innovation in Network-Bound Systems: Implications for the Consumption of Water, Waste Water and Electricity Services. *Journal of Environmental Policy & Planning*, 14, 263–278.

Van Vliet, B., Van Buuren, J., Mgana, S. (Eds.) (2013). *Urban waste and sanitation services for sustainable development: Harnessing social and technical diversity in East Africa.* London, Routledge.

Verbong, G. P. J. & Geels, F.W. (2010). Exploring sustainability transitions in the electricity sector with socio-technical pathways. *Technological Forecasting and Social Change*, 77, 1214–1221.

Van Vliet, B. & Spaargaren, G. (2010). Sense and sanitation. In: B. Van Vliet, G. Spaargaren and P. Oosterveer (Eds.), *Social Perspectives on the Sanitation Challenge.* (pp. 31–47). Dordrecht: Springer.

Wallenborn, G., Orsini, M., Vanhaverbeke, J. (2011). Household appropriation of electricity monitors. *International Journal of Consumer Studies* 35, 146–152.

Wolsink, M. (2012). The research agenda on social acceptance of distributed generation in smart grids: Renewable as common pool resources. *Renewable and Sustainable Energy Reviews* 16, 822–835.

31

Retail sector facing the challenge of sustainable consumption

Mikael Klintman

Introduction

As previous chapters have shown, consumption is anything but an independent activity. It is tightly intertwined with not only social expectations, conventions, and (infra)structures. There is also the relationship between consumer activities and entire sectors of the market. One sector that has a substantial influence on consumer activities is the retail sector. This becomes evident concerning the specific issue that is in focus on this chapter: the role of the retail sector, in light of challenges of moving consumption towards sustainability.

Some scholars argue that retailers occupy a dominating position on the market (Lehner, 2015b). In this role, operating between consumer and producers (via distributors), and with the large financial resources they control, they are often argued to be very powerful. In analyses of the power of the retail sector, it is most often the sector's influence on consumers that is in focus (Oosterveer & Spaargaren, 2011).

Without having to draw conclusions about exactly how influential the retail sector is, there is no need to dispute that they are major players in the market, and by extension in society. Nor is there any need to dispute the retailer sector's priority of making, and even maximizing, economic profit. Although well aware of this priority, scholars, branch organizations, and sustainability-oriented consumer organizations express increasing hope for retailers to channel their influence not merely towards further increased economic profit, but also towards sustainable development. What does the research history look like with regard to the retailing-consumption relationship from a sustainability perspective? In general marketing studies, the relation between retailing and consumer behavior began not long after the development of department stores and standardized retailing, during the first part of the twentieth century (Musso & Druica, 2014). As to research specifically examining sustainability aspects of this relationship, it did not follow directly from the general marketing research mentioned above (an exception is Wood, 1972). Instead, there was first a period where sustainability dimensions of retailing were usually studied separately from consumers. Corporate social responsibility, lifecycle analyses and relationships between retailers, suppliers, and producers were in main focus, often in light of arguments about a competitive advantage of taking sustainable development into account (Carroll, Lewis & Thomas, 1992). The role of consumers for sustainable development (or *environmental friendliness* or *concern*, terms used before *sustainable development*) was in the 1980s and early 1990s seen as something that stems largely from values, attitudes, and an appreciation of nature (Balderjohn, 1988; Burke, Milberg & Smith, 1993). The specific situation created in the store for raising environmental awareness or impacting environmentally oriented consumer practices was consequently not so much in the center of scholarly attention. It is chiefly in the late 1990s and the first decades of the twenty-first century when retailing, consumption, and sustainable development have become integrated into scholarly analyses.

The aim of this chapter is to give an overview of some key challenges, and opportunities for the retail sector to stimulate as well as adapt to a sustainability-oriented consumption. Based on an extensive review of the literature on the retailing-consumption relationship, this chapter focuses on four challenges that have turned out to be crucial to handle to move consumption in the direction towards sustainability. By *sustainability*, the chapter refers particularly to two of the three pillars of sustainable development: ecological and social sustainability. The third pillar, economic sustainability, is indirectly touched upon here, by recognizing its salience both among retailers and consumers, in parallel with ecological, social, and by extension governance-related, concerns.

Analysis: Four challenges

Challenge 1

To strengthen the trustworthiness of the retail sector

The most common issue that emerges when the retailer role for sustainable consumption is discussed concerns trustworthiness. This remains a critical issue involving governments, the OECD as well as environmental and consumer-oriented organizations (OECD, 2010). The questions, to put it bluntly, are, firstly, to what extent actors in the retail sector are inclined to make false or misleading claims about the sustainability performance of their products. The second question is how false or misleading claims should be regulated—a question that places its focus on private, voluntary labels and claims made by, for instance, the retail sector itself. Several global organizations are active in trying to develop internationally consistent regulation that protects consumers and the sustainability cause(s) across countries (Klintman, 2016). Also, various third-party schemes have been developed with the explicit aim of reducing the risk of the most bluntly false or misleading sustainability claims of retailers and other corporate actors (O'Rourke, 2005). Nonetheless, parts of the social science literature on the retail sector's role concerning sustainable consumption are critical from a more structurally oriented perspective. Instead of trying to find better ways for identifying individual retailers that make false or misleading sustainability claims to consumers, and instead of attempting to find concrete measures for how to prevent so-called greenwashing (Chen & Chang, 2013), scholars point to what they perceive as the nature of markets and business (Schor, 2007). Since it will always be within the retail sector's primary interest to maximize economic profits, this sector will always use its power and resources to mislead the rest of society in any issue that does not converge with their primary interest. Parts of, although not all, issues of sustainability may, according to this literature, fall within matters that do not converge with basic retail interests. This skepticism contends that the idea of a socially (or ecologically) responsible retailer is an oxymoron, since the 'nature' of corporations are fundamentally different from those of the norms and mores of the rest of society (Devinney, 2009).

The widened focus of retailer trustworthiness, from a narrow actor-oriented focus to an incorporating of a structural critique, has entailed a deeper and subtler scholarly examination of challenges to trustworthiness. For instance, scholars try to trace shades of sustainability as well as investigate to what extent these shades are fully comprehensible to consumers (Boström & Klintman, 2011). Still, social analysis has moved at least one step beyond this. From having focused on trustworthiness of false, misleading, and unnuanced claims by retailers about sustainability, analyses are increasingly done on cases where sustainability claims of retailers are, to be sure, in line with stipulated sustainability criteria. Yet, scholars and practitioners involved in issues of sustainable development continuously try to identify not just false and misleading retail claims but also claims where the analysts find the sustainability criteria implausible. Examples have in the literature been made concerning various sectors. For instance, assessments of whether a certain automobile (Coad, de Haan, & Woersdorfer, 2009) or certain meat (Klintman & Boström, 2012) corresponds with criteria for eco-cars or organic meat may, to be sure, be correct given the stated criteria. Critics maintain that the criteria themselves have not been enough subject to question and debate (Yanarella, Levine, & Lancaster, 2009), for instance in terms of climate impact. This issue does not concern truth, falseness, or whether something is misleading in the concrete sense. Instead, some scholars hold that retailers at best adopt a light or weak sustainability ideology, by almost entirely ignoring interests among some consumer groups that are oriented towards more thorough and far-reaching versions of sustainable development (Peattie & Crane, 2005).

Challenge 2

To navigate among multiple, sustainability-oriented values

This second challenge is one facing not merely retailers but also consumers. Moisander (2007), among others, has analyzed how consumer motivations and meanings revolving around sustainability are highly multi-faceted. In a similar vein, Klintman and Boström (2012) claim that it is highly insufficient for retailers to invest all of their sustainability efforts into standardized labelling schemes. The reason that this is insufficient is that the meanings and motivations that consumers attach to the vast topic of sustainability are far more diverse than the values that current sustainability labels reflect. Since the very idea of the term *sustainable development* is that it should not be narrowed down to rigid and concrete solutions, Oosterveer and Spaargaren (2011) argue that it be important to allow for multiple sustainability values, not least in stores.

Needless to say, this constitutes a challenge. But it is a challenge that is necessary to handle in part by retailers who work on sustainability issues. Themes that are typically omitted from the conventional sustainability schemes and labels include, for instance, sustainability benefits of a vegetarian diet rather than a meat-based one, through reduced greenhouse-gas emissions and water use. Nor is the theme of modified consumption versus reduced levels of consumption addressed in the conventional sustainability schemes that retailers use.

However, social scientists are continuously exploring niches and alternatives to the mainstream parameters of sustainability schemes (Stripple & Bulkeley, 2013), investigating their preconditions for becoming subject to retail engagement. For instance, the cultures of voluntary simplicity (Elgin, 2010), the sharing economy (Scaraboto, 2015), and product and service systems (PSS) (Mont & Tukker, 2006) are developments to which scholars pay considerable attention. They investigate this on whether and how retailers adopt such developments that previously were perceived by the retail sector as running counter to their business interests.

Scholars who examine such activities from a retail perspective largely agree that a future success of the incorporation of these wider sustainability-oriented consumer values into retail must move beyond idealism and the attraction of specific sustainability-oriented ideas based only on their novelty. Instead, the long-term viability of practices such as the sharing economy as well as product and service systems depend, these scholars hold, on whether retailers and other market actors manage to develop efficient business models to provide consumers with schemes for sharing, lending, and borrowing. In some cases, such schemes may operate in their own right, as the whole business idea, whereas they may in other instances operate in parallel with regular activities of purchasing and selling.

Another key theme here concerns the local and regional levels. Numerous studies have investigated retailer attempts, or omitted attempts, at promoting locally produced goods through the use of sustainability arguments. Even if scientists of ecology are far from in agreement about the pros and cons of local production in various regions and concerning various products, local production has in many studies been shown to resonate with consumer values about sustainability (DuPuis & Goodman, 2005).

Lehner (2015b) moves more in depth with the themes of the local and regional by pointing towards the difficulty of certain large retail chains to accommodate local and regional specificities in their sustainability activities. Some retail chains are simply managed extensively from the national or international headquarters, making it difficult for the local retailer to tailor her sustainability activities to local culture and production. Nonetheless, Lehner suggests ways in which local retailers may take local specificity and culture into better account, and to integrate more into local culture concerning sustainability. This refers to much more than promoting local food production, which is the common focus as soon as retailers are to become locally aware of the local consumer demand and sustainability interests (Lehner, 2015a). A local focus could, for instance, be that retailers recognize and connect to local and regional campaigns for supporting a region in another part of the world. It could also be retail initiatives recognising and promoting environmentally friendly parts of a food tradition of an immigrant population in the local area.

Concerning the broader issue of multiple sustainability parameters, some scholars have found it essential to move to the underlying, latent interests connected to various sustainability values. Trustworthiness of retailers' sustainability claims and the plausibility of various sustainability values do not seem to be sufficient for explaining consumer engagement, or omitted engagement, in sustainability efforts as consumers. These scholars maintain that we must move beneath cognitive and individual perspectives, and instead analyze sustainability consumption for what it is: a fundamental social and cultural phenomenon. For instance, Brown (2009) shows how values surrounding sustainability are connected to moral boundaries that are highly socially embedded in the groups with which people identify themselves. This is a critique of perspectives that elevates the individual belief system and individual moral system (if such a system can even be traced) to the main force driving active choices of purchasing (or not purchasing) the products and goods marketed as sustainable. As Thøgersen and Crompton (2009) explain, only a limited number of consumers can be assumed to carry both the knowledge and the personal involvement to process such information and react accordingly. The retailers' and NGO-spokespersons' step-motherly treatment of social components of consumption motivation is even more surprising given the strong focus on social drivers of consumption in conventional marketing literature. Where 'green' or 'sustainable' marketing literature continues to talk about altruistic (e.g. biodiversity, climate change) versus selfish (e.g. health) motives to consume more sustainably, conventional marketing literature has long ago uncovered the importance of group motivations, 'neo-tribalism' (Cova & Cova, 2002) and value-creation through social interaction (Lusch, Vargo, & Tanniru, 2010).

Challenge 3

To reach a sustainability-oriented dynamic between retailers and consumers

The third challenge moves us more deeply into the relationship between the retail sector and consumers. Who should be the sustainability leader and who should be the follower? Leaving this normative question aside, it is more relevant here to discuss various views of who is the leader and follower in efforts towards sustainable development, in our context retailers or consumers.

In consumer studies, one can draw a fairly straight dividing line between, on the one hand, studies rooted in economics and business studies, and, on the other hand, studies rooted in large parts of the social sciences. The former stresses the active role and great potential of consumers to make sustainability-oriented choices in the store: by consumers' actively requesting sustainable products and services, retailers are highly likely to follow by meeting these requests (Stolle, 2005). Instead, social scientific schools of thought emphasize the limits to active consumer choice. It could be a limited supply of sustainability-oriented products and services, excessive costs of such products and services, or social norms and structures in which consumers are caught that lead them to more resource-demanding consumption.

Whereas scholars agree that consumers, in general, are becoming increasingly aware of sustainability matters, benevolent intentions by consumers are often mere intentions (Thøgersen, 2006). Devinney and colleagues state this issue by portraying consumers as cause-driven liberals when surveyed, but economic conservatives at the checkout line (Devinney, Auger, & Eckhardt, 2010).

Still, despite the bleak results from the social science on consumer proactivity in sustainability issues, the conventional response by retailers has been that they need to wait for signals of an increasing consumer demand for products with a higher sustainability record. To be sure, most scholars who have studied closely the conditions under which retailers work develop empathy for retailers, given the challenges the latter face when trying to bring in sustainability logic into their daily activities (Lehner, 2015c). At the same time, several studies indicate ways for meeting some of these challenges.

For example, some studies have shown how retailers may use sustainability-oriented measures of 'libertarian paternalism' for stimulating sustainable consumption. Advances in behavioral economics have opened new ways for how retailers can be more proactive with regards to the promotion of sustainability-oriented products and services (Ölander & Thøgersen, 2014). Concepts such as nudging, anchoring, and descriptive norms refer to measures that retailers, for instance, can take to stimulate consumers to choose these products.

Further examples of retailer initiatives include recycling schemes, for instance of mobile phones, sometimes distributed by retailers to developing countries and sometimes distributed for recycling of the material to new products (Ongondo & Williams, 2011). Such measures need not be preceded by a certainty that consumers are financially motivated to have their phones recycled.

Also, studies have investigated retailer attempts at becoming engaged in philanthropic activities, and to what extent it meets the strategic, underlying motive behind such activities (Baron, 2007). Scholars usually understand philanthropic activities of retailers as a strategy that takes place between sustainability efforts and explicit efforts of profit seeking. Similar to the philanthropy of any other corporate sector, a key purpose for retailers is here to strengthen the social ties of customers with the retailer. One example is when drug stores initiate campaigns for making medicines accessible to poor groups domestically or abroad. Research suggests that consumer loyalty to the store may increase by such activities of the retail sector (Luo, 2005).

Challenge 4

To handle the possible dominance of retail-based sustainability framings

To be sure, efforts of retailers informing consumers about sustainability, and how it can be pursued, are applauded by many (Jones, Comfort, & Hillier, 2009). Others worry that this information, consciously or not, tends to give prominence to the specific sustainability efforts made by the retailers themselves (Lehner & Halliday, 2014). The fear is that the retail sector, along with the industry in question, will exert too much control over the dominant framing of what consumers conceive of as sustainable consumption. Other possible efforts with superior effect in sustainability terms might as a consequence be ignored, overlooked, or even silenced.

In this light, social scientists have indicated an increase in private standard setting and retail brands that make their own sustainability claims (Chkanikova & Mont, 2012). Still, these scholars hold that this increase is to a lesser extent a risk of outright false or misleading sustainability claims to consumers. At a deeper level, these social scientists maintain that we must examine the role of retail-based sustainability schemes as governance mechanisms as well as of framing devices (Fuchs, Kalfagianni, & Havinga, 2011). Sustainability schemes influence how consumers, policy makers, and retailers themselves think. Several consumer studies have been done of how consumers are influenced by the framings used in marketing, and the same goes for sustainability marketing and media (Halkier, 2010). If certain meat or cars are labelled ecological, this moves our thinking away from searching for sustainability measures beyond car use and meat-based meals.

This might be the most significant challenge about sustainability consumption in relation to retailing. One side of this challenge concerns how to maintain a discursive openness towards alternative and more far-reaching sustainability measures and norm changes than those that retailers typically present. The other side concerns keeping this openness while retaining and strengthening retail sectors to continue their engagement in sustainability issues in dialogue with the rest of us.

Conclusions and discussion

The chapter has shed light on a number of factors that in the literature are treated as key to the role(s) of the retail sector when facing the challenge of sustainable consumption.

Correctness and disambiguity of sustainability claims are the most obvious factor. Although retailers often function as messengers of sustainability claims made by producers, rather than as initiators of such claims, the phenomenon of retail-based brands with sustainability profile makes this factor increasingly relevant to the retail sector. The second factor is the plausibility of sustainability claims. Even if a retailer's claims of greenness or sustainability of a certain product or service may be consistent with currently stipulated criteria, a continuous revision of criteria is needed in order for the claims to be trustworthy. The multi-stakeholder design of many sustainability-oriented certificates and schemes makes the retail sector a major player with potential to increase the plausibility and relevance of the schemes and information that the sector uses.

Thirdly, there is a need for the retail sector to be responsive to the multifacettedness of sustainability concerns in society and among various consumer groups. The notion of sustainable development has since its start been intended to be an unspecific concept in order to be open to new knowledge claims and multiple values. Consumers reflect multiple sustainability-oriented values in their interests in goods and services that move beyond specific schemes and labels. Retailers have a high potential to be responsive to this variety of sustainability concerns, often in connection with occurrences in the local area and region.

A fourth factor is that retailers need not just respond to consumer concerns; retailers may also help to trigger such concerns. The chapter provided several examples of how, in addition to offering sustainability-labelled products, retailers may initiate recycling schemes, philanthropic activities, and campaigns connected to cultural events, not least in multi-ethnic communities, that help to trigger consumer practices in a sustainable direction. A final factor that overlaps the factors mentioned above is the need for the retail sector to balance between being proactive in sustainability endeavors on the market and at the same time not becoming a strongly dominating force. Inconsistent worries are sometimes heard among nongovernmental organizations and scholars of sustainable development, that retailers be both too weak (and passive), not doing as much as they can towards sustainability, and too strong, as in influencing and narrowing, even watering down, the sustainability agenda in society.

Among the research gaps that still exist, the most notable ones are how to take a more intensive interaction between various sustainability concerns of consumers and efforts of mainstream retailing and translate this into a wider, sustainability-oriented 'culture' of stores. Research mainly translates 'sustainability' into eco-labelled products. However, the vegetarian movement and interests in local production are consumer interests to which retailing has found it more difficult to respond. Here, research has a lot to contribute by examining, for instance, what reference points and normality are implied in how products are exposed in the store, what recipes are provided to consumers, and so forth. A related research gap concerns the socio-economic and Bourdieusian 'distinctions' implied in sustainability-oriented marketing in the stores. A working hypothesis would here be that such marketing is still almost entirely directed to the upper-middle class, thus overlooking the above-mentioned multifacettedness of sustainability concerns that transcend the posh, eco-labelled products at a high-price premium. Several promising research tendencies indicate a good preparation for such explorations. The most important of such promises is probably that much of the relevant research has moved beyond the following two positions: on the one hand, naïve beliefs in environmental attitudes of consumers and retailers as a main driving force of sustainability work among these actors, and on the other hand, entirely cynical perspectives on this relationship, where any efforts by retailers and consumers in the name of sustainable development are rejected at the outset as hypocrisy. Current and hopefully future research examines the relationship as one which in turn is embedded in the wider social, political, and cultural structures for which all spheres of society have both stakes and responsibility.

In sum, all this may seem quite daunting as concerns the potential role – with all its potentials and risks – of the retail sector facing the challenge of sustainable consumption. The hope lies in the continuous collaboration and dialogue with consumer groups, nongovernmental organizations and policy agencies about how to better share the responsibility of creating sustainable development.

References

Balderjahn, I. (1988). Personality Variables and Environmental Attitudes as Predictors of Ecologically Responsible Consumption Patterns. *Journal of Business Research*, 17, 51–56.

Baron, D. P. (2007). Corporate Social Responsibility and Social Entrepreneurship. *Journal of Economics & Management Strategy*, 16(3), 683–717.

Boström, M., & Klintman, M. (2011). *Eco-Standards, Product Labelling and Green Consumerism*. Houndmills, Basingstoke: Palgrave Macmillan.
Brown, Keith R. (2009). The Social Dynamics and Durability of Moral Boundaries. *Sociological Forum*, 24(4), 854–876.
Burke, S. J., Milberg, S. J., & Smith, C. N. (1993). The Role of Ethical Concerns in Consumer Purchase Behavior: Understanding Alternative Processes. *Advances in Consumer Research*, 20(1),119–22.
Carroll, C., Lewis, P. M. & Thomas, H. (1992). Developing Competitive Strategies in Retailing. *Long Range Planning*, 25(2), 81–88.
Chen, Y.-S., & Chang, C.-H. (2013). Greenwash and Green Trust: The Mediation Effects of Green Consumer Confusion and Green Perceived Risk. *Journal of Business Ethics*, 114(3), 489–500.
Chkanikova, O., & Mont, O. (2012). *Corporate Supply Chain Responsibility: Drivers and Barriers for Sustainable Food Retailing*. Corporate Social Responsibility and Environmental Management.
Coad, A., de Haan, P., & Woersdorfer, J. S. (2009). Consumer Support for Environmental Policies: An Application to Purchases of Green Cars. *Ecological Economics*, 68(7), 2078–2086.
Cova, B., & Cova, V. (2002). Tribal Marketing: The Tribilisation of Society and Its Impact on the Conduct of Marketing. *European Journal of Marketing*, 36(5/6), 595–620.
Devinney, T. M. (2009). Is the Socially Responsible Corporation a Myth? The Good, the Bad, and the Ugly of Corporate Social Responsibility. *Academy of Management Perspectives*, 23(2), 44–56.
Devinney, T. M., Auger, P., & Eckhardt, G. M. (2010). *The Myth of the Ethical Consumer*. Cambridge, UK: Cambridge University Press.
DuPuis, E. M., & Goodman, D. (2005). Should We Go 'Home' to Eat?: Toward a Reflexive Politics of Localism. *Journal of Rural Studies*, 21(3), 359–371.
Elgin, D. (2010). *Voluntary Simplicity: Toward a Way of Life That Is Outwardly Simple, Inwardly Rich (2nd ed.)*. New York, NY: Harper.
Fuchs, D., Kalfagianni, A., & Havinga, T. (2011). Actors in Private Food Governance: The Legitimacy of Retail Standards and Multistakeholder Initiatives with Civil Society Participation. *Agriculture and Human Values*, 28(3), 353–367.
Halkier, B. (2010). *Consumption Challenged: Food in Medialised Everyday Lives*. Burlington VT: Ashgate.
Jones, P., Comfort, D., & Hillier, D. (2009). Marketing Sustainable Consumption within Stores: A Case Study of the UK's Leading Food Retailers. *Sustainability*, 1(4), 815–826.
Klintman, M. (2016). *A Review of Public Policies relating to the Use of Environmental Labelling and Information Schemes (ELIS)*. OECD Environment Working Papers No. 105. Paris: OECD.
Klintman, M., & Boström, M. (2012). Political Consumerism and the Transition Towards a More Sustainable Food Regime: Looking Behind and Beyond the Organic Shelf. In G. Spaargaren, P. Oosterveer, & A. Loeber (Eds.), *Food Practices in Transition: Changing Food Consumption, Retail and Production in the Age of Reflexive Modernity* (pp. 107–128). London: Routledge.
Lehner, M. (2015a). Retail Store Influence on Sustainable Consumption Behaviour. *International Journal of Quality & Service Sciences*, 7(4), 404.
Lehner, M. (2015b). *Sustainability in Store*. Lund: Lund University, IIIEE Dissertations.
Lehner, M. (2015c). Translating Sustainability: The Role of the Retail Store. *International Journal of Retail & Distribution Management*, 43(4/5), 386–402.
Lehner, M., & Halliday, S.V. (2014). Branding Sustainability: Opportunity and Risk behind a Brand-Based Approach to Sustainable Markets. *Ephemera: Theory & Politics in Organization*, 14(1), 13–34.
Luo, X. (2005). A Contingent Perspective on the Advantages of Stores' Strategic Philanthropy for Influencing Consumer Behaviour. *Journal of Consumer Behaviour*, 4(5), 390–401.
Lusch, R., Vargo, S., & Tanniru, M. (2010). Service, Value Networks and Learning. *Journal of the Academy of Marketing Science*, 38(1), 19–31.
Moisander, J. (2007). Motivational Complexity of Green Consumerism. *International Journal of Consumer Studies*, 31(4), 404–409.
Mont, O., & Tukker, A. (2006). Product-Service Systems: Reviewing Achievements and Refining the Research Agenda. *Journal of Cleaner Production*, 14(17), 1451–1454.
Musso, F., & Druica, E. (2014, Eds). *Handbook of Research on Retailer-Consumer Relationship Development. 1 Edition*. Hershey, PA: IGI Global.
Ölander, F., & Thøgersen, J. (2014). Informing Versus Nudging in Environmental Policy. *Journal of Consumer Policy*, 37(3), 341–356.
OECD (2010). *Enhancing the Value and Effectiveness of Environmental Claims: Protecting and Empowering Consumers*. Report on the OECD workshop [DSTI/CP(2010)18], OECD, Paris, France.

Ongondo, F., & Williams, I. (2011). Mobile Phone Collection, Reuse and Recycling in the UK. *Waste Management*, 31(6), 1307–1315.

Oosterveer, P., & Spaargaren, G. (2011). Restructuring Food Supply: Sustainability and Supermarkets. In G. Spaargaren, A. Loeber, & P. Oosterveer (Eds.), *Food in a Sustainable World. Transitions in the Consumption, Retail and Production of Foodstuffs*. London: Routledge, 129–149.

O'Rourke Dara. (2005). Market Movements: Nongovernmental Organization Strategies to Influence Global Production and Consumption. *Journal of Industrial Ecology*, 9(1–2), 115–128.

Peattie, K., & Crane, A. (2005). Green Marketing: Legend, Myth, Farce or Prophesy? *Qualitative Market Research: An International Journal*, 8(4), 357–370.

Scaraboto, D. (2015). Selling, Sharing, and Everything In Between: The Hybrid Economies of Collaborative Networks. *Journal of Consumer Research*, 42(1), 152–176.

Schor, J. B. (2007). In Defense of Consumer Critique: Revisiting the Consumption Debates of the Twentieth Century. *ANNALS of the American Academy of Political and Social Science*, 611(1), 16–30.

Stolle, D. (2005). Politics in the Supermarket: Political Consumerism as a Form of Political Participation. *International Political Science Review/ Revue Internationale de Science Politique*, 26(3), 245–269.

Stripple, J., & Bulkeley, H. (2013). *Governing the Climate: New Approaches to Rationality, Power and Politics 1 Edition*. New York: Cambridge University Press.

Thøgersen, J. (2006). Norms for Environmentally Responsible Behaviour: An Extended Taxonomy. *Journal of Environmental Psychology*, 26(4), 247–261.

Thøgersen, J., & Crompton, T. (2009). Simple and Painless? The Limitations of Spillover in Environmental Campaigning. *Journal of Consumer Policy*, 32(2), 141–163.

Wood, R. J. (1972). The Challenge of Consumerism and Environmental Concern. *Public Relations Quarterly*, 17(2), 16–28.

Yanarella, E. J., Levine, R. S., & Lancaster, R. W. (2009). Research and Solutions: 'Green' vs. Sustainability: From Semantics to Enlightenment. Sustainability: *The Journal of Record*, 2(5), 296–302.

32

Sexual embodiment and consumption

Sue Scott

Introduction

It is a truism to say that sex and bodies are commodified and differently so on the basis of gender, sexuality, class, ethnicity and age. However, the actual everyday processes and practices of embodied sexuality have been relatively little discussed in consumption studies. For example, a major text on consumer culture has only a passing reference on page 125 to the sexual commodification of the body (Slater, 1997). There are of course exceptions (see Featherstone, 1982), but in the main scholars working on sexuality and the body, outside of the field of consumption, have made connections with consumption rather than the other way around (see Jackson and Scott, 2015). So, while in theory and research bodies and sexuality have been intertwined, the sociology of consumption has tended to develop in parallel but with little physical contact.

While many other disciplines have developed an interest in sexuality and embodiment, sociology led the development of work focusing on the social construction of these aspects of being human (Gagnon and Simon, 1973; Jackson, 1982; Shilling, 1993; Scott and Morgan, 1993). The sociology of sexuality and the body developed over a similar time frame to the sociology of consumption also influenced by the cultural turn. Other contributors to this volume have explored the development of consumption studies; suffice to say here that, as with the body and sexuality there has been a strong emphasis on 'reflexive individualism' (see Warde, et. al., 1.3. in this volume).

I intend to introduce the reader to the development, and importance, of ideas about sexuality and the body as social, and to the notion that sexual and bodily practices are interwoven with our everyday lived experience. I will emphasize gendered power relations and go on to explore some aspects of sexual embodiment important for the study of consumption and deserving of greater attention. I will do this in two ways. First, by discussing aspects of society and culture which shape our understandings of adult sexuality and embodiment in relation to consumption, and secondly, by taking the issue of the 'sexualisation of children and childhood' as a case study in order to emphasize the need for a more nuanced understanding of the relationship between consumer culture and the antinomies of sexuality. Finally, I will suggest how we might integrate ideas about everyday consumption with thinking in relation to the more routine and mundane aspects of embodied sexuality.

Sexuality and the social

Until the 1980s sexuality was not seen as a legitimate object of sociological enquiry and secondly; there was a lack of existing work on which to draw (for a fuller discussion see Jackson and Scott, 2015). There was Freud, of course, and the work of the so-called 'sexual radicals' Reich and Marcuse, as well as feminist political writing. There was some anthropological work on the diversity of human sexual relations and practices, which stressed their socio-cultural origins, but Gagnon and Simon (Gagnon and Simon, ([1973] 2004; Gagnon, 2004) were 'truly the first sociologists to radically question the biologism, the naturalism and the essentialism that pervaded most existing research and study' (Plummer, 2001: 131). Rather than simply asserting the pre-eminence of the social over the natural, they critiqued the idea of repression thus allowing for a positive conception of the social as *producing* sexuality rather than moulding or modifying inborn drives. However, it was not until gender had become much more established as a sociological concept that sexuality came to be more widely seen as amenable to sociological investigation (see Jackson and Scott, 2010a).

The lived body

Prior to the 1980s there was little sociological interest in the body as such (Jackson and Scott, 2014). This neglect is perhaps understandable in terms of sociology's unwillingness to give ground to social Darwinism or biological reductionism, but it 'resulted in a somewhat ethereal conceptualization of our being-in-the world' (Turner, 1984, p. 1). The social world was largely depicted as inhabited by disembodied men – women, where they appeared, were more likely to be considered as embodied, defined by their bodily difference – a tendency that can be traced back to the founding fathers, in particular Weber and Durkheim, both of whom saw women as less social than men and closer to 'nature' (see Sydie, 1987). This is not to say that the body was wholly absent from the disciplinary corpus; there were some earlier sociologists who considered embodied aspects of interaction or practices (for example, Goffman, 1969; Elias [1939], 2000), but it was not the explicit focus of attention.

Significant for discussions of consumption was the work of Mike Hepworth and Mike Featherstone on ageing, exploring embodied everyday experience (Featherstone, 1982; Hepworth and Featherstone, 1982). In *Surviving Middle Age* they focused almost exclusively on the body – primarily bodily aesthetics but also taking in physical fitness and sexual activity. They present a sustained and often witty critique of the pressures to remain youthful in appearance, to resist the process of bodily ageing, including such issues as cosmetic surgery, dieting and fitness. In many respects their analysis was prescient: the pressures they describe have intensified since the book was published, with more anti-ageing products than ever on the market.

Arguably the most significant publication in establishing the field and arguing for an embodied sociology was Bryan Turner's *The Body and Society* (1984). While Turner took Foucault's *The History of Sexuality* (1980) as a starting point, he downplays its originality, arguing for the primacy of Weber's theorization of rationalization in application to modern conditions of embodiment. In much of the work that has been produced since, however, Foucault has been accorded greater significance in sensitizing us to the working of power on bodies at the individual and collective level. His conceptualization of the productive (rather than repressive and coercive) effects of power was further developed in the first volume of *The History of Sexuality* (1978), in which sexuality is conceptualized as having been brought into being as an object of discourse, along with particular categories of sexual subject.

However, in order to understand how bodies are affected by their place in the social order, sociologists turned to Bourdieu in the 1990s. Sociologists were aware that bodies were marked by class, and that individuals were identified as classed, gendered or raced by virtue of bodily attributes and that this was a feature of everyday life. What was lacking was a theoretical language with which to address this. Bourdieu's analyses of habitus and bodily hexis provided a way to theorize how we come to embody our locations within the social in terms, particularly, of class and gender without seeing this as a conscious performance. 'Bodily hexis is political mythology realized, *em-bodied*, turned into a permanent disposition, a durable way of standing, speaking, walking, and thereby of feeling and thinking' (1990, p. 70, emphasis in original). Acquired dispositions associated with particular social locations mark the body internally and externally, affecting both self and social relations.

A further influence noted by some commentators, such as Shilling (1993) and Morgan and Scott (1993), was the North American interactionist tradition, primarily Erving Goffman, whose observations of the minutiae of bodily interaction – eye contact, civil inattention, the placement of bodies in lifts and on buses – and on the arts of impression management, dress and demeanor highlighted the importance of the management of embodied conduct in public space (Goffman, 1969). Goffman also paid some attention to gendered embodiment both in interactional settings (1977) and in representations (1979). Goffman's focus was primarily on the deployment of bodies and their surface appearance, with little attention to experiential embodiment. Other interactionists, however, offer a more nuanced understanding of embodied practices and experience (see for example discussion of Howard Becker's approach in Jackson and Scott, 2007) and provide a useful springboard for rethinking sociological analysis of the gendered and sexual body.

Queer sexuality and the post-modern body

No sooner had the body and sexuality received recognition as important for sociology than they were, to a large extent, disembodied via the cultural turn and the move to more discursive accounts of social construction and post-modern deconstruction.

Foucault's influence on embodied sexuality has probably had its greatest influence through the development of Queer theory from the 1990s onwards (Gamson and Moon, 2004). It emerged as an approach to dissident sexualities framed within deconstructionist, poststructuralist or postmodern perspectives, but has now outlived the latter. Queer theory de-essentialized identity and destabilized the heterosexual/homosexual binary. Perhaps the most influential writer in this context in relation to sexuality and the body is Judith Butler. Butler sees the body as unintelligible without the cultural construction of gender (Butler, 1990), seeing bodies as becoming gendered through the continual performance of gender. This position resonates with Goffman (1969, 1979) and with Garfinkel (1967). She goes on to argue (Butler, 1993) that sex is materialized through citational practices such as 'girling the girl' that begins with the pronouncement 'it's a girl' at a baby's birth. Butler does, therefore, despite much abstraction, discuss the practices through which sexed bodies are brought into being. What is missing is any notion of the social in these processes and practices and, although sexuality appears to be central to her work she actually says very little about the sexual, erotic body. Other influential 'Queer theorists' have gone even further in rendering the social absent from the production and actions of sexual bodies.

Elizabeth Grosz, for example (Grosz, 1995a, 1995b), has contributed to re-conceptualizing desire as positive and productive rather than stemming from lack, as Lacanian psychoanalysis would have it. This is appealing insofar as it resonates with a particularly feminist investment in challenging the conventional sexual order and pushing the boundaries. However, her definition of desire is de-coupled from the social.

This failure, on the part of many recent theorists of sexuality and the body, to recognize either the sociality of embodiment or sociality as embodied and the lack of attention to the 'lived' body, in all its everyday messiness, has been critiqued (see Plummer, 2003; Witz, 2000; Jackson and Scott, 2010a) and greater attention has been paid, by sociologists, to bodily experience and sociality (Crossley, 2001; Jackson and Scott, 2007 and 2014). A focus on the 'lived body' arguably sets the scene in a more appropriate fashion for the development of the relationship between sexual embodiment and consumption.

Gendered sexual embodiment and consumption

It could be argued that if prostitution is the oldest profession then sex is one of human society's oldest commodities. Certainly women's bodies have been bought and sold for sexual purposes in most cultures across recorded time, and this continues globally in the twenty-first century with greater mobility, social media and the internet making the trafficking of women easier than ever. Wives are also bought (and sold); this used to happen in the marketplace and now occurs in cyberspace, but the underlying issue is the same – men have the power to control women's sexuality through the control of their bodies.

In recent years the development of the modern tourist industry (Urry, 1990) has coincided with the increasing commodification of sex and expanded opportunities for what has come to be called sex tourism (Ryan and Kinder, 1996). Sex tourism is not an entirely new phenomenon – Amsterdam's Der Wallen district has a long history – but in recent decades it has developed into a worldwide industry (Enloe, 2000) in which individuals, usually men but sometimes women (Ryan and Kinder, 1996, Hall and Ryan, 2001), from the global North travel to poorer areas of the world in order to purchase a variety of sexual services (primarily from women, sometimes very young girls, but also from young men). It operates at the intersection of ethnicity, gender and age, as well as relative wealth, within the context of the global capitalist tourist industry; it can be seen as an extension of the latter, made possible by discrepancies of wealth and the practices of sexual and gendered power relations. The structure of the wider tourist industry is mirrored to the extent that there are internet sites which enable buyers to customize a complete packaged sex tour online. Stereotyping in advertising is sometimes such that whole populations become sexually commodified.

Another significant aspect of consumption and sexual embodiment is the growth of goods and services for the general public in the context of the widespread shift from sex as primarily tied to reproduction and heterosexual marriage – or even to romantic love – to sex as an aspect of the reflexive project of the self, of self expression, and a leisure activity to be engaged in by freely chosen partners (Giddens, 1992). This shift can be encapsulated in the changing face of the 'sex manual'. These texts also have a long history going back to, at least, the third century BC and appearing in various guises through the centuries, a famous example being the Kama Sutra. The twentieth century saw a growth in the publication of 'how to do it' books such as *The Joy of Sex*, and with increased emphasis on good sex as an essential aspect of the good life there has been a proliferation of books and other media explaining how we can engage in the sexual aspects of the project of ourselves (Giddens, 1992, Jackson and Scott, 1997). Thus sexual consumers are educated in a wide variety of techniques to improve their sex lives, often through the consumption of other goods (from massage oils to sex toys) and services (from sex counsellors to gym membership). The major change, in more recent years, has been the increased focus on heterosexual women as fully engaged embodied actors rather than the passive recipients of male sexual attention. Thus not only are women expected to engage in a good deal of work to be ready for sex, they are supposed to be confident and active as well, thus increasing the pressure to succeed in all sexual contexts and thus the need for more advice and 'self-improvement'.

The twenty-first century has seen the expansion of the sexual marketplace in the form of online dating sites where services are bought in order to facilitate meetings with compatible potential lovers and/or long-term partners (Rosenfeld and Thomas, 2012). This process of commodifying the self via an intermediary is not in itself recent, as there have been 'matrimonial agencies' since the 1700s, and modern dating agencies and 'lonely hearts' columns in newspapers and periodicals developed apace during the twentieth century. This development parallels sociological theorizing about the reflexive project of the self-alongside the increase in long-term relationship breakdown and so the number of individuals seeking a new partner. Much of the research into this phenomenon has been in the form of small qualitative studies of the experience of the process (Barraket and Henry-Waring, 2008), although there are exceptions (see for example Räsänen and Wilska, 2007).

What the topics discussed above have in common is their expansion in the context of the development of the internet. There are examples of sociological theorizing about gendered power relations in the context of the availability of sex via the internet (Brickell, 2012) and research exploring the ways in which sex is merchandised on the web (Pajnik, 2015), but more work is needed to understand the way in which such consumption practices work in the context of sexual embodiment in everyday life.

Bodily adornment with the aim of increasing sexual attractiveness is also nothing new but, as with other aspects of sexual embodiment, it is deeply gendered and also needs to be understood in local social and cultural contexts and in relation to the antinomies which some practices of body transformation produce.

There has been a trend in recent years for increasing degrees of depilation (Herzig, 2015). The 1970s saw a strong feminist critique of the pressure on women to remove body hair, and this certainly had a liberating effect on many women of my generation, but the pressure has redoubled, with ever more techniques available for the removal of hair from every part of the female body (Toerien and Wilkinson, 2003; Hildebrandt, 2003). Some men encourage, or even pressurize, their female partners to remove body hair so as to render them more like women in porn movies (Dines, 2011). It seems that the Brazilian wax, which probably emerged as a response to the 'itsy bitzy' bikinis of Ipanema Beach, has gone global with the porn industry. While the desire on the part of some men to be hairless may likewise be generated by pornography or by a wish to show off a muscular physique, it seems unlikely that they are being pressurized by female partners.

So, women are expected to remove so called 'unsightly' hair in order to look sexier, but ironically this returns them to a pre-pubescent state, and so sexy is equated with looking child-like and all the contradictions that this entails. So, removing pubic hair creates a bodily region ripe for further commodification, for example the vajazzling trend. Women would seem to be unattractive with pubic hair, but still not attractive enough without it. Again we need to understand more about the interrelationship between cultural discourses, consumption practices and embodied sexual interactions.

While other aspects of body adornment and modification could be discussed in the context of consumption and sexual embodiment it would be remiss not to mention the increase in sexual commodification that has accompanied the liberalization of legislation and attitudes in relation to gay sexuality in the global North. The notion of the 'pink pound' has become shorthand for the economics of the gay marketplace, and while this concept existed from the early twentieth century (Bengry, 2009), the possibilities on offer have proliferated in recent years (Kates, 2002, Binnie and Skeggs, 2004). These developments, primarily aimed at gay men, but increasingly at lesbians, included a proliferation of bars and clubs, hotels and holidays, internet sites such as Gaydar and Grindr, sex tourism and sex toys and more recently the paraphernalia surrounding the celebration of civil partnerships and gay marriages.

It is important to understand the development of the 'sexual consumer' and the 'body modifier' as emerging from particular historical and cultural contexts. The wide array of options for changing our bodies – to render them more desirable – which are commercially available need to be interrogated in relation to whether they disrupt or reinforce gendered, racialized and classed definitions of the body. What we need to explore and understand are the continuities and differences between sexual slavery in the context of colonial domination and sexual trafficking in the context of organized globalized crime. Changes in legislation increase the sexual freedom of those previously denied it: the criminalization of rape in marriage; the legalization of gay partnerships and marriages is occurring alongside the increase in the possibilities of pornography via the internet which might be seen to represent freedom of choice for some, mainly men, but mean an increase in objectification, exploitation, violence and even death for others, mainly women. Who makes these changes and what do they mean for everyday lived experience?

The 'market' is very adaptable – blackout tattoos are now seen as an art form in themselves rather than being born of a need to cover up past mistakes, but they are likely to appear more artistic on svelte and youthful bodies both male and female than on older bodies with history written on their surface. So, as with so many aspects of consumption, we are being sold an illusion.

Childhood, consumption and sexualisation: A case study

Over the past thirty years or so, sexualisation, and indeed sexuality itself, has generated anxiety as a threat to children, and to childhood. During the mid 1990s there was much public debate, in the UK, about the sexually explicit content of teenage girls' magazines with an attempt, in 1996, to introduce legislation on providing a minimum age recommendation on the covers of these publications. There was also extensive coverage of the child beauty pageant phenomenon. Unsurprisingly public debate was framed in terms of the threat such phenomena posed to childhood and especially to childhood 'innocence'. Issues were raised about the problem of dressing girls up as mini versions of adult beauty queens, plastering them with make-up and training them to perform for audiences and behave in ways that were age inappropriate (see Jackson, 1999; Scott, Jackson and Backett-Milburn, 1998). Little girls have long enjoyed playing at grown-ups; the difference now is that dressing up has become commodified, and we are presented with mini versions of adult 'dressing-up' clothes in the shops.

The Disneyfication of childhood has expanded in recent years. I have memories of pink, glittery (and impossible to walk in) Cinderella slippers linked to the first Disney Cinderella movie, but these were as nothing compared to the movie-related products now produced by the Disney empire. These outfits tend to be extremely gendered (Auster and Mansbach, 2012) and to render little girls as romantic heroines – although the heroine of the latest Disney craze, *Frozen*, is a much more sturdy character who is in search of her sister rather than romance, she is still described as having a 'wide-eyed' gaze, and the clothes in the merchandise store are made of the stuff of romance and not designed for real-life adventures.

Thus, there are concerns about girls growing up too soon and displaying age-inappropriate traits while wearing 'sexy' clothes. At the same time a widespread acceptance of gender-specific toys, clothes and role models reinforce the idea of girls as little pink princesses in search of a prince. The line between the acceptable and the anxiety inducing is a fine one.

So far the twenty-first century has witnessed increasing public concern about childhood and sexuality (Cook and Kaiser, 2004; Jackson and Scott, 2010a; Egan and Hawkes, 2010; Egan, 2013; Renold, Ringrose, & Egan, 2015; Jackson and Scott, 2015). While there is currently more discussion about boys and (internet) pornography than in previous decades, gender as a social and cultural issue is still rarely addressed explicitly. Such was the concern in the UK that the British government commissioned two reviews on sexualisation. One was for the Home Office, focusing on young people (Papadopoulos, 2010); the other, on children, was for the Department for Education, authored by the Chief Executive of the Mothers' Union (Bailey, 2011). Both called for greater protection of children and young people from sexualisation, and both constructed sexualisation as a threat to 'healthy' sexual development and indeed as a threat to the very essence of childhood, summed up by the title of the Bailey report: 'Letting Children be Children'.

There has also been considerable feminist engagement with the issue of sexualisation, both in terms of critiquing mainstream interpretations of the phenomenon and in providing alternative critical perspectives. In particular, attention has been drawn to the 'limited and commodified vision of active female sexuality' in the media (Attwood, 2006, p. 83), the reinforcement of normative heterosexuality, the classed and racialized dimensions of the imagery and so on (see, for example Attwood, 2006; Gill, 2009). This matters because the representations of sexuality available to children and young people are part of the discourses or cultural scenarios on which they draw in making sense of their own sexuality and locating themselves as competent sexual actors. If these are limited in terms of their representation of gendered sexual practices, this potentially also limits the resources young people can access in constructing a sense of embodied sexual selfhood and in developing future sexual practices.

It is important not to locate children and young people as cultural dopes, as passive recipients of media messages. If we see girls as either 'brainwashed' by the media or as 'rebelling' against dominant discourses, we lose sight of the actualities of girls' everyday experience and practice. As Danielle Egan says: 'In the end, we may demonize, exoticize, or canonize the girl' as 'only a victim' or as 'an agentic warrior' so that 'either way, she becomes a figure frozen in the amber of adult projection' (2013, p. 135).

The objection to the stereotyped conceptions of children, especially girls, as innocent victims, as 'bad girls' (sluts and potential criminals) or as proto-feminist rebels resisting dominant discourse is one reason for drawing on the interactionist perspective of Gagnon and Simon. Developing their perspective allows for a nuanced understanding of the relationship between cultural scenarios, interpersonal interaction and intrapsychic self-reflexivity through which sexual selves are constructed and sexual practices learned and enacted. It enables us to conceptualize agency not as resistance to social forces but as a product of social interaction, involving active intersubjective interpretation of cultural scenarios (such as sexualized imagery). It is this understanding of children as active interpreters of their social world, as engaged in making sense of it with their peers, that is missing from most of the public debate around sexualisation (Jackson and Scott, 2015, King, 2013).

Young women are often deprived of space to develop an autonomous sexuality – and this is becoming increasingly problematic given the contradictions of contemporary Western sexual culture. In the relatively recent past there was assumed to be a transition to a passive sexuality in which women were recipients of men's sexual activity. However, while double standards certainly persist, and young women may still be viewed as sexual gatekeepers, expectations about adequate (hetero) sexual practice have changed. Young adult women are now addressed in popular media as active desiring subjects – within certain limits (see e.g. Attwood, 2006). Performance anxiety is no longer reserved for men; in heterosexual relations women are expected to develop expertise in techniques designed to 'please your man' and also to be 'in touch' with their own bodily pleasure (see Jackson and Scott, 1997). Thus the transition from asexual child to sexually competent adult woman has become more complex.

In many ways contemporary Western sexual mores seem to have been liberalized, with increasing openness about sexuality, more information available about, more opportunities for women's sexual and social autonomy and greater tolerance of sexual diversity (Weeks, 2007). The liberalization of adult sexuality, and the gendering – or not – of the body, there is an increased focus on policing the boundary between childhood and adulthood. In this context, however, the category of 'the child' or 'children' held to be at risk from a sexualized culture has little to do with actual children; it is constructed in terms of an idealized notion of childhood – of children shielded from the world within idealized happy families (Scott et al., 1998; Valentine, 1997). The sexualisation of girls within consumer culture is being flipped over to display childhood innocence, but this very innocence feeds into the potential for certain kinds of male sexual fantasy (Scott and Watson-Brown, 1997).

As Stevi Jackson and I have argued elsewhere (Jackson and Scott, 2010, 2015), this idea of innocence, which entails attempting to keep children ignorant in the name of protection, is no protection. Indeed, it robs children and young people of the means to understand any difficult situations which they might face and gets in the way of the processes they need to go through in order to become competent adult sexual actors. While some young women are clearly at risk, as recent cases in the UK (for example the Jimmy Savile case and organized abuse in Rochdale and Rotherham) have shown, this abuse is not happening as a result of the young women 'knowing too much' or wearing 'inappropriate' clothes, concerns which are the stuff of media and parental risk anxiety.

There is also increasing concern about heterosexual boys and young men not being able to differentiate between pornography and appropriate everyday sexual behavior, and therefore expecting their girlfriends to behave (and look) like porn stars. To the extent that this is the case it is likely to be reinforced by the lack of open discussion of everyday embodied sexuality. However, in the context of media magnification of these anxieties, there is a failure to acknowledge that young people can be competent social and sexual actors who will, in the main, develop their sexual practices in the context of embodied interactions with willing partners. It is important that those of us with an interest in the relationship between sexuality, embodiment and consumer culture develop understandings of these different scenarios and the context within which they occur and that we explore their complexities.

A key point here is that adult anxieties around these issues can serve to render children less safe by potentially depriving them of the knowledge they need to interpret the sexual mores of the world in which they must make the transition to adulthood (see Jackson and Scott, 2010a). Somehow young people who are innocent of desire are expected suddenly to become functioning adult sexual actors engaged in 'healthy' sexual practices.

Conclusion: Understanding sexual embodiment as an everyday practice

There has been a tendency in both academic literature and in media representations to portray and emphasize the more exotic or problematic aspects of sexuality, and it would be tempting to further develop research into sexuality and consumption which continued this focus. I have touched on issues such as sex tourism, and this chapter could have explored many other exotic and/or risky aspects of erotic life. I am not convinced, however that this approach would lead to a better understanding of consumption than can be provided by the study of any other set of specific tastes or interests. Following some other consumption scholars (Gronow and Warde, 2001; Warde, 2015) I would make a plea for a focus on more mundane, routine, everyday practices as an important route to exploring the relationship between embodied sexuality and consumption. I have argued elsewhere for the need to explore mundane sexual practices in order to understand how we make sense of ourselves as sexual actors (Jackson and Scott, 2010a, 2010b, 2015, 2016) and the ways in which we negotiate and compose gendered sexual interactions (Jackson and Scott, 2007, 2010a). If we are to develop a nuanced understanding of consumption in the context of embodied sexuality then we need to explore the ways in which different habits, routines and practices come together to produce sexual scenarios. There are many clichés about candlelight dinners and aphrodisiacs and also a great deal of anxiety about the relationship between alcohol and pressured sex, but we have little systematic knowledge about the way in which scenes are set and props utilized in everyday life. We are presented with images in adverts which suggest that many products are essential to good sex: massage oils, candles, clothing, etc., and we also hear a good deal about Viagra, but what those of us with everyday bodies living in less-than-luxurious surroundings actually do, if anything, by way of preparation for sex with a new or long-term partner is underexplored.

We already know something about the difficulties entailed in disrupting or changing established sexual expectations, practices and routines from research on attempts to change heterosexual practice in the context of sexual risk, specifically HIV transmission. Attempts to encourage condom use came up against embodied and gendered sexual practices, indicating what I have called a 'grammar' of sex (Scott and Freeman, 1995), the sequencing of acts that 'doing sex' conventionally involves, thus indicating that sex is a practice in the sense of being a coordinated entity and also that it is scripted drawing on wider cultural scenarios. To the extent that such practices are routinized they are difficult to (re)negotiate and thus it proved a challenge to punctuate the (hetero) sexual sentence with condoms (see Holland, Ramazanoglu, Scott, Sharpe and Thomson, 1993; Scott and Freeman, 1995).

There is no doubt then that the body and sexuality are at the heart of many consumption practices, but while we know a good deal about media representations of sexualized bodies in the service of consumption, and quite a lot about exotic and more 'extreme' sexual practices, we seem to know relatively little about social differentiation in everyday sexual preferences and their related consumption practices. While we know something about gender and sexual identity in this context (Attwood, 2005; Sonnet, 1999; Westhaver, 2005), there is a lack of sociological research into generational and cohort differences and even less about the relationship between sexual tastes and social class. Is the baby boomer generation's desire to be forever young reshaping sexual practices in older age? We know something about who goes to Anne Summers parties (Storr, 2004), and about the gendered marketing of sex (Attwood, 2005), and market research data will be available on the acquisition of sex toys and other erotic paraphernalia; their appropriation, or the appropriation of more mundane commodities into a sexual context, remains underexplored. We seem to know even less about the social dimensions of the development of sexual tastes and how this leads to the appreciation of particular settings, objects and practices as an integral part of our everyday sexuality. There have been earlier attempts to create a framework for understanding sexuality and consumption – Ken Plummer (Plummer, 2001), makes the case for utilizing Tim Edwards' classification of the meanings of consumption to consumers (Edwards, 2000). While this might work at a general level, I would suggest that by taking Alan Warde's understanding of acquisition, appropriation and appreciation (Warde, 2010) as a starting point we could develop an empirical research agenda which would better embrace the multi-dimensionality of sex, bodies and consumption. This would entail exploring the acquisition of services and equipment for sexual purposes (examples could be clothes, massage oils, hotel rooms, music, etc.) and the ways in which these acquisitions are appropriated by individuals, so as to render them particular, and how they are then introduced and utilized in sexual interactions and embedded within everyday sexual practices. Also of interest would be the development of sexual tastes and how these vary between social groups and across the life course. How do preferences for body shapes emerge and change? How do certain contexts and things come to be understood as sexual for some and not for others? What are the differences between the classic signifiers of the erotic, in a given cultural context, and the actual tastes of sexual actors in negotiation with sexual partners in specific social contexts? Developing research along these lines while taking account of cultural differences and the global context of sexual consumption (Altman, 2000) would have the potential to produce a more nuanced understanding of the relationship between embodied sexualities and the practices of consumption than is currently the case.

References

Altman, D. (2000), *Global Sex*. Chicago: University of Chicago Press.

Attwood, F. (2005), Fashion and Passion: Marketing Sex to Women. *Sexualities* 8(4), 393–407.

Attwood, F. (2006), Sexed Up: Theorizing the Sexualization of Culture. *Sexualities*, 9(1), 77–94.

Auster, C. J. and Mansbach, C. S. (2012), The Gender Marketing of Toys: An Analysis of Color and Type of Toy on the Disney Store Website. *Sex Roles* 67, 375–388.

Bailey, (2011), *Letting Children be Children* Report of an Independent Review of the Commercialization and Sexualisation of Childhood. UK Government.

Bengry, J. (2009), Courting the Pink Pound: *Men Only* and the Queer Consumer, 1935–39. *History Workshop Journal* 68, 122–148.

Binnie, J. and Skeggs, B. (2004), Cosmopolitan Knowledge and the Production and Consumption of Sexualized Space: Manchester's Gay Village, *Sociological Review 52*, 39–61.

Bourdieu, P. (1990), *The Logic of Practice*, Stanford: Stanford University Press.

Brickell, C. (2012), Sexuality, power and the sociology of the Internet, *Current Sociology*, 60, 28–44.

Butler, J. (1990), *Gender Trouble: Feminism and the Subversion of Identity*, New York: Routledge.

Butler, J. (1993), *Bodies That Matter*, New York: Routledge.

Cook, D. and Kaiser S. (2004), Betwixt and be Tween: Age Ambiguity and the Sexualization of the Female Consuming Subject, *Journal of Consumer Culture* 4, 203–227.

Crossley, N. (2001), *The Social Body: Habit, Identity and Desire*. London: Sage.

Dines, G. (2011), *Pornland: How Porn Has Hijacked Our Sexuality*, Boston: Beacon Press.

Edwards T. (2000), *Contradictions of Consumption: Concepts, Practices and Politics in Consumer Society*, Buckingham: Open University Press.

Egan, D. (2013), *Becoming Sexual: A Critical Appraisal of the Sexualisation of Girls*, Cambridge: Polity Press.

Egan, D. and Hawkes, G. (2010), *Theorizing the Child in Modernity*, London: Palgrave.

Elias, N. ([1939] 2000), *The Civilizing Process*, Oxford: Wiley-Blackwell.

Enloe, C. (2000), *Bananas, Beaches and Bases: Making Feminist Sense of International Politics*. Berkeley: University of California Press.

Featherstone, M. (1982), The Body in Consumer Culture, *Theory, Culture & Society* 1, 18–33.

Foucault, (1978), *The History of Sexuality Volume 1*, New York: Random House.

Gagnon, J. (2004), *An Interpretation of Desire*, Chicago IL: University of Chicago Press.

Gagnon, J. and Simon, W. ([1973] 2004), *Sexual Conduct: The Social Sources of Human Sexuality*, Chicago: Aldine Books.

Gamson, J. and Moon, D. (2004), The Sociology of Sexualities: Queer and Beyond *Annual Review of Sociology* 30, 47–64.

Garfinkel, H. (1967), *Studies in Ethnomethodology*, Englewood Cliffs NJ: Prentice Hall.

Giddens, A. (1992), *The Transformation of Intimacy*, Cambridge: Polity PressGill 2009.

Gill, R. (2009), Beyond the 'Sexualization of Culture' Thesis: An Intersectional Analysis of 'Sixpacks', 'Midriffs' and 'Hot Lesbians', in *Advertising Sexualities* 12, 137–160.

Goffman, E. (1969), *The Presentation of Self in Everyday Life*, London: Allen Lane.

Goffman, E. (1977), The Arrangement between the Sexes. *Theory and Society* 4, 301–331.

Goffman, E. (1979), *Gender Advertisements*, London: MacMillan.
Gronow, J. and Warde, A. (2001), *Ordinary Consumption*, London: Routledge.
Grosz, E. (1995a), Animal Sex: Libido as Desire and Death, in E. Grosz and E. Probyn (Eds), *Sexy Bodies: The Strange Carnalities of Feminism*, New York, Routledge, 278–300.
Grosz, E. (1995b), Experimental Desire: Re-Thinking Queer Subjectivity, in E. Grosz (Ed) *Space, Time and Perversion*, New York: Routledge.
Hall, M. C. and Ryan, C. (2001), *Marginal People and Liminalities*, New York: Routledge.
Henry-Waring, M. and Barraket, J. (2008), Dating Intimacy in the 21st Century: the use of online dating sites in Australia. *Australian Journal of Emerging Technologies and Society* 6(1), 14–33.
Hepworth, M. and Featherstone, M. (1982), *Surviving Middle Age*, Oxford: Blackwell.
Herzig, R. (2015), *Plucked: A History of Hair Removal*, New York and London: New York University Press.
Hildebrandt, S. (2003). The last frontier: Body norms and hair removal practices in contemporary American culture. In H. Tschachler, M. Devine, and M. Draxlbauer (Eds.), *The Embodiment of American Culture* (pp. 59-73). Munster: Litverlag.
Holland, J., Ramazanoglu, C., Scott, S., Sharpe, S. and Thomson, R. (1993), "Don't Die of Ignorance" I Nearly Died of Embarrassment: Condoms in Context, in M. Berer and S. Ray (Eds), *Women and HIV/AIDS: An International Resource Book*, London, Pandora.
Jackson, S. (1982), *Childhood and Sexuality*, Oxford: Blackwell.
Jackson, S. (1999), *Heterosexuality in Question*, London: Sage.
Jackson, S. and Scott, S. (1997), Gut Reactions to matters of the Heart: Rationality, irrationality and sexuality. *Sociological Review* 45, 4.
Jackson, S. and Scott, S. (2007), Faking Like a Woman? Towards an Interpretive Theorization of Sexual Pleasure. *Body and Society* 13, 295–313.
Jackson, S. and Scott, S. (2010b), Rehabilitating Interactionism for a Feminist Sociology of Sexuality. *Sociology* 44(5), 811–826.
Jackson, S. and Scott, S. (2010a), *Theorizing Sexuality*, Maidenhead: Open University Press.
Jackson, S. and Scott, S. (2014), Embodying Sociology, in J. Holmwood and J. Scott (Eds), *The History of Sociology*, London: Palgrave.
Jackson, S. and Scott, S. (2015), A Sociological History of Researching Childhood and Sexuality: Continuities and Discontinuities, in E. Renold, J. Ringrose and R. D. Egan (Eds), *Children, Sexuality and Sexualization*, London: Palgrave.
Jackson, J. and Scott, S. (2016), Practice Theory and Interactionism: An Integrative Approach to the Sociology of Everyday Sexuality? in A. King, A. Cristina Santos and I. Crowhurst (Eds), *Sexualities Research: Critical Interjections, Diverse Methodologies and Practical Applications*, London: Routledge.
Kates, S. M. (2002), The Protean Quality of Subcultural Consumption and Ethnographic Account of Gay Consumers. *Journal of Consumer Research* 29(3), 383–399.
King, A. (2013), Recognizing Adulthood? Young Adults' Accomplishment of Their Age Identities. *Sociology* 47, 109–125.
Morgan, D. H. J. and Scott, S. (1993), Bodies in a Social Landscape, in S. Scott and D. H. J. Morgan (Eds), *Body Matters*, Basingstoke: Falmer.
Pajnik, M. (2015), Merchandising Sex on the Web, *Gender Technology and Development*, 19, 181–203.
Papadopoulos, L. (2010), *Sexualisation of Young People Review*, London: UK Government.
Plummer, K. (2001), *Sexualities: Critical Concepts in Sociology*, London: Routledge.
Plummer, K. (2003), *Intimate Citizenship: Personal Decisions and Public Dialogues*, Washington: University of Washington Press.
Räsänen P. and Wilska, T-A (2007), Finnish Students' Attitudes towards Commercialised Sex. *Journal of Youth Studies* 10, 557–576.
Renold, E., Ringrose, J. and Egan, R. D. (Eds.). (2015), *Children, Sexuality and Sexualization*, London: Palgrave.
Rosenfeld, M. J. and Thomas, R. J. (2012), Searching for a Mate: The Rise of the Internet as a Social Intermediary, *American Sociological Review* 77(4): 523–547.
Ryan, C. and Kinder, R. (1996), Sex, Tourism and Sex Tourism: Fulfilling Similar Needs? *Tourism Management* 17(7), 507–518.
Scott, L. and Watson-Brown, L. (1997), The beast, the family and the innocent children, *Trouble and Strife*, 36, 8–12.
Scott, S. and Morgan, D. H. J. (Eds). (1993), *Body Matters*, Basingstoke: Falmer.

Scott, S. and Freeman, R. (1995) Prevention as a problem of Modernity: The Example of HIV and AIDS, in J. Gabe (Ed) *Medicine, Health and Risk*, Oxford: Blackwell
Scott, S., Jackson, S. and Backett-Milburn, K. (1998), Swings and Roundabouts: Risk Anxiety and the Everyday Worlds of Children. *Sociology* 32, 689–705.
Shilling, C. (1993), *The Body and Social Theory*, London: Sage.
Slater, D. (1997), *Consumer Culture and Modernity*, Cambridge: Polity.
Sonnett, E. (1999), Erotic Fiction by Women for Women: The Pleasure of Post-Feminist Heterosexuality. *Sexualities* 2(2), 167–87.
Storr, M. (2004), *Latex and Lingerie: Shopping for Pleasure at Anne Summers Parties*. Oxford: Berg.
Sydie, R. (1987), *Natural Women, Cultured Men: A Feminist Perspective on Sociological Theory*, British Colombia: UBC Press.
Toerien, M. and Wilkinson, S. (2003), Gender and Body Hair: Constructing the Feminine Woman. *Women's Studies International Forum* 26(4), 333–344.
Turner, B. S. (1984), *The Body and Society*, Oxford: Oxford University Press.
Urry, J. (1990), *The Tourist Gaze*, London: Sage.
Valentine, G. (1997), 'My Son's a Bit Dizzy.' 'My Wife's a Bit Soft.': Gender, Children and Cultures of Parenting. *Gender, Place & Culture: Journal of Feminist Geography*, 4, 37–62.
Warde, A. (2010), Introduction XX1-L, in A. Warde (Ed), *Consumption* Volumes 1–4, London: Sage, Benchmarks in Culture and Society Series, xxi–l.
Warde, A. (2015), *The Practice of Eating*, Cambridge: Polity.
Weeks, Jeffrey (2007), *The World We Have Won: The Remaking of Erotic and Intimate Life*. London and New York: Routledge.
Westhaver, R. (2005), "Coming Out of Your Skin": Circuit Parties, Pleasure, and the Subject. *Sexualities*, 8(3), 347–374.
Witz, A. (2000), Whose Body Matters? Feminist Sociology and the Corporeal Turn in Sociology and Feminism, Body *and Society* 6, 1–24.

33

Taste and embodied practice

Melissa L. Caldwell

In *Distinction: A Social Critique of the Judgement of Taste*, Pierre Bourdieu famously wrote that "taste classifies, and it classifies the classifier" (Bourdieu, 1984, p. 6). By focusing specifically on taste as what defined fields of consumption – broadly conceived as consumers, consumer goods, consumer practices, and consumer sensibilities – Bourdieu argued that taste was a form of embodied knowledge about how and what to consume, and that this knowledge was not singular and universal but rather simultaneously multiple and socially and culturally particular. Taste both unified people and the social groups to which they belonged and differentiated them from others. For Bourdieu, this work of classification and differentiation happened through the embedded structuring system of the *habitus* or lifeworld, often rendered simply as "culture," that prefigured all cultural possibilities of a particular society and positioned the people who occupied that society within a self-reproducing system. Because the cultural practices and preferences performed by consumers were already predetermined by and learned from the cultural system that they inhabited (1977), the choices that people made to use particular cultural items were deeply and already internalized within their own consciousness – often so deeply that individuals were not even aware that their actions and preferences reflected cultural constraints.

Bourdieu's argument about internalized, embodied knowledge was not particularly novel, as it had been suggested by other theorists, including Emile Durkheim with his notion of *conscience collective* (1984) and Marcel Mauss's work on "techniques of the body" (1973). What has been most significant from Bourdieu, however, was his specific attention to taste as a recognizable expression of embodied practice.

How, precisely, does taste express embodied practice? Alternatively, how does embodied practice illuminate taste as a cultural phenomenon? Perhaps more importantly, how does taste as a form of embodied practice help us understand consumption? This chapter examines the relationship between taste and embodied practice as a particular aspect of consumption. Of special concern will be the ways in which embodied dimensions of taste reveal systems of cultural classification and distinction in the world at both empirical and analytical scales.

Considered variously as physiological response, act of choice or preference, enactment of knowledge and assessment, and even performance of identity, both actual and aspirational, taste has continuously shifted registers between the biological and the cultural, and between what is presumed to be natural and what is presumed to be learned (Bourdieu, 1984; Korsmeyer, 2005).

As a result, consumption studies have long illuminated, either obliquely or explicitly, the practical and even experiential qualities of taste, such that taste is understood as an embodied practice that links the sensory, the physiological, the psychological, and the cultural. Yet even among scholars working on consumption-related topics, the differences between these different registers have not been convincingly resolved. As Jeffrey Pilcher has pointed out for the specific case of food studies, "One of the great challenges. . . has been to analyze the connections between taste as an individual physical experience and as a collective social category – between what tastes good and who has good taste" (Pilcher, 2016, p. 35; see also Ferguson, 2011; Fitzgerald & Petrick, 2008; Shapin, 2012).

Hence because the embodied dimensions of taste straddle so many registers both within and beyond the human body, and both within and beyond a social or cultural community, my goal in this chapter is not to provide absolute definitions or comprehensive explications of either "taste" or "embodied practice," but rather to discuss some ways in which "taste" and its relationship to embodied practice have been variously recognized and theorized in accounts of consumption. Thus intertwined in this chapter are two related axes: one that explores how scholars have thought about taste and embodied practice, particularly in terms of studies of material culture and consumption, and one that considers what attention to taste and embodied practice illuminates about human nature and social phenomena more broadly.

Recognizing and mobilizing taste

Even as matters of taste are now commonplace in studies of consumption, recognition of taste as a distinct cultural phenomenon was the product of a particular historical moment. As Grant McCracken has documented, the "consumer revolution" that changed how people in Western societies engaged with material goods occurred in the late 1500s as the proliferation of material goods enabled individuals to exercise choice. McCracken notes that these changes promoted differentiation of individuals according to choices and habits, and by extension more subjective attitudes such as fondness and curiosity (1990, pp. 3–14). Since then, ongoing cycles of "consumer revolution" have been inspired by transformations in science, technology, agriculture, and transportation around the world. From changes in manufacturing made possible by the Industrial Revolution in the eighteenth and nineteenth centuries to the increasing speed and reach of distribution made possible by new transportation modes in the nineteenth and twentieth centuries, and from the global spread of cultural habits and goods via the geopolitical networks and markets of colonialism and postcolonial capitalisms to the dramatic political, economic, and cultural restructuring that has occurred via so-called post-socialist transitions in the late twentieth century, the dynamic relationships that have emerged between production, distribution, and consumption have reoriented consumers' abilities to make choices and display preferences.

These changing conditions have inspired new questions about how and why people make the choices they do, most notably in terms of how they understand and experience taste. Thus in the same way that "taste" emerged as a particular historical product, so, too, did recognition of taste as a distinct cultural phenomenon worthy of critical inquiry. Observers' focus on taste was shaped by several overlapping strands of research, most notably from analyses of political economy about the nature and role of commodities. Departing from understandings of consumption as the direct product of geographic location and utilitarian satisfaction of material need, and in which taste was not considered at all or only obliquely implied as a concern of access-driven choice, this emerging scholarship increasingly considered how individuals' decisions about what and how to use material objects were entangled with societal norms and cultural traditions that defined what was and was not permissible. Consumption habits of both excess and modesty were understood as being determined by factors such as social class, cultural background, religious beliefs, political ideologies, and economic access to resources (Goody, 1982; Veblen, 1967 [1899]). From these perspectives, taste as choice was merely an outward expression of one's unique social, cultural, and economic positioning, and not necessarily or exclusively an act of desire or even agency.

By the eighteenth century, with the simultaneous growth of advertising, marketing, and retailing, health and hygiene concerns, and moralist political movements around the world, associations between bodies, goods, and consumption practices became more explicitly recognized as factors to be considered. The physicality of material objects was understood as a means for conditioning particular bodily behaviors, including sensory experiences. Whether it was foodstuffs such as sugar and other spices (Mintz, 1985; Ray & Srinivas, 2012), fabrics such as calico or wool (Eacott, 2012; Rasmussen, 2009), soap, deodorants, and other cosmetics (Jenner, 2011; Weisenfeld, 2004), or other mundane material objects, consumption practices directly shaped the bodies, movements, and experiences of ordinary people as they moved through the world around them. Time, temperature, and space all became lived experiences with palpable structures that shaped visceral experiences (Amato, 2013; Bachelard, 1964; Howes, 2005; Kivelson, 2006; Tuan, 1977). These experiential qualities were then mapped on to cultural and social distinctions, such as age, gender, class, ethnicity, and nationality.

The sensory experiences of taste were especially valuable in the new global capitalist economy, most notably in taste's capacity to encourage more effective labor practices, whether it was by using sweetness to fuel workers' bodies (Mintz, 1985), by providing traditional foods and medicines to comfort and heal indentured servants on their long voyages to plantation colonies (Kumar, 2016), or by transforming food, clothing, and other material goods into global commodities of desire and disdain alongside the slaves, factory workers, and other marginalized workers who were being circulated in this new global economy (Ogundiran, 2009; Stahl, 2002; White, 2011). When taste became a means of fueling labor, it also became a way to protect, preserve, and even punish the human bodies on which colonial and industrial capitalism depended. Pleasure was an especially fraught issue, whether it was promoted as something desirable and productive (Cohen, 2014; Guy, 2002), or as something dangerous and to be avoided, especially by moralizers who sought to promote more ascetic lifestyles that avoided the social, cultural, and existential "problems" of the new modern world (Luker, 1998; Tompkins, 2009).

At a broader level, visceral experiences associated with consumption practices also signaled cultural concerns over demarcations between insiders and outsiders, local and foreign. On the one hand, consumer goods and practices facilitated exploration of the Other, whether it was by satisfying curiosity, enabling adventurism and tourism, both virtual and actual, or marking one as someone with access to non-local experiences (Ching, 2016; Duruz, 2016; Pilcher, 2016). As cultural goods and practices – spices, foods, fabric, languages, art, music, sports, among many other things – circulated via global imperial networks, so, too, did the sensibility to recognize, appreciate, or even to despise them (Gmelch, 1998; Klein, 1993; Nabhan, 2014; Ray & Srinivas, 2012). Consequently, people, cultures, and even geographies became identified with and evoked by particular sensory qualities of taste, smell, sound, sight, and touch.

On the other hand, social, moral, and medical hygiene reformers alike worried that unfamiliar goods and practices might disturb consumers' physiological and emotional sensibilities. Nationalist logics were incorporated into concerns that "foreign" things might upset and damage the psyches, palates, and even digestive systems of the individuals who comprised a particular nation or community (Caldwell, 2014; Earle, 2012). The nascent field of bacteriology contributed to these understandings of taste as intimately connected to sensory and cultural experiences by suggesting that different ethnic or national groups had unique digestive systems that needed to be cultivated – literally and figuratively – by particular foods and sensory experiences (Yotova, 2013). In these logics, tastes were the physical embodiments not just of ideals of Self and Other, but also of the presumed comforts and anxieties associated with each.

By the middle of the twentieth century, choice was more prominent, both as an empirical reality and as an analytical object. Choices increasingly represented opportunities for consumers and the states in which they lived to demarcate and claim the contours of particular lifestyles and worldviews. Appliances, vehicles, home furnishings, clothing, art, architecture, garden styles, and reading materials, among many other aspects of material culture, signaled, individually and collectively, cultural patterns that were believed to indicate a society's status along an evolutionary continuum that ranged from primitive and backward to modern, progressive, or futurist (Buchli, 1999; Jones, 1997).

State governments mobilized consumer preferences and tastes to promote and achieve particular political and economic goals. For instance, the division of the world into two dominant competing ideologies – capitalist democracy and state socialism – was captured via competing consumer ideologies and possibilities that were meant to create particular types of citizens. Representatives from both sides promoted their respective visions through distinct cultural systems that were intended to cultivate particular taste sensibilities – a taste for luxury, a taste for modesty, a taste for science and technology. Soviet reformers promised citizens that in return for surviving times of shortage and outright deprivation, when citizens developed a "taste" for famine foods, physical labor and active leisure, and physical discomfort (Caldwell, 2002, 2014), they would enjoy "tastes" of indulgence and even surplus, such as regular access to ice cream, champagne, recreation parks, rest spas and beach vacations, and appropriately soothing and inspiring architectural styles and home furnishings (Buchli, 1999; Crowley and Reid, 2002; Fehérváry, 2013, p. 3; Gronow, 1997; Haney, 2002). Meanwhile, social reformers in the capitalist West promoted consumer tastes to express and realize what were believed to be uniquely "democratic" or "capitalist" values, goals that became especially significant in post-World War II reconstruction (Gundle, 1999; Schor, 2007). In addition to material goods, organizations of public space, and media, cultures of technology such as those in industry, transportation, and energy were especially prized for their ability to shape consumers' behaviors and, in turn, liberal democratic values (Kroen, 2004; Merelman, 2000).

During the twentieth century, the use of consumption to link physical bodies with political ideologies was not restricted to top-down efforts but also was a bottom-up strategy used by civic groups and other grassroots activist communities. Whether it was 1930s Canadian housewives engaging in milk protests to persuade the state to protect consumers following Canada's Depression era (Guard, 2010), or Lithuanian grandmothers in the 1990s and early 2000s flagrantly violating European Union policies restricting the consumption of raw milk in order to demonstrate public fears over losing Lithuanian heritage (Mincyte, 2009), consumption had clearly emerged as a conduit for ingesting and inscribing larger ideologies, values, and social worlds in the most intimate spaces of consumers' bodies.

Theorizing taste and consumption practice

Coinciding with consumption's role in defining and structuring daily life was greater scholarly attention to the theoretical and methodological insights that could be gleaned from the embodied dimensions of consumption, and consumer tastes in particular. In these shifting conversations about consumption, taste moves in and out of focus as both a topic of inquiry and a product of cultural activity.

One point of departure within this scholarship was inspired by Marcel Mauss's essay "Techniques of the Body" (1973), in which he considered how bodily habits, comportment, and dispositions were shaped by social structures and cultural systems, including material objects and practices. Within anthropology, Mauss's provocations about the interplay between material culture and bodily behavior and experience emerged in numerous other approaches, including the "culture and personality" school associated with Ruth Benedict in the 1940s. According to this theoretical paradigm, societies and their peoples possessed distinctive "personalities" or dispositions that were embedded psychologically and expressed materially. These personalities or dispositions were shaped by and reflected in the unique cultural habits of those societies, including consumer practices. Another direction resonant with Mauss's provocations was that of the structuralist debates of the 1960s. In the logic of structuralism, culture was the external manifestation of deeply internalized, cognitive structures of knowledge and awareness. When applied to the ways in which people interacted with material objects, the structuralist approach framed consumers' preferences and aversions as psychologically, even biologically produced outcomes. Taste preferences as forms of bodily practice were implied by structuralists' ideas that perceptions of color, aroma, taste, and sound, among other sensory registers, were hardwired into the brain and body (Lévi-Strauss, 1969).

For scholars sympathetic to structuralism but not fully inclined to the extreme cognitive determinism proposed by Lévi-Strauss and others, the idea of underlying logics and grammars was useful for explaining cultural patterning, including taste preferences. Mary Douglas was influential in suggesting that material objects operated as "system[s] of communication" (Douglas, 1982). Paving the way for poststructuralist theories, Douglas's insight offered a more nuanced lens for understanding that consumers make selections about the objects and services they consume according to discrete cultural codes that "package" items together in unique ways (Douglas, 1975). This notion that cultures have distinctive patterns that are expressed in unique combinations and recombinations of material objects was picked up by scholars representing several different theoretical orientations, each of which sought to understand how cultural difference was made manifest and experienced as a physical reality.

For poststructuralists such as Baudrillard (1990), cultural patterning resulted from affinities and logics that drew clusters of objects, styles, and practices together, thereby forming discrete sets or even ecosystems of related consumer goods and preferences. Taste as both preference and experience was something channeled and mediated by these predetermined clusters (see also Goffman, 1959). Similarly considering cultural patterns as bounded and discrete entities, Bourdieu's concept of *habitus* further illuminated how bounded entities were perpetually self-producing and reproducing, so that cultural beliefs, values, and behaviors were located both internally and externally (Bourdieu, 1977). With Foucault's explication of the disciplining structures in which those cultural systems were embedded (Foucault, 1978), theorists of consumption, and practice more generally, had new possibilities for understanding not just the power dynamics and coercive dynamics in which Bourdieu's self-reproducing cultural systems were embedded, but also how those cultural practices became internalized and habituated in the most intimate and taken-for-granted spaces of people's bodies and dispositions. For the specific field of consumption, this theoretical turn to practice and discipline offered possibilities for understanding taste preferences as simultaneously culturally conditioned and individually experienced.

Coinciding with these analytical developments were several other theoretical strands that have influenced how scholars make sense of relationships between taste and embodied practice. Drawing on structuralist insights about deep symbolic structures, semiotics approaches considered the ways in which objects and practices could contain and convey multiple meanings. An object or practice was never a singular thing but had a polysemic nature that enabled it to exist with multiple meanings and uses (Lotman, 1990). Not only did this approach shed light on the flexible nature of consumer objects, which allowed them to shift registers and have different meanings for different people and according to different systems, but it also meant that there were no absolute connections between a material object, its value, and the experience it evoked. In other words, semiotics' emphasis on polysemia opened up space for theorists to understand that taste was not an absolute and singular concept or experience but something that had multiple possibilities with effects both within and beyond the body.

Performance theory approaches have similarly disrupted assumptions about connections between consumption and embodied practices. By attending to role-playing activities, performance theorists have productively posed new questions about how consumption practices are performed for different audiences and the criteria by which practices and experiences are deemed authentic or persuasive (Goffman, 1959). This resonates with Baudrillard's ideas about simulacra and the question of what is "real" or "original" when performances produce multiple copies or imitations (Baudrillard, 1994). For matters of taste, these insights rework connections between bodily registers, whether it is by questioning how externally performed roles map on to internally experienced sensations or by investigating how one person's experiences can be transferred to another (Seremetakis, 1993).

In contrast, scholars working on political economy considered the circumstances informing people's interactions with material objects and how value (financial, cultural, symbolic) was created, instituted, and regulated. A key question was how political structures shaped cultural systems: for instance, how have systems of class, race, sex, and age determined which cultural systems exist and who is allowed to access them or participate in them? From this perspective, taste becomes a quality that is limited and accessible only to those with means or abilities (Canclini, 2001). These questions were perhaps raised most effectively by Jack Goody's foundational book *Cooking, Cuisine, and Class* (Goody, 1982), in which he posed a deceptively simple question about what might explain culinary and cultural differentiation by comparing food systems in Africa and Europe. The answer, Goody suggested, had to do with the interrelationship between production and consumption amidst different cultural contexts. By shifting consumption beyond the register of socioeconomic access and into the realm of history and culture, Goody opened up possibilities for thinking about how personal and social values, experiences, and traditions influence the ways in which people both produced and consumed, so that difference was not determined purely by utilitarian or material concerns but was the result of more ambiguous and flexible dimensions of culture. Mary Douglas and Baron Isherwood continued this approach in their book *The World of Goods* (1979). By focusing on the material objects that populate the lives of ordinary people, Douglas and Isherwood illustrated how consumer differentiation occurs, even within the same society. What these approaches have contributed to studies of taste is an understanding of how particular configurations of time and space – of history and geography – have influenced and can explain diverse cultural experiences around the world.

Following both Bourdieu's insights about the classificatory nature of taste and Foucault's arguments about the disciplining nature of cultural forms, by the 1990s taste was understood as something that could discipline and evaluate cultural practice at multiple scales, from the broadest levels of national and global sustainability to the most intimate spaces of the individual body. The globalization/localization debates of the 1990s focused directly on whether entire cultures could or should change their taste preferences for particular styles and objects (Ritzer, 1996; Watson, 1997; Wilk, 1999, 2002). Central to these debates were concerns with whether global circulations of food, music, clothing, languages (English, most notably), and other cultural commodities were eradicating local cultures and producing a generic, meaningless, even bland, global culture (Ritzer, 2004), or whether appropriations of "foreign" cultures were techniques by which local communities articulated their own preferences and distinctive cultural experiences (Caldwell, 2004; Watson, 1997). Even distinctive "taste experiences" identified as being "historical" and "authentic" to a particular society might have been deliberately created for export via the circulation of global trends, as Richard Wilk observed in Belizean inventions of separate food traditions for internal consumption by "locals" and external consumption by "tourists" (Wilk, 1999; 2002).

A related field of critical scholarship, largely pursued by geographers and cultural studies scholars, has seriously attended to the ways in which bodily experiences themselves are subject to classification, organization, and regulation, so that the classificatory nature of taste as an embodied practice has produced categories and standards of normative and non-normative or differently abled bodies (Biltekoff, 2013; Guthman, 2011; Hall, 2000). Once taste became understood as a quality that could be used to discipline and evaluate cultural practice, scholars, policy makers, and practitioners from many different fields harnessed the preferences and choices made by individual consumers into systems of praise or blame for societal-level problems with poverty, inequality, public health, and environmental sustainability. The outcomes of these approaches have inspired studies of perceived health problems like the so-called obesity epidemic and the spread of diabetes, which are largely blamed on consumers not having sophisticated taste preferences that would enable them to make "better" health choices (see Guthman et al., 2014; Guthman, 2014), or analyses of ethical consumption such as fair trade that encourage consumers to channel their taste preferences into practices that support an ethical cause such as labor, trade, or animal welfare (Carrier and Luetchford, 2012). In this logic, taste is a pressure point that encourages or discourages consumer behavior.

Collectively, these scholarly approaches have expanded the criteria defining what counts as the embodied nature of taste, under what conditions and for whom, how taste is taught or learned, how it is valued and by whom, and whether it is universal or particular to historical, political, and economic circumstances. Perhaps most importantly, these approaches have challenged scholars to consider whether taste and embodied practice, as well as taste as a form of embodied practice, are individualized and thus unique to every person, or represent a universally shared aspect of human nature.

Rethinking embodied practice through taste: Future directions

The transformation of taste's embodied dimensions into new states, locations, and experiences poses new challenges and provocative questions for future studies of consumption, beginning with the immediate issue of rethinking relationships between culture and physiology. As the notion of "taste" has expanded, so have the possible embodied practices and sensory experiences associated with taste, whether it is the addition of umami to the category of flavors, the deprivileging of the visual and flavor dimensions of taste with the inclusion of aroma (Herzfeld, 1991), sound (Bakker Kellogg, 2015; Feld, 1982; Helmreich, 2009; Hirschkind, 2006), memory (Sutton, 2011), or even the recognition of kinesthesia as a sensory way of knowing and being in the world (Guerts, 2002). More expansively, scholars have observed how embodied expressions and experiences of taste may exist in other parts of the body – the stomach, the gut, the skin, metabolic systems, limbs, the genitalia, or even implants and prostheses (Caldwell, 2014; Heineman, 2006; Hennion, 2007; Hogle, 2005; Landecker, 2011; Mann, Mol, Satalkar et al., 2011) – and even "cross over" from one bodily register to another, such as with synaesthesia when colors may be experienced as sounds, and temperatures experienced as aromas (Harris, 2015; Sutton, 2001).

Reconfiguring the experiential qualities of taste as forms of practice troubles the relationships presumed to cohere between objects and bodies, and between reality and the imaginary.

Innovative hybrids of art, science, and technology deconstruct conventional forms and experiences of consumer objects and taste, such as with biodegradable or edible clothing (McEachran, 2015) or digital media platforms that displace physical and social experiences onto other registers of bodily awareness (Boellstorf, 2008; Malaby, 2009). Wearable technology allows consumers to monitor their bodily activities and experience them cognitively through numbers rather than viscerally through physical exertion, while social media platforms like videoconferencing enable the immediacy and spontaneity of social intimacy without physical intimacy. Increasingly, the sensory possibilities inspired by rethinking taste are moving consumption experiences into other realms far beyond the here and now of an actual, corporeal body and into more diffuse, flexible, and amorphous spaces beyond the body, and in the process, radically transforming what counts as an embodied practice.

Ultimately, the rearrangement of taste and embodied practice in consumption activities raises profound questions about whether taste truly is a form of embodied practice or is, instead, a metadiscourse on how embodied practice can and should be experienced and understood as something that is simultaneously cultural, sensory, visceral, practical, and even material. If so, then Bourdieu was right in proposing that taste classifies both the classifier and the classified, as well as the classification itself.

References

Amato, Joseph A. (2013). *Surfaces: A History*. Berkeley: University of California Press.

Bachelard, Gaston. (1964). *The Poetics of Space*. Maria Jolas, trans. New York: Orion Press.

Bakker Kellogg, Sarah. (2015). "Ritual Sounds, Political Echoes: Vocal Agency and the Sensory Cultures of Secularism in the Dutch Syriac Diaspora." *American Ethnologist* 42(3): 431–445.

Baudrillard, Jean. (1990). *Selected Writings*. Stanford, CA: Stanford University Press.

___. (1994). *Simulacra and Simulation*. Sheila Faria Glaser, trans. Ann Arbor: University of Michigan Press.

Biltekoff, Charlotte. (2013). *Eating Right in America: The Cultural Politics of Food and Health*. Durham, NC: Duke University Press.

Boellstorff, Tom. (2008). *Coming of Age in Second Life: An Anthropologist Explores the Virtually Human*. Princeton, NJ: Princeton University Press.

Bourdieu, Pierre. (1977). *Outline of a Theory of Practice*. Richard nice, trans. Cambridge: Cambridge University Press.

Bourdieu, Pierre. (1984). *Distinction: A Social Critique of the Judgement of Taste*. Richard Nice, trans. Cambridge, MA: Harvard University Press.

Buchli, Victor. (1999). *An Archaeology of Socialism*. Oxford: Berg.

Caldwell, Melissa L. (2002). "The Taste of Nationalism: Food Politics in Postsocialist Moscow." *Ethnos* 67(3): 295–319.

Caldwell, Melissa L. (2004). "Domesticating the French Fry: McDonald's and Consumerism in Moscow." *Journal of Consumer Culture* 4(1): 5–26.

Caldwell, Melissa L. (2014). "Digestive Politics in Russia: Feeling the Sensorium beyond the Palate." *Food and Foodways* 22(1–2): 112–135.

Canclini, Nestor Garcia. (2001). *Consumers and Citizens: Globalization and Multicultural Conflicts*. Minneapolis: University of Minnesota Press.

Carrier, James G. & Peter G. Luetchford, eds. (2012). *Ethical Consumption: Social Value and Economic Practice*. New York: Berghahn Books.

Ching, May-bo. (2016). "The Flow of Turtle Soup from the Caribbean via Europe to Canton, and Its Modern American Fate." *Gastronomica: The Journal of Critical Food Studies* 16(1), 79–89.

Crowley, David & Susan E. Reid, eds. (2002). *Socialist Spaces: Sites of Everyday Life in the Eastern Bloc*. Oxford: Berg.

Cohen, Joanna. (2014). "Promoting Pleasure as Political Its Economy: The Transformation of American Advertising, 1800 to 1850." *Winterthur Portfolio* 48(2/3): 163–190.

Douglas, Mary. (1975). "Deciphering a Meal." In *Implicit Meanings: Selected Essays in Anthropology*, Pp. 249–275. London: Routledge and Kegan Paul.

Douglas, Mary. (1982). "Food as a System of Communication." In M. Douglas (ed.), *In the Active Voice*. Pp. 82–104. London: Routledge and Kegan Paul.

Douglas, Mary & Baron Isherwood. (1979). *The World of Goods*. New York: Basic Books.

Durkheim, Emile. (1984). *The Division of Labor in Society*. W.D. Halls, trans. New York: Free Press.

Duruz, Jean. (2016). "Love in a Hot Climate: Foodscapes of Trade, Travel, War, and Intimacy." *Gastronomica: The Journal of Critical Food Studies* 16(1): 16–27.

Eacott, Jonathan P. (2012). "Making an Imperial Compromise: The Calico Acts, the Atlantic Colonies, and the Structure of the British Empire." *The William and Mary Quarterly* 69(4): 731–762.

Earle, Rebecca. (2012). *The Body of the Conquistador: Food, Race, and the Colonial Experience in Spanish America, 1492–1700*. Cambridge: Cambridge University Press.

Fehérváry, Krisztina. (2013). *Politics in Color and Concrete: Socialist Materialities and the Middle Class in Hungary*. Bloomington: Indiana University Press.

Ferguson, Priscilla Parkhurst. (2011). "The Senses of Taste." *American Historical Review* 116(2): 371–384.

Fitzgerald, Gerard & Gabriella Petrick. (2008). "In Good Taste: Rethinking American History with Our Palates." *Journal of American History* 95, no. 2 (September): 392–404.

Feld, Steven. 1982. *Sound and Sentiment: Bird, Weeping, Poetics, and Song in Kaluli Expression*. Philadelphia: University of Pennsylvania Press.

Foucault, Michel. (1978). *The History of Sexuality*. Robert Hurley, trans. New York: Pantheon Books.

Gmelch, George. (1998). *In the Ballpark: The Working Lives of Baseball People*. Washington, DC: Smithsonian.

Goffman, Erving. (1959). *The Presentation of Self in Everyday Life*. New York: Anchor Books.

Goody, Jack. (1982). *Cooking, Cuisine and Class: A Study in Comparative Sociology*. Cambridge: Cambridge University Press.

Gronow, Jukka. (1997). *The Sociology of Taste*. London: Routledge.

Guard, Julie. (2010). "A Mighty Power against the Cost of Living: Canadian Housewives Organize in the 1930s." *International Labor and Working-Class History* 77: 27–47.

Guerts, Kathryn Linn. (2002). *Culture and the Senses: Bodily Ways of Knowing in an African Community*. Berkeley: University of California Press.

Gundle, Stephen. (1999). "Feminine Beauty, National Identity and Political Conflict in Postwar Italy, 1945–1954." *Contemporary European History* 8(3): 359–378.

Guthman, Julie. (2011). *Weighing In: Obesity, Food Justice, and the Limits of Capitalism*. Berkeley: University of California Press.

Guthman, Julie. (2014). "Introducing Critical Nutrition: A Special Issue on Dietary Advice and Its Discontents." *Gastronomica: The Journal of Critical Food Studies* 14(3): 1–4.

Guthman, Julie, Broad, Garrett, Klein, Kendra, Landecker, Hannah. (2014). Beyond the Sovereign Body, *Gastronomica: The Journal of Critical Food Studies*, 14(3): 46-55.

Guy, Kolleen M. (2002). "Rituals of Pleasure in the Land of Treasures: Wine Consumption and the Making of French Identity in the Late Nineteenth Century." In *Food Nations: Selling Taste in Consumer Societies*, ed. Warren Belasco and Philip Scranton. Pp. 34–47. New York: Routledge.

Hall, Edward. (2000). "'Blood, Brain and Bones': Taking the Body Seriously in the Geography of Health and Impairment." *The Royal Geographical Society* 32(1): 21–29.

Haney, Lynne A. (2002). *Inventing the Needy: Gender and the Politics of Welfare in Hungary*. Berkeley: University of California Press.

Harris, Anna. (2015). "The Hollow Knock and Other Sounds in Recipes." *Gastronomica: The Journal of Critical Food Studies* 15(4): 14–17.

Heineman, Elizabeth D. (2006). "The Economic Miracle in the Bedroom: Big Business and Sexual Consumption in Reconstruction West Germany." *The Journal of Modern History* 78(4): 846–877.

Helmreich, Stefan. (2009). *Alien Ocean: Anthropological Voyages in Microbial Seas*. Berkeley: University of California Press.

Hennion, Antoine. (2007). "Those Things that Hold Us Together: Taste and Sociology." *Cultural Sociology* 1(1): 97–114.

Herzfeld, Michael. (1991). *A Place in History: Social and Monumental Time in a Cretan Town*. Princeton, NJ: Princeton University Press.

Hirschkind, Charles. (2006). *The Ethical Soundscape: Cassette Sermons and Islamic Counterpublics*. New York: Columbia University Press.

Hogle, Linda F. (2005). "Enhancement Technologies and the Body." *Annual Review of Anthropology* 34: 695–716.

Howes, David, ed. (2005). *Empires of the Senses: The Sensual Culture Reader*. Oxford: Berg.

Jenner, Mark S.R. (2011). "Follow Your Nose? Smell, Smelling, and Their Histories." *American Historical Review* 116(2): 335–351.
Jones, Janna. (1997). "The Distance from Home: The Domestication of Desire in Interior Design Manuals." *Journal of Social History* 31(2): 307–326.
Kivelson, Valerie. (2006). *Cartographies of Tsardom: The Land and Its Meanings in Seventeenth-Century Russia.* Ithaca, NY: Cornell University Press.
Klein, Alan M. (1993). *Sugarball: The American Game, the Dominican Dream.* New Haven, CT: Yale University Press.
Korsmeyer, Carolyn, ed. (2005). *The Taste Culture Reader: Experiencing Food and Drink.* Oxford: Berg.
Korsmeyer, Caroline (2005). "Introduction: Perspectives on Taste." In *The Taste Culture Reader: Experiencing Food and Drink*, ed. Caroline Korsmeyer, Pp. 1–9. Oxford: Berg.
Kroen, Sheryl. (2004). "A Political History of the Consumer." *The Historical Journal* 47(3): 709–736.
Kumar, Ashutosh. (2016). "Feeding the *Girmitiya*: Food and Drink on Indentured Ships to the Sugar Colonies." *Gastronomica: The Journal of Critical Food Studies* 16(1): 41–52.
Landecker, Hannah. (2011). "Food as Exposure: Nutritional Epigenetics and the New Metabolism." *BioSocieties* 6(2): 167–194.
Lévi-Strauss, Claude. (1969). *The Raw and the Cooked.* John and Doreen Weightman, trans. New York: Harper & Row.
Lotman, Yuri M. (1990). *Universe of the Mind: A Semiotic Theory of Culture.* Ann Shukman, trans. London: Tauris.
Luker, Kristin. (1998). "Sex, Social Hygiene, and the State: The Double-Edged Sword of Social Reform." *Theory and Society* 27(5): 601–634.
Malaby, Thomas M. (2009). *Making Virtual Worlds: Linden Lab and Second Life.* Ithaca, NY: Cornell University Press.
Mann, Anna, Annemarie Mol, Priya Satalkar, Amalinda Savirani, Nasima Selim, Malini Sur, and Emily Yates-Doerr. (2011). "Mixing Methods, Tasting Fingers: Notes on an Ethnographic Experiment." *HAU: Journal of Ethnographic Theory* 1(1): 221–243.
Mauss, Marcel. (1973). "Techniques of the Body." *Economy and Society* 2(1): 70–88.
McCracken, Grant. (1990*). Culture & Consumption: New Approaches to the Symbolic Character of Consumer Goods and Activities.* Bloomington: Indiana University Press.
McEachran, Rich. (2015). "Would you wear a wedding dress made from fungus?" *The Guardian*, February 17, 2015, online edition, http://www.theguardian.com/sustainable-business/sustainable-fashion-blog/2015/feb/17/grow-compost-wedding-dress-homegrown-fashion.
Merelman, Richard M. (2000). "Technological Cultures and Liberal Democracy in the United States." *Science, Technology, & Human Values* 25(2): 167–194.
Mincyte, Diana. (2009). "Self-Made Women: Informal Dairy Markets in Europeanizing Lithuania." In *Food & Everyday Life in the Postsocialist World*, ed. Melissa L. Caldwell, Pp. 78–100. Bloomington: Indiana University Press.
Mintz, Sidney W. (1985). *Sweetness and Power.* New York: Viking Penguin Inc.
Nabhan, Gary Paul. (2014). *Cumin, Camels, and Caravans: A Spicy Odyssey.* Berkeley: University of California Press.
Ogundiran, Akinwumi. (2009). "Material Life and Domestic Economy in a Frontier of the Oyo Empire during the Mid-Atlantic Age." *The International Journal of African Historical Studies* 42(3): 351–385.
Pilcher, Jeffrey M. (2016). "'Tastes Like Horse Piss': Asian Encounters with European Beer." *Gastronomica: The Journal of Critical Food Studies* 16(1): 28–40.
Rasmussen, Margaret Byrd Adams. (2009). "Waging War with Wool: Thomas Jefferson's Campaign for American Commercial Independence from England." *Material Culture* 41(1): 17–37.
Ray, Krishnendu, and Tulasi Srinivas. (2012). *Curried Cultures: Globalization, Food, and South Asia.* Berkeley: University of California Press.
Ritzer, George. (1996). *The McDonaldization of Society: An Investigation into the Changing Character of Contemporary Social Life.* Thousand Oaks, CA: Pine Forge Press.
Ritzer, George. (2004). *The Globalization of Nothing.* Thousand Oaks, CA: Pine Forge Press.
Schor, Juliet B. (2007). "In Defense of Consumer Critique: Revisiting the Consumption Debates of the Twentieth Century." *The Annals of the American Academy of Political and Social Science* 611: 16–30.
Seremetakis, C. Nadia. (1993). The Memory of the Senses: Historical Perception, Commensal Exchange and Modernity. *Visual Anthropology Review* 9(2): 2–18.
Shapin, Steven. (2012). "The Sciences of Subjectivity." *Social Studies of Science* 42(2): 170–184.

Stahl, A.B. (2002). "Colonial Entanglements and the Practices of Taste: An Alternative to Logocentric Approaches." American Anthropologist 104(3): 827–845.

Sutton, David E. (2001). *Remembrance of Repasts: An Anthropology of Food and Memory*. Oxford: Berg Publishers.

___. (2011). "Memory as a Sense: A Gustemological Approach." In "The Sensory Experience of Food" with Caroline Korsmeyer. *Food, Culture and Society* 14(4): 461–476.

Tompkins, Kyla Wazana. (2009). "Sylvester Graham's Imperial Dietetics." *Gastronomica* 9(1): 50–60.

Tuan, Yi-fu. (1977). *Space and Place: The Perspective of Experience*. Minneapolis: University of Minnesota Press.

Veblen, Thorstein. (1967). *The Theory of the Leisure Class*. New York: Viking Press.

Watson, James L., ed. (1997). *Golden Arches East: McDonald's in East Asia*. Stanford, CA: Stanford University Press.

Weisenfeld, Gennifer. (2004). "'From Baby's First Bath': Kaō Soap and Modern Japanese Commercial Design." *The Art Bulletin* 86(3): 573–598.

White, Sophie. (2011). "French Colonial Louisiana and a World of Goods." *Winterthur Portfolio* 45(2/3): 229–248.

Wilk, Richard. (2002). "Food and Nationalism: The Origins of 'Belizean Food." In *Food Nations: Selling Taste in Consumer Societies*, ed. Warren Belasco and Philip Scranton. Pp. 67–89. New York: Routledge.

Wilk, Richard. (1999). "'Real Belizean Food': Building Local identity in the Transnational Caribbean." *American Anthropologist* 101(2): 244–255.

Yotova, Maria. (2013). "'Bulgaria, the Holy Land ofYogurt': A Brand Myth and Management Philosophy." *Senri Ethnological Studies* 82: 87–90.

34

Health, bodies and active leisure

Roberta Sassatelli

While Hollywood stars and media personalities routinely appear on the covers of fitness magazines thanking their personal trainers for their toned appearances, medical discourse has been attributing an ever-increasing value to active leisure and physical exercise, both therapeutic and preventive. Fitness activities as offered by commercial gyms, match current governmental public campaigns sponsoring healthy lifestyle and longevity for the entire population in what has recently been termed "mindful fitness" (Markula, 2011; Sassatelli, 2016). In such a guise, fitness may be seen as an apparently all-inclusive territory where functionalized, rationalized and individualized enjoyment must be displayed while working towards a normalized healthy-looking, young and efficient embodied self. Healthism (Crawford, 1980) as a particular form of health promotion has long been recognized as being deeply intertwined with consumer capitalism, commodity culture and the objectification of the self-monitoring self (Lupton, 1994; 2016). It has coated our notions of beauty, just like fitness has given new colors to sport activities. Bodies are intensely under pressure in consumer capitalism, doubly objectified as signs of pleasure as well as instruments of work. This chapter considers how consumer culture contributes to the contemporary politics of health, active leisure and the body. It starts by considering the way body care is organized through fitness culture as a predominantly commercial culture which addresses the sovereign, even choosy consumer. The chapter thereby looks at which kind of symbolic work happens in the gym around ideals of the body, considers the interplay between health and beauty, the emergence of fitness as a central value, closing with a reflection on the politics of active leisure and the fit body.

The commercialization of variety

In contemporary consumer capitalism, the "fit body" has replaced body decoration as a potent symbol of status and character, both for men and women, both for the upper and the middle classes, and it is increasingly promoted as a goal for the aging in what may be termed the global West (Andreasson and Johansson, 2014; Sassatelli, 2016). Fitness gyms and health centers have become highly visible as the sites where, through various forms of active leisure practices, such a body is produced. These commercial institutions at the core of a much-broader fitness culture comprise a variety of commodities: magazines, book and blogs on exercise, diet and health provide advice for DIY well-being; fitness festivals across the global West are increasingly getting media coverage and contribute to the professionalization of trainers, self-monitoring apps help individuals to keep their goals and performances under objectifying control (Lupton, 2016). Blending pop culture, dance and physical education, and initially reserved for women, fitness culture has moved away from body-building, depoliticizing recreational gymnastic. If recreational and sporting physical activities had previously been connected with social values like faith in progress or loyalty to a nation, personal motivations have now become the key factor. Targeted at paying customers who can always decide they no longer have any need or desire for the gym, fitness is presented as an expression of the individual consumer's will.

Terms such as "fitness center" or "health center" have a luxurious feel attached to them, as well as diverge attention from the competitive, harsh and often very masculine world which was originally associated to the term *gymnasium*, and attach themselves more clearly to some form of leisured healthism. Leisured healthism or therapeutic active leisure (Caldwell, 2005; Sassatelli, 2015, 2016) mix pop culture and the iconicity of the fit body with the medicalization of the exercising body. Fitness gyms are non-competitive environments aimed at providing recreational exercise to boost physical form and well-being. Typically located in urban contexts, they are a special breed of leisure institutions (Rojek, 2000). Gyms are different from social clubs – both working class and upper class – in that a set of specific tasks are to be carried out, with sociability being either a by-product or a facilitator of those tasks. In some ways, going to a fitness gym is a form of "serious leisure" (Stebbins, 2009; more generally on the mix of asceticism and hedonism see Sassatelli, 2001) which allows the development of a project and to a degree a "career" within one's own free time. They may be understood under the banner of "rational recreation", which stresses that recreational activities should be morally uplifting for the participant, good for his or her body, and have positive benefits for the wider society (Foucault, 1991); they also incorporate the upbeat positivity which is typical of commercial culture (Hochschild, 2012). At a difference with more informal, spontaneous forms of leisure, or with sub-cultures of commodity appropriation, they appear, at least at a first glance, functional to social order and dominant classifications, rather than "anti-structural" or "subversive" such as boxing (Wacquant, 2004).

Different countries across the globe may work through different forms of provision, with Nordic countries being also influenced by public provision, Italy and Mediterranean Europe being closer to what might be considered the dominant commercial model, with different degrees in the UK and the US. Yet, overall, fitness culture is heavily imbued with promotional culture and commercial relations organized around "clients" (Maguire Smith, 2007, Sassatelli 2010). Managers are keen to structure the variety of activities offered in fitness gyms in time and space as to provide what in their words is a "fulfilling", "total", "complete" experience. The continuous introduction of new techniques and the role of trainers, both as gym employees and as self-employed personal trainers, in pushing innovation and differentiation forward is a feature of today's fitness industry. An impression of variety is reinforced by trainers who insist that all clients are expected to find or discover "their own way" to train, and to do so by using the various alternatives available. In their manner of speech, preference for different techniques is presented as a "personal choice", as a selection from a range of valid techniques of what is "best for each person". This script clearly matches the commercial nature of fitness culture and its provision of what has been called "structured variety" (Sassatelli, 2010). Modern markets thrive on the generation of differences, and consumers as well as producers are quite willing to collaborate in the process. Growth and control by managed, marginal diversification (or structured variety) is a well-known dynamic within consumer capitalism as developed in the large cities of today. The organization of different techniques in spatially differentiated areas helps construct the idea that the fitness gym provides all that is needed for fitness. It thus has a legitimating function as well as mundane commercial scope, broadening the clientele by catering for the whole life course of a prospective client. Much of the generated difference in fitness culture happens through the ever-shifting hybridization and reshuffling of precepts and precincts which once appeared as irreconcilable and distant, thus for example re-negotiating the boundary of sport and gymnastic. Sport leisure pursuits are themselves becoming less competitive and more health-oriented while fitness activities are considered the major sport among the active population, which may instrumentalize the competition element to allow participants to adhere to the exercise (Sassatelli, 2016).

The boom of the fitness industry has been matched by an equal growth in the range of workout options available: aqua exercise, boxing training, cardiovascular machines, circuit training, combat-style workouts, core-stability workouts such as Pilates, exercise to music such as step and aerobics, free weight exercise and indoor cycling including spinning. Replacing the monolithic exercise salons devoted entirely to body building or aerobics, commercial fitness gyms increasingly draw on cognate areas – such as sports, martial arts, dance, meditation – to provide different blends of aerobic and anaerobic, free-body and equipment-based exercises. Fitness is an increasingly hybrid endeavor, mixing Eastern and Western techniques. It draws from a truly global reservoir of body techniques and emotional codes which are thus fast changing: Colombian-born Zumba, a form of exercise-to-music mixing Caribbean dance and aerobic exercises and sustained by a sensuous emphasis on fun and (female) togetherness, has quickly become popular only to leave room to fitness boot camps, mimicking US Marines' military training, emphasizing strength and resistance, harsh and muscular discipline (Andreasson and Johansson, 2014). Originally, fitness boot camps stretched fitness outside the gym into parks and nature, realizing the gym's, and in fact instructors', attempts at extending control of activities well beyond the immured, managerially-driven reality of the club. Yet, these muscular techniques got back into the gym, bringing with themselves new dress codes drawing on military outfits and opening the way for a renewed emphasis on strength training as opposed to aerobic exercise. This is resulting in formats such as body weight training, which, mixing acrobatic elements and an emphasis on bare body performance, somehow mimics the extraordinary stunts of superheroes and superheroines from the movie industry.

Active leisure and body ideals

Fitness culture has attracted contrasting diagnoses from within a host of disciplines, often corresponding to disciplinary specializations in the study of sport and physical activity at large. Physical education, medical practice and, to some extent, even leisure studies have typically played a celebratory tune, stressing the physical benefits of the fitness workout, its emancipation potential and even its psychological paybacks. On the contrary, within sociology and gender studies there has been a tendency to expose the fitness boom, stressing its commercial nature and its disciplinary functions, showing that it may sustain quite a bit of consumers' dissatisfaction and frustration (Frow and McGillivray, 2005). This is especially so as related to gender identities, with aerobics in particular being considered as yet another practice of beautification which subjugates women to hegemonic and male-dominated views of female subjectivity (Dinnerstein and Weitz, 1998; Maguire and Mansfield, 1998). Fitness has thus appeared as the illusory and narcissistic response to a heavily standardized and profit-seeking industry and the perpetuation of heavily gender-biased images of the body, with participants being asked to joyfully take responsibility for their bodies and to invest in body maintenance in order to perform culturally appropriate self-presentation. A similar reading does not account for the specificity of gym practices with respect to other forms of body transformation, with fitness being grouped together with arguably quite different techniques such as plastic surgery. Highlighting the corrosion of character in an era of obsessive self-presentation, this view contrasts markedly with fitness discourse, according to which fitness demonstrates character.

Expert fitness discourse is closer to another set of grand theories which have been drawn upon to understand the fitness boom. They offer a more positive view of individualization and revolve on the notion of "body projects", the idea that in late modernity the self becomes a reflexive and secular project which works on an ever-refined level of body presentation (Giddens, 1991, Sassatelli 2012). These views are further sociologically qualified, and made more critical, by relating reflexive body projects to the particular self-presentation needs of the new middle class, who compete in job and relationship markets where high levels of "physical capital" are required (Bourdieu, 1978). Following this line of thought, fitness culture has been seen as either as a demand-side phenomenon of body transformation (Glassner, 1992) or as a supply-side phenomenon of commercialization (Maguire Smith, 2007) and either traced back to the late-modern subject and its new middle-class incarnations, or is conceived as a leisure industry, the mirror of mounting commoditization with the ensuing individualization of social problems such as obesity.

On another account, coming from post-feminist views and ethnographic approaches, a number of studies have highlighted the creative role of the situated meaningful practices of fitness fans. Fieldwork research which focuses on participants' meanings has proved useful to show that gym going is not motivated by a single motive, static across gym careers and uniform across participants, and that body ideals and hegemonic gender views are negotiated rather than simply taken up by fitness participants (Crossley, 2006; Leeds, Creig and Liberti, 2007). Like other commercial institutions where active leisure is organized, fitness gyms are indeed productive environments. This not only because they produce material effects on the body, but also because they allow participants to negotiate and (re)produce body ideals. This entails a dialectical play between objectified fitness ideals as responding to broad cultural ideals and lived body objectives as negotiated through training.

Body ideals and lived practices

Fitness culture is co-terminus with consumer capitalism, enticing a vast, typically urban, public of consumers to engage, via commercial transactions, with goods and services that are produced to be sold. Yet, my ethnographic journey into the world of the fitness gym in Italy and the UK (Sassatelli, 2010) demonstrated the productive force of consumer practices and the permeability of the division between production and consumption in consumer spaces such as commercial gyms. As participants manage to organize their efforts into a training project, some physical characteristics acquire importance. These, in turn, form the basis for an awareness of the body as being something "useful" and "real", an embodied awareness which can be used to negotiate initial subjective aspirations as related to broad cultural ideals objectified in commercial images and the like. In their verbalization, the "feeling" component acquires relevance for many regulars (see also Crossley, 2006).

This configuration may generate a variety of responses, which are more mixed and articulated than the simple "aesthetic masochism" diagnosed by Frew and McGillivray (2005) as endemic among Scottish gym goers. A sense of frustration may be there, and it is very clearly so among quitters, novices and irregular clients. But it is alleviated by a shift in body objectives among those who stick to a club and become regulars: regular clients typically learn to suspend their initial aspirations, concentrate on performing the exercises, and then re-consider their aspirations in the light of what may be provided by locally organized fitness options. The process which leads to a successful gym career is described as having a circular structure. But rather than having the "vicious" quality of a contradiction, it is portrayed by gym staff and enthusiastic clients alike as a "virtuous circle", a spiral in fact, that in cognitive terms may be seen as reducing dissonance and organizing preferences, thus offering a way forward. In successful gym careers, the gym becomes important not only because participants acquire an insider habitus, but also because they acquire insider agency; they begin to set objectives which the gym can meet. The very variety of keep-fit exercise is taken as a palette of possibilities which circumscribes the body objectives one may aspire to, rendering such objectives more "realistic" indeed – namely both "within reach" and "truthful" to the body as practically known through keep-fit techniques. Tone replaces weight as a concern, and a younger, healthier, more active-looking body becomes beautiful.

For some, buying a fitness pass is like buying a dream of perfection and plasticity. As we know, consumption may allow the cultivation of utopias that may not be realizable in ordinary life (Sassatelli, 2007). Goods represent bridges suspended not only towards others, but also towards broad cultural ideals of a deep mythical force that on average escape us, and which we don't want to give up. Practices of consumption of what may be called utopian goods and services may not so much change the cultural traits of the utopia, but it may change how we relate to it. Working on media representation of the fit and slender body, Bordo (1993) famously identified in a similar mechanism a sort of disempowerment machinery for the reproduction of the gender-laden normative ideal of the slender body. Bordo (1993, p. 191) sees "an important continuity of meaning in our culture between compulsive dieting and body building" and, by extension, fitness bodywork, which are "united in a battle against a common enemy: the soft, the loose, unsolid excess flesh [. . .] simply to be slim is not enough – the flesh must not wiggle". This is ultimately linked to the possibility of demonstrating a disciplined self – which, given that self-control is decisively coded as male and middle class, becomes more demanding for women and the working class. Empirical work in fitness gyms may also reach similar results. For example, Frew and McGillivray (2005) carried out their mentioned study of the Scottish fitness gym mainly amongst personal trainers, with whom they conducted personal interviews, and supplemented these by focus groups with clients solicited to comment on a six-minute video clip representing an array of body shapes. With such objectifying methodology, the study has come up with the result that "desires for the attainment of physical capital is constantly open to objectification in the health and fitness club" (2005, p. 166). Rather than listening to the voices of fitness participants, such a study brings them to focus quite narrowly on official body ideals, allowing for very little attention to the many different mechanisms that different clients put to work to negotiate or appropriate such ideals.

The detail of ethnographic and deep qualitative interviewing with clients has been recognized as fundamental to understand the ambivalence of fitness exercise as commercialized active leisure (Molnar and Purdy, 2016). In her study of Norwegian aerobic classes, Loland (2000, p.118) reports the verbalizations of Ann, an aerobicizer in her early thirties, who thus justifies her participation: "I started with aerobics to do something about this [body] dissatisfaction [. . .] I didn't know that it was that it was that difficult to attain the thin, well shaped model body . . . however, even if I now see it as impossible, I still dream about that body and it is still the reason for taking classes". Loland does not explore how regular, loyal participants such as Ann manage with what appears as a contradiction, nor does she tell us to which extent such contradiction comes to be felt as painful or irrelevant, central or secondary to other rewards in fitness. However, it is precisely such dynamics which need exploring. They have been addressed by Gimlin (2002), who has maintained that aerobics in many ways helps steer the contradiction. Working out with aerobics fans and collecting their narrations, Gimlin (2002) has considered bodywork as something of an empowerment opportunity. "Women" – so she says (2002, p. 52) – "are capable of using aerobics classes to fuel a reconstruction of the self that releases identity from the physical, denies individual responsibility for socially constructed bodily 'imperfections', and provides new resources for identity formation".

Yet, it is arguable that neither disempowerment nor empowerment offer a precise picture. Fitness training is rather almost a classic "coping mechanism" (Goffman, 1963) – a device through which one's own inadequacies with respect to body ideals are negotiated, without necessary implying a shift in those ideals. A gym pass is in many ways a bridge to ideals of beauty, health and fitness, but – to follow the metaphor through – consumers may be able to walk on such a bridge only if they actually use the gym. And by using the gym, they modify their initial body objectives, the ones the bridge was directed to in the first place. At the very least, they learn how to practice "emotion work" (Hochschild, 2003) on body ideals and may emotionally qualify these objectives differently. Regulars often experience a shift in body objectives, with "realistic" aspirations becoming more important, and with ideals becoming less pressing as faults commanding strong dissatisfaction. We should not underestimate such shifts since they are grounded in lived bodily experiences which are described as deeply involving, and which allow fitness fans to devise often quite imaginative patterns of use. But use, involvement and exercise adherence itself become important as stabilizers of a positive attitude which may not be sustainable if we stop training (Burgess et al., 2009). As a coping mechanism, fitness training may need to be continuously activated, opening the way to exercise addiction (Warner and Griffiths, 2005).

We thus should be wary of providing a reconciliatory vision of fitness gym culture. The ongoing surveillance of the body demanded by training adumbrates a likewise constant negotiation of body objectives. We also get a few fitness fans that dangerously linger on the contradictions of fitness culture, with the negotiation of body objectives becoming itself a goal. In other physical pursuits, collectivized as they are through official competition such as body building and boxing (Klein, 1993; Wacquant, 2004), looking at other participants' bodies and focusing on body hierarchies are, as it were, sub-culturally sustained practices in fitness-training clients who become obsessed with the negotiation of their physique and are left much more alone and emotionally trapped.

All in all, patterns of successful initiation shed doubts on the apocalyptic conclusion that fitness is an unsuitable field for the pursuit of health just like they cast doubt on its character as a cure-all for the ills of late-modern sedentary life (Sassatelli, 2015). Yet, like most individualized coping mechanisms, even when successful, keep-fit workouts might more modestly provide consolation for our defects, offering some emotional relief. This, rather than dramatic bodily or life changes, may be the most significant outcome of fitness training for the regular, but not frantic, practitioner. Moreover, a shift in body objectives or their subjective emotional re-qualification does not automatically mean that we actually renounce, once and for all, broader body ideals, and even less that we manage to contribute to their overall change in objectified commercial images.

Let's take gender awareness as an example. A commercial context, so it seems, has the potential to instrumentalize all, including feminism. But commercial contexts may also provide for quite different routes. For example, the study of Leslea Collins (2002) on a group of US self-proclaimed feminist exercisers and their use of aerobics offers an example. Deeply critical of the gendered nature of fitness, the women in her study used strategies for participation that both downplayed oppressive aspects of training (the focus on the look, nonfunctional or embarrassing movements) and enhanced their personal empowerment in aerobic classes (sociability, criticism, refusal to participate). She concludes that their constant adaptation of practice testifies to both the normative gendered views incarnated by keep-fit training and the capacity of fitness participants to take (some) distance from them while practicing fitness. Examples such as this, however, do not represent the bulk of the phenomenon, and feminist notions of empowerment have often been cosmetically incorporated in fitness discourse (Markula, 2011). The development of celebrity fitness chains such as Madonna's Candy Fitness, with her emphasis on empowerment and survival, as well as a deeply instrumental vision of the toned, healthy and young body, largely witness to the ambivalence of the phenomenon.

Health, beauty and the fit body

Let's focus on fitness culture and its body ideals. Beauty is often referred to within fitness discourse. It comprises features within a semantic area that refers to the body as an exterior instrument of self-presentation in everyday life, and in erotic relations in particular. Working towards the surface may be an aim in itself, and indeed, quite a few of the incitements from fitness periodicals deal with such a dimension. In general, they suggest that the gym is to be expected to help clients "look good" and "have a presentable physique from an aesthetic point of view". Slimming down is in this case often quoted together with "problem areas" as a primary target for bodywork. Problem areas are quite obviously heavily gendered: attention is drawn to the lower part of the body for women, to the upper part of the body for men. The ideal is small, round bum and slim, long legs for women; muscled, flat stomach and broad shoulders for men. These differentiated shapes, which evidently stress the complementary relation among gendered bodies sustaining heterosexuality, are paramount in fitness magazines. Sexual attraction, sexual problems, and tips for a better sexual life often feature in dedicated articles in these periodicals, where the beauty and the prowess of a differently gendered fit body is correlated to the capacity to boost the "magic" of sexual intercourse.

Still, in many ways, notions of beauty are weighted against the idea of being in "good physical form" or "being fit". Energy, together with other factors such as strength, resistance, agility, elasticity, vascular capacity, breathing, etc., chart the territory of the "fit body". Fitness, as good physical form, covers a number of broad aspirations which relate to the body as an instrument to be used in sports as in ordinary life. The emphasis placed on functionality has obvious implications for the third semantic area which is paramount in keep-fit discourse, namely health. With the development of self-monitoring devices, fitness activities are increasingly becoming therapeutic (Lupton, 2016). And this, in turn, colours the notion of health which is typical of fitness as commercialized active leisure. The particular notion of health promoted by fitness is evident in fitness manuals which stress efficiency and energy (Sassatelli, 2010). Such a notion of health goes well beyond the absence of illness and may be placed side by side what has been defined, by WHO among others, as "positive health". It may be conceived as a healthy physical form, or a "general functional adequacy to withstand physical challenges without overstrain" (Oja and Tuxworth, 1995, 7). Rather than an environment of function to preserve, the body which can reach such a healthy form is an instrument whose internal functioning is to be stimulated in order for its utility to grow and work submissively for the subject in the world.

A healthy body may work as a sign of a deep internal environment in which organic functions are carried out and either facilitated or threatened by external factors, rather than a body-instrument to be used or presented in an external environment (Park, 1994). Even as an deep set of functions, the body demands an active use of energy, and fitness training is presented as fundamental to the preservation of the physiology of the internal organs. Health may therefore be seen a specific goal of fitness, and it is indeed presented as such in expert discourse, especially insofar as exercise is seen as a means to counter the current increase in obesity on the one hand, and aging on the other.

Of these three semantic areas, the "fit body" is clearly hegemonic, and it is this ideal that – independently of initial aims, age, social standing or gender – the vast majority of regular clients refers to as "normal". To be sure, such a notion is differently modulated by gender. The available literature has stressed the gendered nature of fitness, and more broadly of exercise as related to body modification (Leeds Craig and Liberti, 2007; Maguire and Mansfield, 1998; Markula, 2001). Loland (2000, 119) summarized this quite bluntly in her study of Norwegian women: "[w]hereas many women are concerned about appearing to be too large, men are dissatisfied with areas of the their bodies that are considered too small". Such findings need to be qualified cross-culturally. For example, a strong cultural preference among Japanese women for tiny, slim bodies and a strong aversion for building muscles was precisely found by Spielvogel (2003) as a deterrent to the diffusion of fitness gyms in Japan. When intersected with ethnicity and class, size and muscles matter in quite subtle ways along gender lines (Markula, 2011).

Still, the idea of functionality, and its aestheticization in relation to a choosing, strong and self-controlling self is central across gender. To explore this further, let's take a brief look at the genealogy of the notion of fitness and at its rendering in an ever-evolving expert discourse. Historical studies such as that of Park (1994, p. 61) have shown that "the Victorians thought of fitness in terms of biological adaptability, and from this idea are derived a number of racial, sexual and other differences" to the extent that "athletes were often portrayed as biologically superior males". Adaptability and the capacity to withstand the world and its demands are still central and so is muscularity. Yet, what once might have been a measuring instrument, exercise, is now co-extensive with the notion of fitness, which has itself become "linked to muscularity, the shape of the body, and/or the ability to perform an exercise session of 30 minutes" (1994, p. 62). An instrumental vision of the body lies at the heart of fitness. In keep-fit culture, instrumentality becomes a value in itself, and as such it is signified by external marks that may be used to adorn the self. Functionality today has come to the surface: fitness is predicated on the notion that the body must be kept active, yet energy emanates from the body's shape and becomes a crucial indicator of the subject's worth.

A fit body is appreciated as a "sign" of the subject's energy, vitality and strength. If, as Foucault (1991, 152 and 137) claims, a "disciplined body is the prerequisite of an efficient gesture" and "the only truly important ceremony is that of exercise", a body which has visibly incorporated exercise acquires ceremonial properties; it becomes important at the level of signs as well as function, and tells us something about the subject and its worth. We know that Eastern body-soul techniques, and yoga in particular (Strauss, 2002), have been locally adjusted in various ways through its global penetration, yet their hybridized forms in fitness gyms – such as combat yoga, yoga fitness and power yoga, to mention some of the more popular definitions – emphasize relaxation, feeling and well-being, but ultimately remain framed through the dominant cheerful, self-challenging instrumentality of fitness training.

Concluding remarks

All in all, considering the politics of commercial fitness culture as active leisure we may conclude by bearing in mind a few issues which will need to be addressed by future research. Advantages will certainly be derived from the merging of studies about consumer practices and cultures and the sociology of sport, with its attention to the detail of practice organization and the politics of practice (Markula, 2015).

First, we need to consider the "loose coupling" (Goffman 1983) of the fitness world with the social structure. We thus need focus further on how fitness training is organized in (different) gym environments and how this facilitates successful coping with the body, providing for more than emotional relief and including the transformation of identities and empowerment. We also need to explore how external identities and differences in terms of gender, class and ethnicity impact on gym careers, hindering or favoring the agency of consumers in responding to ever-more-standardized body ideals. McDonaldized fitness (O'Toole, 2009) often brings with itself global Western body ideals, and more research is needed to investigate how this is differently localized, appropriated and possibly subverted in different countries such as India or Brazil where gyms are rapidly expanding.

Second, we should investigate the systemic effects of the diffusion of fitness as a dominant form of active leisure pursuit. That is, we need to focus on what is the social role of the fitness gym in current health and stratification issues (including the impact of a predominantly commercial diffusion on populations differentiated by class, age, gender and ethnicity). Training in the commercial fitness gym may provide some real individual relief for problems – of health and fitness – which are larger and social, remarkably skewed in terms of ethnicity, class, gender, age and education (Bakken and Seippel, 2011). Commercialized fitness culture, with its emphasis on universalized individual choice and will, on the contrary, sustains the impression that a healthy, fit and young-looking body may indeed be simply achieved by anyone, simply individual resolution and the purchase of a fitness pass. The universalistic and individualistic profile of commercial gyms may exacerbate this, contributing to foreclose the possibility that fitness be addressed also by other probably more collectivized, informal or public means, and reach vulnerable populations such as the old, migrants and the working classes. This opens the way for a discussion on fitness promotion and policies tailored to re-consider body care as fully and distinctively part of citizenship.

Finally, we shall address the urban nature of commercial fitness culture as the dominant active leisure pursuit in the global West (Sassatelli 2016). As a leisure pursuit, fitness training may work for individual wellbeing, but this looks very much like therapeutic, solitary copying rather than some kind of empowerment vis-à-vis the ills of urbanization, something that probably would require some form of grass-root participation with a political slant. On the contrary, commercial fitness culture tends to thrive on a rather toxic image of the city and a limited possibility of appropriation of common goods and spaces (Sassatelli, 2015). Research on how to organize urban life and re-think the place of active leisure in more humane and egalitarian urban spaces is very much in need.

References

Andreasson, J. and Johansson, T. (2014), *The Global Gym. Gender, Health and Pedagogies.* Houndsmill: Palgrave, MacMillan.

Bakken Ulseth, A. L. and Seippel, Ø. (2011), "Fitness, Class and Culture: Social Inequality in Fitness", Nordic Sport Science Forum, idrottsforum.org.

Bordo, S. (1993), *Unbearable Weight. Feminism, Western Culture and the Body,* Berkeley: University of California Press.

Bourdieu, P. (1978), "Social Science Information" in *Sport and Social Class,* 17 (6), pp. 819–840.

Burgess, G.R. et als. (2009), "Effects of a 6-Week Aerobic Dance Intervention on Body Image and Physical Self-Perceptions in Adolescent Girls', in *Body Image,* 3, pp. 5–66.

Caldwell, L. L. (2005), "Leisure and Health. Why Is Leisure Therapeutic?" *British Journal of Counselling and Psychology,* 1, pp. 7–26.

Collins, L. H. (2002), "Working Out the Contradictions. Feminism and Aerobics", *Journal of Sport and Social Issues,* 26 (1), pp. 85–109.

Crawford, R. (1980), "Healthism and the Medicalization of Everyday Life", in *International Journal of Health Service,* 10, (3), pp. 365–88.

Crossley, N. (2006), "In the Gym: Motives, Meanings and Moral Careers", *Body and Society,* 12 (3), pp. 23–50.

Dinnerstein, M. and Weitz, R. (1998), "Jane Fonda, Barbara Bush and Other Aging Bodies: Femininity and the Limits of Resistance, in Weitz, R. (ed.) *The Politics of Women's Bodies,* Oxford: Oxford University Press, 189–203.

Foucault, M. (1991), *Discipline and Punish.* London: Penguin [orig. 1975].

Frew, M. and McGillivray, D. (2005), "Health Clubs and Body Politics. Aesthetics and the Quest for Physical Capital", *Leisure Studies*, 24 (2), pp. 161–175.
Giddens, A. (1991), *Modernity and Self-Identity*, Cambridge: Polity Press.
Gimlin, D. (2002), *Bodywork. Beauty and Self-Image in American Culture*, Berkeley: University of California Press.
Glassner, B. (1992), *Bodies. Overcoming the Tyranny of Perfection*, Chicago: Contemporary Books.
Goffman, E. (1963), *Stigma. Notes on the Management of Spoiled Identities*, Englewood Cliffs: Prentice-Hall.
Goffman, E. (1983) "The interaction order" in American Sociological Review, 48, 1, pp. 1-17.
Hochschild, A. R. (2003), *The Commercialization of Intimate Life: Notes from Home and Work*, Berkeley: University of California Press.
Hochschild, A. R. (2012), *The Outsourced Self*, New York: Metropolitan Books.
Klein, A. M. (1993), *Little Big Men. Bodybuilding Subculture and Gender Construction*, New York: Suny Press.
Leeds Craig, M. and Liberti, R. (2007), "'Cause That's What Girls Do. The Making of a Feminized Gym". *Gender and Society*, 21 (5), pp. 676–699.
Loland, N. W. (2000), The Art of Concealment in a Culture of Display: Aerobicizing Women's and Men's Experience and Use of Their Own Bodies, *Sociology of Sport Journal*, 17, pp. 111–29.
Lupton, D. (1994), "Consumerism, Commodity Culture and Health Promotion", *Health Promotion International*, 9 (2), pp. 111–118.
Lupton, D. (2016), *The Quantified Self*. Cambridge: Polity Press.
Maguire Smith, J. (2007), *Fit for Consumption. Sociology and the Business of Fitness*. London: Routledge.
Maguire, and Mansfield (1998) "'No-body is perfect!' Women, Aerobics and the Body Beautiful, *Sociology of Sports Journal*, 15(2), 109–37.
Markula, P. (2001), "Women's Body Image Distortion in Fitness Magazine Discourse", *Journal of Sport and Social Issues*, 25 (2), pp. 158–179.
Markula, P. (2011), "'Folding. A Feminist Intervention in Mindful Fitness, in Kennedy, E. and Markula, P. (eds.) *Women and Exercise. The Body, Health and Consumerism*, London: Routledge, 81–100.
Markula, P. (2015), "Assessing the Sociology of Sport: On Sport and Exercise", *International Review for the Sociology of Sport*, 50 (4–5), pp. 536–541.
Molnar, G. and Purdy, L. (2016) *Ethnographies Is Sport and Exercise Research*, London: Routledge.
Oja, P. and Tuxworth, B. (1995), *Eurofit for Adults. Assessment of Health-Realted Fitness*, Tampere: Council of Europe.
O'Toole, L. (2009), "McDonald's at the Gym. A Tale of Two Curves", in *Qualitative Sociology*, 32, pp. 75–91.
Park, R. J. (1994), "A Decade of the Body: Researching and Writing about the History of Health, Fitness, Exercise and Sport, 1983–1993". *Journal of Sport History*, 21 (1), pp. 59–82.
Rojek, C. (2000), *Leisure and Culture*. Basingstoke: Palgrave Macmillan.
Sassatelli, R. (2001), Tamed Hedonism: Choice, Desires and Deviant Pleasures, in Warde, A. and Gronow, J. (Eds), *Ordinary Consumption*, Routledge, London, pp. 93–106.
Sassatelli, R. (2007), *Consumer Culture. History, Theory and Politics*. London: Sage.
Sassatelli, R. (2010), *Fitness Culture. Gyms and the Commercialization of Discipline and Fun*, Basingstoke: Palgrave Macmillan [2014].
Sassatelli, R. (2012) Consumer Identities in A. Elliott (Ed) Handbook of Identity Studies, Routledge, London, pp. 236-53Sassatelli, R. (2015), "Healthy Cities and Instrumental Leisure: The Paradox Fitness Gyms as Urban Phenomena", *Modern Italy*, 20 (3), pp. 237–250.
Sassatelli, R. (2016), "You Can All Succeed!" The Reconciliatory Logic of Therapeutic Active Leisure, *European Journal for Sport and Society*, 3, 230–45.
Spielvogel, L. (2003), *Working Out in Japan. Shaping the Female Body in Tokyo Fitness Clubs*. Durham, NC: Duke University Press.
Stebbins, R. A. (2009), "Serious Leisure and Work", *Sociology Compass*, 3, 764–74.
Strauss, A. (2002), "Adapt, Adjust, Accommodate: The Production of Yoga in a Transnational World", *History and Anthropology*, 13 (3), pp. 231–51.
Wacquant, L. (2004), *Body and Soul: Ethnographic Notebooks of an Apprentice Boxer*. New York: Oxford University Press.
Warner, R. and Griffiths, M. (2005), "A Qualitative Thematic Analysis of Exercise Addiction. An Exploratory Study", *International Journal of Mental Health Addiction*, 4, 13–26.

Part VII
Culture, media and consumption
Introduction

Topics related to lifestyle consumption, such as cultural participation, cultural preferences and taste have been important themes in consumption research for decades, still maintaining vivid theoretical and methodological debates. The themes also contain research on luxury, fashion and other conspicuous aspects of consumption that have been in the focus of scholarly attention for more than a century, ever since Veblen's and Simmel's seminal works. Studies on the consumption associated with leisure and lifestyle have gained even more momentum recently, as the importance of leisure time has increased in people's lives. In the developed countries, the rising affluence and reducing working hours have enabled individuals to spend more time and money on multiple consumer goods and experiential commodities in their leisure time. Thereby, participation in culture and leisure is increasingly intertwined with consumption and materiality. Simultaneously, symbolic aspects of consumption have overcome material needs, and many socio-cultural divisions and hierarchies are reproduced in cultural consumption. This is particularly obvious in the dynamics of the consumption related to fashion and luxury, but also in many spheres of leisure, such as sports, play, entertainment, and media use.

As the variety of cultural products and services are in constant increase and change, the ways of consuming culture and leisure are also changing. This development has been accelerated with the rapid expansion of digital media. Digital technologies and particularly social media are changing all consumption, not only by generating new technological goods and services, but also by creating new channels and arenas for buying, selling, marketing and socializing. For today's individual consumers, digital technologies infiltrate everyday life in numerous ways, not only mediating, but also (co-)creating lifestyles, consumer cultures and consumer identities. Digital media are also changing the values and roles of consumers, producers and consumable objects in the consumption processes. The symbolic and material values of goods and services in digital environments are determined in novel ways, changing also the roles and hierarchies within consumer groups and between consumers and producers.

The chapters in Part VII: *Culture, media and consumption*, discuss the above-described change, focusing on consumption first from the broader viewpoints of culture, lifestyles and leisure, and then more specifically analyzing the meanings of luxury and fashion in consumer culture. Two last chapters specifically highlight the role of digital technology and social media in consumption.

As cultural preferences, tastes and lifestyles have been among the most popular themes in the sociology of consumption in the past decades, and several conceptual, contextual and methodological questions have arisen. In chapter 35 Tally Katz-Gerro discusses analytically the most recent ones, analyzing first the multi-dimensional concepts of culture and lifestyle. Emphasizing the cross-time and cross-national comparative point of view, she sheds light on the role of economic regimes, responses to globalization processes, varying power relations between the state and the market, and political conditions in accounting for trends in cultural consumption and lifestyle behavior. This emphasis fits perfectly in the handbook's aim of paying special attention to social divisions, constraints and opportunities that characterize the relationship between consumption and social structures.

Chapter 36, authored by Jennifer Smith Maguire, continues the theme of lifestyle consumption by providing an insightful overview of key areas in the research of leisure. First the chapter considers the definition of leisure and its consumption relationship to work. Secondly the chapter analyses the central place that leisure occupies with regard to how individuals construct and perform identities and lifestyles. Analyses of the 'serious,' 'self-improvement' and 'authentic' dimensions of sport call attention to the significance of leisure for self-production and the reproduction of collective identities. Thirdly, the chapter also considers the place of play, fun and non-instrumental activity in cultural notions of leisure and discusses the ways in which a notion of play runs through consumer culture. The chapter concludes by describing the implications of the increasing convergence of leisure and work for the diminishing prospects of play in consumer culture.

In chapter 37, Laurie A. Meamber, Annamma Joy and Alladi Venkatesh highlight the multiple meanings and elements of fashion in consumer culture. The authors present a comprehensive overview of the subject, acknowledging the rich literature on the relations between fashion, culture, marketing, consumption and consumers. The chapter specifically focuses on the fashion system and process, as well as fashion as appearance. The chapter closes with the discussion of fashion, brands and brand culture, global marketing, and consumer agency. It is noted that research on fashion will continue to be an important facet of understanding consumer culture and new avenues for research will open, such as re-examining the definition of fashion in relation to sustainability. Future research can also continue to examine brand management and marketing approaches used by fashion producers and the consequences of this for consumers and society at large.

In chapter 38, Annamma Joy, Russell Belk and Rishi Bhardwaj analyze the fascinating concept of luxury; how the perceptions of luxury have changed over time and how they are related to social and economic divisions in global and local contexts. The chapter pays special attention to the changes in luxury consumption in emerging nations, particularly India and China. Furthermore, the chapter discusses luxury in relation to aesthetics, emotions and situational factors in individual and collective consumer behavior. The authors also limn the evolution of luxury brands over time: how such brands are perceived, what market segments they target and what the implications of current research reveal about brands' impacts on social constructs. In the end, the chapter discusses the specific areas of luxury marketing and consumption deserving of further research. How do conceptions of luxury in the past inform the experience of luxury in the present? How will luxury goods be perceived and consumed in the future?

In chapter 39, Alladi Venkatesh and Duygu Akdevelioglu write about the role of social media in consumption, illustrating social media consumers as digital avatars. The chapter defines and describes thoroughly the concept of social media, and then provides an analysis of the social media culture and social media users from social-psychological, media-centric, and socio-cultural perspectives. The chapter also explores how the consumer in social media is constituted within the socio-historical context, and conceptualizes the consumer in the context of the social media environment with a specific focus on consumer dynamics and digital environments as places for consumer communication. The authors argue that the interplay among social media users, platforms, companies and regulatory parties creates the medium of communication. In conclusion, the chapter stresses the importance of further exploration of digital interactions in the social media arena across consumer segments and different demographic and socio-cultural groups.

Last but not least, in chapter 40, Minna Ruckenstein paves the way to the research of future consumption by discussing how digitalization is shaping consumption practices in ways that commodify people's lives. The chapter demonstrates that research on digital consumption can avoid a narrow market-analysis stance by promoting a more dynamic view of the market and value formation. The chapter introduces findings from empirical research that points towards various different research streams, including research on toys, virtual goods, social media, games and wearables. By bringing to the fore the very intimate ways in which commodities become a part of people's relationship to themselves and others, this emerging research urges scholars to examine how the merging of selves and consumption opportunities might promote studies of consumption. In conclusion, the chapter also suggests that researchers of digitalization could position themselves in relation to digital consumption in order to promote their own value projects in light of longer-term goals of social and economic reproduction.

35

Consumption of culture and lifestyles

Tally Katz-Gerro

Introduction

Cultural preferences, tastes, and lifestyles have been among the most popular concepts in the sociology of consumption in the past decades, giving rise to several theoretical, contextual, and methodological questions, the most recent of which are discussed in this chapter. Since the chapter discusses both cultural consumption and cultural lifestyles, I will first clarify the difference between the two terms.

The consumption of culture refers to one aspect in the process by which individuals reproduce their position within the social structure. This cultural aspect coincides to some extent with material aspects. Resources that are embodied in symbolic abilities and competencies legitimize privilege, and the adoption of certain patterns of cultural consumption enables individuals to maneuver within the social structure.

Lifestyle research, in the sociological rather than marketing sense, refers to identifying the position of individuals on multi-dimensional hierarchies of consumption constituting, for example, lifestyle tribes, status groups, or taste communities. While cultural consumption patterns mark and maintain social distinction (Katz-Gerro, 2011), cultural lifestyles sustain group boundaries (Lamont & Molnár, 2002). Cultural consumption patterns are often sporadic, while lifestyles may form the basis for the crystallization of more concrete social groups such as omnivores, down-shifters, residents in gated communities, or hipsters that objectify certain values through consumption acts.

The concept of lifestyle is not yet fully developed in social science research, which tends to focus on various components of lifestyles rather than on the broader concept as a complete entity. Scholars have generally considered three main components of lifestyle: cultural consumption (e.g., of music, books, or food), cultural participation (e.g., attendance at the theater or a cultural festival), and tastes (e.g., in music, reading, or food). These components have been translated into specific lifestyle indicators, such as leisure time activities (cultural consumption), attendance at arts and cultural events (cultural participation), and tastes in music (tastes) (Bourdieu, 1984; DiMaggio, 1994; Slater, 1997; Sobel, 2013 [1982]). By paying little attention to cultural attitudes and aesthetic dispositions, the existing research falls short of providing a comprehensive account of lifestyles, which includes not only practices but also attitudes and values.

Empirical research on cultural lifestyles has mainly been interested in the distribution and configurations of patterns of cultural consumption, cultural participation, and tastes, in the way they are hierarchized in society, and in the way they are associated with major social cleavages (Katz-Gerro, 2004). Perhaps the most important focal point for lifestyle research has been the relationship between cultural consumption patterns, the competencies they bring with them, and the structures of power and inequality in society.

Before outlining the relationship between lifestyles and contemporary structures of inequality, I will briefly discuss the main theoretical inspirations of studies on cultural consumption among classical sociologists. A good place to start would be the work of Karl Marx (1976) and the distinction between the use value and exchange value of commodities, which provides theoretical rigor to the sociological study of consumption in the context of a market economy. Under capitalism, exchange value trumps use value, because goods are no longer produced for the purpose of exchange in the market place but rather than for personal consumption. One of the results of this shift is the fetishism of commodities. When objects are perceived as commodities that satisfy human needs, their use value, as well as their relation to the laborer who made them, is obscured. Instead, they are laden with value inherent in the objects themselves (Marx, 1976). This shift leads to the greater importance of money and economic exchange in the market. Neo-Marxists, particularly scholars associated with the Frankfurt School, extended Marx's ideas to cultural consumption. There is a direct link between the notion of fetishized commodities and a term coined by Horkheimer and Adorno (2002) – the *culture industry*. This term refers to the way mass culture is produced by institutions and then consumed by individuals who are reduced to the level of being members of a mass group. Thus, through the culture industry, capitalism promotes the generation of false needs, which crystalize into an ideology of consumption. For example, according to Adorno (1941), the consumption of popular music is associated with passive listening habits. Escapism from everyday routine is sought in popular music because, unlike authentic music, which requires more energy and effort, it is simple, repetitive, and predictable.

Just as Marxist scholars linked developments in consumers' behavior to the development of capitalism, Max Weber, Georg Simmel, and Thorstein Veblen saw consumption as part of the modern, urban way of life. Simmel's (1978) major work *The Philosophy of Money* studied the role of money in consumption and inspired research on the cultural consumption of fashion as part of a process of social emulation and differentiation that leads to distinction (Simmel, 1957). Fashion as an expression of pecuniary culture also preoccupied Veblen in his *Theory of the Leisure Class* (2007). For Veblen, pecuniary strength and conspicuous consumption were ways to render honorific the power associated with private property. Conspicuous leisure became the principal means of openly displaying wealth and status. Similarly, in Weber's (1978) work the intricate relationship between power, money, and culture is formalized in the social structure in the form of classes, status groups, and political parties. The multi-dimensional character of social relationships is fully acknowledged, and the separate existence of lifestyles as generators of honor and social hierarchy is articulated. Douglas and Isherwood (1979) took this formulation one step further to argue that cultural consumption is a form of expression that manifests the categories of culture. Consumption has a symbolic and communicative value, which is used to make judgments in classifying persons and events. This argument links us directly to Bourdieu's (1984) theory of taste, explicating how patterns of cultural consumption mark and maintain social distinctions, specifically with regard to social classes, which are discussed in the next section.

Hierarchies of cultural consumption: Highbrow/lowbrow and omnivorousness

The main body of cultural consumption research has two main emphases. The first stems from Bourdieu's (1984) analysis of how the upper class uses highbrow cultural distinctions to produce and reproduce social boundaries. Bourdieu's (1984) seminal work has had a tremendous influence on research on comparative cultural stratification, in which scholars have dealt, almost exclusively, with the contrast between highbrow and non-highbrow (or popular or lowbrow) cultural preferences (Gans, 1974). In particular, they have tested the homology thesis, which maintains a structural equivalence between social class structure and the hierarchy in cultural preferences and practices.

The second emphasis draws on Peterson's (2005) work on the way that the cultural distinction of elite groups in society has shifted from a preference for highbrow culture to embracing omnivorous cultural tastes and activities. Omnivores are typically characterized as high-status individuals who not only like and consume highbrow culture, as highbrow snobs do, but who also like and consume a wide range of middlebrow and lowbrow cultural expressions (Peterson & Simkus, 1992; Peterson & Kern, 1996). High-status individuals are members of specific occupational groupings including professional occupations, higher managers, and senior sales workers (Peterson & Simkus, 1992). Thus, omnivores are inclusive highbrows, as opposed to snobs who are exclusive highbrows (Bryson, 1996). Peterson and Kern (1996) and Peterson (2005) have advanced the hypothesis that rising socio-economic levels of living, broader education, and the wide diffusion of the elite arts via the media, among other reasons, have all made elite aesthetic preferences more accessible to broader segments of the population, devaluing the fine arts as markers of exclusion. The result is that high-status individuals are generally becoming more omnivorous and younger, because more omnivorous age cohorts are replacing older cohorts with a snobbish orientation. Following Peterson's work, scholars have demonstrated the applicability of different variations of eclectic cultural tastes in various cultural domains in different countries (e.g., Bryson, 1997; Warde, Martens, & Olsen, 1999; Holbrook, Weiss, & Habich, 2002; López-Sintas & Garcia-Álvarez, 2002; Fisher & Preece, 2003; Chan & Goldthorpe, 2007; Karademir-Hazir & Warde, 2015).

More recently, the literature on cultural omnivores developed a further nuanced differentiation of cultural omnivorousness related to both the breadth and level of cultural preferences. The result was an ideal type categorization of four groups of cultural consumers: highbrow univores (highbrows with a narrow breadth of tastes), highbrow omnivores (highbrows with a wide breadth of tastes), lowbrow univores (lowbrows with a narrow breadth of tastes), and lowbrow omnivores (lowbrows with a wide breadth of tastes) (Warde et al., 2007). Additional attempts at expanding the conceptual framework of cultural omnivorousness include voraciousness, which reflects a quantitative dimension of out-of-home leisure consumption without distinction between highbrow and lowbrow activities (Sullivan & Katz-Gerro, 2007; Virtanen, 2007; Katz-Gerro & Sullivan, 2010); attitudinal openness, which measures openness to cultural diversity as a new aesthetic associated with cultural omnivorusness (Van Eijck & Lievens, 2008; Ollivier et al., 2009); cultural dissonance, which emphasizes intra-individual behavioral variation in legitimate and illegitimate cultural practices and preferences (Lahire, 2004); and cosmopolitan aesthetic tastes (Cicchelli et al., 2016).

Thus, the research on the consumption of culture and lifestyles has converged on two clusters. The first looks at the factors that condition cultural consumption and lifestyles with a specific interest in class, occupational status, education, and gender (Bourdieu, 1984; Peterson & Kern, 1996). The second cluster emphasizes the significant social consequences of cultural consumption and lifestyle patterns, given that these patterns generate values, attitudes, and behaviors (Ollivier et al., 2009) and also shape life outcomes such as educational attainment (Sullivan, 2001) and the strength of social networks (Lizardo, 2006). These two main clusters of research have benefited from recent developments that have added much to our knowledge, mainly in two areas that will be discussed in the next section. These two areas are cross-national and cross-cultural similarities and differences in the categories of cultural consumption, cultural tastes, and lifestyle preferences, and the intergenerational transmission of consumption patterns.

Cross-national and cross-cultural research on consumption, tastes, and lifestyles

A comparative point of view is adopted in lifestyle research mainly to discern similarities and differences between countries or regions in lifestyle patterns and in the association between such patterns and socio-demographic or economic variables. The findings regarding cultural consumption patterns from a cross-national perspective (e.g., Garcia-Álvarez et al., 2007; Chan, 2010; Jaeger & Katz-Gerro, 2010) point to several generalizable patterns. First, studies in different countries find support for the claim that starting from about the 1990s upper-status individuals have abandoned an exclusively highbrow taste in culture in favor of an eclectic, diverse, culturally omnivorous taste (Peterson, 2005; Alderson et al., 2007; Chan & Goldthorpe, 2007; Coulangeon & Lemel, 2007; Garcia-Álvarez et al., 2007; Torche, 2007; Bennett et al., 2008; Ollivier, 2008; Tampubolon, 2008; Van Eijck & Lievens, 2008; Berghman & Van Eijck, 2009; Ollivier, Gauthier & Truong, 2009; Chan, 2010; Jaeger & Katz-Gerro, 2010; Karademir-Hazir & Warde, 2015), with some exceptions (Rössel, 2006; Heikkilä & Rahkonen, 2011). Recent research has argued that it is not at all certain that the omnivorous aesthetic is more eclectic than in the past, or that it is an entirely new phenomenon, as suggested by surveys conducted in the 1960s in France (Lahire, 2004, 2008). Jaeger and Katz-Gerro (2010) found that a group of eclectic cultural consumers existed in Denmark even in the 1960s. They demonstrated that social stratification in cultural eclecticism has remained remarkably strong over the past forty years. This finding may indicate that the adoption of eclectic tastes and cultural participation habits did not occur through a dramatic change in the zeitgeist of modern, industrialized societies. Rather, it was a slow and gradual process.

Second, much of the comparative research on cultural consumption and lifestyles has been geared toward looking for cross-national similarities or differences in the application of Bourdieu's homology thesis or Peterson's omnivorousness thesis. For example, there seem to be systematic differences between countries with regard to a number of indicators (e.g., cultural participation, artistic activity, and tastes), whereby the highest means of cultural repertoires are found in the Nordic countries, the Netherlands, and Luxembourg. The two lowest means are scored by the Greek and the Portuguese, and the most omnivorous countries in each cultural domain are Sweden, Finland, and Luxembourg (Virtanen, 2007). An analysis of similar indicators collected in Eurobarometer 2007 pertains to a larger sample of twenty-seven countries and reveals that there is a clear pattern of highbrow cultural participation adopted by a small share of the population (Gerhards, 2008).

A third feature appearing in several studies has to do with directly addressing the relevance of the societal context to lifestyle patterns in a comparative fashion (e.g., Kraaykamp & Nieuwbeerta, 2000; Katz-Gerro, 2002, 2006; Chan, 2010; Birkelund & Lemel, 2013). Some of these studies use country-specific survey data (e.g., Bennett et al., 2013) while others rely on international survey programs such as Eurobarometer 2001 (Virtanen, 2007), Eurobarometer 2007 (Gerhards, 2008), or ISSP, 2007 (Katz-Gerro & Jaeger, 2012). Most studies report systematic differences among countries with regard to a number of lifestyle indicators and in the associations of cultural participation or tastes with education and class position. Although most research has focused on single-country analyses, many studies, for example those replicating Bourdieu's methodological choice of the multiple correspondence analyses of consumption items, report quite similar patterns of cultural consumption and taste across national spaces (Bennett, Bustamante & Frow, 2013; Birkelund & Lemel, 2013; Purhonen & Wright, 2013). These similarities might mean that national particularities play a very small role in the theory of cultural consumption. As Kirchberg and Kuchar (2014) observe, there are almost no studies that enable a comprehensive comparative analysis of cultural consumption, which limits the development of a theory that goes beyond the national level. Indeed, some cross-country differences in the correlates of cultural consumption patterns that are detectable from existing data are quite interesting. For example, the effects of gender and age seem to be inconsistent across countries. Some studies report that there are no significant gender differences (Prieto-Rodriguez & Fernandez-Blanco, 2000) while others find that women are less omnivorous than men (Van Eijck, 2001). In Hungary and the Netherlands, women are more likely than men to be highbrows rather than omnivores, while in England women are more likely than men to exhibit higher levels of cross-domain cultural participation, and in Chile there is little gender difference (Chan, 2010). In the United States (Christin, 2012) and in Denmark (Katz-Gerro & Jaeger, 2015) women report more highbrow tastes compared to men. Another example pertains to the effect of age on cultural consumption, which is usually, but not exclusively, negative (Katz-Gerro, 2002). Older people in England and the United States generally report higher levels of cultural consumption, but the opposite is true for the Netherlands, where it is younger people who are more likely to be omnivores rather than inactive individuals or highbrows (Van Eijck, 2001; Chan, 2010). The pattern is different again for Chile and Hungary, where age is associated with higher odds of being culturally inactive (Chan, 2010). Finally, while comparisons between Western and Eastern Europe are scarce (but see Virtanen, 2007), there is substantial evidence of the patterns that characterize Western European countries. Several studies have focused on the differences between countries in the way cultural consumption is associated with class position. Most of these studies report that there are consistent associations between a privileged economic position (based on income, occupational status, or economic class) and highbrow or omnivorous consumption practices (Peterson, 2005; Chan, 2010; Bennett et al., 2013). Comparisons with non-European countries are warranted because of the different social mechanisms that are at work, for example, in less industrialized societies such as Turkey (Üstüner & Holt, 2009); in countries that have experienced significant political changes such as in post-socialist societies (Zavisca, 2005); and in countries with strong regional disparities such as Brazil (Diniz & Machado, 2011) or with a multi-cultural makeup such as South Africa (Snowball, Jamal & Willis, 2010) or Israel (Katz-Gerro, Raz & Yaish, 2009).

Fourth, cultural participation patterns in many societies are socially constructed and parallel a number of demographic and socioeconomic characteristics (Katz-Gerro, 2006; Bennett, Savage, Silva, Warde, Gayo-Cal & Wright, 2008). Higher levels of education, income, occupational prestige, occupational status, and class position tend to be associated with more active and more frequent cultural participation. More than occupational measures, education and age seem to be the dominant correlates of cultural consumption (Van Eijck, 2001; Holbrook, Weiss & Habich, 2002; López-Sintas & Garcia-Álvarez, 2002). Gender is also a persistent, significant correlate of lifestyle (Bihagen & Katz-Gerro, 2000; Katz-Gerro & Sullivan, 2010).

Fifth, in economically advanced societies larger proportions of the population participate in a broad range of leisure and consumption activities, compared with less-affluent societies. Nevertheless, while general trends in media consumption, cultural activities, and cultural participation can be identified, national cultural variations in specific practices do exist. Macro trends in consumption are shared across capitalist societies and are associated with the economic, cultural, and political processes of globalization. However, alongside evident cultural homogenization there are fundamental differences that could be associated with national institutional arrangements that are yet to be explored (Gronow & Southerton, 2010). Such arrangements have to do with the role the educational system plays in fostering cultural heterogeneity, with the degree to which cultural platforms are open to promoting national culture, and more generally with the extent to which a society is open to cultural imports.

This last point leads us to studies that have looked at structural variables among countries. Here we have evidence that highbrow cultural consumption in European countries is affected by a nation's wealth, degree of social mobility, and cultural funding levels and supply (Van Hek & Kraaykamp, 2013). In addition, educational and affluence inequality in cultural consumption is less pronounced in wealthy countries, and educational differentiation in highbrow cultural consumption is less marked in countries with large social mobility. In a similar comparison, Katz-Gerro & Lopez-Sintas (2013) found that a country's mean level of education and political orientation affect individuals' breadth of cultural preferences and that the specific mix of omnivorous cultural tastes varies between countries and depends on the average level of education and political orientation in that country. Interestingly, we also have evidence that over time, changes in cultural policy have had little effect on inequalities in cultural participation in France (Coulangeon, 2013).

Intergenerational transmission of consumption patterns

The literature identifies two major types of variables that shape cultural consumption patterns: economic resources (e.g., income, class) and cultural resources (e.g., education, parental cultural capital). Typically, cultural participation is more heavily constrained by economic resources (e.g., Lahire, 2004; Peterson, 2005; Sullivan & Katz-Gerro, 2007). Through the habitus, cultural resources play a greater role in the development of cultural tastes, which are less associated with spending money (e.g., Bourdieu, 1984; Peterson & Simkus, 1992; Silva, 2005). The habitus is shaped both in the family and at school (Bourdieu, 1984). Parents pass on to their children cognitive capacities and cultural competences that shape cultural dispositions (Bourdieu & Passeron, 1977; Lamont & Lareau, 1988; Bodovski & Farkas, 2008; Dumais & Ward, 2010; Colbert & Courchesne, 2012). These dispositions are translated into cultural preferences that may or may not transform into practices, depending on availability and affordability. While the habitus predisposes actors to do certain things and provides a basis for the generation of practices (Bourdieu, 1984), it operates within specific limits on practices (Jenkins, 2002), for example financial resources. Therefore, Bourdieu proposes that material wealth (economic capital) is a resource that individuals draw upon to make their place in society. In other words, individuals adopt strategies that are the result of an ongoing interaction between the dispositions of the habitus and the constraints and possibilities that are the reality of a given social field (Jenkins, 2002).

Cultural resources such as parental education, parental cultural capital, and level of education shape the cultural preferences that form part of the habitus. As a more active choice, cultural participation is constrained not only by economic resources such as income and infrastructure, but also by cultural preferences. Several studies have looked at the intergenerational transmission of cultural capital (Van Eijck, 1997; Kraaykamp, 2003; Notten, Kraaykamp & Konig, 2012; Gaddis, 2013; Willekens et al., 2014). Many of them were interested in early socialization processes, positing that gendered expectations about the kinds of culture that boys and girls should engage with account for gender differences in cultural participation (Silva, 2005). Girls and women are expected to take charge of everything concerned with aesthetics, and girls are encouraged more than boys to participate in cultural activities (Donnat, 2004; Octobre, 2005). Accordingly, girls outnumber boys in art lessons, music lessons, dance lessons, library visits, concerts, and visits to art museums (DiMaggio, 1982; Dumais, 2002; Christin, 2012). In contrast, it is more socially acceptable for boys to participate in sports, which promote the skills associated with masculinity such as leadership and competitive or group-oriented behaviors (Ridgeway & Smith-Lovin, 1999; Nomaguchi & Bianchi, 2004). Girls rely on artistic lessons to create networks of friends (Pasquier, 2010), and social network characteristics, especially network diversity, are better predictors of women's cultural participation than of men's (Kane, 2004). Studies have documented both how the cultural tastes and behaviors of individuals are shaped by those of their parents and how the educational attainment of individuals is shaped by the cultural resources acquired in the family. Typically, research finds that parents affect their children's cultural participation by providing active guidance and by setting an example. They also influence their children's educational attainment by providing them with the cultural capital that can be converted into advantage and privilege in the educational system (Katz-Gerro & Jaeger, 2015; Van Hek & Kraaykamp, 2015).

Conclusion

This chapter reviewed recent developments in the sociological analysis of cultural consumption and lifestyles, emphasizing a comparative point of view to shed light on patterns of behavior and taste in the context of economic inequalities, cultural stratification, and economic and social regimes.

Cultural consumption relates to attitudes and behaviors that change with individuals' stages of life (age, marital status), environment and socialization (peers), and general political, economic, and social circumstances (time period) (Van den Broek, 2013). Individuals move through different stages of the life cycle and change their tastes and consumption patterns according to these three dimensions. For example, several studies have documented the effect of a partner's cultural preferences on individuals' tastes and behaviors (Upright, 2004; Kraaykamp, Van Eijck, Ultee & Van Rees, 2007; Lazzaro & Frateschi, 2015). However, the degree to which cultural tastes are stable over the course of one's life and are indeed determined to a large extent at an early age is still understudied.

The effect of historical, economic, and political circumstances on changing cultural consumption patterns is also not well explored. The focus on the United States and Europe in data collection and analysis has probably contributed to the scant research in this area. Evidence accumulating in recent years indicates interesting variations in the way the cultural and economic context shapes the relationship between the inequality of access and cultural consumption patterns. Notable examples include the correlates of omnivorousness in performing-arts attendance in Taiwan (Cheng & Wen, 2011), the different correlates of likelihood and frequency of cultural attendance in Taiwan (Wen & Chang, 2013), the experiential aspect of omnivorous consumption and its racial manifestations in Brazil (Hedegard, 2013), intergenerational relationships between cultural capital and parental expectations in urban China (Sheng, 2014), the distinction between traditional omnivores and modern omnivores in multicultural South Africa (Snowball, Jamal & Willis, 2010), and the embodiment of privileged cultural consumption in Turkey (Karademir-Hazir, 2014).

Most importantly, future research should develop approaches to measuring and analyzing cultural competencies acquired through lifestyles by using a variety of quantitative and qualitative methods and by drawing from various societal contexts. Researchers should then analyze the effect of these competencies on variations in education, employment, social networks, and wellbeing to determine the role of culture in the persistence of and change in social inequality.

References

Adorno, T. (1941). On Popular Music. *Studies in Philosophy and Social Sciences*, 9, 17–48.
Alderson, A., Junisbai, A., & Heacock, I. (2007). Social status and cultural consumption in the United States. *Poetics*, 35, 191–212.
Bennett, T., Bustamante, M., & Frow, J. (2013). The Australian Space of Lifestyles in Comparative Perspective. *Journal of Sociology*, 49 (2–3), 224–255.
Bennett, T., Savage, M., Silva, E., Warde, A., Gayo-Cal, M., & Wright, D. (2008). *Culture, class, distinction*. London: Routledge.
Berghman, M., & Van Eijck, K. (2009). Visual arts appreciation patterns: Crossing horizontal and vertical boundaries within the cultural hierarchy. *Poetics*, 37 (4), 348–365.
Bihagen, E., & Katz-Gerro, T. (2000). Culture Consumption in Sweden: The Stability of Gender Differences. *Poetics*, 27 (5/6), 327–249.
Birkelund, G.E., & Lemel, Y. (2013). Lifestyles and Social Stratification: An Explorative Study of France and Norway. *Comparative Social Research*, 30, 189–220.
Bodovski, K., & Farkas, G. (2008). Concerted cultivation and unequal achievement in elementary school. *Social Science Research*, 37, 903–919.
Bourdieu, P. (1984). *Distinction: A social critique on the judgment of tastes*. Cambridge: Harvard University Press.
Bourdieu, P., & Passeron, J. (1977). *Reproduction education, society, and culture*. Chicago: University of Chicago Press.
Bryson, B. (1996). "Anything but heavy metal": Symbolic exclusion and musical dislikes. *American Sociological Review*, 61 (5), 884–899.
Bryson, B. (1997). What about the univores? Musical dislikes and group-based identity construction among Americans with low levels of education. *Poetics*, 25 (2), 141–156.
Chan, T.W. (Ed.). (2010). *Social status and cultural consumption*. Cambridge: Cambridge University Press.
Chan, T. W., & Goldthorpe, J. (2007). Social stratification and cultural consumption: Music in England. *European Sociological Review*, 23, 1–19.
Cheng, T-C., & W-J. Wen. (2011). Determinants of Performing Arts Attendance in Taiwan: A Multivariate Probit Analysis. *Applied Economics Letters* 18, 15, 1437–1442.
Christin, A. (2012). Gender and Highbrow Cultural Participation in the United States. *Poetics*, 40 (5), 423–443.
Cicchelli, V., Octobre, S., & Riegel, V. (2016). After the omnivore, the cosmopolitan amateur: Reflections about aesthetic cosmopolitanism. *The Global Studies Journal*, 9 (1), 55–70.
Colbert, F., & Courchesne, A. (2012). Critical Issues in the Marketing of Cultural Goods: The Decisive Influence of Cultural Transmission. *City, Culture and Society*, 3 (4), 275–280.
Coulangeon, P. (2013). Changing Policies, Challenging Theories and Persisting Inequalities: Social Disparities in Cultural Participation in France from 1981 to 2008. *Poetics*, 41 (2), 177–209.
Coulangeon, P., & Lemel, Y. (2007). Is 'distinction' really outdated? Questioning the meaning of the omnivorization of musical taste in contemporary France. *Poetics*, 35 (2), 93–111.
DiMaggio, P. (1982). Cultural capital and school success: The impact of status culture participation on the grades of US high school students. *American Sociological Review*, 47 (2), 189–201.
DiMaggio, P. (1994). Social Stratification, Life-Style, and Social Cognition. In D. Grusky (Ed.), *Social Stratification* (pp. 458–465). San Francisco: Westview.
Diniz, S., & Machado, A. (2011). Analysis of the consumption of artistic-cultural goods and services in Brazil. *Journal of Cultural Economics*, 35, 1–18.
Donnat, O. (2004). La feminisation des pratiques culturelles. In T. Blo (Ed.), *La dialectique des rapports hommes-femmes* (pp. 423–431). Paris, France: PUF.
Douglas, M., & Isherwood, B. (1979). *The world of goods*. New York: Basic.
Dumais, S. A. (2002). Cultural capital, gender, and school success: The role of habitus. *Sociology of Education*, 75 (1), 44–68.
Dumais, S. A., & Ward, A. (2010). Cultural Capital and First-Generation College Success. *Poetics*, 38 (3), 245–265.

Fisher, T. C. G., & Preece, S. B. (2003). Evolution, Extinction, or Status Quo? Canadian Performing Arts Audiences in the 1990s. *Poetics*, 31 (2), 69–86.

Gaddis, S. M. (2013). The Influence of Habitus in the Relationship between Cultural Capital and Academic Achievement. *Social Science Research*, 42 (1), 1–13.

Gans, H. (1974). *Popular Culture and High Culture*. New York: Basic.

Garcia-Álvarez, E., Katz-Gerro, T., & López-Sintas, J. (2007). Deconstructing cultural omnivorousness 1982–2002: Insights from Americans' musical preferences. *Social Forces*, 86, 417–443.

Gerhards, J. (2008). Die kulturell dominierende Klasse in Europa. Eine vergleichende Analyse der 27 Mitgliedsländer der Europäischen Union im Anschluss an Pierre Bourdieu. Kölner Zeitschrift für Soziologie und Sozialpsychologie, 60, 723–748.

Gronow, J., & Southerton, D. (2010). Leisure and consumption in Europe. In S. Immerfall, & G. Therborn (Eds.), *Handbook of European societies* (pp. 355–384). New York: Springer.

Hedegard, D. (2013). Blackness and Experience in Omnivorous Cultural Consumption: Evidence from the Tourism of Capoeira in Salvador, Brazil. *Poetics* 41, 1, 1–26.

Heikkilä, R., & Rahkonen, K. (2011). 'IT IS NOT A MATTER OF TASTE. . .' Cultural capital and taste among the Swedish-speaking upper class in Finland. *European Societies*, 13 (1), 143–163.

Holbrook, M. B., Weiss, M. J., & Habich, J. (2002). Disentangling effacement, omnivore, and distinction effects on the consumption of cultural activities: An illustration. *Marketing Letters*, 13 (4), 345–357.

Horkheimer, M, & T. Adorno. (2002) [1944]. *Dialectic of Enlightenment*. Stanford: Stanford University Press.

Jaeger, M. M., & Katz-Gerro, T. (2010). The Rise of the Eclectic Cultural Consumer in Denmark, 1964–2004. *The Sociological Quarterly*, 51 (3), 460–483.

Jenkins, R. (2002). *Pierre Bourdieu*. Oxford: Routledge.

Kane, D. (2004). A Network Approach to the Puzzle of Women's Cultural Participation. *Poetics*, 32(2), 105–127.

Katz-Gerro, T. (2002). Highbrow Cultural Consumption and Class Distinction in Italy, Israel, West Germany, Sweden, and the United States. *Social Forces*, 81 (1), 207–29.

Katz-Gerro, T. (2004). Cultural Consumption Research: Review of Methodology, Theory, and Consequence. *International Review of Sociology*, 14 (1), 11–29.

Katz-Gerro, T. (2006). Comparative Evidence of Inequality in Cultural Preferences: Gender, Class, and Family Status. *Sociological Spectrum*, 26, 63–83.

Katz-Gerro, T. (2011). Cross-National Cultural Consumption Research: Inspirations and Disillusions. *Kölner Zeitschrift für Soziologie und Sozialpsychologie*, 51, 339–360. (in English)

Katz-Gerro, T., & Jaeger, M. M. (2012). Religion, Religiosity, and Cultural Stratification: Theoretical Links and Empirical Evidence. *Research in the Sociology of Work*, 23, 337–366.

Katz-Gerro, T., & Jaeger, M. M. (2015). Women's preference for highbrow culture does not begin in the family: comparing cultural participation among brothers and sisters. *Leisure Sciences*, 37 (5), 415–430.

Katz-Gerro, T., & Lopez-Sintas, J. (2013). The Breadth of Europeans' Musical Tastes: Disentangling Individual and Country Effects. *Advances in Sociology Research*, 14, 97–122.

Katz-Gerro, T., & Sullivan, O. (2010). Voracious Cultural Participation: Reinforcement of Gender and Social Status. *Time & Society*, 19 (2), 193–219.

Katz-Gerro, T., Raz, S., & Yaish, M. (2009). How do Class, Status, Ethnicity, and Religiosity Shape Cultural Omnivorousness in Israel? *Journal of Cultural Economics*, 33 (1), 1–17.

Karademir-Hazır, I. (2014). How bodies are classed: An analysis of clothing and bodily tastes in Turkey. *Poetics* 44, 1–21.

Karademir, H. I., & Warde, A. (2015). The Cultural Omnivore Thesis. In L. Hanquinet, & M. Savage (Eds.), *International Handbook of Sociology of Art and Culture* (pp. 77–89). London: Routledge.

Kirchberg, V., & Kuchar, R. (2014). States of Comparability: A Meta-Study of Representative Population Surveys and Studies on Cultural Consumption. *Poetics*, 43, 172–91.

Kraaykamp, G. (2003). Literary socialization and reading preferences. Effects of parents, the library, and the school. *Poetics*, 31 (3), 235–257.

Kraaykamp, G., & Nieuwbeerta, P. (2000). Parental background and lifestyle differentiation in Eastern Europe: social, political, and cultural intergenerational transmission in five former socialist societies. *Social Science Research*, 29 (1), 92–122.

Kraaykamp, G., Van Eijck, K., Ultee, W., & Van Rees, K. (2007). Status and media use in the Netherlands: Do partners affect media tastes? *Poetics*, 35 (2), 132–151.

Lahire, B. (2004). *La culture des individus: Dissonance culturelles et distinction de soi*. Paris: La Découverte.

Lahire, B. (2008). The individual and the mixing of genres: Cultural dissonance and self-distinction. *Poetics*, 36 (2), 166–188.

Lamont, M., & Lareau, A. (1988). Cultural capital: Allusions, gaps and glissandos in recent theoretical developments. *Sociological theory*, 6 (2), 153–168.
Lamont, M., & Molnár, V. (2002). The study of boundaries in the social sciences. *Annual review of sociology*, 5, 167–195.
Lazzaro, E., & Frateschi, C. (2015). Couples' arts participation: assessing individual and joint time use. *Journal of Cultural Economics*, DOI 10.1007/s10824-015-9264-3.
Lizardo, O. (2006). How cultural tastes shape personal networks. *American Sociological Review*, 71, 778–807.
López-Sintas, J., & García-Álvarez, E. (2002). Omnivores Show Up Again: The segmentation of Cultural Consumers in the Spanish Social Space. *European Sociological Review*, 18, 353–368.
Marx, K. (1976). *Capital: A critique of political economy*. New York: Penguin Books.
Nomaguchi, K., & Bianchi, S. (2004). Exercise time: Gender differences in the effects of marriage, parenthood, and employment. *Journal of Marriage and Family*, 66 (2), 413–430.
Notten, N., Kraaykamp, G., & Konig, R. P. (2012). Family Media Matters: Unraveling the Intergenerational Transmission of Reading and Television Tastes. *Sociological Perspectives*, 55 (4), 683–706.
Octobre, S. (2005). La Fabrique Sexuée des Goûts Culturels: Construire son Identité de Fille ou de Garçon à Travers les Activités Culturelles. *Développement culturel*, 150, 1–10.
Ollivier, M. (2008). Modes of Openness to Cultural Diversity: Humanist, Populist, Practical, and Indifferent. *Poetics*, 36 (2–3), 120–147.
Ollivier, M., Gauthier, G., & Truong, A. (2009). Cultural classifications and social divisions: A symmetrical approach. *Poetics*, 37 (5), 456–473.
Pasquier, D. (2010). *Le théâtre, une sortie sociale: Rapport au département des études, de la prospective et des statistiques (DEPS)*. Paris, France: Ministere de la Culture.
Peterson, R. A. (2005). Problems in Comparative Research: The Example of Omnivorousness. *Poetics*, 33 (5–6), 257–282.
Peterson, R., & Kern, R. (1996). Changing highbrow taste: From snob to omnivore. *American Sociological Review*, 61, 900–907.
Peterson, R., & Simkus, A. (1992). *How Musical Tastes Mark Occupational Status Groups. Cultivating differences: Symbolic boundaries and the making of inequality*. Pp. 152–186.
Prieto-Rodriguez, J., & Fernandez-Blanco, V. (2000). Are popular and classical music listeners the same people? *Journal of Cultural Economics*, 24, 147–164.
Purhonen, S., & Wright, D. (2013). Methodological Issues in National-Comparative Research on Cultural Tastes: The Case of Cultural Capital in the UK and Finland. *Cultural Sociology*, 7 (2), 257–273.
Ridgeway, C. L., & Smith-Lovin, L. (1999). The gender system and interaction. *Annual Review of Sociology*, 25, 191–216.
Rössel, J. (2006). Allesfresser im Kinosaal? Distinktion durch kulturelle Vielfalt in Deutschland. *Soziale Welt*, 57, 259–272.
Sheng, X. (2014). Parental Expectations Relating to Children's Higher Education in Urban China: Cultural Capital and Social Class. *Journal of Sociology*, 50, 4, 560–576.
Silva, E. B. (2005). Gender, Home and Family in Cultural Capital Theory. *The British Journal of Sociology*, 56 (1), 83–103.
Simmel, G. (1957). Fashion. *American journal of sociology*, 541–558.
Simmel, G. (1978). *The philosophy of money*. London: Routledge & Kegan Paul.
Slater, D. (1997): *Consumer Culture and Modernity*. Cambridge: Polity Press.
Snowball, J. D., Jamal, M., & Willis, K.G. (2010). Cultural Consumption Patterns in South Africa: An Investigation of the Theory of Cultural Omnivores. *Social Indicators Research*, 97 (3), 467–483.
Sobel, M. (2013) [1982]. *Lifestyle and Social Structure: Concepts, Definitions, Analyses*. Rotterdam: Elsevier.
Sullivan, A. (2001). Cultural Capital and Educational Attainment. *Sociology*, 35, 893–912.
Sullivan, O., & Katz-Gerro, T. (2007). The Omnivore Thesis Revisited: Voracious Cultural Consumers. *European Sociological Review*, 23, 123–137.
Tampubolon, G. (2008). Distinction in Britain, 2001–2004? *European Societies*, 10 (3), 403–428.
Torche, F. (2007). Social status and cultural consumption: The case of reading in Chile. *Poetics*, 35, 80–92.
Upright, C. B., (2004). Social capital and cultural participation: spousal influences on attendance at arts events. *Poetics*, 32 (2), 129–143.
Üstüner, T., & Holt, D. (2009). Toward a theory of status consumption in less industrialized countries. *Journal of Consumer Research*, 37, 37–56.
Van den Broe, A. (2013). Arts participation and the three faces of time: A reflection on disentangling the impact of life stage, period and socialization on arts participation, exemplified by an analysis of the US arts audience. *Cultural Trends*, 22 (1), 46–53.

Van Eijck, K. (2001). Social differentiation in musical taste patterns. *Social forces*, 79 (3), 1163–1185.

Van Eijck, K. (1997). The Impact of Family Background and Educational Attainment on Cultural Consumption: A Sibling Analysis. *Poetics*, 25, 195–224.

Van Eijck, K., & Lievens, J. (2008). Cultural Omnivorousness as a Combination of Highbrow, Pop, and folk Elements: The Relation between Taste Patterns and Attitudes Concerning Social Integration. *Poetics*, 36 (2–3), 217–242.

Van Hek, M., & Kraaykamp, G. (2013). Cultural Consumption Across Countries: A multi-level Analysis of Social Inequality in Highbrow Culture in Europe. *Poetics*, 41 (4), 323–341.

Van Hek, M., & Kraaykamp, G. (2015). How do parents affect cultural participation of their children? Testing hypotheses on the importance of parental example and active parental guidance. *Poetics*, 52, 124–138.

Veblen, T. (2007). *The theory of the leisure class*. Oxford: Oxford University Press.

Virtanen, T. (2007)[1899]. *Across and beyond the bounds of taste: On cultural consumption patterns in the European Union*. Turku: Turku School of Economics.

Warde, A., Martens, L., & Olsen, W. (1999). Consumption and the problem of variety: cultural omnivorousness, social distinction and dining out. *Sociology*, 33 (1), 105–127.

Warde, A., Wright, D., & Gayo-Cal, M. (2007). Understanding cultural omnivorousness: Or, the myth of the cultural omnivore. *Cultural sociology*, 1 (2), 143–164.

Weber, M. (1978). *Economy and society: An outline of interpretive sociology*. Berkeley: University of California Press.

Wen, W.-J., and T.-C. Cheng. (2013). Performing Arts Attendance in Taiwan: Who and How Often? *Journal of Cultural Economics*, 37(2), 309–325.

Willekens, M., Daenekindt, S., & Lievens, J. (2014). Whose education matters more? Mothers' and fathers' education and the cultural participation of adolescents. *Cultural Sociology*, 8 (3), 291–309.

Zavisca, J. (2005). Status of cultural omnivorism: A case study of reading in Russia. *Social Forces*, 84, 1233–1255.

36
Consumption of leisure

Jennifer Smith Maguire

Introduction

This chapter examines key themes in the sociocultural study of the consumption of leisure. To begin, let us consider the relationship between these terms. *Consumption* and *leisure* are often treated synonymously: a reflection of the degree to which leisure has been shaped by commercialization and commodification (Rojek, 1985; Wearing & McDonald, 2015). This is perhaps best exemplified through sport as a genre of leisure activities. The participation in and spectatorship and organization of sport have undergone extensive commercialization over the contemporary period (Andrews & Clift, 2015; Moor, 2007) such that we might refer to a 'sports-industrial complex' (Maguire, 2004). The close alignment of consumption and leisure might even be considered a structural feature of capitalism. As consumer spending increasingly predominates within national economies, a mentality that equates leisure with consumption ensures the reproduction of the social order (e.g. McDonald, Wearing & Ponting, 2008).

While consumption and leisure may be overlapping processes of having and doing, there nevertheless remain leisure forms that require no, or virtually no, commercial consumption (Stebbins, 2009). Moreover, the social phenomenon of leisure predates consumer culture (Burke, 1995): to understand leisure on its own terms offers insights into the social function of the consumption of leisure beyond simply the purchase of leisure goods and services. Three themes related to leisure and consumption provide the chapter's framework. First, we consider the definition of leisure through its relationship to work. While often conceptualized as binary opposites, work and leisure are better understood as interrelated social phenomena; considerations of that interrelationship call attention to the ideological implications of leisure, its historically contingent characteristics and social function. Second, we turn to leisure's significance with regard to how individuals construct and perform identities and lifestyles. Drawing from research on sport, the section touches on notions of conspicuous leisure, serious leisure and lifestyle. Third, we examine the connection between leisure and play. The potential for leisure to afford non-instrumental fun, excitement and 'flow' experiences is examined with regard to societal and individual benefits. The chapter concludes by considering the implications for and of leisure in consumer culture.

Leisure and work

Leisure is typically conceptualized in opposition with work. This binary often hinges on the question of time: leisure amounts to 'time other than that spent in paid employment' (Williams, 1983, p. 336). This 'residual' definition of leisure (Haworth & Lewis, 2005) focuses on what goes on during the time left over from paid (and unpaid) work, and is central to time-use surveys that gather statistics about what people do within their 'free' time. For example, we know that American adults have an average of five hours and five minutes of leisure time per day (Bureau of Labor Statistics, 2014), which are most commonly spent watching television (two hours and forty-nine minutes), socializing and communicating (thirty-eight minutes), and playing games or using the computer for leisure (twenty-seven minutes). Time-use surveys in the UK have similar findings (Seddon, 2012): television watching (four hours and two minutes a day on average) is the most commonly reported free time activity, followed by spending time with friends and family, and listening to music.

Research by The Organisation for Economic Co-operation and Development (OECD) helps to put this into a global and historical perspective. The average time spent on paid work is changing: there is an overall decline in average hours worked in most countries from the 1980s until 2009 (OECD, 2009, p. 25); since 2009, with very few exceptions, the proportion of employees who work more than fifty hours per week has increased (OECD, 2015, p. 75). Within this global distribution of 'free time,' there remain clear national differences (2015, p. 75): for example, Turkey has the highest proportion working very long hours (over 40% working fifty or more hours per week) whereas Netherlands has the lowest (approximately 0.4%). Across OECD countries, people spend an average of fifteen hours per week on leisure and personal care (2015, p. 76), with main activities being personal care (of which activities sleep and eating predominate), and then leisure, which made up 22% of an average day (OECD, 2009, p. 27). Daily leisure time differs between countries, from the high end of Belgium, Germany, Finland and (highest at 27% of the day) Norway, to the low end of Japan, France, New Zealand and (lowest at 16%) Mexico (OECD, 2009, p. 27). Time-use surveys are also useful for identifying inequality in the availability of leisure time, for example in relation to women whose 'second shift' of domestic work entails greater constraints on their available free time (Hochschild & Machung, 2012; see also Mattingly & Bianchi, 2003). Across the OECD countries, men spend more time in broad leisure activities than women in the majority of countries (OECD, 2009, p. 32; 2015, p. 78), with the greatest gender gaps occurring in Italy, (over eighty more minutes per day), Mexico, Poland and Korea (OECD, 2009, p. 32).

Another approach that underpins population leisure statistics hinges not on time, but on an activity-based form of the work/leisure dichotomy. Leisure is constituted by activities assumed to be other than those associated with paid and unpaid work. This approach is central to cultural participation surveys such as the British 'Taking Part' survey (Davies, 2011), which has found that the most common leisure activities for adults are reading for pleasure (64%), visiting historic places (54%), going to the cinema (52%), visiting libraries (45%) and visiting museums and galleries (44%), while the most common sporting activities are indoor swimming (32%) and gym/fitness activities (22%). This approach, too, is useful in revealing inequalities in leisure participation. For example, looking at British visitors to museums and galleries in 2015–16 (Department for Culture Media & Sport, 2015), participation is clearly shaped by social class (approximately 60% of the upper socio-economic group take part, compared with 38% of the lower socio-economic group), somewhat by age (48% of 16–24 year olds, 54–56% of 25–74 year olds, but only 34% of those over 75), but not by gender (51% of men, 52% of women). This approach also reveals variation in patterns of leisure expenditures. For example, British households (Key Note,

2015) increased their spending on leisure activities by nearly 15% between 2010 and 2014. Of the £190.98 billion spent in 2014, nearly 42% was spent on restaurants, cafés and bars, and just over 21% on recreational and cultural services, within which approximately 53% was spent on cultural services (including cinema, theatre, concerts and satellite subscriptions), 27% on games of chance (gaming and gambling, lotteries), and 20% on recreational and sporting services.

Both time- and activity-based statistics underscore the close leisure/consumption link. It is difficult to imagine any of the above activities taking place without being simultaneously linked to activity-specific purchases (such as equipment and entrance fees) or embedded within wider constellations of consumer practices and political economies (from museum gift shops to advertising revenues linked to daily television habits). Time use and participation data are useful for investigating what people do when not otherwise occupied with jobs or routines of self- and household-maintenance, but they also highlight the shortcomings of understanding leisure strictly through an opposition to work. Practices such as updating one's Facebook profile during the workday and checking emails while watching television with one's family remind us there is no firm boundary between work and leisure time. Similarly, many activities fall into both obligatory and discretionary use of time, such as cooking and reading. Meanwhile, research suggests a continuity of dispositions across the work/leisure divide: for example, those with jobs with higher levels of autonomy (such as professional/managerial occupations) are more likely to have an 'extension' pattern to their work-leisure relationship, meaning that work and leisure share at least some common characteristics or style, and that there is no clear demarcation experienced between the two spheres (Parker, 1976). Thus, sociologists of consumption and of leisure (amongst others) have challenged the work/leisure binary, calling attention to the continuities of activities and dispositions that fall between and across the two realms, from the home-based tele-commuting of knowledge workers (Lewis, 2003) to the workplace nap (Baxter & Kroll-Smith, 2005).

If not binary opposites, work and leisure are nevertheless interrelated: the boundary between them is historically specific and must be understood in the context of the dominant political-economic social order (e.g. Bramham, 2002; Elias & Dunning, 1986; Parker, 1976; Rojek, 1985, 1995). One approach to understanding this interrelationship is to focus on the ideological implications of leisure for the reproduction of capitalism (e.g. Baudrillard, 1998). Consider, for example, the British 'Rational Recreation' movement of the nineteenth century. Middle-class reformers promoted particular forms of leisure to the urban working classes (including revised forms of established working-class leisure) in an attempt to encourage orderliness, productiveness and self-improvement (Bailey, 1978). This ideological approach to leisure as a mode of social reform diffused to many societies including the United States, where Henry Ford, for example, adopted principles of rational recreation alongside scientific management in his reformulation of the organization of production (Rojek, 1995). Looked at in this way, leisure may appear as an auxiliary sphere to that of occupational work, ensuring the restoration of individuals' productive and creative capacities, but also an ideological 'bread and circuses' trick played on the masses, disciplining the working classes and pacifying unrest (e.g. Ewen, 1976; Rojek, 1985).

A second approach to the work/leisure interrelationship is to situate both phenomena within the long-term process of modernization (e.g. Elias & Dunning, 1986). The emergence of leisure is bound up with social changes that were both preconditions for and consequences of the Industrial Revolution and its implications for the organization and experience of work – both paid, occupational work and the unpaid labour of households (Burke, 1995). Attentiveness to leisure's historical context suggests distinctions between a pre-industrial world of agrarian work interspersed with occasional festivals, and a modern world of paid labour and paid-for leisure pursuits, and between an industrial producer society dominated by work, and a post-industrial consumer society dominated by leisure. However, these shifts are long term and never absolute. Burke (1995) identifies the emergence in the fifteenth century of an idea of leisure as time that should be shaped with purpose, and traces its institutionalization from the sixteenth century through, for example, educational discourses aimed at training children through appropriate forms of recreation and pastimes; theological-moral discourses that sought to restrict and forbid particular forms of recreation that were regarded as morally corrupting; and medical discourses attempting to evidence and promote the positive, restorative benefits of particular forms of recreation (all of which helped lay the foundations for the nineteenth-century Rational Recreationists).

A socio-historical understanding of leisure and work is thus bound up with an understanding of the very long-term development of human society. Social relations have become increasingly interdependent, allowing for intricate divisions of labour and dense urban agglomerations, but also requiring the control of potentially disruptive emotions and urges. Leisure provides individuals with socially-approved opportunities for 'loosening their armour' in order to experience emotions otherwise excluded from public life (Elias & Dunning, 1986, pp. 124–125). One can safely experience thrills or desire, for example, through the experiences of first-person shooter video games or romantic films, the public outpouring of elation at a sporting event, or the sociability of the pub or café. Elias and Dunning (1986) suggest that through the elements of sociability, motility and imagination, people are able to experience a controlled decontrolling of emotions (themes to which we will return in the final section). From this perspective, leisure is not auxiliary to work, but is the other side of the same coin; highly routinized societies resting on emotional restraint and impersonal interactions require opportunities for a counterbalancing loosening of emotional controls. Thus, leisure – and by implication, consumption – is central to human life; leisure's 'other' is not work, but non-leisure.

Leisure and identity

Leisure is closely related to work with regard to how scholars have defined and measured it, and understood its development and social function. Leisure is also closely related to questions of identity, which has itself become an object of work in contemporary societies. Accounts of individualization draw attention to the ways in which identity has shifted over the course of modernity from a fixed set of characteristics determined by birth and ascription, to a reflexive, on-going project or performance (Bauman, 2000; Beck & Beck-Gernsheim, 2002). Individuals, free to choose their pathways towards self-realization, are then faced with a loss of security; without fixed rules, individuals are constantly at risk of getting it wrong, and anxiety potentially attends each choice. These questions of identity converge with leisure in the concept of lifestyle: the system of practices assembled through individuals' classification of consumer goods and practices – and in turn, themselves – as more or less legitimate or desirable (Bourdieu, 1984). Individualization is a process by which identity has become a problem accompanied the ascendancy of a consuming way of life and a host of countless products, experiences and therapeutic experts aimed at addressing that problem. Consumer culture thus casts leisure time as the sphere for self-work.

According to Elias and Dunning, self-work (self-fulfilment and self-expansion activities such as volunteering, private study, hobbies and self-improvement pursuits) is a major component of the spectrum of activities that make up people's spare time (1986, p. 97). While they consider this as separate from leisure in its proper sense of sociable and mimetic activities (to which we will return in the next section), we can see that the logic of self-expansion pervades much of the representation of leisure time. Self-help media present leisure as a category overwritten by the logic of self-improvement (McGee, 2005). Fitness magazines and exercise manuals exhort readers to discipline their bodies and time in order to address a panoply of risks and problems, from excess weight to inadequate self-confidence. The rewards of such self-work are typically formulated as external pleasures (e.g. looking slimmer, younger) rather than the inherent pleasure of the activity per se (Smith Maguire, 2008). Thus, fitness guides – like the sixteenth-century how-to treatises on leisure (Burke, 1995) – situate leisure as functionally appropriate to a specific societal context. Readers are instructed in the obligations of leisure-time self-work and making oneself fit for a culture dominated by consumption.

This interrelationship between leisure and identity was a focus for Veblen, writing at the turn of the twentieth century in *The Theory of the Leisure Class* ([1899] 1992). Veblen commented upon the 'work' of the nouveaux riches to display and defend their new class position. Social mobility required that the gentleman 'change his life of leisure into a more or less arduous application to the business of learning how to live a life of ostensible leisure in a becoming way' (Veblen, 1992, p. 64). Conspicuous forms of leisure – particular sports, tourism and cultural activities – served as tools in status competition and identity construction. Golf, for example, involves specific skills, equipment, accessories and deportment that explicitly signal an ability to eschew instrumental manual labour and budgetary concerns (Veblen, 1992, p. 76). While participation in golf has arguably democratized since Veblen's time, the sport nevertheless continues to operate in the reproduction of power hierarchies and group identities, as research on the South African context suggests (Cock, 2008).

Since Veblen's time, the concern with performing social identities via leisure and lifestyle choices has expanded beyond the nouveaux riches. This is reflected in research on the significance of participation in physical activities and sport subcultures for individuals' identities. Particularly useful in this regard is Stebbins' notion of 'serious leisure' for activities that are 'sufficiently substantial, interesting, and fulfilling for the participant to find a (leisure) career there acquiring and expressing a combination of its special skills, knowledge, and experience' (2009, p. 14). Six qualities characterise serious leisure and link leisure to identity: the possibility of following a relatively structured career within the pursuit; the need to persevere in the face of challenges; the need to invest personal effort in acquiring specialized skills and knowledge; the possibility of enjoying such durable benefits as self-actualization, a sense of belonging and self-gratification; the shared expression of a distinct ethos or values by the community of participants; and a strong sense of identification with and through the chosen pursuit for participants (Stebbins, 2009, pp. 17–19).

Given those common characteristics, serious leisure pursuits often take the form of subcultures or social worlds with distinctive sets of norms and beliefs, through which participants potentially gain a meaningful sense of identity and belonging. Consider, for example, various forms of 'serious sport tourism' (Green & Jones, 2005, pp. 176–178) such as diving or golfing holidays, or travel for triathlon and adventure racing events. The additional investment of time and effort in travel in order to undertake the activity affords participants enhanced identity benefits, such as the chance to interact with subcultural peers, conspicuously display their identity and mark milestones within their career. Similarly, the positioning of skateboarding and kite-surfing as 'alternative' reinforces identity: participants tend to share a common currency of attitudes and styles of behaviour and dress, and 'describe their activities as "lifestyles" rather than as "sports"' (Wheaton, 2010, p. 1059). As an extreme, high-involvement serious leisure participants may exhibit characteristics of addiction, as research on young Korean players of Massively Multiplayer Online Games (MMOG) suggests (Seok & DaCosta, 2014).

Just as leisure has been shaped by commercialization and individualization, so too is the experience of lifestyle sports inflected by these two processes. Research on lifestyle sports identifies a potential conflict between a counter-cultural ethos and the co-option that accompanies the corporate-driven expansion of these activities (Stranger, 2010; Wheaton, 2010). Commercialization – in the form of the increasing prominence of media and mega events, such as ESPN's X Games and the mainstreaming of once-marginal brands – poses a seeming threat to the self-actualization of lifestyle sport participants, whose authenticity is assumed to rest on a juxtaposition with mainstream sport. However, interpretive research highlights that there is no inherent, authentic identity reserved for subcultural insiders, that notions of authenticity are used to police subcultural boundaries, and that commercial processes and goods are as central as distinctive styles of participation in the lived identities of participants (Donnelly, 2006; Stranger, 2010). For serious lifestyle sport participants, leisure is clearly a sphere for undertaking the considerable effort of self-work, and of consuming in a style appropriate to one's identity.

Leisure and play

The ideal of leisure as fun and pleasurable is largely implicit within the work reviewed thus far, such as in the case of a work/leisure dichotomy juxtaposing the drudgery of work with the pleasure of play. Yet, as we have seen, such a dichotomy is flawed: work and leisure are co-constituted and intertwined phenomena (Burke, 1995; Elias & Dunning, 1986), and they overlap in their dispositions and structures, as with the case of serious leisure (Stebbins, 2009). Rather than regard the association with fun and play as a result of leisure's ideological implications (or as merely a preserve of children), studies of leisure and consumption suggest that the play element of leisure is fundamental to human experience. This idea lies at the heart of *homo ludens*, Huizinga's (1970) conceptualization of an ideal type of human existence for which free, spontaneous, non-instrumental play (as opposed to work) is fundamental to self-development (Rojek, 2000). Put more broadly, leisure and play can only be understood through attention to the interdependencies between society and emotions (Maguire, 2011).

Play features within established typologies of leisure. Stebbins, for example, contrasts serious leisure with 'casual leisure': 'immediately intrinsically rewarding, relatively short-lived pleasurable activity requiring little or no special training to enjoy it' (2009, p. 22), such as playing games, relaxing or socializing, and forms of active and passive entertainment. Elias and Dunning (1986, pp. 97–98), on the other hand, reserve the term *leisure* expressly for those spare-time activities that are sociable and/or mimetic. Mimetic play activities arouse emotions such as fear, desire, laughter or disgust, and transpose them onto a new (leisure) form, thus blunting their sting and making them socially-acceptable to experience (1986, p. 124). In this way, leisure offers a controlled de-controlling of the emotions, as with the pleasure of being 'hunted' within predation-themed video games (Bertozzi, 2014). Formality and routines are not the opposite of play and pleasure but can, in fact, facilitate the loosening of emotional restraints – e.g. the formal socializing of a wedding compared with that of meeting up at the pub; the highly organized format of playing in a football match or being part of a fan group compared with the informal organization of dancing.

The above accounts suggest that the degree of skill, regulation and routinization of the activity is significant to participants' experience of play, and its potential benefits. This dovetails with the work of Csikszentmihalyi (1992), who identifies an experience of 'flow' in various pursuits, including sport, art and music: a deeply meaningful sense of engagement and participation that is completely absorbing. Participants lose track of time, a sense of themselves as separate from the task, and an orientation towards external ends to which the activity might be directed. Being 'in the flow' or 'in the zone' affords a sense of pleasure and happiness, and is associated with a clear sense of purpose, intense concentration and a sense of control (both in relation to risk, and in relation to one's autonomy in choosing to do the activity for its own sake). Comparing across various studies, Csikszentmihalyi suggests that what enables flow experiences is the alignment of a participant's skills and competencies with the challenges of the task; being over-challenged or under-challenged is unlikely to result in a flow experience (1992, p. 74).

Various studies of sport participation identify dimensions of flow. For example, skateboarders' experience of pleasure is closely linked to the autonomous, self-directed and intrinsic aspects of the activity: being able to set their own challenges appropriate to their skill level, and persist in skill improvement on their own terms, is associated with feelings of pride and satisfaction (Seifert & Hedderson, 2010; see also Beal, 1996). Similarly, the potential for 'thrills' is a key motivational factor for participants in sports such as kayaking and ice climbing (Stebbins, 2005) and many other lifestyle sports that combine specialized skills, identities and risk.

It is important to remember that flow, play and pleasure are not limited to leisure participation 'on the field of play,' but extend to spectatorship. This is perhaps most obvious in the case of fans – individuals whose identities are explicitly linked to their appreciation of and involvement in a particular phenomenon. Research on football fans in Belgium, France and Spain finds fandom to be both sociable and mimetic, creating the potential for subcultural identity through shared routines and rituals such as team scarves and paraphernalia, songs and chants, and the sacred place of the stadium (Derbaix & Decrop, 2011). Music fans similarly derive pleasure and identity through their leisure. Research on the fans of the band Phish suggests musical improvisation offers the thrill of risk (for the musicians) and discovery (for the fans), while flow might be found through the immediacy of dancing and being carried away by the music (Blau, 2010). While meaningful leisure can certainly extend to 'casual' spectatorship, the degree of pleasure and emotional release is likely to hinge on the relative presence of one or more of the elements of sociability (e.g. watching alone or with others), motility (e.g. standing vs. dancing) and imagination (e.g. the proximity or distance between the leisure experience and everyday life) within the experience of spectating. Hence, those with a deeper sense of engagement and investment in leisure activities are more likely to experience the emotional release associated with flow or other forms of catharsis – be that the devoted opera enthusiast, transported in imagination while listening alone to a recording of a performance, or the passionate rugby fan, face painted in team colours and crying in despair alongside fellow supporters at the loss of their team. These potentialities for engaged spectatorship, sociability and mimesis are now being extended through digital and social media, such as online video gaming 'clans' (Jansz & Tanis, 2007) or online Turkish football fan sites (McManus, 2013).

Taken together, research from the sociology of consumption, leisure and sport suggests that the potential for flow, play and pleasure is located at the intersection of freedom and constraint. Leisure is not 'free' but is freeing because it is embedded within routines and rules. Leisure potentially offers both a tension release for humans embedded in societies built on emotional restraint, and a form of 'exciting significance' (Maguire, 2011, p. 921) through which self-actualization and identity are achieved and performed. This potential rests on the structures (rules, regulations, conventions, norms) within which the activity sits, the relative alignment between skills, competencies and challenges, and the degree of autonomy and intrinsic motivation underlying participation.

Leisure and consumer culture

In light of the above discussion, what insights does leisure research offer to our understanding of consumer culture? Existing research suggests diminishing prospects for play in consumer culture. Pervasive rationalization and commercialization (Rojek, 1985) constrain the potential experience, and ideal conceptualization of leisure, as suggested by critiques of the 'McDonaldization' (Ritzer, 2013) and 'Disneyization' (Bryman, 2004) of society. Furthermore, in a consumer society, self-work is presented as an obligation. Pleasure is instrumentalized, both as a means of motivating individuals to partake in leisure activities, and as part of the wider reproduction of service economies, consumer cultures and neo-liberal social orders that rely on self-managing, responsible individuals (Rose, 1999). The logic of self-investment potentially transforms even banal, routine care activities into vehicles for self-expression and status-positioning, and thus opportunities for profit. Leisure as a time of doing nothing, of idleness, is a refusal of the obligation of productivity (Dumazedier, 1974), but this radical potential is reserved for the very wealthy (for whom it is sanctioned), or tolerated only in the very poor (with the unemployed expected to actively engage in re-skilling). For the majority, leisure must be a time for the 'production of value – distinctive value, status value, prestige value' (Baudrillard, 1998, p. 157).

Yet, there is also reason to be affirmed in the persistence of the playful – and possibly radical – dimensions of leisure. Indeed, play, spontaneous fun and non-instrumental pleasure remain at the core of the myth of leisure in consumer culture, and of a view of human life as an on-going 'unstable tension-equilibrium between . . . impersonal intellectual activity and . . . pleasurable excitation' of emotion (Elias & Dunning, 1986, p. 120). Beyond the social function of leisure as an antidote to the rationalization and emotional restraints of everyday life, there is also the possibility for leisure to disrupt the social order. As Turner (1988) suggests, it is in the seemingly harmless, innocent danger of fun that leisure and ludic culture have the chance to critique the social order. Consider, for example, the Red Hat Society (RHS), a leisure group for mid-life and elderly women (Stalp, Radina & Lynch, 2008). The RHS members use notions of fun and play as a shield for challenging cultural stereotypes, including the traditional view of women's leisure as secondary to that of men's (Henderson, Hodges & Kivel, 2002), and of older women as invisible both in public space and in the sexualized male gaze (Calasanti & Slevin, 2001). Through extravagant outfits (red hats, flamboyant purple outfits), campy performances (hyper-feminine tea parties; shopping excursions) and deviant behaviour (loud laughter, look-at-me outfits), RHS members assert themselves within public leisure places, challenging their assumed absence from such spaces and practices (Stalp, Radina & Lynch, 2008).

Conclusion

Let us conclude by considering the state of knowledge vis-à-vis consumer culture and leisure, and identifying future directions for research. Signs of a maturing coalescence of research on consumption and on leisure (in general, and oriented around a specific leisure field, such as sport) include recent monographs (Dixon, 2013; Stebbins, 2009) and entries in compendiums of consumption (e.g. Andrews & Clift, 2015; Wearing & McDonald, 2015; this entry). From population surveys, to ethnographic interview-based studies, to textual studies, we can identify a wealth of existing research that has sought to locate and critically unpack the meaning, significance and consequences of leisure forms through a diverse range of epistemological and methodological positions. Such work makes clear that context matters: the lived experience, political economy and cultural norms of leisure times, practices and ideals cannot be understood without reference to the specific societal and historical context of the participants, institutions and practices. Such contextuality has been confirmed through the growing range of studies that look beyond Western settings, traditional leisure forms and typical leisure participants. However, amidst the expansion of our knowledge of the specific, we should not lose sight of the 'big picture' through, for example, cross-cultural, longitudinal and archival research that is able to widen our lens to appreciate the on-going development of dominant, emergent and residual leisure forms (Williams, 1977).

This review thus suggests some emerging directions for future studies of leisure and consumption. First: there remain pressing questions with regard to the unequal distribution of resources (economic and temporal resources, but also cultural tastes and preferences) through which individuals take up consumption and leisure options. Especially for the understudied, rapidly growing and precarious middle classes of emerging economies, leisure inequalities must be traced along various lines (including gender, sexuality, race/ethnicity, age, class, physical disability). Second: insights from the sociology of consumption regarding the rise of an 'omnivorous' taste regime (Warde, Wright & Gayo-Cal, 2007) beg questions of how changing notions of legitimate and illegitimate culture manifest in leisure domains. Such questions are especially pertinent for sport, which – in addition to an internal stratification that positions some sports as more socially esteemed than others – has its own awkward positioning as less legitimate vis-à-vis other 'cultural' leisure activities such as art and music.

Third: the dialogue between the study of consumption, leisure studies and leisure-related sub-disciplines (among them the sociology of sport and of gaming) remains underdeveloped. Digital and social media have created possibilities for new forms and modes of cultural exchange, social community, identity, obligation, creativity, control and co-production; these have yet to be fully assessed in terms of their implications for the reproduction and transformation of dominant, emergent and residual consumption practices. Fourth and finally: historically oriented examinations of leisure highlight the intersection of individual and social structures, and should be a call to take a wide view of the 'institutional field' (Zukin & Smith Maguire, 2004) within which specific consumption practices sit. As Warde argues (2014, p. 295), studies of consumption generally neglect the normalisation of practices and 'pay little attention to the creation of norms, standards and institutions which produce shared understandings and common procedures.' Yet, this is a strength within studies of leisure that foreground the historical contingency and social construction of routines and of their significance for the enactment and experience of emotions, identities and group bonds.

References

Andrews, D.L., & Clift, B.C. (2015). Consumption and sport. In D.T. Cook & M.J. Ryan (Eds.), *The Wiley Blackwell encyclopedia of consumption and consumer studies* (pp. 191–195). Chichester: John Wiley & Sons.

Bailey, P. (1978) *Leisure and class in Victorian England: Rational recreation and the contest for control, 1830–1885*. London: Routledge & Kegan Paul.

Baudrillard, J. (1998). *The consumer society: Myths and structures*. London: Sage.

Bauman, Z. (2000). *Liquid modernity*. Cambridge: Polity Press.

Baxter, V., & Kroll-Smith, K. (2005). Normalizing the workplace nap: Blurring the boundaries between public and private space and time. *Current Sociology*, 53(1), 33–55.

Beal, B. (1996). Alternative masculinity and its effects on gender relations in the subculture of skate-boarding. *Journal of Sport Behavior*, 19, 204–220.

Beck, U., & Beck-Gernsheim, E. (2002). *Individualization: Institutionalized individualism and its social and political consequences*. London: Sage.

Bertozzi, E. (2014). The feeling of being hunted: Pleasures and potentialities of predation play. *Games and Culture*, 9(6), 429–441.

Blau, J.A. (2010). A phan on Phish: Live improvised music in five performative commitments. *Cultural Studies: Critical Methodologies*, 10(4), 307–319.

Boudieu, P. (1984). *Distinction: A Social Critique of the Judgment of Taste*. Cambridge, MA: Harvard University Press.

Bramham, P. (2002). Rojek, the sociological imagination and leisure. *Leisure Studies*, 21, 221–234.

Bryman, A. (2004). *The Disneyization of society*. London: Sage.

Bureau of Labor Statistics. (2014). Leisure and sports activities. *American Time Use Survey*. http://www.bls.gov/TUS/CHARTS/LEISURE.HTM [Accessed January 2016].

Burke, P. (1995). The invention of leisure in early modern Europe. *Past and Present*, 146, 136–150.

Calasanti, T., & Slevin, K.F. (2001). *Gender, social inequality, and aging*. Walnut Creek, CA: AltaMira Press.

Cock, J. (2008). Caddies and 'cronies': Golf and changing patterns of exclusion and inclusion in post-apartheid South Africa. *South African Review of Sociology*, 39(2), 183–200.

Csikszentmihalyi, M. (1992). *Flow: The psychology of happiness*. London: Ryder.

Davies, J. (2011). *Mapping leisure: Visualising the landscape of cultural and sporting participation: An analysis of the Taking Part Survey*. English Heritage. https://content.historicengland.org.uk/content/docs/research/mapping-leisure-rep-jul11.pdf [Accessed January 2016].

Department for Culture Media & Sport. (2015). *Taking Part 2015/16 Quarter 2*. Statistical Release. https://www.gov.uk/government/statistics/taking-part-201516-quarter-2-statistical-release [Accessed January 2016].

Derbaix, C., & Decrop, A. (2011). Colours and scarves: An ethnographic account of football fans and their paraphernalia. *Leisure Studies*, 30(3), 271–291.

Dixon, K. (2013). *Consuming football in late modern life*. London: Routledge.

Donnelly, M. (2006). Studying extreme sports: Beyond core participants. *Journal of Sport & Social Issues*, 30(2), 219–224.

Dumazedier, J. (1974). *Sociology of leisure*. Amsterdam: Elsevier.

Elias, N., & Dunning, E. (1986). *Quest for Excitement: Sport and Leisure in the Civilizing Process*. Oxford: Blackwell.

Ewen, S. (1976). *Captains of Consciousness: Advertising and the Social Roots of the Consumer Culture*. New York: McGraw-Hill.

Green, B.C., & Jones, I. (2005). Serious leisure, social identity and sport tourism. *Sport in Society*, 8(2), 164–181.

Haworth, J., & Lewis, S. (2005). Work, leisure and well-being. *British Journal of Guidance & Counselling*, 33(1), 67–79.

Henderson, K.A., Hodges, S., & Kivel, B.D. (2002). Context and dialogue in research on women and leisure. *Journal of Leisure Research*, 34(3), 253–271.

Hochschild, A., & Machung, A. (2012). *The second shift: Working families and the revolution at home (rev. ed.)*. London: Penguin

Huizinga, J. (1970). *Homo Ludens: A study of the play element in culture*. London: Temple Smith.

Jansz, J., & Tanis, M. (2007). Appeal of playing online first person shooter games. *CyberPsychology and Behaviour*, 10(1), 133–136.

Key Note. (2015). *Trends in leisure activities*. London: Key Note Limited.

Lewis, S. (2003). The integration of paid work and the rest of life. Is post-industrial work the new leisure? *Leisure Studies*, 22(4), 343–355.

Maguire, J.A. (2004). Challenging the sports-industrial complex: Human sciences, advocacy and service. *European Physical Education Review*, 10(3), 299–322.

Maguire, J.A. (2011). Welcome to the pleasure dome?: Emotions, leisure and society. *Sport in Society*, 14(7/8), 913–926.

Mattingly, M., & Bianchi, S.M. (2003). Gender differences in the quantity and quality of free time: The U.S. experience. *Social Forces*, 81(3), 999–1031.

McDonald, M., Wearing, S., & Ponting, J. (2008). Narcissism and neoliberalism: Work, leisure and alienation in an era of consumption. *Loisir et Société/Society and Leisure*, 30(1), 489–510.

McGee, M. (2005). *Self-Help, Inc.: Makeover Culture in American Life*. New York: Oxford University Press.

McManus, J. (2013). Been there, done that, bought the t-shirt: Besiktas fans and the commodification of football in Turkey. *International Journal of Middle East Studies*, 45(1), 3–24.

Moor, L. (2007). Sport and commodification: A reflection on key concepts. *Journal of Sport and Social Issues*, 31(2), 128–142.

OECD. (2009). *Society at a glance*. Paris: OECD iLibrary.

OECD. (2015). *How's life? 2015. Measuring well-being*. Paris: OECD iLibrary.

Parker, S. (1976). *The sociology of leisure*. London: George Allen & Unwin.

Ritzer, G. (2013). *The McDonaldization of society. (20th anniversary ed.)*. Los Angeles: Sage.

Rojek, C. (1985). *Capitalism & leisure theory*. London: Tavistock Publications.

Rojek, C. (1995). *Decentring leisure: Rethinking leisure theory*. London: Sage.

Rojek, C. (2000). *Leisure and culture*. Basingstoke: Palgrave.

Rose, N. (1999). *Powers of freedom: Reframing political thought*. Cambridge: Cambridge University Press.

Seddon, C. (2012). *Measuring national well-being: What we do, 2012*. Office of National Statistics. http://www.ons.gov.uk/ons/dcp171766_258996.pdf [Accessed January 2016].

Seifert, T., & Hedderson, C. (2010). Intrinsic motivation and flow in skateboarding: An ethnographic study. *Journal of Happiness Studies*, 11, 277–292.

Seok, S., & DaCosta, B. (2014). Distinguishing addiction from high engagement: An investigation into the social lives of adolescent and young adult massively multiplayer online game players. *Games and Culture*, 9(4), 227–254.

Smith Maguire, J. (2008). *Fit for consumption: Sociology and the business of fitness*. London: Routledge.

Stalp, M.C., Radina, M.E., & Lynch, A. (2008). "We do it cuz it's fun": Gendered fun and leisure for midlife women through Red Hat Society membership. *Sociological Perspectives*, 51(2), 325–348.

Stebbins, R. (2005). *Challenging mountain nature: Risk, motive, and lifestyle in three hobbyist sports*. Calgary: Detselig.

Stebbins, R. (2009). *Leisure and consumption: Common ground/separate worlds*. Basingstoke: Palgrave Macmillan.

Stranger, M. (2010). Surface and substructure: Beneath surfing's commodified surface. *Sport in Society*, 13(7/8), 1117–1134.

Turner, V. (1988). *The anthropology of performance*. New York: PAJ.

Veblen, T. ([1889] 1992). *The theory of the leisure class: An economic study of institutions*. New Brunswick, NJ: Transaction Publishers.

Warde, A. (2014). After taste: Culture, consumption and theories of practice. *Journal of Consumer Culture*, 14(3), 279–303.

Warde, A., Wright, D., & Gayo-Cal, M. (2007). Understanding cultural omnivorousness: Or, the myth of the cultural omnivore. *Cultural Sociology*, 1(2), 143–164.

Wearing, S.L., & McDonald, M. (2015). Leisure and consumption. In: D.T. Cook & M.J. Ryan (Eds.) *The Wiley Blackwell encyclopedia of consumption and consumer studies* (pp. 381–383). Chichester: John Wiley & Sons.

Wheaton, B. (2010). Introducing the consumption and representation of lifestyle sports. *Sport in Society*, 13(7/8), 1057–1081.

Williams, R. (1977). *Marxism and literature*. London: Oxford University Press.

Williams, R. (1983). *Keywords: A vocabulary of culture and society*. Oxford: Oxford University Press.

Zukin, S., & Smith Maguire, J. (2004). Consumers and consumption. *Annual Review of Sociology*, 30, 173–197.

37

Fashion in consumer culture

Laurie A. Meamber, Annamma Joy and Alladi Venkatesh

Introduction

> Fashion can be considered "... a cultural phenomenon, (as) an aesthetic medium for the expression of ideas, desires and beliefs circulating in society"
>
> (*Wilson, 1985, p. 9*).

This quote by Elizabeth Wilson exploring fashion as an aesthetic mode of expression underscores the importance of fashion in contemporary culture, or more specifically, consumer culture in an aesthetic economy (Gaugele, 2015; Joy, Sherry, Venkatesh, Wang & Chan, 2012; Solomon, 1985). The study of consumer culture is certainly becoming an important area of inquiry. Scholars continue to study how fashion reflects prevailing cultural modes of bodily décor and ornamentation (Batterberry & Batterberry, 1977; English, 2007). Fashion has a long-standing history as a pervasive element in consumer culture, which has continued into contemporary culture (Barthes, 2006; Blumer, 1969; McCracken, 1988; Roche, 1994; Simmel, 1904/1971; Veblen, 1899/1925). The substance of fashion is considered simultaneously ambiguous and challenging because it is multi-dimensional and multi-contextual; it involves aesthetic content and meaning that change with time and space as well as cultural modes of behavior and expression, and elements of social distinction (Crane, 2000; Thompson & Haytko, 1997). Fashion is also equated with bodily adornment, involving more than just clothing and accessories (Ma, Shi, Chen & Luo, 2012), and extending to such elements as body piercing, tattoos, and the like. In this chapter our focus is primarily on (but not limited to) clothing and personal adornment and appearance, what role they play in the daily lives of fashion-conscious consumers, and the breadth of their exposure to fellow consumers (Bruzzi & Gibson, 2013). Just as there are multiple contexts of fashion, there are multiple definitions of fashion. In this chapter, we discuss fashion as a process in which the fashion system and object as well as fashion-related behaviors are aesthetic representations embedded in consumer culture (Entwistle, 2000).

What is fashion?

Fashion can be viewed as a style or appearance to be noticed, embraced, admired, and sometimes regarded critically (Venkatesh, Joy, Sherry & Deschenes, 2010). It can signify age, social status, and gender. For example, concerning social hierarchy, Veblen (1899/1925) and Simmel (1904/1971), taking a critical perspective, discussed novelty in fashion within a Western sociological context and as part and parcel of the consumption imperative of society. Simmel (1904/1971) describes the acceleration of fashion that occurred when the upper classes began to adopt the logic of distinction, and were compelled to engage in constant appearance innovation in order to escape the undermining of status markers by the appearance imitation of the masses.

While Simmel's (1904/1971) orientation was top-down, that is, fashion started at the top of society and moved downward, fashion is shown to operate from both the top-down and bottom-up (i.e., originating with consumers to fashion designers) in studies from around the world (Ma, Shi, Chen & Luo, 2012). While fashion, as noted previously implied status competition, as a display of wealth evolved into a display of style, today, the competitive display of wealth via fashion continues, but also provides the opportunity to mock status seeking.

Fashion-related behavior can represent a conscious effort to be socially provocative (Entwistle, 2009; Sproles, 1979). A way of describing fashion more inclusively is to consider it an object of consumption itself, whether as clothing or bodily adornments (Joy, Sherry, Troilo & Deschenes, 2010). In sum, fashion can simultaneously be considered an aesthetic system or representation in which objects are imbued with meaning and become aesthetically significant or "fashionable," so to speak. Some fashion scholars (e.g. Davis, 1992; Godart, 2012; Kaiser, 1990; Sproles, 1979) view fashion as a dynamic social process by which novel styles are created, introduced first to specific fashion-conscious segments, and then diffused more widely to the public at large. In other words, styles are experimented and promoted first among a select group of people at a particular point in time based on prevailing or novel tastes and cultural dispositions before they are disseminated more widely, resulting in acceptance or rejection (Rocamora & Smelik, 2015; Scott, 2005).

Fashion in a culturally constituted world and meaning transfer

McCracken's (1988) work on meaning transfer suggests that meaning moves from the culturally constituted world via modes of advertising and communication. Accordingly, the fashion system facilitates the diffusion of aesthetic goods and adoption by consumers via rituals of possession, exchange, grooming, and divestment. The culturally constituted world incorporates a system of categories and principles that may vary across sub-cultures of consumers. In essence, fashion as a communication system is dynamic, as meanings can evolve when the system connects consumers to goods or objects. The transfer of consumer objects to eventual adoption also occurs through a variety of rituals and systems of identity formation such as gift exchange.

More recent work on meaning transfer extends McCracken's model of cultural adoption (Venkatesh & Meamber, 2008). Culture and consumption are thus mutually constitutive and account for the constantly changing meaning flow in culture. The cultural production process provides opportunities for consumers to develop and form their own identities by consuming cultural products, such as fashion. Some other examples include the work of Polhemus (1994), which showed that there is freedom to sample a supermarket of styles or consume a pastiche of pluralistic fashion. Accordingly, while advertising and fashion systems may attempt to transfer agreed-upon cultural meanings to objects, the consumer can challenge these in their quest for self-identity within a fashion system. As Banister and Hogg (2007) suggest, fashion provides the consumer the opportunity to accept or reject fashion as "not me." There is thus a perennial tension between fashion discourses created by designers (and marketers) and the consumers whose unique, personal meanings can subvert the intended meaning.

Barthes (1967/1983) conceived of the fashion system as one of signs and language. Examining the written garment as found in fashion magazines, he proposed a relationship between images and text and the dissemination of fashion to individuals. Clothing is communicative and operates like a language, code, or a signaling system we use to convey our feelings, group identities, and sense of selves (Damhorst, 1999; McCracken & Roth, 1989). Accordingly, in this context, fashion becomes a code.

Given the important role of fashion in consumer culture, we approach fashion from an interdisciplinary perspective. Singular approaches and viewpoints on fashion can be questioned as being limited and potentially reductive (Barnard, 2007). To present a comprehensive overview of the subject, one has to consider the relations between fashion culture and marketing practices. Research on fashion cuts across disciplinary boundaries, including scholarly work in the social sciences, humanities, and cultural studies, and is critically examined in feminist discourse (Broby-Johansen, 1953; Flügel, 1930; Scaraboto & Fischer, 2013; Skov, 2002). Thus, for example, some early discourse on feminism has struggled with the subject of fashion (Parkins, 2008; Wilson, 1985), critically focusing on the body and the exploitation of body image (Joy & Venkatesh, 1994). In this chapter, we discuss fashion from a cultural standpoint. Here, for example, the body is central to the notion of fashion, and high fashion becomes wearable art. This in itself is indeed worthy of further inquiry.

Elements of fashion

Clothing styles and bodily adornments

According to Jensen (1999), clothing can be defined as a means of expression of style, and aesthetic appearance as a synthesis of styles of clothing and related accessories. Much of the early research on fashion in consumer culture has focused on clothing and personal adornment as well as psychological functions of clothing (Dearborn, 1918). Scholars consider clothes as integral to the fashion process, and fashion, in turn, as a key element of clothing culture. Jensen (1999) elaborates on the concept of style, which represents how fashion is displayed outwardly and also which is sometimes positioned in opposition to fashion (Östberg, 2011), which is considered intrinsic design.

The notion of fashion also extends beyond clothing to other aesthetic categories and a variety of bodily adornments comprising jewelry, cosmetics, and ornamentation, as well as tattoos and the like (Bloch & Richins, 1992; Langman, 2008). As shown by Bloch and Richins (1992), when considering the history of almost all cultures, such adornments contribute to a pervasive sense of attractiveness and have become indispensable to consumers' quest for beauty. According to Langman (2008), they also enhance consumers' self-esteem and empower them within their social milieu.

Fashion aesthetics

The original meaning of *aesthetics* can be traced back to the Greek word *aesthesis*, which refers to sensory perception (Barilli, 1989/1993). One meaning locates the sensory experience or response in relation to the arts, media, or entertainment, which includes its visual forms (Holbrook & Zirlin, 1985; Venkatesh, Joy, Sherry & Deschenes, 2010). This is especially true of high fashion or luxury fashion. Luxury brand stores are considered hybrids between retail stores and art galleries/museums that sell and display fashion (Joy, Wang, Chang, Sherry & Cui, 2014); fashion is considered a form of aesthetic creativity (Wilson, 1985).

A related meaning of *aesthetics*, which extends the original, refers to the sensorial experience of everyday objects (Forty, 1986; Heilbrun, 2002). Consumer scholars have used the sensorial idea of aesthetics to discuss fashion as adornment and the relation between the body and body image (Venkatesh et al., 2010). A third definition concerns the visual substance of aesthetics such as form, expression, harmony, order, symbolism, and imagery (Carroll, 2001). Sproles' (1979) model of fashion-oriented consumer behavior is premised on the idea that the aesthetics of fashion overwhelm merely utilitarian concerns (Eckman & Wagner, 1995). The perspectives on aesthetics mentioned here are key to understanding fashion.

Fashion, the body, and aesthetic labor

In consumer culture, there is a preoccupation with the body (Joy & Venkatesh, 1994) and adornment to augment physical attractiveness (Bloch & Richins, 1992). In terms of the relationship with the body, fashion not only adorns the body but also accentuates it. As noted by Venkatesh et al. (2010), "It has become a truism in studies of fashion that garments cannot signify without a body, real or imagined, and that even an unworn garment refers to the materiality of an eventual wearer" (p. 462). For some consumers, the pleasure of beautifying the body is to understand oneself as an artist and to exert cosmetic agency, leading to greater self-expression and satisfaction.

Research on the body and fashion integrates and extends work on aesthetics of the body found in marketing and consumer research, fashion theory, and gender studies, among other disciplines. Clothing reformers of the nineteenth century noted the different functions of fashion, which included decoration that in turn contrasted with the elements of modesty and protection for which it was originally intended (Flügel, 1930; Wilson, 1985). Unlike these "clothing reformers," twentieth-century thinkers (e.g., Baudrillard, 1981; Finkelstein, 1991), including psychologists, sociologists, anthropologists (e.g., Dunlap, 1928; Flügel, 1930; Westermarck, 1921), and cultural critics (e.g., Broby-Johansen, 1953), have considered fashion as a false extension of the wearer's true identity, and have argued against the need for such clothing unless it contributes to an honest representation of the body (Jensen, 1999). Sproles (1979) articulated the functions of dress more widely as contributing not only to utility (usefulness), modesty, and adornment (including psychological self-enhancement), but also to sexual attraction, symbolic differentiation, and social affiliation. Taking a communications perspective, Holman (1981) suggested that apparel functions include parasomatic, utilitarian, aesthetic, mnemonic, and emblematic elements. In this regard, the parasomatic, utilitarian, and somatic functions relate to the body. In other words, the parasomatic function of dress can camouflage (hide or alter) the body and/or display (reveal or draw attention away from) bodily elements. That is, the body becomes an object of fashionable attention (Barnard, 2007). While the utilitarian function of dress protects the body, the aesthetic element enhances the alluring element of the body.

Contemporary fashion theorists examine how fashion, particularly clothing and dress, contribute to the intensification of the normative aesthetics of the body. Work on the body and fashion highlights the role of embodiment, the consumer experience, and some socio-psychological elements (Thompson & Haytko, 1997, Venkatesh et al., 2010). These studies focus on attitudes and preferences concerning bodily appearance, as well as on perceptions of the aesthetics of luxury fashion – that is, dress and accessories. The resulting theoretical framework emphasizes the aesthetics of production, reception, and labor. The attention is on fashion as a cultural production process and system, leading to the notion of embodiment of fashion, and identity formation.

Embodiment can be explored at multiple levels (Pettinger, 2004). At the level of the fashion model, it refers to their physical features: the body and face that are carefully manipulated to display clothing and accessories. In this sense, models (as well as the consumers that are inspired by these models) engage in body modification/display practices (e.g., plastic surgery) in order to achieve a certain aesthetic ideal. As Venkatesh et al. (2010) noted, "... we see the body as an externalized object to be worked on by the self, as well as an integral aspect of the self... There is a lot of aesthetic labor that goes into sculpting oneself and one's appearance. Often, negative emotions and dissatisfaction with one's looks trigger aesthetic labor" (p. 467). Likewise, Parmentier & Fischer's (2011) work on fashion models suggests that while the models are operating within the realm of fashion, their identities are inscribed within the fashion system. As a result, models are anxious about conforming to its normative aspects such as maintaining an industry-accepted body weight. Mikkonen, Vicdan and Markkula's (2014) paper on wardrobe self-help literature indicates that consumers who adhere to these practices become self-critical about their bodies and are obliged to follow norms of dressing for their body type. In general, aesthetics and bodily appearance have become critical as fashion culture has begun to evolve and become a visually oriented culture (Schroeder, 2002).

"Fashion labor" or "aesthetic labor" has historically been associated with the production of garments and textiles by factory workers (also known as retail service workers). With the rise of the cotton industry in the West in the nineteenth century and extending to present day "sweat shops," we have witnessed the exploitation of aesthetic labor (for example, it is widely known that workers who toil and produce fashionable items typically work under unsafe and/or unhealthy conditions for low wages, Wilson, 1985).

Fashion, brands, and identity

In the late twentieth century, many social-science disciplines began to explore fashion and its role in understanding cultural phenomena, identity construction, and the role of consumption in the constitution of self and society. Hetzel (1994) suggested that fashion affects all sectors of activity in which a fashion object contributes to the construction of an individual's personality. Sahlins (1976) characterized the system of American clothing as a veritable map of American cultural ambiance. Broby-Johansen (1953) described clothing as a second skin to the self or as a magnification of one's self. Because of its visibility and close connection to the body, clothing creates a bridge between the cultural meaning of objects and the individual consumer's self-concept, signifying associations with brands and lifestyles (Jensen, 1999).

Consumers appropriate cultural products, such as fashion, for their functionality as well as for their symbolism. In the case of fashion objects, symbolism extends to such intrinsic aspects as fabric (Weiner & Schneider, 1989), color (Schneider, 1987), and design (Lurie, 1981). Consumer research suggests that consumption contributes to identity formation (Ekström & Brembeck, 2004; Wattanasuswan, 2005). This is certainly true of fashion. Finkelstein (1991) proposed that the notion of self is often equated with one's fashion image. As Shankar, Elliott, and Fitchett (2009) also noted, identity is no longer thought of as a unitary, fixed, or stable property, but rather that which is constantly assembled, reassembled, produced, and re-reproduced. Fashion therefore contributes to consumers' self-definition. That is, consumers can create meanings for themselves to incorporate or subvert the dominant fashion discourses created by designers and marketers. By extension, consumers are able to appropriate fashion discourses and generate unique fashion identities while at the same time resisting dominant fashion narratives.

This is not to argue that consumer identity is a matter of complete free choice; such identities are also influenced by marketers. The social and historical realities impacting identity projects suggest that different actors play a role in the formation of cultural capital (Bourdieu, 1984). In this regard, we argue that consumers are co-producers of meaning, whether it is personal, identity-related, and/or group-level meaning.

An area of inquiry in consumer research extends to the formation of fashion-consciousness. For example, Gould and Stern (1989) examined gender differences among fashion-consciousness and the relationship to self-identity. Not surprisingly, in terms of clothing, women were found more likely to be fashion-conscious than men. In addition, Wan, Youn, and Fang (2001) found that a diverse set of factors such as brand consciousness, healthy eating, attitudes towards technology, socially sensitive sexual issues, and advertising skepticism also relate to the development of fashion consciousness. Other research has extended this line of inquiry. Auty and Elliott (1998) considered the role of self-monitoring and brand patronage in fashion involvement. Tatzel (1982) considered consumer skill to be related to fashion consciousness, and Gorden, Infante, and Braun (1985) studied communicator styles. Other studies have focused on demographic differences pertaining to engagement with fashion, matters of affluence (Belleau, Haney, Summers, Xu & Garrison, 2008), and materialism (O'Cass, 2004). In this regard, age becomes an important variable because young consumers through to teenagers (Hogg, Bruce & Hill, 1998; Kjeldgaard, 2009) and other age cohorts play a critical role. This research collectively indicates that fashion awareness and preferences begin at an early age and are influenced by exposure to market elements and brands, as well as to social elements that include the influence of family and friendship groups.

Another important variable in the formation of fashion consciousness is the significance and the role of the brand itself. Consumers use brand images to construct and communicate their identities (Elliott & Wattanasuswan, 1998; Wikström, 1996). In related research, Sproles (1979) took an information-processing perspective and proposed that fashion-oriented behavior implies that consumers make decisions based on style and brand-related information. Yet, other more contemporary research indicates that fashion-conscious consumers value brand names and make branded fashion purchases because they are closely related to identity formation (Wan et al., 2001). For example, Hokkanen's (2014) text on Swedish fashion consumers found that consumption of particular fashion brands were used to communicate the personalities and identities of these adults, particularly in social situations.

As proposed by Björkman (2002), consumers incorporate the brand or designer symbolism into their own identities, and thus the meanings are subject to (re)interpretation. In wearing the clothing, consumers communicate its brand symbolism to others, and simultaneously develop, encode, and reinforce the organizational (designer, brand) identity found in the marketplace. Nevertheless, if consumers choose to construct alternate meanings for fashion, this can change or even undermine the intended organizational or marketplace identity (Kozinets, 2002). Therefore, while fashion is communicative, it does not convey or express a single meaning (Barnard, 2007).

Recent fashion trends and future research

More recent work on fashion trends has focused on the interrelated subjects of sustainable fashion, eco-fashion, and ethical clothing (Beard, 2008; Niinimäki, 2010). In general, these topics refer to fashion design, sourcing, manufacturing, and wear that does not do unnecessary harm to the environment and has a positive impact on people and communities (Hethorn & Ulasewicz, 2015). Many of the studies on sustainable fashion consumption underscore that while consumers do care about the origins and production of fashionable items and have strong ethical values, quality and aesthetics are equally or more important in making fashion choices (Joergens, 2006). For example, historical treatments on the origins of ethical or eco-fashion trends do incorporate such elements as "natural" looks (Welters, 2008).

While recent research has attempted to classify sustainable fashion consumers by gender, attitudes, values, or purchasing intentions and behavior in different cultures (e.g, D'Souza, Gilmore, Harmann, Apaolaza Ibáñez & Sullivan-Mort, 2015; Jung & Jin, 2016; McNeill & Moore, 2015), additional work should focus on the lifeworld of these consumers more generally and how fashion is integrated into their lives. Work by Jung & Jin (2016) identifies potentially four distinct sustainable consumer groups in the United States and suggests consumer education approaches to reach them. Future research can extend this work to other cultural contexts and to test communication approaches that were highlighted in the article.

Extensions of research on sustainability include upcycle fashion design (Kwan, 2012), in which consumers (as producers/designers) take clothing and refashion it into something new, and which has contributed to the reinvention of the resale (thrift) industry. Future work can also consider potential parallels between ethical consumption in other arenas and fashion, such as the idea of leasing or renting clothing beyond just high-fashion or for special occasions but on a regular basis, just as car-sharing has been embraced in many parts of the world. More generally, further research on sustainability can examine questions on the potential for societal change in both the production and consumption processes.

Other related areas of study have included fast fashion and slow fashion. Fast fashion involves producing and making low-cost fashion available quickly for consumers in the marketplace (Cachon & Swinney, 2011). Fast fashion mimics current luxury fashion trends, but as with ethical fashion, fast-fashion consumers, while concerned with the environment, often engage in consumption practices that are contrary to this concern (Joy et al., 2012). In contrast, slow fashion refers to fashion that takes into consideration the design, production, and consumption of clothing, and its effects on people and the eco-system more generally (Pookulangara & Shephard, 2013). While fast fashion is both time and taste oriented, slow fashion is usually defined as a philosophical orientation focusing on being attentive to and mindful of all the stakeholders and impacts of fashion, rather than a slowing down of the production process, although this can occur.

The study of slow fashion and its attention to all stakeholders also relates to fashion labor, as discussed previously. Slow fashion has more recently assumed the role of a consumer movement, partly inspired by the Rana Plaza disaster in Bangladesh in 2013 (Fletcher & Tham, 2015) where a building collapsed, resulting in over a thousand workers losing their lives while making clothes for the fashion industry. Slow-fashion consumers are interested in clothing that is eco and labor friendly. As the collection of readings in Fletcher and Tham's (2015) handbook suggests, fashion, while perhaps contributing to the economic empowerment of women globally via employment, can at the same time be exploitative and contribute to pollution, waste, and an overall decline of the eco-system. More attention should be devoted to the study of slow fashion, including consumers' desire to reflect on their fashion choices (Clark, 2008; Fletcher, 2010) and practices which encourage this reflection, such as on the potential of new labeling standards for clothing – including sourcing of materials, compliance with labor practices, etc., similar to discussions on labeling food and other products that have occurred in many countries.

Other studies on fashion focus on global aspects of fashion marketing and consumption, including the visibility and invisibility in fashion globally. Gurova's (2014) volume on the rise of fashion in Russia and its transformation of Russia over the last two decades highlights the role of fashion in constituting consumer culture. Sandikci and Ger's (2010) discussion on veiling in style emphasizes the politics of fashion and how a stigmatized practice of veiling in Turkey becomes fashionable. Sobh, Belk and Gressel's (2014) study of fashion invisibility sheds light on how Middle Eastern consumers engage with global fashion brands and tend to create an identity that incorporates both Western consumer culture and Islamic conservatism. Findings suggest that consumers in this part of the world engage in practices such as layering in order to hide luxurious Western fashion underneath religiously approved outer garments and thus embrace and mimic the Western excess of consumption of luxury brands. These consumers exhibit the conflicting narratives of modesty and vanity in their clothing choices. While these studies focus on relatively affluent consumers in several Middle Eastern countries, other work suggests the emergence of a cross-faith, transnational youth subculture of modest fashion (Lewis, 2015). Future research can explore the relationships and contradictions inherent in the global fashion production and consumption arena. For example, Arvidsson and Malossi's (2011) piece on customer co-creation, and Arvidsson and Niessen's (2015) article on Bangkok fashion markets illustrate alternative approaches to fashion innovation outside of the traditional fashion system.

Conclusions

Research on fashion spanning multiple cultures, multiple disciplines, and multiple centuries will continue to be an important facet of understanding consumer culture. As Kaiser (1990) put it, "the challenge of explaining fashion change across historical and cultural contexts remains" (p. 481). Research gaps include re-examining the definition of fashion in relation to sustainability, linking sustainable fashion studies to how meaning moves in the culturally constituted world, and on global fashion culture. Questions that can be addressed are: Is it possible to reconcile the inherent contradiction between fashion and sustainability from the consumer's perspective – the tension between the emphasis on the new (or in the case of fast fashion – the new and the quick) and the harm associated with fashion production and consumption? Can the global fashion industry influence individual and societal desire for fashion that is more intrinsically sustainable? Does silence on sustainability limit the potential for transforming consumer behavior and the global fashion industry at large? For example, a recent piece by Solér, Baeza, and Svärd (2016) examines fashion brand discourse, and in particular those "muted" sustainable fashion brands that attempt to reduce their negative environmental and social impact, but do not communicate this in their branding and communications. Future research can continue to examine brand management and marketing approaches used by fashion producers and the consequences of this for consumers and society at large. As a dynamic social process, fashion will be discussed and debated for many years to come.

The authors would like to acknowledge receipt of a grant from the Social Sciences and Humanities Research Council of Canada [No: 435-2013-1211].

References

Arvidsson, A., & Malossi, G. (2011). Customer co-production from social factory to brand: Learning from Italian fashion. In D. Zwick & J. Cayla (Eds.), *Inside marketing: Practices, ideologies, devices* (pp. 212–397). Oxford: Oxford University Press.

Arvidsson, A., & Niessen, B. (2015). Creative mass. Consumption, creativity, and innovation on Bangkok's fashion markets. *Consumption Markets & Culture*, 18, 111–132.

Auty, S., & Elliott, R. (1998). Fashion involvement, self-monitoring and the meaning of brands. *Journal of Product & Brand Management*, 7, 109–123.

Banister, E.N., & Hogg, M.K. (2007). Consumers and their negative selves, and the implications for fashion marketing. In T. Hines & M. Bruce (Eds.), *Fashion marketing: Contemporary issues* (pp. 190–202). Oxford, UK: Elsevier.

Barilli, R. (1993). *A course on aesthetics*. (K.E. Pinkus, Trans.). Minneapolis: University of Minnesota Press. (Original work published 1989).

Barnard, M. (2007). *Fashion theory: A reader*. London: Routledge.

Barthes, R. (1983). *The fashion system*. (M. Ward & R. Howard, Trans.). New York, NY: Hill & Wang. (Original work published 1967).

Barthes, R. (2006). *The language of fashion*. Sydney, AU: Power Publications.
Batterberry, M., & Batterberry, A.R. (1977). *Mirror, mirror: A social history of fashion*. New York, NY: Holt Rinehart & Winston.
Baudrillard, J. (1981). *For a critique of the political economy of the sign*. St. Louis, MO: Telos Press.
Beard, N. (2008). The branding of ethical fashion and the consumer: A luxury niche or a mass market reality? *Fashion Theory*, 12, 447–468.
Belleau, B., Haney, R., Summers, T., Xu, Y., & Garrison, B. (2008). Affluent female consumers and fashion involvement. *International Journal of Fashion Design*, Technology and Education, 1, 103–112.
Björkman, I. (2002). Aura: Aesthetic business creativity. *Consumption, Markets & Culture*, 5, 69–78.
Bloch, P.H., & Richins, M.L. (1992). You look 'marvelous': The pursuit of beauty and the marketing concept. *Psychology and Marketing*, 9, 3–15.
Blumer, H. (1969). Fashion: From class differentiation to collective selection. *The Sociological Quarterly*, 10, 275–291.
Bourdieu, P. (1984). *Distinction: A social critique of the judgment of taste*. Cambridge, MA: Harvard University Press.
Broby-Johansen, R. (1953). *Krop og klaer.* Copenhagen, DK: Gyldendal.
Bruzzi, S., & Gibson, P.C. (Eds.). (2013). *Fashion cultures revisited: Theories, explorations and analysis*. London: Routledge.
Cachon, G.P., & Swinney, R. (2011). The value of fast fashion: Quick response, enhanced design, and strategic consumer behavior. *Management Science*, 57, 778–795.
Carroll, N. (2001). *Beyond aesthetics: Philosophical essays*. Cambridge: Cambridge University Press.
Clark, H. (2008). Slow + fashion – an oxymoron – or a promise for the future . . .? Fashion Theory: *The Journal of Dress, Body and Culture*, 12, 427–446.
Crane, D. (2000). *Fashion and its social agendas: Class, gender, and identity in clothing.* Chicago: University of Chicago Press.
Damhorst, M. (1999). Dress as nonverbal communication. In M. Damhorst, K. Miller & S. Michelman (Eds.), *The meanings of dress* (pp. 78–89). New York, NY: Fairchild.
Davis, F. (1992). *Fashion, culture, and identity*. Chicago: University of Chicago Press.
Dearborn, G. (1918). The psychology of clothing. *Psychological Review Monographs*, 26, 1–72.
D'Souza, C., Gilmore, A.J., Hartmann, P., Apaolaza Ibáñez, V., & Sullivan-Mort, G. (2015). Male eco-fashion: A market reality. *International Journal of Consumer Studies*, 39, 35–42.
Dunlap, K. (1928). The development and function of clothing. *Journal of General Psychology*, 1, 64–78.
Eckman, M., & Wagner, J. (1995). Aesthetic aspects of the consumption of fashion design: The conceptual and empirical challenge. In F. R. Kardes and M. Sujan (Eds.), *Advances in Consumer Research* (pp. 646–649). Provo, UT: Association for Consumer Research.
Ekström, K., & Brembeck, H. (Eds.). (2004). *Elusive consumption*. Oxford, UK: Berg.
Elliott, R., & Wattanasuwan, K. (1998). Brands as symbolic resources for the construction of identity. *International Journal of Advertising*, 17, 131–144.
English, B. L. (2007). *A cultural history of fashion in the 20th century: From the catwalk to the sidewalk*. New York, NY: Berg.
Entwistle, J. (2000). *The fashioned body: Fashion, dress, and modern social theory.* Cambridge, UK: Polity Press.
Entwistle, J. (2009). *The aesthetic economy of fashion: Markets and value in clothing and modeling.* Oxford, UK: Bloomsbury Academic.
Finkelstein, J. (1991). *The fashioned self.* Cambridge, UK: Polity Press.
Fletcher, K. (2010). Slow fashion: An invitation for systems change. *Fashion Practice*, 2, 259–266.
Fletcher, K., & Tham, M. (Eds.). (2015). *Routledge handbook of sustainability and fashion*. London: Routledge.
Flügel, J.C. (1930). *The psychology of clothes*. London: Hogarth Press.
Forty, A. (1986). *Objects of desire: Design and society since 1750*. London: Thames and Hudson.
Gaugele, E. (Ed.) (2015). *Aesthetic politics in fashion*. Berlin, DE: Sternberg Press.
Godart, F. (2012). *Unveiling fashion: Business, culture and identity in the most glamorous industry.* Basingstoke, UK: Palgrave Macmillan.
Gorden, W.I., Infante, D.A., & Braun, A.A. (1985). Communicator style and fashion innovativeness. In M.R. Solomon (Ed.), *The psychology of fashion* (pp. 161–176). Lexington, MA: Lexington Books.
Gould, S.J., & Stern, B.B. (1989). Gender schema and fashion consciousness. *Psychology and Marketing*, 6, 129–145.
Gurova, O. (Ed.). (2014). *Fashion and the consumer revolution in Contemporary Russia*. New York, NY: Routledge.

Heilbrun, B. (2002). Alessi: Italian design and the re-enchantment of everyday objects. In M. Solomon, G. Bamossy, and S. Askegaard (Eds.), *Consumer behavior: A European perspective* (pp. 569–673). Harlow, UK: Prentice Hall.

Hethorn, J., & Ulasewicz, C. (2015). *Sustainable fashion: What's next?* New York, NY: Bloomsbury.

Hetzel, P. (1994). The role of fashion and design in a postmodern society: What challenges for firms? In M.J. Baker (Ed.), *Perspectives on marketing management* (pp. 97–118). London: John Wiley & Sons.

Hogg, M., Bruce, M., & Hill, A. (1998). Fashion brand preferences among young consumers. *International Journal of Retail & Distribution Management*, 26, 293–300.

Hokkanen, S. (2014). *Fashion brands and consumption in postmodern consumer culture: The construction of self and social identities* (Unpublished masters thesis). Swedish School of Textiles, University of Boras, Boras, Sweden.

Holbrook, M.B., & Zirlin, R.B. (1985). Artistic creation, artworks, and aesthetic appreciation: Some philosophical contributions to nonprofit marketing. In R.W. Belk (Ed.), *Advances in nonprofit marketing* (pp. 1–54). Greenwich, CT: JAI Press.

Holman, R. (1981). Apparel as communication. In E.C. Hirschman & M.B. Holbrook (Eds.), *Symbolic consumer behavior: Proceedings of the conference on consumer esthetics and symbolic consumption* (pp. 7–15). Provo, UT: Association for Consumer Research.

Jensen, A.F. (1999). *Acknowledging and consuming fashion in the era after good taste* (Unpublished dissertation). Odense University, Odense, Denmark.

Joergens, C. (2006). Ethical fashion: Myth or future trend? *Journal of Fashion Marketing and Management*, 10, 360–71.

Joy, A., Sherry, J.F., Troilo, R., & Deschenes, J. (2010). Re-thinking the relationship between self and other: Levinas and narratives of beautifying the body. *Journal of Consumer Culture*, 10, 33–361.

Joy, A., Sherry, J.F., Venkatesh, A., Wang, J., & Chan, R. (2012). Fast fashion, sustainability, and the ethical appeal of luxury brands. *Fashion Theory*, 16, 273–295.

Joy, A., & Venkatesh, A. (1994). Postmodernism, feminism, and the body: The visible and the invisible in consumer research. *International Journal of Research in Marketing*, 11, 333–357.

Joy, A., Wang, J.J., Chan, T-S., Sherry, J.F., & Cui, G. (2014). M(Art) worlds: Consumer perceptions of how luxury brand stores become art institutions. *Journal of Retailing*, 90, 347–364.

Jung, S. & Jin, B. (2016). From quantity to quality: Understanding slow fashion consumers for sustainability and consumer education. *International Journal of Consumer Studies*, 40, 410–421.

Kaiser, S.B. (1990). *The social psychology of clothing – Symbolic appearances in context*. New York, NY: Macmillan.

Kjeldgaard, D. (2009). The meaning of style? Reflexivity among Danish high school youths. *Journal of Consumer Behavior*, 8, 71–83.

Kozinets, R.V. (2002). Can consumers escape the market? Emancipatory illuminations from Burning Man. *Journal of Consumer Research*, 29, 20–38.

Kwan, J-S. (2012). Based on the perspective of sustainability, the characteristics of upcycle fashion design. *Fashion & Textile Research Journal*, 41, 13–23.

Langman L. (2008). Punk, porn and resistance: Carnivalization and the body in popular culture. *Current Sociology*, 56, 657–677.

Lewis, R. (2015). *Muslim fashion: Contemporary style cultures*. Durham, NC: Duke University Press.

Lurie, A. (1981). *The language of clothes*. New York, NY: Random House.

Ma, F., Shi, H., Chen, L., & Luo, Y. (2012). A theory of fashion. *Journal of Management and Strategy*, 3, 84–92.

McCracken, G.D. (1988). *Culture and consumption*. Bloomington: Indiana University Press.

McCracken, G.D., & Roth, V. (1989). Does clothing have a code? Empirical findings and theoretical implications in the study of clothing as a means of communication. *International Journal of Research in Marketing*, 6, 13–33.

McNeill, L. & Moore, R. (2015). Sustainable fashion consumption and the fast fashion conundrum: Fashionable consumers and attitudes to sustainability in clothing choice. *International Journal of Consumer Studies*, 39, 212–222.

Mikkonen, I., Vicdan, H., & Markkula, A. (2014). What not to wear? Oppositional ideology, fashion, and governmentality in Wardrobe self-help. *Consumption Markets & Culture*, 17, 254–273.

Niinimaki, K. (2010). Eco-clothing, consumer identity and ideology. *Sustainable Development*, 18, 150–160.

O'Cass, A. (2004). Fashion clothing consumption: Antecedents and consequences of fashion clothing involvement. *European Journal of Marketing*, 38, 869–882.

Östberg, J. (2011). Style. In D. Southerton (Ed.), *The encyclopedia for consumer culture* (pp. 1389–1391). Thousand Oaks, CA: Sage.

Parkins, I. (2008). Building a feminist theory of fashion: Karen Barad's agential realism. *Australian Feminist Studies*, 23, 501–515.

Parmentier, M-A., & Fischer, E. (2011). You can't always get what you want: Unsustainable identity projects in the fashion system. *Consumption Markets & Culture*, 14, 7–27.

Pettinger, L. (2004). Brand culture and branded workers: Service work and aesthetic labour in fashion retail. *Consumption Markets & Culture*, 7, 165–184.

Polhemus, T. (1994). *Street style: From sidewalk to catwalk*. London: Thames & Hudson.

Pookulangara, S., & Shephard, A. (2013). Slow fashion movement: Understanding consumer perceptions – an exploratory study. *Journal of Retailing and Consumer Services*, 20, 200–206.

Rocamora, A., & Smelik, A. (Eds.). (2015). *Thinking through fashion: A guide to key theorists*. London: I.B. Tauris.

Roche, D. (1994). *The culture of clothing – Dress and fashion in the "ancien régime"*. Cambridge, UK: Cambridge University Press.

Sahlins, M. (1976). *Culture and practical reason*. Chicago: University of Chicago Press.

Sandikci, Ö., & Ger, G. (2010). Veiling in style: How does a stigmatized practice become fashionable? *Journal of Consumer Research*, 37, 15–36.

Scaraboto, D., & Fischer, E. (2013). Frustrated fatshionistas: An institutional theory perspective on consumer quests for greater choice in mainstream markets. *Journal of Consumer Research*, 39, 1234–1257.

Schneider, J. (1987). The anthropology of cloth. *Annual Review of Anthropology*, 16, 409–448.

Schroeder, J.E. (2002). *Visual consumption*. London: Routledge.

Scott, L. (2005). *Fresh lipstick: Redressing fashion and femininism*. New York, NY: Palgrave Macmillan.

Shankar, A., Elliott, R., & Fitchett, J. (2009). Consumption, identity and narratives of socialization. *Marketing Theory*, 9, 75–94.

Simmel, G. (1971). Fashion. In D.N. Levine (Ed.), *On individuality and social forms, selected writings* (pp. 294–323). Chicago: University of Chicago Press. (Original work published 1904).

Skov, L. (2002). Hong Kong fashion designers as cultural intermediaries: Out of global garment production. *Cultural Studies*, 16, 553–69.

Sobh, R., Belk, R.W., & Gressel, J. (2014). Mimicry and modernity in the Middle East: Fashion invisibility and young women of the Arab Gulf. *Consumption Markets & Culture*, 17, 392–412.

Solér, C., Baeza, J., & Svärd, C. (2016). Construction of silence on issues of sustainability through branding in the fashion market. *Journal of Marketing Management*, 31, 216–246.

Solomon, M.R. (Ed.). (1985). *The psychology of fashion*. Lexington, MA: D.C. Heath.

Sproles, G.B. (1979). *Fashion: Consumer behavior toward dress*. Minneapolis, MN: Burgess.

Tatzel, M. (1982). Skill and motivation in clothes shopping: Fashion conscious, independent, anxious, and apathetic consumers. *Journal of Retailing*, 58, 90–97.

Thompson, C., & Haytko, D. (1997). Speaking of fashion: Consumers' uses of fashion discourses and the appropriation of countervailing cultural meanings. *Journal of Consumer Research*, 24, 15–42.

Veblen, T. (1925). *Theory of the leisure class*. London: Unwin. (Original work published 1899).

Venkatesh, A., Joy, A., Sherry, J.F., & Deschenes, J. (2010). The aesthetics of luxury fashion, body, and identity formation. *Journal of Consumer Psychology*, 20, 459–470.

Venkatesh, A., & Meamber, L.A. (2008). The aesthetics of consumption and the consumer as an aesthetic subject. *Consumption, Markets & Culture*, 11, 45–70.

Wan, F., Youn, S., & Fang, T. (2001). Passionate surfers in image driven consumer culture: Fashion-conscious, appearance savvy people and their way of life. In M.C. Gilly & J. Meyers-Levy (Eds.), *Advances in consumer research* (pp. 266–274). Valdosta, GA: Association for Consumer Research.

Wattanasuswan, K. (2005). The self and symbolic consumption. *Journal of American Academy of Business*, 6, 179–184.

Weiner, A., & Schneider, J. (1989). *Cloth and human experience*. Washington, DC: Smithsonian University Press.

Welters, L. (2008). The natural look: American style in the 1970s. *Fashion Theory*, 12, 489–510.

Westermarck, E.A. (1921). *History of human marriage*. London: MacMillan.

Wikström, S. (1996). The consumer as co-producer. *European Journal of Marketing*, 30, 6–19.

Wilson, E. (1985). *Adorned in dreams: Fashion and modernity*. Berkeley: University of California Press.

38

Luxury consumption and luxury brands

Past, present, and future

Annamma Joy, Russell Belk and Rishi Bhardwaj

Introduction

Luxury – its meaning, accessibility, and desirability – continually evolves, with one seemingly entrenched trend subtly and incrementally (or not so subtly and quite dramatically) replaced by another. Yet through the eras, some venerable luxury brands have retained their allure, even as they incorporate prevailing trends. An Hermès handbag, for example, is as indicative of luxury today as when it was first introduced at the turn of the twentieth century. In this paper, we limn the evolution of luxury and of luxury brands over time: how such brands are perceived, what market segments they target, and what the implications of current research reveal about brands' impacts on social constructs. Additionally, we discuss specific areas of luxury marketing and consumption deserving of further research. How do conceptions of luxury in the past inform the experience of luxury in the present? How will luxury goods be perceived and consumed in the future?

First, to understand current perceptions of luxury, we consider its terminology. As an experiment in the language of luxury, Joy, Wang, Chan, Sherry, and Cui (2014) elide *art* and *mart* to describe the new world of luxury retail environments in which a brand's core narrative defines luxury as art, resulting in the phrase *M(Art)Worlds*. They find that terms such as *market* or *mart* fall short of capturing what such luxury brands as Louis Vuitton, Hermès, and Bottega Veneta, among others, have accomplished in incorporating art within their identities. In the course of their research, they develop additional terms: *luxetecture*, which references the dazzling architecture of luxury stores; *(de)luxe*, which applies to the lighting design that enables visitors to experience luxury stores as exclusive, welcoming, and exciting spaces; and *luxedesigners*, which captures the role of iconic designers in defining a luxury brand. *Luxescapes* defines attention to detail and service, while *luxeart foundations* refers to the alliances of luxury brand corporations with renowned artists.

The terms above represent the experience of luxury brand consumers in the present. What of the future? The Comité Colbert, an association of seventy-eight French luxury brands and fourteen cultural institutions, including the Musée Du Louvre and the Musée d'Orsay, took as its mission to "promote the concept of luxury". Founded in 1954, the association celebrated sixty years in 2013; its efforts in deploying France's "art de vivre, creativity and craftsmanship into economic strength and influence in the world" (Comité Colbert, 2014, p. 2) have effectively positioned France as a global economic powerhouse of luxury brands. In 2014, the association embarked on a social media campaign to envision how the luxury brand industry might appear sixty years in the future, and what new marketing phrases might apply (King, 2014).

Aesthetics, beauty, form, magic, and creativity appear as common themes underlying these terms, with many referring to artistic innovations that encourage indulging in dreams, and experiencing pleasure and transcendence through both materiality and immateriality. The new terms created by the French linguist Alain Rey in collaboration with the Comité Colbert (2014, pp. 272–276) are "portmanteau" words, combining meanings at odds with each other. For example, *noventique* combines innovation with newness ("nouveau") and authenticity, as new and old collide. Such melding of seemingly opposing concepts is exactly what the Comité Colbert and Alain Rey see as inevitable, with their argument in essence already confirmed, as luxury brands evolve to target culture-specific tastes, which can be in opposition to those of other cultures; to meet the needs of the aspirational middle class, which can similarly be counter to those of the upper classes, and to sate the desires of the long-established wealthy versus those of the newly wealthy, who often engage in markedly different consumption patterns (Joy, Sherry, & Wang, 2016). With this document, The Colbert Committee not only has its overall future strategy in place, but also has provoked its members to develop company-based strategies and tactics to take action.

Below, we identify the current state of knowledge regarding luxury consumption and luxury brands, tracing their origins from antiquity through the present trend of Western conceptions of luxury taking root in emerging economies in China and India. We explore the seldom-investigated fundamental concept of consumer dreams of luxury products and experiences (d'Astous & Deschenes, 2005). How do such dreams differ from consumer aspirations and desires (Belk, Ger, & Askergaard, 2003)? Belk (2011) questions consumer envy and distinguishes between benign envy (which he suggests drives luxury purchase behavior in Western contexts) and malignant envy, which occurs when consumers lack the means to personally experience luxury. The concepts of hybridization and mimesis (Sobh, Belk, & Gressel, 2014) uncover the meanings of luxury in India and China. We provide a scholarly perspective on past and extant research on the concept of luxury brands. In conclusion, we summarize our findings and identify areas of potential future research.

The roots of luxury, luxury consumption, and luxury marketing

Luxury is not new. Luxury items appear in the earliest recorded history, when revered political and religious figures were buried with costly jewels and other precious objects (Kapferer & Bastein, 2009). Consumers from various strata of society such as merchants, craftsmen, and money lenders emerged in Europe at the beginning of the thirteenth century with access to luxury (Kovesi, 2015). Romans were the first to use the term *luxury* as a disparaging word for wealthy elites who abandoned Roman virtues of using wealth for public good (Kovesi, 2015). Over time, the industrial classes also discovered discrete worlds of luxury (Veblen, 1899/2007).

Luxury brands are the pinnacle of a hierarchical brand structure, even as the definition of luxury remains highly subjective, varying according to individual tastes, cultures, and socio-economic status, and differing between consumers in emerging economies versus those in the developed world. Heine's (2012, p. 62) definition of luxury brands offers perhaps the most insight: "Luxury brands . . . comprise associations about a high level of price, quality, aesthetics, rarity, extraordinariness and a high degree of non-functional associations". As Brun and Castelli (2013) note, the concept of luxury is fluid, dependent on social and political structures.

To meet the needs of an ever-more-inclusive consumer base, luxury brands now offer a hierarchy of products, starting with affordable luxury (D'Arpizio, 2007) via relatively lower price points targeting middle-class consumers, a tactic that has diluted some luxury brands (Danziger, 2004; Nueño & Quelch, 1998; Silverstein & Fiske, 2003). Truong, McColl, and Kitchen (2009) disagree, concluding that luxury brands can maintain brand prestige while targeting mass markets (e.g., Karl Lagerfeld designing for H&M), as evidenced by mass prestige (termed "masstige") brands. Forty percent of today's luxury goods market comprises aspirational luxury brands, targeting middle- to upper-class consumers, in contrast to absolute luxury, which caters exclusively to those for whom price is irrelevant (Hoffmann & Coste-maniere, 2012, p. 63). Such contemporary struggles are not new and could be identified as powerful forces in earlier centuries.

Mukerji (1983), in her attempt at "excavating the underpinnings of Industrial capitalism" (p. 254), draws our attention to the materialism that preceded and promoted it. She looks at materialism in trade, productive processes, and consumption that promoted accumulation of goods and luxuries in the sixteenth century. McCracken (1988, pp. 14–19) takes this further in identifying the political underpinnings of conspicuous consumption in Queen Elizabeth I's court and its reverberating impact on the localities from which her nobles were drawn. The theater of spectacle, deleterious as it was on family loyalty and consumption, gave way to more individualistic forms of display. Hence, the importance of fashion and not patina is of high import in this process of status competition. The advent of the consumer explosion of the eighteenth century can be found in these beginnings. The trickle-down effect then became a powerful source for conspicuous consumption in the eighteenth and nineteenth centuries, giving rise to the founding of department stores and the escalation of consumption as part of individual and family life.

More recently, with the growth of the middle class in developed and reconstructed nations following WWII, luxury's reach extended farther. Initially limited to cities in Europe, luxury brands gradually expanded, with their goods manufactured on a far larger scale; by the late twentieth century, such brands were targeting a worldwide audience (Kapferer & Bastien, 2009) with their efforts spurred by globalization, communications technology such as e-commerce, and emerging economies in China and India. Today, anyone with online access can experience desire for, and potentially purchase, luxury products. Luxury consumption is in an upward spiral according to Wang (2010, p. 181), with the global luxury market expected to exceed US$400 billion by 2019 (Euromonitor, 2015a).

With the advent of classic brands such as Louis Vuitton (founded in 1854), Cartier (1947), Chanel (1909), Gucci (1921), and Hermès (1837), among others, France and Italy have become recognized as the birthplaces of luxury brands, with the brands serving as silent ambassadors for their respective country of origin. Louis Vuitton's flagship store in Paris, for example, is a heritage store embodying the sense of time conveyed by museum exhibits. Urde, Greyser, and Balmer (2007, p. 5) consider heritage "a dimension of a brand's identity found in its track record, longevity, core values, use of symbols and particularly in an organizational belief that its history is important". Eight of the top ten luxury brands are owned and managed by individual families, with ownership routinely passing from one generation to the next (the Millward Brown Report, 2013). Founders, CEOs, and high-profile designers are also associated with a brand's heritage, essentially serving as honorary family members. Dion and Arnould (2011) identify the importance of the creative director of luxury brands (e.g., Marc Jacobs) as someone who offers an aesthetic brand ideology. "Luxury retail draws on the principles of art and magic to assemble the charismatic persona of the creative director and to diffuse his/her aesthetic ideology to the brand" (p. 502).

Unlike other brands, luxury brands are perceived as art crafted with labour-intensive detail and high-quality materials (Berthon, Pitt, Parent, & Berthon, 2009; Joy, Wang, Chan, Sherry, & Cui, 2014). As with works of art, the dream quality associated with such products is heightened via limited editions or the design involvement of recognized artists such as Takahashi Murakami with Louis Vuitton, enhancing an aura of exclusivity and investment value typically embodied in works of art. Exclusivity implies rarity, whether of rare materials, an artistic use of technology, or limited editions (Catry, 2003). Such products are sold only in certain stores, with limited promotion. While luxury may be sold online, information rarity is not compromised. To construct and sustain the dream, luxury must communicate beyond the target market, even as it offers an exclusive experience, termed *invisible luxury* (Kapferer, 2012, p. 461), such as the presentation of unique items from a store's archives, or entrance to a store's inner sanctum. Ironically, today luxury connoisseurs seek out little-known brands whose desirability lies in their exclusivity (Eckhardt, Belk, & Wilson, 2015).

Luxury is often associated with dream worlds (Dubois & Paternault, 1995; Comite Colbert, 2014). The experience of opulence – a high price that reaffirms rarity, the feel of fine fabrics, and bespoke quality – has significant appeal to consumers and provides them a strong sense of self-worth (Joy et al., 2014). The value of hedonism is intrinsic to luxury goods consumption, just as the symbolic and social value are crucial in understanding what luxury means to consumers (Berthon et al., 2009). The meaning of luxury can differ depending on the consumer. Veblen's (1899/2007) conceptions of conspicuous consumption and status display may apply to the nouveau riche, but "old money" consumers may be less likely to broadcast their wealth.

Vigneron and Johnson (2004) develop a scale to measure the dimensions of perceived luxury (based on Dubois, Laurent, & Czellar, 2001; Kapferer, 1998; Vigneron & Johnson, 1999) and the differences in luxury among brands based on personal and non-personal perceptions of luxury. In the case of the former, the scale considers perceived conspicuousness, uniqueness, and quality; for the latter, the scale allows for perceived hedonism and the extended self; all are essential in sustaining a luxury brand. Kapferer (1998) and Dubois et al. (2001) also create discrete scales for measuring luxury perception; De Barnier, Falcy, and Valette-Florence (2012) and Christodoulides, Michaelidou, and Li (2009) study the validity of these scales in differing circumstances and cultures. All find that the various scales similarly measure luxury perception.

Luxury today: Emerging economies

As Western conceptions of luxury expand globally, particularly in emerging markets, luxury is now more widely experienced and increasingly adopted. As of 2012 and onwards, China has surpassed the US as the world's largest consumer of luxury items (Bain & Company, 2012; Crowe, 2015).

China has a long history associated with luxury. In a traditional feudal Chinese society based on Confucianism, youth were selected from across the country based on national examinations and groomed to become scholar-bureaucrat elites whose educational and cultural accomplishments often led to wealth, forming the first Chinese leisure class (Degen, 2009) and creating a legacy of luxury. Although the merchant class gained wealth during the late Ming dynasty, their luxury consumption was limited by strict sumptuary laws that ranked them below farmers in the Confucian hierarchy, and by the control the elite held over the art market through patronage. Global brands freely entered China once the Chinese economy opened to the West in the 1800s until the establishment of Chinese communism in 1848, and again in the late 1970s as Deng Xiaopeng reopened China to foreigners (Belk, 2016; Belk & Zhao, 2012). These influxes re-ignited ancient Chinese rituals of guanxi gift giving, with luxury gifts proffered as de facto bribes to government officials. Current anti-corruption policy forbids government officials from purchasing luxury goods with public funds (Joy, Sherry, and Wang, 2016), which limits luxury advertising. While this policy, coupled with a slowdown in the Chinese economy, has slightly curtailed the growth of luxury brands in China, the long-term outlook remains positive (Euromonitor, 2015b).

India is also a highly significant emerging market (Bhardwaj, Joy, & Belk, 2015; Schultz & Jain, 2015) with a rapidly growing luxury industry thanks to India's stable economic growth, a rising middle class, and a young, urban market with disposable income. In 2014, luxury goods sales grew over 200% from 2009 (Euromonitor, 2015c).

Historically, luxury consumption in India was mostly limited to royalty, but in the 1990s global brands took hold as Western and Eastern concepts of luxury began to blend. Indian culture has long valued gold and jewellery as sound investments, with weddings and other festive celebrations deemed auspicious days for their purchase. Luxury consumption is inevitably affected by the perception of luxury by consumers in a given culture. Luxury brands in India signal achievement and wealth, with Indian consumers seeking social acceptance through their luxury consumption (Shukla, Singh, & Banerjee, 2015).

The Indian luxury market is poised for luxury consumption: the number of Indian citizens earning above USD$150,000 per annum is expected to almost triple from over 540,000 as of 2013 to just under 1.5 million in 2030 (Euromonitor, 2015a). Yet income alone offers only a simplistic understanding of how global brands adapt to local contexts. Rather, as Mazzarella (2002, p. 2) notes, the luxury brand encapsulates powerful ideas of rationalization and spectacle: "... the brand operates as a kind of insignium of value, decorating and incorporating those loyal retainers who, in turn, consume it." The luxury market in India is expected to grow by double digits every year over the next five years (Euromonitor, 2015c). With the government allowing online sales of goods manufactured in India without requiring official permission, luxury brands are expected to increase manufacturing in India to avoid import tariffs (Euromonitor, 2015c).

The future of luxury consumption and luxury brands: Strands of research

With the increasing spread of luxury, luxury brands face new challenges in marketing strategies, especially of exclusivity. Increasingly, the importance of experience over ownership is touted in the literature (Atwal & Williams, 2009; Hennigs, Wiedmann, Behrens, & Klarmann, 2013; Truong, McColl, & Kitchen, 2009). Joy, Sherry, and Wang (2016) study the consumption of luxury goods by Hong Kong and mainland Chinese residents through the practices of tasting, savouring, and signalling, through which luxury brands – as a variant of contemporary art – serve as emblems of status and refinement.

Just under six percent of total luxury sales in 2014 were conducted online, which has doubled since 2004 (Euromonitor, 2015a). Although close to fifty percent of 2014 online sales were of designer apparel, an extension to other luxury items is inevitable. By being increasingly available online, luxury brands' cachet and focus on personal service may be diluted; however, losing online consumers, who tend to be younger, would be strategically untenable. Moreover, an online consumer has far greater control than in a physical store, particularly in communicating with other customers. Okonkwo (2009) studies the challenges faced by luxury brands online as they confront a changing consumer shopping experience and translate the glamorous atmospherics of their physical stores into their online equivalents. Belk's (1988, 2013) study of the extended and digital self suggests that social media interactions are crucial to today's luxury consumption.

As online sales increase so too do counterfeit luxury goods, which can be hard to distinguish from authentic products and provide the status of luxury without the high cost. There is little consensus on the impact of counterfeit luxury goods, with some research finding a negative impact on genuine brand consumers (Fournier, 1998; Hellofs & Jacobson, 1999) and others indicating no negative impact (Gabrielli, Grappi, & Baghi, 2012; Heike, 2010). Nia and Zaichkowsky (2000) argue that counterfeit luxury items decrease neither demand nor value for authentic luxury goods. Counterfeit products may reduce the luxury brand aura of perceived scarcity simply by being similar yet relatively affordable (Gabrielli et al., 2012), but do not necessarily dilute the value of luxury brands because consumers are aware of fake alternatives; counterfeits may even increase the perceived prestige of the brand, since the latter is sufficiently valued to inspire knockoffs. However, fakes can destabilize distinctions between authenticity and imitation (Lin, 2011). Some luxury brands try to curtail online counterfeits, achieving only limited success. The market for counterfeits will increase as long as luxury brand goods remain aspirational products.

The increase in counterfeits is balanced by a growing trend – especially among the elites – of a lower consumption of goods, a particular distaste for loud logo objects, and a simpler and quieter lifestyle. The resulting effect of this lifestyle, however, is slow despite an increasing emphasis on sustainability and eco-consciousness. A growing number of researchers are working on these topics to link luxury and sustainability, as important as that between luxury and art.

Luxury and art

Luxury and art are closely connected (Joy et al., 2014). A luxury brand watch that is also a piece of art is highly desirable given its exclusivity. A luxury product is linked to art either intrinsically (through aesthetic product design) or extrinsically (when sold in settings that feature or embody art). Joy et al. (2014) study the presence of elements of art galleries and museums in Louis Vuitton stores, which feature elegant architecture, interior design, and lighting similar to that of world-class museums. In such M(art)Worlds, objects for sale are displayed alongside actual art, and employees are both salespersons and curatorial advisors.

Luxury brands also connect to the art world through architecture and art exhibits. To validate high pricing, especially after the 2008 economic crisis, many international luxury brands have been investing in contemporary art and architecture to create an interdisciplinary definition of luxury (Mendes & Rees-Roberts, 2015). For example, the architectural marvel that is the Prada Transformer (a temporary building that can be rotated into different shapes, e.g., when the base is a hexagon, the building can be used for fashion shows) trumpets the Prada brand. Dior bankrolled an exhibit, "Christian Dior and Chinese Artists" (2008–2009), for which artists interpreted the world of Dior; Cartier hosted a temporary museum exhibit within the Forbidden City in Beijing in 2009 (Kapferer, 2012), and Louis Vuitton wrapped the Hong Kong Museum of Art in prints by the artist Richard Prince to advertise its 2009 exhibit, "A Passion for Creation" (Joy et al., 2014). Art is eternal, and the perception of iconic luxury products as art confers a similar disconnect from temporality. While contemporary art is not necessarily positioned as luxury, luxury goods are positioned as contemporary art.

Advertising can further position luxury products as art by communicating the brand dream even as it visually downplays brand products. Fashion magazine editors package intelligence at an accessible and actionable level for consumers (Chadha & Husband, 2010). Vogue China has supported young designers in launching fashion shows abroad, and providing exchange programs for young talent (Karabell, 2011). China is still struggling to create an internationally recognized – and therefore competitive – luxury brand. Shang Xia (Hermès' Chinese brand) creates authentic luxury products inspired by Chinese design and crafted in China (Burkitt, 2014), with stores in Shanghai, Beijing, and Paris. The role fashion publications play in creating and sustaining demand are crucial to the success of Western and local luxury brands. Brand advertisements, whether print or electronic, often use celebrities from the art, film, and music worlds. A luxury brand endorser must be perceived as embodying elements intrinsic to luxury (McCracken, 1989). Film directors Francis Ford Coppola and his daughter, Sofia Coppola, for example, pose with Louis Vuitton products in an LV advertisement. Together, they are emblems of family, generational continuity, and accomplished quality – terms one could also associate with LV products. That they might use LV items in their day-to-day lives seems entirely believable. Such brand ambassadors are the focal point for a series of rituals that may include promotional performances and advertising, designed to achieve cultural enclosure (Mazzarella, 2002, p. 2).

Effective advertising fuses creativity with behavioural research, with luxury coded in multiple ways within a given advertisement and extending a sense of perceived prestige (Schroeder, 2005). More research is needed on how luxury brand ambassadors in contexts other than the culture of origin help to collectively forge an elaborate set of meanings and impressions through promotional performances and advertising that can be used by the brand to establish itself in a new culture. The dynamics of identity and how they affect a luxury brand's image require unpacking to help us understand "how the brand will provide a conduit between the everyday life of the consumer and a rarefied world of transnational glamour" (Mazzarella, 2002, p. 10).

The ever-increasing reach of digital media has enabled consumers to access luxury in everyday life (Armitage & Roberts, 2014) as luxury and the media combine to frame powerful feelings of elation even during sadness, which the authors term "Euphoria in Unhappiness". Such dramatic changes require research on the critical perspectives of how luxury is defined and perceived.

As sustainability becomes ever more essential, luxury brands will by necessity extend their emphasis on sustainable development within different industrial sectors. Moreover, luxury consumption is not based on functionality but on the symbolic values associated with luxury, which include sustainability (Kapferer & Michaut, 2015). Can luxury be simultaneously exclusive and sustainable? How will luxury brands change their strategy to increasingly include sustainability as a measure of quality?

Luxury, aspirations, and mimesis

All luxury products have a symbolic value of achievement, success, and reputation attached to them, which affects consumer pre-purchase behaviour. Consumer aspirations similarly affect such behaviour. The cognitive processing of product images leads the consumer to form a mental image of the desired object, and a change in social status once that desired object is obtained. Belk, Ger, and Askegaard (2003) state that consumers passionately desire "The Luxurious". In emerging post-colonial economies, the desire for Western luxury brands is heightened by mimesis and mimetic desire, with international luxury brands belonging to the "EuroAmerican Culture" (Taussig, 1993), holding an aspirational value among such consumers. Conspicuous consumption by early adopters sets mimetic desire in motion.

Girard (1966, 1977) argues that desires do not originate within an individual but rather are copied from others, defined as models, who serve as mediators between the desirer and the desired object; the actual source of aspiration is to become the model who already possesses the object. Thus, imitation defines consumer desires, fantasies, and aspirations. If this is the case, a more minimalist approach to consumption is also possible with powerful individuals or celebrities serving as models for a less-ostentatious life. This idea of less is more connects with the concepts of sustainability and eco-consciousness and bodes well for the future (Alexander & Ussher, 2012).

The aspects of luxury and luxury brands discussed above – brands as a form of art signalling status and refinement; the interplay between accessible, aspirational, and absolute luxury in terms of values related to the acquisition of social and cultural capital over time; the values associated with various levels of luxury consumption; the dreams and myths engendered by luxury and embodied by brand ambassadors; the impact of e-commerce and the spread of counterfeits, through to the role of mimesis in emerging economies – are deserving of further research to probe the nature, both social and intimate, of luxury's impact on individuals' lives, dreams, and desires.

Dream worlds as strategy

We come full circle from the starting point of luxury terminology, whether of the past, present, or future: luxury brands cannot be viewed separately from art. The creation of the Comité Colbert in 1954, in combination with Dreaming 2074, was a deliberate strategy by the luxury industry to forge new directions, and focuses on elements common to both luxury and art such as innovation and aesthetics. Research using discourse analysis will allow us to decode the brands' collective strategic messages and how they affect consumer actions. The weight luxury carries in shaping social and personal identities and the politics of the self begs for deeper understanding.

Conclusion

From its roots through to the present day and looking to the future, luxury is a culture in itself (Kapferer & Bastein, 2009). To truly understand luxury, we must both identify and immerse ourselves in this culture. As the demand for luxury increases in developing and emerging economies, luxury firms are expanding their reach even as they tailor their brands to specific cultural preferences while recognizing that Western standards of luxury find acceptance in other cultures. This cultural understanding of emerging markets will also help determine luxury brand strategies to further local appropriation of their international appeal. As brands extend their online presence, they must also simultaneously combat counterfeiting, itself spurred by E-commerce, even as they adhere to their core value of maintaining exclusivity.

We must recognize and critically explore the political and cultural contexts intrinsic to understanding luxury and luxury brands; whether through the lenses of consumer aspirations, dreams and desires, or consumer envy, such contexts matter. Luxury has an aspirational value across all cultures, especially post-colonial emerging markets such as India and China, where mimesis and hybridization provide an additional overlay. Context in such economies may be more challenging to decode, and even more essential to our understanding.

Challenges for luxury brands include incorporating sustainable luxury (Joy et al., 2012) into their manufacturing and products. With a growing awareness of sustainability as a necessity, luxury brands risk being perceived as symbols of income inequality. While luxury brands develop their strategies based on brand heritage (Berghaus, Bossard, & Baehni, 2015), they must also develop a strategic foresight (Berghaus et al., 2015) to adjust to changing economic environments. Less-prominent logos and accessible second- or third-tier product lines are increasingly desirable. Further blurring the line between an aesthetic product and actual art may well appeal to brand strategists. These dramatic changes offer new avenues for future research into luxury. As we consider the future of luxury brands, one aspect is certain: they will always embody a dream in which consumers will always take pleasure. However, the move towards a simpler and more sustainable world might alter the course of luxury consumption. Consumers may prefer more quality and refinement over quantity.

The authors would like to acknowledge receipt of a grant from the Social Sciences and Humanities Research Council of Canada [No: 435-2013-1211]

References

Alexander, S., & Ussher, S. (2012). The voluntary simplicity movement: A multi-national survey analysis in theoretical context. *Journal of Consumer Culture*, 12(1), 66–86.

Armitage, J., & Roberts, J. (2014). Luxury new media: Euphoria in unhappiness. *Luxury*, 1(1), 113–132.

Atwal, G., & Williams, A. (2009). Luxury brand marketing – the experience is everything. *Journal of Brand Management*, 16(5–6), 338–346. doi:10.1057/bm.2008.48

Bain and Company. (2012). *Chinese shoppers world's top luxury goods spenders, while China luxury market cools to seven percent growth in 2012.* Retrieved from http://www.bain.com/about/press/press-releases/bains-china-luxury-market-study-2012.aspx

Belk, R. (1988). *Possessions and self.* Chichester: John Wiley & Sons.

Belk, R. (2011). Benign envy. *AMS Review*, 1(3), 117–134. doi:10.1007/s13162–011–0018-x

Belk, R. (2016). China's global trade history: A western perspective. *Journal of China Marketing and Logistics*, 6(1), 1–22.

Belk, R. W. (2013). Extended self in a digital world. *Journal of Consumer Research*, 40(3), 477-500.

Belk, R., Ger, G., & Askegaard, S. (2003). The fire of desire: A multisited inquiry into consumer passion. *Journal of Consumer Research*, 30(3), 326–351. doi:10.1086/378613

Belk, R., & Zhao, X. (2012). Advertising and consumer culture in Old Shanghai. In Shintaro Okazaki (Ed.), *Handbook of Research on International Advertising* (pp. 137–157). Cheltenham, UK: Edward Elgar Publishing.

Berghaus, B., Bossard, C., & Baehni, L. L. (2015). Strategic foresight in the luxury industry: managerial perspectives. *Luxury Research Journal*, 1(1), 76–90.

Berthon, P., Pitt, L., Parent, M., & Berthon, J. P. (2009). Aesthetics and ephemerality: observing and preserving the luxury brand. *California Management Review*, 52(1), 45–66.

Bhardwaj, R., Joy, A., & Belk, R. (2015). Hybridization ofVisual Imagery: A Semiotic Analysis of International Luxury Brand Advertisements in India. Paper submitted for *Consumer Culture Theory Conference.* Lille, France.

Brun, A., & Castelli, C. (2013). The nature of luxury: A consumer perspective: 1. *International Journal of Retail & Distribution Management*, 41(11/12), 823.

Burkitt, L. (2014). Hermès' Chinese brand slow to gain traction. *The Wall Street Journal.* Retrieved from http://www.wsj.com/articles/hermes-chinese-brand-slow-to-gain-traction-1413882677

Catry, B. (2003). The great pretenders: the magic of luxury goods. *Business Strategy Review*, 14(3), 10–17.

Chadha, R., & Husband, P. (2010). *Cult of the luxury brand: inside Asia's love affair with luxury.* Boston, MA: Nicholas Brealey Publishing.

Christodoulides, G., Michaelidou, N., & Li, C. H. (2009). Measuring perceived brand luxury: An evaluation of the BLI scale. *Journal of Brand Management*, 16(5), 395–405.

Comite Colbert. (2014). *Dreaming 2074, A Utopia Created by French Luxury.* Retrieved from: http://www.dreaming2074.com/assets/livre/en/pdf/Dreaming2074.pdf

Crowe, P. (2015). Here are the countries where the ultra-rich are going to be spending even more money. *Business Insider.* Retrieved from http://www.businessinsider.com/countries-with-the-most-luxury-spending-2015–3

Danziger, P. (2004). *Let them eat cake: Marketing luxury to the masses-as well as the classes.* Chicago: Dearborn Trade Publishing.

D'Arpizio, C. (2007). *Monitor Altagamma 2007 on luxury markets.* Retrieved from www.altagamma.it

d'Astous, A., & Deschênes, J. (2005). Consuming in one's mind: An exploration. *Psychology & Marketing*, 22(1), 1–30. doi:10.1002/mar.20044

De Barnier,V., Falcy, S., & Valette-Florence, P. (2012). Do consumers perceive three levels of luxury? A comparison of accessible, intermediate and inaccessible luxury brands. *Journal of Brand Management*, 19(7), 623–636.

Degen, R. J. (2009). Opportunity for luxury brands in China. *Journal of Brand Management*, 6(3/4), 75–85.

Dion, D., & Arnould, E. (2011). Retail luxury strategy: Assembling charisma through art and magic. *Journal of Retailing*, 87(4), 502–520. doi:10.1016/j.jretai.2011.09.001

Dubois, B., Laurent, G., & Czellar, S. (2001). *Consumer rapport to luxury: Analyzing complex and ambivalent attitudes* (No. 736). France: HEC Paris.

Dubois, B., & Paternault, C. (1995). Observations – understanding the world of international luxury brands – the dream formula. *Journal of Advertising Research*, 35(4), 69–76.

Eckhardt, G. M., Belk, R. W., & Wilson, J. A. (2015). The rise of inconspicuous consumption. *Journal of Marketing Management*, 31(7–8), 807–826.

Euromonitor. (2015a). *The rise of luxury spending and high income earners in emerging markets*. Euromonitor Passport Database. Retrieved from http://www.euromonitor.com/the-rise-of-luxury-spending-and-high-income-earners-in-emerging-markets/report

Euromonitor. (2015b). *Luxury goods in China*. Euromonitor Passport Database. Retrieved from http://www.euromonitor.com/luxury-goods-in-china/report

Euromonitor. (2015c). *Luxury goods in India*. Euromonitor Passport Database. Retrieved from http://www.euromonitor.com/luxury-goods-in-india/report

Fournier, S. (1998). Consumers and their brands: Developing relationship theory in consumer research. *Journal of Consumer Research*, 24(4), 343–353. doi:10.1086/209515

Gabrielli,V., Grappi, S., & Baghi, I. (2012). Does counterfeiting affect luxury customer-based brand equity & quest. *Journal of Brand Management*, 19(7), 567–580.

Girard, R. (1961/1966). *Deceit, desire, and the novel*. Trans. Yvonne Freccero. Baltimore: Johns Hopkins University Press.

Girard, R. (1977). *Violence and the sacred*. Trans. Patrick Gregory. Johns Hopkins: Baltimore, MD.

Heike, S. (2010). Effects of counterfeits on the image of luxury brands: an empirical study from the consumer perspective. *Journal of Brand Management*, 18(2), 159–173.

Heine, K. (2011). *The concept of luxury brands*. Retrieved from: http://www.conceptofluxurybrands.com/content/20110907_Heine_TheConceptofLuxuryBrands.pdf

Hellofs, L. L., & Jacobson, R. (1999). Market share and customers' perceptions of quality: When can firms grow their way to higher versus lower quality? *The Journal of Marketing*, 63(1), 16–25.

Hennigs, N., Wiedmann, K. P., Behrens, S., & Klarmann, C. (2013). Unleashing the power of luxury: Antecedents of luxury brand perception and effects on luxury brand strength. *Journal of Brand Management*, 20(8), 705–715.

Hoffmann, J., & Coste-Manière, I. (2012). *Global luxury trends: Innovative strategies for emerging markets*. New York: Palgrave Macmillan.

Joy, A., Sherry Jr, J. F., Venkatesh, A., Wang, J., & Chan, R. (2012). Fast fashion, sustainability, and the ethical appeal of luxury brands. *Fashion Theory*, 16(3), 273–295.

Joy, A., Sherry, J. F., & Wang, J. (2016). *Tasting, Savoring, and Signaling: Articulating the Luxury Brand Experience in Hong Kong and the People's Republic of China.* To be published in M. Jayne (Ed.), *Chinese urbanism: everyday critical perspectives*. London: Routledge.

Joy, A., Wang, J. J., Chan, T. S., Sherry, J. F., & Cui, G. (2014). M (Art) Worlds: Consumer perceptions of how luxury brand stores become art institutions. *Journal of Retailing*, 90(3), 347–364.

Kapferer, J. N. (1998). Why are we seduced by luxury brands? *Journal of Brand Management*, 6(1), 44–49.

Kapferer, J. N. (2012). Abundant rarity: The key to luxury growth. *Business Horizons*, 55(5), 453–462.

Kapferer, J. N., & Bastien, V. (2009). *The luxury strategy*. London, UK: Kogan Page.

Kapferer, J. N., & Michaut, A. (2015). Luxury and sustainability: A common future? The match depends on how consumers define luxury. *Luxury Research Journal*, 1(1), 3–17.

Karabell, S. (2011). Too much demand, Too little space: Chinese Vogue. *Forbes*. Retrieved from http://www.forbes.com/sites/insead/2011/11/30/too-much-demand-too-little-space-chinese-vogue/2/

King, J. (2014). French luxury maisons pen utopian tale for Comité Colbert's 60th anniversary. *Luxury Daily*. Retrieved from http://www.luxurydaily.com/french-luxury-maisons-pen-utopian-tale-for-comite-colberts-60th-anniversary/

Kovesi, C. (2015). What is luxury? The rebirth of a concept in the early modern world. *Luxury*, 2(1), 25–40.

Lin, Y. C. J. (2011). *Fake stuff: China and the rise of counterfeit goods*. London: Routledge.

Mazzarella, W. (2002). Cindy at the Taj: Cultural enclosure and corporate potentateship in an era of globalization. In Diana Mines and Sarah Lamb (Eds.), *Everyday life in South Asia* (pp. 387–399). Bloomington: Indiana University Press.
McCracken, G. (1988). *Culture and consumption: New approaches to the symbolic character of consumer goods and activities*. Bloomington: Indiana University Press.
McCracken, G. (1989). Who is the celebrity endorser? Cultural foundations of the endorsement process. *Journal of Consumer Research*, 16(3), 310–321.
Mendes, S., & Rees-Roberts, N. (2015). New French luxury: Art, fashion and the re-invention of a National Brand. *Luxury*, 2(2), 53–69.
Millwardbrown. (2013). *Top 100 global brands*. Retrieved from https://www.millwardbrown.com/brandz/2013/Top100/Docs/2013_BrandZ_Top100_Report.pdf
Mukerji, C. (1983). *From graven images: Patterns of modern materialism*. New York: Columbia University Press.
Nia, A., & Zaichkowsky, J. L. (2000). Do counterfeits devalue the ownership of luxury brands? *Journal of Product & Brand Management*, 9(7), 485–497.
Nueno, J. L., & Quelch, J. A. (1998). The mass marketing of luxury. *Business Horizons*, 41(6), 61–68.
Okonkwo, U. (2009). Sustaining the luxury brand on the Internet. *Journal of Brand Management*, 16(5), 302–310.
Schroeder, J. E. (2005). *Visual consumption* (Vol. 4). New York; London: Routledge.
Schultz, D. E., & Jain, V. (2015). Discovering India's three levels of luxury consumption: An exploratory research to find a conceptual framework. *Journal of Marketing Communications*, 0(0), 1–20.
Shukla, P., Singh, J., & Banerjee, M. (2015). They are not all same: variations in Asian consumers' value perceptions of luxury brands. *Marketing Letters*, 26(3), 265–278.
Silverstein, M. J., & Fiske, N. (2003). Luxury for the masses. *Harvard Business Review*, 81(4), 48–57.
Sobh, R., Belk, R., & Gressel, J. (2014). Mimicry and modernity in the Middle East: fashion invisibility and young women of the Arab Gulf. *Consumption Markets & Culture*, 17(4), 392–412.
Taussig, M. T. (1993). *Mimesis and alterity: A particular history of the senses.* New York: Routledge.
Truong, Y., McColl, R., & Kitchen, P. J. (2009). New luxury brand positioning and the emergence of Masstige brands. *Journal of Brand Management*, 16(5), 375–382.
Urde, M., Greyser, S. A., & Balmer, J. M. (2007). Corporate brands with a heritage. *Journal of Brand Management*, 15(1), 4–19.
Veblen, T. (1899/2007). *The theory of the leisure class.* Oxford: Oxford University Press.
Vigneron, F., & Johnson, L. W. (1999). A review and a conceptual framework of prestige-seeking consumer behavior. *Academy of Marketing Science Review*, 1(1), 1–15.
Vigneron, F., & Johnson, L. W. (2004). Measuring perceptions of brand luxury. *The Journal of Brand Management*, 11(6), 484–506.
Wang, J. (2010). *Brand new China: Advertising, media, and commercial culture.* Cambridge, MA: Harvard University Press.

39

Social media consumer as digital avatar

Alladi Venkatesh and Duygu Akdevelioglu

Introduction

> We live in a world which is an accumulation of spectacles. There is no greater spectacle than the media world. Images are detached from life . . . The spectacle appears incessantly and constantly. Spectacle is not merely a collection of images, it is a social relationship between people mediated by images.
>
> *(Guy DeBord, 2000, p. 42)*

What is "social media"?

A simple definition offered by Hoffman, Novak, and Stein (2013, p. 29) is as follows: "a set of web-based mobile and applications that allow people to create (consume) content that can be consumed (created) by others and which enables and facilitates connection . . . tools that support social interaction between users." In a similar fashion, boyd and Ellison (2007) regard social media as social networking sites that allow individuals to: a) maintain a public or semi-public profile within a bounded system, b) articulate a list of other users with whom they share opinions and ideas, and c) view the list of connections made by them and those made by the others in the system. It is the third item that allows users to make their social networks visible (Wasserman & Faust, 1994), thus facilitating new connections that render the social networking sites unique and socially compelling. According to boyd and Ellison (2007), the sites are used for social networking activities (e.g., Facebook and LinkedIn), or for sharing videos and photos (YouTube, Pinterest) and thoughts, opinions, and other content through microblogging (Twitter, Tumblr). They all represent transformational network systems that include friends, family members, professional associates, and even strangers as well as local and distant communities (van Dijck, 2013). In addition to user- generated activities, social media platforms permit public and private organizations to post information about their products and services and communicate or promote their activities. Thus social media is practically the first instance in the history of human communication that both organizations and their constituencies are able to share equally and communicate with each other in the same interaction space.

Research on social media shows that scholars and critics are pursuing a wide range of topics regarding social media users and their activities.

In the broader context of social media culture, some developments include the rise of *convergence* culture (Jenkins, 2006), social media and youth perspectives (boyd, 2014), linguistic patterns and semiotic modes (Zappavigna, 2014), social media intelligence (Moe & Schweidel, 2014), the culture of connectivity (van Dijck, 2013), comparative social media usage patterns (PEW Report, 2016), and structures of user participation in social media (Hansen, Shneiderman, & Smith, 2011).

Specifically, in terms of social media consumer culture, some noteworthy issues are digital self and virtual consumption (Belk, 2013), virtual/digital goods (Denegri-Knott & Molesworth, 2013), social commerce (Hoffman & Novak, 2012), netnography and networked narratives (Kozinets, 2015), the role of branding (Gensler et al., 2013; Labrecque, 2014; Singh & Sonnenburg, 2012; Smith, Fischer, & Yongjian, 2012), consumer self-expression and identity representation (Buechel & Berger, 2016), consumer socialization and collaboration (Lowgren & Reimer, 2013), the selfie generation and the rise of selfie culture (boyd, 2014; Murray, 2015), and social media and consumer privacy (Venkatesh, 2016).

The chapter will proceed as follows. We will first provide a preliminary analysis of the social media culture and social media users. This will be followed by a more focused discussion of consumer issues. We will conclude with some final thoughts on social media consumption.

Social media culture – user participation issues

According to Statista (2016), there are currently 2.22 billion social network users worldwide, and the number of users is likely to grow to 2.39, 2.72, and 3.0 billion in 2017, 2018, and 2019, respectively. Similarly, Social Media Examiner (2016) has reported 90% of the marketers consider social media as indispensable to their businesses. Regarding social media trends, according to PEW Research report (2016), "nearly two-thirds of American adults (65%) use social networking sites, up from 7% when Pew Research Center began systematically tracking social media usage in 2005." Thus there is no doubt that social media usage is a global phenomenon and is growing rapidly.

In spite of the growing popularity of social media, there seem to be some holdouts as reported recently by Wayne (2016). He notes that there is a "stubbornly resistant minority" even among the younger age groups that seem uninterested and also quite concerned about privacy erosion on social media sites. The concern expressed by some refers to lurkers who can invade "your avatar in a way that feels invasive." Such concerns give rise to the privacy issues on social media discussed recently by Venkatesh (2016).

At a rather macro level, Jenkins (2006) raises some fundamental concerns regarding (social) media convergence, participatory culture, and collective intelligence. By *convergence*, he means the flow of content across media platforms and media participants, the cooperation between media players and constituencies, and the sharing of their experiences. By *participatory culture*, he means that it is not the traditional media spectatorship where media producers and consumers are separated; the reference is to all individuals who are social media users who interact with each other and produce and share content. Since these individuals share ideas with each other, what emerges is voluntary consumer collaboration (Lowgren & Reimer, 2013).

danah boyd (2014) examines issues concerning how teenagers communicate with each other on Facebook, Twitter, and Instagram. The main question she addresses is: Do social media affect the quality of teens' lives and, if so, how? She explores tropes about identity, privacy, safety, danger, and bullying. Ultimately, boyd argues that society bears heavy responsibility in shaping the lives of teens and making sure they are better informed and thoughtful, and become engaged citizens through their online activities. Based on her analysis, she draws conclusions regarding the impact of emerging technologies on society, culture, and commerce. She concludes on a reassuring note regarding the future of teens in this technologically complex world, finding that they often develop a sense of identity and social purpose. For consumer researchers, teen behaviors constitute a major area of research and inquiry.

Zappavigna (2014) argues that social media platforms give rise to new linguistic patterns and semiotic modes (e.g., online/real-time chat) not encountered before. She proposes that these emerging forms of conversation are not only different from face-to-face encounters (i.e., due to lack of physicality) but give rise to new linguistic patterns of content production and management.

Certainly, social media users not only post their comments but are able to upload pictures of themselves and friends and family members and other items of interest. This has given rise to what is known as selfie culture (boyd, 2014, Murray, 2015). For example, Murray (2015) has shown that social media users post pictures of themselves, often times in a personally daring fashion. Thus social media is emerging as an uninhibited digital/visual culture.

What is the nature of social media interactions? Moe and Schweidel (2014) liken them to "water-cooler conversations" except, of course, the social media exchanges are more-permanent records that are now digitally available for further examination and scrutiny. At a more serious level, they call it "social media intelligence gathering" or "social media monitoring," which permits the researcher to perform computational linguistic analysis and extract underlying themes.

In her work on social media connectivity, van Dick (2013) has shown how users play different roles on social media that include consumers, producers, recipients, friends, critics, citizens and professionals. In these different roles, users voluntarily devote their time and effort to develop and sustain social media content. As a result, user-generated content "creates value for the ecosystem of social media as a whole" (p. 23).

Social media networks and communication issues

In social media networks, consumers interact with each other, build communities, and share opinions. This network notion of communication is somewhat different from offline human interaction. The connected media with its numerous new cultural forms such as tweets and posts enable individuals to access various sources simultaneously, which was not possible in the pre-Internet era. Because of this, social media culture emerges with new behavioral codes and values.

The notion of friendship is also slightly different in social media networks when compared to traditional offline networks. To begin with, social media platforms act as bridges between online and offline connectivity (Hampton, 2007). In the context of social media, the terms *friends* and *friending* express the strength of the relationship between individuals. Thus, both a person with a close relationship and high intimacy as well as a total stranger can be included under the term *friend*. Also, the term *followers* has a connotation that includes both members from neutral groups as well as devotees and believers. In other words, in the context of social media, meanings change to include people who simply follow one's Twitter stream. That is, although most of the contacts in social media networks are *weak* ties in the traditional sense, they are nevertheless significant (Trusov, Bodapati, & Bucklin, 2010).

We are now able to examine social media user participation in terms of some related criteria in the context of networks: asynchronous threaded conversation, synchronous conversation, World Wide Web (WWW) and hyperlinks, collaborative authoring, blogs and podcasts, and social sharing. Here is a brief description of each of these participation categories (extracted from Hansen, Shneiderman, & Smith, 2011).

Asynchronous threaded communication

Asynchronous communication typically starts with a user-communicator and is followed by another user, and this may go back and forth. Typical categories in this sequence are: (i) email and (ii) forums/groups These sources serve as an excellent platform to curate people's sentiments, relationships, and social influence.

Synchronous conversations

Synchronous conversations, on the other hand, allow for communications to take place at the same time or simultaneously. Examples include such categories as: (i) Chat, instant messaging, texting (Yahoo!, Messenger, Facebook, Google Talk, etc.) and (ii) audio and video conferencing.

World Wide Web traditional websites, homepages, and documents

The World Wide Web is the largest public web content platform where the contents are connected through hyperlinks. Network analysis plays a significant role in various activities performed on this platform. Homepages, as well as social media tools such as Facebook, Twitter, Pinterest, and Instagram, are good examples.

Collaborative authoring

Wikipedia and shared documents provide useful sources for collaborative authoring over social media. In Wiki, people not only contribute their own articles but can also fine-tune others'. These signify content relationship and social roles; individuals with expertise in certain areas contribute to relevant contents in those areas.

Blogs and podcasts

Blogs (e.g., Twitter) are a very attractive platform for content presentation and for making comments. Some of them can also be embedded within larger websites. Typically, web crawlers capture these connections, and thus blogs can be mined to develop various social and political insights.

Social sharing

Social sharing sites are content centric. They include video, TV, photos, art, music, bookmarks, news, and books. They help the users save time while searching for any particular topic. Such media aid researchers in analyzing people with shared interests, identifying new information, finding a historical trace, and fostering collaboration in community formation.

Some other social media participation examples would include social networking services, online markets and production, idea generation, virtual world, and mobile-based services (Thompson, 2003). Social networking services such as dating, professional, and niche networks are becoming an integral part of contemporary society and, needless to say, people are choosing these networks to find a friend or like-minded community, look for a job, pursue sales leads, and so on. Financial transactions, user-generated products, and review sites are flourishing in online market and production platforms. Consumers depend increasingly not only on reviews by others (i.e., friends/acquaintances/strangers), but also on the recommendations provided by specific websites to decide on their next set of purchases.

Consumer participation in social media and the digital world

While Jenkins's (2006) notion of convergent culture describes the macro environment, at a micro level, we refer to Belk's (2013) work on extended self in the digital world. In his seminal paper, Belk discusses the notion of digital self, which is a virtual reincarnation of the "extended self" he proposed in his earlier work (Belk, 1989). He identified five characteristics that describe the consumer in the digital environment. They are:

- Dematerialization – Attachment to virtual possessions
- Re-embodiment – The emergence of digital avatar
- Sharing – Referring to virtual space as a shared space
- Co-construction of self – Extended self in the virtual environment
- Distributed memory – Consumer narratives in the virtual world

Thus Belk argues that the technological environment has altered consumer discourses, but the basic concept of "extended self" is still intact. In other words, consumer fundamentals have not changed. One question that arises in this regard is: What kind of objects are consumers dealing with in the social media environment? Denegri-Knott and Molesworth (2013) call them aptly "digital virtual goods."

Members of online communities are active Internet contributors who expend time and creative effort outside their professional routines and produce what Kozinets (2015) calls "network narratives." Their roles are varied and diverse. For example, they are information initiators and recipients, consumers, producers, critics, and participants within the social media culture. In other words, users voluntarily devote time and effort to developing and sustaining social media content and their presence. Users contribute to the content because of the need to communicate, gather information, and express their ideas. As a result, *user-generated content*, a key phrase in social media vocabulary, creates value for the ecosystem of social media as a whole (van Dijck, 2009). Social media platforms (Facebook, Twitter, etc.) reinforce the interaction between users through different forms of user-generated cultural content (e.g., text, photos, and videos) that have become key drivers of people's opinion formation and value judgments. Socially speaking, ties between individuals are also generated through such content production and sharing.

Hoffman, Novak, and Stein (2013) aptly conceptualize social media in terms of four Cs: connect, consume, create, and control. Thus social media represent a significant development in a short time, giving rise to several possibilities and scenarios that involve socializing, information sharing, buying and selling, and interacting with others in significant ways. This also means that consumers are producing and sharing a lot of data about themselves and others.

Consumers are social media users of different platforms that are continuously being modified and updated through user demands and initiatives "via microblogs, pictures, videos and/or private messages to which other users in their network can respond" (Buechel & Berger, 2016, p. 3). What makes this particularly striking is users' ability to create and consume social media content at the same time. These dynamics remind us of the transition of consumers to "prosumers" – a combination of producers and consumers (Kotler, 1986, Ritzer & Jurgenson, 2010).

Along with the emergence of social media come questions about data security and privacy. There is some concern that privacy protections over social media are easy to circumvent. Consumer data is not really protected well enough and can be accessed with sophisticated tools and software. Thus the social media environment raises some critical questions of privacy, security, and net neutrality that are emerging as key issues (see Venkatesh, 2016).

The privacy of the user or the consumer is a major concern in social media given the semi-public nature of the medium. Basically, one expects that the data or information about an individual remains secure, and their right to protection regarding information or data about themselves is guaranteed. So the main concerns relate to: a) secure data, b) imperatives regarding the need to keep data private, c) the need for individuals to have control over data, d) transparency in terms of how data is stored, accessed, and secured, and e) enforcement of compliance in practices regarding data management. To this end, Venkatesh argues for security design and operations, infrastructure protection, network and data protection, transparency, customer control, and third-party compliance.

Conceptualizing the consumer in the social media world

Typically, in the field of consumer research, the general tendency is to study the consumer from different theoretical perspectives – as a psychological being with socio-cognitive and emotional characteristics; from a socio-cultural point of view with an emphasis on cultural values, group affiliations, and social background; or from an economic standpoint with a focus on utility maximization and tradeoffs. We believe there is another but related perspective that is appropriate for our study. That is, the participant in *social* media is a *social* person engaged in social communicative interactions with friends and associates as well as strangers – all in their capacity as social beings. Thus there is an opportunity for us to explore how the individual is constituted within the socio-historical context. To pursue this point of view, we refer to some pertinent literature and begin with relevant work from consumer research, social psychology, and media studies that include: identity theory of planned behavior (Ajzen, 1985), Marshall McLuhan's (1964) and McLuhan and Powers' (1989) work on media imagery, and the notion of digital avatar (Damer, 2007).

A social psychological perspective

Ajzen (1985) proposed that intentions to perform behaviors of different kinds can be predicted with a high degree of accuracy from attitudes towards that behavior under conditions of prevailing subjective norms. Ajzen also proposed a theory of planned behavior, which offers the notion that human behavior is not capricious and that there is a conscious formulation of such behavior. For our purposes, we might say that social media users are very cognizant of the social media environment's benefits and drawbacks and participate in them with due deliberation and not capriciously.

Ajzen's theory is preceded by a well-known theory of reasoned action with a similar logic (Fishbein & Ajzen, 1985). For our purposes, the implication here is that if social media users have positive attitudes towards social media sites and feel a need for involvement, they will have positive dispositions toward social media. Identity theory and social identity theory (Hogg, Terry, & White, 1995; Stets & Bure, 2000) explain how the socially constructed self mediates between the individual and the social environment. Both theories address the social nature of the self as constituted by the environment instead of self as a purely independent construct. This may help explain consumer participation in social media; it contributes to consumers' sense of identity and self-worth or serves as a way to accumulate some level of social capital. Lin (2002) proposes a more sociologically oriented notion of social capital formation. In some early work, Pierre Bourdieu (1984), the French social theorist, popularized the notion of capital formation in the social world by integrating the three forms of capital – social, cultural, and economic. He argued that some elite members of society assume the role of arbiters of social taste, and socially orchestrate the three forms of capital that are combined to form "human capital," which in turn confers "social distinction" on them. The other members become followers of this elite group. Lin (2002) takes this notion further and identifies the dynamics of social capital formation, which include a number of sociological concepts such as social interaction, social cohesion, social norms, and values. Relating social capital to the notion of human capital, Lin (2002) argues that social capital is the outcome of a collective effort built around social networks, trust, and socially oriented contexts. For our purposes, one can make an argument that participation in social media is a way to build social capital. In this context, social capital refers to investment in the social community with some expected returns – economic, social, and cultural (friends, community formation, information exchange, etc.).

A media-centric perspective: Individual in the media age – Marshall Mcluhan

Marshall McLuhan (1964) is very pertinent to our discussion on social media because he was preoccupied with the role of media in contemporary society. His media work had and continues to have a wider appeal globally along with his other well-known joint work on the global village (McLuhan & Powers, 1989). McLuhan was interested in cultural transformation due to media influence/expansion. He proposed the view that cultural change was driven by technological forces and, in particular, by the characteristics of media technologies. He was, of course, referring primarily to television. According to McLuhan, new media are not just novel manifestations of communication technology but are instruments of change in the social structure and formation of social character. Although the Internet and social media (and even email) did not exist in McLuhan's time, his famous thesis regarding new media as instruments of cultural change turned out to be prophetic and has stood the test of time. For example, he stated that all media are extensions of human discourses and sites of human interactions. They are also change agents, for they are technological manifestations of the human world in the form of video and sound (e.g., television). The TV is not merely an entertainment medium; it may appear to act as a visual aid to the external world, but it can also fashion human behavior and influence the way we think. It does this quite effectively while people are watching TV in the privacy of their homes. In other words, it is a *social technology*, par excellence.

By extension we can argue that social media, in the form of social networking sites, play a similar role and are sites of social discourse and instruments of social transformation. But they do represent a fundamental attribute not encountered before because social media users are not passive consumers but active change agents. That is, unlike in the traditional media culture, social media users are both content producers and active initiators of change. Thus they act more like *digital avatars* shaping the social media landscape.

Social media structure – a socio-cultural perspective

For our purposes, we can describe social media in terms of their communication structures and user configuration and participation in a socially constructed environment. There are indeed certain social roles that social media users assume. Members of online communities are active Internet contributors who expend time and creative effort outside their professional routines to produce what Kozinets et al. (2010) call "network narratives." Their roles are varied and diverse. For example, they are information initiators and recipients, consumers, producers, critics, and participants within the social media culture. In other words, users voluntarily devote time and effort to developing and sustaining social media content and configuration. Users contribute to the content because of the need to communicate, gather information, and express their ideas. As a result, *user-generated content*, a key phrase in social media vocabulary, creates value for the ecosystem of social media as a whole. Social media platforms (Facebook, Twitter, etc.) reinforce the interaction between users through different forms of user-generated cultural content (e.g., text, photos, and videos) that have become key drivers of people's opinion formation and value judgments (Wilson, Gosling, & Graham, 2012). Socially speaking, ties between individuals are also generated through such content production and sharing.

According to Christakis and Fowler (2009), the Internet "facilitates interactive multimedia and many-to-many communication"; therefore, it shifts the one-to-many communication of traditional media to many-to-many. Consumers are no longer passive recipients of what is produced for them but are now involved in the process of content generation for social sharing. Unlike traditional mass media such as television and magazines, which deliver content controlled and manufactured by producers without audience input in the construction and sharing of content, social media platforms treat content producers and consumers as collaborative entities, for they do create value jointly (Peñaloza & Venkatesh, 2006). Of course, sometimes the users do generate content independently. This user-generated content is a key to understanding social media platforms that constitute a medium for consumers as initiators of content production. For corporations, on the other hand, this is a great way of promoting their brands since consumers perceive consumer- generated content as more reliable than company-generated content. Additionally, consumers gain agency as they contribute to social media content.

In sum, it is important to emphasize that consumers are both *content providers* and *data generators* for social media platforms (van Dijck, 2009). That is, when consumers create content, they become a rich data source for companies, which can then mine the data for commercial purposes.

Digital persona/avatar – the social persona in the information age

Damer (2007) describes avatars as follows: "Avatars . . . focus on what people do inside (the) virtual worlds . . . navigating through the worlds, and learning digital etiquette and social interaction skills." Meadows (2010) draws upon some literature in development psychology and explains how, as children begin to get socialized with their peers and elders, they begin to acquire a social character that drives their behavior in many settings, especially in the digital arena. Many such interactions involve using computers, mobile phones, and other Internet-based devices. By extension, one can argue that the world of social media presents itself as an appropriate venue for new forms of interactive social behavior not envisioned in traditional media culture.

The construction of digital consumer persona is a foundational concept in the current technological discourse (Clarke, 1994; Solove, 2004). Primarily this has to do with "digital dossiers" that can be generalized to any digital configuration about the individual, whether self-generated or other-generated. Digital dossiers are information banks and involve different aspects of personal data – the production of dossier information, dossier database construction, and dossier updating as well as dossier availability for others to share or take a peek into.

Digital persona/avatar issues become even more complicated given that social media are not limited geographically; the information individuals post can be accessed instantaneously and acted upon globally.

With current technology, many companies and online/offline government agencies are able to construct databases about individuals. Take for example, Amazon. Not only does the company have past records of customer purchases, they can easily construct consumer profiles based on patterns of expenditures, types of products purchased, credit card information, online histories, credit-worthiness, and other personal information. Later, they utilize the customer information to create personalized marketing strategies. Given that consumers continue to provide information to social media sites through IP addresses, it follows that user information can be stored and mined. Additionally, consumers as social media users need to formally sign social media platform agreements (i.e., terms of use) in order to gain further entry into the sites. These data mining practices of social media platforms introduce privacy concerns (see Venkatesh, 2016).

In order to fully understand the digital persona in the context of social media, we will address some issues pertaining to social media platforms and structure.

Social media platforms and consumer content generation

Social media platforms are dynamic objects adjusted through users' needs and owners' objectives, and also in reaction to competing platforms and the larger technological and economic infrastructure. On social media platforms such as Twitter and Reddit, users can post information and create streams while platform owners may adjust their programming (algorithms and interfaces) to affect data traffic (van Dijck, 2013). Platforms gain economic value through marketing activities. It is important to understand the effect of socioeconomic and technological underpinnings of the relationships between social media platforms, users, and marketers. User practices such as *sharing*, *liking*, and *friending* create specific technological and economic meanings in social media networks. Although the definition of social media implies that platforms allow people to have relational connections, different platforms provide different communication patterns and opportunities.

Social media brands – a social discourse

In contrast to traditional media, social media provide continuous, detailed feedback via their participation in online communities, contribute to new product ideas and engage in brand-related conversation enabling better broad positioning based on real-time data. Companies can also use social media for brand promotion. However, according to Fournier and Avery (2011), unlike traditional media structure – where the consumer is a mere recipient of company information and images – the social media user is very much in charge of content management. Therefore, in order to succeed in the social media world, brands attempt to manage user presence differently. Hoffman and Novak (2012) propose an effective system to motivate consumers on social medium platforms that would take into consideration consumers' subjective well-being and their fundamental needs and motives in the context of social media engagement.

An important topic in this context relates to consumers and their brand preferences (Singh & Sonnenberg, 2012). One issue that brand management attempts to understand is why people use social media. This can be addressed in the context of their basic needs for autonomy, competence and relatedness, intrinsic and external motivations, and well-being perceptions. Results show that motivations differentially drive social media goal pursuit, and users with different primary social media goals differ in perceptions of well-being. Using these results, Singh and Sonnenberg (2012) develop a testable, theoretical, brand-oriented framework. They take into consideration social media goals defined by two higher-order dimensions that contrast the primary focus of the online interaction with the primary direction of the online interaction. This framework may be useful in developing further understanding of the relationship between users' social media behaviors and subjective well-being in the context of their fundamental needs and motives. Thus Singh and Sonnenberg argue that consumers participate in social media through the vehicle of brand storytelling; they play an active role in brand marketing through storytelling that focuses on their brand experiences, both positive and negative. The basic concept is experiencing empathy for the brand and engaging in reinterpretation of brand stories. The authors call this improvisational performance. They use the Dove company sites on Facebook and YouTube as an example of this.

Social media consumption – a theoretical integration

The foregoing discussion in this chapter is an attempt to conceptualize the consumer in the context of social media environment with a specific focus on consumer dynamics. As discussed above, Jenkins refers to these developments as the emergence of "convergence culture" (Jenkins, 2006). In this final section, we would like to propose how social media are integrated into consumption practices. We identify several levels of integration. The levels vary according to the specific institutional/group-oriented conditions and user dispositions. Here are examples of social media integration measures or indicators that are pertinent to our discussion:

- Social media are dominated by different consumer/demographic groups (e.g., adults/children, men/women, and other group members)
- User skills develop naturally as well as by practice and engagement
- Social media participation is interest specific and at the same time a contagion
- Familiarity with social media is both intuitive and involves active participation, but may not require formal training
- School/work/social-cultural groups, based on the situation, may play a major role
- Social media characteristics include: communication patterns, user-generated content, information-storage medium, entertainment medium, instant messaging, social learning
- A very important aspect of social media is that it fosters a culture of socialization
- No longer a passing fad, social media are considered a necessity in this information age
- Of course, one realizes too much technology can negatively impact social life, although it varies with contexts and social groupings

The above indicators should help researchers develop appropriate hypotheses and identify topics for further investigation. We will now elaborate on some key ideas.

As social technologies, social media represent cultural phenomena that reflect a number of different characteristics based on specific social relationships (family, friends, consumer segments, and professional associates). In other words, although social media platforms are a technological phenomenon, users employ them to build social networks and to interact with others. Thus social media serve different purposes.

In the context of active social involvement there are a few aspects of social media that are worthy of note. First, they allow for instant communication. Thus they are very effective as networking tools. They also allow users to create personal presence, and are a very powerful medium for establishing social connections near and far. They can be used to convert offline relationships to online ones and online relationships to offline. Social media allow groups to come together and share their opinions and their interests. Content generation and sharing are major characteristics of social media. One can also engage in political discourse and comment on current events and happenings. There is also an opportunity to gather political intelligence.

This is particularly important as consumers share consumption experiences and are able to project their opinions on media sites. That is, as consumers, social media users can become publicly active and express their opinions and preferences. They are sometimes critical of companies and their products, and their opinions can easily be shared with other members. Thus the opportunity to create social content can have both positive and critically constructive overtones. Opinions are expressed, and other social media users either agree or disagree or remain neutral.

Depending on the specific social media platform, communication strategies vary based on the nature of the social media vehicle (Wang, Yu, & Wei, 2012). On the positive side, social media represent a high degree of user friendliness and a spirit of community formation. For example, Facebook is very effective as a community network (Wilson, Gosling, & Graham, 2012). Twitter is for blogs. Professional contacts can be established on LinkedIn. YouTube is a very useful tool for archiving and sharing information and visual material. In other words, different social media play different roles and can be effective in different ways based on their purpose and impact. Unlike traditional media, social medial are built around frequent/constant updates. Since customers use social media regularly and frequently, i.e., several times during the day, their expectations are also tied to novelty of information and currency. Many consumers use mobile devices consistently, and the social media outlets take this into consideration. At the same time, companies try to coordinate social media with traditional media.

Many organizations use social media effectively to advertise their products and gather information about users and their views on various subjects. While companies have a prominent brand presence on, say, Facebook, they are not really *selling*. It is all about providing information and augmenting their brand presence. Yes, they deliver product information, but they are careful not to act aggressively. This, indeed, is an interesting conundrum in social media culture where companies appear to be guarded. Maybe this is because the medium is still new and experimental. Typically, companies do show a lot of activity on their timeline tab. There may be several posts from their customers, but customer complaints are handled separately via email.

Conclusions

In the foregoing, we provided an analysis of user/consumer issues concerning social media. It was directed towards a conceptual analysis of the social character of the consumer and his or her digital persona. Certainly, this is an emerging field and promises much potential for future inquiry. To conclude, the transformation from human connectedness to automated connectivity occurs as social activities are translated into technological codes. The interplay among social media users, platforms, companies, and regulatory parties creates the medium of communication. Therefore, this medium enables the consumer in social media to become *a participant and an active agent* who connects with friends and colleagues as well as acquaintances and strangers in an effort to engage as a *social persona* or *digital avatar* in this emerging global scene. Much potential exists to explore digital interactions in the social media arena across consumer segments and different demographic and socio-cultural groups.

References

Ajzen, I. (1985). From Intentions to Actions: A Theory of Planned Behavior. In J. Kuhl & J. Beckman (eds.), *Action Control*, Berlin: Springer Verlag, 11–40.

Belk, R. (1989). Extended Self and Extending Paradigmatic Perspective, *Journal of Consumer Research*, 16 (1), 129–132.

Belk, R. (2013). Extended Self in a Digital World, *Journal of Consumer Research*, 40 (3), 477–500.

boyd, d. M. (2014). *It's Complicated: The Social Lives of Networked Teens*, New Haven, CT: Yale University Press.

boyd, d. M., & Ellison, N. B. (2007). Social Networking Sites: Definition, History and Scholarship, *Journal of Computer Mediated Communication*, 13 (1), 210–230.

Bourdieu, P. (1984). *Distinction:A Social Critique of the Judgment of Taste*, Cambridge, MA: Harvard University Press.

Buechel, E. C., & Berger, J. (2016). Motivations for Consumer Engagement with Social Media. In Claudiu V. Dimofte, Curtis P. Haufgtvedt, & Richard F. Yalch (eds.), *Consumer Psychology in a Social Media World*, London: Routledge, 3–22.

Christakis, N. A., & Fowler, J. H. (2009). *Connected: The Surprising Power pf Social Networks*, Boston, MA: Little Brown & Company.

Clarke, R. (1994). The Digital Persona and Its Application to Data Surveillance, *The Information Society*, 10 (2), 77–92.

Damer, B. (2007). Avatars! Exploring and building Virtual Worlds on the Internet, http://www.digitalspace.com/avatars/book/, Accessed March 5, 2016

Debord, G. (2000). *The Society of Spectacle*, Cambridge, MA: MIT Press.

Denegri-Knott, J., & Molesworth, M. (2013). Redistributed Consumer Desire in Digital Virtual Worlds of Consumption, *Journal of Marketing Management*, 29 (13–14), 1561–1579.

Fishbein, M., & Ajzen, I. (1985). *Belief, Attitude, Intention, and Behavior: An Introduction to Theory and Research*, Reading, MA: Addison-Wesley.

Fournier, S., & Avery, J. (2011). The Uninvited Brand, *Business Horizons*, 54 (3), 193–207.

Gensler, S., Volckner, F., Liu-Tompkins, Y., & Wietz, C. (2013). Managing Brands in the Social Media Environment, *Journal of Interactive Marketing*, 27, 242–256.

Hampton, K. N. (2007). Neighborhoods in the Network Society: The E-Neighbors Study, *Information, Communication & Society*, 10.

Hansen, D. L., Shneiderman, B., & Smith, M. A. (2011). *Analyzing Social Media Networks: Insights from a Connected World*, Burlington, MA: Elsevier – Morgan Kaufman.

Hoffman, D. L., & Novak, T. (2012). Toward a Deeper Understanding of Social Media, *Journal of Interactive Marketing* (Editorial), 26, 69–70.

Hoffman, D. L., Novak, T., & Stein, R. (2013). The Digital Consumer. In Russell Belk & Rosa Llamas (eds.), *The Routledge Companion to Digital Consumption*, London: Routledge, 28–38.

Hogg, M. A., Terry, D. J., & White, K. (1995). A Tale of Two Theories: A Critical Comparison of Identity Theory and Social Identity Theory, *Social Psychological Quarterly*, 56 (4), 255–269.

Jenkins, H. (2006). *Convergence Culture: When Old and New Media Collide*, New York: New York University Press.

Kotler, P. (1986). Prosumers: A New Type of Customer," *Futurist*, September–October), 24–28.

Kozinets, R. (2015). *Netnography*, 2nd Edition, Thousand Oaks, CA: Sage.

Kozinets, R., de Valck, K., Wojnicki, A. C., & Wilner, S. C. (2010). Networked Narratives: Understanding Word-of-Mouth Marketing in Online Communities, *Journal of Marketing*, 74 (2), 71–89.

Labrecque, L. (2014). Fostering Consumer-Brand Relationships in Social Media Environments: The Role of Parasocial Interaction, *Journal of Interactive Marketing*, 28, 134–148.

Lin, N. (2002). *Social Capital*, Cambridge: Cambridge University Press.

Lowgren, J., & Reimer, B. (2013). *Collaborative Media: Production, Consumption, and Design Interventions*, Cambridge, MA: MIT Press.

McLuhan, M. (1964). *Understanding Media: The Extensions of Man*, Cambridge, MA: MIT Press.

McLuhan, M., & Powers, B. R. (1989). *The Global Village: Transformation in World Life in the 21st Century*, Oxford: Oxford University Press.

Meadows, S. (2010). *The Child Social Person*, London: Routledge.

Moe, W. W., & Schweidel, D. A. (2014). *Social Media Intelligence*, Cambridge: Cambridge University Press.

Murray, D. C. (2015). Notes to Self: The Visual Culture of Selfies in the Age of Social Media, *Consumption, Markets & Culture*, 18 (6), 490–516.

Peñaloza, L., & Venkatesh, A. (2006). Further Evolving the New Dominant Logic of Marketing: From Services to the Social Construction of Markets, *Marketing Theory*, 6 (3), September, 299–316.

PEW Research Report (2016). News Use Across Social Media Platforms. Retrieved from: http://www.journalism.org/2016/05/26/news-use-across-social-media-platforms-2016/, Accessed March 5, 2016.

Ritzer, G., & Jorgenson, N. (2010). Production, Consumption, Prosumption, *Journal of Consumer Culture*, 10 (1), 13–36.

Singh, S., & Sonnenburg, S. (2012). Brand Performances in Social Media, *Journal of Interactive Marketing*, 26 (4), 189–107.

Smith, A. N., Fischer, E., & Yongjian, C. (2012). How Does User-Generated Content Differ across YouTube, Facebook and Twitter, *Journal of Interactive Marketing*, 26 (2), 102–113.

Social Media Examiner (2016). Social Media Marketing Industry Report. Retrieved from: http://www.socialmediaexaminer.com/, Accessed May 5, 2016

Solove, D. J. (2004). *The Digital Person: Technology and Privacy in the Information Age*, New York: New York University Press.

Statista (2016). Statistics and Facts about Social Networks. Retrieved from: http://www.statista.com/statistics/272014/global-social-networks-ranked-by-number-of-users/, Accessed May 5, 2016

Stets, J. E., & Bure, P. J. (2000). Identity Theory and Social Identity theory, *Social Psychological Quarterly*, 63 (3), 224–237.

Thompson, G. F. (2003). *Between Hierarchies and Markets: The Logic and Limits of Network Organization*. Oxford, UK: Oxford University Press.

Trusov, M., Bodapati, A.V., & Bucklin, R. E. (2010). Determining Influential Users in Internet Social Networks, *Journal of Marketing Research*, 47 (4), 643–658.

van Dijck, J. (2009). Users like You: Theorizing Agency in User-Generated Content, *Media, Culture and Society*, 31 (1), 490–516.

van Dijck, J. (2013). *The Culture of Connectivity: A Critical History of Social Media*, Oxford: Oxford University Press.

Venkatesh, A. (2016). Social Media, Digital Self and Privacy: A Socio-Analytical Perspective of the Consumer as the Digital Avatar, *Journal of the Association for Consumer Research*, 1 (3), July, 23–33.

Wang, X., Yu, C., & Wei, Y. (2012). Social Media Peer Communication and Impacts on Purchase Intentions: A Consumer Socialization Framework, *Journal of Interactive Marketing*, 26, 198–208.

Wasserman, S., & Faust, K. (1994). *Social Network Analysis: Methods and Applications*, Cambridge: Cambridge University Press.

Wilson, R. W., Gosling, S. D., & Graham, L. T. (2012). A Review of Facebook Research in the Social Sciences, *Perspectives in Psychological Science* 3, 203–220.

Wayne, T. (2016). Holdouts of the Social Media Age, *New York Times*, http://www.nytimes.com/2016/03/27/fashion/not-on-facebook-twitter-social-media.html?rref=collection%2Fcolumn%2Ffuture-tense&action=click&contentCollection=style&region=stream&module=stream_unit&version=latest&contentPlacement=1&pgtype=collection&_r=0, Accessed March 27, 2016

Zappavigna, M. (2014). *Ambient affiliation: A linguistic Perspective on Twitter*, London: Bloomsbury.

40
Digital consumption

Minna Ruckenstein

Introduction

The era of digitalization is shaping consumption practices in ways that continue to blur the boundaries between business initiatives and the everyday. Opportunities to commodify ordinary people's lives are plentiful in digital culture: sociability, friendship, rivalry, sleeping, health histories, personal preferences, and distributed knowledge can all be converted into sources of value for Facebook, Google, Amazon, Apple, and comparable companies. Meanwhile, market developments are becoming ingrained in daily experiences through the promotion and modeling of self-presentation, intimate encounters, and social interactions.

"Digital consumption" emerged over the past half century with the transition from analog to digital coding, permitting a greater transmission speed of information at a much lower cost. In the 1980s, Alvin Toffler's (1980) notion of the "Third Wave" propagated the new order of computerized society, pointing to improved global communication regardless of time and space. The newly gained communicative freedom was then limited, however, by the nature of the Internet as a corporate battleground, commodifying communicative forms. Digital consumption has matured at the intersections of various kinds of cultural forces, ranging from the managerial to technological and artistic, underlining the complexity of the field (Allison, 2006; Kline, Dyer-Witheford, & De Peuter, 2003). The scholarly work on digital consumption mirrors this complexity: digital consumption is defined as online retail, marketing approaches, or seen as an expanding field of technological platforms and mobile applications that advance various forms of production, distribution, and consumption. In this chapter, the emphasis will be on the latter kind of digital consumption, exploring how consumption-related activities integrate with new business models and strategies that rely on people's involvement and digital contributions, rather than mere purchasing behaviors. The aim is to promote a research agenda designed to detect the linking and merging of everyday aims, technological devices, and market-making efforts. From this perspective, markets connected with digital consumption do not exist as stable formations, but rather reveal themselves in the very act of their making (Knorr-Cetina & Preda, 2007; Pantzar & Ruckenstein, 2015). Companies operate in an interconnected and personalized world, becoming part of people's lives through forms of social networking, sharing, and knowledge formation that promote new kinds of interactions, collaborations, and divisions of labor between commercial agents and consumers (Bruns, 2008; Jenkins, 2006).

Research approaches presented in this article build on studies conducted in the fields of consumer culture research, media and communication research, science and technology studies, anthropology, history, and digital sociology, all of which share an alertness to forms of value promoted in corporate practices and entangled with everyday aims and imaginaries (Arvidsson, 2005; Brembeck, 2008; Miller, 1998; Ruckenstein, 2010; Zelizer, 1985). The aim is to demonstrate the parasitic and fluid nature of the digital consumption phenomenon rather than to delimit its scope. This method enables observation of how digital encouragement to consume follows people in their daily lives, reacting to, shaping, transforming, and exploiting the everyday. The empirical findings used to argue for this kind of approach are drawn, for instance, from research on toys, social media, virtual worlds, and self-tracking technologies. Consumer research which explores consumer involvement and empowerment can be framed as an advanced form of market analysis, complicit in the expansion and deeper penetration of market forces into people's lives. The goal of this chapter is to demonstrate that research on consumption can avoid the market analysis stance by promoting a more dynamic view of the market and value formation. The aim throughout is to stay attentive to the defining features of digital consumption, while introducing research findings that treat digital consumption as an emergent and constantly transforming area of interactions with an uncertain, even erratic, flavor to it: technological platforms fail, and users disappear from social media sites. These frictions and tensions surrounding consumption are critically relevant to its understanding, because they remind us that consumers do not reside in some place "outside the market", but are active contributors in processes whereby entities like markets come into being.

A focus on prosumption

Researchers have tackled digital consumption by describing a larger shift in the consumption landscape that requires that production and consumption be studied as thoroughly intertwined. Although processes of production and consumption have been equally important to economic value formation, the scholarly attention given to them has not been similarly balanced: usually the focus has lain either on one or the other. From the perspective of digital consumption, it is crucial to work on approaches that are attentive to both and, with this in mind, the hybrid term *prosumption* (Ritzer & Jurgenson, 2010; see also Toffler, 1980; see also chapter 8 in this volume) used in this chapter works as a sensitizing concept. Although prosumption is by no means unique to digital consumption, the way in which digital consumption arrangements take advantage of user involvement and user participation underline the tight intertwining of the spheres of production and consumption. Communication scholar Axel Bruns (2008) describes a continuum, distinctive to digital services, that links the dichotomies of production and consumption, work and play. Users of digital services move along it, hardly noticing or concerning themselves with the fact that their participation contributes to the overall corporate process of content creation and profit making. Participation, sharing, communication, and creativity interweave with commercial aims; production melts into leisure activities. It is thus no wonder that digital media interactions, including blog entries, comments and photograph sharing on websites, and interactions on social media platforms are difficult to define in terms of consumption. People's doings merely become an integral part of the production of consumption: of the communication, content creation, and interaction that they and others consume.

The focus on prosumption advocates that in order to understand emerging consumer culture, analyzing how people enact and internalize the possibilities that digital consumption opens for them is of utmost importance. Useful in this regard is research that traces historical developments and identifies key actors, ideological shifts, materialities, and technologies in the making of consumption and consumers (Buckingham, 2011; Pugh, 2009). The children's clothing industry – its rise, growth, and segmentation – provides a telling historical example of the commodification of childhood, for example, including the introduction of a new kind of child consumer, the toddler, with a designated style (Cook, 2004). New consumer personas, needs, and opportunities are developing with the aid of innovative market devices and technological and spatial solutions; the segmentation of retail spaces, offers important clues to how consumers are approached in terms of gender or age. Conceptualizations of selves, others, and social aims are thus a vital part of the making of the market. Illustrating this is the recent emergence of the notion of the Quantified Self in *Wired* magazine which has paved the way for the market of self-tracking devices and applications by promoting a notion of the self that ties in with market-making efforts (Ruckenstein & Pantzar, 2015). At the heart of the notion lies a computational logic that emphasizes the revelatory power of personal data, asserting that self-knowledge is established with data flows and data analysis.

In terms of digital consumption, prosumers are empowered and exploited in ways that depend on the situation and perspective. Consequently, scholars need to ask questions that go beyond dualistic either/or stances that regard consumers as either entirely free to make their own choices, or as victims of the market (Cook, 2004). Only through a comprehensive understanding of the ways in which corporate offerings participate in and promote prosumption, and the everyday conditions connected with it, can we tackle their effects and influences. Therefore, digital consumption research should never be removed from the lifeworld experiences of users. By bringing to the fore the very intimate ways in which commodities become a part of people's relationship with themselves and others, research into digital consumption urges scholars to examine how the merging of selves and consumption opportunities challenge our notions of what consumption is and could be.

Dimensions of value

In the last decade, professionals in fields from financial services to government agencies and from social media to design have talked extensively about value, value creation, and added value (see Miller, 2008). Value talk is symptomatic of the contemporary corporate culture that is eager to produce value, but also uncertain about how exactly new kinds of value should be generated at a time when established business models are being disrupted and digital technologies are promoting new modes of profit-making. One of the great insecurities lies in the concept of value itself, in the difficulties of pinning down the properties and dimensions of value. Consequently, as economic value is by far the easiest to measure, it tends to dominate corporate and societal understandings and obscure the importance of integrating more social or imaginative perspectives into the assessment of value formation, given that it is difficult to imagine and appreciate the relationship between social aspirations and desires and their economic consequences (Flynn, 2010). Consequently, the focus is directed towards the most sacred goal of all, the return on investment, resulting in stereotypical and false ideas of customers' aspirations and desires. Corporate ethnographer Donna Flynn (2010) recounts how corporate executives in Microsoft launched a series of initiatives to increase the priority of the customer experience across multiple levels of business strategy and product development as early as the late 1990s. Despite these efforts, Flynn suggests that product decisions are still based on erroneous assumptions about how people interact with technologies and incorporate them into their daily lives: the user-experience community jokes about this by talking about how "Microsoft builds products for Microsoft" (2010, p. 51). In many technology companies users are treated as more technology savvy than they actually are. People's relationship to technologies is seen as instrumental and utilitarian, poorly reflecting the ways in which products and services become included into everyday aims and needs.

Consumption scholars who are interested in finding more sophisticated and dynamic ways to explore value formation have relied on approaches to value that do not locate it in objects, consumer segments, or financial measurements, but in the various ways that relations between people, materialities, and technologies are arranged and mediated (Arvidsson, 2005). In this kind of approach, attention is paid to at least three dimensions of value (see Graeber, 2001, pp. 1–2), beginning with value in the economic sense, or the degree to which objects are desired, particularly as measured by how much people are willing to give up to obtain them. Measurement of value is fairly unambiguous when it is translated into revenue and profit. Yet even if economic value is measured separately from other dimensions of value, its production is closely tied to social and cultural aspects of value formation. Values in the sociological sense cast light on conceptions of good, proper, and desirable in human life; they have to do with the organization of daily lives in terms of spheres such as work, the pursuit of wellbeing, notions of kinship, or preferred presentations of the self. Finally, value in the linguistic-symbolic sense communicates cultural differences understood not only as meaningful, but also as worth pursuing. Such differences cover all aspects of sociality, tying in with notions of gender, religion, sexuality, age, or local identity. The different aspects of value should not be separated, however, because they are "refractions of the same thing" (Graeber, 2001, p. 2). In order to accurately pin down what is of value and how such value guides people's doings, consideration should be given to all three aspects.

Successful services and products align and pool symbolic, social, and economic aspects of value in a manner that benefits commercial aims while, from the consumer perspective, it promotes shared understandings and interests. They make consumer actions meaningful by placing them "in some larger social whole, real or imaginary" (Graeber, 2001, p. 254). Such real and imaginary orientations facilitate and direct value formation, steering people towards pursuing and desiring specific things, shared practices, and communication. Popular digital services support people in various everyday aims in fields as varied as daily communication, exercise regimens, partner search, or affordable accommodation. From the production and design perspectives, the processes of value formation entail that companies or organizations engage in detailed explorations of their customers' doings and desires, thereby implicating a renegotiation of ways to approach people as customers or users of products and services (Cefkin, 2010; Lehdonvirta & Castronova, 2014).

Whenever possible, digital services use unpaid rather than paid labor, meaning that digital consumption is characterized by subtle, seductive, and indirect manipulative processes. Commercial agents take advantage of people's digital input to the extent that such labor becomes barely noticeable (Terranova, 2000). The relentless production of new content does require work, however, and the provision and curation of pictures and quotations for Facebook and Instagram, for example, depends on users' efforts, so promoting digital consumption in this context means understanding how and why people react, participate, and share. The aim of the host company is thus to push and manipulate people to behave in a certain manner in order to translate their content creation and behavioral patterns into company resources and deliverables.

Residents of the digital world

In order to capture how corporations approach consumers and take advantage of their digital participation, digital consumption researchers need to understand dynamic processes of value formation and also the various translations and conversions of value. Research on virtual worlds, games, and social media has explored how digital consumption extends and multiplies consumption opportunities by creating possibilities for intimate encounters, social interaction, and spatial permanence. Ethnographic research on virtual worlds describes how digital encounters and playfulness enable and pin down spatial orientations and social ties, and strengthen and expand them (Boellsstorf, 2008; Malaby, 2009). Users of digital services not only participate in the creative production, but make services appealing and inviting to others; therefore, the mere presence of users is important for the promoters of digital consumption because it enhances the value of products and services. For instance, Snapchat, a picture-sharing application where images permanently disappear after seconds, tempts potential users by offering them more control over the use and circulation of their pictures. By sharing photographs and messages, leaving digital traces that are consumed and measured by others, users build a more-or-less permanent presence in the digital world.

Empirical studies of children and young people are particularly instructive in terms of how people become residents of online spaces (Lehdonvirta, Wilska, & Johnson, 2009; Ruckenstein, 2011, 2013). The digital world is characterized by playgrounds where children and teenagers are "freed from the yoke of adult rules, norms, forms of social propriety and the physical scale of the adult world" (Cook, 2007, p. 45). For example, at the peak of its popularity, with millions of users, a stunning range of interactions and spatial arrangements characterized Habbo, one of these virtual worlds (Lehdonvirta et al., 2009; Ruckenstein, 2011). For many children and teenagers, attraction to digital services is linked to the spatiality of the service. Digital platforms meet children's needs by inviting them into places that can be modified through building new kinds of social and spatial realities. The desire to spend time online, and to create content for the service, emerges not only in relations between people, but also in relations between people and digital objects. The possibilities of action are maintained with various kinds of digital objects: weaponry, clothing, virtual pets, or in the case of Habbo, furniture in particular. In addition to decorating their own private rooms, users of Habbo build theme rooms, including hospitals, schools, model agencies, orphanages, dating rooms, cruise ships, and discos.

The exchange economy of children is commercially valuable because it helps to keep items interesting and desirable (Cook, 2007). In the Habbo world, new, limited batches of items are regularly produced for children to consume with the aim of generating sales and exchange. Although they change ownership from one child to another, these digital objects can be owned by children who never buy anything: anybody can purchase rare items, but the most skillful Habbo residents do not pay for them. Thus, children have their own ways of distancing the commercial underpinnings by valuing their own actions over those of the host company. When children exchange and trade items, transactions are typically based on the social value of things: the age, rarity, previous owner, and how the item is originally acquired all matter (Lehdonvirta et al., 2009). The more self-expression, comparison, and rivalry generated between children, the more users buy digital objects for making and marking social distinctions. In terms of digital consumption, social interactions generated by digital objects gain a corporate value. The desire to own, collect, and trade items emerges in social relations and aspirations that are mediated and supported by digital objects. In practice, this means that concept designers and service developers must try to understand how relations between children and objects emerge and expand and how they advance processes of content creation.

Consumption of personal data

The recent expansion of digital consumption has taken advantage of new forms of data gathering and analysis in the personal sphere, which can further clarify the close connection between digital consumption and the most intimate aspects of daily lives (Lupton, 2016; Ruckenstein & Pantzar, 2015; Van Dijck, 2014). Both public and private sector organizations are seeking to capitalize on data analytics to improve products, personalize services, or target advertising more effectively. Moreover, a stunning variety of self-tracking applications and devices, taking advantage of innovative engineering and design approaches, have been developed to capitalize on personal data streams for consumption purposes. Commercial products and services that promote self-tracking – understood as gathering and sharing personal data about oneself in order to reflect on some aspect of life including diet, sleep, posture, blood chemistry, genetics, heart rate, body temperature, and exercise patterns – offer yet another form of prosumption. This is facilitated by the collection of increasingly detailed personal information through a growing range of digital devices, such as smart phones, tablets, watches, cameras, and blood pressure monitors. Self-tracking devices might also be designed as wearables, clip-on devices, or jewelry with embedded sensors able to measure bodily functions, everyday movements, or social encounters.

In light of digital consumption, self-tracking devices and applications are a telling example of the value formation processes that shape the economy, communication, social life, and identities. Drawing on the capacities of digital technologies to generate increasing quantities and diverse forms of information about daily lives, self-tracking expands the area of digital consumption by offering opportunities to understand lives as sets of numerical phenomena that can be examined and acted upon. As a consumption form, self-tracking takes advantage of personal data streams in an attempt to slice life into comprehensible and controllable units, including the number of steps taken in a specific period, stress levels, eating patterns, or sleep cycles. Mundane practices, such as sitting or using a fork, are datafied and transformed into an arena of calculation and, through that calculation, into potential areas for consumption (Schüll, 2016).

Self-tracking adds a layer of complexity to digital consumption, raising questions about how data streams that concern the self, the body, or sociality transform into consumption forms, and who benefits as a result. Direct-to-consumer (DTC) genetic testing is a particularly controversial area of digital consumption that reveals tensions concerning the commodification of personal data. Tens of companies offer genetic testing, covering areas such as "deep ancestry", "ethnicity", "health", and "relationships", operating in the fields of biomedicine, information technology, consumer culture, social media, and health (Harris, Kelly, & Wyatt, 2014; Harris, Wyatt, & Kelly, 2013; O'Riordan, 2011, 2013), and pushing the market in a direction that blurs professional boundaries and lacks ethical and regulatory oversight (Saukko, Reed, Britten, & Hogarth, 2010). When the genetic testing company *23andMe* was launched in 2007, the high-end DNA saliva test cost $999. Gradually, however, the test began to be advertised as a more mainstream lifestyle add-on, and its price dropped to just $99. Typically, people do not seek validated medical or clinical utility when they purchase a *23andMe* test; they tend to be purchased more light-heartedly, as gifts, out of curiosity, or perhaps as a group order put together in the workplace or among friends. The genetic findings are then pre-packaged by the testing company into consumable reports offering cultural framings of personal data, producing "data materializations" (Lupton, 2015): that is, graphs and visualizations, including personal traits and ancestry maps, designed to represent data in manner accessible to the consumer.

Users of such services generally do not comprehend what this kind of consumption means in the long run in terms of the implications of sharing personal information. Social media and information technology professionals might communicate light-heartedly about their genetic cousins without being aware that they have given away control of sensitive personal information that extends to other people (Ruckenstein, 2016). New consumption forms might offer consumers baits, such as genetic testing and participation, in order to take advantage of people's contributions and participation elsewhere. For instance, a less public agenda on the part of the

23andMe is to get consumers involved in the production of a database that may be used in service development and corporate partnerships. The profit-making efforts of companies are rarely entirely transparent, underlining the need to follow market developments critically. The rhetoric of sharing and participation suggested by platforms such as *23andMe* contrasts with the lack of transparency regarding company outputs and uses of personal information; the economic value of health data, for example, is never shared with the test takers whose samples make up the database.

The production of human beings

The reactive and responsive nature of digital technologies provides commercial companies with the means to develop products and services that become a part of self-discovery and sociality, and are embedded in everyday routines and temporal rhythms. Self-tracking and related data gathering and uses provide unforeseen opportunities for combining different data sets to identify patterns in consumer behavior. Commercial agents have never before been so intimately and seamlessly involved in people's daily lives. Digital devices and applications provide the opportunity to access personal details quickly and efficiently, opening a new kind of vista of the everyday life of the consumer. Smart phones, with their hundreds of applications, have become our new companions. Digital consumption, along with its enabling technologies, has become part of the ordinary. Children play with techno toys that allow them to enter interactive gaming worlds, while virtual pets are valued and desired because they sustain sociality, and open new kinds of imaginary possibilities (Ruckenstein, 2015). Young people maintain a presence on platforms including Facebook, Instagram, Snapchat, and Whatsapp which facilitate contemporary methods of connecting with their friends. People everywhere are co-constructing – in tandem with corporate offerings, objects, and technical specifications – who they are and who they want to become in relation to others.

With the ubiquity of digital technologies that sense and trace people's movements, enable social interactions, and then participate in them, daily lives are becoming increasingly entangled with market-making efforts. As data contributors, consumers are constantly emitting data as they move around in consumption spaces. Taken together, current developments suggest that digital consumption has penetrated the most intimate sectors of everyday life. Anthropologist David Graeber (2007, p. 77) even argues, provocatively, that we should stop talking about consumption altogether and rename the consumption sphere "the sphere of the production of human beings", and, undoubtedly, emerging consumption forms such as self-tracking resonate powerfully with the conflation of the two. With their data-gathering and analysis capabilities, self-tracking devices are designed to help their users in quotidian tensions and struggles; they are supposed to aid in making comparisons, judgments, suggestions, and decisions about what exactly is desirable, balanced, or healthy in the everyday as it unfolds over time. Tracking sleep, emotional reactions, or stress levels offers an opportunity to relate one's behavioral aspects to company-specified target levels. By doing so, self-tracking devices and applications offer a powerful technique to become recognized as a certain kind of sleeper, runner, or stress subject.

Digital consumption leads to its becoming a part of, while commodifying, individual and social aims – a parasitic relationship, in other words – yet its promoters' rhetoric continues to embrace playfulness, empowerment, sharing, and participation. Opportunities for closeness and intimacy are sought by paying attention to people's behavior, perspectives, and experiences as users of online services. Self-tracking devices enable the capturing, detailing, and recording of everyday behavior and events that might otherwise go by unrecognized and unattended, documenting patterns of sleeping, eating, having sex, or even labor contractions before giving birth. By taking advantage of technological possibilities, commercial agents have found a way to be present in the most intimate moments of people's daily lives. Yet consumption is still not the only force that makes consumer activities worthwhile. The production of human beings is a process that takes advantage of various kinds of powers, commercial and non-commercial, and it is important not to exaggerate the role of commercial endeavors in defining actions and identities. While commodification is typically a process that seeks new kinds of intimacies and conditions of oneness, users also ignore and avoid such unity of aims, constantly bending digital services to their own ends and searching out alternatives to company offerings. Despite digital consumption practices, people continue to have their own ways of distancing and critiquing commercial efforts by valuing their own doings over those of corporations (Nafus & Sherman, 2014; Sharon & Zandbergen, 2016).

Digital divides and shortcomings

Digital services and products recognize and engage people, but also fail to engage them, while digital consumption, as more in-depth and nuanced research on consumption suggests, is not free of tensions, frictions, and shortcomings. The latter are important, because they can expose and explain the shortcomings, vagaries, and limits of digital consumption. A study by media scholar Eran Fisher (2015), focusing on a class-action lawsuit by Facebook users against the company over its Sponsored Stories advertising program, details the users' plea for full control of the information they generate on the company platform. The study suggests that users are increasingly aware of the economic value of their online activities: suing Facebook, they were demanding ownership of a greater share of the economic surplus value the company produces by taking advantage of the content that they produce.

As with all forms of consumption, digital consumption is defined by various kinds of divides linked to economic, political, and social inequalities and differences, which have consequences for the ways in which people behave in terms of consumption (Chin, 2001). Social determinants such as gender, age, or education continue to matter and shape technology uses and consumption, while the resources, capabilities, work, and care that new technologies require can lock out those who lack the means or technological competence (Oudshoorn & Pinch, 2003). Meanwhile, consumers can express their discontent by not using applications and platforms or by abandoning them and moving elsewhere. A focus on failures, on products and services that find no users or are used only in the short term, highlights the asymmetries and tensions in technological possibilities (Scheldeman, 2010; Suchman, 2007), revealing how people ignore, reject, or openly challenge market offerings (Wyatt, 2005). People can, for instance, resist self-tracking or, having tried it, become disenchanted or bored with the practice. Tracking devices offer visualizations and interpretations based on personal data streams for consumption purposes, but these might find no space, support, or context in people's lives. Direct-to-consumer genetic testing can be perceived as irrelevant, or uninteresting, and some of those purchasing tests do not even log into the service to see their test results but leave their accounts to be managed by others, typically those who convinced them to take the test in the first place (Ruckenstein, 2016).

The digital world is defined by speed, and technologies become outdated at an accelerated pace, while the overflow of technologies underlines the excess that accompanies market-making efforts. Paying attention to such overflow can aid in the exploration of the performative character of market making, including hype cycles (Alvial-Palavicino, 2016), and explaining how entities like markets evolve or fail to do so. Ultimately, market-making efforts depend on identifying and attracting people who have the time, interest, and patience to become involved, although the active work of translation and contextualization conducted by users of products and services often goes unnoticed. In terms of research, it is important not to replicate the invisibility of users' unpaid labor, but, rather, to acknowledge and broadcast it. Digital consumption forms become possible because users dedicate time and effort to get value out of products and services, and prosumption materializes because people are ready to learn new skills and promote practical and communicative engagements that generate conditions for current and constantly renewed consumer practices.

Conclusion

Digital consumption is characterized by an intertwining of the personal and social aims of consumers and the economic aims of companies, a model that is often reliant on mobile technologies which enable, direct, and exploit self-reflection and social relations. Yet, while the consumer agency and involvement promoted by digital services is a key to their success, the format allows people to feel that, despite interactions taking place on commercial platforms, they are operating independently. The aim of this chapter has been to demonstrate that research on consumption can promote a more dynamic view of the market, driven by exploration of the comprehensive dynamics of value formation. Such a view demonstrates that market developments connected with digitalization do not homogenize or flatten social relations, but create new ones that are just as complex, imaginative, and exploitative (see Maurer, 2006). Even as digital services and gaming platforms seduce children and teenagers into consuming more digital items, they also allow them to use digital spaces as extensions of everyday lives where users can explore, manipulate, and interact with other spatialities, people, and objects. Self-tracking, on the other hand, presents the interior of the human body, the tiniest details of it, for consumption purposes as the search for self-knowledge converts into emotionally appealing exploration supported by personal data flows and data analysis.

Investigation of consumer culture can help us to re-theorize the economy that surrounds us and produces the infrastructure of the everyday, yet as self-exploration, sociality, and knowledge production become economically more valuable, a whole new array of political and ethical questions is emerging. Current developments call for a new kind of reflexivity from researchers, as well as novel and perhaps even controversial research perspectives to help us to navigate emergent forms of digital consumption (Thrift, 2005, 2011). Dialogue and research collaboration between companies, consumer agencies, and researchers interested in steering digital consumption in a more consumer-friendly direction is suggesting possibilities for promoting and cultivating corporate and societal processes that disrupt conventional market making. In the course of this initiative, consumption scholars could become influential in redefining the market along the lines suggested, for instance, by the human economy project (Hart, Laville, & Cattani, 2010). This kind of move would open opportunities for thinking about how researchers are positioning themselves in relation to digital consumption, and how they might promote their own value projects in light of longer-term goals of social and economic reproduction. Digital consumption research can be guided by notions of ecologically sustainable production processes, concentrate on uncovering how digital platforms harvest value by using unpaid labor, or aim at protecting consumers' rights over personal data. It can thus also be defined as a value project that not only exposes the global inequalities of digital consumption, but shapes the digitalization era by reproducing and recreating a more desirable social, economic, and political order.

References

Allison, A. (2006). *Millennial monsters: Japanese toys and the global imagination.* Berkeley, CA: University of California Press.

Alvial-Palavicino, C. (2016). The future as practice: A framework to understand anticipation in science and technology. *Technoscienza: Italian Journal of Science & Technology Studies, 6*(2), 135–172.

Arvidsson, A. (2005). Brands: A critical perspective. *Journal of Consumer Culture, 5*(2), 235–258. doi: 10.1177/1469540505053093

Boellstorff, T. (2008). *Coming of age in second life: An anthropologist explores the virtually human.* Princeton, NJ: Princeton University Press.

Brembeck, H. (2008). Inscribing Nordic childhoods at McDonalds. In M. Gutman & N. de Coninck-Smith (Eds.), *Designing modern childhoods: History, space, and the material culture of childhood* (pp. 269–281). New Brunswick, NJ: Rutgers University Press.

Bruns, A. (2008). *Blogs, wikipedia, second life and beyond: From production to produsage.* New York: Peter Lang.

Buckingham, D. (2011). *The material child.* Cambridge: Polity Press.

Cefkin, M. (2010). Business, anthropology, and the growth of corporate ethnography. In M. Cefkin (Ed.), *Ethnography and the corporate encounter: Reflections on research in and of corporations* (pp. 1–37). New York: Berghahn Books.

Chin, E. (2001). *Purchasing power: Black kids and American consumer culture.* Minneapolis, MN: University of Minnesota.

Cook, D. (2004). *The commodification of childhood: The children's clothing industry and the rise of the child consumer.* Durham, NC: Duke University Press.

Cook, D. (2007). The disempowering empowerment of children's consumer "choice": Cultural discourses of the child consumer in North America. *Society and Business Review, 2*(1), 37–52. http://dx.doi.org/10.1108/17465680710725263

Fisher, E. (2015). Class struggles in the digital frontier: Audience labour theory and social media users. *Information, Communication & Society, 18*(9), 1108–1122. doi: 10.1080/1369118X.2015.1018300

Flynn, D. K. (2010). "My customers are different!" Identity, difference, and the political economy of design. In M. Cefkin (Ed.), *Ethnography and the corporate encounter: Reflections on research in and of corporations* (pp. 41–57). New York: Berghahn Books.

Graeber, D. (2001). *Toward an anthropological theory of value: The false coin of our own dreams.* New York: Palgrave.

Graeber, D. (2007). *Possibilities: Essays on hierarchy, rebellion, and desire.* Oakland, CA: AK Press.

Harris, A., Kelly, S. E., & Wyatt, S. (2014). Autobiologies on YouTube: Narratives of direct-to-consumer genetic testing. *New Genetics and Society, 33*(1), 60–78. doi: 10.1080/14636778.2014.884456

Harris, A., Wyatt, S., & Kelly, S. E. (2013). The gift of spit (and the obligation to return it): How consumers of online genetic testing services participate in research. *Information, Communication & Society, 16*(2), 236–257. doi: 10.1080/1369118X.2012.701656

Hart, K., Laville, J.-L., & Cattani, A. D. (Eds.). (2010). *The human economy: The citizen's guide.* Cambridge: Polity Press.

Jenkins, H. (2006). *Convergence culture: Where old and new media collide.* New York: New York University Press.

Kline, S., Dyer-Witheford, N., & De Peuter, G. (2003). *Digital play: The interaction of technology, culture, and marketing.* Montreal & Kingston, London, Ithave: McGill-Queen's Press-MQUP.

Knorr Cetina, K., & Preda, A. (2007). The temporalization of financial markets: From network to flow. *Theory, Culture & Society, 24*(7–8), 116–138. doi: 10.1177/0263276407084700

Lehdonvirta, V., & Castronova, E. (2014). *Virtual economies: Design and analysis.* Cambridge, MA: MIT Press.

Lehdonvirta, V., Wilska, T.-A., & Johnson, M. (2009). Virtual consumerism: Case Habbo hotel. *Information, Communication & Society, 12*(7), 1059–1079. doi: 10.1080/13691180802587813

Lupton, D. (2015). Personal data practices in the age of lively data. Available at SSRN: http://ssrn.com/abstract=2636709

Lupton, D. (2016). The diverse domains of quantified selves: Self-tracking modes and dataveillance. *Economy and Society, 45*(1), 101–122. doi: 10.1080/03085147.2016.1143726

Malaby, T. (2009). *Making virtual worlds: Linden lab and second life.* Ithaca, NY: Cornell University Press.

Maurer, B. (2006). The anthropology of money. *Annual Review of Anthropology, 35*, 15–36. doi: 10.1146/annurev.anthro.35.081705.123127

Miller, D. (1998). *A theory of shopping.* Ithaca, NY: Cornell University Press.

Miller, D. (2008). The uses of value. *Geoforum, 39*, 1122–1132. doi: 10.1016/j.geoforum.2006.03.009

Nafus, D., & Sherman, J. (2014). Big data, big questions. this one does not go up to 11: The quantified self movement as an alternative big data practice. *International Journal of Communication*, 8, 11.

O'Riordan, K. (2011). Revisiting digital technologies: Envisioning biodigital bodies. *Communications, 36*(3), 291–312. http://dx.doi.org/10.1515/comm.2011.015

O'Riordan, K. (2013). Biodigital publics: Personal genomes as digital media artefacts. *Science as Culture, 22*(4), 516–539. doi: 10.1080/14636778.2013.764069

Oudshoorn, N., & Pinch, T. (Eds.). (2003). *How users matter: The co-construction of users and technology.* Cambridge, MA: MIT Press.

Pantzar, M., & Ruckenstein, M. (2015). The heart of everyday analytics: Emotional, material and practical extensions in self-tracking market. *Consumption, Markets and Culture, 18*(1), 92–109. doi: 10.1080/10253866.2014.899213

Pugh, A. (2009). *Longing and belonging: Parents, children, and consumer culture.* Berkeley: University of California Press.

Ritzer, G., & Jurgenson, N. (2010). Production, consumption, prosumption: The nature of capitalism in the age of the digital prosumer. *Journal of Consumer Culture, 10*(1), 13–36. doi: 10.1177/1469540509354673

Ruckenstein, M. (2010). Toying with the world: Children, virtual pets and the value of mobility. *Childhood, 11*(4): 501–512. doi: 10.1177/0907568209352812

Ruckenstein, M. (2011). Children in creationist capitalism: The corporate value of sociality. *Information, Communication & Society, 14*(7), 1060–1076. doi: 10.1080/1369118X.2011.565781

Ruckenstein, M. (2013). Spatial extensions of childhood: From toy worlds to online communities. *Children's Geographies, 11*(4), 476–489. doi: 10.1080/14733285.2013.812309

Ruckenstein, M. (2015). Playing Nintendogs: Desire, distributed agency and potentials of prosumption. *Journal of Consumer Culture, 15*(3), 351–370.

Ruckensten, M. (2016). Keeping data alive: Talking DTC genetic testing. *Information, Communication and Society.*

Ruckenstein, M., & Pantzar, M. (2015). Beyond the quantified self: Thematic exploration of a dataistic paradigm. *New Media & Society*. doi: 10.1177/1461444815609081

Saukko, P. M., Reed, M., Britten, N., & Hogarth, S. (2010). Negotiating the boundary between medicine and consumer culture: Online marketing of nutrigenetic tests. *Social Science & Medicine, 70*(5), 744–753. doi: 10.1016/j.socscimed.2009.10.066

Scheldeman, G. (2010). Technokids? Insulin pumps incorporated in young people's bodies and lives. In J. Edwards, P. Harvey, & P. Wade (Eds.), *Technologized images, technologized bodies* (pp. 137–160). New York. NY: Berghahn Books.

Schüll, N. D. (2016). Data for life: Wearable technology and the design of self-care. *BioSocieties*. Retrieved from: doi:10.1057/biosoc.2015.47

Sharon, T., & Zandbergen, D. (2016). From data fetishism to quantifying selves: Self-tracking practices and the other values of data. *New Media & Society*. Advance online publication. doi: 10.1177/1461444816636090

Suchman, L. A. (2007). *Human-machine reconfigurations: Plans and situated actions.* Cambridge: Cambridge University Press.

Terranova, T. (2000). Free labor: Producing culture for the digital economy. *Social Text, 18*(2), 33–58. doi:10.1215/01642472-18-2_63-33

Thrift, N. (2005). *Knowing capitalism.* London: Sage.

Thrift, N. (2011). Lifeworld Inc – and what to do about it. *Environment and Planning D: Society and Space, 29*, 5–26. doi:10.1068/d0310

Toffler, A. (1980). *The third wave.* New York: Bantam Books.

Van Dijck, J. (2014). Datafication, dataism and dataveillance: Big data between scientific paradigm and ideology. *Surveillance & Society, 12*(2), 197–208.

Wyatt, S. (2005). Non-users also matter: The construction of users and non-users of the internet. In P. Trevor & N. Oudshoorn (Eds.), *How users matter: The co-construction of users and technology* (pp. 67–79). Cambridge, MA: MIT Press.

Zelizer, V. (1985). *Pricing the priceless child: The changing social value of children.* New York: Basic Books.

Index

For Product Safety Concerns and Information please contact our
EU representative GPSR@taylorandfrancis.com Taylor & Francis
Verlag GmbH, Kaufingerstraße 24, 80331 München, Germany

Sustainable Artificial Intelligence-Powered Applications

IEREK Interdisciplinary Series for Sustainable Development

The interdisciplinary series "Sustainable Artificial intelligence Powered Applications," (SAIPA) aims to cover a wide range of Artificial Intelligence applications with a specific focus on sustainability to further support the sustainable development goals. AI systems are able to perform a wide range of tasks, including high-level image and video recognition, perspective modeling, smart automation, advanced simulation, and complex analytics among many others, and has high learning and improvement potential through machine learning and deep learning. These capabilities have many uses and provide many benefits in all industries applications. SAIPA includes a diverse range of these applications, perspectives, and expertise, where it seeks to advance the understanding and implementation of sustainable AI-powered solutions across various scientific disciplines. Its aim is to become a comprehensive guide to different experimental sciences. The "Sustainable AI-Powered Applications" publishes conference proceedings, monographs, and textbooks that address the intersection of artificial intelligence, sustainability, and advanced technologies. Authors, researchers, contributors, and scientists from all scientific disciplines related to AI and advanced technologies, are all invited to contribute to this series to shape the future of AI in a sustainable and responsible manner. Thus, the series represents an excellent endeavor that promotes a collaborative and interdisciplinary strategy for the development of sustainable AI-driven applications. The scope of this series includes, but is not limited to: Promoting sustainability and human well- being, health and medical use, optimizing smart cities planning, transportation systems management, infrastructure development, creating livable urban environments, renewable energy, agricultural Innovations, precision agriculture, weather agriculture, sustainable food production, crop & animal monitoring, and agricultural robotics, Socio-Economic Impacts, optimizing energy consumption in buildings, factories in energy usage and lower carbon, smart grids applications, smart grids management, climate modelling, environmental monitoring, waste management, Internet of things (IOT) and other domains related to the use of AI applications that improve overall environmental impact.

Series Editor: Mourad Amer **editor@saipa-series.com**

Velliangiri Sarveshwaran · P Karthikeyan ·
Vani Rajasekar
Editors

Responsible AI for Smart Cities

Empowering Ethical Urban Innovation Through Responsible AI Deployment

Springer

Editors
Velliangiri Sarveshwaran
Department of Computer Science
and Information Engineering
National Chung Cheng University
Chiyai, Taiwan

P Karthikeyan
School of Computer Science and Engineering
RV University
Bengaluru, Karnataka, India

Vani Rajasekar
School of Computer Sciecne and Engineering
Vellore Institute of Technology
Vellore, Tamil Nadu, India

ISSN 3005-1762 ISSN 3005-1770 (electronic)
Sustainable Artificial Intelligence-Powered Applications
IEREK Interdisciplinary Series for Sustainable Development
ISBN 978-3-032-26900-3 ISBN 978-3-032-26901-0 (eBook)
https://doi.org/10.1007/978-3-032-26901-0

This Springer imprint is published by the registered company Springer Nature Switzerland AG
The registered company address is: Gewerbestrasse 11, 6330 Cham, Switzerland

Contents

Responsible AI for Smarter Cities: Empowering Ethical Urban Innovation Through Responsible AI Development

J. Manoranjini, M. Gayathri, S. Sowjanya Chintalapati, Swathi Gowroju, and Satyanarayana Nimmala

Abstract

A robust healthcare system is essential for a prosperous society. For a nation's healthcare system to earn a positive reputation, it must cultivate trust, integrity, and medical expertise, fostering dynamic relationships between patients and medical institutions. Hospitals function as the physical representation of the overall healthcare system. When these facilities effectively demonstrate efficiency and progress in their structure, operations, and foundational infrastructure, they significantly enhance the community's physical and mental well-being. To achieve this elevated standard, hospitals and healthcare systems must fully integrate with modern industrial and technological advancements. The "smart hospital" concept represents one critical step in this direction. Recognizing the profound significance of digital transformation in modern medicine, this research integrates the principles of Industry 6.0 with smart hospital systems to introduce and define the concept of Hospital 6.0.

J. Manoranjini
Department of Computer Science and Engineering, Rajalakshmi Engineering College, Chennai, TamilNadu, India

M. Gayathri (✉)
Department of Computer Science and Engineering, SCSVMV Deemed University, Kanchipuram, Tamilnadu, India

S. Sowjanya Chintalapati
Department of Computer Science and Engineering, Sreyas Institute of Engineering and Technology, Hyderabad, Telangana, India

S. Gowroju
Department of CSE (Artificial Intelligence and Machine Learning), Sreyas Institute of Engineering and Technology, Hyderabad, Telangana, India
e-mail: swathigowroju@sreyas.ac.in

S. Nimmala
Department of CSE (Data Science), CVR College of Engineering, Hyderabad, Telangana, India

Keywords

Healthcare · Precision medicine · CPS monitoring · Digital twin · Internet of medical things

1 Introduction

Historically, the desire for long life has been a powerful motivator, captivating royalty, scholars, and the wealthy who sought elixirs, specific treatments, and specialized lifestyles to postpone death (Adibi 2023). While the elite focused on extending life or even achieving immortality, most people simply struggled for survival and fought off diseases with limited means. This universal human drive to maintain well-being and preserve life has been a persistent theme across all civilizations, leading naturally to the formal organization of medical services and the founding of healthcare institutions (Volkov and Averkin 2023).

Hospitals, initially established as basic care and refuge centers, have gradually grown into sophisticated, structured organizations dedicated to protecting individual health and promoting longevity (Mohammed et al. 2022). Meeting the ever-increasing societal demand for healthcare required that this evolution be supported by ongoing collaboration with various industrial and technological sectors.

Indeed, the last few decades have seen the healthcare sector undergo a massive transformation. We have moved past traditional approaches, which relied heavily on personal experience and basic interventions, toward sophisticated, advanced technological systems (Sandulescu et al. 2021a). Furthermore, major breakthroughs in genomics, customized medicine, and analytics allow providers to customize treatments based on a patient's genetic makeup, lifestyle, routine and environment, resulting in significantly improved therapeutic outcomes and fewer negative side effects (Dhirani et al. 2023). These innovations have clearly done more than just improve patient care; they've also boosted oper-

V. Sarveshwaran et al. (eds.), *Responsible AI for Smart Cities*, Sustainable Artificial Intelligence-Powered Applications,
https://doi.org/10.1007/978-3-032-26901-0_1

ational efficiency, streamlined resource management, and broadened overall access to medical services.

Despite these tremendous strides, the healthcare environment is constantly grappling with persistent and emerging hurdles ([Online]. 2023). Worldwide, global healthcare systems are facing immense pressure from rapidly growing populations, an increasing elderly demographic, and the rising rates of chronic, non-communicable illnesses like cancer, diabetes, and cardiovascular disease (Chataut et al. 2024a). Moreover, the recent COVID-19 pandemic starkly emphasized the essential nature of resilient healthcare structure, exposing serious weaknesses in public health preparedness, crisis response, and international cooperation. The pandemic forcefully emphasized the necessity for real-time data exchange, flexible treatment protocols, and proactive disease monitoring to lessen the impact of future health crises (Ong 2023).

Given this complex environment, the continuous evolution of healthcare systems is both a societal responsibility and an absolute necessity (Sahi et al. 2018). We must strategically utilize technological integration, evidence-based practices, and preventive care strategies to achieve a model of sustainable healthcare delivery that successfully balances quality, efficiency, and affordability. Essential to nurturing systems that can effectively respond to developing health threats are significant investments in health education, the development of the medical workforce, and interdisciplinary research. Furthermore, as the focus of healthcare shifts toward being more patient-centric, all policy development and technological implementation must be guided by ethical considerations around data privacy, equitable access, and cultural sensitivity (Bajwa et al. 2021). This chapter, therefore, intends to comprehensively explore the many facets of healthcare's evolution, reviewing its historical foundations, current technological innovations, and the strategic necessities for building durable and robust systems. By synthesizing key insights from clinical practice, biomedical research, and health policy, this work offers a holistic view of how healthcare can successfully address the complex requirements of modern societies. Ultimately, our goal is to ensure that healthcare remains a fundamental pillar of human well-being, enhancing the quality of life, not just the duration, and preparing future generations to flourish in an increasingly intricate world (Alowais et al. 2023).

2 Transition and Its Impact

The world is now entering the next era of industrial and technological advancement, aptly named Industry 6.0, which is characterized by the incorporation of distributed intelligence, instantaneous decision-making capabilities, and hyper-connectivity (Nankya et al. 2023). This forthcoming transition is being powered by several key technologies: advanced AI, blockchain, edge computing, and what is termed bio-digital convergence. As a result, the healthcare sector is poised for a series of profound transformations:

1. AI-Driven Predictive Healthcare: By leveraging AI and real-time health data, predictive models will enable early-stage diagnosis and highly tailored treatments based on an individual's hereditary factors, environment, and lifestyle.
2. Autonomous and Self-Learning Systems: We can expect AI-driven robotic systems to autonomously manage monitoring, assist in surgical procedures, provide patient care, and even conduct medical research, thereby decreasing the need for human intermediation and lowering the rate of medical errors.
3. Quantum Computing for Drug Discovery: The field of pharmaceutical research is set to be revolutionized by quantum computing, which will allow for extremely rapid testing and discovery of new drugs, drastically shortening the time required to bring new treatments to market.
4. Decentralized and Secure Healthcare Systems: Blockchain technology is the answer for secure, decentralized management of healthcare data, guaranteeing patient privacy while simultaneously ensuring seamless interoperability between various medical institutions.
5. Digital Twins and Bio-digital Convergence: The utilization of digital twins (virtual, precise replicas of patients) will make it possible to simulate personalized treatments before they are applied in a real-world setting. This capability is expected to optimize patient outcomes and dramatically minimize risks.

The shift from Industry 5.0 to 6.0 signifies a true paradigm shift where healthcare is becoming increasingly independent, flexible, and fundamentally focused on the patient. Technologies such as artificial intelligence (AI), the Internet of Medical Things (IoMT), and digital twins, medical care will become more accurate, readily accessible, and proactive ("Leveraging AI and Machine Learning for Robust Cybersecurity in Healthcare" 2024). Crucially, this evolution is anticipated to do more than just improve treatment precision; it is also expected to decrease overall healthcare expenditures and help close the global disparity in medical service availability, ultimately creating a more intelligent and interconnected healthcare ecosystem (Wolf 2024).

3 Core Concepts and Technologies

a. **Cyber-Physical Systems (CPS): a Foundation for Integrated Healthcare**

Cyber-Physical Systems (CPS) are the backbone of this new era, merging digital intelligence with physical components like medical devices to facilitate both real-time oversight and extensive automation. Within the healthcare context, CPS significantly boosts the capabilities of remote surgery, automated diagnostic tools, and interconnected medical equipment, leading to greater efficiency and a reduction in human error. These networks allow for effortless communication among sensors, actuators, and computational systems, which is vital for guaranteeing operational precision in complex medical procedures. Ultimately, CPS is the enabling technology behind the concept of smart hospitals, where networked systems streamline operational workflows, continuously monitor patients, and utilize predictive analytics to guide emergency responses (Paul et al. 2023).

b. **Artificial Intelligence (AI) and Machine Learning (ML): Enabling Instantaneous Decisions**

AI and Machine Learning (ML) represent the bedrock of Industry 6.0, providing the capacity to process massive patient datasets instantaneously. While ML models focus on anticipating patient outcomes using historical data, AI-driven diagnostic tools actively support clinicians in the early detection of diseases (Mishra and Singh 2023). These powerful tools are crucial for improving hospital resource allocation, minimizing diagnostic mistakes, and creating superior treatment strategies. The ability of machine learning algorithms to constantly learn from new data allows them to deliver personalized treatment precisely adapted to each patient's needs. Beyond clinical use, AI-powered virtual assistants are instrumental in managing administrative tasks, supporting patient engagement, and automating various hospital processes.

c. **Blockchain Technology: Ensuring the Security of Medical Records**

Blockchain technology offers a crucial result by providing a decentralized, absolute ledger that is fundamentally designed to guard the security and integrity of medical data. This technology ensures full transparency in all healthcare transactions, dramatically enhancing patient privacy, speeding up the safe transfer of medical records between separate institutions, and acting as a powerful deterrent against fraud (Sachdeva 2024). Furthermore, smart contracts—self-executing agreements built on the blockchain—allow for secure management of patient consent, reducing bureaucratic delays and ensuring smooth information exchange between care providers. An added benefit is the technology's ability to reinforce drug traceability, which plays a vital role in combating counterfeit medicines within the supply chain (Chenthara et al. 2019).

d. **Robotics and Automation: Greater Precision in Surgery and Routine Tasks**

Robotic-assisted surgeries have transformed complex procedures, offering a level of precision that leads to faster recovery times. The automation of hospital workflows, seen in examples like intelligent inventory management and robotic dispensing systems, maximizes operational effectiveness, allowing medical staff to dedicate more time to direct patient care. AI-powered robots are also deployed to assist with elderly care, rehabilitation therapies, and minimally invasive surgeries, ensuring exceptional accuracy and fewer complications. Improving healthcare logistics through automation is essential for optimizing resource utilization throughout hospital management (Chataut et al. 2024b).

e. **Quantum Computing: Accelerating Data Analysis and Predictive Modeling**

Quantum computing introduces an unparalleled level of processing power, making it possible to conduct real-time analysis of extremely complex genetic data, facilitate accurate disease modeling, and drive personalized medicine initiatives. This innovative technology is set to dramatically accelerate the process of drug discovery and allows for highly accurate simulations of human physiology, leading to more effective treatment protocols. By analyzing multidimensional datasets, quantum-enhanced AI can significantly improve diagnostics, providing valuable insights into rare diseases and medically challenging cases. Crucially, quantum cryptography is also used to strengthen cybersecurity within healthcare, guaranteeing the secure communication of sensitive patient information (Alhammad et al. 2022).

f. **Internet of Medical Things (IoMT): Continuous, Seamless Monitoring**

The Internet of Medical Things (IoMT) is responsible for establishing an intelligent healthcare network by connecting a variety of sensors, wearables, and dedicated medical devices. This ecosystem facilitates real-time patient monitoring, utilizing smart implants and AI-driven diagnostics to boost preventive care, decrease hospital readmissions, and ensure interventions are delivered when they are most needed. The capability of IoMT to support remote healthcare services means that patients can receive consistent, ongoing care without the need for frequent hospital visits. Furthermore, when IoMT data is combined with AI, it enables predictive analytics that can alert medical professionals to potential health crises before symptoms fully manifest (Seh et al. 2020).

4 Digital Twins in Healthcare: Virtual Models of Patients and Medical Systems

Digital twins imitate real-world medical conditions in a simulated environment, enabling doctors to simulate treatments before applying them to patients. This innovation minimizes risks, enhances surgical planning, and provides tailored treatment approaches based on real-time patient data (Guerra 2023). By mirroring a patient's physiological responses, digital twins allow precise drug testing, optimizing medication dosages, and improving patient outcomes. In hospital management, digital twins optimize workflows by predicting equipment maintenance needs and enhancing resource allocation.

Industry 6.0, the next phase of technological progress, incorporates enhanced artificial intelligence (AI), cyber-physical systems (CPS), autonomous systems, and the Internet of Things (IoT) to enhance a range of industries. Industry 6.0 is transforming medical research, patient care, and hospital management through automation, real-time data processing, and intelligent decision-making (Chaudhary and Yousafzai 2022a). AI, IoT, and robotics are used by smart hospitals to provide constant, real-time patient monitoring. These hospitals use sensors and networked equipment to monitor patient vitals, forecast health concerns, and notify medical staff of urgent circumstances. AI-driven systems monitor patients without human intervention, reducing the burden on healthcare staff. While smart hospitals increase efficiency by automating mundane operations like inventory management, patient record updates, and scheduling, continuous tracking guarantees that any abnormalities in vital signs prompt quick medical intervention ("Credential Stuffing Attack Exposed United Healthcare Member Data" n.d.).

Healthcare systems can respond more quickly to global health emergencies and therapies thanks to continuous innovation. To prevent the spread of diseases, they can also implement public health initiatives.

5 Evolution of Healthcare

The development of healthcare can be broken down into a series of distinct, cumulative stages, each one propelled by evolving societal demands, policy changes, and technological breakthroughs. Analyzing this historical progression is crucial, not only for recognizing how technology has fundamentally changed care delivery, but also for gaining foresight into how we can build patient-centric, sustainable systems in the future ("HIPAA Network Compliance and Security Requirements Explained" 2024) (Fig. 1).

a. **Healthcare 1.0: The Traditional Manual System**

Healthcare 1.0 defines the earliest organized model of medical care, characterized by primarily manual processes, record-keeping based on physical paper, and highly centralized institutions. In this environment, hospitals and clinics typically functioned as isolated entities, meaning patient information was scattered and fragmented across various individual providers ("What is an Electronic Health Record (EHR)" 2024). This lack of standardized protocols and

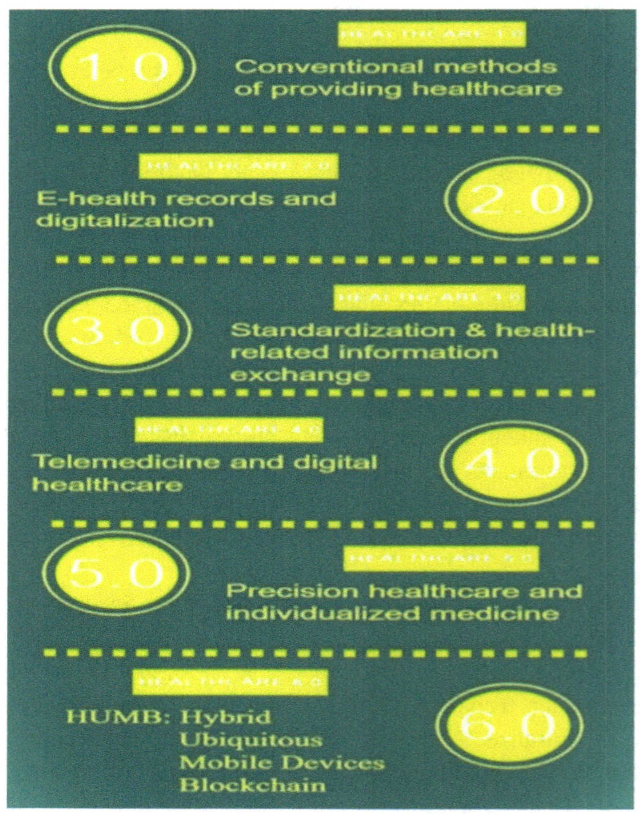

Fig. 1 Evolving Healthcare 1.0 to 6.0

systems capable of working together often resulted in significant care delivery inefficiencies, delayed diagnoses, and poor coordination among different practitioners. While defined by the twentieth century, this model was foundational, nonetheless, as it highlighted the critical need for organized procedures, structured documentation, and better patient record management, paving the way for the digital revolutions that would follow (Alanazi 2023).

b. **Healthcare 2.0: The Leap to Digitization**

The movement into Healthcare 2.0 began in the early 2000s, heralded by the widespread adoption of digital technologies, most notably Electronic Health Records (EHRs). This phase directly addressed the core drawbacks of paper-based systems, facilitating the much faster storage, retrieval, and sharing of patient data. Healthcare providers prioritized digitizing patient records to boost operational efficiency and enable data exchange across different systems. EHRs were transformative, giving clinician's immediate access to full patient histories, which in turn reduced errors and ensured a seamless continuity of care. This digitization was far more than an internal organizational change; it created the necessary framework for advanced analytics and new decision-support systems, completely redefining how patient care was managed and delivered (Zhang et al. 2020a).

c. **Healthcare 3.0: Focus on Information Exchange**

Healthcare 3.0 came into focus around the mid-2010s, with a strong emphasis on achieving true interoperability and enabling fluid data exchange among all healthcare stakeholders. The introduction of Health Information Exchanges (HIEs) was key, allowing for secure, real-time sharing of data between hospitals, labs, clinics, and pharmacies. This period was characterized by a focus on coordinated treatment, continuous care, and improving health outcomes across entire populations. By effectively linking previously disconnected systems, Healthcare 3.0 successfully reduced redundancies, minimized medical mistakes, and empowered providers to make data-informed choices, leading to significant improvements in patient outcomes. In essence, this stage established the technical and organizational prerequisites for modern, patient-centered care and predictive health management (Kumar and Patel 2021a).

d. **Healthcare 4.0: Digital Tools and Patient Empowerment**

The late 2010s marked the emergence of Healthcare 4.0, a stage defined by the mainstream use of telemedicine, remote patient monitoring tools, mobile health apps, and wearable devices. This model deliberately empowered patients by giving them direct access to their real-time health data, which facilitated proactive management of long-term conditions and encouraged healthier personal habits. By integrating Internet of Things (IoT) devices into the healthcare framework, continuous tracking of vital signs became possible, which is essential for early intervention and highly personalized care. This era also fundamentally altered the dynamic between patient and provider, positioning patients as active partners in their own healthcare decisions (Ramesh and Saini 2023a). Ultimately, the digital transformation of Healthcare 4.0 boosted both accessibility to medical services and overall operational efficiency, while simultaneously driving down costs.

e. **Healthcare 5.0: Individualized and Precision Medicine**

The early 2020s ushered in Healthcare 5.0, representing a dramatic shift away from a "one-size-fits-all" model toward highly individualized care. This phase capitalizes on breakthrough developments in genomics, biomarker research, artificial intelligence, and big data analytics to fully realize the potential of precision medicine. Healthcare 5.0 enables clinicians to customize interventions based on a patient's precise genetic blueprint, life history, and unique environment, thereby significantly boosting treatment effectiveness and reducing unwanted side effects. Predictive modeling, personalized therapeutic strategies, and risk stratification became core practices during this phase, effectively addressing the growing complexity and prevalence of chronic diseases ("Emerging Trends in AI-Powered Healthcare and Industry 6.0" 2023). By seamlessly merging patient-centric strategies with state-of-the-art technology, Healthcare 5.0 laid a strong foundation for more targeted, preventive, and proactive medical approaches.

f. **Healthcare 6.0: Decentralization and Transparency**

Healthcare 6.0 is the current, emerging frontier of innovation, which is expected to become fully established after 2024. This stage is defined by the integration of blockchain technology, tokenization, and decentralized systems to create an ecosystem that is uniquely transparent, secure, and focused on the patient. In contrast to earlier phases, Healthcare 6.0 places a heavy emphasis on trust, actively incentivizing patient behavior, and ensuring total interoperability among all parties involved ("The Future of Healthcare: AI, Robotics, and Digital Transformation" 2022).

1. Blockchain for Data Security and Integrity: The use of blockchain ensures that patient health data is both unchangeable and traceable, offering a powerful defense

against fraud, unauthorized access, and data tampering. Because the blockchain ledger is decentralized, it instills greater confidence in healthcare transactions and allows for secure sharing of sensitive data among researchers, providers, patients, and insurers ("AI and Block chain in Smart Healthcare Systems: Challenges and Solutions" 2021).

2. Tokenization and Patient Incentivization: Through tokenization, patients are given a mechanism to be active participants in managing their own health via a reward system that encourages positive health habits (Health and "The Rise of Intelligent Healthcare: How Industry 6.0 is Shaping the Future of Medicine" 2023). Patients can earn tokens for activities like adhering to treatment plans, participating in wellness programs, or taking preventive health measures, fostering deeper engagement and promoting lasting health results.
3. Enhanced Efficiency and Interoperability: By harnessing blockchain and tokenized systems, Healthcare 6.0 ensures seamless integration across diverse healthcare platforms, which improves coordination, reduces unnecessary administrative load, and optimizes how resources are utilized. The inherently transparent nature of this health data exchange guarantees accountability, eliminates redundant efforts, and enables truly evidence-based decision-making (Vincent and Huang 2020).

Healthcare 6.0 takes the principles of precision and personalization from 5.0 and applies them while simultaneously solving critical security, transparency, and patient empowerment issues. This vision is of a healthcare future where patients are not passive recipients but active collaborators, supported by powerful technology that guarantees sustainable practices, equitable access, and better overall population health. By combining new technologies with deeply patient-centered principles, Healthcare 6.0 represents a crucial stride toward a more resilient, inclusive, and highly efficient medical future.

6 Applications of Industry 6.0 in Healthcare

The integration of Industry 6.0 technologies is not merely an upgrade; it is a fundamental re-engineering of the healthcare paradigm. It orchestrates a pivotal shift away from generalized, reactive treatment models toward highly personalized, predictive, and precision-based medicine. By synergistically utilizing artificial intelligence (AI), advanced robotics, and hyper-connected systems, this new industrial era is poised to fundamentally enhance patient care, streamline operations, and ultimately raise the universal standard of medical practice ("AI-driven Diagnostics and Personalized Medicine: A Future Perspective" 2022).

a. **Autonomous Monitoring and Real-Time Patient Care in Smart Hospitals**

The advent of the Smart Hospital represents the physical manifestation of Industry 6.0's capabilities. These facilities are designed for constant, real-time patient monitoring through the strategic deployment of the Internet of Things (IoT) sensors and networked medical equipment. By continuously tracking patient vital signs and physiological parameters, these systems not only identify but also preemptively forecast potential health crises, immediately alerting medical staff to subtle changes that signal an urgent circumstance.

AI-powered solutions play a critical role in minimizing the workload on clinical staff by assuming responsibility for perpetual, automated patient oversight, reducing the need for continuous human presence. Beyond bedside care, Smart Hospitals leverage automation to significantly boost efficiency by managing repetitive and time-consuming administrative functions, such as inventory control, scheduling, and updating patient records. The continuous data streams ensure that any anomaly in a patient's condition triggers prompt, targeted medical intervention. For instance, institutions like the Mayo Clinic have successfully implemented AI-based monitoring systems that evaluate high-dimensional patient data in real-time, drastically reducing response times and noticeably improving clinical outcomes by recognizing minor, critical shifts in patient status ("Blockchain for Secure Healthcare Data Management: Policy and Implementation Challenges" 2021).

b. **Personalized Medicine: AI-Driven Patient-Specific Treatments**

Industry 6.0 is the driving force behind the transition to personalized medicine. In this model, generalized treatment protocols are replaced by customized therapies derived from in-depth analysis of patient-specific data via AI ("Blockchain for Secure Healthcare Data Management: Policy and Implementation Challenges" 2021). Predictive analytics allows AI to comprehensively assess individual disease risk based on a confluence of genetic markers, environmental exposure, and lifestyle factors. Concurrently, sophisticated machine learning models are crucial in determining the most effective medications, adjusting dosages, and selecting optimal treatment pathways uniquely suited for each individual. This hyper-personalized approach is proven to significantly enhance therapeutic efficacy while simultaneously mitigating the risk of adverse side effects. A prime example of this is the application of IBM Watson in oncology. Watson analyzes enormous volumes of patient genomic data and relevant medical literature to recommend tailored cancer therapy options, leading to greater treatment accuracy and improved success rates in complex cancer care ("Healthcare 6.0: The Convergence of AI, Robotics, and Data Analytics" 2023).

c. **Robotic Surgery: Enhancing Precision and Minimizing Error**

The widespread adoption of robotic surgery, powered by AI and sophisticated Cyber-Physical Systems (CPS), marks a groundbreaking application of Industry 6.0 principles. These integrated robotic systems dramatically increase surgical accuracy, substantially reduce the incidence of human error, and deliver superior patient outcomes. AI-driven robots augment the surgeon's capabilities by providing exceptional visualization and maintaining rock-steady stability throughout procedures, while the robotic instruments themselves execute intricate operations with microscopic precision, thus minimizing collateral tissue damage. The result of this technological synergy is the proliferation of less invasive surgical techniques, which translate directly into shorter hospital stays, less post-operative pain, and markedly faster patient recovery times. The Da Vinci Surgical System, a well-known robotic assistant, epitomizes this trend, facilitating minimally invasive procedures across numerous specialties and revolutionizing the patient recovery process (Singh and Verma, 2021a).

d. **Telemedicine and Remote Healthcare: Leveraging CPS for Monitoring**

Telemedicine, already established, is now substantially enhanced by Industry 6.0 technologies, effectively extending high-quality healthcare beyond the traditional hospital walls. This capability facilitates remote consultations, diagnostic procedures, and continuous monitoring, thereby making medical services readily accessible, particularly to patients residing in remote or medically underserved areas. The interaction between doctor and patient is streamlined by AI-powered chatbots and advanced video conferencing platforms. Crucially, wearable devices and IoT sensors track vital health parameters in real time, creating a consistent data stream for clinicians. Remote healthcare offers tangible benefits: it reduces the necessity of physical hospital visits, leading to lower overall healthcare expenditures, and minimizes the risk of exposure to infections, as highlighted during the recent global pandemic. Initiatives like eSanjeevani, launched by the Indian government, successfully demonstrate this, enabling patients in rural regions to obtain specialist consultations without the undue burden of long-distance travel ("Smart Hospitals and the Future of Healthcare: A Roadmap for Industry 6.0, Boston Consulting Group 2022).

e. **Genomics and Drug Development: A Revolution in Precision**

The merging of AI and big data analytics in the field of genomics is fundamentally redefining precision medicine by identifying patients' genetic predispositions to specific diseases and tailoring customized preventive care strategies. AI is uniquely capable of processing colossal genomic datasets to identify complex disease markers and potential therapeutic targets. Furthermore, predictive healthcare strategies built upon comprehensive genetic profiling significantly improve the potential for early disease detection. The efficiency of drug development, testing, and distribution is also being accelerated by AI and automation, drastically reducing both the associated time and financial outlay ("Japan's AI-Powered Smart Hospitals: Improving Patient Outcomes" 2023). Intelligent pharmaceutical manufacturing facilities utilize advanced robotics for ultra-precise medication formulation and packaging, while specialized AI models rapidly evaluate extensive biological data to swiftly pinpoint promising therapeutic candidates. Finally, AI-driven supply chain management ensures the highly efficient and secure delivery of pharmaceuticals to pharmacies and hospitals.

Taken together, Industry 6.0 is actively transforming healthcare through a profound, comprehensive integration of AI, advanced robotics, the IoT, and vast data analytics. These developments are paving the way for a medical landscape that is more accurate, profoundly effective, and universally available, ultimately ensuring a substantial elevation in patient outcomes and the general standard of medical care worldwide.

7 Case Studies and Real-Life Implementations

The healthcare industry is currently undergoing a radical transformation, fueled by the swift development of Industry 6.0 technologies. These include artificial intelligence (AI), robotics, the Internet of Medical Things (IoMT), and blockchain, all of which are changing the way care is delivered. Across the globe, various nations have taken the lead in pioneering creative implementations designed to secure patient data, maximize efficiency, and ultimately elevate the standard of patient care ("The Role of Machine Learning in Disease Prediction and Prevention" 2022).

1. **Smart Hospitals in Japan**

Problem Statement: Many hospitals worldwide are struggling with prolonged patient wait times, ineffective scheduling practices, and serious delays in emergency response. These issues stem largely from outdated manual processes and a lack of real-time monitoring capabilities, which negatively affect both patient outcomes and satisfaction.

Solution: Leading Smart Hospitals in Japan, such as the Fujita Health University Hospital, are using an advanced combination of AI-driven diagnostics, automated patient tracking, and specialized robotic assistants to streamline their entire workflow. This comprehensive strategy has achieved impressive results: wait times have been cut by 30%, and early disease detection rates have improved by 25%, leading to faster treatment and a superior patient experience.

1. Japan has long been at the forefront of technological integration in healthcare. Its smart hospitals have seamlessly merged AI and sophisticated robotics to improve clinical care and optimize operations. These state-of-the-art medical facilities rely on extensive automation, robotic assistance, and real-time data analytics to establish environments that are both highly efficient and deeply patient-focused. A prime example of this innovation is the Fujita Health University Hospital, which has set a global benchmark by implementing a fully automated patient care system.
2. Central to the success at Fujita is the integration of AI-powered diagnostic technologies. These systems are indispensable in supporting radiologists and other medical specialists. By analyzing complex medical images—such as X-rays, MRIs, and CT scans—the AI can accurately identify irregularities at an unprecedented scale. This efficiency not only reduces the chance of human error but has significantly increased early disease diagnosis rates. For example, AI models trained on vast datasets are capable of spotting subtle patterns in images that might be missed by human eyes, ensuring quicker and more precise diagnoses. Furthermore, AI-based predictive analytics aid physicians in constantly evaluating patient status and recommending individualized treatment strategies to guarantee the best possible care.
3. Robotics has become another major game-changer in Japan's smart hospitals, particularly for patient care and elderly support. Humanoid robotic assistants like Pepper and Paro are routinely deployed to manage mundane tasks, offer companionship to older patients, and enhance the overall hospital experience. Pepper, an interactive robot, uses natural language processing to communicate with patients, answer basic questions, and provide emotional reassurance. Meanwhile, Paro, a therapeutic robotic seal, is designed to comfort elderly patients and those with dementia by responding to physical touch and sound, mimicking the soothing behavior of a real animal. These robotic companions have proven highly effective in boosting the mental well-being of patients, combating feelings of loneliness, and creating a more interactive and positive hospital setting.
4. A third vital component of these smart hospitals is the automation of medication management. Automated dispensing systems have been installed to ensure drug distribution is precise, thereby minimizing the risk of critical human errors. Utilizing AI and robotics, these systems deliver the correct medication dosage at the optimal time, lowering the probability of inaccurate prescriptions and dangerous drug interactions. Hospitals also benefit from effective inventory management, which helps avoid shortages and reduces waste by maintaining appropriate stock levels. Crucially, these automated systems also lighten the workload of healthcare professionals, allowing them to focus their energy on more complex facets of direct patient care.
5. The benefits of smart hospitals extend far beyond clinical care and operational effectiveness. Studies indicate that incorporating AI and robotics into these environments has led to a notable drop in patient wait times, with some facilities reporting a 30% reduction in delays. Additionally, the 25% increase in early disease identification rates ensures prompt interventions and significantly improved health outcomes. Patient satisfaction also rises because AI-driven solutions offer healthcare services that are more responsive and tailored to individual needs. Despite these impressive advancements, the widespread adoption of smart hospital technology faces several challenges. The high cost of implementation remains a primary obstacle. Smaller healthcare providers often find it difficult to justify the significant financial investment required for AI-driven diagnostic suites, robotic assistants, and automated drug dispensers. Furthermore, integrating new digital solutions with existing, often antiquated, IT systems presents a substantial technical hurdle. Finally, the ethical implications of using AI-driven diagnostics and robotic care are still under discussion. To ensure that smart hospitals maintain a

necessary balance between technological efficiency and human compassion, issues of data privacy, accountability for AI decisions, and the potential loss of the "human touch" in patient interactions must be thoroughly addressed.

The future of smart hospitals in Japan is undoubtedly promising, driven by continuous innovation in AI, robotics, and digital health. As technology progresses, we can anticipate even greater improvements in hospital productivity, overall patient care, and health outcomes. By resolving current implementation challenges and ensuring strict ethical and legal compliance, these intelligent hospitals are poised to establish the global benchmark for the healthcare industry, ushering in a new era of patient-centered medical treatment.

b. **Blockchain for Secure Data Management in Europe**

Problem Statement: Patient health records in many countries are scattered across multiple providers, which results in inefficient data sharing, unnecessary duplication of medical tests, and prolonged treatment delays. Security fears further inhibit the open exchange of this vital information ("Regulatory Challenges in AI-Enabled Healthcare Devices" 2023).

Solution: Estonia's pioneering blockchain-based National Health System offers a robust solution. It securely stores patient data on a decentralized ledger, granting authorized providers instantaneous access while rigorously protecting privacy. This system successfully eliminates data redundancy, accelerates treatment, and guarantees full compliance with demanding GDPR standards.

1. Europe has taken a decisive lead in utilizing blockchain to enhance the security, transparency, and interoperability of managing medical data. The decentralized nature of blockchain inherently reduces the risk of fraud, data breaches, and unauthorized manipulation by ensuring patient records are inaccessible to unauthorized parties. The Estonian National Health System (ENHS) provides one of the best examples of blockchain deployment in healthcare, using the technology to securely manage and store patient health records.
2. Estonia's system has fundamentally revolutionized medical data handling. By deploying blockchain, the country ensures that all patient information is encrypted and permanently held on a decentralized ledger, actively thwarting cyber-attacks and unauthorized access. The use of smart contracts within the system allows patients to control precisely who can view their health data, enabling selective information sharing only when necessary with specific healthcare providers. This degree of patient control instills confidence in the security of their private medical data. Furthermore, blockchain's immutability ensures that medical records cannot be altered or corrupted, substantially improving data integrity and reliability.
3. Beyond Estonia, other European nations have also begun exploring blockchain for secure data management. In the United Kingdom, several hospitals have initiated blockchain solutions to smooth the sharing of medical records among different healthcare providers. Historically, patient files resided in isolated databases within individual institutions, making seamless information transfer challenging. With blockchain, authorized providers gain instant access to up-to-date patient records, thereby reducing errors from missing information, eliminating redundancy, and increasing overall treatment efficiency. This technology is particularly beneficial in emergency settings, where immediate access to a patient's medical history can be life-saving. European law requires patients to have dominion over their personal data, including the right to view, correct, and even request the removal of information. Blockchain's architecture facilitates these requirements by using privacy-preserving techniques, such as cryptographic hashing and zero-knowledge proofs. These features allow patients to verify their identity and access records without revealing sensitive information, enabling healthcare organizations to meet GDPR standards while maintaining both security and operational efficiency.
4. Clinical trials and medical research are two other critical areas where Europe is implementing blockchain. Guaranteeing the integrity and validity of clinical trial data is vital for medical advancement and the creation of new treatments. Blockchain provides a transparent and unchangeable record-keeping mechanism for clinical trials, preventing data manipulation and verifying the authenticity of study results. Pharmaceutical companies and research institutions now use blockchain to securely store patient consent forms, trial outcomes, and drug development data. This application not only boosts confidence in clinical research by reducing fraud but also accelerates the release of new medications by fostering better collaboration among researchers.
5. Despite its numerous advantages, the widespread implementation of blockchain in European healthcare faces significant hurdles. Scalability is the primary challenge. Given the enormous volume of data generated daily by the healthcare sector, maintaining an ever-expanding blockchain ledger can become highly resource-intensive, demanding substantial storage space and processing power. Researchers are actively working on innovative

solutions like sharding and off-chain storage to mitigate these limitations and ensure blockchain remains a viable option for high-volume data management. Another obstacle is the inherent resistance from traditional healthcare professionals who are comfortable with centralized data management systems. Integrating blockchain with existing healthcare IT systems requires considerable financial outlay, specialized technological expertise, and regulatory approval. The decentralized nature of blockchain also raises complex questions regarding legal accountability in the event of system failures or disputes. Addressing these multifaceted issues is crucial for the broad adoption of the technology in the healthcare sector.

The future of blockchain technology in European healthcare appears extremely promising. With continued advancements in blockchain protocols, enhanced security measures, and growing regulatory support, its adoption is expected to broaden considerably. As more research institutions, pharmaceutical companies, and hospitals embrace blockchain, the potential for vastly improved patient data security, streamlined medical processes, and enhanced trust in healthcare services will continue to grow. By overcoming existing barriers and strategically combining blockchain with innovations like the Internet of Medical Things (IoMT) and artificial intelligence, Europe is establishing the foundation for a more transparent, effective, and secure healthcare system.

c. **IoMT-Based Real-Time Patient Monitoring in the USA**

Problem Statement: Patients residing in rural or medically underserved areas frequently lack timely access to specialized care, which often leads to higher readmission rates and poorer outcomes, particularly for those managing chronic diseases.

Solution: Mount Sinai Hospital in the USA is utilizing IoMT wearables and biosensors for continuous remote monitoring of patients' vital signs. AI-powered algorithms generate real-time alerts that notify doctors of critical anomalies, a system that has successfully reduced hospital readmissions by 40% and enables proactive, personalized interventions ("Revolutionizing Drug Discovery with AI and Quantum Computing" 2022).

1. The Internet of Medical Things (IoMT) has profoundly reshaped healthcare in the United States by enabling remote medical interventions, continuous patient monitoring, and predictive analytics. IoMT describes a network of interconnected sensors, wearables, and medical devices that constantly collect, transmit, and analyze health data. This technology has brought significant improvements to chronic illness management, post-operative care, and emergency response. By integrating IoMT data with cloud computing and AI, healthcare providers can deliver proactive, individualized care, improving patient outcomes while reducing hospital readmission rates.
2. Mount Sinai Hospital in New York is a leading institution implementing IoMT for real-time patient monitoring. The hospital has seamlessly integrated smart wearables and biosensors into its care model which collect data in real time and send it to cloud-based systems where artificial intelligence (AI) algorithms analyze patterns and identify potential health risks. If abnormal readings are detected, automatic notifications are immediately dispatched to both the patient and their healthcare providers. For instance, in patients with cardiac conditions, a wearable ECG monitor can detect subtle arrhythmias and alert doctors before a critical event occurs, which is potentially life-saving.
3. Furthermore, IoMT has transformed remote patient care, a vital necessity in rural and impoverished areas where access to medical facilities is limited. Telemedicine platforms, coupled with IoMT, enable physicians to monitor patients remotely, drastically reducing the need for frequent hospital visits. Patients managing chronic conditions such as high blood pressure or diabetes can use linked glucose and blood pressure monitors at home, sharing real-time data with their physicians. This constant oversight allows for timely adjustments to treatment plans, effectively reducing complications and hospitalizations. The Veterans Health Administration (VHA) in the USA runs one of the largest remote patient monitoring programs, leveraging IoMT to track the health status of veterans with chronic illnesses. This program has achieved a 40% decrease in hospital readmissions and significantly improved patient adherence to recommended therapies.
4. IoMT is also widely used in post-operative care to prevent complications and ensure a smooth recovery. Smart bandages with integrated sensors track wound healing by detecting infection-related changes, including elevated temperature, moisture levels, or pH fluctuations. These devices automatically alert medical teams if a patient is at risk of infection, facilitating early intervention and reducing recovery times. Hospitals like the Mayo Clinic have incorporated IoMT-based solutions for post-surgical patients, which has led to improved recovery metrics and shorter hospital stays.
5. Despite its benefits, the widespread adoption of IoMT in the USA faces several barriers. Data security and patient privacy are paramount concerns. IoMT devices generate enormous volumes of sensitive health data,

making them attractive targets for cybercriminals. Unauthorized access to these systems can compromise patient information and disrupt essential health services. To mitigate these risks, hospitals and technology providers are implementing advanced cybersecurity measures, including multi-factor authentication, robust encryption techniques, and blockchain solutions. Interoperability is another significant challenge, as IoMT devices from different manufacturers often operate on proprietary, incompatible platforms, hindering seamless data exchange. Standardization efforts are underway to ensure that healthcare providers can integrate various IoMT solutions into a unified digital ecosystem. The creation of universal health data exchange protocols, like Fast Healthcare Interoperability Resources (FHIR), is crucial for increasing compatibility between IoMT systems and Electronic Health Records (EHRs). The future of IoMT in the USA is exceptionally bright, driven by ongoing advancements in artificial intelligence, edge computing, and 5G connectivity. AI-driven predictive analytics will soon be integrated to further improve early disease identification, allowing clinicians to act before symptoms worsen. Additionally, the expansion of 5G networks will provide faster and more reliable data transmission, greatly improving the effectiveness and accessibility of real-time monitoring, even in remote areas.

d. **Comparative Analysis and Future Prospects**

A comparative examination of these implementations clearly reveals the diverse and powerful applications of Industry 6.0 in global healthcare. Japan's Smart Hospital model demonstrates how AI-driven automation can enhance efficiency and the patient experience. Europe's proactive blockchain system successfully addresses fundamental concerns about data transparency and security. Meanwhile, the USA's focus on IoMT solutions is revolutionizing remote monitoring and patient care.

While these technologies offer transformative advantages, they all share common implementation challenges that must be overcome for smooth adoption, including exorbitant start-up costs, persistent cybersecurity risks, and various regulatory and ethical obstacles. Looking ahead, the critical step will be the strategic integration of these established technologies with emerging innovations like quantum computing and 6G networks. This unified approach promises to dramatically enhance global healthcare solutions, making them more secure, efficient, and universally accessible for the future.

8 Literature Survey

The synergy between Industry 6.0 and Hospital 6.0 is establishing a new paradigm in healthcare, promising significant societal and clinical benefits. Existing research underscores the profound influence of Industry 6.0 on the medical sector, noting how its technological advancements are fundamentally enhancing global healthcare services. This evolution is instrumental in facilitating the transition toward more efficient and patient-centric healthcare models. Historically, every industrial revolution has redefined various sectors, and healthcare is no exception. The strategic collaboration between industry and clinical institutions aims to usher in an advanced era of medical solutions, focusing on systematically improving service quality, guaranteeing patient safety, optimizing clinical outcomes, elevating the overall patient experience, and streamlining healthcare delivery processes. Notably, the technological foundations of Industry 5.0, building upon Industry 4.0 innovations, have already contributed substantially to improved hospital quality. The deployment of advanced automation technologies, which characterizes the impact of Industry 5.0, clearly illustrates the close alignment between industrial and healthcare transformations in boosting overall service efficacy ("5G and IoMT: Transforming Connected Healthcare Systems" 2023).

Further discussion must address the foundational concept of industrial transformation within the health sector. This transformation necessitates the adoption of cutting-edge methodologies to enhance both service quality and productivity. By integrating advanced technologies and data-driven approaches, healthcare facilities can significantly elevate clinical care standards and optimize operational workflows, leading directly to improved patient outcomes. These technological advancements are also critical in alleviating systemic burdens, such as financial constraints and inconsistencies in service quality. Moreover, governmental support, particularly through increased funding for medical centers, can accelerate these transformations. Technological innovation also dramatically expedites patient access to necessary care. The application of artificial intelligence (AI) and data analytics is instrumental in facilitating evidence-based clinical decision support within hospitals. Machine learning, AI, and data analytics collectively address complex medical challenges, proving particularly valuable in the diagnosis and treatment of critical illnesses, such as various forms of cancer. For instance, an advanced hospital management system utilizing AI can swiftly assess emergency room conditions, enabling prompt and effective decision-making under duress ("The Impact of Artificial Intelligence on Global Health Equity" 2021).

Hospital 6.0 embodies the capability for real-time, automated healthcare processes, which significantly improves time management for both staff and patients. Despite these technological strides, patient dissatisfaction with healthcare services remains a challenge, even in technologically developed nations. In the diagnostic domain, advanced imaging techniques, such as Magnetic Resonance Imaging (MRI) scans, demonstrate high specificity, underscoring the continuous need for sophisticated medical imaging solutions, especially in emergency scenarios. Furthermore, technological innovation extends clinical capabilities beyond the physical hospital premises. Virtual healthcare platforms, exemplified by applications such as Huma, allow patients to access medical assistance from their homes. These digital solutions are crucial for fostering supportive patient communities, thereby enhancing morale and engagement in treatment. In summation, the integration of Industry 6.0 with the Hospital 6.0 framework underscores the immense, transformative potential of science and technology in modern healthcare ("Robotic Surgery: The Next Frontier in Minimally Invasive Procedures" 2022).

9 Core Components of Healthcare Industry 6.0

Industry 6.0 is conceptualized as an emerging stage that builds upon the principles of Industry 5.0, with a central focus on developing intelligent healthcare facilities. This phase of industrial evolution emphasizes enhanced sustainability and profoundly individualized patient care. By effectively leveraging Industry 6.0 principles, hospitals can achieve heightened levels of operational agility and productivity, fundamentally restructuring internal decision-making processes. The realization of the Hospital 6.0 model is predicated on these technological advancements, which optimize clinical processes and operational efficiency ("Deep Learning and Computer Vision in Medical Imaging" 2023).

The following components represent the key technological pillars of this transformative concept:

a. **Digitalization of Hospital Processes:**

The foundation of Hospital 6.0 rests on a smart network infrastructure that facilitates fully digital hospital operations. This involves the integration of advanced technologies, intelligent devices, and digital networks to optimize management, enhance efficiency, and provide data-driven clinical and administrative decision support (Sathyamoorthy et al. 2026).

b. **Digital Pain Monitoring**:

This involves capturing and analyzing the onset, duration, and intensity of patient-reported pain via digital means, utilizing Electronic Health Records (EHRs), specialized mobile applications, or connected wearable devices ("Ethical Considerations in AI-powered Healthcare Systems" 2022). This continuous data stream significantly aids in the diagnosis and effective management of various health conditions.

c. **Automation of Healthcare Services:**

Automating core hospital procedures is essential for minimizing human errors, drastically increasing operational efficiency, and enhancing patient satisfaction ("The Future Workforce in AI-Driven Healthcare: Opportunities and Challenges" 2023). Automation streamlines complex medical processes and data management, enabling more precise and strategic resource allocation.

d. **AI-Based Personalized Treatment Suggestions:**

AI systems analyze vast and complex patient datasets to discern predictive patterns, calculate risk scores, and develop highly tailored treatment recommendations. The use of AI in conjunction with Internet of Things (IoT) facilitates continuous remote monitoring, which significantly enhances patient care and medical decision-making quality (Nankya et al. 2024).

e. **Machine Learning for Medical Staff Training**:

Machine learning algorithms are applied to improve the analytical capabilities of hospital staff, notably by refining disease diagnostic accuracy and optimizing the allocation of patient-specific resources.

f. **IoT-Enabled Patient Monitoring**:

IoMT facilitates the real-time, continuous monitoring of patient vital signs. This functionality provides medical staff with instant data streams, which are critical for making informed, time-sensitive decisions. Wearable sensors, in particular, improve patient assessment and are instrumental in the management of chronic diseases.

g. **Smart Software for Post-discharge Monitoring:**

Implementing dedicated smart software ensures continuous health surveillance and maintains a crucial communication link between discharged patients and healthcare providers. This continuous engagement helps reduce post-operative complications and accelerates recovery.

h. **Predictive Healthcare Solutions:**

The combination of continuous monitoring with advanced predictive analytics enables the proactive identification of potential future health risks, allowing for timely medical interventions before conditions escalate ("AI and Automation in Healthcare: Bridging the Global Digital Divide" 2022).

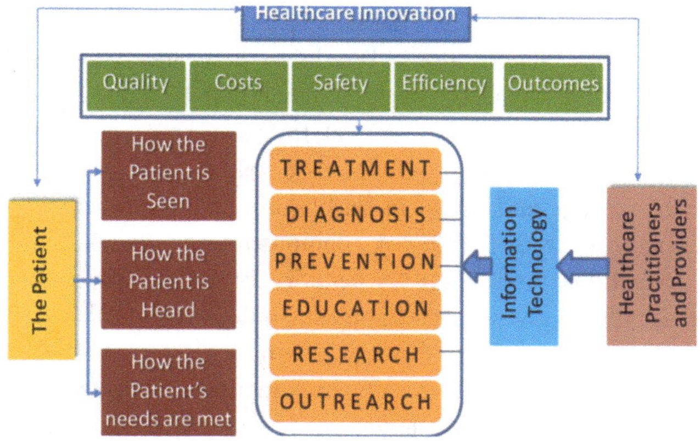

Fig. 2 Theoretical framework for advancing innovation in healthcare

10 Research Methodology and Conceptual Validation

a. **Delphi Method for Consensus Building**

To ensure the rigor and validity of the proposed concepts regarding the Industry 6.0 and Hospital 6.0 interplay, the Delphi Method was employed. This established, consensus-driven technique systematically gathers expert opinion through multiple rounds of structured feedback. The iterative process allows for the refinement of research components and the validation of the theoretical framework by integrating the collective expertise of field specialists. This methodology is crucial for establishing the robustness of emerging concepts where empirical data may still be limited.

b. **Conceptual Framework and Patient-Centric Innovation**

The developed conceptual framework provides a visual and theoretical representation of the symbiotic relationship between Industry 6.0 and Hospital 6.0. This model illustrates how the integration of advanced technological innovations directly leads to enhanced healthcare accessibility, improved clinical efficiency, and the delivery of highly personalized patient experiences (Refer to Fig. 2).

The fundamental operations of any healthcare organization can be categorized into six main functions: therapy, evaluation, early detection, training, investigation (research), and public relations. To successfully execute these core functions, healthcare institutions must demonstrate adept management across five critical domains: quality, costs, safety, efficiency, and clinical results. The patient—alongside the healthcare professionals and providers—remains the central focus of all innovation efforts. Successful innovation in the healthcare ecosystem is therefore characterized by its prioritization of three essential, patient-centric outcomes (Smaldone 2024):

1. Perception of the Patient: The manner in which the patient is viewed and understood by healthcare providers and all other personnel involved in their care continuum.
2. Efficacy of Patient Voice: The degree to which the patient's concerns, feedback, and perspectives are effectively communicated, acknowledged, and integrated into the clinical interaction and decision-making processes within the hospital setting.
3. Fulfillment of Needs: The extent to which the patient's specific needs, expectations, and concerns are comprehensively addressed and satisfied throughout their entire journey within the healthcare system. Refer Fig. 2.

11 The Successful Diffusion of Healthcare Innovation

The ultimate success of novel healthcare innovations is critically dependent not just on the quality of the invention itself, but on the effectiveness of its dissemination and widespread adoption throughout the healthcare system. As outlined by Berwick (2003), there are seven key factors that collectively enable the successful diffusion of innovation in diverse healthcare settings:

- Establish Structured Processes for Identifying Effective Innovations: To ensure valuable breakthroughs reach a broader audience, formal, and rigorous mechanisms must be instituted to identify, assess, and prioritize innovations based on their proven effectiveness. This necessitates robust evaluation, clinical research, and coordinated efforts among policymakers, healthcare professionals, and researchers.
- Recognize and Support Innovators: The genesis of healthcare innovation often lies with individuals or orga-

nizations willing to challenge traditional methods and develop new solutions. Providing dedicated support—including financial backing, mentorship, and institutional resources—is essential for sustaining continuous improvement and progress in the field.

- Encourage and Invest in Early Adopters: Early adopters play a crucial role by demonstrating the practical feasibility and tangible benefits of new innovations. Targeted investment in these pioneering individuals and organizations, through incentives, resources, and specialized training, significantly increases the likelihood of successful implementation and subsequent, broader adoption.
- Increase Visibility of Early Adoption: When early adopters achieve success, their experiences serve as powerful, real-world examples for others. Making these successes highly observable through platforms like professional networks, case studies and conferences helps to dismantle resistance to change and encourages others to follow suit.
- Build Trust and Allow Adaptation of Innovations: Overly rigid implementation models can severely impede widespread adoption. By fostering trust in providers and allowing flexibility in application, innovations can be adapted to fit the unique requirements of different clinical settings and patient needs. This practical modification capability enhances their relevance and long-term sustainability.
- Allocate Resources to Support Change: Successful implementation requires an appropriate allocation of resources, including funding, adequate workforce capacity, protected time, and supportive infrastructure. Without these necessary resources, even the most promising innovations may fail due to practical limitations. Creating systems that provision for resource allocation and "slack time" eases the transition and improves long-term success.
- Demonstrate Strong Leadership Commitment: Committed leadership is vital for driving and sustaining innovation within a healthcare organization. By actively championing and implementing new ideas, leaders set a clear example for their teams, establish a culture of continuous improvement, and ensure that innovation becomes an integral, rather than peripheral, part of the healthcare system's operation.

The trends in heathcare technology are detailed in Fig. 3. These innovations are shaping the future of healthcare by enhancing diagnosis, treatment, and patient care. Despite the presence of ground breaking innovations, their success ultimately depends on whether the healthcare system, market, or environment is ready for adoption. Berwick emphasizes that while developing new healthcare solutions is inherently challenging, the process of spreading and embedding these innovations across healthcare settings is even more difficult. Overcoming these barriers requires strategic planning, collaboration, and a commitment to ongoing improvement.

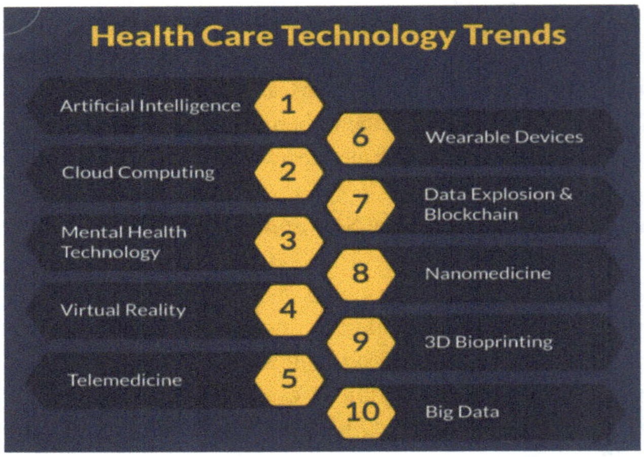

Fig. 3 Tends and technologies in healthcare

12 Challenges and Limitations of Industry 6.0 in Healthcare

While Industry 6.0 technologies—including AI-driven automation, robotics, IoMT, and blockchain—present a revolutionary shift in healthcare, their broad, successful adoption is met with significant challenges and limitations. Overcoming these hurdles, which span from severe budgetary constraints to critical data security issues, is essential to ensure the seamless integration of cutting-edge technology into the clinical ecosystem.

a. **Data Security and Patient Privacy**

One of the most pressing concerns surrounding Industry 6.0 in healthcare is data security and patient privacy. The immense volume of sensitive patient data generated by IoMT devices, smart hospitals, and AI diagnostics necessitates absolute confidentiality and integrity. The interconnected nature of Industry 6.0 systems makes healthcare organizations highly susceptible to cybersecurity threats, such as data breaches, ransomware attacks, and unauthorized access, which can compromise patient information and disrupt medical services.

While blockchain technology is often proposed as a solution to enhance data security through tamper-proof storage and controlled access, its widespread implementation faces barriers including scalability, technical complexity, and navigating regulatory compliance. To safeguard sensitive data, institutions must make substantial investments in advanced cybersecurity solutions, including encryption, multi-factor authentication, and continuous monitoring. Furthermore, establishing strict access controls and conducting frequent security audits are mandatory to proactively identify and address vulnerabilities before malicious actors can exploit them.

b. **Ethical Dilemmas and Human-Centered Care**

Another critical challenge is the ethical dilemma of balancing technology-driven automation with the necessity of human-centered care. While AI-powered decision support, robotic assistants, and automated diagnostics improve accuracy and efficiency, they raise profound questions about the evolving role of human healthcare professionals.

There is a risk of over-reliance on AI in clinical decision-making, which presents ethical concerns, particularly when AI recommendations conflict with human medical judgment. Furthermore, the efficacy of AI systems is fundamentally limited by the quality of their training data. Pre-existing biases within medical datasets can be amplified by algorithms, potentially leading to disparities in healthcare outcomes for specific patient groups. Clear guidelines are required to ensure that AI algorithms remain unbiased and that the technology serves to augment, rather than replace, human expertise. Finally, establishing clear lines of liability and accountability remains a complex issue in the event of AI-related surgical errors or misdiagnoses.

c. **Interoperability and System Integration**

Interoperability stands as a significant barrier to the widespread adoption of Industry 6.0. The healthcare industry is a fragmented landscape of diverse systems, including Electronic Health Records (EHRs), IoMT devices, AI platforms, and management systems, often developed by different vendors using incompatible standards. This lack of seamless communication between systems hinders efficient data exchange, resulting in fragmented care delivery.

For example, incompatible data formats can prevent a patient's medical history from being instantly shared between different hospital systems, leading to treatment delays, duplicate diagnostic tests, and overall inefficiency. While efforts like the Fast Healthcare Interoperability Resources (FHIR) are working toward standardization, achieving full interoperability demands collaborative effort from technology providers, regulatory bodies, and healthcare institutions to develop and widely adopt unified standards. Until universal standards are adopted, integrating complex Industry 6.0 solutions will continue to be a considerable challenge.

d. **High Implementation Costs**

The substantial financial burden of implementation is another major limitation, particularly for smaller healthcare facilities and institutions in developing regions. Deploying the required infrastructure—AI-powered systems (Smaldone et al. 2409; Yempally et al. 2025), IoMT devices, robotics, and blockchain solutions—requires massive upfront financial investment.

Advanced Industry 6.0 solutions demand high-end computing power, specialized technical personnel, and continuous system maintenance, all of which contribute to elevated operating costs. The transition from traditional systems also requires extensive retraining of both clinical and administrative staff, further increasing expenses. This financial disparity risks widening the gap in access to advanced care between large, well-funded urban hospitals and under-resourced rural centers. To bridge this financial gap and promote equitable access, government initiatives, public–private partnerships, and the development of cost-effective solutions like cloud-based AI services and flexible funding models (e.g., pay-as-you-go services) are essential.

Despite these critical limitations, Industry 6.0 retains immense potential for transforming global healthcare. By strategically addressing data security, refining ethical frameworks, enhancing interoperability, and focusing on cost-effective solutions, the sector can fully harness these emerging technologies. The future of healthcare relies on a balanced approach that successfully integrates technological advancements while preserving the vital human element necessary for compassionate medical care.

13 Recommendations and Best Practices

To fully and responsibly harness the transformative potential of Industry 6.0 in healthcare, strategic planning and focused action across organizational, professional, and policy levels are mandatory:

- Strategic Planning and Implementation: Healthcare institutions must develop clear long-term roadmaps that align the adoption of new technologies with core patient care objectives, financial viability, and regulatory compliance. Organizations should utilize pilot programs to rigorously assess the impact and adaptability of new solutions before wide-scale deployment. Furthermore, establishing innovation hubs within hospitals and research centers can foster a culture of agility, continuous technological evaluation, and seamless integration.
- Workforce Training and Skill Enhancement: Successfully adopting Industry 6.0 requires a technologically

proficient workforce. Institutions must invest heavily in professional development programs that equip staff with the skills necessary to operate AI systems, robotic tools, and data-driven platforms. Integrating AI literacy and advanced analytics training into medical curricula is crucial. Moreover, fostering interdisciplinary collaboration among clinicians, data scientists, and engineers through cross-functional training will be vital for driving future innovation.

- Policy Formulation and Ethical Governance: Governments and regulatory agencies play a critical role in establishing clear, comprehensive legal frameworks that govern the application of AI and automation in clinical decision-making. These frameworks must address ethical issues such as data privacy, algorithmic bias, and ensuring adequate human oversight to maintain transparency and accountability. Additionally, policymakers should establish funding initiatives specifically designed to support the adoption of advanced technologies in under-resourced regions, thereby bridging the digital divide and ensuring equitable access to high-quality medical services. This proactive policy-making is essential for fostering an environment of responsible, sustainable healthcare innovation.

14 Conclusion

The convergence of Industry 6.0 and Hospital 6.0 presents a revolutionary model for current healthcare. By strategically including the power of AI, IoMT, automation, and predictive analytics, this paradigm promises to significantly enhance both medical services and operational efficiency. Aligning healthcare systems with these cutting-edge industrial advancements ensures a future defined by efficient, highly patient-centric, and technologically driven medical care. This evolution has the potential to elevate healthcare innovation into a structured, multidisciplinary discipline, attracting diverse research communities. The theoretical framework and operational elements discussed highlight both the environmental and operational factors that shape healthcare development, offering crucial insight into the strategic and practical steps organizations must take to effectively implement new developments. This knowledge is invaluable for policymakers, providing a deep understanding of the various forces driving the healthcare improvement, which can support informed decision-making and lead to policies that promote and sustain this vital transformation.

References

"5G and IoMT: Transforming Connected Healthcare Systems", Cisco Healthcare, 2023.

Anthony M. Smaldone et al., "Quantum Machine Learning in Drug Discovery: Applications in Academia and Pharmaceutical Industries," arXiv: 2409.15645v1, 2024.

Accenture Health, "The Rise of Intelligent Healthcare: How Industry 6.0 is Shaping the Future of Medicine," 2023.

S. Adibi, "The mPOC framework: An autonomous outbreak prediction and monitoring platform based on wearable IoMT approach," *Future Internet*, vol. 15, no. 8, p. 257, Jul. 2023.

Alanazi, "Clinicians' Perspectives on Healthcare Cybersecurity and Cyber Threats," 2023.

Alhammad, M. M., Yusof, D. I., and Jambari, D. I., "A review of cyber threats to medical devices integration with electronic medical records," in *Proc. Int. Conf. Cyber Resilience (ICCR)*, vol. 13089, Dubai, UAE, Oct. 2022, pp. 1–6, https://doi.org/10.1109/iccr56254.2022.9995984.

S. A. Alowais et al., "Revolutionizing healthcare: The role of artificial intelligence in clinical practice," *BMC Med. Educ.*, vol. 23, no. 1, p. 689, Sep. 2023, https://doi.org/10.1186/s12909-023-04698-z

Assistant Secretary for Public Affairs (ASPA), "HHS' Office for Civil Rights Settles Ransomware Cyber-attack Investigation," 2023. [Online]. Available: https://www.hhs.gov/about/news/2023/10/31/hhs-office-civil-rights-settles-ransomware-cyberattack-investigation.html

"AI and Automation in Healthcare: Bridging the Global Digital Divide", WHO Digital Health Report, 2022.

"AI and Block chain in Smart Healthcare Systems: Challenges and Solutions", IBM Research, 2021.

"AI-driven Diagnostics and Personalized Medicine: A Future Perspective", National Institute of Health (NIH), 2022.

"Blockchain for Secure Healthcare Data Management: Policy and Implementation Challenges," European Commission, 2021.

J. Bajwa, U. Munir, A. Nori, and B. Williams, "Artificial intelligence in healthcare: Transforming the practice of medicine," *Future Healthcare J.*, vol. 8, no. 2, pp. e188–e194, Jul. 2021,https://doi.org/10.7861/fhj.2021-0095

R. Chataut, Y. Usman, and F. Scholl, "Unveiling Cyber Threats: A Comprehensive Analysis of Connecticut Data Breaches Paper," 2024.

"Credential Stuffing Attack Exposed United Healthcare Member Data." [Online]. Available: https://www.hipaajournal.com/credential-stuffing-attack-exposed-united-healthcare-member-data/

R. Chataut, Y. Usman, and F. Scholl, "Unveiling Cyber Threats: A Comprehensive Analysis of Connecticut Data Breaches," 2024. [Online]. Available: https://peer.asee.org/unveiling-cyber-threats-a-comprehensive-analysis-of-connecticut-data-breaches

R. Chaudhary and A. Yousafzai, "Industry 6.0 and the evolution of smart healthcare systems: A review," *J. Med. Syst.*, vol. 46, no. 9, pp. 88–102, 2022.

S. Chenthara et al., "Security and privacy-preserving challenges of e-Health solutions in cloud computing," *IEEE Access*, vol. 7, pp. 74361–74382, 2019, https://doi.org/10.1109/ACCESS.2019.2919982.

"Deep Learning and Computer Vision in Medical Imaging", University of Cambridge AI Lab, 2023.

L. L. Dhirani, N. Mukhtiar, B. S. Chowdhry, and T. Newe, "Ethical dilemmas and privacy issues in emerging technologies: A review," *Sensors*, vol. 23, no. 3, p. 1151, Jan. 2023, https://doi.org/10.3390/s23031151

"Emerging Trends in AI-Powered Healthcare and Industry 6.0," Gartner Research, 2023.

"Ethical Considerations in AI-powered Healthcare Systems", Stanford University AI Lab 2022.
Guerra, "HC3 Breaks Down Types of Actors Threatening Healthcare," 2023. [Online]. Available: https://healthsystemcio.com/2023/06/09/hc3-breaks-down-types-of-actors-threatening-healthcare/
"Healthcare 6.0: The Convergence of AI, Robotics, and Data Analytics," McKinsey & Company, 2023.
"HIPAA Network Compliance and Security Requirements Explained," 2024. [Online]. Available: https://www.algosec.com/resources/hipaa-compliance/
"Japan's AI-Powered Smart Hospitals: Improving Patient Outcomes," Fujita Health University, 2023.
S. Kumar and N. Patel, "The role of quantum computing in precision medicine and genomics," *Nat. Comput. Sci.*, vol. 1, no. 3, pp. 125–134, 2021, https://doi.org/10.1038/s43588-021-00030-6.
"Leveraging AI and Machine Learning for Robust Cybersecurity in Healthcare," 2024. [Online]. Available: https://emag.medicalexpo.com/leveraging-ai-and-machine-learning-for-robustcybersecurity-in-healthcare/
P. Mishra and G. Singh, "Internet of Medical Things healthcare for sustainable smart cities: Current status and future prospects," *Appl. Sci.*, vol. 13, no. 15, p. 8869, Aug. 2023,https://doi.org/10.3390/app13158869
S. Mohammed, T.-H. Kim, R.-S. Chang, and C. Ramos, "Guest editorial: Data analytics for public health care," *IEEE J. Biomed. Health Informat.*, vol. 26, no. 4, pp. 1409–1410, Apr. 2022, https://doi.org/10.1109/JBHI.2022.3159347
Mary Nankya, Allan Mugisa, Yusuf Usman, Aadesh Upadhyay, Robin Chataut, "Security and Privacy in E-Health Systems: A Review of AI and Machine Learning Techniques," *IEEE Access*, 2024, https://doi.org/10.1109/ACCESS.2024.3469215.
M. Nankya, R. Chataut, and R. Akl, "Securing industrial control systems: Components, cyber threats, and machine learning-driven defense strategies," *Sensors*, vol. 23, no. 21, p. 8840, Oct. 2023,https://doi.org/10.3390/s23218840
R. Ong, "Factors affecting patient and public perceptions of the adoption of electronic health record sharing: A Hong Kong study," *Int. J. Med. Informat.*, vol. 178, Oct. 2023, Art. no. 105193, https://doi.org/10.1016/j.ijmedinf.2023.105193.
M. Paul, L. Maglaras, M. A. Ferrag, and I. Almomani, "Digitization of healthcare sector: A study on privacy and security concerns," *ICT Exp.*, vol. 9, no. 4, pp. 571–588, Aug. 2023,https://doi.org/10.1016/j.icte.2023.02.007
A. Ramesh and S. Saini, "The impact of robotic-assisted surgeries on healthcare efficiency: A systematic analysis," *J. Surg. Robot.*, vol. 11, no. 2, pp. 99–115, 2023.
"Regulatory Challenges in AI-Enabled Healthcare Devices", U.S. Food and Drug Administration (FDA), 2023.
"Revolutionizing Drug Discovery with AI and Quantum Computing", Deloitte Insights, 2022.
"Robotic Surgery: The Next Frontier in Minimally Invasive Procedures", Royal Society of Medicine, 2022.
"Smart Hospitals and the Future of Healthcare: A Roadmap for Industry 6.0", Boston Consulting Group, 2022.
S. Sachdeva, "Unraveling the role of cloud computing in the health care system and biomedical sciences," *Heliyon*, vol. 10, no. 7, pp. 1–24, 2024.
M. A. Sahi et al., "Privacy preservation in e-Healthcare environments: State of the art and future directions," *IEEE Access*, vol. 6, pp. 464–478, 2018, https://doi.org/10.1109/ACCESS.2017.2767561.
V. Sandulescu, S. Pucoci, M. Petre, M. Dumitrache, V. Bota, and A. Garlea, "MHealth application for remote health monitoring useful during the COVID-19 pandemic," in *Proc. IEEE Int. Symp. Med. Meas. Appl. (MeMeA)*, Lausanne, Switzerland, Jun. 2021, pp. 1–6.
Sathyamoorthy, M., Rajasekar, V., Krishnamoorthi, S., & Pamucar, D. (2026). Ensemble deep learning approach for traffic video analytics in edge computing. *Scientific Reports*.
H. Seh et al., "Healthcare data breaches: Insights and implications," *Healthcare*, vol. 8, no. 2, p. 133, May 2020,https://doi.org/10.3390/healthcare8020133
Singh, P., & Verma, K., "Internet of Medical Things (IoMT) and Real-time Patient Monitoring: A Systematic Review," *IEEE Trans. Biomed. Eng.*, vol. 68, no. 7, pp. 1482–1495, 2021.
"The Future of Healthcare: AI, Robotics, and Digital Transformation", World Economic Forum 2022.
"The Future Workforce in AI-Driven Healthcare: Opportunities and Challenges," PwC Health Research Institute, 2023.
"The Impact of Artificial Intelligence on Global Health Equity," Microsoft AI for Health, 2021.
"The Role of Machine Learning in Disease Prediction and Prevention", Harvard Medical School, 2022.
Vincent, R., & Huang, J., "Cyber-Physical Systems (CPS) in Telemedicine: Enhancing Remote Patient Care with AI," *Telemed. E-Health J.*, vol. 26, no. 4, pp. 382–397, 2020.
E. N. Volkov and A. N. Averkin, "Explainable artificial intelligence in clinical decision support systems," in *Proc. IV Int. Conf. Neural Netw. Neurotechnologies (NeuroNT)*, Jun. 2023, pp. 3–6.
"What is an Electronic Health Record (EHR)?," 2024. [Online]. Available: https://www.healthit.gov/faq/what-electronic-health-record-ehr
Wolf, "Biggest Healthcare Industry Cyber Attacks," 2024. [Online]. Available: https://arcticwolf.com/resources/blog/top-healthcare-industry-cyberattacks/
Yempally, S., Singh, S. K., & Sarveshwaran, V. (2025). A secure authorization in Multi-WSN based on Blockchain_SecAuth approach for secure data communication. *Blockchain: Research and Applications*, 100331.
X. Zhang, P. Chang, and H. Li, "Blockchain for healthcare data security: A systematic review," *Comput. Biol. Med.*, vol. 121, 103774, 2020, https://doi.org/10.1016/j.compbiomed.2020.103774.

Additional Reading

Bajwa, J., Munir, U., Nori, A., & Williams, B. (2021). Artificial intelligence in healthcare: Transforming the practice of medicine. Future Healthcare Journal, 8(2), e188–e194. https://doi.org/10.7861/fhj.2021-0095
Chaudhary, R., & Yousafzai, A. (2022). Industry 6.0 and the evolution of smart healthcare systems: A review. Journal of Medical Systems, 46(9), 88–102.
Kumar, S., & Patel, N. (2021). The role of quantum computing in precision medicine and genomics. Nature Computational Science, 1(3), 125–134. https://doi.org/10.1038/s43588-021-00030-6
Mishra, P., & Singh, G. (2023). Internet of Medical Things healthcare for sustainable smart cities: Current status and future prospects. Applied Sciences, 13(15), 8869. https://doi.org/10.3390/app13158869
Ramesh, A., & Saini, S. (2023). The impact of robotic-assisted surgeries on healthcare efficiency: A systematic analysis. Journal of Surgical Robotics, 11(2), 99–115.
Sandulescu, V., Pucoci, S., Petre, M., Dumitrache, M., Bota, V., & Garlea, A. (2021). MHealth application for remote health monitoring useful during the COVID-19 pandemic. In Proceedings of the IEEE International Symposium on Medical Measurements and Applications (MeMeA) (pp. 1–6). IEEE. https://doi.org/10.1109/MeMeA52024.2021.9478714

Singh, P., & Verma, K. (2021). Internet of Medical Things (IoMT) and real-time patient monitoring: A systematic review. IEEE Transactions on Biomedical Engineering, 68(7), 1482–1495. https://doi.org/10.1109/TBME.2021.3070135

Stanford University AI Lab. (2022). Ethical considerations in AI-powered healthcare systems. Stanford Ethics & AI Policy Brief.

World Economic Forum. (2022). The future of healthcare: AI, robotics, and digital transformation. WEF Global Report Series.

Zhang, X., Chang, P., & Li, H. (2020). Block chain for healthcare data security: A systematic review. Computers in Biology and Medicine, 121, 103774. https://doi.org/10.1016/j.compbiomed.2020.103774

Key Terms and Definitions

Artificial Intelligence (AI): The simulation of human intelligence by computer systems, enabling machines to perform tasks such as decision-making, learning, and problem-solving in healthcare.

Block chain Technology: A decentralized, tamper-proof digital ledger system used in healthcare to secure patient data, ensure transparency, and improve trust among stakeholders.

Cyber-Physical Systems (CPS): Integrated networks that combine computing, communication, and physical processes to enable automation and real-time monitoring in healthcare environments.

Digital Twins: Virtual representations of patients or medical systems that simulate real-world conditions for diagnosis, treatment planning, and predictive healthcare.

Electronic Health Records (EHRs): Digitized versions of patients' medical histories, stored securely and accessible to authorized healthcare providers for improved decision-making.

Healthcare 6.0: The next stage of healthcare transformation that leverages advanced technologies like AI, IoMT, block chain, and quantum computing to create efficient, patient-centred medical systems.

Internet of Medical Things (IoMT): A network of connected medical devices, wearables, and sensors that continuously collect and share patient data for remote monitoring and real-time care.

Personalized Medicine: A medical approach that tailors treatments and therapies based on an individual's genetic makeup, lifestyle, and environment for more effective outcomes.

Quantum Computing: An advanced form of computing that uses quantum-mechanical principles to solve complex medical problems, such as drug discovery and genomics, faster than traditional computers.

Smart Hospitals: Healthcare facilities that integrate automation, AI, IoMT, and robotics to enhance efficiency, reduce errors, and provide real-time patient care.

AI-Driven Sustainable Consumption Framework for Urban India: A Citizen-Centric Approach to Eco-Conscious Living

T. Sridevi, Jhansi Gonuguntla, and Srishti Turki

Abstract

The rapid urbanisation in India has furthered environmental challenges, resource constraints, and unsustainable consumption patterns, which involve intelligent and data-driven solutions that can facilitate sustainable urban development. Sustainable consumption in India is considered a premium lifestyle choice; therefore, its adoption by middle- and low-income households, which comprise the majority of the population, is limited. This paper introduces an AI-enabled sustainable consumption ecosystem aimed at making eco-friendly living affordable, inclusive and economically beneficial for citizens across socio-economic strata in India. The proposed system utilised budget-sensitive recommendation models, which identified affordable, sustainable alternatives that matched individual financial capabilities and served to reframe sustainability as a cost-saving practice rather than a luxury preference. AI-driven behavioural insights further facilitated household practices and product choices that reduce recurring monthly expenses through reusable and refill-based solutions, sharing community resources, and waste-to-income models, including monetising household compost. This work makes a very valuable contribution to integrating sustainability into livelihood enhancement by providing a digital marketplace to connect small entrepreneurs, women self-help groups, artisans, street vendors and informal recyclers with urban consumers. It creates income opportunities for marginalised communities and strengthens the local green economy in India. Identifying AI as a driver of affordability, inclusiveness and the creation of circular value, this study extends the socio-economic responsiveness of the model for sustainable urban consumption in India.

Keywords

Sustainable consumption · Affordable sustainability · Artificial Intelligence (AI) · Urban India · Eco-inclusive innovation · Small business · Community-based sustainability

1 Introduction

Sustainability has become a defining priority for modern cities, which face rapid urbanisation, changing consumption habits and increasing waste generation that exerts unprecedented pressure on environmental and resource systems. India is experiencing one of the fastest urban expansions in the world; its urban population is projected to surpass 600 million in the coming years. While cities are engines of economic growth, they contribute disproportionately to air pollution, waste production and greenhouse gas emissions. Shaping urban lifestyles towards more sustainable consumption in this context is not merely desirable but an imperative for achieving environmental, social and economic goals.

However, the sustainability narrative in India has traditionally been couched in luxury and exclusivity. Green products, ethical brands and eco-services are often priced well beyond the reach of lower- and middle-income households, making the notion very strongly held that sustainability is only for the privileged. This is especially problematic in India, given that a large segment of the population needs to make highly cost-conscious decisions about their purchases. Thus, sustainability remains aspirational rather than accessible, even though Indian cultural values are deeply entrenched in reuse, repair, repurposing and resource

T. Sridevi · J. Gonuguntla · S. Turki (✉)
Department of Computer Science and Engineering, Chaitanya Bharathi Institute of Technology (A), Hyderabad, India
e-mail: srishtiturki@gmail.com

T. Sridevi
e-mail: tsridevi_cse@cbit.ac.in

J. Gonuguntla
e-mail: jhansignet@gmail.com

V. Sarveshwaran et al. (eds.), *Responsible AI for Smart Cities*, Sustainable Artificial Intelligence-Powered Applications,
https://doi.org/10.1007/978-3-032-26901-0_2

efficiency. What is missing is a system that translates eco-friendly choices into economically viable decisions for everyday urban citizens.

Coupled with the socio-economic challenges mentioned above, Indian smart cities are rapidly evolving digitally, enabled by emerging technologies in AI, IoT, blockchain, data analytics and mobile connectivity. Government initiatives under the Smart City Mission, Swachh Bharat Abhiyan and AMRUT have accelerated urban modernisation within a framework of better governance, infrastructure and citizen services. However, sustainability has mostly been pursued through policy and infrastructure measures rather than by bringing consumer-level behavioural transformation, which is crucial for long-term environmental resilience.

Responsible AI has become a strategic enabler in smart city ecosystems. It drives data-informed decision-making with fairness, transparency, affordability and inclusivity principles. Responsible AI applied in the context of sustainable consumption can help democratize access to eco-friendly options, especially if it factors in local availability and citizen budget constraints, among other environmental considerations. Through guiding choices of individuals at the moment of purchasing a product, disposing of waste or finding services, AI can impact and optimise behavioural change at scale.

Despite progress in sustainability technologies globally, there is a significant research and implementation gap in India related to:

1. **AI-driven systems that consider affordability as a core sustainability metric**: Most AI sustainability solutions centre around environmental performance only. There is a lack of intelligent systems that would emphasise cost-effectiveness and aid economically constrained citizens in choosing environmentally responsible options without adding to their financial burden.
2. **Digital platforms that enable citizen-centric sustainable consumption**: The existing sustainability platforms are oriented towards premium consumers. Several gaps persist, like the platforms that should cater to diverse urban populations, with recommendations tailored for real lifestyle needs, cultural practices and household constraints.
3. **Formal inclusion of small-scale vendors, artisans, SHGs and recyclers in urban supply chains**: The local eco-friendly producers are not connected to formal digital markets. They include self-help groups, rural artisans, waste collectors and repair workers whose products and services are sustainable but lack discoverability and fair-market access.
4. **Transparency tools that help users trust the origin and ethics of products and vendors**: However, mechanisms for verification of such claims of sustainability, like eco-certification, ethical sourcing and recycling authenticity, are few and far between. Thus, this often leads to consumer distrust of "greenwashed" brands.
5. **Circular economy models that are accessible to everyday households**: Circular economy models that can be accessed by everyday households. Reuse, repair and recycling are circular practices that are not integrated into mainstream marketplaces. In general, urban consumers still lack easy-to-use online platforms for reselling items, exchanging goods or arranging repair and refill services in their own neighbourhood.

Existing eco-marketplaces or sustainability platforms offer pieces of the solution but fail to integrate affordability, accessibility and accountability in a single system designed specifically for Indian urban communities.

To address this gap, this chapter proposes an AI-Driven Sustainable Consumption Framework for Urban India. This citizen-focused digital ecosystem connects consumers with environmentally responsible and economically feasible products and services. The proposed system leverages:

1. **AI-powered recommendation models that match products to budgets, sustainability ratings and personal preferences of each individual**: This citizen-focused digital ecosystem provides suggestions by balancing environmental impact with affordability, so that eco-friendly decisions remain economically viable for every citizen.
2. **Vendor discovery mechanisms that widen access to markets for local, low-income and community-driven enterprises**: Mechanisms for vendor discovery that extend market access to local, low-income and community-driven enterprises. Through onboarding underrepresented vendors into the digital marketplace, the model leads to economic inclusion by strengthening local green supply chains in urban communities.
3. **Circular economy enablement, including resale, exchange and repair options**: Resale, exchange or repair. This enables peer-to-peer reuse models and community-driven repair networks to turn waste into value, reduce household expenditure and unlock resource efficiency.
4. **Impact analytics that help users track cost savings, carbon savings, and waste reduction**: Impact analytics that enable users to monitor cost savings, carbon savings and waste reduction. The platform offers a means by which to quantify eco-friendly actions into measurable sustainability insights that motivate long-term behaviour change and support evidence-based policymaking.

To put it simply, to make Indian cities sustainable, there should be appropriate technology for the creation of social equity and economic viability, along with digital systems in which all citizens, irrespective of their socio-economic background, will be able to contribute to sustainability. It will integrate financial viability with environmental responsibility, integrating principles of Circular Economy, AI, Community Marketplace and Circular Economy into one seamless system that will redefine what consuming sustainably is. This is by offering it as a daily, affordable, desirable lifestyle choice, not a luxurious, expensive one. The research contained in this chapter will add to the growing body of literature related to smart cities. It offers a conceptual framework that aligns with the socio-economic realities of urban India, along with those technologies that empower people from marginalised groups to rebuild local green economies. The remaining chapters will review the current state of research with regard to the topic at hand and give a description of the architectural design for the proposed system, along with the potential for substantial environmental and socio-economic impacts within rapidly changing environments in urban India.

2 Literature Review

In India, the urban sustainability discussion has advanced rapidly along with the country's vision for smart cities. Although many global studies have focused on responsible AI and green consumption (providing useful frameworks), they cannot be readily applied to urban Indian populations due to vast social and economic diversity and negligible affordability. A thorough review of the literature has shown that most studies have focused on sustainable infrastructure, mobility systems, and energy systems. However, there are far fewer studies that address sustainability as a practice for consumers, even though consumers' behaviour has an impact on their purchasing decisions based on available household budgets, prevailing behavioural norms in society and dynamics of local markets.

The majority of urban residents in India belong to a low- or middle-income strata where sustainable products are considered to be lifestyle enhancements that cannot be incorporated into the consumer's household decisions. Therefore, the inability to afford sustainable products creates an economic gap regarding the adoption of sustainable products. Yet, current models of technology-driven sustainability do not often consider the impact of price sensitivity on purchasing decisions as well as socio-economic motivations for adopting sustainable behaviour.

However, if a person's perception of sustainability varies based on income segments, and if there are currently digital sustainability tools available, it becomes necessary to understand the digital tools and their effectiveness by determining where stakeholders lie in the circular economy.

Together, this review establishes a clear justification for an AI-enabled, affordability-first sustainable consumption ecosystem, aligning with India's social needs, digital growth and circular economy goals.

2.1 Sustainable Consumption Challenges in Urban India

The rapid growth of urbanisation in India has created several problems for the environment and people. For example, the problems of environmental degradation, increased consumption and the rise of unsustainable behavioural patterns are all consequences of the combined effects of rapid urbanisation and rapid urban population growth (Imam and Banerjee 2016). The phenomenon of increasing waste generation, developing shorter product life cycles and increasing resource-intensity in urban lifestyles, among many other urban consumption patterns, is indicative of the rapid urbanisation process in India.

It has been indicated by the literature that the primary reason for the lack of resource-efficient lifestyles is limited awareness of sustainable options (Prakash and Pathak 2017) and a lack of availability of sustainable options on the market. Many authors believe that sustainability is often confused with the lifestyle of affluent individuals; therefore, there has been little change in the level of sustainability understood by the middle and lower classes of the majority of the urban population of India (Imam and Banerjee 2016; Prakash and Pathak 2017).

The assessments made by various levels of government and institutions are a clear indication of the immediate necessity to integrate city-level circular economy practices into a comprehensive plan of action and integration into the economy, rather than placing the entire responsibility for implementing sustainable consumption practices on individuals (Aayog and MOSPI 2022; Rajasekar et al. 2024).

2.2 Affordability and Behavioural Barriers

Cost was identified as the main barrier to eco-friendly product options in India by multiple sources of research (Prakash and Pathak 2017). Eco-friendly product options generally have a higher price point than what consumers are used to seeing for conventional products. As a result, consumers who are price-sensitive may choose not to consider purchasing an eco-friendly product option because of the price difference. Additionally, it has been suggested in existing literature that sustainability is viewed as a 'moral choice' by most households rather than something that would benefit them economically; therefore, they would be less likely to make a change unless an economic incentive was introduced (Imam and Banerjee 2016; Prakash and Pathak 2017)

Behavioural nudges (e.g. gamification, savings feedback, peer influence) can help improve eco-friendly product adoption, according to research conducted on consumer psychology; however, these nudges must be tailored to what is most important to Indian consumers (Garg et al. 2025). Recurring household purchases (i.e. cleaning products, groceries and personal care items) have the opportunity to serve as low-cost entry points into sustainable options via refillable, reusable product types (Rajasekar and Sarvehswaran 2025).

A recent study conducted in India showed that household waste behaviours are not driven solely by knowledge of proper waste disposal practices; this study also identified the need for households to know what economic value can be derived from changing their behaviours (Suthar and Singh 2015).

2.3 Circular Economy and Local Green Markets

The circular economy model that promotes the reuse, repair and sharing of materials and goods is being acknowledged as an important model of sustainability for Indian cities (Pandey and Gautam 2025). According to government publications, the transition to this new system must be inclusive of small-scale stakeholders, informal recyclers and local market participants for inclusive green growth to occur (Aayog and MOSPI 2022; Bhuvaneswari et al. 2025).

The opportunity for economic development in the area of Community-Based Waste-to-Wealth Systems in hyperlocal areas, neighbourhood-based Sharing Economies and frugal lifestyle choices has been highlighted by previous research (Pandey and Gautam 2025; Rajasekar and Sarvehswaran 2025). Urban India has a strong historical claim to Repairing Goods, however in order to increase the Rate of Repairing Goods, what is needed is an Infrastructure to support rapid deployment of Technology by Digital Enablement of Repair Services (Chauhan et al. 2024).

According to specialists, the lack of organisations that connect citizens with Circular Service Providers (Refill Sellers, Scrap Collectors and Repair Artisans) adds to the barriers to a "widespread" adoption of recycling (Hande 2019; Chauhan et al. 2024).

2.4 AI for Sustainable Behaviour Change

Artificial Intelligence has been identified as an important component of the transition to sustainable practices by helping to influence decision-making (in real time) of consumers through Artificial Intelligence Systems (i.e. AI Systems) (Garg et al. 2025; Soni and Sharma 2025). These systems use data from the household level and use that data to determine the limitations, the behavioural patterns and the financial preferences of the consumers in the household to create viable, economically feasible and environmentally friendly alternatives for purchasing goods and services (Garg et al. 2025; Soni and Sharma 2025). The use of AI Systems enables consumers to make sustainable choices that are more suited to their day-to-day lifestyles, as opposed to relying solely on their level of Environmental Awareness or Ethical Reasons.

Ways in which AI Systems assist in promoting sustainable consumption are through various formats. For example, the use of Predictive Analytics helps identify products and services that provide both the best overall financial savings and the least Negative Environmental Impact (Garg et al. 2025; Soni and Sharma 2025). The use of personalised nudges such as 'Reminders', 'Habit-Tracking' and 'Feedback on Savings' has shown promise for enhancing consumers' commitment to, or establishing long-term adoption of, Greener Household Practices by facilitating Behavioural Commitment (Garg et al. 2025). AI Digital Marketplaces provide urban consumers with greater access to eco-friendly products through connection with Local Vendors (typically greater participation on the part of urban consumers) and by providing greater visibility, greater affordability and greater context for the supply of and accessibility of eco-friendly products (Hande 2019; Chauhan et al. 2024). By employing optimisation models, AI Systems also reduce material waste, promote reuse and help to reduce the recurring financial costs of households by providing Intelligent Resource Planning (Soni and Sharma 2025; Francis and Sarangi 2022).

Together, these capabilities transform sustainability from a value or philosophy to a strategic cost-saving initiative, particularly important in economies, such as India, that are sensitive to pricing (Garg et al. 2025). However, for AI to effectively promote sustainable living in an Indian context, there needs to be a clear focus on citizens—creating solutions tailored to diverse socio-economic conditions, an interdisciplinary approach in their design, as well as being attuned to the specific market characteristics in each neighbourhood. Scholars note that the simple application of Western-based sustainability technologies does not account for affordability, the lack of Infrastructure, as well as informal market conditions (Chauhan et al. 2024). This reinforces the importance of developing AI innovations not only to promote responsible consumption, but to reflect India's cultural, economic and behavioural conditions.

2.5 Digital Inclusion and Socio-economic Equity

Green innovation in India should not only be considered from an environmental or technological standpoint, but it also needs to take into account the decades of socio-economic inequities that exist within the country today. The sustainability models that are presently being developed do not necessarily include and recognise the contributions of the many workers that constitute the informal economy. Even though informal labour is a key player in creating circular value (Aayog and MOSPI 2022; Bhuvaneswari et al. 2025), much of the current focus on sustainability and sustainability policy is on the formal retail sector. Waste pickers, street vendors, local artisans and other forms of micro-entrepreneurship play an essential role in supporting city reuse, repair and efficiency efforts, yet they continue to remain largely unrecognised within the dominant marketing ecosystems and sustainability policy frameworks.

Recent research has highlighted the critical importance of technology-enabled marketplace design, as well as digitally inclusive ways to empower these communities and improve their economic status (Hande 2019; Demaria 2023; Kaushik et al. 2030). By integrating women's self-help groups (SHGs) that have been established, informal recyclers, the growing base of small-to-medium-sized green businesses and street level sustainable enterprises into a structured value chain, we can better position these businesses to increase their market reach, improve their compensation and access to social security provisions. These alternative forms of marketplace create not only a means for a form of marketplace for sustainable consumption but also provide avenues for new livelihood creation, especially for low and middle-income people, as well as other marginalised communities.

The support of local production, circular entrepreneurship and resilient community networks as the foundation of all aspects of sustainable development in India. Because of the linkages between climate change, social and economic justice, economy (through job creation), the most relevant way to build a better world is through inclusive innovation (Sengupta et al. 2023). By connecting these two components, it demonstrates how inclusive innovation can create the connection between environmentally responsible product and socio-economic welfare and how inclusive innovation creates an opportunity to increase local economic development and build community resilience through creating sustainable livelihoods by strengthening the local.

The approach provides a foundation for inclusive innovation through creating solutions that support both environmental and economic inclusion as we progress towards the future of smarter, climate-adaptive cities in India. The most effective and contextually appropriate transformation strategies in India are those that support both types of innovation in collaboration (Aayog and MOSPI 2022; Bhuvaneswari et al. 2025).

2.6 Gaps in Existing Literature

While the growth of AI-powered sustainability options is gaining momentum, there remain some significant gaps in both academia and industry regarding AI-powered sustainability options. To begin with, India's current view of sustainability, which has been labelled as a choice associated with an 'elite' or 'lifestyle' mentality, continues to be preventing significant participation from those who fall into the middle and low-income population category, even though the majority of urban consumers reside in these categories (Imam and Banerjee 2016; Prakash and Pathak 2017). Thus, the current platforms and policies are mostly focused on higher-priced eco-products, and this focus will create socio-economic exclusion and not the widespread change of behaviour that occurs with other forms of sustainable consumption. Secondly, although smart services are frequently studied in relation to their use of AI-driven decision support technologies, there is currently a lack of focus on affordable recommendation systems that guide citizens towards finding low-cost, eco-friendly alternatives that are within their financial means (Garg et al. 2025; Soni and Sharma 2025). This is a continuing trend in the majority of digital sustainability solution providers, where the perceived need to be environmentally responsible is associated with increased cost.

Finally, in the area of providing citizens with access to digital sustainability solutions, very few companies are currently offering integrated digital ecosystems that connect product recommendations with circular economy services. In fact, the majority of the existing digital sustainability solutions can only offer a limited form of awareness and commerce, without a common platform for citizens to engage in multiple forms of sustainable consumption (Hande 2019; Chauhan et al. 2024).

In addition to those already identified, there are many more informal green actors/micro-enterprises that should be included within an expanded definition of the 'smart city' economy (Aayog and MOSPI 2022; Bhuvaneswari et al. 2025). Waste workers, self-help groups, local artisans and street vendors provide much of the raw materials used in the process of creating low-carbon products and recovering resources; yet they have little to no access to either digital tools, visibility or growth opportunities through mainstream sustainability programmes.

Behavioural research has primarily focused on understanding motivation, social norms and attitudes towards

Table 1 Comparison of sustainability perception across income groups in urban India

Factor	High-income group	Middle-income group	Low-income group
View of sustainable products	Lifestyle upgrade	Aspirational but costly	Low priority; affordability first
Spending willingness	High	Moderate	Very low
Access to eco-friendly options	Wide availability	Limited access	Very limited access
Awareness of sustainability	High	Improving	Lower
Key barrier	Availability	Cost	Accessibility

sustainable consumption; however, economic empowerment has not received enough attention as a potential outcome (Suthar and Singh 2015; Rajasekar and Sarvehswaran 2025). Currently, the literature does not link the adoption of environmental practices with increased savings or income generation potential for households, meaning that these could serve as strong motivators to change behaviours sustainably over the long term.

The issues outlined above create a strong foundation for the proposed development of an AI-based ecosystem for sustainable consumption as a way of redefining sustainability as not just a moral obligation but rather an economically viable, inclusive and citizen-driven process of transformation. Given India's rapidly transforming urban economy and accompanying social issues associated with this transformation, there is an urgent need to develop such an AI-based sustainable consumption ecosystem.

2.7 Comparison of Sustainability Perception Across Income Groups in Urban India

Households in urban India have different perceptions about sustainability, depending on their income class. As identified from Table 1, high-income groups perceive sustainable products to be an upgrade to a better lifestyle and therefore have greater purchasing intent due to increased access and awareness. For middle-class consumers, sustainability is desirable but not affordable, while for low-income classes, affordability takes precedence. Each segment thus presents different reasons tied to both financial and accessibility limitations; interventions for sustainability should be targeted appropriately.

Table 2 Digital sustainability interventions and their limitations in India

Intervention type	Strength	Limitation
Eco-product marketplaces	Wide variety of sustainable options	High price barriers for the majority of users
Recycling Apps	Awareness generation	Poor monetisation; limited user motivation
Carbon footprint trackers	Educates users on environmental impact	No direct economic incentive to change behaviour
Mobility Greentech	Strong adoption in the transport sector	Focused mainly on vehicle emissions only
Smart City dashboards	Government-driven sustainability insights	Weak link to citizen consumption and purchase choices

Table 3 Contribution of local informal stakeholders to sustainability

Stakeholder group	Contribution	Systemic challenge
Waste Pickers	Major recycling backbone in cities	Zero digital visibility or recognition
Women SHGs	Sustainable handmade products	Poor market access; low scaling opportunity
Local Artisans	Low-carbon traditional production	Low monetisation and inconsistent demand
Street Vendors	Affordable goods with low waste	Lack of trust, certification, and formal support
Small Recyclers	Essential circular economy agents	Not integrated into formal supply chains

2.8 Digital Sustainability Interventions and Their Limitations in India

Table 2 summarises current digital sustainability interventions in India, showing that although they provide awareness and access to green solutions, user participation remains limited due to cost, weak incentives and narrow focus areas.

2.9 Contribution of Local Informal Stakeholders to Sustainability

Table 3 highlights the crucial sustainability role played by informal local actors, while emphasising that a lack of recognition and market integration limits their wider contribution.

Table 4 AI functionalities proposed in the system

AI capability	System role	Expected sustainability outcome
Budget-aware Recommendations	Suggests affordable sustainable alternatives	Higher adoption across all income groups
Behavioural Analytics	Guides habit changes based on user patterns	Reduced household waste and expenses
Vendor Discovery Algorithms	Promote nearby sustainable and informal vendors	Strengthens local economy and job creation
Impact Estimation Model	Tracks carbon reduction and savings	Motivates long-term sustainable behaviour
Transparency Scoring (Future Blockchain)	Reduces greenwashing by validating claims	Builds trust among citizens and buyers

2.10 AI Functionalities Proposed in the System

Table 4 presents the AI capabilities integrated into the proposed system, targeted at encouraging accessible, transparent and impactful sustainable consumption.

2.11 Proposed Circular Economy Service Integration

Table 5 showcases service integrations that encourage reuse and resource efficiency, helping consumers save money while promoting circular economy practices.

Table 5 Proposed circular economy service integration

Service	Consumer benefit	Sustainability impact
Product resale	Earn money back on unused items	Extends product lifespan
Repair ecosystem	Cheaper than new purchases	Reduces material waste
Refill + Reuse	Lower recurring expenses	Decreases plastic consumption
Community sharing	Cost-free/low-cost item access	Higher resource efficiency
Household compost Monetisation	Additional income or savings	Waste-to-value transformation

3 AI Components

The proposed AI-enabled sustainable consumption ecosystem involves a suite of interdependent Artificial Intelligence components, which collaborate in support of the three-pillar objectives of affordability, inclusiveness, and behavioural change for urban Indian consumers. Each AI component is theoretical and envisioned to work within the socio-economic and cultural milieu of Indian households, especially those of middle- and lower-income classes. Because the system aims to impact responsible, transparent and fair results, the design specifications for the AI components are described in theoretical, algorithmic terms without detailing aspects related to implementation or computation.

These components comprise the core intelligence of the ecosystem, which will enable the system to make budget-sensitive recommendations, generate behavioural insights, perform sustainability matching and facilitate a circular economy. The general aim of these components using AI is, therefore, to lead users towards choices that are affordable and eco-friendly to meet their household constraints while reinforcing local green economies and strengthening informal recycling networks.

3.1 A Budget-Tech-Based Recommendation System

The Budget Allocation and Eco-Friendly Solutions recommendation engine is a component of AI that illustrates the concept of searching for, and supplying, the most cost-effective and environmentally conscious buying opportunities available to different socio-economic classes.

Mathematical Model

To determine the best sustainable option within a user's budget, the model selects:

$$R_i = \arg\min(C_i + \lambda E_i)$$
$$p_i \leq B \tag{1}$$

where

- R_i = recommended item,
- p_i = price of item i,
- B = user's budget,
- C_i = cost component,
- E_i = environmental impact score,
- λ = weight representing user or policy priority for sustainability.

Conceptual Algorithmic Logic

1. **User Financial Profiling**: A household's income, monthly expenses, past spending behaviours, price sensitivities and savings objectives can all be examined by the system to determine what is affordable for the household.
2. **Sustainability Cost Map**: By mapping sustainable product and service offerings against their initial costs, recurrent costs and usage costs, the Sustainable Map also compares the potential long-term savings of each product/service category.
3. **Sustainability-Affordability Matching**: A process of eliminating unsustainable options will match a household's affordability threshold (number 1 above) with the position of each sustainable option in the sustainability cost map (number 2 above). Therefore, potential sustainability choices will be limited by the affordability of the household.
4. **Recommendation Score**: Each sustainable option, based on the above criteria, will be assigned an overall score reflecting the product cost vs. the potential long-term savings; Secondly, the environmental benefits; Thirdly, how well the product fits into the individual's behaviour; Fourthly, including how many products will be available locally for each option.
5. **Individualised Final Recommendation Lists**: A system will generate individualised lists of cost-effective sustainable products (for reuse); Refillable Products; Low-Energy Appliances; Options for Collaborative Resource Sharing; Waste-to-Income Opportunities.
6. **Expected Outcome**: Consequently, the above will provide assurance to users of having references for low-priced cost-effective products along with visible savings as opposed to luxe products available for purchase as a result of sustainable behaviour.

3.2 An Adaptive Learning Approach to Behavioural Insights

The Behavioural Insights Module allows families to understand how they make decisions and gives them the knowledge needed to provide custom-tailored advice to develop positive behaviour changes that will benefit them over time.

Mathematical Model

The AI System changes the sustainability preference of a user dynamically based on the usefulness gained from adopting a sustainable behaviour.

$$P_{t+1} = P_t + \alpha(U_t - P_t) \tag{2}$$

where

- P_t = user preference at time step t,
- U_t = utility gained from the chosen sustainable action,
- α = learning rate controlling how quickly preferences adapt.

The Behavioural Modelling Process is Done in Four Steps

1. **Data Abstraction About Households Habits**: This gives us an overview of household spending, waste disposal, energy/water consumption and if they've ever considered changing their habits to more environmentally friendly options.
2. **Generating Archetypes Based on the People's Behaviour**: Each type of household falls under a certain category based on what they primarily do with their home (cost-driven, occasional eco-adopter, habitual householders, environmentally mindful).
3. **Apply Nudge Theory**: Based on each archetype's characteristics, they're nudged towards behaviour changes through personalised messages. For example, a household that wants to save money may receive a reminder about saving money through water conservation, while an occasional eco-adopter may receive ideas about switching products to better options.
4. **Adaptive Learning Mechanism**: Monitoring user reaction to the nudges and analysing seasonal influences on user behaviour and their engagement in the community as well as available products in the community.

Behaviour Modification through AI Logic: This module will help families save money, transition towards the use of reusable items, decrease the commonness of single-use products, and work collaboratively with other families to utilise the resources each family possesses, as well as contribute to the long-term sustainability of the planet at the household level.

3.3 Waste-to-Income Analytics and Circular Value Creation

Through this component, households can participate in circular economy systems by creating money through the recycling of their waste.

The Following is a Basic Conceptual Flow of the Algorithm

1. **Household Waste Profiling**: Profiles the types and quantity of organic and recyclable waste a household generates, how often they dispose of it, as well as identifies the potential value of these resources.
2. **Mapping to Local Recycling Networks**: Utilises Artificial Intelligence to match the types of waste generated by households to informal recyclers or sellers of compost and compost hubs in their neighbourhood.
3. **Value Estimation Algorithm**: Estimates the potential financial return a household could achieve from selling compost produced from their organic waste, selling any recyclable materials, lending tools or trading other items.
4. **Circular Opportunity Recommendations**: Recommendations on how to generate income from composting, partnering with recyclers, sharing yard tools typically not used frequently or trading reusable items.

Goal of Component: This feature provides access to small income-producing opportunities for low-income households that can provide the ability to participate in sustainable practices while being part of the circular economy model.

3.4 Sustainability Scoring and Prioritisation

Every product and service will be assigned a sustainability score with the assistance of the new AI layer.

Mathematical Model

The formula for the sustainability score S is a weighted sum of major features and environmental impact factors.

$$S = \beta_1 R_e + \beta_2 Rw + \beta_3 Rc$$

where

- R_e = resource efficiency,
- R_w = represents the potential of waste reduction,
- R_c = carbon reduction impact,
- β1, β2, β3 = Weights according to the rules of the user that satisfy a policy. (3)

Scoring Parameters: The scoring criteria include reusable, reduce carbon footprint, save money, produce locally, support circular economy and reduce waste.

Multi-Level Scoring Logic: The AI layer includes multiple levels of scoring logic. The scores are theoretical and have a weighted value of environmental impact, financial benefit, social inclusion and the like included in the final recommendations.

3.5 Optimisation Based on Affordability

The affordability maximiser AI layer consists of recommendations of sustainable solutions.

Conceptual Optimisation Objective: The effectiveness of achieving the conceptual minimisation of household financial expenditures while improving the adoption of sustainably-produced products.

The constraints for this concept are:

- Financial limitations of the household.
- Accessibility to sustainable products.
- Cultural preferences.
- Ecosystem limitations.

Expected Behaviour: The expected behaviour of this system is to focus on low-cost, sustainable solutions, to give special consideration to the recommendation of high-impact sustainable behaviour modifications, and to provide inclusive recommendation logic to assist financially vulnerable users.

3.6 Ethical Use of Artificial Intelligence

All AI layers are designed to be explicit, equitable, secure and to cover the needs of all users. The AI System should not recommend high-priced sustainable products, and it should ensure equitable recommendations of low-cost sustainable products that benefit low-income families.

4 Use Cases

This section provides the conceptual use cases showing the functioning of the proposed AI-enabled sustainable consumption ecosystem in the daily life of Indian urban households. These use cases imagine a story being told, with behaviour and economics grounded in reality as well as culture. The examples focus on middle-class and lower-middle-class families, as these two demographic groups form the bulk of urban India and face limited financial resources to adopt sustainable alternatives. The use cases exemplified here show the interaction between the AI components to deliver affordability, accessibility and actionable recommendations through responsible and inclusive AI-driven decision support.

4.1 Use Case 1: A Case Study of a Monthly Budget for a Middle-Class Family

The Verma Family is in Pune and has a middle-class income. Due to rising food, fuel and day-to-day purchases, the monthly cost of the Verma Family is still climbing. They are determined to buy environmental-friendly. They will receive more savings but this is what makes them buy the products a month, compared to having an environmentally friendly lifestyle.

Interaction with the Recommendation Engine: After using the platform the budget-sensitive recommendation engine reviews the financial information and recurring expenses of the family. It provides members with recommendations for environmentally friendly alternatives that are cost-effective. Examples of some of these include:

- Replacing kitchen rolls with reusable microfiber cloths.
- Using refillable local eco-cleaning alternatives in place of branded chemical cleaners.
- Using LED bulbs in high-traffic areas of the house.

Through the estimated monthly savings presented with each recommendation, members of the family are primarily motivated by their ability to save money.

Behavioural Insights: The Behavioural Insights Module conceptually identifies that families prefer to use products that are most convenient for them. As such, families are likely to resist making any changes that are inconvenient or require significant behaviour change. As a result of this, nudges will provide less of a behaviour change push than has historically been demonstrated. Examples of behaviour change nudges include.

- 'This month, consider switching two of your regular cleaning products for quick savings'.
- 'With a slight change in your kitchen habits, you can save money'.

4.2 Use Case 2: A Lower-Income Family Seeking Refill Solutions

The second example of this case is for the Shaikh Family. The Shaikh Family belongs to the lower-middle class and lives off a gig economy. The primary concern of this family is affordability and stability. Sustainable products will not be affordable and accessible to them.

Affordability Matching and Nudge Activation: The system will see that regularly the family purchases some household items (small sizes) such as detergent sachets at the cheapest price but are more expensive over time. The recommendation engine is suggesting the following:

1. Purchasing detergent from a local supplier, which is one-third of the per-wash cost.
2. Buying cooking oil using a bulk refill service through a local self-help group at a cheaper price.
3. Utilising a low-cost aerator that can save water on their taps with a payback speed.

The nudges provide financial logic rather than environmental messages to this household because this household is primarily motivated by cost.

Behavioural Outcome: The monthly grocery expense of the family decreased after two weeks and will continue to decrease due to the affordability and availability of a sustainable lifestyle. From the above-mentioned use case, it is clear that individuals can use AI without requiring an extensive amount of technical knowledge to make use of changes.

4.3 Use Case 3: Energy-Efficient Practices Adopted by a Dual-Income Family

The Menon Family, a dual-income family unit, struggles to find enough time for household decision-making due to their busy lifestyle. While they are financially stable, their purchasing and spending habits reflect impulse buying and a lack of awareness of the long-term costs associated with those purchases.

Energy Usage Habits: The system has identified that the majority of energy is being consumed during peak hours through the use of inefficient lighting and cooling systems. However, the system also makes suggestions for improvement:

- Use LED lights instead of incandescent light sources.
- Use timers on air conditioning units to more effectively manage their cycling.
- Install energy-efficient kitchen appliances.

Along with suggestions for how the Menon Family could save money, the system will provide Menon Families with estimated monthly and annual savings. This information appeals to the Menon Family's reliance on data to drive their decision-making processes.

Influencing Long-Term Habits with AI: The behavioural module of the system employs a personalised approach, using personalised nudges to help influence lasting changes in habit. Examples of nudges the system might use are:

> Your new energy-efficient LED bulbs will cover all of your living room lighting for a whole weekend!

By creating a direct link between sustainable living practices and the Menon Family lifestyles, the system helps to ensure that the Menon's develop behaviours that will lead to long-term change.

4.4 Use Case 4: Waste-To-Income by a Family

The fourth use case is for 'Circular Economy Participation' of the Reddy Household, which generates a lot of organic waste through their daily food preparation, grocery shopping and consumption; however, they do not know that this waste can create an opportunity for earning money.

Circular Value Creation: The waste-to-income analytics module is the conceptualisation of:

1. Profiling the amount of household organic waste produced on a weekly or bi-weekly basis.
2. Mapping local compost buyers and urban aggregation networks.
3. Calculating the potential income and savings through the sale of the organic waste.

The system suggests starting a small-scale composting operation for the household. The household then accesses the digital marketplace and connects with a local urban farmer who buys the compost from them on a regular (monthly) basis.

Outcome: The household earns supplemental income and also decreases the amount of waste being sent to landfills, and therefore is contributing to a circular economic value chain that creates additional business opportunities for local agriculture.

4.5 Use Case 5: Sharing and Pooling Resources at a Community Level

The last use case is identified as one outside of the household and demonstrates that the effects of the system can be viewed at a larger community level. Within an apartment complex located in Hyderabad, India, a number of families collectively own items and tools such as ladders, drill machines, garden tools that go unused for extended periods of time (in some cases, months).

Using AI to Identify New Sharing Opportunities: The system captures patterns such as:

- Seasonal use of kitchen cooking tools, party decorating items and kettles.
- Some people use things like ladders and drill machines infrequently or periodically.
- Multiple homes that are purchasing the same product that they use infrequently (e.g. rarely used garden tools).

The platform can also recommend establishing a 'community-sharing' pool that could be provided by the marketplace ecosystem powered by the platform's technology.

Economic Impact: By using shared resources:

- Each family saves both money and space.
- In addition to giving local craft makers and service providers greater visibility.
- The social aspect of sustainability becomes an integral part of a family, making it easier for the community to embrace sustainable behaviours.

This final use case provides an example of how the information obtained from AI could enhance the ability of consumers to adopt sustainable consumption habits on a broader scale, resulting in the community becoming more inclined to modify their purchases to take into consideration environmental factors.

4.6 A Summary of Insights from the Five Use Cases Described in This Report

The use cases represent a collective illustration of how the proposed AI Ecosystem will support affordability, behaviour modification, accessibility to affordable services and circular value generation through the development of practical, actionable options for low-cost and sustainable living, meeting the household at their current point in terms of financial, emotional and behavioural reality. Examples reinforce that it is possible to positively transform consumption behaviours throughout urban India by leveraging Responsible AI as an enabling tool for social-economic transformation.

5 Case Studies

Sustainable urban consumption in India is not starting from zero. There is a vibrant ecosystem of green start-ups, social enterprises, circular economy innovators, etc., that have demonstrated the possibilities of using eco-friendly business models to create both environmental and livelihood benefits. Examples of such initiatives include waste upcycling enterprises, digitally enabled resource recovery platforms and more. These initiatives demonstrate that integrating sustainability into everyday economies offers an opportunity for economic viability and social inclusion.

The following case studies spotlight representative organisations from India's sustainable marketplace. Each case demonstrates a unique route to green value creation, while collectively highlighting the need for a unified, citizen-centric digital infrastructure to expand their impact.

5.1 Phool.Co: Upcycling Floral Waste into Eco-Products

Phool.co is a Kanpur-based biomaterials start-up that was founded in 2017. It addresses a very unique waste issue in India: the wasted temple and ritual flowers. Instead of letting such flowers reach the rivers or landfills, Phool.co collects them and transforms them into eco-friendly products, such as incense sticks/cones, compost, biodegradable packaging ('Florafoam') and a new plant-based leather alternative branded 'Fleather.'

Important Contribution

1. It has recycled several thousand metric tonnes of floral waste so far, changing what was hitherto considered waste into useful, environment-friendly products.
2. The enterprise model is socially inclusive, wherein many of the workers are women coming from marginalised backgrounds. This engages labour in the informal sector, supports livelihoods and addresses waste.
3. Phool.co products are better-priced and more accessible compared to many of the high-end 'green' products, and make sustainable choices more attainable by a broader consumer audience.

Phool.co epitomises a circular economy company with its combination of waste-to-resource conversion, social inclusion, affordability and scalable eco-products aligned to a conceptual AI-enabled sustainable consumption ecosystem.

5.2 Recykal: Digitising Waste Management and Circular Marketplace

Recykal is based in Hyderabad and was founded in 2016. It's a digital Waste Management and Recycling Tech Company whose goal is to formalise waste recycling in India by creating a digital marketplace that connects waste generators (Households and Businesses) and informal waste collectors (Kabadiwalas and Aggregators) with Recyclers.

Important Contribution

1. All over India, Recykal's platform is successfully growing rapidly by processing and channelling high volumes of Plastic, Metal, Paper and Electronics Waste from Waste Generators to Recyclers.
2. Recykal's platform provides support for EPR compliance, a Digital Deposit-Refund System (DRS) for returning packaging, and incentives to motivate households and businesses to recycle.
3. With the introduction of digitisation of workflows/tracing waste supply chains connecting informal waste collectors to a formal circular supply chain, Recykal enhances fair treatment of waste workers, provides transparency and offers a better livelihood option.

Recykal has established itself as a model for a circular economy marketplace with a large supply of waste and demand for recycling/reusing. It demonstrates how a Tech-Based Platform can connect various stakeholders (households, informal workers, recyclers) to create a foundation for an inclusive, scalable ecosystem.

5.3 Without (by Ashaya): Recycling Hard-To-Recycle Plastic Waste into Consumer Goods

Without is an Indian circular economy company with the aim of converting hard-to-recycle plastic waste into reusable materials for consumer and industrial products, especially flexible multi-layer plastic packaging.

What Stands Out

1. The company is on a mission to provide high-recycling solutions for obstinate waste streams that typically evade traditional recycling processes, such as MLPs. This broadens the concept of the circular economy outside of conventional materials.
2. It integrates informal waste pickers into formal value chains, providing them with structured opportunities rather than marginal, unorganised work.

Without's model demonstrates that the circular economy and eco-consumption need not be confined to common materials alone (plastic bottles, paper); there is ample scope for innovation in handling those streams of waste that are otherwise considered valueless. On your platform, such businesses can be signed up as specialised vendors and can facilitate greater reuse of materials to offer a larger range of sustainable products/services.

5.4 Thaely: Turning Plastic Waste into Sustainable Footwear

An Indian sustainable fashion start-up called Thaely turns used PET bottles and plastic bags into vegan trainers. ThaelyTex, the signature invention, is produced without the use of additional chemicals or water-intensive procedures. Single-use plastic pollution and material overconsumption are the two main urban waste issues it addresses. According to reports, each pair upcycles ten plastic bags and 12 plastic bottles, demonstrating the scalability of the process to transform waste into a product.

What Stands Out

1. In order to transform a traditionally waste-generating process into a regenerative one, the brand also incorporates circularity into the packaging system by allowing the seed-embedded recycled paper shoe boxes to be planted after delivery.
2. By working with waste management systems and guaranteeing fair labour practices throughout its supply chain, Thaely further emphasises ethical employment.

While the enterprise targets urban youth through a fashion-forward product, it simultaneously promotes the idea that sustainability can be appealing, functional, and not limited to, premium luxury markets. Thaely's model highlights how sustainability can be integrated into everyday consumer products, encouraging responsible purchasing behaviour in urban India.

6 Expected Results

The expected outcomes of implementing the proposed AI-based system in the daily life of a middle-class family include providing families with more meaningful information when making financial and operational decisions, behavioural and social decisions and providing families with improved opportunities to make better and more efficient decisions. The anticipated impacts based upon the proposed theoretical design of the system, its algorithmic components, and its connection to real-life domestic situations are summarised in the sections that follow.

6.1 How Decision-Making Efficiency Will Be Improved

The model is anticipated to enhance the speed and quality of decision-making for the family. Middle-class families are faced frequently with budget, selected household purchases, utility management, health plans, education plans and plans for future savings. Traditionally, family decisions have typically been made based upon the intuition of individuals or using limited, fragmented information and often result in less than optimal results. Conversely, the AI-based framework will assess multiple options systematically by utilising Probabilistic Modelling, Constraint Satisfaction, Predictive Analytics and Multi-Criteria Decision-Making (MCDM).

The proposed model can help reduce cognitive effort by providing users with recommendations that are relevant to the user's needs and in the form of well-organised recommendations, versus having the user interpret raw data. Over the course of time, this will lead to more efficient decision-making and ultimately result in considerable monetary savings, reduced negative emotions from making decisions, and a more uniform decision-making style within a family or household. Additionally, households that have difficulty comparing prices, un-understanding the impact of decisions over a period of time, and/or prioritising future objectives will gain the greatest degree of benefit from this change.

6.2 Improved Financial Optimisation and Stability

The AI model has many anticipated effects, especially when it comes to improved financial optimisation for middle-class households who usually have several competing expenses (food, living expenses, tuition, health care, transportation and occasional company outings). The AI System determines the optimal expenses for each household by analysing factors like the price fluctuations of groceries, the historical spending patterns of the household, the seasonal trends of specific groceries, and the unique circumstances faced by each family.

The AI programme provides data on: How closely or differently a family may budget their earnings each month,

- which expenses are truly necessary for a family, and how to determine if those expenses are being impulsively or inefficiently spent,
- new ways for families to utilise their existing resources more efficiently,
- how early a family should notice that they are spending money in a wasteful manner and
- how families should save more money over time.

In addition to enhancing families' ability to forecast spending over time, the predictive modelling aspect of the AI programme allows families to plan their future finances more effectively. With the ability to predict what types of expenses will occur in the near future, families will be able to determine when it is best to make a purchase and will have access to cost-saving suggestions to help maintain a balanced budget over the long term. As such, families will be able to build up a healthy spending history and avoid experiencing any of the financial 'shock' from an unexpected expense.

6.3 Behavioural Change and Better Planning at Home

The proposed system not only assists in making recommendations to the users, but it also affects the manner in which they make decisions depending on how they use the system. Along with the continued use of the system, one can assume that individuals will start adopting a more evidence-based attitude towards the manner in which they make their daily decisions compared to the lack of social influence, reliance on uncertainty and unfinished knowledge.

Examples of the types of behaviour that may change are:

- Increased understanding of their consumption behaviour,
- a better understanding of long-term consequences,
- more attention paid to long-term needs instead of short-term wants,
- creation of more sustainable habits and
- the development of a data-driven society and culture for making decisions.

For households with many decision makers (e.g. parents and adult children), a further benefit of using an AI intelligent system could be to provide a platform for coordinating decisions and reducing conflict between multiple decision-making parties. Through the use of transparency and structured recommendation scoring, the family will have a shared basis of discussion to make planning decisions more effective, consistent and harmonious.

6.4 Resource Consumption with Less Environmental Impact

An AI System can help improve the way we use resources within our household by finding ways to optimise our energy, water and grocery consumption; identify ways we are wasting our resources; suggest actions to take and show us patterns of excess in the usage of resources. Households that have class-level income are at risk of wasting their resources without knowing it because they do not monitor their resource usage or have a good system for scheduling household tasks and activities.

Here are a few improvements that are expected to be made if the model is implemented:

- Reducing the amount of electricity used in the home by optimising how appliances are used,
- meals in the household will be planned better, leading to a reduction in food waste,
- household chores scheduled intelligently for maximum efficiency,
- household shared items will be better utilised as a result of our recommendations,
- over time, households will reduce their carbon footprint by implementing our recommendations.

We build the AI recommendations into a sustainable way of living by providing a framework to evaluate our recommendations against sustainability metrics. This enables us to motivate people to make eco-friendly decisions in an easy and practical manner. This also allows us to provide individuals with a personalised sustainability coach that can help them to reduce their carbon footprint and adopt sustainable practices into their lives without compromising their way of living.

6.5 Household Productivity Increased and Time Saved

The middle-class American family has many demands on its limited amount of time, particularly for working parents or when family members are elderly or are in school. By automating many of the decisions the average American family has to make with its spending through an AI model, this will create a large amount of free time for consumers to use in ways that don't require comparing different types of services or products, gathering research and resolving confusion.

Some Examples of the Types of Time-Saving that This May Produce Include

1. Automated product and service comparison capabilities,
2. simplified service selections based upon the list of household-related alternatives available,
3. automatic ranking of tasks based upon priority using intelligent mechanisms,
4. reminders and optimised schedules for daily activities and
5. decreasing the number of repeatedly or redundantly made decisions.

As a result of these time savings, households will become increasingly productive by creating a greater need to establish a better work-life balance and allowing for greater opportunities for quality family interactions in a more relaxed atmosphere.

6.6 Increased Preparedness for the Future and Long-Term Stability of the Household

A long-term planning capability of this model utilises Predictive Analytics, risk assessment model scenarios and simulation scenarios to help households foresee future uncertainty. A household can make informed decisions about how to prepare for and respond to future risks through understanding how a decision made today could influence a future situation.

Examples of Expected Future Benefit Include

1. improved ability to prepare for unexpected financial obligations,
2. structured plans for Educational resources, Health resources, and Retirement resources,
3. an ability to identify high-risk spending and/or behavioural patterns,
4. improving the resilience of the household to react to major disruption economically or through changes in their lifestyle.

The AI will continue to learn from new household inputs, which means that the AI will continue to grow with the family and have more advanced and personalised recommendations in the future.

6.7 Potential Socio-Economically Positive Effects of New Programmes Used by Households to Save Money Through Resource Consumption

As the AI model is implemented in many households, it demonstrates as a micro-level agent of economic and social improvement. The middle class creates many of the economic engines of countries; thus, when households are successful in making better decisions, this has a collective positive impact on savings and the overall stability of economies, along with the jobs created to facilitate marketplaces for their products.

In addition to promoting household financial and social stability, the use of the AI model can lead to greater levels of academic performance and higher levels of social mobility for children who grow up in households that are supported with financial stability. The AI model serves as a detailed guide on how to successfully manage the decisions made at the household level, but also how this can influence the economic and social development of the nation as a whole.

7 Summary of Expected Results

A summary of some of the specific outcomes that are anticipated will result from the implementation of the AI decision support system are as follows:

1. More efficient decision-making based on data,
2. financial optimisation and savings,
3. the changing of behaviour and managing the planning of future investment,
4. increased use of household resources,
5. greater productivity and time efficiency,
6. prepare you for future savings and goals,
7. provides a foundation for wider economic and social benefits.

The cumulative outcomes noted above represent a transformative ability of information-based decision support systems to provide benefits to the family unit supporting the middle class while offering the ability for them to achieve their goals within a stable environment, as well as a path towards sustainable living.

References

Bhuvaneswari, A., Sumathi, K., Sarveshwaran, V., & Sivasangari, A. (2025). Hybrid deep learning and similarity measures for requirements-driven composition of semantic web services. *Knowledge and Information Systems, 67*(2), 1627–1649.

S. Chauhan, O. Bansal, and A. Puriya, "Innovating Urbanity: The Synergy of Smart Cities and Circular Economy in India," in *Smart Cities. S.M.A.R.T. Environments*, S. Majumdar, V. Kandpal, and L. G. Anthopoulos, Eds. Cham: Springer, 2024.

F. Demaria, *The Political Ecology of Informal Waste Recyclers in India: Circular Economy, Green Jobs, and Poverty*. Oxford, UK: Oxford Univ. Press, 2023. https://doi.org/10.1093/oso/9780192869050.001.0001

A. Francis and G. K. Sarangi, "Sustainable consumer behaviour of Indian millennials:Some evidence," *Current Research in Environmental Sustainability*, vol. 4, p. 100109, 2022. https://doi.org/10.1016/j.crsust.2021.100109

V. Garg, S. Bohara, and A. Srivastav, "AI-driven sustainability marketing transformingconsumers' perception toward eco-friendly brands," *Discover Sustainability*, vol. 6, p. 984, 2025. https://doi.org/10.1007/s43621-025-01934-y

S. Hande, "The informal waste sector: a solution to the recycling problem in developing countries," *Field Actions Science Reports*, Special Issue 19, pp. 28–35, 2019.

A. U. K. Imam and U. K. Banerjee, "Urbanisation and greening of Indian cities: Problems, practices, and policies," *Ambio*, vol. 45, no. 4, pp. 442–457, 2016. https://doi.org/10.1007/s13280-015-0763-4

P. Kaushik, H. Sharma, and A. Sarna, "Why AI for India 2030 is a blueprint for inclusive growth and global leadership," *World Economic Forum, Forum Stories*, Jan. 14, 2025. Available: https://www.weforum.org/stories/2025/01/ai-for-india-2030-blueprint-inclusive-growth-global-leadership/

NITI Aayog and MOSPI, *Achieving Circular Economy: Resource Efficiency and Circular Economy — Status Paper*. Govt. of India, 2022.

NA, I. S., Rajasekar, V., & Sarvehswaran, V. (2025). Real-time fire risk classification using sensor data and digital Twin-Enabled deep learning. *IEEE Journal of Selected Topics in Applied Earth Observations and Remote Sensing*.

S. Pandey and S. Gautam, *Towards Zero Waste: Innovations in Circular Economy Models for Indian Cities and Towns*. TERI, Sept. 12, 2025. Available: https://www.teriin.org/article/towards-zero-waste-innovations-circular-economy-models-indian-cities-and-towns

G.Prakash and P. Pathak, "Intention to buy eco-friendly packaged products among young consumers of India: A study on developing nation," *Journal of Cleaner Production*, vol. 141, pp. 385–393, 2017.https://doi.org/10.1016/j.jclepro.2016.09.116

Rajasekar, V., Sathya, K., Santhosh, A., Saran, S., & Senthilvel, K. (2024, April). An intelligent system for skin cancer detection using deep learning techniques. In *2024 International Conference on Advances in Data Engineering and Intelligent Computing Systems (ADICS)* (pp. 1–5). IEEE.

D.Sengupta, I. M. S. K. Ilankoon, K. D. Kang, and M. N. Chong, "Circular economy and household e-waste management in India. Part II: A case study on informal e-waste collectors (Kabadiwalas) in India," *Minerals Engineering*, vol. 200, p. 108154, 2023. https://doi.org/10.1016/j.mineng.2023.108154

P. Soni and S. Sharma, "AI Recommendations and Consumer Awareness: Drivers of Eco-Friendly Behavior," *International Journal of Scientific Development and Research*, vol. 10, no. 5, 2025. Available: https://ijsdr.org/papers/IJSDR2505157.pdf

S. Suthar and P. Singh, "Household solid waste generation and composition in different family size and socio-economic groups: a case study," *Sustainable Cities and Society*, vol. 14, pp. 56–63, 2015.https://doi.org/10.1016/j.scs.2014.07.004

AI for the People: Citizen Engagement and Participatory Design

H. J. Vrishank, Samarth Kadam, K. R. Harish, and Karthikeyan Periyasami

Abstract

The Citizen Engagement and Participatory Artificial Intelligence(AI) Design is a form of designing AI systems that engages ordinary people in decision-making concerning the way AI should be constructed and utilized. This method also allows citizens to contribute their ideas and enhance AI to suit the community values and needs instead of AI being developed by experts alone. The activities such as coming together to collect data, participating in workshops, and joining groups where they can have discussions with the developers and make decisions on how AI can be used within the society make people involved. New technology simplifies AI and makes it more just. The human-centered computing theory is aimed at designing AI to assist humans and user-friendly AI. Explainable AI (XAI) is what makes people understand why AI takes a specific decision and trust it. Value-sensitive design ensures that AI does not violate major human values such as fairness and privacy tree-ring. People who are involved in the development of AI systems, such as smart cities, health care, or environmental initiatives, feel safer that AI is just and reliable. Such issues as the inclusion of everybody, the security of data, and access to people without technologies remain. This chapter will seek to discuss the idea that citizen engagement in AI design will help to make AI more democratic, fair, and acceptable. It also considers the most recent tools and approaches that can be used to facilitate participation, talks about practical cases, and analyzes problems and future prospects of developing AI that can benefit everyone.

Keywords

Participatory AI design · Citizen engagement in AI · Responsible AI for smart cities · Explainable AI (XAI) · Human-centered computing · Value-sensitive design · Ethical AI development · Digital inclusion · AI governance · Trustworthy AI systems

1 Introduction

AI has quickly become a pervasive socio-technical infrastructure affecting policing, welfare, health care, mobility, agriculture, and digital identity management, reshaping how individuals access the state and interact with institutions (Eubanks, 2018).

Figure 1 illustrates how AI systems operate as a hub connecting multiple public domains that directly affect citizens' everyday lives. A central circle labeled "AI Systems" is linked by spokes to surrounding bubbles representing Policing, Welfare, Healthcare, Mobility/Transport, Education, Digital Identity/Public, and Agriculture. The diagram emphasizes that AI is not confined to a single sector but functions as shared socio-technical infrastructure embedded across key state and societal functions.

As governments and organizations deploy AI at scale, these systems increasingly mediate citizen government interactions, transform decision-making processes, alter resource distribution, and redefine civic responsibilities.

Although AI has broad social reach, it is still frequently imagined and developed with limited involvement from communities most affected by its decisions. Development is often guided by technical experts, corporate interests, or

H. J. Vrishank (✉) · S. Kadam · K. R. Harish · K. Periyasami
School of Computer Science and Engineering RV University, Bengaluru, India
e-mail: vrishank62@gmail.com

S. Kadam
e-mail: kadam.samartha@gmail.com

K. R. Harish
e-mail: k.r.harish025@gmail.com

K. Periyasami
e-mail: karthikeyanp@rvu.edu.in

V. Sarveshwaran et al. (eds.), *Responsible AI for Smart Cities*, Sustainable Artificial Intelligence-Powered Applications,
https://doi.org/10.1007/978-3-032-26901-0_3

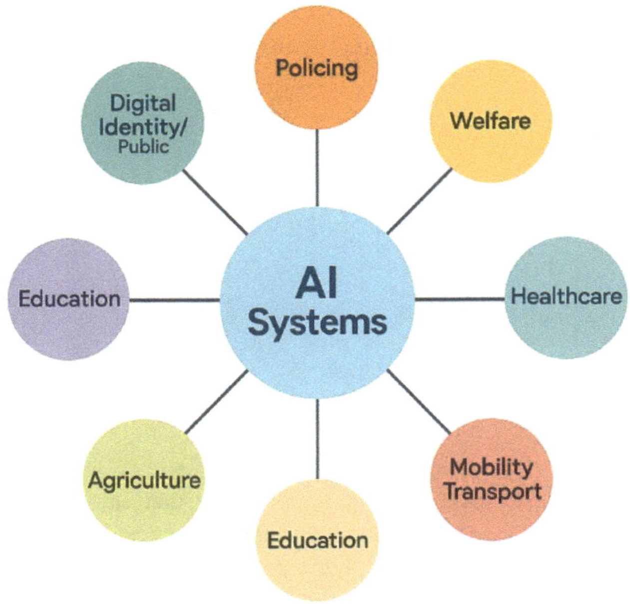

Fig. 1 Domains impacted by ai systems

state agencies whose priorities may not reflect the lived realities, vulnerabilities, or cultural contexts of diverse populations (Longworth, 2021). This detachment creates a democratic deficit: algorithmic systems shape key aspects of everyday life while citizens have very little say in how these systems are designed or governed. In such settings, AI can reproduce historical inequalities, institutionalize structural injustices, and deepen harms for marginalized or under-represented groups.

Growing awareness of these issues has driven interest in PAI, which positions citizens as collaborators, critics, and co-designers throughout the AI lifecycle (Jobin et al., 2019). This perspective recognizes that communities hold contextual knowledge and moral insight that are essential for building equitable, trustworthy, and socially grounded AI systems. PAI reframes technological development as a democratic, community-anchored process rather than a purely expert-driven, technocratic activity.Background: AI as Socio-Technical Infrastructure.

The expansion of AI in public governance has unfolded alongside the growth of digital public infrastructure worldwide. As states modernize service delivery, AI systems become embedded in routine institutional operations, influencing decisions in criminal justice, welfare administration, public health, education, and urban management. Smart-city platforms integrate AI into mobility, energy, waste management, and emergency response, restructuring how civic life is organized.

These systems are often presented as neutral tools that increase efficiency, yet research shows that AI is shaped by social, cultural, and political contexts. Historical inequalities are encoded in training data, design choices reflect particular notions of fairness or efficiency, and deployment conditions determine who benefits and who bears risk (Organisation for Economic Co-operation and Development, 2022). AI should therefore be understood not only as a technical artifact but as a governance apparatus that affects rights, opportunities, and representation, requiring democratic engagement and oversight rather than mere optimization.

Figure 2 contrasts a traditional, expert-driven AI pipeline with a participatory AI pipeline to highlight the democratic deficit in conventional development.

1.1 Problem Statement: Why Traditional AI Development Is Not Enough

Eubanks shows how automated welfare and policing tools can deepen existing inequalities when they are built without input from the communities they target (Eubanks, 2018). Training data often fails to reflect the diversity and lived experience of affected groups, leading to biased or inaccurate predictions, especially for marginalized communities.

Citizens also have limited understanding of how models work or why decisions are made, which weakens trust and accountability. Moreover, communities most exposed to AI systems are rarely involved in scoping, development, deployment, or evaluation, leaving them few avenues to contest harmful outcomes or demand changes. These limitations mean that expert-driven AI development is insufficient both ethically and practically: systems that ignore local knowledge and priorities are more likely to fail in practice, generate resistance, or create unintended harms.

1.2 Why Participatory AI Now?

PAI has gained urgency as failures and abuses of AI systems become more visible in areas such as facial recognition, hiring, credit scoring, and welfare governance. High-profile cases of bias have illustrated the risks of opaque, black-box systems deployed without meaningful public oversight. At the same time, many governments are experimenting with citizen assemblies, participatory budgeting, and deliberative forums, creating institutional precedents for involving the public in AI governance.

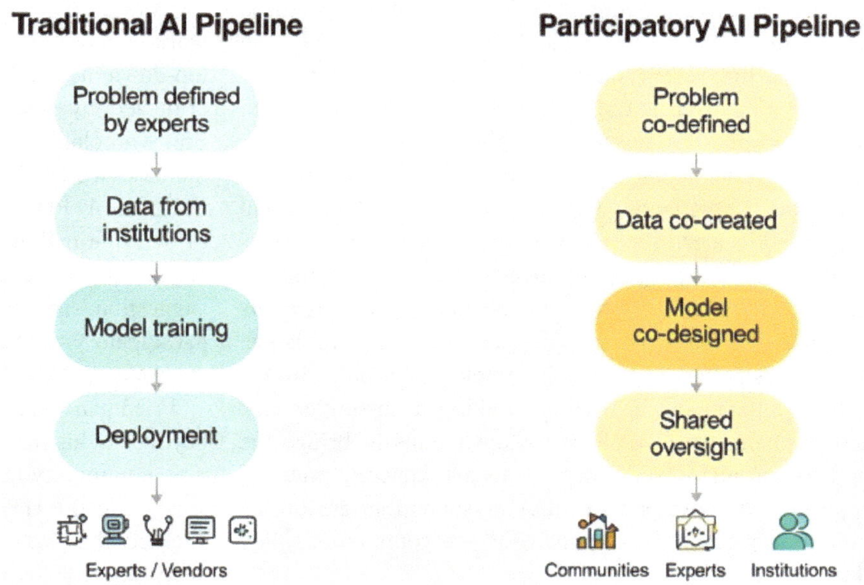

Fig. 2 Traditional AI pipeline versus participatory AI pipeline

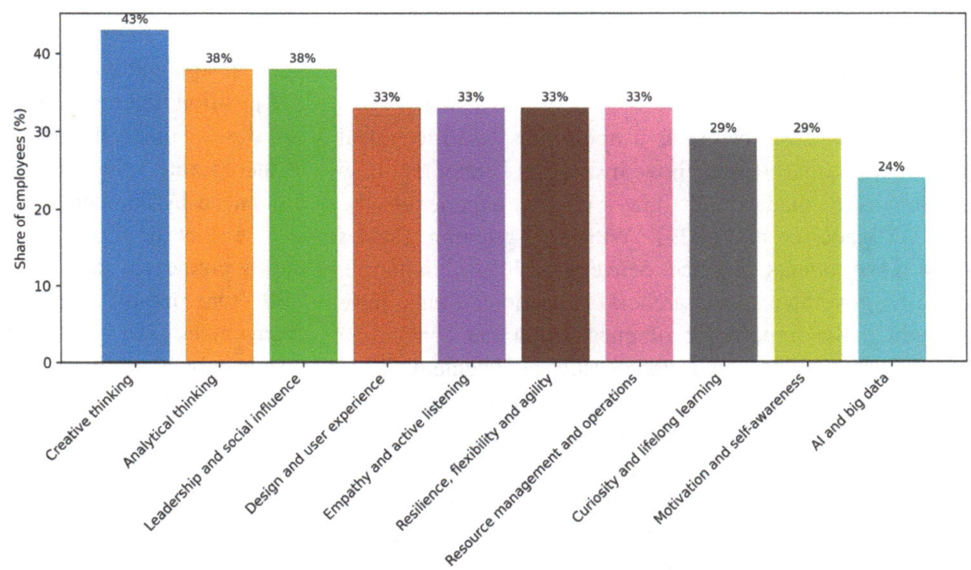

Fig. 3 Prioritized reskilling areas in the global public sector (2023) (World Economic Forum. (June 13 2023). Prioritized reskilling focus in the government and public sector worldwide in 2023, by skill [Graph], 2023)

The broader digital transformation of public services has intensified demands for transparency, reliability, and fairness in automated decision-making. International frameworks from bodies such as UNESCO, the OECD, and the EU emphasize human-centered, rights-respecting, and participatory principles for AI, and highlight the importance of contextual factors in achieving these goals. Against this backdrop, participatory methods are increasingly framed not as optional enhancements but as core mechanisms for responsible AI governance.

Figure 3 illustrates prioritized reskilling needs in the global public sector for 2023, emphasizing creative, analytical, and design skills as essential for AI integration in governance. This underscores the shift toward human-centered competencies in PAI, where public sector workers must develop skills to collaborate with citizens in AI design, ensuring systems align with community values rather than purely technical expertise (World Economic Forum (June 13, 2023). Prioritized reskilling focus in the government and public sector worldwide in 2023, by skill [Graph], 2023).

1.3 Contributions of this Chapter

This chapter contributes to debates on responsible AI by offering an extended analysis of PAI, its core principles, practical methods, and implications for public-sector innovation. It situates PAI within broader traditions of AI ethics, participatory design, and socio-technical governance, and proposes a lifecycle framework describing how communities can be involved at each stage of AI development, from problem scoping to long-term oversight.

Drawing on examples from settings such as India, Kenya, Brazil, the Netherlands, Japan, the European Union, and the United States, the chapter shows that participatory practices can be adapted to diverse cultural and institutional contexts. It identifies key enablers and constraints for embedding participatory approaches in AI governance, and outlines policy directions and implementation pathways for governments and institutions seeking to institutionalize such mechanisms. Overall, the chapter aims to bridge the gap between high-level ethical ideals and concrete practice, supporting the development of AI systems that are democratic, transparent, and responsive to the communities they affect.

2 Literature Review and Conceptual Foundations

Delgado et al. describe AI as a ubiquitous socio-technical infrastructure that shapes how institutions function, how decisions are made, and how citizens experience the state (Delgado et al., 2023). With the growing use of AI in governments, service delivery and administration, and city governance, researchers in various fields have highlighted the importance of questioning the connection between AI, society, and democratic engagement. It is observed that the literature shows an increasing awareness that AI cannot be satisfactorily described using technical measures like accuracy or computational efficiency. Instead, AI should be considered in the larger political, cultural, and ethical frameworks, where it is engrained. This area summarizes the historical backgrounds, theoretical discussions, and integrated paradigms, which define the new paradigm of PAI. The review of literature traces some of the most important concepts of the Participatory Design, socio-technical systems theory, and digital governance, and Responsible AI to show how various academic traditions are converged towards the necessity of more inclusive, democratic approaches to AI development and governance.

2.1 History: Participatory Design and Democratization of Technology

The intellectual roots of PAI date back to the Participatory Design (PD) movement that had appeared in 1970s Scandinavia. The technologies were fast being introduced at the. workplaces without the participation of the actual workers whose daily activities would be transformed. This top-down account of technological change was strongly criticized by researchers like Kristen Nygaard and Pelle Ehn who claimed that computational technologies ought to increase worker autonomy instead of improving managerial control. PD thus attempted to decentralize the process of decision-making by engaging the workers in the design and review of the technological systems. This was a radical suggestion since it redefined design as the political and participatory process that was rooted in the experiences of the communities affected in their lived experiences.

Friedman and Hendry show that PD has expanded beyond industrial workplaces into public-sector innovation, community technology projects, education, and digital service design (Friedman and Hendry, 2019). Researchers stressed that individuals had contextual expertise, which is the knowledge that is stored in both local experience, cultural practices as well as everyday routine and it is indispensable when developing systems reflecting real world requirements. PD therefore not merely provided techniques of co-design and collaborative prototyping, but a philosophical position that disputed expert-based model of technological development. It was aware that technologies are bound to incorporate values and assumptions, and thus have to be influenced by democratic participation.

Warne et al. argue that as digital systems become more tightly connected to government, participatory design must shift from one-off workshops toward long-term, sustained engagement (Warne et al., 2021). This need was aggravated by the advent of AI since algorithmic systems can make permanent effects on communities even after first usage. The contemporary participatory theorists contend that AI opens up its secrecy, fluidity and scale necessitate novel participatory governance, one that transcends the existing design stages. This historical path of PD to participatory co-governance creates an essential intellectual point of contact with modern PAI which extends the principles of PD to the lifecycle of AI systems in general and presupposes more overall questions of power, justice, and institutional responsibility.

Table 1 compares the Historical development between early PD and modern PAI. It shows that participation has grown over the years, initially worker involvement in Scandinavian workplaces, to wider civic-community involvement in the provision of public services, and finally inclusive and democratic involvement in AI systems controlling the provision of public infrastructures. The table represents the changes in the settings, participants, and goals, demonstrating how the participatory methods have gradually transitioned, to challenge top-down technological control to integrating fairness, accountability, and justice throughout the entire lifecycle of AI systems.

Table 1 From participatory design to participatory AI

Period/Concept	Main setting	Who participates	Main goal
1970s–1980s Participatory design (PD)	Scandinavian Workplaces and unions	Workers, trade unions	Counter top-down technological control and increase worker autonomy
1990s–2010s Participatory design	Public services, community technology projects, education, and digital service design	Citizens, communities, public-sector professionals	Align digital systems with everyday practices and local contextual knowledge
Today—Participatory AI (PAI)	AI in governance, smart cities, welfare, healthcare, and other public infrastructures	Broad publics, especially affected and marginalized groups, alongside experts and Institutions	Build fair, accountable, and Democratic AI systems across The full lifecycle, linking design with questions of power, justice, and institutional responsibility

2.2 AI as a Socio-Technical Governmental Architecture

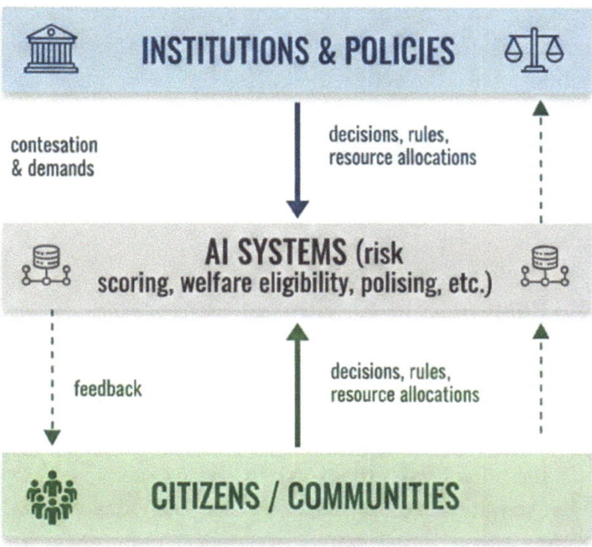

Fig. 4 AI as socio-technical governmental architecture

There is growing literature acknowledging AI as a governance infrastructure beyond a computational tool, that is influencing the manner in which institutions engage with citizens and how social resources are allocated. In the last ten years AI has found its way into many government systems, such as welfare eligibility scoring, police and risk analysis, medical diagnosis, pandemic prediction, smart city traffic control, and government bureaucracy. These systems affect the choices traditionally made by human officials and therefore assume the same sphere of power as the public policies.

Figure 4 shows how political decisions and policies flow downward into AI systems, which then shape how resources, opportunities, and sanctions are distributed to people in everyday life.At the same time, the dashed arrows going upward highlight that citizens are not just passive recipients: they can provide feedback on AI systems and contest decisions at both the technical and policy levels. The diagram therefore visualizes the core argument that AI is a governance infrastructure that must be subject to democratic oversight, community voice, and institutional accountability, rather than being treated as a neutral technical tool.

According to scholars, this change is a sign of change in the way governance works: automated systems are becoming more and more involved in the distribution of rights, opportunities and services.

Crawford shows AI systems aren't neutral tools but models trained on biased data simply recreate past inequalities. She also highlights how their 'black box' nature blocks citizens from grasping or challenging how categories form, which variables matter most, or why predictions happen (Crawford, 2021).

The socio-technical approach dictates that AI should be looked at as a part of the political, institutional, and cultural contexts in which it is implemented. The AI systems used in the public sector encode the assumptions of efficiency, risk, fairness, and legitimacy: They could or could not correspond to the community values or lived experiences. In cases where AI is implemented without participatory regulation, it has the potential to cloud or strengthen the existing systemic inequalities, especially to marginalized groups who, already, experience disproportionate institutional attention. Theorists thus propose the need of governance models that incorporate democratic engagement and community based supervision to counter the dangers of technocratic decision-making.

This literature lays the foundation as to why the traditional AI governance models are inadequate. Conventional strategies are more inclined to use technical auditing, regulatory standards or ethical principles, but these systems of checks do not work until systems have been created and implemented. The AI systems will lose touch with the values and needs of the communities in which they operate without the participatory processes that are introduced in all the lifecycle stages, such as problem definition, data creation, model development, evaluation, and deployment. The notion of AI as a socio-technical infrastructure, therefore, creates a rationale behind the implementation of PAI.

2.3 Citizen Participation in the Digital Age and Democratic Participation

PAI is also highly informed by the existing studies which demonstrate a strong relationship between citizen engagement in governance and trust in institutions. In the context of AI and algorithmic systems, participatory mechanisms can increase the transparency and understanding of how automated decisions are made and who bears responsibility for their consequences. Citizens can contribute their perspectives on what fairness, accountability, or safety mean in their specific contexts, ensuring that AI systems align with locally held values rather than imposing a singular conception of these principles.

The broader digital transformation of public services has intensified demands for transparency, reliability, and fairness in automated decision-making. International frameworks from bodies such as UNESCO, the OECD, and the EU emphasize human-centered, rights-respecting, and participatory principles for AI, and highlight the importance of contextual factors in achieving these goals. Against this backdrop, participatory methods are increasingly framed not as optional enhancements but as core mechanisms for responsible AI governance.PAI within broader traditions of participatory design, and socio-technical governance, proposes a lifecycle framework describing how communities can be involved at each stage of AI development, from problem scoping to long-term oversight. Drawing on examples from settings such as India, Kenya, Brazil, the Netherlands, Japan, the European Union, and the United States, participatory practices can be adapted to diverse cultural and institutional contexts.

The literature also underlines that participation should not be only an adjunct to the technical advancement, but a root of the responsible governance. Community involvement will reveal the local knowledge and tacit knowledge that would be unnoticed by conventional sources of data. It also creates trust and the feeling of common proprietorship of public technologies. The closer digital systems are linked to the administration, the more scholars demand participatory mechanisms, which are deliberate, planned, inclusive, and persistent, which the notion of PAI puts in the spotlight.

Figure 5 reveals the concentration of AI expertise in larger Indian organizations as of December 2019, highlighting a critical skills gap that limits PAI adoption in smaller public entities and SMEs. This distribution reinforces the need for democratized AI development, where citizen engagement bridges technical shortages by incorporating local knowledge, making AI systems more accessible and equitable across organizational scales (India TV. (December 24, 2019). Employment share of artificial intelligence (AI) professionals in India as of December 2019, by company size [Graph], 2019).

2.4 Responsible AI, Human-Centered Computing, and the Case of Participatory AI

Responsible AI (RAI) has gained prominence in the world given the increased use of AI in diverse sectors and the growing awareness of associated risks. The concept of RAI encompasses a broad range of concerns: fairness, transparency, accountability, privacy, and security. It seeks to

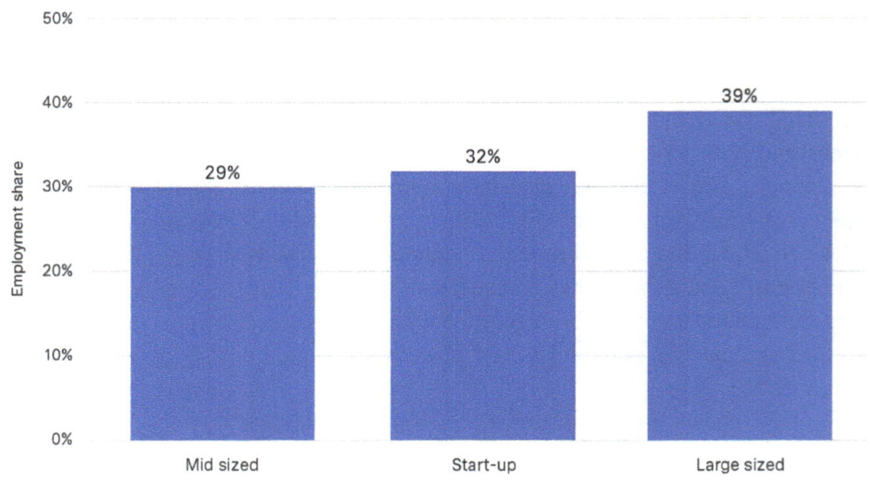

Fig. 5 AI expertise concentration by company size in India (2019) (India TV. (December 24, 2019). Employment share of artificial intelligence (AI) professionals in India as of December 2019, by company size [Graph], 2019)

ensure that AI systems are developed and deployed in ways that respect human rights, promote equity, and mitigate potential harms.

Lee et al. define human-centered computing as a research and design approach that prioritizes human values, needs, and well-being over pure technical performance in system development (Lee et al., 2020). This approach contrasts with technology-centric development paradigms that focus primarily on technical performance or efficiency. Human-centered approaches recognize that technology is not value-neutral and that the design decisions embedded in systems reflect particular worldviews and priorities.

PAI represents a synthesis of these traditions-responsible AI, human-centered computing, and participatory design-applying them to the context of AI systems in governance and public services. Rather than treating citizen participation as an afterthought or consultation exercise, PAI embeds community engagement throughout the entire lifecycle of AI development and deployment. This includes stages such as problem definition, data collection and labelling, model training, evaluation, deployment decisions, and ongoing monitoring and oversight.

The rationale for this comprehensive participatory approach stems from recognition that the most affected communities possess essential knowledge about local contexts, needs, and values that should inform AI system design. Communities can identify potential unintended consequences or misalignments with their priorities, contribute to defining fairness and accountability in culturally appropriate ways, and help establish oversight mechanisms that ensure systems remain responsive to their needs over time. In this way, PAI bridges the gap between high-level ethical principles and on-the-ground implementation, creating concrete pathways for making AI systems more democratic, transparent, and accountable to the communities they affect.

3 A Participatory Artificial Intelligence (PAI) Conceptualization

PAI is a strategic rebranding of the idea of AI, its development, and the way it is regulated (Kaminski, 2020) than viewing AI as a strictly computational product designed by professionals and pushed to passive consumers, PAI defines AI as a socio-technical product that is being formed by shared knowledge, values in the marketplace and democracy. This school of thought acknowledges that AI does not exist beyond the society; it is engrained in the institutions, cultures, power practices, and life activities. This is why both technical knowledge and civic engagement and social acceptability should guide the creation of AI.

With the growing role of algorithmic systems in the delivery of services, city infrastructures, and governmental decision making, there has been a better understanding that the classical approach to developing AI involving top down and expert knowledge is no longer sufficient. The issues of justice, equity, autonomy, and representation are now completely inseparable with AI. PAI is one response to these realities, which aims to find systematic means to involve citizens, and most particularly those most impacted by AI, in the process of the AI lifecycle. This section will outline the conceptual basis of PAI, define the meaning of participation in an AI environment, and place the paradigm in the context of the larger theoretical discussions in computing, design, and governance.

3.1 Defining Participatory AI

Despite the various definitions that are used with regard to PAI, it is broadly accepted that communities must actively and organized participate in the creation of AI systems (Cheong, 2024). Business benefits of AI according to retail executives worldwide in 2023 [Graph], 2023). PAI is not simply consultation or a collection of feedback as it is a practice that focuses on shared decision-making, joint design and long term monitoring. It is a sign of reality that AI systems have a considerable impact on social outcomes hence should be formed by individuals whose lives are affected by them.

PAI is based, at its most fundamental level, on the assumption that humans have important contextual knowledge which cannot be substituted by data or by technical information. The citizens know the specificities of their real-life surroundings, the specifics of interpersonal relations, and the possible threats posed by automated decisions. Their perspective can be used to make sure that the AI systems capture the local cultural standards, moral demands, and social priorities. Participation, in turn, can serve as a tool of influencing the technical and normative aspect of AI.

Figure 6 illustrates how citizens can play different roles at every stage of the AI lifecycle, from co-defining problems and co-creating data to reviewing models during evaluation and monitoring deployment and governance over time.

One of the most important components in this definition is the concept of involvement throughout the lifecycle of AI. The citizens are able to play their role in formulating problems, which problems need technology interventions and which do not. They have the ability to influence the practices of data by determining what is either missing or wrong, or what is considered sensitive or inappropriate

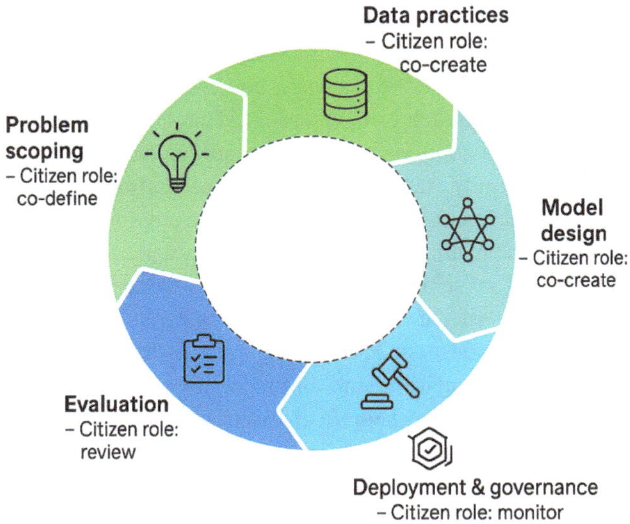

Fig. 6 Citizens across the AI lifecycle

data. They could affect the goals of the models, fairness-related goals, interpretability-related goals, and deployment-related requirements. Notably, the communities might also continue to monitor the effects of AI, oppose decisions, and assist in determining when systems require updating or discontinuation.

Lastly, PAI is not merely a methodology it is a normative commitment. It instills values of democracy including transparency, accountability, equity and the right to challenge algorithmic results. In this way, it is also providing a challenge to the notion that AI must be expert-centred and rather makes AI a subset of a larger social contract between the governments and the people.

3.2 The Reason AI Systems Are Better with Participation

The positive aspects of the involvement go well beyond the ethical issues. Researchers in the fields of computing, social sciences, and governance are increasingly putting forward the argument that participatory processes result in superior, stronger, and more situational AI systems. Involvement makes the definition of problems more relevant, risks that could be missed by the technical teams may be made known, and the outputs of the models may be made fair and interpretable. Since AI systems are going to work in multifaceted settings, the variety of voices becomes a rational requirement instead of an imaginary aspirational one.

Figure 7 shows retail executives' perceived business benefits of AI worldwide in 2023, with dominant emphasis on productivity, profitability, and customer management. This highlights how PAI can extend these corporate gains to public governance by incorporating citizen input, ensuring AI delivers equitable societal value beyond efficiency metrics alone (Chain store Age (February 28, 2023)).

The argument of data quality enhancement is one of the most compelling ones in favor of participation. Most of the failures in AI are because of biased, incomplete, or non-representative data. Systems are characteristically more productive of equitable results when communities are engaged in the data collection process design, the locating of missing categories, or the emboldening of harmful labels. Annotation by community and participatory data governance are able to uncover cultural undertones that are usually hidden in traditional datasets.

Fig. 7 Perceived AI business benefits in retail (2023) (Chain storage Age (February 28, 2023))

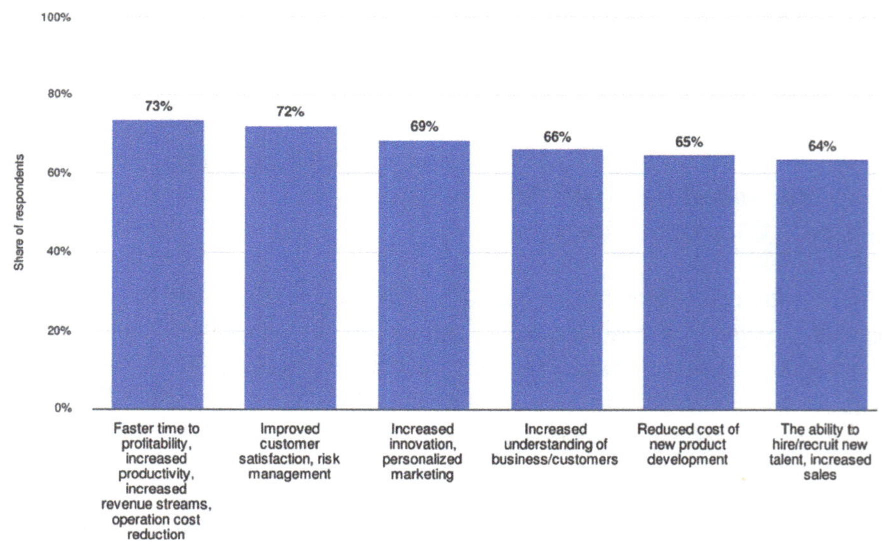

The involvement also enhances the trust of the people. AI systems that are implemented in a non-transparent and non-engaged manner are often met with opposition, mistrust, and allegations of injustices (Ada Lovelace Institute, AI Now Institute & Open Government Partnership, Algorithmic accountability for the public sector 2021). Conversely, acceptance and legitimacy become greater when the citizens know how a system operates, why decisions are taken, and what checks and balances are involved. Trust is not a social good in itself; it also has been useful in terms of adoption, compliance, and long-term sustainability of AI systems.

The other element that makes participation important is the fact that it can help in uncovering the unintended consequences. Social groups usually expect the real-life issues like stigmatising, privacy, or behavioural modification, which technical teams do not anticipate. Such lessons would be useful in making certain systems resilient, ethical, and sensitive to dynamic social contexts. Through participation, AI development is iterative and it can be continuously refined as situations change.

Lastly, participatory governance is based on accountability. Communities should be allowed to challenge, debate and affect the development of AI systems. Accountability institutions can be citizen councils, grievance institutions, transparency services and ways in which people can withdraw their consent. These mechanisms make AI a social entity that is to be controlled instead of an unregulated technological power. Involvement will make AI promote the common good, as opposed to institutional utility or market interests.

3.3 Participatory AI Guiding Principles

Despite the fact that participatory methodology differs depending on locations and organizations, there are a number of guiding principles that come out (Open Government Partnership, Participatory data Governance 2022a). Such principles are not merely used to choose the methodology, but they also point to the more significant philosophical commitments of PAI.

The first principle is inclusivity. PAI aims to engage individuals and groups that have not been technologically involved in decision making in the past. This encompasses marginalized populations, people with low-income, people of diverse cultural groups, and those that are disproportionately impacted by algorithmic harms. Inclusivity will mean AI does not reinforce the differences that already exist in society but rather reflects diversity.

A second principle is transparency, which allows participation that is meaningful. Unless communities are aware of what the system is, how it works and what data it utilizes, they will not be able to engage in communities. Openness towards the purposes of AI deployment, potential risks, governing structures, as well as modes of contestation is also referred to as transparency, not restricted solely to algorithmic explainability.

The third principle is shared power, which is one of the main points of the distinction between participatory design and symbolic engagement. Sometimes the citizens are considered to participate only because one is given a chance to express the opinions, which is not enough to call participation a possibility (Open Government Partnership, What makes participatory data initiatives successful? 2022b). Shared power is reflected in participation in the co-design sessions, auditing with participation, citizen supervisory organizations, and co-creation of policies. In the absence of means of moving power, the participation will be tokenistic.

Another principle that is imperative is contextual grounding. AI systems have to be placed within social, cultural, historical, and political environments in which they are placed. This involves acknowledging and appreciating local knowledge systems, that is whether they be in regard to urban practice, local norms, or local culture-based definitions of fairness. Participation will make sure that AI solutions are more tailored to local realities than imposing universalized and abstracted ones.

Lastly, participatory governance is based on accountability. Communities should be allowed to challenge, debate and affect the development of AI systems. Accountability institutions can be citizen councils, grievance institutions, transparency services and ways in which people can withdraw their consent. These mechanisms make AI a social entity that is to be controlled instead of an unregulated technological power.

The combination of these principles provides a conceptual roadmap of developing AI systems that are fair, transparent, and based on democratic principles.

Table 2 summarizes the main principles of participating AI and how they can be put into practice in terms of AI development and deployment. It shows how abstract normative commitments, i.e. inclusivity, transparency, shared power, contextual grounding and accountability are applied to concrete practices across AI projects. Collectively, these principles stand in favor of a change based on technical optimization to participatory governance, such that the AI systems are influenced by the most vulnerable and are sensitive to the social context, power imbalance, and systems of democratic accountability.

Table 2 Guiding principles of participatory AI

Principle	Practical implication in AI projects
Inclusivity	Proactively involve marginalized and historically under-represented groups in workshops, data annotation, user testing, and advisory councils so that those most affected help shape system goals and constraints.
Transparency	Provide clear, accessible information about why the AI system is being built, what data it uses, how decisions are made, and what risks or trade-offs are involved, enabling informed participation and critique.
Shared power	Create formal mechanisms—Such as citizen panels, participatory audits, and co-governance boards—Where community representatives have real influence, including the ability to delay, modify, or veto deployments.
Contextual grounding	Adapt model objectives, fairness metrics, and interface designs to local social, cultural, historical, and political contexts, drawing on community knowledge about what harms and benefits matter most.
Accountability	Establish accessible channels for appeal, redress, independent audits, and periodic review so that citizens can challenge outcomes and ensure that AI systems can be corrected, suspended, or retired when necessary.

3.4 Theory Underpinning Participatory AI

It has a number of intellectual traditions that participatory AI builds on to offer various insights into how technology is to be designed and regulated. The knowledge of such theoretical backgrounds can explain why involvement is not a luxury in modern AI development but a prerequisite.

A prime one is that of socio-technical systems theory, where the society and technology are shaping each other. This view suggests that AI systems are inseparable to the institutional, cultural, and social relations in which they exist. AI is never technical per se, but a part of human conditions. PAI builds on this observation by suggesting that communities should be involved in determining what socio-technical configurations cover them.

Critical data studies is yet another vital foundation and it notes that data is not neutral. Numbers represent political backgrounds, social injustices, and authority. Data sets, labels, and categories usually contain biases, leaving out the views of groups that are marginalized. The participatory practices can be used to offset these trends, engaging communities in the definition of the categories of data, identifying problematic assumptions, and building governance models like data trusts or cooperatives.

Human-centered design also affects participatory AI and emphasizes the role of user requirements, engaging in steps, and focusing on people-centered outcomes rather than technological features alone. It is therefore imperative to ground participatory AI in the perspectives of those who are most affected by algorithmic systems. Finally, PAI is informed by the concepts of value-sensitive design, which seeks to proactively integrate human values into the technological design process itself from the beginning rather than as an afterthought to the technical development.

4 Procedures and Systems of Deploying Participatory AI

Operationalizability Part PAI can not be operationalizable using principle only, but needs tangible methodologies, organized processes, and governance systems to convert the abstract ideals of participation into long-term and repeatable practices (Rosella et al., 2025). With the proliferation of AI systems into the fabric of the state machinery, smart city systems, and the institutional level of decision-making, the systematic participatory structures are particularly essential. The section presents the methodological ground of PAI, models from which ethical and inclusive development should be implemented, and the practical tools that can be utilised by researchers, administrations of a city and institutes.

It is not about technical processes but the creation of the space in which a community can significantly influence the development and management of AI.

4.1 Participatory AI Lifecycle (PAI -L)

he PAI Lifecycle offers an organized system of integrating the community during the entire lifetime of an AI system.

Figure 8 provides a high-level visual overview of the Participatory AI Lifecycle (PAI-L), emphasizing that participation is built into every major stage rather than added at the end.

In contrast to the classical AI pipelines, where the definition of the problem, data curation, modeling, evaluation, and deployment are performed in technocratic environments to a greater degree, the PAI-L focuses on open decision-making, co-design, and shared control (Parthasarathy et al., 2024). In the lifecycle, there is appreciation of the fact that the community knowledge is needed not just in the initial design but also during the final monitoring and system development.

In addition to determining the priorities of the community, the structural issues that are not reflected by the traditional technical processes can be revealed by participatory problem scoping. An example is mobility-related AI systems, where residents might raise the issue of safety, gender relations with the public transportation system, or accessibility issues that are not reflected in the municipal datasets. Communities can offer localized ecological information, like seasonal pollution trends or risk of flooding, which automated sensors are unable to identify in environmental sensing projects. These lessons redefine not only the definition of the problem, but also the suitability of AI as a tool in the first place. Participatory scoping in most situations assists in avoiding the implementation of unneeded and perilous algorithmic systems by uncovering the socio-political causes of the problem that ought to be addressed with policy response in lieu of prediction modeling.

Table 3 contrasts the normal AI development processes with the PAI -L, which demonstrates how PAI distributes power, decision-making, and governance that was once under technocratic control to community-based, democratic engagement throughout the entire AI lifecycle.

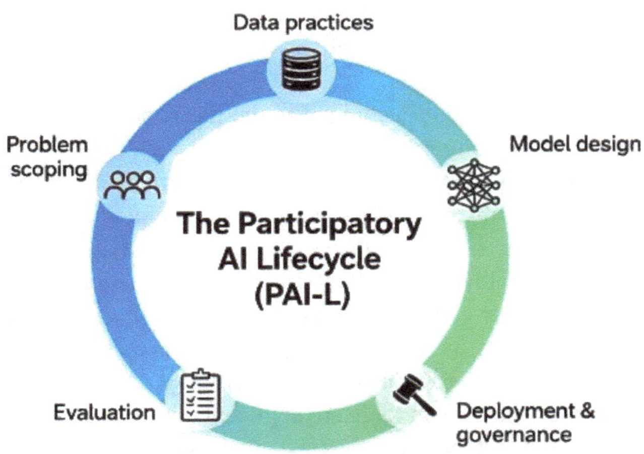

Fig. 8 The Participatory AI lifecycle (PAI-L)

Participatory problem scoping is the initial step and it entails collaborating with communities to establish the social problem that the AI system is aimed at solving. This is essential since inappropriate or limited definitions of problems are usually associated with technological solutions that fail to capture structural inequalities or local realities. Community assemblies, data walks, workshops and co-ideation platforms are useful in eliciting lived experiences and bringing out competing interpretations of the problem. This will make sure that AI is not an optimization of administrative efficiency, but in line with the community priorities.

The second stage, participatory data practices, is concerned with the idea of making sure that the practices of data collection, labelling, and governance represent the views of the community. The citizens will be able to recognize culturally sensitive features, disarm malicious labels, engage in annotation, and influence the decision on consent, access, and data security (Jungherr & Rauchfleisch, 2025). The equitable allocation of rights of data ownership and data use can be ensured through the participation data stewardship model (e.g. community data trusts or citizen councils).

The third phase, participatory model design, enables local individuals and domain specialists to influence model assumptions, criteria of fairness, evaluation metrics, levels of interpretability and levels of risk. This phase indicates that there is a necessity to encode social values into computational artifacts. Stakeholders aid in identifying fairness, order of preferences, and trade-offs by ranking the harm to be addressed. This can be assisted by such

Table 3 Participatory AI lifecycle

Lifecycle stage	Purpose	Primary stakeholders	Key outputs
1. Engaging in problem scoping.	Develop social Problems together; bring out local priorities.	Citizens, leaders of the community, policymakers, experts in the social domain.	Value statements, problem maps, Needs of stakeholders.
2. Ensuring that customers have a participatory role In the production of their data.	Definitely make data representative, ethical and community approved.	People, people with annotations, people with data knowledge, lawyers.	Consent Approaches consent Frameworks community-verifi ed. datasets.
3. Participatory model design	Transform social values into model Constructs, measures and equity requirements.	Professionals, field professionals, citizen groups.	Fairness criteria, model prototypes, interpretable.
4. Participatory evaluation	Holistic assessment of AI performance through social impact measures.	Researchers, citizen auditors, agencies of the city.	Impact reports, Bias audit reports, iterative reports on evaluation.
5. Participatory deployment as well as governance.	Provide permanent supervision and responsibility systems.	Community boards, control agencies, nongovernmental organizations.	Alerts of performance, supervisory boards, complaint systems.

methodologies like participatory prototyping and model cards.

Participatory evaluation is the fourth stage which broadens the concept of model validation beyond accuracy measures. Communities are used to test system outputs, unintended consequences as well as social impact. The system audits which involve the independent citizen panels reviewing the system behavior, known as participatory audits, establish accountability frameworks that are not limited to self-evaluation by institutions.

Lastly, the fifth phase, participatory deployment and governance, has guaranteed long-term supervision by keeping track of monitoring committees, grievance systems, ongoing consent models, and avenues of system parameter revision. AI is dynamic, and the frameworks governing it need to be the same. Participatory approaches make sure that communities have power even after first implementation.

4.2 AI Design Communities Engagement Tools and Techniques

The participatory AI cannot solely be described as conceptual buy-in but, instead, it necessitates instruments capable of bringing the high-level values to the daily routine of design. Such tools facilitate the gap between the technical teams and the communities to get in touch, cooperate and make decisions together. The practices outlined here are global studies and practice in participatory technology design.

In Co-design workshops, citizens, technologists, policy makers, and domain experts come together to mutually design AI features, interfaces, data practices, and governance requirements. Through these workshops, the stakeholders are given an opportunity to tell what they expect, what concerns them and what their values are. They also disclose any possible user damages or structural disparities that could be ignored by engineers. Co-design sessions, based on the use of visual aids, scenario mapping and speculative prototyping, assist non-technical participants to express complicated socio-technical understandings.

Participatory data annotation enables the involvement of community individuals in data-labelling. The old labelling systems use outsourced labellers that have little context and hence they are not interpreted as they should be or local cultural meanings omitted. Participatory annotation can address this through participation of citizens who have some knowledge of contextual details, like local dialects, social dynamics, or local categories (Jungherr & Rauchfleisch, 2025). This approach improves the relevance of data sets and minimizes bias, particularly in smart city solutions such as surveillance, mobility prediction algorithms, and the public service algorithms.

Civic deliberation platforms Digital tools that are intended to facilitate massive involvement among people can be used to engage people that cannot physically reach the workshops. Surveys, deliberation forums, participatory polling, argument mapping and interactive scenario simulations may be supported through platforms. Properly implemented, they can expand the limits of participatory AI not just to small groups but thousands of residents can influence AI policies.

Non-expert explainable tools play an important role in increasing transparency and meaningful involvement. Dashboards that are user-friendly, counterfactual explanation, simplified model visualization, and interactive what-if simulation can enable a user to test, explore the decision path, and comprehend the model behaviour. These instruments put sophisticated technical ideas into understandable interfaces, and the communities are able to analyse and improve AI systems.

Another important technique is the participatory impact assessments. Contrary to the usual regulatory assessment which is usually done by a technical expert or a lawyer, participatory impact assessment entails communities in deciding potential risks, ethical issues, and societal impacts before the deployment of a system. These evaluations unite sociologists, lawyers, technologists and the groups impacted to jointly review the effects like invasion of privacy, disproportionate effect, and dangers of surveillance.

On the whole, such tools are applicable in democratising AI development because they establish tangible means in which citizens shape the direction of AI systems.

Alongside these tools, hybrid engagement structures or structures that incorporate both online and offline engagement have shown to be the most successful. The cities that have implemented multi-layered participation ecosystems are Barcelona, Taipei and Amsterdam which encompass neighbourhood meetings, mobile participation kiosks, citizen juries and open-source civic platforms. These hybrid systems assist in closing the digital divides because those who have less access to the internet, or those who are less digitally literate can still play a significant role. Moreover, hybrid infrastructures embrace sustained participation: citizens can contribute to it online asynchronously, visit periodic town halls, or participate in thematic workshops when interested, when they are available. This multimodality approach makes the participation not limited to one space, time, and form and therefore increases the democratic reach.

4.3 Governance Models and Institutional Approaches

A PAI should be governed with mechanisms that are institutionalized. In the absence of long-lasting structures, the participation is likely to be intermittent or symbolic, and will be subject to the goodwill of the architects, rather than institutionalized. Various forms of governance have been developed across the globe, which could provide the model that may be followed by the cities, governments, and other organizations.

The citizen oversight committee is one of the promising frameworks, in which the members of the community are engaged in the AI systems review, audit results, and policy direction. These committees operate in a similar manner to that of ethics boards or advisory panels but include a broader membership of civil society, advocacy groups and populations affected. They assist in keeping the accountability of algorithms and their suitability to the values of the population.

The other strategy is the participatory regulatory sandbox, in which experimental AI systems are run in controlled conditions and also evaluated by communities. This allows on-the-job testing and still has the oversight and safeguards. Sandboxes combine technical experimentation and feedback loops to the public, enabling policy refinement by the regulators and responsible iteration by developers.

The structures of governance of data are also in the spotlight. The community data trusts, data cooperatives, and collective consent models give the citizens the authority to decide how their data may be used and what type of oversight is available. Those structures criticize the traditional extractive data practices by identifying data as a shared resource to be governed democratically, and not be controlled by corporations and governments unilaterally.

One of the most innovative governance systems that are emerging in the world is the idea of the algorithmic citizen assemblies. Based on the climate and constitutional assemblies, these forums convene randomly chosen, but demographically proportional citizens to discuss the ethical and social consequences of the proposed AI systems. The participants are briefed by experts in a structured manner, they have facilitated discussions and come up with recommendations to policymakers. Pioneering pilots in the United Kingdom, France and Canada prove that citizen assemblies can give rise to more advanced policy knowledge, which tends to be more inclusive and morally based than the one produced by the technical committees alone. This model shows that even with the right instruments and information the ordinary citizens can actually lead the complicated socio-technical decisions.

The institutional level cross-sectoral partnerships, which include universities, civil society, municipal governments, and community organizations, can assist in the establishment of PAI based on interdisciplinary knowledge (Robles & Mallinson, 2025). Such partnerships give the social scientists and the ethicists an opportunity to collaborate with engineers, which stops such technocratic decision-making.

Lastly, the legal and policy frameworks like transparency laws, algorithmic accountability acts and participatory rights charters establish formal requirements of engaging with the public. These frameworks can be used to make PAI move beyond ideation practice and into enforceable standards that are integrated within governance frameworks.

4.4 Problems and Constraints of Participatory Implementation of AI

Even though participatory approaches have great advantages, they are difficult to apply on large scales. The participation demands time, resources, facilitation skills and institutional commitment. Unless well supported, the initiatives might turn out to be tokenistic or unavoidable to the marginalized groups (Mushkani et al., 2025).

Participation Mediation Participation fatigue is one of the major challenges. Governments and society might request communities to give suggestions many times without significant transformation, and this causes frustration and lack of interest. In order to avoid this, participation processes should be designed to generate concrete impact and should not overwork the same groups over and over again.

One of the other limitations is related to power imbalances. In even more participative contexts, individual voices, including those of experts, policymakers or eloquent members of the community can prevail in discussions. Inclusive design should also be facilitated well to avoid hierarchies and other existing hierarchies being strengthened.

Barriers can also be caused by the technical complexity of AI systems. Lack of explainability tools or educational support may mean that communities cannot easily comprehend the behavior of the system and thus cannot make a contribution. This problem can only be overcome by investing in the digital literacy of the populace, available explanation tools, and continuous orientation programs.

The other challenge is the institutional resistance. Companies that are used to making decisions centrally might be afraid of delegating power to communities. The participation might be viewed by developers as a slowdown in the timelines or as a process making work more complex. The solution to these barriers includes proving the long-term value of the participation which may be decreasing the number of system failures, enhancing trust, and facilitating compliance with regulations.

5 Participatory AI in Practice Case Studies

PAI is as much a concept as a practice that is actively embraced in cities, in governmental structures and in civil-society-technology alliances around the globe (Delgado et al., 2023) The practical example of case studies shows that participatory approaches can make the process more transparent, offer community legitimacy or turn to structural inequities that are reproduced by an algorithm system. Although the contexts are different—public health and mobility versus welfare, agriculture, and urban governance, the common trends are evident: communities have local and experiential knowledge, which can greatly enhance AI applicability; participatory models can enhance institutional trust; and shared governance can reduce risk levels of opaque and technocracy. In this section, successful applications in various parts of the world are discussed as well as the limitations and lessons, which can be used in future implementations. The chosen case studies also indicate differences in political culture, digital infrastructure and institutional maturity, with how one can implement PAI in different governance ecosystems.

5.1 Lessons Learned about Participatory AI in Smart Cities: European and Asian Learning

The most apparent examples of AI-powered public infrastructure are smart city deployments and therefore can be fruitful sites of participatory practices (Ada Lovelace Institute, AI Now, and Open Government Partnership. Algorithmic accountability for the public sector 2021). The Amsterdam city was the first in the Netherlands to launch a system called the Algorithm Register, a transparent storehouse where local citizens get to see and challenge, as well as assess, municipal algorithms. The register was supported by comprehensive public deliberation meetings where the residents jointly worked on transparency requirements and risk categories. The following considerations demonstrated that the kind of contextual explanations of algorithm systems was more important to residents than technical details, which makes the city redesign its communication strategy. Amsterdam model proved that the transparency is not enough, participatory involvement is required to form the picture of what the transparency should be and to make sure that disclosures can be available to the common people.

Figure 9 depicts the regional distribution of global smart-city initiative spending, with concentrations in the United States, Western Europe, China, and Asia-Pacific regions. This geographic imbalance underscores the urgency of PAI in guiding concentrated investments toward inclusive urban governance, ensuring citizen engagement prevents elite-driven AI deployments that overlook local needs in under-represented regions (IDC. (February 10, 2020). Smart city initiatives spending share worldwide in 2020.

An example of using AI as a participatory tool in mobility governance is found in Tokyo or Kyoto. When Japanese cities added AI-based pedestrian flow optimization and prediction of public transportation systems to their infrastructure, the local neighbourhood councils were invited to test earlier models. The cultural-specific patterns of movement, including the significance of paths to shrines and movement patterns at festivals, were identified in the residents, but could not be represented in the typical mobility data. Such understandings resulted in different assumptions of the model and culturally more consistent predictions. Notably, the concerns related to surveillance and the loss of privacy also emerged during the participatory process, and so the cities have started to exercise more stringent rules in minimizing the data and reformulate the rules on sensor placement. These examples demonstrate the fact that PAI can be able to bring to the forefront contextually based social conventions, like community rituals or expectations of privacy, which cannot be discovered by technical systems alone.

Another educational case study is the smart city programs in India. The citizen feedback platforms have been utilized on a large scale in cities such as Pune and Surat, to test the civic AI tools on waste management, flood warning, and traffic monitoring. Meetings in the community wards enabled the residents to challenge misclassification, point to disparities in system implementation, and report harms perceived. As an example, the flood prediction models did not initially fully represent informal settlements because of absence of data, shear feedback through communities indicated the absence and participatory mapping and sensor positioning guided by local inhabitants was included. These case studies illustrate how participation in correction can fill in the data blind sips and how the system could avoid causing harm to the marginalized groups disproportionately.

5.2 Public Health and Social Welfare: Algorithmic Systems that Are Community-Centered

Public health forecasting and welfare distribution as well as resource allocation have become major areas where AI can be involved in algorithmic decisions that have the potential to have a profound effect on vulnerable groups of people. The system of welfare fraud prediction in Denmark was met with criticism on the part of the population, which was not based on discrimination; the government responded by initiating participatory hearings, during which the communities in question consulted the logic of the model and discovered discriminatory associations. Although the system was later suspended, the participatory process created new national standards that must be publicly consulted on the high-risk algorithmic instruments. The case represents how participatory oversight may be used as a corrective mechanism in cases where systems are harmful.

An example of participating AI within the structures of the general health services is found in Brazil. When there were dengue outbreaks, community health workers worked together with the data scientists to label risk factors, have geospatial predictions validated, and find the missing indicators which were not captured in the official datasets like informal water storage practices. The process of participatory annotation generated better models and demonstrated the socio-spatial disparities of disease risk. The community feedback also had an impact on the methods of communicating alerts to the community in terms of making them more accessible and more prone to adopt preventative measures. The example of Brazil shows that lived experience, particularly in low-income communities, enhances the effectiveness of the model and policy.

In Kenya, AI systems that involve participation have been incorporated in the agricultural and health systems. Smallholder farmers were involved in the data collection of crop disease forecasting models, local soil condition, practice of indigenous knowledge, and environmental variables that are not contained in the commercial datasets. The process enhancing model relevance as well as producer confidence, boosted AI-suggested intervention adoption in farmers. These practices help emphasize the need to have culturally responsive and locally centric AI systems in the Global South because, in many cases, standardized datasets do not reflect environmental and social complexity.

5.3 Participatory AI in Governance and Civic Decision Making

Governments all over the world are testing algorithmic decision-support instruments and at the same time dealing with democratic pressures of transparency and engagement. The pilot program of the Fundamental Rights Impact Assessment of the European Union integrated the public consultations into the assessment of the high-risk AI systems. The citizens and civil society organizations were involved in the examination of the impact of the systems, human rights issues, and offering mitigation measures (Papagiannidis et al., 2025). These participatory assessments impacted changes to the EU AI Act, which illustrates that PAI can not only influence the form of the system but also the rules.

Public algorithmic accountability hearings have been implemented in a number of municipalities in the United States, such as New York City, and San Francisco. In these hearings, people and advocacy organizations discuss AI

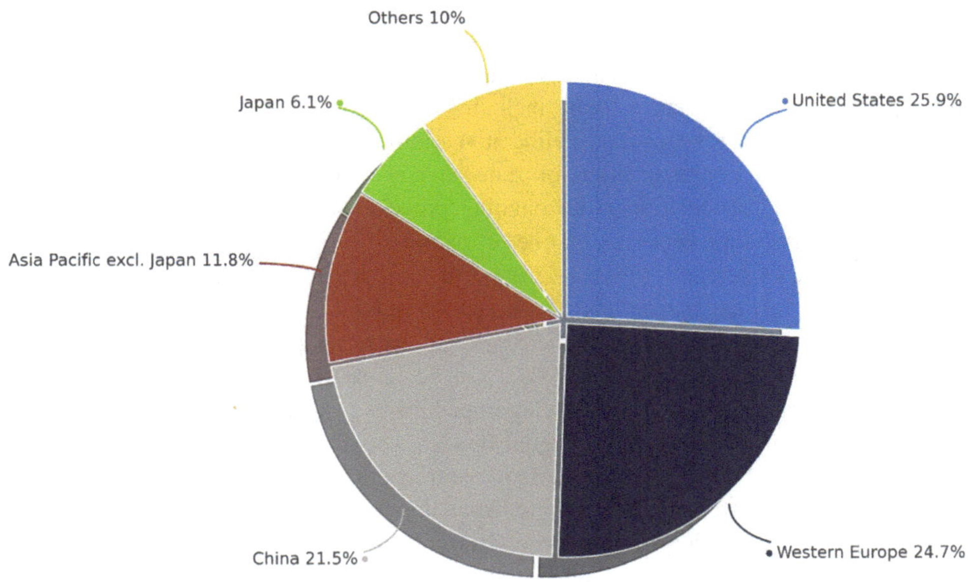

Fig. 9 Regional smart-city investment distribution (IDC. (February 10, 2020). Smart city initiatives spending share worldwide, 2020)

municipal tools such as tenant risk scoring and predictive policing. Systems considered harmful or too opaque have been changed or even banned through public testifying. Although it is possible that these processes are adversarial, they are essential accountability mechanisms that can help AI development be consistent with democratic principles.

The example of Taiwan can provide one of the most developed models of participatory digital governance (Batool et al., 2023). By means of the Taiwan, citizens discuss and influence technology policies in a structured manner with the help of online tools. It is not limited to AI, but the platform has been adopted to test proposals of algorithmic moderation, digital identity systems, and data governance. The Taiwan model shows that deliberation can be scaled at a high level with the help of digital participation, which does not have to jeopardize the depth and inclusivity. Lessons of this model are that facilitation is important, documentation is transparent and deliberation ought to be iterative combining knowledge of experts and citizen wisdom.

With these governance centered case studies, the emphasis has been on the fact that PAI is not a design approach but a democratic tool. Participatory structures contribute to the balance of institutional power, the reduction of power asymmetries, and the increase in the chances of effective civic participation.

5.4 Cross Case Synthesis: Lessons, Lapses and New Trends

Various things across the regions have some similar understanding. First, participatory procedures contribute to the contextual validity of AI systems by including local knowledge that cannot be incorporated into the traditional modelling techniques. Second, PAI enhances the legitimacy of the population, particularly when systems impact the provision of basic services like health, welfare or mobility. Third, participatory governance tools, including oversight committees, algorithm registers and deliberative platforms, contribute to the institutionalization of transparency and accountability, and participation is an ongoing process as opposed to a consultation process of a one-off nature.

However, gaps persist. Most of the participatory processes are either small-scale, project-based, or reliant on funding cycles, which constrain the ability to have a long-term impact. The participation is likely to be imbalanced, with the marginalized groups having impediments to meaningful participation because of digital divides, socio-economic factors, or language lockout. Also, it is frequently introduced at a late stage in the AI lifecycle, when important decisions, including problem framing and data collection, have already been made, which diminishes the potential of PAI to be a transformative technology. Lastly, little standardization exists between models of participation making it difficult to evaluate or attempt to replicate models.

Figure 10 presents global technology spending on smart-city initiatives from 2018 to 2023, revealing rapid growth in investments that highlights the critical need for PAI approaches to steer large-scale urban AI deployments responsibly (IDC Technology Spending on smart city initiatives worldwide from 2018 to 2023, 2020).

The new trends notwithstanding, the direction of developing AI appears to be globally shifted towards the direction of democratization. Cities, governments, and networks of civil societies are coming to realize that AI will not be able to rule infrastructure without the participation of the population. Overall, it is evident in the case studies that PAI is not just possible but advantageous, as it provides a way to a fair, open, and socially-based AI ecosystem.

6 Conclusion

PAI is a reshaping of the principles of AI systems construction, their implementation, and regulation in modern societies, specifically, in the context of smart cities where algorithmic decisions start to dominate the life of ordinary people. The chapter has shown that PAI is not an ethical add-on but an element of structure that is necessary in making sure that AI systems are held accountable, contextually embedded, and in accordance with the democratic principles. PAI, through incorporating a variety of local knowledge and community level knowledge, along with deliberative systems, can overcome the long-standing vulnerabilities of previous AI pipelines including biased data, limited framing of the problem, a lack of transparency, and technocratic dominance.

The reviewed conceptual bases of Participatory Design, socio-technical theory, Responsible AI, and deliberate governance note that participation is epistemic and political requirement. The approaches to methods, such as the Participatory AI Lifecycle and community-engagement approaches show how participation may be applied in real-world contexts. Still case studies that are based on international geographical areas also indicate that participatory methods result in AI systems which are more legitimate, fairly, and robust in the real world.Nevertheless, institutional inertia, power balance, resource availability and the complications of scaling participation among different populations continue to pose a challenge to the implementation of PAI. To deal with such problems, long-term investment in participatory infrastructure, inclusive governance, the socialization of people to digital literacy, and institutive regulatory norms are needed. Finally, this is the promise of the PAI: AI should not be perceived as a technological object that

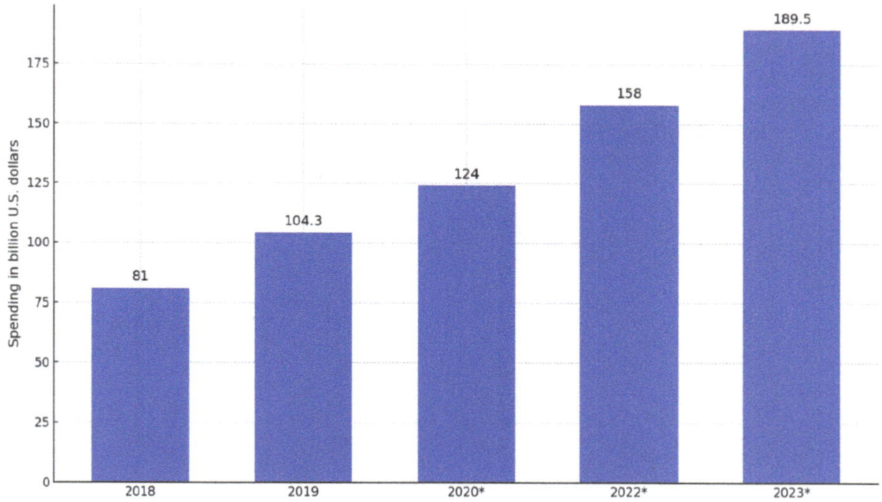

Fig. 10 Global smart-city technology spending (2018–2023) (IDC Technology Spending on smart city initiatives worldwide from 2018 to 2023, 2020)

needs optimization but as a community institution that will be co-created. By providing meaningful citizen participation, AI can also become a system that will reinforce democratic governance, social justice, and be genuinely in the best interests of the collective good.

References

Ada Lovelace Institute, AI Now, and Open Government Partnership. (2021). Algorithmic accountability for the public sector

Ada Lovelace Institute, AI Now Institute, & Open Government Partnership. (2021). *Algorithmic accountability for the public sector*. Open Government Partnership.

Batool, A., Zowghi, D., & Bano, M. (2023). Responsible AI governance: a systematic literature review. https://arxiv.org/abs/2401.10896

Chain Store Age. (February 28, 2023). Business benefits of AI according to retail executives worldwide in 2023 [Graph]. In Statista. Retrieved December 12, 2025, from https://www.statista.com/statistics/1374052/ai-benefits-according-to-retail-businesses/

Cheong, B. C. (2024). Transparency and accountability in AI systems: safeguarding wellbeing in the age of algorithmic decision-making. *Frontiers in Human Dynamics*, *6*, 1421273.

Crawford, K. (2021). *The atlas of AI: Power, politics, and the planetary costs of artificial intelligence*. Yale University Press.

Delgado, F., Yang, S., Madaio, M., & Yang, Q. (2023, October). The participatory turn in ai design: Theoretical foundations and the current state of practice. In *Proceedings of the 3rd ACM Conference on Equity and Access in Algorithms, Mechanisms, and Optimization* (pp. 1–23)

Eubanks, V. (2018). *Automating inequality: How high-tech tools profile, police, and punish the poor*. Macmillan+ ORM

Friedman, B., & Hendry, D. G. (2019). *Value sensitive design: Shaping technology with moral imagination*. Mit Press.

IDC. (February 10, 2020). Technology spending on smart city initiatives worldwide from 2018 to 2023 (in billion U.S. dollars) [Graph]. In Statista. Retrieved December 12, 2025, from https://www.statista.com/statistics/884092/worldwide-spending-smart-city-initiatives/

IDC. (February 10, 2020). Smart city initiatives spending share worldwide in 2020, by region [Graph]. In Statista. Retrieved December 12, 2025, from https://www.statista.com/statistics/884181/worldwide-smart-city-investment-region/

India TV. (December 24, 2019). Employment share of artificial intelligence (AI) professionals in India as of December 2019, by company size [Graph]. In Statista. Retrieved December 12, 2025, from https://www.statista.com/statistics/1134299/india-employment-share-of-ai-profession als-by-company-size/

Jobin, A., Ienca, M., & Vayena, E. (2019). The global landscape of AI ethics guidelines. *Nature machine intelligence*, *1*(9), 389–399

Jungherr, A., & Rauchfleisch, A. (2025). *Artificial Intelligence in Deliberation: The AI Penalty and the Emergence of a New Deliberative Divide*

Kaminski, M. E. (2020). Understanding transparency in algorithmic accountability. *Forthcoming in Cambridge Handbook of the Law of Algorithms, ed. WoodrowBarfield, Cambridge University Press (2020)., U of Colorado Law Legal Studies Research Paper*, (20–34)

Lee, M. K., Grgić-Hlača, N., Tschantz, M. C., Binns, R., Weller, A., Carney, M., & Inkpen, K. (2020, April). Human-centered approaches to fair and responsible AI. In *Extended Abstracts of the 2020 CHI Conference on Human Factors in Computing Systems* (pp. 1–8)

Longworth, J. (2021). Benjamin Ruha (2019) Race After Technology: Abolitionist Tools for the New Jim Code. Medford: Polity Press. 172 pages. eISBN: 9781509526437. *Science & Technology Studies*, *34*(2), 92–94

Mushkani, R., Berard, H., Ammar, T., Chatonnier, C., & Koseki, S. (2025, October). Co-Producing AI: Toward an Augmented, Participatory Lifecycle. In *Proceedings of the AAAI/ACM Conference on AI, Ethics, and Society* (Vol. 8, No. 2, pp. 1785–1799)

Open Government Partnership. (2022a). *Participatory data governance: How small changes can lead to greater inclusion*. Open Government Partnership

Open Government Partnership. (2022b). What makes participatory data initiatives successful?Research & practitioner guide

Organisation for Economic Co-operation and Development. (2022). *OECD Framework for the Classification of AI systems*. OECD Publishing

Papagiannidis, E., Mikalef, P., & Conboy, K. (2025). Responsible artificial intelligence governance: A review and research framework. *The Journal of Strategic Information Systems*, *34*(2), 101885

Parthasarathy, A., Phalnikar, A., Krishnan, G. S., Jauhar, A., & Ravindran, B. (2024). Participatory Approaches in AI Development and Governance: Case Studies. https://arxiv.org/abs/2407.13103

Robles, P., & Mallinson, D. J. (2025). Advancing AI governance with a unified theoretical framework: a systematic review. *Perspectives on Public Management and Governance*, gvaf013

Rosella, L. C., Shaw, J., Guha, S., Abejirinde, I. O. O., Gibson, J. L., Lipscombe, L., ... & Itanyi, I. U. (2025). A participatory approach to deploy responsible artificial intelligence for diabetes prediction and prevention. *Digital Health*, *11*, 20552076251358541

Warne, H., Dencik, L., & Hintz, A. (2021). Advancing civic participation in algorithmic decision-making: A guidebook for the public sector.

World Economic Forum. (June 13, 2023). Prioritized reskilling focus in the government and public sector worldwide in 2023, by skill [Graph]. In Statista. Retrieved December 12, 2025, from. https://www.statista.com/statistics/1239251/public-sector-reskilling-needs/

Importance of Privacy-Preserving AI and Secure Data Management in Urban Systems

U. S. Abhiram, C. Saravanan, and Shapun S. Poonja

Abstract

With the increasing use of technology in smart cities, artificial intelligence (AI) is now used to manage everyday systems like traffic control, healthcare, public safety, and citizen services. However, this heavy reliance on data brings serious challenges related to privacy, data misuse, and security. Large amounts of personal information—such as names, addresses, locations, and habits—are collected to improve city services, but this also increases the risk of data leaks and unauthorized access. In addition, unfiltered or offensive data shared through public platforms can damage the reputation of smart city systems and reduce public trust. Therefore, it is essential to develop secure and privacy-preserving methods to protect citizens' personal information while allowing smart cities to function efficiently and responsibly. The proposed chapter explores privacy-preserving AI and secure data management in urban systems, aligns with global data protection regulations such as the General Data Protection Regulation (GDPR) and India's Digital Personal Data Protection (DPDP) Act. These laws highlight the importance of safeguarding personal information and ensuring responsible data handling in digital ecosystems. In accordance with these principles, the proposed platform aims to address the privacy and security challenges faced by smart cities. It protects citizens' personal information by automatically hiding or removing sensitive details such as names, addresses, or ID numbers before they are stored or analyzed. Using advanced methods like data masking and pseudonymization, the system keeps data secure while still enabling meaningful analysis for city operations. Additionally, it incorporates AI-powered filters to detect and block offensive, biased, or harmful content in smart city applications. By adhering to these data protection standards, the proposed solution builds citizen trust, enhances data security, and supports the ethical and responsible use of AI for smarter urban governance.

Keywords

Smart city · Data management · Responsible AI · Privacy

1 Introduction

1.1 The Role of AI in Modern City Living

1.1.1 Rise of AI in Smart Urban Systems

Cities around the globe are turning to artificial intelligence to keep pace with rapid growth. As urban populations swell and infrastructure feels the strain, AI helps bridge the gap by providing real-time solutions for everyday challenges. Today, AI is the engine behind smoother traffic flow, more efficient power grids, and faster emergency responses. It powers everything from telemedicine to smarter public health monitoring, transforming the way we interact with our physical environment.

However, for these "smart" systems to work, they need a constant stream of information. They rely on data gathered from street cameras, environmental sensors, mobile apps, and public service portals. This creates a massive, interconnected web of "multimodal" data that must be processed in the cloud at lightning speed. As these systems become

U. S. Abhiram (✉) · C. Saravanan · S. S. Poonja
Department of MCA, RV College of Engineering, Bengaluru, India
e-mail: abhiramus.mca24@rvce.edu.in

C. Saravanan
e-mail: saravananc@rvce.edu.in

S. S. Poonja
e-mail: shapunspoonja.mca24@rvce.edu.in

V. Sarveshwaran et al. (eds.), *Responsible AI for Smart Cities*, Sustainable Artificial Intelligence-Powered Applications,
https://doi.org/10.1007/978-3-032-26901-0_4

more deeply woven into the fabric of city life, we face a pressing challenge: how do we harness this technology while keeping our data private and secure? This expansion of technology means that security is no longer just a technical requirement—it is a fundamental pillar of modern urban design.

Furthermore, the sheer scale of these AI applications introduces a level of complexity that traditional city management was never designed to handle. When we link traffic lights to emergency sirens or connect home energy meters to regional power plants, we create a digital ecosystem that is as fragile as it is powerful. Every new sensor added to a street corner represents a new opportunity for innovation, but it also represents a new potential vulnerability that must be defended against increasingly sophisticated cyber threats.

1.2 Data-Driven Governance and Citizen Services

Modern smart cities are built on a foundation of data. By treating information as a vital asset, city leaders can make better decisions—predicting where a new bus route is needed, automating public services, and ensuring resources like water and electricity are used wisely. These insights even help policymakers understand community needs, leading to more effective and personalized public programs. Data-driven governance allows a city to "breathe" and react to the needs of its residents in real time, moving away from slow, bureaucratic processes toward a more agile and responsive form of leadership.

But there is a catch. The data required to run a smart city is often deeply personal. It includes where we go, our health history, our financial habits, and our private identities. Without ironclad security and clear privacy protections, this wealth of information is vulnerable to breaches and misuse. Ultimately, the success of any smart city depends on the trust of its citizens. If people feel that their daily movements are being watched or that their private lives are being commodified, the technology meant to improve their lives could instead undermine their sense of safety and freedom.

To bridge this gap, cities must move beyond mere data collection and focus on "data stewardship." This involves creating transparent frameworks where residents are not just subjects of data collection, but active participants who understand and consent to how their information is used. True progress lies in finding the balance between the efficiency of a high-tech city and the fundamental human right to privacy. Without this balance, the digital transformation of our urban centers risks alienating the very people it was designed to serve.

Table 1 Challenges in handling data

Challenge	Description
Data sensitivity	Citizen data often includes identifiable information such as names, addresses, IDs, and biometric markers
Large attack surface	Millions of endpoints—sensors, IoT devices, and cloud services—create multiple vulnerabilities
Cross-platform data sharing	Data flows between agencies (transport, health, policing), raising integration risks
Unfiltered public input	Smart city apps may receive harmful, offensive, or misleading content
Opaque AI models	Automated decisions without transparency reduce user trust

1.3 Challenges of High-Volume Personal Data Collection

The expansion of data-collecting infrastructure introduces several operational challenges (Table 1).

Due to these challenges, privacy-preserving AI becomes essential for sustainable urban governance (Elma et al. 2025).

1.4 Importance of Privacy and Trust in Smart City Adoption

Citizens must feel confident that their information is handled responsibly, as trust is the foundation of any technology-driven urban system. This trust can be easily broken when data breaches expose personal or behavioral profiles, when AI systems operate in ways that seem unfair or opaque, or when surveillance infrastructure is perceived as intrusive rather than protective. To prevent such loss of confidence, smart city systems must be designed with strong, transparent safeguards. This includes adopting data-minimization principles so that only essential information is collected, applying encryption and anonymization techniques to protect sensitive data, and ensuring audit transparency so that system operations can be independently verified (International Organization for Standardization 2013). Together, these practices support both privacy and reliability, allowing smart city technologies to function effectively while maintaining public trust.

1.5 Chapter Overview

This chapter introduces a practical framework for deploying privacy-focused AI solutions in urban systems. It covers regulatory compliance, core privacy technologies, secure system architectures, AI-driven content filtering models, and future opportunities in secure urban computing. A technical case study demonstrates how these principles apply to real-world smart city deployments.

2 Background and Motivation

Smart cities operate as highly interconnected ecosystems where citizens, devices, sensors, and digital service platforms continuously exchange information. As artificial intelligence becomes deeply embedded in these urban systems, concerns related to privacy, fairness, and security have grown from isolated technical issues into complex governance challenges. The increasing dependence on real-time data for decision-making demands a strong foundation of responsible data management. This section provides the context that motivates the need for privacy-preserving AI and secure data governance in modern urban environments.

2.1 Role of Data in Modern Urban Systems

Modern urban infrastructures rely heavily on high-volume, real-time data streams that enable automation and intelligence across critical public services. In mobility and transport, for example, adaptive traffic lights respond to vehicle counts and speed data while navigation and mobility apps capture user locations, travel routes, and behavioral patterns. Public health and emergency systems depend on digital platforms that store patient identifiers, health records, diagnostic histories, and even location-linked outbreak information to provide timely interventions (International Organization for Standardization 2013). Energy and utility networks use smart meters that record consumption at fine granularity, which, while useful for efficiency, can inadvertently reveal household routines and behavioral habits (Elma et al. 2025). Similarly, citizen service portals used for grievances, identity verification, and welfare schemes require submission of personal details, addresses, and documents, all of which generate substantial amounts of sensitive data (Haddad Pajouh et al. 2020). As these systems expand, protecting such information from misuse becomes an increasingly critical responsibility.

2.2 Privacy Concerns in Smart Cities

The transition toward data-driven governance raises serious privacy concerns (Ghosh and Rajagopalan 2020). The widespread deployment of CCTV networks, facial recognition systems, and IoT sensors creates an environment of continuous surveillance that many citizens find intrusive (Organization for Economic Co-operation and Development (OECD) 2019). Moreover, digital interactions leave behind identifiable data trails—location histories, service usage logs, and transactional patterns—that form detailed behavioral profiles capable of revealing daily routines, work locations, personal associations, and even health conditions. Many urban applications tend to collect more data than required, violating purpose limitation principles and increasing risks of misuse. Adding to this is the lack of transparency around how data is collected, stored, shared, and used by AI systems, leaving citizens uncertain about how their information is handled. This lack of clarity significantly undermines confidence in public digital systems (Organization for Economic Co-operation and Development (OECD) 2019).

2.3 Cybersecurity Challenges in Public Infrastructure

Because smart cities function through a complex network of cloud infrastructures, servers, mobile platforms, and IoT devices, they face an expanded cybersecurity threat landscape (HaddadPajouh et al. 2020). IoT devices such as sensors, smart meters, and cameras often operate with weak authentication measures, outdated firmware, and insecure communications, making them susceptible to hacking. Poorly secured APIs used by public service platforms expose large volumes of citizen data (Ghosh and Rajagopalan 2020), while ransomware attacks have demonstrated the capacity to disable transportation networks, water systems, and administrative portals (HaddadPajouh et al. 2020). Insider threats also pose substantial risks, as individuals with legitimate access may misuse data knowingly or accidentally. Additionally, AI models that rely on real-time inputs can be compromised through data poisoning, where fake sensor readings or bot-generated submissions distort outputs. Failures in these areas can compromise not only privacy but the functioning of entire city systems.

2.4 Public Trust and Ethical Implications

Trust forms the backbone of successful smart city adoption. When privacy breaches or opaque AI operations occur, citizens may become reluctant to engage with digital platforms, reduce participation in public services, and develop concerns regarding surveillance (Scientific and Cultural Organization (UNESCO) 2021). Ethical issues deepen this problem. Algorithmic bias can result in unfair classifications, uneven service recommendations, or misinterpretation of behaviors among minority groups, potentially embedding systemic discrimination into automated systems. The lack of explainability in AI decisions further weakens accountability, leaving citizens unsure why certain requests are flagged or why eligibility decisions for services or subsidies are made. Data sovereignty adds another dimension, as governments must ensure that sensitive citizen information is not stored or processed in jurisdictions lacking strong legal safeguards (International Organization for Standardization 2013).

2.5 Case Reports of Data Breaches in Smart City Deployments

Real-world incidents highlight the scale of risks associated with improper data protection. In Barcelona, attackers exploited an unsecured API to manipulate smart traffic systems, demonstrating how cyber intrusions can threaten public safety (Ghosh and Rajagopalan 2020). India's Aadhaar ecosystem suffered major leaks where the personal data of millions became exposed due to misconfigured databases and external application vulnerabilities. In the United States, intercepted smart meter data revealed patterns that showed when homes were unoccupied, posing significant security risks. In another case, a citizen mobile application was compromised by malware, leading to unauthorized extraction of sensitive data from a municipal resident database. These examples collectively illustrate the urgent need for privacy-by-design principles, secure data governance frameworks, and ethically responsible AI practices.

Figure 1 represents various facts about privacy and security concerns to be addressed in the context of smart cities.

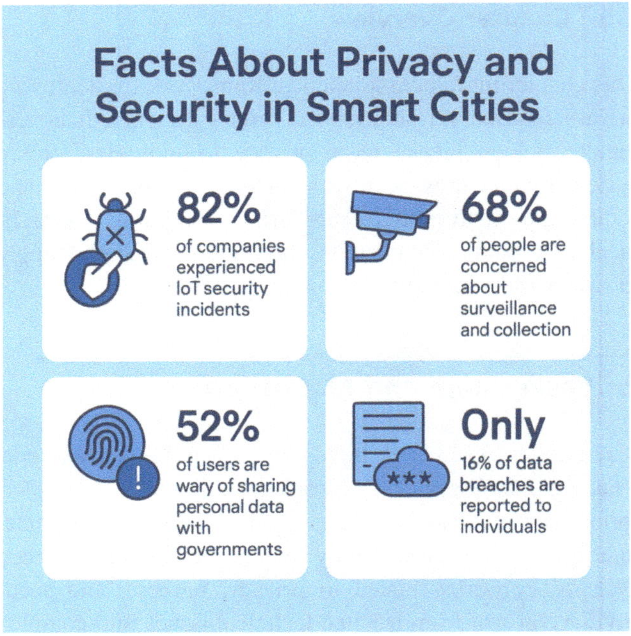

Fig. 1 Facts about privacy and security in smart cities

3 Regulatory and Ethical Landscape

Smart cities must operate within strict legal and ethical frameworks to protect citizen data, maintain trust, and ensure responsible AI governance (Organization for Economic Co-operation and Development (OECD) 2019). This section outlines the major regulations and principles shaping privacy-preserving systems globally, with emphasis on GDPR and India's DPDP Act, as well as international ethical guidelines.

3.1 Global Data Protection Regulations (GDPR, CCPA)

3.1.1 General Data Protection Regulation (GDPR)

The GDPR is the world's most influential data protection law. It applies to any system processing personal data of EU citizens, regardless of geography. Key principles relevant to smart cities include:

- Lawfulness, fairness, and transparency: Data collection must be legal and clearly communicated.
- Purpose limitation: Data must be collected only for specific, stated purposes.
- Data minimization: Only the minimum required information should be collected.
- Accuracy: Systems must ensure data is accurate and up to date.
- Storage limitation: Personal data cannot be stored longer than necessary.
- Integrity and confidentiality: Encryption, access controls, and secure storage are mandatory (International Organization for Standardization 2013).
- Accountability: Cities must document compliance and implement technical safeguards.

GDPR violations can lead to significant fines, making compliance essential for EU-connected digital infrastructure.

3.1.2 California Consumer Privacy Act (CCPA)

CCPA grants citizens rights similar to GDPR but focuses strongly on transparency and selling of personal data (Ghosh and Rajagopalan 2020).

Key rights include:

- The right to know what data is collected.
- The right to delete personal data.
- The right to opt-out of data being sold.
- The right to non-discrimination for exercising privacy rights.

While U.S. laws are sector-based, CCPA lays groundwork for urban data governance in American smart city deployments.

3.2 India's Digital Personal Data Protection (DPDP) Act

The DPDP Act (2023) is India's first comprehensive data protection legislation and is extremely relevant for Indian smart cities (International Organization for Standardization 2013).

Key provisions

- Consent-based data processing: Citizens must provide clear consent before data collection.
- Right to correction and erasure: Individuals may request corrections or deletion of their data.
- Data Fiduciary Responsibility: Smart city organizations become Data Fiduciaries and must ensure secure storage, controlled access, and responsible processing.
- Significant Data Fiduciaries (SDFs)
- Larger entities face stricter requirements: Data protection officers, data audits, and impact assessments
- Cross-border data transfer controls: Sensitive citizen data can only be sent to trusted jurisdictions.
- Strict penalties for data breaches: Fines can exceed 250 crore INR depending on severity.

The DPDP Act directly influences how city administrations must design data workflows, cloud architectures, and AI-based systems.

3.3 Privacy Principles for Smart Cities

Even beyond legal requirements, smart cities must follow established privacy engineering principles, including:

1. Privacy-by-Design (PbD): Systems must embed privacy from the start, not as an afterthought.
2. Data Minimization: Collect only what is absolutely necessary.
3. Purpose Specification: Explicitly declare why data is collected and restrict secondary usage.
4. User Consent and Control: Citizens must have control over data sharing and withdrawal of consent.
5. Secure Data Lifecycle Management: Data must be protected during collection, transmission, processing, storage and deletion (International Organization for Standardization 2013).
6. Transparency and Explainability: AI systems should provide clear decision logs, audit trails, model explanations when needed (Scientific and Cultural Organization (UNESCO) 2021).
7. Accountability and Governance: Policies, audits, logging, and role-based access help ensure responsible data handling.

3.4 Ethical AI Guidelines (OECD, UNESCO, ISO Standards)

Organization for Economic Co-operation and Development (OECD) AI Principles (Organization for Economic Co-operation and Development (OECD) 2019):

- Inclusive growth and well-being.
- Human-centered values.
- Transparency.
- Robustness and security.
- Accountability.

United Nations Educational, Scientific, and Cultural Organization (UNESCO) Ethical AI Framework.

Focuses on (Scientific and Cultural Organization (UNESCO) 2021):

- Fairness.
- Explainability.
- Non-discrimination.
- Human oversight.

ISO Standards for Smart Cities (International Organization for Standardization 2013).

- ISO/IEC 30,141—IoT Reference Architecture.
- ISO 37120—Sustainable city indicators.
- ISO/IEC 27,001—Information security management.

These standards help cities create interoperable, safe, and ethically compliant systems.

3.5 Compliance Requirements for Smart City AI Systems

To comply with global and national data protection frameworks, smart cities must implement a combination of technical, procedural, and AI-specific safeguards that ensure data is handled responsibly at every stage. On the technical side, strong security measures such as encryption of personal data both in transit and at rest, pseudonymization, data masking, and strict least-privilege access controls are essential to prevent unauthorized exposure. These systems must be supported by comprehensive logging and traceability mechanisms, secure APIs, and in some cases, privacy-enhancing techniques like federated learning or on-edge processing to keep sensitive data local (Communication-Efficient Learning of Deep Networks from Decentralized Data 2017). Equally important are procedural requirements, including conducting Data Protection Impact Assessments (DPIAs), performing regular cybersecurity audits and penetration tests, appointing Data Protection Officers (DPOs), and ensuring that all vendors and third-party providers adhere to established privacy and security standards. In addition, AI systems deployed in urban environments require specialized governance measures such as continuous monitoring for bias, implementing fairness checks, ensuring explainability of automated decisions, and applying filters to detect harmful or inappropriate content (Qin et al. 2021). Safeguards must also be in place to prevent advanced threats like model inversion or reconstruction attacks that could expose sensitive information. Together, these technical, procedural, and AI-oriented controls establish the foundation for safe, lawful, and trustworthy AI deployment within smart city ecosystems.

4 Privacy-Preserving AI: Concepts and Frameworks

As smart cities transition toward large-scale automation and real-time analytics, the volume and sensitivity of citizen data being processed increases significantly. Traditional security measures such as firewalls and encryption are no longer sufficient on their own. Modern urban ecosystems require privacy-preserving AI techniques that not only protect data but also ensure that analytics and decision-making remain accurate, explainable, and trustworthy. This section presents the core privacy-enhancing technologies (PETs) that enable smart cities to benefit from AI without compromising individual privacy.

4.1 Overview of Privacy-Preserving Machine Learning

Privacy-preserving machine learning refers to techniques that allow AI models to learn from data without exposing raw personal information. These methods are particularly useful for:

- Healthcare data from hospitals.
- Smart meter energy readings.
- CCTV and sensor-based analytics.
- Citizen service platforms and grievance portals.

The goal is to maintain analytical performance while ensuring data confidentiality and regulatory compliance.

4.2 Differential Privacy

Differential privacy (DP) is one of the most widely adopted methods globally, used by organizations such as Google, Apple, and the U.S. Census Bureau. DP works by introducing statistically calibrated noise into datasets or model outputs, ensuring that individual records cannot be reverse-engineered. Even if an attacker knows most of the dataset, they cannot identify a single person's contribution.

Key benefits:

- Extremely useful for population-level analytics.
- Prevents identification of individuals from aggregate results.
- Works well for smart city dashboards and trend analysis (Table 2).

Table 2 Advantages of AI in various domains

Smart city domain	Example application	Privacy advantage
Transportation	Traffic flow prediction	Prevents exposure of individual vehicle paths
Healthcare	Outbreak mapping	Individual patient data hidden with noise
Utilities	Energy consumption trends	Household identity protected
Citizen services	Public feedback analytics	Prevents tracing comments to individuals

4.3 Federated Learning

Federated learning has become one of the most practical and impactful approaches for privacy-preserving AI, especially in distributed environments like smart cities. Instead of collecting all data into a central server for training, federated learning enables individual devices or local systems—such as hospitals, traffic controllers, utility providers, or municipal kiosks—to train a model locally on their own data. Only the resulting model updates or gradients are transmitted to a central aggregator, where they are combined to form an improved global model. In this way, sensitive citizen data never leaves the originating system. This significantly reduces the risk of data leakage, unauthorized access, or exposure during transmission. The approach also ensures compliance with privacy regulations because raw data remains under the control of the organization that collects it. For smart cities, federated learning provides an effective mechanism for joint analytics across multiple departments or agencies while maintaining strict privacy boundaries.

4.4 Homomorphic Encryption

Homomorphic encryption offers a powerful way to process data securely by allowing computations to be performed directly on encrypted information. This means that AI models and analytics systems can operate on data without ever decrypting it, ensuring that the underlying raw information remains inaccessible even to system administrators or cloud operators. In a smart city context, this becomes particularly valuable when dealing with highly sensitive datasets such as medical records, citizen identities, or financial information. By ensuring that encrypted data can be used for meaningful computation, homomorphic encryption eliminates several insider threats, minimizes the risk associated with cloud-based processing, and aligns well with the security expectations of modern data protection laws. Although computationally intensive, it remains a strong option for high-risk domains requiring maximum confidentiality.

4.5 Data Masking, Tokenization, and Pseudonymization

Smart city ecosystems often integrate multiple administrative services—transportation, utilities, healthcare, public safety, and citizen service platforms—each of which requires access to different types of data. Sharing full, identifiable records across different city systems can create serious privacy risks and widen the potential attack surface. To prevent this, techniques like data masking, tokenization, and pseudonymization help reduce how much sensitive information is exposed, while still allowing the data to be useful for analysis and day-to-day operations. Data masking hides specific personal details—like names, addresses, or identification numbers—so that even if someone accesses the data, they cannot trace any record to an individual. It can be applied permanently (such as displaying only the last digits of an ID on a dashboard) or dynamically, where only the minimum necessary information is shown based on the task or the user's role.

Tokenization offers a stronger layer of security by substituting sensitive data with random tokens that bear no direct connection to the original information. The actual data is kept separately in a secure token vault that only authorized systems can access. While tokenization is often linked to financial transactions, it is equally valuable in smart city systems such as billing, permit approvals, or complaint management, where citizen references are needed without revealing their true identities. By storing tokens and the original data in entirely separate locations, cities can ensure that even if a dataset is compromised, attackers cannot retrieve any meaningful personal information from it.

Pseudonymization offers a balanced approach suitable for analytical tasks where data must be tracked over time without revealing who the data belongs to. In this technique, direct identifiers are replaced with artificial keys or pseudonyms, enabling systems to study trends such as healthcare patterns, service usage frequency, or energy consumption while keeping individual identities hidden. Although pseudonymized data can potentially be re-identified when combined with other information, this risk can be reduced through strong governance practices, strict access controls, and cryptographically separating datasets. In smart cities—where large-scale analytics guide policy decisions and infrastructure planning—pseudonymization preserves data usefulness while maintaining privacy-by-design principles. Together, these methods create a multi-layered defense strategy that promotes responsible data sharing, reduces exposure, and ensures compliance with regulatory standards across complex urban systems.

4.6 Secure Multi-party Computation

Secure multi-party computation allows multiple entities to jointly perform analytics or train models without ever revealing their individual datasets to one another. Each party contributes encrypted or mathematically transformed data, enabling the system to compute collective outputs such as predictions or statistical metrics without compromising confidentiality. For smart cities, this is particularly beneficial when different departments—such as health, traffic, and utilities—or even different municipal regions want to collaborate on shared insights while respecting privacy boundaries. It allows organizations to maintain compliance with privacy regulations while still benefiting from combined analytics that would otherwise require centralizing sensitive data.

4.7 Responsible Data Lifecycle Management

Privacy-preserving AI depends not only on advanced algorithms but also on a disciplined and secure data lifecycle. Responsible data lifecycle management ensures that information remains protected from the moment it is collected until it is eventually deleted. This includes minimizing the volume of data collected, validating and transforming it securely, restricting access through role-based controls, encrypting all sensitive information during storage and transmission, and maintaining strong audit trails for accountability. As data ages, it should be archived in a masked or pseudonymized form and eventually deleted using secure erasure methods when it is no longer required. For smart cities, following such a structured lifecycle is essential for regulatory compliance and to maintain public trust, especially when dealing with large, continuous data streams from sensors, mobile applications, and citizen service portals.

Figure 2 represents an example of how data masking and pseudonymization works on sample data.

5 Secure Data Management in Smart Cities

Secure data management is a foundational requirement for ensuring trust, safeguarding citizen privacy, and maintaining resilience in AI-driven smart city ecosystems (Ghosh and Rajagopalan 2020). Modern urban infrastructures continuously generate data from millions of interconnected sources—including IoT sensors, surveillance systems, public service apps, utilities, and healthcare platforms. As a result, cities face the dual challenge of protecting data at scale while ensuring that it remains usable for real-time analytics and decision-making. The complexity of smart city architecture means that security cannot rely on a single mechanism; instead, it must be embedded throughout the entire lifecycle of data, from collection to storage, processing, sharing, and deletion. This section outlines the essential practices and architectural strategies required to achieve secure and compliant data management in contemporary urban systems.

5.1 Secure Data Collection and Access Control

Secure data management begins at the point of collection, where devices and applications must be verified, authenticated, and connected through trusted channels. Smart cities use a variety of edge devices—traffic sensors, environmental monitors, water meters, and healthcare kiosks—that often operate unattended and therefore become prime targets for cyberattacks. Ensuring device authenticity through secure certificates, cryptographic keys, or hardware-backed trust modules prevents impersonation and injection of malicious data. Once data is collected, it must be transmitted through encrypted communication protocols, which protect it from interception and tampering. Access control policies also play a major role; by assigning permissions based on user roles and functional requirements, cities can limit unnecessary exposure and reduce the risk of insider misuse. Through strict authentication and authorization mechanisms, the integrity of collected data remains intact as it moves into the city's processing ecosystem.

5.2 Identity Management and Zero-Trust Architecture

Identity management becomes increasingly important as smart cities integrate multiple departments, third-party vendors, and cloud-based service platforms. Traditional perimeter-based security models are ineffective in such distributed environments because they assume that internal

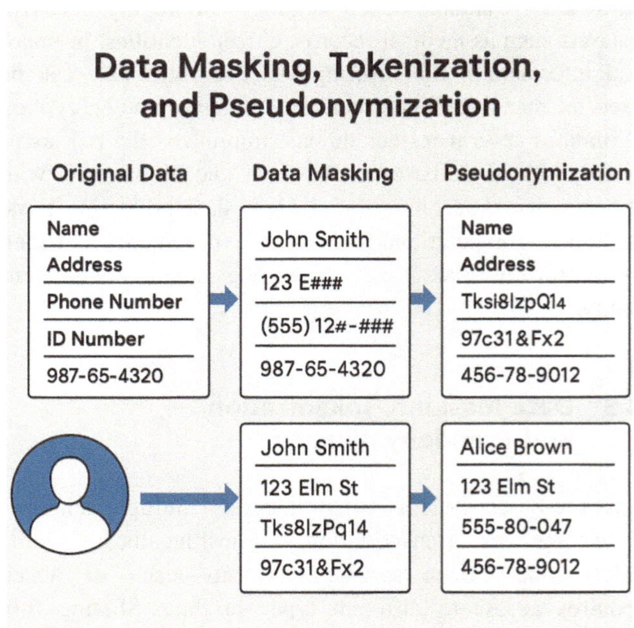

Fig. 2 Example for data masking and pseudonumization

networks are inherently safe. Zero-trust architecture (ZTA) addresses this challenge by enforcing the principle of "never trust, always verify." Every user, device, and service—regardless of physical or network location—must continuously validate its identity before gaining access to data or system components. This validation is often risk-based, considering factors such as device health, user behavior, and contextual indicators. By implementing zero-trust policies, municipal systems significantly reduce the likelihood of lateral movement in the event of a breach, thereby containing threats before they escalate (Gartner Research 2020). ZTA also helps ensure compliance with data protection regulations by enforcing strict, auditable access governance.

5.3 Blockchain-Based Data Integrity and Auditability

Blockchain enhances integrity and traceability in smart city operations by offering a tamper-resistant ledger for recording interactions, transactions, and system events (Dhanaraj et al. 2022). While not designed to store bulk citizen data, blockchain is highly effective for maintaining transparent logs that cannot be altered retroactively. This is valuable when multiple independent agencies—such as transport, healthcare, and utilities—need to collaborate while maintaining accountability. For example, access records, permissions, and policy changes can be stored on a blockchain to ensure that every action is verifiable and traceable (Dhanaraj et al. 2022). This strengthens trust between departments and provides strong forensic evidence in the event of a breach or dispute. By integrating blockchain into the city's governance layer, administrators can achieve higher levels of transparency, reduce fraud, and support compliance with audit requirements imposed by privacy regulations.

5.4 Role of Zero-Knowledge Proofs in Data Security

Zero-knowledge proofs (ZKPs) offer a sophisticated method for validating information without disclosing the underlying data itself. This is particularly beneficial in urban systems that require frequent verification of citizen eligibility or compliance. For instance, residents may need to prove that they fall within a certain age bracket to access benefits, or businesses may need to verify environmental compliance to obtain permits. ZKPs allow these validations to occur without exposing sensitive information such as full identities or detailed operational data. This significantly reduces the amount of personal or proprietary information shared between departments, thereby lowering privacy risks and meeting the principles of data minimization and purpose limitation (Dwork and Roth 2014). As smart cities continue to expand digital services, ZKPs will play a crucial role in enabling secure, privacy-aware interactions between citizens, service providers, and government agencies.

5.5 Threat Detection, Monitoring, and Incident Response

Advanced threat detection and continuous monitoring are essential for protecting the vast networks of interconnected systems within a smart city. AI-driven anomaly detection systems can identify unusual patterns such as unexpected spikes in sensor activity, abnormal login attempts, or deviations in network traffic (Qin et al. 2021). These early warnings enable city administrators to respond quickly to potential cyberattacks or data leaks. Effective incident response frameworks include clear procedures for isolating affected components, notifying relevant authorities, restoring system functionality, and conducting post-incident analysis. Smart cities must also maintain backup and recovery mechanisms to ensure operational continuity even in the face of ransomware or infrastructure failures. By integrating monitoring tools with automated incident response workflows, cities can significantly reduce reaction time and minimize the impact of security breaches on public services.

5.6 Secure Multimodal Data Fusion for Urban Systems

Smart cities depend heavily on multimodal data fusion, where information from various sources—such as video streams, sensor data, citizen feedback, and administrative records—is combined to support city-wide decision-making. However, integrating data from multiple domains introduces unique security challenges, as each dataset may carry different sensitivity levels and originate from systems with varying security standards. Ensuring secure fusion requires strong preprocessing mechanisms, including validation, cleaning, encryption, and anonymization. Access permissions must be carefully structured so that data from highly sensitive domains, such as healthcare, is not improperly exposed to unrelated departments. Additionally, the fusion process must maintain consistent metadata and adhere to compliance rules to prevent accidental cross-linking of personal data. Secure data fusion enables cities to generate accurate, holistic insights while preserving privacy and minimizing systemic vulnerabilities.

5.7 Governance and Policy Frameworks for Secure Data Management

Technical safeguards alone are insufficient without strong governance frameworks that define responsibilities, data ownership, retention policies, and compliance mechanisms. Smart cities need strong, well-defined policies that outline how data should be classified, when consent is required, how information can be shared with third parties, how long it should be stored, and how it must be securely deleted using cryptographic methods. Routine internal audits, security assessments, and compliance checks help ensure that all systems continue to meet legal requirements and follow established best practices. Managing vendors is equally important, since many external partners handle sensitive city data. Their contracts must clearly specify security expectations, incident reporting procedures, and regular review cycles. It is also essential to train municipal employees so they understand how to handle data responsibly and avoid accidental leaks. Ultimately, good governance ensures that secure data management becomes an ongoing, organization-wide practice—not just a one-time technical task.

6 AI Safety, Bias Prevention, and Content Moderation

As AI systems become deeply embedded in smart city operations, ensuring their safety, fairness, and responsible behavior becomes a critical requirement. Urban environments rely on AI for sensitive and high-impact tasks such as facial recognition, emergency response prediction, healthcare triaging, crime analysis, infrastructure optimization, and public feedback processing. These tasks involve complex datasets that may inadvertently contain biases, offensive content, or sensitive personal information (Scientific and Cultural Organization (UNESCO) 2021). Without proper safeguards, AI models can amplify these issues, leading to unfair outcomes, exclusionary policies, misinformation, or loss of public trust. Therefore, smart cities must incorporate robust AI safety mechanisms, continuous monitoring, and strong content moderation systems to ensure ethical and reliable service delivery.

6.1 Detecting Harmful, Biased, or Sensitive Content

AI systems deployed in public-facing applications often process unstructured data such as text submissions, voice interactions, CCTV footage, and social media posts (Ghosh and Rajagopalan 2020). Such data may include offensive language, hate speech, harmful misinformation, or content targeting specific communities. If left unfiltered, these inputs can degrade the quality of public services and damage citizen confidence in government technology. Modern smart city platforms integrate AI-based content classifiers that detect toxic language, personal threats, sexually explicit material, extremism, and disallowed political content (Qin et al. 2021). These models are trained on large datasets and continuously refined to identify evolving behavior patterns. Importantly, the content moderation layer ensures that harmful data is never stored or forwarded to downstream systems, reducing both reputational and regulatory risks.

6.2 Fairness and Bias Mitigation in AI Systems

Bias in AI models can arise from skewed training data, disproportionate representation of demographic groups, or historical inequalities embedded in public datasets. In critical domains like policing, credit eligibility, welfare distribution, or hiring portals, biased AI systems may result in unfair treatment or discriminatory outcomes. Smart cities must adopt bias-mitigation practices such as rebalancing datasets, removing sensitive attributes from model inputs, and using fairness constraints during training. Periodic audits help identify unintended discrimination by evaluating model outputs across gender, age, socio-economic status, language groups, and geographic zones. Additionally, cities may deploy adversarial testing techniques to assess how models behave under edge cases or adversarial inputs (Qin et al. 2021). By prioritizing fairness, urban AI systems become more transparent, equitable, and trustworthy for all citizens.

6.3 Explainability and Transparency in Automated Decision-Making

Smart city AI models often influence decisions that directly impact residents—for example, determining risk levels for emergency dispatch, flagging anomalies in utility usage, or prioritizing healthcare services during outbreaks (Ghosh and Rajagopalan 2020). Without transparency, such automated decisions may appear arbitrary or discriminatory. Explainable AI (XAI) techniques help address this concern by providing human-readable explanations for model outputs. These explanations may highlight which features contributed most to a decision or show how similar past cases were resolved. Cities can integrate dashboards that display model logic, validation metrics, and audit logs, enabling administrators to understand how systems behave under different conditions. Explainability improves accountability, supports regulatory compliance, and enhances citizen trust by ensuring that AI-driven decisions remain interpretable rather than opaque.

6.4 Human-in-the-Loop Moderation in Government AI

While automation accelerates service delivery, complete reliance on AI for sensitive decisions can be risky. Human-in-the-loop moderation offers a balanced approach by combining the efficiency of AI with the judgment of trained personnel (Abadi et al. 2016). In scenarios such as threat detection, resource allocation, legal documentation processing, or critical citizen complaints, AI systems act as preliminary filters, highlighting cases that require human review. Human experts then validate, approve, or override AI-generated decisions. This hybrid approach prevents errors caused by misclassification or incomplete data while also reducing workload for city employees. Human oversight is especially important when decisions involve ethical implications, subjective interpretation, or potential harm to individuals.

6.5 Preventing Model Overexposure and Privacy Attacks

AI models themselves can become targets of privacy attacks, such as model inversion, membership inference, or data reconstruction. These attacks attempt to extract sensitive information from trained models by exploiting patterns learned during training. Smart cities must therefore adopt protective techniques such as differential privacy, adversarial regularization, and limiting model exposure through restricted APIs. By ensuring that internal machine learning models cannot be queried in ways that reveal training data, cities reduce the risk of confidential citizen information leaking through AI behavior. Regular red-team testing and model security evaluations help identify vulnerabilities and strengthen defenses over time.

6.6 Safe Handling of Public Feedback and Citizen Opinions

Public feedback systems—complaint portals, city surveys, helpline chatbots, and community discussion platforms—capture large volumes of user-generated content. This content often includes sensitive personal stories, emotional expressions, or politically charged sentiments. AI-driven systems must process such information carefully to avoid misinterpretation or unsafe automated actions. Moderation mechanisms classify content based on sensitivity, urgency, or privacy level, ensuring that only authorized personnel handle highly sensitive information. Context-aware analysis also helps detect sarcasm, emotional distress, or implicit threats, enabling cities to respond appropriately. Safe handling of public feedback not only protects citizen privacy but also ensures that urban governance decisions are informed by accurate, meaningful data.

6.7 Building Trust Through Ethical and Safe AI Practices

Ultimately, smart cities must view AI safety and content moderation not merely as technical requirements but as foundational pillars of ethical governance. Transparent policies, consistent monitoring, open communication with citizens, and demonstrable fairness all contribute to building confidence in AI-enabled public services. When residents trust that AI systems are safe, unbiased, and respectful of privacy, they are more likely to engage with digital services, contribute meaningful data, and support broader smart city initiatives. Responsible AI practices therefore play a critical role in achieving inclusive, sustainable, and future-ready urban development.

7 System Architecture and Integration Model

Modern smart cities operate through a complex digital ecosystem that integrates IoT devices, data ingestion platforms, AI analytics engines, identity management systems, and secure storage environments. As the volume and sensitivity of urban data increase, the system architecture must balance performance, scalability, and real-time analytics with strict privacy and security guarantees. A well-designed architecture ensures that data flows through trusted components, is processed by privacy-preserving AI mechanisms, and remains protected throughout its lifecycle. This section outlines a practical architectural model suitable for secure, AI-driven smart city deployments, with emphasis on modular design, secure communication, access governance, and layered privacy controls.

7.1 High-Level Architecture Overview

A typical privacy-preserving smart city architecture consists of four major layers: data collection, data protection, AI processing, and service delivery. The data collection layer gathers information from sensors, citizen applications, and public service platforms. This raw data is

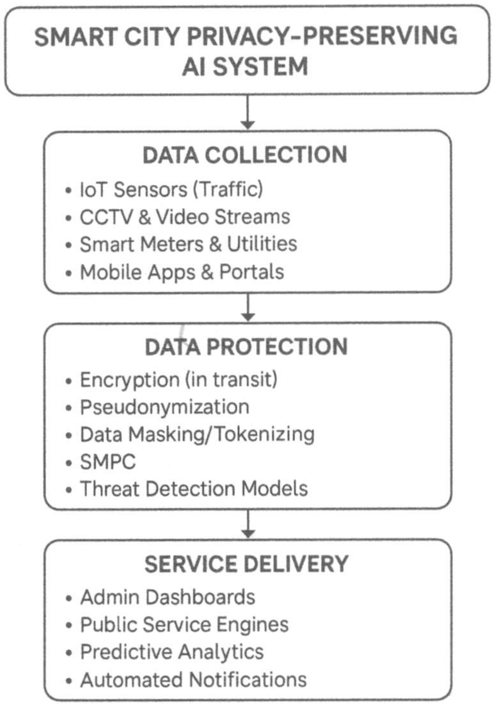

Fig. 3 Privacy-preserving AI system in smart cities

passed through a protection layer that enforces encryption, masking, pseudonymization, and access control. The AI layer then uses privacy-enhanced techniques such as federated learning, differential privacy, or homomorphic encryption to generate insights without exposing sensitive details. Finally, the service delivery layer provides dashboards, automated alerts, or decision-support tools to administrators, while ensuring that only minimal and necessary information is displayed. This layered structure minimizes risk by ensuring that sensitive data is protected at every stage of processing.

Figure 3 represents an overview of privacy-preserving AI systems in smart cities which takes care of Data Collection, Protection, and Service Delivery concepts, which in turn ensures secure data handling.

7.2 Data Pipelines and Secure Storage

Within this architecture, the data pipeline is designed to prevent unauthorized access and maintain the confidentiality and integrity of information. Data from edge devices is transmitted through encrypted channels and stored in secure repositories equipped with access controls, audit logs, and anomaly detection mechanisms. The storage layer is often divided into structured, semi-structured, and unstructured data zones, allowing each type of dataset to be managed with appropriate security policies. Sensitive information is stored in encrypted form, while less sensitive data may be anonymized or aggregated for analytical use. A key component of the pipeline is the data governance module, which monitors compliance with data retention policies and ensures adherence to privacy regulations.

7.3 Privacy-Aware AI Decision Modules

AI components within smart cities must operate in a manner that respects privacy constraints while still delivering accurate and real-time insights. Privacy-aware models incorporate safeguards such as differential privacy to prevent leakage of individual information, federated learning to enable decentralized training, and encryption-based computation to protect data during processing. Decision modules also include bias detection and fairness evaluation techniques, ensuring that automated outputs are equitable and legally compliant. The system continuously monitors the performance of AI models, updating them as new data becomes available while ensuring that model integrity is preserved. These safeguards collectively ensure that AI-driven services operate in an ethical and transparent manner.

7.4 Identity Management and Access Governance

Identity management systems serve as the foundation of trust within smart city architectures. Through strong authentication mechanisms—including multi-factor authentication, biometrics, and cryptographic credentials—cities ensure that only authorized users access sensitive dashboards or operational systems. Access governance frameworks enforce the principle of least privilege, granting users only the minimum permissions necessary for their roles. Administrators use audit logs and periodic access reviews to detect misuse or unauthorized account activity. Integration with zero-trust architecture ensures that every access request is continuously evaluated based on risk, behavior, and context, minimizing the likelihood of insider threats or credential compromise.

7.5 Monitoring, Feedback Loops, and Audit Trails

Modern smart city architectures rely heavily on continuous monitoring to ensure that systems remain secure, efficient, and compliant. Monitoring mechanisms track system performance, access activity, potential intrusions, and unusual data patterns that may indicate cyberattacks or technical failures. Automated feedback loops provide real-time alerts to administrators, enabling swift corrective action. Audit trails record every significant operation—data access, configuration changes, login attempts, or AI decisions—creating a transparent and reliable historical record. These logs are essential for compliance with regulations such as DPDP and GDPR, and they support investigations and policy improvements when incidents occur.

7.6 Cloud, Edge, and Hybrid Deployment Models

Smart cities often use a combination of cloud and edge environments to achieve both scalability and low-latency performance. Edge deployments handle real-time decision-making close to the source of data, reducing response time for applications such as traffic control or emergency alerts. The cloud provides extensive computing resources for large-scale analytics, AI model training, storage, and inter-departmental collaboration. Hybrid architectures offer the best of both worlds by enabling sensitive data to remain on-premise or on-edge devices while leveraging the cloud for high-level computation. This approach ensures optimal performance while maintaining compliance with privacy and sovereignty requirements.

8 Use Cases and Implementation Scenarios

Smart cities rely on AI-driven systems to optimize public services, improve infrastructure efficiency, and enhance overall quality of life. However, these systems must be deployed in a manner that respects privacy, ensures data security, and maintains fairness for all residents. This section presents practical use cases that demonstrate how privacy-preserving AI and secure data management practices can be applied to real-world urban scenarios. Each example shows how privacy techniques—such as federated learning, differential privacy, pseudonymization, and secure data fusion—can be integrated into operational workflows to deliver effective and trustworthy solutions (Communication-Efficient Learning of Deep Networks from Decentralized Data 2017; Dwork and Roth 2014)).

8.1 Smart Healthcare and Secure Telemedicine

In modern cities, healthcare facilities increasingly use AI-enabled systems for disease surveillance, patient triaging, appointment scheduling, and teleconsultation.

Table 3 Domains for application of privacy-preserving AI

Smart city domain	Example use cases	AI methods applied	Privacy-preserving techniques used
Healthcare and telemedicine	Disease prediction, teleconsultation, digital records	Predictive modeling, anomaly detection	Federated learning, differential privacy, encryption, pseudonymization
Mobility and transportation	Traffic optimization, route prediction, congestion control	Computer vision, time-series forecasting	Edge processing, anonymized GPS data, aggregation techniques
Citizen service portals	Grievances, permit processing, document uploads	NLP-based classification, sentiment analysis	Data masking, role-based access, automated content moderation

These services require access to highly sensitive medical information, such as diagnostic reports, prescriptions, and biometric data. Privacy-preserving AI techniques help hospitals collaborate on population-level analytics without sharing identifiable patient records. For instance, federated learning allows different hospitals to train disease prediction models locally, while only sharing encrypted updates with a central server. Differential privacy ensures that aggregated health statistics do not expose individual information, making it suitable for public dashboards used during outbreaks. Combined with secure data storage and access control, this approach enables cities to deliver efficient digital healthcare while complying with medical privacy laws.

Table 3 represents the application of AI methods to preserve privacy in various domains along with some use cases.

8.2 Smart Mobility and Transportation Systems

Transportation systems generate massive amounts of real-time data, such as vehicle movement logs, traffic camera feeds, GPS traces from public transit, and app-based ride patterns. AI models rely on traffic and mobility data to adjust signal timings, ease congestion, and enhance road safety. But because location data can reveal a person's daily habits and movement patterns, it needs to be handled very carefully. Privacy-preserving analytics make it possible to remove identifying details while still allowing accurate insights. For instance, transport authorities can use pseudonymized identifiers to study how routes are performing without knowing who is traveling where. Differential privacy adds another layer of protection by ensuring that aggregated travel statistics cannot be traced back to any individual. Meanwhile, secure edge processing allows devices placed along the roads—such as cameras or sensors—to analyze basic information like vehicle counts or unusual activity directly on-site, without sending raw footage to central servers. By combining these techniques, cities can build smarter mobility systems that improve transportation efficiency while still respecting citizen privacy.

8.3 Urban Surveillance and Public Safety Analytics

Smart cities often rely on surveillance systems, including CCTV networks, facial recognition, and emergency detection sensors, to enhance public safety. While these tools can support crime prevention and incident response, they also raise significant ethical and privacy concerns. Privacy-preserving AI offers safer alternatives through techniques like on-device face blurring, object-only detection, and role-based access to sensitive video feeds. Instead of transmitting raw video to a central server, edge AI systems can extract anonymized metadata—such as object counts or movement patterns—while discarding identifying features. Moreover, secure audit trails ensure that only authorized personnel can access sensitive footage and that every access is logged (International Organization for Standardization 2013). This approach balances the need for public safety with the protection of civil liberties.

8.4 Citizen Service Platforms and Grievance Portals

Digital service portals allow residents to submit complaints, request permits, pay utility bills, and access government schemes. These platforms often collect personal information, photographs, documents, and detailed descriptions of issues. Privacy-preserving data management ensures that sensitive identifiers are masked or pseudonymized before analysts or AI systems process them. Automated content moderation tools detect offensive language, threats, or misinformation in user submissions while preserving legitimate feedback. Secure workflows ensure that only the departments responsible for resolving a particular request can access the relevant information (Narayanan and Shmatikov 2008). By protecting citizen data at every stage, cities can improve service efficiency while maintaining public trust.

8.5 Environmental Monitoring and Smart Utilities

Smart utility systems—such as water distribution networks, electricity grids, and pollution monitoring stations—use IoT sensors to collect consumption and environmental data. While this information is generally not personally identifiable, certain patterns (like utility usage at specific times) can indirectly reveal private details about household behavior. Privacy measures like aggregation, data minimization, and edge analytics reduce the risk of exposing such patterns. For example, smart meters can transmit only summarized or anonymized data for billing and forecasting, while retaining detailed logs locally. Secure data fusion enables city administrators to combine utility data with weather models, population density, and industrial activity to optimize resource allocation. These systems support sustainability goals while ensuring that resident data remains protected.

8.6 Public Engagement and Community Decision-Making

Smart cities are increasingly bringing residents into the decision-making process by using digital tools such as online surveys, participatory budgeting platforms, and community discussion forums. These systems give people an easy way to share their views, highlight local problems, and vote on proposed initiatives. AI tools like sentiment analysis and trend detection help city officials understand this feedback and make better policy decisions. However, user-generated content often includes sensitive personal details or political opinions, which must be handled carefully. Privacy-preserving NLP models help by removing identifiable information and anonymizing submissions before any analysis takes place. At the same time, bias-mitigation techniques ensure that feedback from different language groups, income levels, or communities is interpreted fairly. With these protections in place, digital engagement tools can support more inclusive and democratic decision-making while still safeguarding citizen privacy.

9 Evaluation and Performance Metrics

Evaluating privacy-preserving AI systems in smart cities requires going beyond traditional notions of technical performance. These systems must comply with legal requirements, adhere to ethical standards, and operate dependably in real-world conditions. Metrics such as accuracy or response time alone are insufficient. Smart city AI must also demonstrate its ability to safeguard citizen privacy, withstand security threats, minimize algorithmic bias, and remain accessible and easy to use for both administrators and the public (Qin et al. 2021). Thus, a comprehensive evaluation framework becomes essential. This section outlines the key metrics and assessment methods used to determine how effectively privacy-preserving AI functions within complex urban environments.

9.1 Privacy–Utility Trade-Off Analysis

A core challenge in privacy-preserving AI is balancing protection with performance. Techniques like differential privacy, encryption-based computation, or heavy anonymization may reduce data precision, affecting the accuracy of AI predictions (Nakamoto 2008). Smart cities must therefore evaluate the privacy–utility trade-off, ensuring that privacy measures do not compromise essential service quality, such as emergency response alerts or disease prediction models. Evaluations typically compare model accuracy, recall, and latency under different privacy configurations to identify optimal settings. The goal is to maintain strong privacy guarantees while ensuring that AI-driven decisions remain reliable and actionable.

9.2 Security Compliance and Risk Assessment Metrics

Security evaluation focuses on ensuring the confidentiality, integrity, and availability of data throughout its lifecycle. Smart city systems undergo periodic penetration testing, vulnerability assessments, and configuration audits to verify compliance with standards such as ISO 27001, GDPR, and the DPDP Act. Key performance indicators include encryption strength, access control enforcement rates, API security posture, and incident response time. Systems are also evaluated on their ability to detect and contain intrusions, using metrics such as false-positive rates in threat detection models or time-to-detection for anomalous behaviors. These metrics help administrators verify that cyber risks are minimized and that the city's digital infrastructure remains resilient.

9.3 Algorithmic Fairness and Bias Monitoring

Ensuring fairness is essential for AI models that influence public-facing decisions such as resource allocation, risk prediction, or citizen service prioritization. Fairness evaluation involves comparing model outcomes across demographic groups to detect disparities based on gender, age, income, language, or geography. Metrics such as disparate impact, equal opportunity difference, or demographic parity are used to identify unintended discrimination. Cities must implement continuous monitoring to account for model drift, changing population behaviors, or biases introduced through new data sources. Regular fairness assessments increase transparency and ensure that AI systems support equitable service delivery.

9.4 Explainability and Transparency Metrics

Smart cities often deploy AI systems that administrators must understand and justify, especially when decisions impact public welfare. Evaluating explainability involves assessing the clarity and comprehensibility of model explanations provided by Explainable AI (XAI) tools. Metrics include the interpretability of decisions, explanation accuracy, and user satisfaction among human reviewers. Dashboards displaying feature importance, decision pathways, or model confidence scores improve trust and accountability. Transparent AI systems not only meet regulatory expectations but also enhance confidence among city officials and citizens who rely on these decisions.

9.5 System Resilience and Operational Reliability

Operational reliability is essential in smart city environments where system failures can impact public safety or essential services. AI systems and data pipelines must be evaluated for uptime, fault tolerance, failover mechanisms, and recovery times. Stress testing and load simulations help determine whether the architecture can handle peak data volumes—such as during festivals, emergencies, or extreme weather conditions. Metrics like mean time to recovery (MTTR), system availability percentages, and error propagation rates are critical for assessing resilience. Privacy-preserving mechanisms should also be tested to ensure they function correctly under stress and do not degrade performance during high-demand periods.

9.6 User Trust, Adoption, and Usability Metrics

Despite strong technical performance, AI systems cannot succeed without user trust. Smart city platforms must therefore be evaluated based on citizen satisfaction, transparency of operations, ease of use, and perceived fairness. Surveys, feedback analytics, and user experience testing help assess whether residents feel comfortable with data handling practices and whether services are intuitive to interact with. Higher adoption rates indicate greater acceptance of digital governance. Metrics such as task completion time, error rate on citizen portals, and engagement levels provide valuable insight into usability. Prioritizing trust and usability ensures that smart city systems remain inclusive, accessible, and widely adopted.

10 Future Directions and Research Opportunities

As smart cities continue to expand in scale, complexity, and digital sophistication, the need for advanced privacy-preserving AI techniques and secure data management practices will only grow stronger. While current approaches already offer powerful tools for securing information and ensuring ethical AI behavior, significant opportunities exist for enhancing these systems further. Future developments must balance innovation with societal values, regulatory compliance, and evolving security threats. This section presents emerging research directions that could reshape privacy-preserving AI and reinforce the foundations of secure urban governance.

10.1 Next-Generation Privacy-Preserving Technologies

Privacy-enhancing technologies (PETs) are rapidly evolving, creating new possibilities for secure computation in smart cities. As quantum computing progresses, traditional encryption schemes may become vulnerable, increasing the importance of post-quantum cryptographic algorithms (Institute and of Standards and Technology (NIST) 2022). Researchers are also working on improving the speed and practicality of homomorphic encryption, as well as developing hybrid models that pair secure computation techniques with trusted execution environments (TEEs) for additional protection (Lindell 2021). Another promising avenue is the extension of federated learning into decentralized, cross-city collaboration networks, enabling multiple cities to train shared AI models without ever exchanging raw data. Continued research in these areas will support the development of future-ready AI systems that deliver strong privacy protections while still enabling advanced analytics and informed decision-making (Dwork and Roth 2014).

10.2 Self-Regulating and Autonomous Ethical AI Systems

Another promising research direction involves developing AI systems that can monitor their own behavior and maintain ethical alignment without continuous human oversight. These systems would incorporate built-in modules to evaluate fairness, track transparency, and identify privacy risks, enabling them to continually verify that their actions stay within ethical boundaries. Such self-regulation could significantly reduce the need for manual audits and accelerate the deployment of responsible AI technologies. Capabilities like real-time bias detection, automatic rollback when harmful behaviors emerge, and on-demand explainability tools would further strengthen system reliability. In addition, ongoing exploration of reinforcement learning-based governance models and AI-generated audit trails may allow AI systems to adjust and correct themselves in real time while remaining compliant with legal and ethical standards (Organization for Economic Co-operation and Development (OECD) 2019).

10.3 Cross-City Data Collaboration and Federated Urban Intelligence

As cities become increasingly interconnected, new opportunities arise for developing shared analytical models that function across multiple urban regions. This idea—referred to as federated urban intelligence (FUI)—allows cities to collaborate on analytics without ever sharing raw data. For example, municipalities can jointly train predictive models for disease outbreaks, disaster response, or traffic optimization by combining federated learning with secure multi-party computation (Lindell 2021). This approach enables cities to leverage large, diverse datasets while retaining full ownership and control of their local information. This area presents numerous research possibilities, such as enhancing communication efficiency between participating cities, minimizing delays in federated learning workflows, and designing governance frameworks to guide how multi-city collaboration should be organized, monitored, and regulated.

10.4 Quantum Threats and Post-Quantum Security Models

With the rapid advancement of quantum computing, many commonly used cryptographic algorithms may soon become vulnerable (Institute and of Standards and Technology (NIST) 2022). Smart cities—heavily dependent on large-scale data systems and cloud-based infrastructures—are particularly at risk from emerging quantum threats. Future research must prioritize the development of post-quantum cryptographic protocols that work effectively on IoT devices, edge nodes, and low-power sensors. In addition, quantum-resistant communication channels and lightweight encryption techniques are essential to safeguard the vast number of connected devices operating in urban environments. Researchers are also beginning to investigate quantum-safe federated learning and hybrid classical-quantum privacy frameworks as part of the next generation of secure smart city architectures ("Communication-Efficient Learning of Deep Networks from Decentralized Data" 2017).

10.5 Policy Evolution and Regulatory Harmonization

As technology evolves, the policies that regulate it must adapt in parallel. Smart cities often struggle with fragmented regulations that vary across regions, departments, and service sectors. To overcome these challenges, future efforts should aim to harmonize data protection standards across jurisdictions—especially for systems that use cross-border cloud storage or involve data sharing among multiple agencies. Research into adaptive regulatory frameworks, where rules automatically adjust based on factors such as system risk level, data sensitivity, or AI behavior, could significantly improve governance efficiency. Additionally, cities will need updated auditing practices and new certification procedures to properly assess whether AI systems meet emerging standards for safety, fairness, and privacy.

10.6 Open Challenges and Research Gaps

Despite progress, numerous open challenges remain. Privacy-preserving AI techniques often introduce computational overhead, reducing real-time performance. Balancing accuracy with privacy continues to be an unresolved issue, particularly in time-critical applications such as emergency response or traffic control. Another unresolved challenge is designing explainable AI systems for complex deep learning models, especially those integrated with privacy-preserving techniques like differential privacy or homomorphic encryption. Ensuring fairness across diverse demographic groups is also complicated by the lack of high-quality, unbiased datasets. Finally, the increasing sophistication of cyberattacks—such as model inversion, membership inference, and adversarial manipulation—demands ongoing research into robust, attack-resistant AI architectures (Elma et al. 2025).

10.7 Toward Holistic Safe and Ethical Smart Cities

The long-term vision for future smart cities is to create systems that integrate privacy, security, fairness, and transparency into the core of every technological component. Achieving this requires interdisciplinary collaboration between AI researchers, cybersecurity experts, policymakers, urban planners, and civil society. Future research should explore socio-technical approaches that incorporate human values, ethical reflection, and participatory governance into the design of AI-driven public infrastructure. By aligning technological advancements with human-centric principles, cities can evolve into safer, more inclusive, and more trustworthy digital ecosystems.

11 Conclusion

Privacy-preserving AI and secure data management are essential pillars of modern smart city infrastructure. As urban systems continue to expand and rely on interconnected IoT devices, cloud services, and automated decision-making, safeguarding citizen data becomes critical not only for regulatory compliance but also for maintaining public trust. The chapter demonstrated that privacy is not an obstacle to innovation; rather, it is a foundational enabler that supports trustworthy, scalable, and ethically responsible smart city ecosystems.

By integrating technologies such as federated learning, differential privacy, homomorphic encryption, and secure multi-party computation, smart cities can analyze large-scale data while minimizing exposure of sensitive information. Secure data pipelines, identity management frameworks, zero-trust architectures, and blockchain-based audit mechanisms together create a layered defense model that ensures end-to-end protection. At the same time, AI safety measures—including fairness monitoring, content moderation, explainability tools, and threat detection—ensure that automated systems operate transparently and equitably for all residents.

Ultimately, the successful deployment of privacy-preserving AI requires a combination of robust technical safeguards, forward-looking policy frameworks, continuous monitoring, and citizen-centric governance. As research continues to advance in areas such as post-quantum security, autonomous ethical AI, and cross-city collaborative intelligence, the future of smart cities will increasingly rely on systems that are secure by design, privacy-preserving by architecture, and accountable by governance. This chapter provides a blueprint for building such systems and highlights the research pathways required to shape safer, more inclusive, and more resilient urban environments.

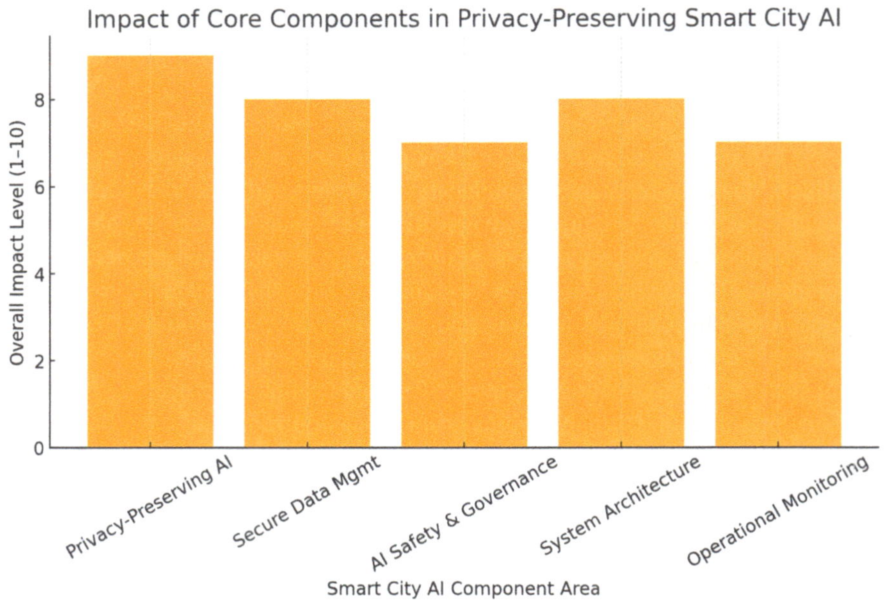

Fig. 4 Impact of privacy-preserving AI in core components

Figure 4 represents the impact of the core components of privacy-preserving AI in smart cities.

References

H. Brendan McMahan, Eider Moore, Daniel Ramage, Seth Hampson, and Blaise Agüera y Arcas, "Communication-Efficient Learning of Deep Networks from Decentralized Data," in Proceedings of AISTATS, 2017.

International Organization for Standardization, "ISO/IEC 27001: Information Security Management Systems Requirements," ISO Standard, 2013.

Keith Bonawitz, Vladimir Ivanov, Ben Kreuter, Antonio Marcedone, H. Brendan McMahan, Sara Patel, Daniel Ramage, Aaron Segal, and Karn Seth, "Towards Federated Learning at Scale: System Design," in Proceedings of SysML, 2019.

Martín Abadi, Andy Chu, Ian Goodfellow, H. Brendan McMahan, Ilya Mironov, Kunal Talwar, and Li Zhang, "Deep Learning with Differential Privacy," in Proceedings of the ACM Conference on Computer and Communications Security, 2016, pp. 308–318.

Dhanaraj, R. K., Islam, S. H., & Rajasekar, V. (2022). A cryptographic paradigm to detect and mitigate blackhole attack in VANET environments. *Wireless Networks*, *28*(7), 3127-3142.

C. Dwork and A. Roth, "The Algorithmic Foundations of Differential Privacy," Foundations and Trends in Theoretical Computer Science, vol. 9, no. 3–4, pp. 211–407, 2014.

Elma, K. J., Britto, P. I., Sarveshwaran, V., & Sankaran, S. (2025). Design and development of healthcare data classification with Gannet Geese migration optimisation. *International Journal of Ad Hoc and Ubiquitous Computing*, *49*(2), 75-91.

Gartner Research, "Zero Trust Security Model," Gartner Technical Report, 2020.

Anupam Ghosh and Raju Rajagopalan, "Smart Cities: A Survey on Data Management, Security, and Privacy," ACM Computing Surveys, vol. 53, no. 6, pp. 1–41, 2020.

Hamidreza HaddadPajouh, Ali Dehghantanha, Reza M. Parizi, Kim-Kwang Raymond Choo, and Ali Mahmoud, "A Comprehensive Survey on IoT Security: Emerging Threats and Countermeasures," IEEE Communications Surveys & Tutorials, vol. 22, no. 3, pp. 1646–1685, 2020.

National Institute of Standards and Technology (NIST), "Post-Quantum Cryptography Standardization," NIST Report, 2022.

Yehuda Lindell, "Secure Multiparty Computation," Communications of the ACM, vol. 64, no. 1, pp. 86–96, 2021.

Satoshi Nakamoto, "Bitcoin: A Peer-to-Peer Electronic Cash System," 2008. [Online]. Available: https://bitcoin.org

Arvind Narayanan and Vitaly Shmatikov, "Robust De-Anonymization of Large Sparse Datasets," in Proceedings of the IEEE Symposium on Security and Privacy, 2008, pp. 111–125.

Organisation for Economic Co-operation and Development (OECD), "OECD Principles on Artificial Intelligence," OECD Legal Instruments, 2019.

Zhan Qin, Yuncheng Yang, Tong Yu, and Iqbal Khalil, "Privacy-Preserving Machine Learning: Methods, Challenges, and Directions," IEEE Internet of Things Journal, vol. 8, no. 13, pp. 10430–10444, 2021.

United Nations Educational, Scientific and Cultural Organization (UNESCO), "Recommendation on the Ethics of Artificial Intelligence," UNESCO Publications, 2021.

Role of Responsible AI in Healthcare for Smart Cities

V. S. S. V. Surya Ganesh, Ajith Mathew, C. Saravanan, and Mohan Aradhya

Abstract

India's high urban migration rate has created a large number of rural-to-urban migrants unable to avail themselves of equitable and quality healthcare services in changing smart city platforms. Even though smart cities purport to provide top-line healthcare technology and infrastructure, migrants are most often left on the margins of these services through monetary, linguistic, and systemic impediments. This initiative, "Responsible AI for Inclusive Smart City Healthcare," seeks to use the potential of Artificial Intelligence to fill this gap in healthcare and make technological advancement equate to social equity. The central issue is the disjointed access to healthcare services for migrants who experience increased out-of-pocket costs, disconnection from urban insurance programs, and poor health awareness. With 70% of India's population living in rural locales but with an access of only 36.5% to hospital beds, the imbalance takes a greater dimension in the migration to urban areas. The proposed AI-enabled solution will harness responsible AI practices—transparency, accountability, and fairness—to detect high-risk migrant clusters, schedule mobile healthcare unit deployment for optimal impact, facilitate multilingual telehealth consultations, and process insurance eligibility for streamlined access using intelligent automation. The proposed chapter examines the principal stakeholders in this smart city eco-system and their interactions in providing the best solutions for the society. Through promoting co-operation between these parties, the chapter explores critical real-world problems of healthcare inequity, resource misallocation, and policy blind spots in migrant welfare. In the end, the chapter focuses on the role of responsible AI in the health care system for providing all feasible solutions in addressing the challenges faced by migrants in smart cities.

Keywords

Responsible AI · HealthCare · SmartCity · AI Practises

1 Introduction

Cities promise opportunity, but for millions of migrant workers, urban life is a daily struggle for dignity, security, and health. Behind the glitter of Smart Cities lies an invisible workforce building homes, roads, and economies while living in fragile conditions. Their journey from villages to megacities is not just a story of migration—but of survival in unequal urban spaces.

1.1 The Century of the City: Urbanization, Migration, and the "Invisible" Majority

The twenty-first century is growing as the century of cities. The world in the brink of urban millennium which united nation has mentioned. Because close to 68% world's population is migrating to urban thank to this population in urban center is increased to 2.5 billion people mainly 90% of growth will be seen especially in Asia and Africa before the industry drove growth in the developed country and cities are developed to meet the demand (Fig. 1).

This has resulted in a huge divide in modern cities. Smart city which is characterised by its technology and global

V. S. S. V. Surya Ganesh (✉) · A. Mathew · C. Saravanan · M. Aradhya
Department of MCA, RV College of Engineering®, Bengaluru, India
e-mail: vissapragadasv.mca24@rvce.edu.in

A. Mathew
e-mail: ajithmathew.mca24@rvce.edu.in

C. Saravanan
e-mail: saravananc@rvce.edu.in

M. Aradhya
e-mail: mohanaradhya@rvce.edu.in

V. Sarveshwaran et al. (eds.), *Responsible AI for Smart Cities*, Sustainable Artificial Intelligence-Powered Applications,
https://doi.org/10.1007/978-3-032-26901-0_5

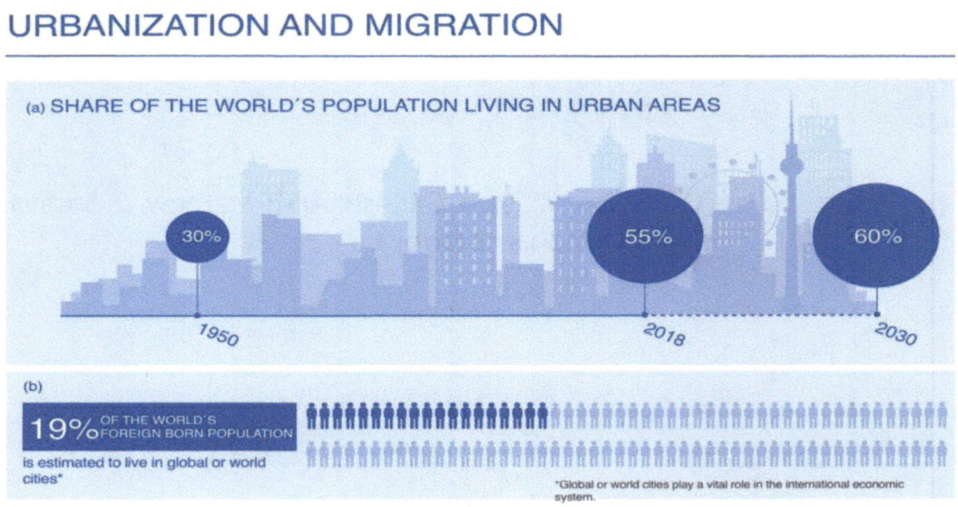

Fig. 1 Urban population growth from 30% (1950) to 60% (2030) *source* http://migrationdataportal.org/

connectivity. The other side of the coin is the invisible city filled with slum and unauthorized colonies of workers in even though the smart cities are built on their shoulder they are being ignored. while these people are important for development of cities they have very poor living conditions.

The health complications are severe. The migrants are forced to live in confined areas with no proper water, sanitation and medical care and not to mention they are at high risk of diseases such as TB, malaria, dengue, and waterborne diseases. This is the same smart city which consists of state of the art health facilities. This is because of invisibility not lack of access and they are becoming invisible.

1.2 The Smart City Paradigm: A Data-Driven Promise and Its Limits

The Government has taken the approach to developing and managing growing urban complexity using the Smart City model. Smart City basically uses technologies such as IoT, Big Data, and Cloud Computing to enhance the efficiency of urban services. There is "Smart Health" in this vision that will logistically enable planning, resource distribution, and emergency response in health with real-time data.

Key smart health technologies include:

Predictive Epidemiology: The machine learning models analyze health records for predicting the outbreak of a certain disease, thus helping the preparation of resources in advance by the authorities.

IoT-based surveillance: Sensors monitor environmental health metrics-air quality or viruses in wastewater, for example.

Digital triage and telemedicine refer to connecting patients to doctors through mobile apps and remote medical devices, easing pressure on the hospitals.

The philosophy of the Smart City is optimisation, crunching data to make sure that scarce resources—ambulances, hospital beds, and vaccines—go where demand for them is greatest. But this relies on one key assumption: the data being collected truly represents the population as a whole. In most developing cities, this simply isn't the case, given that much of urban life happens beyond formal systems.

Much of their health behavior occurs outside of formal institutions, relying on local pharmacists, informal clinics, or self-medication. Because of this, their health experiences remain largely invisible in official databases. In cases when Smart City systems rely on formal data alone, they optimize only for those who are visible and documented.

1.3 The Core Challenge: The Trilemma of Data Invisibility

Where Smart City technologies meet migrant populations, the failure is not technical-it is human invisibility."Smart cities operate on data," notes Arundhati Roy, "yet migrants leave no data trail, not because they don't exist but because services are tailored to exist within middle-class life." As long as they appear on official documentation, receipts, or health records, migrants exist and toil in the smart city unnoticed.

The result of this is invisibility from three interlocking barriers; the first one is digital limitation due to lack of access to smart phones and health apps. Second not proper coordination between government officials and insurance providers and finally, threat of losing their job and getting harassed for complaining which make them to remain invisible.

1.4 Problem Statement: The Algorithmic Divide

The central challenge addressed in this chapter is the Algorithmic Divide—the growing risk that uncritical use of AI in urban governance will reinforce existing health inequalities. While AI offers powerful tools for improving efficiency, it is currently deployed with an "efficiency-first" mindset rather than an "equity-first" one.

There is a clear gap in both policy and research: existing Smart City and AI governance frameworks rarely account for the mobile, undocumented, and vulnerable nature of migrant populations. Key questions remain unanswered. How can AI systems include migrant communities without turning them into targets of surveillance? How can fairness be built into resource allocation algorithms rather than added as an afterthought?

This chapter argues that the answer lies in the principles of Responsible AI (RAI). It introduces frameworks which ensure AI systems are Fair, Accountable and Transparent. It will not solely check on technical accuracy but real world social impact as well and their effects on migrant population.

Chapter overview

This chapter bridges the gap between AI ethics and health care realities of the migrant population living in smart cities. Its main contribution is introduction of a Responsible AI Framework for Migrant Health which combines privacy, fairness aware machine learning frameworks with community driven systems to make sure technological advancement does not increase existing health care inequalities.

The chapter starts by examining socioeconomic, infrastructure barriers that migrant communities face accessing the health care in their daily life. It reviews the existing research on smartcities, AI ethics and try to identify the gaps that are there in the existing system.

The following chapter maps stakeholders and data that is essential for the framework. Building on this groundwork, the proposed Responsible AI Framework is presented in detail, including mechanisms for privacy-preserving cluster detection and equity-based resource allocation.

The technical architecture and system workflow are subsequently outlined, demonstrating how data flows from sensing to decision-making within a responsible design paradigm. The effectiveness of the framework is then evaluated through a comprehensive case study simulation.

Finally, the chapter concludes with a discussion of the ethical implications, policy recommendations, and future research directions, offering a forward-looking vision for inclusive, accountable, and equitable urban healthcare systems.

2 Healthcare Challenges for Migrant Populations: The Paradox of Proximity

Although urbanization is often associated with improved health outcomes at the population level, migrant communities experience the opposite reality—what is widely described as the "urban penalty." For migrant workers, cities function not as zones of opportunity but as environments where economic insecurity, overcrowding, and environmental risks combine to produce a disproportionate burden of disease. Unlike the urban middle class, whose health risks are largely lifestyle-related, migrants face a double burden: persistent infectious diseases driven by poverty alongside rising exposure to pollution, occupational hazards, and stress (Fig. 2).

Fig. 2 Migrant health shaped by socio-economic risks, system failures, and dual disease burden

2.1 Socio-Economic and Epidemiological Characteristics of Disadvantage in Urban Areas

The struggle to meet the higher demand for healthcare could worsen if, for instance, immigration rises because.

For most migrant workers, the city is not a place that mitigates risks of ill-health but rather multiplies them incrementally. Life is lived in slums and serviced housing areas that are overcrowded and lacking the rudimentary services that most humans take for granted, like cleaning and sanitation and the use of toilets and water. In such environments, illness like cholera and tuberculosis spreads quickly through communities. However, the insecurity that migrant workers experience for financial reasons means that illness is something they live with and not something that they get treatment for because going for treatment means they forgo the day's income if they get services from the informal sector that has no benefits at all.

But beyond these apparent challenges lies a more hidden and structural challenge generated by migration and exclusion. Migrants are always moving from one village to another city in order to get health checkups, while the health systems of the city are developed for people who are staying in the city itself with proper knowledge of finding and navigating the hospitals. Due to this, many migrant people end up lost in the city's extensive mechanisms. The condition of Tuberculosis depicts this scenario clearly. A person who works in the city might begin his TB treatment, but then move to his village when the season of labor comes. As soon as the person stops coming to the clinic, the person is considered to be "lost to follow-up." TB itself does not get lost, it just spreads further and ceases to be treated due to resistance to medications.

This is the same case with malaria and dengue diseases, where the lack of attention is seen in rural areas. Construction sites create pools of stagnant water, which act as breeding centers for mosquitoes as they thrive in clean water. Moreover, these spots are not monitored regularly by the people, and thus the diseases remain under the radar. On paper, the city is healthy, but the reality is hidden in the numbers.

Refugee women and children find themselves in similar predicaments. Many women are unable to access antenatal care because of the lack of necessary documents and addresses. This leads to child deliveries taking place within homes and restricting basic healthcare options for both mother and child. Children miss vaccinations because mothers relocate with their children from place to place across different regions when they move for searching daily wage jobs. They end up in new regions while migrating, where the vaccination levels remain low; this is why some diseases like measles continue to make appearances even in those areas when everything seems to be okay in big cities.

Finally, poor migrant health is not an issue of "poor decision-making" or "bad luck." Rather, it is a system that was never intended for "mobile" people. "Illness follows migrant patients, but a 'health system' does not." This leads to a kind of 'invisible city.'

This is a great way to describe a situation: "Poverty follows migrant patients. Illness follows migrant patients. Illness follows migrant patients. A 'health system' does not."

2.2 Health Metrics Comparison: "Data Gap"

To put this disparity into perspective, key findings of comparable health indicators for both registered city residents and vulnerable migrant groups are compiled in Table 1 below, using findings of various urban health studies.

Table 1 Comparative health indicators: documented urban residents versus migrant populations

Health indicator	Urban non-migrant (Reference)	Migrant/slum dweller (Vulnerable)	Key structural barrier
TB prevalence	~150 per 100,000 population	~350–500 per 100,000 population	Overcrowding; Discontinuous treatment due to mobility
Institutional delivery	>90%	<55%	Lack of local ID/ANC registration; Cost of private care
Full immunization	>85%	<45%	Missed immunization drives due to relocation; Lack of awareness
Malaria/ dengue risk	Moderate (Seasonal)	High (Occupational)	Living on construction sites (breeding grounds); Lack of nets
Health expenditure	Mostly covered (Insurance/ CGHS)	High out-of-pocket (>60%)	Exclusion from state insurance; Reliance on private "quacks"
Treatment delay	<2 days from symptom onset	>7 days from symptom onset	Loss of daily wages (Opportunity Cost); Fear of system
Digital access to health	High-App-based booking	Close to zero	Language barriers, Lack of SmartphonesandDigital Illiteracy

2.3 Exclusion in the System and Administration

Apart from disease contact, the biggest challenge associated with accessing healthcare is administrative.

The identity paradox underlies this exclusion. Healthcare services usually have criteria for local residence, and migrants do not have access to these. It is even difficult for the national identity service to make national healthcare portable. As a result, there are 'stateless citizens' who are eligible for neither rural nor urban welfare services.

Health data fragmentation makes it even more difficult for there to be a smooth continuum of care. Medical records don't travel from city to city. A result is repeated testing because medical records aren't available, excessive antibiotics prescriptions, and ineffective control of chronic conditions. It directly leads to antimicrobial resistance and ineffective health care.

Linguistic and cultural factors aggravate the situation of exclusion. Miscommunication between migrant patients and city medical services leads to misunderstandings, devaluing complaints, and a loss of dignity. As a consequence, migrants turn to unregulated alternative medical systems.

2.4 Section Conclusion

The healthcare challenges faced by migrant populations are not accidental—they are structurally produced by an urban system that treats migration as temporary rather than permanent. Digitizing this exclusion through Smart City platforms, without correcting these foundational inequalities, risks deepening the urban health divide. A truly Smart City must first become a Just City, one that redesigns healthcare systems around mobility, informality, and inclusion rather than permanence and documentation alone.

3 Literature Review: The Gap Between Smart Cities and Responsible AI

3.1 Smart City Healthcare: The Technocratic Dominance

The academic discourse on Smart Cities has historically been based on a technocratic narrative, which sees the city as a "system of systems" to be optimized through cyber-physical integration. Early definitions (Giffinger et al. 2007) emphasized the role of ICT (Information and Communication Technology) in enhancing the competitive profile of a city. In the health domain, this means "Smart Health", defined as in Solanas et al. (2014), referring to the provision of health services by intelligent agents - sensors, actuators, and network devices.

A large literature is focused on IoT-driven Epidemiology. Works, such as that described in Pramanik et al. (2017), illustrate architectures in which wearable sensors and environmental monitors stream continuous data to cloud-based systems to forecast cardiac events or respiratory distress. In the realm of infectious disease, in another example, Big Data Analytics has been applied to social media feeds (e.g., Twitter/X) to identify flu trends more rapidly than traditional sentinel surveillance (Ginsberg et al. 2009).

A critical review of the literature on such frameworks reveals a "data positivist" bias underlying most of them. A baseline of digital connectivity is assumed to be the norm. For example, mHealth interventions discussed in Silva et al. (2015) assume that patients own smartphones and are sufficiently digitally literate to navigate through complex interfaces. There is a dearth of research in "low-resource" Smart City environments where the target demographic has no digital footprint. Indeed, as pointed out in Kitchin (2014), Smart City technologies often "deepen the digital divide" since services are optimized for the data-rich (documented citizens) while making the data-poor (migrants) invisible to the algorithmic gaze.

3.2 The Ethics of AI in Urban Governance

Parallel to the technical literature, a robust field of AI Ethics has emerged. The transition from "Big Data" to "Responsible Data" is marked by high-level frameworks such as the Montreal Declaration for Responsible AI and the EU High-Level Expert Group Guidelines. These documents establish the normative standards for AI deployment, emphasizing human autonomy, privacy, and prevention of harm.

In the urban context, "Algorithmic Governance" research has highlighted the risks of automated inequality. Eubanks, in her seminal work *Automating Inequality*, illustrates how automated eligibility systems for welfare in the US systematically purged poor families from rolls due to minor data errors. Similarly, in the Global South, scholars like Arora have critiqued the "Datafication" of development, arguing that digital identity systems (like Aadhaar) often act as tools of exclusion rather than inclusion for itinerant populations.

Despite these critical voices, there remains a disconnect between the *technical* Smart City literature and the *sociological* Critical Data Studies literature. Most technical papers propose novel algorithms (e.g., "A genetic algorithm for ambulance routing") without discussing fairness constraints. Conversely, most ethical papers critique bias without proposing technical architectures to fix it. This chapter aims to bridge this specific gap.

3.3 Comparative Analysis: The "Migrant Gap" in Existing Research

To visualize the deficit in current research, Table 2 presents a comparative analysis of prominent Smart City healthcare frameworks. The analysis evaluates these studies based on three criteria:

- Technological Focus: The core AI/IoT mechanism used.
- Target Demographic: Who the system is designed to serve.
- Inclusion of Transients: Whether the framework accounts for undocumented or mobile populations.

Comparative Analysis of Existing Smart Health Frameworks and the "MigrantGap".

3.4 Operationalizing FAT: Fairness, Accountability, and Transparency

For a Smart City to be truly "smart" for all its residents, it must operationalize the principles of FAT (Fairness, Accountability, Transparency) specifically for the migrant context (Fig. 3).

3.4.1 Fairness: Beyond Statistical Parity

In standard ML, fairness is often defined as "statistical parity" (e.g., ensuring the error rate is equal for men and women). However, for migrant health, we must adopt Counterfactual Fairness. We must ask: "If this high-risk migrant settlement were a wealthy gated community, would the algorithm have dispatched an ambulance?".

Furthermore, we must address allocative harm. If a routing algorithm ignores a slum because "the roads are unmapped," it is maximizing efficiency at the cost of equity. A "Fair" algorithm in this context is one that accepts a "cost penalty" (e.g., longer travel times) to ensure service coverage for the most vulnerable.

3.4.2 Accountability: The Human-In-The-Loop

Who is accountable when an AI system fails to predict an outbreak in a migrant camp? Is it the software vendor, the city municipality, or the data scientist? Responsible AI requires Algorithmic Auditing. There must be a "Human-in-the-Loop" mechanism where decisions taken by the AI-say "Do not deploy mobile vans to Zone C"-can be reviewed and overruled by community health workers, ASHAs/ NGOs, who possess ground truth knowledge. Accountability also implies Redressal: if a migrant is denied insur-

Table 2 Comparative analysis of prominent Smart City healthcare frameworks

Reference no	Core technology	Primary objective	Target population	Gap analysis (migrant inclusion)
Hossain and Muhammad (2019)	IoT and cloud computing	Real-time monitoring of elderly patients	Geriatric population with fixed residence	High Exclusion: Requires stable Wi-Fi/Sensors in the home. Irrelevant for homeless/migrants
Combi et al. (2016)	Machine learning (ML)	Predicting COVID-19 hotspots using urban density data	General urban population	Data Bias: Relies on census data which undercounts slums. Misses high-density unauthorized colonies
Rathore et al. (2018)	Big data & hadoop	Detecting waterborne diseases via social media sentiment	Social media users (Digital Natives)	Selection Bias: Migrant laborers rarely post health status on Twitter/X. Leads to "silent" outbreaks
Francis et al. (2024)	Blockchain	Secure Electronic Health Record (EHR) sharing	Insured patients in private hospital networks	Access Barrier: Migrants lack the "Health ID" anchor required to create the blockchain wallet
Dash et al. (2021)	Telemedicine	Remote diagnostics for chronic diseases	Rural patients connecting to city specialists	Linguistic Gap: Interfaces typically in English/Main languages. Ignores dialect barriers of interstate migrants
Proposed framework	Privacy-preserving AI and fairness constraints	Equitable resource allocation and "Invisible" cluster detection	Transient, undocumented, & "floating" populations	Inclusive Design: Specifically targets data-sparse zones using satellite/aggregated inputs

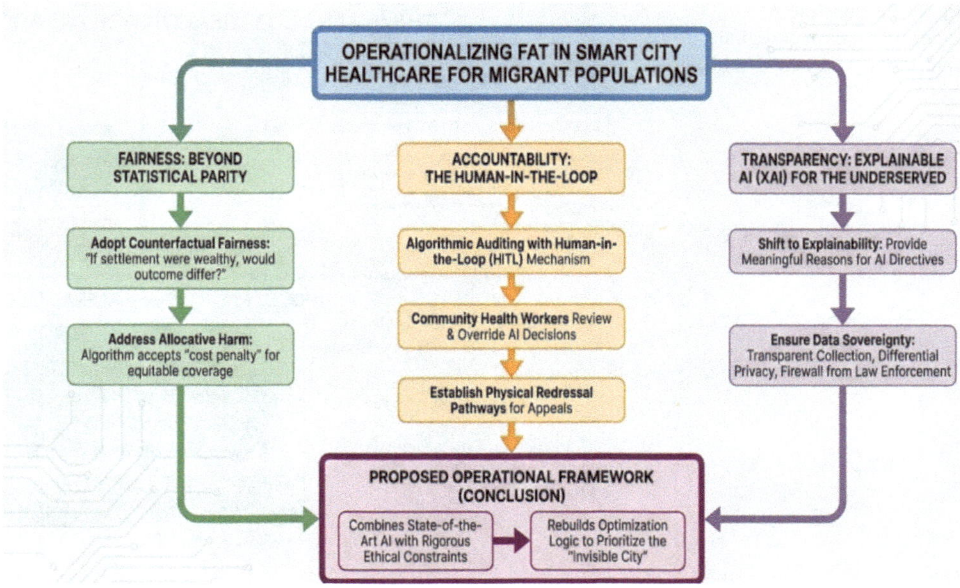

Fig. 3 Proposed human-centered AI framework for just healthcare delivery in smart cities

ance by an automated system, there must be a physical pathway to appeal that decision.

3.4.3 Openness: Explainable AI (XAI) for the Underprivileged

Transparency is commonly misconstrued as making source code available. To a migrant worker who cannot read or write very well, open-source code means absolutely nothing. Here, Transparency means Explainability. If a health application routes a worker to a particular clinic, then it needs to explain why, such as "This clinic speaks your dialect and it is open now."

Furthermore, transparency involves Data Sovereignty: Immigrants are suspicious often that health data collections are thinly veiled deportation operations; a Responsible AI framework needs to be clear as to what is being collected (Allam and Jones 2020; Rajasekar et al. 2022), how it is anonymized-Differential Privacy-and guarantee that it is firewalled from law enforcement agencies.

3.5 Conclusion of the Literature Review

The review of existing literature establishes a clear dichotomy. On one hand, sophisticated Smart Health frameworks exist but are designed for the "data-rich" formal city. On the other hand, ethical frameworks exist but remain abstract and high-level. There is a distinct lack of operational frameworks that combine state-of-the-art AI (like Computer Vision or Spatiotemporal Clustering) with rigorous ethical constraints (like Fairness Optimization) specifically for transient, data-sparse populations.

The proposed framework in this chapter addresses this specific lacuna. It does not merely "add" ethics to an existing model; it rebuilds the optimization logic of the Smart City to prioritize the "Invisible City" described in Sect. 1.4. Smart City Healthcare Ecosystem: Architecture and Gaps.

3.6 The Stakeholder Landscape: A Complex Adaptive System

A Smart City is not merely a collection of sensors and servers; it is a complex adaptive system composed of interacting agents with distinct, often conflicting, incentives. To understand why healthcare delivery fails for migrant populations, we must first map the ecosystem of stakeholders governing the urban health domain. The ecosystem can be divided into four major quadrants (Fig. 4):

- Governance Layer (Municipal Corporations & Public Health Departments):
- This layer is responsible for policy formulation, disease surveillance, and management of public hospitals. Their key incentive is Population Health Management-assuring aggregate morbidity is reduced and epidemics avoided

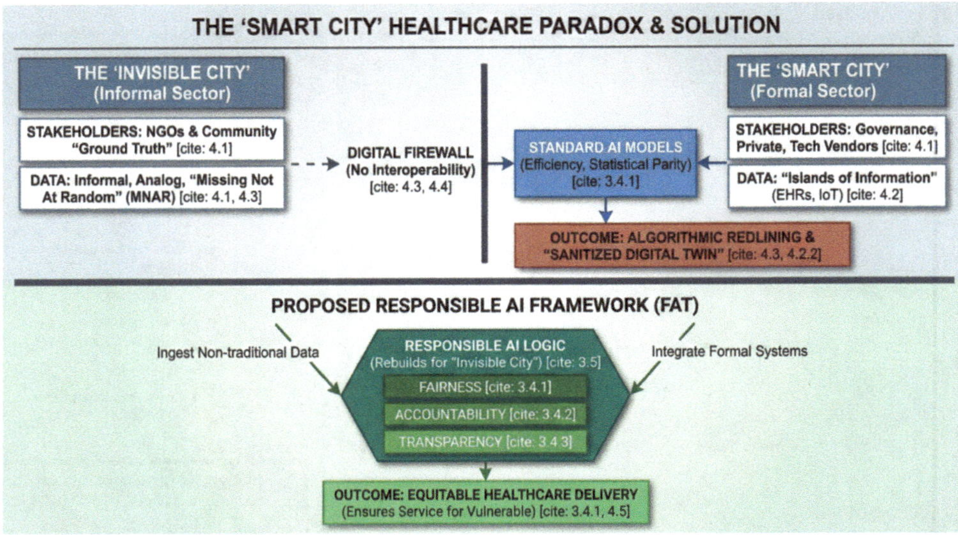

Fig. 4 Responsible AI framework to correct digital exclusion in smart city healthcare

to maintain economic stability. But on the ground, their mandate is often structurally constrained by ward boundaries, resulting in jurisdictional friction in the case of transient populations shifting across wards.

- The Service Provider Layer (Private Hospitals & Clinics):
- In many developing economies, the private sector delivers up to 70% of outpatient care (Floridi et al. 2018). Their incentive structure is Revenue Maximization. Consequently, their digital infrastructure - appointments, billing, Electronic Health Records - is optimized for the insured or paying customer. Migrants, possessing neither insurance nor high purchasing power, are largely invisible to this layer's sophisticated data systems.
- The NGOs & Community Health Workers Layer:
- This "last mile" of healthcare delivery in slums and construction camps is operated by organizations such as Doctors Without Borders, or local non-profits. They have the best "ground truth" data of migrant health—knowing exactly where the dengue outbreak is starting or which family is malnourished. However, their data is analog (paper registers), unstructured, and siloed from the central municipal database.
- The Technological Layer System Integrators & IoT Vendors:
- These are the architects of the Smart City—multinational technology firms deploying command-and-control centers, surveillance cameras, and cloud platforms. Their incentive is Scalability and Standardization. They design systems for the "average" citizen often failing to build edge cases for undocumented or linguistically diverse users.

3.7 The Current Data Infrastructure: Islands of Information

The architecture that is currently deployed in most cities for "Smart Health" relies on a flow of data that is fundamentally broken for the informal sector. Distinct "Islands of Information" characterize the infrastructure and simply do not talk to each other.

3.7.1 Formal Health Data—EHRs

Large tertiary care hospitals use standard HIS, such as HL7 or FHIR. These capture relatively granular clinical data: vitals, lab history, and imaging. This data is, however, strictly "facility-based." It captures the patient only after they have actually entered the hospital system. Since migrants often delay their care until the terminal stage, the EHR system captures the mortality but misses the morbidity trajectory, rendering it useless for preventive modeling.

3.7.2 IoT and Environmental Sensing

Smart Cities deploy environmental sensors to monitor air quality (PM2.5), noise, and water quality. While technologically advanced, the deployment topology of these sensors is biased: normally, sensors are installed in formal commercial districts, IT parks, and planned residential zones to protect high-value assets. Informal settlements and peripheral labor camps rarely get instrumented. The "environmental digital twin" of the city is thus a sanitized version of reality, blinding authorities to the toxic exposures faced by the migrant workforce.

3.7.3 Administrative Registries

Civil registration systems, or birth and death registries, form the backbone of public health planning. These systems are porous for migrants: a birth in a migrant camp often goes unregistered because parents may lack documentation, or fear approaching the authorities means that the child simply fails to show up in the algorithm used to plan vaccination stocks. The outcome is "statistical invisibility".

3.8 The Critical Failure Mode: Data Sparsity and "Missingness"

It is one of the major technical challenges that Data Sparsity issues have prevented effective AI deployment. In data science, there are three categories of missing data, and the migrant context describes the most severe form: Missing Not At Random (MNAR).

MNAR refers to a condition where data are missing because of the value of that very data. For instance, a migrant has no health record because they are ill, indigent, and fear deportation. Contrast this to missing at random: for example, the battery dies in a sensor.

The current AI models trained on city-wide health data assume the absence of a signal means the absence of an event.

The algorithm sees zero reported malaria cases in Zone X - the migrant camp.

Algorithmically inferred: Zone X is healthy. Low risk.

Fact: Zone X has 50 cases, but they are seeing unregistered "quacks" who do not upload data to the central server. This "False Negative" is the most dangerous failure mode of Smart City logic, in which Algorithmic Redlining takes automated resource allocation systems away from the areas that need them most simply because the data pipeline is dry.

3.9 The Institutional Void: Lack of Interoperability

Why does this data gap persist? It is not merely a lack of sensors, but a lack of Semantic and Structural Interoperability.

3.9.1 Semantic Barriers

Even when data is collected by NGOs in slums, it lacks standardization. One NGO might record "Fever" while another records "Pyrexia." Without a unified medical ontology (like SNOMED CT) enforced at the grassroots level, this data cannot be ingested by the central AI brain. The "Smart City" speaks English/Code, while the "Invisible City" speaks in vernacular/narrative, creating a translation failure.

3.9.2 The "Data Trust" Deficit

There is a profound lack of trust mechanisms for data sharing. Private providers hoard health data to maintain competitive advantage. NGOs are hesitant to share vulnerable migrant data with the government, fearing it might be repurposed for eviction drives or surveillance. Without a secure, privacy-preserving protocol—a Data Trust—the ecosystem remains fragmented.

3.10 Conclusion of the Ecosystem Analysis

The current Smart City ecosystem is a "Walled Garden." It functions exceptionally well for the documented, insured, and digital-native population, creating a positive feedback loop of better data leading to better services. Outside the walls, the migrant population exists in a digital void.

The challenge, therefore, is not just to build better algorithms, but to build better bridges. We need a framework that can ingest non-traditional, sparse, and noisy data from the informal sector and translate it into actionable intelligence without violating privacy. This necessitates the "Responsible AI Framework" proposed in the following section.

4 Proposed Responsible AI Framework: The RAI-MH Architecture

4.1 Conceptual Shift: From Efficiency to Equity

The central thesis of this chapter is that current Smart City paradigms suffer from "blind optimization." Standard algorithms optimize for visible variables (e.g., registered traffic flow) while implicitly penalizing invisible ones (e.g., migrant health needs). To rectify this, we propose the Responsible AI Framework for Migrant Health (RAI-MH). This framework represents a fundamental architectural shift from an *Efficiency-First* logic (minimizing cost) to an *Equity-First* logic (maximizing coverage).

The RAI-MH framework operates on three concentric layers:

1. The Detection Layer: Utilizing privacy-preserving data proxies to identify "invisible" population clusters.
2. The Optimization Layer: Re-engineering resource allocation algorithms to include "Fairness Constraints."
3. The Interaction Layer: Deploying dialect-aware NLP interfaces to bridge linguistic divides.

4.2 Module I: Privacy-Preserving Spatio-Temporal Cluster Detection

To identify undocumented populations without violating privacy, we rely on Proxy Indicators via Satellite Imagery $(S_{i,j})$ and Aggregated Call Detail Records $(M_{i,j})$.

4.2.1 Mathematical Formulation of Density Estimation

We model the city as a grid G consisting of cells $c_{i,j}$. The objective is to estimate the population density $\hat{D}_{i,j}$ as a weighted fusion of proxies:

$$\hat{D}_{i,j} = \alpha \cdot f(S_{i,j}) + \beta \cdot g(M_{i,j})$$

where α and β are weighting coefficients determined by ground-truth calibration, and $f(\cdot)$ and $g(\cdot)$ are normalization functions.

4.2.2 The Privacy Guarantee: Differential Privacy (ε-DP)

To prevent re-identification attacks ("Surveillance Capitalism"), we inject Laplacian noise. The released density value $D^*_{i,j}$ satisfies ε-Differential Privacy:

$$D^*_{i,j} = \hat{D}_{i,j} + Lap\left(\frac{\Delta f}{\varepsilon}\right)$$

We propose a dynamic ε that increases during health emergencies (higher utility needed) and decreases during normal periods (higher privacy maintained).

4.3 Module II: Fairness-Constrained Resource Allocation

Once clusters are identified, Mobile Medical Units (MMUs) must be deployed. Standard algorithms (like Traveling Salesman) deprioritize peripheral migrant camps to save fuel. We propose a Fairness-Constrained Multi-Objective Optimization (FCMOO) model.

4.3.1 The Objective Function

We utilize the Gini Coefficient (G) of Service Access Time as a penalty metric. The objective is to minimize a composite loss function L:

$$\text{Minimize}\, L = (1 - \lambda) \cdot \frac{C_{total}}{C} + \lambda \cdot G$$

Subject to:

1. Max Latency: $\forall k,\ T_k \leq T_{critical}$ (e.g., 48 h).
2. Capacity: $\sum_{k \in Route} P_k \leq Cap_{vehicle}$.

The Equity Parameter (λ) is the critical policy lever. Setting $\lambda \leq 0.4$ ensures the algorithm accepts higher operational costs to guarantee coverage for vulnerable zones.

4.4 Module III: Dialect-Native Interaction Layer (NLP)

To address linguistic exclusion, the framework integrates a Fine-Tuned Transfer Learning NLP model. Unlike standard models, this is trained on rural dialect voice data. The input audio X_{audio} is mapped directly to Clinical Intent:

$$\text{Intent} = \text{Softmax}(W \cdot \text{Encoder}(X_{audio}) + b)$$

This classifier is designed to recognize colloquial descriptions of symptoms (e.g., "body is burning" for fever) rather than formal medical terminology.

Table 3 The responsible AI fairness engine logic

Component	Responsible AI processing logic	Responsible output
Ingestion	Imputation and Anonymization: Checks for data sparsity. If data < Threshold, triggers synthetic data injection to prevent under-fitting. Applies ε-DP noise	Anonymized "Risk Heatmap" highlighting need without revealing identity
Prediction	Bias Mitigation: Runs "Counterfactual Testing" (flipping socio-economic labels of a zone). If the risk score changes significantly, weights are adjusted to remove bias	Bias-Corrected Disease Forecast (e.g., flagging high risk in unreported zones)
Allocation	Equity Optimization: Solves the Multi-Objective function ($minCost, minInequality$). Enforces strict latency constraints for peripheral zones	Fair Route Plan: Ambulances visit high-need/low-access zones first
Delivery	Explainability (XAI): If service is denied, generates a Natural Language Explanation (e.g., "Denied because Document A is missing")	Transparent Service Interaction with appeal mechanisms

4.5 The "Fairness Engine": Governance Logic

The core innovation is the "Fairness Engine"—middleware that audits every algorithmic decision (Table 3).

4.6 Algorithmic Impact Assessment (AIA)

To prevent "Technological Solutionism," we mandate a pre-deployment Algorithmic Impact Assessment (AIA).

1. Representation Gate: Does the training dataset include >15% representation from informal settlements?
2. Error Rate Parity: Is the False Negative Rate difference <5% between migrant and settled populations?
3. Purpose Limitation: Is there a legal guarantee that location data is firewalled from law enforcement?

This framework converts abstract ethical principles into executable code, ensuring the Smart City becomes an engine of redistribution rather than exclusion.

5 System Architecture and Methodology

5.1 Architecture Overview: The 4-Layer "Fairness Stack"

To operationalize the Responsible AI Framework defined in Sect. 5, we propose a four-tier service-oriented architecture (SOA). This architecture is designed to decouple the data ingestion (which is noisy and unstructured) from the decision logic (which must be precise and fair).

Layer 1: The Sensing and Ingestion Layer (The "Eyes")

This layer is responsible for gathering raw data from the heterogeneous urban environment. It employs a "Multi-Modal Sensor Fusion" approach to overcome data sparsity.

- IoT Stream: Input from air quality monitors (PM2.5/PM10) and water quality sensors (pH, turbidity) installed in pilot slum clusters.
- Digital Stream: Aggregated Call Detail Records (CDRs) from telecom partners to estimate real-time population density.
- Human-in-the-Loop Stream: Unstructured data from NGO field workers via mobile applications (ODK/KoboToolbox), including text notes and geotagged photos of potential breeding sites.

Layer 2: The Privacy and Data Lake Layer (The "Shield")

Raw data is never processed directly by the AI models to prevent re-identification attacks.

- De-Identification Module: All Personally Identifiable Information (PII)—such as names, phone numbers, and exact GPS coordinates of households—is stripped at the point of ingestion.
- Differential Privacy Injector: As mathematically defined in Sect. 5.2.2, Laplacian noise is injected into the spatial data.
- Data Lake: The sanitized data is stored in a non-relational database (e.g., MongoDB) to handle the schema-less nature of the input.

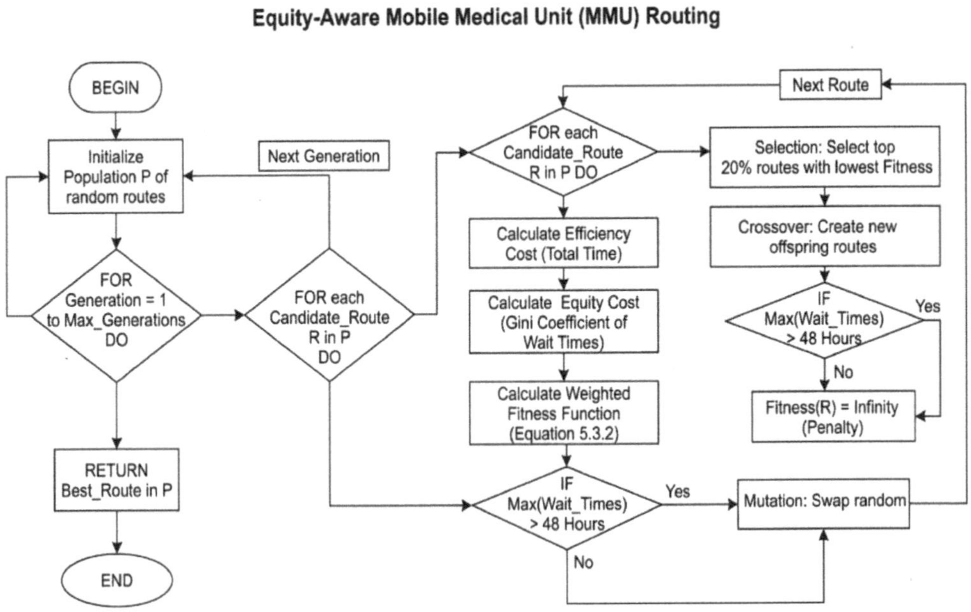

Fig. 5 Flowchart of an equity-aware genetic algorithm

Layer 3: The Intelligence Layer (The "Brain")

This is where the core logic resides. It consists of three independent microservices:

1. Cluster Detection Engine: Runs DBSCAN (Density-Based Spatial Clustering of Applications with Noise) on the satellite/CDR data to identify unmapped settlements.
2. Risk Prediction Model: An Ensemble Tree model (XGBoost) trained on historical epidemiological data to forecast disease outbreaks.
3. Fairness Optimizer: The routing engine that calculates MMU paths based on the Gini-Coefficient penalty function.

Layer 4: The Action and Interaction Layer (The "Hands")

The intelligence is converted into actionable formats for distinct user groups:

- City Administrators: A Web Dashboard (React.js) showing a "Heatmap of Vulnerability" rather than just a heatmap of cases.
- Field Workers: A Mobile App providing optimized route maps and the Multilingual Chatbot interface for patient screening.
- Beneficiaries: SMS/IVR alerts sent to high-risk clusters in their local dialects (e.g., "Boil water today, high cholera risk detected").

5.2 Implementation Logic: Fairness-Constrained Routing

To ensure reproducibility, we present the algorithmic logic for the Fairness-Constrained Resource Allocation module. Unlike standard routing which utilizes Dijkstra's algorithm for shortest paths, this implementation utilizes a Genetic Algorithm (GA) to solve the Multi-Objective Optimization problem (Fig. 5).

Algorithm: Equity-Aware Mobile Medical Unit (MMU) Routing

```
INPUT:
  C = {c_1, c_2, ..., c_n}  // Set of detected Clusters
  V = {v_1, v_2, ..., v_m}  // Fleet of Mobile Medical Units
  Risk(c_i)              // Normalized Health Risk Score for cluster i
  Dist(c_i, c_j)          // Distance Matrix (Travel Time)
  Lambda                  // Equity Parameter (0.4)

OUTPUT:
  Routes R = {r_1, ..., r_m} // Optimized Schedule
BEGIN
  1. Initialize Population P of random routes.
  2. FOR Generation = 1 to Max_Generations DO:
     FOR each Candidate_Route R in P DO:

       // Calculate Efficiency Cost (Total Time)
       Cost_Eff = Sum(Dist(u, v) for all edges in R)

       // Calculate Equity Cost (Gini Coefficient)
       Wait_Times = []
```

```
            FOR each cluster c_i in R DO:
                Wait_Times.append(Time_of_Arrival(c_i))
            Gini_Score = Calculate_Gini(Wait_Times)

            // Calculate Weighted Fitness Function (Equation 5.3.2)
            Fitness(R) = (1 - Lambda) * Normalize(Cost_Eff) + Lambda * Gini_Score
            // Apply Hard Constraints
            IF Max(Wait_Times) > 48 Hours THEN Fitness(R) = Infinity (Penalty)

        END FOR
        // Selection, Crossover, Mutation
        Select the top 20% of routes with the lowest Fitness score.
        Perform Crossover to create new offspring routes.
        Apply Mutation (Swap random stops) to prevent local minima.
        P = New_Population
    END FOR
    RETURN Best_Route in P
END
```

5.3 Technical Stack and Feasibility

The proposed architecture utilizes open-source technologies to ensure cost viability for developing nations:

- Backend: Python (FastAPI) for microservices.
- ML Libraries: Scikit-learn for clustering; PyTorch for the NLP dialect model.
- Database: PostgreSQL (PostGIS) for geospatial queries.
- Visualization: Kepler.gl for high-performance geospatial data rendering.

6 Case Study: Migrant Healthcare in Smart Cities

To validate the RAI-MH framework, we present a simulated implementation based on real-world urban data parameters typical of a "Tier-1" Indian metropolis (e.g., Bengaluru or Pune). This case study compares the outcomes of a Standard Smart City Approach versus the Proposed Responsible AI Framework.

6.1 Context: "MetroCity" Simulation Parameters

"MetroCity" is a rapidly urbanizing agglomeration with the following profile:

- Total Population: 8.5 Million.
- Migrant Population: 1.2 Million (~14%), primarily residing in 450 + unmapped settlements.
- Healthcare Assets: 50 Primary Health Centers (PHCs) and 20 Mobile Medical Units (MMUs).
- The Crisis Scenario: A pre-monsoon Dengue outbreak. Historical data suggests cases spike in July. The city aims to deploy MMUs for preventative screening and fumigation.

6.2 Implementation Scenario a: Standard Smart City (Baseline)

The city utilizes a standard Predictive Analytics model trained on Hospital Information System (HIS) data from the previous 5 years.

- Input Data: Documented hospital admissions and registered residential addresses.
- Prediction: The model identifies "Hotspots" in high-density, lower-middle-class wards where reporting is high.
- Allocation: MMUs are routed to maximize "Patient Outreach per Hour." They stick to main roads and mapped neighborhoods to minimize travel time.

6.3 Implementation Scenario B: Responsible AI Framework (Proposed)

The city deploys the RAI-MH framework described in Sect. 5 (Fig. 6).

- Input Data: Satellite Night Lights + Aggregated Cellular Activity + NGO inputs.
- Prediction: The Cluster Detection Engine identifies 40 "Hidden Clusters" near construction zones on the periphery. The Fairness Engine flags them as "High Vulnerability" despite zero historical cases.
- Allocation: MMUs are routed using the Algorithm 1 (Genetic Algorithm) with $\lambda = 0.4$. The system accepts a 15% increase in fuel costs to reach the peripheral camps

6.4 Comparative Results and Impact Analysis

The simulation was run for a 30-day operational cycle. Table 4 details the quantitative outcomes.

6.5 Lessons Learned

The simulation highlights a critical trade-off: Efficiency versus Equity.

The Responsible AI Framework was less efficient in terms of fuel consumption and operational speed (18% cost increase). However, it was vastly more effective in terms of public health outcomes (preventing a widespread outbreak by catching it in the hidden clusters).

- Lesson 1: Smart Cities must budget for the "Cost of Fairness." Equity is not free.
- Lesson 2: Algorithms work best when they optimize for *impact*, not just *throughput*.

7 Ethical, Social, and Policy Implications

7.1 Beyond Bias: Addressing "Allocative Harm"

The most significant ethical implication of this research is the shift from discussing "Representational Harms" (e.g., offensive stereotypes in AI) to "Allocative Harms" (e.g.,

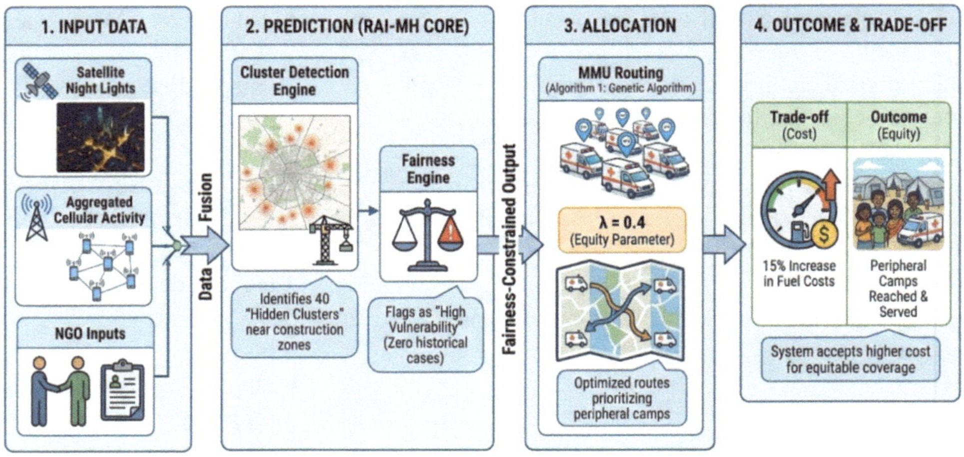

Fig. 6 Equity-aware AI pipeline for fair mobile healthcare routing

Table 4 Comparative outcomes—standard model vs. responsible AI framework

Metric	Standard smart city approach	Responsible AI framework	Impact analysis
Detection of vulnerable clusters	12 Clusters identified	52 Clusters identified	+333% Visibility. The Standard model missed 40 camps due to lack of addresses
Total travel distance (Fleet)	12,500 km	14,800 km	18% Cost Penalty. Reaching the periphery required more fuel/time
Patient coverage (Migrants)	450 individuals	2,800 individuals	+522% Coverage. The RAI model actively targeted the excluded demographic
Cases detected (early stage)	85 cases	310 cases	3.6 × Improvement. Early detection prevented secondary transmission
Gini coefficient (wait time)	0.65 (High Inequality)	0.32 (Moderate Inequality)	Fairness Improvement. Service distribution was significantly more equitable
Data privacy violations	N/A (Data not used)	0 (Proven)	Differential Privacy ($\varepsilon = 1.5$) prevented re-identification

denial of life-saving resources). In the context of Smart Cities, an algorithm that ignores a migrant slum is not just biased; it is an agent of structural violence.

Policymakers must recognize that neutrality is a fallacy. An AI system that maximizes efficiency within an unequal society will simply optimize inequality. Therefore, "Affirmative Action" must be coded into the algorithmic logic (as demonstrated by our λ parameter).

7.2 Data Sovereignty and the "Right to be Forgotten"

For migrant populations, data visibility is a double-edged sword. While visibility brings healthcare, it also brings the risk of surveillance.

- The Risk: If the geolocation data of illegal immigrant settlements is shared with the police or land revenue department, it could lead to eviction drives. This would permanently destroy trust in public health initiatives.
- The Policy Fix: We propose a "Purpose Limitation Protocol." Legislation must mandate that data collected for public health cannot be cross-referenced with criminal or civil registries. Furthermore, migrants must have a specific "Right to be Forgotten"—once the health crisis (e.g., pandemic) is over, the granular location data of their settlements must be purged from the system.

7.3 The Role of the "Algorithmic Auditor"

To govern these powerful systems, cities need a new institutional role: the Algorithmic Auditor. This independent body would be responsible for:

1. Pre-Deployment Vetting: Checking the training data for representational gaps (as per Sect. 5.6).
2. Continuous Monitoring: Tracking the Gini Coefficient of service delivery in real-time.
3. Redressal: Acting as the ombudsman for communities who feel they have been "redlined" by the smart city logic.

7.4 Sustainability and Scalability

The RAI-MH framework supports the United Nations Sustainable Development Goals (SDGs), specifically SDG 3 (Good Health) and SDG 11 (Sustainable Cities and Communities). By integrating the migrant workforce into the preventative health grid, the city reduces the long-term economic burden on its tertiary hospitals. A healthy migrant workforce ensures the continuity of the urban infrastructure projects they build, creating a virtuous economic cycle that justifies the initial investment in Responsible AI.

8 Conclusion

The 21st-century Smart City stands at a crossroads. It can evolve into a digital panopticon that serves only the documented elite, or it can become a platform for radical inclusion. This chapter has argued that the current trajectory of "blind optimization" risks creating a permanent underclass of the "algorithmically invisible."

We identified the trilemma of digital, administrative, and trust deficits that exclude migrant populations from modern healthcare. In response, we proposed the Responsible AI Framework for Migrant Health (RAI-MH). This framework fundamentally re-engineers the Smart City stack. It uses privacy-preserving proxies to see the invisible, fairness-constrained algorithms to route resources equitably, and dialect-native interfaces to listen to the voiceless.

Future Scope

The journey does not end here. The next frontier is Federated Learning, which would allow models to be trained on patient data *on the edge device* (e.g., a health worker's tablet) without the data ever leaving the slum. This would offer the ultimate guarantee of privacy. Furthermore, this framework can be extended beyond healthcare to other domains of exclusion, such as access to rations, education, and legal aid.

Ultimately, a city is only as "Smart" as its ability to care for its most vulnerable residents. Responsible AI provides the blueprint to build that city.

References

Arora, P. (2019). *The Next Billion Users: Digital Life Beyond the West.* Harvard University Press.

Allam, Z., & Jones, D. S. (2020). "On the Coronavirus (COVID-19) Outbreak and the Smart City Network: Universal Data Sharing Standards Coupled with Artificial Intelligence (AI) to Benefit Urban Health Monitoring and Management." *Healthcare*, 8(1), 46.

Benjamin, R. (2019). *Race After Technology: Abolitionist Tools for the New Jim Code.* Polity.

Combi, C., Pozzani, G., & Pozzi, G. (2016). "Telemedicine for Developing Countries: A Survey and Some Design Issues." *Applied Clinical Informatics*, 7(4), 1025-1050.

Corburn, J., & Sverdlik, A. (2017). "Slum upgrading: Can it improve health and equity for the urban poor?" *American Journal of Public Health*, 107(9), 1362-1365.

Chakraborty, P., Majumder, S., & Samanta, T. (2020). "Migration and Health in India: A Study of the Literature." *Indian Journal of Public Health*, 64(2), 105.

Crawford, K. (2021). *Atlas of AI: Power, Politics, and the Planetary Costs of Artificial Intelligence.* Yale University Press.

Dash, S., Lahiri, P., & Mitra, S. (2021). "A Review on Blockchain in Healthcare: Application, Challenges, and Future Trends." *International Journal of Wireless Information Networks*, 28, 1-17.

Dwork, C. (2008). "Differential privacy: A survey of results." *International Conference on Theory and Applications of Models of Computation*, 1–19. Springer.

Eubanks, V. (2018). *Automating Inequality: How High-Tech Tools Profile, Police, and Punish the Poor.* St. Martin's Press.

Floridi, L., Cowls, J., Beltrametti, M., Chatila, R., Chazerand, P., Dignum, V.,... & Vayena, E. (2018). "AI4People—An ethical framework for a good AI society." *Minds and Machines*, 28(4), 689-707.

Francis, S. F. V., Gopi, P., Sarveshwaran, V., & Ponnupillai, A. (2024). An intelligent system using deep learning-based link quality prediction and optimization enabled secure communication in UAV network. *Cybernetics and Systems*, *55*(8), 2013-2040.

Giffinger, R., Fertner, C., Kramar, H., Kalasek, R., Pichler-Milanović, N., & Meijers, E. (2007). *Smart cities: Ranking of European medium-sized cities.* Vienna: Centre of Regional Science.

Ginsberg, J., Mohebbi, M. H., Patel, R. S., Brammer, L., Smolinski, M. S., & Brilliant, L. (2009). "Detecting influenza epidemics using search engine query data." *Nature*, 457(7232), 1012-1014.

Government of India. (2017). *Economic Survey of India 2016–17: India on the Move and Churning: New Evidence.* Ministry of Finance, New Delhi.

Hossain, M. S., & Muhammad, G. (2019). "Emotion-Aware Connected Healthcare Big Data Towards 5G." *IEEE Internet of Things Journal*, 6(6), 2346-2353.

International Institute for Population Sciences (IIPS). (2021). *National Family Health Survey (NFHS-5), 2019–21: India Report.* Mumbai: IIPS.

Jobin, A., Ienca, M., & Vayena, E. (2019). "The global landscape of AI ethics guidelines." *Nature Machine Intelligence*, 1(9), 389-399.

Kusner, M. J., Loftus, J., Russell, C., & Silva, R. (2017). "Counterfactual fairness." *Advances in Neural Information Processing Systems*, 30.

Kitchin, R. (2014). "The real-time city? Big data and smart urbanism." *GeoJournal*, 79(1), 1-14.

Mittelstadt, B. D., Allo, P., Taddeo, M., Wachter, S., & Floridi, L. (2016). "The ethics of algorithms: Mapping the debate." *Big Data & Society*, 3(2).

Obermeyer, Z., Powers, B., Vogeli, C., & Mullainathan, S. (2019). "Dissecting racial bias in an algorithm used to manage the health of populations." *Science*, 366(6464), 447-453.

Pramanik, M. I., Lau, R. Y., Demirkan, H., & Azad, M. A. K. (2017). "Smart health: Big data enabled health paradigm within smart cities." *Expert Systems with Applications*, 87, 370-383.

Rajasekar, V., Predić, B., Saracevic, M., Elhoseny, M., Karabasevic, D., Stanujkic, D., & Jayapaul, P. (2022). Enhanced multimodal biometric recognition approach for smart cities based on an optimized fuzzy genetic algorithm. *Scientific Reports*, *12*(1), 622.

Rathore, M. M., Paul, A., Ahmad, A., & Jeon, G. (2018). "IoT-Based Health Monitoring Architecture for Smart Cities Using Big Data Analytics." *IEEE Communications Magazine*, 56(2), 2-10.

Reiter, P. (2001). "Climate change and mosquito-borne disease." *Environmental Health Perspectives*, 109(suppl 1), 141-161.

Silva, B. M., Rodrigues, J. J., de la Torre Diez, I., Lopez-Coronado, M., & Saleem, K. (2015). "Mobile-health: A review of current state in 2015." *Journal of Biomedical Informatics*, 56, 265-272.

Solanas, A., Patsakis, C., Conti, M., Vlachos, I. S., Ramos, V., Falcone, F.,... & Martinez-Balleste, A. (2014). "Smart health: a context-aware health paradigm within smart cities." *IEEE Communications Magazine*, 52(8), 74-81

Stop TB Partnership. (2021). *Key Populations Brief: Refugees, Internally Displaced Populations, and Migrants*. Geneva: WHO.

Subramanian, S. V., Smith, G. D., & Subramanyam, M. (2006). "Indigenous health and socioeconomic status in India." *PLoS Medicine*, 3(10), e421.

Taddeo, M., & Floridi, L. (2018). "How AI can be a force for good." *Science*, 361(6404), 751-752.

UN-Habitat. (2022). *World Cities Report 2022: Envisaging the Future of Cities*. Nairobi: United Nations.

United Nations Department of Economic and Social Affairs (UN DESA). (2018). *World Urbanization Prospects: The 2018 Revision*. New York: United Nations.

Vlahov, D., Freudenberg, N., Proietti, F., Ompad, D., Quinn, A., Nandi, V., & Galea, S. (2007). Urban as a determinant of health. *Journal of Urban Health*, 84(3), 16-26.

World Health Organization (WHO). (2016). *Global Report on Urban Health: Equitable, Healthier Cities for Sustainable Development*. Geneva: WHO.

World Bank. (2020). *Data for Better Lives: World Development Report 2021*. Washington, DC: World Bank.

Zuboff, S. (2019). *The Age of Surveillance Capitalism: The Fight for a Human Future at the New Frontier of Power*. PublicAffairs.

Building Trust in Smart Cities: Responsible AI and Blockchain for IoT–Edge–Twin Integration

Cynthia Jayapal

Abstract

Convergence of emerging technologies such as internet of things (IoT), digital twins and edge artificial intelligence in today's urban infrastructure is redefining the development of smart cities. Integration of these technologies helps build a smart city ecosystem that is capable of sensing, analyzing and making real-time decisions for providing better citizen specific services. Smart city governance spans across domains such as intelligent transportation, smart grids, healthcare, environmental monitoring, citizen safety and e-governance. Large volume of data generated from multiple sensors, actuators and devices challenge the centralized cloud processing. Hence, the data acquired is filtered in edge using federated AI intelligence. By integrating the digital twin technology, a virtual simulation of any cyber physical system or asset is done for predictive maintenance and swift decision making. In order to provide a sustainable smart city governance, a technology framework that integrates responsible AI features such as accountability, transparency and explainability is proposed. The framework proposed ensures trust by integrating blockchain to store the data acquired in an immutable, distributed ledger with timestamp and also to provide role-based access, audit trails and authorization and authentication. The technology synergy proposed in this chapter paves way for a transparent, sustainable and inclusive smart city governance.

Keywords

Smart cities · Internet of things · Edge AI · Digital twin · Responsible AI · Blockchain trust · Ethical governance

1 Introduction

Developing countries are creating smart cities integrated with digital technologies in order to enhance sustainability, citizen experience, optimize resources and efficient e-governance. Every urban city exercise cyber physical system for real-time decision making with integration of advanced technology. Convergence of technologies like internet of things (IoT), edge AI, predictive analytics and digital twin is redefining the urban landscape by provisioning automatic responses based on real time data availability.

IoT and industrial IoT devices help in sensing real time environmental and physical parameters from different cyber physical systems such as intelligent traffic, healthcare, smart grids, water distribution, garbage collection and public safety systems. The data acquired are either processed in edge or fog or cloud storages or federated environments to transmit either all of the data captured or filtered data for further analysis or prediction. These reports are used for e-governance. However, this large scale deployment of IoT devices pose additional challenges due to large volume and velocity. It is also exposed to various cyber attacks. In order to overcome these challenges paradigm shift from centralized to decentralized processing is adopted.

Edge AI is a disruptive technology that relocates the computational intelligence from cloud to edge where the data is generated. The data acquired from edge nodes are processed in embedded processors for providing real time inference, detect any anomaly and to make context-

C. Jayapal (✉)
School of Computer Science and Engineering, RV University, Bengaluru, India
e-mail: cynthiaj@rvu.edu.in

V. Sarveshwaran et al. (eds.), *Responsible AI for Smart Cities*, Sustainable Artificial Intelligence-Powered Applications,
https://doi.org/10.1007/978-3-032-26901-0_6

aware decision making. Edge processing also helps in reducing latency, enhances network resource utilization and improves privacy and trust. Federated processing further aids in providing distributed processing and training and reduces centralized day = ta processing risks (Khan et al. 2022).

Digital twin is a modern technology that uses the features of augmented reality (AR) and virtual reality (VR) to simulate, visualize and perform predictive analytics. A digital twin represents every asset present in real time environment. The real time IoT system is integrated to virtual model in a digital twin for remote monitoring. Simulations can be performed to predict failure situations by changing the real-world parameters. Digital twins use real time data to for actual predictive maintenance. They serve as a control system including edge AI and actual IoT systems.

This chapter proposes an urban intelligence architecture that incorporates IoT data acquisition layer, edge computing layer, digital twin simulation layer and governance feedback layer. Smart city governance utilized AI for various model training, analysis and prediction. Considering the sustainability and citizen trust, responsible AI (RAI) is recommended in order to ensure transparency, inclusivity, fairness, accountability and explainability (Dignum 2019). Integrating IoT, edge, digital twin in smart city governance involving data collection, aggregation, analytics, prediction and authentic report generation involving devices and stake holders who are heterogeneous and distributed needs a trust platform. Blockchain enabled trust framework is proposed in order to ensure integrity, role-based access control, immutable recording of transactions with time stamping and audit trails.

This chapter aims to provide the following:

- Comprehensive understanding of integration of IoT, edge and digital twin for effective smart city governance.
- Justify the use of responsible AI for sustainability.
- Demonstrate how blockchain is integrated to provide trust and resilience in smart city governance.

2 Urban Data Ecosystems for Smart City Governance

Urban cities have a digitalized eco system with a complex cyber physical data framework. Urban cities have continuous, heterogeneous data generated from multiple digital infrastructures that are aggregated for real time decision making. The data collected lays the foundation for effective e-governance.

2.1 Data as the Foundation of Smart City Governance

Continuous stream of data is generated from multiple digital infrastructures. The data collected from sensors fixed in environment is used to measure the pollutants present in air is used for protecting citizen health by taking preventive actions. Data from smart meters is used to analyse the demand for electricity or water and accordingly schedule the fair distribution. Data from patients are used by health care centers to monitor and protect health of citizens. The data collected from industries are used for effective increase in productive by fostering preventive maintenance and disaster management. The data collected from vehicles and traffic signals is used for intelligent transportation by controlling traffic and preventing congestion.

Urban city planning and effective governance relies on these data collected for effective prediction, anomaly detection and resource optimization (Batty 2021). AI enabled decision making aids in efficient data aggregation, noise reduction, model training and prediction using the raw data (Kitchin 2021).

2.2 IoT–Edge–Twin Synergy for Data Governance

Data governance evolves in each phase. It starts with data acquisition. Heterogeneous data spread across urban city has to be collected in real time. Different sensors such as temperature, humidity, PM 2.5, cameras and garbage levels are acquired (Ng and Wakenshaw 2017). Edge nodes perform the role of data aggregation and filtering with aid of AI. Centralized processing has limitations of latency and network bandwidth to transmit real time images and videos. Hence edge nodes aggregates the data collected, performs noise removal, distributed AI model training and federated computing to do edge analytics and notification. The aggregated data with meta data such as context information is send to cloud for further centralized analytics, model training, prediction and visualization reports. The centralized AI processing is still required in order to avoid skewed training of model for certain geographic location or context (Khan et al. 2022).

Digital twin is used to simulate the real world parameters in remote for virtual representation of physical systems. Visualization, predictive maintenance and scenario simulation for unforeseen circumstances are done at this end. The final reports are used for e-governance with aid of responsible AI to ensure sustainability and transparency. The data stored from multiple stake holders need to be stored and shared only after ensuring privacy and trust. Blockchain supplements e-governance by storing data records in ab immutable distributed digital ledger ensuring transparency, trust and security.

Figure 1 illustrates the smart city governance wherein the sensor data acquired is collected by the governance regulatory authority to perform traffic management, pollution control, smart parking, data analytics and prediction for citizen wellbeing. This lifecycle enables smart cities to progress from reactive to proactive governance.

3 Internet of Things (IoT) for Smart Cities

Smart cities are connected by internet of things (IoT) that forms backbone. The IoT comprises of sensors, actuators, edge devices and gateways that aids in monitoring the smart city. IoT network aids in monitoring traffic flow, health parameters and air quality for effective e-governance.

3.1 IoT Architecture and Urban Infrastructure Integration

IoT architectures for smart city governance include the following.

1. **Sensing Layer**

The sensors in sensor layer sense various environment parameters such as temperature, pollution, humidity, images, videos and GPS location. This helps to monitor the traffic flow health condition, smart meter energy usage. The edge devices acquire these data and are either processed in edge layer or are forwarded to cloud through the network layer.

2. **Network Layer**

The data captured from sensing layer is communicated to the network layer via network protocols such as LoRaWAN, Zigbee, Wi-Fi and MQTT. The protocol is chosen based on the distance, data rate, speed, bandwidth requirement so as to have high reliability, low latency and scalable connectivity (Gubbi et al. 2013).

3. **Middleware Layer**

The middleware layer captures the data received from network layer to provide device management, interoperability administration to provide fog computation or integration with edge or cloud platforms. This layer manages data received from heterogeneous network to manage inconsistent data.

4. **Application Layer**

The application layer is used to monitor the measured parameters and perform e-governance by performing analytics and visualisation dashboard. This helps in prediction and proactive or reactive maintenance.

3.2 IoT Applications Across Urban Domains

Smart Mobility and Intelligent Transportation Systems (ITS).

Intelligent transport systems are aimed at achieving smart mobility in urban cities. The vehicles are currently enabled with Vehicular Ad hoc Network (VANET) capability for communication from Vehicle to Infrastructure (V2I), Infrastructure to Vehicles (I2V) and Vehicle to Vehicle (V2V). The sensors and cameras in the vehicle capture the real time environmental parameters like disaster occurrence, traffic flow, vehicle congestion and prevent vehicles from reaching the disaster area (Chen et al. 2020).

3.2.1 Smart Energy and Utilities

Energy is most important resource which is depleting and is not able to cater to growing population. Hence it is very important to measure the need and consumption, IoT enabled smart meters are required to measure consumption of electricity, gas and water. This data acquired is used for performing data analytics, predictive maintenance and load balancing, preventing wastage and ensuring fair allocation.

3.2.2 Environmental Monitoring

In growing urban cities, pollution is a serious concern causing major health hazard. It is important to measure constantly the presence of pollutants such as No2, greenhouse gases, PM2.5, carbon content in air in order to create awareness to general public in order to take preventive measures for citizens with chronic breathing issues and governance models to plan traffic and other propose other measures to avoid massive pollution and provide healthy environment to citizens.

3.2.3 Healthcare and Public Welfare

Sensors are implanted in patients with chronic illness and heart issues to monitor health parameters in real time. This helps to monitor the patient and trigger alerts whenever

Fig. 1 Smart city e-governance

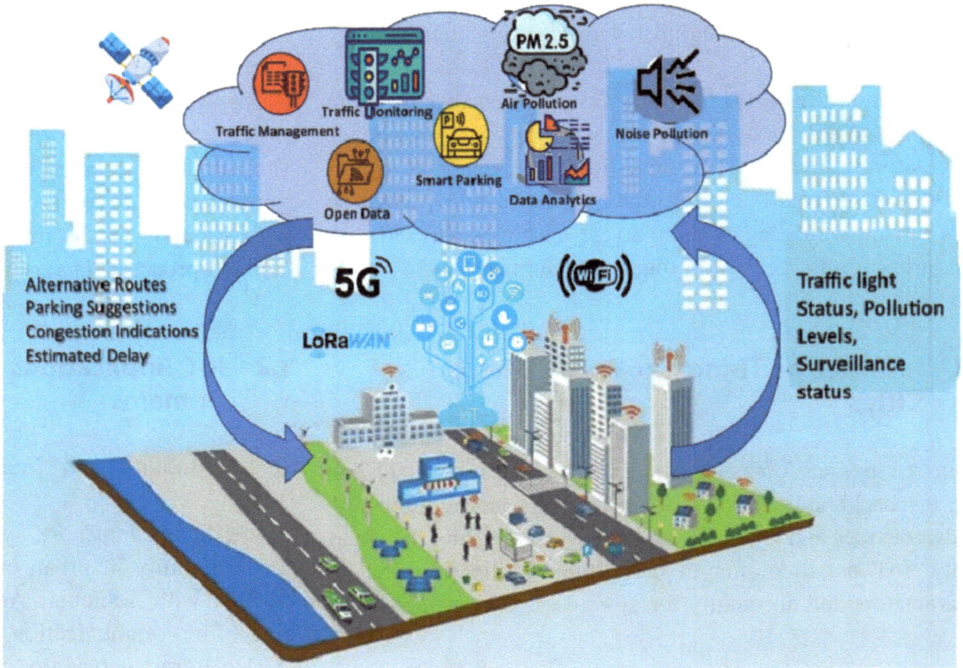

the vital parameter readings crosses the threshold limits. These wearable and telemedicine sensors are increasingly becoming prevalent (Aman et al. 2019).

3.2.4 Public Safety and Surveillance

In order to provide a safety living community, cameras are fixed in all public places and communities to continuously monitor the safety and deduct any cause of crimes after occurrence. The IoT powered surveillance enables rapid incident response.

3.3 Communication Protocols and Interoperability

The communication protocols used for IoT are MQTT, OPC-UA, NGSI-LD and other wireless protocols such WI-FI, Zigbee and Bluetooth low energy. These standard protocols enable consistent, scalable and secure communication between various heterogeneous IoT devices. Few major protocols are as follows.

MQTT (Message Queuing Telemetry Transport)

It is a very light weight protocol that enables communication among battery constraint IoT devices that operate in an unreliable condition. It enables transmission of real time sensor data to edge or cloud platforms (Banks and Gupta 2014).

OPC-UA (Open Platform Communications Unified Architecture)

This protocol is used in Industrial IoT environments where high security and data modelling is required. This protocol can also be used for urban city resource measurement and monitoring such as energy or water distribution (Mahoney and Ward 2020).

Constrained Application Protocol (CoAP)

CoAP is an application layer protocol designed for battery constrained low power devices that operates over UDP protocol on a request-response basis. This protocol was helpful in multicast protocol Because of its light weight nature it is effective for battery constrained IoT nodes deployed in large numbers across urban cities.

LoRaWAN (Long Range Wide Area Network)

LoRaWAN is a low powered communication protocol that is used for transmission of small amount of data over long distance. This protocol is used widely for smart city applications such as smart parking, waste management and environment monitoring where the devices operate with battery and transmit less data.

Narrowband IoT (NB-IoT)

This NB-IoT is a protocol developed for cellular networks in order to provide large scale IoT communication with LTE network as a backbone infrastructure. It is used for transmitting continuous real time data such as smart metering, traffic monitoring and other applications that demand reliability with less latency.

NGSI-LD (Next Generation Service Interface—Linked Data)

NGSI-LD protocol is used where context-based data transmission is required in urban context demanding semantics interoperability. This protocol can be used for digital twin synchronization for IioT or e-governance applications. It is used where cross domain analytics is required wand edge intelligence for real time decision making is demanded.

4 Edge AI for Distributed Urban Intelligence

Smart city applications are increasingly using IoT sensors that capture real-time continuous data. It is technically difficult to transmit these large volumes of data to cloud platform for further processing because of network bandwidth and reliability to take real time decisions. Hence, edge computing is preferred over centralised cloud computing. The heterogeneity of IoT data is also a major challenge to provide secured data transmission. Edge computing merged with AI intelligence termed as Edge-AI is increasingly being used to provide decentralised intelligence closer to the source of data. This Edge AI assures context—based access control and role—based trust and authentication within the short range of data source. Edge AI also enables real time decision making, prediction and preventive maintenance for effective governance.

4.1 Edge AI

Edge AI infrastructures typically involve a three-tier architecture.

1. **Device Layer**

The IoT sensor captures data from the environment such as images, video, environment parameters, GPS logs. The edge device is embedded with light weight AI models such as TinyML that performs basic data filtering, threshold—based detection, binary classification and basic computation (Banbury et al. 2021).

2. **Edge Layer**

The edge layer comprises of edge gateways, minor data centers and mini servers which are meant to execute light weight ML algorithms that are capable of making inference based on the training of optimised ML models. These models perform basic pre processing, filtering, noise reduction, security enforcement and anomaly deduction.

3. **Cloud Layer**

Even though the basic tasks are performed in edge, still centralised training and large scale analytics can be performed only in cloud side. Hence the data must be forwarded to cloud for long term storage, large scale data training, knowledge prediction and coordination amongst multiple edge nodes (Shi et al. 2016).

4.2 Benefits of Edge AI in Smart Cities

4.2.1 Low Latency and High Responsiveness

Centralized cloud servers have limitations for transmission of continuous IoT data streaming. The delay for transmission is also high. Wherein, edge computing reduces the network latency and increases responsiveness. This facilitates real time decision making for smart city applications such as disaster management, IIoT applications, Intelligent Transport systems (Li et al. 2018).

4.2.2 Network Bandwidth Efficiency

Transmission of continuous real time data including images and videos requires consistent large bandwidth for transmission to remote cloud which incurs high cost and is also inefficient reducing throughput and reliability. Edge AI reduces the total cost of filtering, pre-processing and performing real time analytics and sends only meta data to the cloud for centralized analytics and prediction (Zhang et al. 2020).

4.2.3 Enhanced Security and Trust

IIoT data transmitted to the cloud over the network using various wireless protocols is subjected to security breaches such as hacking, privacy, and trust. The owner of data does not have control of with whom their data is shared by the cloud administrator. Edge AI prevents such breaches as the private data is kept with the owner preventing sharing of sensitive data of patients and industry ensures data privacy and security by preventing sending of all personal data of patients or industry. This ensures stakeholder trust and legal compliance (Khan et al. 2022).

4.2.4 Robustness and Sustainability

Edge processing also ensures robustness and is resilient. This is very much essential to make real time decision to ensure public safety and emergency responses. Proactive alerts helps in continuity of operations. This reduces computation overhead of cloud servers promoting sustainability and energy efficiency (Strubell et al. 2019).

4.2.5 Support for Responsible AI

Cloud processing does not ensure transparency. Responsible AI (Shahat et al. 2021) at edge facilitates more transparency as it can enable local audit, tracing and access control through technology such as blockchain.

4.3 Federated Edge Intelligence: Privacy-Preserving Urban Analytics

Federated learning and federated intelligence in edge aids in distributed training of AI models across edge devices. Every edge node can train a model locally with its private data. The updates of the model are sent to central aggregator where a global model is updated and is again shared with the edge nodes. The centralised training is infeasible using sensitive data that a stake holder will not share. This approach has the advantages of privacy preservation, reduced network bandwidth and facilitates cross-organizational collaboration. There are works that have demonstrated the use of federated learning for anomaly detection, prediction and forecasting (Velliangiri et al. 2021).

4.4 Edge AI Applications in Smart Cities

Few of edge AI applications for smart cities are as follows.

Intelligent Transport System

Using federated AI the edge nodes acquire data from cameras to perform real-time classification, traffic flow and congestion detection, adaptive traffic management by changing signals dynamically, performing pedestrian analytics (Chen et al. 2020).

Smart Energy

Energy demand and distribution is a major challenge in urban cities. Edge AI be used to detect faults, sense and predict future fluctuations, automate energy resource distribution as per demand and perform orchestration (Mahmoud et al. 2020).

Public Surveillance

Edge processing aids swift detection of threat to public safety from data captured from surveillance cameras by enabling real-time weapon detection, fire and flood detection, Local edge processing allows real-time weap crowd management in public gatherings (Roman et al. 2018).

Assistive Technologies

Assistive technologies have multiple wearable devices with implanted or embedded sensors. The vital data from assistive devices or healthcare monitoring devices are captured by the edge devices located near to the patient. This data can be used to send alert messages either to the care taker of the patient or nearest health care center for preventive action. This data can also be used for providing proactive health care before occurrence of any distress.

5 Digital Twins for Smart City Governance

Digital twin (DT) is a virtual representation of real world physical objects, process or system. The digital twin is synchronized with real world data from actual counterpart. This DT has emerged as a disruptive technology in evolution of smart city. The DT can be used for e-governance for applications such as water management, smart energy or IioT applications for real time monitoring, analytics or prediction. These twins can be used to monitor either macro- or micro-level assets of smart city (Batty 2021).

The characteristics of digital twin includes real-time data synchronization, dual interaction to and from the physical systems, context awareness of the behaviour of data monitored, performing predictive and prescriptive analytics for future scenarios with recommendations and also enable building a close feedback loop with IoT.

5.1 Digital Twin Architecture for Smart Cities

A digital twin architecture typically involves five core layers:

1. **Data Acquisition Layer**

The physical layer is data acquisition layer that includes data acquired from every physical sensor from smart cities including buildings, traffic lights, vehicles, hospitals, government infrastructures, pipelines, smart meters. This also includes spatio-temporal meta data and behavioural (Krishnamoorthi et al. 2021).

2. **Data Aggregation Layer**

The data aggregation layer operates in edge devices by aggregating the data received from sensors and other third part APIs (Gupta and Gupta 2022). Central aggregation can be performed at cloud server. The protocols such as MQTT,

NGSI-LD and OPC-UA are used for data exchange and provide inter operability.

3. **Simulation Layer**

The simulation layer operates in the digital twin where models are simulated and trained. Agent-based simulations are also done. Advanced ML model is used to model complex dynamics of a smart city (Lee et al. 2015).

4. **Analytics Layer**

The analytics layer can be activated either in edge, DT or Cloud. In DT the AI/ML algorithms perform forecasting, anomaly detection, optimization, and real-time decision approximation. Edge AI feeds pre-processed insights to the DT, reducing latency and bandwidth costs.

5. **Visualization and Control Layer**

Interactive dashboards, 3D/VR environments, and simulation consoles enable planners and decision-makers to explore various scenarios and outcomes.

5.2 Applications of Digital Twins for Smart Cities

DTs provide real time simulation environment for remote monitoring of vital smart city applications to provide strategic planning and operational intelligence. Any urban assets or systems can be represented virtually to monitor performance and think of alternative governance policies.

Intelligence transport systems are simulated by creating a digital twin depicting real time traffic flows, pedestrian movements, congestion avoidance, disaster and accident management. This enables real time traffic management, emergency rerouting for ambulance and predictive decision making.

Digital twin for water and energy requirement can be simulated to monitor the consumption, availability, requirement and distribution. This is used for effective planning of future demand supply optimization and proactively maintain infrastructure reducing losses, and increase resilience.

DT can be used for effective monitoring of health care centers for any emergency response. DT combined with RAI can model hospital capacity, pandemic spread like COVI, ambulance allocation and rerouting by combining with traffic twin and optimize any resource allocation for emergencies.

DT can simulate all physical infrastructures in smart cities to optimize heating, air conditioning, ventilation and air conditioning. By modeling usage patterns and demand prediction. This can be used by smart city governance authority to plan city expansion, infrastructure investments and urban planning.

6 IoT-Edge-Digital Twin Integrated Architecture for Smart Cities

Smart city Governance demands an integrated framework that comprises a technical stack combining multiple technologies. It requires the data acquired from various IoT sensors to be aggregated and filtered at edge layer and then monitored in real time by remote digital twin. This enables acquiring real time insights for fast analytics, prediction and sustainable governance. This facilitates a real-time feedback loop for effective maintenance and proactive prediction.

6.1 IoT-Edge–Twin Convergence

The IoT-Edge-Twin convergence is conceptualized as a cyber physical system in which,

- IoT enables device level sensing, monitoring and actuation.
- Edge AI enables filtering, aggregation, federated processing, model training, analytics and prediction ensuring privacy and trust.
- Digital twin provides virtual simulation of environmental parameters in real-time for proactive maintenance, alert and prediction.

This combined synergy builds a resilience smart city governance system that is sustainable (Lee et al. 2015).

6.2 IoT-Edge-DT Integrated System Architecture

6.2.1 IoT Sensing and Actuation Layer

This layer senses various environmental parameters and actuates the associated alert system. This sensing and actuation effectively monitors the urban infrastructure such as transportation, energy grid, buildings, health care, traffic flow and industries. This layer acquires various heterogeneous data from multiple vendors at different velocity and frequency.

6.2.2 Edge AI Layer

Edge AI layer enables edge processing combined with edge intelligence performing data filtering, aggregation, cleaning, classification, anomaly detection, processing, analytics and prediction. This layer ensures security and trust by preventing sensitive data to be shared to cloud servers. Edge AI enables high responsiveness (Shi et al. 2016). Edge processing reduces latency and optimizes network resources by sending only the aggregated or meta data rather than continuous streaming of real time IoT data including text, images and videos.

6.2.3 Communication Layer

The data aggregated or meta data has to be sent either to cloud servers or digital twin using effective communication protocol depending on nature of communication, type of messages, volume, security demand. This layer facilitates interoperability across platforms. The protocol used can be MQTT, OPC-UA, NGSI-LD or any other wireless communication protocols and wired protocols.

6.2.4 Digital Twin Simulation Layer

The digital twin simulation layer receives the real time data transmitted by edge nodes with real time synchronization for effective system monitoring, prediction and forecasting. Digital twin are used for risk-free testing risk-free scenario testing, optimized resource allocation and real time visualization. The digital twin combined with augmented and virtual reality features can provide better visualisation experience of real time environmental parameters.

6.2.5 Governance Layer

The governance layer is user or application layer with dashboards and automated controls. This is used for smart city governance providing a better quality of life for urban citizens by providing a consolidated holistic view of the realistic scenarios. It provides a better quality of life by using AI enabled model optimization to improve the quality of lifestyle. It is used to provide alerts to stakeholders on disaster occurrence, traffic congestion, pollution levels, optimized decision making, and planning. Responsible AI adds an ethical insight to decision making, building trust on the system with more transparency and accountability (Dignum 2019). Figure 2 illustrates integration of ioT, edge and digital twin for smart city governance.

6.3 Responsible AI as the Middleware of Trust

The middleware for the synergy is responsible AI as it ensures transparency and trust which is essential for successful deployment of any heterogeneous system involving multiple stake holders. The key features of responsible AI are as follows:

- Explainability—The edge decisions made are transparent and are interpretable. Anomaly thresholds are defined

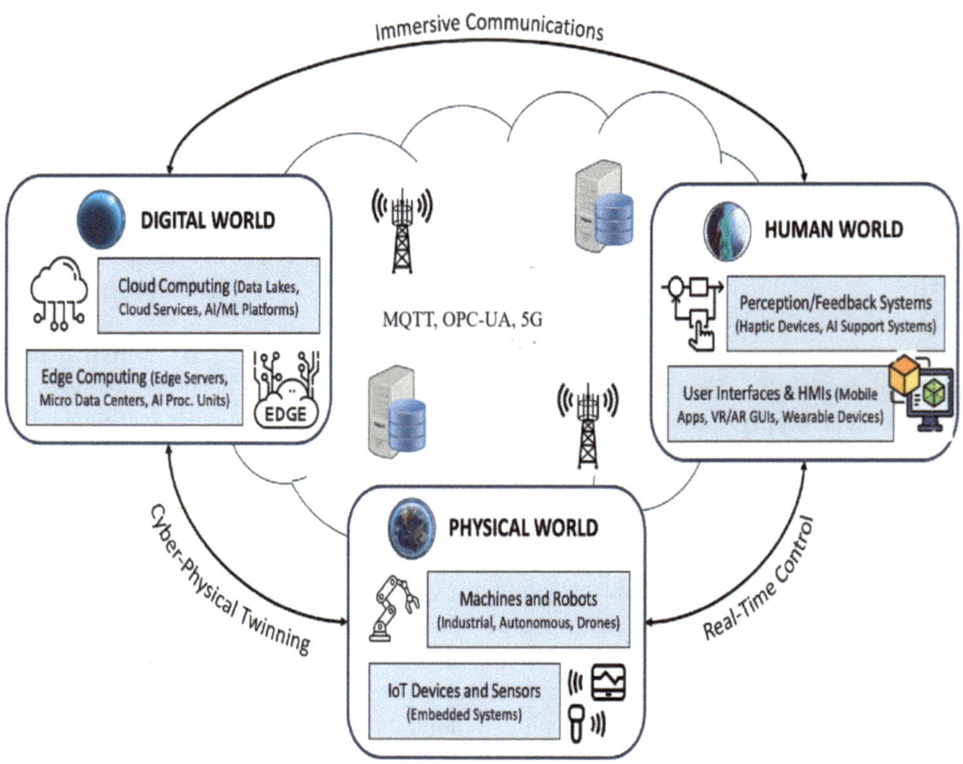

Fig. 2 IoT-Edge-Digital Twin System model for Smart City Governance

and standard models trained on large scale generic context sensitive data are used.

- Fairness—AI models are not trained only by the edge data of a specific system, but rather the model is shared to central cloud.
- Inclusive Governance—As edge nodes are involved in training the model it paves way for inclusive governance of multiple stake holders and trains data along with the context.
- Privacy and Trust—Reducing data movement from source of generation instills trust and privacy amongst the stake holders (Khan et al. 2022).

6.4 Blockchain as a Trust Layer in IoT–Edge–Twin Integration

Blockchain has features built in to ensure trust, security, privacy and transparency. It supplements authentication, authorization and integrity with its architecture. The following are associated traits of blockchain,

6.4.1 Immutable Record

Every data fetched from IoT sensors are immutable. The records are timestamped Each IoT event can be securely timestamped and recorded. These records are stored in a distributed ledger.

6.4.2 Decentralized Identity and Access Management

Blockchain enables decentralized identity and access management by using a wallet. The credentials are not given by centralized entity but are rather issued from wallets. The smart contracts automate access rules. The users have control over their identity termed as Self sovereign identity. The certificate authority issues the certificate to a user's wallet that is linked to the users digital identity. Whenever a verification is required, the user presents his digital identity without sharing any other proof. This is termed as Zero Knowledge Proof. This ensures trust and integrity.

6.4.3 Edge Model Verification

Blockchain ensures that edge models are authentic from any tampering. Inter Planetary File System (IPFS) can be used to store the AI models and the hash of same can be stored in blockchain. The blockchain provides an audit trail which prevents tampering and unauthorized access to the model.

6.4.4 Distributed Access Control

Blockchain enables all stakeholders to have role-based access to data stored in blockchain. This access control policy is defined in the smart contract and hence there is no centralized delegation of access. This build trusts among various stake holders, authorities and administrators.

6.5 Challenges in IoT–Edge–Digital Twin Integration

There are multiple technical challenges foreseen in integration of multiple technologies such as heterogeneity, latency, security, scalability and governance.

- Urban applications that are synchronized in real time with the DT demands low latency for real-time decision making. Intermittent connectivity results in delay in processing and hence remains a major challenge.
- The IoT devices spread across the smart city are heterogeneous in nature. They have different computational abilities, communication protocols and security features. Standardizing this heterogeneity demands an edge middleware that is capable of translation. Edge processing must handle the scalability challenge by performing edge aggregation.
- Even though edge computing increases privacy and trust, the data processed in edge is subjected to security challenges such as DoS attack, malware injection, hardware and firmware protection with strong Intrusion Detection Techniques.
- Smart city governance has unique challenges adhering to the law of the land and ensuring privacy, authorization, ownership and regulatory compliance. Ethical data sharing must be ensured.

7 Blockchain-Enabled Trust and Governance for Smart Cities

Smart cities digital eco system has continuous flow of data from IoT networks, edge network, digital twins and cloud platforms. This synergy demands real time responsiveness but is subjected to serious security threats. Hence it is important to prevent data tampering, authorization, identity management and access control. In urban governance decision making is automated and is distributed.

Blockchain technology is the best fit for the urban governance for providing trust, authentication, verification, validation, distributed data sharing. The technology inherently embeds these features.

7.1 Blockchain Applications for Smart Cities

Blockchain is foundation for providing a trust framework for smart city governance creating a synergy of multiple technologies involved for distributed sensing, multiple stake holder participation and autonomous decision making.

Smart mobility demands vehicle identity management, trusted V2X communication in VANET environment. Storing immutable traffic violation records. Edge AI technology when integrated with blockchain can be used to store as immutable records the traffic violations, accidents and disaster detection. These records stored are available for tamper proof recording and retrieval of data used for further analytics, prediction and governance decisions.

Smart water and energy utilization can be recorded in blockchain for energy trading in decentralized, distributed environment involving multiple stakeholders. This can be used for automated billing and transparent governance policies. This eliminates any involvement of intermediaries and transaction overheads.

Blockchain distributed ledgers can also be used to store health care records, public infrastructure records, waste management, public safety, urban planning as it can be used to facilitate secure, auditable trains that ensures trust, identity management and access controls. The smart contracts can be used to automate digital warning system like water leakage, waste management, pollution control and resource allocation.

7.2 Blockchain for Responsible AI Governance

Blockchain also facilitates RAI usage for smart city governance. When AI is used for decision making transparency and explainability is required to ensure trust amongst all stakeholders. AI models influence decision making. Therefore the immutable audit trails available in distributed ledger is used to record the details of AI models used, the training data source, also the metadata depicting the context and location.

The AI decision pathway is recorded as immutable audit trails. This helps in evaluation of automated decisions to get a holistic insight on regulatory and governance policies. When a new decision is recommended by edge node or a DT the audit logs can be verified for automated decision making and anomalies can also be recorded in ledgers. This enables policy refinements and ensures preserving accountability.

The recording of meta data and context mitigates any bias and ensures fairness. This enables fairness correction leading to citizen trust. Public dashboards with verifiable records gains trust amongst stake holders and leads to acceptance by public.

8 Responsible AI Framework for Sustainable Smart Cities

Smart cities use AI for automated decision making. Use of AI involves privacy violations and bias. The need for trust, privacy, explainability, accountability and security is essential for sustainability of integrated smart city governance could be achieved through Responsible AI (RAI). RAI aims to bring fairness, transparency, explainability, privacy, data protection and human oversight that is aimed to build sustainable e-governance model that is sustainability, inclusiveness and citizen participation with trust.

8.1 Responsible AI for IoT–Edge–Twin Systems

RAI needs to be integrated in every layer of smart city governance.

8.1.1 Role of RAI in IoT Layer

IoT layer acquires a large amount of environmental and specific personal data. RAI is required for

- Data Minimization: Collect minimal data that is required to train the model or make real time decisions.
- Stakeholder Consent: Stakeholders need to be informed about the data that is being collected and with appropriate reasoning.
- Bias-Free Sensing: The IoT data acquired must not be biased only from certain IoT networks.

8.1.2 Role of RAI in Edge Layer

RAI role in edge layer must be fair, explainable and privacy preserving.

It requires

- An explainable AI model customised for edge device.
- Federated learning AI model for efficient network resource utilisation.
- Monitor bias across distributed nodes.
- Ensure robustness against tampering.

8.1.3 Role of RAI in Digital Twin Layer

The role of RAI in digital twin layer is to ensure transparency and accountability. It requires

- Transparency in DT simulation.
- Validate the data that are received by the twin.
- Context of model assumptions are documented.
- Transparent review before any automated critical action.

8.1.4 Role of RAI in Governance Layer

The role of RAI in Governance layer is for ethical decision making. It requires intervention of human at each level for

- Efficient decision making.
- Audit and evaluate the performance of any model.
- Intervention before any alert is sent.
- Democratic accountability for the decision made.

8.2 Blockchain for Responsible AI Governance

RAI features as discussed demands a technology to ensure the same. Blockchain is the distributed peer to peer network that ensures accountability and trust.

8.2.1 Transparency and Traceability

Digital ledger of a blockchain reveals details about the AI model used for execution, the data stream used for training, when a model was last updated and who had authorised a particular action (Dignum 2019).

8.2.2 Fairness and Equity

Blockchain enables fairness for decentralised decision making in order to ensure distributed decision making without any bias or manipulation of data.

8.2.3 Stakeholder Accountability

Utility providers, government agencies, private vendors, and citizens can be held accountable for their interactions with smart city infrastructure.

8.3 Institutional and Policy Frameworks for Responsible Smart Cities

Few countries and global forums have formulated guidelines for responsible AI governance frameworks for urban systems. These frameworks emphasize on human centric AI that ensures transparency, inclusiveness and sustainability. Global principles are aimed at using a controllable responsible AI that has inclusivity for long-term societal benefit. Such framework is aimed to integrate AI ethics for exchanging data across platforms with regulatory compliance and cross sector coordination.

At national level also the AI framework for smart city should ensure that responsible AI principles inculcated in order maintain operational consistency between multiple domains and jurisdictions to build trust worthy smart city governance.

8.4 Human-Centric AI Governance

RAI governance should enable human centric governance with citizens as active participants rather than being a data source. RAI Governance needs to have a transparent dashboard that informs citizens of the data collected from them and how it is utlilized to provide a better quality of life and for making Responsible smart cities must position citizens as active participants rather than passive data sources. Human-centric AI governance requires transparency, engagement, and inclusivity.

Transparency dashboards allow citizens to understand what data is collected, how AI systems influence policy decisions, and how digital twins simulate urban environments. Any misconception of trust breach. Digital literacy to citizens will enable them to engage and understand the role of AI in governance. The framework should be ethical and socially responsible to include the marginalized society and ensure they are not affected by the algorithmic decisions. Responsible AI in foundation of trust and sustainability.

9 Future Research and Emerging Opportunities

Rapid development of IoT, Edge AI and Digital Twin augmented with blockchain and Responsible AI opens new paradigm in e-governance of smart cities. Implementation of these technologies is feasible but operationalization in urban environment and legal compliance and policy decisions for e-governance is a major challenge.

Distributed collaborative intelligence across federated edge processing is much promising potential in urban environment as centralized processing will lack trust and sustainability and is not suitable for smart city data acquisition, modelling, analytics and prediction leading to effective decision making for e-governance. Heterogeneous urban data raises new research challenges in terms of bias mitigation and training of RAI models for real time prediction.

Research advances in smart mobility, distributed energy grids, autonomous infrastructure management paves pathways for multi-agent reinforcement learning. New ways for ensuring safe data exchange, coordination and ethical law reinforcement has scope for research. Blockchain provides solution for audit trails, trust, decentralized identity and access control the transaction throughput and latency for large scale urban eco system is still a challenge. Modifying blockchain protocols for federated environment is a research challenge. So light weight trust and privacy preserving protocols with minimal overhead is to be developed.

The Digital Twin systems are to evolve as an autonomous system capable of learning and adapting to real-time challenges. This should ensure inter-operability across multiple domains with un interruptive synchronization between physical and virtual twin. The DT must enable simulations for unforeseen failures in order to plan proactive smart city planning. Responsible AI has lots of scope for research to enhance the explainability, fairness and human insight to gain the trust of urban population. This EAI must be able to integrate with edge and DT environments to handle real-time synchronous data and federated AI models training that is not skewed.

Interdisciplinary research integrating multiple computing domains, ethical governance, regional policies and urban planning is expected to be an integral part of smart city innovation.

References

Aman, M. N., Snekkenes, E., & Jøsang, A. (2019). A trust-based flood early warning system. Sensors, 19(18), 3824.

Banbury, C. R., et al. (2021). Micromachine learning on edge devices: TinyML. IEEE Micro, 41(5), 23–30.

Banks, A., & Gupta, R. (2014). MQTT Version 3.1.1. OASIS Standard.

Batty, M. (2021). Digital twins for smart cities. Environment and Planning B: Urban Analytics and City Science, 48(8), 1963–1975.

Chen, X., Xu, Y., Zhang, X., & Li, W. (2020). IoT-based traffic management systems: A survey. IEEE Internet of Things Journal, 7(5), 4715–4730.

Dignum, V. (2019). Responsible Artificial Intelligence: How to Develop and Use AI in a Responsible Way. Springer.

Gubbi, J., Buyya, R., Marusic, S., & Palaniswami, M. (2013). Internet of Things (IoT): A vision, architectural elements, and future directions. Future Generation Computer Systems, 29(7), 1645–1660.

Gupta, V., & Gupta, M. (2022). Improved PSO Algorithm-Based Convolutional Neural Network Approach for Ship Detection and Classifications. *SN Computer Science*, *3*(4), 318.

Khan, L., Khan, S., & Abbas, S. (2022). Federated learning for smart city environments: Taxonomy, applications, challenges, and opportunities. IEEE Access, 10, 46735–46756.

Kitchin, R. (2021). Data Lives: How Data Are Made and Shape Our World. Bristol University Press.

Krishnamoorthi, S., Jayapaul, P., Dhanaraj, R. K., Rajasekar, V., Balusamy, B., & Islam, S. H. (2021). Design of pseudo-random number generator from turbulence padded chaotic map. *Nonlinear Dynamics*, *104*(2), 1627-1643.

Lee, J., Bagheri, B., & Kao, H. (2015). A cyber-physical systems architecture for industry and smart manufacturing. Manufacturing Letters, 3, 18–23.

Li, Y., Dai, Y., Tian, L., & Bian, K. (2018). Edge computing for smart cities: Applications, technologies, and research challenges. IEEE Communications Magazine, 56(5), 27–33.

Mahmoud, M. S., Mohamad, A., & Pan, J. (2020). Edge-based smart energy management systems in smart cities. Energy Reports, 6, 46–52.

Mahoney, W., & Ward, J. (2020). Applications of OPC-UA in industrial IoT systems. IEEE Transactions on Industrial Informatics, 16(1), 620–628.

Ng, I., & Wakenshaw, S. (2017). The Internet-of-Things: A review and research agenda for marketing. International Journal of Research in Marketing, 34(1), 3–21.

Roman, R., Najera, P., & Lopez, J. (2018). Securing the Internet of Things. Future Internet, 10(12), 114.

Shahat, E., Hyun, C. T., & Yeom, C. (2021). Digital twins and smart cities: A review of applications, challenges, and future directions. Sustainable Cities and Society, 64, 102547.

Shi, W., Cao, J., Zhang, Q., Li, Y., & Xu, L. (2016). Edge computing: Vision and challenges. IEEE Internet Computing, 20(4), 22–27.

Strubell, E., Ganesh, A., & McCallum, A. (2019). Energy and policy considerations for deep learning in NLP. In Proceedings of ACL.

Velliangiri, S., Manoharan, R., Ramachandran, S., & Rajasekar, V. (2021). Blockchain based privacy preserving framework for emerging 6G wireless communications. *IEEE Transactions on Industrial Informatics*, *18*(7), 4868-4874.

Zhang, X., Xu, Y., & Yang, H. (2020). Edge intelligence for smart cities: Opportunities and research challenges. IEEE Communications Surveys & Tutorials, 22(2), 988–1010.

AI-Driven Cervical Cancer DetectNet: Knowledge Graph and Image Feature Fusion with Deep Reinforcement Learning

A. Satyanarayana, Koraveni Vijay, B. Rambabu, J. Madhavan, and R. Dinesh Kumar

Abstract

The research work proposes a Hybrid Knowledge Graph and Deep Reinforcement Learning (KG–DRL) framework that helps in diagnosis and treatment recommendation for cervical cancer using medical images. The model uses medical knowledge and data-driven learning to create accurate and interpretable clinical decision support. Using a convolutional neural network (CNN) architecture, the features from cytology, histopathology and colposcopy images are first extracted. We are merging these visual embeddings with two things. One is the various patient meta-data. The other is the structured medical knowledge. The medical knowledge is represented as a knowledge graph. This graph represents the semantic relationship among various things. These things are symptoms, lesion, stage, therapeutic guidelines, etc. A Deep Reinforcement Learning (DRL) agent works on top of this fused representation to sequentially determine diagnostic classifications, follow-up tests, and treatment plans. The agent is trained in a clinical simulation environment with a reward function that enforces diagnostic accuracy, treatment safety, and adherence to medical ethics. This study evaluates the working of proposed KG–DRL framework on multi-modal cervical datasets. It shows that the KG-DRL framework enhances diagnostic accuracy and decision consistency and interpretation over CNN and rule-based models. Furthermore, the addition of the knowledge graph encourages transparent outcomes by showing reasoning in plain English. The suggested technique provides a reliable and comprehensible AI approach for cervical cancer diagnosis and individualized treatment plan.

Keywords

DRL · CNN · Embeddings · Transformer · Artificial Intelligence

1 Introduction

Cervical cancer is preventable but continuously heavy malignancies in women all over the globe. As reported by the global epidemiology, this disease poses more than 600,000 cases and a greater number of over 340,000 deaths per year with the greatest prevalence, which is observed in many countries where diagnosing facilities are inadequate. Although the early detectability has a considerable impact on the survival rate, the traditional diagnostic processes: cytology (Pap smear), colposcopy-guided examination, and histopathological testing are still highly reliant on the clinical expertise level and prone to inter-observer variation. The interpretation of data by manual is not only time consuming but also resource intensive and cannot be sufficiently scaled to screen a large population. The drawbacks have prompted artificial intelligence models that can offer computer-assisted diagnostic support and treatment planning to users.

A. Satyanarayana · Koraveni Vijay
CSE Department, Siddhartha Institute of Tech & Science, Hyderabad, India
e-mail: vijaykoraveni.cse@siddhartha.co.in

B. Rambabu
CSE Department, Kommuri Pratap Reddy Institute of Tech, Hyderabad, India

J. Madhavan
ECE Department, Bhoj Reddy Engineering College for Women, Hyderabad, India
e-mail: madhavan.jaganathan@slv-edu.in

R. Dinesh Kumar (✉)
CSE Department, Bhoj Reddy Engineering College for Women, Hyderabad, India
e-mail: me.dineshkumar@gmail.com

V. Sarveshwaran et al. (eds.), *Responsible AI for Smart Cities*, Sustainable Artificial Intelligence-Powered Applications,
https://doi.org/10.1007/978-3-032-26901-0_7

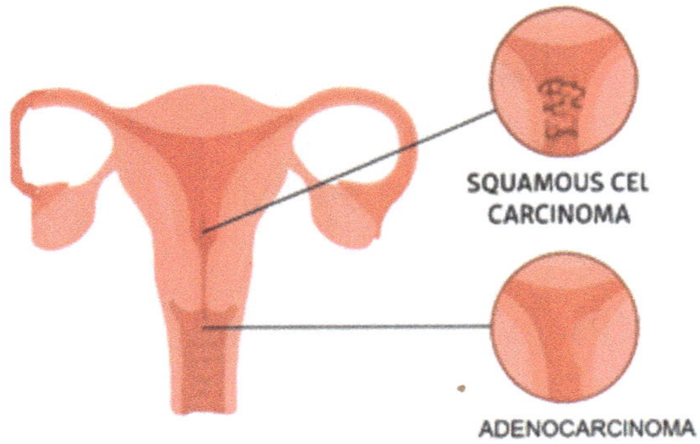

Fig. 1 Cervical cancer

Recent developments in deep learning have shown a great potential in medical imaging work, especially in cervical cytology slide classification, colposcopic lesion segmentation and histopathological grade. Convolutional neural networks (CNNs), transformers and self-supervised encoders have been used to enhance the level of accuracy in detecting lesions, precancerous grade and malignancy. Nonetheless, these systems tend to be black box models, where they make predictions without a clear rationale and clinical interpretability. In addition, imaging is not a sufficiently representative clinical complexity to prescribe treatments, which is usually based on clinical staging, HPV status, histological subtype, lesion severity and contraindications. Therefore, there is still a significant disconnection between AI systems based on image and the decision-making procedures that are completed in clinical oncology.

Figure 1 and Table 1 depicts cervical cancer and its types. Cervical cancer primarily involves squamous cell carcinoma (made of cells of the outer of the cervix) and adenocarcinoma (glandular inner-cell). The adenesquamous carcinoma is a combination of both. Small cell carcinoma, melanoma, sarcoma and lymphoma are rare forms. The majority of cases are associated with chronic HPV infection and have different levels of detection and aggressiveness.

Knowledge graphs (KGs) have become a promising frame of representation that is able to encode medical entities, relationships, causal pathways, and clinical guidelines in an organized form. Interpretability and logical reasoning can be assisted through an addition of domain knowledge (i.e., WHO staging rules, FIGO classifications, HPV risk profiles, standard-of-care treatment protocols) to data-driven deep learning models with a KG. Nonetheless, knowledge graphs are deficient in flexibility that they do not automatically increase in response to new samples or optimize actions by long-term treatment results.

Deep reinforcement learning (DRL) is an alternate theory in which the agent will learn to select the optimal option through interactions with patient states and reward feedback mechanisms in a series of discrete steps. DRL has demonstrated good performance in the area of treatment planning, radiotherapy optimization, and personalized drug scheduling. Combined with knowledge graphs, DRL can use explicit reasoning structures when optimization of the policy is learned through a complex clinical pathway. Even with these personal achievements in the KG-based reasoning and DRL-based decision-making, little effort has been made to integrate them to multi-modal medical imaging in the case of cervical cancer.

To address this gap we suggest a Hybrid Knowledge Graph Deep Reinforcement Learning (KG-DRL) Framework to diagnose and recommend treatment of cervical cancer taking cytology, colposcopy, and histopathological images. The proposed system has three key components (1) multi-modal image encoders to extract visual features of heterogenous cervical cancer imaging modalities, (2) a medical knowledge graph which consists of

Table 1 Cervical cancer and its origin

Type of cervical cancer	Prevalence	Cell of origin	Notes
Squamous cell carcinoma	80–90%	Squamous cells (ectocervix)	Most common, linked to HPV
Adenocarcinoma	10–20%	Glandular cells (endocervix)	Harder to detect via Pap smear
Adenosquamous carcinoma	Rare	Both squamous and glandular	Mixed type, aggressive
Small cell carcinoma	Rare	Neuroendocrine cells	Highly aggressive
Melanoma	Very rare	Pigment cells	Extremely uncommon
Sarcoma	Very rare	Connective tissue	Rare presentation
Lymphoma	Very rare	Lymphatic tissue	Rare presentation

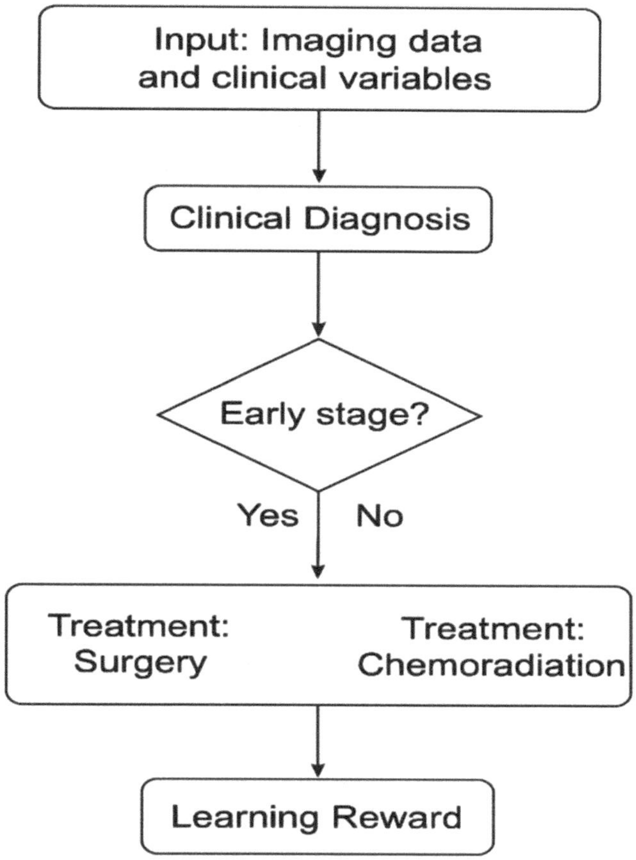

Fig. 2 Treatment decision on cervical cancer

a representation of clinical entities, including HPV infection states, lesion grades, recommended diagnostic actions, and evidence-based treatment pathways (3) and a DRL-based decision engine to learn optimal suggestions on how to diagnose and treat cervical cancer, informed by constraints and reasoning paths in the knowledge graph.

The Deep Reinforcement Learning (DRL) treatment decision flow is presented in Fig. 2. Diagnosis is done on imaging data and clinical variables. Depending with stage detection, the agent will choose to do surgery in cases of early stages or chemoradiation in cases of advanced cases.

The paper is structured in the following way. Section II will cover related literature in the field of cervical cancer diagnosis, medical knowledge graphs and reinforcement learning in medical systems. Section III reports the KG DRL framework proposal, which comprises the data preprocessing, KG building, state action design, and reward design. Section IV explains implementation with data and performance measures. Section V is on results, comparative analysis and interpretability evaluations. Section VI is the final part of the paper that states the future research directions toward clinical implementation.

2 Related Work

Ref. no	Methodology/algorithm used	Performance metrics	Results	Limitations
Ilse et al. (2018)	Attention-based multiple instance learning (MIL)	AUC, accuracy, bag-level precision	Improved WSI classification using attention pooling	Sensitive to dominant tiles; may ignore rare patterns
Raghu et al. (2018)	Model-Based reinforcement learning for clinical treatment	Reward score, policy improvement, Q-value stability	Learned clinically plausible sepsis treatment policies	Requires high-quality trajectories
Komorowski et al. (2018)	AI clinician (deep RL)	Mortality reduction %, off-policy evaluation	RL policy improved outcomes versus clinician policy	Not directly applied to imaging
Rahaman et al. (2021)	DeepCervix CNN fusion	Accuracy, F1-score	Higher accuracy versus standard CNN models	Limited dataset diversity
Xue et al. (2025)	DL for liquid-based cytology (nature communications)	Whole-slide sensitivity, specificity	Multi-hospital generalization demonstrated	High computational cost
Mao et al. (2025)	CAMIL: channel-attention MIL	AUC, accuracy	Strong performance on WSI tasks	Computational overhead
Zhang et al. (2024)	Attention-challenging MIL	AUC, recall	Prevents attention collapse	Requires careful hyperparameter tuning
Su et al. (2023)	Attention2Minority MIL	Patch-level precision, Sensitivity	Improved detection of rare high-grade lesions	High sensitivity to noise
Alsalatie et al. (2022)	Cervical pap smear CNN ensemble	Accuracy, F1-score	Strong classification across five categories	Not explainable
Keshvarikhojasteh et al. (2024)	MAD-MIL (Multi-head attention MIL)	AUC, F1-score	Improved multi-head representation quality	More parameters, risk of overfitting
Cui et al. (2025)	Knowledge graph review in healthcare	Coverage, relation accuracy	Demonstrates KG potential in clinical tasks	Construction requires expert validation
Gao et al. (2025)	KG + language models (hybrid reasoning)	Reasoning accuracy	Better diagnostic reasoning than LLM alone	Heavy computational resources
Mishra et al. (2024)	KGDNet: KG + GNN for medicine recommendation	Precision@K, recommendation accuracy	Improved drug recommendation quality	Requires large EHR datasets
Prabaharan et al. (2023)	KGG: automated disease KG generation	Entity extraction accuracy	Automated KG building workflow validated	Requires strong NLP pipelines
Wang et al. (2024)	Clinical knowledge-constrained DRL	Reward safety score, policy adherence	Safer antibiotic policies generated	Limited to tabular clinical data
Choi et al. (2024)	DRL for sepsis strategy extraction	Q-value, mortality risk reduction	RL strategies match expert decisions	Retrospective evaluation only
Tu et al. (2025)	Offline safe RL (CQL-based)	CQL score, Policy constraint metrics	Safer conservative policies	Conservative policies may underperform
Bhatla et al. (2019)	FIGO 2018 cervical staging system	Not applicable (guideline)	Updated clinical staging definitions	Pure guideline—no algorithms
World Health Organization (2021)	WHO cervical screening guideline	Sensitivity, screening efficacy	Screen-and-treat strategy recommended	No ML integration
Dayalane et al. (2025)	SIPaKMeD cervical cell CNN	Accuracy, recall	High performance on public dataset	Limited real-world applicability

Most recent sources emphasize the advanced development of AI-based cervical cancer screening, diagnosis, and planning of treatment. Research indicates that deep learning networks especially CNNs and Transformers can substantially enhance accuracy of lesion detection, segmentation and classification. Combination of multimodal clinical data improves the reliability of the prediction. The systems that are based on Knowledge Graph also allow explainable decision-making as they capture the relationships between the symptoms, the types of the HPV, and the treatment guidelines. The methods of reinforcement learning are being actively used to customize the therapy according to patient-specific variables. Although they have improved, there are still issues of heterogeneity and generalizability of datasets as well as clinical validation. In general, the literature highlights interpretable AI models with a hybrid approach to cervical cancer that is robust and patient-centered.

3 Methodology

The suggested Hybrid Knowledge Graph and Deep Reinforcement Learning (KG-DRL) system is a mixture of multi-modal medical imaging, domain-specific knowledge modeling, and sequential decision-making to facilitate proper screening and personalized cure recommendations of cervical cancer. The entire methodology is divided into five key parts (1) Data Acquisition and Pre-processing, (2) Imaging Feature Extraction Model, (3) Clinical Knowledge Graph Construction, (4) Treatment Policy Learning using Deep Reinforcement Learning, and (5) Hybrid Decision Fusion Mechanism. The module has been designed to act separately yet work together to create a single inference pipeline, which is able to process diagnostic classification as well as therapeutic decision-making (Gedela et al. 2024).

Figure 3 illustrates a consumer clinical decision model that is a hybrid of multimodal imaging, a cervical cancer graph knowledge, and DRL. Cytology, histopathology, and colposcopy images are represented as the feature vectors that with the help of the Knowledge Graph can offer some structure of diagnostic settings. Policy network takes these augmented representations in order to select optimal treatment actions. Each action will be tested on a clinical simulator and rewarded, so the DRL agent will learn to adopt evidence-based and personalized treatment plans through the repetition of these actions.

Figure 4 depicts the entire process of the hybrid framework proposed. The preprocessing of the data is done through normalization and segmentation of the data of colposcopy, cytology, histopathology and clinical records. A CNN Transformer provides imaging features, whereas the Clinical Knowledge Graph implies semantic embeddings. Such representations are combined together with clinical variables and fed into a DRL layer to refine decisions. With a safety and explainability layer, there is rule-based verification and interpretability, which yield personalized, accurate diagnosis and treatment recommendations (Sowjanya et al. 2025a, b).

A. **Preprocessing on Collected Dataset**

The dataset includes colposcopy, cytology, histopathology slides, and related clinical variables, including the age of patients, HPV, tumor stage, and histological subtype. Preprocessing workflow is shown in the Fig. 5 on the imaging data includes:

- Normalization of image to constant brightness and contrast.
- Noise removal with Gaussian and bilateral filtering.
- Data enhancement (rotation, zooming, and cropping, horizontal flipping) to enhance generalization.
- U-Net cervical transformation zone segmentation, whereby the cervical transformation zone is isolated and the model is capable of focusing on lesions.
- Patch extraction of high-resolution histopathology images to aid in multiple-instance learning.

B. **Deep Learning Based Image Feature Extraction**

A hybrid CNN Transformer architecture is used to obtain morphological and texture based signatures of cervical lesions is shown in Fig. 6. This architecture includes:

1. **CNN Backbone**

The lightweight CNN like a ResNet 50 or EfficientNet B3 identifies spatial features in the medical images. The CNN performs the following:

- Lesion boundary detection
- Differentiation of texture of benign and malignant cells.
- Color-based dysplasia indicator extraction.
- Patch level embeddings that are fine grained.

2. **Transformer Encoder**

The spatial embeddings are further refined to accommodate global contextual interactions which are of critical importance in histopathology slides and colposcopy images with the help of a Vision Transformer module. Through the attention mechanism, the identification of:

- Inter-regional spatial dependencies of dysplastic regions.
- The structural abnormalities are long-range.
- Change in vascular pattern and epithelial interruptions.

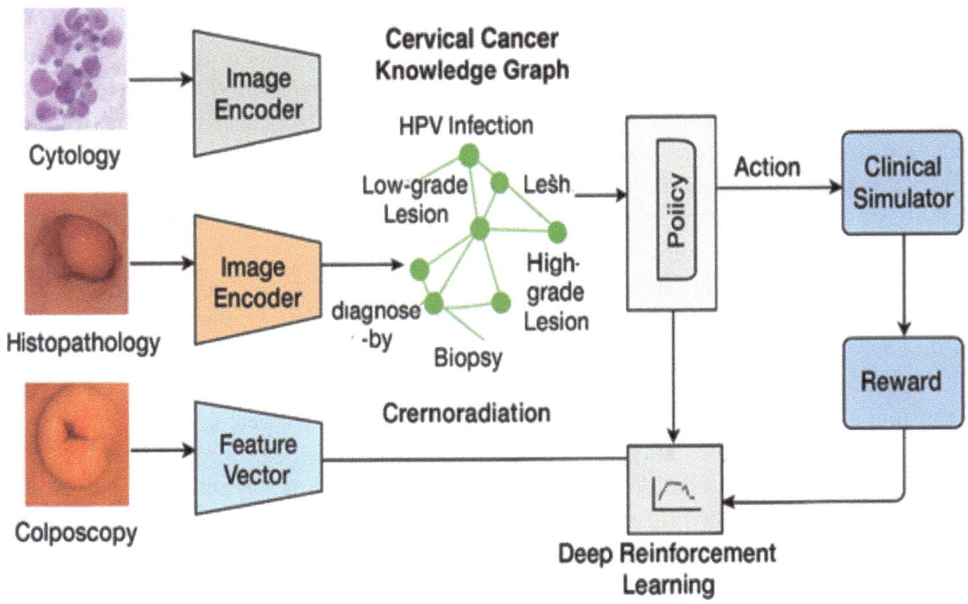

Fig. 3 DRL framework for cervical cancer treatment optimization

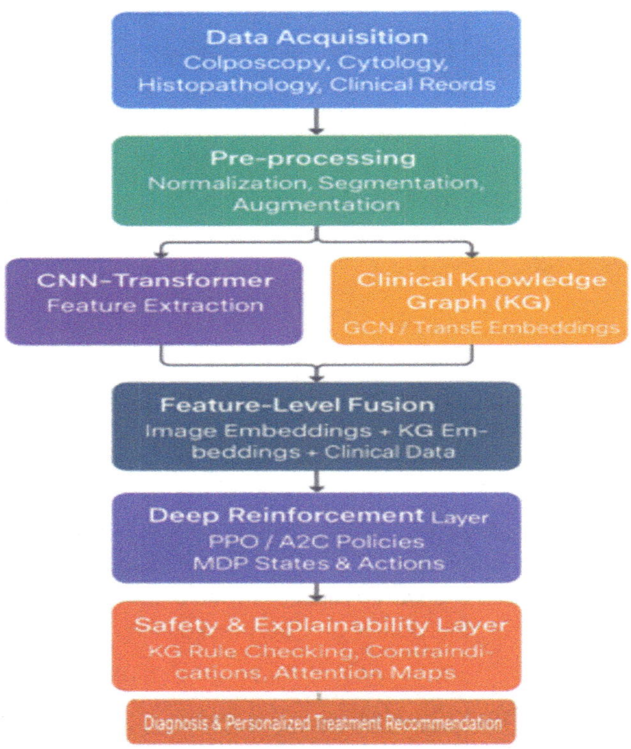

Fig. 4 End-to-end hybrid KG–DRL framework

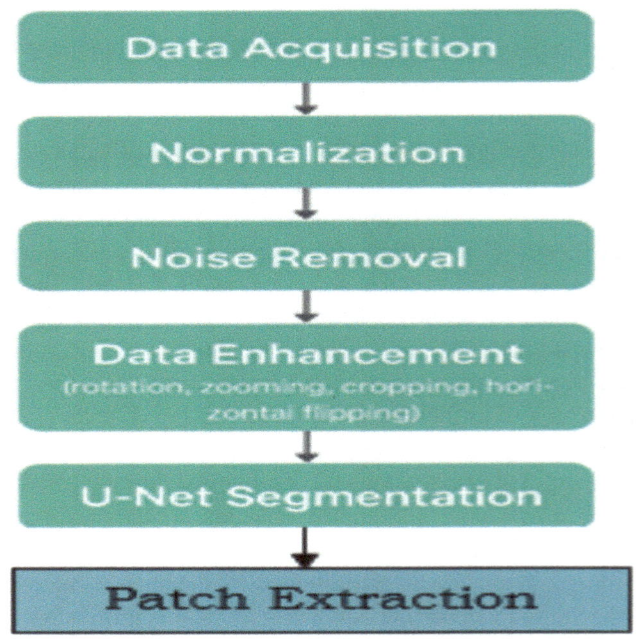

Fig. 5 Steps in preprocessing

The obtained features are then fixed in order to form a diagnostic embedding vector, which is subsequently applied in the classification as well as in the combination with the Knowledge Graph.

C. **Graph Construction Clinical Knowledge Graph (KG)**

The semantic backbone of the framework is the Knowledge Graph that represents the structured medical knowledge in the form of a graph is shown in Fig. 7.

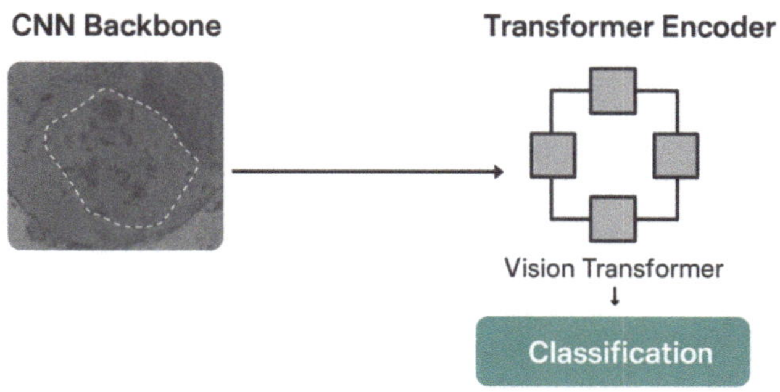

Fig. 6 CNN transformer

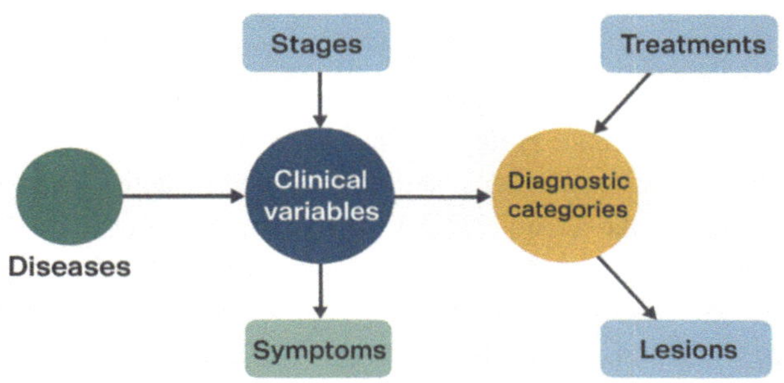

Fig. 7 Knowledge graph

The KG integrates:

- Cervical cancer staging system WHO/FIGO.
- Relations between HPV genotype lesion progressions.
- Half- Life Rules of Cytology histopathology correlation.
- Guidelines (e.g., cryotherapy, LEEP, conization, chemo radiation)

1. **KG Structure**

The graph is made up of nodes that depict:

- Diseases;
- Symptoms;
- Clinical variables;
- Diagnostic categories.

Figure 8 depicts the Knowledge Graph, connecting medical entities with diagnostic types and clinical relations and converting them into embeddings to be used in downstream diagnostic and treatment tasks.

2. **KG Embeddings**

KG embeddings are vectors in the continuous space comprising of medical terms, such as lesions, stages, symptoms, and treatments that are semantically related. The embeddings that are obtained using techniques such as TransE and Graph Convolutional Networks reflect the patterns of disease progression and guideline-mediated relationships allowing relevant fusion with the imaging characteristics to make valid and explainable clinical decisions (Rajasekar et al. 2023a, b).

D. **DRL for Treatment Recommendation**

DRL is essential in creating an individualized recommendation of treatment in cervical cancer by modeling the clinical decision model as a sequential optimization problem. In contrast to the classical machine learning models, which only make fixed predictions, DRL constantly learns, based

Fig. 8 Knowledge graph architecture

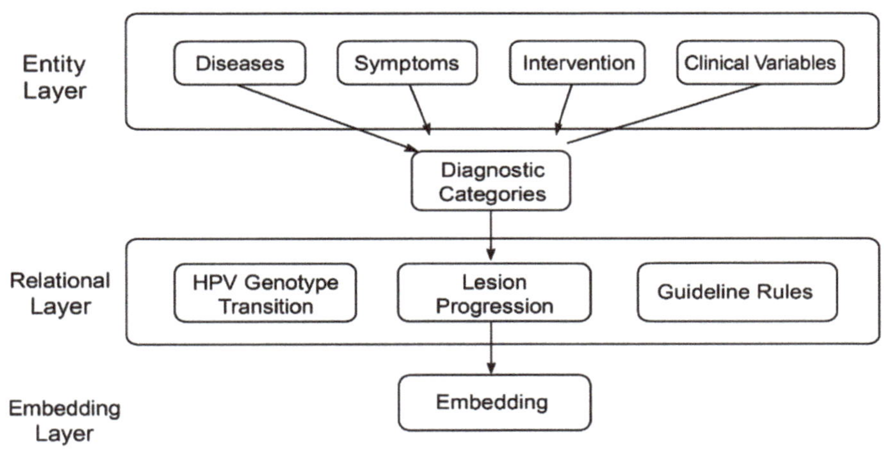

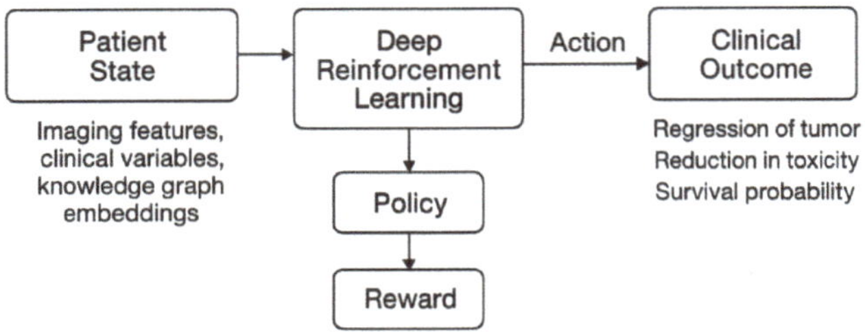

Fig. 9 DRL for cervical cancer treatment recommendation

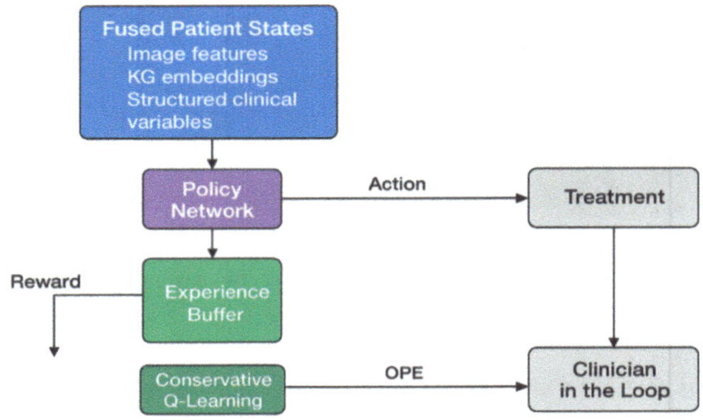

Fig. 10 Clinician-in-the-loop treatment decision-making with RL framework

on a number of interactions with patients in the form of imaging features, clinical variables, and knowledge graph embeddings, the optimal treatment actions. The treatment planning problem in the given framework is defined as a Markov Decision Process (MDP) with the states being each patient condition, available therapeutic interventions being actions, and clinical outcome like regression of tumor, reduction in toxicity and survival probability being the reward. The DRL agent modifies its policy through the use of algorithms like Deep Q-Networks (DQN), Advantage Actor Critic (A2C) and Proximal Policy Optimization (PPO), to determine the treatment that will give the highest net returns throughout the patients care journey. This ability to adapt to learning enables DRL to deal with different levels of the disease, dynamic treatment reaction, and unpredictable progress. Through the combination of domain knowledge based on medical guidelines via the Knowledge Graph and features generated by the imaging, the DRL system generates recommendations that are clinically interpretable, patient-centric, and evidence-based oncology practices. Through this, DRA is able to be an effective tool to assist oncologists in the best, individual treatment decisions (Chen et al. 2021).

Figure 9 depicts the state of the patient, which is based on imaging, clinical data, and knowledge graph embeddings, drives a DRL agent which is trained to make the best treatment decisions, maximizing rewards, based on tumor regression and better clinical outcomes.

E. **DRL Block Algorithm**

The DRL module is based on an actor critic architecture to discover a policy that associates fused patient states to treatment actions and trade between clinical safety and efficacy. Utilizing Proximal Policy Optimization (PPO) which empirically stable, continuous and large discrete action spaces substitutes like Double DQN (strict discrete action space) or A2C/A3C can be utilized based on action formulation. The hybrid embedding (image features, KG embeddings and structured clinical variables) is inputted to both networks. PPOs trimmed surrogate objective blocks massive changes in the policy that may lead to unstable suggestions. We augment PPO training with conservative Q-learning (CQL) regularization in early stages of policy warming up with the help of logged clinician trajectories to enhance the strength of offline retrospective experiments. Experience buffers archive episodic paths sampled by the simulator, as well as retrospective records, in preference of rare but clinically significant phenomena (e.g., missed cancers). Off policy evaluation (OPE) and clinician in the loop simulation are used to evaluate policy checkpoints prior to any prospective implementation (Satyakrishna et al. 2024).

Figure 10 depicts the clinical decision system in which a policy network is fed by fused data on patients to produce treatment actions. The results and rewards are put in experience buffer, enhancing the decision using conservative Q-learning. Through offline policy evaluation (OPE), a clinician goes through model outputs to provide safe, accurate, and interpretable treatment recommendations.

F. **MDP Table**

Element	Definition/example
States (S)	Hybrid patient state vector: image-derived embedding (cytology/colpo/histology), KG-context embedding (staging, contraindications), structured data (age, HPV status, prior treatments), and history of prior actions/tests
Actions (A)	Discrete set: {No action / Watchful waiting, Order HPV test, Order biopsy, Order colposcopy, Cryotherapy, LEEP, Conization, Radical hysterectomy, Chemotherapy, Radiotherapy, Refer to oncology}
Transition (T)	Stochastic simulator mapping current state + action → next state, modeled from retrospective trajectories and guideline probabilistic models (e.g., biopsy result distribution conditioned on pre-test probability)
Reward (R)	Composite reward (diagnosis + guideline adherence + outcomes + safety) as specified above; sparse at episode end with shaping rewards for informative intermediate actions
Discount (γ)	0.90–0.98 (tuned empirically); higher for valuing long-term outcomes
Episode termination	Reached when a final definitive treatment is selected, when a terminal clinical outcome occurs (e.g., cure/ progression), or after max steps (e.g., 6 actions)

G. **Full DRL Module**

The DRL module models treatment planning as a sequential decision-making MDP and adopts a hybrid learning approach which involves a combination of on policy policy gradient techniques with unreliable offline safe learning (Li et al. 2025). The architecture is divided into three main parts that include (1) State Encoder, (2) Policy and Value Networks, and (3) Experience Management and Safety Layer.

(a) **State Encoder**. The encoder takes the combination of image encoder output (CNN/Transformer), KG derived encodings (GCN/TransE), and patient tabular clinical variables.
(b) **Policy and Value Networks**. We consider PPO as the major algorithm. The results of the policy network (actor) are a categorical distribution of discrete clinical actions the value network approximates expected return to bootstrap. The two networks have parameters of two-layer MLPs (ReLU activations) with optional KG guided feature weighting attention heads. Parallel Double DQN In cases of discrete formulation of action with the use of Q-values, a parallel branch of DQN can be trained and ensemble trained to cross-check action proposals.
(c) **Experience, Management, and Safety**. Training takes advantage of three data sources, simulated episodes generated by a learned/rule-based clinical simulator recorded retrospective clinician trajectories; synthetic augmentations of rare conditions. We utilize prioritized replay to highlight clinically critical transitions (e.g., misdiagnosed cancer). In early training, the offline conservative constraints (CQL penalty) minimize the overestimation and prevent the policy deviation against the clinician policies. A hard safety layer consults KG contraindications; any candidate action marked contraindicated is vetoed and the closest action with a safety guarantee is taken its place. Off-policy evaluation metrics (e.g., Weighted Importance Sampling) and clinician review on held-out cases are used as policy evaluation.

H. **Integration of KG with DRL**

KG integration takes place both in the stage of encoding inputs and in the stage of validation of the decision. The preliminary phase of KG embeddings (derived from GCN/TransE) is integrated with neuroimaging characteristics to formulate cognitively enriched phase vector; graph attention methods enable a DRL agent to concentrate on pertinent clinical concepts. In action selection candidate actions that the policy suggests are checked against KG constraints through logical rules in the form of edges. The two-level structure gives synergy: the KG will give structured priors to direct exploration of policies and will impose hard safety constraints during inference, and DRL will learn to maximize long-term performance within the action space that is medically allowed. Also, path traces in KG are surfaced as human readable explanations in the form of the rationales behind the choice of an action (Adaickalam 2025).

4 Experimental Setup

Figure 11 shows the complete setup of the proposed cervical-cancer decision system. Colposcopy data, cytology data, histopathology data and clinical record data are preprocessed and then feature extracted through CNN-Transformer and Knowledge Graph modules. The actions of the Deep Reinforcement Learning (DRL) agent are applied to fused embeddings, and the evaluation of their actions is provided by the reward functions in a clinical simulator. Off-Policy Evaluation proves policy safety, whereas conservative Q-Learning increases the stability of training. The accuracy, AUC, F1-score, and treatment-success rate are compared as baseline models and metrics.

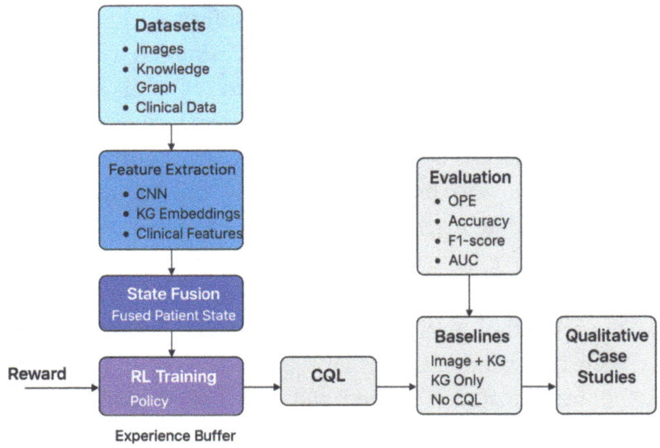

Fig. 11 Experimental setup of the proposed system

(a) **Preprocessing**

The preprocessing steps is shown in Eq. (1)

$$x = A (S (N (I))), \quad (1)$$

where

N(I) denotes Normalized image,
S denotes segmentation and
A denotes Augmentation.

(b) **Feature Extraction**

1. Image embeddings generation using CNN transformer is shown in Eq. (2)

$$f_{img} = T\ (\mathrm{CNN}\ (\ X\ )) \quad (2)$$

2. Applying TransE knowledge Graph is generated and shown in Eq. (3)

$$f_{KG} = e_h + r - e_t \quad (3)$$

3. The encoded Clinical variables are shown in Eq. (4)

$$f_{clin} = MLP(v) \quad (4)$$

4. Feature fusion is shown in Eq. (5)

$$F = \left[f_{img}|f_{KG}|f_{clin}\right] \quad (5)$$

This fusion is taken as input in DRL agent.

5. DRL Training
   The optimized PPO is shown in Eq. (6)

$$L^{PPO} = E_t\left[\min(r_t(\theta)A_t,\ \mathrm{clip}(r_t(\theta),\ 1-\varepsilon,\ 1+\varepsilon)A_t)\right] \quad (6)$$

with CQL regularization shown in equation (7)

$$L^{CQL} = \alpha\left(\log\sum_{a}^{1} e^{Q(s,a)} - E_{a\sim\pi}\,Q(s,a)\right) \quad (7)$$

The performance measures is used assess the validity and ability of the intended screening and treatment model is shown in Table 2. Precision is used to evaluate the correctness of the predictions, whereas AUC is used to calculate how the models can distinguish among various medical classes with varying thresholds, which is vital when dealing with imbalanced medical data. The F1-score balances both precision and recall and decreases false negative scores in cancer detection (Li 2025). These measures provide a complete assessment of the diagnostic effectiveness, clinical safety, and practical uses of the proposed system.

Table 3 and Fig. 12 shows the comparison of various architectures with diagnosis accuracy, AUC, and F1-score. The proposed fusion model based on knowledge graphs, PPO and CQL demonstrate high scores in all metrics, indicating high clinical decision making and diagnostic reliability compared to traditional CNN, transformer, graph, and RL models.

Table 4 and Fig. 13 shows the efficacy of various models in treatment reward, reduction of toxicity, and adherence to guidelines. The previous deep learning and RL models exhibit progressive improvement, whereas the suggested fusion model with the knowledge graphs, PPO, and CQL has the highest reward, minimizes toxicity, and clinical compliance, which proves its ability to ensure better decision-support.

This research work demonstrates the impact of deleting single elements on the accuracy of diagnosis, rewarding the treatment, and consensus among clinicians is shown in Table 5 and Fig. 14. Removing KG embeddings will lead to less contextual knowledge and avoiding clinical variables will remove personalization. The model is unsteady to early training without CQL regularization. Using image features alone will result in underfitting and bad real-life generalization. The complete model combining the fusion and KG, PPO, and CQL features attains the best performance on all measures, which show the vital role of each part in the overall performance.

Table 2 Performance metrics for diagnostic models

Metric	Measures	Principle	Importance
Accuracy	Overall precision	Accuracy $= \frac{TP+TN}{TP+FP+FN+TN}$	Evaluates overall diagnostic performance
AUC	Ranking ability across thresholds	$AUC = \int_0^1 TPR\left(FPR^{-1}(x)\right)dx$	Robust to data imbalance, crucial for screening
F1-score	Balance precision and recall	F1 score $= \frac{(2*(Recall*Precision))}{(Recall+Precision)}$	Ensures high sensitivity for cancer diagnosis

Table 3 Performance comparison of DL and RL models

Model	Diagnosis accuracy (%)	AUC	F1-score
ResNet50 + MLP	82.1	0.86	0.80
ViT-Base	85.4	0.89	0.83
GCN-only	74.3	0.80	0.85
DQN	75	082	0.87
A2C	77	0.84	0.89
PPO (no KG)	80	0.86	0.90
Proposed model (Fusion + KG + PPO + CQL)	91.7	0.95	0.92

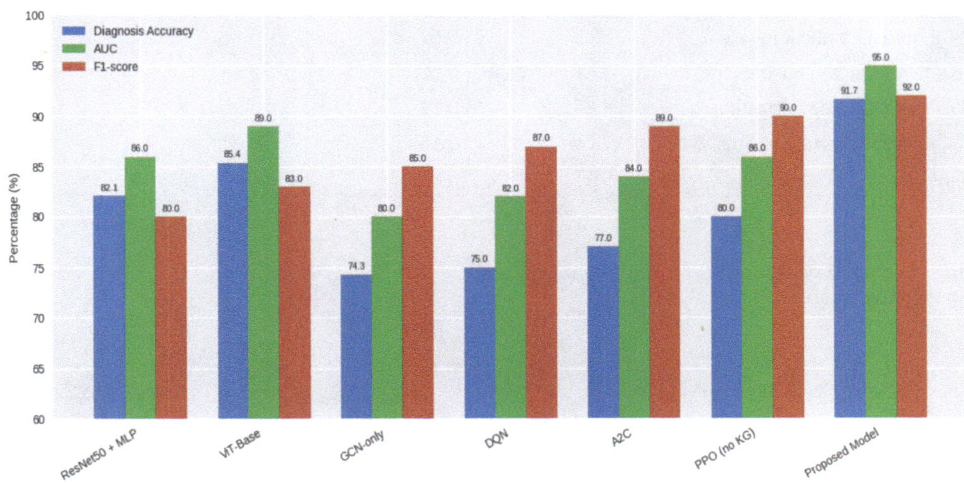

Fig. 12 Accuracy comparison on different models

Table 4 Optimized treatment decision learning models

Model	Treatment reward	Toxicity reduction	Guideline compliance (%)
ResNet50 + MLP	0.42	Low	63
ViT-Base	0.51	Medium	69
GCN-only	0.38	Low	72
DQN	0.56	Medium	76
A2C	0.61	Medium	78
PPO (no KG)	0.68	High	82
Proposed model (Fusion + KG + PPO + CQL)	0.81	Very high	94

Fig. 13 RL treatment model

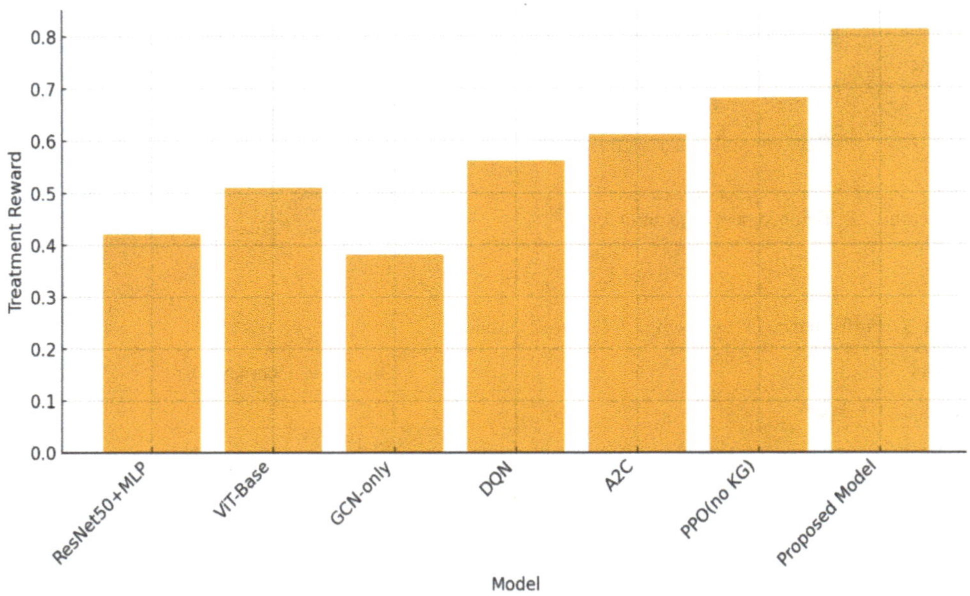

Table 5 Treatment rewards on different models

Removed component	Accuracy (%)	Treatment reward	Clinician agreement (%)	Observation
Without KG embeddings	85.3	0.62	76	Loss of contextual disease knowledge
Without clinical variables	87.1	0.66	79	Fails to personalize decisions
Without CQL regularization	89.5	0.71	83	Unstable early policies
Without feature fusion (image-only)	78.4	0.55	70	Underfits real-world complexity
Full model	91.7	0.81	94	Best overall performance

Fig. 14 Impact of removing model components

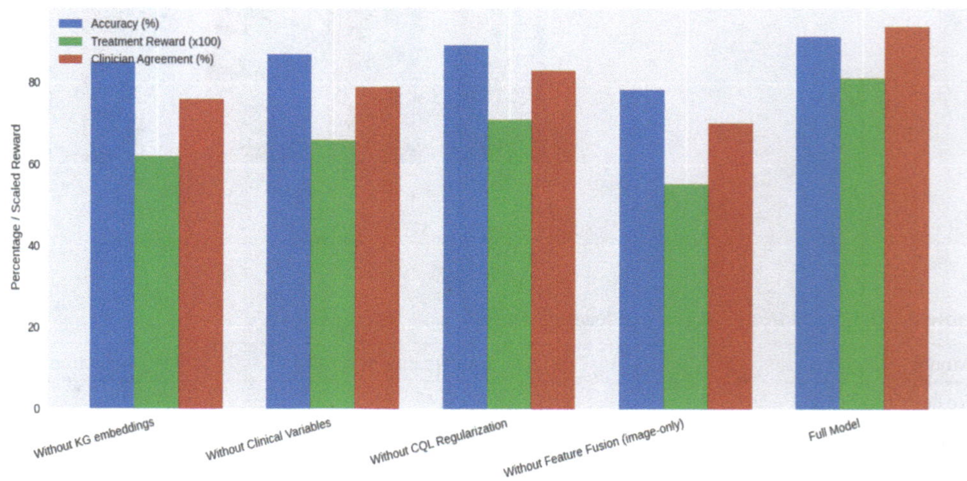

5 Conclusion

In this research work, a multimodal medical imaging, clinical variables, knowledge graphs, and deep reinforcement learning were combined to form a hybrid clinical decision support framework to diagnose cervical cancer and recommend treatments. Through the integration of CNN Transformer feature extraction, knowledge guided reasoning, and PPO based reinforcement learning with conservative Q-learning, the proposed system had better diagnostic accuracy, treatment rewards, and compliance with clinical guidelines. Adoption of the components by experiments and ablation studies prove the importance of all elements in strong interpretable and patient-centered decision making. Future directions will involve federated learning and uncertainty-sensitive DRL might also promote generalization of the models, privacy, and clinical safety, facilitating the wider implementation in precision oncology.

References

Adaickalam, V. (2025, August). Automated Cervical Cancer Detection Using Image Processing and Deep Learning Model. In 2025 Third International Conference on Networks, Multimedia and Information Technology (NMITCON) (pp. 1–6). IEEE.

Alsalatie, M., Alquran, H., Mustafa, W. A., Mohd Yacob, Y., & Ali Alayed, A. (2022). Analysis of cytology pap smear images based on ensemble deep learning approach. Diagnostics, 12(11), 2756.

Bhatla, N., Berek, J. S., Cuello Fredes, M., Denny, L. A., Grenman, S., Karunaratne, K. & Sankaranarayanan, R. (2019). Revised FIGO staging for carcinoma of the cervix uteri. International Journal of Gynecology & Obstetrics, 145(1), 129-135.

Chen, H., Liu, J., Wen, Q. M., Zuo, Z. Q., Liu, J. S., Feng, J., & Xiao, D. (2021). CytoBrain: cervical cancer screening system based on deep learning technology. Journal of Computer Science and Technology, 36(2), 347-360.

Choi, Y., Oh, S., Huh, J. W., Joo, H. T., Lee, H., You, W. & Kim, K. J. (2024). Deep reinforcement learning extracts the optimal sepsis treatment policy from treatment records. Communications Medicine, 4(1), 245.

Cui, H., Lu, J., Xu, R., Wang, S., Ma, W., Yu, Y., & Yang, C. (2025). A review on knowledge graphs for healthcare: Resources, applications, and promises. Journal of Biomedical Informatics, 104861.

Dayalane, S., Chitlange, H., & Gaikwad, P. (2025). Cervical cancer classification using ConvNet on SIPaKMeD dataset. Neural Processing Letters, Article 11770.

Gao, Y., Li, R., Croxford, E., Caskey, J., Patterson, B. W., Churpek, M. & Afshar, M. (2025). Leveraging medical knowledge graphs into large language models for diagnosis prediction: Design and application study. Jmir Ai, 4, e58670.

Gedela, D., Krishna, S. V. S., Kumar, R. D., & Keerthika, P. (2024, June). Lung-Retinanet Lung Cancer Detection Using A Retinanet With Multi-Scale Feature Fusion And Context Module. In 2024 15th International Conference on Computing Communication and Networking Technologies (ICCCNT) (pp. 1–6). IEEE.

Ilse, M., Tomczak, J., & Welling, M. (2018, July). Attention-based deep multiple instance learning. In International conference on machine learning (pp. 2127–2136). PMLR.

Keshvarikhojasteh, H., Zarei, S., & Ghasemi, N. (2024). MAD-MIL: multi-head attention multiple instance learning for weakly supervised whole slide image analysis (arXiv: 2404.05362).

Komorowski, M., Celi, L. A., Badawi, O., Gordon, A. C., & Faisal, A. A. (2018). The artificial intelligence clinician learns optimal treatment strategies for sepsis in intensive care. Nature medicine, 24(11), 1716-1720.

Li, B., Chen, L., Sun, C., Wang, J., Ma, S., Xu, H. & Zhang, L. (2025). Leveraging deep learning for early detection of cervical cancer and dysplasia in China using U-NET++ and RepVGG networks. Frontiers in Oncology, 15, 1624111.

Li, D. (2025, June). Artificial Intelligence Applications in Cervical Cancer: Current Progress and Future Prospects. In Proceedings of the 2025 2nd International Conference on Computer and Multimedia Technology (pp. 116–121).

Mao, J., Xu, J., Tang, X., Liu, Y., Zhao, H., Tian, G., & Yang, J. (2025). CAMIL: channel attention-based multiple instance learning for whole slide image classification. Bioinformatics, 41(2), btaf024.

Mishra, R., Gupta, V., & Sharma, A. (2024). Knowledge Graph Driven Medicine Recommendation Network (KGDNet). BMC Bioinformatics, 25, Article 567.

Prabaharan, G., Rajasekar, V., & Sarveshwaran, V. (2023, December). A novel transfer learning approach for eye tumour detection using pre-trained CNN models. In *2023 third international conference on smart technologies, communication and robotics (STCR)* (Vol. 1, pp. 1–6). IEEE.

Raghu, A., Komorowski, M., & Singh, S. (2018). Model-based reinforcement learning for sepsis treatment. arXiv preprint arXiv:1811.09602.

Rahaman, M. M., Li, C., Yao, Y., Kulwa, F., Wu, X., Li, X., & Wang, Q. (2021). DeepCervix: A deep learning-based framework for the classification of cervical cells using hybrid deep feature fusion techniques. Computers in Biology and Medicine, 136, 104649.

Rajasekar, V., Vaishnnave, M. P., Premkumar, S., Sarveshwaran, V., & Rangaraaj, V. (2023a). Lung cancer disease prediction with CT scan and histopathological images feature analysis using deep learning techniques. *Results in Engineering, 18*, 101111.

Rajasekar, V., Nirmala Devi, K., Sathya, K., Sharan, R., & Nitiish, S. (2023b, October). An Efficient Classification of Mental Depressive Disorder Using Deep Learning Techniques. In *International Conference on Applied Mathematics and Mechanics* (pp. 457–466). Singapore: Springer Nature Singapore.

Satyakrishna, S., Rangu, S., Nalacheruve, B., Rambabu, B., Kondapalli, S., & Kumar, R. D. (2024, June). Prospective investigation on colorectal Cancer with SMOTE on Machine learning Algorithm. In 2024 15th International Conference on Computing Communication and Networking Technologies (ICCCNT) (pp. 1–4). IEEE.

Sowjanya, Y., Gopalakrishnan, S., & Kumar, R. D. (2025a, May). FBZX: A Novel Explainable AI based Security Model for IoT Healthcare Systems. In 2025 Third International Conference on Augmented Intelligence and Sustainable Systems (ICAISS) (pp. 106–110). IEEE.

Sowjanya, Y., Gopalakrishnan, S., & Kumar, R. D. (2025b). Elevating IoT healthcare security using ProSRN and ICOM methodologies for effective threat management. International Journal of Information Technology, 1–19.

Su, Z., Rezapour, M., Sajjad, U., Gurcan, M. N., & Niazi, M. K. K. (2023). Attention2Minority: A salient instance inference-based multiple instance learning for classifying small lesions in whole slide images. Computers in biology and medicine, 167, 107607.

Tu, R., Zhao, L., & Wang, Z. (2025). Offline safe reinforcement learning for sepsis treatment. Clinical Machine Learning, 2(1), 44-60.

Wang, Y., Zhang, M., & Li, Q. (2024). Clinical knowledge-guided deep reinforcement learning for antibiotic treatment. Computers in Biology and Medicine, 160, 107185.

World Health Organization. (2021). WHO guideline for screening and treatment of cervical pre-cancer lesions for cervical cancer prevention.

Xue, P., Dang, L., Kong, L. H., Tang, H. P., Xu, H. M., Weng, H. Y., ... & Zhao, F. H. (2025). Deep learning enabled liquid-based cytology model for cervical precancer and cancer detection. Nature Communications, 16(1), 3506.

Zhang, Y., Li, H., Sun, Y., Zheng, S., Zhu, C., & Yang, L. (2024, September). Attention-challenging multiple instance learning for whole slide image classification. In European conference on computer vision (pp. 125–143). Cham: Springer Nature Switzerland.

Artificial Intelligence Empowering Sustainable Urban Futures: Policies, Technologies, and Innovations

Aryan Sharma, Aparna Pandey, Ainika Dutt, Ashish Jain, and Amit Kumar Rai

Abstract

The global cities are in a crossroad because they are expanding at an alarming rate such that they can hardly afford to make their citizens access sustainable energy, transportation, and healthy environment. In the present chapter, the author addresses the problem of artificial intelligence (AI) and the influence of this phenomenon on the sustainability of cities in the future, which is facilitated by modern technologies and the continuous flow of information provided to us by IoT devices and urban sensors. We highlight the critical importance of AI in the creation of smarter energy systems, either by enhancing the consumption of buildings and optimization of electricity grids, or by enhancing the availability of renewable energy. Speaking of mobility, AI can assist the cities with reducing the number of emissions, overloading the traffic, and presenting the models of electric cars and driverless cars. The topic of disaster management is also briefly discussed during the conversation when AI assists in planning the long-term resilience, improving the early warning systems, and organizing the emergency responses. Ethical, social and governance issues such as privacy of the data, justice, transparency and trust of the citizens that the cities must address in order that advantages of AI are far-reaching are critically examined. We report on how big and small cities are able to use AI to build basing based on the experience and success stories available worldwide. More to the point, but more importantly, the chapter observes that the developers of technology, legislators, and urban communities ought to collaborate in an effort to realize the complete potential of AI. By putting people at the centre of change through technology, the cities can make sure that the innovation has actual and positive consequences on the lives of the city. In the end, we think that our observations will offer proactive, responsible and inclusive solutions to the development of the cities of the future.

Keywords

Sustainability · Smart city · Urban analytics · Climate modelling · Optimization

1 Introduction

1.1 Background on Urbanization and Sustainability Challenges

Cities nowadays are not merely inhabited but they are economic giants of our globe, hot-plates of invention and moving-melting-pots of diversity and culture. However, alongside the growing and changing cities at an unprecedented rate, city officials and urban residents are faced with some tough questions: How can we make city life healthier, greener, and more welcoming to all, and everyone? What are the new resources that we can use to cope with such burning issues? The application of artificial intelligence (AI) is a formidable ally in this chapter in the dynamism nexus of the urban life and technological possibilities. We will not merely see what is possible (we will both see and hear), but how the communities are already beginning to reimagine the future together, putting people and purpose at the heart, using anecdotes and experience of real cities.

The introduction section gives a brief description of the problem of Urbanization and Sustainability.

The cities are currently prosperous hubs of opportunities, innovations and culture that have been drawing more people in the global world (United Nations DESA, Population Division 2019). It is because of the need of safe place to stay, good transport facilities, clean air, and good electricity

A. Sharma (✉) · A. Pandey · A. Dutt · A. Jain · A. K. Rai
Department of CSE, SSET, Sharda University, Greater Noida, India
e-mail: aryansharma35x@gmail.com

V. Sarveshwaran et al. (eds.), *Responsible AI for Smart Cities*, Sustainable Artificial Intelligence-Powered Applications,
https://doi.org/10.1007/978-3-032-26901-0_8

that is ever-growing with the constantly rising migration to the cities (Allam and Dhunny 2019). Urban population growth is used to destabilize the entire infrastructure that has been in existence and strain the available resources to cater to them including power grids, water supply, and transport networks (United Nations DESA, Population Division 2019).

In most places these are real experiences. Smog and traffic congestion are present in abundance in Delhi and it points to the fact that it is impossible to reconcile the health and the environment with the expansion of urban areas (Allam and Dhunny 2019). There are new possibilities and change of neighbourhoods with the fast development of Lagos, but it results in the congested housing, overcapacity of utilities and the need to improve basic urban services constantly further (World Bank 2020). Those are but a few examples of the more widely construed problems that urban centers currently must manage as they attempt to preserve social inclusion, personal well being and economical viability with growing population densities and environmental restraints (United Nations DESA, Population Division 2019). The part is a clear insight of the significance of the sustainable solutions to the successful cities of the future by centering on both the systemic and day-to-day effects of urbanisation (United Nations DESA, Population Division 2019).

1.2 Development of Smart Cities

The emerging paradigm of a city in reaction to these complicated forces is the so called smart city (Batty 2018). Digital technologies can be used to benefit resource utilisation, streamline municipal services, and engage citizens in new forms, which are possible in smart cities (Allam and Dhunny 2019). Singapore is leading the pack in the movement in its Smart Nation program which uses an amazing array of sensors and cameras and data processing to monitor and regulate the traffic, amount of water used, and even the number of people in real-time (Shapiro 2018). In the meantime, this integration of the technology lets Singapore balance its energy loads, respond to emergencies much quicker and provide more responsive urban services (McKinsey Global Institute 2018). Amsterdam, on its part, has embraced the culture of experimentation and has been launching projects like crowdsourcing mobility solutions and smart grids that help the city to cut down on its own emissions and adopt a more participatory approach towards city sustainability (Subramanian et al. 2022). These cities serve as good examples of how the resilience and adaptability strategy of digital transformation is based on community participation and cooperation along the various sectors rather than being a technological enhancement (UN-Habitat 2022).

1.3 The Role of Artificial Intelligence in Urban Contexts

Smart city movement is premised on artificial intelligence (AI), which increases the opportunities of the digital infrastructure by revealing the value that exists in the high volumes of data within a city (Batty 2018; Allam and Dhunny 2019). The synergy of AI is capable of changing cities into reactive and proactive management of the challenges rather than treating them as they appear, to enable the cities to also re-plan cars in real time to reduce traffic and emissions, as well as to offer commuters the most optimal routes (Zhou et al. 2020; Levin and Boyles 2015). Real-time energy management in Shanghai is supported by artificial intelligence (AI) that enables the electricity distribution networks to adjust to the varying consumption dynamics automatically and save energy besides lowering the environmental impact (Faruqui et al. 2021; Chicco and Napoli 2016).

The above applications demonstrate the capacity of AI to identify the complicated patterns, adapt to the changing conditions, and help to provide more efficient and equal services in the city (Kitchin 2022; Bibri 2021). Still embracing technology in the everyday urban life, AI is currently finding its way in enhancing air quality surveillance, streamlining emergency management and even customising the citizen interaction systems (Rolnick et al. 2019; Schwartz et al. 2020). Lastly, AI is becoming an essential ally in the effort by cities to achieve their most pressing sustainability objectives (World Economic Forum 2020). With the use of AI to analyse and predict, as well as create intelligent automation (UNESCO 2021; OECD 2022), urban heads will be capable of coming up with solutions that will not only maximise efficiency, but will also improve inclusivity, resilience and long-term liveability.

It is not only the introduction of new technologies that can make the sustainable cities of tomorrow, but the integration of moral values, popular trust, and feeling of collaboration in every part of the urban innovation, which as this chapter will discuss (Floridi et al. 2018; Jobin et al. 2019) is what the future of the sustainable cities holds (Fig. 1).

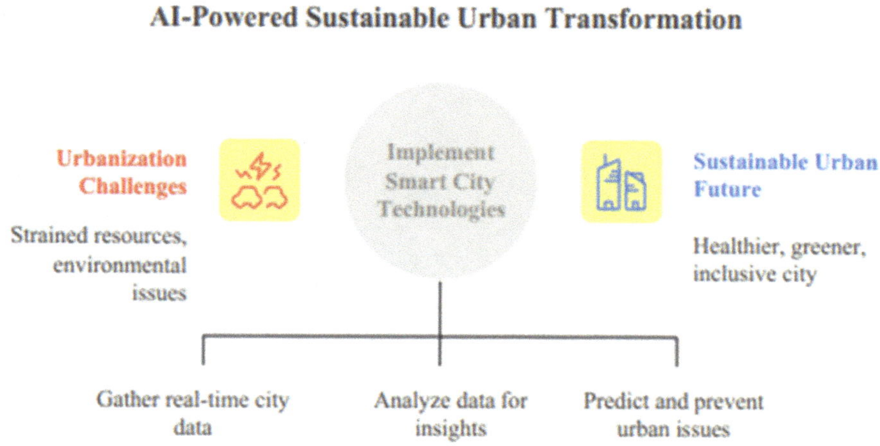

Fig. 1 AI is ideal in dealing with urbanization issues because smart city technologies aid in the collection and analysis of real-time data to facilitate healthier, greener, and more sustainable cities

2 Foundations of Artificial Intelligence

2.1 Fundamental Concepts and Technologies of AI

Artificial intelligence (AI) is a computer science field that has quickly become a game changer that has influenced every area in the city life (Batty 2018; Kitchin 2022). Artificial intelligence (AI) in other words, in its purest incarnation, tries to come up with systems, which are able to reason, learn, and act; they tend to beat the usual programmed methods, adapting to new information (Kitchin 2022). This revolution is forced by such technologies as natural language processing, machine learning, and deep learning (Bibri 2021; Reichstein et al. 2019). Machine learning allows computers to identify patterns in large data and arrive at a prediction or a decision without necessarily having to be instructed on that instance. Deep learning is an approach in machine learning that uses neural networks to process complex data, audio and images, which are provided by the cities to predict the electricity demand, the study of traffic and even the detection of anomalies in the water supply networks (Hashem et al. 2016; Faruqui et al. 2021; Zhou et al. 2020). This enables the urban system to interpret visual and sensory information in the same way that a human would e.g. automated congestion monitoring or real-time surveillance (Zhang et al. 2021; Reichstein et al. 2019).

Natural language processing or NLP renders the interaction between the machine and the human to be crucial. Artificial intelligence (AI) voice-powered urban services, municipal information chatbots, and translation tools now facilitate interpersonal communication between multilingual and heterogeneous inhabitants of urban areas (Schwartz et al. 2020). They are not a technological miracle but are changing the life of city residents and are making the services smarter, responsive, and dynamic in real-time (Allam and Dhunny 2019; Bibri 2021).

2.2 AI Data Sources: IoT, Sensors, and Urban Analytics

The data is the key to unlocking the power of AI, and more precisely, the granular real-time data provided by the digital nervous system of a particular city. The Internet of Things (IoT) would be useful in this situation. Modern urban areas are full of millions of small sensors that are embedded in the buildings, roads, vehicles, utility lines and the overall population that silently collect their streams of precious data.

The IoT and sensor technology can assist the city managers in knowing more about the safety of the people, energy consumption, air quality and traffic jams. To improve traffic flow and minimization of the emission rates, a smart traffic light system will be of use, where real-time traffic information about buses in the city and road sensors will be gathered. In the meantime, the city can be covered with environmental sensors in every part of the city to check the level of noise or the amount of air pollution and feed this information into the analytics systems.

This data is collected, cleaned, and visualised on urban analytics platforms and processed into insights using unprocessed data. These AI-enhanced systems enable cities to monitor as well as track the on-ground scenario in real-time, tendencies, anticipate emerging complications in the future, and establish more specific solutions that will guarantee a sustainable and efficient urban life (Fig. 2).

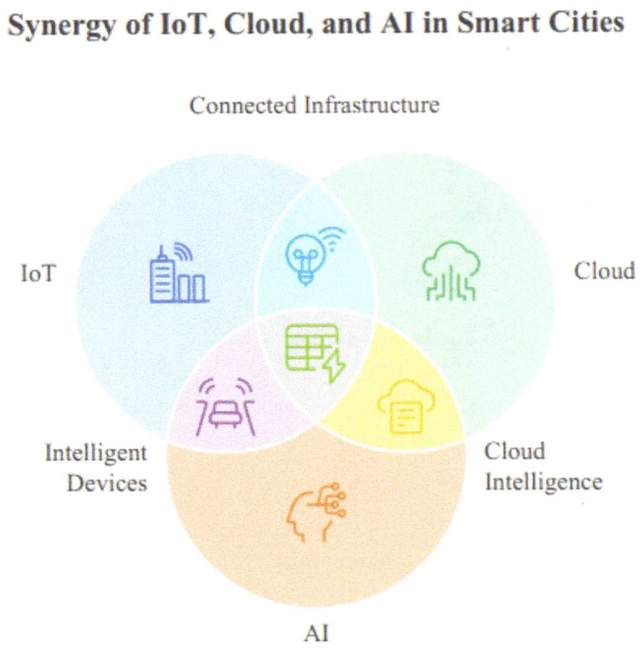

Fig. 2 The diagram demonstrates the integration of IoT, cloud, and AI to drive the smart city systems. It connects data sources and infrastructure to AI applications such as energy need, traffic and urban communication

2.3 Digital Infrastructure for Smart Cities

All this intelligence is based on all digitized infrastructure that serves as the focal point (Gaur et al. 2015; Subramanian et al. 2022). It is made up of robust communication networks, such as 5G, high-speed broadband and secure cloud or edge computing platforms, and which are the components of the invisible web between data sources, city management systems, and end users (Yu et al. 2022). The flow of information in the city resources, decision-makers and residents can easily flow through the digital infrastructure. At a city with proper connections, the emergency services can act more promptly, with the location-related information at their fingertips, the waste collection crews can optimize their route depending on the actual state of the bins, and transportation can reroute, depending on the updated information about the traffic (Zanella et al. 2014; Zhou et al. 2020). The only section of really smart infrastructure is the interconnectedness. It embodies such values as security, scalability and resiliency. Systems are also scalable and are built in such a way that they have redundancy in case of any unforeseen failure.

These aspects, combined together with the variety of sources of data in urban areas, the well-developed digital capabilities, and advanced AI softwares have the potential to enable urban populations to construct intelligent and adaptable systems capable of meeting the needs of their citizens and securing their privacy and trust (Viveha et al. 2024; UNESCO 2021). These foundations augment day-to-day endeavors in the city, comprehensive growth, and innovative innovativeness of the future cities, among other things, (UN-Habitat 2022; OECD 2022).

3 AI Applications in Urban Energy Management

Due to the fast pace of urbanization process, energy management emerges as an important element of sustainable development (United Nations DESA, Population Division 2019). The generation, delivery and use of energy in urban areas is turning out to be a revolution of artificial intelligence (AI) (Faruqui et al. 2021; Chicco and Napoli 2016). By means of AI usage to analyze data, cities will become more efficient and will have comparatively lower environmental impact and will find it easier to adopt renewable resources (Faruqui et al. 2021; Rolnick et al. 2019). Artificial intelligence is transforming the urban energy management in the three primary areas just mentioned in the subsections below, namely, building power optimization, demand response and smart grids, and integration of renewable energy sources with storage options (Chicco and Napoli 2016; Lu 2020).

3.1 AI-Powered Demand Response and Smart Grids

The traditional power generation frameworks were installed to deliver energy in a unidirectional flow of the centralized power stations to the consumers (Faruqui et al. 2021). The city of the present day demands a much more sophisticated system, the one that will react instantly to the fluctuating patterns of consumption, the one that would be dynamically mobilized in between the supply and demand and provide multiple sources of energy, including renewable ones (Chicco and Napoli 2016).

The electrical grids of the future are referred to as the smart grids that will be equipped with a high set of sensors, Internet of Things connectivity, and a control system based on artificial intelligence (Zanella et al. 2014; Faruqui et al. 2021). These grids are artificial intelligent (AI) grids that allow them to run their grids in an optimum manner at any given time by gathering immense amounts of real-time data, which includes weather, power generation, and consumer demand (Faruqui et al. 2021; Lab 2021).

This information is used by demand response systems (based on AI) to predict the energy demand and increase consumption (Faruqui et al. 2021). Informing industrial users or smart appliances to reduce or postpone their use of electricity during peak hours in order to make the load on the grid less is just one example of how AI can be used. However, the excess renewable energy can be stored or diverted when there is a low need (Chicco and Napoli 2016).

Smart grids reduce carbon emissions, decrease costs and power reliability by applying machine learning models to analyze past and current data (Faruqui et al. 2021; Chicco and Napoli 2016). The other aspect AI enhances grid resilience is by identifying anomalous conditions and the problems that a grid is prone to before they develop (Berkeley Lab 2021).

The sustainable cities of the future are not simply in the introduction of new technologies, but in the integration of moral values, popular trust and the perception of collaboration in all elements of the urban innovation, which this chapter will discuss (Floridi et al. 2018; Jobin et al. 2019).

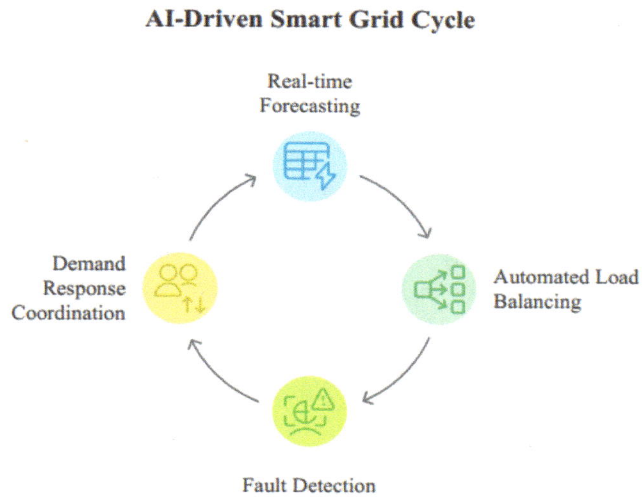

Fig. 3 This illustration demonstrates how smart grid systems for urban energy management are enhanced by artificial intelligence (AI). Among its essential components for reliable and efficient energy distribution are real-time forecasting, automated load balancing, fault detection, and demand response coordination

4 Basic Elements of Artificial Intelligence

4.1 Foundational Principles and Technologies of AI

Artificial intelligence (AI) is a branch of computer science that has been discovered at a very high rate as a game changer that has influenced every part of the city life (Batty 2018; Kitchin 2022). Artificial intelligence (AI) in its simplest form tries to come up with systems, which can think, learn and take action; they usually beat the conventional programmed methods, as they modify themselves to new information (Kitchin 2022). Natural language processing, machine learning, and deep learning are such technologies (Fig. 3).

4.2 Optimizing Building Energy

Nearly 40% of urban energy consumption occurs in buildings worldwide, making them an ideal target for AI-driven efficiency gains (Lu 2020). AI provides a far more flexible and accurate method of controlling lighting, ventilation, and air conditioning (HVAC), even though many urban buildings still rely on manual settings or set schedules (Lu 2020).

AI-powered building management systems (BMS) continuously learn and modify building operations in real time by monitoring occupancy, temperature, humidity, lighting levels, and energy consumption through a network of Internet of Things (IoT) sensors (Kumar et al. 2020; Zanella et al. 2014). These data streams are analyzed by machine learning algorithms to maximize energy use without sacrificing occupant comfort (Lu 2020).

Table 1 AI-driven building energy optimization techniques

Technique	What it does	Urban benefits	Real-world example
Occupancy-based control	Adjusts lighting/ HVAC based on presence	Reduces unnecessary energy use	Smart lighting systems in office buildings
Weather-adaptive HVAC	Prepares HVAC systems using forecasts	Saves energy, maintains comfort	Pre-cooling during summer peak hours
Predictive equipment maintenance	Forecasts failures and schedules fixes	Prevents unplanned outages, saves energy	Monitoring HVAC filter status
Energy usage analytics	Identifies inefficiencies and improvement areas	Supports energy-saving retrofit decisions	Usage dashboards for building managers

An AI system, for instance, can recognize when a room is empty and adjust the lighting or turn it off appropriately (Lu 2020). Additionally, it can automatically preheat or precool spaces during off-peak hours and predict temperature changes based on weather forecasts, which lowers expenses and energy waste (Lu 2020).

Additionally, by tracking the condition of equipment and anticipating possible malfunctions, AI helps predictive maintenance by minimizing downtime and preventing energy inefficiencies brought on by broken HVAC or electrical systems (Lab 2021) (Table 1).

4.3 Renewable Integration and Storage Solutions

Buildings make a perfect target to attain efficiency with the help of AI since nearly 40% of the global urban energy consumption is consumed in buildings (Lu 2020). Even though these control features of the technology are still applied in various buildings in cities as they are manually controlled or in some cases, pre-programmed, artificial intelligence (AI) offers a far more accurate and flexible way to switch on and switch off the lights, vent, or air conditioning (HVAC) (Lu 2020).

AI-based building management systems (BMS) continuously adjust the building processes in real time with a system of sensors on the Internet of Things (IoT) to monitor occupancy, temperature, humidity, intensity of the light and energy consumption (Kumar et al. 2020; Zanella et al. 2014). Machine learning algorithms analyze these streams of data in order to maximize the energy consumed without mitigating the comfort of occupants (Lu 2020).

Using the example of an AI system, it can observe the scenario, in the case when the room is empty, and turn off or regulate the lights (Lu 2020). It can also predict the changes in temperature based on weather prediction and can automatically cool or heat rooms during off-peak times which will save money and energy consumption (Lu 2020).

The transition to the sustainable energy cannot be effective without adding intermittent renewable energy sources, i.e. solar and wind, to the energy mix of the city without interfering with its reliability (Faruqui et al. 2021; Rolnick et al. 2019).

Artificial intelligence (AI) has played a critical role in addressing this complexity by forecasting the availability of renewable energy, based on weather conditions and past trends and reorganizing energy storage equipment (like batteries) to align the demand and supply (Faruqui et al. 2021; Berkeley Lab 2021).

Using the example of AI algorithms, the storage systems are planned, and excesses in renewable production during sunny or windy days are predicted. To ensure that the supply stays constant, generation reduces and the stored energy is emitted. In this process, it saves on the reliance on the utilization of the backup generators that are fossil fuel-powered and release greenhouse gases (Rolnick et al. 2019).

A resilient and flexible energy system with the assistance of organizing distributed energy resources (DERs), i.e., rooftop solar panels, electric vehicles acting as mobile batteries, and demand-side management devices, is created by AI. More optimization of grid operations is derived (Faruqui et al. 2021; Meng et al. 2021).

5 AI for Sustainable Urban Mobility

The coordination of distributed energy resources (DERs) of rooftop solar panels, electric vehicles capable of functioning as mobile batteries and demand-side management devices can be used to improve AI in the operation of the grid and make the energy ecosystem resilient and flexible.

5.1 Smart Traffic Management and Intelligent Transportation System

The modern cities have several issues, including road safety, traffic congestion, delays, and there is an urgent need to attain equitable mobility to all citizens (Zhou et al. 2020). Traffic management in traditional manners becomes inefficient due to the high regulation and intervention of human beings (Levin and Boyles 2015). Intelligent Transport Systems (ITS) that use artificial intelligence (AI) are making roads, lights, and transit systems dynamic, responsive, and adaptive ecosystems (Zhou et al. 2020; Zhang et al. 2021).

- **Real-time Traffic Optimization:**

AI-based systems use the latest reports on traffic on weather services, connected cars, sensors, and traffic cameras (Zhou et al. 2020; Zhang et al. 2021). Machine learning models invariably analyse this data to forecast traffic, detect collisions and adjust the timing of signals in a dynamically fashioned manner (Levin and Boyles 2015; Zhang et al. 2021). Some examples of them are AI-based adaptive traffic lights that can cut wait time and other delays at the time of traveling by 25 per cent in congested streets in the city (Zhou et al. 2020).

- **Predictive Analytics:**

It is possible to predict traffic accumulations in the future and reroute the cars before they occur or inform the city managers due to the use of neural networks and other sophisticated learning algorithms (Zhang et al. 2021). Such a predictive ability is required in the resources allocation of the construction, events, and emergencies (Zhou et al. 2020).

- **Smarter Public Transport Planning:**

It is applied to estimate the demand of the passengers and optimize the schedule of buses and metro, besides planning more sensible public transportation with the help of AI.

5.2 Emissions Reduction Through AI Optimization

More than 30% of city carbon emissions come from urban mobility, which is mostly caused by fossil fuel-powered vehicles, ineffective public transportation, and traffic congestion (Liu et al. 2022). AI provides strong tools for modeling, analyzing, and actively lowering these emissions (Zhou et al. 2020; Liu et al. 2022):

- **Congestion and Idle Reduction:**

AI reduces stop-and-go driving by synchronizing signals and guiding traffic away from bottlenecks. Pollutant emissions and fuel consumption are directly reduced. AI-based traffic management can lower city-level CO_2 emissions by 10–30%, according to studies and recent implementations. The potential is even greater when AI-guided policies encourage a shift to public transportation and active modes.

- **Public Transport Efficiency:**

AI reduces operating costs and emissions per passenger by anticipating passenger demand and optimizing schedules to prevent empty buses and unnecessary trips.

- **Targeted Shared Mobility and Policy Planning:**

Smarter infrastructure and regulatory actions are made possible by advanced artificial intelligence (AI) tools that assist public authorities in determining where shared e-scooters, bikes, or EV ride-shares will significantly reduce urban carbon footprints and replace private vehicle use.

6 AI in Urban Disaster and Climate Risk Management

Early Warning Systems: Forecasting and Alerting:

AI is already making cities much better at detecting threats prior to their emergence (Gupta et al. 2021; United Nations Office for Disaster Risk Reduction (UNDRR) 2021). Just imagine having a system that can quickly filter through massive amounts of data, ground sensors and satellites monitoring the skies, and pinpoint the most basic, initial signs of heatwaves, floods, or storms (Reichstein et al. 2019; Rolnick et al. 2019). AI does precisely that. It delivers custom-made alerts to specific communities or neighborhoods once it becomes familiar with identifying minute patterns that would otherwise be undiscovered by humans (Gupta et al. 2021). It is really impressive that these alerts may be delivered through radio announcements, apps, or texts to the people who are far or hard to reach in any way (United Nations Office for Disaster Risk Reduction (UNDRR) 2021). The AI enhances the preparation, helps to keep people safer, and in the end, it saves lives because each person can get the necessary information at the necessary time (Gupta et al. 2021; United Nations Office for Disaster Risk Reduction (UNDRR) 2021).

Disaster Response Coordination Using AI:

When disaster strikes, it is often difficult to find out where help is most required (United Nations Office for Disaster Risk Reduction (UNDRR) 2021). To give a vivid image of what is going on and where, artificial intelligence (AI) will analyze live feeds, such as social media posts by people on the ground and drones flying overhead (Gupta et al. 2021; United Nations Office for Disaster Risk Reduction (UNDRR) 2021). Consequently, rescue and relief efforts will be conducted more promptly and efficiently through the dispatching of emergency teams straight to the worst-hit locations (United Nations Office for Disaster Risk Reduction (UNDRR) 2021). In the case when humans are too much in danger, AI-equipped drones and robots can even access the unsafe zone in search of victims or to inspect the damage (Rolnick et al. 2019; United Nations Office for Disaster Risk Reduction (UNDRR) 2021). Also, through accurate guidance and updates, AI chatbots reassure the affected families (Schwartz et al. 2020). What's the best part? These systems become effective as time goes by through learning with every event.

Urban Climate Modeling with AI:

One cannot be sure of the way climate change is going to affect our cities, but AI can alleviate uncertainty (Reichstein et al. 2019; Rolnick et al. 2019). AI can provide a complete view of risks such as heatwaves, rising moments, and floods by combining information obtained with satellites, weather stations, and years of climate history, even to the extent of individual neighborhoods or streets (Reichstein et al. 2019). Consequently, the planners of cities will be able to make smarter choices regarding the ways of building safer infrastructure or the number of trees to plant (UNESCO 2021; OECD 2022). Even hypothetical scenarios can be modeled by AI to observe how adjustments in the city may affect such factors as temperature or the risk of floods (Rolnick et al. 2019). We should keep these AI systems transparent and equitable in order to facilitate the benefits of these systems to all communities, particularly those, which are less connected (Floridi et al. 2018; Jobin et al. 2019).

Integrated Example: Urban Flood Risk Management:

Using weather forecasts, city construction maps, sensor data, and resident reports, AI can offer ground-based emergency responsers with accurate warnings of floods

(Gupta et al. 2021; United Nations Office for Disaster Risk Reduction (UNDRR) 2021). Rapid storm recovery, smarter deployment of resources and the benefits of previous alerts have already been witnessed in such cities as Jakarta and Mumbai (United Nations Office for Disaster Risk Reduction (UNDRR) 2021). This form of AI-based coordination reduces damage not only when an event (disaster) takes place but also helps to save lives and has faster recovery rates of cities (Gupta et al. 2021; United Nations Office for Disaster Risk Reduction (UNDRR) 2021). Overall, AI is transforming our cities to be more robust and smart. It is a powerful weapon that is changing the way we face the growing demands of climate and disaster risk, whether it be the early recognition of threat and the coordinated response of saving lives or getting cities ready to face climate change (Rolnick et al. 2019; UNESCO 2021).

7 Ethical, Social, and Governance Challenges

7.1 Data Privacy and Security Considerations

- The issue of data privacy and security is also on the front burner of organizations and regulators as the extent of data breach continues to rise and cybercrime is taking its toll on the financial front (Viveha et al. 2024; UNESCO 2021). The best 2025 foresees and statistics include.
- Consumer Concern: 92% of Americans are concerned about their privacy online and only 3% of those have an idea about privacy regulations (Viveha et al. 2024).
- Growth of Regulation: Is being passed in countries including India, Japan, the UK, and the US, and at least eight new state-level privacy laws in the US are coming into effect by the year 2025. Breach of Data and Cost: The average cost of a breach of data was 4.62 million dollars in the year 2024, and by 2025, cybercrime expenses are projected to be 10.5 trillion dollars across the globe. In 44% of breaches, personal customer data are exposed, and the phishing is currently the cause of about 30% (UNESCO 2021).
- Security Investment: The global spending on security and risk management by end-users will reach 212 billion in the year 2025—a 15% increase on the 2024 spending (OECD 2022).
- Data Privacy Technologies More than two out of three enterprises will be using one or more privacy-enhancing technologies by the end of 2025. It is estimated that the market of data privacy software will grow at a 35.5% CAGR over the time up to 2032 (Viveha et al. 2024; UNESCO 2021).

It is important that the board of directors remains impartial and transparent in their actions, human Bias, Accountability, and Transparency It is crucial that the board of directors is unbiased and accountable in their acts (Fig. 4).

Ethical deployment of AI is mainly about algorithmic bias, responsibility and explainability (Floridi et al. 2018; Jobin et al. 2019).

Algorithmic Bias: AI bias arises due to biased or non-representative training data and can lead to increased social inequalities, especially in hiring, lending, and medicine (Binns 2018).

Actions against Lack of responsibility: Firms will be requested to institute AI ethics boards and draw clear principles of AI decision-making, and conduct bias audits and minimization audits (Floridi et al. 2018).

Transparency and Explainability: As AI is generally a black box, it is proposed to use such solutions as SHAP (Shapley Additive Explanations) and LIME (Local Interpretable Model-agnostic Explanations) to make decisions more comprehensible to stakeholders. Open procedures are a source of regulatory and general trust.

Legal and Regulatory Background: The introduction of EU AI Act and the changes to the data protection laws around the globe point to the growing regulatory interest in the fairness, explainability, and risk management in AI (UNESCO 2021; OECD 2022) (Fig. 5).

7.2 Public Trust, Policy Frameworks and Inclusivity

Sustainable digital technology adoption is all about trust in the government by the populace and the involvement in the government (UNESCO 2021).

Trust Erosion: There is a historic low of trust in both the public and the private institutions since the fear of data abuse and deployments of dark technology are high (Viveha et al. 2024).

Stakeholder Engagement: The policy making process is also shifting to participatory mechanisms, engagement of the citizens and e-participation to ensure that the marginalized voices are heard and considered when it comes to digital governance (UN-Habitat 2022; Schwartz et al. 2020).

Policy Invention: Global leaders include moving to full AI ethics, citizen participation initiatives (e.g., the Finland AI Challenge), and continuing impact measurement systems (e.g., in Canada Directive on Automated Decision-Making) (Floridi et al. 2018; Jobin et al. 2019).

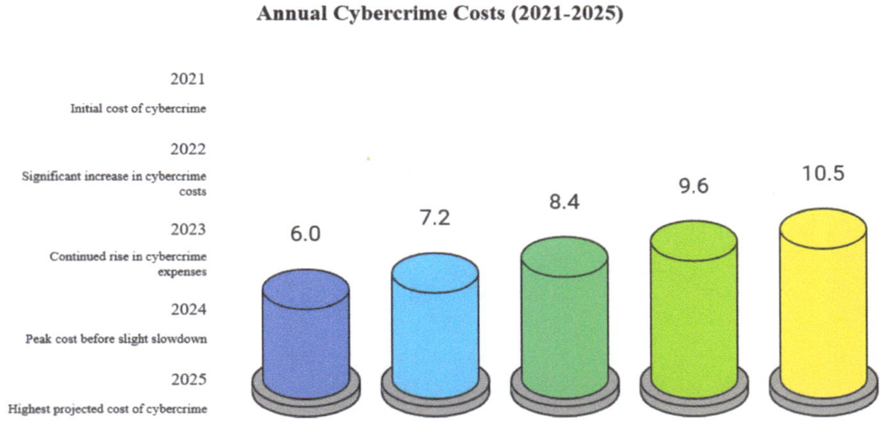

Fig. 4 The bar chart illustrates the projected annual global cost of cybercrime from 2021 to 2025. It shows a steady rise from $6 trillion in 2021 to an estimated $10.5 trillion by 2025, reflecting the growing financial impact of cyber threats worldwide

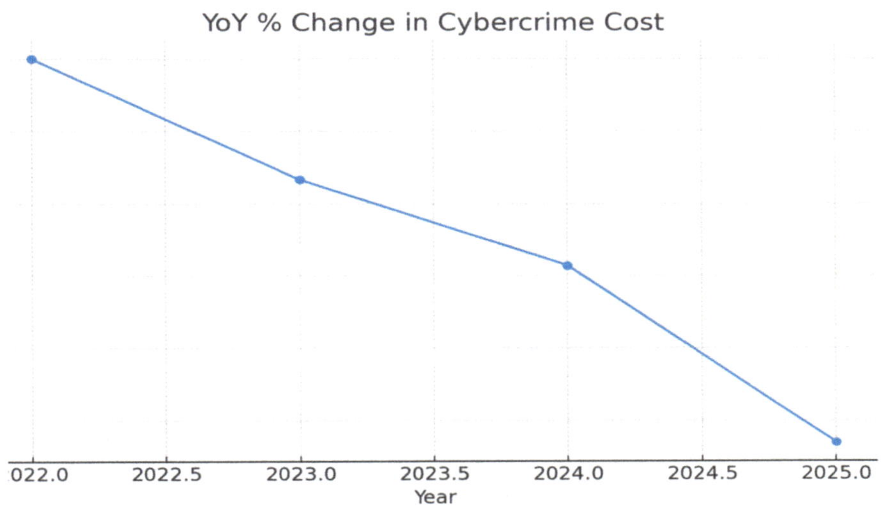

Fig. 5 The graph forecasts the Year-over-Year (YoY) percentage change in global cybercrime cost from 2022 to 2025. This rate of change is shown to decline, while the underlying text notes the total cost is projected to surge to $10.5 trillion by 2025

Inclusivity and Equity: A policy priority is to respond to digital equity through the lens of the so-called universal design and by considering different communities. Improved public trust is also promoted by improved transparency and frequent review mechanisms (UN-Habitat. 2022) (Fig. 6).

8 Case Studies and Global Best Practices

In this chapter, the author explains how the pioneering cities across the globe are utilizing artificial intelligence (AI) to drive sustainability initiatives (Subramanian et al. 2022; UN-Habitat 2022). By use of excellent case studies, incorporating practical-lessons towards a large cross section of urban settings, and providing a comprehensive comparative analysis of strategies embraced in the Global North and South, this chapter illuminates the main pathways to copycat, inclusive, and scalable urban sustainability solutions (World Bank 2020; OECD 2022).

8.1 Leading Cities Leveraging AI for Sustainability

1. **Amsterdam, the Netherlands (Global North)**

Smart Infrastructure and Circular Economy: The Amsterdam-based AI-based Digital Twin model simulates the city transport trends, energy consumption, and waste to enable the municipal body and corporations to optimize the logistics process, reduce emissions, and expedite the process of circularity implementation (Subramanian et al. 2022; Franco et al. 2022).

AI in Mobility: Real time AI analytics can be used to support adaptive traffic management and optimize the use of public transit to reduce congestion and NO_2 emissions (Zhou et al. 2020).

Nature-based Solutions: Artificial intelligence can be used to map urban biodiversity and trace green areas to inform urban greening efforts and carbon neutrality planning efforts (Subramanian et al. 2022).

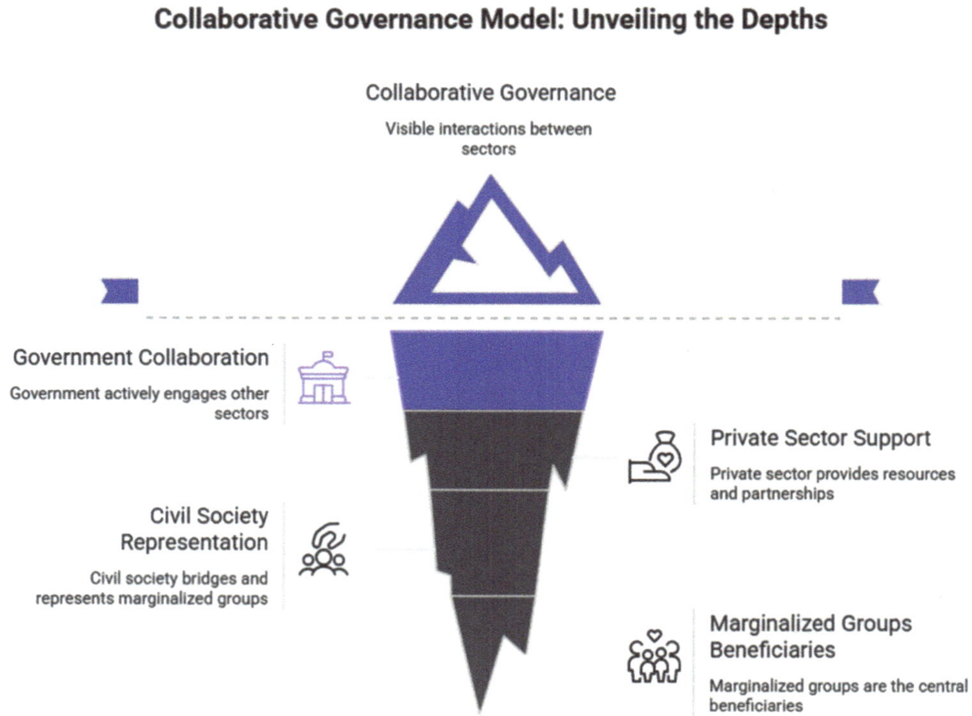

Fig. 6 Simplified stakeholder network showing key collaboration among Government, Private Sector, Civil Society, and Marginalized Groups in inclusive digital governance. Arrows indicate the main engagement pathways that build trust, shape policies, and promote inclusivity

2. **Singapore (Global North/Asia)**

Urban Environment Analytics: "Smart Nation Singapore" is an implementation of AI-based sensors and analytics into waste management, water supply, and energy grids, serving to optimize the resources in real-time (McKinsey Global Institute 2018).

Sustainable Construction: AI will be used to predict energy requirements in new buildings and guide retrofitting to achieve efficiency in buildings, which will contribute to the Green Mark certification in Singapore (Lu 2020; Shapiro 2018).

Policy Convergence: Government, academia, and industry have close coordination and, as such, have enabled effective AI solutions in sustainability to be piloted and scaled rapidly (UNESCO 2021).

3. **Kigali, Rwanda (Global South)**

AI in Mobility and Air Quality: Kigali is an AI-based application of demand-based optimization of bus routes and reduction of emissions. AI-based air quality monitoring systems identify areas of pollution and direct city development (World Bank 2020).

Waste Management: The AI-powered mobile apps can allow citizens to report illegal dumping, and predictive analytics can optimize the routes to collect waste.

Renewable Energy: Strategic partnerships with technological firms have enabled the application of AI in mini-grid operations to optimize the level of renewable penetration and coverage in the community (World Bank 2020).

4. **Curitiba, Brazil (Global South)**
   - Urban Environment Analytics: To make Singapore a smart country, the sensors and analytics of the waste management, water supply, and energy grids are optimized with the help of AI in order to streamline resources in real-time (McKinsey Global Institute 2018).
   - Sustainable Construction: The Green Mark certification program that covers the issue of sustainability is supported by the AI applications in Singapore to predict the energy needs in new buildings and the process of retrofitting (Lu 2020).
   - Policy Convergence: The close connections between government, academia, and business have enabled successful AI solutions to become piloted and scaled rapidly when it comes to sustainability (UNESCO 2021).
   - 3. AI in Mobility and Air Quality in Kigali, Rwanda (Global South): Kigali uses AI-based methods to minimize the emissions and optimize the bus routes based on the demand. The air quality surveillance systems based on AI inform urban planning by revealing the polluted regions (World Bank 2020).
   - Waste Management: AI-driven mobile applications can enable residents to report cases of their neighbors improperly disposing of waste, and predictive analytics can optimize the waste collection routes.

8.2 Lessons Learned and Replicability

Key Lessons from Leading Cases:

Information Fusion is important: Successful AI sustainability takes interoperability and cross-sector data sharing (e.g. Amsterdam, Singapore).

Public–Private Partnerships Form Scale: Governments, academic and technology businesses collaborate to develop most of the high-impact projects (e.g. nationwide deployment in Singapore, renewable grids in Kigali).

Contextual Adaptation: The solutions of Singapore utilize state-of-the-art infrastructure, but the AI in Kigali has a low cost and is open-source transportation.

Community Engagement: It seems to be more legitimate, relevant and able to uncover concealed sustainability concerns through the involvement of the citizens such as in the case of Curitiba.

Replicability Considerations:

Scalability: The resource-poor cities are likely to adopt Open-source AI models and modular instruments (as in Kigali and Curitiba).

Capacity Building: City managers and local technical talent Capacity-building training programs are essential to sustainable adoption- most Global south cities partner with universities to increase capacity.

Digital Infrastructure: Preinvestment in sound networks and data standards is needed in order to transform AI-led transformation.

8.3 Comparative Assessment: Global North and South

1. **Artificial Intelligence Readiness and Technology:**

Global North:

Has well developed urban digital infrastructure (data, IoT, and broadband) as the base of the real-time AI applications, predictive analytics, and digital twins of city governance (Subramanian et al. 2022).

Invests in AI research and development clusters and pilot projects integrated into city planning to enable city-wide solutions (e.g. Amsterdam Digital Twin, Smart Nation Singapore) (Shapiro 2018).

Global South:

Utilizes pragmatic, mobile-based and open-source AI applications to bypass infrastructure gaps and reach (e.g. mobile waste reporting in Kigali, adaptive flood management in Curitiba (World Bank 2020).

Shows flexible capability- difficult to adaptive, scrupulous systems frequently outrun the housing restrictions of the North.

2. **Investment, Resources, and Expansion.**

Global North:

Large per capita governmental and non-governmental investment, and institutionalized innovation systems.(Alawadhi et al. (2019))

Continuous funds streams are the common advantage of projects, as they make it long-term sustainable and fast to advance pilots into systemic solutions (McKinsey Global Institute 2018).

Global South:

The projects often require the involvement of the government with business (World Bank 2020), short-term foreign assistance, and donor interventions.

Scalability requires advancement of the effects which are practical, should develop local capacity and give continuous technical support.

3. **Management and Structures of Policy**

Global North:

Combined national and urban AI strategy operations, incorporating innovation along with strict data governance and regulatory applications (adherency to GDPR, city AI regulations) (UNESCO 2021; OECD 2022).

Embedded technology mitigates measures and social responsibility.

Global South:

Utilizes the adaptive, flexible government- in most instances it regionalizes and adapts the international forms to the realities on the ground (World Bank 2020).

Works with repetitiveness of policy-making, in most cases, trying to experiment with new technologies and regulations simultaneously (UNESCO 2021).

4. **Engagement and Inclusion of Citizens.**

Global North:

Encourages openness, through online consultations and open data, but privacy of data, online disparities, and innovation fatigue could limit engagement (Viveha et al. 2024).

Global South:

Demands participatory rule, and participates in the design of projects and provides feedback on it via community-based

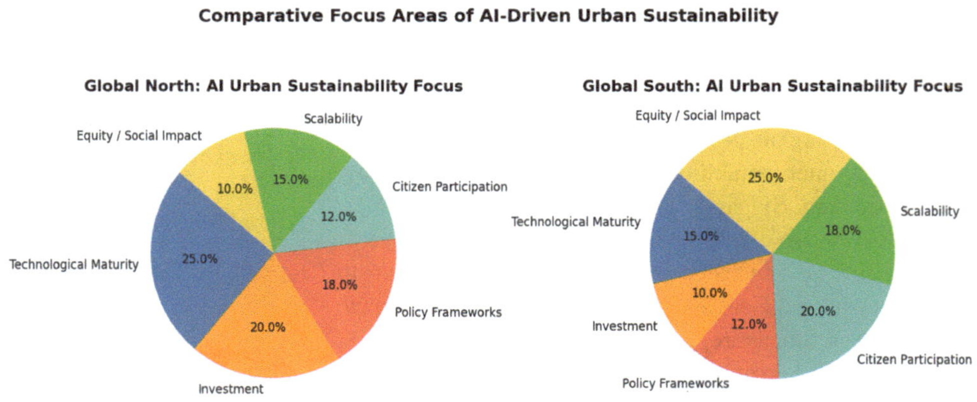

Fig. 7 Relative pie charts of the focus of key areas of attention of AI-driven urban sustainability in the Global North and the Global South. Each section reflects the various priorities in the tech, investment, policy, participation, scalability, and equity

forums (e.g., participatory budgeting, civic apps (Schwartz et al. 2020).

Social equity is not a marginal objective of offering maximum benefits to underprivileged people and underserved communities (World Bank 2020).

5. **Obstacles and Implementation Openings**

Global North:

At other times, AI system enrichment has been halted because earlier infrastructure and regulatory mandate was complex and inflexible (UNESCO 2021).

Perhaps have more barriers to aging out old systems and the introduction of new systems is slow.

Global South:

Can integrate customizable and cutting-edge AI solutions that are highly lower complexities without necessarily having to move to giant legacy systems.

Its key obstacles are low levels of digital literacy, insufficient resources, and access to technical skills (World Bank 2020).

6. **Social Impact and Equity Urban Outcomes**

Global North:

Evolutionary changes according to which the overemphasis on efficiency, resources, and reduction of emissions are substituted with the increased emphasis on environmental justice and equity (UNESCO 2021; World Economic Forum 2020).

The artificial intelligence solutions are shifting away to the lapses in accessibility and underserved areas.

Global South:

Equity-based in its principles to the core: projects will seal the weaknesses in core services (waste, air, mobility), jobs and livelihoods, and environmental health (UN-Habitat. 2022; World Bank 2020).

It is impossible to talk about AI interventions outside of the context of socio-economic development and the resilience-building initiatives (Fig. 7).

7. **Cross-Regional Learning and Knowledge Transfer**

Global North:

Suggests new technical expertise, policy values, regimes or even standardized digital systems.

New receptivity to participatory and responsive practices was introduced by him as a consequence of Global South experience.

Global South:

Low-cost innovation, grass-root government and fast to-scale.

Shows how malleable and prepared artificial intelligence solutions can deliver outcomes utilizing lesser and lesser resources, provides instances on how the same may be replicated in other locations.

9 Future Direction and Future Innovations

The end of the chapter contains the description of the strategic orientations of AI-enabling city sustainability (UNESCO 2021; World Economic Forum 2020). It greatly values circularity of asset circulations, democratic and trustful AI governance, and the integration of AI with the state-of-the-art technologies in the city centres to develop resilient, low-carbon and fair city systems (Floridi et al. 2018; Franco et al. 2022; Yu et al. 2022).

The paper explains how AI is implemented to the Circular Economy and Resource Efficiency.

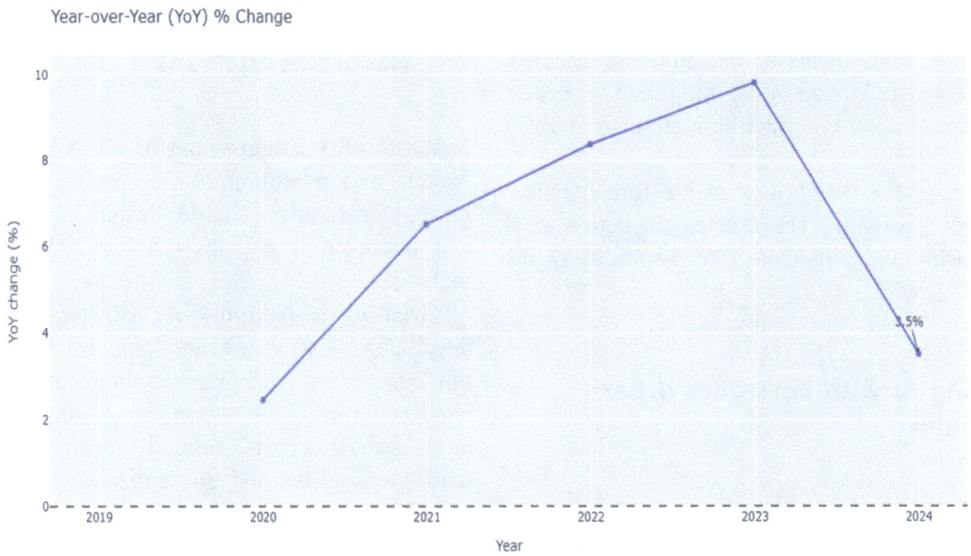

Fig. 8 A percentage change (2019–2024–year-over-year) scatterplot of the momentum of the circular economy per annum. A value of greater than 0% is a sign of improvement and a value of less than 0% is a sign of slowdown. It is the annotation of the last point and 0% that indicates the current direction

9.1 Strategic Vision

Regenerative urban metabolism: Transforming linear take-make-waste systems to regenerative material intelligence through AI-based systems (Franco et al. 2022). This will reduce embodied and operational emissions and value in the urban stocks will be held.

Key Skills:

Smart recovery and reverse logistics: Computer vision and spectroscopy to separate the things of a high purity; routing and bin positions should be aware; and uncertainty aware optimization of fleet operations and placement of where to install the facilities.

Circular design and procurement: assisted AI-aided life-cycle assessment to identify the most good products i.e. low carbon, repairable, can be re-used in other applications; predictive maintenance to ensure buildings, fleets, and the infrastructure in the public can last longer.

Track of materials and markets: The priority of materials flows (steel, cement, batteries, electronics); the secondary-materials exchange with provable characteristics and price discovery and discovery through the assistance of AI.

Where utilities and manufacturing symbiosis: prediction of demand to decrease food waste and permit redistribution; knowledge graphs to support trades in by-products; artificial intelligence (AI) control to recycle water in district thermal networks, and wastewater energy extraction.

Equity and Governance:

Interoperability standards of data and citywide ontologies; customer-specific KPI of contractual (reparable, reused content, and recovery rate).

Co-designed inclusion: data deserts inhibited through disaggregated and privacy preserving-circularity indicators: publication; formalization and protection of informal waste workers where needed (Fig. 8).

9.2 Citizen Engagement and Participatory AI

Normative underpinnings: In AI in the delivery of the service of the population and city planning, legitimacy, inclusiveness, transparency, and sustainability accountability should exist Institutional systems.

Tiered access of research and entrepreneurship consists of Tiered access: civic data trusts/commons, purpose limitation, and benefit-sharing.

Co-design and deliberation: structured sprints and meetings to formulate goals, equity policies, and achievement of AI systems measures in the safety, housing, mobility, and climate resiliency area.

Involvement of sensing, feedback: federated learning to descend raw information to the location; in-app error reporting, community participatory labelling, community deployed sensors and smartphone campaigns (air, heat, noise, accessibility).

Algorithmic Impact Assessments (AIAs): Publicly available mandatory assessments of the high-risk systems, which contain a distributional analysis, mitigation measures, audit and decommissioning criteria which are also publicly available.

The interaction of the two brings to the fore the likelihood of the two coexisting. The connection between AI and new urban technologies indicates the possibility of the coexistence of the two.

9.3 Integrating AI with Emerging Urban Technologies

AI & Digital Twins:

Prior to deployment, simulating and optimizing city-scale twins relying on physics and data on optimal congestion pricing, emergency routing, and climate adaptation (heat/flood) can be simulated and optimized (Kamalam and Rajasekar 2023).

Such technical practices are quantification of uncertainty, ground truth validation, model versioning, public sandboxes, hybrid physics-ML surrogates, and standardized data layers (geospatial, BIM/IFC, IoT/SCADA, and mobility (Kamalam and Rajasekar 2023)).

A healthy existence requires edge artificial intelligence:

Building, real-time user privacy inference, plant, intersection (near sensor redaction, adaptive signal, leak/anomaly signal, micro-grid/HVAC control).

Some of the examples of engineering patterns are: attestation, zero-trust security, fleet-scale MLOps, split computing, compression/quantization, and safe-degradation fallbacks (Yu et al. 2022).

Robotics and autonomous systems:

Emergency duty, repairs and maintenance of the parks, sidewalk logistic and sanitation, inspection (bridges, roofs, powerlines) (UNESCO 2021).

These are wrappings of policies such as common curb/ sidewalks structure of governance, incident report, audit and access control/protect.

Interoperability and openness:

Open data models and open interfaces to enable others Vendors: Open data models and APIs to enable the use of application ecosystems and city sandboxes (International Telecommunication Union 2016) (Fig. 9).

10 Policymakers and Practitioners Recommendations

Sustainability Suggestions of AI Adoption: The policymakers and practitioners who would achieve sustainable AI implementation should design coordinated, inclusive, and future-proof policies (OECD 2022). Key approaches include.

Creating a National AI Strategy: Nations need to develop a clear vision and plan of AI development and implementation with priorities in sectors, ethical concerns, legal supervision, infra structure, and labor preparedness. Such strategies have already been published in more than 75 countries and this underlines their significance in the national competitiveness and sustainable development (OECD 2022).

Policy Coherence: The policies should be aligned with the existing cybersecurity, data, and digital efforts. Such coordination enhances chances of successful policies in various sectors and avoids scattered efforts (Viveha et al. 2024; Susha et al. 2019).

Stakeholder Engagement: Inclusion of public, private, academic and civil society stakeholders ensures that there is an increase in buy-in and ensures that policies address the variety of needs. As an example, the national AI strategy of Nigeria is participatory in nature (Jong et al. 2020; Schwartz et al. 2020).

Context-Specific Adaptation: There is no universal answer and the strategies must consider the strengths of the institution, the social values, local development priorities, and the condition of the digital infrastructure (UN-Habitat. 2022).

Capacity Building and Workforce Development: The organization has developed a strategic plan to enhance staff skills and capabilities to ensure the achievement of strategic goals and objectives. Human Building: The organization has established a four-year strategic plan to build the skills and ability of the staff members in order to realize strategic goals and objectives.

The human capital and organizational preparedness is key to the sustainable adoption of *AI* recommendations include:

Skill Training and Upskilling: To make sure that the future workforce is AI literate, invest in general education, in particular in STEM and AI-related areas. This includes partnerships with learning institutions to revise curricula and promote life long learning (OECD 2022).

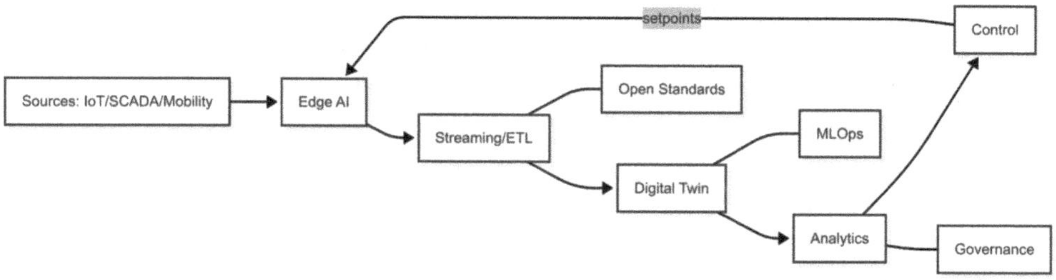

Fig. 9 The data of city systems are transmitted to Edge AI (low-latency actions), to a Digital Twin (simulation), to Analytics and to Control (sending setpoints to the edge). Interoperability is ensured and enhanced by Open Standards, Governance and MLOps

Enhancing Organizational Capacity: Enhance organizational culture and preparedness towards AI adoption by means of digital capability tests and specific training. Promote evidence-based decision-making, experimental learning and innovation-driven attitudes (Susha et al. 2019).

Inclusive and Equitable Access: Attend to the digital and AI literacy gender, regional, and socio-economic disparities, and provide opportunities to the underserved and marginalized communities key to sustainable development in general (UN-Habitat 2022; UNESCO 2021).

11 Conclusion

Computer-Assisted Urbanism: Thinking About AI in Sustainable Cities

Artificial intelligence (AI) is already emerging as a revolution in the effort to create more welcoming, sustainable, and dynamic metropolitan areas. Unlike earlier times of technological advances, AI provides cities with a special chance to collect, compute, as well as act upon large volumes of real-time data, making it feasible to achieve an urban understanding and reactivity previously unthinkable. The AI-powered systems provide cities with efficient resource distributions, predicting issues and addressing the needs of more citizens in the future in the fields of energy management, transportation, waste reduction, and emergency responses, among others.

The use of AI can improve the way the population accesses the services provided by the government by becoming more dynamic and approachable. In the healthcare industry, AI is being used to detect disease outbreaks early and minimize healthcare provision among undeserved individuals. Adaptive learning platforms can enhance the achievement and opportunity gap in education through a personalized experience of each learner. The safety of the city also increases, since AI-based surveillance and predictive policing systems allow more prompt and more precise responses to the situation, yet such options introduce valuable ethical issues that include privacy and civil rights.

One of the key benefits of AI is that AI can be used to enhance the sustainability of the environment. Algorithms have the potential to track the quality of air and water in real-time, anticipate areas of pollution, and improve the use of infrastructure in cities such as lighting, heating, and transport. Such dynamic control of these systems can help cities to save energy, decrease emissions, and decrease their ecological footprint. This intelligence-based stewardship advocates greater climate objectives, as well as, safeguards that city development does not take place at the cost of environmental well-being.

Moreover, AI enhances resilience of the city systems. Predictive analytics are used to enable cities to prepare in case of natural disasters by predicting extreme weather and responding effectively and promptly to such events. With the potential to combine information between departments, AI can help authorities in cities discover weak points in a matter of seconds, distribute resources and safeguard urban citizens, especially the most vulnerable.

Regardless of these advantages, making AI a reality in the cities will require careful, active governance. There should be an effort to make sure that technological advancement does not enhance the current inequalities nor does it bring new divisions. The issue of digital inclusion should be given priority because the underprivileged communities should be able to receive the benefits of AI-driven innovation, and contribute to its development. Privacy and strong data management and continuous evaluation of risks should be put in place to avoid abuse and discrimination due to discriminative algorithms and unregulated surveillance.

The most important thing is the effective governance structures, which need to be formed between the government, industry, academia, and civil society. Cities may promote trust, transparency, and responsiveness to urban AI systems by engaging a wide group of stakeholders in the design and management of these systems. The rules and codes of ethics need to be used to ensure not only security and privacy, but inclusivity, fairness, and transparency to the population.

Overall, AI can be seen as an effective set of tools that can be used to tackle one of the most urgent problems of modern urban areas and make them more renewable, inclusive, and resilient. But these benefits can only be achieved by the way of inclusive policies, close monitoring and a common desire to see to it that the digital future is beneficial to all citizens. With the city growing and becoming more and more complex, AI can be turned into the power of good, and the human and environmental welfare can be prioritized in the values guiding the development of cities.

Significant Implications and Recommendation

AI as a catalyst to achieve Sustainable Urban Transformation: Well-managed AI has the potential to enhance energy consumption, minimize pollution, enhance mobility, and enhance quality life of urban residents.

Critical to Governing, Ethics, and Inclusion: The implementation of AI in cities has to consider transparency, equity, ethical consideration, and open discussion as the only ways to gain trust in people and guarantee that everyone can be heard.

Capacity Building is Necessary: Sustainable adoption implies long term investment into digital infrastructure, training in AI skills and life-long learning of city officials and citizens.

Monitoring and Adaptation: To ensure that cities adapt to rapidly changing technologies and meet changing urban demands, continuous evaluation, open reporting, and adaptive strategies can be useful.

Cooperation is the key to success: Governments, technology providers, researchers, and community groups should cooperate to co-invent and exchange best practices at the international level.

Call to Action: Policymakers, practitioners, and city stakeholders have been encouraged to play a direct role in determining the path of AI towards the greater good. Invest in non-discriminatory, ethical, and future-proof artificial intelligence systems; consult and hear different people; and pay attention to new threats. Cities need to open up the transformative opportunities of AI that can help them achieve a more sustainable, equitable, and resilient urban future through strategic leadership and cross-sectoral collaborations.

References

Alawadhi, S., Aldama-Nalda, A., Chourabi, H., Gil-Garcia, J. R., Leung, S., Mellouli, S., et al. (2019). Measuring smart city performance: Comparative experiences from urban regions. *Cities*, 92, 25–34. https://doi.org/10.1016/j.cities.2019.03.004

Allam, Z., & Dhunny, Z. A. (2019). On big data, artificial intelligence and smart cities. *Cities*, 89, 80–91. https://doi.org/10.1016/j.cities.2019.01.032

Batty, M. (2018). Artificial intelligence and smart cities. *Environment and Planning B: Urban Analytics and City Science*, 45(1), 3–6. https://doi.org/10.1177/2399808318760329

Berkeley Lab. (2021). AI and Machine Learning for Modern Grid Management. Lawrence Berkeley National Laboratory, LBNL-2001358. https://eta-publications.lbl.gov/sites/default/files/lbnl-2001358.pdf

Bibri, S. E. (2021). Big data and AI analytics for smart sustainable cities: A systematic review of practices, techniques, and frameworks. *Sustainable Cities and Society*, 71, 102945. https://doi.org/10.1016/j.scs.2021.102945

Binns, R. (2018). Fairness in machine learning: Lessons for urban AI. *Communications of the ACM*, 61(4), 22–24. https://doi.org/10.1145/3190521

Chicco, G., & Napoli, R. (2016). Smart Grids with AI-based solutions. *IEEE Transactions on Smart Grid*, 7(2), 666–679. https://doi.org/10.1109/TSG.2015.2023120

Chui, M., Manyika, J., & Miremadi, M. (2018). Notes from the AI frontier: Insights from hundreds of use cases. *McKinsey Global Institute Discussion Paper*. https://www.mckinsey.com/capabilities/mckinsey-digital/our-insights/notes-from-the-ai-frontier-applications-and-value-of-deep-learning

de Jong, M., Hoppe, T., & Noori, N. (2020). Participatory AI for urban sustainability transitions. *Environmental Innovation and Societal Transitions*, 34, 267–285. https://doi.org/10.1016/j.eist.2019.12.004

Faruqui, A., Sergici, S., & Palmer, J. (2021). AI-enabled smart grids and urban sustainability. *Renewable and Sustainable Energy Reviews*, 146, 111151. https://doi.org/10.1016/j.rser.2021.111151

Floridi, L., Cowls, J., Beltrametti, M., Chatila, R., Chazerand, P., Dignum, V., et al. (2018). AI4People—An Ethical Framework for a Good AI Society. *Minds and Machines*, 28(4), 689–707. https://doi.org/10.1007/s11023-018-9482-5

Franco, J., Ruiz, M. D., Garcia, J. M., & Saenz, J. (2022). AI-enabled circular economy in urban systems. *Waste Management*, 138, 220–230. https://doi.org/10.1016/j.wasman.2021.12.020

Gaur, A., Scotney, B., Parr, G., & McClean, S. (2015). Smart City Architecture and its Applications based on IoT. *Procedia Computer Science*, 52, 1089–1094. https://doi.org/10.1016/j.procs.2015.05.122

Gupta, J., Prakash, A., & Yadav, A. (2021). AI for urban flood risk management. *International Journal of Disaster Risk Reduction*, 53, 101957. https://doi.org/10.1016/j.ijdrr.2020.101957

Hashem, I. A. T., Yaqoob, I., Anuar, N. B., Mokhtar, S., Gani, A., & Khan, S. U. (2016). The role of big data in smart city. *International Journal of Information Management*, 36(5), 748–758. https://doi.org/10.1016/j.ijinfomgt.2016.05.002

International Telecommunication Union (ITU). (2016). Smart Sustainable Cities: AI, Standards and the Role of ICT. https://www.itu.int/en/ITU-T/ssc/united/Pages/default.aspx

Jobin, A., Ienca, M., & Vayena, E. (2019). The global landscape of AI ethics guidelines. *Nature Machine Intelligence*, 1(9), 389–399. https://doi.org/10.1038/s42256-019-0088-2

Kamalam, G. K., & Rajasekar, V. (2023). Digital twin meets artificial intelligence: AI-augmented industrial automation systems using intelligent digital twins. In *Digital Twin for Smart Manufacturing* (pp. 145–159). Academic Press.

Kitchin, R. (2022). Urban intelligence and smart cities: The future of urban AI. *Philosophy & Technology*, 35, 1–26. https://doi.org/10.1007/s13347-021-00492-3

Kumar, A., Mallick, P. K., & Mallick, R. C. (2020). Role of IoT and AI in Smart City Applications. *Sensors and Actuators A: Physical*, 303, 111913. https://doi.org/10.1016/j.sna.2019.111913

Levin, M. W., & Boyles, S. D. (2015). A Review of AI in Real-Time Urban Traffic Control. *Transportation Research Part C: Emerging Technologies*, 57, 440–453. https://doi.org/10.1016/j.trc.2015.04.009

Liu, F., Wang, L., & Zhang, H. (2022). AI-based approaches for reducing transport emissions in smart cities. *Sustainable Cities and Society*, 76, 103371. https://doi.org/10.1016/j.scs.2021.103371

Lu, Y. (2020). AI-driven optimization in building energy management. *Applied Energy*, 272, 115220. https://doi.org/10.1016/j.apenergy.2020.115220

Lundberg, S. M., & Lee, S. I. (2017). A Unified Approach to Interpreting Model Predictions. *Advances in Neural Information Processing Systems*, 30, 4765–4774. https://proceedings.neurips.cc/paper/2017/hash/8a20a8621978632d76c43dfd28b67767-Abstract.html

McKinsey Global Institute. (2018). Smart Cities: Digital Solutions for a More Livable Future. https://www.mckinsey.com/capabilities/operations/our-insights/smart-cities-digital-solutions-for-a-more-livable-future

Meng, F., Zhang, Y., & Fang, X. (2021). Integration of electric vehicles and AI in urban mobility. *IEEE Access*, 9, 145758–145771. https://doi.org/10.1109/ACCESS.2021.3122606

OECD. (2022). The Impact of AI on Cities and Urban Policy. OECD Urban Policy PaperNo.04. https://www.oecd.org/publications/the-impact-of-ai-on-cities-and-urban-policy-17b3b9d5-en.htm

Reichstein, M., Camps-Valls, G., Stevens, B., Jung, M., Denzler, J., Carvalhais, N., et al. (2019). Deep learning and process understanding for data-driven Earth system science. *Nature*, 566(7743), 195–204. https://doi.org/10.1038/s41586-019-0912-1

Rolnick, D., Donti, P. L., Kaack, L. H., et al. (2019). Tackling Climate Change with Machine Learning. *arXiv preprint* https://arxiv.org/abs/1906.05433

Schwartz, H. A., Giorgi, S., Sap, M., Crutchley, P., Ungar, L. H., & Eichstaedt, J. C. (2020). AI and citizen engagement in urban governance. *Government Information Quarterly*, 37(4), 101507. https://doi.org/10.1016/j.giq.2020.101507

Shapiro, J. (2018). The Impact of Smart Cities on Urban Sustainability: Evidence from Singapore. *Urban Studies*, 55(4), 813–828. https://doi.org/10.1177/0042098017724820

Subramanian, M., Rajasekar, V., VE, S., Shanmugavadivel, K., & Nandhini, P. S. (2022). Effectiveness of decentralized federated learning algorithms in healthcare: a case study on cancer classification. *Electronics*, *11*(24), 4117.

Susha, I., Grönlund, Å., & Van Veenstra, A. F. (2019). Data governance for sustainable smart cities. *Government Information Quarterly*, 36(4), 101400. https://doi.org/10.1016/j.giq.2019.06.002

UNESCO. (2021). Artificial Intelligence and Cities: Risks, Opportunities, and Good Governance. https://unesdoc.unesco.org/ark:/48223/pf0000374927

United Nations, DESA, Population Division. (2019). World Urbanization Prospects: The 2018 Revision. https://population.un.org/wup/Publications/

UN-Habitat. (2022). People-Centered Smart Cities: Case Studies and Best Practices. https://unhabitat.org/people-centered-smart-cities-case-studies-and-best-practices

United Nations Office for Disaster Risk Reduction (UNDRR). (2021). Leveraging Artificial Intelligence for Disaster Risk Reduction in Cities. https://www.undrr.org/publication/leveraging-artificial-intelligence-disaster-risk-reduction-cities

Viveha, C., Rajasekar, V., Sowmiya, S., Devi, K. N., Dhivyanchali, M. N., & Varshni, M. (2024, February). Point of care noninvasive screening tool for early detection of anemia using smartphone. In *2024 Second International Conference on Emerging Trends in Information Technology and Engineering (ICETITE)* (pp. 1–5). IEEE.

World Bank. (2020). Smart Cities for Sustainable Development in Africa and Asia. https://openknowledge.worldbank.org/entities/publication/bc5b6f50-8ba6-4e3b-a3a3-9eff3b710d00

World Economic Forum. (2020). Artificial Intelligence and the Future of Urban Sustainability. https://www.weforum.org/agenda/2020/01/artificial-intelligence-and-the-future-of-urban-sustainability/

Yu, S., Buyya, R., & Thulasiraman, P. (2022). Edge computing for AI in smart cities: Challenges and opportunities. *Future Generation Computer Systems*, 129, 411–422. https://doi.org/10.1016/j.future.2021.11.002

Zanella, A., Bui, N., Castellani, A., Vangelista, L., & Zorzi, M. (2014). Internet of Things for smart cities. *IEEE Internet of Things Journal*, 1(1), 22–32. https://doi.org/10.1109/JIOT.2014.2306328

Zhang, J., Zheng, Y., & Qi, D. (2021). Deep learning in intelligent transportation systems: A review. *IEEE Transactions on Intelligent Transportation Systems*, 22(7), 3831–3845. https://doi.org/10.1109/TITS.2020.3040820

Zhou, J., Ma, Y., & Fadlullah, Z. M. (2020). AI in intelligent transportation systems: A review. *IEEE Transactions on Intelligent Transportation Systems*, 21(9), 3632–3651. https://doi.org/10.1109/TITS.2019.2958751

Chanakya Shield: A Responsible AI-Oriented Security Framework for Ethical and Secure Smart City Networks

S. Sathya Bama, G. Harsha Varthan, D. Logit Prasath, and N. Vishnu Prahalathan

Abstract

Cities are changing fast because of new technologies. In order to improve cities, these smart city technologies combine sensors and computers. They have features like energy-saving techniques, traffic lights, and safety measures. All of these things are supposed to make cities work better be kinder to the earth and make people happier. When you connect all of these things together it can also make it easier for bad people to hack in and cause problems. This can stop services from working and make people lose trust in the city. Smart city technologies are still really important. Cities need to make sure they are safe, from cyberattacks. Smart cities have to be careful to keep peoples trust and make sure everything keeps working. When we talk about digital infrastructure it is not like other computer systems that are not connected to people. Failures in digital infrastructure can affect people who live in the city the people who help in emergencies and the way the city is managed Failures in urban digital infrastructure may affect residents, first responders, and city officials. Cybersecurity is really important for keeping city systems safe. Intrusion Detection Systems are used to monitor network activity and identify human activity. We have made some progress with these systems they can detect things more accurately and handle a lot of traffic. But many of these systems do not think about what's right and wrong they just care about how well they work. So, when Cybersecurity systems are always watching and collecting a lot of data and we do not know how they make decisions that is a problem. It is a problem because we worry about our privacy and who is responsible when something goes wrong and if the system is being fair, to everyone. As artificial intelligence is used more and more in Cybersecurity for cities we have to think about these problems it is not something we can just ignore. Cybersecurity systems have to be fair and transparent. We have to think about Cybersecurity and how it affects people. This chapter is about the CHANAKYA SHIELD. The CHANAKYA SHIELD is a system that uses intelligence to detect problems in smart cities and urban areas with internet connected devices. The CHANAKYA SHIELD's primary objective is to strike a balance between being fair and identifying threats. It does this by watching the network all the time. Machine learning models that are positioned at the network's edge are used by the CHANAKYA SHIELD. This means it can react quickly to problems. Additionally, the CHANAKYA SHIELD strives to minimize system workload and delays. By doing the work at the edge of the network the CHANAKYA SHIELD does not have to rely much on big central systems. This makes it easier to use the CHANAKYA SHIELD in different urban areas. To keep citizen privacy safe the CHANAKYA SHIELD system only looks at the information in the packet headers. It does not go into the packets to get more details. This way the CHANAKYA SHIELD system reduces the chance of information getting out.

S. Sathya Bama (✉)
Department of Computer Science and Engineering (AI/ML Specialization), Sri Krishna College of Engineering and Technology (SKCET), Coimbatore, Tamil Nadu, India
e-mail: sathyabama.s@skcet.ac.in

G. Harsha Varthan · D. Logit Prasath · N. Vishnu Prahalathan
Sri Krishna College of Technology (SKCT), Coimbatore, Tamil Nadu, India
e-mail: 727822tucy018@skct.edu.in

D. Logit Prasath
e-mail: 727822tucy028@skct.edu.in

N. Vishnu Prahalathan
e-mail: 727823tucy603@skct.edu.in

V. Sarveshwaran et al. (eds.), *Responsible AI for Smart Cities*, Sustainable Artificial Intelligence-Powered Applications,
https://doi.org/10.1007/978-3-032-26901-0_9

Keywords

Edge computing · Ethical AI · Intrusion detection systems · IoT security · Privacy-preserving monitoring · Responsible AI · Smart cities · Urban cybersecurity

1 Introduction

1.1 Smart Cities and Urban Digital Transformation

Cities around the world are using computers and technology to manage things like transportation and energy. They are also using it to control water and take care of waste. Even healthcare and keeping people safe are becoming more digital.

Numerous devices must be connected to one another for these smart city initiatives. This includes things like sensors and special communication devices. For instance, depending on how congested the roads are, traffic lights may change. There are also cameras that help prevent crime. The amount of power consumed by individuals at any given time can be adjusted by the electrical system. The city needs these systems to be connected to the internet all the time so that they can work properly. The city also needs to be able to send and receive data reliably. Cities like these are called cities because they use digital technologies, like these. Cities are depending more on digital infrastructure. This means that when the network fails it can have bad consequences. For example, if someone carries out a cyberattack on the systems that control traffic, it can create a lot of congestion or even accidents. If they attack the smart grids, it can turn off power to crucial places like hospitals and emergency services. The thing about city systems is that they are out in the open in public so when they fail it affects people directly. This is different from computer networks that are inside a company. So, it is very important that we make sure the networks, in cities are secure. This is something that modern cities really need to do.

1.2 Cybersecurity Challenges in Smart City Environments

Smart city networks have a lot of problems when it comes to keeping things safe from cyber-attacks. This is because they are really big and have a lot of parts.

The city's infrastructure is made up of devices from companies, old systems and new internet connected devices. Many devices connected to the internet lack strong processing power. They are often placed in areas where people can easily reach them. This makes them easy targets for attacks.

Smart city networks also make an amount of traffic in real time so it is not possible for people to watch everything that is happening. This is why it is difficult to protect smart city networks from cyber-attacks. Smart city networks need care to stay safe.

Cybersecurity tools that people use today are usually made for companies and do not work well in cities. These tools can send out a lot of alarms, which can cause problems with services that people need. If these tools do not find a problem away it can spread to other connected systems. In cities we cannot have these problems. So, the systems that watch for intruders in cities must be correct work well and be trustworthy all the time especially when things are happening fast. Smart cities need these systems to be good at what they do because cybersecurity is very important, for cities.

1.3 Ethical Considerations and Responsible AI

Cybersecurity solutions used in cities have to think about what is right and wrong too. When people are in cities the internet traffic can have information about the people who live there the services they use and the important things that keep the city running.

Intrusion detection systems that look closely at what is being sent over the internet or that store secret information may not be okay with people who want their privacy protected and they may also not follow the rules about protecting data.

Cybersecurity solutions like these can be a problem.

The way that automated systems make decisions is not clear. That makes people not trust them and that is a big issue, for Cybersecurity solutions and the cities that use them. The principles of AI are very important. They are all about being transparent and accountable. We also need to make sure that AI systems are fair and that they protect people's privacy. They have to be sustainable too. When we use AI systems in infrastructure these principles are not just nice to have, they are necessary.

We need to have security measures in place that can find threats. We also need to ensure that these measures respect citizens' rights and help people trust the system. Responsible AI principles like transparency and fairness and privacy protection are crucial, in this case.

1.4 Motivation and Objectives

The reason we are doing this work is to create an intrusion detection framework that is effective and responsible. Smart city infrastructures need systems that can identify new cyber threats. These systems have to work on devices that do not have a lot of resources. At the time intrusion detection systems must keep data safe reduce fake alerts and provide clear decisions. Intrusion detection systems like this have to balance how well they work with being responsible which is very important, for city infrastructures and intrusion detection systems. The main goal of this chapter is to discuss CHANAKYA SHIELD. CHANAKYA SHIELD is a system that helps keep city networks safe from bad people. It uses machine learning and puts it on the edges of the network. This way CHANAKYA SHIELD can look at data without sharing information. CHANAKYA SHIELD is designed to be fair and safe. It wants to protect the computer systems of cities in a way that people can trust. CHANAKYA SHIELD does this by being open and honest, about what it does.

2 Literature Review

2.1 Cybersecurity in Smart Cities

Smart city infrastructures are getting more and more vulnerable to cyberattacks. This is a problem because cities have things like smart traffic systems and smart grids that people depend on. These systems are like targets for people who want to cause trouble. They can use tools like distributed denial-of-service attacks or malware to disrupt the city's operations. When this happens, it can be really hard for the city to keep everything running smoothly. The security systems that are, in place often have a time detecting these problems when the city's networks are really busy. Smart city infrastructures and their security systems need to handle these kinds of threats.

2.2 Signature-Based Intrusion Detection Systems

Signature-based intrusion detection systems are based on rules that we already know and attack patterns that have happened before. We use tools like Snort and Suricata because they are effective at detecting known threats. But these systems have a problem. They cannot find attacks or attacks that are changing. They need to be updated all the time with rules. This is an issue in smart city environments where attack patterns can change very quickly. Signature-based intrusion detection systems are not effective, in these situations because they cannot keep up with the attack patterns.

2.3 Machine Learning-Based Detection

Machine learning is really helpful for finding intruders. It can look at things that have happened before and learn from them. This way it can find guys who are trying to get in. There are two types of machine learning. One type uses examples to learn. The other finds things that are not normal. Machine learning techniques are good at finding intruders. They need a lot of power to work. They also need to be run from a location. This makes it hard to use machine learning techniques in cities where things need to happen fast and, on the edge, like in a smart city deployment with machine learning techniques. Machine learning techniques are important for intrusion detection, with machine learning.

2.4 Ethical and Responsible AI Research

Recent studies show that it is very important to have Artificial Intelligence in public sector applications. Artificial Intelligence frameworks that are point out that it is necessary to be transparent and fair and to protect people's privacy when designing these systems. A lot of cybersecurity solutions only think about the technical side of things and do not really consider how to use Artificial Intelligence in a way that is ethical. This is a problem, especially, in smart city contexts, where Artificial Intelligence makes decisions that affect citizens of the city directly. Artificial Intelligence is used in these cities. It is important to think about how it is used.

2.5 Research Gap

The literature shows a need for intrusion detection systems that are effective and ethically responsible. Few existing methods combine machine learning detection with privacy-preserving design, explainability, and edge deployment. This gap drives the creation of CHANAKYA SHIELD as a responsible AI-focused solution for smart city networks.

3 Problem Definition and System Scope

3.1 Problem Statement

The main issue talked about in this chapter is that there are not intrusion detection systems that can find threats in real time and also follow good artificial intelligence rules in smart cities. Most systems that exist today. Focus on finding threats accurately but do not care about privacy and being open or they think about doing the right thing but are not good enough, from a technical point of view.

3.2 Objectives

The goals of this work are:

1. To create a real-time intrusion detection system for smart city networks.
2. To minimize privacy risks by avoiding intrusive data inspection
3. To reduce false positive rates and operational disruptions
4. To enable deployment on resource-constrained edge devices
5. To support transparency and accountability in automated decision-making

3.3 System Scope and Limitations

This work is about finding intrusions at the network level, for cities and Internet of Things systems. It does not cover checking what is being sent over the network or monitoring devices. The main goal of this work is to detect intrusions in a way that's ethical and only looks at the network not trying to manage all of the security.

4 Proposed System Architecture

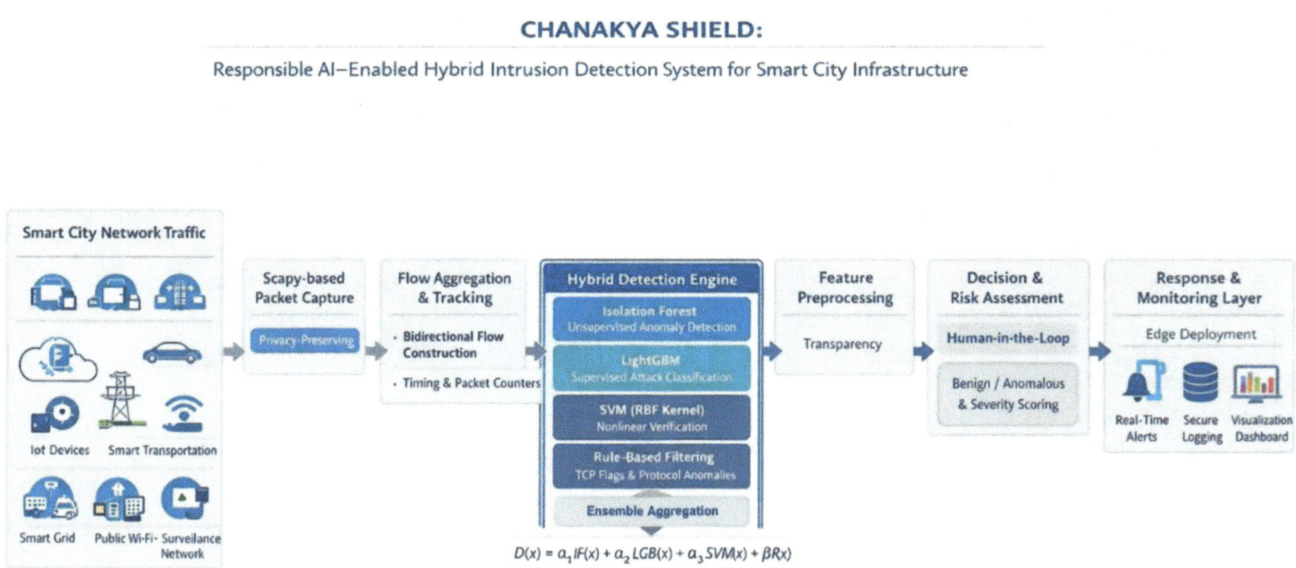

4.1 System Overview

The CHANAKYA SHIELD consists of components that function together. It has parts that capture packets extract features, from them detect things send out alerts and keep logs. Each part of the CHANAKYA SHIELD works on its own. This means the CHANAKYA SHIELD can be changed and made bigger if it needs to be. The CHANAKYA SHIELD is meant to keep working all the time in time. The CHANAKYA SHIELD always has to be ready to capture packets and detect things.

This way of doing things means that the actual content of the packets is not looked at which helps to keep people's information safe. The features that are extracted from the network packets show how the traffic is behaving than what the users are actually doing with the Network packets.

4.2 Packet Capture and Feature Extraction

The system captures live network packets directly from network interfaces by using a packet sniffing method. Each packet is examined to pull out header-level information. This includes the source and destination addresses, details about the transport protocol, the packet length, and the TCP control flags Instead of looking at packets separately, the system combines packets into bidirectional flows to capture behaviour patterns over time. Feature extraction happens in real time. It changes raw packet data into structured numerical forms that are suitable for machine learning-based intrusion detection. These features describe traffic volume, flow behaviour, protocol usage, and time-based characteristics.

4.2.1 Packet Size and Length-Based Features

Packet size–related features provide insight into traffic behaviour and application patterns. The system maintains cumulative statistics within each flow, including:

- Total Forward Packet Length
- Total Backward Packet Length
- Mean Forward Packet Length
- Mean Backward Packet Length

These features differentiate between interactive applications, bulk data transfers, and automated traffic. Malicious traffic often shows unusual patterns in packet sizes or an uneven amount of forward and backward traffic when compared to legitimate applications.

4.2.2 Temporal and Flow Duration Features

Temporal features capture the timing behaviour of network flows. The system computes:

- Flow Duration: Total lifetime of a bidirectional flow
- Packets per Second: Rate of packet transmission within the flow

Legitimate user-driven traffic typically demonstrates variable timing patterns, whereas automated attacks generate highly regular or extremely bursty traffic. These temporal indicators are effective in distinguishing human activity from scripted or malicious behaviour.

4.2.3 Flow Rate Features

Packet Rate: $R_{pkt} = \frac{N_{pkt}}{T_{flow}}$

Packet rate measures the number of packets transmitted per unit time within a flow, characterizing traffic intensity. DDoS attacks show very high packet rates. In contrast, legitimate bulk transfers have moderate, steady rates.

Byte Rate: $R_{byte} = \frac{\sum_{i=1}^{n} pi}{T_{flow}}$

Byte rate quantifies bandwidth consumption, distinguishing between high-volume data transfers and lightweight control traffic.

4.2.4 Protocol and TCP Flag Features

Protocol-level features describe how network protocols are used within traffic flows. The system extracts:

- Transport protocol identifiers (TCP/UDP)
- TCP control flags including SYN, ACK, FIN, RST, PSH, URG, and ECE

Unusual flag combinations (e.g., SYN–FIN) and abnormal flag frequencies are strong indicators of scanning activity, malformed packets, or attack attempts.

4.2.5 Connectivity and Directional Features

Connectivity features characterize communication patterns between hosts:

- Total Forward Packets
- Total Backward Packets
- Bidirectional flow symmetry

Malicious traffic often exhibits asymmetric flow behaviour, such as a large number of outbound requests with minimal responses, which is typical of scanning and command-and-control communication.

4.3 Hybrid Detection Engine

The detection engine uses a different method to find problems. It looks for traffic patterns on its own. It also uses supervised classification to identify known attack behaviours. It has rules to flag things that seem suspicious. By using all these methods, the detection engine is more reliable in many different situations. The detection engine is better, at finding problems because it uses anomaly detection and supervised classification and rule-based analysis.

4.3.1 Isolation Forest (Unsupervised Anomaly Detection)

The Isolation Forest works like this: it figures out that weird points have paths when you make random trees to separate the data. The Isolation Forest does this by looking at how it takes to get to the weird points.

$$\frac{E[h(x)]}{c(m)}$$

$$s(x) = 2$$

where:

$$E[h(x)] = \text{average path length of sample x across all isolation trees}$$

$$c(m) \approx 2H(m = 1) - \frac{2(m-1)}{m} = \text{average path length for unsuccessful searches}$$

$$H(m-1) = \text{harmonic number}$$

Lower scores indicate higher anomaly likelihood. Isolation Forest's linear runtime complexity ((log)) makes it particularly suitable for high-dimensional network traffic data and edge computing environments.

4.3.2 LightGBM (Supervised Gradient Boosting)

LightGBM works to make a kind of function better this function is used to tell the difference between good and bad traffic patterns on the internet. It learns about these patterns from information that people have already looked at and labelled as good or bad. LightGBM uses this information to improve how it can tell the difference between traffic and malicious traffic. This helps LightGBM to be really good, at figuring out what kind of traffic is good and what kind is bad.

$$Obj = \sum_{i=1}^{n} L\left(y_i, \hat{y}_i\right) + \sum_{t=1}^{T} \Omega(f_t)$$

where:
$L\left(y_i, \hat{y}_i\right)$ = loss function measuring prediction error

$$\Omega(f_t) = \gamma T + \frac{1}{2}\lambda w^2 = \text{regularization term penalizing model complexity}$$

$$\text{Gradients} : g_i = \frac{\partial L}{\partial \hat{y}_i}$$

$$\text{Hessians} : h_i = \frac{\partial^2 L}{\partial \hat{y}_i^2}$$

LightGBM implements Gradient-based One-Side Sampling (GOSS) to select high- gradient instances during training and Exclusive Feature Bundling (EFB) to reduce dimensionality, achieving 20× faster training compared to standard gradient boosting while maintaining accuracy.

4.3.3 Support Vector Machine with RBF Kernel (Supervised Nonlinear Classification)

The Support Vector Machine or SVM creates the line to separate things in a special kind of space called feature space. It does this by trying to reduce something called hinge loss. This helps the Support Vector Machine find the hyperplane that separates the data. The Support Vector Machine uses this method to make the hyperplane, in the feature space.

$$\min\left(\frac{1}{2}\|w\|^2 + C\sum_{i=1}^{n}\xi_i\right)$$

subject to: $y_i(w^T\phi(x_i) + b) \geq 1 - \xi_i, \xi \geq 0$

The decision function utilizes Radial Basis Function (RBF) kernel enabling nonlinear feature space mapping:

$$f(x) = \text{sign}\left(\sum_{i=1}^{n}\alpha_i y_i K(x_i, x) + b\right)$$

where:

$$K(x_i, x) = \exp\left(-\gamma\|x_i - x\|^2\right.$$

$$\alpha_i y_i K(x_i, x) + b$$

RBF kernels enable effective discrimination of complex attack patterns that are not linearly separable in the original feature space.

4.3.4 Rule-Based Filtering

A lightweight rule-based component supplements machine learning detection by flagging known malicious indicators including:

- IP addresses on threat intelligence blacklists
- Reserved or invalid port numbers indicating reconnaissance

- Unusual TCP flag combinations (e.g., SYN + FIN)
- Protocol anomalies (e.g., TCP traffic on port 53)

4.3.5 Ensemble Aggregation

The three models independently score each packet, and their outputs are combined through weighted averaging:

$$D(x) = \alpha_1 IF(x) + \alpha_2 LGB(x) + \alpha_3 SVM(x) + \beta R(x)$$

where:

- $IF(x)$, LGB, $SVM(x)$, $R(x)$ = normalized outputs from Isolation Forest, LightGBM, SVM, and rule-based filter
- α_1, α_2, α_3, β= model weights optimized through grid search on validation data
- Final classification: Attack if $D(x) > \theta$, Benign if $D(x) \leq \theta$
- Threshold θ tuned to achieve target false positive rate

Ensemble aggregation enables complementary strengths: Isolation Forest detects novel anomalies, LightGBM captures known attack signatures, and SVM identifies nonlinearly separable patterns. Rule-based filtering allows for clear knowledge integration and quick identification of known threats.

4.4 Alert Management System

When the system finds something, with the traffic it right away sends out alerts in many different ways:

Email Alerts: SMTP integration delivers detailed alert summaries including timestamp, source/destination IPs, protocol information, detected anomaly type, and confidence scores from individual models.

Telegram Integration: Real-time notification via Telegram Bot API enables immediate operator awareness regardless of physical location, with alert suppression mechanisms preventing notification flooding during sustained attacks.

Alert Severity Classification: Alerts are given severity levels of Critical, High, Medium, or Low based on confidence scores from the ensemble and rule-based threat indicators. This helps operators prioritize their response to incidents.

4.5 Data Logging and Persistence

All detected anomalies and supporting feature vectors are logged to a lightweight SQLite database, enabling:

- Comprehensive audit trails for post-incident forensic analysis
- Dataset generation for model retraining and performance evaluation
- Statistical analysis of attack patterns and trends
- Correlation analysis identifying attack campaigns spanning extended time periods

Each database record includes packet-level metadata (timestamp, source/destination IPs, protocol), extracted features (all 91 features), model confidence scores, and classification result.

4.6 Visualization Dashboard

A PyQt5-based graphical user interface provides security operators with real-time visibility into network security posture:

Dashboard Components:

- **Live Traffic Statistics**: Real-time packet rate, byte rate, and protocol distribution graphs
- **Alert Log**: Chronological listing of detected anomalies with searchable/filterable interface
- **Feature Distribution Visualizations**: Histograms showing feature distributions for comparison with historical baselines
- **Model Confidence Heatmaps**: Visual representation of model agreement on suspected malicious traffic
- **System Status Indicators**: CPU utilization, memory consumption, database size metrics
- **Attack Timeline**: Graphical representation of attack frequency and intensity over time

5 Experimental Methodology

We want to ensure our tests are realistic and can be repeated. So, we used two known datasets to detect intrusions. These datasets were collected in environments but they look a lot, like the traffic patterns we see in cities with lots of Internet of Things devices, public networks that people use to communicate and smart city services that use edge computing.

5.1 Datasets and Smart City Relevance

To ensure realistic and reproducible evaluation, two widely accepted intrusion detection datasets were used. Although collected in controlled environments, these datasets closely resemble traffic patterns observed in urban IoT ecosystems, public communication networks, and edge-enabled smart city services.

CIC-IDS2017 Dataset

The CIC-IDS2017 dataset, developed by Sharafaldin et al. (2018), contains network flow features extracted from realistic benign and malicious traffic scenarios representative of smart city network usage.

- Benign traffic: Web browsing, email services, file transfers, and interactive applications commonly used in public digital services
- Attack traffic: Distributed Denial-of-Service (DDoS), brute-force authentication attempts, Heartbleed exploits, botnet activity, and infiltration attacks, which pose significant risks to smart city infrastructure
- Total records: 2,830,743 network flow instances
- Attack distribution: 225,745 attack instances (8%) and 2,605,998 benign instances (92%)

This imbalance reflects real-world urban networks, where malicious events are rare but highly impactful, making responsible handling of false positives essential.

NSL-KDD Dataset

The NSL-KDD dataset was improved by Tavallaee et al. (2009) from the KDD'99 benchmark, was used to validate model generalization across different traffic characteristics.

- Total records: 125,973 instances
- Attack categories: Denial of Service (DoS), Probe, Remote-to-User (R2U), and User-to-Root (U2R)
- Feature set: 41 network features

Using multiple datasets supports Responsible AI evaluation principles, reducing dataset-specific bias and improving trustworthiness for urban deployment.

5.2 Data Preprocessing and Ethical Considerations

Data preprocessing is made to help make sure the model is fair works and protects people's privacy, which is what the Responsible AI guidelines say should happen for smart city systems. The main goal of data preprocessing is to make the model behave in a way that's fair and stable and that also protects people's privacy just like the Responsible AI guidelines say it should, for smart city systems.

- Feature Scaling: Min–max normalization scaled all features to a uniform range, preventing dominance of high-magnitude features and ensuring balanced learning across heterogeneous traffic attributes.
- Missing Value Handling: Records with missing values (less than 0.1%) were discarded to avoid introducing artificial patterns that could bias model decisions.
- Class Imbalance Handling: Stratified k-fold cross-validation preserved attack-to-benign ratios across training, validation, and test sets, preventing skewed performance that could disproportionately impact legitimate urban services.
- Categorical Encoding: Non-numeric features were one-hot encoded to maintain interpretability and avoid ordinal bias in machine learning models.

These preprocessing steps make sure that detection results stay consistent, fair, and repeatable across different smart city network conditions.

5.3 Model Training and Hyperparameter Optimization

We chose the model configurations to get the balance between finding things accurately using computer power wisely and being mindful of the rules for using these models in smart cities where resources are limited. This is important for city edge environments where we have to be careful, with what we have.

Isolation Forest:

- Number of trees: 100
- Subsample size: 256

LightGBM:

- Boosting rounds: 100
- Learning rate: 0.1
- Maximum depth: 7

LightGBM offers high accuracy and low inference latency. This makes it a good fit for real-time smart city applications.

Support Vector Machine (RBF Kernel):

- Kernel parameter $\gamma = 0.001$
- Regularization parameter $C = 1.0$
- Training subset: 20% of data to control computational cost SVM contributes nonlinear discrimination capability while respecting edge resource constraints.

5.4 Performance Metrics

- Accuracy : $\frac{TP+TN}{TP+TN+FP+FN}$
- Precision : $\frac{TP}{TP+FP}$
- Recall (Sensitivity) : $\frac{TP}{TP+FN}$
- False Positive Rate (FPR) : $\frac{FP}{FP+TN}$
- F1-Score : $2 \times \frac{\text{Precision} \times \text{Recall}}{\text{Precision} + \text{Recall}}$

5.5 Evaluation Methodology

We found a method to see how well our system works. This is called five-fold cross- validation. It helps us make sure the results are real. We split the data into groups. Each group has data for training, data for validation, and data for testing. We made sure that each group has 60% of the data for training 20% for validation and 20% for testing. The data was split in a way that keeps the number of each type of data in each group. This is what we mean, by 5fold stratified cross-validation. It helps us trust that our system is working well with the data we have.

6 Experimental Results

6.1 Individual Algorithm Performance

See Table 1.

Key Observations:

- LightGBM achieved the highest individual accuracy at 96.7% with lowest FPR among individual algorithms at 4.1%
- Isolation Forest achieved 93.5% accuracy, effective for detecting novel anomalies despite lower performance than boosting methods
- SVM achieved competitive performance at 95.1% accuracy with 5.8% FPR
- Simple classifiers (Naïve Bayes, K-NN) exhibited notably lower performance, emphasizing the importance of complex nonlinear models for network intrusion detection

6.2 Hybrid Ensemble Performance

The tri-model ensemble significantly outperformed all individual algorithms:

The ensemble achieved 98.3% accuracy, representing 1.6 % point improvement over the best individual algorithm (LightGBM 96.7%). FPR dropped from 4.1% for LightGBM to 2.6% for the ensemble. This cut false alarms by 37%.

6.3 Ensemble Weight Optimization

Grid search optimization identified optimal ensemble weights:

- $\alpha_1 = 0.25$ (Isolation Forest)
- $\alpha_2 = 0.40$ (LightGBM)
- $\alpha_3 = 0.25$ (SVM)
- $\beta = 0.10$ (Rule-based filter)

Weight distribution reflects LightGBM's superior individual performance while allocating substantial weight to Isolation Forest and SVM for their complementary detection capabilities.

6.4 Comparative Analysis Against Existing IDS

See Table 2.

The CHANAKYA SHIELD is really good at finding things. It does a better job than Suricata, which is the best system we have right now for detecting things in real time. The CHANAKYA SHIELD is 10.9 percentage points better at detecting things than Suricata. It also makes a lot mistakes. The CHANAKYA SHIELD reduces the positive rate by 73 percent compared to Suricata. This is a deal because it means the CHANAKYA SHIELD works a lot better and is more helpful. The CHANAKYA SHIELD has an impact, on how well things run.

6.5 Performance Under Varying Network Loads

The system was tested to see how it works when the network is really busy. We looked at how it performed when the network was sending information at rates, from 0 to 2.5 Gbps.

Algorithm	Accuracy (%)	Precision (%)	Recall (%)	F1-Score (%)	FPR (%)
Hybrid ensemble	98.3	97.5	97.9	97.7	2.6

Table 1 Presents performance metrics for individual algorithms evaluated on the CIC-IDS2017 dataset

Algorithm	Accuracy (%)	Precision (%)	Recall (%)	F1-Score (%)	FPR (%)
Isolation forest	93.5	91.8	92.6	92.2	7.2
LightGBM	96.7	95.9	96.2	96.0	4.1
SVM (RBF)	95.1	94.3	93.7	94.0	5.8
Random forest	94.8	93.2	94.1	93.6	5.4
Decision tree	89.3	87.6	88.9	88.2	10.7
Naïve Bayes	85.4	83.1	84.8	84.0	14.6
K-NN	87.1	85.4	86.7	86.0	12.9
AdaBoost	93.2	91.5	92.3	91.9	6.8
Gradient boosting	94.6	93.1	93.8	93.4	5.9

Table 2 Benchmarks CHANAKYA SHIELD against widely-deployed IDS platforms

Tool/Method	Detection rate (%)	False positive (%)	Real-time	Edge ready
Wireshark	N/A	N/A	No	No
Tcpdump	N/A	N/A	No	Limited
Snort	87.4	12.3	Yes	No
Tool/method	*Detection rate (%)*	*False positive (%)*	*Real-time*	*Edge ready*
Suricata	89.7	9.8	Yes	Limited
CHANAKYA SHIELD	**98.3**	**2.6**	**Yes**	**Yes**

Key metrics under maximum load (2.0 Gbps):

- Detection accuracy: 97.9% (minimal degradation from baseline 98.3%)
- Response latency: 35.2 ms average
- CPU utilization: 65% on 4-core processor
- Memory consumption: 340 MB
- False positive rate: 3.1% (slight increase from baseline 2.6%)

The minimal performance degradation under extreme network loads demonstrates the system's suitability for high-speed network monitoring and validates the effectiveness of lightweight ensemble implementation.

6.6 NSL-KDD Dataset Validation

The system was additionally evaluated on the NSL-KDD dataset to assess generalization:

- Accuracy: 97.8%
- FPR: 3.2%
- F1-Score: 97.5%

Performance on NSL-KDD comparable to CIC-IDS2017 results indicates robust generalization across different network traffic characteristics and attack distributions.

7 Comparative Analysis and Responsible AI Novelty

This section is about the CHANAKYA SHIELD. It looks at where the CHANAKYA SHIELD fits in with systems that detect intrusions. The CHANAKYA SHIELD is not just about how it works from a technical standpoint. It is also about the CHANAKYA SHIELD having attributes of AI. These attributes are very important, for city deployments. The CHANAKYA SHIELD needs to be able to preserve people's privacy. The CHANAKYA SHIELD should be fair and clear. The CHANAKYA SHIELD needs humans monitoring it to ensure it is working properly.

7.1 Comparison with Existing Intrusion Detection Approaches in Smart City Contexts

Signature-Based Systems (Snort, Suricata).

Strengths:

Fast and deterministic detection of previously known attack signatures, making them suitable for well-characterized threats in controlled environments.

Limitations in Smart Cities:

Inability to detect zero-day attacks and adaptive threats targeting urban IoT ecosystems; high false positive rates (9.8–12.3%) can disrupt critical public services and overwhelm municipal security teams.

CHANAKYA SHIELD Advantage:

Combines rule-based detection with adaptive machine learning, significantly reducing false positives (2.6%) while enabling detection of novel and evolving threats—an essential requirement for responsible AI deployment in city-scale infrastructure.

Packet Analysis Tools (Wireshark, tcpdump) Strengths:

Provide detailed packet-level visibility useful for forensic analysis and post-incident investigation.

Limitations in Smart Cities:

Operate primarily in offline or manual modes, lack automated decision support, and are impractical for real-time protection of large-scale urban networks.

CHANAKYA SHIELD Advantage:

Enables continuous, real-time monitoring with automated yet interpretable alerting, supporting timely human intervention in smart city operations.

Machine Learning–Based IDS (Published Research) Strengths:

"Show better detection accuracy than traditional rule-based systems."

Limitations:

Many approaches emphasize accuracy alone, neglecting false positive rates, latency constraints, explainability, and operational usability—factors critical for ethical and trustworthy AI in public-sector systems. Additionally, evaluations often depend on single datasets. This limits their general applicability.

CHANAKYA SHIELD Advantage:

Incorporates cross-dataset validation, prioritizes low false-positive operation, integrates visualization and alerting, and is designed for edge deployment—addressing practical and ethical considerations often absent in prior work.

7.2 Responsible AI-Driven Contributions of CHANAKYA SHIELD

CHANAKYA SHIELD advances the state of the art by integrating high-performance cybersecurity analytics with Responsible AI design principles, tailored for smart city environments.

1. Tri-Model Ensemble Architecture with Ethical Robustness

The integration of Isolation Forest (unsupervised anomaly detection), LightGBM (supervised classification), and SVM (nonlinear decision boundaries) provides complementary detection capabilities while mitigating bias inherent in single-model approaches. This combined strategy improves fairness and resilience in different urban traffic conditions.

2. Edge-Optimized and Sustainable Urban Deployment

The system is intentionally engineered for resource-constrained edge devices commonly used in smart cities. Algorithm selection, lightweight feature extraction, and Docker containerization enable sustainable, energy-efficient operation on platforms such as Raspberry Pi, supporting scalable and environmentally responsible urban AI deployment.

3. Operational Transparency and Human-Centric Design

CHANAKYA SHIELD integrates real-time alerting, persistent logging, and an interactive visualization dashboard, enabling city administrators to understand, verify, and contextualize AI-driven detections. This transparency helps ensure responsible decision-making and stops blind trust in automated systems.

4. Privacy-Aware Feature Engineering

The 91-feature extraction framework relies exclusively on packet headers and flow-level statistics, avoiding payload inspection. This privacy-preserving design aligns with Responsible AI principles and data protection requirements in smart city networks handling citizen communications.

5. Demonstrated Performance with Societal Risk Minimization

Achieving 98.3% detection accuracy with a low false positive rate of 2.6%, CHANAKYA SHIELD minimizes unnecessary alerts that could disrupt essential urban services. The balance between performance and reliability underscores its suitability for ethical AI deployment in critical public infrastructure.

8 System Implementation and Responsible Deployment in Smart City Environments

This section describes the implementation and deployment of CHANAKYA SHIELD as a Responsible AI–enabled cybersecurity solution designed for smart city digital infrastructure. The system architecture focuses on protecting privacy, being open about operations, promoting sustainability, and ensuring compatibility with edge technology. These factors are crucial for using AI ethically in urban public-sector settings.

8.1 Technology Stack for Responsible Urban AI Deployment

The technology stack was selected to balance performance, transparency, portability, and ethical deployment constraints typical of smart city ecosystems.

Programming Language: Python 3.8+.

Chosen for its readability, wide range of tools, and support for clear, checkable AI development.

Packet Capture: Scapy.

Enables low-level access to network headers while supporting privacy-preserving traffic analysis without payload inspection.

Machine Learning Frameworks:

scikit-learn (Isolation Forest, Support Vector Machine).

LightGBM

These frameworks provide interpretable model behaviour, reproducibility, and efficient inference suitable for edge-based urban infrastructure.

Alerting Mechanisms:

SMTPlib (Email)

python-telegram-bot (Telegram)

Multi-channel alerting ensures inclusive and timely notification of municipal network administrators, supporting human-in-the-loop oversight.

Data Persistence: SQLite3

Lightweight, auditable storage enabling traceability, forensic analysis, and regulatory compliance in public-sector deployments.

Visualization: PyQt5

Provides transparent, real-time dashboards enabling administrators to interpret AI-driven detections and system health metrics.

Containerization: Docker

Ensures consistent, portable, and policy-compliant deployment across different smart city infrastructures.

Testing Platform:

Raspberry Pi Model 4B (4 GB RAM), Ubuntu 20.04.

Represents typical edge devices used in urban IoT gateways and municipal data collection nodes.

8.2 Deployment Architecture and Ethical Engineering Considerations

CHANAKYA SHIELD is deployed using a containerized architecture to support secure, scalable, and maintainable smart city operations. Docker-based deployment ensures consistent execution environments, simplifies updates, and reduces configuration drift—critical for accountable AI lifecycle management in public infrastructure.

FROM python:3.8-slim

RUN apt-get update && apt-get install -y \ libpcap-dev \ build-essential

COPY requirements.txt.

RUN pip install -r requirements.txt COPY src/.

CMD ["python", "chanakya_shield.py"] This deployment approach supports:

- **Portability** across municipal data centers and edge nodes
- **Isolation** between AI components and other city services
- **Auditable software configurations** aligned with Responsible AI governance frameworks

8.3 Edge Deployment Results and Sustainability Assessment

Deployment experiments on Raspberry Pi hardware demonstrate that CHANAKYA SHIELD is operationally viable for real-world smart city environments, where computational efficiency and energy awareness are critical.

- **Startup time**: 8.3 s
- **Sustained operation**: 24 + h without memory leaks
- **CPU utilization**: 15–20% during normal operation, 65% under maximum load
- **Memory footprint**: 180 MB baseline, 340 MB under 2 Gbps load
- **Network throughput capacity**: 1.2 Gbps sustained, 2.0 Gbps peak

These results confirm that CHANAKYA SHIELD achieves high-performance cybersecurity monitoring while adhering to Responsible AI principles of sustainability, reliability, and equitable access, making it suitable for deployment across diverse smart city infrastructures.

9 Responsible AI Principles in Design

9.1 Privacy Protection

Only non-sensitive packet header data is analyzed. No payload content is stored or processed. This design reduces the chance of exposing personal or confidential information.

9.2 Transparency and Accountability

Detection decisions are logged with supporting indicators, allowing operators to review and audit system behaviour. This transparency supports trust and responsible operation.

9.3 Fairness and Reliability

The hybrid detection method lowers reliance on one model and makes it stronger against various traffic patterns. Lower false positives help prevent unnecessary service disruptions.

9.4 Sustainability

Efficient algorithms and edge deployment reduce computational overhead and energy consumption, supporting environmentally sustainable operation.

10 Smart City Use Cases

Smart cities depend on complex digital systems. These systems connect Internet of Things (IoT) devices, edge computing platforms, communication networks, and artificial intelligence to provide essential public services. As these systems rely more on data and operate independently, real-time, reliable, and ethically deployed AI-based cybersecurity is essential. It helps ensure service continuity, citizen safety, and public trust. CHANAKYA SHIELD serves as a Responsible AI–enabled security layer that can be adapted across multiple smart city domains.

10.1 Intelligent Transportation Systems (ITS)

Intelligent Transportation Systems rely on real-time data exchange among traffic sensors, connected vehicles, smart traffic lights, and centralized traffic management platforms. These systems are vulnerable to cyberattacks like DDoS attacks, fake sensor data, and unauthorized access attempts. These issues can cause traffic congestion, accidents, or disruptions in emergency vehicle routing.

CHANAKYA SHIELD can be deployed at transportation network edge nodes to continuously monitor traffic-related communication flows. By detecting unusual traffic patterns in real time, the system helps maintain smooth operation of traffic control systems. It also reduces false alerts that could lead to unnecessary interventions. Its privacy-preserving analysis keeps vehicle and commuter data safe. This follows Responsible AI principles in public mobility systems.

10.2 Smart Energy Grids and Utility Networks

Smart grids and utility management systems use distributed sensors, smart meters, and automated control systems to improve energy distribution and consumption.

Cyberattacks on these networks can lead to power outages, data changes, or financial losses.

CHANAKYA SHIELD improves the resilience of smart grids by spotting unusual communication patterns between substations, control centres, and field devices. Its edge-based deployment allows for quick detection of threats near the source. This cuts down response time and limits the spread of attacks. The system's low false positive rate is important because unnecessary interruptions to power or water supply can lead to serious social issues.

10.3 Public Surveillance and Smart Monitoring Systems

Urban surveillance systems, such as smart cameras and sensor networks, are essential for public safety, managing crowds, and preventing crime. These systems produce large amounts of network traffic and are often used in distributed settings with limited resources.

CHANAKYA SHIELD can monitor network traffic generated by surveillance infrastructure to detect malware propagation, unauthorized access attempts, or coordinated attacks. Importantly, the system does not analyze video or content payloads, ensuring ethical deployment that respects citizen privacy while safeguarding the integrity and availability of public safety systems.

10.4 Emergency Response and Critical Communication Infrastructure

Emergency response systems depend on secure and dependable communication channels among first responders, control centres, hospitals, and public safety agencies. Any disruption caused by cyber threats can directly endanger lives.

By offering real-time anomaly detection and instant alerts, CHANAKYA SHIELD helps quickly identify cyber incidents that impact emergency communication networks. Human-in-the-loop alerting allows trained staff to evaluate and respond as needed. This process stops automated actions that might disrupt important decisions during emergencies.

10.5 Smart Public Wi-Fi and Digital Citizen Services

Many cities offer public Wi-Fi and online platforms for citizen engagement, e-governance, and access to city services. These networks attract attackers because they are open and easy to access.

CHANAKYA SHIELD can be deployed at Wi-Fi gateways and service access points to detect abnormal traffic patterns indicative of misuse, botnet activity, or denial-of-service attacks. Its scalable, edge-compatible design helps cities provide public digital services without major infrastructure investment. This approach promotes fair and inclusive access to smart city technologies.

10.6 Responsible AI and Governance Across Urban Use Cases

Across all smart city domains, CHANAKYA SHIELD supports Responsible AI deployment by:

- Preserving privacy through header-only traffic analysis
- Reducing societal risk via low false positive rates
- Enabling transparency through logging and visualization
- Maintaining human oversight in security decision-making

These attributes ensure that AI-driven cybersecurity enhances urban innovation without compromising ethical standards, public trust, or regulatory compliance.

11 Limitations and Future Work

While **CHANAKYA SHIELD** demonstrates strong performance and practical viability as a Responsible AI–enabled cybersecurity framework for smart city infrastructure, certain limitations remain. Identifying these constraints and outlining future research directions is important. This helps guarantee the ethical, transparent, and sustainable use of AI-driven security systems in complex urban environments.

11.1 Current System Limitations

11.1.1 Network-Level Visibility Constraints

CHANAKYA SHIELD operates primarily at the network and flow level, analyzing packet headers and statistical traffic features. Although this design maintains privacy and follows data minimization principles, it restricts the system's ability to detect application-layer attacks that need deep payload inspection. Certain complex threats, like encrypted command-and-control channels or specific protocol attacks, may still go unnoticed.

11.1.2 Dependence on Benchmark Datasets

Experimental validation relies on widely used datasets such as CIC-IDS2017 and NSL-KDD. While these datasets allow for reproducible evaluation, they might not completely reflect the variety and changing nature of actual smart city traffic patterns. This includes new IoT protocols and local usage behaviours.

11.1.3 Residual False Positives and Human Oversight

Despite achieving a low false positive rate, some legitimate traffic may still be flagged as anomalous. In smart city environments, such alerts could impact essential services if acted upon automatically. This limitation highlights the need for human oversight and context-based decision-making.

11.1.4 Resource Constraints in Ultra-Low-Power Devices

Although optimized for edge deployment, extremely constrained devices with minimal memory or processing capability may not support full model execution. This can limit deployment in certain legacy or ultra-low-power urban IoT nodes.

11.2 Future Research Directions for Responsible Urban AI

11.2.1 Federated Learning for Privacy-Preserving Collaboration

Future work will look into federated learning methods. These methods will allow model training to happen collaboratively across several smart city edge nodes, all without centralizing data. This approach improves privacy protection, lowers data governance risks, and supports knowledge sharing between cities while keeping local data sovereignty intact.

11.2.2 Policy-Aware and Regulation-Compliant Detection

Integrating policy-aware AI mechanisms that adapt detection behaviour based on regulatory requirements, municipal policies, or service-level agreements represents a critical future direction. Such mechanisms could adjust thresholds, logging detail, or alerting strategies to match governance frameworks and legal requirements.

11.2.3 Explainable AI for Public Accountability

Improving explainability with clear model outputs, visualizing feature importance, and providing natural-language explanations can build public trust. Explainable AI techniques would help city administrators justify security decisions to stakeholders, auditors, and citizens.

11.2.4 Adversarial Robustness and Resilience

Future research should look into how well systems withstand adversarial attacks meant to bypass machine learning detection systems. Developing resilient ensemble strategies and adaptive learning mechanisms will be essential to protect AI-driven urban infrastructure from sophisticated attackers.

11.2.5 Integration with Urban Governance Frameworks

CHANAKYA SHIELD can be expanded to work with larger smart city governance platforms, including digital twins, urban security operation centres, and policy management systems. Such integration would help with coordinated response strategies, accountability, and long-term risk assessment at the city level.

11.2.6 Quantum-Inspired Optimization and Advanced Threat Analysis

As an exploratory research direction, future versions of CHANAKYA SHIELD may investigate quantum-inspired optimization techniques for offline feature selection and traffic analysis. Quantum-inspired methods created with classical optimization models, like QUBO-based approaches, can help improve feature relevance selection and lower redundancy in high-dimensional network data. Additionally, quantum-inspired clustering techniques could help with offline grouping of unusual traffic patterns. This would improve threat intelligence and post-incident analysis. These approaches would complement existing classical machine learning models without introducing dependencies on quantum hardware.

12 Conclusion

This chapter is about the CHANAKYA SHIELD. The CHANAKYA SHIELD is a system that helps keep city digital infrastructure safe. It uses a kind of artificial intelligence called Responsible AI. This system has a few ways to find problems. It can look for things on its own it can learn from people. It can follow rules. The CHANAKYA SHIELD system is better than systems because it can find problems that other systems might miss. It also does things in a fair and easy-to-understand way. This matters for cities because they must ensure their digital infrastructure is safe and secure. The CHANAKYA SHIELD system is designed to work in cities and to help people who live there. It follows principles that're good for people and, for cities. The system was. It worked really well. It was able to detect things 98.3

percent of the time. It also did not make false accusations, which is good.

This is much better than systems like Snort and Suricata. CHANAKYA SHIELD is not just about being good at detecting things. It also makes sure that people's private information is safe when it looks at traffic. It is also clear about what it's doing and it lets people check its work. This makes CHANAKYA SHIELD a good choice for situations, like city applications, where safety is very important.

12.1 Key Technical and Responsible AI Achievements

Hybrid Ensemble Architecture with Ethical Robustness:

We can use math to make a system that combines three methods, Isolation Forest, LightGBM and Support Vector Machines to work together. This system is really good, at finding threats even if we have not seen them before. It also helps to avoid problems that can happen when we only use one method to make decisions. The combination of Isolation Forest, LightGBM, and Support Vector Machines offers a method to detect threats.

Edge-Ready and Sustainable Urban Deployment:

Docker is a tool for containerization. It helps things run smoothly on devices like the Raspberry Pi. This means we can use these devices in cities for things like IoT gateways and municipal networks. The Raspberry Pi is a good option because it is small and uses little energy. This is important, for city projects because they need to be able to work well and not use too much power. The Raspberry Pi work well together to make this happen.

Privacy-Aware Feature Engineering:

A comprehensive 91-feature extraction framework based exclusively on packet headers and flow-level statistics ensures effective detection without inspecting payload content, aligning with privacy-by-design and data minimization principles.

Transparent and Human-Centric Operations:

Integrated multi-channel alerting, persistent logging, and visualization dashboards support explainability, accountability, and informed human decision-making in urban network operations.

Validated and Generalizable Performance:

Evaluation across CIC-IDS2017 and NSL-KDD datasets demonstrates robustness and generalization, supporting trustworthy AI deployment in heterogeneous smart city network environments.9.2 Practical Impact.

12.2 Practical Impact on Smart City Ecosystems

CHANAKYA SHIELD bridges the gap between high-accuracy research prototypes and responsibly deployable AI systems for urban infrastructure. By combining machine learning with operational reliability and ethical safeguards, the framework helps cities and urban service providers protect essential services like public Wi-Fi, intelligent transportation systems, smart utilities, and emergency communication networks. The system has a low false positive rate and includes a human-in-the-loop design. This reduces the risk of unnecessary service disruptions and helps build public trust in AI-driven urban security solutions.

12.3 Limitations and Ethical Considerations

Encrypted Payload Limitation:

To preserve privacy, the system analyzes packet headers only and does not inspect encrypted payloads, which may limit detection of certain application-layer attacks.

Dataset Representativeness:

Evaluation on benchmark datasets may not capture all real-world urban threat scenarios, highlighting the need for continuous model adaptation and contextual validation.

Residual False Positives:

Although minimized, a small number of false alerts may occur, underscoring the importance of human oversight in Responsible AI deployment.

12.4 Future Research Directions for Responsible Urban AI

Quantum-Enhanced Anomaly Detection

Exploration of quantum and quantum-inspired machine learning techniques to improve scalability and detection in high-dimensional urban network data.

Federated Learning for Municipal Privacy:

Development of decentralized training frameworks enabling collaborative learning across multiple city edge nodes without centralizing sensitive traffic data.

Blockchain-Enabled Trust and Governance:

Integration with blockchain-based threat intelligence platforms to support transparent, tamper-resistant sharing of attack indicators across urban stakeholders.

Adversarial Robustness:

Investigation of ensemble resilience against adversarial attacks targeting AI-based security systems in smart city environments.

Zero-Trust Smart City Integration:

Extension of the framework to support zero-trust architectures requiring continuous authentication and authorization across urban services.

12.5 Contribution to Responsible AI and Smart City Cybersecurity

CHANAKYA SHIELD demonstrates that Responsible AI principles can be practically embedded into high-performance cybersecurity systems for smart cities. By prioritizing privacy, transparency, fairness, and human oversight alongside detection accuracy, the framework contributes to ethical urban innovation and resilient digital governance.

The open and extensible design provides a foundation for future research and real-world adoption, supporting the development of trustworthy AI-driven security solutions critical to the sustainability and safety of next-generation smart cities.

Bibliography

L. Zhou, Q. Li, and M. Zhang, "Real-time traffic analysis with Wireshark for network security monitoring," J. Network Computer Applications, vol. 145, pp. 102–115, Nov. 2019.

F. Hirsi, F. Ullah, S. Kumar, and I. A. Khan, "Detecting DDoS threats using supervised machine learning for traffic classification in software defined networking," IEEE Access, vol. 12, pp. 65044–65057, 2024.

M. Roesch, "Snort: Lightweight intrusion detection for networks," in Proc. 13th USENIX Conf. System Administration, Seattle, WA, USA, 1999, pp. 229–238.

Open Information Security Foundation, "Suricata IDS/IPS and Security Monitoring engine," 2023. [Online]. Available: https://suricata-ids.org/

S. Ness, R. Gopalakrishnan, and T. L. Maheswaran, "Anomaly detection in network traffic using advanced machine learning techniques," IEEE Access, vol. 13, pp. 113722–113739, 2025.

A. Javaid, Q. Niyaz, W. Sun, and M. Alam, "A deep learning approach for network intrusion detection system," in Proc. 9th EAI International Conference on Bio-inspired Information and Communications Technologies, New York, USA, 2016, pp. 21–26.

F. Ullah, M. A. Shah, S. Zhang, and M. Imran, "Cyber security threats detection in Internet of Things using deep learning approach," IEEE Access, vol. 6, pp. 39800–39813, 2018.

T. F. Liu, K. M. Ting, and Z.-H. Zhou, "Isolation Forest," in Proc. 8th IEEE International Conference on Data Mining (ICDM), Pisa, Italy, 2008, pp. 413–422.

G. Ke et al., "LightGBM: A highly efficient gradient boosting decision tree," in Proc. 31st International Conference on Neural Information Processing Systems (NIPS), Long Beach, CA, USA, 2017, pp. 3149–3157.

I. Sharafaldin, A. H. Lashkari, and A. A. Ghorbani, "Toward generating a new intrusion detection dataset and intrusion traffic characterization," in Proc. 4th International Conference on Information Systems Security and Privacy, Funchal, Portugal, 2018, pp. 108–116.

M. Tavallaee, E. Bagheri, W. Lu, and A. A. Ghorbani, "A detailed analysis of the KDD CUP 99 data set," in Proc. IEEE Symposium on Computational Intelligence for Security and Defense Applications, Ottawa, ON, Canada, 2009, pp. 1–6.

R. Schummer et al., "Intrusion detection with change-point detection and Random Forest," in Proc. International Conference on Information Security, 2015, pp. 145–158.

B. B. Tama and K. H. Lim, "Ensemble learning for intrusion detection systems: a systematic review," J. Network Computer Applications, vol. 113, pp. 95–113, Apr. 2018.

M. Bagaa, T. Taleb, and A. Ksentini, "Optimal network slicing for 5G core network," IEEE Communications Magazine, vol. 55, no. 12, pp. 90–97, Dec. 2017.

Y. Wu, H. Dai, Z. Tang, and B. Liu, "A deep learning approach for network traffic generation," in Proc. International Conference on Network Computing and Communications, 2018, pp. 190–200.

C. Evangelou and B. Adams, "Statistical machine learning hybrids for anomaly detection," International Journal of Network Security, vol. 15, no. 3, pp. 234–245, 2017.

X. Zhao, Y. Liu, and Z. Wang, "Lightweight intrusion detection system for edge computing environments," IEEE Transactions on Network and Service Management, vol. 18, no. 2, pp. 1456–1468, Jun. 2021.

L. Breiman, "Random forests," Machine Learning, vol. 45, no. 1, pp. 5–32, Oct. 2001.

Y. Freund and R. E. Schapire, "A decision-theoretic generalization of on-line learning and an application to boosting," J. Computer and System Sciences, vol. 55, no. 1, pp. 119–139, Aug. 1997.

J. H. Friedman, "Greedy function approximation: A gradient boosting machine," Annals of Statistics, vol. 29, no. 5, pp. 1189–1232, Oct. 2001.

T. Cover and P. Hart, "Nearest neighbor pattern classification," IEEE Transactions on Information Theory, vol. 13, no. 1, pp. 21–27, Jan. 1967.

D. D. Lewis, "Naive (Bayes) at forty: The independence assumption in information retrieval," in Proc. 10th European Conference on Machine Learning, Chemnitz, Germany, 1998, pp. 4–15.

C. E. Shannon, "A mathematical theory of communication," Bell System Technical Journal, vol. 27, no. 3, pp. 379–423, Jul. 1948.

H. HaddadPajouh, A. Dehghantanha, R. Khayami, and K. K. R. Choo, "A deep recurrent neural network-based approach for Internet of Things malware threat hunting," Future Generation Computer Systems, vol. 85, pp. 88–95, Aug. 2018.

R. Vinayakumar, K. P. Soman, and P. Poornachandran, "Evaluating deep learning approaches to characterize and classify malicious URLs," J. Cybersecurity, vol. 4, no. 1, pp. 1–22, 2018.

H. Kim, Y. Park, J. Lee, and K. Park, "Federated learning for edge intelligence: applications and challenges," IEEE Transactions on Industrial Informatics, vol. 17, no. 6, pp. 4222–4234, Jun. 2021.

R. Doriguzzi-Corin et al., "LUCID: A lightweight deep learning model for detecting DDoS attacks at line rate," IEEE Transactions on Network and Service Management, vol. 18, no. 4, pp. 4397–4410, Dec. 2021.

DeepGallery: An AI-Enabled Photography Platform for Accessibility, Organization, and Responsible Smart-City Innovation

Savita Sheelavant, Aditi Narasimhan, and Ananya Ganapati Hegde

Abstract

This chapter discusses DeepGallery, an AI-powered photography portfolio platform that embeds responsible AI into its core to foster ethical digital interaction and inclusion. The system utilizes machine learning for automated image classification in broad thematic categories and similarity- based browsing, illustrating how AI can support inclusive and explainable media organization while bridging technology and creativity. Automatically generated captions from pre-trained vision-language models (BLIP, CLIP) create context-sensitive descriptions that address pressing issues of web accessibility, in which nearly 60% of online images do not include alternative text, furthering notions of social responsibility and equal digital inclusion. The extended vision for the platform positions DeepGallery as a participatory urban storytelling hub; citizens upload photographs that reflect themes of sustainability, mobility, and social inclusion. These images are sorted by thematic similarity using unsupervised AI clustering techniques that generate visual narratives of collective urban experiences and diverse citizen perspectives. As the smart cities market is set to grow from $877.6 billion in 2024 to $3.76 trillion by 2030, the present research underlines the critical role of ethical AI design, transparency, and data governance within creative civic platforms. DeepGallery represents one concrete model for responsible AI deployment, improving both accessibility and civic engagement with human-centered smart city innovation.

Keywords

Deep gallery · Vision language · Smart city · Artificial intelligence

1 Introduction

Over the past decade, artificial intelligence (AI) has changed from an experimental capability to a foundational infrastructure, which has a strong influence on the way societies create, communicate, and govern. AI algorithms operate as aesthetic mediators more and more in digital media ecosystems, which include the creation of art, curation of content, and engagement of the audience. Generative and analytic models are now used to support creative processes in a wide variety of applications from automated photo enhancement and caption generation to intelligent recommendation and retrieval (Ramesh et al. 2021). Concurrently, city administrations and civic organizations are integrating analogous algorithmic logics into smart-city systems: platforms that manage mobility, public safety, and environmental monitoring through data-driven insights (Bibri and Krogstie 2017).

The merging of these two worlds, creative media and urban intelligence, implies a common socio-technical trajectory: both fields aim to understand complex visual, textual, and spatial data to improve human experience. Computer-vision models used, for instance, to identify elements in a photographer's portfolio can also be used, in another governance scenario, to recognize scenes from citywide surveillance networks. The technological link between these different uses calls for an equally continuous ethical reflection. Hence, responsible designing of AI in smart cities should not focus only on the accuracy and efficiency of algorithms, but also on their cultural, aesthetic, and participatory effects (Kitchin 2014).

S. Sheelavant · A. Narasimhan (✉) · A. G. Hegde
Department of MCA, RV College of Engineering, Bangalore, India
e-mail: aditin.mca24@rvce.edu.in

S. Sheelavant
e-mail: savitas.sheelavant@rvce.edu.in

A. G. Hegde
e-mail: ananyaghegde.mca24@rvce.edu.in

V. Sarveshwaran et al. (eds.), *Responsible AI for Smart Cities*, Sustainable Artificial Intelligence-Powered Applications,
https://doi.org/10.1007/978-3-032-26901-0_10

Within the larger scenario, visual data are the main protagonists of today's digital life. Pictures are one of the primary means through which people tell their identity, record space, and engage in social interchange. However, despite their prevalence, visual content is still hard to be managed and accessed in a responsible manner on a large scale. The increasing amount of personal and communal images demands new ways of annotation, discoverability, and inclusivity. It is exactly in this field that the system DeepGallery, which is presented in this chapter, makes its contribution: an AI-driven photography portfolio platform that not just serves as a model for responsible AI practices but also promotes digital inclusion and civic creative engagement.

1.1 Importance of Responsible and Human-Centric AI Systems

The idea of responsible AI is not limited to technical robustness but also includes social accountability, transparency, and equity (Jobin et al. 2019; Shneiderman 2020). It requires that algorithmic systems should support human judgment, not replace it; they should respect user autonomy and not have the effect of amplifying existing bias. In case of smart-city development, these principles mean that AI systems should enable citizens to be data contributors and decision-makers instead of just being passive data points (Cardullo and Kitchin 2019).

DeepGallery is an example of a platform that integrates the concept of responsibility in its system design rather than considering it superficially. Its features like captioning and category-classification show that AI can be used to help and not watch over users. The automated image descriptions are a step towards the goal of making the content accessible by providing textual alternatives for visually impaired users, as they account for a major divide whereby a large portion of web images is without descriptive alt text (WebAIM 2023). The explainable organization of the system and user-editable metadata are the means to transparency and trust.

1.2 Challenges in Image Accessibility, Organization, and Digital Inclusion

Although computer vision has made great strides, images in digital form are still among the least accessible types of content on the web. The automated tagging systems have been prioritizing commercial personalization or surveillance for a long time without considering inclusivity (Buolamwini and Gebru 2018). As a result, a large part of online visual culture is not accessible for reading software and thus people who use assistive technologies are left out.

Another issue originates from the fact that AI-based media platforms frequently do not reveal how they categorize or rank images. This lack of transparency lowers the level of trust and gives rise to the problem of fairness in algorithmic decisions. In urban scenarios, similar invisibility is evident in the case of predictive policing, traffic optimization, or public-space analytics, where people usually do not know in what way visual data about their environment are being used (Eubanks 2018).

Third, digital inclusion is not only about technical accessibility; it also involves representation and participation. Several current AI systems have cultural biases because their training data poorly represent the perspectives of the marginalized (Noble 2018). Solving these problems requires the presence of responsible intermediaries: platforms that can communicate the technological potential and the social benefits to each other. DeepGallery is one such intermediary. It utilizes AI not for surveilling or exploiting but for helping people in a transparent way to manage and share their creative work.

1.3 Motivation for Developing DeepGallery

DeepGallery's creation motive was the crossing point of three converging needs: to improve image accessibility by the use of automated yet clear descriptions, to responsibly manage quickly expanding personal and public photo archives, and to find out how the use of participatory visual data could lead to ethical smart-city innovation. On the less theoretical side, photographers and digital artists are often confronted with the challenge of keeping their portfolios well annotated. Manually captioning and tagging is very labor-intensive, and present AI tools are either non-transparent or stylistically constrained, thus, authorship level gets decreased.

From the ethical perspective, DeepGallery is participating in the debate about AI explainability and user-autonomy. To support traceability both in production and operation, we decided to use open pre-trained models (for example, vision-language architectures) instead of closed ones for our applications (Dourish and Bell 2011).

2 Background and Literature Review

2.1 AI Applications in Visual Media Management

Artificial Intelligence has significantly changed the way digital media is created, curated, and shared. AI-powered media management solutions have become indispensable instruments in the digital economy. Their range of applications extends from systems for automatic tagging and retrieval to tools providing creative assistance to photographers and designers (Radford et al. 2021). The advent of multimodal architectures which integrate text and image understanding has completely transformed the field thus paving the way for contextual captioning, visual question answering, and semantic search functionalities (Chen et al. 2015).

DeepGallery, in this example, is a thoughtful repositioning of a tool that doesn't aim at the staff's creative abilities elimination but rather at their ethical support by the automation of organizational tasks that are repetitive in nature while respecting user autonomy and data ownership. By using pre-trained multimodal models, the platform ensures transparency and lessens the chances of bias arising from the use of closed or proprietary datasets (Mitchell et al. 2019).

2.2 Accessibility Gaps in Image-Based Platforms

Studies have shown that generally, images found online do not have alternative descriptive texts which means that users of screen readers, or other assistive devices are left with limited access to these images (Gleason et al. 2020). Insufficient textual support also hampers the potential of semantic search because untagged or wrongly labeled images are inaccessible in any substantial way (Morris et al. 2018).

DeepGallery's captioning feature employs vision-language models (BLIP and LLaVA) to generate concise but informative and accurate image descriptions. Moreover, the platform allows users to change or humanize the caption texts, thus emphasizing human supervision, which is one of the principal aspects of responsible AI design (Amershi et al. 2019).

2.3 Vision-Language Models for Captioning

The conventional approach to machine comprehension and description of visual content has been significantly altered by vision-language models such as BLIP and LLaVA. In order to attain richer semantic alignment, the contemporary ones learn joint embeddings between texts and images (Li et al. 2022). To generate natural and contextually relevant descriptions, LLaVA (Large Language and Vision Assistant) combines instruction-tuned language models with large-scale vision encoders.

Using BLIP and LLaVA for caption generation at DeepGallery allows for adaptable, user, focused descriptions rather than standard labels, which is in line with the principles of explainability and contextual relevance. In addition, since both models are open source, they permit community driven enhancements and transparent model auditing, which are two of the most important elements of the ethical AI deployment process (Shunmugesh et al. 2026).

2.4 Image Classification and Semantic Tagging

Conventional approaches of image classification are heavily reliant on supervised learning where the models are trained on datasets that already have categories labeled (Crawford and Paglen 2019). Vision Transformers (ViT) have been recognized as the most potent structures for image classification and they utilize the self-attention mechanisms to identify the overall image features (Dosovitskiy et al. 2020).

Through a fine-tuned ViT model, DeepGallery is capable of sorting images into six semantic categories: Architecture, Food, Nature, Portrait, Wildlife, and Miscellaneous. Unlike unsupervised techniques, supervised classification offers clear, interpretable categories with which users can familiarize themselves and gain their trust (He et al. 2016).

2.5 Responsible AI Principles for Modern Digital Systems

The frameworks put forward by organizations like the OECD, UNESCO, and the European Commission suggest that AI should be used and developed in a manner that is respectful of human rights, that provides equitable access, and that allows for the disclosure of the decision-making process (OECD 2019). DeepGallery emphasizes voluntary involvement, user agency, and the interpretability of automated outputs. The platform refrains from using biometric recognition or identity tracking to bring privacy protection to the forefront (Garvie et al. 2016).

2.6 Smart City Frameworks Emphasizing Citizen Engagement

It is now more common to define smart cities by the characteristics of civic participation ecosystems, in which citizens become co-producers of knowledge and value through their data-driven interactions (Rajasekar et al.

2023). These visual materials, if properly collected and processed, can serve as a source of city planning, local community storytelling, and digital heritage conservation. The incorporation of participatory visual materials into smart-city analytics frameworks changes the interaction between technology and citizenship (Certomà et al. 2017).

3 Problem Definition and Objectives

3.1 The Need for Automated Image Captioning to Enhance Accessibility

Despite the massive use of digital images, visual content on the internet is still not very accessible to a large number of people. Research shows that alt text is often not available or is insufficient for images on the web (Bigham et al. 2010). Most photography and portfolio platforms treat accessibility as an optional feature that can be turned on, rather than as a design principle that is integrated.

DeepGallery attempts to solve this issue by combining vision-language models BLIP and LLaVA to automatically generate sophisticated and context-sensitive descriptions of the images that users have uploaded. The automatically generated captions serve as alternative text for accessibility tools, which are directly supporting social inclusion and digital equity (Gurari et al. 2018).

3.2 The Need for Automated Semantic Classification of Photography Collections

With the massive spread of digital photography, the trend of people accumulating pictures has risen among individuals and communities, but most of them do not have structured organization of their photo collections. The conventional ways of manually categorizing are slow, prone to errors, and limited in terms of subjective labeling (Luo and Savakis 2001).

DeepGallery uses supervised image classification through fine-tuned Vision Transformers to help users automatically sort their photos into semantic classes like Architecture, Nature, Portrait, Food, Wildlife, and Miscellaneous. Rather than merely providing a black box sorting, the platform focuses on explainable classification, thus aligning it with responsible AI frameworks that call for transparency, interpretability, and user agency (Lipton 2018).

3.3 Challenges in Creating Transparent, User-Controlled AI Systems

It has been observed that it is a challenge to create AI-powered platforms that abide by ethical and human-centric values. Most AI systems in the media domain use a lot of personal or contextual data to make recommendations and do classifications better (Zuboff 2019). This dependence on data raises issues like data privacy, algorithmic bias, and lack of explanation of automated decisions.

We intentionally do not incorporate surveillance-like practices such as facial recognition or identity tracking. DeepGallery is focused on human control over AI where users have the power to decide what to upload, what to share, and whether to keep or edit the automatically generated metadata. These challenges become more critical when considering DeepGallery's potential urban applications.

3.4 Justification for Smart-City Relevance

The deeper meaning of DeepGallery aside from being just a tool for personal use is linked with the idea of participative smart-city innovation. DeepGallery's semantic classification in such a scenario can be like collective urban sensing where photos from citizens depict different views of public spaces, transport, and environment (Hollands 2015; Townsend 2013; Sathyamoorthy et al. 2026).

3.5 Research Objectives

The objectives of our research are the following:

1. Create a prototype for an artificial intelligence-powered photography website featuring automated image captioning functionalities and semantic classifications based on the captioned images.
2. Improve web accessibility using vision-language models for captioning.
3. Enquire into responsible AI integration through the promotion of transparency, control, and protection.
4. Evaluate the use of AI-enabled visual media as participatory technologies for the construction of smart cities.
5. Set up principles for ethical, human-centered AI-systems for creative applications as well as civic technologies.

4 System Overview: The DeepGallery Platform

4.1 Conceptual Vision

DeepGallery is designed as an intelligent and responsible AI-powered platform that combines visual creativity with digital inclusion. This system empowers users from photographers and graphic artists to common people to upload, arrange, and discover their photographic materials in a well-organized and significant way. DeepGallery utilizes advanced vision-language models to generate image captions and semantic categories automatically.

The concept is grounded in two objectives that work parallel to each other: to solve the mental and time challenge of handling images manually and to ensure that digital visual materials are accessible, searchable, and understandable by various users, including those with limited visual or technical skills.

4.2 Key Features

4.2.1 AI-Generated Captions

The main part of DeepGallery is an automated captioning module supported by pre-trained vision-language models (BLIP from Salesforce and LLaVA 1.5). Descriptions in natural language are automatically generated by the system for each picture, thus providing contextual captions in a human-readable format that essentially translate visual information into text without any user intervention. Such captions make images more discoverable and may be treated as metadata for indexing, searching, and filtering large repositories. Users can edit the generated captions in order to maintain control and ensure the transparency of the AI, generated outputs. Besides that, CLIP scoring serves as a quality measure for captions by checking image, text similarity, thus low quality descriptions that are under certain thresholds can be filtered out.

4.2.2 Semantic Category Classification

DeepGallery is equipped with a supervised classification unit in addition to the captioning module that determines the class of pictures. It separates pictures into six semantic classes: Architecture, Food, Nature, Portrait, Wildlife, and Miscellaneous. To decide the best fit category, the software passes each photo through a fine-tuned Vision Transformer (ViT) model. This tool is the way photo collections can be orderly structured so users can dive into their works by themes instead of just chronological order or manual tagging.

4.2.3 User Authentication and Secure Storage

DeepGallery users have no worries, knowing their details are secured through verified access and encrypted cloud storage. Only authorized users can view or modify the content that they have uploaded and all AI-generated outputs must be in the environments controlled by the users. The system refrains from collecting any personally identifiable information or geolocation metadata unless the user explicitly discloses them.

4.3 Responsible AI Considerations Embedded into the Platform Design

Responsibility, inclusiveness, and openness are not supplementary things in DeepGallery: they are deeply incorporated in its structure and methods. It is up to a human to check that all the captions and categories are editable. In this manner, users can change or amend the AI outputs which ensures that the system is a creative facilitator, rather than a judge-automator.

By data minimization, only the pictures that have been voluntarily uploaded by users are taken care of by the system and it does not reason or extract sensitive personal data from them. Facial recognition, demographic classification, or surveillance are not happening. Being transparent allows the users to realize that the captions and categories are the outputs of AI models trained on public datasets.

5 Methodology

5.1 System Architecture

The architecture of DeepGallery is a modular pipeline system that has integrated image processing, multimodal caption generation, supervised classification, and responsible AI governance. When a user uploads an image, it automatically undergoes two parallel AI components: a captioning module and a classification module. The outputs are stored as metadata linked to the user's secure cloud repository.

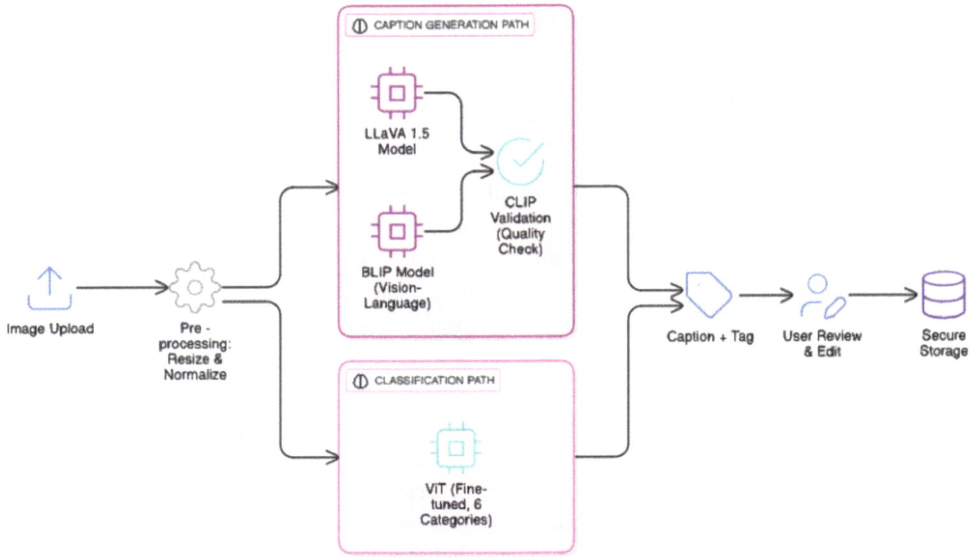

Fig. 1 DeepGallery's captioning and tagging pipeline

System architecture at the conceptual level comprises five stages: input acquisition, feature extraction, caption generation, category classification, and output storage with user feedback. The design ensures scalability, modularity, and ethical traceability (Fig. 1).

5.2 AI Caption Generation Module

5.2.1 Vision-Language Model Selection

Two vision-language architectures were used for caption generation: BLIP (Bootstrapped Language-Image Pre-training) and LLaVA 1.5 (Large Language and Vision Assistant). Both models are transformer-based and known for their complex reasoning abilities. BLIP connects an image encoder with a text decoder. LLaVA merges vision encoders with instruction-tuned large language models that help in more conversational and contextually rich descriptions (Li et al. 2023).

5.2.2 Caption Pipeline Design

The captioning pipeline comprises several sub-stages: pre-processing resizes and normalizes the input image; caption generation produces a token sequence that is converted into text; post-processing removes repetitive parts; quality validation employs CLIP to obtain similarity scores and filters low-quality captions; metadata integration stores the final caption.

CLIP scoring ensures that only those captions which have a strong semantic relation with the corresponding images are retained, leading to caption reliability enhancement and manual review work reduction.

5.2.3 Editable Captions and Human Oversight

DeepGallery has added an editorial layer in response to the reality of pre-trained models being sources of inaccuracy and biased text. Users are permitted to correct the AI-generated text with human-in-the-loop capability.

5.3 Semantic Category Classification Module

5.3.1 Model Architecture and Training

For multi-class image classification, the classification module uses a Vision Transformer (ViT) that has been fine-tuned. ViT employs self-attention mechanisms to acquire the global features of an image more efficiently than traditionally used convolutional architectures. It was pre-trained on ImageNet and then fine-tuned on a custom dataset containing six semantic categories: Architecture, Food, Nature, Portrait, Wildlife, and Miscellaneous.

The process of fine-tuning included the addition of a classification head to the pre-trained ViT backbone and training of the model on labeled images by standard supervised learning techniques. To get better model generalization and less overfitting, data augmentation methods such as random horizontal flips, color jitter, and affine transformations were used.

5.3.2 Category Taxonomy

The designed six-category taxonomy was intended to cover the most common photographic themes while being interpretable and actionable by users: Architecture (buildings, urban structures, architectural details), Food (culinary subjects, meals, food photography), Nature (landscapes, flora, natural environments), Portrait (human subjects, face-focused imagery), Wildlife (animals in natural or semi-natural habitats), and Miscellaneous (images that cannot be easily placed into other categories).

5.3.3 Classification Pipeline

The classification workflow is made up of image preprocessing (resize, normalize), feature extraction via the ViT encoder, classification head inference for category probabilities, and post-processing for choosing the class with the highest probability as the final prediction.

5.4 Ethical and Responsible AI Design Choices

Several methodological choices explicitly embody responsible AI principles. Data sovereignty is the main guarantee that users will remain the owners of all the pictures uploaded and the captions generated. Privacy preservation is the reason why no biometric identification or facial recognition is done. Transparency is the obligation to inform users about the source of the model (BLIP, LLaVA, ViT) used for them along with the possible biases. Accountability can be tracked via editable captions and categories through which users can make corrections. Inclusivity becomes more efficient by means of the automatic captions and tags that are friendly to visually impaired individuals.

6 Implementation

6.1 Development Environment and Tools

DeepGallery is a modular, reproducible environment implementation, which is aimed at being transparent and scalable. All AI components were developed with Python 3.10 in Google Colab Pro, which provided GPU acceleration by the NVIDIA T4 hardware. The main dependencies were the Transformers library (Hugging Face), PyTorch, Pandas, Pillow, and scikit-learn. The integration of Google Drive made data storage and sharing very easy and efficient.

6.2 Integration of Captioning Models

The image-captioning system was realized with two pre-trained vision-language models: Salesforce's BLIP (Large) and LLaVA 1.5, both accessible via the Hugging Face Transformers API (Liu et al. 2023). Each image was passed through this pipeline: image acquisition, pre-processing, caption generation with contextual prompts, quality validation using CLIP, post-processing, and storage.

The described procedure led to quite rapid GPU times for inference, and as a result, the text was in most cases grammatically correct and semantically coherent. Besides that, the captions were given an option to be modified by the end users before they were saved permanently, hence the human-in-the-loop principle was still at the core of the platform's ethics framework.

6.3 Fine-Tuning the Classification Model

The semantic category classifier was realized when a pre-trained Vision Transformer (ViT-base-patch16-224) was fine-tuned on a custom dataset. The dataset was made up of 280 training images (with 30 images in the Miscellaneous category, 50 images for the rest of the categories) and 20 test images, divided into six semantic categories. The training modified the last layer of the loaded pre-trained ViT model. Several data augmentation techniques were used during training like random horizontal flips, color jitter, random affine transformations, and standard normalization.

The model was trained with the cross-entropy loss function and AdamW optimizer for several epochs. The model, with very high training accuracy (95.83%) was obtained, was drastically less effective on the test set (55% accuracy), thus indicating the problem of overfitting, which is a highly common issue with small datasets. This difference points to the requirement for more and varied training data and maybe also for increasing the regularization strength in the forthcoming versions.

6.4 Cloud Integration and Data Handling

During the experiments, all the caption and classification metadata were saved in secure storage. The entire data handling operation was based on privacy-respecting design principles. No biometric identifiers were obtained or stored.

6.5 Security Practices and Ethical Safeguards

Following responsible AI and smart-city data-ethics guidelines, the implementation took several protective mechanisms. Access control ensures authentication tokens allow only authorized users to have access to their data. Model transparency is ensured through open documentation of exact model checkpoints and configurations. User agency is promoted by the caption and category editing interface. Bias mitigation is addressed by the usage of pre-trained models which were audited for open-domain fairness (Kim et al. 2024).

7 Results and Evaluation

7.1 Overview

The Evaluation phase of DeepGallery revolved around gauging the model on three key aspects: technical capability of AI for image captioning and image classification, user-centric values of improved usability and accessibility, and responsible AI practices followed by the system. In contrast to simply dwelling on accuracy figures, we lay a lot of accent on the quality of the results obtained—the linguistic correctness of the descriptions, semantic accuracy of the categories, and overall user experience of image collections sorted by AI.

Being a prototype with an exploration type and having a relatively small number of data samples for training (280) as well as for testing (20), the focus of the evaluation is on insight gathering rather than on benchmarking.

7.2 Caption Quality Analysis

7.2.1 Qualitative Assessment

The AI description components (BLIP & LLaVA) were successful in producing natural-sounding and contextually adequate captions in diverse visual domains such as landscapes, architecture, urban settings, and objects. Some such instances are (Table 1).

Captions were rated by users as semantically appropriate and linguistically fluent in the majority of cases. Errors primarily occurred in scenes with abstract compositions, low lighting, or ambiguous objects, where the pre-trained models struggled to infer the subject matter with confidence.

Table 1 Generated captions and human assessment

Image type	Generated caption	Human evaluation
Street scene	"A crowded market street during sunset"	Accurate and contextual
Modern architecture	"A tall glass building reflecting the blue sky"	Highly descriptive
Everyday object	"A ceramic mug on a wooden table"	Accurate
Portrait	"A person smiling in front of a bright background"	Coherent but generic

7.2.2 CLIP-Based Quality Validation

To ensure caption quality, CLIP (Contrastive Language-Image Pre-training) was employed to compute similarity scores between generated captions and their corresponding images. Here are the CLIPScore results for 20 sample images (Table 2).

Key Findings: Average normalized CLIPScore of 0.576 indicates generally good semantic alignment between images and captions. Top-performing captions reached perfect normalized scores (1.0) which is proof of the models high-quality output capability. The large variance ($\sigma = 0.22$) shows that the quality of captions fluctuates for different images and their complexities. These figures serve as a confirmation of the necessity for CLIP-based quality control in the captioning pipeline.

7.2.3 Limitations and Error Patterns

Analysis of captions with low scores has uncovered various types of failures that occurred repeatedly across the data. For example, in the case of abstract or artistic imagery (the models produced generic descriptions without providing local contextual details), low-light conditions (bad visibility led to uncertain or incorrect identification of objects), cultural specificity (models sometimes failed to recognize culturally important elements that were under-represented in the training data), and multi-subject complexity (the pictures having several focal points were sometimes given oversimplified captions).

7.3 Semantic Category Classification Performance

7.3.1 Quantitative Metrics

The fine-tuned Vision Transformer model was evaluated on training and test datasets, with the latter having the following category distribution (Fig. 2).

The evaluation of the fine-tuned Vision Transformer model resulted in the following performance metrics.

Table 2 CLIPScore results

Metric	Raw CLIP score	Normalized CLIP score
Mean	2938.02	0.5761
Std Dev	295.78	0.2195
Minimum	2161.80	0.0000
Median	2935.48	0.5742
Maximum	3509.23	1.0000

Fig. 2 Label distribution of test images

Training Performance:

- Accuracy: 95.83%
- Precision: 97.22%
- Recall: 95.83%
- F1-Score: 95.95%

Test Performance:

- Accuracy: 55.00%
- Macro Precision: 48.61%
- Macro Recall: 41.71%
- Macro F1-Score: 43.51%

Analysis: The substantial gap between training (95.83%) and test (55.00%) accuracy indicates significant overfitting—the model memorized training examples over learning generalizable features. This is a predictable outcome given the small dataset size (280 training images across 6 categories) and highlights a critical limitation of the current prototype.

7.3.2 Per-category Performance Analysis

Preliminary findings are as follows.

Nature and Architecture categories have been relatively better in terms of accuracy, presumably because of the distinct characteristics of the objects belonging to those categories. Miscellaneous category has been poor, as it should be because it contains all other objects. Food and Portrait objects have been confused. Classification of objects belonging to the category of wildlife has not been consistent, especially in the case of animals in the background (Table 3).

The confusion matrix highlights several flaws in the model's results. In particular, it appears that the Food type had no representation in the test set, meaning the model's ability to classify food images could not be evaluated at all, a significant gap given it is one of the six defined categories. It seems that it has been unable to pick out characteristic traits about food photos from its training samples. The Wildlife category's 0% also made it a poor performer, since it labelled a lone photo of the type as Architecture. The best-scoring type was the Portrait with a 80% success rate (4/5). It is probably because human faces possess a set of recognizable compositional traits for a human face. While the Misc category performed miserably, with a mere 29% accuracy level, it is to be expected. The model preferred to default to Architecture and Misc classes for its predictions.

7.3.3 Addressing Overfitting

The reason for the overfitting is attributed by a number of reasons: lack of data in training (since the model has been trained with only 50 pictures in each class, it has not been exposed to the intra-class variations), quality of data (variations in image quality can have led to some noise in the data).

Mitigation Strategies: Increase the size of the dataset to 500 to 1000 images per category; implement strong regularization techniques; reduce the model size and resort to few-shot learning methods; perform transfer learning and pre-train the model on the domain-specific data. Implement cross-validation.

7.3.4 Qualitative Category Assignment

Although it lacks quantity, the classification system proved its application in organizing photography collections on a thematic basis. The users also found value in the ineffi-

Table 3 Confusion matrix

Actual ↓/Predicted →	Architecture	Food	Miscellaneous	Nature	Portrait	Wildlife
Architecture	3	0	0	0	0	0
Food	0	0	0	0	0	0
Miscellaneous	0	0	2	2	0	3
Nature	0	1	3	0	0	0
Portrait	1	0	0	0	4	0
Wildlife	1	0	0	0	0	0

cient system when organizing portfolios, as it did not require computational processing.

7.4 Performance and Efficiency Considerations

The implementation demonstrated efficient performance under modest computational resources.

Captioning Performance:

- Average caption generation time: 3.4 s per image (NVIDIA T4 GPU)
- Memory footprint during inference: ~6 GB
- CLIP scoring overhead: ~1.5 s per caption

Classification Performance:

- Average prediction time: 0.8 s per image (NVIDIA T4 GPU)
- Memory footprint: ~4 GB

Storage Requirements:

- Metadata per 1000 images (captions + categories + scores): ~25 MB (CSV format)
- Optimized JSON storage: ~18 MB per 1000 images

Scalability for the future might involve optimization methods like quantization or pruning of the network, batch processing (simultaneous processing of images), lightweight models (integration with efficient models such as BLIP-2 base or MobileViT), or edge computing (possibility of execution on mobile devices for faster response or privacy preservation).

7.5 Responsible AI Compliance Evaluation

The assessment of DeepGallery also covered ethical audits, benchmarked for responsible AI use. The model had to comply with these design principles for operation (Table 4).

Table 4 Implementing responsible AI compliance in DeepGallery

Responsible AI principle	Implementation in DeepGallery
Transparency	Usage of BLIP, LLaVA, and ViT models in the public domain and open-source models
Fairness	No use is made of the face recognition technique or the inference of demographic attributes
Accountability	An editable captions practice to ensure the required quality
Privacy	User data is encrypted and made available for voluntary sharing only and does not involve the extraction of personally identifiable information
Inclusivity	Screen-reader friendly captions and structured metadata enhance accessibility
Explainability	Easy-to-read category labels and intuitive captions can ensure understandable results

7.6 Comparative Analysis: Model Selection Insights

Although direct comparison between BLIP and LLaVA was not the main objective, based on observations during the process of development, it has been identified that:

- BLIP has more descriptive captions with better performance accuracy in simple scenes, faster inference times, and more consistent formatting.
- LLaVA has more conversational and descriptive captions with improved performance accuracy in complex scenes involving elements, verbosity that requires post-processing, and semantic interpretations of ambiguous scenes.

7.7 Discussion of Limitations

While the prototype successfully validates its conceptual objectives, several limitations remain: small dataset size (280 training, 20 test images) restricts generalization and statistical reliability; significant overfitting in classification (95.83% train, 55% test accuracy); variable caption quality requiring CLIP-based filtering; pre-trained models may generate culturally skewed captions; absence of quantitative benchmarking against established datasets (COCO, Flickr30k); current implementation tested on small collections (<500 images); and energy efficiency and carbon footprint of model inference not measured.

7.8 Summary

The results obtained show that DeepGallery performs image captioning and semantic categorization in an autonomous way in a responsible and inclusive fashion. Though faced with challenges of overfitting and the size of the data, resulting in some quantitative limitations, the qualitative results show the potential of using pre-trained vision-language models and classifiers in improving accessibility, engagement, and semantics.

The key accomplishments include: CLIP-evaluated caption production with an average semantic similarity of 0.576, functional system of six categories for classification tasks (although needing data augmentation), evidence of improved accessibility using automated alt-text writing, integration of human oversight mechanisms, and compliance with responsible AI practices related to dimensions of transparency, privacy, and inclusivity.

8 Discussion

8.1 DeepGallery and the Ethos of Responsible AI

The creation of DeepGallery was in accordance with the principal objectives of responsible artificial intelligence, i.e., a system that tries to be fair, transparent, accountable, and inclusive. We didn't just maximize predictive accuracy; rather, we have positioned the system as an ethical instrument to augment human creativity. Deep learning techniques captioning and classification are viewed as good instruments that facilitate the accessibility and user-friendly interpretation of the visual data, instead of the human decision being completely handed over to them.

We are addressing the issue of how users could have complete control over their uploaded content and the metadata generated by the system, which is definitely one of the biggest challenges in AI deployment - maintaining agency in the interaction between humans and AI. DeepGallery is a socially positive AI application and unlike most AI applications that are mainly used for surveillance purposes or to exploit customers, DeepGallery is a responsible design at its core, therefore, the main function of the automation is to promote inclusion, transparency, and civic engagement. Such a strategy is fully in line with the OECD Principles on AI (2019) and the European Commission's Ethics Guidelines for Trustworthy AI (2020), which both point out human oversight, social welfare, and explainability as the key features of AI system design (Commission 2019).

8.2 Ethical and Social Impacts

DeepGallery socially is a tech demo that shows one of the ways AI tech can be thoughtfully created to empower people rather than exploiting them. A platform employed a method for the indirect dissemination of image captioning to a large part of the visually impaired community, and that was automated image captioning, for those who have cognitive challenges and they can now easily participate in visual content.

Automatically creating alternative texts for images is a very straightforward move towards compliance with web accessibility standards (e.g., WCAG 2.2) which is a major step in breaking down the inclusion barrier that has been there for a long time (Trewin et al. 2010).

The platform's inclusive captioning pipeline is an example of how AI can be intentionally used to lessen the digital equity divide. The content does not only support the functioning of the assisted devices but is also semantic; hence users can receive images via text queries, thus opening the way of creative content to the general public.

DeepGallery is a user-involved AI design example, the end-users are not simply the subjects but the co-creators of meaning with the system.

The feature of editing captions and changing categories is a demonstration of this collaborative model, which empowers the users to become the interpreters of AI output and hence, keep human authority of interpretation.

8.3 Urban and Civic Implications

DeepGallery is an urban storytelling tool and a data ecosystem for citizen-generated data, which is smart city innovation that deeply understands its socio-political context. As cities become smarter via the integration of digital sensing and analytics, visual data emerge as one of the most powerful mediums people use to record, criticize, and shape their shared experiences.

By empowering people to take pictures and describe them in terms of the environment, transport, and social inclusion, DeepGallery is putting forward a model of participatory democracy through photography. The use of an optional GPS-based system to organize these contributions could make a spatial representation of them—turning them into visual stories of city life that complement and enrich traditional data-driven urban planning (Goodchild 2007).

These kinds of participatory media platforms feed the social layer of smart cities, where citizens are not mere data providers, but narrators and co-creators of urban knowledge. It is in line with UN-Habitat's view of human-centered smart cities that stress aspects such as inclusion, cultural representation, and open data governance. DeepGallery can move from the software of the artist to the civic domain where the creative process is linked to digital citizenship through the execution of ethical AI practices.

8.4 Explainability and Transparency in Visual AI Systems

Explainability remains a major issue for AI systems that interpret images to words or categories.

DeepGallery brings about transparency by means of traceability and editability. All captions and category predictions are open to users for checking, changing, and redoing, thus providing interpretive transparency which is generally not present in closed generative systems.

Besides this, architectural transparency is a result of employing well-documented pre-trained models (BLIP, LLaVA, ViT) for which training data, limitations, and intended uses are not hidden, thus allowing the user to make an informed judgement.

In responsible AI, explainability should not be regarded as just another technical feature, but rather as an ethical prerequisite, which provides interpretive freedom. DeepGallery regards every AI-generated result as tentative, thus necessitating human involvement and, hence, locates explainability at the point of co-authorship between machine intelligence and human sensibility (UN-Habitat 2020).

Later editions could have features like attention visualization or embedding-space mapping that could help users understand why the model came up with certain descriptions or predictions thereby giving them more trust and making the system more accountable.

8.5 Addressing the Overfitting Challenge: Dataset Quality and Size

The large discrepancy of the classification module's performance between training (95.83%) and test (55%) accuracy is a clear indication of the overfitting problem which is at the core of the challenge of building AI systems with limited data. Overfitting is not only a technical issue; it is also a concern of ethics since its application in practice has the effect of producing results that are unreliable, which would result in the decrease of the user's confidence in the system's usefulness.

The overfitting issue with DeepGallery is mostly due to the size and quality of the dataset. The fact that there were only 280 training images divided into six categories (with an average of 47 images per class) means that the model was not fed enough examples from which to extract robust and generalizable features. Moreover, the differences in image quality, content, and lighting of the small dataset could have increased the noise, which the model attempted to memorize rather than generalize from.

This discovery leads to the principle of responsible AI development that data quality and quantity should be regarded as moral obligations and not just technical necessities. Small datasets may be enough for demonstration purposes, but they cannot be trusted for production systems, especially in scenarios that affect accessibility and user experience. The next versions will need to extensively focus on systematically expanding the dataset by:

- Planning collection activities that ensure balanced representation of categories and other relevant factors
- Working with photography communities for sourcing diversified and quality images
- Using synthetic data generation or advanced augmentation techniques
- Learning with few-shot or zero-shot methods that leverage large pre-trained models

8.6 Limitations and Critical Reflections

DeepGallery's present prototype points out several significant areas for further work:

The system was tested on a dataset that was not sufficiently large, limiting its ability to reflect visual diversity globally. New datasets need images representing different cultures, various aesthetic styles, and rare cases to eliminate bias and enhance generalization.

The pre-trained models used in captioning and classification may carry linguistic and cultural assumptions from their training data. For example, architectural styles or food presentation common in the non-Western world may be misclassified or described in very general ways.

The qualitative outputs seem positive; however, the system needs to be benchmarked against well-known datasets such as COCO or Flickr30k to obtain quantitative metrics for validation and comparison with state-of-the-art systems.

Performance optimization, energy efficiency, and carbon footprint are important ethical and environmental concerns for large-scale civic deployment but have not been tested at scale (10,000 + images).

The initial usability study ($n = 15$) was very informative, but it lacked the statistical significance to make conclusive claims about the impact of accessibility on usability.

For these reasons, we can understand, therefore, that responsible AI is a process of review, adjustment, and engagement, involving human beings to oversee AI. The value of AI systems can be considered not only within the context of what can be achieved, at a given time, through the use of AI, but also through the capability of responsible AI to evolve responsively with data, technology, and emerging needs.

8.7 Synthesis: From Ethical AI to Ethical Cities

DeepGallery in its design and final impact aligns with the overarching narrative that urban areas can adopt ethical urbanism practices with the aid of responsible AI. Urban areas have the potential to develop a system that embraces human diversity and at the same time honors people's digital rights through co-creating accessibility, observability, and participation in the digital realm.

DeepGallery is a small-scale implementation of the ethical AI governance model. The project is an "experiment at the level of the community", showing the feasibility of applying these values within a civic system.

Such frameworks will be essential for keeping technological intelligence at the service of human values and collective well-being as smart cities become more dependent on AI-powered sensing and representation. This platform demonstrates that ethical AI development is challenging from a technical perspective and requires equal focus on performance, user experience, and social responsibility. Achieving excellent results on benchmark datasets is insufficient if the system cannot serve diverse users fairly and if outputs cannot be understood and corrected by those affected.

DeepGallery is thus centered at the intersection of creative AI, responsible design, and civic innovation. It aligns with the academic discussion on explainable and accessible AI and offers a concrete urban application model for ethical AI deployment in participatory smart city ecosystems.

9 Future Scope

9.1 Dataset Expansion and Model Refinement

It is important to pursue the systematic extension of the training data in a systematic manner. In order to increase the classification performance to a production quality level and to avoid overfitting, we propose.

Quantitative Objectives

- Reach a number of 500 to 1,000 images for each category, meaning at least a total of 3,000 training images
- Ensure class distribution is representative to prevent class bias
- Incorporating different photography genres, lighting, and settings

Qualitative Improvements

- Acquire photos from professional as well as amateur photographers all over the globe
- Add edge examples that test the boundaries of these categories
- To ensure the quality of the dataset, expert review and inter-annotator agreement tests can be conducted

Model Optimization:

- Use cross-validation for fine-tuning classification models on larger data sets
- Attempt few-shot learning approaches for maximum knowledge transfer from pre-trained models
- Use ensemble methods based on the combinations of predictive models to enhance stability
- Explore the use of smaller models (Mobile ViT, EfficientNet) designed to be resource-friendly

9.2 Geographic and Spatial Organization Features

Today, the organization of images in DeepGallery is carried out semantically. A major improvement in the system can be achieved with the inclusion of geotagging metadata. Most modern cameras, as well as mobile phones, tend to store GPS information in the EXIF data of images. With this functionality, images can be organized based on location in DeepGallery.

This utility may also be employed to demonstrate graphically various parts of a city that may be explored in alternative ways by citizens. Geospatial patterns may assist in identifying trends in urban development, architecture photography trends, and activities of the social community in these spaces. The above activities shall be undertaken in an opt-in data sharing framework to ensure user privacy is considered.

9.3 Expansion into Participatory Urban Storytelling Platforms

DeepGallery's next stage shows the transition from the individual portfolio app to a user-driven storytelling platform. The expansion highlights the communal value of street photography—giving the locals, artists, and academics the means to record their surroundings and hence, be a part of the shared, constantly evolving story of their cities.

By using AI-generated captions and semantic classification, DeepGallery might be a curator of the visual stories of the communities about the local culture, climate change, and urban diversity. In this way, photography becomes a means of data democratization where each contributor holds the key to determining how the city is viewed and understood (Shelton et al. 2015).

9.4 Smart City Integration and Thematic Urban Mapping

DeepGallery's integration into smart city networks creates new avenues for research and experiential learning. Even though smart cities heavily rely on sensor data and real-time analytics, the core of urban life is still a human-centered, qualitative visual narrative. DeepGallery, being an AI-interpreted visual supplement to quantitative datasets, has the potential to generate detailed thematic maps illustrating urban dynamics.

The general categories like Architecture, Nature, or Food could be utilized to reveal the patterns of the city development, the availability of the green areas, or the local culinary diversity of different neighborhoods. By implementing proper anonymization and data aggregation, local government officials and researchers might be able to use these visual datasets for the purposes of sustainable planning and community designing (Batty 2013).

9.5 Potential for Community-Driven Datasets

A possible pathway would be the development of community-supported AI datasets. This can be facilitated by involving users to provide a selected data set of images along with suitable verified captions and labels for categories, so that DeepGallery can establish a vibrant dataset environment. This dataset can form a resource pool for computer vision, urban studies, and digital humanities researchers, especially computer vision researchers who require a diverse dataset for training. User contribution to data creation ensures diversity and can eliminate biases due to geographically limited datasets (Gebru et al. 2021).

Involving users in data generation ensures that users become not just users but dataset co-producers for a responsible AI environment instead. AI datasets generated from the community can be as diverse as the community itself, so transparency is not a concern. Hence, users become responsible for generating a responsible AI environment instead. This goal is attained through transparency among diverse individuals to ensure a responsible AI environment.

9.6 Advanced Explainability and Transparency Mechanisms

Future versions of DeepGallery could take into consideration the integration of advanced techniques for explainability, ensuring that these would increase user understanding regarding the decision-making processes behind the AI, such as:

Caption Generation Transparency:

- Attention visualization, showing where in the image the most discriminative features for certain words appeared in the captions
- Scores representing confidence levels in the model for the generated descriptions of the data
- Some possible alternative captions based on giving the user the ability to choose from a number of options

Classification Explanability:

- Class Activation Mapping (CAM) which highlights the areas of an image responsible for a particular category prediction
- Similarity visualization highlighting training examples most similar to classified image
- Uncertainty Quantification: Illustrating situations where the model is uncertain between two categories.

These will boost user confidence, facilitate support for informed editing decisions, and will thus meet the overall objective of developing interpretable AI systems.

9.7 Cross-Disciplinary Research Opportunities

The roadmap of DeepGallery opens up huge avenues for research in ethics and explainability in AI, such as.

Technical Research

- Improving the Effectiveness of Vision and Language Models for Culturally Diverse Images
- Designing few-shot learning approaches for fast category extension
- Enhancing energy efficiency and reducing carbon emissions for models

Human–Computer Interaction

- Long-term analyses of user engagement and behavior change with AI-assisted organization
- Usability comparison studies among various demographic populations
- Design patterns for Human-AI collaboration in creative activities

Urban Studies And Digital Humanities

- Application of visual narratives produced by citizens in urban planning analysis

- Studies across cultures: Photography subjects, aesthetics, or both?
- Support for digital heritage through community-driven photo collections

Through the incorporation of ethics, fairness, and empowerment in each level of technology advancement, DeepGallery is set to become an exemplary model for sustainable and human-oriented design principles of smart city AI systems for the next generation.

10 Conclusion

10.1 Summary of Contributions

In this chapter, the DeepGallery photography service utilizing AI is presented, which aims to offer digital accessibility, semantic structuring, and public engagement in a responsible manner using artificial intelligence. In this context, the utilization of vision-language architectures (BLIP & LLaVA) for the task of composing descriptive captions for images can reduce the required human attempts for human labeling and provide greater assistive benefits for the visually impaired in the community. In DeepGallery, the fine-tuned classification of the Vision Transformer enables semantic labeling of images in six themes.

In bringing together these features with a transparent and user-driven design, DeepGallery represents a paradigm of AI application that is cutting-edge and responsible. Where others might focus on AI for surveillance purposes or predictive analytics, this AI tool is focused on creativity and accessibility, taking a human-centered view of how AI can be a tool of inclusion and empowerment.

Primary Technical Contributions:

- Dual model captioning pipeline (BLIP + LLaVA) with validation of quality on the basis of CLIP
- Word-level classification into six classes using Vision Transformers
- Modular, reproducible architecture enabling the evaluation of individual components.
- Integration of Accessibility-Focused Design in AI Systems Development

Key Ethical Contributions:

- Application of human-in-the-loop AI governance with editable outputs
- Privacy-preserving architecture that does not support face recognition and inference of demographics
- Transparency regarding model selection and documentation in line with open science standards
- Proof-of-concept regarding the use of visual data systems for participation

10.2 Advancing Accessibility in AI-Driven Platforms

DeepGallery's biggest achievement is its role in digital accessibility and inclusivity. The automatically generated captions are beneficial for the visually impaired, those who have lots of visual archives to deal with, and communities who would like to share their cultural heritage with the world. The explainable design of DeepGallery provides an opportunity for users to control the results with their own understanding, especially for captions and categories which can be checked and edited or refused to ensure human judgments are based in the interpretative stage. The balance of the participatory equilibrium within automation and agency is based on the model of responsible and human-focused AI that uses the power of machine intelligence to extend and complement human creativity. With the increasing popularity of visual media within digital environments, such models would be paramount in maintaining a balance of accessibility and transparency.

10.3 Reflection on Responsible AI Practices

DeepGallery, in developing AI, aligns with the moral norms that contemporary responsible AI frameworks emphasize, such as transparency, accountability, privacy, and fairness. It uses pre-trained, publicly accessible models. Thus, it does not involve any kind of privacy-invasive activities in model training. The AI components of DeepGallery are designed to be bias-minimizing and interpretable.

The project demonstrates several key principles in practice:

- Transparency: The model structures for each model: BLIP, LLaVA, ViT are transparent; their capabilities and limitations are clearly stated. The user is also informed that the output may come from an AI model and may be incorrect.
- Accountability: Structures with human involvement enable the checking of all machine-made output. Nothing irrevocable is decided by the system without the input of the users.
- Privacy: This system resists the processing of any private information from images. There is no face recognition. All data is under user control.

- Inclusivity: Captions are useful as alternative texts for the deaf or blind while semantic categories enable different navigation mechanisms.
- Fairness: The pre-trained models chosen are openly documented and subject to community audits. The system is sensitive about functions like surveillance that can end up harming marginalized groups disproportionately.

By harmonizing these principles with real-world application, the initiative demonstrates that responsible AI is not only a regulatory requirement but a design philosophy that leads to sustainable innovation in digital media.

10.4 Lessons Learned: The Importance of Data Quality and Quantity

One of the most important lessons from DeepGallery's development is the relationship between dataset characteristics and model performance. The biggest instance of overfitting in the classification module (95.83% training accuracy versus 55% test accuracy) is an indication that data is paramount in ensuring that an ethical AI model is deployed.

- Ethical Issues: In case of trained models with inadequate data provision to the artificial intelligence models, they may provide poor service to users. This is particularly true in instances where users mostly use accessibility features.
- Resource Implications: In small projects, data considerations can impact innovation strategies. To that end, Proof-of-concept demos need to ensure a resonance between their innovation vision and their data needs.
- Methodological Implications: AI research related to creativity and civic engagement must adopt an attitude of data quality and diversity as issues not only of significance to outcomes, but as ethical necessities.

The DeepGallery prototype is not only a technical demonstration but also a warning: even AI systems with good intentions need robust data infrastructure to fulfill their ethical promises.

10.5 Closing Remarks on DeepGallery's Role in Human-Centered Smart Cities

As the use of AI systems is on the rise in urban infrastructures, there is an increasing requirement to balance the human element in the progress that comes with technological advancements. DeepGallery is one such balance that seeks to integrate the values of creativity, inclusiveness, and transparency from images that can blend the urban space with the concept of intelligence.

These tools have the potential of becoming a part of the culture infrastructure, documenting the experiences of people. They differ from the sensors used for place-making in the sense they show the qualitative experience of place-making.

DeepGallery is not only an advancement for responsible AI applications related to pictorial media but is also a means to conceptualize a smart city that is still quite human. It shows that technology can improve life in a city instead of monitoring it, structure it instead of restricting it, and help it creatively instead of hindering it. The future levels of the platform-from personal portfolio management to collaborative civic storytelling-point to a direction of AI development that prioritizes public benefit, openness, and empowerment over extraction, secrecy, and automation.

10.6 Recommendations for Future Development

Some of the recommendations that we would like to give to the researchers working on such AI systems for creative/civic purposes, based on our experiences in this project, are the following:

1. Data Infrastructure First: Invest in data collection before investing in model development.Small and high-quality varied datasets are always preferred over noisy, large datasets.
2. Design for Editability: User interfaces should be designed to make it easy for users to review and correct the output of the AI. Human oversight should be facile, not optional.
3. Communicate Uncertainty: The system should provide confidence scores, alternative suggestions, and indication of model uncertainty. Transparency about the limitations helps build trust.
4. Testing with Diverse Users: Should include testing with users having varied abilities from high to low technical know-how, users from diverse cultures. Accessibility testing is a process not a stage to be completed.
5. Scalability planning must be responsible, allowing factors such as energy efficiency and the environment to be taken into account.
6. Engage stakeholders: When it comes to civic tech, the system design should incorporate elements of the city, including the citizens, urban planners, and policymakers. This makes the system useful for its intended purpose.

Final Synthesis

DeepGallery is a step towards the next generation of AI systems which can be not just benevolent but also ethics-oriented. This evolution from generating gallery text to semantic classification to other applications for urban storytelling is a reflection on how AI can enhance the digital world as well as the lives of city-dwellers when motivated by the tenet of responsibility, inclusiveness, and transparency.

On one hand, technological advancements (captioning capabilities verified by CLIP, semantic categorization) are evidence of the possibility of the task, but insufficient performance (overfitting, variability in captions) confirms the paramount role of data infrastructure, realistic scope definition.

DeepGallery illustrates that responsible AI development is not concerned with the highest level of accuracy, but with people being able to "retain control over their decisions, enjoy respect for their dignity, and derive concrete benefits from technology." The project illustrates how people's abilities can be enabled by technology without diminishing their judgment, helping organize information in a way that is user-centered, and enabling the creation of a community without the element of surveillance.

DeepGallery will remain a strong example of good AI potential. It is the type of technology that does not mute the human voice but unshackles it.

Rather, it seems likely that true benchmarks for success in AI application, not only for smart cities but also for creative ecologies, will steadily migrate from rapid calculation performance to its capacity to support human flourishing.

DeepGallery is far more a new beginning than an ending, truly the first step on the way to proving that it is both necessary and possible to use AI for the creation of responsible AI for the visual media sector for civic engagement. This project will involve a good deal of research and development on our part to engage with the questions we ought to take into consideration on the way to a truly helpful development of AI that can support the vital concepts of transparency and human dignity.

References

Amershi, S., Weld, D., Vorvoreanu, M., Fourney, A., Nushi, B., Collisson, P., Suh, J., Iqbal, S., Bennett, P. N., Inkpen, K., Teevan, J., Kikin-Gil, R., & Horvitz, E. (2019). Guidelines for human-AI interaction. *Proceedings of the 2019 CHI Conference on Human Factors in Computing Systems*, 1–13. https://doi.org/10.1145/3290605.3300233

Batty, M. (2013). Big data, smart cities and city planning. *Dialogues in Human Geography*, 3(3), 274–279. https://doi.org/10.1177/2043820613513390

Bibri, S. E., & Krogstie, J. (2017). Smart sustainable cities of the future: An extensive interdisciplinary literature review. *Sustainable Cities and Society*, 31, 183–212. https://doi.org/10.1016/j.scs.2017.02.016

Bigham, J. P., Jayant, C., Ji, H., Little, G., Miller, A., Miller, R. C., Miller, R., Tatarowicz, A., White, B., White, S., & Yeh, T. (2010). VizWiz: Nearly real-time answers to visual questions. *Proceedings of the 23nd Annual ACM Symposium on User Interface Software and Technology*, 333–342. https://doi.org/10.1145/1866029.1866080

Buolamwini, J., & Gebru, T. (2018). Gender shades: Intersectional accuracy disparities in commercial gender classification. *Proceedings of Machine Learning Research*, 81, 1–15. https://doi.org/10.1145/3287560.3287596

Cardullo, P., & Kitchin, R. (2019). Being a 'citizen' in the smart city: Up and down the scaffold of smart citizen participation in Dublin, Ireland. *GeoJournal*, 84(1), 1–13. https://doi.org/10.1007/s10708-018-9845-8

Certomà, C., Dyer, M., Pocatilu, L., & Rizzi, F. (2017). *Citizen empowerment and innovation in the data-rich city*. Springer. https://doi.org/10.1007/978-3-319-47904-0

Chen, X., Fang, H., Lin, T. Y., Vedantam, R., Gupta, S., Dollár, P., & Zitnick, C. L. (2015). Microsoft COCO captions: Data collection and evaluation server. *arXiv preprint* arXiv:1504.00325.

European Commission. (2019). *Ethics guidelines for trustworthy AI*. High-Level Expert Group on Artificial Intelligence. https://doi.org/10.2759/177365

Crawford, K., & Paglen, T. (2019). Excavating AI: The politics of images in machine learning training sets. *AI & Society*, 36(4), 1105–1116. https://doi.org/10.1007/s00146-021-01162-8

Dosovitskiy, A., Beyer, L., Kolesnikov, A., Weissenborn, D., Zhai, X., Unterthiner, T., Dehghani, M., Minderer, M., Heigold, G., Gelly, S., Uszkoreit, J., & Houlsby, N. (2020). An image is worth 16x16 words: Transformers for image recognition at scale. *International Conference on Learning Representations*. https://doi.org/10.48550/arXiv.2010.11929

Dourish, P., & Bell, G. (2011). *Divining a digital future: Mess and mythology in ubiquitous computing*. MIT Press. https://doi.org/10.7551/mitpress/9780262015554.001.0001

Eubanks, V. (2018). *Automating inequality: How high-tech tools profile, police, and punish the poor*. St. Martin's Press. https://doi.org/10.1177/0094306119872496h

Garvie, C., Bedoya, A., & Frankle, J. (2016). *The perpetual line-up: Unregulated police face recognition in America*. Georgetown Law Center on Privacy & Technology. https://doi.org/10.2139/ssrn.3092366

Gebru, T., Morgenstern, J., Vecchione, B., Vaughan, J. W., Wallach, H., Daumé III, H., & Crawford, K. (2021). Datasheets for datasets. *Communications of the ACM*, 64(12), 86–92. https://doi.org/10.1145/3458723

Gleason, C., Pavel, A., McCamey, R., Low, C., Carrington, P., Kitani, K. M., & Bigham, J. P. (2020). Twitter A11y: A browser extension to make Twitter images accessible. *Proceedings of the 2020 CHI Conference on Human Factors in Computing Systems*, 1–12. https://doi.org/10.1145/3313831.3376728

Goodchild, M. F. (2007). Citizens as sensors: The world of volunteered geography. *GeoJournal*, 69(4), 211–221. https://doi.org/10.1007/s10708-007-9111-y

Gurari, D., Li, Q., Stangl, A. J., Guo, A., Lin, C., Grauman, K., Bigham, J. P., et al. (2018). VizWiz grand challenge: Answering visual questions from blind people. Proceedings of the IEEE Conference on Computer Vision and Pattern Recognition, 3608–3617. https://doi.org/10.1109/CVPR.2018.00380

He, K., Zhang, X., Ren, S., & Sun, J. (2016). Deep residual learning for image recognition. Proceedings of the IEEE Conference on Computer Vision and Pattern Recognition, 770–778. https://doi.org/10.1109/CVPR.2016.90

Hollands, R. G. (2015). Critical interventions into the corporate smart city. *Cambridge Journal of Regions, Economy and Society*, 8(1), 61–77. https://doi.org/10.1093/cjres/rsu011

Jobin, A., Ienca, M., & Vayena, E. (2019). The global landscape of AI ethics guidelines. *Nature Machine Intelligence*, 1(9), 389–399. https://doi.org/10.1038/s42256-019-0088-2

Kim, D., S, V., NG, B. A., & Lee, D. (2024). Class Scatter Ratio Based Mahalanobis Distance Approach for Detection of Internet of Things Traffic Anomalies. *Mobile Networks and Applications, 29*(2), 373–384.

Kitchin, R. (2014). The real-time city? Big data and smart urbanism. *GeoJournal*, 79(1), 1–14. https://doi.org/10.1007/s10708-013-9516-8

Li, J., Li, D., Xiong, C., & Hoi, S. (2022). BLIP: Bootstrapping language-image pre-training for unified vision-language understanding and generation. *Proceedings of the 39th International Conference on Machine Learning*, 162, 12888–12900. https://doi.org/10.48550/arXiv.2201.12086

Li, J., Li, D., Savarese, S., & Hoi, S. (2023). BLIP-2: Bootstrapping language-image pre-training with frozen image encoders and large language models. *Proceedings of the 40th International Conference on Machine Learning*, 202, 19730–19742. https://doi.org/10.48550/arXiv.2301.12597

Lipton, Z. C. (2018). The mythos of model interpretability. *Communications of the ACM*, 61(10), 36–43. https://doi.org/10.1145/3233231

Liu, H., Li, C., Wu, Q., & Lee, Y. J. (2023). Visual instruction tuning. *Advances in Neural Information Processing Systems*, 36, 34892–34916. https://doi.org/10.48550/arXiv.2304.08485

Luo, J., & Savakis, A. E. (2001). Indoor vs outdoor classification of consumer photographs using low-level and semantic features. *Proceedings 2001 International Conference on Image Processing*, 2, 745–748. https://doi.org/10.1109/ICIP.2001.958595

Mitchell, M., Wu, S., Zaldivar, A., Barnes, P., Vasserman, L., Hutchinson, B., Spitzer, E., Raji, I. D., & Gebru, T. (2019). Model cards for model reporting. Proceedings of the Conference on Fairness, Accountability, and Transparency, 220–229. https://doi.org/10.1145/3287560.3287596

Morris, M. R., Johnson, J., Bennett, C. L., & Cutrell, E. (2018). Rich representations of visual content for screen reader users. *Proceedings of the 2018 CHI Conference on Human Factors in Computing Systems*, 1–11. https://doi.org/10.1145/3173574.3173633

Noble, S. U. (2018). *Algorithms of oppression: How search engines reinforce racism.* NYU Press. https://doi.org/10.18574/nyu/9781479833641.001.0001

OECD. (2019). *Recommendation of the Council on Artificial Intelligence.* OECD Legal Instruments. https://doi.org/10.1787/0e5df5a3-en

Radford, A., Kim, J. W., Hallacy, C., Ramesh, A., Goh, G., Agarwal, S., Sastry, G., Askell, A., Mishkin, P., Clark, J., Krueger, G., & Sutskever, I. (2021). Learning transferable visual models from natural language supervision. *Proceedings of the 38th International Conference on Machine Learning*, 139, 8748–8763. https://doi.org/10.48550/arXiv.2103.00020

Rajasekar, V., Devi, K. N., Sathya, K., Sabarnika, S., Raagul, N. S., & Logeshwar, R. (2023, October). An Intelligent System for Nutrition Deficiency Detection Using Deep Learning Techniques. In *International Conference on Applied Mathematics and Mechanics* (pp. 39–47). Singapore: Springer Nature Singapore.

Ramesh, A., Pavlov, M., Goh, G., Gray, S., Voss, C., Radford, A., Chen, M., & Sutskever, I. (2021). Zero-shot text-to-image generation. *Proceedings of the 38th International Conference on Machine Learning*, 139, 8821–8831. https://doi.org/10.48550/arXiv.2102.12092

Sathyamoorthy, M., Rajasekar, V., Krishnamoorthi, S., & Pamucar, D. (2026). Ensemble deep learning approach for traffic video analytics in edge computing. *Scientific Reports.*

Shelton, T., Zook, M., & Wiig, A. (2015). The 'actually existing smart city'. *Cambridge Journal of Regions, Economy and Society*, 8(1), 13–25. https://doi.org/10.1093/cjres/rsu026

Shneiderman, B. (2020). Human-centered artificial intelligence: Reliable, safe & trustworthy. *International Journal of Human–Computer Interaction*, 36(6), 495–504. https://doi.org/10.1080/10447318.2020.1741118

Shunmugesh, K., Biju, B., Reji, A., Rajasekar, V., Hiremath, S., Anne, G., & Vishwanatha, H. M. (2026). Optimizing 3D printing parameters for enhanced tensile strength and efficiency using machine learning models. *Progress in Additive Manufacturing*, 1–16.

Townsend, A. M. (2013). *Smart cities: Big data, civic hackers, and the quest for a new utopia.* W. W. Norton & Company. https://doi.org/10.5860/choice.51-2388

Trewin, S., Cragun, B., Swart, C., Brezin, J., & Richards, J. (2010). Accessibility in the enterprise: Challenges and opportunities. *Proceedings of the 12th International ACM SIGACCESS Conference on Computers and Accessibility*, 83–90. https://doi.org/10.1145/1878803.1878821

UN-Habitat. (2020). *People-Focused Smart Cities: A guide for city leaders.* United Nations Human Settlements Programme. https://doi.org/10.18356/9789211326549

WebAIM. (2023). The WebAIM Million: An annual accessibility analysis of the top 1,000,000 home pages. https://doi.org/10.1145/3308561.3353786

Zuboff, S. (2019). *The age of surveillance capitalism: The fight for a human future at the new frontier of power.* PublicAffairs. https://doi.org/10.1177/0263276419856861

Challenges, Opportunities, and Future Directions in Ethical AI

R. Saurabh, S. Srikanth, and C. Saravanan

Abstract

According to the United Nations, by 2050, nearly 68% of the global population is expected to live in urban areas, compared to 55% in 2020. In India alone, the urban population might reach 600 million by 2036, putting immense pressure on education, infrastructure, water, energy, and housing systems. Greater migration to cities like Delhi, Mumbai, and Bengaluru is causing a lot of obstruction, increasing pollution growth, and high demand for basic needs. These various challenges need ethical and effective management by integrating artificial intelligence into urban governance in ways that are transparent and responsible. Population growth has placed a burden on city infrastructures, often manifesting in overcrowded public places, inadequate housing, and poor waste disposal. Ethical AI tools can support predictive urban planning, optimize traffic flow, and monitor environmental conditions within frameworks that respect privacy and avoid bias. Similarly, educational systems in developing cities reflect important disparities in both access and quality. AI-driven learning platforms will help tailor instruction and resource allocation more effectively, but must be designed to safeguard data security and fairness to avoid reinforcing social inequalities. Most water and electricity utilities in cities are under tremendous pressure due to consumption beyond sustainable levels and a generally aging infrastructure. Some cities, like Chennai, have suffered from serious water shortages, while others are regularly load-shedding during peak demand for electricity. AI will further enhance efficiency through smart grids, predictive maintenance, and water-usage forecasting that guarantee sustainability of urban operations. But ethical deployment shall demand transparency, equity in access, and accountability in decision-making. This chapter examines various challenges associated with smart city, opportunities for people staying in smart city compared to rural regions. The proposed chapter also focuses on arriving at feasible solutions for the challenges faced in the smart city involving the usage of responsible AI technology.

Keywords

Ethical AI · Smart governance · Responsible AI · Smart city

1 Introduction

The unprecedented global shift to urban living presents a crisis of complexity that traditional systems of governance are failing to manage. It frames artificial intelligence (AI) not as a mere technological tool, but as a potentially transformative force for this new urban age. However, it immediately introduces the central tension and research question that the chapter will explore: that this technological potential is inextricably linked to profound ethical risks. The introduction argues that the true challenge for twenty-first-century cities is not just adopting AI, but doing so responsibly—harnessing its power to solve acute problems like housing, transportation, and environmental degradation while safeguarding human rights, equity, and democratic values.

R. Saurabh · S. Srikanth (✉) · C. Saravanan
Department of MCA, RV College of Engineering, Bengaluru, India
e-mail: srikanths.mca24@rvce.edu.in

R. Saurabh
e-mail: saurabhr.mca24@rvce.edu.in

C. Saravanan
e-mail: saravananc@rvce.edu.in

V. Sarveshwaran et al. (eds.), *Responsible AI for Smart Cities*, Sustainable Artificial Intelligence-Powered Applications,
https://doi.org/10.1007/978-3-032-26901-0_11

1.1 Background and Motivation

The twenty-first century is the moment in human civilization when the preponderance of our species shifts from largely rural to overwhelmingly urban (United Nations, Department of Economic and Social Affairs, Population Division. World Urbanization Prospects: The 2018 Revision 2019a). This change comes with breath taking rapidity and is fundamentally reshaping the ways that billions of people live, work, and interact with one another. Unfortunately, this trend does not represent an unmixed blessing but a complicated challenge that severely tests the capacity of existing systems of governance, infrastructure, and social organization.

Now, consider the scale of change: every week, about 1.5 million people move to cities worldwide (United Nations, Department of Economic and Social Affairs, Population Division. World Urbanization Prospects: The 2018 Revision 2019b). In India, this transformation is seen even more dramatically: cities such as Bengaluru absorbed more than 110 percent population growth between 2001 and 2011 (Census of India, 2011); Delhi's population topped 30 million in recent estimates. More than 7.5 million passengers ride Mumbai's suburban trains every day—far over their designed capacity. But these numbers are not just statistics; they are human lives in pursuit of opportunity, fighting for a decent roof over their head, being squashed in impossibly crowded commutes, and competing for meager resources.

Enter artificial intelligence—a suite of technologies that seem almost purpose-built for the complexity of the urban condition. Machine learning algorithms detect patterns in datasets too vast for human analysis. Computer vision systems monitor infrastructure continuously without fatigue. Optimization algorithms balance a host of competing objectives across multiple constraints at one time. Natural language processing enables automated citizen engagement at scales previously impossible.

Yet technology alone provides no panacea. History is riddled with cautionary tales of innovations deployed with insufficient regard for social consequences, creating new problems while solving old ones. The question facing contemporary cities therefore exceeds mere technical capability: How can we harness AI's transformative potential while safeguarding human rights, promoting equity, ensuring accountability, and preserving democratic values? This chapter addresses that question.

1.2 Urban Challenges Magnified by Migration

Migration to cities is the result of rational individual decisions; economic opportunities, schools, healthcare, and cultural activities are available within urban confines. What is individually rational, however, is collectively problematic when millions make the same decision at the same time (see Fig. 1).

This figure quantifies the defining demographic shift of the century, projecting an immense influx of 2.5 billion new urban residents globally by 2050, with nearly 90% occurring in Asia and Africa. It specifically underscores India's pivotal role in this trend, accounting for a staggering 416 million

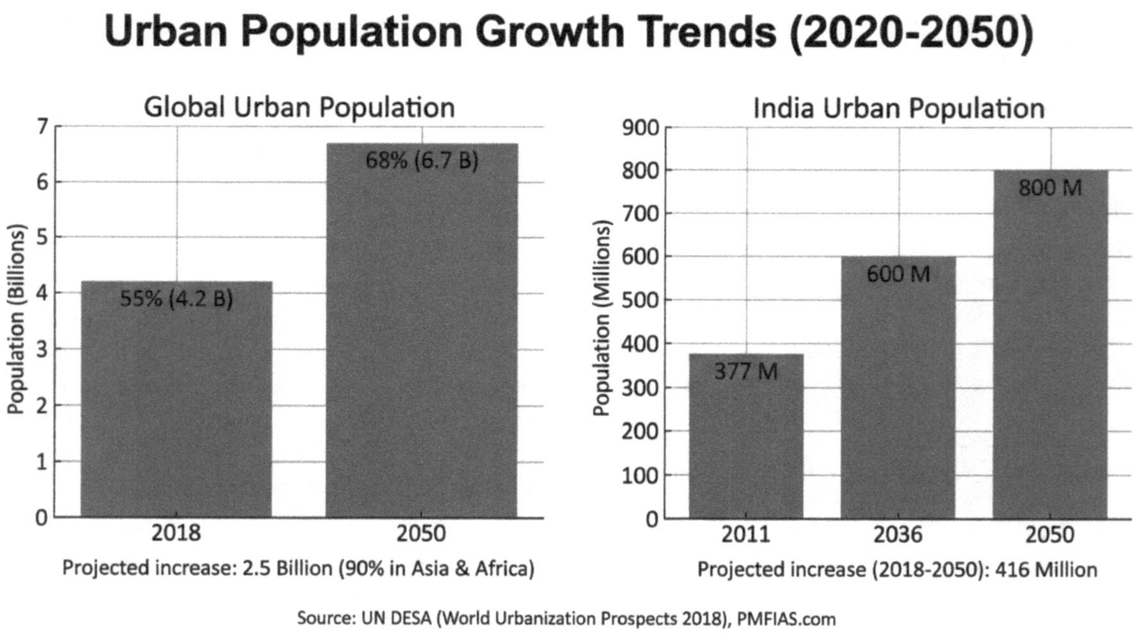

Fig. 1 Global and national urbanization projections (2020–2050)

of this growth, which illustrates the unprecedented scale of urban management challenges and opportunities facing the nation.

Housing Crisis Deepens: Urban land is a fundamentally finite resource, but demand keeps on expanding. In Mumbai, this tension reaches an extreme form where densities range above 100,000 residents per square kilometer in some neighborhoods—arguably the highest in the world (Kundu 2016). Property prices surge beyond the reach of middle-class citizens, who have to move into ever-suburban locations or informal settlements. The slum population is growing despite government efforts at re-development. Up to 30% of Chennai's population lives in informal settlements bereft of basic services such as piped water, sewage connections, or legal tenure security.

Gridlocked Transportation Systems: The challenge of infrastructure is probably best personified by the conditions of urban mobility in Bengaluru. Commuters spend an average of 71% longer in traffic (TomTom 2024) than free-flow travel times would require, making it one of the most congested cities in the world. Such bottlenecks impose enormous costs in terms of lost productivity, extra fuel consumption, and higher levels of air pollution, all combining to reduce quality of life. The problem compounds as rising incomes enable private vehicle ownership while public transit investment lags population growth.

Delhi's case thus represents the problem and partial solutions. Despite unparalleled investment in metro rail that has created one of the largest systems in the world, private vehicle use keeps rising. The road space stays limited while vehicle registrations accelerate. Peak-hour traffic turns arterial roads into parking lots. Consequences regarding pollution are severe when vehicular emissions account for a substantial share of air quality that often exceeds the safe threshold multiple-folds.

Accelerating Environmental Degradation: Cities concentrate people and, therefore, pollution. Industrial emissions, vehicular exhaust, construction dust, and burning of garbage culminate in air quality crises. Delhi's episodes of winter pollution epitomize the extremes: PM2.5 concentration sometimes exceeds WHO guidelines by 30–40 times (Guttikunda and Goel 2013), forcing the closure of schools and emergency measures. The health consequences prove severe and inequitable: children, elderly, and economically disadvantaged populations suffer disproportionate impacts.

Water bodies are contaminated from various sources. Untreated sewage is discharged into them even in places where such practices are forbidden by regulations. Industrial effluents with pollution control measures go into water courses. Solid wastes of all types on river and lake banks. Lakes in Bengaluru, said to be the pride of the city, were so badly contaminated with chemicals that they foamed and, worse still, catching fire. The Adyar and Cooum rivers in Chennai became synonymous with pollution and resembled open sewers rather than living water courses.

Changing consumption patterns are making waste management increasingly problematic. Greater incomes lead to increased wastes generated. Packaging materials, electronic waste, and plastic proliferate. However, the pace of generation is far outstripping the growth in facilities for collection, segregation, and processing. Landfills are reached to their capacity; new sites face community opposition. Informal waste pickers perform essential recycling services without safety equipment, fair compensation, or social recognition.

Service Delivery Strains: The healthcare, education, and public safety systems are experiencing overwhelming demand. Most government hospitals operate beyond their capacity, with treatment in corridors not an uncommon sight. Treatment for non-emergency cases may require waiting lists extending up to several months. The urban poor seldom hold health insurance, and illness is often catastrophic. Preventive care is not suitably matched to acute treatment. Mental health, though demand is increasing, is one of the largest shortfalls in services.

Educational inequality between private and public schools continues to widen. Resource-starved, public schools are barely able to maintain infrastructure, retain quality teachers, or invest in modern learning tools. The learning environment suffers due to overcrowding. Students of underprivileged backgrounds cannot afford extra resources, such as tutoring or learning gadgets. Consequently, educational achievement becomes closely tied to family socioeconomic status—a far cry from meritocratic ideals.

Public safety evolves with the cities: sophisticated patterns of crime are growing, cybercrime is becoming increasingly problematic, traffic congestion delays emergency responses, falling police-to-population ratios below recommended levels are experienced, and the fire services face difficulties reaching narrow lanes within the informal settlements. Disaster response capacity is inadequate for major events of floods, earthquakes, or industrial accidents.

1.3 Rise of AI in Managing Urban Systems

Fortunately, AI technologies are reaching maturity. The capabilities they offer address severe limitations in urban management. The abundance of data, powerful computation, and advanced algorithms together create opportunities little more than science fiction a few decades ago.

From Reactive to Predictive: Traditional infrastructure management uses a reactive approach, responding after failures occur. Water main breaks disrupt service before the repair crews arrive. Potholes are allowed to develop before road crews address them. Equipment failures knock operations offline before maintenance occurs. In addition, this reactive approach tends to be expensive both financially and in terms of service disruption.

Basically, AI enables fundamental transformation toward predictive maintenance. Sensors implanted in infrastructure assets continuously monitor condition parameters like vibration, temperature and pressure, and flow rates. Machine learning algorithms analyze this data alongside historical failure patterns for subtle changes that serve as signs of impending problems. Maintenance teams get alerted before failures actually happen, thus enabling proactive intervention at scheduled windows rather than emergency responses.

It does this in Singapore through predictive maintenance of lifts in public housing. Sensors monitor operating parameters, and algorithms run pattern analyses that show component degradation. The system schedules preventive maintenance before failures, which cuts breakdowns by more than 50% while actually lowering overall maintenance costs (Housing and Development Board, Singapore 2021). Residents get more reliable service, and the housing authorities can better allocate resources.

Real-Time Optimization: Urban systems involve myriads of interconnected decisions. Traffic signal timing, energy generation dispatch, water pressure management, and deployment of emergency units form just a partial list. Each of these affects the performance of the system, while traditional approaches have relied on fixed schedules or simple rules incapable of adapting to dynamic conditions.

AI-based optimization algorithms approach real-time conditions across complete systems all at once, finding configurations that maximize performance against multiple objectives. Traffic management systems adjust timing based on actual vehicle presence, not according to fixed schedules, in order to reduce congestion and improve flow. Smart grids balance supply of electricity coming from multiple sources—including intermittent renewables—against fluctuating demand, maintaining stability while minimizing costs and emissions.

The best example of such functionalities is smart traffic in Barcelona. Computer vision cameras monitor the flow of vehicles and pedestrians across the junctions. Machine learning algorithms forecast traffic based on time, weather, events, and other historical data. Optimization algorithms dynamically change the timing of the signals, prioritizing the direction with heavier flow while ensuring adequate crossing times for pedestrians. Implementation reduced average travel times by 21% in pilot areas, with a drop in intersection accidents by 17% (Barcelona City Council 2023).

Pattern Recognition at Scale: Cities produce tremendous volumes of data from sensors, transactions, social media, and administrative records. This holds a wealth of information on urban dynamics, service quality issues, and emerging problems, but it outstrips human analytical capacity.

Machine learning excels at finding patterns in large datasets. Infrastructure damage will be detected with computer vision analyzing images that would take months for human inspection; natural language processing analyzes citizen complaints for issues about service quality and emerging concerns. Anomaly detection algorithms flag abnormal patterns suggesting fraud, waste, or system malfunction.

Automated Decision Support: Urban managers have to make hundreds of decisions every day regarding permit applications, allocation of resources, implementation of policies, and other responses to emergencies. Most of the decisions use well-defined rules but nevertheless require human judgment. This volume of decision-making uses up a great deal of time while introducing delays and potential inconsistencies.

These AI systems support decisions by reliably applying the rules, flagging cases that require attention, and making recommendations based on relevant precedent and data. Applications for building permits automatically pre-review for missing information and potential code violations before humans take over. Service requests are routed to the proper departments. Budget variance analyses draw attention to areas requiring managerial attention. In this way, human decision-makers can tackle complex situations that require judgment but know that matters of routine are handled consistently.

1.4 Why Responsible AI Matters in Cities

Deployments in urban contexts differ fundamentally from many other deployments of AI. These differences create unique ethical imperatives that need careful attention.

Involuntary Exposure: Unlike applications in consumers, where people can decide whether to use the services powered by AI or not, urban AI systems affect all residents irrespective of consent. Traffic management systems impact everyone using the roads. The public spaces watched by surveillance systems are practically unavoidable for citizens. Utility management systems decide the quality of service for all customers. Air quality monitoring affects the health of all residents. This involuntary exposure requires much higher ethical standards than voluntary-use consumer applications.

- Vulnerable Populations: Cities are made up of diverse populations, including those groups that require special protection, such as children, the elderly, people with disabilities, economically disadvantaged communities, linguistic minorities, and recent migrants. These populations lack the capacity to understand the AI systems affecting them, to advocate for their interest, or to seek redress when harmed. Ethical AI deployment must ensure protection for vulnerable populations rather than optimize for the preferences of the majority.

- Scale of Impact: AI systems in urban areas will be deployed at scales involving millions of people at once. Algorithmic errors scale across an entire population; biased systems discriminate against whole demographic groups; privacy violations impact whole cities, and cascading system failures are magnitudes larger in their disruption. This scale demands robust testing, validation, and governance before deployment.
- Long-Term Consequences: Urban infrastructures are multi-decade investments that shape and mold cities for generations. Infrastructure-embedded AI systems create path dependencies limiting choices in the future. Data collection practices set today define privacy expectations for years to come. The algorithmic decision-making norms set precedents that will shape democratic governance. These long-term consequences demand careful ethical consideration beyond immediate functionality.
- Democratic Accountability: Democratic systems are based on the right of citizens to exercise political power through voting, advocacy, and participation. AI systems that obscure decision-making processes, concentrate power among technical experts, or otherwise operate without meaningful oversight undermine democratic accountability. Responsible AI deployment needs to preserve and enhance democratic governance rather than eroding it.
- Public Trust: Effective governance is critically dependent upon citizen trust in institutions. The latter is cultivated over decades and lost suddenly when egregious violations occur. Of course, AI systems biased to expose privacy to violation or giving rise to unexplained harm will undermine institutional credibility. When public trust is lost, it will be very hard to regain. So, the confidence in such transparency needs to be fostered from the very beginning.

2 Understanding Smart Cities and Their Challenges

This section provides the core context of modern urban environments and transcends specific challenges of migration to look at systemic burdens and inherent limitations defining today's cities. It frames the "smart city" not simply as a technological upgrade but as a necessary evolution in order to meet deep-seated infrastructural and operational frailties. By enumerating physical deterioration, capacity constraints, and the reactive nature of traditional urban management, this section provides the backdrop for understanding why technologies such as AI have to intervene to bring about an urgently called-for paradigm shift.

2.1 Urban Infrastructure Burdens

Infrastructure is the circulatory system of cities—visible only when it fails. Contemporary Indian cities carry infrastructure legacies created by colonial priorities, post-independence development philosophies, and decades of postponed maintenance. This bequeathal is proving increasingly inadequate to meet current demands while it requires massive investment for preservation.

Many Indian cities operate infrastructure built during colonial times for populations a fraction of today's size. Mumbai's water system from the 1860s now serves 20 million instead of its designed one million. Post-independence development prioritized rapid expansion over quality, resulting in infrastructure showing premature aging.

Physical Deterioration: Aging infrastructure is exhibiting accelerating failure rates as components exceed design lifespans. Water distribution networks in several cities lose from 40 to 50% of supply due to leakage—an enormous waste amidst scarcity. Corroded pipes burst often enough to disrupt service and damage roads frequently. Sewer lines crack, collapse, and back up, causing environmental contamination. Electrical transformers fail under peak loads and create outages. Road surfaces deteriorate into crater-filled hazards that damage vehicles and cause accidents.

The Financial Ramifications are Huge: Emergency repairs are many times more costly than preventive maintenance; service disruptions damage productivity; infrastructure failures pose significant threats to public health and safety. Yet, infrastructure maintenance competes with politically more visible projects for limited budgets. The result is that maintenance gets deferred while problems compound, ultimately requiring far more expensive comprehensive replacement.

Constraints on Capacity: In fact, even the well-maintained infrastructure in the country was designed for smaller population sizes. For instance, Chennai required water supply infrastructure that would serve 8.5 million residents but was serving more than 10 million. During the acute water crisis in 2019, the four main reservoirs serving Chennai fell to less than 1% capacity. The crisis brought out a systemic inadequacy that includes over-extraction of ground water, insufficient rainwater harvesting, lacking recycling and desalination capacity, and leakage in the distribution network.

Technological Obsolescence: Many infrastructure systems rely on obsolete technologies incompatible with modern monitoring. Full replacement is prohibitively expensive, while piecemeal retrofitting requires managing compatibility during prolonged transitions.

2.2 Limitations of Traditional City Systems

Traditional urban management is based on periodic planning, reactive maintenance, and manual monitoring. It cannot handle city complexities and dynamism in the present day.

Reactive, Not Proactive: Most older systems only react to a problem after it has occurred instead of preventing the problem in the first place. Water main breaks disrupt service before repair takes place. Road potholes develop before maintenance takes place. Outbreaks of diseases spread before public health intervention begins.

Limited Data Collection: Manual data collection means information on system status is sporadic and incomplete. Census data become outdated rather quickly. Condition assessments of infrastructure are infrequent. Citizen feedback channels capture just a fraction of service quality issues.

Isolated Operations: City departments operate in isolation with little coordination amongst themselves. Transport planning lacks linkage to land use planning, energy systems are not integrated with building management systems, and healthcare delivery operates without coordination with environmental monitoring.

Inflexibility: Fixed planning cycles do not readily accommodate changed circumstances. Five-year plans become obsolete as events unfold. Budget allocations set at fiscal year beginning cannot adjust to rising needs. The regulatory regimes cannot keep pace with technological and social changes.

3 Role of AI in Addressing Urban Problems

This would be a pivotal section in that it would switch from diagnosing urban ailments to presenting AI as a transformative toolkit of solutions. It articulates well how artificial intelligence transcends the mere hype of being a buzzword into an operational enabler that alters the governance model from being reactive to predictive and adaptive. The section is structured to show how AI, integrating continuous monitoring, predictive analytics, complex system optimization, and automated decision support, constitutes the new "central nervous system" of the city, thus directly confronting the limitations described above.

3.1 AI as an Enabler of Smarter Cities

See Fig. 2.

AI is transforming urban management by surmounting its conventional boundaries along three converging trends: proliferating sensor data, advanced computation, and sophisticated algorithms. It empowers the transformation of city governance from being reactive to proactive and adaptive.

1. **Continuous Real-Time Monitoring**: IoT sensors provide continuous, city-scale monitoring of air/water quality, traffic, infrastructure health, and energy consumption. The large streams of generated data are analyzed in real-time by machine learning algorithms that detect anomalies and trigger alerts. For instance, Barcelona has implemented a 500-sensor network to monitor hotspots of pollution and automatically adjust the flow of traffic, thus reducing emissions.
2. **Predictive Analytics**: AI models predict future urban challenges by analyzing past trends in data sets. Major areas of use:
   - Predictive Maintenance: Anticipating when infrastructure will fail and scheduling repairs before a disruption can occur.
   - Demand Forecasting: Optimizing utilities, traffic, and healthcare resources.
   - Public Health: Systems like the Singapore dengue outbreak predictor analyze weather and case data for the purpose of targeting vector control preemptively.
3. **Optimization of Complex Systems**: AI operates the complex interdependent infrastructure of cities, including competing objectives for transport-priority scheduling in intersections. Specific algorithms leverage real-time data to optimize trade-offs in traffic flow, emissions, and safety. Decentralized AI agents in each intersection coordinate with Pittsburgh's Surtrac system to produce 25% travel time reduction and 21% emissions reduction while learning continuously from changing patterns.
4. **Automated Decision Support:** AI automates routine administrative processes, such as permit application review or routing of citizen requests, using natural language processing and rule-based automation. This accelerates services, ensures consistency, and reserves human experts for complex judgments. AI-driven chatbots and sentiment analysis enable better citizen engagement and improvement in service quality across diverse

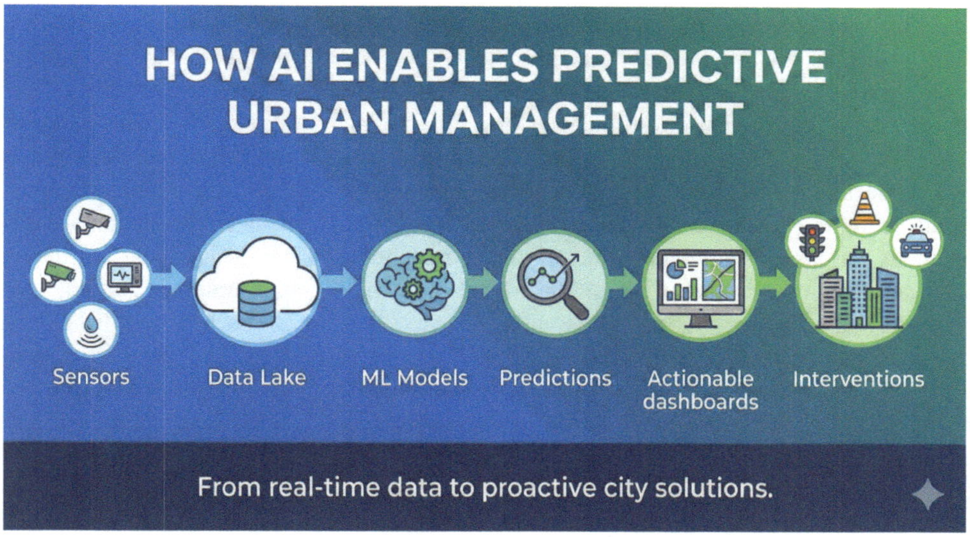

Fig. 2 The AI-enabled predictive management pipeline for smart cities

populations. This integration of monitoring, prediction, optimization, and automation positions AI as the central nervous system for smarter, more responsive, and efficient cities.

3.2 AI in Education and Healthcare

Adaptive Learning Platforms: Traditional classroom teaching cannot meet the needs of its diversified students. Teachers managing 30–40 students simply cannot provide fully personalized instruction. AI-driven adaptive learning systems address this by adapting content, pace, and approach to each student's level and learning style. The systems continuously assess understanding and automatically adjust difficulty—students who grasp concepts quickly move to more challenging material, while those who struggle receive extra practice and alternative explanations.

Carnegie Learning's math platform demonstrates this effectively. It generates problems adapted to each student's mastery level, providing hints and worked examples when needed. In controlled studies, students using the platform showed learning gains 30–50% greater than traditional instruction (Learning 2022). Beyond individualization, these platforms provide teachers with dashboards showing all students' progress, struggle areas, and skill mastery, enabling targeted interventions without replacing the teacher's role.

Early Warning Systems: Student dropout rarely occurs suddenly—warning signs accumulate through declining attendance, falling grades, and disengagement. Machine learning algorithms analyze student data to identify predictive patterns in dropout risk, flagging at-risk students early when interventions are most effective. The Karnataka Project to Address Learning Trajectories integrates school data to assess dropout risk, enabling timely interventions like counseling and tutoring. Pilot implementations achieved a 40% reduction in dropout rates compared to control schools.

Medical Diagnosis: AI diagnostic assistance systems compare patient data against enormous medical knowledge bases, providing potential diagnoses with supporting evidence. These systems augment physician judgment in complex or rare cases. Apollo Hospitals' Cardiac Risk Prediction System assesses patient data to predict cardiac events with over 90% accuracy, enabling targeted preventive interventions that reduced cardiac events by 30% among high-risk patients (Apollo Hospitals Group 2020). Computer vision AI applied to medical imaging achieves specialist-level accuracy in specific tasks. AI screening for diabetic retinopathy matches ophthalmologist performance, while chest X-ray AI identifies tuberculosis with higher sensitivity than human readers. These tools prove especially valuable in resource-limited settings with restricted specialist access.

Telemedicine Enhancement: Geographic barriers limit healthcare access, particularly for specialized services. AI makes telemedicine more effective through medical chatbots for initial symptom assessment, translation systems for cross-language communication, and remote monitoring systems that analyze wearable device data. During COVID-19, AI-enhanced telemedicine sustained care access while reducing infection risk through symptom checkers, remote monitoring, and 24/7 mental health chatbot support—extending rather than replacing human healthcare resources.

Resource Optimization: AI optimization algorithms enhance healthcare resource utilization by considering complex, competing demands. Operating theater scheduling accounts for procedure duration variation, surgeon availability, and emergency cases. Emergency room staffing aligns with predicted patient patterns, while smart ambulance dispatch considers traffic and hospital capacity. A 2% gain in operating room utilization equals adding an entire room—avoiding millions in capital costs—while reduced emergency wait times improve outcomes and patient satisfaction.

Population Health Analytics: AI analytics process electronic health records, insurance claims, socioeconomic indicators, and environmental data to identify high-risk populations and health determinants beyond individual behavior—air pollution exposure, food deserts, lack of parks, and social isolation. Predictive models identify communities where disease outbreaks are likely, enabling proactive public health measures. Environmental health monitoring detects conditions affecting health outcomes, such as air pollution episodes triggering asthma attacks or heat waves threatening older persons, allowing protective advisories and targeted outreach to vulnerable populations.

3.3 Risks and Constraints

The potential for transformation through AI in urban contexts carries with it tremendous risks and constraints that call for active management.

Data Quality Dependencies: The performance of a machine learning system depends entirely on the quality of the training data. If this data contains errors, biases, or gaps, then these are inherited and amplified by the resulting AI—garbage in, garbage out is still true. Historical data often represents discriminatory practices: predictive policing systems trained on arrest records take on geographic and demographic biases from discriminatory enforcement, credit-scoring systems perpetuate redlining effects, and hiring recommendation systems replicate gender and racial imbalances. Deploying these kinds of systems without addressing the underlying bias automates and legitimates discrimination.

Data Incompleteness Creates Blind Spots Where AI Fails: Neighborhoods without sensors can't be monitored, populations underutilizing digital services stay invisible, and rare events with few historical examples can't be predicted. These gaps correlate with disadvantage and hence make systems work worst for those needing most support. Performance also degrades over time due to data drift: models trained on historical data fail when patterns shift because of urban development, climate change, pandemics, or economic changes—a process that requires continuous monitoring and retraining.

Implementation Complexity: Most cities, especially smaller ones with limited budgets and staff, often lack the substantial technical capabilities, infrastructure investments, and organizational change required by most AI deployments. Secondly, integrating this into legacy infrastructure poses a huge challenge: modern AI requires digital streams of data from sensors, yet cities operate much pre-digital infrastructure. Retrofitting sensors is costly, their total replacement is not practical, and building interfaces between old and new requires extensive engineering.

Organizational change is equally difficult as the technical implementation. AI-enabled processes represent a significant break with traditional workflows and demand staff training, cultural changes from reactive to proactive approaches, and from intuition-based to data-driven decisions, and continuous adaptation rather than fixed procedures. Data governance becomes critical but complex since AI systems require data integrated across traditionally separate domains; privacy regulations constrain beneficial uses, while interagency sharing faces bureaucratic obstacles.

Adversarial Vulnerabilities: Several AI systems are vulnerable to different forms of attack with the aim of forcing malfunction or eliciting various weaknesses. It is possible for adversarial examples—those designed to mislead systems—to force misclassifications in computer vision, errors in speech recognition, or the mistake of an autonomous vehicle in interpreting subtly modified road signs. Poisoning attacks compromise the integrity of training data by modifying it in such a way that it biases models, inserts backdoors, or degrades performance—the risks of which are increasing as more systems continue to train on crowdsourced public data. Model extraction attacks steal proprietary models through the observation of inputs and outputs, allowing for intellectual property theft and vulnerability analysis. Privacy attacks extract sensitive information through model inversion—the reconstruction of training data—or membership inference—determining if individuals were in training datasets.

Trade-Offs Between Explainability and Performance: The most accurate machine learning models-deep neural networks-operate as "black boxes" where even the developers cannot explain individual predictions. Simpler interpretable models, such as decision trees, sacrifice accuracy. In applications where accuracy is critical and errors create grave harm-medical diagnosis, structural safety, financial fraud-maximizing accuracy may justify opacity. Where explanation enables learning, builds trust, or is legally required-loan denials, criminal sentencing, school admissions-interpretability outweighs marginal accuracy gains.

In the context of urban governance, opacity undermines accountability, blocks the identification of bias or error, and destroys public trust; yet requiring full explainability will also block beneficial uses where complex patterns exceed human comprehension. As discussed in more detail later, recent research developing techniques for explanations such as saliency maps showing influential input features, counterfactual explanations describing required input changes, and local approximations for individual predictions are partial solutions to this ongoing challenge.

4 Responsible AI and Ethical Urban Innovation

Here, the narrative introduces a most critical framework of caution and principle, realizing that technological power does indeed require ethical imperatives that control and guide it. Fairness, transparency, accountability, privacy, and human oversight are core principles of Ethical AI that this section outlines with crucial explanations for why those principles are non-negotiable in an urban context. It looks at unique ethical issues arising in cities—including involuntary exposure, impacts on vulnerable populations, and threats to democratic accountability—but puts forward that without this ethical backbone, AI solutions run the risk of further exacerbating the very problems they seek to solve.

4.1 What Is Ethical AI?

Ethical AI is defined as the development and deployment of artificial intelligence systems in ways that respect human rights, foster fairness, operate with transparency, and are accountable for their impacts. The tenet of ethical AI represents more than mere compliance with regulation; it embodies guiding principles for responsible innovation (Jobin et al. 2019) (see Fig. 3).

Fundamental Principles:

1. **Fairness and Non-discrimination**:

AI systems should not discriminate due to race, gender, religion, or socioeconomic status. Ensuring fairness involves both procedural equity in how decisions are made and distributional equity of the outcomes. There are many definitions of fairness, which brings in the further challenge of choice among them as appropriate for a particular context.

2. **Explainability and Transparency**:

Stakeholders should understand how AI systems make decisions, in particular when those decisions significantly affect individuals. Explainability helps detect errors or biases. Transparency creates trust, which allows for accountability.

3. **Privacy and Data Protection**:

This requires AI systems to collect, store, and process personal data without violation of the privacy of a person. Data minimization allows collection only up to that which is necessary. Purpose limitation prevents use of the data beyond the original stated purposes. Security against unauthorized access.

4. **Accountability and Responsibility**:

There should be clearly defined chains of responsibility for the impacts of AI systems. When systems cause harm, affected individuals deserve recourse. Where AI systems

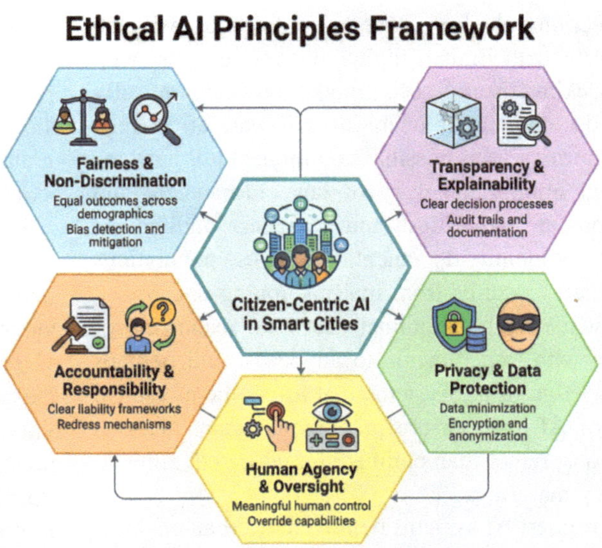

Fig. 3 A framework for operationalizing ethical AI principles

cause harm, the organizations that deploy these systems are responsible, even for unintended consequences.

5. **Human Agency and Oversight**:

AI should enhance but not replace human judgments, especially in decisions involving consequences. Humans must retain meaningful control over AI systems. Override capabilities ensure that humans can intervene in case of malfunction or inappropriate recommendations from the systems.

4.2 Why Responsible AI is Critical for Cities

The applications of urban AI differ fundamentally from consumer applications in ways that demand increased ethical attention.

Involuntary Exposure: Unlike voluntary consumer applications, urban AI systems affect all residents independent of consent: traffic management affects all road users, surveillance tracks unavoidable public spaces, utility management AI affects the service quality for all customers, and air quality monitoring affects everyone's health information. This involuntary exposure involves asymmetrical power relations; residents cannot opt out without extraordinary sacrifices such as relocation. Consent models developed for choice-based consumer applications prove seriously wanting. Democratic legitimacy based on public consultation and oversight from elected representatives, through transparency making informed public discourse possible, becomes necessary.

Exposures to Vulnerable Populations: Cities contain complex, multifaceted populations with groups that require special protection: children unable to provide informed consent, elderly with limited digital literacy, persons with disabilities seeking special accommodations, economically disadvantaged communities unable to advocate effectively, linguistic minorities with possible communication barriers, undocumented immigrants wary of law enforcement and other government authorities, and homeless individuals devoid of regular identity documentation. These populations are typically left to suffer from malfunctioning and biased AI systems while having minimal access to resources for legal redress, with impediments to advocacy, and perhaps without knowledge of the systems that affect them. Ethical deployment of AI must ensure protections against vulnerable populations, rather than optimize for educated, affluent, digitally savvy majorities.

Scale of Impact: AI systems deployed in urban environments operate at an enormous scale, where results may be presented to, or impact, millions of individuals at once. A biased criminal justice algorithm may be applied to thousands of defendants, discriminatory loan approval systems may impact tens of thousands of applications, and flawed traffic management disrupts millions of commuters. This scale multiplies individual algorithmic errors across whole populations. Large-scale deployment concentrates power: the companies or agencies in control of urban AI make technical decisions about algorithms, data collection, and system design that might affect the lives of millions of people. Strong governance becomes critical for ensuring technical decisions align with democratic values and public interest, rather than narrower organizational interests.

Long-Term Consequences: Urban infrastructure represents multi-decade investments in shaping cities for generations. AI systems establish path dependencies and lock-in effects. Today's data collection practices define tomorrow's privacy expectations and technical possibilities. The norms of algorithmic decision-making establish enduring precedents for democratic government. Proprietary system vendor dependencies can persist for decades. Long-term implications involve taking a view on consequences beyond immediate functionality: what will this system enable or constrain in twenty years, how may future governments or administrators misuse it, and what precedents does deployment establish? These temporal considerations are integral to responsible innovation.

Democratic Accountability: Cities are the fundamental units of democratic government in which citizens exercise political power through voting, advocacy, public comments, and civic participation. AI systems that obscure processes for decision-making, concentrate power in the hands of technical experts, or operate without meaningful oversight erode democratic accountability. Algorithmic governance-transferring decisions from democratically elected officials and democratically accountable administrators to automated systems-shifts power from democratic to technocratic control. While AI contributes usefully to decision-making inputs, preserving space for human judgment, value-based choice, and political contestation is imperative. Technical optimization cannot substitute for democratic deliberation about priorities and tradeoffs.

Public Trust Imperatives: Urban governance depends vitally on citizen trust of institutions. Hard-won trust, built incrementally through better performance and transparent communication, is rapidly lost when transgressions occur. AI systems tainted by bias, invasions of privacy, or other unexplained noxious outcomes shred institutional credibility. As will be seen, trust is even more fragile in communities suffering from institutional discrimination or abuse, especially regarding AI systems from agencies implicated in policing or welfare services. Building trust involves authentic engagement, equity commitment, transparency enabling verification, and also accountability arrangements allowing redress to occur. Without trust, even the best-designed systems face resistance that undermines their effectiveness.

4.3 Ethical Issues

Algorithmic Bias in Urban Contexts: Machine learning systems, trained on historical data, reflect embedded biases from discriminatory practices, unequal enforcement, differential service quality, reporting biases, and disparate sampling. Predictive policing epitomizes these risks: systems predict future locations of crime based on historical arrest data biased by racial profiling, disparate minority neighborhood enforcement, and differential arrest rates across racial groups. Areas with greater past enforcement have more recorded crimes not because there were more crimes, but because there was more enforcement being carried out there (Buolamwini and Gebru 2018).

Algorithms trained on biased data reinforce and amplify discrimination, guiding disproportionate enforcement at minority neighborhoods, creating more arrests that become the training data that reinforces the bias. Such feedback loops are self-fulfilling prophecies: predicted high-crime areas become high-arrest areas through enforcement directed by predictions based on historical arrests. Algorithms to predict building code violation, credit scoring, employment screening, and housing allocation pose similar risks when they are trained on biased historical data.

Addressing algorithmic bias requires several interventions: data curation done carefully to identify and correct historical biases; tracking of fairness metrics in outcomes across demographic groups; diverse development teams with varied perspectives; stakeholder engagement to ensure design is informed by communities affected; frequent audits that can spot emerging bias; accountability mechanisms allowing redress when discrimination occurs.

Surveillance and Privacy: Many smart city technologies support unprecedented scales of surveillance. Facial recognition cameras track the movement of public citizens, license plate readers monitor vehicles, WiFi and Bluetooth sensors also detect devices for apparent movement patterns, smart meters record energy use and hence infer occupancy and activities, and mobile applications generate location and behavior data. Integrating many data streams creates comprehensive profiles of citizen behavior (Crawford 2021).

This surveillance capability raises fundamental questions: Do people have reasonable privacy expectations in public spaces? What constraints should limit government monitoring? Who accesses collected data for what purposes? How long should data be retained? Can individuals discover what data exists about them and challenge inaccuracies? Different jurisdictions reflect varied cultural values: European approaches emphasize protection of privacy, Chinese approaches privilege security and social stability, American approaches balance security and civil liberties, and Indian approaches evolve through judicial decisions and proposed legislation.

Responsible surveillance systems require legible legal authority defining permissions, purpose limitations preventing mission creep, data minimization, access controls, retention policies guaranteeing deletion when data becomes unnecessary, transparency enabling public oversight, and accountability mechanisms investigating abuses.

Digital Exclusion: AI-powered services are likely to generate two-tier cities in which the quality of the service is related to one's level of digital capabilities. Apps for reporting issues on a mobile device take away from those without smartphones or knowledge of basic skills in digital literacy. Such automated systems fall short of addressing disabled peoples' needs. People who are non-native speakers face a barrier in language, leading to a lack of access to AI-powered services. Elderly populations find themselves at odds with clunky digital interfaces. Poor residents are without reliable internet connectivity. All these forms of exclusion correlate with disadvantage, and the AI systems are working worst for people who need most support, and, in fact, enhance inequality between digitally connected and excluded populations.

In its design, universal design addresses issues of digital exclusion by providing multichannel access: phone, in-person, and mail; language support through translation services and multilingual interfaces; accessibility for people with visual, auditory, motor, or cognitive impairments; reduced complexity in interfaces; and functionality while offline without constant connectivity. Digital exclusion is more than a technical accommodation; rather, it involves universal affordable internet access, digital literacy training, and traditional service channels for those unable or unwilling to adopt digital alternatives.

Accountability Deficits: Complex AI systems create accountability problems when decisions prove harmful or wrong. Automatic permit denials based on AI assessment may not yield explanations enabling appeals. Utility service disruptions from AI optimization algorithms leave no one clearly responsible. Credit denials informed by machine learning models may inadequately justify legally required adverse action notices. These accountability gaps particularly offend government applications where principles of administrative law demand explanation, due process, and appeal opportunities. Where algorithmic decision-making is opaque, these principles are frustrated—citizens cannot mount meaningful challenges without understanding decision rationales, officials cannot defend decisions without explaining system logic, and judges cannot assess the appropriateness of administrative decisions.

Accountability deficits will have to be addressed by explanation interfaces that provide human-understandable rationales for individual decisions; audit trails that record decision inputs, outputs, and intermediate states enabling retrospective review; human oversight so that consequential decisions involve human review rather than rubber-stamping; clear organizational responsibility in terms of assigning specific individuals accountable for system performance; and redress mechanisms through which affected individuals can contest the decisions and obtain corrections.

Data Ownership and Consent: Smart city sensors collect individual data without explicit consent or realistic opt-out opportunities. Visiting cities with smart infrastructure means non-volitional data collection. Residents performing basic activities, such as walking streets, using public transit, and consuming utilities, create data gathered without affirmative consent. Traditional consent models cannot cover involuntary collection at scale. Getting individual consent from millions is not feasible. The notice-and-consent model allows for unbridled use of data in unreadable, lengthy terms. Opt-out models place burdens on the individual to protect privacy. None satisfactorily address the issue of involuntary ambient data collection.

Alternative models of governance involve democratic legitimacy through public consultation and oversight by elected representatives, rather than individual consent; data trusts that manage data collectively on behalf of communities; robust purpose limitations preventing use other than for specified public purposes; aggregate analyses that prevent identification of individuals; differential privacy, which provides mathematical guarantees; and public transparency that enables oversight. These collective approaches together constitute governance appropriate for collective, involuntary data collection.

4.4 Citizen-Centric AI Design

Ethical AI requires centering citizen interests throughout design, development, deployment, and operation processes.

Participatory Design Processes: The articulation of citizen participation in the design of AI systems ensures that systems reflect community values, solve real needs, and do not convey external priorities. This would be done by early engagement to outline priorities and requirements through public consultations, community meetings, and even digital platforms with answers to the following questions: Which problems are to be prioritized? Which trade-offs are tolerable? What concerns need to be addressed? Design-phase engagement also gauges alternatives as communities provide feedback regarding acceptability, usability, and potential impacts before major investments. Pilot programs engage communities in testing systems prior to wide-scale deployment and are able to give feedback on actual use rather than an abstract description.

Ongoing engagement continues post-deployment via citizen advisory boards, which provide ongoing input into systems as they evolve; mechanisms for feedback, through which issues can be reported and improvements suggested; and public performance reporting, enabling transparency and accountability. This sustained engagement means the systems will evolve in tandem with the needs and values of that community. The Decidim platform in Barcelona embodies participatory smart city governance: the free and open-source digital direct democracy platform enables citizens to propose technology initiatives, debate alternatives, and vote on priorities. Thousands of active citizens shape technology decision-making processes that otherwise would remain under the full control of administrators and vendors. This helps ensure that smart city investments reflect community priorities rather than technology-driven agendas or vendor interests.

Privacy by Design: The privacy protection built into the design is much more effective than it is added later. Key principles include the following:

- Minimizing data reduces collection to what is required for specified purposes instead of collecting all that could be useful later, thus reducing privacy risks, storage costs, and breach consequences.
- Edge processing analyzes sensitive data in a locality without gathering it into a central repository. The processing is done on devices or neighborhood gateways and only the aggregate statistics are transmitted.
- Anonymization: Personal data may be anonymized before storage or analysis. K-anonymity ensures that each record is indistinguishable from k-1 others, while l-diversity ensures the diversity of sensitive attributes within anonymous groups.
- Differential privacy adds calibrated statistical noise to provide mathematical guarantees that individual records remain unidentifiable, while enabling accurate aggregate analysis, even against well-informed adversaries.
- Purpose limitation protects against any uses exceeding the specified purposes without new authorization. Smart meter billing data should not enable surveillance, and collection of health data for public health should not inform immigration enforcement.
- Retention policies ensure data gets deleted automatically when no longer needed; the retention period, however, should be appropriate to balance operational needs against protection of privacy.

Algorithmic Transparency: Making intelligible the AI decision-making process develops trust and accountability at a number of levels. For general audiences, system cards document capabilities, limitations, and performance characteristics: what the system does, what data it uses, accuracy levels, known limitations, operators, and ways of giving feedback. Model cards provide detailed technical documentation of training data characteristics, model architecture, key performance metrics across various demographic subgroups, known biases, and failure modes.

Explanation interfaces provide human-understandable rationales for individual decisions, showing which input factors most influenced the predictions, how decisions would change with different inputs, and why similar cases received different decisions. Audit trails capture extensive system operation information for retrospective investigation: what data entered, what processing occurred, what outputs produced, who accessed results. Public reporting provides aggregate performance information, including decision counts, outcome distributions across demographic groups, prediction accuracy, and appeal results that enable democratic oversight.

Equitable Access: Universal design ensures AI-enabled services remain accessible regardless of digital capability, language, disability, or economic status. Multichannel service delivery provides alternatives to digital interfaces through telephone hotlines, physical service centers, and postal mail for populations unable or unwilling to use digital services. Language support entails translation services, multilingual interfaces, and in-person interpretation—particularly important in cities with dozens of spoken languages. Accessibility features enable disability access through screen readers, video captioning, wheelchair-accessible physical locations, and disability awareness staff training. Digital literacy support through library and community center computer training, plain language step-by-step guides, and inclusion programs enables residents to gain successful technology use skills.

Meaningful Human Oversight: Human judgment shall remain central to consequential decisions, informed but not determined by AI. Decision architecture explicitly defines human versus AI roles: routine decisions based on clear-cut rules may use automation with human exception handling; complex decisions requiring judgment remain with human decision-makers informed by AI analysis; and critical decisions affecting fundamental rights require multiple human reviewers. Override: Where systems make inappropriate recommendations, capability for human override exists, with justification documented and regular review of override rates illuminating systematic problems.

Ongoing review processes examine system performance regarding stated objectives and equity metrics: Are predictions meeting expected accuracy? Do outcomes show demographic disparities? Do users understand and trust the system? Informed by this review, decisions are made about continuing or adjusting systems. Training for human operators builds effective oversight skills, understanding of system capabilities and limitations, appropriate trust calibration—neither excessive trust nor unjustified skepticism—development of critical evaluation skills, and spotting of edge cases needing special attention, to provide meaningful rather than merely perfunctory oversight.

5 Opportunities Enabled by Ethical AI in Smart Cities

The section underscores the positive vision and tangible benefits that responsibly deployed AI can unlock, building on the ethical framework. Moving the focus from risks to rewards in light of how a principled approach to AI can lead to more effective and equitable outcomes, the section organizes opportunities across three key urban domains: planning, service delivery, and sustainability. It underlines very specific examples of how ethical AI leads to better, evidence-based decisions, more responsive citizen services, and a reduced environmental footprint, thus turning the promise of a smart city into a reality for all residents.

5.1 Better Urban Planning

Data-Driven Land Use Optimization: AI-based analytics will better inform planning by considering data on mobility patterns, economic activity, and residential preferences, thus grounding decisions in reality. Machine learning identifies optimal locations for schools, healthcare facilities, parks, and commercial development based on real usage patterns and accessibility analyses. Simulation models assess the impacts of the proposed developments before any building construction: street traffic effects, environmental impacts, demands on infrastructure, and social consequences. Generative design algorithms create alternatives for development with optimizations across multiple objectives, including housing density, green space, transport access, and community cohesion.

This has aptly been showcased in Amsterdam's smart city planning (Amsterdam Smart City 2022). Taking data from sensors, administrative records, and surveys, Amsterdam understands urban dynamics. Machine learning models forecast how development proposals are affecting traffic, air quality, and community character. Evidence-based approaches uplift quality in planning decisions, reduce costly errors, and increase public engagement with visualization of proposed changes.

Prioritization of Infrastructure Investments: Constrained capital budgets mean prioritization of infrastructure investments against competing needs such as road repairs, upgrades of the water system, school facilities, and parks.

Traditional methods tend to be based on the squeaky wheel principle where the visible problem areas or those with political pressure lead allocations. AI can enable more systematic evidence-based prioritization.

Predictive asset management systems forecast infrastructure deterioration and the probability of failure. That way, they enable investments to be prioritized so as to avoid catastrophic failures or high-consequence problems. Cost-benefit algorithms evaluate returns on different investment options considering multiple factors: user impacts, lifecycle costs, environmental effects, equity implications. Optimization algorithms allocate budgets to maximize overall benefit subject to constraints.

These methods have been applied to the infrastructure management system of Singapore (Land Transport Authority, Singapore 2020). Sensors monitor infrastructure condition continuously. Machine learning came into play for predicting deterioration and failure risks. Scheduling of maintenance using optimization algorithms is done in a manner that provides maximum asset lifespan with minimum disruption of service. This systematic approach reduced infrastructure failure rates by 40%, while actually shrinking maintenance expenditure through preventive rather than reactive methods.

Community Impact Assessment: Different communities are affected differently by proposed development and policies. Impact assessment tools facilitate evidence-based evaluation before implementation.

Traffic microsimulation models predict the development impacts on congestion at a very fine spatial and temporal resolution. The environmental models project air quality, noise, and ecological effects. The economic impact models estimate employment, tax revenue, and business impacts. Equity analysis identifies populations that would be affected by disproportionate benefits or harms. This is a complete assessment that will lead to balanced decision-making by taking into consideration many factors.

5.2 Better Public Service Delivery

Intelligent Citizens' Engagement: Natural language processing lets AI-powered chatbots handle routine inquiries by citizens 24/7 without waiting. Systems answer frequently asked questions about services, operating hours, procedures, forms, and application status. They route more complex issues to human staff and resolve the routine matters efficiently.

Sentiment analysis of citizens' feedback, complaints, surveys, and social media would look at finding issues in service quality and arising concerns. Text mining extracts themes from unstructured feedback at scales impossible through manual review, hence allowing political staff to identify areas for service improvements and policy adjustments.

Fraud Detection and Prevention: Machine learning brings suspicious patterns in government transactions, benefit programs, and procurement to the fore. Anomaly detection flags strange activities for scrutiny, such as duplicate payments, impossible travel claims, bid rigging indicators, and identity fraud. Network analysis will illustrate the relationships between entities that would point to a coordinated fraud scheme.

These are capabilities that protect public resources while ensuring the benefits reach their intended recipients. The fraud detection system of the Indian government FCI really shows promise (Ministry of Consumer Affairs, Food and Public Distribution, India 2021). Employing machine learning algorithms on the data related to ration distribution, ghost beneficiaries, duplication, and diversion were detected. Implementation resulted in the recovery of millions spent toward fraudulent disbursals while augmenting the services among genuine beneficiaries (Census of India 2011).

Emergency Response Optimization: Each second being crucial in an emergency, AI optimization has brought significant efficiency in such responses.

Predictive models anticipate emergency incidents based on historical patterns, weather events, and real-time indicators, enabling the prepositioning of resources at possible incidents. Optimal dispatch algorithms select response units to minimize arrival time, taking into account location, traffic, and unit capability. Dynamic routing adjusts the path in real time by using real-time traffic conditions to route around congestion. Coordination systems enable better multi-agency responses during major incidents that involve fire, police, medical, and utility coordination.

In Pittsburgh, AI-optimized emergency response shaved up to 30% off the average ambulance arrival time, directly improving outcomes of medical emergencies for which every minute counted.

5.3 Sustainability Benefits

Energy Efficiency and Demand Response: Energy efficiency increases tremendously due to smart grid technologies with AI optimization using integration with renewables.

Demand forecasting predicts consumption at high temporal and spatial resolution. Generation dispatch optimizes multiple sources, including intermittent renewables while maintaining grid stability. Automated demand response shifts non-essential loads to off-peak periods or times of high renewable generation. Building management systems optimize HVAC and lighting based on occupancy, weather, and electricity pricing.

Pune's smart grid pilot demonstrates the various benefits: AI-driven systems brought down distribution losses from 23% to 15% through intelligent monitoring and theft detection (Pune Smart City Development Corporation Ltd 2022). Peak demand reduced 18% with automated demand response engaging large consumers. This would bring greater sustainability and lower cost.

- Water Conservation: Leak detection systems use pressure and flow analysis, combined with machine learning pattern recognition, to detect losses in the distribution system. Early leak detection prevents major breaks and associated water waste. Smart metering provides detailed consumption data, enabling the detection of customer-side leaks and other wastes. Predictive maintenance prevents infrastructure failure. Irrigation optimization maintains healthy parks and green spaces while minimizing the amount of water applied.
- Reduction of Waste: The AI-driven route optimization curbs fuel consumption and resultant waste in collection. Computer vision monitors illegal dumping to enable prompt cleaning. Waste sorting robots enhance efficiency in recycling and curb contamination. Fill-level sensors make it possible for demand-based collection instead of fixed schedules, thus reducing superfluous trips. Analytics identify patterns in waste generation that inform reduction strategies.

Sensor networks offer high-resolution real-time air quality monitoring across cities. Source apportionment algorithms identify major contributors of pollution. Predictive models forecast episodes of pollution, thereby enabling proactive measures like construction restrictions, traffic management, and public health advisories. Optimization of traffic flow minimizes congestion and optimizes flow in order to reduce emissions from vehicles. Industrial monitoring for compliance with emission regulations.

6 Challenges of Adopting Ethical AI

This section serves as a crucial reality check, shifting the discussion from theoretical frameworks and potential benefits to the practical, on-the-ground obstacles that cities must navigate. It acknowledges that the path to implementing ethical AI is fraught with multifaceted hurdles. The analysis is structured to provide a systematic inventory of these barriers, categorizing them into technical limitations, policy vacuums, social resistance, and infrastructural deficits. By detailing these challenges—from data quality issues and legacy system integration to regulatory uncertainty and the digital divide—this section provides a sobering balance to the optimistic vision, arguing that recognizing and strategically planning for these impediments is a prerequisite for any successful and responsible smart city initiative.

6.1 Technical Challenges

- Data Quality and Availability: Ethical AI needs high-quality representative data. Infrastructure for collecting data is incomplete in most cities, or it doesn't exist at all. There are biases in existing data created during historical practices. Data silos impede horizontal integration across departments. Well-meaning privacy regulations forbid some uses. Solutions to these challenges will involve systematic investment in sensor networks, data integration platforms, bias detection and mitigation techniques, and methods that preserve privacy.
- Legacy System Integration: AI retro-fitting on several decades-old infrastructure is expensive and technologically challenging. Overall replacements are hardly viable. Developing the interfaces between the old and the new demands appreciable engineering. Gradual migration strategies require longer transition periods with continuity.
- Scalability: Many successful small-scale pilot projects do not scale well across the city. The volume of data expands exponentially. The system becomes complex. Performance suffers. Architecture design needs to consider scalability requirements right from the outset.
- Model Drift: Unless continuously updated, models will degrade in performance as conditions change. For example, urban development patterns change, climate change shifts weather patterns, and social dynamics change. Continuous monitoring and retraining prove essential to maintain accuracy.
- Adversarial Robustness: AI systems are under threat, especially from active adversaries who try to make AI malfunction. In particular, adversarial examples mislead computer vision, while data poisoning corrupts training and model extraction enables theft and vulnerability analysis. Defenses depend on continuous research and vigilance.

6.2 Policy and Governance Challenges

- Regulatory Uncertainty: While the development of AI races ahead, the evolution of regulatory frameworks lags behind. While existing regulations may not satisfactorily address concerns specific to AI, there is also regulatory fragmentation across jurisdictions, which poses some challenges in compliance. Needless to say, regulatory clarity is a must for responsible innovation, yet tough to achieve when the technology changes so fast.

- Procurement Challenges: AI systems are beyond traditional procurement processes. Uncertain capabilities make it difficult to define fixed requirements; vendor evaluation should consider ethical issues besides technical performance. Relationships for ongoing maintenance and updates are required rather than one-off purchases.
- Liability Frameworks: When AI causes harm, determining liability among developers, deployers, and operators is complicated. Current legal systems struggle to deal with algorithmic harms. Insurance mechanisms remain underdeveloped. Well-balanced liability frameworks should incentivize safety without deterring beneficial innovation overly.
- Intergovernmental Coordination: Different governments and their departments need to be coordinated in implementing a smart city. Federal, state, and local governments have different priorities. The tendency of departments guarding authorities and data creates an obstacle in integration. Clear governance structures and aligned incentives will ensure effective coordination.

6.3 Social Issues

- Digital Divide: Poorer digital capability creates two-tier cities. Older populations are less digitally literate. Low-income residents may not have a smartphone or internet access. Recently migrated residents may face issues of language barriers. Disabilities require accommodation. Universal design and multi-channel access remain key considerations.
- Public Trust Deficits: Privacy-violating and biased technologies deplete citizen trust. Certainly, deployed surveillance without consultation does face opposition; suspicion is engendered by the algorithms that are not transparent. Transparency, community engagement, and demonstrated fairness help build trust.
- Job Displacement: Automation can displace municipal jobs. For example, smart meters eliminate meter readers. For customer service, there is a risk that chatbots will take over from representatives. In areas where automation frees up resources, transitioning workers is paramount.
- Algorithmic Literacy: A mismatch in expectations due to a lack of understanding about the possibilities and limitations of AI on the part of citizens is bound to occur. Unrealistic expectations lead to disappointment. Furthermore, insufficient risk awareness prevents informed consent. Education will have to create algorithmic literacy.

6.4 Infrastructure Challenges

- Connectivity requirements: AI-enabled systems require ubiquitous robust connectivity. Most areas lack good broadband. Mobile capacity may be insufficient. The cost of connectivity may exclude some users from access. Public WiFi programs address the gaps in access but require investment.
- Power Infrastructure: Sensor networks require reliable power. In most of the locations, electrical infrastructure is not available. Battery-powered sensors need periodic maintenance. The investments in power infrastructure need to be developed in tandem with the sensor deployment.
- Physical Infrastructure Challenges Exposed sensors face vandalism and theft risks, requiring protection and redundancy for critical systems. Infrastructure requires continuous maintenance—calibration, software updates, component replacement—demanding cities build maintenance capacity through training and resource allocation.

7 Future Directions: Ethical AI in Smart Cities

This forward-looking section explores the horizon of technological and governance innovation. It looks at the emerging technologies, such as edge AI and digital twins that will shape the next generation of urban solutions, in concert with parallel innovations in data governance, such as data trusts and differential privacy, created to protect citizen rights. Notably, it also outlines the long-term systemic risks—like algorithmic governance and surveillance creep—that cities must vigilantly guard against. The section concludes with a roadmap for action, emphasizing multi-stakeholder collaboration, adaptive regulation, and capacity building as the key pathways to realizing a sustainable and humane urban future.

7.1 Emerging Technologies

With Edge AI, the computation moves to the edge devices, improving privacy, reducing latency, and hence improving resilience. Such examples include edge processing, which analyzes sensitive data locally instead of transmitting it. Reduced latency provides the capability of creating real-time applications. A distributed architecture improves resilience. As edge capabilities improve, more applications are feasible with less privacy risks.

- Federated Learning: It is a new approach that allows different parties to collaborate on model training with distributed data, which never actually centralizes sensitive information. Several organizations, therefore, train the models while maintaining the data locally. Individual records are protected by privacy-preserving techniques. Federated learning enables desirable AI while addressing data governance concerns. Digital Twins are virtual replicas of cities that allow option simulations well in advance of their actual implementation in the physical world. With this, urban planners test scenarios without disrupting daily life; infrastructure managers predict behavior under different conditions; and realistic simulations train emergency responders. Putting it all together, it greatly enhances the capacity for planning and operations.

7.2 Data Governance Innovations

Data trusts are legal arrangements for the handling of data in the interest of beneficiaries. In a similar way to how financial trusts work, they govern smart city data to ensure that use is appropriate and in tune with community values. They provide professional trustees who balance multiple stakeholders' interests. Data trusts offer governance mechanisms.

Data trusts concepts have been piloted as part of the DECODE project in Barcelona (Decode Project 2020). Individual citizens are in control of the sharing of personal data, including time-limited access for specific purposes. Preliminary results show technical feasibility but also bring out issues related to governance that would need continuing attention.

Personal Data Stores: These applications put the individual in control and let organizations access their data for explicit purposes. It is not up to the organization to collect data; rather, the individual is in control. For the AI system, access to the data is temporary, and no copy of the data is retained. Personal data stores reverse the power dynamic in data relationships.

Differential Privacy: The mathematical framework enables aggregational analytics with the protection of individual privacy. No single record could be identified because of statistical noise. Therefore, the organizations could extract analytical insights without compromising privacy. Differential privacy finds increasing practical deployment.

Data Integrity with Blockchain: Distributed ledgers maintain the veracity of data without unauthorized modification. Audit trails track the access and use of data. Smart contracts automatically enforce agreements concerning the use of data. Blockchain offers solutions for specific data governance challenges.

7.3 Long-Term Risks to Watch

Algorithmic governance risks come from heightened dependence on AI, which will tend to shift authority from elected representatives to technical systems. Democratic accountability does require retaining meaningful human control over consequential decisions. Governance frameworks should leave space for political judgment.

- Vendor Lock-in: Proprietary AI systems create dependencies from which it is hard to escape. The switching costs increase over time. Requirements of open standards and interoperability avoid much lock-in but may prevent access to some state-of-the-art capabilities.
- This might be called surveillance creep: Sometimes, the spread of monitoring is surreptitious; infrastructure put in place for one purpose gets repurposed. That requires governance frameworks to exert firm limits on surveillance to prevent erosion of privacy.
- Inequality Amplification: the efficiencies of AI can make benefits accrue mostly to already-advantaged populations. The explicit attention to equity makes sure the technology does not further exacerbate disparities.
- Environmental Impacts: The artificial systems involve a great deal of energy usage, especially during the training process. Data centers require cooling and power. Electronic waste resulting from sensors creates disposal problems. The environmental footprint has to be weighed against sustainability benefits.

There is dependence on technology where over-reliance on AI may cause the skills in humans to atrophy. Workers will no longer be able to operate manually. Cascading disruption due to system failures: Therefore, keeping backup capability provides resiliency.

7.4 Roadmap

The collaboration of government, civil society, academia, technology providers, and citizens makes for effective ethical AI. All bring different types of perspective and capacity. Formal coordination mechanisms underpin regular dialogue. Public–private partnerships distribute costs but ensure benefit to all.

- Regulatory Frameworks: These need to be laid down by governments so that innovations are allowed to serve the greater good, with safety and the prevention of harm being considered. Clear-cut criteria are required for transparency, accountability, and fairness. Risk-based Approaches: The requirements will have a direct relationship with criticality. Supervised experimental deployments may have regulatory sandboxes granted.

- Ethics Review Processes: AI ethics review boards are to be set up in cities to review proposed deployments for population impacts, privacy implications, and concerns about fairness. It is a way of having accountability, while community representation ensures diversity in those views.
- Capacity Building: Successful AI deployment needs the building of organizational and societal capacity. This means that training is required among the staff of governments, and educational institutions must build curricula for this. Public education informs and builds algorithmic literacy, while technical assistance facilitates smaller cities lacking expertise.
- International Cooperation: Cities share similar challenges, making knowledge sharing through networks like the G20 Global Smart Cities Alliance valuable for establishing interoperability standards and cross-border data governance frameworks (G20 Global Smart Cities Alliance 2023)."

8 Conclusion

Cities around the world are being challenged on an unparalleled scale as the population concentrates and demands become more insistent. The conventional approaches of managing cities fall woefully short of confronting the current scale and sophistication that urbanization poses today. Artificial intelligence offers functionalities that are game-changing and involves intelligent automation, predictive analytics, and efficient resource management.

But that is not all, for the issue at stake is not only one of technological capability. Ethical deployment of AI, particularly in urban contexts, requires a keen emphasis on issues related to fairness, transparency, privacy, and accountability. Irresponsible deployments could accentuate inequalities, enable discrimination, breach privacy, and even undermine democratic governance. The way forward puts citizen interest at the front in design, development, and deployment processes.

This chapter assessed the interaction of responsible AI development with smart city innovation. We have analyzed major urban challenges that have been intensified by migration, explored AI's capability for addressing such challenges, and identified ethical considerations that must guide implementation. Technical, policy, social, and infrastructure challenges in the path of ethical AI adoption have been systematically examined together with opportunities for improved urban planning, enhanced public services, sustainability benefits, and better education and healthcare delivery.

New capabilities will emerge from technologies such as edge AI, federated learning, and digital twins, but they will also require continued ethical vigilance. Innovations in governance—including data trusts, personal data stores, and differential privacy—offer mechanisms that protect rights while enabling important uses. Long-term implications of risks include algorithmic governance, surveillance creep, and inequality amplification, and these themes will continue to demand attention.

It is still possible to envision truly smart cities—such that the deployment of technology improves quality of life, respects human dignity, and promotes equity. Turning this vision into reality will take commitment from government leaders, technology developers, civil society organizations, academic institutions, and engaged citizens. Responsible AI deployment rests on multi-stakeholder collaboration, thoughtful regulation, robust ethical review, continuous capacity building, international cooperation, and adaptive governance.

With rapid urbanization and complex challenges, Indian cities have a particular opportunity to demonstrate ethical leadership in the development of smart cities. These cities can learn from international experiences, yet stay firmly rooted in their local contexts and values to chart a path toward efficient, sustainable, equitable, and humane urban futures. The journey towards truly "smart" cities has only just begun; making this journey an ethical one does need continuous commitment, vigilance, and democratic participation.

The technologies discussed in this chapter represent tools-powerful tools, but tools nonetheless. Their impact depends entirely on how they are designed, deployed, and governed. If cities keep their gaze fixed on human flourishing, social equity, democratic accountability, and environmental sustainability, they can tap AI capabilities while eschewing dystopian outcomes. A choice that is ours to make: the stakes simply could not be higher. Future generations will judge not just our technical sophistication but our wisdom in wielding these powerful capabilities responsibly.

References

Amsterdam Smart City. Amsterdam City Data: The Key to Smarter Urban Planning. Amsterdam: Gemeente Amsterdam, 2022.

Apollo Hospitals Group. AI in Cardiology: The Apollo Experience. Chennai: Apollo Hospitals, 2020.

Barcelona City Council. Barcelona Smart City Report 2022: Transforming Urban Mobility. Barcelona: Ajuntament de Barcelona, 2023.

Buolamwini, J., and T. Gebru. Gender Shades: Intersectional Accuracy Disparities in Commercial Gender Classification. Proceedings of the 1st Conference on Fairness, Accountability and Transparency, 2018, 77–91.

Census of India. Primary Census Abstract for Cities. New Delhi: Office of the Registrar General & Census Commissioner, India, 2011.
Crawford, K. Atlas of AI: Power, Politics, and the Planetary Costs of Artificial Intelligence. New Haven: Yale University Press, 2021.
Decode Project. Decode: Data Sovereignty for Citizens. Barcelona: Decode Consortium, 2020.
G20 Global Smart Cities Alliance. G20 Smart Cities Action Plan. Geneva: World Economic Forum, 2023.
Guttikunda, S. K., and R. Goel. Health Impacts of Particulate Pollution in a Megacity: Delhi, India. Environmental Development 6 (2013): 8–20.
Housing & Development Board, Singapore. Smart HDB: Transforming Towns Using Technology. Singapore: HDB, 2021.
Jobin, A., M. Ienca, and E. Vayena. The Global Landscape of AI Ethics Guidelines. Nature Machine Intelligence 1, no. 9 (2019): 389–399.
Kundu, A. Trends and Processes of Urbanisation in India. Urbanisation 1, no. 1 (2016): 1–17.
Land Transport Authority, Singapore. Predictive Maintenance for Railway Systems: A Case Study. Singapore: LTA, 2020.
Carnegie Learning. Efficacy Research: Meta-Analysis of Carnegie Learning Math Solutions. Pittsburgh: Carnegie Learning, 2022.
Ministry of Consumer Affairs, Food and Public Distribution, India. Automated Fair Price Shop Monitoring System: Impact Assessment. New Delhi: Government of India, 2021.
Pune Smart City Development Corporation Ltd. Smart Grid Pilot Project: Final Report. Pune: PSCDCL, 2022.
TomTom. TomTom Traffic Index 2023. Amsterdam: TomTom International BV, 2024.
United Nations, Department of Economic and Social Affairs, Population Division. World Urbanization Prospects: The 2018 Revision. New York: United Nations, 2019a.
United Nations, Department of Economic and Social Affairs, Population Division. World Urbanization Prospects: The 2018 Revision. New York: United Nations, 2019b.

Advanced Fusion of Hybrid Cryptography and Steganography for Socio-Technical Harmony in Secure Digital Voting Using Blockchain

S. Sathya Bama, S. Abirami, B. Mugil, and A. Nathisha

Abstract

Keeping democratic integrity in elections means we need a voting systems that are very safe and reliable. Digital platforms for elections face numerous technical challenges though. Public trust is declining. Procedures stay opaque a lot of the time. There are risks from centralized weak spots. Cyberattacks keep posing threats too. Traditional blockchain setups boost security in some ways. They struggle with scaling up. Voter privacy gets compromised often. That holds them back from real widespread adoption. This paper puts forward a blockchain framework that mixes in hybrid cryptography and steganography to tackle those issues. For encrypting votes solidly, it relies on the Elliptic Curve Integrated Encryption Scheme, or ECIES. Then, the Least Significant Bit method hides that encrypted stuff inside regular photos. It shields voter identities that way. Current blockchain-based voting systems face challenges such as limited scalability and compromised voter privacy. This work proposes a multi-layered approach combining hybrid cryptography and steganography to overcome these limitations. The blockchain ledger stays decentralized. It logs hashes of each stego-image. Auditability comes through clear. Immutability holds strong. Voter anonymity stays protected. This layered setup provides defense in depth. It balances secrecy with transparency. Centralized failures drop way down. Tests show high marks for confidentiality. Data integrity checks out well. Steganography blends in without notice. The approach hits a good socio-technical sweet spot. It delivers a practical solution that verifiable and scales for modern digital voting. Security gets better overall. Public trust builds up from there.

Keywords

Blockchain · Digital voting · Hybrid cryptography · Steganography · Socio-technical harmony

1 Introduction

Safe and reliable voting is the base of any democratic society. Digital assets in elections is evolving up more in these days. That makes it really important to lock down transparency, dependability, and protection from cyber attacks. Traditional digital voting runs into trouble with making voters anonymous, weak central spots that can get hit, and people losing trust in the whole thing. Blockchain looks promising because it spreads things out and anyone cannot change the records once set. Still, it has problems with handling big loads and keeping privacy very secured. So embedding the cipher text in steganography with high secured crypto methods seems like a fresh path forward. The idea here is to make sure elections are transparent enough to check, run smoothly and keep data highly confidential.

The plan to secure digital voting pulls together steganography, blockchain, and some hybrid crypto approach. Votes get locked up with ECIES, which is the Elliptic Curve Integrated Encryption Scheme. That gives strong secrecy and holds up against attacks. Then they use LSB steganography, the Least Significant Bit method, to hide the encrypted vote inside a regular cover image. Attackers cannot even spot it that way to exploit the vulnerability. Keeps the voters name highly secured (Benabdallah et al. 2022). The blockchain side handles a spread-out ledger for every stego-image hash. That means you can audit,

S. Sathya Bama (✉)
Department of CSE (AI/ML), Sri Krishna College of Engineering and Technology, Coimbatore, TN, India
e-mail: sathyabama.s@skcet.ac.in

S. Abirami · B. Mugil · A. Nathisha
Department of CSE (Cyber Security), Sri Krishna College of Technology, Coimbatore, TN, India

V. Sarveshwaran et al. (eds.), *Responsible AI for Smart Cities*, Sustainable Artificial Intelligence-Powered Applications,
https://doi.org/10.1007/978-3-032-26901-0_12

trace, and nothing changes once its there. This multi-layer setup balances privacy, the ability to scale, and openness. It gets rid of those single weak points and make sure that each single votes are integrated. These implementation along with the block-chain makes elections dependable.

This whole effort builds a secure digital voting system. It mixes LSB steganography, blockchain, and hybrid crypto based on ECIES. Cover images hide the encrypted votes. Blockchain makes sure its auditable and unchangeable. The approach gives a solid, spread-out, checkable base for modern digital elections. It tackles privacy issues, transparency needs, and scaling issues. Blockchain really changes things up as a replacement for those central, fragile systems that have worn down trust in digital government. Its a distributed ledger, decentralized all the way. No one entity runs the show. Instead, a bunch of computers keep copies of the ledger. That kills off the single failure point you see in old-school setups (Liu et al. 2022). Its pretty much impossible for a bad actor to take down or control the network. The built-in toughness handles that. For voting, this setup brings two big wins. First off, immutability. Once a vote hits the blockchain as a transaction in a block, its linked to the one before. Makes an unbreakable chain. Trying to mess with an old vote would take insane computing power you just can't get. Second, transparency. Everyone can see the transaction happened. But the vote details stay hidden thanks to encryption. That lets anyone verify the count of encrypted votes matches the public tally (Ramyadevi and Priya 2024). Blockchain builds trust on shared facts you can check yourself. Not some central boss calling the shots.

The first security layer comes from a hybrid crypto protocol. At its heart is a mathematical function called as AES-GCM, which stands for Advanced Encryption Standard that operates in Galois/Counter Mode. It is an AEAD method, Authenticated Encryption with Associated Data. This method does two jobs. It encrypts the vote into gibberish ciphertext for confidentiality and it adds a tag that spots any tampering right away. Makes unauthorized changes obvious mathematically. For each transaction, you need a secure high-entropy symmetric key shared between voter and election folks. We handle that with Elliptic Curve Cryptography, or ECC. Its a modern public-key system. ECC gives the same or better security as older ones like RSA, but with way smaller keys. That cuts down on computing needs and data bloat. ECIES puts it all together nicely. It creates a temporary key pair for every single vote. Ensures forward secrecy that way. If the authorities long-term private key gets compromised later, past votes stay safe. Each one uses its own one-time key (Reddy et al. 2024).

Steganography layers on extra privacy protection. It hides the presence of the encrypted vote in the steganography image. Works on that security through obscurity idea. The encrypted string will be get embedded in the crypto payload into the pixels of a normal digital image. So sending the vote looks like everyday network chatter. Gives voters some deniability if questioned. Also blocks traffic analysis that could reveal voting patterns or turnout. Steganography pairs up with ECIES for a deep defense. Any attacker has to detect it first, which is tough. This method secure from the any kind of brute force attacks that has the ability to decrypt the secure message.

Figure 1 shows how blocks link one after another to form a blockchain. Inside each block are some very important parts. The block index simply tells where that block stands in the entire chain. The previous hash is a pointer that references the hash of the block before it, which essentially keeps the system linked and immutable. The timestamp keeps the order straight by marking the exact moment when the block was created. Transactions are the values that will be get stored within, things like votes in the setup discussed. Then comes the proof or nonce-the cryptographic value used in the consensus mechanism, be it proof of-work or something else.

2 Literature Review

Research on blockchain-based voting has gained momentum over the past few years, mainly because traditional digital voting systems still struggle with trust and tamper-resistance. The work of G. Rathee, R. Iqbal, O. Waqar and A. K. Bashir (Rathee et al. 2021) is one of the early attempts to show how blockchain can support e-voting in smart-city environments. Their system uses a decentralized structure so that no single authority can alter votes, which helps build public confidence. Along this, A. Benabdallah, A. Audras, L. Coudert, N. El Madhoun and M. Badra (Benabdallah et al. 2022) reviewed various blockchain voting solutions and pointed out how features like transparency and immutability can improve election integrity. A broader view was then provided by M.-V. Vladucu, Z. Dong, J. Medina and R. Rojas-Cessa (Vladucu et al. 2023), who surveyed blockchain voting models and noted that scalability and performance are still major barriers to adoption.

Parallel to voting security, there has also been strong interest in protecting user privacy. Y. Zhao, C. Chi, H. Zhang, W. Song, J. Zhao and X. Yan (Zhao et al. 2021) introduced a system that tracks differential-privacy budgets on the blockchain, making data-usage more accountable. A similar emphasis on privacy appears in the work of Z. Liu, C. Hu, H. Xia, T. Xiang, B. Wang and J. Chen (Liu et al. 2022), who proposed a blockchain model for power-data trading that prevents sensitive data from leaking. Privacy within distributed learning systems was further improved

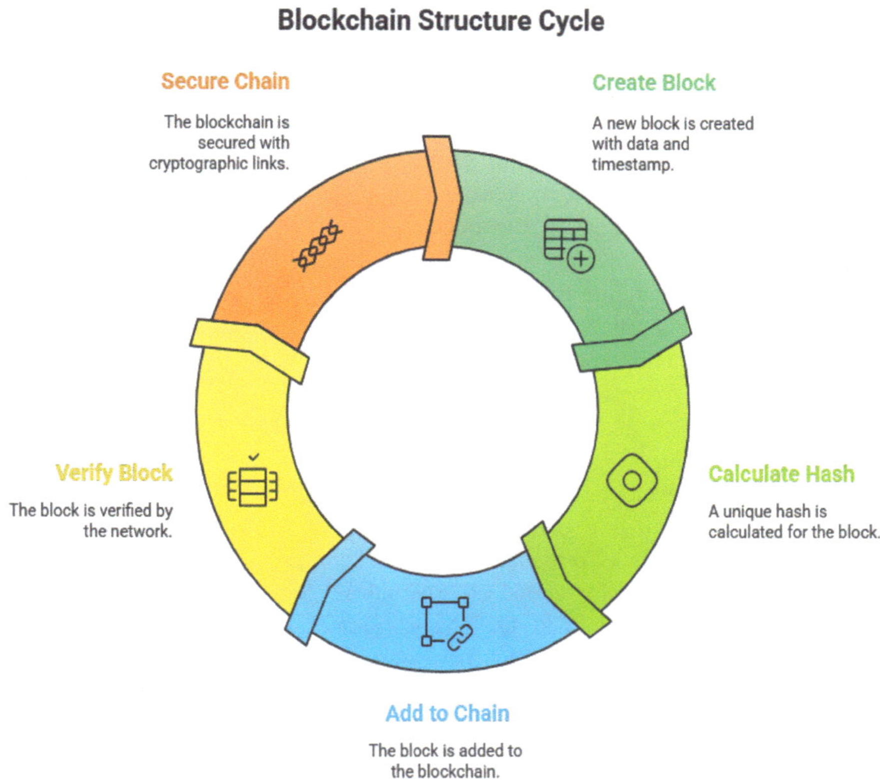

Fig. 1 Secure vote storage in blockchain

by S. De Chaudhury, S. Podder, A. Sharma, S. Islam, S. Chakraborty and M. Masud (De Chaudhury et al. 2024), who combined blockchain with federated learning so that user data never needs to leave local devices.

Smart contracts also play an important role in secure digital systems. Y. Wang, J. Ali, J. Arshad and Y. Liu (Y. Wang, J. Ali, J. Arshad and Y. Liu, "A Proxy-Layer Approach to Secure Smart Contract Deployment on Private EVM-Based PoA Blockchains," 2023) developed a proxy layer to make smart-contract deployment more secure, especially in permissioned blockchains. In the financial domain, N. Legowo, N. Hawari, T. Karlina, E. Tanuwijaya and K. Mahendra (N. Legowo, N. Hawari, T. Karlina, E. Tanuwijaya and K. Mahendra, "Design Smart Contract Based on Blockchain for Peer-to-Peer Lending Platform," 2023) designed a smart-contract system for peer-to-peer lending. Smart grids also benefit from blockchain-based automation, as discussed by M. A. Saleh, S. P. Khatri, A. Ghrayeb and S. S. Refaat (Saleh et al. 2024), who reviewed several applications of smart contracts in energy networks. Identity has become another critical topic, and M. R. Ahmed, A. K. M. M. Islam, S. Shatabda and S. Islam (Ahmed et al. 2022) examined different blockchain identity frameworks, placing strong focus on self-sovereign identity (SSI). Supporting this idea, M. Popa, S. M. Stoklossa and S. Mazumdar (Popa et al. 2023) proposed an IoT-linked SSI architecture called ChainDiscipline. A related study by E. Zeydan, L. Blanco, J. Mangues, S. Arslan and Y. Turk (Kim et al., 2024) explored the use of SSI within federated-learning environments.

Privacy for e-voting continues to receive attention. Z. Xu and S. Cao (Z. Xu and S. Cao, "Efficient Privacy-Preserving Electronic Voting Scheme Based on Blockchain," 2020) presented a lightweight privacy-preserving e-voting system using blockchain. Also, S. B and P. E (S. B and P. E 2020) discussed different privacy techniques that can be applied in blockchain-based systems. To strengthen voter anonymity, Y. Gu and Z. Shen (Y. Gu and Z. Shen, "An Accountable Anonymous Voting Scheme Based on One-time Ring Signature," 2023) designed a voting scheme using one-time ring signatures, which hides voter identity while still keeping the system accountable.

Several studies have explored how stronger cryptography can reshape digital voting. S.-V. Oprea, A. Bâra, A.-I. Andreescu and M. P. Cristescu (Ganeshan et al. 2023) proposed a blockchain model for university elections, mainly focusing on transparency. S. Majumder, S. Ray, D. Sadhukhan, M. Dasgupta, A. K. Das and Y. Park (Majumder et al. 2024) introduced an e-voting system called ECC-EXONUM-eVoting, which makes use of elliptic-curve cryptography and zero-knowledge proofs. In another contribution, J. Yao, B. Yang, T. Wang and W. Zhang (Premalatha and Rajasekar 2020) developed a self-tallying voting method using smart contracts so that results can be counted without relying on a central authority.

Identity and privacy continue to intersect in various application domains. E. Zeydan, L. Blanco, J. Mangues, S. Arslan and Y. Turk (Zeydan et al. 2023) applied SSI to vehicular networks to secure federated learning. Another privacy method was presented by M. Bi, Y. Wang, Z. Cai and X. Tong (Bi et al. 2020), who introduced a local-differential-privacy mechanism for edge computing. M. Kumar and S. Bhatt (M. Kumar and S. Bhatt, "Blockchain-Driven Federated Learning Based Differential Privacy in Decentralized Supply Chain," 2025) combined differential privacy with blockchain to protect supply-chain data. Smart-contract-based SSI frameworks were proposed by K. Gilani, F. Ghaffari, E. Bertin and N. Crespi (Gilani et al. 2022), while C. Hu, Z. Liu, R. Li, P. Hu, T. Xiang and M. Han (Hu et al. 2024) developed a privacy-preserving aggregation scheme for smart-grid data. A broader overview of decentralized identity was provided by Š. Čučko and M. Turkanović (Sathyamoorthy et al. 2026), and E. Samir, H. Wu, M. Azab, C. Xin and Q. Zhang (Samir et al. 2022) introduced a trustworthy SSI framework for secure authentication.

There have also been several practical implementations of blockchain voting. A. Kumar, M. Choudhary, A. R. Singh, S. Kumar and A. Thakur (Kumar et al. 2025) created a permissioned blockchain voting system for university settings. R. Ramyadevi and V. Priya (Ramyadevi and Priya 2024) strengthened e-voting security further by adding a three-tier OTP verification mechanism.

Decentralized identity continues to evolve, as shown in the work of C. N. Butincu and A. Alexandrescu (Butincu and Alexandrescu 2024), who examined the essential design factors of decentralized identifiers. Y. Ding, J. Yu, S. Li, H. Sato and M. G. Machizawa (Ding et al. 2024) studied SSI in decentralized data-aggregation environments and highlighted its benefits for secure communication.

More blockchain voting research is seen in E. J. Reddy, D. R. Kumar and T. V. Babu (Reddy et al. 2024), who developed another blockchain-based e-voting system supported by smart contracts. M. Mahalakshmi, V. Bhatnagar and K. A. Pandita (Mahalakshmi et al. 2024) proposed an Ethereum-based voting model focusing on transparent processes. The legal aspect of smart contracts was examined by E. Kafeza, S. J. Ali, I. Kafeza and H. AlKatheeri (Kafeza et al. 2020), who explored how legal rules can be integrated into blockchain agreements.

Research on smart-contract applications has also expanded beyond voting and identity systems. P. J. Bustamante, M. M. Gomez, M. B. H. Weiss, I. Murtazashvili and A. Palida (Bustamante et al. 2023) made an experiment how blockchain and smart contracts can support spectrum sharing, a domain where efficient and transparent allocation is essential. They showed that blockchain can reduce disputes between stakeholders by maintaining a clear, tamper-proof record of resource distribution. This work highlights how decentralized technologies can be applied even in highly regulated communication environments.

Security within distributed and mobile networks has also been a focus. K. N. Qureshi, H. Nafea, I. Tariq Javed and K. Zrar Ghafoor (Qureshi et al. 2024) developed a blockchain-based trust and authentication model aimed at detecting malicious nodes in flying ad-hoc networks. Their model uses blockchain to maintain a reliable trust record for each node, making it harder for attackers to hide their behavior.

3 Existing System

People still point out the two big types of digital voting setups we have going these days. Each one comes with some real problems. The first kind involves server-based centralized systems. Basically, a main server run by the election folks collects and holds all the votes. One good cyber hit could mess up the whole thing. It might swap votes around or wipe out data. Or just crash everything. The setup is super open to that kind of trouble. Thing is, folks need to totally trust those election authorities. Independent groups can't really check the results on their own. It completely vanishes the transparency of the digital asset.

Those early blockchain voting systems count as the second type pretty much. Figure. 2 breaks it down. They did improve openness and integrity by adding decentralization. Still their setups were often way too basic. People logged encrypted ballots right onto the blockchain even if protected. That left the whole voting process and voter identities out in the open for anyone. An attacker could link an anonymized voter ID to a specific transaction time. Voters end up at risk for coercion that way. These systems stuck to

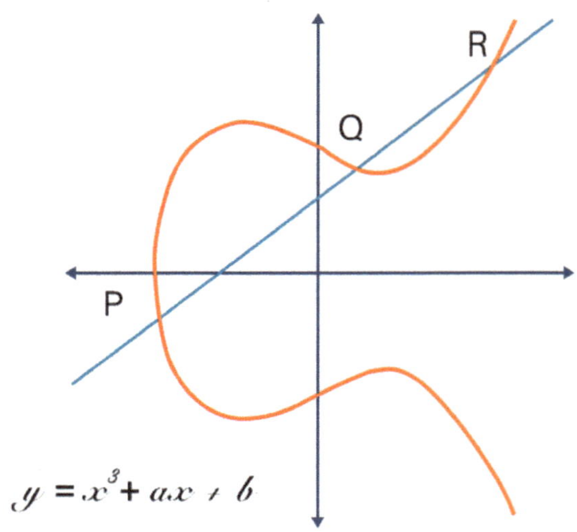

Fig. 2 Hybrid cryptography module

just one encryption method most of the time. It might not stand up to really complex attacks. They also skipped hiding the vote transmission process itself. All these limits mean we need a more layered approach. Something complex to guard both the vote's context and its content.

4 Proposed System

4.1 The ECIES Cryptographic Protocol

We go with the Elliptic Curve Integrated Encryption Scheme, or ECIES, to make sure security stays top level. It covers integrity and efficiency too. Our setup mixes different crypto approaches, so votes get strong confidentiality along with real authenticity. Forward secrecy applies to every single vote. Thing is, ECIES fits large electronic voting just right. Keys end up smaller than what you see in old public-key stuff like RSA. Security holds up the same, or even beats it sometimes. That cuts down on computing load and the amount of data flying around. Pretty crucial for handling thousands, or even millions, of votes.

Right from the protocol start, the election authority sets its crypto identity through Elliptic Curve Cryptography, ECC. The private key, k_{Auth}, picks a random integer. Then the public key, Q_{Auth} (1), pairs with it to form the long-term key set the authority puts together. They derive the public key from the equation.

$$Q_{Auth} = K_{Auth} \cdot G \tag{1}$$

G serves as the base point on the mathematical elliptic curve they selected. The public key Q_{Auth} (1) goes out to all the voters openly. The private key stays locked down in the authorities secure setup. A voter submits their ballot M. The client app handles ECIES encryption right there. It covers confidentiality and keeps everything intact. They start by creating a temporary key pair, r and R. Its single-use only. That setup provides forward secrecy. Even if private keys get leaked down the line, it stops long-term damage. The end-uses the Elliptic Curve Diffie-Hellman protocol next. It combines the ephemeral private key with the authorities public key Q_{Auth}. From that, they derive the shared secret S. This secret feeds into a Key Derivation Function. The KDF spits out the symmetric encryption key K_E.

$$(C, T) = AES - GCM - Encrypt(K_E, N, M) \tag{2}$$

N stands for a unique nonce. It makes sure things do not repeat over successive encryption sessions. The encrypted payload (2) includes R, C, T, and N. That whole thing gets transmitted on to the steganography module next. Over there, it lies inside some digital cover medium. This gives another layer of safety. It guards against traffic analysis quite well. The vote message gets safeguarded with AES-GCM. That is an authenticated encryption technique. It does more than merely encrypt the message. The function also checks for integrity. That verifies nothing has been tampered with. The process puts out a ciphertext C. It also makes an authentication tag T.

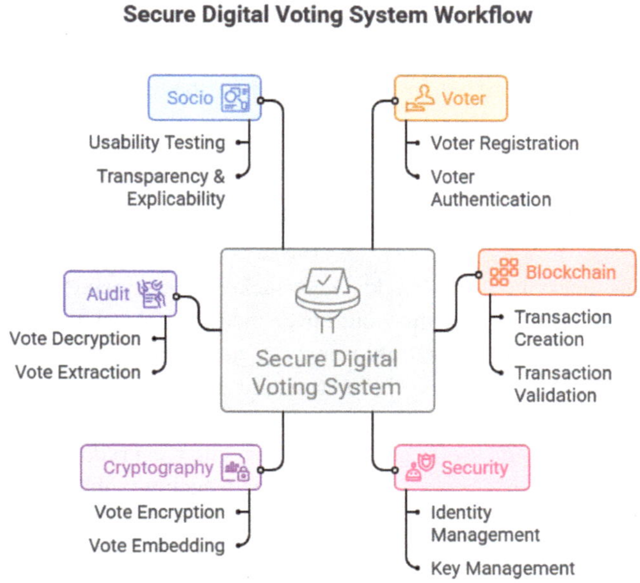

Fig. 3 Proposed system block diagram

Figure 3 visualizes the setup for this proposed system. It has several layers that handle security and different functions. The whole thing is built to protect everything from start to finish. That helps build trust with the public when it comes to voting.

It starts off with checking who the voter is. People use their approved digital IDs to prove it's them. After that gets done, they can get into the system and vote safely through the interface. Once the vote is sent in, it goes through some crypto parts. Those make sure it's kept secret, stays the same as sent, and can't be denied later. Then the function consist of encryption happens. Next, the steganography part hides the encrypted vote inside a regular-looking image. That way, sending it over looks like any other digital stuff, nothing special. The part which contains the blockchain takes over after that. It records the vote in a way that can't be changed. So it's resistant to messing around, and everyone can see what's going on. All these pieces work together to create a solid setup against problems like changing votes, replay tricks, or leaking info without permission. Putting ECC crypto, hiding with steganography, and blockchain's unchanging nature all in one spot means the system runs efficiently. It's easy to use too. And it gives real security promises.

This tackles a big issue in today's online elections. Votes which are polled by the voters remains stay private and can be checked, all while keeping trust in the whole process intact.

4.2 Steganographic Encoding Using LSB

The encrypted data packet gets tucked away inside what looks like a totally innocent cover medium. That helps cut down on risks from traffic analysis and boosts privacy in the process. It turns out pretty hard for any bad guy to spot the sensitive stuff hiding there. The whole transmission just comes off like swapping regular everyday files, nothing weird. You see, out of all the steganographic tricks people use, the Least Significant Bit method, or LSB, stands out because it is so simple. And it works well too. Basically, you pick a cover image for this. Could be some neutral graphic or a logo. Or really any plain digital picture that fits. Those pixel values in the image show up in binary. Each pixel breaks down into bits that handle the color intensity. The LSB way swaps out the least significant bit in each pixel. It gets replaced with bits from that encrypted data packet. Changes to those least bits do not mess up how the image looks at all. You would not notice a thing with your eyes. The tweaks stay hidden, visually speaking.

Figure 4 shows how this embedding thing works. It creates what they call a stego-image. That image looks just like the original cover one. You can't tell them apart visually. But unlike the plain original. The stego-image hides the encrypted vote or data packet right inside its structure. Pretty discreet. This setup means the image can travel openly through communication channels. Still. Only folks with the right extraction key get to pull out the hidden info. The real plus here is the two-layer security it provides. Say someone intercepts the stego-image. They have to spot the hidden message first. Then they need to crack the decryption. All that makes the whole system way more confidential. And tougher overall.

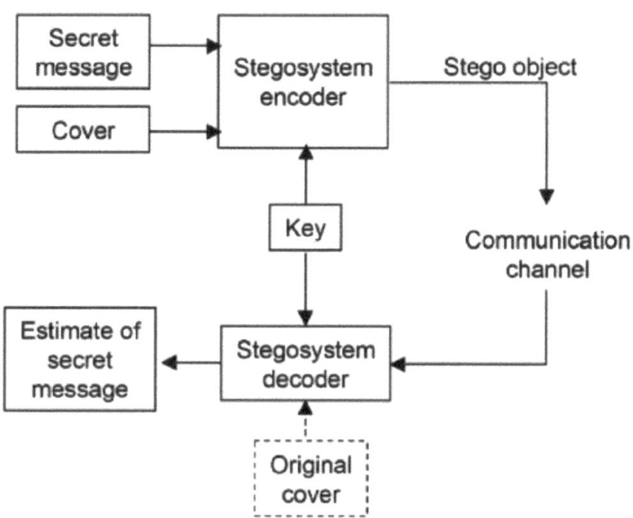

Fig. 4 Data hiding using steganography

$$\text{Capacity}_{\text{bytes}} = \frac{\text{Width} \times \text{Height} \times 3}{8} \tag{3}$$

People still mention the least significant bit substitution method is a popular method. It is a basic technique in spatial domain steganography. The method replace the least significant bits of the image in the form of the pixels in a cover image with bits from the secret message for your typical 24-bit color image. Take a pixel with RGB values like 200, 155, 88. That shows up in binary as 11,001,000, 10,011,011, 01011000. Seems like you can hide a 3-bit message, say 101, just by tweaking those LSBs. The new pixel turns into 201, 154, 89. Kind of hard for the human eye to notice any change. Now, the biggest amount of data you can hide in something like that. It comes down to this formula. Capacity(3) in bytes equals image width times height times 3, all divided by 8.

4.3 Blockchain Integration and Vote Tallying

They keep the blockchain light by not storing the stego-image directly on it. That also helps with voter privacy. So instead, they put it in a secure off-chain setup. Like IPFS, you know, the InterPlanetary File System. In IPFS everything gets addressed using its hash value. Access stays limited to the election authority. That way, no unauthorized eyes see those stego-images before the tally. Then a transaction goes out to the network. It includes the hash, a timestamp, and the voter's anonymized public identifier. Nodes run it through consensus to validate. After that, it lands permanently in a block on the ledger. All of this creates an audit trail that's immutable. Pretty much impossible to alter without crazy computation.

After the stego-image gets made from the vote, it heads out to the network. That way, it can get recorded and tallied up later. The system crunches a cryptographic hash of that image, using SHA-256. This acts like a permanent, unique fingerprint you cant mess with. Figure. 5 shows the whole workflow for this secured voting setup. The blockchain picks up a broadcast transaction from the network. Inside that transaction, there's a timestamp, the hash of the picture, and the voters anonymized public ID number. To keep things private and not bog down the ledger, the actual voting data and the image stay off the chain entirely. The stego-

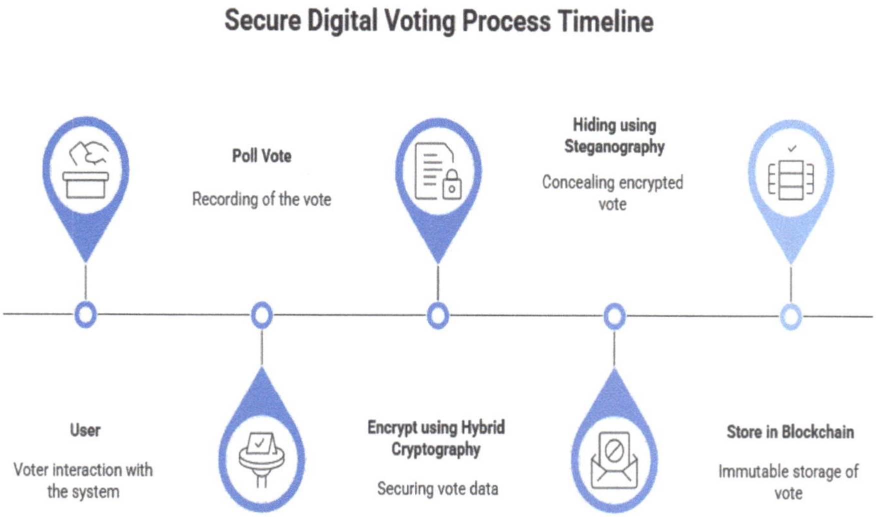

Fig. 5 System flow diagram

images sit in a distributed file system. Only the election authority can get to them.

Once voting wraps up, the authority starts the tallying process. For each transaction on the blockchain, they pull the matching stego-image. Then they extract the ECIES payload and run the decryption algorithm. On top of that, the voters ephemeral public key, which is single-use and called R, adds forward secrecy. It is a key security feature even if the authorities long-term private key, k_{Auth}, gets compromised down the line, old votes stay safe. This is because those one-time ephemeral keys get tossed after use. The authority combines the voters R with its own k_{Auth} to recreate the shared secret S.

$$S = k_{Auth} \cdot R \quad (4)$$

The authority gets that same symmetric key, K_E, out of the shared secret S (4). It does this by running it through a key derivation function, or KDF. This is the key part of the process. It turns the plain shared secret into something solid and secure, a key that's just the right length for AES. Then it goes ahead and uses AES-GCM for the decryption. AES-GCM mathematical function works in a well secured manner by ensuring the primary goals of the cyber security. It is efficient and tough against attacks. People call it an authenticated encryption with associated data scheme, or AEAD for short. Basically, it handles two heavy processes at once. It keeps things confidential with the decryption. And it checks the integrity and authenticity too, through some validation step.

$$M \text{ or FAIL} = AES - GCM - Decrypt(K_E, N, C, T) \quad (5)$$

So before it lets out the plaintext message M (5), this function grabs the authentication tag T. It checks to see if the vote got changed at all since encryption happened. The tag works like a cryptographic checksum. Only folks with the key K_E can whip up the right one. Now if somebody tries to manipulate with the ciphertext C or that unique nonce N, say during sending or keeping it stored, then validation will be invalidated. The function gets returned and holds back the decrypted message. All that setup gives solid guard against any fiddling around. It makes sure just the real deal votes, the ones not touched, end up getting tallied.

5 Result and Discussions

They check how well this system works by looking at performance stuff, security, and keeping things intact. You know, before we surf into the details on those metrics. Figure 6 gives a look at the main user interface. That's where a voter picks an ongoing election. It kind of sets the scene for what we're evaluating here. The mix of technologies really handle up against all sorts of threats. Things like voter coercion or messing with the data. Pretty much covers a lot. The whole setup protects privacy using steganography. It handles integrity and making sure you can audit with that blockchain ledger. And confidentiality comes from hybrid encryption.

Once someone casts their vote, you can spot the transaction right there on the network's monitoring page. It gives this real-time look into how the whole electoral thing is going. Like in Fig. 7. That interface pulls up key stats from the network. Plus it shows the flow of those anonymized transactions. They get validated one by one. Then added to the ledger.

The final count stays transparent that way. Combination of results come out in a straightforward graphical setup. Check Fig. 8 for an example. It lays out a real-time tally of total votes per candidate. This kind of visualization matters

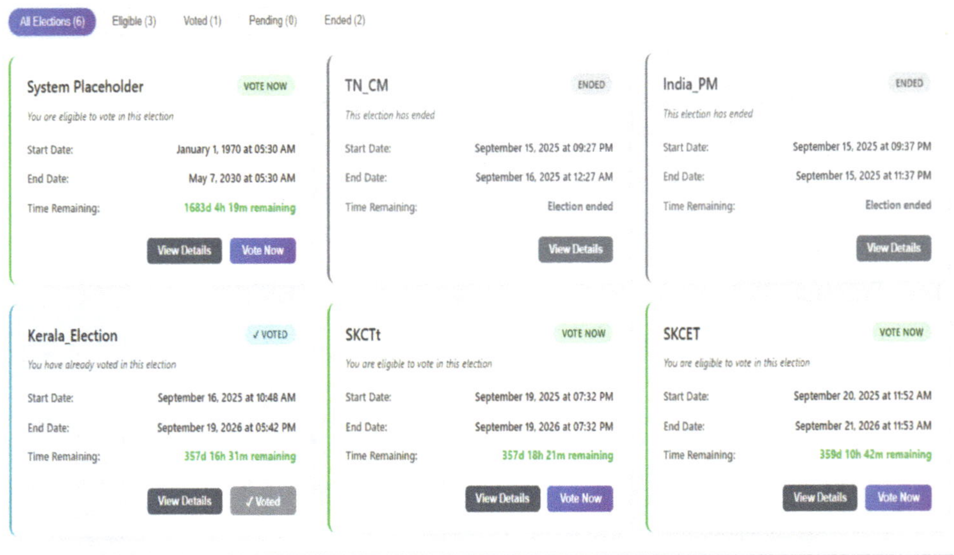

Fig. 6 Main dashboard for election selection

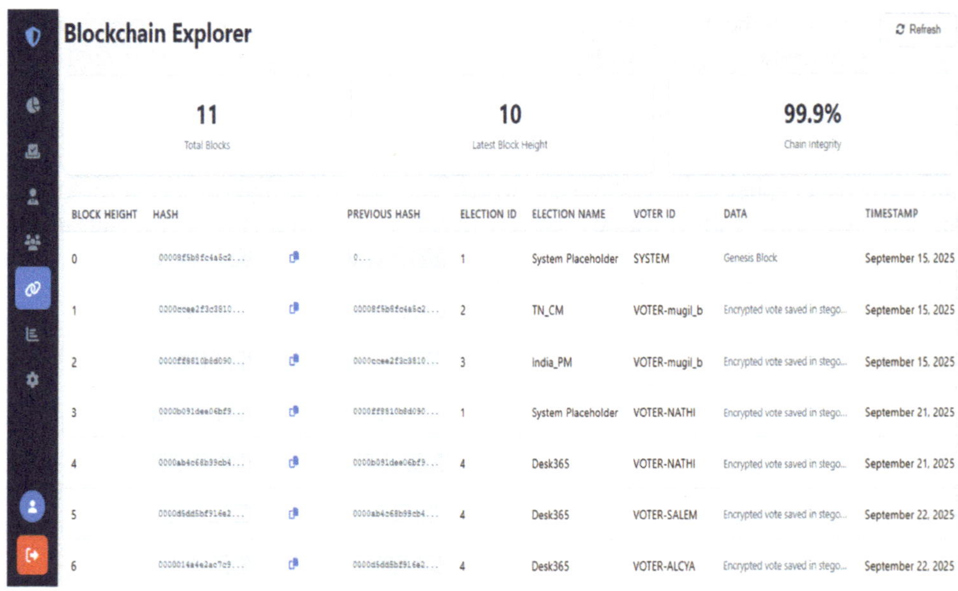

Fig. 7 Real-time blockchain monitoring

a lot for public audits. Stakeholders can keep an eye on results as they build up. It help to trust in the end result of the election.

Performance Metrics

Encryption strength, that is lambda basically. It measures the bits of security in a cryptographic protocol. You figure it out from the toughest part of the system to crack computationally. For our ECIES setup, the security level comes from the weaker one between the symmetric cipher (6) and the elliptic curve.

$$\lambda = \min(\lambda_{ECC}, \lambda_{AES}) \quad (6)$$

The method hits around lambda equals 128 bits of security. It does this with AES-256 and a 256-bit elliptic curve, like secp256r1. Thing is, this lines up with what the field accepts as a standard for protecting sensitive data on classical computers. You know, against serious threats like nation-states.

PSNR handles the steganographic imperceptibility (7). Its the peak signal-to-noise ratio. That measures distortion between the original cover image I and the stego-image K. Higher PSNR means better quality for the stego-image. Less distortion overall.

$$\mathrm{PSNR} = 20 \cdot \log 10(\mathrm{MAXI}) - 10 \cdot \log 10(\mathrm{MSE}) \quad (7)$$

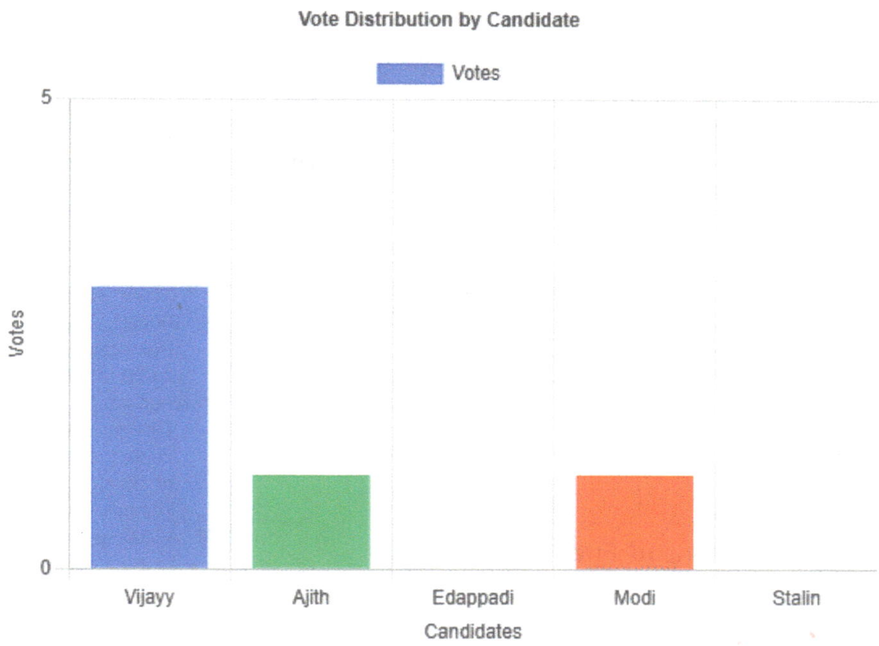

Fig. 8 Graphical representation of total votes

The formula involves mean squared error (8) between the images. And MAXI is the max pixel value, 255 for eight-bit stuff. Our LSB implementation usually gets PSNR over 40 dB. Thats seen as really hard to notice.

$$\mathrm{MSE} = \frac{1}{\mathrm{m} \times \mathrm{n}} \cdot \sum_{\mathrm{i}=0}^{\mathrm{m}-1} \sum_{\mathrm{j}=0}^{\mathrm{n}-1} \left[\mathrm{I}(\mathrm{i}, \mathrm{j}) - \mathrm{K}(\mathrm{i}, \mathrm{j})^2 \right] \tag{8}$$

Our LSB setup keeps pushing those PSNR values past 40 dB. Which puts it well into territory where the human eye doesn't pick up on changes visually.

Table 1 lays out the electoral stuff pretty clearly. It shows how the on-chain ledger ties into the off-chain data. Each row is one vote transaction. The system generates unique hash to establish integrity in the blockchain and also the previous hash links it to the one before, making this whole blockchain that cannot be same as other. Key bits like the anonymized voter id show up too. Along with the nonce from consensus all those digital assets gets locked into the blockchain. The stego-image is just here to show what it actually looks like. But in the actual setup, only its hash goes on-chain. This table puts together the full record as what the election folks would pull up. It mixes those solid on-chain pointers with the secure off-chain parts. That way, everything stays transparent. You can audit it all. Still, voter privacy holds up and the blockchain doesn't get exploited.

Table 2 makes it pretty clear how the suggested system stacks up. They assess its efficacy based on performance, security, and integrity measures. You know, from stuff like voter coercion all the way to data tampering, this mix of technologies puts up a strong defense. It covers a bunch of different threats. The solution handles privacy protec-

Table 1 Secure blockchain format

Id	Hash	Previous_hash	Nonce	Voter_id	Stego_image
1	a3f5c9...	000000...	102,345	9b74c9...	stego_img_001.Png (iVBORw0KG...)
2	d4b2e6...	a3f5c9...	204,800	2f7766...	stego_img_002.Png (R0lGODlhPQ...)
3	f0e1d2...	d4b2e6...	409,601	7c4a8d...	stego_img_003.Png (iVBORw0KGgoAAAAN...)
4	0a1b2c...	f0e1d2...	512,000	3a7bd3...	stego_img_004.Png (UklGRigAAABXRUJ...)

Table 2 Result analysis

Existing	Precision	Recall	F1-score	Support
0	0.7	0.7	0.8	50
1	0.7	0.7	0.8	50
Accuracy			0.77	90
Macro avg	0.78	0.78	0.78	90
Weighted avg	0.78	0.78	0.78	90

tion through steganography. It takes care of integrity and auditability with the blockchain ledger. Confidentiality gets covered by hybrid encryption.

Transaction Throughput, or Ttps, basically tells you how many votes the blockchain can handle in a second. That is with respect to the reference of 7. In that elections, it turns out to be a very serious thing.

$$T\ tps = \frac{\text{Total Votes Processed}}{\text{Total Time (Seconds)}} \tag{9}$$

Early tests on a private Ethereum network. They show throughput that handles municipal elections pretty well. Growth paths look obvious through layer-2 solutions.

6 Conclusion and Future Work

This whole method embedded blockchain tech with steganography and highly secured hybrid cryptography setup. It lays out a pretty unique way to make digital voting safe and reliable. The democratic country know, the key stuff like anonymity, keeping everything intact, confidentiality, and being able to verify it all. That gets handled pretty well in this proposed solution. We build up these layers of protection. They push back against tech attacks and even the social doubts people might have. Basically, you hide the vote inside something, encrypted using ECIES, which is this elliptic curve integrated encryption scheme. It fetches in ECC for setting up keys and AES-GCM for that authenticated encryption part. Then you anchor the hash right to the blockchain, so nothing can mess with it. The procedures stay transparent, easy to audit makes the availability of the data. This socio-technical approach really aims to build up voter trust at the same time, it locks down the voting process tight.

References

G. Rathee, R. Iqbal, O. Waqar and A. K. Bashir, "On the Design and Implementation of a Blockchain Enabled E-Voting Application Within IoT-Oriented Smart Cities," in IEEE Access, vol. 9, pp. 34165–34176, 2021, doi:https://doi.org/10.1109/ACCESS.2021.3061411.

A. Benabdallah, A. Audras, L. Coudert, N. El Madhoun and M. Badra, "Analysis of Blockchain Solutions for E-Voting: A Systematic Literature Review," in IEEE Access, vol. 10, pp. 70746–70759, 2022, doi:https://doi.org/10.1109/ACCESS.2022.3187688.

M. -V. Vladucu, Z. Dong, J. Medina and R. Rojas-Cessa, "E-Voting Meets Blockchain: A Survey," in IEEE Access, vol. 11, pp. 23293–23308, 2023, doi:https://doi.org/10.1109/ACCESS.2023.3253682

Y. Zhao et al., "A Blockchain-Based Approach for Saving and Tracking Differential-Privacy Cost," in IEEE Internet of Things Journal, vol. 8, no. 11, pp. 8865–8882, 1 June1, 2021, doi:https://doi.org/10.1109/JIOT.2021.3058209

Z. Liu, C. Hu, H. Xia, T. Xiang, B. Wang and J. Chen, "SPDTS: A Differential Privacy-Based Blockchain Scheme for Secure Power Data Trading," in IEEE Transactions on Network and Service Management, vol. 19, no. 4, pp. 5196–5207, Dec. 2022, doi:https://doi.org/10.1109/TNSM.2022.3181814

S. De Chaudhury et al., "Blockchain Based Secure Federated Learning With Local Differential Privacy and Incentivization," in IEEE Transactions on Privacy, vol. 1, pp. 31–44, 2024, doi:https://doi.org/10.1109/TP.2024.3487819.

Y. Wang, J. Ali, J. Arshad and Y. Liu, "A Proxy-Layer Approach to Secure Smart Contract Deployment on Private EVM-Based PoA Blockchains," 2023 IEEE International Conference on Blockchain (Blockchain), Danzhou, China, 2023, pp. 109–112, doi:https://doi.org/10.1109/Blockchain60715.2023.00027

N. Legowo, N. Hawari, T. Karlina, E. Tanuwijaya and K. Mahendra, "Design Smart Contract Based on Blockchain for Peer-to-Peer Lending Platform," 2023 10th International Conference on ICT for Smart Society (ICISS), Bandung, Indonesia, 2023, pp. 1–5, doi:https://doi.org/10.1109/ICISS59129.2023.10291985.

M. A. Saleh, S. P. Khatri, A. Ghrayeb and S. S. Refaat, "A Review on the Applications of Blockchain-Based Smart Contracts in the Smart Grid," 2024 4th International Conference on Smart Grid and Renewable Energy (SGRE), Doha, Qatar, 2024, pp. 1–6, doi:https://doi.org/10.1109/SGRE59715.2024.10428798

M. R. Ahmed, A. K. M. M. Islam, S. Shatabda and S. Islam, "Blockchain-Based Identity Management System and Self-Sovereign Identity Ecosystem: A Comprehensive Survey," in IEEE Access, vol. 10, pp. 113436–113481, 2022, doi:https://doi.org/10.1109/ACCESS.2022.3216643

M. Popa, S. M. Stoklossa and S. Mazumdar, "ChainDiscipline - Towards a Blockchain-IoT-Based Self-Sovereign Identity Management Framework," in IEEE Transactions on Services Computing, vol. 16, no. 5, pp. 3238–3251, Sept.-Oct. 2023, doi:https://doi.org/10.1109/TSC.2023.3279871.

Kim, D. J., Amma, N. B., & Sarveshwaran, V. (2024). A novel split learning-based consumer electronics network traffic anomaly detection framework for smart city environment. *IEEE Transactions on Consumer Electronics*, *70*(1), 4197–4204.

Z. Xu and S. Cao, "Efficient Privacy-Preserving Electronic Voting Scheme Based on Blockchain," 2020 IEEE International Conference on Smart Internet of Things (SmartIoT), Beijing, China, 2020, pp. 190–196, doi:https://doi.org/10.1109/SmartIoT49966.2020.00036.

S. B and P. E, "Methods and Techniques for Privacy Preserving in Blockchain," 2020 3rd International Conference on Intelligent Sustainable Systems (ICISS), Thoothukudi, India, 2020, pp. 1346–1351, doi:https://doi.org/10.1109/ICISS49785.2020.9316115

Y. Gu and Z. Shen, "An Accountable Anonymous Voting Scheme Based on One-time Ring Signature," 2023 3rd International Conference on Frontiers of Electronics, Information and Computation Technologies (ICFEICT), Yangzhou, China, 2023, pp. 51–57, doi:https://doi.org/10.1109/ICFEICT59519.2023.00019

Ganeshan, A., Jayagopalan, S., Perumal, B., & Sarveshwaran, V. (2023). Secure identity key and blockchain-based authentication approach for secure data communication in multi-WSN. *Concurrency and Computation: Practice and Experience*, *35*(28), e7861.

S. Majumder, S. Ray, D. Sadhukhan, M. Dasgupta, A. K. Das and Y. Park, "ECC-EXONUM-eVOTING: A Novel Signature-Based e-Voting Scheme Using Blockchain and Zero Knowledge Property," in IEEE Open Journal of the Communications Society, vol. 5, pp. 583–598, 2024, doi:https://doi.org/10.1109/OJCOMS.2023.3348468.

Premalatha, J., & Rajasekar, V. (2020). Industrial Internet of Things Safety and Security. In *Internet of Things* (pp. 135–152). CRC Press.

E. Zeydan, L. Blanco, J. Mangues, S. Arslan and Y. Turk, "Blockchain-Based Self-Sovereign Identity for Federated Learning in Vehicular

Networks," 2023 19th International Conference on Network and Service Management (CNSM), Niagara Falls, ON, Canada, 2023, pp. 1–7, doi:https://doi.org/10.23919/CNSM59352.2023.10327817.

M. Bi, Y. Wang, Z. Cai and X. Tong, "A privacy-preserving mechanism based on local differential privacy in edge computing," in China Communications, vol. 17, no. 9, pp. 50–65, Sept. 2020, doi:https://doi.org/10.23919/JCC.2020.09.005.

M. Kumar and S. Bhatt, "Blockchain-Driven Federated Learning Based Differential Privacy in Decentralized Supply Chain," 2025 International Conference on Networks and Cryptology (NETCRYPT), New Delhi, India, 2025, pp. 1291–1294, doi:https://doi.org/10.1109/NETCRYPT65877.2025.11102516.

K. Gilani, F. Ghaffari, E. Bertin and N. Crespi, "Self-sovereign Identity Management Framework using Smart Contracts," NOMS 2022–2022 IEEE/IFIP Network Operations and Management Symposium, Budapest, Hungary, 2022, pp. 1–7, doi:https://doi.org/10.1109/NOMS54207.2022.9789831.

C. Hu, Z. Liu, R. Li, P. Hu, T. Xiang and M. Han, "Smart Contract Assisted Privacy-Preserving Data Aggregation and Management Scheme for Smart Grid," in IEEE Transactions on Dependable and Secure Computing, vol. 21, no. 4, pp. 2145–2161, July-Aug. 2024, doi:https://doi.org/10.1109/TDSC.2023.3300749.

Sathyamoorthy, M., Rajasekar, V., Krishnamoorthi, S., & Pamucar, D. (2026). Ensemble deep learning approach for traffic video analytics in edge computing. *Scientific Reports.*

E. Samir, H. Wu, M. Azab, C. Xin and Q. Zhang, "DT-SSIM: A Decentralized Trustworthy Self-Sovereign Identity Management Framework," in IEEE Internet of Things Journal, vol. 9, no. 11, pp. 7972–7988, 1 June1, 2022, doi:https://doi.org/10.1109/JIOT.2021.3112537.

A. Kumar, M. Choudhary, A. R. Singh, S. Kumar and A. Thakur, "Permissioned Smart Contract Based e-Voting System for University," 2025 International Conference on Networks and Cryptology (NETCRYPT), New Delhi, India, 2025, pp. 1339–1343, doi:https://doi.org/10.1109/NETCRYPT65877.2025.11102528.

R. Ramyadevi and V. Priya, "Block Chain-Powered E-Voting System: A Secure and Transparent Solution with Three-Tiered OTP Security Mechanism," 2024 IEEE International Conference on Computing, Power and Communication Technologies (IC2PCT), Greater Noida, India, 2024, pp. 728–731, doi:https://doi.org/10.1109/IC2PCT60090.2024.10486507.

C.N. Butincu and A. Alexandrescu, "Design Aspects of Decentralized Identifiers and Self-Sovereign Identity Systems," in IEEE Access, vol. 12, pp. 60928–60942, 2024, doi:https://doi.org/10.1109/ACCESS.2024.3394537.

Y. Ding, J. Yu, S. Li, H. Sato and M. G. Machizawa, "Data Aggregation Management With Self-Sovereign Identity in Decentralized Networks," in IEEE Transactions on Network and Service Management, vol. 21, no. 6, pp. 6174–6189, Dec. 2024, doi:https://doi.org/10.1109/TNSM.2024.3451995.

E. J. Reddy, D. R. Kumar and T. V. Babu, "E-Voting System Using Block Chain," 2024 2nd International Conference on Artificial Intelligence and Machine Learning Applications Theme: Healthcare and Internet of Things (AIMLA), Namakkal, India, 2024, pp. 1–4, doi:https://doi.org/10.1109/AIMLA59606.2024.10531437.

M. Mahalakshmi, V. Bhatnagar and K. A. Pandita, "Decentralizing Voting: Block Chain based E-Voting System Using Ethereum Smart Contracts," 2024 International Conference on Intelligent Systems for Cybersecurity (ISCS), Gurugram, India, 2024, pp. 1–7, doi:https://doi.org/10.1109/ISCS61804.2024.10581197.

E. Kafeza, S. J. Ali, I. Kafeza and H. AlKatheeri, "Legal smart contracts in Ethereum Block chain: Linking the dots," 2020 IEEE 36th International Conference on Data Engineering Workshops (ICDEW), Dallas, TX, USA, 2020, pp. 18–25, doi:https://doi.org/10.1109/ICDEW49219.2020.00-12.

P. J. Bustamante, M. M. Gomez, M. B. H. Weiss, I. Murtazashvili and A. Palida, "A Techno-Economic Study of Spectrum Sharing with Blockchain and Smart Contracts," in IEEE Communications Magazine, vol. 61, no. 2, pp. 58–63, February 2023, doi:https://doi.org/10.1109/MCOM.001.2200317.

K. N. Qureshi, H. Nafea, I. Tariq Javed and K. Zrar Ghafoor, "Blockchain-Based Trust and Authentication Model for Detecting and Isolating Malicious Nodes in Flying Ad Hoc Networks," in IEEE Access, vol. 12, pp. 95390–95401, 2024, doi:https://doi.org/10.1109/ACCESS.2024.3425153.

Ethical Principles and Frameworks for AI in Smart Cities

Mohanaradhya, C. Saravanan, and Savita Sheelavant

Abstract

A rapid increase in the urban population worldwide due to migration from rural to urban areas needs transformation of traditional cities into smart cities. According to the statistics from United Nations, by the year 2050, around 70% of the world population is expected to lead life in urban areas up from 56% in the year 2023. This may lead for placing significant strain on existing infrastructure, essential public services and natural resources. It requires adoption of automation for resource conservation and in providing various services to the society in order to improve the life style. Integrating Artificial Intelligence (AI) in automation may lead to better management, decision making, and predicting infrastructure requirement for growing population, in advance. Traditional cities become smart cities by adopting Internet of Things (IoT) applications along with Responsible AI for effective utilization of resources optimally. However, adoption of technology in transforming traditional cities to smart cities raises ethical challenges related to transparency, accountability, fairness, privacy, and inclusivity. This chapter exhibits how ethical principles and governance frameworks can be effectively integrated into AI-driven smart city systems. It determines major ethical models, including principle-based, rights-based, and participatory approaches, and analyzes their implications for responsible AI governance. By considering real-world examples from both emerging and established smart cities, the chapter highlights the dual nature of AI: its potential to enhance urban efficiency and its capacity to deepen social inequalities.

Keywords

Smart city · Cybercrime · Data protection · Sustainability · Human errors

1 Introduction

Digital technologies are structuring and experiencing urban life considerably. In traditional cities, human judgment, regulated schedules, and manual labor are the major sources of administrative services and activities. Fortunately, automated systems powered by real-time data are now driving it more and more. Smarter, more responsive systems are required since traditional urban infrastructures such as traffic lights, rubbish collection, and public services often cannot keep up with the city's growing complexity and rapid population growth.

The rising needs of urban systems have resulted in the evolution of a smart city. Citizens of present-day cities are able to track their environment with a series of sensors and cameras connected to devices and platforms online. They can predict challenges that shall await them in the future and make their services optimized to a level that could not have been imagined a few decades back. AI is a decisive force behind this revolution that helps a huge amount of data processed that helps cities make faster and more accurate judgments with respect to their day-to-day tasks like public security and traffic congestion, managing energy consumption levels, and so on.

But as AI becomes more integrated into public governance, it creates new ethical challenges, such as how a fair, transparent, and accountable approach can be devel-

Mohanaradhya (✉) · C. Saravanan · S. Sheelavant
Department of MCA, RV College of Engineering, Bengaluru, India
e-mail: mohanaradhya@rvce.edu.in

C. Saravanan
e-mail: saravananc@rvce.edu.in

S. Sheelavant
e-mail: savitassheelavat@rvce.edu.in

V. Sarveshwaran et al. (eds.), *Responsible AI for Smart Cities*, Sustainable Artificial Intelligence-Powered Applications,
https://doi.org/10.1007/978-3-032-26901-0_13

Table 1 Smart city across the globe

Position	Smart city name	Population (in millions)	Sector	Technical partner	Smart city since
10	Barcelona, Spain	1.6	Digital democracy	Cisco	2011
9	Singapore	5.9	Urban mobility	ST engineering	2014
8	Amsterdam, the Netherlands	0.92	Energy efficiency	Philips	2009
7	Copenhagen, Denmark	0.63	Public transport	Siemens	2014
6	Tokyo, Japan	9.73	Disaster resilience	Hitachi	2016
5	New York city, USA	8.26	Data-driven governance	IBM	2013
4	London, UK	8.86	Open data innovation	Arup	2013
3	Seoul, South Korea	9.41	Digital connectivity	Samsung SDS	2011
2	Dubai, United Arab Emirates:	3.3	Artificial intelligence	Core42	2014
1	Helsinki, Finland	0.65	Citizen-centric innovation	Nokia	2011

Source https://sustainabilitymag.com/top10/top-10-smart-cities December 04, 2024

oped for AI that affects decision-making with a significant impact on people's opportunities, rights, and safety. Hence, it becomes a challenge for smart cities because it is not only the delivery of the technology, but it is also the development and use of AI in an ethical, non-biased, and rights-respecting fashion; it is a matter of decision-making, personal data, and the accountability of the automated systems to society; it is a challenge for trust, preventing misuse, and ensuring smart city innovations serve all people. Hence, it becomes more important as it creates an ethical and responsible governance structure for smart cities that are not only technology-based, technologically advanced, but also people-centered and people-friendly. There are many cities around the globe who are named as smart city focusing on many areas for development. The table below contains the top 10 smart cities around the world along with their details, such as the population, sector, technical partners, and year of implementation (see Table 1).

1.1 AI in Urban Environments: Key Areas of Integration

There is gradual rise in the role of AI in urban environment as depicted in Fig. 1.

Public Safety

Additionally, cities are also using AI-driven safety solutions like smart surveillance, video analytics, motion sensors, and audio threat alerts for supporting law enforcement and emergency services in order to identify unusual events, track missing individuals, and streamline emergency responses. However, the misuse of such technologies can lead to over-

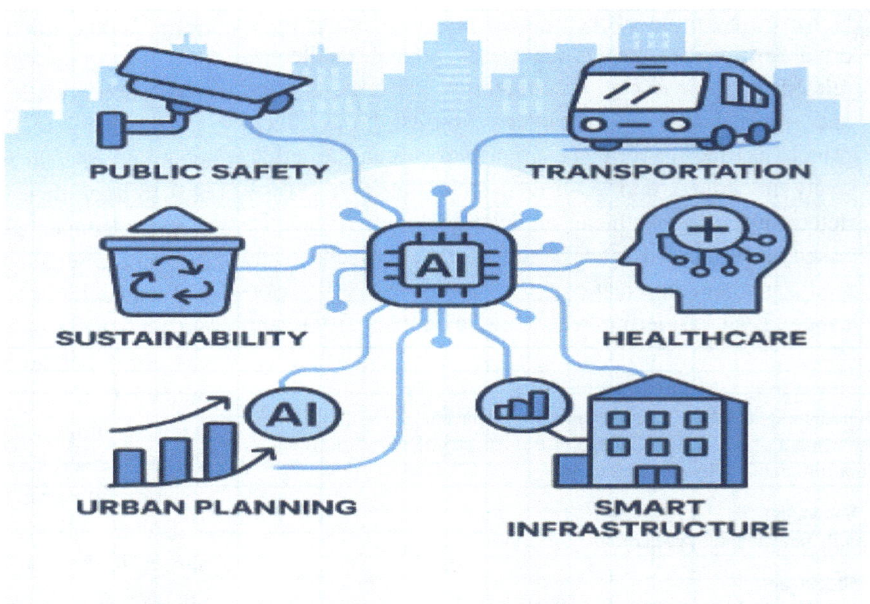

Fig. 1 Rise of AI in urban environments

surveillance, discriminatory identification, and even threats to privacy rights on the part of cities as they have to strike a balance between public safety and freedoms while using responsible AI practices like transparency, fairness, and accountability.

Transportation and Mobility

AI is transforming the way cities manage mobility. Real-time traffic predictions, adaptive signal control, and intelligent routing systems reduce congestion and travel time. Intelligent parking solutions guide vehicle riders to available spaces, cutting fuel consumption and emissions, and some cities test AI-based public transport and self-driving vehicles as steps toward more efficient, sustainable mobility systems that are equitable, reliable, and unbiased-because of Responsible AI-in terms of who gets priority for routes or access to the service.

Sustainability and Resource Management

Another area where AI finds immense implementation in urban sustainability involves analyzing consumption patterns of energy, waste, and environmental factors to optimize smart energy grid distribution, simulating future environments based on digital twin technology concepts to provide planners insightful information prior to major infrastructure development measures, and environmental sensors providing updates on environmental changes supported by AI technology to detect air quality, water levels, and pollution risks, and thus Responsible AI becomes imperative to ensure that environmental policies based on data are not only up to date and credible but serve the cause of the people and not used as a marketing or political tool.

Healthcare and Emergency Response

AI helps urban healthcare systems to predict patient arrivals, detect outbreaks of diseases for early diagnosis, and optimize routes taken by the ambulance during emergencies. In particular, in emergent high-stress situations such as pandemics, these capabilities enhance preparedness and enable quick responses. However, medical information remains among the most sensitive personal data type. Responsible AI protects this by ensuring adequate protection of privacy, secure handling of data, fair decision-making, and interpretable generation of diagnostic or predictive outcomes. This ensures AI enhances healthcare without compromising the rights of a patient.

Urban Planning and Governance

Administrators will be able to understand the needs of the communities, usage of utilities, mobility, and growth of populations with the help of AI. This is possible due to data-driven insights that help in proper planning for services, housing, and mobility. AI helps the government in properly allocating resources and developing policies for addressing the current issues through the prediction of expected demands. Integration of Responsible AI in city planners helps ensure that policies and allocations remain just and transparent. It prevents the abuse of data for the unequitable allocation of resources, zoning, and implementation of policies.

Smart Infrastructure

AI strengthens urban infrastructure by adopting the systems that monitor building stability, detect structural faults, optimize street light utilization, and manage electricity grids. Smart infrastructure systems reduce operational costs and increase reliability across essential services. At this time, automated infrastructure also requires strong safeguards. Adoption of Responsible AI allows cities to ensure critical infrastructures remain secure, resilient, and free from vulnerabilities that could lead to failures or exploitation. The data gathered from the utilities in the buildings and public domain is handled in a secure and responsible manner by adopting ethical monitoring practices.

1.2 Ethics in Technology-Enabled Governance

Ethics is emerging or becoming an integral part of modern governance due to cities' rapid adoption of AI systems. The conventional nature of governance relied highly on accountability by sight, formal rules of procedure, and human discretion. Nevertheless, ethical governance in today's digital age must concern itself not only with issues of data gathering and algorithmic behavior but also accountability in the instance of an error or failure on the part of a system. This shift makes responsible AI an essential component of ensuring that AI systems are reliable, just, and aligned with values.

Why Ethics Matters

If technology-based governance fails to carry out its processes and operations in a responsible and ethical manner, there may arise new sources of harm, such as discriminatory decision-making in AI systems, privacy issues in AI systems, or discriminatory provision of services to different communities. Responsible AI can thus help in ensuring that the mere fact of technological innovation has not been at the expense of human rights and social justice, such that technologies used in smart cities keep the trust of the citizens and their rights intact in order to gain the public's confidence in technology, which would mean that ethics, and consequently responsible AI, can make technology subject to society's control and not vice versa.

Core Ethical Principles

Transparency

Citizens must be able to comprehend how decisions are made in the automated system, what information AI is considering, and how the result influences public services. The role of responsible AI is assisting AI principles, such as transparency via explainable models, by reducing incorrect information and trust.

Accountability

In computerized environments, human beings are also held responsible for outputs created by AI systems. The governments need to clarify who is responsible for system errors and misuse of data and other accidental consequences. Responsible AI gives importance to humans in the design of the system and overrides the decisions of the AI System when required.

Privacy and Data Protection

Information handled by a Smart City AI system is of sensitive nature and relates to personal or behavioral data. Ethical governance using Responsible AI should thus support strict data minimization, secured storage of data, and constraints on data. This helps public to strengthen and avoid misuse of digital rights.

Fairness and Non-Discrimination

The design of an AI system can unconsciously perpetuate social biases should it not be properly designed. Fairness by bias detection, audits of algorithms, and inclusively constructed datasets are emphasized in Responsible AI. This results in equal access to services regardless of gender, geographical location, socio-economic factors, or ethnicity.

Inclusiveness and Accessibility

Digital governance should help all of us—urbanites and rural dwellers, younger generations and senior or physically challenged citizens. Inclusive design and accessibility are values that responsible AI promotes.

Security and Reliability

Cyber-attacks and failure of operations should be highly secured by the AI-powered public systems. This should promote continuous monitoring of systems in place by ensuring safe implementation procedures and reliability through continuous improvement.

Public Trust

Also, trust between people has an important role in digital transformation. City authorities should be transparent and just with their AI application. This helps people embrace change and utilize digital technologies. AI ethics help in building this trust so that the technology always stays trustworthy and justified to people's needs.

Figure 2 represents Core Ethical Principles in technology enabled governance.

1.3 E-Governance: Transforming Public Administration

E-governance uses Information and Communication Technology (ICT) tools—online portals, mobile apps, digital records, and automated workflows as shown in Fig. 3—to make public administration more efficient, transparent, and citizen-friendly. It transforms interactions across key domains:

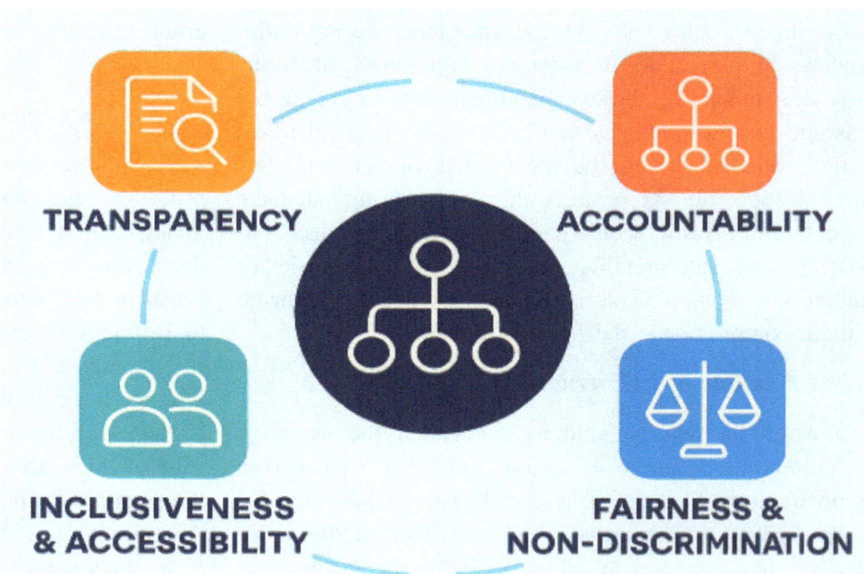

Fig. 2 Core ethical principles

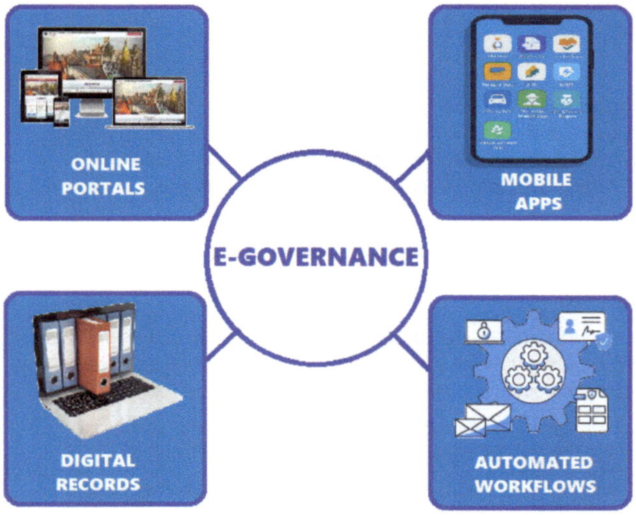

Fig. 3 ICT tools for E governance

- **G2C**: Citizens can access essential services such as certificates, bill payments, and healthcare information.
- **G2B**: Businesses benefit from digital licensing, taxation, procurement, and compliance platforms.
- **G2G**: Government departments exchange data securely and collaborate more effectively.
- **G2E**: Employees access digital HR services, payroll, training, and communication tools.

Objectives of E-Governance includes Improve administrative efficiency, increase transparency, strengthen accountability, reduce operational costs, empower citizens, promote inclusive, equitable service delivery and Support data-driven policy making.

Ethical Dimensions of E-Governance

Although e-governance makes it quite easier, it should be done in an ethical manner. The principle of responsibility by AI assists and promotes this by having respect for privacy, being transparent, preventing any form of discrimination, and being accountable by using technology.

Ethical e-governance means:

i. Protecting citizens' personal data
ii. Preventing algorithmic biases
iii. Maintaining accessibility for all communities
iv. Ensuring fair distribution of digital services
v. Avoiding surveillance misuse or political manipulation

Responsible AI helps attain these goals by incorporating fairness, accountability, and transparency directly into the digital governance system's design.

1.4 Challenges in Data-Rich Smart City Ecosystems

Smart cities rely on data that is continuous in nature and is collected through highly interlinked networks. However, this enhances efficacy as well as the ability to make decisions in real time; simultaneously, it also generates complex vulnerabilities. RA stands as an important means to mitigate such vulnerabilities by promoting safe, trustworthy, and morally sound data practices. Table 2 highlights some challenges that emanate due to massive data production in smart cities.

2 Ethical Foundations for AI in Smart Cities

Worldwide, the integration of cities, intelligence, and data continues to intensify. One such revolutionary technology is the use of AI. This technology has managed to attract significant focus which in turn affects the life, movement, and interaction of human beings. AI has a significant role in regulating the flow of traffic and predicting energy demand. AI systems for smart cities ensure safer, cleaner, and more efficient city operations. However, such enormous potential hides a very essential question: How can there be assurance that the technology in control of our lives meets these objectives in a trustworthy, just, and ethical manner, which directs itself in terms of human values? At this juncture, the ethical foundations of AI in smart cities assume great importance. Apart from performing mundane tasks, smart city technology has a significant influence on decision-making that has a very immediate impact on the lives of millions of people. For instance, algorithms in smart city technology can determine what neighborhoods receive priority in terms of access to public services, how quickly emergency services reach a place in case of an accident, how congested junctions are dealt with by traffic lights, and finally, how citizens' personal information should be collected and processed. These systems can cause unintended inequality in society, affect privacy, and render.

In ethical AI and intelligent cities, it means being a responsible developer as it goes beyond creating best-performing technology because it represents a responsibility to society as well and acts as a bridge between what technology is capable of and what should happen with what technology can do to make people's lives better. Building a good foundation in ethics involves being transparent and taking responsibility for a decision as it ensures that there is fairness and inclusivity throughout the process

Table 2 Challenges in data rich smart cities

Challenges	Description
Cybercrime and vulnerabilities	With their vast, exposed digital surfaces, smart cities will be a tempting target for cyber criminals. Risks include unauthorized access to IoT devices, ransomware attacks on vital services, data theft from public databases, manipulation of smart home systems, infrastructure sabotage, and intrusion into autonomous vehicles. Responsible AI would encourage threat detection systems, robust cybersecurity procedures, and secure-by-design architectures
Weaknesses in IoT devices	Many IoT devices are still employing outdated software and/or insecure security settings. To ensure that vulnerabilities are reduced to the lowest level, the use of responsible AI emphasizes secure configuration, secure communication, and continuous monitoring
Attacks on critical infrastructure	Facilities for the transportation of people, the provision of electricity, the supply of water, and the delivery of health care can all be enhanced by AI, which means these can all be considered as possibilities for attack by the opponents. Well-behaved AI ensures that there are mechanisms for rapid response and redundancy
Interconnected systems and cascading failures	As smart cities form interrelated systems, damage to one part might cascade rapidly. In this manner, responsible AI uses explainable models or risk-aware design to help predict the ripple effects
Legacy infrastructure	Contemporary security patches are not compatible with traditional infrastructure. Multi-layered protection approaches and secure modernization techniques are enabled through responsible AI
Human error and cyber hygiene	Configuration errors, phishing, and weak passwords continue to be serious risks. The focus of responsible AI is on secure default settings, automated error detection, and user education
Lack of standardized governance	There is an intensification of risk due to the divergent roles of telecom firms, private firms, and the government. There is an emphasis on clear lines of accountability, ethics, and governance through responsible AI
Real-time data and limited downtime	As smart city infrastructure functions continuously, it can prove challenging to implement a patch or update. As AI helps adaptive systems that can be safely updated without affecting essential infrastructure and other activities, AI becomes necessary

of developing artificial intelligence. But most importantly, it promotes interaction between policymakers and citizens because technology must progress along with ethics and morals and not vice versa.

2.1 Transparency and Explainability

Transparency and explainability are two foundations that make AI in smart cities more trustworthy and accountable. When we talk about transparency with respect to AI in cities, we essentially ask cities and developers to "show their work." This means they need to clearly explain the source of the data, how models are constructed, what models were trained with, how models are evaluated, and what constraints there may be. It's this level of transparency that would allow regulators, auditors, and even lay people, for that matter, to understand how a particular AI system arrived at a particular conclusion, most especially for decisions related to critical operations such as managing traffic flow, disaster relief, and allocation. It should be noted, as (Cheong 2024) mentions, that there's more to accountability than just documenting. It's a trail that becomes important work when there's a dispute over performance requirements.

Explainability is the next step after transparency. Transparency is to describe the actions of the system, while explainability is to explain the rationale behind those actions. For instance, in smart transportation, explainable AI, referred to as heatmaps or saliency methods, is used to enable users to interpret why an autonomous traffic system selected that particular route or detected that potential danger. XAI tools not only enable better decision-making through inclusion in smart transportation systems but also increase public trust, which is an essential aspect to create within any smart system based on AI technology, as found in research studies concerning smart transportation enabled through AI technology.

However, openness and explainability are not always easy to achieve in smart cities. Many of the most performant models, especially deep learning systems, are notoriously hard to interpret. Urban data is also spread over departments, sensors, and private suppliers, making it difficult to maintain a coherent view of how information flows through the system (Sanchez et al. 2024). Commercial secrecy limits what can be openly disclosed in public-private collaborations, adding another layer of complexity.

To overcome these challenges, cities need an effective balanced approach using the key principles of responsible AI. By this, cities need to adopt hybrid models of transparency methods, where model-explanation AI is used alongside robust data-related guidelines. Additionally, it involves developing policy guidelines on how cities can be transparent without exposing their critical infrastructure data. By implementing AI services like traffic regulation, waste services, and citizen safety, cities need transparent explanations on multiple levels depending on the audience, ranging from simple language descriptions for citizens to technical reports for technical staff and auditors.

Finally, openness and explainability help to ensure that AI systems in smart cities are not just strong, but also ethical, intelligible, and in line with the public good.

2.2 Accountability and Responsibility

Responsible AI for Smart Cities is sorely dependent on accountability. This is because it ensures that when AI systems affect daily living patterns, such as managing control signals, allocating public resources effectively, or helping law enforcement agencies to detect areas where crimes tend to occur—they do so with clear accountability of people and entities that remain responsible for their outputs. This means that accountability helps to ground AI systems in moral values. This is because sophisticated algorithms do not remain operational in a vacuum.

AI is not designed and operated by a sole party in smart cities. It is because, for the development of the AI lifecycle, smart cities depend on data providers, system integrators, private technology companies, as well as city authorities. Because of such complexity, it becomes important that accountability should be shared and clear from the onset until the implementation of design (Goldsmith and Yang 2025). According to recent studies, AI is altering the definitions of accountability in urban administration. To stay updated with technology, it is important that governments change their processes for overseeing accountability (Sanchez et al. 2024).

In reality, Responsible AI should focus on three essentials of accountable implementation: Firstly, there should be a clear definition of roles and responsibilities. Secondly, to contribute to helping researchers identify why an AIs decision occurred and if errors occurred due to data issues or human misuse of AIs, traceability of an AI should occur through audit trails and histories (Cheong 2024). Thirdly, redress should exist. In order to make an AI contestable and not a "black box" technology that citizens are forced to accept without questioning, citizens should have the opportunity to contest or appeal on behalf of the accuracy of computerized decisions (Sanchez et al. 2024).

Predictive police tools and other practical applications of technology might, through unintended consequences, give renewed forms of previously existing prejudice within law enforcement. For example, as the speed of public transit is degraded within poorer neighborhoods, traffic-routing software might give preference to those in which the median income is higher. Existing inequities hidden within historical data might be replicated within resource-allocation models.

Responsible AI in smart cities requires much more accountability frameworks than compliance to avoid this. Some examples of responsible AI include pre-deployment risk assessments, continuous performance and fairness monitoring, mandatory third-party audits for high-risk applications, and public transparency reports (Goldsmith and Yang 2025; Cheong 2024). Most of the recent proposals for governance demand multilayered oversight structures, embedding independent ethics committees, public advisory boards, and real-time bias, accuracy, and system behavior dashboards. This helps ensure that decisions made by AI are rational, understandable, and aligned with the bigger goal of improving people's welfare.

Lastly, accountability is also about maintaining trust rather than pointing fingers. When cities are able to develop AI systems that are traceable and explainable and can be connected to human accountability. Additionally, innovation in cities should never be solely dependent on being technological wizards but also socially and ethically inclusive.

2.3 Privacy and Data Protection

Since AI-assisted smart cities require a constant stream of data from sensors, transport systems, public infrastructure, and even day-to-day online activities, privacy and protection of this data become a prime focus of such systems. If cities are to win and then maintain the trust of their citizens, this sensitive and highly personal data must be handled with great caution (Hamarsheh 2025). This requires effective privacy-by-design processes, effective governance that keeps their citizens well-informed and in control of their data collection and use processes.

Data handling is evolving alongside smart-city technologies, where once massive volumes of information were transmitted to central servers for processing, more data today is handled closer to its point of creation—on the sensors and devices themselves or on nearby local systems. In this way, through what has come to be called edge analytics, cities can respond more rapidly and more accurately, with less risk of having massive volumes of data in one place. Of course, new responsibilities arise, such as the requirement for robust measures to block unauthorized access and misuse of data, for secure communication, as well as for security of the devices themselves (Konda 2025).

Data protection in an interconnected urban ecosystem, involving many government departments, private vendors, and service providers, is very complex. The drawing of attention to the protection of data will have associated risks: inconsistent security controls, unclear data-sharing arrangements, and regulatory gaps. Thus, smart cities have to adopt interoperable security standards and conduct regular audits to maintain resilience and compliance across the entire ecosystem (Rajasekar et al. n.d.).

A stronger privacy may be realized, without undermining analysis, through the implementation of distributed IoT networks for the sustainability of cities using federated learning and secured model updates aided by FPGA edge acceleration so as to prevent the primary data from migrating out of local regions and still achieve quality analysis. This indicates that cities of the future are embracing decentralized and privacy-respecting architectures for AI so as to preserve the data of their citizens while promoting innovation (Sanlı 2025).

2.4 Safety, Security, and Reliability

Therefore, with cities increasingly relying on AI to manage critical services such as power, transport, water, and emergency services, safety, security, and reliability will be increasingly under threat. This is because any small bug in any system or any cyberattack can completely bring down any city. Because of adoption in digital technology in cities, risk probability has also decreased as vulnerability has increased in cities. The role of AI can be to mitigate this increased risk with increased detection and response speeds to make transport and utility infrastructure cyber-resilient (Yedalla and James 2025).

However, purely digital protection strategies are not sufficient for a thorough understanding of AI safety in more complex city settings. AI systems in urban contexts should thus be carefully designed to produce durable alignment—enough to ensure that their objectives are in line with human values and the well-being of society. This would include developing adequate, fail-safe systems, model monitoring for unintended changes in performance, and scenario-based testing of models that are reflective of real-life city circumstances. Such strategies can empower city residents to depend on AI systems for safe performance even in challenging contexts, and also help in anticipating how autonomous systems would possibly behave in unpredictable human activities. For AI in smart city contexts to be both safe and reliable, adequate cyber protection has to be merged with durable AI safety considerations in order to address both technological failure and human complexities (Han 2025).

2.5 Inclusiveness, Accessibility, and Citizen-Centric Values

AI systems need to be designed for everyone and not only for people with high technological expertise or financial strength so that a smart city can be facilitated effectively. To make a technology inclusive, technological needs and abilities of people need to be considered. This research study revealed that AI systems can make a huge difference in effectively managing energy and transport for citizen services. If not planned properly, existing technological differences may continue (Prabakaran et al. 2025). To make a smart and inclusive city, trust needs to be built using AI systems, which should not be demanded but earned. IEEE has proposed a strategic framework on how public trust can be boosted for AI systems of a country's governance (Tsarouhas 2024).

Another important key point is accessibility. Accessible technology matters, and a report offers a holistic analysis of AI-based accessibility approaches, which categorizes the technology based on computer vision, speech processing, natural language processing, and automated auditing. Various studies demonstrate how these technologies, incorporated into design processes and combined with a human-centered assessment, can help alleviate digital exclusion. Supporting the needs of people with disabilities, as well as other users who may not know a particular language, AI serves as a bridge, rather than a barrier (Yedalla and James 2025). "Smart cities are not just smart technology, smart cities are for people. When inclusiveness, accessibility, and people-centered principles are considered, AI's role in a smart city becomes even more empowering, meaningful, and fair."

3 Ethical Frameworks for Smart City AI

The adoption of artificial intelligence technology in smart solutions for cities requires a framework of guiding principles that ensure the marriage between technological development and societal responsibility. Rather than just identifying the challenges and limitations posed by the regulations and technologies, stakeholders can work towards identifying and fixing both regulatory and technological hurdles to enable the rapid responsible development and use of artificial intelligence technology in cities. While cities around the world gear towards a world that will be defined and shaped by the development and use of artificial intelligence technology, the European experience proves that it's absolutely feasible to do things the right way to ensure a world that prioritizes the health and well-being of its citizens and not just the development and use of technology, which, in the long run, could result in the deterioration and downfall of society and human life itself. Frameworks serve as guiding documents that ensure the responsible, just, and fair use of technology, including artificial intelligence. They are meant to remind those who design and create technology that just like the air that sustains life, the development and use of technology must not compromise the human rights, dignity, and trust of the very people who need the technology. It's undeniable that the development and advancement of artificial intelligence are happening at a pace that's just remarkable, and within the last ten years, the corresponding regulation and legislation related to the use and development of AI are not only occurring, but they are dynamic and concurrent. The regulation and legislation related to the development and use of AI not only apply to the use and processing of data, and now there's the added focus and interest related to the decisions that the systems make, the prejudices that the system might carry and cultivate, and the moral dilemmas that arise when interacting with human society and other technologies.

Here, regulation of AI is considered as an approach meant to cover the different ethical and social concerns linked to the increasingly more autonomous nature of AI. Across the world, different approaches are used in the regulation of AI because each country has its different sets of values and concerns, and some may look at innovation and human rights regarding AI, while others try and balance the two. Collectively, all the approaches demonstrate the global effort in ensuring that AI is doing the least amount of harm and the maximum amount of good.

AI regulation is now a need for a variety of reasons such as protecting individual privacy rights, upholding ethical uses of AI to minimize risks of AI to societies, and assuming accountability for AI development and applications. AI regulation was initially required for ethical purposes and individual privacy matters. AI regulation is required for a variety of reasons.

Biased AIs can contribute to the exacerbation of some of the greatest problems in society, including jobs and finance and the criminal justice system in any country. As a result, legislation is required that ensures AIs are developed and utilized in a manner that is good for everyone in society. By minimizing biases, encouraging transparency and protecting the rights and dignity of everyone in society, they assist in ensuring that these technologies serve everyone and not just a select few.

This makes it imperative to develop guidelines regarding who to hold responsible when the AI outcome affects people or a community negatively, especially when the subject area involves sensitivity, such as the medical, financial, or legal sectors. This will ensure that the public knows who to hold responsible: the entities operating the AI system or the individuals or entities that built the AI system or the application of the said AI system. Otherwise, public trust will deteriorate quickly.

These regulations are considered vital as they help in providing specific parameters in the collection, processing, storage, as well as the transfer of data. This is because the confidentiality of a person's security could be threatened in the event of the abuse or unauthorized use of the data (Sun et al. 2024).

3.1 Responsibility of Stakeholders in Framing Regulatory AI Guidelines

A smart city is an endeavor involving the collective efforts of many people and entities instead of the technology itself. Businesses build, governments plan, innovators invent, and citizens help shape the future of the city through their needs. All the parties involved have special roles to play in ensuring that solutions in smart cities not only have the most up-to-date technology but are also long-lasting and inclusive.

The Fig. 4 represents various stake holders involved in building smart city following regulatory AI guidelines. Table 3 represents different stake holders and their responsibility in framing AI regulations for Smart cities.

By considering the responsibilities of stakeholders, Fig. 5 represents the proposed steps to frame AI Regulations that can be adopted in smart city for efficient and ethical surviving of the citizens.

3.2 Best Practices and Strategies for Implementing AI Regulations

The use of Artificial Intelligence to manage services in smart cities calls for the highest urgency to ensure these systems work safely, transparently, and ethically. Confidence is required among people that AI respects privacy, does not create scope for misuse in the form of deepfakes or digital arrest scams, and facilitates fair decision-making. Gaining such confidence has to be entrusted with the undertaking of clear strategies and best practices by smart cities while framing Regulatory AI Guidelines, focusing on the following: human-centric design, responsible data usage, strong governance, risk-based controls, and continuous monitoring. Such well-formulated guidelines will ensure that governments, tech companies, and people collaborate in making an ecosystem for smart cities that are embracing innovation while safeguarding Rights, Security, and Human Dignity. Table 4 depicts some best practices and strategies that will go a long way toward better smart city management imbued with ethical elements.

Regulatory frameworks are systematic frameworks that offer structure and guidance to rules that govern and monitor activities in smart cities. Sensor networks, data hosting services, AI-based services, digital mobility solutions, and smart energy infrastructure can be termed as some sort of

Fig. 4 Smart city stakeholders

Table 3 Different stake holders and their responsibility in framing AI regulations for smart cities

Stakeholders	Responsibility
Government & Policymakers	The government's job in AI regulation is to make sure technology is used safely and fairly. To safeguard public data, avoid biased or unfair decisions and guarantee the accountability of AI systems, policymakers establish explicit regulations
Citizens & communities	Through grievance platforms, smart governance portals, citizen forums, and mobile apps, they participate in the formulation of regulations and offer input on public needs, accessibility, and satisfaction
Technology providers	Companies that provide sensors, networks, software, AI tools, cybersecurity systems, and internet of things solutions ensure smart system interoperability and dependability in the long run
Urban planning authorities & infrastructure developers	This would, however, call for architects, civil engineers, environmental planners, and transport planners to be able to design sustainable buildings, smart systems of mobility, green open spaces, energy grids, and roads
Private Sector & Businesses	In terms of investing in innovation and creating jobs and enhancing productivity through intelligent infrastructure, large-scale intelligent cities can be facilitated by public-private partnerships
Utility providers	Using smart meters, grids, and analytics, services such as waste management, energy producers, water, and sewage, as well as electricity boards, manage critical infrastructure
Academic & Research Institutions	Besides providing analysis, audit, and training services for staff, institutions of higher learning and research facilities design innovative solutions in the area of artificial intelligence, sustainability, transportation, and urban analysis
Financial institutions & investors	Invest capital into infrastructure, innovation, and sustained urban developments
Regulators & legal bodies	In order to track levels of compliance and resolve any disputes, there needs to be a framework for public safety, cyber security, and AI, and data protection

inter-related systems that join to form a smart city. These systems might need to handle various challenges that come their way, like air pollution, cyber threats, health pandemics, climate change, and economic threats. The various inter-related systems go beyond national borders, regions, and even the international body. Hence, local rules and regulations cannot be applied for governance to a smart city. At national, local, and international forums, frameworks need to work in conjunction with each other. National Governments can formulate rules for privacy and cyber issues, while local authorities can handle mobility and data issues in cities, with international bodies giving directions on handling climate issues and ethics on digital issues.

International regulation frameworks result from the collective requirement for dealing with global issues. At the national level, laws and regulation frameworks are

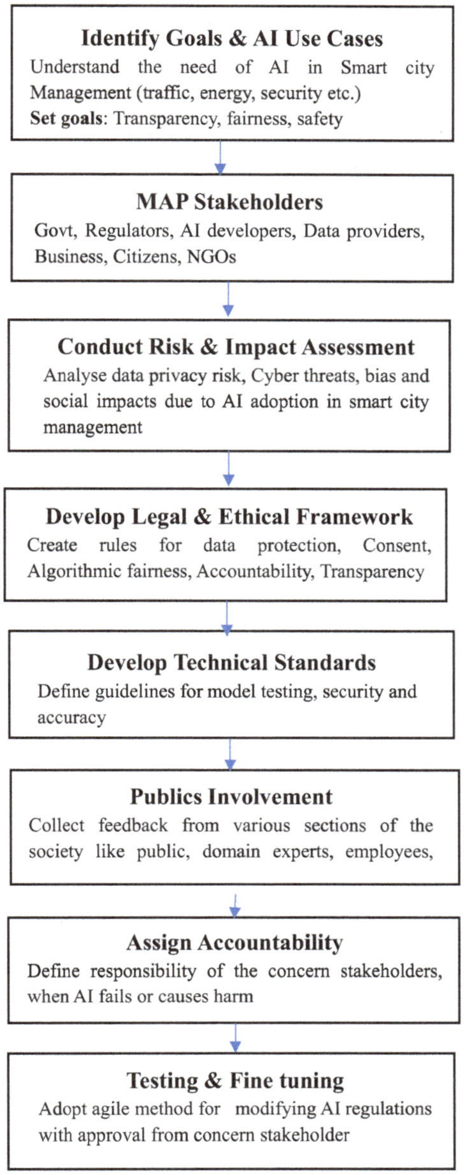

Fig. 5 Proposed steps for framing AI regulation

developed by the government according their political, economic, and cultural environment. National regulation frameworks enable the conversion of international frameworks regarding pertinent laws in the country. Significant frameworks include The European Union's AI Act, which has been accepted by the authorities in order to safeguard the rights of the people and ensure transparency. Other countries, for example China, United States, and United Kingdom, have accepted the laws, whose scope is limited (Górski and Ramakrishna 2025).

3.3 Challenges Faced by Smart Cities Due to Lack of Standard AI Regulations

Smart cities encounter various challenges in the absence of regulatory bodies. It leads to.

The Loss of Trust and Fairness: AI systems used in policing, resource allocation, or public service delivery can unintentionally discriminate if they are not audited or regulated. People who live in smart cities may lose faith in smart city initiatives if there are no regulations to ensure fairness and transparency and the public does not understand how AI systems work. Low adoption of digital services and public opposition may result from this

Security Vulnerabilities: IoT components, digital infrastructure networks, and sensors using AI or machine learning algorithms are integral to the implementation of the cities. Without appropriate cybersecurity and AI safety standards, these systems become easy targets for hacking, data breaches, manipulation of energy or traffic systems, and disruption of vital services.

Expensive Smart city: If appropriate standards are not followed, different vendor companies or departments may use different AI models, making it challenging for systems to communicate. This could result in "locked in," with a single technology supplier and a vendor lock issue that raises prices and prevents the city from implementing newer, better technologies.

Fragmented Legal Landscape: Where there is an ambiguity regarding regulations to utilize AI, smart cities face confusion. Instead, they have to comply with diverse regional laws, specifically with respect to data utilization, monitoring, or fairness of algorithms. Thus, the deployment of AI in an entire city becomes difficult and full of legal hazards.

4 Use Case Scenarios of AI for Smart Cities

For smart cities to support effective resource and infrastructure utilization, AI-monitored and managed services are necessary. The following use cases the necessity of both regulatory frameworks and AI technology.

4.1 AI-Monitored Traffic Management System

In situations where traffic flow suddenly rises, AI can automatically provide longer green lights to ensure that traffic flow can proceed smoothly. This happens without

Table 4 Best practices and strategies for implementing AI regulations

Metrics	Best practices/Strategies
Adopt a human-centric, rights-first approach	• Prioritize citizens' privacy dignity, and digital rights in all AI deployments and include special safeguards for vulnerable groups
Establish clear governance structures	• Mandate third-party audits for high-risk applications such as surveillance, facial recognition, and predictive policing
Safeguard responsible data life-cycle management	• Implement rules on the collection of lawfully collected data, define rules for the retention periods, encryption of all citizen data and secure deletion • Limit needless departmental data sharing without clear ethical and legal justification
Adopt risk-based classification of AI systems	• Classify AI applications into low-risk, medium-risk, and high-risk categories based on potential harm to society
Encourage open standards and interoperability	• Leverage interoperable frameworks, use open data standards, and employ open APIs for all smart city applications. • Avoid vendor lock-in and ensure that the long-run viability of the AI model
Support innovation within ethical boundaries	• Provide regulatory sandboxes for the safe testing of novel AI solutions • Support startups and academic institutions that are developing AI solutions for smart cities, and ensure that these developments comply with social, legal, and ethical standards
Implement agile way of review and adaptive regulation	• Since AI is developing quickly, guidelines need to be dynamic documents that are updated on a regular basis • Local AI regulations need to be updated to comply with international AI regulations

responding to events taking place on roads. To predict regions where traffic congestion is expected to happen, AI uses predictive analytics by drawing data from sourced patterns of traffic flow, weather, and other data. This is very useful to cities. Rather than dealing with traffic jams and preventing traffic congestion, traffic agencies can effectively handle traffic congestion by adjusting traffic lights, routing the vehicles, and allocating more resources. By keeping the roads free from trouble before hand and maintaining smooth flow of roads, AI assists in smart management of the flow of roads in the city. The following operations are carried out by the AI roads, control system in the smart city.

Dynamically adjusts traffic signals: Traffic lights are controlled through an automatic mechanism which is constantly fed data from traffic cameras, road sensors, and connected cars. Reduces unnecessary stops at traffic lights signals, adding towards ensuring there is an unbroken flow of traffic.

Manages congestion: The AI system can quickly divert vehicles to other routes, provide information about other better routes, and even temporarily alter speed limits by identifying traffic problems or sudden incidents. This helps in maintaining an adequate flow of traffic movement within the city, making it easier to avoid traffic-congested routes.

Provides priority routing for emergency vehicles: The moment an approaching emergency-usually a fire truck or ambulance-can be detected, the AI system instantly detects and changes the lighting at this crossing to allow it to pass. An AI system will help the emergency teams reach their destination safely as soon as possible by making the road ahead free and preparing a smooth, green-light corridor in their movement.

Anticipates Upcoming Peak Hour Spikes: It analyzes the history of patterns of traffic flow along with the current road condition using machine learning algorithms and predicts where congestion might occur. Based on these predictive results, the city can take proactive measures to not let any problems further deteriorate.

Because of the above functionalities it leads to:

Fuel Efficiency and Emission Reduction: Vehicles are compelled to remain stationary due to the congesting of roads, resulting in the wastage of fuel and the emission of pollutants in the atmosphere. Contributing to the seamless flow of vehicles, AI-based traffic management technologies ensure that the waiting time of vehicles at crossroads is reduced, reducing fuel consumption and the emission of harmful pollutants, thus paving the way for clean air conditioning in the atmosphere and smart ecologically favorable environments in smart cities.

Enhanced Commuter Experience: AI-run traffic systems ensure that people can move from one place to another faster. This technology enables people to reach their destinations without unnecessary delays and suggests a better route for them to avoid traffic jams. As a result, the system reduces the stress associated with urban traffic.

Enhanced Road Safety: Intelligent and adaptable traffic lights, however, shall greatly improve the safety of the roads by decreasing the traffic flow and preventing the occurrence of wait-and-go traffic accidents. Intelligent traffic lights cause an improvement in the safety of drivers as well as pedestrians by increasing the effectiveness of the coordination of the traffic lights and reducing the risk of high-speed accidents.

The following issues must be resolved for the implementation of AI-Powered Traffic Control to be successful.

Data Quality and Availability: AI-powered traffic systems require efficient operation based on accurate and timely information. This means cities need to invest in good cameras, sensors, and V2I communication. Bad or incomplete data will lead AI to make poor decisions; in simple words, inefficient traffic control translates to longer delays for commuters.

System Integration: It can be difficult to integrate AI-powered traffic control into the current city infrastructure. New AI technologies may not work well with older traffic lights, sometimes necessitating significant upgrades or complete replacements. Smooth communication and interoperability are also necessary to ensure the system operates smoothly when coordinating numerous intersections and connecting with other transportation systems, such as buses or trams.

Scalability: In fact, deploying AI-powered traffic systems across a city or metropolitan area involves considerable effort and many resources. Scaling the technology up to manage hundreds of intersections, while maintaining reliable and continuous operation, can become challenging. Furthermore, the system must adapt to the altered flow of traffic during different day cycles, seasons, or during events; hence, constant observation and cautious tuning of the variables involved are required.

Ethical and Privacy Concerns: There is an issue of privacy with the use of sensors and cameras. Of importance is the role of cities in managing people's data. Ensuring that the data is processed in the right way is important. An aspect of ensuring that the right to the privacy of the people is achieved is protecting the data from breaches and ensuring that it is anonymized where possible and coming clean with them (Shunmugesh et al. 2026).

Urban transport systems are undergoing changes from the application of AI-based intelligent traffic light control systems. These systems optimize traffic flow, minimize congestion, conserve fuel, and reduce the stress of commuting by leveraging the capabilities of machine learning and predictive models based on real-time information. Although challenges in the quality of the data used, system interoperability, and technology scalability still persist, innovations based on artificial intelligence and smart city technology hold great promise. These intelligent traffic control systems will play pivotal roles in the effective and sustainable transport of people and goods in expanding urban sprawls.

4.2 AI-Based Smart Healthcare & Emergency Response

Healthcare services like patient monitoring, managing chronic illness, and emergency response are greatly impacted by developments in AI technologies and IoT sensor networks (Arslanoğlu and Karaköse 2024). The following tasks are carried out by the AI system used for healthcare management in smart cities.

Predictive Analytics: In the identification and prediction of possible outbreaks of disease and significant incidents in the area of health, such as heart attack complications, the AI algorithm processes enormous amounts of health-related data in the form of EHRs and the latest data from the Internet of Things. In this case, it becomes very easy for the health department and experts in managing the preventive aspects of maintaining good health in the community. The AI algorithm applies machine learning in the prediction process.

Improved Diagnostics and Treatment: AI is helpful in both diagnosing and treating ailments at an early stage.

Medical Imaging: With the help of deep learning techniques enabled by AI, it is possible to examine various types of images from the medical realm, including X-ray images and mammography images. This is accomplished by detecting defects in the images in the form of tumors or lesions. They do so more quickly than human professionals.

Personalized Medicine: AI can be used to develop treatment plans tailored to an individual's requirements by combining the effects of genetics, lifestyle, and medical histories. Not only can these plans improve health, but they can also make healthcare both effective and affordable.

Wearable Health Tracking: Wearables, such as biosensors and smartwatches, continuously track vital signs, including blood pressure, pulse rate, and glucose level. The AI analyzes the real-time data from such wearables and then alerts healthcare providers to problems. Such proactive monitoring enables a patient to steer clear of unnecessary hospital admissions or readmissions. It is particularly useful in the management of chronic diseases.

Drug Discovery: AI fast-tracks the discovery of promising candidates for drugs, hence fostering quicker developments in new drugs. Again, optimization in the clinical process also ensures a faster, cheaper, and efficient process, thereby facilitating a quicker delivery to patients.

Because of the above functionalities it leads to:

Improved Patient Outcomes: AI is revolutionizing healthcare by speeding up and improving the accuracy of diagnosis, particularly through sophisticated image analysis that can identify diseases like diabetic eye disease or cancer earlier than with conventional techniques. It also encourages personalized medicine because it analyzes the genetic makeup, lifestyle, and medical history of every patient to create treatments specifically suited to the needs of every individual. AI is also capable of identifying any health risks a patient may have before they develop any symptoms because of its ability to analyze data through predictive analytics. AI-enabled wearables, for example, monitor a patient's vitals continuously and alert caregivers to any emerging conditions while also motivating a patient to take control of his or her own health.

Improved Efficiency in the Healthcare Industry: Performing activities like recording observations of patient conditions, fixing appointments, and handling matters of health insurance claims, the use of artificial intelligence is helping to increase efficiency in the healthcare industry by giving more attention to the patients as well as enhancing the functionality of the hospitals by knowing the admission of the patients and the availability of beds for their use without the presence of long waiting lines. Additionally, AI is playing an important role in the reduction of medical and drug-related errors in the healthcare industry by providing an independent interpretation of the information in this sector that makes the sector safe and trustworthy.

Accelerated Medical Innovation: AI is currently revolutionizing the healthcare industry by accelerating and enhancing the efficiency of medicinal research, helping scientists identify potential drugs and modeling clinical trials much faster and at a much lower cost than before. The use of AI-enabled robots in surgeries gives surgeons greater accuracy and stability to conduct safe and minimally invasive surgeries with faster turnaround times for patients to recover. Additionally, AI increases efficiency in medical research by analyzing massive amounts of complex data, like genetic and medical data, to identify trends and patterns that would have gone unnoticed otherwise, thus helping humanity increase its knowledge and comprehension of diseases and their treatments (Rao et al. n.d.).

To implement AI-Powered Health care Management System, the implementors may face the following challenges, which has to be addressed for their successful deployment:

Maintaining human clinical skills: When clinicians have constant access to AI-generated insights, there's a risk that their own diagnostic and critical-thinking skills may weaken over time—especially for medical trainees still learning the basics. When the AI system malfunctions, yields inaccurate results, or is unavailable, it becomes a major issue that makes clinicians less confident in their ability to make decisions on their own.

Preventing Errors in AI Systems

Additionally, AI models can introduce other mistakes such as

- ***Biased or Low-Quality Data***: Since AI technology is a result of learning from previous healthcare information, if such information is not scrutinized, it might unconsciously absorb even reinforce inequities in healthcare.
- ***The "Black Box" Problem***: It may be difficult for the clinician to understand and verify a recommendation due to a lack of transparency in sophisticated AI systems to explain the reasoning behind reaching a specific conclusion. The clinician may find it difficult to point questions to an AI system as it lacks transparency.
- ***Algorithm Malfunctions or Hallucinations***: While working on unique patients compared to the data the algorithms have been trained on, the AI system can sometimes produce incorrect or misleading data, which could go on to produce inappropriate or incorrect diagnoses or treatment regimens.
- **Accountability and Liability**: Determining who should be held accountable when AI makes a mistake that causes harm to a patient is a significant concern. Is it the doctor who used the tool, the developer who built it, or the healthcare institution that deployed it?

  This uncertainty creates significant legal and ethical challenges.

Evidence base and evaluation of effectiveness of AI: The trustworthiness of AI systems is in their training datasets. The AI system may actually generate biases unconsciously. This can lead to inequitable and misleading results in the medical field due to un-diverse training datasets. The AI system may actually fail to work in an efficient manner in other races and classes, for instance, due to the training it has been subjected to in relation to the particular social classes. There may also be misleading medical diagnoses and improper medical advice. There is a need to counteract the biases by using a variety of datasets and making the AI system undergo continuous validation and following appropriate approaches to counteract the biases and ensure fairness in the provision of medical services to everyone (Akila et al. n.d.).

Regulatory and Legal Challenges: There are several legal and regulatory matters that arise in the increasing usage of AI in the medical domain. It has become rather difficult to formulate specific rules and regulations in regard to the usage of these technologies, as most of the rules and regulations in the medical domain that exist today have not been designed in consideration of the usage of AI in medical diagnoses and treatment suggestions. In order to ensure that these medical devices that employ AI are safe, effective, and ethical, the FDA and the European Medicines Agency are working on specific frameworks. The most difficult aspect is to ensure the right balance between innovation and the safety of patients.

Integration with Existing Healthcare Systems: In most hospitals, obsolete IT infrastructure, which may not be easily integrated with modern AI solutions, continues to be common. The integration of AI with existing work environments or with health record systems may need overhaul and new software infrastructure. The integration of AI into existing environments at healthcare facilities could be made simpler, with a need to improve communication between most healthcare facilities since they may not have a proper interface with each other. This could be achieved by adopting standards to ensure AI works effectively within the entire health system infrastructure (Razai et al. 2024; Akila et al. n.d.).

4.3 AI Driven Energy Management

In smart cities, energy management plays an integral role in lowering costs, increasing productivity, and minimizing environmental impact. In regards to monitoring and managing energy consumption effectively, simple solutions tend to come up poorly, especially in more complex urban and buildings settings. But AI solutions can provide more intelligent and dynamic means of monitoring energy consumption, optimizing energy efficiency, and maximizing energy use, where more conventional solutions simply cannot keep up.

Smart city AI systems can be used in a variety of fields to maximize energy use. The following are possible outcomes of using AI techniques for energy management.

Predictive Maintenance: Even the smallest malfunction in equipment, such as a transformer overheating or a fault in a power line, can cause the energy supply of thousands in a smart city to go nonfunctional. Predictive maintenance, powered by AI, prevents these breakdowns. Sensors deployed along the smart grid constantly monitor the health of all critical components, and machine-learning models analyze this data to find early signs of wear or failure.

Instead of waiting for something to break, city utilities can plan repairs in advance, avoiding unexpected outages and extending the life of grid infrastructure to provide more reliable energy for its citizens. This proactive approach saves a great deal of energy across the smart city in addition to the lower levels of downtown.

Energy Demand Forecasting: Knowing how much electricity will be demanded at the peak office hour during a heat wave and/or during the night of the festival at such a smart city is of utmost importance to maintain power stability and cut costs. AI does this by analyzing past electricity demand trends, weather, industry production levels, and even market trends.

Because of this knowledge, AI systems can generate exact predictions of what their future energy requirements will be. Essentially, this will enable urban power suppliers to optimally utilize renewable resources, know exactly what their electricity needs to generate or procure, and take advantage of dynamic pricing. Smart grids are going to help eliminate unnecessary waste of energy, decrease their dependence on fossil fuels, and deliver cheap electricity to every urban zone.

Grid Management: The grid is becoming more complicated with the increased use of renewable energy sources in smart cities, such as solar panels placed on roofs. Cities require more intelligent control systems to facilitate the functionality of the grid since renewable energy sources may be clean sources of energy; however, they are unreliable sources of energy. AI helps in predicting the amount of renewable energy that can be produced and varying the electric flows. It ensures that clean energy is used first and effectively by automatically balancing supply and demand. With AI guiding the smart grid, cities can rely more on renewable power, reduce carbon emissions, and provide residents with a cleaner, more sustainable energy experience (Melike Sultan Karasu Asnaz, Balikesir University 2024).

To implement AI-Powered Energy Management System, the implementors may face some of the following challenges, which has to be addressed for successful deployment:

Integration with existing systems: The integration of Artificial Intelligence technology in the current energy infrastructure of a city involves modernizing the outdated equipment and redesigning the control mechanisms and work coordination between the various departments of the city. As most of the current energy infrastructure is not built with Artificial Intelligence in mind, the integration of the most advanced technology in the equipment that keeps the whole city running is essential.

The need for a deep understanding of the existing infrastructure in order to facilitate such a transition arises; integrating this technology of Artificial Intelligence would provide a smarter energy system for the entire city. It would also be efficient and ready for the future because of good planning by all involved.

Cyberthreats: In order to protect energy networks from any threat of insecurity and unreliability, these energy AI networks should be made safe from cyberattacks. These networks not only command energy-infrastructure assets, but they also handle confidential data. This means that if there is even a small threat of insecurity, it might result in something big going terribly wrong. Frequent security audits help in identifying these areas of vulnerability before being exploited by cyber attackers. An effective incident response plan is also as important, as employees should know exactly what is expected of them in case of a threat.

Regulatory Compliance: There has to be rigid regulation for the energy infrastructure in order to ensure environmental sustainability, reliability, and safety. Bringing AI into the picture makes the situation more complicated. Questions about the processing of data, automated decision-making, or interaction of the technology with the existing infrastructure may be asked. Regulations and guidelines will be closely scrutinized by the city and the energy industry to make sure their own AI is safe and compliant with all the requirements. They would be able to ensure the added safety of the energy infrastructure by being compliant.

Human intervention in AI Driven Energy System: It is essential that human beings are well-informed when using AI to control energy resources. Even the brightest computers are prone to neglecting context and details that experienced personnel are able to notice easily. That is why human oversight and ability to correct at all times are necessary. Decisions taken by AI systems are subject to review and override or human guidance that ensures the entire process stays safe, fair, and transparent. The knowledge that decisions are not left in the hands of computers but in human hands that are in a position to respond to unexpected scenarios and have a bigger picture is responsible for trust building too (Zhong-Lin et al. 2025; Rajasekar et al. 2023).

5 Conclusion

Smart cities are emerging from conventional cities due to the resultant need for human resourcefulness in response to the unprecedented pressure from the growing number of citizens on services and infrastructure. This is more than an infrastructure or technological advancement. AI plays a pivotal role in this process due to its ability to make decisions faster and predict infrastructure demands.

Although there is the possibility for massive improvements in the efficiency of cities through the help of AI, there is also the danger of worsening the already existing social injustices if it is applied improperly. Smart city solutions have a core impact on the decisions taken by millions of people in a range of ways, including the selection in urgent responses or the allocation of resources. It is imperative for guidelines on ethics -more specifically, Responsible AI—to be highly valued in the event the implementation of AI is so profoundly rooted in public governance. Technology-driven governance could emerge as a source of pain if it did not have a solid foundation in ethics.

In conclusion, the development of an ethical framework for AI in smart cities involves human commitment to connecting technological capability with social obligation. The basis comprises fundamental ethical values like transparency, accountability, non-discrimination, privacy, and inclusivity to protect the citizens it serves. For example, accountability ensures that people remain responsible for outcomes, which demands mechanisms like human-in-the-loop design, while transparency demands that citizens understand how decisions are reached through automated systems and what data is involved. To ensure access to services is on par with socioeconomic status and locational lines, responsible AI must also have fairness and nondiscrimination with algorithmic audits and inclusive datasets among their most valued priorities.

This requires accountability frameworks that must be explicit, as well as flexible regulatory models, among all stakeholders, including both the research community as well as technologists, in effectuating these principles. In dealing with complex issues of cybersecurity, as well as data, in these networked systems, these frameworks require constant monitoring of bias as well as regular audits. The ultimate purpose of all these is, of course, to address social issues, as well as technological issues, ensuring, in effect, that all members of society reap benefits from technology. Communities reap the public trust essential in ensuring long-term digital adoption when they govern their artificial intelligence systems ethically, ensuring that they protect data, rights, as well as security.

The success of these systems is going to be a function of how much they adhere to a strong set of moral principle, as opposed to purely technological success as cities around the world go further down their rapid digital trajectory. If the future of cities is going to see real improvement within them via the use of artificial intelligence, then what is needed is a system that is not merely advanced technologically, but is instead compassionate, just, and very much human.

References

K. Akila, R. Gopinathan, J. Arunkumar, B. Sree Bavai Malar "The Role of Artificial Intelligence in Modern Healthcare: Advances, Challenges, and Future Prospects", European Journal of Cardiovascular Medicine, Volume 15 Issue 4, Pages 615–624.

K. Arslanoğlu and M. Karaköse, "Artificial intelligence based explainable smart healthcare: integration and analysis of IoT data," *8th IET*

Smart Cities Symposium (SCS 2024), Hybrid Conference, Bahrain, 2024, pp. 810-815, doi:https://doi.org/10.1049/icp.2025.0903.

Cheong, B. C. (2024). *Transparency and accountability in AI systems: Safeguarding wellbeing in the age of algorithmic decision-making.* Frontiers in Human Dynamics, 6, 1421273

Goldsmith, S., & Yang, J. (2025). *AI and the transformation of accountability and discretion in urban governance.* arXiv preprint https://arxiv.org/abs/2502.13101.

L. Górski and S. Ramakrishna, "Right to Explanation in Large Language Models: Lessons from the European Union AI Act and General Data Protection Regulation," in *IT Professional*, vol. 27, no. 1, pp. 34–40, Jan.-Feb. 2025, doi:https://doi.org/10.1109/MITP.2024.3518917

A. Hamarsheh, "Building Trust in AI-Driven Urban Environments: Privacy, Accountability, and Ethical Frameworks," Arab American University Repository, Apr. 17, 2025. Available: https://repository.aaup.edu/handle/123456789/3494.

S. Han, "Bridging Today and the Future of Humanity: AI Safety in 2024 and Beyond," https://arxiv.org/abs/2410.18114, Jan. 11, 2025. Available: https://arxiv.org/abs/2410.18114

Kim, K.; Alshenaifi, I.; Ramachandran, S.; Kim, J.; Zia, T.; Almorjan, A. Cybersecurity and Cyber Forensics for Smart Cities: A Comprehensive Literature Review and Survey. Sensors 2023, 23, 3681. https://doi.org/10.3390/s23073681.

R. Konda, "AI at the Edge of Urban Intelligence: Real-Time Awareness and Precision Diagnostics for Resilient Smart Cities," Int. J. Emerging Trends in Comp. Sci. & IT, Sept. 2025. Available: https://ijetcsit.org/index.php/ijetcsit/article/view/382.

Melike Sultan Karasu Asnaz, Balikesir University, "AI-driven energy management: innovative solutions for achieving green deal targets in industry", 5th International Eurasian Conference on Science, Engineering and Technology (EurasianSciEnTech 2024) June 26–28, 2024

P. Prabakaran, Y. H. Bhosale, P. Mudholkar, M. Mudholkar, R. Rajeswaran, and S. P. Dillibabu, "AI-Powered Urban Infrastructure: A Multidisciplinary Approach to Smart City Development and Social Inclusion," Eksplorium, Vol. 46 No. 02, Jun. 2025, pp. 685–695. Available: https://eksplorium.com/index.php/journal/article/view/274.

Rajasekar, V., Devi, K. N., Sathya, K., Sabarnika, S., Raagul, N. S., & Logeshwar, R. (2023, October). An Intelligent System for Nutrition Deficiency Detection Using Deep Learning Techniques. In *International Conference on Applied Mathematics and Mechanics* (pp. 39–47). Singapore: Springer Nature Singapore.

Rajasekar, V., Devi, K. N., Sathya, K., Sharan, R., & Nitiish, S. Depressive Disorder Using Deep Learning Techniques. *Applied Mathematics and Mechanics: ICAMM 2023, Indore, India, October 18–20*, 457.

B. D. Rao, G. Madhukar, B. N. Reddy, S. K. Voni and N. S. V. Kumar, "Comprehensive AI-Powered Healthcare Management System," *2025 International Conference on Intelligent Computing and Control Systems (ICICCS)*, Erode, India, 2025, pp. 1017–1022, doi:https://doi.org/10.1109/ICICCS65191.2025.10984436

Razai MS, Al-Bedaery R, Bowen L, Yahia R, Chandrasekaran L, Oakeshott P. Implementation challenges of artificial intelligence (AI) in primary care: Perspectives of general practitioners in London UK. PLoS One. 2024 Nov 21;19(11):e0314196. doi:https://doi.org/10.1371/journal.pone.0314196. PMID: 39570873; PMCID: PMC11581230.

Sanchez, T. W., Brenman, M., & Ye, X. (2024). *The ethical concerns of artificial intelligence in urban planning.* Journal of the American Planning Association, 91(1), 1–14.

M. Sanlı, "Privacy-Preserving AI for Distributed IoT in Urban Sustainability Networks," Arab. J. Sci. Eng., Nov. 21, 2025. DOI: https://doi.org/10.1007/s13369-025-10864-w.

Shunmugesh, K., Biju, B., Reji, A., Rajasekar, V., Hiremath, S., Anne, G., & Vishwanatha, H. M. (2026). Optimizing 3D printing parameters for enhanced tensile strength and efficiency using machine learning models. *Progress in Additive Manufacturing*, 1–16.

Sun, Nan & Miao, Yuantian & Jiang, Hao & Ding, Ming & Zhang, Jun. (2024). From Principles to Practice: A Deep Dive into AI Ethics and Regulations. https://doi.org/10.48550/arXiv.2412.04683.

P. Tsarouhas, "Building Trust in AI for Public Administration: A Strategic Framework for Transparency, XAI, Participation, and Digital Literacy," IEEE Conference/Proceedings, 2024. Available: https://ieeexplore.ieee.org/document/11017116.

J. Yedalla and A. James, "Building Cyber-Resilient Smart Cities: The Role of AI and Big Data in Urban Security," Int. J. Sci. Res., Feb. 2025

Zhong-Lin Fu, Can Cao, Feng Gao, "Current status, problems and promotion strategies of AI application in industrial energy management: A case study from China", Journal of Cleaner Production Volume 506, 2025, 145533, ISSN 0959-6526.

Integrating Responsible AI and Facial Emotion Recognition to Prevent Digital Arrest Scams in Smart City Ecosystems

C. Saravanan and Preethi N. Patil

Abstract

The Cyber Crime Coordination Centre (I4C) of India documented 45,000 digital arrest scam cases during 2024 which resulted in more than ₹1200 crore financial loss. In the emerging landscape of smart cities, digital arrest scams—where fraudsters impersonate law enforcement officers using AI-generated voices, videos, or digital warrants have become a growing social and ethical threat. The system requires an immediate solution because of its fast growth. The framework presents a proactive solution which combines Responsible Artificial Intelligence (AI) with Facial Emotion Recognition (FER) technology to create an ethical defense system. FER systems can capture and analyze real and forced emotions by detecting subtle micro-expressions and facial cues, enabling the identification of deceptive behavioral patterns commonly exhibited by fraudsters during digital interactions. Smart city governance systems need to implement emotion-based systems which support AI decision-making through clear systems that humans can understand while following Responsible AI principles of fairness, accountability and human control. The chapter presents a research study which unites Facial Emotion Recognition with Responsible AI systems to achieve early detection of fraudulent activities while safeguarding digital platforms and protecting everyday users from harm. The proposed framework establishes an ethical system which enables smart cities to become secure and trustworthy by using technology to protect human dignity while maintaining public safety and justice through technological solutions.

Keywords

Responsible artificial intelligence (AI) · Facial emotion recognition (FER) · Digital arrest scams · Smart city governance · Ethical AI · Emotion-aware systems

1 Introduction

Digital infrastructures work together to make living in a modern smart city easier, more accessible, and more responsive. In the last few years, governments, businesses, and researchers have all been very interested in Smart Cities. The Indian government is also spending a lot of money to build its own smart cities because it sees the potential (Singh et al. 2022). People today often use smart platforms to do things like book public transportation, get medical care, pay taxes, apply for government documents, and even talk to local officials. These systems have made things a lot easier, cut down on paperwork, and got more people involved. But the same digital connections that make these good things possible have also made things more dangerous.

Increase in population growth in Indian Cities is due to several reasons—Increase in Birth rate, Migration of Citizens from rural region to urban regions and rapid urbanization. As per the Census information of India, there is tremendous and significant increase in India Urban population. About 31.16% of the population lived in cities in 2021. This number is expected to go up to almost 50% by 2050. The Ministry of Housing and Urban Affairs (MoHUA) says that by 2031, there will be about 60 crores people living in cities. The NITI Aayog's Final Report on Reforms in Urban Planning Capacity in India, which came out in September 2021, says that India has the second largest urban system

C. Saravanan (✉)
Department of MCA, RV College of Engineering, Bengaluru, India
e-mail: saravananc@rvce.edu.in

P. N. Patil
Department of MCA, Ramaiah Institute of Technology, Bengaluru, India
e-mail: preethinpatil@msrit.edu

V. Sarveshwaran et al. (eds.), *Responsible AI for Smart Cities*, Sustainable Artificial Intelligence-Powered Applications,
https://doi.org/10.1007/978-3-032-26901-0_14

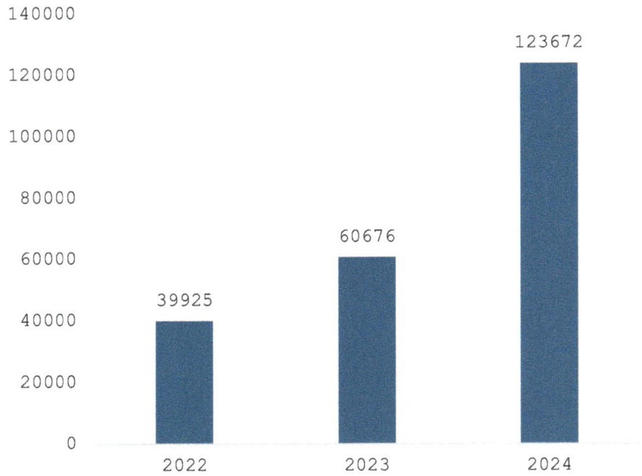

Fig. 1 Number of digital arrest scam incidences

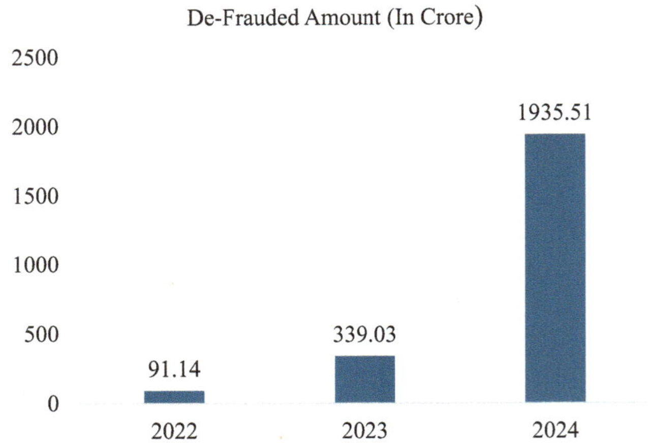

Fig. 2 Financial losses caused by digital arrest scams

in the world. Indian cities are home to about 11% of the world's urban population. In a few decades, half of the country will be "urban."

By 2050, India's urban population will grow by about 400 million people, according to the United Nations World Urbanization Prospects (2018). This makes India one of the fastest growing countries in the Asia and also in the entire world with major countries competition.

As more and more people move to cities, India has both problems and opportunities. It costs a lot of money to make things like transportation, infrastructure, housing, healthcare, security, and education better. It also gives us the chance to build smart, long-lasting cities that can help the economy grow while also solving social, environmental, and economic problems.

The year 2024 observed a surge in cyber scams, particularly those involving digital arrest Schemes (Babu 2025). According to National Crime Records Bureau (NCRB), there is increase in number of digital arrest scam incidence from 2022 to 2024 as represented in Fig. 1.

Figure 2 represents dramatic and accelerating rise in the financial losses caused by digital arrest scams (or related cyber-fraud categories) across India from 2022 to 2024.

The impact of digital arrest scams is being felt across multiple Indian states, leading to significant financial losses and emotional distress for victims.

Figure 3 represents pie chart that shows financial loss (in crores) in different Indian states in 2024. Karnataka has lost the most money compared to other states. In the first four months of 2024, Karnataka had the most cases, with 641 (Jain et al. n.d.).

These scams work not because digital systems fail, but because people behave differently when they are stressed out. They hesitate, panic, doubt their ability to check facts, and act on their feelings instead of their brains. Traditional cybersecurity tools like firewalls, intrusion detection systems, and spam filters are not made to find people who are in pain, scared, or being forced to do something. So, even people who are very tech-savvy can be tricked by these kinds of schemes that play with their emotions.

The current problems demonstrate why organizations need to develop Responsible AI (RAI) frameworks which serve as fundamental management tools. AI systems obtain moral rules from these frameworks which also provide operational guidelines and safety protocols to protect human interests while following community standards. The system functions as a protective mechanism which safeguards human life from dangerous technology threats. The RAI principles require FER tools to maintain transparency while providing equal treatment and complete responsibility and they must defend user privacy through monitoring systems which involve relevant human authorities. The system needs to provide users with increased control instead of taking away their existing authority.

The chapter demonstrates how Responsible AI systems protect smart cities from cyber threats which use Facial Emotion Recognition technology in a correct operating system. The tools enable us to detect situations where people experience forced actions while providing immediate help to those who need it and reducing the damage from digital arrest scams without violating any laws or damaging public confidence. The human-centered security framework exists as an introduction which unites digital protection systems with moral principles to create an equal protective framework.

1.1 Techniques Used by Fraudsters in Digital Arrest Scams

Digital arrest scammers use a mix of psychological tricks and new technology to scare, confuse, and make people do

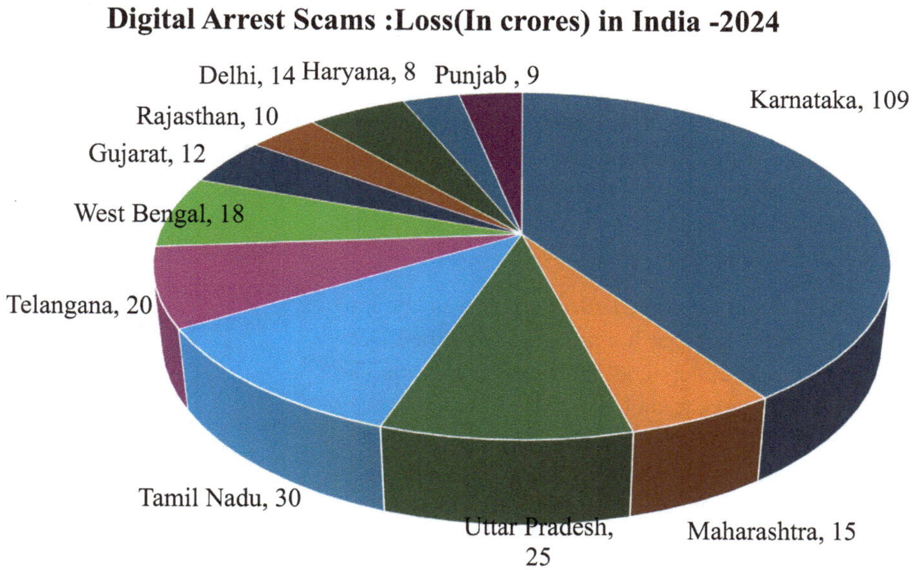

Fig. 3 Financial loss across various states of India-2024. (*Source* Jagran josh)

what they want. Their plan is to scare people, make them stop thinking clearly, and get them to act quickly without checking anything. Three common ways to do this are to scare people, threaten them with legal action, and use AI to make fake identities.

Fear Induction

The first thing that scammers do is scare people for no reason. They usually start by making a scary and shocking claim, like saying that the victim's Aadhaar or bank account is linked to a crime, that a package sent in their name has illegal items in it, or that a police report has been filed against them. The goal is to scare the victim so they can't think straight or check the facts.

Threats of Legal Action

Scammers are getting better at what they do because they use advanced AI tools to support their lies. They use AI to make fake videos that look like real police or officials, clone voices to sound like they know what they are talking about, and use fake virtual backgrounds that look like police control rooms. They also send out fake digital ID cards and papers that look real, which makes it harder for victims to believe what they see or hear. These tools make it look like scammers are real people you can trust. People naturally let their guard down when they see something on screen that looks like a real officer or get a document that looks official. In that moment, doubt fades, questions stop, and the scam becomes far more effective.

Even a careful person can get stuck when all of these things happen at the same time. This is why it's so important in detecting emotional distress early and use AI tools that are safe. They can help you identify if someone is being pressured or manipulated before the fraud goes too far.

1.2 Sample Scenarios of Digital Arrest Scams in India

(a) *The Bengaluru "Parcel Containing Illegal Items" Scam (2024)*

A woman received a sudden call stating that a package in her name had been stopped at Mumbai Airport. The person on the other end of the line said it had drugs and illegal documents in it. She was shocked and scared, and right away she was connected to someone who said he was a "Cyber Crime Officer.". He spoke with authority and told her that she was in big trouble and could be arrested if she didn't "verify her financial activity" right away. After that, there was a six-hour video call during which the scammers showed her fake police IDs, spoke in a way that sounded official, and kept her emotionally overwhelmed. They told her not to hang up or talk to anyone because it could make her "case" worse.

She was scared and wanted to prove she was innocent, so she did what they said and sent ₹15 lakh to what they called a "verification account." She did not realize she had been tricked into a digital arrest scam until she finally talked to her family. She then went to the police and made a complaint.

(b) *"Your Aadhaar is linked to money laundering"—Delhi (2023)*

A young IT professional in Delhi received an unexpected call from someone claiming to be from the Delhi Police. The caller sounded official and serious, saying that the man's Aadhaar number had been used to open fake bank accounts linked to money laundering.

The caller told him that a non-bailable warrant was about to be issued in his name and that his passport could be blacklisted before he could understand what was going on. The tone, the sense of urgency, and the fear of being falsely accused were too much for him. He felt stuck and was desperate to clear his name, so he listened as the scammer told him he could "temporarily secure" his identity by sending money for verification. He sent ₹4 lakh as a "security deposit" because he was afraid of getting in trouble with the law. He didn't realize he had been tricked by a digital arrest scam until later, when he talked to friends and double-checked the information.

(c) *"CBI Video Call Investigation" in Chennai (2024)*

A businessman in Chennai got a WhatsApp call from someone who said he was a CBI officer. The man on the video call seemed to be sitting in what looked like a CBI "virtual office room," complete with badges and files. The backgrounds were made with AI so they looked official.

The person on the other end of the line said he was being looked into for connections to an international drug ring. They showed him a fake FIR on the screen and told him he could be arrested right away if he didn't cooperate. He didn't have time to react. The businessman felt trapped because he was scared and shocked. The scammers kept pushing him, saying he had to send them money to "resolve the matter" and avoid being arrested. He ended up sending ₹32 lakh because he was scared and confused. When he later got in touch with the real authorities, he found out that the whole thing—the video background, the FIR, and the officer's name—had been made up as part of a digital arrest scam.

(d) *International Courier Scam"—Mumbai (2024)*

The student received a phone call which revealed that her passport together with bank details appeared inside a box which authorities discovered in Taiwan. The scammers used AI technology to clone voices which they applied for their police officer impersonation in India. The people who watched her told her that they needed her assistance for help. She transferred an amount of ₹3.8 lakh because she wanted to avoid getting caught by cybercrime authorities.

(e) *Targeted with AI Voice Cloning in Kerala (2024)*

Recently, a medical student in Kerala fell for a disturbing digital arrest scam that used AI voice cloning. The student got a call that sounded just like a relative they knew, which made the situation seem real and urgent. Not long after, the scammers switched to a video call and pretended to be police officers, saying that the student was involved in a serious case. They made the student panic and confused by using a fake voice and a video setup that looked official. This made the student feel like they had to do what they said. The incident shows how scammers are now using advanced AI tools to emotionally manipulate young people and make their threats feel completely believable.

(f) *Senior Citizen Coerced Through False Charges and Intimidation—Hyderabad (2024)*

A senior citizen in Hyderabad had a scary experience when scammers posing as Customs and Cyber Crime officials called him and made a shocking claim. They said that a package connected to his Aadhaar had illegal things in it and that he could get a non-bailable warrant if he didn't help. He was kept on the phone for a long time and told not to talk to anyone else, which made him scared and confused. The scammers used official-sounding language and fake documents to make everything feel real, slowly pushing him into believing he had no choice but to transfer money to "verification accounts." Out of fear of being arrested, he ended up losing ₹1.2 crore before realizing it was all a scam.

(g) *Retired Fire Brigade officer Loses Rs 21 Lakh—Ahmedabad (2024)*

A retired Fire Brigade officer in Maninagar, who is 78 years old, got a WhatsApp video call from an unknown number. The caller on the other end of the line pretended to be a Mumbai Crime Branch sub inspector. He sent a fake police ID card with official seals and signatures to make himself look real, even though the video was off. He said that the complainant's Aadhaar card was found during a raid on a businessman's bungalow and was supposedly connected to a money laundering case. The person on the other end of the line said that if he didn't do what they said, a police team would arrest him, keep him in jail for 90 days, and even "give him the third degree." He sent a fake PDF called "Arrest and Freezing Orders" with the logos of the ED, CBI, and the Supreme Court on it to back up his claims. It was said to have been issued under PMLA and FEMA.

The retired officer was so scared that he talked to the caller again the next day, when the caller again pretended to be a crime branch officer. This time, he wanted private information about the officer and his family, saying that a Supreme Court judge needed it to confirm something. The officer was then told to move money from his accounts to "check whether it was white or black," all in the name of following the law.

The victim sent Rs 20.90 Lakh through several bank accounts that the scammer gave them. After each transfer, the scammer sent fake receipts with the words "Government of India-Enforcement Directorate" on them. Two con artists from Mysuru pretended to be Bangalore Police and Karnataka police Crime Branch officers. They stole more than Rs 1 crore from a 74-year-old man in Rajarhat while keeping him "digitally arrested" in a hotel in New Town for three days. They were taken from Karnataka and brought to Kolkata on a transit remand. The victim got a call from people pretending to be Bengaluru Police officers. They said that his SIM card was used to send out illegal ads and that he was involved in human trafficking. Someone sent him a fake Supreme Court order to scare him. The callers told him to come in for "interrogation," and the victim stayed at the hotel for three days, making payments in several transactions.

(h) *Senior Citizen Trapped in a Sophisticated Digital Arrest Scam: Chandigarh (2024)*

A 73-year-old man from Chandigarh, Shashi Kumar Sahai, went through a deeply distressing experience after cybercriminals trapped him in a "digital arrest" scam. Pretending to be officials from TRAI and the Enforcement Directorate, the fraudsters frightened him with false accusations of money laundering. They even created a fake courtroom over video call and kept him under constant video watch for more than two weeks, isolating him and preying on his fears as a senior citizen. Terrified of being arrested, Sahai followed their instructions and transferred a total of ₹52 lakh, believing he was cooperating with real authorities. The truth came out only when his son noticed something was wrong and discovered the ongoing manipulation. The family immediately reported the scam on the National Cyber Crime Reporting Portal.

Based on analyzing various patterns across all real cases in the scenarios, the scammers:

1. Create instant fear (drugs, crimes, warrants, etc.)
2. Impersonate authorities (Police, CBI, Customs, RBI, Banks, Courier Services)
3. Use AI tools (deepfake backgrounds, voice cloning, fake video rooms)
4. Keep victims under continuous pressure on long video calls
5. Demand "verification" or "security" payments.

Modus Operandi (MO), is a "method of operating." In criminology, cybersecurity, and investigative studies, it refers to the distinctive pattern or systematic approach used by an individual or group while committing an act—whether it is a crime, scam, attack, or any recurring activity. The MO describes the typical behaviors, techniques, tools, and sequence of actions that define how a particular operation is carried out (Anisha 2024; Li et al. 2019).

Understanding the modus operandi is crucial because it helps investigators, researchers, and security professionals identify patterns, anticipate future actions, and develop effective prevention and detection strategies. In modern digital environments, analyzing MO has become essential for recognizing emerging cyber threats such as phishing attacks, financial fraud, and digital arrest scams. Figure 4 represents Modus of operandi for Digital Arrest Scam Process.

A digital arrest scam operates through a multi-stage social engineering pipeline designed to induce fear, enforce isolation, and enable financial coercion.

Fig. 4 Modus of operandi for digital arrest scam process

1.3 Digital Arrest Scam Process

A digital arrest scam usually starts with a sudden call from someone pretending to be from the police, CBI, Customs, or a courier company, claiming that your ID, SIM, or a parcel in your name is linked to a crime. Before you can process anything, they pass you to a so-called senior officer who speaks very formally to make it sound official (Vaswani 2025). They then push you onto a video call that looks like a police station or control room, sometimes using AI-made backgrounds or fake officer faces. Once you're on the call, they keep you scared and isolated—telling you not to talk to anyone, threatening warrants or arrest, and insisting you stay online. In that pressure, they convince you to transfer money to a "verification" or "safe" government account. Only after the call ends do most victims realize it was a scam and rush to report it to the 1930 helpline or the cybercrime portal. Figure 5 represents digital arrest scam process.

1.4 Proposed Methodology

Most digital arrest scams rely on emotional manipulation of their victims. Scammers play the role of powerful authorities, keeping the victim engaged in hours-long video calls to intimidate them and create a feeling of urgency. The proposed approach utilizes FER backed by Responsible AI principles to detect signs related to stress or panic on the victim's face during such video calls. If the system detects that someone is becoming frightened or overwhelmed, it can quickly trigger helpful alerts or warnings, giving the person a chance to realize something is wrong before they fall victim to the scam.

(a) **Responsible AI**

Responsible AI is all about making sure that artificial intelligence is used in a way that is safe, fair, and beneficial for people. AI is changing rapidly, and the notion of Responsible AI has helped to transform regular cities into smart cities that are more efficient, ethical, and tech-savvy (Navarathna and Malagi n.d.). AI systems are becoming part of our lives for navigating cities, using public services, and even keeping us safe online. It is important that they act fairly and openly. Responsible AI does not think about what AI can do; it thinks about what AI should do. It wants to ensure that smart technologies help people, keep their communities safer, and build trust rather than hurting them or causing confusion.

(b) **FER or Facial Emotion Recognition System**

A system with FER can tell how someone is feeling by looking at their face. The development of AI systems which understand and speak with humans naturally depends heavily on FER as their core essential component. The statement applies to various fields which include security and healthcare and affective computing and human-computer interaction (Salah and Hayder 2026; Chen et al. 2020). The system introduces another level of security-related awareness. The system enables systems to identify when users show signs of fear or stress or confusion or physical pain. The system tracks both spoken words and emotional responses which users show during their conversations. The tool shows its usefulness when people need help because they face stressful situations or experience threats or lose their freedom.

By reading emotional cues in real time, FER can help security platforms identify unusual or high-risk situations faster. The system detects fear during video calls and distress signals from suspected scammer conversations which it uses to create preemptive security alerts. The main purpose of this method focuses on protecting human beings instead of monitoring system activities or data storage. Users should beware digital spaces according to FER because it searches for emotional risk indicators which people typically fail to identify.

The objective of the proposed methodology uses Facial Emotion Recognition (FER) and Responsible AI (RAI) to identify emotional distress in real time and trigger specific early-warning actions to prevent victimization. Figure 6 represents the flow chart of the work proposed. The proposed workflow consists of six major phases:

1. Input acquisition (call/video monitoring)
2. Preprocessing and face detection
3. FER-based emotional assessment
4. Responsible AI language and behavior analysis
5. Risk classification and decision layer
6. Intervention and user safety response.

Phase 1: Input Acquisition (Call/Video Monitoring).

The system will automatically trigger itself when a user enters into voice or video calls, acting like a protector in the background. Temporarily capturing the video and audio streams on the user's device only, the system ensures that privacy is never compromised. Nothing becomes uploaded

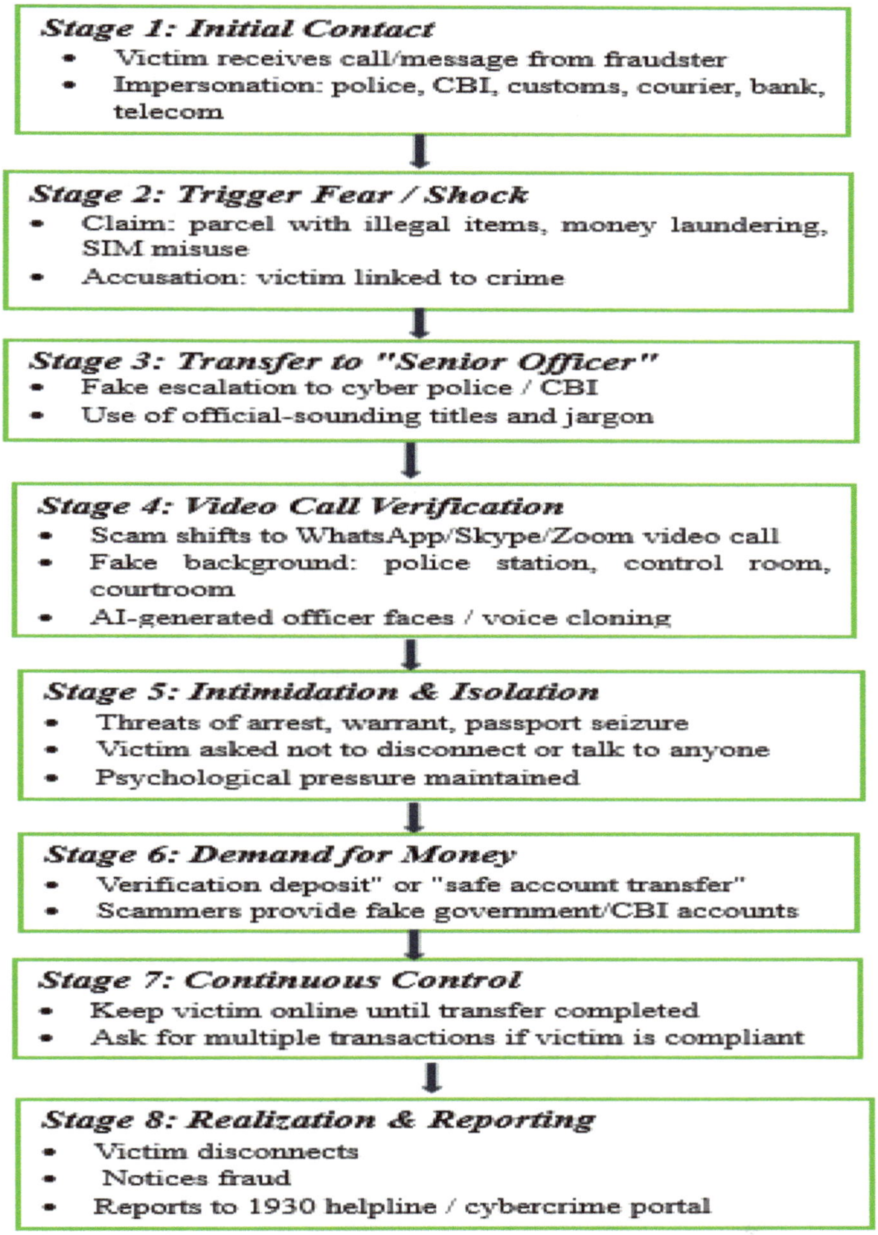

Fig. 5 Digital arrest scam process

or shared anywhere; every piece of processing happens locally, so the user remains fully in control of their data. In this process, the system pays heed to natural cues such as facial expressions from the video frames and the tone of one's voice if enabled. These inputs tune the system to feel and sense whether the person might be under stress or emotional pressure, thus enabling it to extend support in a manner that would make it safe, respectful, and human-centered.

The system captures video and audio streams in real time:

$$F_t = \text{VideoFrame}(t),\ A_t = \text{AudioSegment}(t)$$

$$\mathbf{x}_{\text{input}}(t) = [F_t, A_t].$$

where

- $F_t \in \mathrm{R}^{H \times W \times 3}$ is the video frame at time t
- $A_t \in \mathrm{R}^{N_a}$ is the audio segment
- $\mathbf{x}_{\text{input}}(t)$ is the combined raw input vector

No cloud transfer occurs: $D_{\text{cloud}} = 0$.

Phase 2: Preprocessing and Face Detection

FER requires clean and normalized input for accurate emotion prediction.

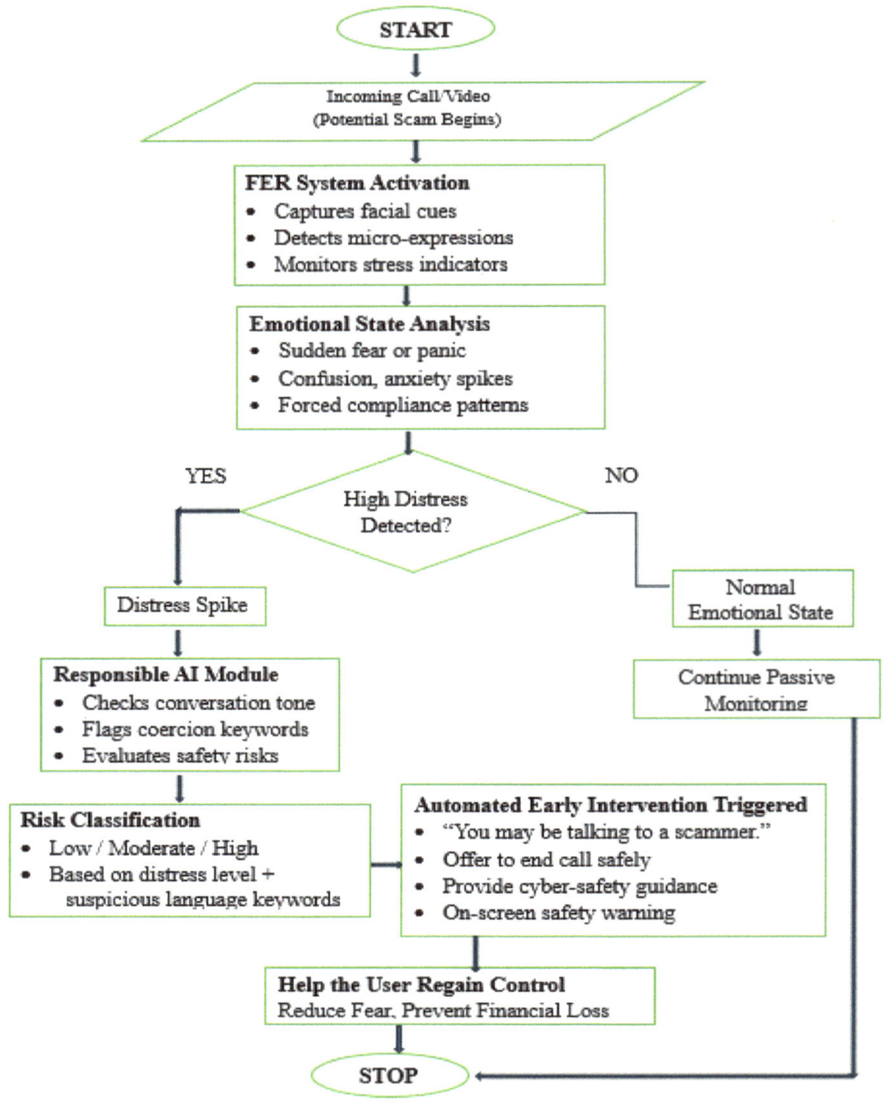

Fig. 6 Flowchart of proposed methodology

Steps

(a) **Frame Extraction**: Frames are captured at 5–10 FPS.

Just like people can listen more efficiently when the environment is clear and calm, this FER system would require clean and well-prepared input at first to understand the right emotions. It begins by softly picking key frames from the video-about 5–10 per second-so it can follow along the user's expressions without clogging up the system.

(b) **Face Localization**: It identifies the region of the face using MTCNN/Haar Cascade/

Retina Face. Then it focuses on the face itself by utilizing some reliable detectors like MTCNN, Haar Cascade, or Retina Face to make sure that it is looking at the right region.

(c) **Landmark Detection**: It detects key points-eyes, eyebrows, mouth.

It then maps significant facial landmarks: the eyes, eyebrows, and mouth, which are important features that would be recognized during conversation by humans.

(d) **Normalization**: These frames are then normalized into standard-sized frames of 48 × 48 or 224 × 224, grayscale or RGB, and lighting conditions are made in such a way that emotions are not distorted due to shadows or brightness.

(e) **Noise Filtering**:

Removes motion blur and poor-quality frames.

These frames are then normalized to a standard size of 48 × 48 or 224 × 224, changed to grayscale or RGB, and fixed for lighting to remove any shadows or brightness that may distort the emotions. Finally, it filters out noisy or blurred frames caused by either movement or poor quality cameras. This will help the FER model get clean, stable input so it can read the emotions with greater precision and respect.

Extract face bounding boxes and normalize frames:

$$B_t = \text{FaceDetector}(F_t)$$

$$F_t' = \text{CropResize}(F_t, B_t) \in \text{R}^{h \times w \times 3}$$

Optional feature extraction for audio:

$$\phi_a(A_t) = \text{MFCC}(A_t) \in \mathbb{R}^{d_a}$$

Phase 3: FER-Based Emotional Analysis

The FER model works like a real-time emotional observer, quietly analyzing facial cues to understand what a person might be feeling during a call. It uses advanced AI techniques—such as CNN-based models, transfer-learning networks like VGGFace, ResNet, or Mobile Net, and sometimes LSTM layers to follow emotional changes over time. The practice of using transfer learning facilitates in developing fast prototype new machine learning models using pre-trained models (R. Ribani and M. Marengoni, "A Survey of Transfer Learning for Convolutional Neural Networks," 2019). With these tools, the system can recognize emotions such as fear, anger, sadness, stress, confusion, surprise, or even a neutral state. Beyond basic emotions, it also pays attention to subtle behavioral signals: sudden spikes in fear, long periods of stress, forced nodding, tense eyebrows, tightly pressed lips, or an unusual fixed gaze. Based on all these observations, the model produces probability scores for each emotion and combines them into a single "distress index." This index helps indicate whether the person might be under pressure, scared, or being manipulated—allowing timely support in situations like digital arrest scams.

Compute stress/emotion score from video frames using facial expression recognition (FER):

$$\phi_v(F_t') = \text{FeatureExtractor}(F_t') \in R^{d_v}$$

$$s_v(t) = \sigma\left(f_v\left(\phi_v\left(F_t'\right)\right)\right)$$

where

- $f_v(\cdot)$ = FER model (MLP or CNN head)
- $\sigma(\cdot)$ = sigmoid function mapping score to [0,1]
- $s_v(t)$ = visual stress score

Similarly, audio-based stress score:

$$s_a(t) = \sigma(f_a(\phi_a(A_t)))$$

Phase 4: Responsible AI Language and Behavior Analysis

The FER system operates to determine user emotional states through their detection of emotional expressions. The Responsible AI (RAI) module operates by processing both the verbal content and the vocal characteristics of human speech. The system begins by transforming the caller's spoken words into written text. The system searches for specific terms which might create problems, including "arrest," "warrant," "verification deposit," "money laundering," and the commands "do not disconnect," and "you are under investigation." The system analyses the language patterns to detect threatening or coercive, or overly dramatic, or scary content in the speech. The system detects hidden risk indicators which include false legal power claims and secretive behavior requirements, and sudden financial payment requests from users. The RAI framework mandates systems to operate under moral standards which stop them from creating false alarms or producing discriminatory results. It also stops them from making unjust choices. The module analyzes both the discussion content and emotional expressions to produce two distinct results, which include a Coercion Score that measures conversation forcefulness, and a Conversation Risk Score which identifies potential scam or high-pressure situations.

If text or linguistic cues are available:

$$T_t = \text{SpeechToText}(A_t)$$

$$\phi_l(T_t) = \text{LanguageFeatureExtractor}(T_t) \in \text{R}^{d_l}$$

$$s_l(t) = \sigma(f_l(\phi_l(T_t)))$$

$s_l(t)$ = language/coercion stress score.

Phase 5: Risk Classification and Decision Layer

The system unites FER and RAI data to build an intelligent risk model which identifies user feelings and analyzes communication patterns between users. The system analyzes multiple elements at once by checking user distress levels and forced speech detection and suspicious phrase frequency and emotional changes from baseline and stress duration tracking. Based on these signals, the system places the situation into one of four levels:

(a) Low risk—where everything seems normal;
(b) Moderate risk—where early signs of fear or pressure begin to appear;
(c) High risk—where emotional distress and threatening language clearly show up; and
(d) Critical risk—where the user may be in immediate danger of financial manipulation.

To make these decisions, the system uses a mix of rule-based thresholds, machine-learning classifiers, weighted scoring, and time-based pattern tracking. Together, these techniques help the system respond in a calm, human-centered way, aiming to protect the user before any harm occurs.

Combine modalities into a single risk score:

Fusion:

$$E_{\text{inst}}(t) = w_v s_v(t) + w_a s_a(t) + w_l s_l(t),\ w_v + w_a + w_l = 1$$

Temporal smoothing:

$$E_{\text{smooth}}(t) = (1 - \gamma)E_{\text{smooth}}(t - 1) + \gamma E_{\text{inst}}(t)$$

Contextual risk function (optional metadata):

$$R(t) = \psi(E_{\text{smooth}}(t), \mathbf{c}_t)$$

Decision rule (alert trigger):

$$\text{Alert}(t) = \begin{cases} 1, & R(t) \geq \theta \\ 0, & R(t) < \theta \end{cases}$$

Phase 6: Intervention and Safety Response

When the system detects a critical or high-risk scenario, it triggers responsible and non-intrusive warnings.

When the system realizes that the user may be in real danger—feeling scared, pressured, or pushed into something harmful—it steps in gently, almost like a concerned friend. It doesn't interrupt harshly; instead, it shows a calm on-screen message saying that the call might be unsafe and that the user may be under emotional stress. It also offers simple, reassuring choices: the user can end the call safely with one tap or instantly access trusted cyber-safety guidance. Helpful reminders appear too—such as the fact that real government officers never ask for money over a phone call—so the user can regain confidence and think clearly. If the situation feels overwhelming, the system can, with the user's permission, alert a trusted person or connect directly to official support like 1930 or the cybercrime portal. And through all of this, it never crosses personal boundaries: everything is processed privately on the device, nothing is recorded without permission, and every response is designed with emotional care to make the user feel protected rather than watched.

Select the best intervention based on alert and context:

$$a^*(t) = \arg\max_{a \in \mathcal{A}} U(a \mid R(t), \mathbf{c}_t)$$

where

- $\mathcal{A}$ = set of possible interventions (e.g., soft nudge, exit call, contact trusted person)
- $U(a \mid \cdot)$ = utility of action (soft, human-centered)
- Execute the selected intervention:

$$\text{Execute}\big(a^*(t)\big)$$

Figure 7 represents the block diagram representing the various phases involved and the corresponding mathematical equations associated with each of the phases.

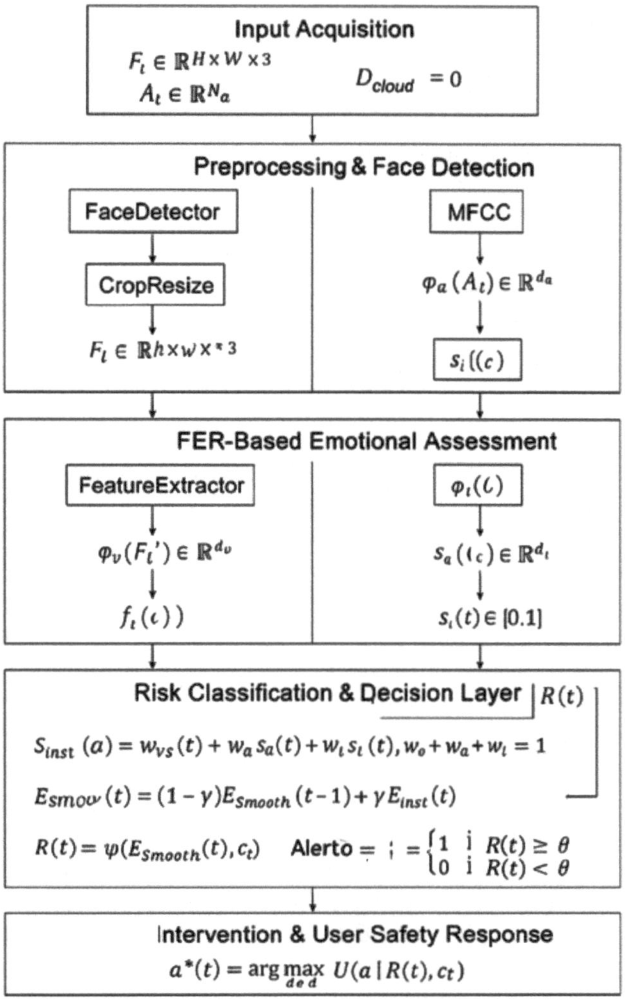

Fig. 7 Mathematical equations associated with each of the phases

Pseudocode: FER_RAI_Early_Intervention

Input: VideoStream V, AudioTextStream T

Output: RiskLevel, SafetyIntervention

```
INITIALIZATION
Load FER_Model
Load RAI_Language_Model
Set Distress_Threshold = θ_d
Set Coercion_Threshold = θ_c
Set Risk_Threshold_High = θ_h
Initialize Distress Index = 0
Initialize Coercion_Score = 0
REAL-TIME MONITORING LOOP
while Call_Is_Active do
   // Stage 1: Facial Expression Recognition
   Frame ← CaptureFrame(V)
   FER_Output ← FER_Model.Predict(Frame)
   Distress_Signal ← Extract_Distress(FER_Output)

   Update Distress_Index:
     Distress_Index ← Smooth(Distress_Index, Distress_Signal)

   // Stage 2: Emotional State Decision
   if Distress_Index > Distress_Threshold then
      Emotional_State ← "High_Distress"
   else
      Emotional_State ← "Normal"

   // Stage 3: Responsible AI Conversation Analysis
   TextChunk ← Transcribe(T)
   Tone, Keywords ← RAI_Language_Model.Analyze(TextChunk)
   Coercion_Score ← Calculate_Coercion(Tone, Keywords)

   if Coercion_Score > Coercion_Threshold then
      RAI_State ← "Suspicious_Conversation"
   else
      RAI_State ← "Safe"

   // Stage 4: Multimodal Risk Classification
   RiskLevel ← Classify_Risk(Emotional_State, RAI_State,
                  Distress_Index, Coercion_Score)

      // Stage 5: Early Intervention Decision
   if RiskLevel ≥ Risk_Threshold_High then
      Trigger_Intervention()
      DisplayWarning("You may be talking to a scammer.")
      OfferSafeExitOptions()
      ProvideCyberSafetyTips()
      LogEvent(RiskLevel, Distress_Index, Coercion_Score)
      break
   // Stage 6: Continue Passive Monitoring Otherwise
   else
      ContinueMonitoring()
end while
RETURN RESULTS
return RiskLevel, SafetyIntervention
```

1.5 Indian Government Initiatives to Prevent Digital Arrest Scam in Smart City Ecosystem

Digital arrest scams have become a worrying problem in India, where scammers pretend to be police or government officers and use fear to trick people—often over video calls or WhatsApp (Babu 2025). These scams lead to severe emotional suffering which results in numerous unsuspecting victims experiencing fear that drives them to lose their financial resources. The Indian Government has established multiple essential security measures to protect citizens because these frauds are spreading at a fast pace. The government has established helplines which people can access quickly while running public education initiatives and they have strengthened their cyber surveillance systems and develop methods to identify and stop fake phone calls to build public trust for digital platform security. The Government of India has established measures which defend the entire country against Digital Arrest Scam attacks.

(a) ***Indian Cyber Crime Coordination Centre (I4C)***

The Ministry of Home Affairs operates I4C to defend citizens from digital arrest scams and all types of online fraud activities. The system creates a connection between state cybercrime teams which enables them to share information at high speeds for better scam network detection. The combination of modern tools with Responsible AI systems at I4C enables them to track fake VoIP phone numbers while they identify suspicious banking operations which scammers use and they discover unlawful call centers that conduct victim attacks. The AI systems help investigators through their ability to identify unusual patterns which protect user privacy and prevent wrong identification of innocent people. I4C achieves digital security for all Indians through its implementation of intelligent solutions which combines their data protection system with dedicated team members.

(b) ***1930 — National Cybercrime Helpline***

The 1930 cybercrime helpline provides an immediate response to victims who discover their online scam and threat situations after they have already identified themselves as victims. People who experience a digital arrest scam can reach out to this number for immediate assistance while they explain their situation. The helpline team works with banks and digital payment services to track down fraudulent transactions which attempt to vanish into untraceable accounts. Smart Cities operate control centers which unite modern technological systems with command infrastructure to strengthen their operational management and their cyber defense teams receive improved support. The Responsible AI tools function as scam pattern detectors while they perform threat signal analysis and maintain protected communication systems. Together, these efforts give victims confidence that a reliable, technology-driven system is ready to help the moment they need it.

(c) ***National Cybercrime Reporting Portal (NCRP)***

The National Cybercrime Reporting Portal (cybercrime.gov.in) provides users with an easy platform to file complaints about digital arrest scams together with other impersonation frauds (Gupta et al. n.d.). People can now report digital arrest scams and impersonation frauds through The National Cybercrime Reporting Portal which functions as an online platform. Users can submit their evidence which includes call logs and screenshots and audio recordings to help authorities understand what occurred. The portal directs all received complaints to their proper state cyber police team which starts the investigative process. Smart Cities operate their systems through command-and-control centers which merge various data streams to detect patterns and activate instant response systems. The system receives additional improvements through Responsible AI which performs complaint sorting and suspicious behavior detection and urgent case identification while protecting both privacy and fairness standards. The portal allows citizens to take action while improving the nation's ability to fight against emerging cyber threats.

(d) ***Ministry of Home Affairs Advisory***

The Ministry of Home Affairs (MHA) maintains a regular schedule for releasing digital arrest scam warnings which help citizens stay protected from falling into these deceptive schemes. These advisories explain how scammers pretend to be officials from agencies like the CBI, Police, NCB, Customs, or even the RBI, and how they use fake arrest warrants or video calls to scare victims into compliance. The government advises citizens to reject any contact with unidentified callers who assert they work for official government entities. Smart Cities use command-and-control centers and public display boards and community awareness initiatives to increase their advisory messages which spread quickly to more residents. The government has started using Responsible AI tools to detect scam operations and track new fraud methods while showing immediate warning messages to the general public through safe and ethical communication channels. The combination of these activities enables people to develop better handling abilities for suspicious phone calls and messages which they encounter.

(e) ***DoT Blocking Fraudulent Numbers and Apps***

The Department of Telecommunications (DoT) blocks fraudulent numbers and suspicious apps before they reach people to achieve their mission of stopping digital arrest scams. Through the Sanchar Saathi portal, citizens can check whether their Aadhaar is linked to unknown SIM cards, report scam numbers, and even help track SIM misuse. The Department of Telecommunications operates advanced artificial intelligence systems which identify fake caller identification and detect major patterns of fraudulent telecommunication activities through Voice over Internet Protocol services. Multiple Smart Cities run their systems through command-and-control centers which enable them to spot unusual call activities for immediate response. Organizations achieve threat detection through Responsible AI because this system performs threat analysis operations which protect user data during its threat identification process. The combined efforts between these groups create a challenging environment for scammers to operate while they work to defend everyday communication from security threats.

(g) ***RCERT-In Warnings and Circulars***

The main cybersecurity agency of India known as CERT-In distributes security alerts and official notices which help citizens defend themselves against developing digital threats including digital arrest scams. The advisories present typical scam methods which they use to fight and they show users how to protect themselves during video calls and when they use remote access applications and share OTPs. Smart City ecosystems depend on technology to link their residents with their built environment and public facilities so they need Responsible AI systems to send proper warning messages which protect people and build digital trust. Smart City ecosystems depend on technology to link their residents with their built environment and public facilities so they need Responsible AI systems to send proper warning messages which protect people and build digital trust.

(f) ***RBI & Banks' Cyber Fraud Mitigation Measures***

The Reserve Bank of India (RBI) protects digital environments from digital arrest scams through its advanced cyber fraud prevention systems. The banking system detects strange account operations through Hawk-Eye tracking technology which blocks suspicious accounts after customers file complaints. The public learns to identify fake police threats through educational programs which the RBI runs under its "RBI Kehta Hai" initiative. The Smart City network depends on Responsible AI (RAI) to improve its protection systems through advanced pattern recognition which detects digital arrest threats and produces ethical warning messages that defend people while developing trust in digital financial systems.

(g) ***State Cyber Police Awareness Drives***

State Cyber Police across India are actively running awareness drives—such as Mumbai Cyber Safe, Hyderabad Cyber Warriors, Delhi Cyber Cell Alerts, and Tamil Nadu Cyber Crime Wing advisories—to protect citizens from evolving threats like digital arrest scams. These initiatives use classroom sessions, WhatsApp alerts, and media campaigns to help people understand real-world cyber risks in simple, relatable ways. In a growing Smart City environment, where citizens rely heavily on connected services, integrating Responsible AI (RAI) can strengthen these efforts by offering timely, ethical, and personalized safety alerts, ensuring people stay informed and feel supported in their daily digital interactions.

1.6 Digital Safety in Smart City Environments: How RAI Principles Help Victims to Respond for Digital Arrest Scams

Smart cities depend on their digital networks which connect public services to surveillance systems and online payment systems and mobility applications and citizen communication platforms. The technological progress has made life easier for people but it has created new ways for criminals to perform digital arrests by pretending to be police officers who demand money and personal information. Smart cities use digital services which operate as their fundamental foundation. The system brings better convenience to users but it creates higher risks for people to become victims of fraudulent activities. Key vulnerabilities include:

High Digital Dependence: People now send most of their messages through digital platforms which include apps and chatbots and online systems that allow others to impersonate them. The system allows users to send messages through digital platforms which makes restating the trust system difficult to achieve.

Trust in Digital Authorities: Scammers take advantage of people who believe in official smart city messages that come from authorized sources. Smart city databases store vital information which hackers could try to steal by breaking into these systems.

Rapid Information Flow: Fake emergency notices and legal warnings spread more quickly through digital channels which operate as their primary distribution method.

Applying Responsible AI (RAI) principles like Accountability, Transparency, Privacy and Data Governance, Societal and environmental well-being (Papagiannidis et al. 2025) strengthens public safety and empowers individuals to respond effectively. Below are practical, actionable solutions built around RAI and smart city security frameworks. Table 1 represents Responsible AI principles, how it prevents the victims and how victims can avoid from being trapped into digital arrest scam.

Table 1 represents How RAI principles—Transparency, Accountability, Data Privacy, Safety and Security are involved in ensuring the protection and steps that can be taken by the victims to safeguard themselves from the digital arrest scam.

Responsible AI (RAI) principles help people stay calm and informed when facing digital arrest scams. Instead of reacting out of fear, victims are encouraged to pause, verify the information through trusted sources, and never share personal or financial details with unknown callers or messages. RAI promotes transparency and human oversight, reminding individuals that genuine authorities do not threaten or pressure people online. By reporting such incidents to cybercrime cells and digital platforms, victims not only protect themselves but also help prevent others from being targeted. In this way, RAI supports safer digital behavior and builds confidence in handling online threats wisely.

2 Future Directions

The increasing incidence of Digital Arrest scams, where cybercriminals exploit fear and authority through video-based impersonation of law-enforcement agencies, necessitates intelligent and ethical technological countermeasures.

The future will see Facial Expression Recognition (FER) systems working together with Responsible Artificial Intelligence (RAI) principles to establish a protective environment for Smart City residents. The future of Smart Cities depends on the combination of Facial Expression Recognition (FER) systems with Responsible AI (RAI) principles to create better urban environments. The city operates through its technological system which detects emergency situations by identifying distress signals that include fear and anxiety and coercion indicators. The systems need designers to work with them because they must protect personal privacy and preserve human dignity and all rights that belong to individuals.

Future FER-enabled systems will focus on real-time detection of emotional distress indicators such as fear, anxiety, panic, and confusion during live video calls. These emotional states are commonly triggered during digital arrest scams and serve as reliable behavioral signals of coercion. By detecting such anomalies early, the system can assist users before irreversible harm occurs.

There is still a lot of room to do better in protecting people from digital arrest scams. In the coming years, technology can become more caring and user-friendly, giving clear and calm warnings when a scam is suspected instead of confusing alerts. Banks, mobile networks, and apps can work together to send instant alerts or temporarily block risky transactions to protect users. More local, language-friendly awareness programs can help reach people who may not be comfortable with technology. By continuing to learn from real experiences and putting people first, the future holds strong potential to make the digital world safer and more reassuring for everyone.

3 Conclusion

The security system of smart cities will become more effective because they combine Responsible AI principles with Facial Emotion Recognition technology to protect their citizens from digital arrest scams. The design of AI system should help to recognize signs of fear, stress, or pressure, doing so in a fair, transparent, and privacy conscious way. Smart cities can identify potential digital arrest scam circumstances earlier and support citizens before they face financial loss or fall into emotional distress.

The solution needs more than technology to solve the problem. These systems need three essential components to work properly which include established rules and public education and continuous monitoring to prevent unintentional damage and maintain proper usage. People can achieve security through responsible AI and emotion-aware technology usage because these systems function as reliable support systems which provide digital safety and emotional comfort and increased trust in virtual environments.

The future development of FER systems within Smart City Ecosystems will focus on ethical systems which protect privacy and center their design on human needs to stop digital arrest scams while protecting citizen privacy and maintaining public trust.

Table 1 RAI principles—how victims can respond to digital arrest scams

RAI principles	How it protects victims	What victims can do
Transparency	Scammers thrive on confusion. Smart city systems using RAI ensure official communication is transparent, consistent, and verifiable	Verification of any officer or agency contacting you through official apps, verified websites, or government helplines QR-code–based verification or digital ID systems provided by your smart city
Accountability	RAI-based systems keep traceable record of every complaint, ensuring accountability	Report scams immediately via your city's citizen service portal or cyber grievance platform In India, use National Cybercrime Portal (www.cybercrime.gov.in), Cybercrime Helpline (1930), Smart-city complaint trackers like SacharSathi. Save call logs, screenshots, and transaction information as evidence.
Data privacy	Smart cities following RAI ensure citizen data is encrypted, access-restricted, and monitored	Never share Aadhaar, PAN, bank OTPs, or account details with anyone over the phone Disable unnecessary app permissions—Camera, mic, storage—On suspicious apps Install apps only from trusted Smart City or government app stores
Safety and security	RAI encourages secure-by-design technologies and awareness tools	Update passwords and enable two-factor authentication across all accounts Use antivirus tools and regularly update device software Check for suspicious apps or remote-access tools scammers may have installed

References

Anisha M., Identification of Patterns in Crimes: A Study on Principle of Modus Operandi and Its Attributes, 7 (1) IJLMH Page 2028–2039 (2024). https://doi.org/10.10000/IJLMH.116963

Japan Babu, Dr. Vikalp Shrivastava, "The Evolution of Digital Arrest Cyber-Crimes in India: Trends and Patterns Preventive Measures", International Journal of Environmental Sciences, ISSN: 2229-7359 Vol. 11 No. 15s, 2025

A. Chen, H. Xing and F. Wang, "A Facial Expression Recognition Method Using Deep Convolutional Neural Networks Based on Edge Computing," in *IEEE Access*, vol. 8, pp. 49741–49751, 2020. https://doi.org/10.1109/ACCESS.2020.2980060.

Vaibhav Gupta & Vidhi Mittal, "Digital Arrests and the Law: A Comparative Analysis of Regulatory Frameworks in India, the European Union, and the United States", National Journal for Legal Research and Innovative Ideas, ISSN(0): 2582-8665, Volume 3, Issue 5, 2025

Aman Jain, S Nitin, Kishandeep KJ, S Ridhi, Varalakshmi, The rise of digital arrests: Implications for cybercrime and justice, Journal of International Research for Engineering & Management, Volume: 05 Issue: 04 2025

Yu-Sheng Li, Ming-Liang Qi, An approach for understanding offender modus operandi to detect serial robbery crimes, Journal of Computational Science, Volume 36, 2019, 101024, ISSN 1877-7503. https://doi.org/10.1016/j.jocs.2019.101024.

Mallick, Saroj Shekhar, (2024) "Digital Arrest Scams in India: Challenges and Solutions Under the IT Act, 2000", December 25, 2024. Available at SSRN: https://ssrn.com/abstract=5076535 or https://doi.org/10.2139/ssrn.5076535. 2024

P. J. Navarathna and V. P. Malagi, "Artificial Intelligence in Smart City Analysis," *2018 International Conference on Smart Systems and Inventive Technology (ICSSIT)*, Tirunelveli, India, 2018, pp. 44–47. https://doi.org/10.1109/ICSSIT.2018.8748476.

Emmanouil Papagiannidis, Patrick Mikalef, Kieran Conboy, "Responsible artificial intelligence governance: A review and research framework", Journal of Strategic Information Systems, Published by Elsevier B.V, 2025. https://doi.org/10.1016/j.jsis.2024.101885

Archana Singh Parmar, Monika Sharma, "A New Frontier in Cybercrime and Its Repercussions: Digital Arrest", International Journal for Multidisciplinary Research, Volume 7, Issue 1, January–February 2025

R. Ribani and M. Marengoni, A Survey of Transfer Learning for Convolutional Neural Networks, 2019 32nd SIBGRAPI Conference on Graphics, Patterns and Images Tutorials (SIBGRAPI-T), Rio de Janeiro, Brazil, 2019, pp. 47–57. https://doi.org/10.1109/SIBGRAPI-T.2019.00010.

Salah, S., Hayder, S. (2026). Advancing Real-Time Facial Expression Recognition: A Deep Learning-Based Video Stream Analysis. In: Al-Mamory, S.O., *et al.* Cybersecurity and Artificial Intelligence Strategies. CAIS 2025. Communications in Computer and Information Science, vol 2693. Springer, Cham. https://doi.org/10.1007/978-3-032-07244-3_13

T. Singh, A. Solanki, S. K. Sharma, A. Nayyar and A. Paul, "A Decade Review on Smart Cities: Paradigms, Challenges and Opportunities," in IEEE Access, vol. 10, pp. 68319-68364, 2022. https://doi.org/10.1109/ACCESS.2022.3184710.

Preesha Vaswani, "Digital Arrest Scam: Navigating Legal Challenges and Solutions within the Indian Criminal Justice System", Journal of Emerging Technologies and Innovative Research (JETIR), Volume 12, Issue 3, March 2025.

Vijay, Bhawna. (2025). The evolution of digital arrest cyber-crimes in India: Trends and patterns preventive measures. International Journal of Sociology and Humanities. 7. 01–05. https://doi.org/10.33545/26648679.2025.v7.i1a.113.

Explainable and Responsible AI for Diabetic Maculopathy Grading: A Smart Healthcare Perspective for Future Cities

Savita Sheelavant and Preethi N. Patil

Abstract

Increased urbanization and changed lifestyle practices have shown a substantial increase in the incidence of diabetes across the globe, with over 500 million adults being diagnosed with the disorder, which is estimated to increase over 640 million by 2030. In the Indian scenario, 12% of adults above the age of 50 have been found to be suffering from diabetes with one out of six having diabetic retinopathy, despite the ratio of one ophthalmologist to 100,000 people. This chapter will describe the Explainable AI(XAI) and Responsible AI (RAI) framework for automatic grading of Diabetic Maculopathy using Optical Coherence Tomography (OCT) images. The proposed framework combines interpretable classifiers with deep learning algorithms for lesion segmentation. In turn, Grad-CAM/SHAP visualization methods are used for interpretability in the diagnosis of the mentioned disease. The proposed framework will incorporate in-built principles of Explainable AI. Through the inclusion of transparency and ethics, the framework aligns with the vision of inclusive smart healthcare. This includes the use of AI to support healthcare professionals. The framework also embraces the vision for future cities where technology is leveraged to improve efficiency while increasing responsibility in urban healthcare.

Keywords

Pathophysiological · Global rise · Data augmentation · Normalization · Optimization

S. Sheelavant (✉)
Department of MCA, RV College of Engineering, Bengaluru, India
e-mail: savitas.sheelavant@rvce.edu.in

P. N. Patil
Department of MCA, Ramaiah Institute of Technology, Bengaluru, India
e-mail: preethinpatil@msrit.edu

1 Introduction

The global rise in diabetes mellitus has been accompanied by a parallel increase in secondary retinal complications, with diabetic maculopathy emerging as one of the foremost causes of irreversible central-vision loss. Maculopathy usually results from a gradual process of microvascular damage to the retina. As weak blood vessels starting to leak fluid, fluid tends to accumulate in and around the retina where the macula is situated. As a consequence of this process, the vision in this part of the retina gets distorted. This is a serious threat to vision in future. Demographic factors like an aging population, a change in lifestyles, and increasing urbanization all contribute to increasing cases of diabetic retinopathy, which makes this disease a serious concern in international health streams.

Although conventional screening approaches remain clinically robust, they rely heavily on specialist expertise, manual image assessment, and subjective grading criteria. These dependencies make it increasingly difficult for healthcare systems to cope with the rising patient load, particularly in resource-limited settings where trained ophthalmologists are scarce. The diabetes population is growing in number, thereby continuing to put immense pressure on the service for screening and diagnosis. This warrants a need for developing automated, quick, and accessible techniques that offer early detection of maculopathy.

As shown in Fig. 1, the prevalence of diabetes mellitus remains a growing concern across the globe, which remains more in urban areas as compared to rural areas. Urbanization has reshaped global health patterns, with diabetes emerging as one of its most significant consequences. In 2021, an estimated 360 million people living in urban areas were affected by diabetes, compared with 176.6 million in rural communities. Projections indicate that by the year 2045, these numbers are expected to increase to 596.5 million and 186.7 million, respectively. The disparity in these numbers shows that it represents more than simple

V. Sarveshwaran et al. (eds.), *Responsible AI for Smart Cities*, Sustainable Artificial Intelligence-Powered Applications,
https://doi.org/10.1007/978-3-032-26901-0_15

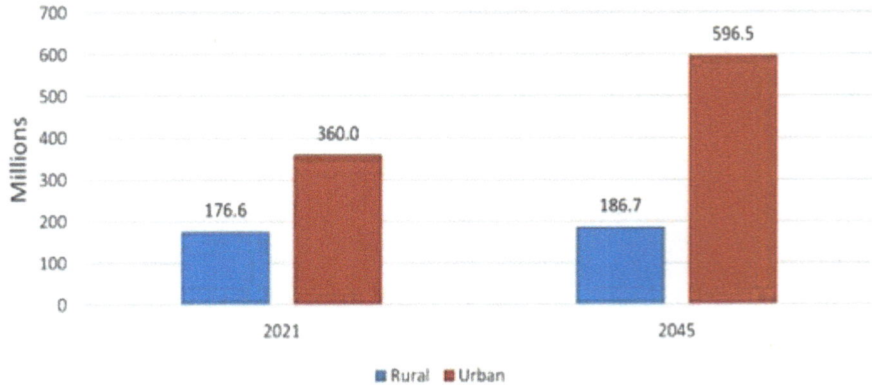

Fig. 1 IDF diabetes atlas: estimated prevalence of diabetes in different regions and nations in 2021 and projected prevalence for 2045 (Osman 2025)

demographics. These numbers are closely associated with the transition of lifestyles that come with urbanization. This includes less exercise, more consumption of saturated foods, as well as disparities in access to preventative care. These variables combine to create an environment that results in the early progression of the disease as well as the development of diabetic retinopathy (Jukić et al. 2025). The expanding diabetic population within cities has placed sustained pressure on ophthalmic services. Although early detection of diabetic eye disease is widely recognized as one of the most effective strategies for preserving vision, screening capacity has not expanded at the same pace as demand (Li et al. 2023; Ting et al. 2021b). Referral and diagnosis delays are frequent as urban healthcare systems become more overburdened, especially for asymptomatic patients. These delays directly result in preventable visual impairment and long-term disability in the absence of systematic screening and clearly defined care pathways (Ting et al. 2017; Abràmoff et al. 2018).

Artificial Intelligence in Ophthalmology

Over the past years, artificial intelligence has been emerging as a major area of research within the field of ophthalmology. Today, the use of AI-based systems has been widely identified as a means of auto-interpretation of retinal images, objective measurement of biomarkers indicative of the disease, and algorithmic grading of the retinal disease (Li et al. 2022; Alzubaidi et al. 2024; Yao et al. 2024). A number of studies have indicated the potential use of Deep Learning models in achieving a level of diagnosis similar to that of an expert within the field, in relation to diabetic maculopathy (Choi et al. 2024; Ting et al. 2017; Gulshan et al. 2016).

Despite these advances, wide clinical adoption has remained cautious. One of the main barriers is the opaque nature of many high-performing models. In a clinical setting, a numerical output or probability score is rarely of use per se. Ophthalmologists must be able to evaluate whether a model's decision is supported by anatomic features rather than by image artefacts, noise patterns, or dataset biases (Selvaraju et al. 2017; Sundararajan et al. 2017; Bendaoud et al. 2023). This need has driven growing interest in Explainable Artificial Intelligence (XAI). Techniques like Gradient-weighted Class Activation Mapping (Grad-CAM) visualization, attention-based maps, and feature attribution methods enable clinicians to review how and where a model is paying attention, enabling verification of predictions with the aim of fostering trust in the AI-assisted assessments. (Osman 2025; Selvaraju et al. 2017; Sundararajan et al. 2017; Bendaoud et al. 2023).

Responsible AI and the Question of Generalizability

The use of AI in healthcare must also align with broader ethical, social, and regulatory expectations (Fan et al. 2023; Abràmoff et al. 2018). Responsible AI frameworks emphasize fairness, accountability, patient privacy, transparency, and rigorous clinical validation alongside predictive accuracy (Osman 2025; Arunkumar et al. 2022). Without these safeguards, automated maculopathy grading systems risk introducing bias, generating misleading recommendations, or undermining clinician confidence (Jukić et al. 2025; Elsharkawy et al. 2025).

Data representativeness is a recurring technical issue. A limited patient population is frequently reflected in the datasets used in the development of many current models, which are gathered from a single facility or imaging platform (Ting et al. 2021a; Wu et al. 2021). Such models may perform worse when used in various clinical settings because of differences in scanner features, acquisition procedures, or disease manifestation. Federated learning and multi-center studies have been brought into focus to counter such a limitation. These techniques enhance robustness and help in improving the generality of models to learn from data geographically distributed across various areas under institutional oversight with preservation of data privacy (Bendaoud et al. 2023).

Digital Health and Distributed Models of Eye Care

At the same time, there is a more significant structural shift in diabetic eye care. There is an increasing shift away from specialist care delivered through center-based services for diabetes care to more scattered approaches for screening and diagnosis because of advances in digital infrastructure for healthcare, tele-ocular care, or smart city initiatives. To cope with an increasing number of cases, there is an increasing requirement for these community clinics, mobile screening stations, or tele-health clinics to rely upon automated retinal scans for diabetic maculopathy grading diagnostics.

Artificial intelligence-assisted grading systems for diabetic maculopathy may aid early detection, hasten referrals, or unload work for ophthalmologists if these systems can be developed on an accountable foundation. The accountability can then safeguard improved liability to care for diabetic eyes. These systems also promote more efficient technologies or approach to handle similar cases with fewer resources/costs.

Within this context, the chapter presents a comprehensive examination of explainable and responsible AI methodologies for diabetic maculopathy grading. It begins by outlining the clinical basis of diabetic maculopathy, followed by a review of retinal imaging modalities and computational techniques commonly used for disease assessment. The chapter then discusses key XAI approaches, responsible-AI principles, and federated learning strategies that underpin current research in ophthalmic AI. A conceptual pipeline is subsequently introduced to support transparent decision-making, secure data handling, and deployment aligned with regulatory standards. Finally, the chapter addresses real-world implementation challenges, highlights emerging research directions, and considers the evolving role of AI-enabled ophthalmic systems within future smart healthcare ecosystems.

2 Clinical Background of Diabetic Maculopathy

Diabetic maculopathy develops as a gradual consequence of long-standing microvascular injury associated with chronic hyperglycaemia, leading to structural and functional compromise of the retinal tissues responsible for central vision (Vujosevic and Cunha-Vaz 2020; Wong et al. 2016). The macula, situated near the posterior pole of the retina, contains a high density of cone photoreceptors that support fine visual acuity and color discrimination (Early Treatment Diabetic Retinopathy Study Research Group (ETDRS) 1991). Even subtle pathological alterations within this region can therefore have a pronounced impact on visual function. Accumulation of intraretinal fluid, increased retinal thickness, and deposition of lipid-rich exudates disrupt the normal macular architecture, making maculopathy one of the most vision-threatening manifestations of diabetic retinopathy. In clinical practice, macular disease is classified according to the pattern and extent of fluid accumulation, the degree of retinal layer involvement, and whether the central fovea is affected, as these factors are closely linked to disease severity, visual prognosis, and therapeutic decision-making (Silva et al. 2014).

2.1 Retinal Anatomy and Macular Vulnerability

The retina consists of highly organized layers of photoreceptors, interneurons, and ganglion cells, supported by a finely regulated microvascular network. The paracentral macula and especially the fovea have few prominent retinal vessels. Though this retinal anatomy allows for excellent visual acuity, it also puts this region at greater risk in cases where microvascular dysfunction exists in diabetes mellitus. Under physiological conditions, the blood-retinal barrier ensures that fluid exchange across the retinal tissues remains tightly regulated. When this barrier is compromised, plasma components leak into the retinal tissue, leading to fluid accumulation and the development of macular edema.

The fovea, measuring approximately 1.5 mm in diameter, contains the highest concentration of cone photoreceptors and is therefore critical for tasks requiring fine spatial resolution, such as reading and detailed visual discrimination. Even minor structural disturbances in this region can result in noticeable functional impairment. Optical Coherence Tomography (OCT) provides high-resolution cross-sectional visualization of the retina, allowing clinicians to detect micrometer-scale abnormalities such as intraretinal cystoid spaces, subretinal fluid, and hyper-reflective exudates that are characteristic of diabetic maculopathy (Ghosh et al. 2020; Groen et al. 2020).

2.2 Pathophysiological Mechanisms

Sustained hyperglycaemia initiates a cascade of microvascular alterations, including endothelial disfunction, loss of pericytes, and thickening of the capillary basement membrane (Early Treatment Diabetic Retinopathy Study Research Group (ETDRS) 1991). Such changes destabilize the retinal vascular structure, increase vascular permeability, and promote leakage of plasma into surrounding tissue (Silva et al. 2014). The thickening of the retina tends to initially occur in the parafoveal area and eventually may involve the central fovea, with this condition resulting in symptoms of vision problems.

Inflammatory processes and upregulation of vascular endothelial growth factor (VEGF) further exacerbate capillary leakage and edema formation. The advent of anti-VEGF therapies has markedly improved visual outcomes, particularly when treatment is initiated during the early stages of disease (Choi et al. 2024; Deodhar et al. 2024; Lin et al. 2025). However, early pathological changes may be subtle or entirely asymptomatic, reinforcing the value of objective, image-based screening and computational assessment tools (Ghosh et al. 2020; Groen et al. 2020).

2.3 Clinical Manifestations and Assessment

Clinically, diabetic maculopathy may present with blurred central vision, visual distortion, or difficulty with reading and near tasks. Importantly, many patients remain asymptomatic during the early stages, making routine screening essential for preventing irreversible damage. Diagnostic assessment typically combines color fundus photography with OCT imaging. OCT has become the cornerstone of macular evaluation, as it enables detailed inspection of retinal layers, identification of intraretinal fluid pockets, assessment of photoreceptor integrity, and quantitative measurement of macular thickness. While modern OCT systems support automated layer segmentation, segmentation accuracy may decline in advanced disease, necessitating expert review and interpretation.

2.4 Clinical Grading of Diabetic Maculopathy

Clinical grading schemes generally categorize maculopathy based on the presence and extent of retinal thickening, involvement of the central macula, and distribution of exudates. Central-involving macular edema is typically regarded as a more advanced and vision-threatening stage, requiring prompt therapeutic intervention. Quantitative OCT-derived parameters, such as central subfield thickness, provide objective support for grading decisions. Nevertheless, interpretation of structural patterns remains partly subjective, and inter-observer variability is well recognized. Automated grading algorithms have therefore been explored to improve consistency and efficiency; however, their clinical acceptance depends on the ability to provide clear visual evidence that predicted severity levels correspond to recognizable anatomical abnormalities within OCT scans (Osman 2025; Selvaraju et al. 2017; Bendaoud et al. 2023).

2.5 Importance of Early Detection

Early identification of macular involvement allows timely initiation of treatment and is strongly associated with improved long-term visual outcomes (Choi et al. 2024; Lin et al. 2025). Despite this, many healthcare systems, particularly in resource-constrained urban and semi-urban settings, face shortages of trained ophthalmic specialists, resulting in delays in diagnosis and referral (Li et al. 2023). In this context, automated grading systems supported by explainable and responsible AI offer a practical means to prioritize high-risk cases, streamline clinical workflows, and reduce the burden on ophthalmic services (Deodhar et al. 2024; Ting et al. 2024). When thoughtfully integrated into care pathways, such systems have the potential to support sustainable and equitable eye-care delivery in growing populations (Arunkumar et al. 2022; Fan et al. 2023).

3 Imaging Modalities and Data Acquisition

The reliability of diabetic maculopathy detection is strongly influenced by the quality of retinal imaging, the inherent properties of the imaging modality, and the uniformity of acquisition protocols (Ghosh et al. 2020; Groen et al. 2020). Today, the eye care field becomes increasingly image-based, wherein the findings from the images are used both for diagnosis and treatment. The various imaging modalities that are currently possible, among which the best-known reference standard modality is the OCT modality. OCT is capable of resolving the micro-structure of the retinal layer at histological resolution. The various imaging modalities offer complementary information and, hence, the definitions are directly influenced (Li et al. 2022; Alzubaidi et al. 2024).

3.1 Color Fundus Photography

Color fundus photography offers a two-dimensional view of the retinal surface, allowing visualization of features such as hemorrhages, microaneurysms, and hard exudates. It remains a cornerstone of diabetic retinopathy screening, particularly in large scale community programs, due to its relatively low cost and wide availability. However, fundus images do not capture depth information and therefore cannot directly reveal intraretinal or subretinal fluid, which is central to maculopathy assessment. As a result, computational models trained solely on fundus photographs often show limited performance when tasked with grading maculopathy severity, especially when compared with OCT based approaches (Li et al. 2022; Yao et al. 2024).

3.2 Optical Coherence Tomography

Optical Coherence Tomography uses low-coherence interferometry to obtain high-resolution cross-sectional images of the retina and has become an indispensable tool for the evaluation of macular pathology. OCT allows for the direct visualization of thickening within the retina, the development of cystoid spaces, the accumulation of fluid beneath the retina, and disruptions to the photoreceptor layers, thus providing the most informative non-invasive modality for assessment in diabetic macular edema. Computationally, this detailed structure provided by OCT better enables discrimination of disease severity and progression.

Nevertheless, differences in scanner manufacturers, acquisition protocols, and signal processing introduce variability across datasets. Addressing these domain shifts is therefore a critical consideration in the development of robust and generalizable algorithms (Alzubaidi et al. 2024; Yao et al. 2024).

3.3 Multimodal Imaging

Combining multiple imaging modalities can offer a more comprehensive view of macular pathology. Fundus photographs capture surface level changes, OCT reveals volumetric fluid distribution and layer integrity, and fluorescein angiography highlights areas of vascular leakage and capillary non perfusion. While such multimodal data can enhance diagnostic confidence, routine acquisition is often constrained by cost, procedural complexity, and limited availability, particularly in high throughput or resource limited settings. Consequently, the use of multimodal imaging remains challenging for population scale screening and large deployment of automated systems (Guo et al. 2024).

3.4 Dataset Acquisition and Annotation

The process of developing credible datasets for maculopathy is quite challenging and requires synchronization and expert knowledge. Creation of high-quality datasets is dependent on annotations, which need to be drawn in terms of the extent of the disease, delineating the lesion areas, and identifying the layers in the retina. The variation in image reconstruction instruments makes the task even harder, with differing resolutions and characteristics. Notably, cases where the diagnosis is uncertain are likely to produce divergent opinions among retinal specialists, and thus it is important that their opinions be sought to create credible ground truths (Silva et al. 2014). Privacy concerns and regulatory restrictions further limit dataset sharing, motivating federated and privacy-preserving alternatives for large-scale AI development.

3.5 Pre-processing for Machine Learning

Image preprocessing is very essential prior to applying machine learning algorithms to the images. Commonly, this includes noise removal, illumination normalization, retinal image layer segmentation, as well as removal of artifacts (Ghosh et al. 2020). Speckle noise or shadows can make relevant anatomical boundaries invisible; hence necessitating careful enhancement strategies. Pre-processing pipelines for XAI-compatible systems must remain transparent and reproducible, ensuring that clinically relevant features are not inadvertently distorted.

3.6 Ethical and Legal Considerations

Medical imaging involves personal data, so ethical principles must be kept foremost in mind. Ethical machine learning development involves strict data anonymization, data accessibility, as well as healthcare regulatory compliance (Arunkumar et al. 2022; Fan et al. 2023). Datasets also need to be examined to avoid demographic representativeness, which may cause the model to disproportionately affect specific subpopulations (Jukić et al. 2025; Elsharkawy et al. 2025).

3.7 Imaging Biomarkers for Diabetic Maculopathy

Certain important biomarkers identified in diabetic maculopathy are:

- Hard exudates: Lipid deposits, look bright on scans
- Intraretinal cystoid spaces: fluid-filled pockets within the retina
- Retinal thickening
- Subretinal fluid.

OCT technology also has applications in accurately determining these variations, which proves beneficial in machine-learning-based grading systems. The ability to focus on such significant features helpful for clinicians will always result in reliable approaches accepted by ophthalmologists, allowing them to see what key structural elements their predictive tools focus on. By making visible the structural cues used for prediction, such models support the differentiation of subtle anatomical variations that often characterize early or borderline stages of disease (Yao et al. 2024; Selvaraju et al. 2017; Bendaoud et al. 2023).

4 Explainable Artificial Intelligence for Retinal Disease Assessment

Artificial Intelligence (AI) systems have demonstrated enormous potential in automating the detection and grading of retinal diseases. However, if AI systems have to translate from the laboratory to practical applications in the clinic, it is imperative to ensure that AI systems explain their reasoning to medical personnel. In the field of ophthalmology, where the outcome of a decision can result in visual impairment or affect the quality of life of a patient, explainability is mandatory rather than a desirable ingredient.

4.1 Need for Explainability

Deep learning models can significantly limit errors in the analysis of retinal images but rely on an opaque decision-making process that gives a prediction without showing any rationale for that prediction. This will undoubtedly restrict the adoption and use of models by clinical practitioners (Shahriari et al. 2022; Yao et al. 2024). This question will be answered by applying eXplainable Artificial Intelligence. This approach helps to identify areas and/or features of an image that helped to take a decision. This will ensure that decisions are based on actual pathological findings and not artifacts or noise.

Explainability in the medical field is more than a simple explanation of previous predictions. For medical professionals to be comfortable with AI systems, their explanations must be traceable and routable according to the medical knowledge behind disease, standard diagnosed terms, and what is medically feasible and acceptable (Arunkumar et al. 2022; Fan et al. 2023).

4.2 Categories of XAI Techniques in Medical Imaging

There are methods that are used in the explainability of medical imaging, depending on the nature of the knowledge revealed. These methods include:

- *Saliency-Based Visualizations* highlight regions of an image that most influence the output.
- *Gradient-Based Attribution* techniques measure how small changes in pixel intensity affect predictions, generating detailed importance maps (Bendaoud et al. 2023).
- *Feature Importance Methods* identify higher-level latent features that contribute most strongly to a decision.

Other strategies include:

- *Decision Rule Extraction*, which approximates complex neural networks with simpler, interpretable models.
- *Counterfactual Explanations*, which explore how hypothetical changes in input could alter outcomes.
- *Confidence-Aware Monitoring*, which provides estimates of uncertainty or reliability for predictions.
- *Perturbation-Based Methods,* such as occlusion or region masking, which test model sensitivity by systematically removing parts of the image.

Attention mechanisms are distinct in the sense that they explicitly incorporate the aspect of interpretability into the model and emphasize the appropriate parts during the training and inference phases.

4.3 Post Hoc Visualization for OCT

Most of these are supported by using post hoc explainability techniques in the interpretation of OCT data within the retinal AI pipeline. Among these, Grad-CAM gives a spatial heatmap which points out the exact region responsible for the highest contribution to the model output prediction (Ghosh et al. 2020). Overlaying these kinds of maps on OCT B-scans or volumetric slices will provide clinicians with a way to confirm if the model focuses on important features like intraretinal cysts, fluid pockets, and/or hyper-reflective exudates.

SmoothGrad is an improved version of gradient-based saliency by averaging the results over multiple slightly perturbed inputs, leading to sharper and more stable visualizations. Occlusion-based sensitivity analysis calculates a model's confidence changes while masking parts of the retina. These two approaches together provide insights into model behavior, complementary in nature, and are standard during validation for clinical interpretation and error analysis.

4.4 Attention-Driven Explainability

Attention models provide a native explainability mechanism that identifies which aspects of the image the model is interested in during training. In the context of OCT analysis, self-attention functions might focus on the edges of the macular area, minute irregularities in the layers, and small changes that might indicate pathology in the vicinity of the fovea. In contrast, region-of-interest analysis depend on human intuition and do not adjust their focus on the image as the patient's disease evolves. When layer information is incorporated through attention functions, their activations closely correspond with human analyses during clinical OCT image reviews.

4.5 Trust, Clinical Responsibility, and Algorithmic Transparency

Simply achieving high accuracy levels is insufficient for AI systems to be trusted in a real-world setting. It requires that AI systems offer understandable evidence, indicate their level of confidence or uncertainty, and record their reasoning in a way that aligns with traditional standards in the clinical community. The regulations and principles regarding AI-assisted diagnosis continue to recognize the significance of transparency in this regard and continue to consider it a key part of this concern in relation to AI systems in achieving enhanced clinician and AI system trustworthiness (Osman 2025; Shahriari et al. 2022).

4.6 Human-Centric Interpretation Principles

Human-based explanations target the physician primarily as the user. Explanations need to be carried out in a language familiar to ophthalmologists and described within the context of the anatomy and pathology of the eye. An appropriate AI system should clearly identify related areas of interest with recognized signals, such as exudates, cystoid spaces, or anomalies within distinct layers of the retina, using standard grading methods. Generic heatmap information that generally points out broad areas of the retina does not contribute meaningfully to identification. Anatomically accurate and disease-specific explanations enable the physician to effectively analyze AI output and challenge decision-making.

5 Proposed Methodology/Conceptual Framework

This section introduces the conceptual end-to-end pipeline developed for explainable and responsible diabetic maculopathy assessment using OCT imaging. A central design objective of the proposed system is modularity. Each stage of the pipeline is constructed as an independent component, allowing it to be optimized, updated, validated, or replaced without disrupting the integrity of the overall framework. This design choice is particularly important in clinical settings, where individual modules may need to evolve in response to new imaging devices, updated clinical guidelines, or regulatory requirements.

Conventional machine learning approaches for retinal disease analysis often rely on global image features and deliver a single end point classification. Although these algorithms work reasonably well, they do not provide any clear explanations about the reasoning behind the classification results and do not work on a scale that relates well to the human interpretation and evaluation of retinal images.

Conversely, the proposed approach adopts a hybrid perception and reasoning architecture that closely resonates with human cognition. The initial component of this architecture is anatomical segmentation that provides a systemic representation of the retina based on its layers. Further, lesion-aware feature encoding facilitates the identification of points that are pertinent to the pathology and enhances the learning objectives based on meaningful lesions. Importantly, the architecture is specifically integrated with explainability to enhance visual and structural explanations of each inference based on its decision.

Under this approach, OCT B-scans are considered three-dimensional anatomical signals that encode subtle details of retinal microstructure. By undergoing a series of processing steps, these signals are converted to higher-level representations that describe recognizable features from a clinical perspective. Instead of a black-box approach to classification, this tool presents itself as an aid for clinician decision-making. It focuses attention on those retinal layers that are most relevant to a case, identifies significant pathological markers, indicates areas that deserve closer scrutiny, and expresses an associated level of confidence in each prediction, which helps clinicians in responsible decision-making (Arunkumar et al. 2022).

By combining interpretability, modular design, and uncertainty awareness, the pipeline fits naturally into established clinical workflows. This makes it well suited for real-world screening, and tele-ophthalmology settings, where transparency, reliability, and clinician trust are central to patient care.

The maculopathy grading system in Fig. 2 is conceptualized to be an extensive and aligned system for appropriate use in clinical practice. Rather than functioning as a single monolithic model, the framework integrates a sequence of clearly defined components, each addressing a specific requirement for reliable diagnostic support. These components include image enhancement, retinal region localization, maculopathy feature extraction and severity classification, explainability and attribution mechanisms, responsible AI safeguards, and clinician-informed feedback loops that support continuous refinement.

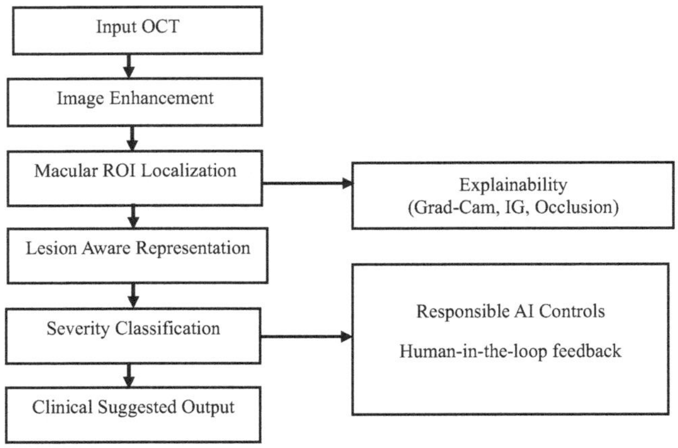

Fig. 2 Proposed pipeline system and architectural overview

While this heterogeneity is essential for developing models that generalize beyond a single clinical setting, it also introduces substantial variation in image resolution, noise characteristics, illumination profiles, and acquisition protocols. In order to tackle these issues, a robust anonymization and preprocessing approach was employed. Noise reduction, intensity normalization, spatial resize, and a well-crafted data augmentation technique were used so that all images fed into the learning models were of a consistent, overall good quality, and suitable for training.

Dataset and Preprocessing

Accurate automated analysis of retinal OCT data depends fundamentally on careful dataset preparation. This section describes the dataset characteristics, the measures taken to protect patient privacy, and the preprocessing workflow used to manage variability across imaging sources.

Dataset Description and Anonymization

The dataset comprised volumetric OCT B scans acquired from multiple Spectral Domain OCT platforms. Using data from different devices and institutions enhances model robustness and supports the principles of responsible AI, but it also introduces notable technical heterogeneity. Importantly, this variability is not limited to differences between manufacturers. Even scans acquired on the same device may exhibit considerable fluctuations in image appearance.

Three recurring sources of variation were observed. First, intra device inconsistency is common, with subtle changes in speckle noise, illumination, and layer definition occurring across scans acquired under similar conditions. These fluctuations require the model to tolerate a degree of natural variability that is inherent to OCT imaging. Second, inter device disparity arises when combining data from different vendors, each of which employs distinct scanning geometries, signal processing pipelines, and resolution settings. In effect, each device produces images with its own characteristic appearance, which the model must learn to interpret consistently. Third, patient related factors introduce additional complexity. Mild motion during acquisition, shadowing from retinal vasculature, reduced contrast caused by blinking or ocular surface conditions, and pathology dependent changes in reflectivity can all obscure subtle lesions such as small cystoid spaces or early exudates.

To safeguard patient privacy, all OCT volumes were fully anonymized prior to analysis. Identifiable metadata, including patient identifiers, acquisition times, and device specific tags, were removed in accordance with established data protection standards. In scenarios where longitudinal tracking or auditability was required, secure hashing techniques were used to generate pseudo identifiers. This approach preserves traceability for clinical governance and quality assurance while ensuring that patient confidentiality is maintained.

By carefully addressing both technical variability and ethical considerations at the dataset level, the preprocessing pipeline establishes a reliable foundation for downstream modeling and supports responsible deployment in real world clinical environments.

Image Enhancement and Preprocessing Pipeline

The preprocessing stage represents a digital restoration and normalization suite that prepares each OCT image such that the data is faithfully representative of underlying retinal pathology, rather than device-specific artefacts.

Noise Removal: Speckle noise is intrinsic to OCT imaging and can render minute pathological details, microaneurysms, and cystoid spaces unseen. The processing sequence therefore begins with the conversion of the acquired OCT images into grayscale, making it easier to interpret the data without compromising the structural details. This is followed by anisotropic diffusion filtering, which reduces noise while preserving the natural boundaries of retinal layers, a property that is particularly important for subsequent segmentation tasks.

To address speckle artefacts that manifest across different spatial scales, wavelet based despeckling is employed. This approach separates noise components from true anatomical signals, enabling targeted suppression of artefacts without degrading clinically relevant structures. In parallel, denoising autoencoders are trained to reconstruct cleaner representations of OCT scans, using data driven priors to further enhance image quality.

In the final step, structure-preserving filters such as Non-Local Means and BM3D are applied. By leveraging the similarities among patches of pixels within an image, these techniques are able to effectively eliminate the residual noise while, at the same time, preserve fine structural details. Overall, this entire process of preprocessing turns raw OCT scans into reliable inputs for segmentation and classification.

Retinal Region Localization

Volumes from OCT images include the periphery of the retina, which is not necessarily related to the evaluation of the maculopathy. Region localization isolates the central macular area, ensuring computational resources are directed toward diagnostically meaningful structures.

Contrast Enhancement: After the denoising phase, Contrast Limited Adaptive Histogram Equalization (CLAHE) is used to emphasize minute details of the pathology. The method helps to enhance the features such as exudate borders, cyst borders, and layers borders by enhancing the contrasts of small regions to avoid enhancement of noise (Ting et al. 2021a; Wu et al. 2021).

Normalization: To standardize intensity ranges across devices, images are normalized into a standardized intensity range of [0, 1]. Features depending on intensity cannot become intensity biases when training models.

Image Resizing and Spatial Standardization: All the scans undergo resampling at a resolution of 512x512 pixels with bicubic interpolation. Standardization of size makes input data handling, learning of the model, and the deployment of the models in hardware devices of varying capability easier.

Data Augmentation: To strengthen the model's ability to generalize across different devices, clinics, and patient conditions, a carefully designed augmentation pipeline was applied. The first set of transformations involves geometric modifications—including controlled rotations, elastic deformations, and subtle scaling—which mimic the natural variability introduced during patient positioning or slight misalignment of the OCT examination.

Next, photometric adjustments such as gamma correction and intensity jitter simulate differences in illumination and contrast that commonly arise across imaging systems. To help the model remain resilient to missing or obscured information, cutout masks are introduced, reproducing realistic shadowing or partial occlusions caused by eyelid interference or vessel shadow artefacts.

Finally, spatial distortions are incorporated to reflect minor patient movements during acquisition, a frequent challenge in real-world clinical settings. Together, these augmentations expose the model to a broad spectrum of plausible imaging conditions, equipping it to perform reliably despite the complexity and variability inherent in routine OCT scanning.

Maculopathy Feature Extraction and Severity Classification

The proposed architecture shown in Fig. 3, adopts a two-stage learning strategy that mirrors the reasoning pathway of retinal specialists.

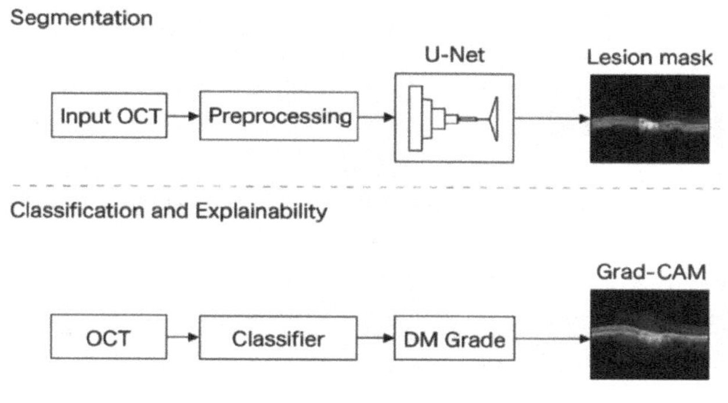

Fig. 3 Multi stage learning pipeline and model architecture

Stage 1: U-Net–Based Lesion Segmentation

The first stage of the framework is dedicated to accurately identifying diabetic lesions in OCT B-scans. The reason for choosing a U-Net model is its proven capacity to merge the information of small-scale detail and high-level semantics, which is a required characteristic for the demarcation of small structures such as microaneurysms and cystoid cavities.

The encoder is made up of five hierarchical convolutional layers with the ReLU function as the activation function. In the middle of the network, the dilated convolutional bottleneck layer leads to a significant increase in the size of the receptive field of the network, which enables it to capture more widespread retinal pathologies such as macular edema, which results in structural changes in the retinal region.

The final segmentation mask

$$\hat{S} \in \{0, 1\}^{H \times W}$$

is generated according to

$$\hat{S} = f_{\theta_{\text{seg}}}(X_{\text{norm}}),$$

where X_{norm} denotes the fully pre-processed and normalized OCT input.

To promote accurate delineation of both small and spatially dispersed lesions, a hybrid loss function is employed:

$$L_{\text{seg}} = \alpha \cdot BCE\left(Y, \hat{S}\right) + (1 - \alpha)(1 - Dice).$$

The binary cross-entropy (BCE) component weighs pixel-level differences, whereas the Dice loss component deals with regional overlap issues. Such a combination is very effective for ensuring proper segmentation of exudates or cystoid fluid regions and other biomarkers with subtle appearance characteristics (Groen et al. 2020; Silva et al. 2014).

Stage 2: ResNet-Based Severity Classification

The second stage of the framework focuses on translating structural cues into a clinically meaningful severity grade using a ResNet-50 classifier. To support flexible and context-aware decision-making, the classifier can operate in three modes: it may analyze the raw OCT slice directly, receive a lesion-masked version that highlights only segmented pathological regions, or process a composite representation that fuses both types of information.

This selective input strategy mirrors the way clinicians review OCT scans—first observing the global structure and then focusing more closely on regions where pathology is suspected. By allowing lesion-specific information to guide the network's attention, the classifier is encouraged to prioritize anatomically relevant features rather than incidental noise or artefacts. As a result, the system achieves a more stable, transparent, and clinically grounded interpretation of disease severity.

The classifier estimates:

$$P(y \mid X) = f_{\theta_{\text{cls}}}\left(\hat{S} \odot X\right),$$

where the element-wise product $\hat{S} \odot X$ directs the classifier's focus to the most clinically relevant regions. Training is optimized using the Adam algorithm with cyclical learning-rate schedules and weight-decay regularization, a combination that stabilizes convergence and reduces overfitting.

Rationale for a Multi-Stage Architecture

Designing the system as two modular components closely reflects the diagnostic reasoning used by ophthalmologists. In clinical practice, specialists first scan the OCT image for structural abnormalities such as cysts, pockets of fluid, or deposits of exudates, and only then determine the severity of maculopathy. By computationally duplicating this sequential procedure, the framework allows for easy decision-making pathways. Moreover, every procedure in this framework can be assessed, refined, and then verified separately, allowing for its long-term use.

By concentrating the classification function on the lesion area, the effect of noise is further diminished and the model is prevented from incorrectly correlating irrelevant patterns in the images. In the context of the proposed health intelligent city framework, such robustness is critical for its successful execution at the larger, city-wide level, where the imaging modalities might differ considerably.

Explainability and Attribution

Explainability is a critical component that helps ensure that the model results are reliable and medically relevant. In this model, the XAI components are seamlessly connected to the inference process to offer end-to-end explanations of the model's decision-making.

Grad-CAM–Based Spatial Attributions

Gradient-weighted Class Activation Mapping (Grad-CAM) is applied at the final convolutional layer to highlight regions that most strongly influence the predicted severity. For a target class c, the Grad-CAM map is calculated as:

$$L^{c}_{\text{Grad-CAM}} = ReLU\left(\sum_{k} \alpha^{c}_{k} A^{k}\right)$$

where A^k is the activation for channel k, and the weights:

$$\alpha^{c}_{k} = \frac{1}{Z} \sum_{i,j} \frac{\partial y^{c}}{\partial A^{k}_{ij}}$$

represent the contribution of each feature map to the class prediction. The resulting heatmaps provide intuitive visual cues, enabling clinicians to confirm whether the network concentrated on disease-relevant structures such as intraretinal cysts or foveal contour distortions.

SHAP-Based Feature Attribution

SHAP values offer a complementary, model-agnostic explanation by expressing predictions as additive contributions:

$$f(x) = \phi_0 + \sum_{i=1}^{n} \phi_i.$$

Each ϕ_i quantifies the influence of a specific feature or superpixel region. For OCT analysis, SHAP helps contextualize how individual layers, reflectivity patterns, or lesion morphologies contribute to the final grading—making the model's logic more interpretable for ophthalmologists.

Lesion-Consistency Overlays

To assess agreement between segmentation-derived and classifier-derived explanations, a composite visualization is produced:

$$M_{\text{overlay}} = \hat{S} \cup L^{c}_{\text{Grad-CAM}}.$$

This overlay allows clinicians to verify that the classifier emphasizes anatomically meaningful lesions, rather than noise, shadow artefacts, or non-pathological retinal layers. The resulting alignment between segmentation and attribution helps build confidence in the model's consistency.

Mathematical Formulation of Attribution Methods

Let $f(x)$ denote a trained maculopathy-grading network that outputs a prediction $y = f(x)$ for input OCT volume x. Explainability aims to derive a relevance distribution $R(x)$ such that:

$$\sum_{i=1}^{n} R_i(x) \approx y$$

where $R_i(x)$ represents the contribution of pixel i to the model's prediction.

(a) *Gradient-based Saliency*

For a target class y_k, the saliency at pixel i is defined as:

$$S_i = \left| \frac{\partial y_k}{\partial x_i} \right|$$

This highlights locations where small input changes cause large variations in the output, signaling important features for the network.

(b) *Grad-CAM*

Given a convolutional activation map A^l at layer l, Grad-CAM computes weights:

$$\alpha_l = \frac{1}{Z} \sum_i \sum_j \frac{\partial y_k}{\partial A^l_{ij}}$$

The corresponding heatmap is:

$$H = \mathrm{ReLU}\left(\sum_l \alpha_l A^l \right)$$

ReLU ensures that only positive (evidence-supporting) contributions appear in the explanation, producing intuitive visualizations linked to pathological regions (Selvaraju et al. 2017; Groen et al. 2020).

(c) *Integrated Gradients (IG)*

For a baseline input x' and an interpolation parameter $\lambda \in [0, 1]$:

$$IG_i(x) = \left(x_i - x_i'\right) \int_0^1 \frac{\partial f\left(x' + \lambda\left(x - x'\right)\right)}{\partial x_i} \, d\lambda$$

IG approximates cumulative contributions along a path from baseline to input, mitigating issues such as gradient saturation (Selvaraju et al. 2017).

(d) *Occlusion Sensitivity*

Let $x^{(i)}$ denote the input with region i occluded. The relevance is:

$$R_i = y - f\left(x^{(i)}\right)$$

A large decrease in output after occlusion indicates that the masked region is critical for prediction (Bendaoud et al. 2023).

Figure 4 provides an overview of the typical explainability workflow applied to OCT-based maculopathy assessment. In the left panel, a raw grayscale B-scan is presented, with annotations highlighting key anatomical landmarks such as the macular center and the foveal pit. The middle panel shows the corresponding retinal-layer segmentation map, where major layers—including the RNFL, GCL, INL, OPL, ONL, and RPE—are depicted using color-coded overlays to aid visual interpretation (Vujosevic and Cunha-Vaz 2020; Silva et al. 2014). Pathological structures such as cystoid cavities are delineated with dotted boundaries, and hard exudates appear as hyper-reflective yellow deposits. The right panel illustrates the Grad-CAM attribution map superimposed on the OCT slice. The red–yellow heatmap signifies regions with the strongest contribution to the predicted maculopathy grade, complemented by a color bar indicating the relative relevance intensity.

The heatmap super-imposed on the raw cross-section highlights regions with high relevance scores (red–yellow) corresponding to intraretinal cystoid cavities and adjacent hyper-reflective exudative foci, while lower-weight areas appear in cooler colors (green–blue) as shown in Fig. 5. The spatial concentration of saliency over fluid pockets and

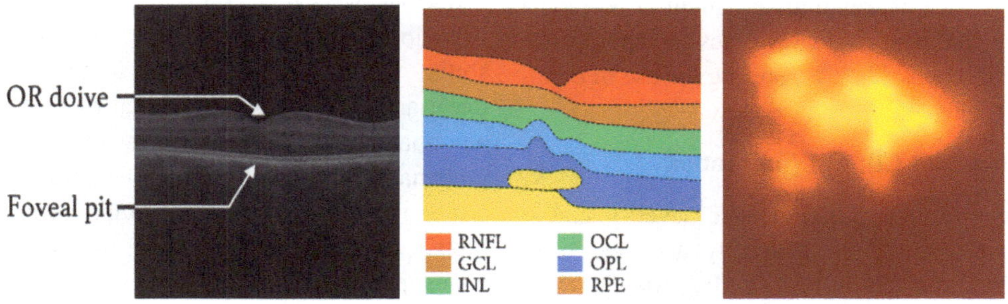

Fig. 4 Raw OCT B-scan, corresponding retinal-layer segmentation with highlighted pathological structures, and Grad-CAM–based attribution overlay demonstrating model-derived spatial relevance for diabetic maculopathy assessment

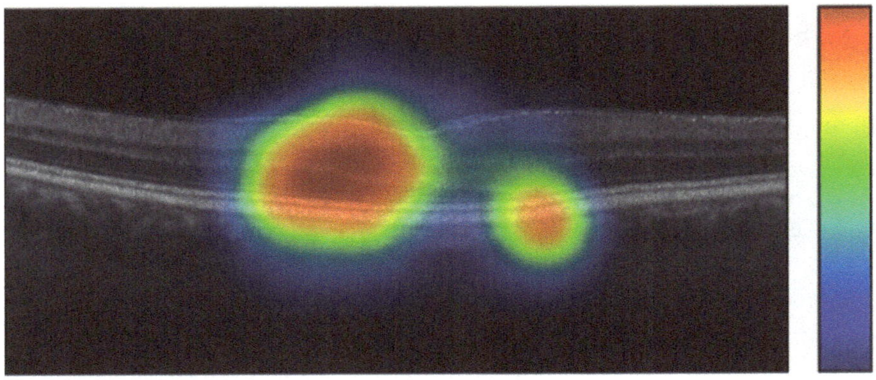

Fig. 5 Grad-CAM attribution overlay on OCT B-scan for diabetic maculopathy interpretation

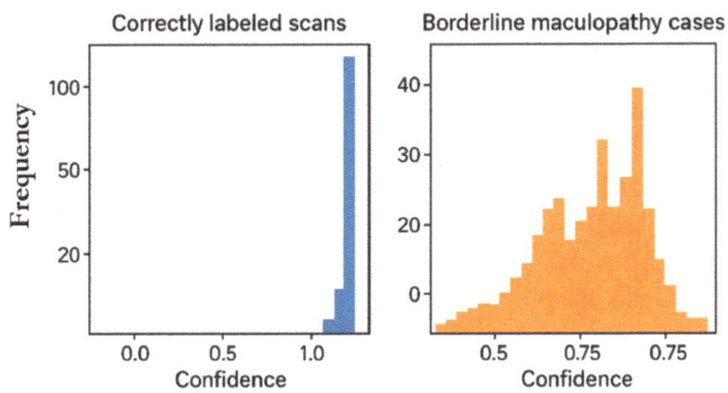

Fig. 6 Confidence distributions for diabetic maculopathy grading

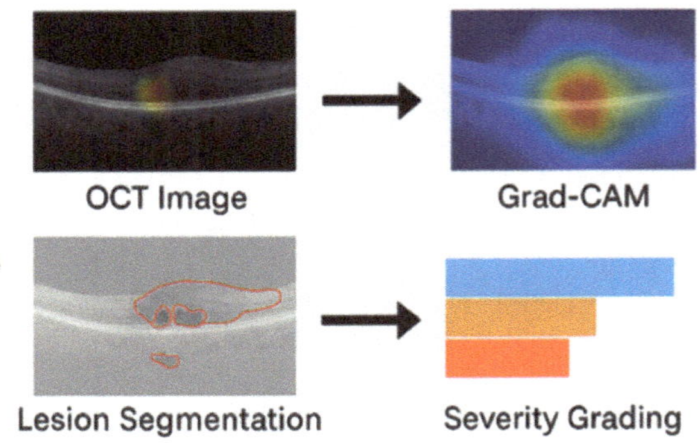

Fig. 7 AI for diabetic maculopathy grading

reflective deposits indicates that the classification network's discriminative cues are anatomically and pathologically meaningful, rather than distributed across background tissue or noise.

Figure 6 shows how prediction confidence varies across clinical scenarios. In the correctly classified OCT scans (left histogram), the confidence values congregate at the top of the range from 0.98 to 1.0. This shows that they make reliable decisions when the structure of the retinal imaging is either normal or pathologically abnormal. The values in the borderline cases of the maculopathy images (right histogram) spread out from 0.45 to 0.85. This shows the diversity of values due to the subtle alterations in the structure of the images, the low contrast exudates, and the intraretinal fluid. Taken together, the two distributions highlight good model calibration: strong confidence for clear cases and appropriate uncertainty for ambiguous ones, supporting the use of confidence scores for triage and clinician review.

Severity Prediction and Clinical Calibration

The extracted features are passed to the severity classifier, which assigns one of the clinically accepted categories—No Diabetic macular edema (DME), MILD-DME, Moderate-DME, or severe DME as shown in Fig. 7. Each model prediction is reported together with a calibrated confidence score, obtained using established techniques such as temperature scaling and Monte Carlo dropout. The resulting confidence distributions are an integral component of the responsible AI layer, as they provide an explicit indication of whether a decision is supported by stable, well-defined evidence or arises from ambiguous and borderline input patterns. In a healthcare context, this is a valuable tool since it helps to identify data that is uncertain for human scrutiny while also enabling confident predictions for efficient patient flow during a triage process.

Responsible AI Controls

For use in routine clinical settings, the framework includes a responsible AI layer that continuously monitors model behavior to ensure reliability over time. It tracks data shifts, uncertainty, out-of-distribution cases, and defers uncertain predictions to clinician review rather than acting autonomously. Bias checks, audit logs, and strict data governance are built in to meet clinical and regulatory requirements. This oversight helps ensure that AI outputs remain trustworthy, transparent, and safe for clinical decision support.

Figure 8 illustrates how the model distinguishes between normal retinal OCT images and those affected by diabetic

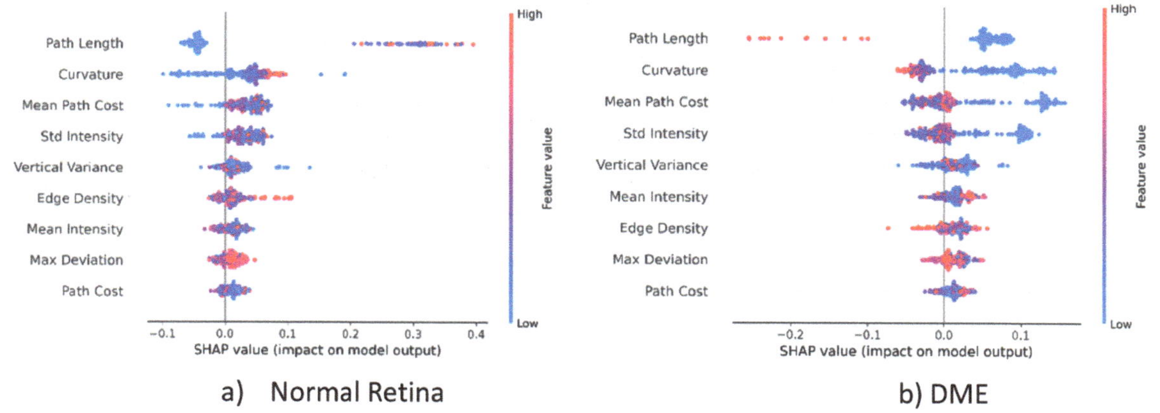

Fig. 8 Comparison of normal retina and DME using SHAP analysis

maculopathy by examining structural and intensity-based features of retinal layers.

In the normal OCT image, a longer path tends to have a positive influence on the result obtained from the model's output. This implies that there are ordered layers found in a normal eye that are characteristic in the healthy eye. In diabetic maculopathy, these paths will often be disrupted as a result of swelling in the retinal regions.

Curvature is the next critical consideration. A normal retina exhibits a smooth boundary corresponding to low curvature, promoting positive predictions. On the other hand, the presence of diabetic maculopathy brings about the concept of curvature or distortion in the retinal layers.

Variations can also be found in path cost, as well as intensity variation. In a normal retinal image, there is likely to be a low traversal cost, along with high intensity. This implies a stable retinal tissue structure. However, the diabetic maculopathy has a high intensity variation of exudates and intraretinal fluid that is expected to affect the model negatively.

Other features such as vertical variability, edge density, and max deviation are of less significance. All the above are descriptions of local variability, and these are small in amount in the regular retinas but are always present, although to varying extents, in the diabetic maculopathy retinas.

Overall, the model identifies normal retinal OCT images by the presence of smooth, continuous, and structurally consistent retinal layers, while diabetic maculopathy is characterized by disrupted geometry, increased curvature, and greater intensity heterogeneity. These differences align well with known clinical changes observed in diabetic retinal disease and support the interpretability of the model's predictions.

The two SHAP bar plots shown in Fig. 9 tells about how different features contribute to the model's decisions for normal and DME retinal OCT images.

Concerning diabetic maculopathy, it can be noticed that the path length and the curve are the dominant factors. This means that the algorithm is driven primarily by the geometric modifications within the retinal layer. In the case of the diseased images, the retinal layer will often be altered due to fluid accumulation. The average path cost and the intensity variation are the second most important aspects,

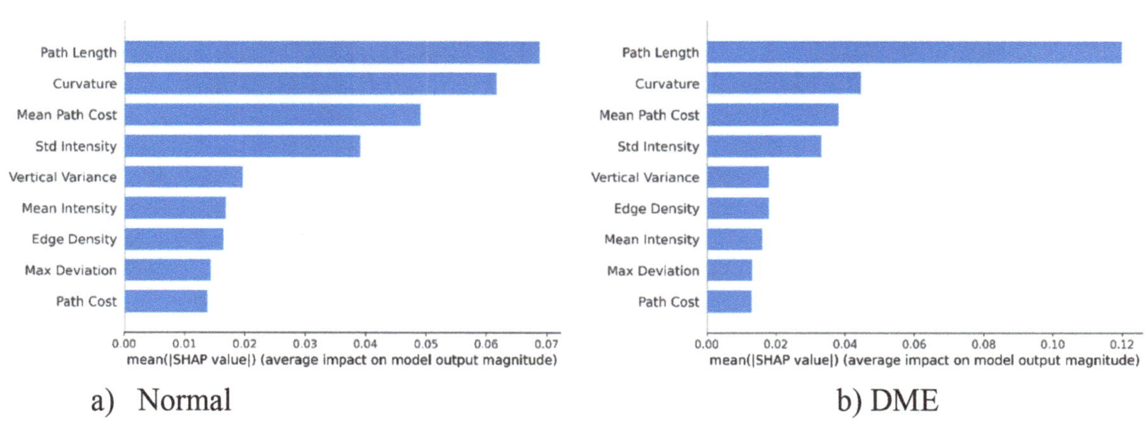

Fig. 9 Comparison of feature importance in normal and DME OCT images

pointing toward the existence of heterogeneous areas caused by fluid accumulation and exudates. A moderate importance has the vertical variance, edge density, and maximum deviation. For the normal OCT images, path length comes out as the prominent factor, although its weight is greater than that in diabetic maculopathy. This is an indication that the model heavily relies on the correlation of normal images to a long, continuous, and unbroken pattern of the retina. Curvature, mean path cost, intensity, and deviation are less important, which is in conformity with the normal, smooth, and healthy nature of the retina.

The comparison shows that the model relies more on geometric irregularities and intensity variability to identify diabetic maculopathy, while structural continuity and smoothness are the key indicators of normal retinal anatomy. These findings align well with known clinical differences between healthy retinas and those affected by diabetic maculopathy, supporting the interpretability of the model's predictions.

The force plots generated by SHAP shown in Fig. 10 can also explain how each feature contributes individually to the model's prediction for a particular OCT scan image. The force plots allow comparisons to be made between patients that present Diabetic Maculopathy and patients that present normal retinal scans, which can also serve to explain disease severity and evolution.

In the DME, the main factors that influence the prediction are vertical variance and elongation of the path length. These indicate dislocations of the retinal layers and the breakdown of normal retinal structures, which are often evident in cases of moderate to severe macular edema. The curvature and maximum deviation work to counter this effect and indicate that there is some retinal distortion that is not uniform, an indication of active disease where there is accumulation of fluid and edema.

In the normal OCT scan, decision-supporting attributes include low path cost, fixed mean intensity, small vertical variability, and smooth curvature. These attributes, taken together, suggest good layering and reflectivity patterns. The presence of low pathcost in the opposite direction further adds to the idea of continuous and unbroken layering of the retina. Such an attribute set is typically found in normal eyes or in treated patients where resolution of edema might have occurred.

In the clinical context, irregularity and geometry anomalies suggest severe disease, whereas a smooth geometry or intensity map indicates a positive course and positive therapeutic response.

The Table 1 summarizes how key structural features change with increasing severity of diabetic macular edema and how strongly they influence the model's predictions. Mild DME shows mostly preserved retinal structure with low SHAP impact, reflecting early or limited edema. As the disease progresses to a moderate stage, retinal layers become more distorted and heterogeneous, with a noticeable rise in feature contributions that typically corresponds to clinically active disease requiring treatment. In severe DME, all features show strong SHAP influence, indicating marked structural disruption, pronounced thickening, and highly irregular reflectivity, consistent with advanced disease and a high risk of visual loss.

Clinician-Informed Feedback Loops

Clinical practice and imaging conditions continue to change, so AI tools must be able to evolve with them. The proposed framework includes a clinician-driven feedback loop in which ophthalmologists review, correct, or override model outputs, and these expert-validated cases are periodically used to refine the model. This process helps maintain reliable performance as patient populations, devices, and proto-

a) Normal

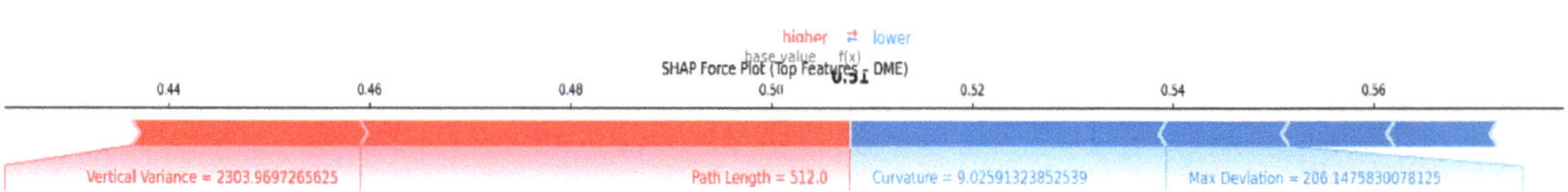

b) DME

Fig. 10 Interpreting SHAP force plots in the context of disease severity and treatment response

Table 1 Feature–severity mapping with corresponding SHAP value ranges

Feature	Mild DME (*Low SHAP impact*)	Moderate DME (*Medium SHAP impact*)	Severe DME (*High SHAP impact*)
Path length	Mostly continuous paths SHAP $\approx \pm 0.05$–0.10	Shortened or fragmented paths SHAP $\approx \pm 0.10$–0.15	Very short or irregular paths SHAP $\geq \pm 0.15$
Curvature	Mild layer bending SHAP $\leq \pm 0.05$	Visible distortion SHAP $\approx \pm 0.10$–0.20	Pronounced folding SHAP $\geq \pm 0.20$
Vertical variance	Low-to-moderate thickening SHAP ≈ 0–± 0.05	Increased thickening SHAP $\approx \pm 0.05$–0.15	Severe macular thickening SHAP $\geq \pm 0.15$
Mean path cost	Slightly elevated SHAP $\leq \pm 0.05$	High structural complexity SHAP $\approx \pm 0.10$–0.20	Extreme disruption SHAP $\geq \pm 0.20$
Intensity variation	Mild heterogeneity SHAP $\leq \pm 0.05$	Mixed fluid and exudates SHAP $\approx \pm 0.10$–0.15	Highly heterogeneous reflectivity SHAP $\geq \pm 0.20$
Clinical interpretation	Early edema with minimal disruption; usually observed or conservatively managed	Active disease with clear anatomical impact; treatment typically required	Advanced disease with high visual risk; aggressive or repeated treatment needed

cols change, while keeping the system aligned with everyday clinical reasoning.

Rather than producing rigid labels, the pipeline presents findings in clinical terms, such as subtle intraretinal cysts, early hyper-reflective foci, or localized changes in the foveal contour. These observations can be directly verified on the OCT image, supporting transparent review and informed judgment. In this way, the system functions as a decision-support aid that complements, rather than replaces, clinical expertise.

6 Experimental Evaluation

The proposed approach was assessed in terms of many aspects such as retinal structure segmentation, gradable severity of maculopathy, explanation, fairness, etc. Performance-wise, the system is found to work well in all conditions. High Dice coefficients are obtained for segmentation, while good accuracy is achieved in grading too. Receiver operating characteristic and interobserver agreement statistics also show similar performances in both datasets. The explainability analysis using Grad-CAM and SHAP showed the model was interested in relevant biomarkers, thus making the model more interpretable and gaining trust among clinicians. The analysis of fairness and transfer testing demonstrated robustness against demographics and OCT devices. Feedback analysis among practicing ophthalmologists affirmed the beneficial use of the system, especially for triage applications and remote ophthalmology.

6.1 Experimental Setup

All experiments were conducted using an NVIDIA RTX A5000 GPU with 24 GB of memory. Model development and training were carried out using PyTorch version 2.2, with support from TorchXRayVision and OpenCV. The segmentation network was trained for 150 epochs, while the classification model was trained for 100 epochs. A hybrid loss function combining Dice loss and focal loss was used for segmentation to balance class imbalance and boundary precision. For classification, label-smoothed cross-entropy loss with a smoothing factor of 0.05 was employed. Optimization was performed using the AdamW optimizer with an initial learning rate of 10^{-4}. Learning rate scheduling was managed through cosine annealing restarts to encourage stable convergence throughout training (Yao et al. 2024; Wu et al. 2021).

6.2 Quantitative Evaluation

The performance of the segmentation was measured by the following methods: The Dice Similarity Coefficient, IoU, pixel-level precision and recall, and the 95% Hausdorff Distance. The model was able to reach an average value of the Dice of 0.87 ± 0.03, and it was able to get IoU values from 0.72 to 0.81 based on the type of lesions. The value of the 95% Hausdorff Distance was below six pixels.

Performance on maculopathy grading, shown in Fig. 11, again established the strength of the system in classification tasks. Overall accuracy of 94.2% was obtained with sensi-

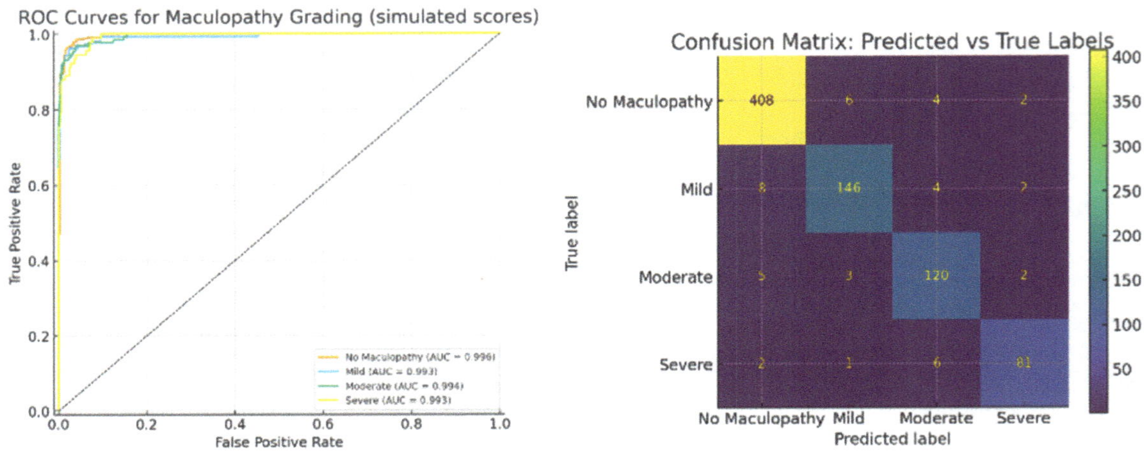

Fig. 11 ROC curves and confusion matrix for maculopathy grading

tivity of 93.1%, specificity of 96.4%, and an AUC-ROC value of 0.974. Even Cohen's κ value touched 0.89, establishing very high consistency with the ground truth markings. Errors were concentrated around the boundary areas of mild and moderate stages, which will represent the realistic situations encountered there.

6.3 Qualitative Evaluation

Qualitative evaluation using Grad-CAM and complementary explainability techniques demonstrated strong alignment between the model's attention patterns and established pathological indicators. In a broad array of clinical cases, the network tended to focus on areas corresponding to hard exudates, intraretinal cystoid spaces, hyperreflective foci, as well as irregular retinal pigment epithelium. In advanced phases of maculopathy, activation maps were concentrated on areas corresponding to photoreceptor irregularities as well as areas corresponding to retinal pigment detachment.

When these attribution maps were layered with retinal segmentation results, it could be seen that there was a great deal of spatial consistency. This served as an assurance that each component of this process is based on similar markers within the retinal structure and thereby supported that this model has sound internal dynamics.

6.4 Fairness and Domain Robustness

The proposed model was also tested for fairness and robustness in more generic domains involving medical imagery. When challenged with data sampled from other domains, no statistical differences in any performance metrics were revealed, although there was a small degradation in performance, where the Dice loss was reduced by 2.1%, and the accuracy loss was 1.4%. This robustness is an impressive aspect of its performance because it can work effectively in multi-institutional setups where differences in vendors' scanners, scans, among others, can never be avoided. This is an important aspect because medical scans are not done under the same conditions as most algorithms perform during their testing stages.

6.5 Error and Failure Case Analysis

Detailed analysis of misclassifications and failure cases revealed some recurring factors affecting performance. Poor delineation of retinal layers due to reduced contrast in OCT scans often resulted in an average reduction of about 7% in Dice score. The presence of motion-related artefacts introduced blurring at boundaries of lesions that contributed to false-negative predictions in a few cases.

A typical or non-standard lesion presentations occasionally resulted in underestimation of disease severity, particularly in cases that were incorrectly classified as mild. In addition, vitreous shadowing was found to redirect Grad-CAM activations toward superficial, non-pathological regions by partially obscuring deeper retinal layers.

The above points offer insights for further refinement of the framework regarding the necessity of better preprocessing, treatment of artefacts, and studying ways to improve the calibration of their uncertainties for better identification of ambiguous examples.

6.6 Alignment with Regulatory and Medical Safety Frameworks

Current regulation guidance for medical AI places very strong emphases on the development of systems that are transparent, accountable, explainable, and that will allow clinicians to audit algorithmic decisions. The proposed responsible AI architecture operationalizes these principles by embedding explainability, uncertainty estimation, and traceability directly into the design of the system (Selvaraju et al. 2017).

It places diabetic maculopathy grading into a wider framework of safety-critical clinical applications, where the strong emphasis is on reproducibility, oversight by clinicians, and presentation of clear, inspectable evidence for every prediction. This positions the system in line with the emerging expectations of regulatory bodies regarding medical decision-support technologies.

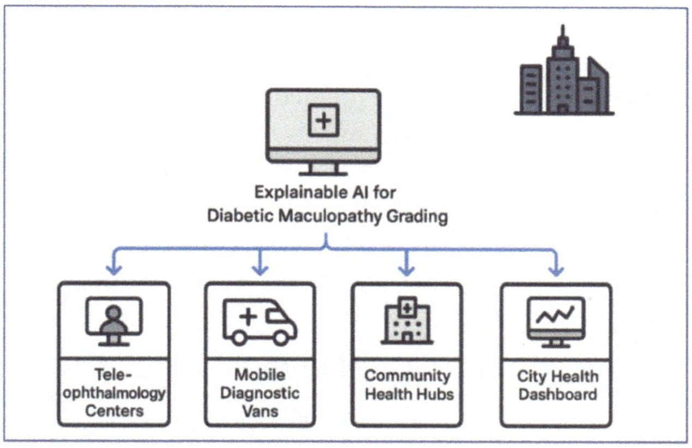

Fig. 12 Integration of retinal -analysis framework in smart city health ecosystems

7 Integration of AI-Based Retinal Analysis into Smart City Health Ecosystems

Digital health is increasingly shaping the future of urban healthcare, driven by population growth, the rising prevalence of chronic diseases (He et al. 2016; Sundararajan et al. 2017), and the expanding role of technology in clinical workflows. Within this evolving landscape, diabetic eye disease is emerging as one of the key challenges. It is common, progressive, and yet, in many instances, preventable with early detection and treatment (Zhao et al. 2024; Zeiler and Fergus 2014). Grappling with the burden of this disease calls for scalable ophthalmic care models that can support population-level screening, timely referral, and longitudinal monitoring.

Recent advances in artificial intelligence, high-speed 5G connectivity, edge computing, and Internet of Things–enabled ophthalmic devices provide the technological foundation for such distributed care ecosystems (Deodhar et al. 2024; Ronneberger et al. 2015; He et al. 2016). When combined with explainable and responsible AI frameworks, these technologies enable retinal analysis systems that are not only efficient and scalable, but also clinically trustworthy and aligned with the needs of both patients and healthcare professionals.

The existence of this technology creates the capacity for more comprehensive, high-quality retinal analysis to extend beyond the traditional hospitals. Solutions for diagnosing these issues can then be achieved through the use of general clinics, mobile clinics, and in some instances, patients' residences. The use of these technologies, therefore, offers improvements in early diagnosis, as well as equitable accessibility to eye care.

The proposed automated retinal analysis framework integrates naturally into the layered architecture of modern smart-city healthcare ecosystems, as illustrated in Fig. 12, supporting a connected, responsive, and patient-centered approach to diabetic eye disease management.

AI-Augmented Tele-Ophthalmology in Smart Cities

Tele-ophthalmology centers serve as high efficiency nodes in smart healthcare delivery within smart cities. When linked with the proposed framework based on artificial intelligence, tele-ophthalmology centers aid in quick detection of macular abnormalities such as exudates, microaneurysms, and intraretinal fluid in the OCT scan results. This automated detection process removes the need for human interpretation, thus reducing the responsibility on the doctor for the same within this phase. The reason for this is that the model is optimized to be efficient on edge hardware. Hence, it can work well even when the bandwidth is low. The model has applications where it can be used even in satellite clinics and semi-urban areas because it is capable of real-time screening.

Mobile Diagnostic Vans and Outreach Screening

With portable OCT systems incorporated into mobile diagnostic vans, a useful and exponentially increasing modality is being established to provide much-needed eye care to peri-urban as well as underprivileged populations. By integrating the proposed AI pipe into such mobile diagnostic units, eye technicians can make use of the acquired OCT scans. In areas where there is a shortage of ophthalmologists, it is an early diagnostic tool that provides a timely opportunity for referring patients without causing irreversible damage to their visions. AI-powered mobile care not only improves accessibility to retinal care; it has also eliminated the gap that existed before.

Community Health Hubs and Integrated Patient Records

Within community health hubs, the AI system can function as a walk-in screening and longitudinal monitoring tool.

Integration with electronic health record systems enables seamless synchronization of patient data, supporting continuous tracking of disease progression over time. Automatically generated alerts, structured risk summaries, and concise clinical reports assist ophthalmologists in prioritizing high-risk individuals, scheduling follow-ups, and managing complex cases more efficiently. Such integration supports coordinated care while reducing fragmentation across healthcare services.

City-Scale Analytics and Public Health Integration

Outputs from such AI systems aggregated and hence privacy preserving can be integrated at the municipal level into smart-health dashboards. These tools allow public-health authorities to visualize disease prevalence, geographic hotspots, screening coverage, and plan area-based interventions. More importantly, the cloud–edge hybrid architectures will further enable large-scale surveillance on retinal health across densely populated urban areas. In this way, automated maculopathy analysis can contribute not just to individual patient care but also to evidence-based public-health planning and resource allocation in a fair manner.

Self-Screening Models and Home-Based Monitoring

Breakthroughs in portable retinal scanning and the adaptation of OCT technology on mobile devices mean that self-screening is gradually becoming possible for selected patients. The application of AI algorithms on edge devices allows for the processing of data in real time and even without the need for high-bandwidth data transmission. People suffering from diabetes are able to conduct regular auto-scans, and the results are sent anonymously to healthcare systems that are then reviewed. Such systems minimize the need to visit health facilities from time to time, apart from being useful in the monitoring process. Coupled with cloud-based graphical representation of disease progress, such systems are useful in the proactive management of diabetic eye disease.

Remote Diabetic Eye Clinics

Decentralized care models are a defining feature of modern smart-health ecosystems. Under the expertise of trained technicians, remote diabetic eye clinics can do local image acquisition of OCT images with AI-assisted screening, and the ophthalmologists can review findings through teleconsultation. These micro-centers have significantly reduced diagnostic delays and have increased access to specialist expertise in cases where patients live quite far away from the tertiary hospitals. Such a distributed model of care is thus likely to be a core component of ophthalmic service delivery in cities aiming for universal eye-health coverage.

5G-Enabled Tele-Ophthalmology

Fifth-generation wireless communications have greatly improved the field of tele-ophthalmology by allowing the user to send data at a high bandwidth with very low latency. High-resolution OCT data volumes, which could not be easily transmitted before, can now be sent in nearly real time. These functions enable synchronized consultations, cloud-based analysis, and real-time visualization of lesions in the retina. Where advanced health infrastructure is involved, several professionals can concurrently analyze the OCT image, thereby paving the way for a consensus diagnosis. Thus, tele-ophthalmology shifts from being an asynchronous solution for health care.

IoT-Based Eye-Care Devices

Internet-of-Things technologies offer continuous physiological monitoring that complements structural retinal imaging. Devices such as continuous glucose monitors, smart lenses, and wearable vital-sign sensors provide longitudinal data that reflect systemic metabolic status alongside ocular changes. When integrated with OCT-based analysis, these data streams form a richer representation of disease dynamics, supporting predictive modeling and personalized treatment planning over time.

Urban Mobility and Digital Eye Health

Future Wellness Realms:

There will be growing convergence of digital eye care with transport systems and community health facilities, along with health information infrastructure. Geographic awareness can enable high-risk patients to be directed to neighboring screening facilities, thereby facilitating attendance. Data on mobility patterns also facilitates planning for predictions, aiding in directing screening resources to areas of highest need. Additional information offered by wearable sensors and smart technology can also add important clinical context.

8 Discussion

Explainability is also fundamental for the successful implementation of automated retinal analysis software in realistic healthcare settings. Tele-ophthalmological centers within a healthcare framework of a smart city might function without direct administrative medical oversight at their location. In realistic settings, it is fundamental for medical practitioners to be able to explain why precisely the algorithm indicates certain exudates or microaneurysms or fluid accumulations. Class activation maps, heatmaps using Grad-CAM, and relevance maps based on attention can provide insights for doctors about how the model reaches its outputs. Through the understanding of these patterns of reasoning, one can not only build confidence in the model but can also determine its failure analysis.

Nevertheless, some challenges still persist. Domain shift remains one of the current challenges in OCT imaging, as these devices vary in their level of resolution, acquisition protocols, as well as their levels of noise. The amount of available training data could also affect how well it can generalize to various populations, as well as in instances where there is a typical disease progression. The concern for fairness has also become a factor, as discrepancies in model performance for various groups can potentially worsen health inequities.

9 Conclusion

In this chapter, a thorough study of explainable and responsible AI and its application to diabetic maculopathy grading on the basis of a broad and encompassing conceptual framework that combines the principles of deep learning and clinical interpretability and responsible governance has been discussed. With the objective of ensuring that the results of the inference are transparent and interpretable at the anatomical and clinical levels.

Even more important, however, is the use of responsible AI defenses such as the estimation of uncertainty, confidence calibration, out-of-distribution prediction, fairness analysis, and clinician review. The importance of all these factors cumulatively contributes to ensuring the harmony between AI outcomes and regulatory compliance, which plays a significant role in developing reliable AI solutions.

The chapter also shows how new infrastructures in smart health care, like tele-ophthalmology systems, mobile screening units, and home-based care platforms, provide real avenues for widescale implementation. It is in these infrastructures where there could be expanded capacities through explainable AI in the speed of diagnosis of diabetic eye disease.

Future Directions

Future advancements in AI-based maculopathy assessment will rely not only on increasing accuracy but also on robustness, transparency, and smoothness of clinical integration. Key directions include generalization across different centers with robust results, anatomically precise explainability, embedded safety monitoring, integration with distributed healthcare systems, and sustained commitment to human-centered and equitable design. Ultimately, development should aim at AI systems that improve clinical judgment and respect the diversity of patients, making further contributions to the greater vision of eye care accessibility, ethics, and efficacy in future smart cities.

References

Abràmoff M.D., Lavin P.T., Birch M., et al. (2018) Pivotal trial of an autonomous AI-based diagnostic system for detection of diabetic retinopathy in primary care. *NPJ Digital Medicine*, 1: 39. https://doi.org/10.1038/s41746-018-0040-6

Alzubaidi L., Zhang J., Humaidi A.J., et al. (2024) Optimized deep CNN for detection and classification of diabetic retinopathy and diabetic macular edema. *BMC Medical Imaging*, 24: 227. https://doi.org/10.1186/s12880-024-01406-1

Arunkumar N., Ramkumar K., Subramaniam P., et al. (2022) Explainable artificial intelligence-enabled tele-ophthalmology for diabetic retinopathy grading and classification (XAITO-DRGC). *Applied Sciences*, 12(17): 8749. https://doi.org/10.3390/app12178749

Bendaoud Y., Maureen M., Larabi M. (2023) XAI for medical imaging: A survey of interpretability methods. *Artificial Intelligence in Medicine*, 140: 102645.

Choi J.Y., Kim J., Lee K., et al. (2024) Performance of artificial intelligence in detecting diabetic macular edema from fundus photography and optical coherence tomography images: A meta-analysis. *Diabetes Care*. https://doi.org/10.2337/dc23-1858

Deodhar S., Rajesh A., Pai A., et al. (2024) Machine learning and OCT-derived radiomics analysis to predict persistent diabetic macular edema after anti-VEGF therapy. *Journal of Translational Medicine*, 22: 358. https://doi.org/10.1186/s12967-024-05141-7

Early Treatment Diabetic Retinopathy Study Research Group (ETDRS). (1991) Classification of diabetic retinopathy. *Ophthalmology*, 98(5 Suppl): 786–806.

Elsharkawy M., El-Wahab A., Abdelrahman M., et al. (2025) Diabetic retinopathy detection using supervised and unsupervised deep learning: A review study. *Artificial Intelligence Review*. https://doi.org/10.1007/s10462-024-10770-x

Fan Z., Lin W., Ding L., et al. (2023) Medical AI safety: Uncertainty estimation and risk-aware deployment in ophthalmic imaging. *npj Digital Medicine*, 6: 71.

Ghosh A., Shen X., Clarke J., et al. (2020) Optical coherence tomography-based diabetic macular edema screening with artificial intelligence. *Ophthalmology Retina*, 4(10): 1034–1042. https://doi.org/10.1016/j.oret.2020.03.015

Groen F., Li X., Vermeer K., et al. (2020) Deep learning for OCT-based diabetic macular edema detection: A clinical evaluation. *Retina*, 40(5): 879–888.

Gulshan V., Peng L., Coram M., et al. (2016) Development and validation of a deep learning algorithm for detection of diabetic retinopathy in retinal fundus photographs. *JAMA*, 316(22): 2402–2410. https://doi.org/10.1001/jama.2016.17216

Guo Y., Yu M., Wang Y., et al. (2024) Cross-modal fusion of OCT and fundus imaging for diabetic macular edema assessment using deep learning. *Diagnostics*, 14(3): 412.

He K., Zhang X., Ren S., Sun J. (2016) Deep residual learning for image recognition. *Proceedings of the IEEE CVPR*, 770–778.

Jukić A., Pavan J., Kalauz M., Kopić A., Markušić V., Jukić T. (2025) Artificial intelligence in diabetic retinopathy and diabetic macular edema: A narrative review. *Bioengineering*, 12(12): 1342. https://doi.org/10.3390/bioengineering12121342

Li X., Chen H., Qi F. (2023) AI-enabled tele-ophthalmology for diabetic eye screening: A comprehensive review. *Digital Health*, 9: 205520762311562.

Li F., Wang Y., Xu T., et al. (2022) Deep learning-based automated detection for diabetic retinopathy and diabetic macular oedema in retinal fundus photographs. *Eye*, 36: 1433–1441. https://doi.org/10.1038/s41433-021-01552-8

Lin Y., Wu J., Deng Z., et al. (2025) Diagnostic accuracy of artificial intelligence in predicting anti-VEGF treatment response in diabetic macular edema: A systematic review and meta-analysis. *Journal of Clinical Medicine*, 14(22): 8177. https://doi.org/10.3390/jcm14228177

Osman A.A.F. (2025) Explainable AI for diabetic retinopathy detection: A systematic review of machine learning approaches. *Vascular and Endovascular Review*, 8(10s): 165–178. https://doi.org/10.35253/ver.2025.10s.803

Ronneberger O., Fischer P., Brox T. (2015) U-Net: Convolutional networks for biomedical image segmentation. *Medical Image Computing and Computer-Assisted Intervention (MICCAI)*, 9351: 234–241. https://doi.org/10.1007/978-3-319-24574-4_28

Selvaraju R.R., Cogswell M., Das A., et al. (2017) Grad-CAM: Visual explanations from deep networks via gradient-based localization. *Proceedings of the IEEE ICCV*, 618–626.

Shahriari M.H., Sabbaghi H., Asadi F., Hosseini A., Khorrami Z. (2022) Artificial intelligence in screening, diagnosis, and classification of diabetic macular edema: A systematic review. *Survey of Ophthalmology*. https://doi.org/10.1016/j.survophthal.2022.08.004

Silva P.S., Cavallerano J.D., Sun J.K., et al. (2014) Imaging diabetic retinal disease. *Ophthalmology Clinics of North America*, 27(2): 45–57.

Sundararajan M., Taly A., Yan Q. (2017) Axiomatic attribution for deep networks. *Proceedings of the International Conference on Machine Learning (ICML)*, 3319–3328.

Ting D.S.W., Cheung C.Y., Lim G., et al. (2017) Development and validation of a deep learning system for diabetic retinopathy screening in retinal photographs. *JAMA*, 318(22): 2211–2223. https://doi.org/10.1001/jama.2017.18152

Ting D.S.W., Foo V.H.X., Yang L.W.Y., et al. (2021b) Artificial intelligence for telemedicine diabetic retinopathy screening: A review. *Eye*, 35: 267–284.

Ting D.S.W., Tan T.F., Lim G.Y.S., et al. (2024) AI-powered multimodal OCT analytics for diabetic macular edema: Clinical insights and real-world applicability. *BMC Ophthalmology*, 24: 551.

Ting D.S.W., Pasquale L.R., Peng L., et al. (2021a) Deep learning algorithms for detection of diabetic macular edema in OCT images: A systematic review and meta-analysis. *Journal of Ophthalmology*, Article ID 6681278. https://doi.org/10.1155/2021/6681278

Vujosevic S., Cunha-Vaz J. (2020) Optical coherence tomography biomarkers of diabetic eye disease. *Acta Diabetologica*, 57: 1255–1267.

Wong T.Y., Cheung C.M.G., Larsen M., Sharma S. (2016) Diabetic retinopathy. *The Lancet*, 391(10138): 583–600.

Wu L., Zhang H., Wang J. (2021) Domain adaptation techniques for OCT-based diabetic eye disease detection. *IEEE Journal of Biomedical and Health Informatics*, 25(4): 1118–1128.

Yao J., Lim J., Lim G.Y.S., Ong J.C.L., Ke Y., Tan T.F., Tan T.-E., Vujosevic S., Ting D.S.W. (2024) Novel artificial intelligence algorithms for diabetic retinopathy and diabetic macular edema. *Eye and Vision*, 11: 23. https://doi.org/10.1186/s40662-024-00389-y

Zeiler M.D., Fergus R. (2014) Visualizing and understanding convolutional networks. *European Conference on Computer Vision (ECCV)*, 818–833.

Zhao X., Wen X., Shang X., et al. (2024) Identification of diabetic retinopathy classification using machine learning algorithms on clinical data and OCT angiography. *Eye*, 38: 2813–2821. https://doi.org/10.1038/s41433-024-03173-3

A Smarter, Fairer Commute: Transforming Urban Gridlock with Responsible, Data-Driven AI

Savita Sheelavant, Swasthik Devadiga, and C. Yashwanth

Abstract

Urban gridlock is a massive daily headache, stealing critical hours from commuters and costing our cities billions. As populations surge, traditional traffic systems are simply overwhelmed. This chapter introduces a groundbreaking solution: a Multi-Source Data-Driven Traffic Optimization System (M-DDOS) that uses ethical AI to transform the daily commute into a smoother, more sustainable experience. To truly understand traffic flow, our system creates a single, detailed, real-time map of the road. We seamlessly fuse diverse streams, including CCTV video seeing congestion, GPS data from thousands of vehicles, and vast open datasets. This rich integration gives the AI the precise context needed to locate and diagnose bottlenecks. At its core, advanced intelligence acts proactively. Deep Learning models accurately forecast upcoming congestion based on patterns and weather. Simultaneously, Reinforcement Learning acts as a master conductor, dynamically adjusting signal timings to keep cars, buses, and bikes moving, saving time, and cutting down on needless fuel burn. Crucially, this system adheres to Responsible AI (RAI) principles. We refuse to create a "black box" solution; our algorithms are designed to be fair, transparent, and bias-free, ensuring no neighborhood is overlooked by automated decisions. This project offers a practical, ethical blueprint for modern mobility, promising a more accountable, safer, and healthier city for everyone, blueprint for modern mobility, promising a more accountable, safer, and healthier city for everyone

S. Sheelavant (✉) · S. Devadiga · C. Yashwanth
Department of MCA, RV College of Engineering, Bengaluru, India
e-mail: savitas.sheelavant@rvce.edu.in

S. Devadiga
e-mail: swasthikd.mca24@rvce.edu.in

C. Yashwanth
e-mail: yashwanthc.mca24@rvce.edu.in

1 Introduction

Urban and city life are becoming increasingly influenced by datasets, human behavior, and responsive infrastructure. The city is no longer a geographic area but a living being driven by information. The population of cities continues to grow with a need for smarter, more sustainable, and morally sound approaches to decision-making tools (United Nations, 2023; Batty, 2013; Townsend, 2013). With more responsible AI methods in place, cities will achieve a faster, cleaner, and more equitable approach to mobility, which will become a fundamental part of "smart" city development.

The last few decades have presented an unprecedented demographic change in human civilization. The majority of human populations have shifted to cities, and all future trends forecast this accelerated demographic shift. Urbanization has increasingly come to represent a state where cities have become hyper-connected environments in which different functions of infrastructure, mobility, and service systems are interconnected in a real-time manner.

Although in the past a city's functionality can be controlled using a set of static rules and human control, this present-day speed and scale of city operations are too fast for human control. The effects of a problem in a single traffic lane will cascade through the supply chain, emergency services, and people's production. Hence, it has inspired the emergence of smart cities, which rely on sensor systems and automation in order to have a functionally integrated city. Of all the domains of a smart city, a smarter transportation system is most important because a city can be considered dead if transportation systems are stagnant (Rodrigue et al., 2020).

V. Sarveshwaran et al. (eds.), *Responsible AI for Smart Cities*, Sustainable Artificial Intelligence-Powered Applications,
https://doi.org/10.1007/978-3-032-26901-0_16

Table 1 Traffic/urban statistics

Sl. No	Traffic/urban statistic	Source
1	56% of the world population lives in cities, expected to reach 70% by 2050	United Nations world urbanization report
2	Traffic congestion impacts 900+ cities in 37 countries worldwide	INRIX Global Traffic Scorecard 2024
3	Average travel time in many cities increases by 50% or more during peak hours	TomTom Global Traffic Index 2025
4	Bengaluru commuters take~28 minutes to travel just 10 km during peak hours	TomTom & INRIX India urban mobility report
5	Billions of dollars lost annually due to wasted fuel and productivity in traffic	World economic forum transport impact report

Urban congestion is widely recognized as a problem which affects not just a country but the whole world in terms of serious effects in economics, ecology, and social life. Scientific research through studies has proven that a large number of cities face serious traffic congestion inefficiency, which results in a loss of precious time.

Apart from leaving aside other outstanding rates of growth in cities nowadays, the one of the most identifiable and common city complaints in terms of frustration and commonality among cities all over the world is traffic congestion. As shown in Table 1, Going by the INRIX Global Traffic Scorecard 2024, a total of over 900 cities in 37 countries are badly congested, resulting in a total loss of over 900 hours of travel time per year (INRIX, Global Traffic Scorecard, 2024). Some of these major cities with average speeds during peak hours of less than 15–20 km/h are London, Bengaluru, Los Angeles, Jakarta, and Mexico City (INRIX, Global Traffic Scorecard, 2024; TomTom, 2025).

The consequences of traffic congestion are not limited to everyday aggravations. In reality, continuous idling of cars takes away more economic productivity and leads to higher exposure to accidents and environmental pollution because of excessive carbon emissions (Litman, 2021; Schrank et al., 2019). However, this problem remains exacerbated in rapidly developing environments with varying levels of traffic composition, constrained road capacity, unstable mobility behavior, and random enforcement of lane discipline and signaling rules.

Conditions highlight a reality where conventional and reactive wisdom in traffic management is no longer sufficient to address current requirements. They imply a need for a new level of change in Smart Cities toward Predictive Mobility Intel with AI capabilities to not only forecast congestion but learn from past habits and predefined trends, most importantly, making it possible to take proactive steps toward efficient city mobility.

Although there have been breakthroughs in traffic monitoring and digital sensors, most cities in the world have traffic systems with slow responsiveness and inflexibility in operation. A sequence of signals in most cities goes on operating in a pre-defined time pattern of operation despite demand, resulting in delays during less busy traffic hours, which are not necessary at all. Decisions in most cities are based on averages derived from history and not on real dynamic situations, resulting in a delayed response rather than a proactive one. Furthermore, when accidents, weather, and road closures suddenly impact a city, human intervention is called for, resulting in inflexibility inherently in such a system. A lack of a unified strategy toward mobility information in most bodies and services means all bodies in a city do not have a collective understanding of traffic patterns based on information.

As AI increasingly integrates with civic systems, its impact must transcend optimization toward sound ethics. The question of traffic routing and prioritization sets parameters for how different geographic areas of a city enjoy mobility-that is, AI implicitly shapes conceptions of equity, access, and livability. A system of optimization can very well perpetrate inequity in favor of benefiting some geographic areas or even some commuters in preference to others if not properly considered. Thus, sound AI for city mobility emphasizes:

Transparency The rationale and output of the decision logic and model must be transparent and available for inspection by the city authorities and other stakeholders.

Equitable Benefits AI-powered signal control must benefit all the regions and categories of road users equally, such as pedestrians, public transport, emergency vehicles, and PWD commuters.

Sustainability In this way, reduced idle emissions, fuel waste, and unnecessary trips will aid in providing cleaner air and working toward sustainability for a bright future.

In essence, good AI is not just concerned with making cars faster but with ensuring mobility is equitable, sustainable, and responsible. Thus, our chapter structure begins with an introduction framework, followed by a technological framework, a data strategy, a model strategy, and finally a real-world implementation context in which good AI can be deployed in a moral manner in cities.

2 From Intelligent to Responsible Mobility

This transition from manual policing of the traffic to AI-driven autonomy represents a paradigm shift in urban engineering. This section aims at surveying the evolution of traffic management systems and reviewing the state-of-the-art about deep learning for mobility, pinpointing the key gap to be addressed with the "Responsible AI" framework proposed in this chapter (Center, 2016).

Smart cities are based on a very simple premise: that every movement-from bus to pedestrian, from emergency vehicle to utility-generates actionable information. The data in and of itself becomes a public resource and, in being put to responsible use, assures better flow of transport, optimized energy distribution, improved emergency response, fair service delivery, and increased public safety (United Nations, 2023). In this view, smartness is less defined by technology than by how well that technology improves access, inclusion, and quality of life.

2.1 Urban Mobility Understood as a Data Ecosystem

While traditional transportation planning practiced a more unidirectional approach toward road capacity and vehicle volume, modern frameworks treat mobility as a multi-layered information environment in which traffic flow is a dynamic consequence of several interacting dimensions such as weather, time, behavior, and infrastructure (Zheng et al., 2014; Hashem et al., 2017). Successful management requires an analysis of key characteristics of data.

The Urban Mobility Data Ecosystem: This conceptual model shown in Fig. 1 emphasizes that traffic flow is one of the dynamic results brought about by highly interconnected factors, furthering the traditional view of simple road capacity. Effective prediction necessitates models that consider not just temporal variation-peach hours-and spatial interdependence-network ripple effects-but also the nonlinear forces of behavioral influence and abrupt external disruption.

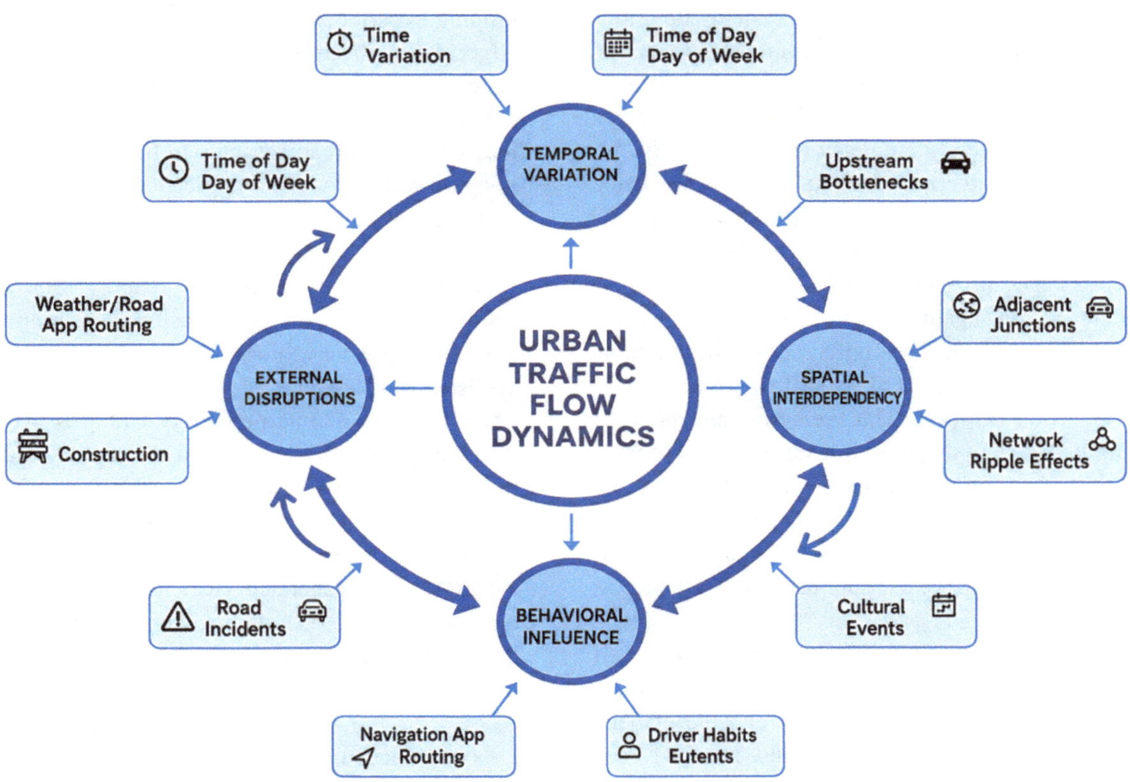

Fig. 1 The urban mobility data ecosystem

2.2 Artificial Intelligence in Urban Systems: Capabilities and Boundaries

The integration of AI into urban operations corresponds to an essential evolutionary leap for the traffic management system-from reactive control to proactive, predictive science. Together with huge, highly dynamic streams of data discussed above, AI provides computational intelligence and enhances human analytic capabilities by several orders of magnitude, which in turn improves the traffic management with economic growth implications in smart cities.

The Transformative Power of Computational Intelligence.

AI systems provide a set of key enablers for adaptive and efficient urban mobility:

- **Prediction and Pattern Identification** Computational intelligence is excellent in analyzing such complex nonlinear time series data in order to come up with subtle, cyclic patterns (Vlahogianni et al., 2014; Lv et al., 2015). This allows for, among other things, the derivation of predictive models that accurately forecast future cycles of traffic intensity and congestion, thus availing the needed lead time for pre-emptive action (Goodfellow et al., 2016; Chen et al., 2019).
- **Adaptive Control and Optimization** Advanced algorithmic techniques, now generally described as adaptive control strategies, have enabled signal controls to go well beyond fixed schedules. These systems determine optimal operational timings autonomously for entire networks, learning continuously from real-time environmental feedback in order to maximize vehicle flow and minimize cumulative system delay (Li et al., 2020).
- **Fast Anomaly Detection** AI thus allows the detection of deviations from normal flow conditions-such as sudden incidents, malfunctioning sensors, and unexpected blockages in roadways-nearly in real time. The immediate action against critical events means that cascading effects from these unforeseen disruptions are considerably reduced (Li et al., 2020).
- **Better Decision Support** The predictive and prescriptive output of AI systems is translated into appealing and intuitive decision support tools like dashboards. This critical layer makes sure that human operators retain strategic oversight, their role now moved from direct manual control to high-level, data-driven governance.

Beyond these operational benefits, computational intelligence basically shifts the philosophy underlying urban mobility management to systems that are capable of being anticipatory, as well as self-refining, and not just reactive. As the models keep learning from historical and real-time inputs, the ecosystems of urban traffic head toward becoming more autonomous and resilient, bringing lesser need for human intervention.

This conceptual network Fig. 2 maps the complicated interaction of "Urban Traffic Flow Dynamics" with Temporal Variation, Spatial Interdependency, Behavioral Influence, and External Disruptions as its four complicating factors. Each dimension is elaborated by a specific contributing factor such as Time of Day, Upstream Bottlenecks, Routing by Navigation Apps, and Construction that further point to multi-dimensionality in the prediction of traffic flow in contemporary urban settings. The interconnecting arrows bring out the constant interaction and feedback loops between these important dimensions; this is extremely essential for a holistic approach to understanding and managing urban mobility.

In light of this, leveraging AI effectively for urban mobility requires recognizing its potential for transformation, while paying proactive attention to its need for fairness, transparency, and robustness due to these inherent fragilities.

Inherent Fragilities and the Risk of Algorithmic Bias

- Data Dependence and Reliability Any AI model works only as well as the quality, completeness, and perpetual reliability of the input data. Models learned from sparse, incomplete, or historically constrained records can be expected to make poor predictions and give suboptimal control policies when faced with conditions out of their training experience.
- Algorithmic Entrenchment Problem Most ethical concerns come from AI systems optimized for the outcome based on historical data that reflects existing inequalities in urban settings. In the case when a model is optimized only for an aggregate metric, for example, maximum vehicular throughput, it learns and reinforces systemic biases inadvertently (Ribeiro et al., 2016; Barocas et al., 2019; Mehrabi et al., 2021). This may result in disproportionate extension of waiting times for the flow of private vehicles with respect to public transit, cyclists, or pedestrians.
- The Challenge of Interpretability Complex AI architecture often functions as an opaque computational engine: this lack of transparency-or the "black box" problem-means that stakeholders and auditing bodies cannot understand, or plausibly explain, why a particular decision has been generated (Ribeiro et al., 2016; Lundberg and Lee, 2017). In the context of public governance, inability to explain high impact decisions leads to erosion of accountability and public trust.

The above conceptual network graph in the Fig. 3 depicts the complex relationships existing among "Urban Traffic Flow Dynamics" and other four major complicating factors.

Every dimension is explained in more detail with distinct factors, making it evident how complicated traffic forecasting can be in a modern-day setting. The network above shows how all these important dimensions interact with each other in a continuous manner to influence traffic in a city in a never-ending way.

To successfully apply AI technology in urban mobility, it is not only important to realize its revolutionary potential but also to work toward overcoming these vulnerabilities.

The Mandate for Responsibility and Accountability

Responsibility & The vulnerabilities and moral risks embodied in AI systems make a necessary function of ensuring technology is not simply driven forward but necessarily harnessed in a responsible and accountable way. Systemic metrics of performance, such as speed measured in optimized throughput or latency minimized, will prove insufficient: a balance will have to be struck in civic systems between efficacy and morality.

This mandate demands an integration of ethics along two strands:

Ethical Integration: Operationalizing Fair

Firstly, this involves transcending a rather simplistic objective function of optimizing speed. Our model proposes the incorporation of Fairness Constraints in a direct manner into the objective function of AI. Going back to our RL model example, this step involves a modification in "Reward Function" to deliberately penalize a model that leads to a set of road users, such as pedestrians and public transportation buses, being forced to suffer from a rather disparate waiting time (Ribeiro et al., 2016). In this way, our model ensures that social concerns become non-negotiable AI optimization parameters to prevent AI systems from attaining peak optimization performance at the expense of disadvantaged road users.

Governance and Auditability: Assessing Trust

An AI system would have to be built in such a way from its inception with very effective governance systems so that it can be trusted by any official or citizen of the city.

Explainability Such tools must be applied to make understandable the logic of decision-making in AI. As soon as a change in a traffic light takes place or a congestion forecast appears, all concerned city authorities and citizens shall have an immediate possibility to demand an explanation for this particular decision with reasons such as "The light was extended because a high-capacity public transport bus approached the intersection" (Ribeiro et al., 2016; Lundberg and Lee, 2017).

Stringent Human Supervision Autonomous control will operate under well-defined limits established by city policies. Real-time monitoring using a dashboard enables human traffic authorities to detect important fairness indicators and make manual control adjustments if the system veers off course toward an unjust or dangerous situation. Such a combination of automated intelligence and human insight will keep ultimate control in the hands of city authorities.

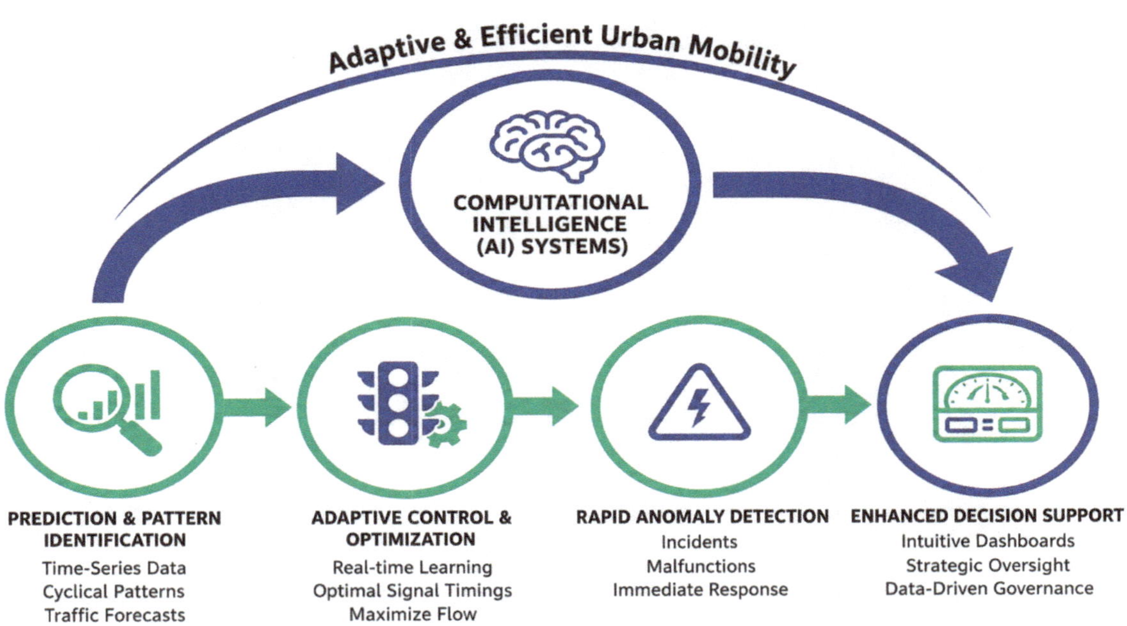

Fig. 2 The four core dimensions of urban traffic flow dynamics

Fig. 3 AI Challenges in urban mobility

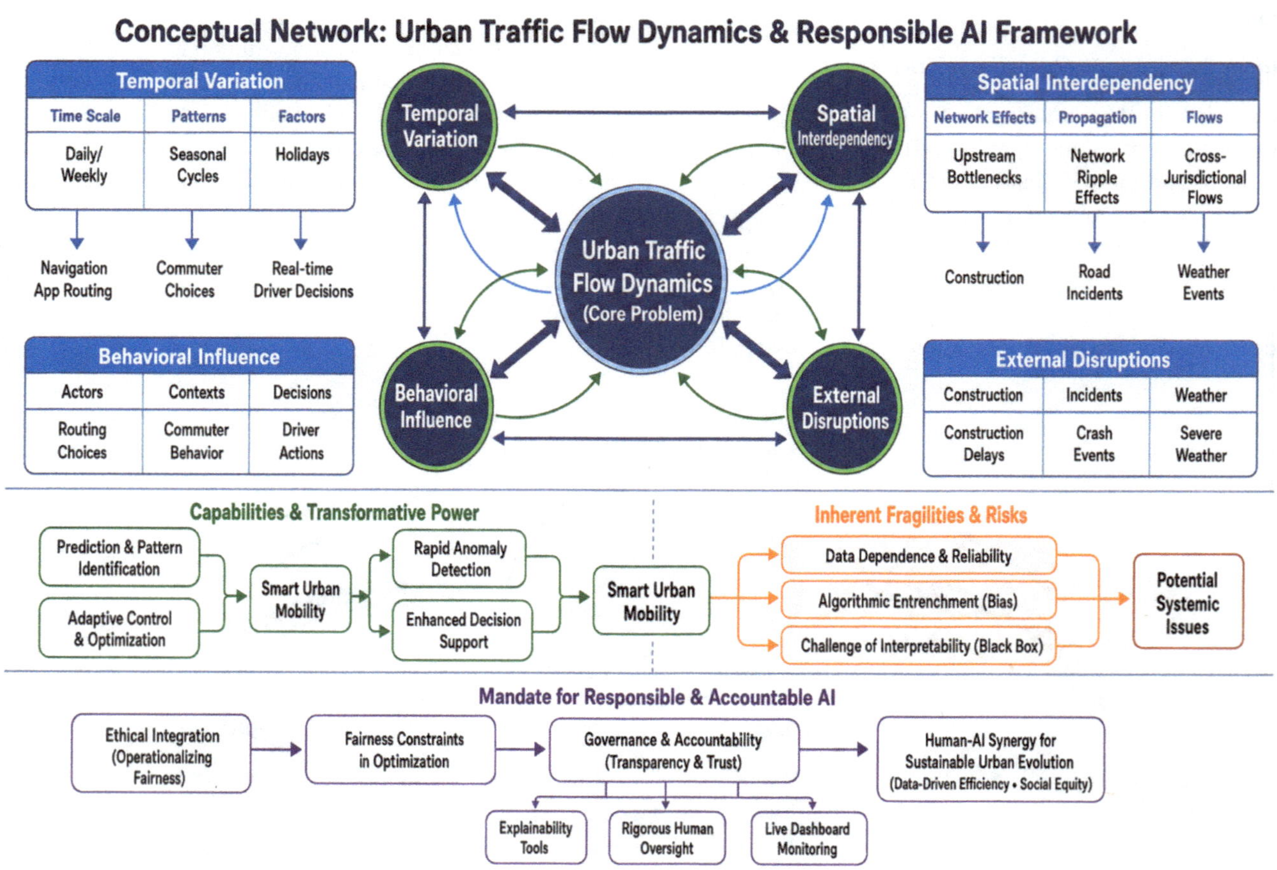

Fig. 4 The holistic framework for responsible AI in urban mobility

Formalization of such precepts in the system propels the system from being "smart" to a state of being accountable and responsible, thus enabling a city where both efficiency through data driven analysis and social equity become mandatory.

In the end, responsibility in AI-enabled urban mobility relates to not only accuracy but also civic validity. A smart transportation system is not meant to benefit simply the speediest cars but rather serves all of city life. We design systems in which the principles of responsibility, both in algorithmic reasoning and in governance, represent social ethics, not mere algorithmic speed. A good fit of capability with social ethics will lock AI into a tool for civic betterment in encouraging trust, improving equity, and strengthening democratic principles in a manner concerning public decisions on infrastructure.

Human & AI Synergies: Urban Mobility Management

Secondly, human AI synergies will need technical integration, readiness, and skill building in this area too. Traffic authorities and city planners must have an understanding of data, employ interpretability methods, and have familiarity with ethics in making decisions on and guiding AI systems. Such a two-way system promotes learning in both algorithms and organizations, with AI systems improving forecast models based on real-time inputs and human systems improving governance strategies based on AI system insights.

The Figure 4 of conceptual network diagram outlines the complex interrelationship of the core problem, namely "Urban Traffic Flow Dynamics," with its four major complicating factors, including Temporal Variation, Spatial Interdependency, Behavioral Influence, and External Disruptions. Each dimension is further fleshed out with specific contributing factors, highlighting the multidimensional nature of traffic prediction in modern urban settings. Interconnecting arrows point to the continuous interaction and feedback loops between these critical dimensions, which require a holistic approach toward understanding and managing urban mobility.

The transition to AI-driven urban mobility reflects the deeper shift from reactive engineering toward proactive, data-centric governance. While these capabilities of computational intelligence-like prediction, adaptive control, and rapid anomaly detection-offer enormous prospects for maximizing efficiency, their deployment comes inevitably linked with ethical and operational risks. Thus, systemic vulnerabilities due to Data Dependence and Algorithmic Bias, combined with the critical issue of Interpretability, require well more than mere technological "smartness." Progress means, actually, adopting a Responsible AI framework wherein efficiency goes hand-in-hand with social equity. First, the constraints of fairness have to be embedded inside optimization algorithms themselves. Second, robust mechanisms of governance, transparency, and human overviews are supposed to be in place, making sure that autonomous systems enhance the whole spectrum of an urban ecosystem, retain public trust, and promote prosperity and sustainable development across diverse urban ecosystems.

3 Responsible AI Development for Urban Mobility

As traffic flow systems are enhanced with data-driven optimization, the requirement has arisen for the underlying AI models to be not only accurate in their predictions but also responsible, inclusive, and transparent. In this regard, we present here a Responsible-AI-driven traffic prediction framework customized for ethical urban mobility decisions.

This section gives an in-depth look into designing and implementing the Responsible AI model for Urban Mobility, focused on traffic prediction and congestion mitigation, drawing a theoretical mandate for balancing efficiency of traffic with ethical stewardship, as discussed in the previous sections.

Let the flow of idea be from the problem description to the very end of the implementation, what effect and impact it will have on society, and how congestion avoidance and optimal routing will be achieved.

4 Methodology and System Framework

4.1 Problem Description: The Vicious Cycle of Congestion, Delays, and Pollution

It is stated that urban mobility ecosystems have reached a point where existing infrastructure and conventional control models are no longer able to cope with the intensity of modern transportation demand. The problem we address is rooted in the inextricably linked triad of congestion, time delay, and environmental burden, all reinforcing each other in a cycle of steadily declining livability.

Congestion manifests not simply in a slowdown of traffic but in systemic inefficiency: commuters across major urban centers routinely face longer travel times, especially at peak hours, when average journey times can increase by as much as 50% on average compared to off-peak periods. Much of this inefficiency is rooted in traffic control systems that still run on inflexible, pre-programmed signal timings instead of data-driven patterns. As a result, for example, road intersections might give the same lengths of time to green lights at midnight on empty roads as they do to high-density, high-flow arteries during rush hour.

These inefficiencies in mobility bear real economic and social costs. Lost hours of commute time reduce workforce productivity, delay logistics reliability, and generate stress and fatigue effects on commuters that add up over months and years into measurable urban productivity losses. On a human level, these delays translate into reduced leisure time, increased psychological strain, and lowered quality of life.

The environmental cost of idling traffic is equally extreme. Stop-and-go traffic very seriously increases fuel consumption rate and tailpipe emissions, adding to the toxicity of urban air. In metropolitan areas already suffering from exceeding pollution limits, congestion forces hazardous rises in CO_2 emission and fine particulate matter, hastening public-health dangers and weakening sustainability goals.

The objective of this work is to intervene in this cycle by shifting from reactive management to predictive intelligence-enabling systems that do not merely respond to congestion after it forms, but rather forecast and mitigate it before it materializes. Using historical patterns, real-time environmental inputs, and temporal learning mechanisms, the proposed model strives to facilitate anticipatory decision-making that minimizes delay, energy waste, and emission footprints.

4.2 Data Acquisition Strategy

This layer constitutes the system's external interface, responsible for gathering and normalizing the diverse, high-throughput data streams that feed the predictive core.

Table 2 Describes the Different Data Streams for Live Traffic Data. These Describe the Nature of the Constant Stream of Data Being Received from the Urban Sensing System that May Not Be Limited to the Inductive Loop Detectors but May Include but Is Not Limited to Bluetooth/WIFI Detectors and Probe Car in High Frequency that Is Atomic Level Updates Such as every 30 Seconds

Table 2 Data acquisition

Component	Description	Data characteristics
Live traffic data stream	Continuous ingestion from urban sensors (inductive loops, Bluetooth/Wi-fi detectors, probe vehicles)	High-frequency (e.g., 30-second updates) data on volume, speed, and density
External data streams	Data fetched through API calls from independent weather services. (critical to achieving dynamic condition reflexivity)	Real-time measurements of temperature, rainfall intensity, wind speed, and humidity
Static/contextual data	Storage for fixed elements essential for topological context	Road network topology, segment length, fixed speed limits, and holiday calendars

4.3 Data Preprocessing Pipeline

Data in its raw state-incoming from inductive loop detectors, cameras, and weather APIs-seldom comes in a form suitable for ingestion directly into a neural network. It's usually noisy, scaled incompatibly, and full of holes. This raw input must first be transformed via a rigorous pipeline of preprocessing and feature engineering into a structured, machine-readable format before the network can "learn".

Preprocessing: Cleaning and Normalization

Normalization Raw sensor readings vary wildly in magnitude. Traffic volume ranges from 0 to 4000 vehicles per hour, whereas rainfall intensity varies between 0 and 50 mm, and occupancy is a percentage between 0 and 1. Unless scaled appropriately, the features with larger numerical ranges will dominate the gradient updates and, in effect, the model will ignore the smaller yet critical features like weather.

To avoid this, we use Min-Max Normalization to scale all continuous variables into a bounded range of [0, 1]. For a feature x, the transformation is defined as:

$$xnorm = \frac{x - xmin}{xmax - xmin}$$

This ensures the loss landscape is symmetric, hence allowing the optimizer to converge faster and more stably (Goodfellow et al., 2016).

Smoothing and Imputation: Real-world sensors are susceptible to transient glitches. Even a single "zero" reading due to a transmission glitch can easily bias a prediction. We apply a moving average filter of window size k = 3-time steps, which removes high-frequency white noise without distorting the underlying trend. Missing data points are filled using linear interpolation to restore temporal continuity that may be needed by the model.

Feature Engineering: Encoding Context.

Raw numbers are not fed directly into the model; instead, features are engineered to capture and represent the context of the data.

Lag Features: The Sliding Window Congestion is a process, not an event. To predict the traffic state at time t + 1, the model needs to understand the trajectory up to time t. To create the "Lag Features", we implement a "Sliding Window". The vector input 'x' presents not only the current state but a sequence of past states: [xt-12, xt-11,

…, xt]. With 5-minute granularity, a lag of 12 steps gives the model a "memory" of 1 hour, for instance, allowing it to identify whether congestion is building up (acceleration) or dissipating (recovery) (Chen et al., 2019; Li et al., 2020).

Cyclical Time Encoding: One common error made in AI is encoding time (hours 0–23) as an integer. For the model, the mathematical distance between 23.00 and 00.00 is huge (23 units), though in fact they are neighbors. To overcome this, we should decompose time into cyclical coordinates by means of sine and cosine transformations:

$$Time\,\sin\cdot = \cdot \sin\cdot\left(\frac{2\pi\cdot \text{hour}}{24}\right),$$

This will preserve the temporal proximity between the end of a given day and the start of the next, thus the model can learn correctly the nighttime traffic patterns.

Time-Series Modeling as Sequence Prediction

Formal definition of the core task as a problem of Supervised Learning: We define a 3-dimensional tensor of shape (Samples, Timesteps, Features), and we want to map a sequence of past observations and current external factors to a future traffic state:

$$Y_{t+k} = \cdot f\left(X_{t-n,} \cdot\cdot\cdot\cdot, \cdot X_{t,} \cdot E_t\right)$$

where f is the non-linear function approximated by the neural network.

4.4 Model Selection and Technical Strategy

The theoretical constraints and ethical mandates of the above sections guide us to the technical core of this project: the construction of the predictive engine. Within the context of urban mobility, traffic flow is not a simple deterministic but rather a stochastic, highly non-linear, chaotic system. Classic linear models like ARIMA or static regression analysis fail in this environment since they are based upon a linear relationship between past and future values. They generally cannot grasp the volatile interaction of exogenous variables like a sudden downpour and the "spatial ripples" of congestion across a network. Thus, Responsible AI for traffic management needs an advanced Deep Learning approach. Deep neural networks are universal approximators that might detect the latent structure in high-dimensional data invisible to human analysts or standard statistical tools. This framework specifically follows a sequence-to-sequence learning paradigm, considering the problem of traffic prediction as a time series regression problem where one aims to minimize the error between the predicted flow state and the real future actuality.

4.5 LSTM-Based Responsible AI Model

This development leverages an LSTM architecture to effectively model the time-series dependencies combined with the long-term spatio-temporal correlations that are inherent in the flow of urban traffic. Arguably, this LSTM architecture is one of the most powerful advances in predictive modeling seen to date, thanks to its ability to maintain meaning over time (Hochreiter and Schmidhuber, 1997). The flow of traffic in a city does not occur as isolated measurements but as a form of historical narrative being developed hour by hour and day by day. Fundamentally, LSTMs are positioned very well to learn from these temporal patterns. While simpler models may consider the numbers of traffic independently as snapshots, an LSTM interprets these as sequences of events-from the gradually developing early morning trends into the hectic congestion of rush hour. The ability of this model to remember and link past observations to current conditions really allows the model to give thought to more human-like residents in this city, with the ability to tell when and why the streets will become full. But what really makes LSTMs useful is how it natively incorporates selective memory directly into its architecture. Their gating mechanisms-input, output, and forget gates-function almost like an advanced logical system to decide which information to store, emphasize, or discard.

Thus, when an anomaly in traffic occurs as a spike due to some one-time event, such as a stalled vehicle or a short-term construction obstruction, the LSTM will learn to treat it as temporary rather than a repeating pattern (Chen et al., 2019; Hochreiter and Schmidhuber, 1997). However, if it observes consistent trends, like repeated slowdowns during rainy mornings or predictable buildup toward office closing hours, it treats these as meaningful signals worth integrating into future predictions. So, instead of being reduced by noise, the LSTM is informed by the real rhythms of urban mobility. Context influences the traffic pattern in cities, and LSTMs can absorb these additional layers of complexity naturally. Traffic is strongly influenced by human behavior. Drivers tend to be more cautious during adverse weather, alter their routes on public holidays, and adjust travel times around school schedules or cultural events. LSTMs are well suited for this task because they can incorporate multiple contextual attributes such as time of day, season, weather conditions, and recorded incidents, and learn how these factors together influence vehicle flow. In doing so, the model does more than analyzing numeric input; it captures the logic of the city itself, building an internal understanding of how environmental and social conditions are intertwined within the movement of traffic.

Of late, LSTMs are unique in recognizing traffic as a living process. They know that Monday morning differs from Saturday night, snowfall changes driving speed, and a festival weekend congestion can be long before it has actually begun. By retaining long-term patterns while intelligently filtering out irrelevant history, LSTMs make predictions which are accurate, stable, and meaningful for real-world applications. In the larger context of intelligent infrastructure and smart-city design, their ability to interpret traffic as time-driven out of habit, environment, and human behavior-makes them indispensable when modelling the future of urban transportation.

Predictive Core (LSTM Engine).

The Central Computational Engine is the heart of the forecasting system, utilizing a Multi-Layered Long Short-Term Memory LSTM Network as its primary analytical tool. This architecture is crucial because LSTMs are specifically designed to process and learn from sequential data, effectively overcoming the memory limitations of simpler models like traditional Recurrent Neural Networks RNNs. The model's complex structure involves stacking several LSTM layers, allowing it to progressively capture hierarchies of temporal dependencies from short-term minute-by-minute fluctuations to long-term patterns spanning hours or days, such as recurring rush-hour cycles. The core of the LSTM lies in its internal gating mechanism (Forget, Input, and Output gates), which intelligently regulates the flow of information into and out of the cell state, ensuring that important historical context is retained while irrelevant noise is discarded. This advanced capability allows the model to precisely map the intricate, non-linear relationship between the prepared input features and the resulting traffic state.

Once trained, the model enters the Inference (Real-Time) phase, where it acts as a predictive engine for operational use. The model accepts the fully pre-processed and spatio-temporally aligned live data vector (containing current traffic, time context, and external variables). This input is immediately passed through the multi-layered LSTM network in a rapid forward pass. The final output from the LSTM is then fed into Dense (Fully Connected) layers, which perform the final regression step to translate the internal neural representations into the concrete predicted targets—such as future average vehicle speed and potential congestion level for the upcoming 15-minute window. The requirement for low latency in this process means the computation is optimized for speed, ensuring the output, which is immediately forwarded to the Interpretability layer, provides timely, actionable intelligence essential for effective real-time traffic management and decision-making.

4.6 Integration of Live Weather Data for Enhanced Responsiveness

Secondly, this pattern of traffic is inextricably linked to external factors in the environment such as rainfall, reduced visibility, or effects of thermal stress not only because they are contributing to additional external noise but because they alter fundamentally the volume-speed relationship (Chung & Rosalion, 2015).

It serves two most critical functions for this system by making a call to an independent weather service API in order to get the current readings pertaining to temperatures, rain intensity, humidity, and wind speed based upon a forecast.

Dynamic Condition Reflexivity

This assists the model in acting immediately if any unusual or abnormal delay is caused by weather.

- **Speed and Delay Adjustment** Suppose the output of a model predicting travel time was 10 minutes based on historical inputs, but in this case, heavy rainfall was indicated in the current weather API output. The model can adjust this output in real time, such as by increasing travel time to 15 minutes, based on correlations derived from learning such factors as rain intensity and historical speed deviations.
- **Infrastructure Effects** Heat damages the road or affects the railways, and snow prevents roads from being used because of heavy snowfall. The model will be taught to factor in all these environmental elements which make unusual delays not accounted for by the normal average delays in history.
- **Behavioral Realism** Such an inference implicitly enables the model to detect and forecast human behavior under negative circumstances.

Risk Adverse Driving

Naturally, a driver is more risk averse during rainfall or when he or she cannot see properly. A driver accelerates slower, follows other cars further, and makes fewer lane changes. The model understands this because it has been trained on historical data where this occurred in conjunction with particular weather information.

Situational Awareness

For example, it learns that in high-intensity rainfall with a wet road surface, congestion grows with less stability in contrast to a dry surface with an equal number of cars. Therefore, this will make the prediction engine have better situational awareness in order to predict the emergence of congestion.

Infrastructure Impact

Extreme heat leads to degradation of roads, and heavy snow saturates roads or impacts railroads. The model must be able to learn to factor in such a constraint imposed by the environment, leading to unusual delays not accounted for in standard historical averages.

This will allow the model to factor in not only driver behavior but also the condition of the transport infrastructure into delayed traffic predictions.

Anomaly Detection & Validation

Having access to real-time weather information is a critical validation step for real-time anomalies in traffic. When it finds an unusual sudden slow speed event without event schedule data available, it will realize a natural event such as heavy weather is happening simultaneously and will thus attribute an automatic delay based on this being a natural event, rather than some random sensor problem or car crash.

Urban traffic flow is largely affected by external environmental factors such as rainfall, low visibility, and temperatures. Such factors do not only amount to system noise but affect the interdependence of vehicle density, allowed speed, and actual time delays. To cater to this need, an interface for real-time access to environmental factor measurements, such as temperatures, rain intensity, humidity level, and wind speed, at the time of making a forecast, is incorporated in this system via an external API.

Such immediate infusion of environmental information into the model enables a reflexive capability to be exercised, which can be termed dynamic condition reflexivity, in order to adjust the model's output based on observed deviations in environmental circumstances from precedent paths.

Access to real-time weather information serves as a critical validation layer in the process of detection and interpretation of traffic anomalies. Whenever the system notices an abrupt and abnormal fall in vehicle speed with no event data scheduled accordingly, it cross-checks concurrent weather conditions. In the case of detecting adverse weather conditions like heavy rainfall or fog at that time, the system will correctly identify the delay to a natural environmental cause and not misclassify it as a sensor malfunction or an accident. It enhances contextual awareness, thereby improving the reliability and accuracy of the traffic anomaly classification. Weather Impact on Urban traffic plays a vital role which can be see in the Fig. 5.

4.7 Output Layer

The Output or Dissemination Layer is the final layer of the system architecture. It takes the complex numeric results from the predictive core-such as the LSTM engine-and turns them into actionable, interpretable, and compliant intelligence for the end-users and administrative systems. Important as such, the power of the system is made to translate into tangible utility and transparency, and it will meet requirements toward Model Explainability and Public Communication.

Core Functions and Ethical Observance

Interpretability Module Techniques of post-hoc explainability like SHAP or LIME are applied based on the model's prediction before data leaves the back-end. This module calculates the weighted contribution of top input features, namely rainfall intensity and time-of-day to the final forecast (Ribeiro et al., 2016; Lundberg and Lee, 2017). This shall create the needed Causal Classification such as Weather-Driven, Temporal-Driven, etc. that explains why a prediction was made which directly counters the "black-box" aspect.

Trace logging and compliance All final predictions, together with the computed feature weights and congestion classification, are directly logged to a secure, auditable database. This is important for providing critical analysis traces that may be used for internal auditing and compliance by the traffic authorities in ensuring the accountability of AI-driven decisions in the public sector (Lundberg and Lee, 2017).

Formatting Results The layer translates the raw numerical outputs-predicted speed, volume, density-to a user-friendly output in metrics such as definitive Estimated Travel Times and clear color-coded severity indicators. It converts raw data into actionable metrics suitable for direct decision-making by citizens and operators.

Dashboard API Finally, the robust API will publish the processed, interpreted, and formatted results. This will supply the necessary data stream for both the Citizen-Facing Prediction Dashboard-public use-and the administrative control systems, including automated signal re-timing and resource allocation.

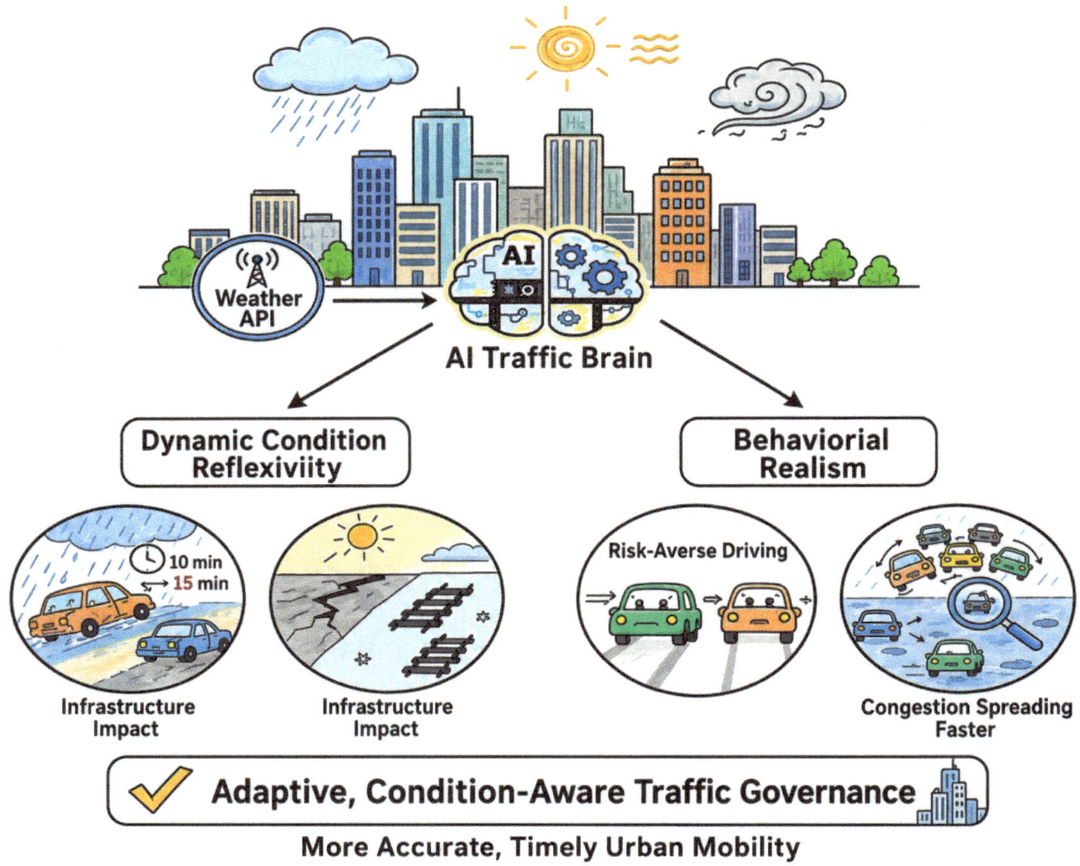

Fig. 5 Impact of Weather Conditions on Traffic Flow

Dataset Characteristics and Ethical Considerations

The integrity and real-world utility of any urban traffic prediction system depend fundamentally on the quality and ethical curation of its training dataset. As outlined above, the impacts of congestion are global, multi-dimensional, and unequally distributed. In order to produce a model that will be effective, equitable, and trustworthy, the dataset will have to meet rigorous criteria for representativeness and ethical safeguards.

Ensuring Representativeness and Avoiding Bias

A key pre-requisite is ensuring that the dataset is representative of the whole urban environment, so that the model does not inherit or amplify pre-existing biases present in society. This has been achieved by:

- **Avoid Demographic Bias:** Data collection protocols have to be developed that do not bias toward rich neighborhoods since these very often tend to have newer infrastructure with more sensors while ignoring socioeconomically disadvantaged regions or areas with weaker infrastructure. A biased dataset leads to a biased model-one that can give high-quality predictions and service to one segment of the population but fails at or misrepresents conditions in another, further exacerbating mobility inequalities.
- **Full Infrastructure Coverage**: Variations in road type, complexity of intersections, and the presence and aging/maintenance status of public transit infrastructure should be representative of all city segments.

Protecting Privacy, Ensuring Public Trust

To achieve the continuing of public acceptance and to be in line with recent regulations concerning data protection, strict standards concerning privacy need to be set:

Protection of Privacy: Stringent care must be taken by the system not to store personally identifiable information. That means active elimination or anonymization of data points involving vehicle IDs, license plates, or particular GPS-based individual movement patterns. The focus needs to be restricted to aggregate flow characteristics such as volume, speed, and density, never on the tracing of individual vehicles. This is indeed an ethical commitment necessary to retain legitimacy and public trust.

Data Integrity and Reliability

Model accuracy is related to the reliability of the data it was trained on. Poor quality, even with comprehensive coverage, can introduce distortion in the model:

Integrity and Reliability: The dataset has to undergo heavy data cleansing. Defective or extreme outliers due to malfunctioning sensors, errors in communications, or short-duration, non-recurring events should be detected and neutralized. For instance, when a sensor is malfunctioning for a moment and reports 100 Km/h speed or zero volume on a busy highway, this kind of unreliable information must be excluded to avoid distorting the model and to ensure that the resulting predictions are based on actual and repeatable traffic physics.

Model Explainability and Transparency

Although deep learning models, such as Long Short-Term Memory LSTM network architecture, possess unmatched capabilities for forecasting intricate nonlinear events such as city traffic, they have historically received criticism for being "black box" decision-making systems. A lack of transparency in such a system remains a serious obstacle in their adoption in public safety and infrastructure administration contexts, where authorities require traceable and verifiable justification for decisions of critical importance. Our solution integrates such layers of interpretability with a goal of making this model's thought process transparent and comprehensible. Through this approach, not only will this system announce a resulting forecast but will do so with a justification, which is an important prerequisite in satisfying hefty demands for transparency.

Model Interpretability in Traffic Governance

The forecasting decisions of AI systems have immediate effects in relation to resource allocation, traffic signal control, and safety in traffic regulation. Through this, an AI forecasting tool lacks explanatory capabilities in regards to:<dl

- **Trust and Adoption** The traffic authorities and city planners will not install systems they cannot audit. In case a model predicts heavy congestion, authorities must be able to establish causality in order to support or act on a prediction manually.
- **Debugging & Improvement** Every time a model fails or makes a wrong prediction, AI engineers would want to know which particular feature went wrong with the model.
- **Compliance & Auditing** Most rules these days state that an auditable model is a requirement when generating decisions using AI in a public sector, which basically means these models have to be able to trace all factors affecting a particular output.

Execution: Layers of Interpretability

Several post-hoc methods of explanation, such as SHAP or LIME, adjusted for time series forecasting tasks, can make this LSTM a transparent tool by transforming it from a "black box" to a transparent "white box."

- **Detailed Prediction Dashboard**

The primary interface, which is referred to as a dashboard, is meant to be a transparent viewing tool into the model processing.

Output Decomposition.

The dashboard shows not only where the main predictions, the predictive traffic volume, and congestion level are, but more importantly, an output decomposition of this output. They show which are the main contributors to this current prediction output.

Features with Examples: "Rainfall intensity", +25% delay weighting, "Morning peak-hour pattern", +40% volume weighting, and "multi-junction spill-over effect", + 15% delay weighting.

Weighted Contribution: A visualization of the percentage/contribution degree of each input variable to arrive at a final prediction offers immediate context awareness to traffic control.

operators. They can use this information to validate a prediction via tangible real-world occurrences rather than relying solely on the hard numbers spewed out by the model.

- Causal Classification of Congestion Drivers

Apart from estimating the degree of influence that each feature contributes to a given problem, this model is also able to categorize the final cause of a predicted event.

Weather congestion can be referred to as a congestion pattern in which the key cause of congestion is a real-time snow or fog factor.

Temporal-Driven Congestion: Road traffic congestion explained based on time-driven temporal elements such as but not limited to fixed morning peak hours, time of school dismissal, and pre-holiday rushes.

"Pattern-Driven Congestion"—a consequence of "learned dependencies," such as a "multi-junction spill-over effect" or "unusual traffic wave propagation pattern."

Such a categorization will allow traffic management systems to make decisions on an intervention strategy based on an event type, such that events driven by weather demand speed variation, while events driven by time demand retiming of signals.

Trust and Traceability: While this commitment to openness ends in relation to the user interface, it continues in regards to the operational internals of this system.

- **Analytical Trace**

Every important model output corresponds with complete analytical traces. They are recorded and stored. This is very important when it comes to forensic analysis and government requirements.

- Data Recording: the input vector used in making a prediction, the computed influence weight among the top N features, the computed congestion class based on weather, temporal, or pattern-driven methods, and the output value.
- Internal Auditing: Internal auditing by traffic authorities can be facilitated, which will allow a forecasted event to be assessed for retrospective analysis and make sure that the model's logic is good because it took a reasonable forecast. A possible forecast leading to an expensive and ineffective strategy will make it possible to see where exactly the model went wrong using the trace log.
- **Compliance & Equitable Performance**

Through the constant affirmation of these different moral safeguards, these two important aspects necessary for proper continued functioning become integral to this system:

Compliance Such analytical trails serve as evidence to make AI-driven decisions in public infrastructure transparent, which is a requirement in governance standards.

Equitable Performance Openness indirectly assists in ensuring equitable performance in the system. The perception by the dashboard of a lower number of reliable features being used in predicting one urban segment because of poor sensor coverage indirectly informs an area requiring improvements in the infrastructure, thus ensuring equitable performance in the system among all segments.

As a consequence, this system not only articulates what can be predicted but articulates why so because it aims to be in accordance with the guidelines of transparency and foundational trust required when dealing with critical infrastructure.

The Figure 6 describes the final stage of the predictive framework involves the clear, ethical, and multi-faceted dissemination of the processed results via a central dashboard, which acts as the culmination of all preceding efforts, integrating ethical principles, data preprocessing, handling, and the complex algorithm implication from the LSTM and its explainability layers. This dashboard is designed as a critical interface for actionable intelligence, serving distinct user groups: Vehicle Drivers receive highly accurate, condition-aware routing and travel time predictions that account for weather-related delays.

Traffic Police and Transportation Authorities gain a command center displaying not only the forecast but also the reasoning behind it (example, "Congestion is 70% Weather-Driven"), enabling proactive deployment and intervention; and Pedestrians/Public Transport Users gain visibility into transit delays and safety risks. Crucially, the dashboard's design reflects the system's ethical commitment by displaying top contributing features and the causal classification of congestion, thereby avoiding the "black-box" nature, ensuring transparency, and building public trust necessary for effective urban mobility governance.

Front-End and Public Communication

A genuinely smart and responsible city AI must not be judged complete if it consists solely of intelligence locked inside government servers but must instead proactively connect with and impact the lives of citizens. The Citizen Facing Predictions Dashboard is an essential interface with which citizens interact with the massive forecasting model, interpreting advanced LSTM model results, ethics, and situational awareness in a manner that is comprehensible and sensible to them. The web interface serves as the last mile of this system, which is meant not just to display but to enable citizen-driven mobility solutions toward achieving maximum benefit from this system in the whole city network.

Design Principles: Accessibility & Trust

The principles behind the design of this dashboard lie in two major aspects that allow a connection to be bridged from complicated algorithms to public application: accessibility and transparency.

a) **Reducing Complexity into Simplicity**

The calculations performed by this model using cell state in LSTM, SHAP, and correlations with real weather are not relevant to a commuter. As a dashboard, it serves a purpose of taking this immense complexity and making it immediately understandable.

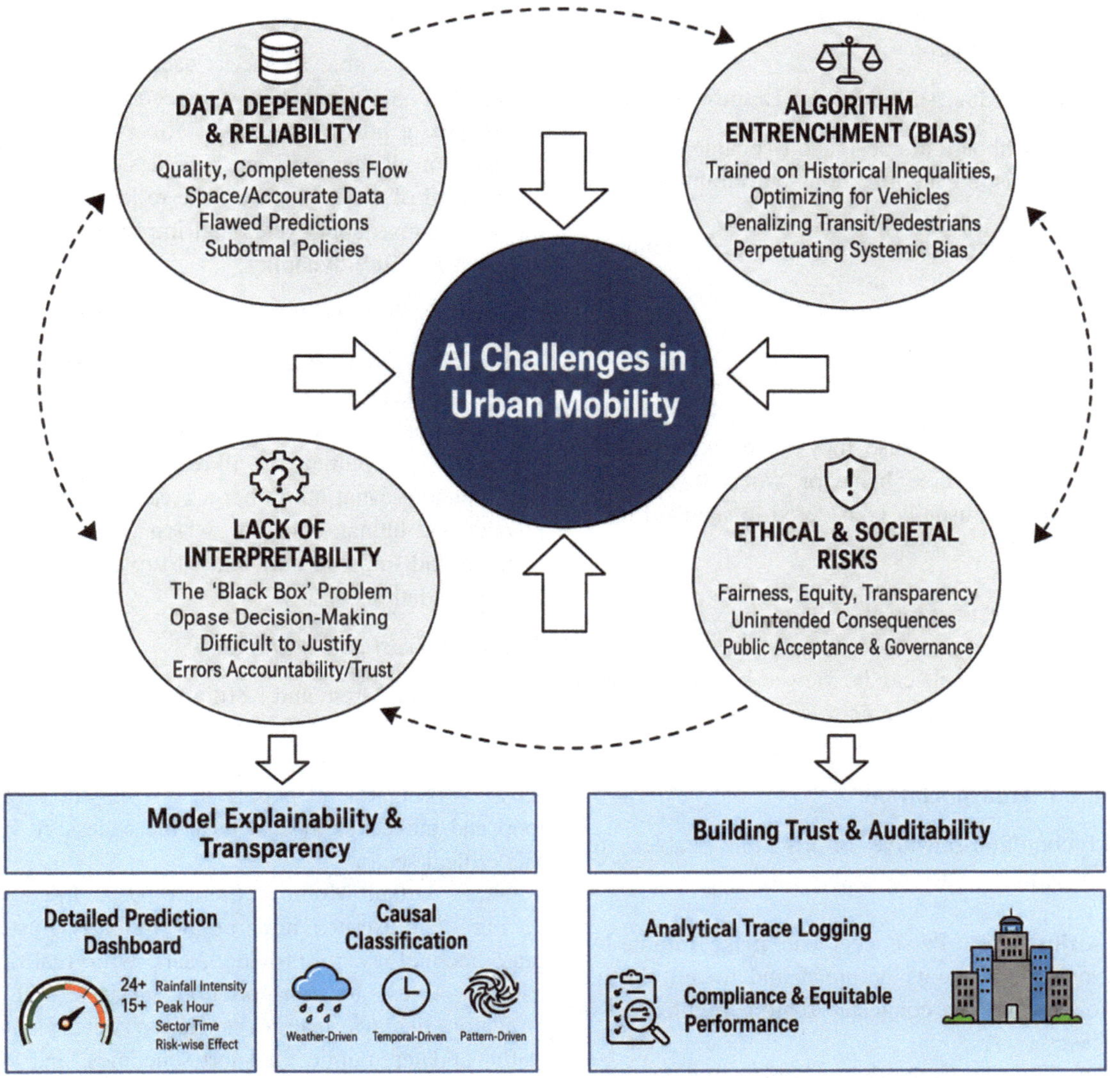

Fig. 6 AI challenges in urban mobility

- **Color-Coded Severity Indicators:** The status of traffic is conveyed immediately and universally using a simple color-coding system in which green progresses to yellow to orange to red. A quick glance can inform a driver of the level of danger using this system without necessarily reading messages.
- **Location Specificity:** Forecasts are offered using geographic location, sometimes in conjunction with a map widget, targeting specific intersections, key routes, or geographic areas of interest related to a driver's common travel route.

b) **Brief General Commentary**

The requirement for transparency is met by using explanatory statements in plain language. Such a characteristic is important when it comes to matters of accountability and understanding why a particular prediction is being made, based on the principles highlighted in Sect. 3.7.

"Direct" Causal Statements:

Rather than simply showing "Expected delay: 20 minutes," a direct causal statement is given, which relates an output to a set of dominating input variables. Some examples include:

- "Heavy congestion expected due to rainfall + morning peak hour pattern."
- "Moderate delay expected because of a localized multi-junction spill-over effect (Pattern-Driven

Accessibility for All: Through using non-technical language in making predictions, this technology makes sure that the information can be understood not only by engineers and city planners but by all people.

Important Features for Active Public Empowerment

Features on the dashboard are designed to enable citizens to make proactive transport modifications before they become part of the problem.

The most important information for a commuter is future-oriented:

- **Travel Time Estimations ETAs**

Travel time estimations are offered. More importantly, these ETAs are very reliable because they factor in behavioral models such as risk-averse behavior when it comes to driving, which are not usually considered in standard travel apps.

- **Estimated Congestion Levels**

Estimated congestion levels can be viewed by the user for a given choke point, thus being able to see into the future for a given time horizon (say 30 or 60 minutes).

Investing in our transportation.

Timely and condition-sensitive information enables this dashboard to support decisions in this way:

- **Route Adjustment**: Passengers can make minute-by-minute route adjustments before actual travel, shifting traffic flow away from congested regions highlighted in the forecast.
- **Departure Time Optimization:** People can adjust their departure time using reliable information, leaving a little late to evade congestion points or leaving early to prevent congestion from happening.
- **Transportation Mode Choice:** When abnormally high congestion levels or protracted peak hours are forecasted, it will be suggested to switch to other transport modes such as using public transport, cycling, or working from a distant site, thus resulting in less traffic on the network.

4.8 Maximizing System Utility and Ethical Compliance

The dashboard is not a mere function but rather a means by which the AI system will maximize utility and fulfill its ethics problem-solving role.

Feedback Loop for System Improvement

As citizens are able to access accurate and trusted information and adjust their behavior accordingly, they automatically have a positive feedback effect on the system. The behavior of all these citizens modifies the traffic pattern in an unheard-of way, which can be re-learned by the LSTM model in subsequent cycles and improve its understanding of urban mobility dynamics.

Common Responsibility as a Policy Option

The system promotes a sense of collective responsibility through education of the user on causality of congestion, such as "Heavy rain is reducing the road's effective capacity." The commuters will realize that this congestion is not a random event but rather a predictable consequence of physics and human behavior, which will promote patience in them and improve adherence to dynamic traffic control recommendations.

Finalizing Trust and Legitimacy

With this transparent and justifiable information, it not only gives meaning to all the huge investments put into this initiative but also shows in a very transparent way that this AI is working for all people in this city to complete this loop and make this system have the necessary viability in this critical sector.

Smart Urban Mobility Sample User Interface shown in Fig. 7 illustrates how urban mobility systems integrate technology to provide users with real-time, user-friendly access to transportation services. The interface typically displays features such as route planning, live traffic updates, public transport schedules, and availability of shared mobility options like bikes or cabs. By presenting data in a clear and interactive manner, the system helps users make informed travel decisions, reduces congestion, saves time, and promotes efficient use of urban transport resource.

The implementation of the Adaptive Traffic Prediction Engine demands a robust, multi-layered system architecture shown in Fig. 8 is designed specifically to handle high-velocity, real-time data streams and ensure continuous model adaptability. This design guarantees integrity from initial data ingestion through to final, explainable forecasts.

5 Comparison of Traditional Models Versus. Responsible AI Approaches for Urban Mobility

Comparative study of two fundamentally different paradigms-traditional traffic forecasting models and state-of-the-art AI-based models are discussed in Table 3. Traditional models, generated with the use of ARIMA,

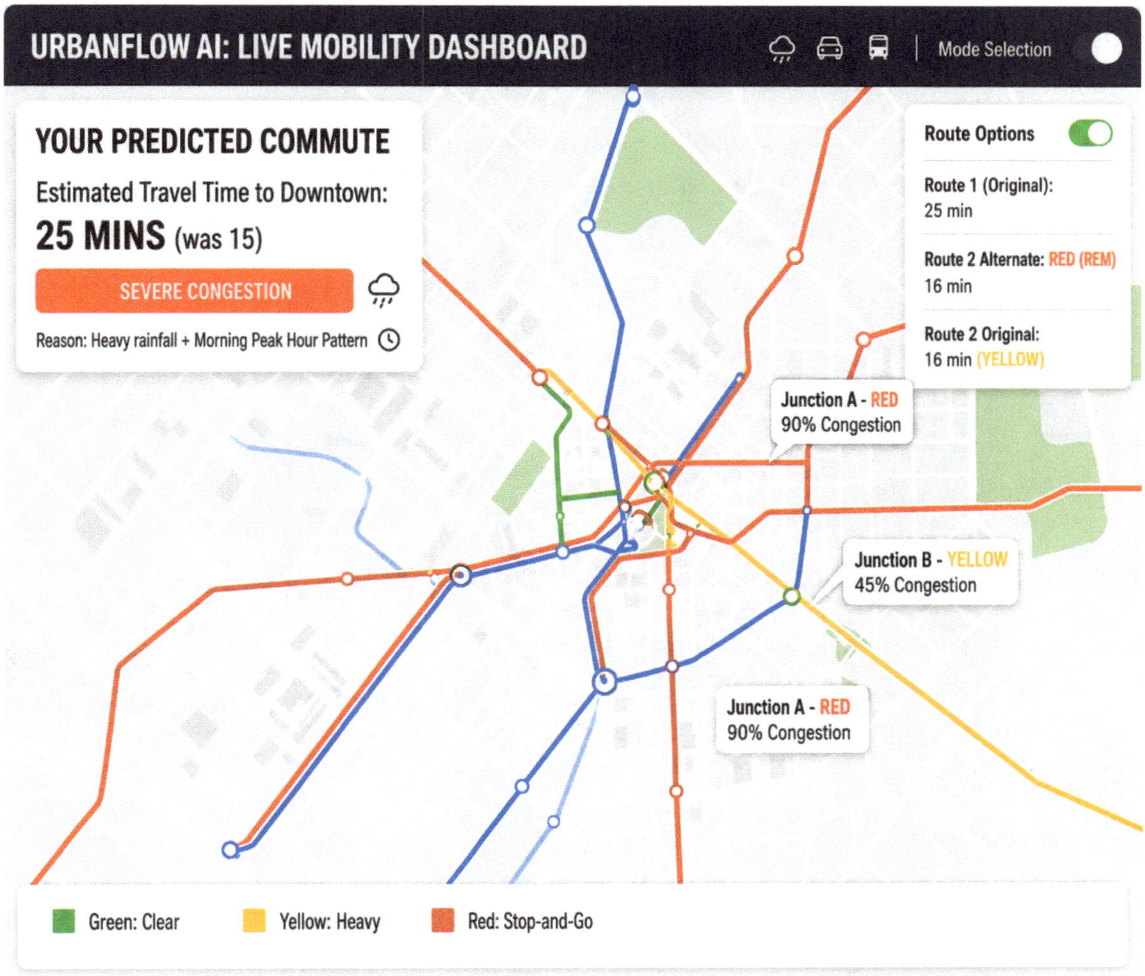

Fig. 7 Smart urban mobility sample user interface

Holt-Winters, or simple exponential smoothing, belong to the class of statistical, linear, and "glass box" systems. The term "glass box" here indicates that their internal mechanics are transparent, mathematically interpretable, and easy to audit. Under strong linearity, stationarity, and stable temporal pattern assumptions, these models rely on the historical time series data to perform trend continuation and seasonality extrapolation (Center, 2016). The constraint imposed by a single dimension drastically restricts them too low to moderate levels of complexity, whereas most performances degrade in the presence of sharp anomalies, nonlinear interactions, and drastic changes in the urban traffic environment. Due to these shortcomings, they are generally less accurate, especially for modern cities where traffic is extremely dynamic and influenced by multiple factors in real time.

By contrast, sophisticated models like LSTM networks, GRUs, and Deep Neural Networks are Machine Learning–driven, Non-linear, and "Black-Box" systems (Center, 2016; Goodfellow et al., 2016). They are "black-box" since their decision processes include complex layers and transformations not easily interpretable. The non-linear architecture makes them powerful for grasping high-dimensional, complex relationships in data that may not be reachable by traditional models. These systems use a huge heterogeneous data source, including long-term historic data and real-time sensor inputs, GPS traces, weather feeds, incident reports, and IoT-based traffic measurements. One of the biggest advantages is automatic feature learning: they find the pattern themselves without much human engineering. Such architecture, like LSTMs, may use memory cells that capture long-term temporal dependencies and thus provide insight into how past conditions affect future congestion. Because of these features, advanced AI models can promise much higher accuracy in predictions, much stronger adaptability, and strong resilience against sudden urban changes such as accidents, rain spikes, lane closures, or unexpected traffic demand surges. Refer Fig. 9 for visual understanding of Traditional and AI model.

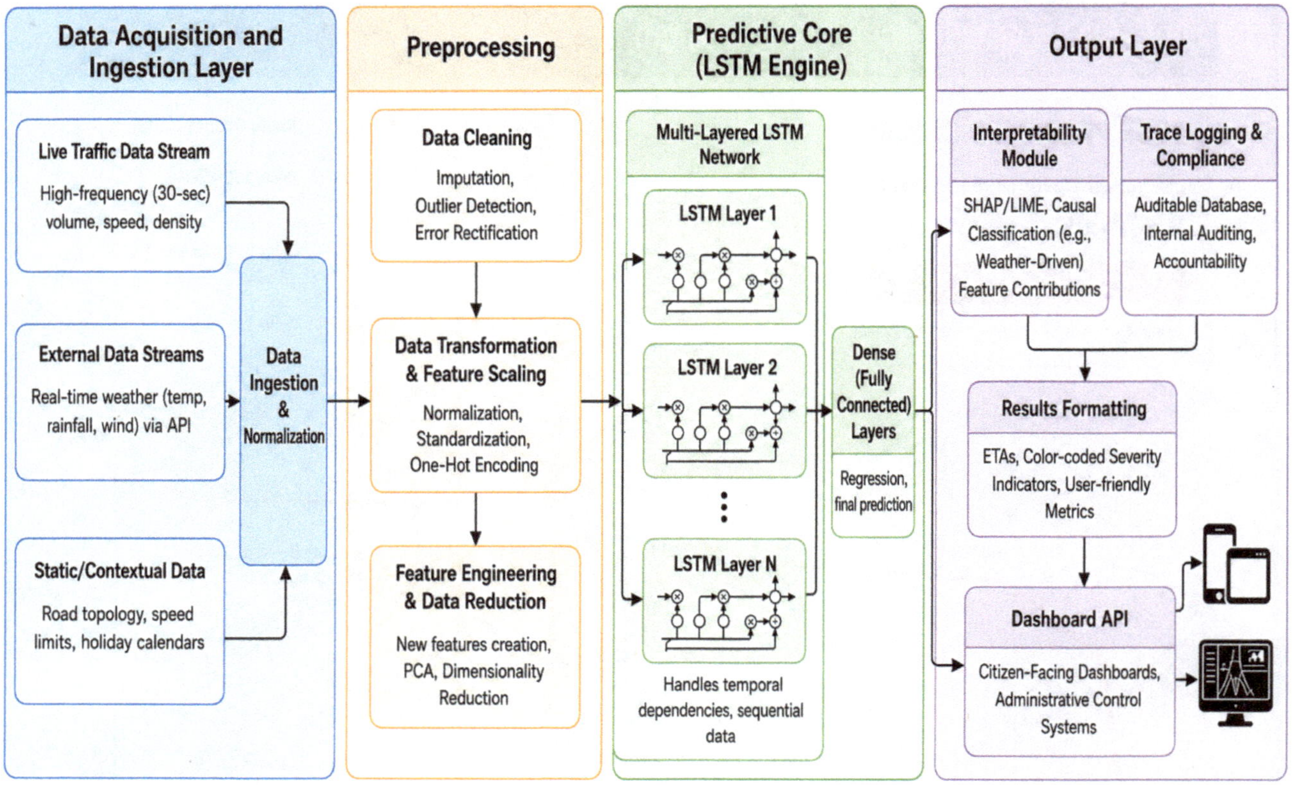

Fig. 8 System architecture for adaptive traffic prediction engine

6 Conclusion

With cities increasing in scale and complexity, the challenge of safe, efficient, and equitable mobility is increasingly a function of emergent intelligence in urban systems. This shift from reactive traffic control to predictive, AI-driven mobility governance stands out as a transformational way in which the urban environment conceives, predicts, and oversees movement. Newer state-of-the-art traffic prediction frameworks make use of multisource data, newer time-series learning models such as Long Short-Term Memory networks, and real-time environmental sensing. These go beyond the limitations of a post-event approach in ways that enable cities to look ahead at disruptions imminent well in advance and manage mobility with even greater precision and foresight (Chen et al., 2019; Hochreiter and Schmidhuber, 1997).

It is a strong commitment to Responsible AI that marks this new generation of mobility systems, where high-accuracy predictive models-like LSTM-are placed alongside powerful explainability layers such as SHAP and LIME, which shine a light on the underlying rationale beneath each prediction. This merger resolves the long-standing trade-off that existed between predictive performance and interpretability. In effect, such hybrid systems ensure that decision pathways across mobility governance remain transparently visible and auditable hence maintaining accountability, interpretability, and conformance with emerging regulatory standards. Such clarity is meaningful in generating public trust amidst burgeoning automated decision-making embedded in the urban fabric (Ribeiro et al., 2016; Lundberg and Lee, 2017).

The application of this responsible AI-enabled framework shifts the focus from mere congestion management to empowering citizens with personalized, reliable, and justified mobility insights. This lays the building blocks for smart cities, fully advanced in technology but also ethical and human-oriented in approach. Meeting predictive intelligence with transparency and fairness makes the future of urban movement resilient, inclusive, and in deep resonance with the needs of the people it will serve.

Table 3 Comparison of tradition model versus ai approaches

Feature	Traditional models	Advanced AI models
Model type	Statistical, linear, "glass-box"	Machine learning, non-linear, "black-box"
Complexity handled	Low-to-moderate (assumes linearity and stationarity)	High (captures non-linear, multi-dimensional complexity)
Data sources	Primarily historical time series data (e.g., past traffic counts)	Vast & Diverse: Historical data+real-time sensor feeds, weather, social media trends, GPS data.
Key capability	Trend & Seasonality Extrapolation	Feature Learning & Long-Term Dependency Capture (via memory cells)
Prediction accuracy	Lower (prone to high errors during anomalies)	Significantly higher (adapts to sudden changes and complex patterns)

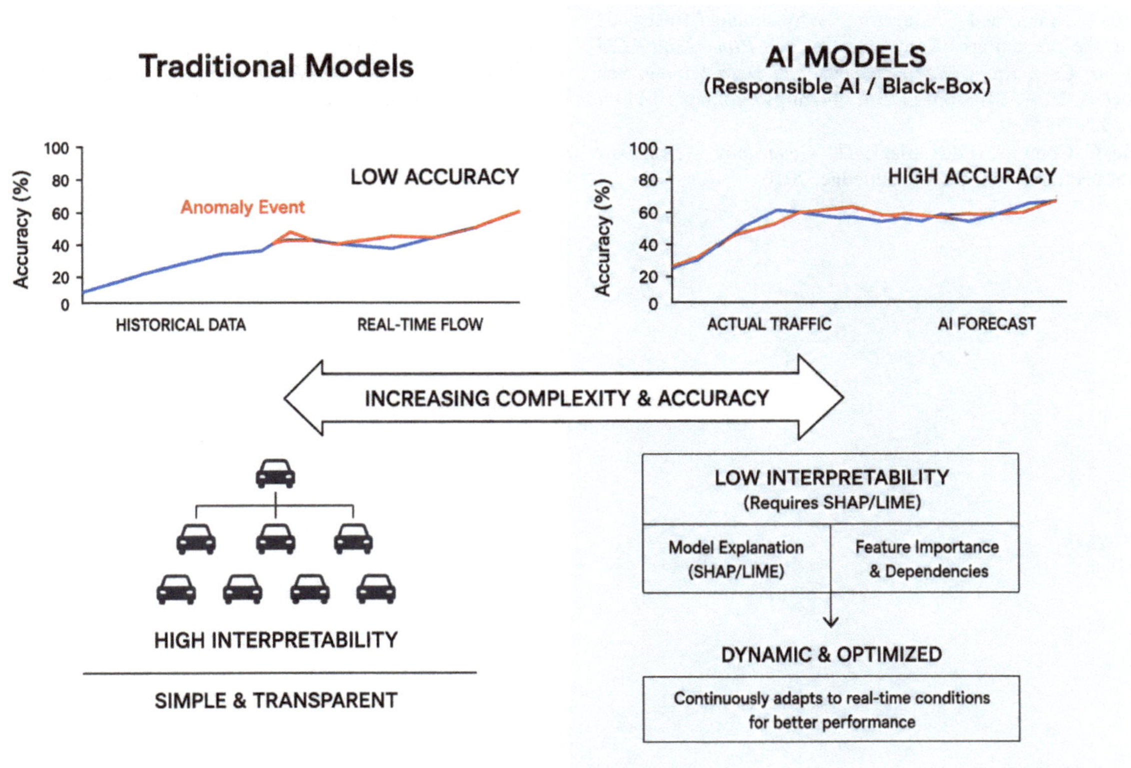

Fig. 9 Traditional and AI model

References

S. Barocas, M. Hardt, and A. Narayanan, *Fairness and Machine Learning: Limitations and Opportunities*, 2019. [Online]. Available: https://fairmlbook.org

M. Batty, *The New Science of Cities*, Cambridge, MA, USA: MIT Press, 2013.

National Transportation Systems Center, *Traffic Flow Theory: A State-of-the-Art Report*, U.S. Department of Transportation, Federal Highway Administration, Washington, DC, USA, 2016.

C. Chen, Y. Lin, S. Wang, and X. Li, "LSTM networks for traffic speed prediction," *IEEE Transactions on Intelligent Transportation Systems*, vol. 20, no. 6, pp. 2001–2013, Jun. 2019, https://doi.org/10.1109/TITS.2018.2877356

E. Chung and S. Rosalion, "Weather effects on traffic congestion and incident detection," *IEEE Transactions on Intelligent Transportation Systems*, vol. 16, no. 5, pp. 2799–2808, Oct. 2015, https://doi.org/10.1109/TITS.2015.2419617

I. Goodfellow, Y. Bengio, and A. Courville, *Deep Learning*, Cambridge, MA, USA: MIT Press, 2016.

I. A. T. Hashem, I. Yaqoob, N. B. Anuar, S. Mokhtar, A. Gani, and S. U. Khan, "The role of big data in smart city," *Future Generation Computer Systems*, vol. 70, pp. 1–24, Apr. 2017, https://doi.org/10.1016/j.future.2016.08.030

S. Hochreiter and J. Schmidhuber, "Long short-term memory," *Neural Computation*, vol. 9, no. 8, pp. 1735–1780, Nov. 1997, https://doi.org/10.1162/neco.1997.9.8.1735

INRIX, Global Traffic Scorecard *2024*, INRIX, Kirkland, WA, USA, 2024.

Y. Li, S. Chai, Z. Ma, and G. Wang, "Deep learning for urban traffic prediction: A survey," *IEEE Access*, vol. 8, pp. 11264–11271, 2020, https://doi.org/10.1109/ACCESS.2020.2969817

T. Litman, "Congestion costs and mobility evaluation," *Transport Policy*, vol. 98, pp. 1–11, 2021, https://doi.org/10.1016/j.tranpol.2020.08.001

S. M. Lundberg and S.-I. Lee, "A unified approach to interpreting model predictions," in *Advances in Neural Information Processing Systems (NeurIPS)*, Long Beach, CA, USA, 2017, pp. 4765–4774, https://doi.org/10.48550/arXiv.1705.07874

Y. Lv, Y. Duan, W. Kang, Z. Li, and F.-Y. Wang, "Traffic flow prediction with big data: A deep learning approach," *IEEE Transactions on Intelligent Transportation Systems*, vol. 16, no. 2, pp. 865–873, Apr. 2015, https://doi.org/10.1109/TITS.2014.2345663

N. Mehrabi, F. Morstatter, N. Saxena, K. Lerman, and A. Galstyan, "A survey on bias and fairness in machine learning," *ACM Computing Surveys*, vol. 54, no. 6, pp. 1–35, Oct. 2021, https://doi.org/10.1145/3457607

M. T. Ribeiro, S. Singh, and C. Guestrin, "Why should I trust you? Explaining the predictions of any classifier," in *Proc. 22nd ACM SIGKDD Int. Conf. Knowledge Discovery and Data Mining*, San Francisco, CA, USA, 2016, pp. 1135–1144, https://doi.org/10.1145/2939672.2939778

J.-P. Rodrigue, C. Comtois, and B. Slack, *The Geography of Transport Systems*, 5th ed., London, U.K.: Routledge, 2020.

D. Schrank, B. Eisele, T. Lomax, and J. Bak, *Urban Mobility Report*, Texas A&M Transportation Institute, College Station, TX, USA, 2019.

TomTom N.V., *TomTom Traffic Index Report 2025*, Amsterdam, Netherlands, 2025.

A. M. Townsend, *Smart Cities: Big Data, Civic Hackers, and the Quest for a New Utopia*, New York, NY, USA: W. W. Norton & Company, 2013.

United Nations, Department of Economic and Social Affairs, Population Division, *World Urbanization Prospects: The 2022 Revision*, United Nations, New York, NY, USA, 2023.

E. I. Vlahogianni, M. G. Karlaftis, and J. C. Golias, "Short-term traffic forecasting: Where we are and where we're going," *Transportation Research Part C*, vol. 43, pp. 3–19, May 2014, https://doi.org/10.1016/j.trc.2014.01.005

Y. Zheng, L. Capra, O. Wolfson, and H. Yang, "Urban computing: Concepts, methodologies, and applications," *ACM Transactions on Intelligent Systems and Technology*, vol. 5, no. 3, pp. 1–55, Jul. 2014, https://doi.org/10.1145/2629592

FSC
www.fsc.org
MIX
Papier | Fördert gute Waldnutzung
FSC® C083411

Kolibri 360 GmbH
Ferdinand-Jühlke-Straße 7
99095 Erfurt, Deutschland
produktsicherheit@kolibri360.de